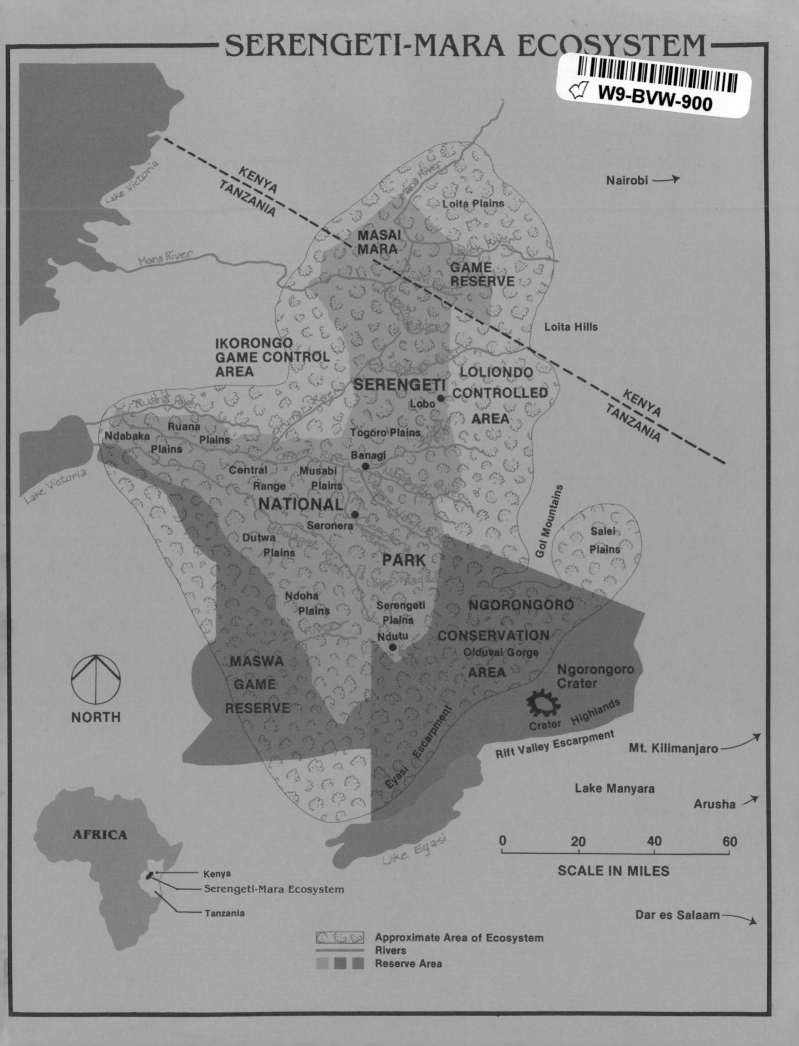

SERENGETI-MARA ECOSYSTEM

W9-BVW-900

Nairobi →

Lake Victoria

KENYA
TANZANIA

Mara River

MASAI
MARA

Loita Plains

GAME
RESERVE

Loita Hills

IKORONGO
GAME CONTROL
AREA

SERENGETI

LOLIONDO
CONTROLLED
AREA

KENYA
TANZANIA

Lobo

Togoro Plains

Ruana
Plains

Ndabaka
Plains

Lake Victoria

Banagi

Central
Range

Musabi
Plains

Gol Mountains

Salei
Plains

NATIONAL

Seronera

Dutwa
Plains

PARK

Ndoha
Plains

Serengeti
Plains

NGORONGORO

Ndutu

CONSERVATION

Olduvai Gorge

MASWA

AREA

Ngorongoro
Crater

GAME

Crater Highlands

RESERVE

Rift Valley Escarpment

Eyasi Escarpment

Mt. Kilimanjaro →

Lake Manyara

Arusha →

Lake Eyasi

NORTH

AFRICA

Kenya
Serengeti-Mara Ecosystem
Tanzania

Dar es Salaam →

0   20   40   60

SCALE IN MILES

Approximate Area of Ecosystem
Rivers
Reserve Area

Baringo Giraffe

Cover: Display by Young Elephants in Samburu

THE AFRICAN SAFARI

The Ultimate Wildlife and Photographic Adventure

P. JAY FETNER

Foreword by George Plimpton

*Cape Buffalo and Tick-Bird
in Early Morning Mist*

Marsh Lioness

THE AFRICAN SAFARI

The Ultimate Wildlife and Photographic Adventure

P. JAY FETNER

Foreword by George Plimpton

St. Martin's Press
New York

THE AFRICAN SAFARI

●

Published by St. Martin's Press, New York, New York

●

Photocomposition by Acu-Graphics, Inc., Hyattsville, Maryland

Color Separations by Graphics III, Ltd., Forestville, Maryland

Printed by Shepard Poorman Communications Corporation, Indianapolis, Indiana

Bound by Hoster Bindery, Hatboro, Pennsylvania and Distinctive Bookbinding, Washington, D.C. and New York

Technical Coordination by GNG Communications, Washington, D.C., and Maury Boyd and Associates, Indianapolis, Indiana

●

This book was designed and produced by P. Jay Fetner.

●

Library of Congress Cataloging-in-Publication Data
Fetner, P. Jay
    The African safari.
    1. Zoology — Africa.   2. Safaris — Africa.
    3. Photography of animals — Africa.   I. Title.
QL336.F47   1987   916.76'044   87-9606
ISBN 0-312-00969-0 (HBK)
        0-312-01173-3 (PBK)

To Joye, who reminded me of the awe and magic experienced by all first-timers, and to my mother, who instilled in me, by genes and by example, my love for animals.

AWF

AFRICAN WILDLIFE FOUNDATION

1717 Massachusetts Avenue, NW, Washington, DC 20036   Telephone: (202) 265-8393   Telex: 1504 TEMBO

Dear Reader:

Here at AWF, where we are charged with the task of protecting all the wonderful "beasts" (in our Trustee Mr. Plimpton's words) pictured in these pages, we enjoy all the African wildlife books published. Indeed, in rushes of recognition, the volumes often seem very nearly like our own children. And like good parents everywhere, we do not easily admit to favorites: we love them all.

But this glorious book is a special example, one in which the magic of safari, the magnificence of the animals, is captured in ways that rarely emerge from the relatively cold pages of type and ink.

We must never forget, however, that behind these evocative pictures and challenging text live the real thing. Stimulating, breathing, loving creatures who earn a living, mate, rear families, build homes, and travel widely and who at the most profound level share this earth with man. It is not enough to enjoy—not even to appreciate.

If we want the next generation to share our enjoyment—and there could scarcely be anything of greater value to pass on—we must preserve as well. That effort takes money, commitment, understanding, time, expertise—and more. AWF has always been a leader in this endeavor. Ultimately, the real value in the volume that you are holding is that, when you have finished it, you will have come to share our commitment.

Cordially,

Paul T. Schindler

Paul T. Schindler
President

Burchell's Zebra Mare and Foal

Acknowledgements

My warmest appreciation to all who participated in producing this book, but special thanks go to:

Cynthia Abramson, who with loyalty and dedication labored with the author to produce the manuscript, draft after draft (after draft), and *Joye Vailes,* who stayed on to help finish the job;

Ann Maurice, who years ago started all this craziness;

Jack Whittemore and *Tommy Hinds,* who had the courage to stand behind a worthy project;

William Fetner, my father, for funding one particularly fruitful photo-safari and for rescuing the project at the eleventh hour;

Jessica Schaffer, who assisted in layout, proofreading, and many other ways, and without whom this volume would still be a year away from publication;

The African Wildlife Foundation, particularly *Diana McMeekin,* for constant help and encouragement;

World Wildlife Fund, for the use of their resources, and *Rick Weyerbaeuser,* for his special assistance;

The Explorers Club and its librarian, *Janet Baldwin,* for the kind use of its library;

the staff at the library of *The American Museum of Natural History,* New York City, a superb collection;

Ron Goldfarb and *Gail Ross,* who provided wise counsel;

Jacky Parmar of "Big Five Tours and Safaris" in Nairobi, Kenya, who has worked out the details of many a successful safari;

the staff at the *Library of Congress,* surely the greatest research facility in the world;

ADG interns who did legwork on the research effort;

Nancy Holmes of *Acu-Graphics, Inc.* typographer (this edition contains nearly one million words!);

Nick Finamore and *Pat Reidy* of *Graphics III, Ltd.,* who along with their people consistently produced the finest separations and stripping — and, equally important, were always a real pleasure with whom to work;

Lincoln Child and the staff at *St. Martin's Press,* a publisher who has taken more than a passing interest in Africana;

everyone at *Shepard Poorman,* a *superb* company (which, incidentally, printed this book on a basis financially competitive with the finest Far East printers), but special mention should go to *Bob Poorman, Cindy Fred,* and the press foremen *Bob Burger, Lee Phillips, Walt Lee, John Coleman,* and *Ron Richardson,* all whom are artists;

Joel Bender, in Philadelphia, who was always there in the beginning to help with equipment needs;

Les Greenberg of *GNG Communications* and now also Graphics III, who freely lent his valuable technical expertise;

Dick Dodge and his people at *Dodge Color;*

Steve Vance of *Distinctive Bookbinding,* a friend and colleague in the struggle to produce work of quality, and *Downey Hoster* of *Hoster Bindery,* an exacting craftsman;

Martin Dial of *Four Color Graphics* in Indianapolis for the fine cover and Chapter X separations;

Joan Engelhardt, who taught me a thing or two (or twenty) about proofreading;

Rick Boyd and *Noble Hatfield* of *Maury Boyd and Associates* in Indianapolis — Noble is one of those rare individuals who gets things done and remains a gentleman in the bargain;

Ricardo Sanchez, a good friend and *enthusiastic* fellow traveler, who provided several photographs of the author (taken on what had to be one of the best safaris of all time);

George Plimpton, for his fine Foreword;

Jack Fornaciari, the "peacemaker" (blessed are . . . etc.); and

all the many naturalists, researchers, and kindred spirits stationed in or wandering through the African bush who over many years have been accosted by the author and subjected to my queries, challenges, comments, and theories.

I trust that this volume will, in some small way, repay everyone's patience, trust, and understanding.

Table of Contents

Foreword

On our first safari to East Africa in 1968 my wife and I — though it was a shooting expedition — took cameras and not untypically we clicked away at everything we saw that moved and at a lot which didn't. On our return we spent evenings looking through the slides and putting the ones we especially liked into carousel trays. I remember coming home one evening with a shopping bag of extra trays to handle the selection.

The first victims of our enthusiasm were my aunt and uncle, the Amyas Ameses (a section of my Aunt Evelyn's graceful book, *A Glimpse of Eden,* is included in this volume), who had invited us over to have dinner and afterwards to show them our "Africa pictures." We carried the trays to their apartment in that same shopping bag.

The fidgeting began along about the fourth tray — very likely at the sixth view of the safari field-kitchen utensils, along with one or two of the cook himself standing holding a black frying pan.

I hurried on to the animals. I stood up to point at the screen. "Right behind that bush on the left is the lion — that tawny patch? See?"

A sequence of bird pictures began. I am a bird-watcher. I stood up again and pointed at a blur on the screen. "This flurry here is the whydah, fluttering up over the female in a kind of dance display. It's a bit out of focus."

"Oh yes," my aunt said.

Both she and my uncle are extremely cultivated and polite — and nowhere was the evidence of the latter more pronounced as the evening wore on. To this day I cannot imagine why a common snort of laughter or even dismay did not go up at yet the sixth frame of a pictorial essay on the Arthur Rackham distortions of an average-sized baobab tree. I suspect even they were hard-pressed: their exclamations of wonder at an acacia tree festooned with gourd-like weaver finch nests, so exultant at first, had died away by the fifth view of the same tree.

All of this registered, of course. I remember my uncle standing by the elevator and saying as we left (it was after midnight), "Perhaps, if you don't mind my saying so, a little pruning might be considered — here and there," and I became very conscious of the *weight* of that large shopping bag.

And yet, when my wife and I sat down to go through that vast collection, we found it hard to discard very much. We may have removed one or two from the baobab sequence but the slides were never actually thrown out: they were relegated to a carousel tray carefully labelled *Reserve* . . . just in case. The fact was that it was anguishing to destroy any evidence that might recall the wonder and pleasures of an African safari.

I am reminded of an experience Mrs. Dillon Ripley, the widow of the collector and benefactor of the New York Zoological Society, described to me — that on safari with Isak Dinesen she had lost a hearing aid while taking a bath in a canvas tub. The next morning Dinesen asked her if she had heard the roaring of the lions the night before. Mrs. Ripley despaired that she hadn't, she'd lost . . . and so forth . . . and from that time on, she told me, when she went on safari she always carried a *spare* hearing aid.

Absolutely! Teddy Roosevelt in a nine-month safari was so anxious for keepsakes of his experience there that he sent home 4800-odd hides, heads, and horns — which works out to a daily average of twenty specimens, ranging in size from dik-dik to elephant, which left the plains of Africa for Washington and the floors and cases of the Smithsonian. Rather large potatoes, it occurs to me, certainly compared to a shopping bag of carousel trays (something I might have reminded my aunt and uncle)!

Each safari has its distinctive features. Teddy Roosevelt flew a large American flag above his safari tent — itself surrounded by enough tents to resemble an army encampment. Martin and Osa Johnson had a gibbon that accompanied them on theirs: he sat at the camp table for meals and used a tiny fork. Johnson writes about the safari-workers singing, which was apparently customary in his day (the '20s and '30s) — ". . . a stimulant to trial," he called it. "The men sing, no matter [in] what task they are engaged, handling luggage, thatching grass huts, sharpening spears, skinning game . . . they always stress particularly the notes that accompan[y] the heave or lift, and when any task is done they wind up with a sibilant *pssssttttt.*"

In those pre-Land Rover days a safari employed enough people to provide quite a chorus. Then, the make-up of a safari (the word means "expedition" in Arabic in case you'd forgotten) for two hunters (the most allowed by the law) was as follows: in charge (after the professional hunters, of course) was the headman, upon whom the success of the safari perhaps most depended. Immediately under him were four gunbearers, then four second gunbearers. The first gunbearers were responsible for field glasses and a light long-range rifle, the second gunbearers for cameras, water bottles, and a heavy double-barreled rifle. The procedure when game was sighted was for one of the first gunbearers to kneel behind the hunter and press the barrel of a second rifle against his right leg so it could be reached in case of a misfire or a bad shot. The gunbearers had instructions never to fire unless "the bwana was disarmed and under the beast."

Once the "beast" was secured, the gunbearers were responsible for the skinning.

Next in the social hierarchy came the *askari* — Swahili for scout — who were usually in uniform. Teddy Roosevelt's askaris wore red fezzes, blue blouses, and white knickerbockers — colors quite in keeping with the flag above his tent. The function of the askaris was twofold — to guard the camp from marauders and to keep disaffected parties from bolting camp and sneaking back to Nairobi.

The Big Male Cheetah

Who next? The cook, of course, distinguished in camp invariably for his polka dot apron. His helpers were recruited from the *totos* — *toto* can mean "boy" or "infant" in Swahili—for whom Nairobi was a place to escape. They watched the caravan being formed out in front of the Norfolk Hotel and followed it off the line of march, out in the bush, until a few days had passed and the chances of being sent back to Nairobi were remote. Once incorporated into the safari the totos carried small loads and worked around the camp. The most interesting of the totos were the self-proclaimed clowns — court jesters — who would caper up and down the line of porters to keep their spirits up with one-liners and jokes, the varieties in their considerable repertoires, apparently, being obscene.

Next down the scale were the tent boys, whose functions were to wait on tables, take care of the bedding, look after personal effects, and so forth. Then came the porters, eighty of them for the size safari of this sort (Johnson's — Roosevelt, of course, had hundreds more on his expedition some twenty years before), each of whom carried a 60-pound load on his head. Lowest in the social order were the grooms, or *saises,* each of them paid 12 rupees a month for his work, an amount which is just under four dollars. The porters actually got paid less ($3.33 a month) but the law required that in addition they had to be outfitted with a water-bottle, a blanket, and a sweater.

One might assume that the safaris of the '20s and '30s had much more activity and spectacle than the expeditions that go out into the bush these days. Possibly. Scale, however, is not the point . . . but rather the rush and novelty of what is seen and experienced. Both my wife and I agree that the most memorable sounds of an African safari were not the dramatic — for example, the coughing roars of lions at night that the loss of Mrs. Ripley's hearing aid had denied her — but rather the sounds of approaching footsteps in the pre-dawn, the knock on the canvas, the rasp of the big-clasped zipper being drawn up, and the cheerful voice, *"Jambo . . . nikupe chai?"* The smell and warmth of tea filled the tent, and because it was the procedure by which each day was introduced, these sounds, especially the zipper, seemed to epitomize the anticipation that any day in Africa brings.

And it's not only travellers on safari who are affected by the African experience. In *Out Of Africa* Isak Dinesen writes of the Masai: ". . . when they moved from their old country, north of the railway line, to the present Masai Reserve, [they] took with them the names of their hills, plains and rivers, and gave them to the hills, plains and rivers in the new country. The Masai were carrying their cut roots with them as a medicine, and were trying, in exile, to keep their part by a formula."

Dinesen is writing, of course, about a tribal equivalent of what was in that heavy shopping bag . . . and more to the point what this present volume supplies — extraordinary words and photographs to keep us (to use one last phrase from Dinesen) from ". . . feeling the shame of extinction falling . . ."

George Plimpton
January 1987

Full Bellies in a Hot Sun

SAFARI DESTINATIONS*
East, Central & Southern
AFRICA

Area of
United States
compared to that
of Africa

ZAIRE

Brazzaville

Kinshasa

Luanda

ANGOLA

NAMIBIA

Namib-
Naukluft

Windhoek

**SOUTH
AFRICA**

Lake Baringo — Lake Bogoria
Lake Turkana/Sibiloi — Aberdares
Samburu-Buffalo Springs-
Shaba
Lake Nakuru — Lewa Downs
Lake Naivasha
Masai Mara — Kampala
Serengeti
Kagera
RWANDA — Kigali
Virunga — Volcans
Kahuzi-
Biega
BURUNDI
Bujumbura

UGANDA

Meru
Mount Kenya
Nairobi
KENYA
Nairobi National
Amboseli Masai
Ngorongoro
Crater
Lake Manyara — Tsavo
Tarangire

Dar es Salaam

TANZANIA

Selous

Luangwa Valley

Nyika

ZAMBIA

Kafue — Lusaka
Kasungu

Lake Malawi
Lilongwe
MALAWI
Liwonde

Okavango Delta/
Moremi Wildlife
Chobe
Lake Kariba/
Matusadona
Mana Pools
Harare
Lengwe
Etosha

Nxai Pan
Makgadikgadi Pans
ZIMBABWE
Hwange
Victoria Falls
(Mosi-oa-Tunya)
Zambezi
River

MOZAMBIQUE

Central
Kalahari
BOTSWANA
Gaborone
Gemsbok
Pretoria
Klaserie
Timbavati
Sabi Sand — Kruger
Maputo
Mlilwane
Kalahari
Gemsbok
Hluhluwe
Ndumu
Mkuzi
Umfolozi — **SWAZILAND**
Mbabane

LESOTHO
Maseru

Cousin Island
Bird Island
Praslin Island/
Vallée de Mai
La Digue

SEYCHELLES IS.
Victoria

La Montagne
d'Ambre

Antananarivo
Eastern
Rain
Forests

MADAGASCAR

*See the chart accompanying
Chapter I. The locations shown
here are approximate only, and no
attempt has been made to show
the exact size, actual or relative,
of each reserve.

I. Introduction

This is the world as it was in the beginning.

Sign at Entrance to Serengeti
National Park

"Safari!" The word, Kiswahili for "journey,"[1] once conjured up images of a trek through unknown and exotic territory. A vision of adventure and possible danger far away in some steamy, sweltering jungle or along the great sweeps of immense plains. Long, single-file lines of sweating native porters, usually dressed in little more than loincloths and always balancing huge bundles on their heads, followed white hunters (themselves undoubtedly decked out in the obligatory pith helmets), the ever-loyal trackers, and stoic gun-bearers. Most of all, wild and exciting animals dominated the picture. Today, the reality of safari is altogether different. The natives — the Africans — are the hosts. And the only remaining constant from the past is the still splendid, though certainly less mythical, wildlife. Fortunately for the animals, the camera has nearly everywhere replaced the gun. Indeed, the modern African safari is far more than another colonial relic. And more people than ever before are, in fact, visiting Africa to see the longest-term inhabitants on earth.

Once long and arduous, requiring stamina and significant investments of time and money, the safari today is within the reach of many and is reasonably safe and comfortable. The visitors return home more often than not with pictures as 'trophies,' instead of the skins, horns, and heads formerly treasured. Moreover, the safari itself yields valuable tourist revenues, in the form of desperately needed hard currency, to the host countries and thus provides the economic justification for safeguarding the vast game preserves[2] necessary for the animals to survive in their natural environments. Accordingly, the African wildlife sanctuaries appear destined to endure awhile longer, because people in large numbers are paying to go.

It is unlikely, however, that the game-viewing will ever be better than what exists today. Quite possibly, it will deteriorate, as many observers expect. The pressures of human civilization, and the resulting tensions between man and wild animals in Africa, are undeniable. We can only speculate just how long the demand for more

---

1. Kiswahili is the *lingua franca* of East Africa; despite the zealous champions of something called "fanagalo" (or fanakalo) and other candidates, no comparable language exists in Central or Southern Africa. The use of Kiswahili reaches all the way from Ethiopia to Zimbabwe and west as far as the Congo. The prestige of the Swahili culture in Africa is relatively recent. The white settlers used the term Kiswahili in a mildy perjorative sense, incorrectly believing it to be a contraction of "kitchen Swahili" — a sort of corrupted "up-country" Swahili learned initially from native servants. Actually, "ki" had an old etymology and was the normal prefix meaning "from" and customarily applied to anything pertaining to a country, especially its language. Thus, Kiswahili originally meant, literally, "language of the coastal people." The Swahili culture itself resulted from the Arab-African mixture on the East African coast and islands, but the term "Swahili" was initially considered, if not an epithet, a sociological "pointer" denoting negative characteristics, such as slave descent, low occupational position, laziness, or rude behavior. Today, the ethnic overtones have faded, and the language has earned official status (as a language of administration and instruction), research centers, and widespread accep-

tance as an acquired speech of daily life of "detribalized" Africans. The language has a musical ring; most safarists find it appealing and quickly adopt a phrase or two. *'Jambo'* somehow draws one closer under the African spell.

2. Throughout the text, the terms "game preserve," "reserve," "park," and the like are used interchangeably — to signify a wildlife sanctuary, where the interests of the animals are officially and strictly protected, but which is nevertheless open to visitors. Within Africa, different terms distinguish the degree of local human intrusion allowed. The International Union for the Conservation of Nature and Natural Resources has set forth a unified system of classification, but the individual countries do not always use the terms in such conformity. Strictly, a "national park" is supposed to be run by the national government and offers complete protection to its fauna and flora, while forbidding any human utilization of the land. A "reserve" on the other hand is controlled by the local government, and, although the preservation of wildlife is a primary purpose, certain human activities impacting on the land, such as the grazing of cattle, are allowed. In any event, the distinctions, mostly political in nature, have little practical significance for the safarist.

farmland will be resisted. People are hungry, the population is exploding, and the governments are young. Poaching, as serious as it is or was, has never posed the threat represented by that other economic activity — agriculture. Loss of habitat, not bullets, constitutes the heart of the problem for most endangered species. Furthermore, drought and other natural phenomena also threaten environmental damage that in today's crowded world may not be as self-correcting as nature eons ago. Thus, wildlife sanctuaries everywhere are under pressure. And, since the turn of the century, African wildlife has disappeared at an accelerated pace. The future, then, of these remaining magnificent inhabitants is not at all assured.

But the visitor to Africa today still confronts an enduring vision — a vision firmly rooted in the past. Much of what one sees was there long before civilization. Certain paleoanthropologists tell us that man orginated in East Africa, but his successors have dominated the earth for a relatively short time compared with the tenure of the wild animals. To be sure, most modern-day vacation-goers do not arrive on the African Continent primed with scientific lore, nor, admittedly, focused on philosophical concerns. Nevertheless, it is impossible for most of us to reach out to Africa and fail to touch the past. And not just yesterday, as an American visiting Europe perhaps, but the distant past. In viewing the game, one inevitably comes to reflect on the relationship of modern man — always an intruder, but now guarantor as well — to the virtually timeless African tableau stretched out before him. An exciting adventure, without a doubt, a safari also turns into a journey of self-examination. The late actor William Holden, who devoted much of his adult life to African conservation, phrased that thought as follows: ''In the vast savannahs of Africa there is a dimension of space and time that is an echo of our own beginnings and which remind us that we were not born initially to live in the concrete jungle.''[3]

Everyone undergoes a private, personal reaction to the wildlife roaming free before him, to nature's triumph of abundance, but few can fail to *feel* the renewal and confirmation of life that the animals provide. Somehow, the lunacy and destructiveness that often characterize human existence temporarily fade from consciousness, as the awesome scenic grandeur of vast herds of game extending across the savannah grasslands as far as the eye can see furnishes nature's reassurance that life will endure. At the end of the day, when twilight ushers in the hush that precedes the changeover in the animal kingdom, the visitor stands amid the solitude of the immense African plains and reflects on those universal feelings that draw the earth's animals (including man) and the land all together into an essential unity. Spiritual refreshment is guaranteed. The African experience enriches our lives.

This book is first about safaris and photographic ''seeing.''[4] The author's goal is to provide the serious picture-taker with enough information and encouragement to enable this latter-day Ernest Hemingway-with-a-camera to return home with trophies that reliably reflect what has been seen — and felt. Trophies, to repeat, that are far superior to their old counterparts: could a cheetah's stuffed and mounted head, for example, ever reveal what a photo does of the fastest animal on land launching into full stride? For those who will go without camera, they should discover that ''seeing'' like a photographer — at least as described here and without exaggerating the point — will often reward extra dividends in understanding and appreciating the animals and thus make the trip that much more enjoyable.

Furthermore, the emphasis in these pages remains squarely on the animals themselves. To be sure, geographical superlatives on this ancient continent abound: the largest desert in the world (Sahara); the longest river (the Nile); in volume, next to the Amazon, the second greatest river (the Congo); the second largest freshwater lake (Victoria); the largest unflooded volcanic caldera (Ngorongoro Crater) — the list goes on and on. But Africa is unique in the richness and variety of its fauna — and this is so even though perhaps as much as ninety percent of the wild game that roamed Africa 100 years ago is gone today. Indeed, in spite of this drastic loss, the savannahs, scrublands, and forests of Africa support many times the number and variety of animals found in North or South America or in Asia.

Some people — primarily, well-meaning Africanists — denigrate animal photography as essentially demeaning to 'modern' Africa, as perpetuating a touristy, ''picture-book'' view of a continent that in reality is struggling with issues considerably more important. From what has already been said, it should be clear that the author regards this view as hopelessly confused. In the final analysis, the wild animals inhabit our earth and only secondarily belong to Africa.[5] The safari represents an opportunity to recapture, however momentarily, a past that has nearly slipped from our grasp forever in only a couple of lifetimes. On the other hand, perhaps a few words are required to justify the absence in this book of photographs taken of the remarkable peoples found in Africa, some of whom will almost certainly be encountered on any photographic safari.

In truth, ''people'' photography, particularly the illumination of tribal cultures, can be a ticklish and ultimately unrewarding pursuit in Africa for the average

---

3. Taken from the ''Introduction'' written by William Holden to Mohamed Amin, Duncan Willets & Brian Tetley, *Journey Through Kenya* (The Bodley Head, 1982), p. 8.

4. This book is, obviously, *not* about hunting. For practical advice, hunters should consult Peter Hathaway Capstick's books, principally *Safari: The Last Adventure* (St. Martin's Press, 1984), *Death in the Long Grass* (St. Martin's Press, 1977), and *Peter Capstick's Africa* (St. Martin's Press, 1987).

5. The author returns to this theme in Chapter X.

tourist, even an accomplished photographer. Most people whom we know in the West enjoy being photographed or at least enjoy having their families photographed. As Susan Sontag has perceptively noted, "good manners" in a photographic society such as the United States requires that the subject pretend not to notice when he is being photographed by a stranger in a public place, so long as the photographer stays at a discreet distance. That is, the subject neither poses nor objects. In Africa, many people still feel apprehensive about being photographed, which act is variously regarded as a kind of personal invasion or an act of disrespect or possibly even the robbing of one's personality. Consequently, the attempt to take a picture may easily lead to problems for which the visitor is not at all equipped. For which a simple, well-meant apology will not suffice. In still other 'African' contexts, highly artificial and essentially unsatisfactory, photography becomes a way to squeeze more money from tourists. Negotiating with a Maasai *moran* (warrior) to take his picture is, for example, going to be one of the most unpleasant experiences on safari. Guaranteed. The basic advice: skip it. In sum, one should leave the tribal cultures to those prepared to invest the time and resources necessary to do them justice.

The text also focuses upon what one is likely to see: those animals most prevalent and doing what comes naturally. Our knowledge — and new and intriguing theories — concerning the wild animals increases nearly daily, and this volume does not accept the often-heard assumption that the typical safarist wants only watered-down science, diluted to triviality and free of challenge. The author hopes to guide the safarist to understand what he is seeing and further to guide him to look for those things that he should be seeing. At that point, the photographer swings into action. Literally millions of pictures have been taken of African animals — but not very many worth looking at more than once. We begin and end with this simple truth: nature photography is primarily representative. The object is to say something significant about the animal in its natural habitat. Photographing a lion in a toilet might show considerable ingenuity, but the result would not be much of a statement about lions. Beyond purely faithful representation, one would then do well to recollect the "mottoes" of some great, non-wildlife photographers: "startle the eye" (Irving Penn); "pull my heart-strings" (Minor White); and "capture the decisive moment" (Cartier-Bresson).

The author is not a professional photographer but professionally is concerned with developing private-sector business in Africa. I have spent some seven to eight months a year in Africa for nearly a decade and, as frequently as possible, have managed to add extensive wildlife viewing to the itineraries. I have accumulated some highly sophisticated photographic equipment along the way, though the exigencies of business do not always permit carrying it along. Only those animals that the author has himself seen or photographed are incorporated

here. And, without exaggeration, these same or similar opportunities represented by the photographs here await the reader. On safari!

All the pictures used in this volume were taken by the author personally, of *wild* animals under strictly natural conditions. The information supplied in the animal chapters that follow comes from my own considerable (in terms of time) observations, supported by the scientific literature and countless lengthy discussions held with those who are spending their lives studying and living amid the fauna. At the end of the book, a selected bibliography for the animals is also supplied. The references given are, for the most part, written for popular consumption. Again, it is worth emphasizing, the material provided here centers on what the safarist himself — properly educated — is most likely to see. If there is a bias, the book favors Kenyan animals, but Kenya is probably the most popular destination for game-viewing.

Having personally covered the territory numerous times, the author could easily describe his own version of the "ideal safari." Such an exercise would be relatively useless for the first-timers or even second- or third-timers. Compromises have to be made. On the other hand, the traveler who hopes to realize the full value of the trip, spend a not inconsiderable amount of money wisely, and return with decent and (dare one hope) one or two breathtaking photographs will avoid the "package tour" at all costs. Every trip, insofar as possible, should instead be planned in detail to satisfy the visitor, who in turn should not hesitate to try to organize the safari to suit best his own goals, means, and companions. The remainder of this chapter is devoted to a discussion — and recommendations, where warranted — of those factors that contribute to planning a successful safari.

The author has read some absolutely shocking advice offered by supposedly knowledgeable individuals encouraging tourists to hop over to Africa without reservations and wing it — an *ad hoc* safari! Promising cash savings (as well as, one assumes, a little special irritation), such an approach seems predicated on a shortage of tourists — a decidedly non-event in safari Africa. For all but the most experienced pros (who are themselves prepared to accept certain disappointments), anything less than detailed planning and preparation is suicidal.

Where To Go

The author takes no firm position on exactly where to go. The possibilities are many and varied; the most prominent destinations are set forth in the chart accompanying this chapter. The chart itself is not meant to be definitive or all-inclusive — only the most accessible reserves or those known personally to the author are described. Moreover, only East, Central, and Southern Africa are represented. Populous West Africa does not have comparable game reserves, though several nations (*e.g.,* Ivory

Coast, Ghana, and Cameroon) are beginning to develop serious parks. Furthermore, political considerations have caused the deletion for now of the Central African Republic, Mozambique, Angola, Ethiopia, Sudan, Somalia, and Uganda. The last —Uganda — is a tragedy. Before Idi Amin, that spectacularly beautiful country and arguably the most hospitable people in Africa had fine animal reserves: Murchison Falls (renamed ''Kabalega,'' but now reverted to its former name), Queen Elizabeth National Park (''Ruwenzori''), and Kidepo Valley National Park. Someday, one fervently hopes, Uganda will rebuild. Certain straws are in the wind. By the time of publication, the process may indeed have begun.

For first-timers, Kenya is difficult to beat. Within a relatively small geography, one can encounter the full range of African habitats: picturesque lakes, stately mountains, apparently endless plains, and dense rain forests. The diversity of wildlife is without equal, and the tourist is valued and encouraged. Travel organization is relatively (for Africa) efficient, and safari standards are generally high; the country has a good road network and efficient charter-air flying; and the guest facilities range from comfortable to superb. The food is frequently excellent. In other words, the Kenyan combination of civilized life and raw nature preserved in the parks is enviable.

At one time, the author could also unreservedly recommend Tanzania as a destination. The Serengeti and Ngorongoro Crater there are still without peer as wildlife reserves. But Tanzania, chronically short of foreign exchange, has not in recent years plowed back a fair portion of its tourist revenues into its safari facilities or supporting infrastructure. Even the main roads are in dangerous disrepair; petrol is frequently sparse; spare parts for the vehicles are simply non-existent; the hotel and lodge rooms lack heat or hot water; light bulbs, soap, and tissue paper are maddeningly unavailable — the list goes on and on and evidences a decline that would put a strain on many visitors. Perhaps, if more of those who love Tanzania would speak out, this extremely short-sighted policy could be reversed. In fact, there is some very recent evidence that Tanzanian facilities are staging a comeback.

Actually, many visitors who now embark on the ''trip-of-a-lifetime'' find themselves returning again (and again) to Africa. An old Arab proverb — ''He that hath drunk of Africa's fountains will drink again.'' — has indeed proved prophetic. Subsequent trips could then be devoted to more difficult or adventurous areas.

When To Go

When to go is dictated in great part by weather considerations, though many destinations are rewarding all year round. In general, the fairly predictable weather patterns permit the tourist to avoid the rainy seasons, usually the best thing to do. For planning purposes, one should also be cognizant of certain local conditions that cause

changes in the animal populations from time to time. An obvious example is the phenomenon of the massive annual wildebeest and (to a lesser extent) zebra, gazelle, and topi migration in the Serengeti ecosystem (which includes Masai Mara in Kenya) that varies according to rainfall. Such factors naturally affect the character of the reserves throughout the year. Some hints as to the ''best times to go'' are also found in the accompanying chart. The single most reliable general rule for good viewing is to visit toward the end of the local dry season: the grass is short, and the animals tend to congregate at the remaining waterholes. But, as the chart makes clear, other factors may be more significant and may dictate a more desirable choice.

Group Tours

As previously indicated, the author believes that the average group tour is a disaster waiting-to-happen. Certainly, this opinion is unequivocally true for the serious photographer. The pressure to ''move on,'' to satisfy everyone's checklist, is the antithesis of the patience and intensity needed to concentrate on photographic seeing. In fact, no serious photographer relishes losing his flexibility and freedom to the collective will, but a safari is likely to prove especially painful in this regard. Moreover, most group tours tend to pack tourists into vehicles like proverbial sardines, making picture-taking difficult and haphazard at best, whatever one's views on basic comfort. On the other hand, a great many people simply will not travel without the security offered by a group. This part of the population should at least try to find a compatible crowd (with ''crowd'' defined as ''as few as possible''), who share similar goals (at a minimum, photography or serious game-viewing). In particular, large mammal devotees have to be on the alert for the ''birders,'' and vice-versa. Many travelers believe that preset tours will save a lot of money. Actually, a good agent can set up comparable custom travel very nearly in the same price range. Nor should the customer allow himself to be bullied by some of the rather snooty operators sitting at the top of the industry who cannot be bothered to explain or discuss a proposed package and who refuse to mend set itineraries.

Aside from the crowd in his own vehicle, the traveler at this time does not have to worry unduly about crowds in the reserves themselves. By necessity, the degree of human intrusion is severely restricted — there simply are not enough beds to accommodate really large numbers of visitors. Even in the biggest and most frequented reserves, and despite anecdotes to the contrary, one is not likely to find more than thirty to forty vehicles on the move at any given time, including the busiest times, and within striking distance of one another.[6] The corresponding draw-

6. With the possible exception of Kruger, Amboseli, and, even less likely, Nairobi National.

back here, is, needless to say, that early booking is always essential.

Getting There

Getting to Africa is relatively easy and reliable. Direct flights (via Europe) leave from New York, and one can also reach much of Africa from the major European capitals. Most of the flights operate, however, only once or twice a week. Once there, flying between African countries is an experience that everyone ought to have — once, to put the rest of life's trials into their proper perspective.[7] A late plane becomes a joy; the alternative is cancellation. "As the crow flies" is a painful euphemism: African crows fly devious patterns. To save time (often, a great deal of time), it is frequently advisable to fly from one country in Africa to another via Europe! The moral, except for the more adventurous: pick a single-country destination, fly there on an international carrier, enjoy, and return. In any event, one should *never* plan on American-type air connections on the continent.

Moving Around on Safari

Moving around on safari is accomplished predominantly by vehicle; most safaris are motorized. Foot safaris are, however, taken in some areas, and "hides" are sometimes used. Boats, horses, and even camels are infrequent but possible exotic options. Most visitors will view nearly everything from their vehicles, which become, in effect, mobile hides and which, despite their noise, the animals have come to regard as relatively benign (and certainly as less of a threat than a human being on foot). There is little doubt that the average safarist will see far more animals from a vehicle than on foot. Consequently, it is critically important that the vehicle used be adequate for the task. A poor vehicle is one of the very few problems that will absolutely ruin a safari.

Two basic types of vehicles are used, with several variations. The tour operators favor the minivan or microbus, which can seat as many as nine. Reputable operators limit the seating to six or seven passengers, thereby assuring everyone a window seat. Modified for safari purposes, the minivans are equipped with pop-up roofs for game-viewing and photography. In fact, most photography on safari is taken from a position standing through the roof of a vehicle, allowing a 360° view and easy camera panning, even when the subject quickly changes direction. During an entire safari, no other perspective is so satisfying, despite the occasional unhappiness over the looked-down-upon perspective that close-up photos may have. One problem experienced with the minivan is that the full complement of passengers cannot use the roof opening at the same time and, from some seats in the vehicle, the passengers cannot use it at all. Another problem concerns the configuration of the pop-up roof itself, which in every commercially used microbus that I have seen does not sit high enough off the roof proper to allow readily the employment of mini-tripods or other similar supports needed to steady telephoto lenses. Of course, some photography is still possible (in many instances, even preferable) through the windows, but it is also quite impracticable to set up a tripod in a fully loaded minivan. In essence, a minivan full of photographers is destined to become a genuine morass. If one is chosen, the safarist should insist that the passengers be limited to a maximum of six.[8] Finally, the microbus cannot go everywhere, despite the extravagant assertions of tour operators and notwithstanding the fancy zebra-striping — crossing streams is difficult; rocky terrain is impassable (and there are animals that seek out such terrain purposely to avoid the tourists); rainy-season travel can be severely limited; and any number of forest tracks are simply off-limits altogether.

In all respects, except seating capacity, the better vehicle is a roof-modified, four-wheel Landrover-type *(1 & 2)*. The best examples have individual roof openings over

Plate 1. The Better Alternative. The all-purpose four-wheel-drive vehicle, ideal safari transportation.

---

7. Whenever frequent African travelers — be they businessmen, journalists, diplomats, or international civil servants — gather, the talk inevitably turns to the misadventures of point-to-point air travel undertaken on the continent. Like their 19th-century counterparts, these contemporary travelers try to outdo their colleagues in recounting the rigors endured. Some of the more harrowing experiences or more complicated routings take a good half-hour or longer to relate.

---

8. In a minivan, the seat next to the driver is the most comfortable but it rarely offers access to the rooftop hatch.

each seat. Four photographers with full gear can comfortably be accommodated, and a fifth passenger can easily sit with the driver. The roof hatches fold away completely, allowing unimpeded access. Most parks forbid passengers from leaving the vehicles, but some allow passengers to climb up onto the roofs. Of course, in inclement weather, the hatches have to be closed, but the same is true with the pop-up roofs found on the minivans, which roofs are not designed to afford more than a little rain protection. The wide-open hatches also provide no sun protection,

one will, however, suffice to give entrepreneurism a bad name.[9]

Whatever the vehicle chosen, the traveler at the beginning of the trip must discuss its condition *on the spot* with the local agent. The agent should know of the tourist's concern and should be present for a visual inspection. The vehicle should be sturdy and obviously well maintained, clean, with good tires and a brand-new spare, and water-tight. Each vehicle should have its own cold box (for refreshments and possibly film) and a fully stocked

Plate 2. Early Morning Drive Spots a Lion.

but one should always take intelligent precautions against the sun (see below), no matter what vehicle is used. Finally, the four-wheel-drive vehicles can go nearly anywhere, rainy season or not, and simply have no equal for total photographic access.

It is a real piece of foolishness for a serious photographer to drive into a game reserve in a normal automobile and expect the same opportunities afforded by vehicles specially designed and modified for safari purposes. And yet, for some reason, one sees the practice all the time. A normal automobile can easily navigate the tarmacs of Kruger, where off-road driving is discouraged anyway, but excellent photographs have little in common with the ability to drive 30 mph. An even more startling choice, favored by some European budget operators, is a large, open flatbed-type truck, into which as many as twenty to thirty poor souls crowd together to see the sights. The reader can well imagine the effect that these leviathans have upon the wildlife. Fortunately, the stupidity of this transportation is (still) evident, and one does not see very many such vehicles in the reserves. Just

first-aid kit. The battery should be in good shape — this last item is most important, as drivers do not always look after their batteries properly and too frequently find themselves in the position of not being able to turn off the engines during safari for fear of not being able to get them started again. As the author will discuss below, good picture-taking periodically requires killing the engine. If the visitor begins the journey with a vehicle that has *any* difficulty in starting, he should quickly climb out and refuse to continue, until the battery is charged or replaced and all connections thoroughly checked. Many a safari has been dampened by sitting for what always seems an eter-

9. This criticism is not meant to include the specially modified, four-wheel-drive Bedford expedition trucks used by at least one reputable operator in Tanzania for carrying the many facilities needed for camping safaris. But these vehicles are never ideal for photography: the perspective is unrelentingly 'aerial,' maneuverability is limited, and, understandably enough, several animals refuse to allow the trucks to approach to a decent viewing range.

nity with a flat tire (and no spare) or dead battery or (no pun intended) under a leaky roof.

A note to all (but especially to women) about to commence a game drive: toilet facilities are scarce to nonexistent in the bush. On long drives, a pit-stop at a lodge or camp facility has to be factored into the day's logistics.

Park Accommodations

The safarist has a choice of accommodations in most parks. For the low-budget traveler or student, designated camping areas or modest huts (called "bandas") are frequently available — in both, the safarist cooks his own meals. Most overseas visitors will choose one of three less Spartan possibilities. The tour groups invariably favor the safari lodges, which vary from tasteful, rustic resorts to garish, tourist-processing centers. All are comfortable; a few have truly memorable charm and character (3). Many now provide swimming pools, beautifully appointed dining rooms, well-stocked bars, and terraces overlooking the game and scenery. Some also offer a round of lectures with local researchers and scientists, wildlife films, and other pertinent activities. The best examples are noted on the accompanying chart.

The second choice is the tented camp. The safarist is housed in permanent, huge canvas sleep tents — very much like what one imagines Civil War field generals lived in — that are established on concrete slabs (4). Each tent has its own attached full bathroom, including a shower and flush (usually) toilet, and a spacious living area (ten feet square or more). Electricity is provided by generators, hot water by a fire. The individual tents also have shaded porches with campaign chairs and tables for outdoor relaxation. A central tent or permanent dining

Plate 4. Luxurious Tent. The author and his mother sitting in front of a tent located in Masai Mara. Each tent accommodates two, sometimes three, guests, has electricity (so long as the generator is turned on), and provides on demand running water that is heated by a wood fire — all the comforts of home, plus the romance of living under canvas in the bush. The experience of staying in a tented camp while on safari should not be missed. The tents that some lodges use for overflow traffic or cheaper beds are, however, not the same and are not included in this recommendation (though adequate for the purposes intended).

facility contains a dining room, bar, and shops and the like. Some camps also have nature walks and nearby hides. Tented camps can be luxurious, accented to standards of considerable comfort and indulging the tourist with superb food. Most are located on the banks of a river or in some other highly scenic position; all are sited in wildlife-favored areas. They can easily cost more than the lodges but more than repay the visitor with their classical safari romance, especially at night. When the heat of the day gives way to the cool of the evening, nothing beats sitting around a campfire when suddenly the deep roar of a lion rolls through the tents and the assembled company.

The third option is the deluxe tented safari, in which the tents are pitched every day as the group moves about; the itinerary is custom-tailored to the specific terrains encountered and the goals of the safarist, though most operators offering this type of safari have preferred sites in mind. Normally, these excursions are

Plate 3. Masai Serena Lodge, Amboseli. A successful harmony between man and nature.

provided only by the more experienced operators,[10] and the best try to recreate the genuine old-time safaris, formerly the almost exclusive preserve of the hunting fraternity. A truck carries the staff and camping equipment (including a complete bath or shower tent and a dining tent; the toilets are not flush but unfailingly hygenic and private) and always precedes the client, who has his own cruising vehicle for transportation. One leaves the campsite for a day of game drives, the staff breaks camp and travels to a new destination, and the safarist arrives at the end of the day to find cold drinks, a hot bath, and exquisite food waiting. The visitor often has an opportunity to develop a personal relationship with his congenial guide and the other company. Such satisfaction does not come cheap — this is the most expensive of all possible safaris — but an adventure of this kind is surely one of the most memorable of all travel experiences.

A special example of the lodge experience should also be singled out — the so-called "Tree Hotel." There are several variations to the theme, but most are modeled after the original, world-famous Treetops located deep in the Aberdare forest of Kenya (5). Typically, the tourist arrives at a related facility outside the reserve where the Tree Hotel is found, has lunch, and is later transported to his destination by bus. The game-viewing lodges are built next to permanent waterholes and salt-licks (natural or man-made), have various viewing platforms and rooms,

and invariably have a ground-level station that directly abuts the land surrounding the waterhole and from which the safarist can, in the wee hours of the morning, safely come eyeball-to-eyeball with a forest denizen. The viewing areas outside are lit by bright spotlights all night long, to which extra 'moons' the animals have long since become accustomed. A visit to a Tree Hotel really must be included in a first-timer's itinerary. If the safarist can manage to stay up all night, he may well have an experience worth repeating to his children and grandchildren:

20 March 'In the viewing lounge about thirty guests were sitting, drinking, talking, or just staring out into the glade. The time was 10 pm. By the floodlit water's edge six buffalo stood placidly grazing or wallowing. Suddenly four hyenas came loping out of the dense bush, passed in front of the now excited spectators and went on to the far side. As they neared cover a cow rhino stepped out and scattered them. She then continued on to chase the nearest buffalo for a hundred yards or so. In the light of subsequent events it would appear that this was her big mistake.

'At this stage a fifth hyena appeared following in the wake of the others, but found it difficult to get past the buffalo and had to change direction several times. The cow rhino then returned to the bushes. The last hyena had gone, the six buffalo started to graze or wallow

Plate 5. The Ark and Elephant Herd in Late Afternoon. The Ark, built in the early 1970s, is the author's favorite Tree Hotel.

10. This trip requires considerable expertise to bring off properly. Therefore, the traveler must thoroughly investigate the *bona fides* of those offering such a vacation. The size of the firm is not necessarily relevant; several ex-hunters and their wives

operate small concerns, with staffs for whom serving the tented safari has become a family tradition. The visitor should generally beware of the operator who has jumped on the "Out of Africa" bandwagon and is offering such a safari for the first time.

again and peace reigned in the glade. One or two guests retired for the night.

'Suddenly the bush across the rush-fringed pool exploded with activity. At first it was thought that a warthog was running, surrounded by the pack of five hyenas, but as they neared, it was seen to be a baby rhino with a "pimple" horn just showing. Each time a hyena got in front the baby howled it over, but twice others were seen to run in and bite at the rear. The milling group had just reached the muddy area on the right of the water when the first buffalo bull arrived, galloping fast. The spectators were now all standing ready to cheer. He waded straight in through the milling pack, lowered his head — and the baby [rhino] was hurled for many yards, rolling over and over in the mud like a barrel. There he lay still.

'The bull then began chasing hyenas in a lunging, pent-up fury. It is easy to bestow upon animals emotions which they do not possess. Probably the buffalo would have treated any species other than his own in the same way, regardless of age. A viewer on the open deck reported later that he heard the impact and a shrill squeal. Doubtless the mother [rhino] heard this too. At all events she burst out of cover at that moment, moving very fast indeed for such a large and heavily built animal. For a few moments it appeared that even now the pack would finish the baby off for, as fast as the old bull chased hyenas away, others were sneaking back for a quick snatch at the prostrate body.

'But the picture was now changing fast as other buffalo arrived upon the scene. The mother was standing over the body, pivoting continuously as she faced each hyena sneaking in. Even so she found it difficult and might have failed had not the buffalo kept up their chasing. At this point, three hyenas came very close to the building and lay down panting before resuming the attack. When the last hyena had been chased from the

glade the baby was seen to be on its feet and no serious injury could be detected through powerful binoculars. Shortly after this both rhinos moved away, our last view being of two rounded posteriors melting into the bush.'[11]

One hint to the safarist looking to improve the usual tour fare: skip the lunch at the outlying facility and the interminable bus ride to the Tree Hotel. The primary consideration originally in locating such a lodge was undoubtedly the density and special character of the neighboring wildlife. The safarist should therefore spend the day investigating the surrounding area by vehicle, managing the itinerary so as to arrive at the Tree Hotel by the end of the afternoon. *No* operator offers such a game drive in lieu of the standard approach (as part of a fixed tour), but, should the safarist insist, an adjustment can easily be made. It is important that the safarist arrive at the lodge well before sunset — in time for late afternoon tea is best. The elephants and buffalos put on their most spectacular show then, and sunset is normally the busiest time at such waterholes.

Travel Between Reserves

Between game parks, the usual mode of travel is by vehicle, either the same safari vehicle employed in the reserves themselves or another used especially for the open road. As yet one more way of justifying what is at heart an economic decision in their favor, tour operators will assert that the minivan provides a smoother ride when compared with the four-wheel-drive vehicles. In truth, the minivan does give a marginally better ride on a smooth road. But, as the vast majority of African roads are rough (or worse, more like Armageddon), the difference is hardly noticeable. (On a really rough road, riding in the back seat of a minibus is comparable to taking a turn at Gilley's on amateur night.) Thus, the question of comfort or discomfort basically relates to the number of passengers along. The question is not academic; drives between parks or between cities and parks sometimes take the better part of a day.

Where feasible, the author strongly urges charter-flying over long distances. The planes are normally reliable and well piloted *(6)*. Arguably, flying is far safer anyway than traveling

Plate 6. Modern Charter Aircraft. Flying by charter aircraft is often the best way to reach a reserve. Most parks have landing strips inside their boundaries or nearby.

11. Taken from the daily log at The Ark, R.J. Prickett, *The African Ark* (Drake, 1974), pp. 108-9.

by road. Nevertheless, the safarist is not in Africa to relive "Tales of the Gold Monkey" and he should fly only in modern aircraft. The expense of flying is obviously greater, but the wear-and-tear saved on the visitor has to be worth a great deal. Indeed, the visitor will receive all the jostling that he might care to have in the parks themselves. The oftentimes bumpy rides experienced between the parks just seem, to this author at least, to add insult to injury. Only a true masochist, for example, would willingly drive from Nairobi to Masai Mara. Yet tour operators schedule the trip all the time. Equally important is the time saved by flying, particularly for the tourist trying to crowd several local destinations into a limited schedule. On the other hand, some road travel would encourage the visitor to see more of the country. This last is certainly desirable and suggests that a balance needs to be reached. In fact, this entire transportation element of the safari should be thoroughly reviewed with the travel agent. As is true with many other features to be elaborated below, the extra expense of charter-flying is a relative matter. An African safari is going to be expensive: the basic costs are unavoidable. It has always seemed to the author false economy to pay these basic costs and to travel all that distance, on what for many will be a once-in-a-lifetime adventure, only to pass large chunks of time driving (uncomfortably, at that) outside the game reserves. But, even if one schedules charter-flying, stand-by land transportation ought to be available in the event of inclement weather or poor visibility caused by fog.

Driver-Guides

First- or even second-timers should never try to take a safari without using a driver-guide supplied through the travel agent or tour operator. The visitor will need the local clout to ensure that the travel scheduled between points is guaranteed and that reservations previously made are, in fact, honored. In addition, driving in these countries, sometimes on the "wrong side" (a legacy from Great Britain), is very much a cultural affair. Finally, a good guide will often prove to be an invaluable ranger in the parks themselves. Some parks have their own rangers, and it is frequently smart (and at times mandatory) to use them as well, especially if one's ordinary driver is unfamiliar with that particular park or comes from a different part of the country. Local rangers know many of the local animals as individuals, not just as lions, or cheetahs, or whatever. This point is discussed in greater detail in the next chapter. In general, the provision of an able driver-guide is another one of those subjects about which the tourist should have a thorough discussion with the travel agent in advance. The driver-guide should be highly experienced (preferably having worked in this capacity for ten or more years), speak and understand English fluently, and know the country, local cultures, and wildlife in detail. A good guide will do no less than ensure the success of the safari.

What Length

On the question of how long should the safari last, the author recommends at least three weeks, preferably four. The reader should keep in mind that a fair portion of the total time will be allotted to traveling. Once in Africa, there is an intoxicating amount to see and do. And Africa is a long way to go to take just ten days or two weeks. Furthermore, a properly designed trip would be broken into several parts, mixing game drives with experiencing (and shopping in) the main cities and even visiting other tourist attractions, including some marvelous seashores. A few days spent at Lamu in Kenya or a week in the Seychelles, for example, cannot be recommended too highly. But the most important point to stress here is that the safarist should take advantage of the full variety of attractions that the game parks themselves have to offer. This approach means visiting a park for days, not hours; staying in tented camps, as well as at lodges; going up in hot-air balloons, where available; and generally trying other means of intra-park transport to change one's perspective — by foot, horseback, or boat, for example. Ballooning especially is an experience that no one should miss (7-9). The trip begins shortly after dawn, when the early morning

Plate 8. Aloft. Once aloft, only the air currents determine in what direction the balloon will go. The pilot can raise or lower the altitude, essentially by heating or cooling the air inside the balloon, but he can choose or guide the path only by seeking different winds at different heights. The ride itself could not be smoother — like floating in suspended animation. Landing is the roughest part of the trip; passengers must take a firm hold in the event that the basket tips over (it often does).

Plate 9. Ready To Land. A "chase vehicle" follows the balloon. If the flight conforms to a predictable pattern, the vehicle will be waiting at landing. When the wind currents carry the balloon into new areas, a not infrequent occurrence, the chase vehicle catches up in due course.

Plate 7. Preparation. The propane-fired hot-air balloons go up at early dawn, but only if the winds are mild and permit a safe flight (and, more important, landing). The baskets each comfortably hold six. As the day progresses and the air is heated by the sun, strong thermal currents form — the skies are then better left to the birds. The season for ballooning in East Africa lasts from July to the end of the following March. A balloon ride is always a memorable experience, but going up over a migration is a particular treat.

breezes are mildest, and lasts little more than an hour. The ride is as smooth as the silk overhead[12] and is ordinarily followed by a champagne breakfast *(10)*. Drifting some 10 mph in utter silence high above the plains, as first light gradually illuminates the landscape stretched out in every direction below, one experiences a sense of primal Africa never duplicated on the ground. The safarist will not forget a balloon ride.

Plate 10. Breakfast on the Plains. The traditional end to the ride, which lasts approximately one hour, is a champagne breakfast. Here, the author offers a toast to the pilot, the diplomatic thing to do.

Above all, a motorized safari is not — or is not meant to be — a window-shopping excursion in a taxi. The purpose rather is to stay with the animals; they will reward the visitor in *their* time. Too many tourists, for example, find a pride of lions, watch them sleep for five minutes, and then rush off to locate the next animal on their list. Had they lingered longer, they would have learned something of the lion and his world. It is during the long, still moments, when the engine is turned off, that nature's richest canvas comes to life all around the vehicle.

_____

12. The temptation of the simile proved irresistible, but the balloons today are made of nylon, like a spinnaker sail. Because the balloons used in Kenya start their journeys high above sea level, where the air is thinner, large balloons are needed to carry passengers. Averaging some 4,000 cubic meters, these are among the largest commercial balloons in the world. Moreover, the strong ultraviolet rays of the sun at the equator take their toll on the nylon — the balloons must be replaced each year.

Health

Certain health precautions are critically important. Many people labor over planning the logistics and itinerary of a trip but develop an unfortunate mental blank concerning their health needs. Yet the medical realities of travel — strange and perhaps unhealthy food, uncertain water, foreign bugs, and jet lag together with other forms of stress — can always sabotage even the best-planned journey. The visitor presumably does not want to waste days confined to a hotel room holding his head or stomach; nor does he want to pick up something abroad that will strike when he returns home. Most of the travel-related health problems are readily preventable, if appropriate precautions are followed. And those infections most commonly acquired abroad are either short-lived or easily cured, once properly diagnosed.

The two primary recommendations are 1) to discuss the trip with one's doctor and 2) to exercise common sense. Prevention of disease is, of course, the intelligent approach to health, and sensible precautions should enable almost anyone to visit Africa without undue concern. The family physician can probably provide most of the immunizations required, but he may not have up-to-date information on exactly which are needed or he may require time to obtain them. The traveler should check with the United States Public Health Service, who will specify what immunizations are currently required for any country in the world. These regulations change frequently. Periodic ''advisory'' memoranda are also issued by the Centers for Disease Control, a free service to travel agents. The United States does not currently require any immunizations for American residents returning to the United States. But, for travel to Africa, as a minimum, cholera, typhoid, poliomyelitis, and tetanus immunizations should be kept current. Possibly yellow fever as well, depending upon where one goes. The traveler should not wait until the trip is upon him to see a physician. Some vaccines can be administered in a single visit, assuming that they are in stock, but others require more than one dose or cannot be given concurrently. A health card, signed by the innoculating physician and validated, must be carried along with one's passport.

Malaria is prevalent in tropical Africa and even increasing in some areas. High-altitude spots like Nairobi are relatively safe, but any trip into the bush risks exposure. Thus, the importance of taking regular antimalarial medication two or three weeks before entering Africa, each week while there, and for five to six weeks after returning home cannot be overemphasized. The usual drug is Aralen or some other chloroquine. A second (sulfa) drug, Fansidar, has, in the past, been added to the regimen for some areas that proved resistant to chloroquine-based antimalarials. The status of Fansidar today is unclear and may no longer be recommended. Both medicines can have potentially serious side-effects, so a physician must be consulted. Wearing long-sleeved shirts and long trousers during mosquito hours, using insect repellent, and sleeping under mosquito netting (as well as using an insecticide bomb — often provided by the lodge — in the room before retiring) should also help.

Hepatitis is often a major health problem in Africa. A gamma-globulin shot administered just before leaving for Africa is one way to safeguard against hepatitis A (the most common form), though there is no absolute prophylactic against its occurrence.[13] Of greater importance than any shot is caution concerning what to eat and drink. The same basic advice applies to the prevention of diarrhea. From his own experience and the wise counsel of others, the author recommends the following:

- *Do* wash hands frequently and always before eating.

- *Do not* drink tap water, even in the best hotels (brushing teeth with tap water in good hotels is probably safe, provided that no water is swallowed; it is always safer, however, to use bottled water).

- *Do* drink bottled water, carbonated soft drinks (carbonation increases acidity, thereby lowering the possibility of contamination), bottled beer, and other bottled or canned beverages with well-known brand names. Wine is generally safe.

- *Do* drink boiled water, but *only* if it has been boiled for at least ten to twenty (preferred) minutes. Chemical treatment (*e.g.*, halogen or iodine tablets left standing in water for thirty minutes[14]) will kill most of the resident bacteria, but not the agents that cause amoebic dysentery. One should also be especially cautious about tea, which is popular and

which has a reputation for being safe because it is "boiled." Very often, however, the water is simply brought to a boil and immediately used. This practice may suffice for locals, who have built up certain resistances; it does not help the tourist.

- *Do not* use ice, unless the water was previously boiled as described. Ice in well-known restaurants is probably safe, but it never hurts to ask. Unfortunately, not even a high-proof drink will kill the bacteria that survive freezing.

- *Do not* eat food or drink juices bought from street vendors or roadside stands.

- *Do not* eat raw fruit and vegetables already peeled, unless served in a reputable restaurant. Even then, it is wise to limit the eating of salads. Fruits peeled by the tourist are fine, as are vegetables washed in good water.

- *Do not* eat dairy products (including cheese), unless pasteurized and kept cold.

- *Do not* eat shellfish. This particular recommendation is, perhaps, too cautious. The author regularly eats shellfish in all the fine restaurants, and depriving anyone of the experience of indulging in the Tamarind (in Nairobi) seems a bit harsh. Nevertheless, a great many people react negatively to shellfish eaten in exotic locales.

- *Do* eat well-cooked foods (meats, fish, poultry). Never eat raw meat. High-acid foods are good for keeping the stomach in an acidic state. In general, eat lightly.

- *Do* eat only at establishments that have a reputation for cleanliness.

Traveler's diarrhea, the notorious 'turista,' in some degree is probably unavoidable. Dining restrictions definitely cramp one's style (especially while "on vacation"); everyone succumbs to one or more dietary improprieties on safari. And even the most prudent precautions will not prevent all attacks. Fortunately, nearly all diarrheas are self-limiting and will clear up in forty-eight hours without antibiotics. Patience is better counsel than the indiscriminate popping of tetracycline. It is important at these times to compensate for fluid loss and prevent dehydration by increasing liquid intake. The author has had success in reducing symptoms with acidophilus pills containing pectin or even Pepto-Bismol tablets.[15] Others

---

13. A vaccine exists for hepatitis B, but it is given in three shots taken over a six-month period. Only those who anticipate intimate contact with the local population should consider this precaution. Moreover, gamma-globulin may offer some protection against hepatitis B.

14. Liquid chlorine laundry bleach or tincture of iodine may also be used as an adequate treatment. The exact dosage depends upon the percentage of chlorine or iodine found in the solution and whether the water is clear or cloudy — for example, a four to six percent chlorine solution common in commercial liquid laundry bleach requires two drops per quart of clear water and four drops per quart of cloudy water; a two percent tincture of iodine solution under the same conditions requires five or ten drops per quart, respectively.

15. The tablets are as effective as the liquid but take a few hours to work; in either form, Pepto-Bismol should not, however, be taken with aspirin.

recommend Lomotil (sold by prescription only), a bowel tranquilizer, or paregoric. Dysentery that does not improve after seventy-two hours or which is accompanied by a fever more than 101°F (with shaking chills) or blood or mucus in the stool should be diagnosed by microscopic examination at a local medical clinic. Blind treatment with antibiotics should be tried only when such clinics are unreachable. Among the most recommended antimicrobials are trimethoprim/sulfamethoxazole, trimethoprim alone, or doxycycline (a tetracycline antibiotic). Some doctors believe that drugs such as vibramycin or neomycin may actually decrease the incidence of diarrhea (the drugs do have side effects), and others believe that tetracycline can actually limit attacks to less than thirty hours by killing the offending organisms.

Adequate rest just before embarking on a trip will pay dividends. Moreover, resting sufficiently during safari is also important in preventing fatigue and stress that could undermine resistance to disease. Maintaining a sensible pace, leaving enough time to make plane and other connections, and avoiding excesses of food and drink are all reliable precautions to follow.[16] If one first arrives in a high-altitude destination, like Nairobi, he should relax for a day or two to recover from jet lag and acclimate himself to the effects of a high altitude. One trick to minimize the debilitating effect of jet lag is to choose a flight that arrives at night, allowing the passenger to retire immediately and adjust more quickly to the new time zone.

Cuts and wounds should be treated promptly in the tropics. Washing with a good antiseptic soap, followed by applying a topical skin ointment such as Neosporin, and then bandaging is the proper regimen. Anyone — even the most meticulous traveler — can contract lice. A bottle of Kwell shampoo is the recommended treatment. One should *never* bathe in a stream or lake in Africa and swim or wade only in salt water or chlorinated swimming pools. Medical studies available at the time that this is being written indicate that AIDS is widespread in parts of Africa — and recently arrived in force in East Africa. Rather than debate the fine points of AIDS transmittal, visitors are simply cautioned to avoid sexual relations with the native populations (black or white), strangers, and especially prostitutes of either sex. Such abstinence is, incidentally, probably the best way also to avoid hepatitis B, the most serious form of hepatitis.

Finally, should a returning traveler become ill, it is imperative that the attending doctor be told exactly where in Africa the patient visited, irrespective of the actual complaint or the length of time elapsed since returning. Doctors are not mind-readers, and some tropical diseases have long incubation periods and vague symptomatology.

The prospective traveler might consider joining the International Association for Medical Assistance to Travelers. "IAMAT" is an extensive network of English-speaking physicians resident in more than 120 countries and 450 cities around the world. Membership is free, though a donation is suggested. IAMAT will supply a wealth of health tips and preventive information, including a world immunization chart that is updated twice a year and a pocket-sized world directory of participating physicians. If a problem develops, the member simply telephones a twenty-four-hour answering service of the local IAMAT center. IAMAT doctors are experts in treating the special ailments that plague foreign travelers. For membership information, write to IAMAT, 736 Center Street, Lewiston, New York, 14092, or call (716) 754-4883.

The author also recommends taking out a membership in the Flying Doctors' Society of Africa. The society exists primarily to supply emergency medical help to rural Africans; membership authorizes the tourist to free air transportation should he become sick or injured in a remote area and require air evacuation. Tour agents can supply current details concerning this service.

Almost parenthetically, it should be noted that Africa is not famous for quality (or reasonably priced) dentistry: before going, visitors would be well warned to have their teeth checked and treated, if necessary.

All travelers should take a spare pair of prescription glasses or contact lenses, if used; contact-lens wearers may be bothered by the excessive dust on safari and may want to have glasses along as well. Any medication regularly used, including contraceptive pills, should be taken in adequate dosages to last the entire trip. For extra safety, really important medicine should be doubled up and kept in separate containers tucked away in different pieces of luggage. To satisfy any challenge by the authorities — the Africans are not sympathetic toward illicit substances — all prescription drugs should be accompanied by the actual prescription itself. A word or two of serious warning: only an imbecile would attempt to smuggle marijuana, cocaine, or the like into or out of Africa; an African jail is a rough experience and a bad place to squander the remainder of one's life. Finally, heart patients should take along a tape of their last electrocardiogram.

Clothing

Clothing requirements are dictated mostly by weather. Safaris basically are highly informal affairs. East Africa is in the tropics, but many safari destinations have high altitudes, where the early mornings and evenings are cool. A wool sweater or two and even a jacket are imperative when out-of-doors at these times. Dressing in layers is the best way to handle the cool hours. A light raincoat and a collapsible umbrella are prudent additions. Clothes generally should be comfortable, lightweight, absorbent (cotton or cotton-synthetics), and in neutral colors. Com-

---

16. Alcohol, like the atmosphere in airplane cabins, has a drying effect on the traveler's body and can increase the chance of contracting a respiratory infection.

fort is especially critical during long game drives; the clothes should fit loosely and permit easy movement. Laundering is usually available at the hotels, lodges, and camps, but dry cleaning can be a bit risky. Laundering facilities can and do break down, however, and not all the tented camps or other bush accommodations offer reliable laundering. In any event, bringing several sets of clothing is recommended. Moreover, the dust on safari is omnipresent, and the safarist will want to change clothes at the end of the day before going to dinner. Comfortable, soft-soled walking shoes are preferred by the author — heavy footwear is not necessary, as there is usually not that much walking on safari. When walking safaris are actually planned, however, boots or shoes with high tops should be included (tennis shoes are not sufficient). A change of shoes at the end of the day is always a good thought as well.

Southern Africa has seasons reversed from those in the United States or Europe — thus, winter in the northern hemisphere means summer in the southern hemisphere. The climate is, however, basically temperate and sunny most of the time. Nevertheless, during our own summer months, warm clothes should be included on safari to Southern Africa.

For evening, casual clothes are worn at the lodges or camps in the reserves. In the cities, a sports jacket for men and a simple dinner dress for women will be needed for dining in the better hotels and restaurants. At some establishments, a tie is required for dinner. Conservative dress is always in the best taste in town.

A hat (crush-proof), sunglasses, and a sun lotion or screen are recommended for sun protection; the African sun is bright, especially near the equator, and deceptively so in the cool air prevailing at high altitudes. And the vehicles are all substantially 'open' to the sun. Another item that might prove useful during game drives is an athletic headband to control one's hair. The author, in common with many safarists, likes to ride standing through the roof hatch for a panoramic view while the vehicle is moving — a sure way to lose a hat (in the wind), but not a headband. The latter also helps to keep perspiration from the camera's eyepiece. Swimsuits are needed, most of the lodges have swimming pools, and a dip taken at midday can prove most refreshing. A lightweight robe and slippers would probably also be appreciated.

Other necessary accessories include: a good pair of binoculars; a small, lightweight flashlight (the electric generators at most lodges and camps are turned off late at night); a transformer kit complete with various plugs, if electric razors, dryers, or other electrical units are used — the usual voltage throughout Africa is 220-240AC[17]; insect repellent (Cutter's is the best, but whatever is used should contain at least thirty percent DET[18]); Wash 'n Dry

towelettes; eye-drops; Kleenex packets; Chapstick; moisturizing creams; vitamins; salt tablets; candles; a bottle opener; a clinical thermometer; foot powder; and a travel alarm clock. The author would like to emphasize that insect repellent will come in especially handy in the presence of African buffalos, who always manage to draw an unimaginable number of flies. Moreover, the bite of a tsetse fly is similar in intensity to that of a horsefly.

Most travelers want to dress the Ernest Hemingway part: this vanity is natural and not necessarily a cause for embarrassment. If one does not have a bush jacket or the like, he can find the "real thing" in shops located in the big African cities. Quality and price vary considerably. An even safer bet, believe it or not, is to buy safari clothing available in the United States at such stores as Banana Republic, Hunting World, Polo-Ralph Lauren, Abercrombie & Fitch, Orvis, and Willis & Geiger (and the stores that feature their clothes). While Willis & Geiger is justifiably known as the Cartier of outerwear, the author has found the safari clothing at Banana Republic to be both "authentic" and durable.

The safarist will want to travel as light as possible. Particularly if camera equipment has to be checked, clothing and accessories need to be held to a reasonable level. In West Africa, with the possible sole exception of Abidjan, clerks at airports forbear assessing fees for overweight baggage in exchange for receiving a slight consideration. In Southern Africa, the airports are, at least as often as not, reasonably lenient. But East African airport officials, the Kenyans especially, are always very strict; excess baggage is recorded, and full direct payment, not "tips," is required — in dollars. Flying to Africa, the *airlines* employ the "piece" system — one is allowed to take a certain number of conforming bags, no matter what the aggregate weight. Returning home, the *airports* in Africa calculate the "basic allowance" strictly by aggregate weight. In some instances, usually when an official is annoyed, hand luggage will also be weighed in order to arrive at the total "check-in" weight. These stratagems, or strict adherences to the rules, depending on one's interpretation, cost the "heavy" traveler a bundle; extra pounds are very expensive. Even those who conscientiously begin their safari well under all limits sometimes find themselves, after purchasing a wood carving or this or that curio, dramatically overweight when flying back home. And considerably poorer.

Documentation/Money

All documentation must be in order. African customs and immigration officials are quite inflexible in the face of documentation problems. Most African countries require a visa upon arriving. Unfortunately, it is often necessary to apply for this visa at the African embassy or consulate here far in advance of the trip. Experienced travel agents and tour operators can usually help break down the bottlenecks, or handle the matter altogether. Equally

---

17. The use of batteries is more reliable.
18. Di-ethyl-toluamide.

important, African countries have strict currency regulations. Travelers should pay as much of the cost of the safari as possible in advance. The remaining currency required should be carried in the form of traveler's cheques. Small denominations are preferable; only as much money as needs to be exchanged for shopping or restaurants should be converted into local currency. There is little point in accumulating currency that is worthless outside the country, and poor rates and bureaucratic hassles greet attempts to re-exchange local currency back into dollars or another hard currency. In all instances, the instructions on the money-declaration forms obtained when entering the country should be obeyed to the letter. It is obligatory to declare how much foreign currency (in cash or traveler's cheques) one is bringing into the country. All exchange transactions thereafter have to be logged on the form. (Incidentally, the best-known credit cards are widely accepted.) Despite the apparent 'with-it' hints dropped by some trendy travel books and the equally *savant* anecdotes spun by returning movers and shakers of various stripes, the author advisedly warns tourists strictly to avoid black-market currency deals; currency problems with the authorities are the last difficulty that anyone needs in Africa. The protection of valuable foreign exchange and the integrity of the national currency are matters of serious concern.

The traveler should also keep in his possession at all times the return airline ticket (at a hotel, all valuables may be checked with the desk clerk for maximum security). Return tickets, incidentally, will be required to show officials at entry points into some African countries.

Before leaving on a trip, one should make two photocopies of one's passport, tickets, first and last traveler's cheques in each batch purchased, credit cards, and identification (driver's license, and so forth). One copy accompanies the traveler, via suitcase; one is left at home with a secretary, relative, or friend. Having adequate identification (and some extra passport pictures) is the key to seeing that a lost or stolen passport is quickly replaced. Replacing a lost or stolen airline ticket is more difficult and varies widely, depending upon the airline and where and from whom the ticket was purchased. Regarding traveler's cheques, the author recommends purchasing only those that can be replaced locally — it obviously makes sense to research this matter and be sure.

A word to the wise: it never pays to show customs and immigration officials one's irritation with the prevailing long bureaucratic procedures. Such 'neocolonial' behavior will only make matters (considerably) worse. To take the psychological stress out of dealing with these officials, one should simply smile and stick methodically to the rules. Some expediting tips: memorize one's passport number and date of issue; for "address" on the arrival form, when in doubt, merely insert the name of a local big hotel; and, in the "occupation" space, journalists or photographers (by profession) should write in something possibly less controversial. The latter are invariably charged special licensing fees.

Insurance

Travel insurance may be a wise precaution.[19] Travel policies often compensate for deductibles in current insurance and protect travelers against risks that are uninsured altogether in current policies. On the medical side, many health plans at home stop short of providing sufficient coverage on a safari. Fortunately, a variety of insurance plans have been designed just for travel emergencies. In addition to accident and illness coverage, these short-term policies also have special travel-related features, like provisions covering emergency evacuation, the cost of a tour if one has to cancel for medical reasons or other unforeseen circumstances, legal assistance, among many other terms. The traveler is also urged to check into the availability of plans that will *prepay* these emergency expenses; most plans are reimbursable only, which fact means that the tourist must pay the bills first — an expense, no matter how temporary, that could be substantial and highly inconvenient. The author recommends an article on this subject found in *American Health Magazine,* July/August 1984. Companies to check include Prudential, Travelers, Mutual of Omaha, Sentry, and AIG (through Berkeley Care), among others.

The second major insurance question is the coverage afforded camera equipment under one's homeowner policy or the like. The photographer should discuss with his insurance agent (it helps to provide a complete, itemized list of all equipment to be insured, its retail values new, the dates of purchase, and the serial numbers) the following:
- protection overseas generally;
- protection against all types of loss and damage, including dropping the cameras and scratching or simply losing a lens;
- a common exclusion concerning damage by customs inspectors (for example, by taking a camera apart looking for contraband);
- provisions that require proof of forced entry into a car from which a camera was stolen; and
- the usual exclusion for damage resulting from "hostile or warlike action" and "civil uprising."

Normal care should, of course, be exercised against thievery. Camera thieves hang out at airports and hotels in Africa, as elsewhere, looking for the telltale aluminum shipping cases and big, flashy camera bags signaling

---

19. The author is not trying to push unnecessary insurance, even to promote "peace of mind." Existing life and homeowner insurance may be adequate, and deductibles usually exist because the insurer prefers to carry the risk himself. In addition, tour packagers and travel agents often include trip-cancellation and other insurance in the cost of their tours. Nevertheless, one should investigate thoroughly exactly what coverage is currently provided by existing insurance. Some major credit cards now offer various emergency aid.

SPECIAL FEATURES

Mt. Kilimanjaro, Africa's tallest mountain, is just across the border in Tanzania, a magnificent backdrop (best views are during the rainy season in early morning). Observation Hill. Olokenya Swamp. Engongo Narok Swamp Circuit. Excellent for cheetah and elephant. Maasai* giraffe. Bat-eared fox. Oryx. Once famous for Black rhino — no longer. Over 400 species of birds recorded. Weavers and starlings around lodge. Amboseli Serena Lodge. Buffalo Lodge (new).
[*When reference is made to the reserves, the official names are used, and the linguistically preferred "Maasai" is, therefore, given as "Masai." At all other times, the longer form is used.]

A miniature Serengeti and the finest all-round reserve in Africa. Breathtaking panoramas. All the plains animals (mostly in the eastern half of the park). Huge lion prides and the finest black-maned lions in Africa. A fair opportunity to see leopard. Millions of migratory herbivores. Ground hornbills. Birds of prey. Mara River. "Mara Triangle." Hippos near Mara Serena. Rhinos at Rhino Ridge. Superb tented camps. Excellent lodges (Mara Serena and Keekorok). Hot-air ballooning.

Second largest park in East Africa. Not particularly recommended for game-viewing. Spectacularly sited lodges (Kilaguni, Ngulia, and Voi Safari). Mzima Springs (hippo viewing). Chyulu Hills. Poacher's Lookout. Occasional huge elephant herds; "red" elephants. Some gerenuk. Mudanda Rock. Tsavo, Athi, and Galana Rivers. Baobab trees. Aruba Dam. Lugard Falls (crocodile). Much of Tsavo East closed to normal visitors. Nearby Hilton Lodges: Taita Hills and Salt Lick.

Variety of rare animals not usually seen elsewhere: gerenuk (antelope), Grevy's zebra, and Reticulated giraffe. Some of the best bird-watching in Africa. Picturesque river. Dik-Dik. Crocodile. Beisa oryx. Banded mongoose. Somali ostrich. Monitor lizard. Vulturine guinea fowl. Sundowner at Samburu Lodge.

Unique and surprisingly pristine montane rain forest, bamboo forests, and rich alpine and sub-alpine flora. Treetops and the Ark ("Tree Hotels" — nocturnal viewing). Rare bongo antelope. Great bird-watching (over 200 species recorded). Black-and-white Colobus monkey. Elephant. Buffalo. Bushbuck. Giant forest hog. Bush pigs. Black rhino. White-tailed mongoose. Chance to see black leopard. Serval. Sunbirds. Birds of prey. Outspan Hotel in Nyeri. Cool climate.

Montane and bamboo forests. Mountain Lodge ("Tree Hotel" — nocturnal viewing). Birds. Colobus monkey. Large buffalos. Climbing. Nearby Mount Kenya Safari Club — unique, superb resort, with peacocks and other exotic birds, luxurious grounds, and a not-to-be-missed animal orphanage (closed to non-members for three-week period around Christmas).

On the very outskirts of Nairobi; easy day, morning, or afternoon trip. Wide variety generally, except elephants. Warthog. Good opportunity for Black rhino. Cheetah. Ostrich. Eland. Zebra. Baboon. Secretary bird. Animal orphanage.

(Jonathan Leakey's Snake Farm is basically defunct.) Island Camp on Ol Kokwe/Gibraltar Island. No flamingoes. Lake Baringo Club and Terry Stevenson.

Birds. Rift Valley views. Hot springs (geothermal activity). Greater kudu.

Birds (nearly 400 species). Hippo. Most beautiful of Kenya's Rift Valley lakes. Hell's Gate. Colonial atmosphere. Crescent Island (birds, antelopes, pythons). Safariland Lodge.

Birds (nearly 300 species). Famed ornithologist Roger Tory Peterson has called the flamingoes here "the most fabulous bird spectacle in the world." Waterbuck. Reedbuck. Rothschild's giraffe. Lion Hill Camp. Lake Nakuru Lodge. New Black rhino sanctuary. Pythons.

Home of the lioness Elsa of "Born Free" fame. White rhino (introduced from South Africa). Giraffe. Tana River. Foot safaris. Similar to Samburu but not nearly as satisfying. Meru Mulika Lodge.

Aquatic and terrestrial birds (nearly 400 recorded species). Nile crocodile (world's largest colony on the eastern shore and on Central Island). Hippo. Volcanic formations. Mammal life on lake shores not abundant. Largest permanent desert lake in the world (and mildly alkaline). Lokitaung Gorge. Lake Turkana Fishing Lodge.

COUNTRY	ANIMAL RESERVES	BEST TIMES TO GO
	Lewa Downs (private ranch)	Anytime but closed May-June and November.
TANZANIA	Lake Manyara (soda)	June-October and December.
	Selous	June-October. Closed March-May (heavy rains).
	Ngorongoro Crater	Anytime.
	Serengeti	June-November (best weather). December-May is wet season. Migration moves the vast herds around (see Chapter VII — Wildebeest).
	Tarangire	June-December.
SEYCHELLES	Cousin Island	May-October is best (most pleasant weather). November-January are rainy months. Islands lie outside cyclone belt, and high winds and thunderstorms are rare.
	Bird Island	
	Praslin Island/ Vallée de Mai	
	La Digue	
MADAGASCAR	La Montagne d'Ambre/ Eastern Rain Forests	Anytime, but April-October is driest.

II. CENTRAL AND SOUTHERN AFRICA

ZIMBABWE	Hwange (formerly "Wankie")	Dry season (April-November). September-October best.
	Lake Kariba/ Matusadona/ Mana Pools	May-November.
	Victoria Falls- Zambezi River	Dry season for best view of falls (mist and spray from falls too strong for viewing during heavy rains), especially August-November.

SPECIAL FEATURES

The Craigs (proprietors). Chance to view game on horseback and on foot. Tented camp (Spartan). Superb food.

Tree-climbing lions. Elephant. Baboon. Hippo. Buffalo. Reptiles. Birdlife on beautiful lake (flamingoes — no way to predict arrival; pelicans; herons; etc.). Sykes monkey. Chance of seeing leopard. Baobab trees. Lake Manyara Hotel (spectacular views from edge of Great Rift Wall). Maji Moto picnic area.

Africa's largest wildlife sanctuary (second largest in the world; over three times larger than Serengeti), bigger than the State of Maryland or the Kingdom of Denmark — six percent of Tanzania. Tanzania's best-kept secret: one of the last great real wilderness areas left in Africa. Animals are truly wild (little contact with man). Outstanding landscape: woodlands, marsh, savannah, and open plains. Largest elephant population in the world. Hippo. Rhino. Buffalo. Crocodile. Wild dog. Nyassa White-faced wildebeest. Sassaby antelope. Few tourists. Boat and walking safaris. Dense foliage not always ideal for photography. Rufiji River and tributaries. Mbuyu Safari Camp. Beho Beho Camp.

The Eighth Wonder of the World. World's largest intact, unflooded, collapsed cone of an extinct volcano. Spectacular setting, Africa's most beautiful reserve. More or less permanent self-contained wildlife concentration and probably the densest in Africa (35,000 mammals for 126-square-mile floor). A natural paradise — as a one-stop animal experience, only Masai Mara in Kenya can compare. Black rhino. Hyena. Cheetah. No giraffes. Lake Makat (also called Crater Lake or Magadi Lake) (soda) and flamingoes. Laiyanai and Lerai forests. Enkoitoktok Springs. Wildlife Lodge.

Most celebrated national park in the world. All the predators. Greatest concentration of plains game in the world. World-famous annual migration depends upon the rains. Animals (wildebeest, zebra, gazelles, topi, and assorted other antelopes) usually leave the southern plains in May and June, moving north and west in search of water and green grass. They begin to return in November. Extensive calving takes place in the short plains (southern) in January-February. Huge concentration of plains animals (over two million) in the central and southern plains from December to May. Fair opportunity to see leopard, especially along Seronera River in Seronera Valley. Lobo (particularly) and Seronera Wildlife Lodges.

After three separate visits, the author cannot strongly recommend: primitive facilities (often uncomfortable), poor food, and sparse animal life. Most numerous mammal was impala. Tsetse flies in abundance. Please note, however: the author has not returned in several years and is reliably informed that the permanent tented camp is now "lovely," "good" food is being served, a swimming pool is being built, and that the oryx, pythons, and other features of the reserve deserve a visit.

Bird sanctuary (internationally sponsored). Fairy terns.

Sooty terns. Seabirds.

Black parrot. Coco-de-mer. Château de Feuilles. La Réserve.

Paradise flycatcher. L'Union (beach).

Lemurs. Orchids. Reptiles. Birds. Unique flora and fauna. Andasibe (Perinet) Reserve. Nosy Be (Lokobe Reserve). Nosy Komba.

Most game species in abundance. Largest and premier park in Zimbabwe. One of the densest animal populations anywhere. Elephant (especially) and other large mammals. Sable antelope. Night drives and foot safaris. Over 400 bird species. Artificial waterholes and hides. Fine accommodations (including luxurious Wankie Safari Lodge). Alan Elliott.

Bumi Hills, one of the great resorts of Africa. Night-hides (Starvation Island). Ume River Expedition (Water Wilderness). Water wildlife. Elephant. Kudu. Fish eagle. Boat and foot safaris. Fothergill and Spurwing Islands. Sanyati Gorge. Jeff Stutchbury and Chikwenya Camp at Mana Pools. Sunsets.

Victoria Falls is twice as high and one-and-a-half times as wide as Niagara. The grandest sight in Africa, with surrounding rain forest (Zambezi National Park) devoid of commercialism. The mile-wide Zambesi is beautiful (launch cruises). Air flights over the falls ("Flight of Angels"). Spencer's Creek Crocodile Ranch. Sable antelope. Victoria Falls Hotel. The Big Tree (baobab).

COUNTRY	ANIMAL RESERVES	BEST TIMES TO GO
I. EAST AFRICA AND THE INDIAN OCEAN		
KENYA	Amboseli Masai	Rainy season ("long rains" anytime from mid-March to early June; possible "short rains" in November, December, and January) is best because of the extreme dust during dry season; moreover, game is more prolific when the two large, permanent swamps, fed year-round by underground springs from Kilimanjaro, are at their wettest. But the rainfall is seldom really heavy in Amboseli, and dust is unavoidable. Calving in March-April.
	Masai Mara	Annual migration from Serengeti crosses and recrosses the Mara, usually from late June to November. Best weather is September-November. Great viewing anytime.
	Tsavo (East & West)	Dry season (July-October [often overcast]; January to mid-March [hot, dusty]), when animals congregate at waterholes. Too lush in wet season for good viewing.
	Samburu-Buffalo Springs-Shaba	End of rainy season (June-July), when shallow Uaso Nyiro River has the most water, is best; but recommended anytime.
	Aberdares (Nyandarna)	"Dry season" (rains occur intermittently year-round); many tracks impassable during heavy rains. Unlike most other environments, early-morning viewing (that is, up to two hours or so after sunrise) is not recommended in rain forests; the fog and mist are too heavy. January, December, and February tend to be best months.
	Mount Kenya	Dry season. Mid-December to mid-March best for climbing.
	Nairobi National	Anytime is fine. February-March and August-October are best (months immediately before rains).
	Lake Baringo	
	Lake Bogoria (Hannington) (soda)	The congregation of birds (especially flamingoes, which are seen in dense flocks only on alkaline, or soda lakes) on any particular lake is subject to a number of fluctuating environmental factors, not all which are completely understood. Visitors are advised to rely only upon up-to-date reports.
	Lake Naivasha	
	Lake Nakuru (soda)	
	Meru	Anytime. Perhaps December is best month.
	Lake Turkana (formerly Rudolf)/ Sibiloi	Anytime not in severe drought. April-May is seasonal high water; September-November breeding season for crocs.

SPECIAL FEATURES

Birds (well over 500 species). Hippo. Rhino. Buffalo. Reptiles. Unspoiled area and most interesting park in Rwanda. Kagera River. Rusumu Falls.

Albert was Africa's first national park (1925). Contiguous with Kigezi gorilla sanctuary in Uganda and Virunga in Zaire. Lower vegetation zones contain variety of montane life: birds, elephant, buffalo, bushbuck, duiker, giant forest hog, leopard, and hyrax. Rare Golden monkey. Most noteworthy animal: Mountain gorilla — the object of a rare and spectacular (but difficult to arrange) safari. Mahabura Volcano.

Full wildlife. Huge, superb area. Night game-viewing tours. Unique Red lechwe antelope. Large mammals. Boat trips on Kafue River. Walking Tours. Chunga Safari Lodge (Village). Musungwa Safari Lodge. Birds.

One of the best parks in Africa. Elephant (made famous by artist David Shepherd). Walking safaris. Hippo. Black rhino. Birds. Luangwa River, a tributary of Zambezi. Thornicroft's giraffe. Primates. Chichele Lodge. Chinzambo. Chibembe. Kapani Safari Camp (Norman Carr).

(See Zimbabwe; the best views are from the Zimbabwe side.) Fenced zoological park.

Off beaten tourist track, but Malawi's most developed park. Unusually warm hospitality. Zebra. Elephant. Antelopes. Lions. Lifupa Lodge.

Beautiful scenery. Off beaten track. Unusually warm hospitality. Rare Nyala antelope. Primates. Basic accommodations. Specially built hides.

Antelopes. Sable antelope. Birds. Unusually warm hospitality. Shire River. Boadzula Island. No satisfactory accommodations. Unspoiled but declining game.

First and best reserve in Malawi. Eland. Birds. No lions or elephants. Flora. Unusually warm hospitality. Basic accommodations. Chelinda Camp. Unspoiled. Chowo Forest. Magnificent scenery. Walking allowed.

Huge lake — ninth largest (surface area) in world and third deepest — is dominant tourist feature. Birdlife. Elephant. Hippo.

Excellent park (formerly part of Albert National Park). Unspoiled countryside. Tropical rain forest to extensive grasslands of open plains to snows on the "Mountains of the Moon" (Ruwenzori). Mountain gorilla. Hippo. Birds. Active volcanos. Unique combination of elephant and buffalo forest and savannah varieties. Lake Edward.

Eastern Lowland gorilla (and pygmy guides). Managed by Frankfurt Zoological Society.

Hides. Birds. White rhino. General variety of game. Mantenga Falls. Horseback tours. "Africa's Switzerland." Gardens. No elephants or carnivores.

COUNTRY	ANIMAL RESERVES	BEST TIMES TO GO
BOTSWANA	Chobe	Dry season only (April-October, but rains can start as early as September); June-September is best.
	Okavango Delta/ Moremi Wildlife (private)	Dry season only. Late May to August best, when Delta is flooded by Okavango River. December-March wet season not recommended, and rains sometimes close Moremi.
	Nxai Pan	Rainy season (November-April; slight rains in May).
	Makgadikgadi Pans	Rainy season. January-April is best.
	Gemsbok	February-May.
	Central Kalahari	June-August. "Kalahari" means "thirst," but the Kalahari is not a desert like the Sahara, only a desert in that it has little permanent water and no permanent surface water. Rainfall is highly unreliable, but, in non-drought years, rains nourish rich vegetation, especially in the northern parts. December-February often sees torrential rain.
SOUTH AFRICA	Kruger/Sabi Sand (private)/ Timbavati (private)/ Klaserie (private)	July to mid-September, when grass is low and animals better seen. This is South Africa's winter (50° F). Weather is best September-November. Rainy season is December-February. Kruger, including the north, is now open year-round.
	Hluhluwe	Mid-May to mid-September.
	Umfolozi	Mid-May to mid-September.
	Kalahari Gemsbok	March-October are good (other months are too hot); March-May are best months. Calving in October.
	Mkuzi	April-October. Others recommend September-May!
	Ndumu	Anytime. Hottest month is February. Coldest is July. May-September are best months.
NAMIBIA	Etosha	Mid-March to October; August-September is best (animals congregate at waterholes). Park is closed to tourists in rainy season (from November).
	Namib-Naukluft	March-October.

SPECIAL FEATURES

Botswana's most accessible park. Unique combination of swamp and savannah. Chobe River and waterways of Linyanti, including Savuti Channel. Gubatsa Hills. Acacia parkland south of Savuti Marsh. Most game in abundance. Several rare species of antelope; rare Chobe bushbuck. Unspoiled area, a great park, and few tourists. Birds of prey. Carmine bee-eaters. Special accommodations, including Chobe (Safari) Game Lodge. Allan's Camp. The Grahams (Linyanti). Elephants.

Largest private game park in the world (Moremi), owned by the Tawana tribe. Spectacular reserve. Khwai River Lodge in Moremi. Delta is the greatest single wildlife wilderness in Southern Africa and arguably the "last frontier in Africa." Boat (including canoeing —in *mekoros*) safaris. Waterbirds. Like Chobe, spectacular combination of swamp and savannah. Red lechwe antelope. Hippo. Crocodile. Baboon. Lake Ngami (birds). Maun. Sitatunga (the boar). Xugana and Tsaro Camps. Xaxaba Lagoon and Xaxaba Camp (Rawsons). San-Ta-Wani Lodge. Khwai River Lodge. Crocodile Camp.

Pans are shallow ponds that collect surface water, which evaporates under intense sun. The ponds turn to mudholes, then dry out altogether and crack. Large herds; wildebeest, zebra, and giraffe. Bat-eared fox. No accommodations.

Largest salt pans in the world. Oryx. Predators. Nighttime safaris. Possible huge concentrations of flamingoes (May-October, when water in pans). No accommodations.

Even larger than sister sanctuary in South Africa but unfortunately generally closed to visitors (need special permission).

Everything but elephants. Over one million herbivores. Kongoni, wildebeest, gemsbok, giraffe, eland, springbok, and ostrich in profusion. Difficult to get permits to visit. Trips must be carefully planned. No accommodations.

Kruger was among the first national parks founded in Africa. Immense — it is bigger than the Serengeti (260 miles south to north) — Kruger is one of the great natural sanctuaries in the world but completely man-managed (for example, most of park is fenced, artificial waterholes are everywhere, and the roan antelopes are vaccinated *each* year against anthrax). Competes with Kenya for tourists. Can accommodate 3000 people in a day; often completely booked, leading to a shortage of rangers. 1000 miles of tarmac and gravel roads; many back roads closed to tourists; and no off-track driving. Many roads are designed (unfortunately) to skirt natural animal congregations at a considerable distance. Many animals acclimated to vehicles. Northernmost part (Lebombo ironwood, primeval baobab forests of Mashikiri Plateau, Hlamalala Plains, etc.) the most interesting. Uitkykpunt overlook. Olifants, Wolhunter, or Nyalaland Wilderness Trails: foot safaris. Olifants Rest Camp. Virtually all the animals of Southern Africa. Big-tusk elephant, White rhino, Nyala antelope. Luxurious camps in the three private reserves to the west of Kruger, especially Mala Mala in the Rattray Reserves of Sabi Sand. Vartys' Londolozi and the small Inyati of Sabi Sand. White lions of Timbavati. Tsessebe. Spotlight nighttime safaris. Hot-air ballooning.

White rhino. Big game and antelopes. Nyala. Lion. Zululand Safari Lodge.

(Linked to Hluhluwe by "wilderness corridor.") Foot safaris: Wilderness Trail and Primitive Trail. All big game but elephant. World's largest concentration of White rhino. Small park — advance reservations required. Dumisani Ngobese (ranger).

Unspoiled and remote, one of the great parks of Africa. Adjoins Botswana's Gemsbok. Gemsbok. Vast herds.

Beautiful Reserve. Excellent hides. Bube Pan. Nhlonhlela Pan and Trail. Hides. Birdlife. Impala. Petrified forest.

"Pocket-sized Okavango." Limited accommodations. Hippo. Birdlife.

Once the world's largest (at four times the current size). Lion. Elephant. Huge numbers of various antelopes. Mountain zebra. Rhino. Wild, hot, and dusty. Okaukuejo waterhole (floodlit at night). Ombika waterhole. Much of park closed to tourism. Flat landscape. Namutoni Camp.

Even larger than Etosha. Namib sand dunes. Kuiseb River Canyon. Sandvisa (Sandwich Harbor). Naukluft Mountains (limited access). Mountain zebra. Limited accommodations.

COUNTRY	ANIMAL RESERVES	BEST TIMES TO GO
RWANDA	(A)Kagera	Dry season (June-August).
	Albert/Volcans (Parc National des Volcans)	Dry season (June-August). Avoid rainy seasons (October-November "short rains"; February-May), during which rain can be heavy.
ZAMBIA	Kafue	Mid-June (end of rains)-October.
	Luangwa Valley (South Luangwa)	May-October.
	Mosi-oa-Tunya (Victoria Falls)	June-October.
MALAWI	Kasungu	May-December.
	Lengwe	June-December. Closed in March.
	Liwonde	May-December. Second half of dry season, when animals congregate along Shire River. Closed in rainy season.
	Nyika (Malawi National)	August-November.
	Lake Malawi	May-October.
ZAIRE	Virunga (Parc National des Virungas)	December-June.
	Kahuzi-Biega	December-June.
SWAZILAND	Mlilwane	Dry season (April-September).

expensive equipment. The author returns to this last point in Chapter II. The traveler should also consider registering his photographic equipment with U.S. customs before going, especially should he travel, leaving or returning, via Europe. The author has never encountered the problem, but the horror stories of paying duty on new-looking equipment upon returning should perhaps be heeded.

The Safari Operator

The best — or the worst — for last. In the final analysis, it is not terribly difficult to plan and achieve a first-class safari: go with good people and choose a good operator. Choosing a good operator is like selecting any major contractor — one relies on recommendations, reputation, and the responsiveness of the operator to serious probing by the potential client. The reader should talk to several operators and do so well before a planned trip. It helps to let them know that one has reasonable expectations. It may help to let them know that one has read this book. Unfortunately, the good reputation of some operators is not deserved. Many people know so little about the full potential of a safari that they happily settle for something far less. Indeed, the animals will probably do their part even on the most ill-conceived safari. Too many operators try to sneak by on a *de minimis* basis; the typical client has only a vague sense of anything missing and chalks up his disappointments to "Africa."

On the other hand, a great many operators can put together a superb safari package — if so encouraged by their clients. But the client must educate himself before he can realistically hope to ask the right questions and evaluate the answers.

A final cautionary note: one should understand in detail the cancellation terms of any prepaid trip.

. . . .

Generally, the tourist must approach Africa, from a travel perspective, with patience and flexibility. One should always expect a hitch or two, at a minimum, to arise in the execution of travel plans, even the best laid plans. Maintaining a sense of humor is always invaluable. The author also recommends that every traveler attempt to memorize a few simple words and phrases in the indigenous language ("please," "thank you," and "good-bye," at least). On the other hand, one should not try to be anyone other than a good American, Britisher, Frenchman, or whoever, as the case may be; the Africans, if shown proper respect and honesty, are prepared to accept the tourist for what he is. It is certainly recommended that the traveler read something about the recent history, culture, and politics of the country or countries to be visited. An important aside: photographers must avoid shooting photographs at the airport or of harbors, soldiers, or anything else remotely "sensitive."

A final introductory tip concerns reading materials and other items of an educational nature. There are some fine picture books on African animals. A few even contain intelligent texts. Reading one or two, in addition to this volume, cannot help but further a visitor's understanding and appreciation for what he is going to see. And a photographer cannot learn too much about his subject. One caveat to virtually all "diary" books, as good as the pictures may be: the format seemingly tends to promote "exaggerating" the connection between the text and pictures. A frequent (and infuriating, to those who know better) liberty, for example, is to label a lion "roaring," when it is actually yawning. Notwithstanding many other examples, the author recommends and hereby acknowledges his own debt (as indicated) to the following:

Leslie Brown, *Africa: A Natural History* (Random House, 1965) (an old standard; comprehensive but superseded in many parts by later knowledge);

Maitland A. Edey & John Dominis, *The Cats of Africa* (Time-Life, 1968) (good information and superb pictures, but many of the latter taken artificially, using bait or pets, and sometimes at zoos);

F. Rodriguez de la Fuente *et al.*, *World of Wildlife: Africa*, 3 vols (in English translation) (Orbis Publishing, 1971-72) (difficult to find; encyclopedic, but text now seriously outdated; surprisingly good pictures for the time);

Peter Matthiessen & Eliot Porter, *The Tree Where Man Was Born/The African Experience* (Collins, 1972) (poetic);

Norman Myers, *The Long African Day* (Macmillan, 1972) (the "bible"; if one could read only one book on African wildlife — and there are few enough books of this distinction on any subject — this would be it);

Harshad C. Patel, *Vanishing Herds* (Stein and Day, 1973) (fine, memorable pictures taken with a Hasselblad format but all in black-and-white, an impossible medium to capture wildlife in all its glory);

Hugo van Lawick, *Savage Paradise: The Predators of Serengeti* (Collins, 1977) (noted African wildlife photographer and many unique pictures);

Peter Johnson, Anthony Bannister, & Creina Bond, *Okavango: Africa's Last Eden* (Country Life Books, 1978) (beautiful book on what may well be the last frontier of wildlife Africa);

Brian Jackman & Jonathan Scott, *The Marsh Lions: The Story of an African Pride* (Elm Tree Books/Hamish Hamilton, 1982) (a special book, to be read and reread for a moving portrayal of life in the African bush; with superb photographs);

Günter Ziesler & Angelika Hofer, *Safari: The East African Diaries of a Wildlife Photographer* (Facts on File, 1984) (magnificent pictures);

Elspeth Huxley & Hugo van Lawick, *Last Days in Eden* (Amaryllis Press, 1984) (good book, with many controversial assertions);

Tom Brakefield, *The African Book* (African Heritage

Book, Amwell Press, 1984) (privately printed, expensive volume, with excellent photographs and a particularly good section on often-neglected antelopes; the text is disappointing, in part just absurd);

Jonathan Scott, *The Leopard's Tale* (Elm Tree Books, 1985) (Scott continues to define what great wildlife photography is all about — this volume contains pictures that most of us can only aspire to achieve[20]);

Isak Dinesen's Africa: Images of the Wild Continent from the Writer's Life and Words (Sierra Club Books, 1985) (enjoyable book, but 1985 is too late in the day to confuse a giant forest hog with a warthog — at pp. 46-7 — and several of the photographs have been published in the other books listed here); and

Allain Bougrain-Dubourg (writer) & Yann Arthus-Bertrand (photographer), *Tender Killers* (English translation) (Vendome Press, 1985) (this book should be enjoyed entirely for its remarkable photographs, though the best lion shots were previously published in Anne & Yann Arthus-Bertrand, *Lion* (Hachette Realites, 1981); from its title to its picture captions, the text is so scarred by inaccuracies and unrelenting *bêtises* as to be virtually useless — at least, the endless grammatical difficulties presumably can be traced to a careless translation from the French).

These titles are all books whose photographs go well beyond a single species — the reader should consult the bibliography for picture books on a particular animal.

As satisfying as reading (or at least looking at) any of the preceding books would be to see one (or more) of Alan Root's justly acclaimed wildlife films: *Serengeti Shall Not Die* (Root was the cameraman); *The Great Migration: Year of The Wildebeest*; *Mysterious Castles of Clay*; *The Mysterious Spring: Africa's Mzima*; and *Secrets of The African Baobab*. Root is a rare commodity operating in a tricky medium. Unfortunately, many moviemakers, in addition to showing wildlife in faked situations (that may or may not occur in nature), also disturb the animals, even to the point of injuring or killing them. Indeed, it has been stated by one well-known filmmaker that "faking is a fundamental tool of the wildlife film industry."[21] Although

Root has tried to avoid manipulating animals, he has occasionally filmed scenes under controlled conditions. And the film is not always edited honestly. Nevertheless, Root *is* good. I can also recommend Simon Trevor's films, perhaps the best-known being *Orphan Animals of Tsavo*.

A final, preparatory visual suggestion: the Akeley Hall of African Mammals in the American Museum of Natural History located in New York City has twenty-eight different displays, on two levels, habitat groupings known as "dioramas," that are truly windows to nature. Recently cleaned and revamped, these three-dimensional, naturalistic presentations enjoy great realism and are accurate down to the leaves of the plants amid which the animals stand.

Useful field guides and guides particularly devoted to the game reserves have been prepared:

Michael Gore, *On Safari in Kenya* (Kenway, 1984) (a reasonably up-to-date guide);

David Western, *A Wildlife Guide and a Natural History of Amboseli* (David Western, 1983) (excellent guide by an outstanding authority, with fine drawings, but unfortunately available — and sparingly — only in Kenya);

Denise E. Costich & Joseph L. Popp, *Mara — A Field Guide to Masai Mara Reserve* (Man and Nature Press, 1978) (brief, but one of the best guides to an African animal park ever done — highly recommended);

Reader's Digest Illustrated Guide to the Game Parks and Nature Reserves of Southern Africa (Reader's Digest Association of South Africa, 1983) (a thorough and informative volume, with the added feature of excellent photographs);

Three serviceable general guidebooks to birds: John G. Williams & Norman Arlott, *A Field Guide to the Birds of East Africa* (Collins, 1980), Jonathan P. Scott, *African Birds* (Kensta Nairobi, 1981), and Ian Sinclair, *A Field Guide to the Birds of Southern Africa* (Collins, 1984);[22]

Jean Dorst & Pierre Dandelot, *A Field Guide to the Larger Mammals of Africa* (Collins, 1972) (standard);

T. Haltenorth & H. Diller, *A Field Guide to the Mammals of Africa Including Madagascar* (Collins, 1980) (standard);

Reay H.N. Smithers, *The Mammals of Rhodesia, Zambia and Malawi: A Handbook* (Collins, 1966) (standard); and

John G. Williams, *A Field Guide to the National Parks of East Africa* (Collins, 1981) (standard, but somewhat dated).

Many parks have small pamphlets on their environs. The best examples perhaps were those published by the

---

20. As the text in Chapter IV will emphasize, leopards are the most difficult of animals to photograph. Of course, the reader should realize that the Scotts and van Lawicks of the world spend their working lives among the animals that they are photographing. Scott, for example, has spent the better part of the last eight or so years in Masai Mara. A bonus with Scott's books are the drawings. Several years ago on safari in Kenya, my mother, an artist of note, met Jonathan at Kichwa Tembo Camp in Masai Mara. When she saw his drawings that were soon to be published in the *Marsh Lions,* she commented, "I don't know what you are doing with a camera, when you can draw like this."

21. A Canadian Broadcasting Corporation documentary entitled "Cruel Camera" that was recently shown on public television looks at the cruelty inflicted on animals by some filmmakers

---

and some actual fraud as well. As one film critic has observed, the great outdoors is a staple on public television, and this documentary is an eye-opener!

22. For additional and more specialized titles, the reader should consult Chapter IX and the Bibliography.

Tanzania National Parks. These truly excellent, charmingly illustrated guides are today virtual collector's items: when the last editions ran out, new copies, in typical fashion, were not printed. Surely, they would pay for themselves.

While this volume was being written, a book entitled *The Wildlife Parks of Africa,* written by Nicholas Luard in conjunction with the World Wildlife Fund, was published (Salem House, 1985). A curious effort, the book is divided into two parts. Part I, after a fairly gratuitous eleven pages on the "History of the Continent," contains a general discussion on conservation and the growth and management of national parks in Africa. Although Chapter 6 is eloquent in its defense of conservation, Part I generally is not impressive for 1985, considering all that has been written on the subject. The reader would do better to concentrate on Myers, *The Long African Day,* previously mentioned. Part II is a list, compiled with the aid of the World Wildlife Fund and the International Union for the Conservation of Nature and Natural Resources, of 161 national parks south of the Sahara. Remarkably, the list is *filled* with inaccuracies. For example, the rainy and dry seasons are sometimes reversed (Botswana), basic closure policies of some parks are incorrectly given (Kruger), and this author at least disagrees with many of the recommendations for when is the "best time to visit" particular parks. Mr. Luard apparently has spent some time in Africa, but one is, however, entitled to wonder about a book that places Zaire and Sudan (!) in "West Africa." The point to be emphasized here is simply this: safarists, who inevitably will spend thousands of dollars in great anticipation of their trip, are entitled to correct, up-to-date information and recommendations based, insofar as possible, on firsthand experience. "Official data" is rarely a satisfactory substitute. *The African Safari* represents an attempt to fill a significant gap in this regard.

Finally, a few general guidebooks for tourists can be recommended. Perhaps, the best series on Africa is that published by International Communications in London, of which these two volumes are pertinent: *Traveller's Guide to East Africa and the Indian Ocean* (1986) and *Traveller's Guide to Central and Southern Africa* (1986). A well-informed addition, whose more limited perspective is announced in its title, is Hilary Bradt and Kriegor Conradt, *Backpacker's Africa* (Bradt Enterprises, 1983). The section on "natural medicine" is, however, a little difficult to swallow. Three other possibilities are Alan and Kerstin Magary, *East Africa: A Travel Guide* (Harper and Row, 1975); Nina Casimati, *Guide to East Africa* (M. Haag, 1986); and Jeffrey Lance, *Overland Through Africa* (Capital Press, 1983). Fodor has recently (1985) produced a truly excellent volume on Kenya, though some of its information on safaris is a little flaky.

The Hildebrand series, handy to carry and with concise and valuable texts far better than most, has produced volumes on the Seychelles, Mauritius, Kenya, and South Africa. The Berlitz series is not recommended. A good guide for the budget-conscious visitor but relevant here mostly for its generally fine descriptions of the countries and game parks is J.R. Yogerst, *East Africa with Zambia and Malawi* (Roger Laselles, 1985). The recently published *Insight Guide: Kenya* (APA Publications, 1985), edited by Mohamed Amin and John Eames, is a beautifully produced guide — with fine pictures by Amin and Duncan Willetts — that contains a challenging but not always accurate text. The safari information is disappointing. Finally, Sherry A. Suttles and Billye Suttles-Graham, *Fielding's Africa: South of the Sahara* (William Morrow, 1986) is comprehensive but far better on West Africa than East, not particularly up-to-date, and contains scarcely any useful safari information. Of course, a major problem with all guides that purport to be comprehensive is the inevitable errors that appear. Pity, for example, the poor tourist who expectantly turns up at "The Secret Valley Lodge. . .located in dense forest on the slopes of Mt. Kenya. . .which offers glimpses of leopard, rhino, elephant and buffalo, as well as other forest animals clustered around the Ondari waterhole" (Yogerst, p. 118) and which burned down several years prior to publication of the guide.

For information concerning conservation efforts in Africa and on behalf of African wildlife, the reader is advised to consult the leading group in the United States, The African Wildlife Foundation, whose headquarters are found at 1717 Massachusetts Avenue, N.W., Washington, D.C. 20036, telephone (202) 265-8394.[23] Major recent AWF projects concern the Mountain gorilla, the rhinoceros, and rehabilitation efforts in Uganda. The Foundation is known for its training programs and the contribution of equipment and spare parts to national parks, its handbooks and field guides, research projects and surveys, and financial support for African colleges of wildlife training.

The safarist should be aware that strict laws are in force in the United States (and elsewhere) governing the import of animal skins and any products made from animals. Some of the most beautiful and interesting souvenirs, offered for sale in safari Africa are made from the furs, hides, shells, feathers, teeth, and so forth of animals threatened with extinction and protected by the International Convention on International Trade in Endangered Species of Wild Fauna and Flora (CITES). It is illegal to import many of these into the United States. Obviously, assurances by the vendors are unreliable, and, if a purchase is confiscated by Customs, no refunds are guaranteed. Moreover, monetary penalties apply in some instances. Useful information in this regard is available from the U.S.

---

23. The entire staff at AWF is uniformly cooperative, but the author wishes to express special thanks to the Vice President of AWF, Diana E. McMeekin, for sharing her library, lending her general encouragement, stimulating our several discussions, and reading this volume in manuscript.

Department of the Interior, but an interested reader should also contact the World Wildlife Fund-U.S. at 1255 23rd Street, N.W., Washington, D.C. 20037, (202) 293-4800. Part of a worldwide network of twenty-three national World Wildlife Fund organizations, WWF (now associated with The Conservation Foundation) actively monitors commerce in flora and fauna.

Plate 11. Marabous over the Mara.

II. Taking Photographs on Safari

Nowadays great sportsmen hunt with cameras. The practice started while I was still in Africa; Denys as a white hunter took out millionaires from many countries, and they brought back magnificent pictures, the which however to my mind (because I do not see eye to eye with the camera) bore less real likeness to their object than the chalk portraits drawn up on the kitchen door by our Native porters. It is a more refined sport than shooting, and provided you can make the lion join into the spirit of it you may here, at the end of a pleasant, platonic affair, without bloodshed on either side, blow one another a kiss and part like civilized beings.

Isak Dinesen, *Shadows on the Grass*[1]

At a relatively high level of abstraction, taking successful photographs on safari requires three different abilities. One must first find and then approach the animals, for which knowledge, information, and planning, as well as skill, are needed. Second, one must be able to rely upon experience to handle the appropriate photographic equipment quickly and confidently. In the face of fleeting phenomena, technique must be sharp. And, third, one must summon the visual ability to see a good picture — a not entirely learned process, but one toward which a few pointers can go a long way.

At the outset, the author ought to express some basic prejudices and choices that underlie and influence his approach to safari photography and hence this chapter. First, I believe that only color film can fully convey the safari message. For greater realism and emotional impact and to give that extra measure of atmosphere and immediacy, color seems indisputably the preferred medium. I simply would not consider taking black-and-white film on safari. Second, and without denying the benefits of creativity generally, I have always subscribed to the philosophy that the basic criterion of good nature photography is realism. Although perhaps not as strictly limiting as traditional botanical and zoological illustration, realism depends, for the most part, on both definition and "correct" color. Definition is primarily sharpness of detail and the general clarity of a photograph resulting from accurate focusing and other good techniques, on the one hand, and the quality and resolving power of the lens

used, on the other. "Correct" color varies, of course, with the lighting, but the indiscriminate recording of color does not automatically make a color appropriate. Moreover, a photograph can be pleasingly color-saturated and can show desirable color contrast and still fall short. Careful esthetic control is required to reproduce faithfully what the naked human eye sees and thus what we call "natural color."

Third, I prefer slide film to print film and shoot very few negatives. Nonetheless, both film types are discussed in this chapter. Fourth, I can recommend only the 35mm single-lens-reflex camera for the field — no adequate substitute really exists. Rugged, lightweight, and relatively silent, with a broad range of interchangeable lenses, the sophisticated 35mm SLR system is unmatched for convenience and performance on safari. With mirrors eliminating the possibility of parallax error, the photographer can see through the lens exactly what will appear on film. I have, on occasion, used a medium-format camera with a prism finder that operated like an SLR (corrected image, with action going in the right direction) with good results. All else being equal, of course, the larger format will produce better finished prints, with better contrast and tonal quality, less grain, and less magnification of focusing errors. But "all else" is rarely equal on safari. And recent improvements in film have all but eliminated the lack of sharpness that used to characterize enlargements of 35mm film.

Today, one may argue that the unprecedented revolution in camera technology, especially as represented by the newer "point-and-shoot" cameras or by the auto-focusing lenses now available, has made obsolete much of the equipment discussed below or advice that follows. It is true that a technology that allows a photographer to

---

1. Originally published by Random House, 1961; Vintage Books Edition, 1974, p. 58.

concentrate on composition, while his equipment automatically decides the technical questions of exposure and focus, will at least occasionally today achieve results that rival those produced by the older professional cameras. But the author, who trusts technology (old and new) only up to a point, prefers a more manual approach. Nevertheless, it must be admitted that the auto-focusing technology now available undoubtedly represents a quantum leap in 35mm SLR photography. The two leading auto-focusing systems are Minolta's Maxxum and Nikon's 2000 series. Minolta (9000, 7000, or 5000, with the 9000 being the "professional" version and the 5000 the less expensive "popular" camera) was first off the block and probably remains the leader. The Minolta system has fifteen different interchangeable lenses, including several compact macro/zooms and a 60mm telephoto. Nikon (the 2020 is the professional version) has also produced a wide selection of AF lenses but additionally has invented a converter that makes auto-focusing possible with more than thirty current manual-focus Nikkor and Nikon Series E lenses. Both systems allow for auto-exposure as well and have several features that mechanically make exposure adjustments. In fact, what we now have in camera technology is a highly sophisticated point-and-shoot capability. The author has not tried this new gear in the field and, after studying the technology, I have reservations about the *speed* and *accuracy* of these systems on safari. And what I have seen is fairly complex to operate. I do, however, frequently use the automatic exposure features on my cameras, which features allow me to set the aperture and the camera automatically to match the "correct" shutter speed (so-called "aperture-priority" type). Other automatic cameras allow the photographer to set the speed, and the camera then sets the f-stop. Some fully programmed cameras will work either way. Experience has proved, however, that even here the judgment of the photographer is often superior to the averaging or programmed exposure features of the camera itself. Esthetic judgment can be aided by technology but is swallowed up by it only at significant cost.

Actually, what can be called "conventional" (that is, non-automatic) technological improvements for some time now have been transforming wildlife photography. On safari, shots are possible today to the average first-timer that were unthinkable to professionals only ten to fifteen years ago. In addition to the improvements in film already noted and further elaborated below, cameras are increasingly sophisticated, yet simpler to use, both results a function of electronics. Lenses give brighter and sharper images. And accessories are keeping pace. Altogether, picture-taking technologies today have opened up unparalleled opportunities to the safarist.

The amateur movie camera has been undergoing a revolution of its own, frequently in advance of what has been going on in still photography. For those whom video technology is the preferred tool, only part of this chapter is relevant.

Equipment and Film

The initial step always is to prepare a checklist, first, to help organize for the trip and, second, to maintain a constant reference during safari to ensure that nothing is missing. The invariable alternative to such planning before a safari is distracting chaos later when least appreciated. The total photographic kit should be as light as possible, sturdy enough to withstand the rigors of safari transportation and use, and inclusive enough to do justice to what the photographer will see. The trouble with eliminating all equipment that is unlikely to be used is that the photographer on safari will desperately want to be prepared for that special unexpected picture. And the difficulty of leaving behind a favorite piece of equipment (albeit in another context) is too well-known to emphasize. Certainly, the photographer must arrive completely self-sufficient; he cannot plan on picking up *anything* in Africa.

Those African countries likely to be safari destinations place no restrictions on bringing in reasonable equipment, though some do charge a special fee at customs for movie gear.

1. Cameras.

At the top of the checklist belongs a super-sophisticated professional camera that is "ruggedized" — that is, all its mechanisms are gasketed against dust, cushioned against shock, and equipped with adequate backup systems (it will work, for example, without its electronic systems, should the camera batteries fail). In addition, a critically important criterion on which to focus in selecting a particular camera for inclusion, and the same consideration applies to any other piece of equipment, is familiarity: a safari is not the place to learn how to use photographic equipment. Travel time is just too precious to deplete practicing with unfamiliar gear. The temptation to pick up a new lens, for example, just before taking such a trip is often great but must be resisted — unless the photographer can manage to use the lens extensively beforehand. Moreover, this principle applies to more than just brand-new equipment. The author well remembers one poor man in Masai Mara who struggled for days trying to figure out how to open his son's camera and change the film. (The older camera, which no doubt suited his son, had some esoteric opening device.) The results ultimately were part of a vacation wasted (photographically speaking) and an exposed roll of film destroyed.

A corollary of the advice offered earlier in this chapter is to choose a camera that is but a starting point for a totally integrated system. From what follows, it will also become obvious that many of the photographic problems encountered on safari are best overcome by using equipment and accessories that were manufactured specifically to match the camera (and lens) in question.

Most equipment should be professionally cleaned and owner-tested before the trip. Again, this recommendation, as obvious as it might seem, applies to old and even familiar, as well as newer, equipment. Cameras have been knowingly compared to athletes: they need regular exercise. Moreover, certain equipment faults that may have developed since the camera was last used can be discovered only after taking some pictures and processing the film.

The serious photographer will want to take more than one camera body. A malfunction or some other problem can always develop with a camera, especially given all the jolting and vibration on safari, and no opportunity for any reliable major repair exists on the trip. The security afforded by bringing an additional camera is well worth the additional weight and packing inconvenience. Furthermore, using different camera bodies with different lenses attached during the safari may mean the difference between capturing a fleeting shot or missing it altogether. And the convenience of skipping frequent lens-changing cannot be denied. Alternatively, a second camera can carry a second speed of film for exposure changes and variations.

If the camera batteries are older than six months, they should be changed before the trip begins. In addition, one should always carry a complete set of spare batteries — the correct battery is rarely available on safari.

Rubber eyepieces are needed to keep out stray light under the bright African sun. Unless screwed on (and checked periodically), eyepieces are always falling off and crawling into inaccessible hiding places, so it is smart to keep several handy.

Neck straps, at least one-inch wide for comfort, are good aides for holding the cameras while rewinding and changing film and serve as well as any other method for controlling a camera generally during game drives. A refinement that has recently appeared on the market is a rubber camera strap made from the tough neoprene-and-nylon blend used in scuba-diving wetsuits. These soft, springy straps act as a cushion to all the jostling and seem to reduce the "felt weight" of a camera/lens.

2. Lenses.

A photographer needs, ideally, at least three lenses on safari: a standard (45 to 58mm), a zoom (for example, 80-200mm), and a super-telephoto (minimum of 300mm). Lenses are the heart of a picture-taking system and definitely not where the photographer should try to reduce his personal budget deficit. Quality means everything here, and the photographer will have to pay a decent price to find a lens that retains image quality at the wide-open apertures necessary to take action shots on safari.

The standard lens represents, in effect, a compromise and hence can be a good general-purpose lens. A wide-angle lens is of little use on most safaris, even though its fast speed is undeniably useful when especially rapid motion is present and its considerable depth of field is welcome when insufficient time remains for accurate

focusing. Wide-angle lenses, as held by many of us, produce subject distortion, and the effective subject-distance-to-the-camera is too great for safari purposes, causing compositional problems (among others). Moreover, because the tremendous vista of the wide-angle often includes on safari large areas of brightness far different from the main subject, the camera's built-in meter may produce poor results. On the other hand, the standard lens, lightweight and fast, works reasonably well for landscapes and for animals up close or in low-light situations. Traditionally, a wide-angle is often used for landscapes that contain a strong visual element in the foreground or to create dramatic pictures with both foreground and background elements in focus. But skillful use of a standard lens can duplicate all but the extreme examples of both situations.

A good zoom lens[2] is one of the safarist's most critical tools. I cannot imagine embarking on a serious photo-safari without taking one. Basically, despite the obvious mobility allowed by the safari vehicle, the photographer is stationary relative to his subject, which for its part generally is moving around. The ability to change focal length as the animal moves, or simply to change perspective for another shot before the animal does move, is often the difference between catching a good photo and wasting an opportunity. Even if one could carry all the major fixed-focal-length lenses that a zoom encompasses, a practical impossibility, and then all the camera bodies necessary to save the time and trouble of changing lenses all the while, an absurdity, a photographer would still miss many of the best shots. For example, I would never set out to photograph birds in flight without a good zoom.

That a zoom is a great convenience in the field and an important aid to those seeking good photographs can hardly be doubted.[3] But the special features of zoom lenses make for special problems as well, some acute on safari. These disadvantages can soon offset any convenience, unless the photographer exercises due care. First, the zoom lens contains more glass than other lenses and is therefore more susceptible to damage from rough handling, shocks, and vibration. Extra caution should be taken to prevent such damage, a subject discussed in greater detail under "Special Problems" below.

Second, the photographer who is hand-holding a zoom must regularly review the shutter speed that he or the camera's auto exposure system has selected. A shutter speed that yields sharp images at the short end of the

---

2. The only zoom considered here is the "one-touch" variety: the same ring that focuses by turning also zooms by moving forwards or backwards. The focus never changes while strictly zooming.

3. Zooms can also be used as relatively effective spot meters in difficult lighting conditions simply by taking the exposure reading at the longest focal length — that is, "close-up" — and then zooming to the shooting length.

zoom range could prove inadequate at the maximum focal length. Thus, for example, 1/60 might work at 80mm but rarely at 200mm. Whenever possible, the photographer should select a shutter speed suited to the longest focal length that the lens offers. One guide is to use the old but reliable rule of picking a speed equivalent to the fraction of a second formed by placing "1" over the longest possible focal length expressed in millimeters. This formula gives the slowest speed at which one is liable to produce sharp hand-held pictures. An even faster speed is, of course, recommended, if conditions permit. Zooms are usually slower than comparable fixed-focal-length lenses — that is, their widest apertures are one or more stops smaller. Moreover, most zooms seem to be sharpest at apertures of f/16 or higher. These smaller apertures and the faster shutter speeds needed to compensate for hand-holding do not make zooms good choices for poor lighting conditions. Fortunately, this limitation is frequently not critical on safari, unless the photographer is working very early in the morning and late in the afternoon.

Third, because zooms are complex lenses, incorporating several optical elements, they are inherently more prone to problems of flare and internal reflections. Consequently, they need maximum lens shading. The problem is that the lens hood employed has to accommodate the minimal focal length as well, without cutting off part of the picture or causing vignetting at the corners — and therefore cannot be as long as it should be for use with the longer focal lengths. The best compromise is to purchase the hood made especially for the particular zoom lens in question.

Fourth, contrast and sharpness can be a problem with zooms. For this and indeed some of the other concerns listed, the photographer is urged not to try to save a few dollars but to buy a good zoom. To repeat, one receives what one pays for when purchasing lenses, and the better zoom lenses have now solved most problems of sharpness, brightness, and vignetting.[4] Nevertheless, the multiplicity of lens elements and air-to-glass interfaces practically guarantees that a zoom will produce lower image contrast,[5] and the photographer might want to use higher-contrast films and experiment with processing techniques to increase contrast.

Fifth, the complex innards of the zoom scatter enough

_____

4. Even the best zooms will probably never provide the same quality image as comparable fixed-focal-lengths, but the difference today is scarcely noticeable.

5. Lower image contrast today is predominantly caused by flare, or non-image-forming light, that strikes the film's emulsion during exposure. Flare can be produced by light reflected from the lens surface or, as suggested above, from the interior lens elements; light diffracted off the edges of the shutter and aperture blades (mostly at small apertures); or light diffused by scratches, dust, moisture, and so forth on the lens or filter surface.

light so that what finally reaches the film might be substantially less than the f-stop read. The resulting underexposure is rarely welcome. The problem is not so difficult to correct with color slide film. Otherwise, the photographer must bracket a great deal and experiment extensively with the lens before going on safari.

Finally, anything that moves externally on a lens acts as a vacuum for fine dust. As compact as some are, no zoom "zooms" purely internally. Helical focusing, which is rapidly becoming obsolete, causes the identical problem. Dust is a more general concern and is discussed below.

A zoom lens is undoubtedly the answer for the photographer who needs to conserve weight and room in his camera bag. By itself, a zoom tends to be a "heavy" lens but one zoom is, of course, many times lighter than the several lenses that it replaces. But, most of all, the zoom should appeal to the artist inside the photographer. With a zoom, he can combine camera-to-subject distance and focal length in a way that would be impossible with conventional lenses. As the photographer zooms while looking through the view-finder, he achieves a certain affinity with his subject and gains tremendous freedom of composition according to the various magnifications and angles of view. The changes in perspective made possible, in the face of limited maneuverability and relatively fixed lighting, make the zoom the greatest creative tool on safari. The author prefers the 80-200mm zoom range.

On the other hand, a super-telephoto is equally important for wildlife photography, reaching as it does even beyond the photographer's visual boundaries. If man wants to photograph the world of the cheetah, he should perhaps see like one. There are many animals and birds to which the photographer just cannot hope to maneuver very near. There are others who would change their behavior if man did move too near. Scientists are only too aware of Heisenberg's uncertainty principle: what is being scrutinized is changed by that very scrutiny. Safarists contend with a similar problem, for which the telephoto is the only practical solution. In addition, a telephoto can profitably be used to throw the background out of focus and make the main subject stand out sharply. Or the compressed perspective can be employed to emphasize the density of animal or bird groups, such as a flock of flamingoes.

Like zooms, the super-telephotos taken on safari should be products of high quality. Longer telephoto lenses customarily have had trouble bringing all the colors of light to focus at a single point on the film, thus in the past producing color aberrations and focusing errors (particularly when used at wide-open apertures).[6] New

_____

6. Aberrations can often be corrected (or improved) simply by using smaller apertures. But the use of small apertures, even if exposure and subject conditions would so permit, sometimes leads to problems of diffraction and flare. The telephoto usually has a relatively small maximum aperture and therefore requires longish exposures.

materials used today in manufacturing the good telephoto lenses have, however, significantly reduced these chromatic problems. The real drawbacks — or requirements to the profitable use of super-telephotos — remain as previously: first, they always need some reliable form of extra support, and the effects of camera shake and subject movement are considerably exaggerated; and, second, they need extremely careful focusing, which characteristic is definitely hindered by their relatively small maximum aperture and thus limited *focusing* light, on the one hand, and by the atmospheric haze and other problems affecting visibility over long distances, on the other hand. The author accordingly recommends that the reader purchase the fastest telephoto lens available, even though the extra glass will cause it to be physically larger and weigh more than its slower (and, of course, less expensive) counterpart. Furthermore, the average photographer would be wise to limit the length of his telephoto to 600mm or less. The author believes that most safarists will do quite well with a good 400mm lens.

Some photographers prefer a compromise to the standard telephoto called a mirror or catadioptric lens — "cat" for short. Lighter and physically considerably shorter than a conventional telephoto of the same focal length, a "cat" is advertised as easier to handhold. The author has had little experience with "cats" — and the ones that he has tried were somewhat difficult to focus. "Cats" seem to be even slower than their rating, and the light transmitted is not optimum by any means for critical focusing. More important, "cats" have fixed apertures (typically, f/8 for a 500mm lens), which characteristic I find a real hindrance. For example, I cannot choose a wider aperture to separate an animal from its background or to help provide the exposure necessary with high speeds to capture animal movement.

A more promising compromise is the teleconverter (or "tele-extender" or "multiplier"), which furnishes the extra focal length — usually double — with minimum bulk. Teleconverters can therefore prove very useful on safari. The most common powers are 1.4x, 2x, and 3x. Cheap teleconverters reduce the image quality of a good lens and often produce vignetting on all four corners of the frame. Good converters specially designed by the *lens* manufacturers to match their own lenses of specific focal lengths produce, however, high-quality images. (Conversely, a teleconverter is only as good as the lens attached.) Teleconverters do reduce the amount of light reaching the film — a 2x converter, for example, halves the effective aperture,[7] and slower shutter speeds must be used to compensate. Thus, using a teleconverter on a telephoto (already "slow") should be limited to the middle of the day, when fast film may be used, and preferably to situations in which a tripod or other support can be employed.

As when using zooms, hand-holding is made tricky by the extra focal-length compensation in shutter speed necessary. Another fact to emphasize is that the use of teleconverters really makes sense, optically speaking, on telephotos only — when converting, say, a 200mm or 300mm to a 400mm or a 600mm; that is, to make a long focal length longer — and not on converting standard lenses. As might be expected, a 1.4x converter yields better results than a 2x, which in turn surpasses a 3x. In fact, the author does not recommend using a 3x converter. Finally, teleconverters do not work very well on zooms, unless the lens is stopped all the way down (*i.e.*, the smallest aperture opening is used).

Newer lenses in the more sophisticated systems have so-called "internal focusing" (IF) that permits rapid and smoother changes in focusing by altering the configuration of optical elements *within* the lens itself. The older, helical thread system actually lengthened or shortened the physical length of the lens. Whenever possible, the safarist is strongly recommended to use IF lenses, which catch far less dust than the older lenses and which have metering advantages that are discussed in the text below.

3. Filters.

All lenses should be permanently protected by either a skylight or ultraviolet filter: replacing a scratched filter is preferable to replacing a scratched lens.[8] The skylight filter, faintly amber- or light pink-tinted, also reduces the bluish cast of color shots taken in open shade, of distant landscapes, and on overcast days to produce a more natural effect. Furthermore, a skylight filter reduces the effect of haze and ultraviolet radiation to reveal more details. The ultraviolet or haze filter, a colorless filter, does much the same, eliminating invisible ultraviolet light and haze that would be recorded by film. Neither filter, it should be emphasized, allows the photographer to penetrate visible haze — they simply cause the film to record subjects as the eye sees them. The skylight filter is preferred when using slide film, the UV filter for print film. Spare filters for each lens should be carried as well. If it needs to be said, one should not risk ruining the optics of an excellent lens by attaching a cheap filter. The safer, if more expensive, course is to buy the filters made by the camera/lens manufacturer.

A polarizer filter, the photographer's 'sunglasses,' so to speak, may be used to good advantage to darken a blue sky, penetrate atmospheric haze, and add richness to colors. Increasing color saturation is an overly fine point relative to most animals — the filter will have the greatest effect on those animals with fur — but good landscapes frequently deserve a polarizer. Every smooth or semi-

---

7. Thus, a 2x converter converts a 200mm f/4 lens to 400mm f/8.

8. Occasionally, the author will read counsel from some *soi-disant* expert who insists that protective filters are superfluous. To the contrary, such a precaution is mandatory on safari. Moreover, a good filter will *not* produce a loss of sharpness.

smooth object — for example, leaves, flowers, rocks, or water — has a surface sheen that diffusely reflects the light, thereby masking some of the color beneath the sheen. Using a polarizer effectively is, however, a subject of some complexity to photographers. Both camera angle and filter orientation are critical. The polarizer is most effective when the photographer is positioned at a right angle to the sun (the sun is directly overhead) and can be employed to varying strengths by rotating it in its mount. Normally, a photographer can simply look through the camera's finder to see the effect of the filter, which effect will change markedly with the angle of the sun. When using a polarizer, the photographer should bracket extensively, especially as TTL exposure readings through a polarizer are not always reliable. Full polarization cuts the light reaching the film by two stops.

Neutral density filters can prove very useful under the bright African sun. ND filters effectively are "dimmer switches" that reduce the transmission of all visible light rays, but cause no appreciable change in color balance. The ND filter allows the use of wide apertures (with shallow depth of field) in strong light — when the photographer wants to throw a distracting background out of focus and concentrate on the main subject.[9] These filters also permit attempting longer shutter speeds — for example, to blur purposely a moving subject — under bright conditions or allow fast films to be adapted to high light situations.

Using color correction filters, which the author believes have only a limited value on safari, is discussed further in the text below.

4. Motor Drive.

Many photographers regard a motor drive as a luxury. The author himself resisted using one for many years but now would not consider going on an African safari without taking at least one, probably two. A motor drive is more than a luxury when using a long telephoto and a tripod or other support. Set on "slow" or "single frame," it frees a hand for additional camera-support duty and, on "fast" or "burst," it gives needed photo firepower in countless wildlife situations. A motor drive is probably most beneficial when photographing birds, but its value in shooting several other fast-moving animals is not to be ignored. The main detriment to its use, putting aside the extra expense of the unit itself, is the tendency to take too many pictures, particularly when the excitement caused by the subject matter leads one to forget (even for a second) to relax the pressure on the shutter release. (It happens! I have ten identical shots of my first leopard.) A motor drive is relatively noisy, and its sound may therefore occasionally disturb animals, especially the birds. In the author's experience, this last consideration is

not a major disadvantage once fast action has started; the extra noise caused by a motor drive is unlikely to affect appreciably an animal's immediate behavior.

5. Tripods and Other Supports.

For the heavier zooms and super-telephotos, special support is required. On the conventional safari, the photographer for the most part is confined to his vehicle, where setting up a large tripod is simply not practicable, unless few persons are along. Fortunately, a veritable arsenal of small tripods, monopods, chest pods, shoulder pods, clamps, and so forth are sold in camera stores. The author recommends a small "table" tripod, seven to eight inches high, that can be set up directly on the roof of the vehicle. A separate but small ball-and-socket swivel head should be added to provide the full range of adjustments necessary.[10] Used with a pistol grip (and attached cable release) screwed into the camera body, this system gives good stability. Recently, a new product has hit the market that deserves trying: a small, foldable plastic tripod that weighs only two ounces and can be tucked into virtually any equipment bag. The "Ultra-Pod" also has velcro strips for mounting the pod to various objects. A window clamp is another useful tool, and there is now even a support bracket available that resembles the old serving trays used in drive-in fast-food places.

All supports must be of the highest quality — even so, the swivel head will probably break over time, especially if it supports the weight of a long lens and a motor drive. The photographer will often not have the time properly to loosen and retighten the head for each change; in a hurry, one tends to force the swivel head to a new position. Eventually, such mishandling results in snapping its neck, and carrying a back-up unit is highly recommended.

The serious photographer will still want to take along a sturdy full tripod for those circumstances in which it might prove very useful — for example, back at the lodge, in a vehicle with few persons, and outside the vehicle on a game drive where disembarking is permitted. Lightweight amateur tripods are the cause of many ruined pictures and not a few ruined cameras. A few dollars more spent for a good tripod will provide peace of mind. The legs should be steady when extended; joints and locks must be tight; and the entire unit has to be built to withstand rugged handling. In addition, the legs should be independently variable, the center column adjustable,[11] and a pan-and-tilt head employed that allows speedy adjustment from

---

9. An ND filter is handy to have when one is using a "cat" in the bright sun.

10. Some small tripods have built-in swivel heads, which invariably are weaker than independent units. Relative strength is important, for the reason given in the text, but the integrated product does save height.

11. When using a tripod at full height, as little of the centerpost as possible should be extended for maximum steadiness. Thus, a good tripod should come to eye-level without the need for extending the centerpost.

horizontal to vertical and a 360° pan. Obviously, the head *must* remain steady once the controls are locked, whatever lens size is used. A monopod, though not offering rock-steady support, can also come in handy when a tripod would be too clumsy or impractical — for example, in a balloon basket.

The old standby — a bean bag or its equivalent — can often replace other supports, especially when used on the roof of a vehicle or on a window glass. Actually, a great variety of "equivalents" can be used, so long as they 'give' to conform to the shape of the lens. For example, plenty of sand can be found on safari to fill any bag. A bulky sweater furnishes another possibility. For obvious reasons, the bean-bag principle does not easily work with a zoom lens. Nor wholly convenient is any older lens that employs a helical-turning focusing system (in which the entire lens barrel moves). Finally, when using a bean bag, one must take care not to jar the focusing ring when resting the lens barrel or changing the direction of view. Although the author supports the acquisition of IF lenses, I should also warn the reader that some IF lenses are extremely sensitive in this regard — the slightest contact can throw off the focus. I personally use a Nikon system, and several of the Nikon IF lenses react this way.

6. Accessories.

The following accessories are strongly recommended:

- If working with a tripod or similar support, a photographer ought to use a *cable release* as well; otherwise, the jar of hand-releasing could well negate the utility of the tripod. Cable releases are easy to break on safari (insofar as possible, they should not be left on the camera when the latter are not in use), and more than one ought to be taken. The shortest-type cable release is usually preferred.

- A *hand grip* or *pistol grip* is a good tool for providing extra support, especially when used with a tripod.

- A set of *jeweler's screwdrivers* is essential for the inevitable minor repairs and tightening of screws after returning from game drives.

- A roll of *black masking tape* will enable the traveler to effect a fast repair of any light leaks.

- The photographer should take a *black engraver's stick* (available from graphic art supply houses) to apply to scratched lenses to keep light from scattering or reflecting.

- A *rainhood*, made from transparent PVC, to cover the camera for use in a shower.

- All the items referred to under the discussion found below on "Special Problems."

7. Carrying Cases.

The safest procedure for the traveling photographer is to use a well-padded, soft camera bag and hand-carry his basic equipment. Two camera bodies, at least one carrying a motor drive, a basic 50mm lens, an 80-200mm zoom lens, a 400mm telephoto, a 2x teleconverter, filters, a miniature tripod and ball-jointed tripod head, and the basic accessories will all fit into one of the larger shoulder bags. Soft lens cases, which take up little more room than the lenses themselves, are ideal for lens protection; if a lens manufacturer does not make soft cases, padded wraps are independently available and recommended. A large tripod that telescopes will fit in a good-sized suitcase or can be secured to the outside of the checked luggage. Other miscellaneous gear can also be packed with one's clothes. Carrying the basic equipment cuts down on the risk of theft or damage. Moreover, the same kit can be taken right into the safari vehicle.

If more equipment is brought along or carrying the large camera bag is impractical, equipment must be shipped in a strong, waterproof, and relatively shock-proof aluminum case. All the gear should be securely embedded in plastic foam lining, with at least half-inch margins left between pieces of equipment. The drawback to taking these cases is that they are loud advertisements to would-be thieves. Vigilance is especially required at airports and in hotel lobbies. Africa is, however, not worse in this regard than, say, Europe. Reasonable attentiveness will more than likely suffice. The author has shipped camera equipment to and throughout Africa many times and has never lost so much as a filter. One helpful trick: tie an old army surplus bag around any aluminum case being sent.

8. Film.

Color film is faster today than its predecessors, without the corresponding sacrifice in additional grain usually associated with fast film. Color accuracy, balance, and purity are more assured, though it should also be noted that processing technology today is more consistent as well. And both image sharpness and color saturation are much improved in recent films. In sum, film technology is improving right along with the hardware. Of course, no one has invented a perfect color film — all show approximations of reality.

As stated earlier, the author shoots mostly transparency film. The pictures in this book were, with only a few exceptions, made from slides. Choosing the "right" film can be troublesome but is, in any event, often a matter of personal taste (and conditioning). The basic rule is to use color negative film if the goal is to produce many prints for easy viewing and transparency (color reversal) film when one is going to organize slide shows, make enlargements, or sell to publications. In general, slide film (especially if slightly underexposed) offers a greater degree of color saturation and contrast and therefore produces the most natural color. Transparencies tend to generate sharper images than negative film and provide a higher degree of permanence. And a greater variety of transparency films exists. On the other hand, print film has more latitude, and printing from negatives permits easier correction of exposure errors. And acceptable slides can be made from the best negatives. Ultimately, the test for a good film is whether the color reproduction is clean, believable, and devoid of any cast.

The full range of film speed should be taken on safari — slow, medium, and fast films.[12] The bright African sun ensures that slow film can often be used. Indeed, in many situations, one must shoot slow film, unless strong neutral density filters are employed. And a very high-speed lens also encourages the use of slow films, even when attempted under less than ideal lighting conditions. And, from the perspective of seeking enlargements, slow film still offers the least grain and the most color saturation. In the author's view, nothing beats Kodachrome 25 for color and clarity. Both Kodachromes have, in fact, extremely fine grain and are ideal choices for wildlife photography. On the other hand, there are numerous times when faster film, even the fastest film, must be substituted.[13] Early morning and late-afternoon game drives — low light conditions — often provide the most productive game-viewing. Subject movement at this time frequently requires the fastest film available (in addition to a motor drive and maximum camera support). Moreover, the necessity for frequent hand-holding during safari also requires that the photographer carry at least a good supply of medium-fast film. If great depth of field is desired and is to be combined with high shutter speeds, fast film will be needed even in bright light. And using telephotos, zooms, and teleconverters calls for faster film, other factors being equal. Of course, midday in the harsh African sun, 25 ASA can be used with a telephoto and teleconverter combined (depending upon subject movement). In this regard, it should be further noted that all slide film can be "pushed" at least twice (doubling or quadrupling its assigned value). The higher-speed print films can also be pushed.

The photographer must pay attention to the fact that all film is perishable and that certain precautions are needed to reduce the rate of deterioration in contrast and sensitivity that takes place in all film. These precautionary measures are discussed in the text below. When buying slow film, the photographer should inquire whether it has been aged — low-speed films often need to age at room temperature before refrigerating. Moreover, Ektachrome 400 is manufactured with a built-in aging process and needs to sit without refrigeration for a certain amount of time before exposure. "Professional" film should generally be left behind,[14] because it is intended for exposure and

---

12. The author uses only Kodak film, a preference that is more the product of inertia and lifelong conditioning than strict comparison shopping, though the results speak for themselves. Kodachrome 25 is an extremely fine-grained film (with smooth, even grain distribution ensuring edge-sharpness) that has superb color saturation and purity. Its high contrast may block up shadow details, something to watch out for under the bright African sun, but is useful when shooting under low-contrast conditions or low-contrast subjects such as scenics or foliage. Kodachrome 25 is a warm film that works notably well on the browns and yellows encountered on safari. There is no better film for enlargements; the emulsion is capable of very high magnifications. Kodachrome 64 is a "high speed" version of and very similar to Kodachrome 25. Essentially, Kodachrome 64 expands the hand-holding and depth of field possibilities available with Kodachrome 25. Slightly more contrasty (and thus perhaps better under flat lighting) and with greens marginally more accurately rendered (and hence perhaps better for nature photography, though some photographers prefer the brighter greens of 25), Kodachrome 64 is sometimes preferred by photographers. Ektachrome 64 is a cooler film (which can easily go "blue" in open shade or under overcast lighting) and should normally be used on safari with a skylight filter. The film should be used cautiously with bright highlights or deep shadows but is a good choice under strong lighting. It also produces spectacular skies (blues). At high magnification, however, it does not show good edge-sharpness. The newer Ektachrome 100 has proved to be a very successful fine-grained color film, closer to the warmer color balance of Kodachrome than the other Ektachromes. Color saturation and purity are both high, and Ektachrome 100 yields a stronger and brighter blue than even Ektachrome 64. Indeed, underexposing 100 can add considerable color exaggeration: bright rich reds, yellows, greens, and blues. The author is now using Ektachrome 100 as his first choice for medium-speed film. Kodak is reportedly improving (warming) its Ektachrome 64; why is difficult to imagine, given the success of Ektachrome 100. For faster speed, I rely on Ektachrome 200 and 400, with a preference for the latter. Ektachrome 400 is the warmer of the two (Ektachrome 200 is the coolest Ektachrome), though both will balance the extreme warmth of early morning or late-afternoon light, under which they are, in fact, most likely to be used on safari. At high magnification, Ektachrome 400 gives reasonable detail and sharpness. The higher-speed films have very narrow latitudes (all color transparency films begin with limited latitudes, compared with negative films) and thus can be used in bright sunlight only with precise handling, or washed-out highlights and black shadows will result.

13. Kodak is preparing a 200 Kodachrome, which is first likely to appear in a professional version.

14. The author occasionally makes an exception and tries a few rolls of Ektachrome P 800/1600. (The ASA/ISO rating is probably more accurately stated as 600/1200.) Although Ektachrome 400 can be pushed to 800 and 1600 (and even 3200 in an emergency!), the former's emulsion is specifically designed for push-processing. The author will use the film for recording fast action with long lenses or a slow zoom under low lighting; when operating long lenses with apertures of f/11 and smaller; and for shooting late on a cloudy day. The results, despite the lack of refrigeration for up to three weeks or more, have been surprisingly good — better color purity, higher saturation, and usually higher image quality than with a pushed 400. Indeed, the grain of P 800 seems no worse than that of a normal Ektachrome

processing within a relatively short time of purchase and should be refrigerated or frozen until shooting. A serious photographer should plan to shoot three to four rolls of 36-exposure film a day, minimum. There will be days when he will use three or four times that amount. Shooting eighty full rolls in two weeks is not uncommon.

The photographer may *not* plan on buying any film in Africa. Despite what tour operators will promise, the desired film is all too frequently unavailable on safari (even in the large cities) or too old. If forced to buy film there, the photographer should carefully check the film dates and buy only from the largest shops or at major hotels. If one has to use some outdated film, it is always preferable to do so late in the day, when "true" color is not invariably critical. But this last solution results in a poor compromise, at best, and a real greenish cast, at worst!

Exposed film deteriorates faster than unused film. But film should be processed as promptly as possible *after* safari and *not* in Africa, unless really extensive travel lies ahead. Furthermore, the author strongly recommends that valuable film (whose true worth for the amateur might be figured, say, by amortizing the total cost of safari over the number of exposed rolls!) be processed only at the best custom labs, where quality control is the rule. Small labels come in handy on safari for keeping track of any problems or any pushing about which the processing technician must be told.

All film, new or exposed, should be hand-carried together in a separate shoulder bag on safari. One should also keep the fresh film in its original package, unopened (and thereby protected against humidity) until just before use, and always in a lead-lined pouch with a silica gel dessicator thrown in at the bottom. Film needs careful handling throughout a safari — thus the importance of keeping it all together in one place to guard against overheating and high humidity. Exposed film should also be kept in a sealed plastic bag, each with its own packet of silica gel to guard against humidity (though the latter must not be kept with used film extending for long periods of time). The lead-lined pouch provides limited protection against low-dosage airport x-ray inspection. X-ray equipment can fog unprocessed film when the radiation level is high *or* if the film receives several low-level doses (the effect of exposure to x-rays is cumulative). In the United States, up to three exposures is believed to be tolerable, but, abroad, the dosages are much higher and vary too significantly to feel safe. Moreover, high-dose x-ray units are used by British Airways at Heathrow in Great Britain,

at all departure points for Concorde, throughout the Far East, and spottily elsewhere, where no protection is adequate. One should forget completely the reassuring signs on the machines themselves. Increased political terrorism has ensured even further onslaughts against the innocent, unsuspecting film roll. Wherever feasible, the photographer should insist on hand-inspection for all film and loaded cameras. Furthermore, it should be obvious that it is highly convenient to unload film from cameras before going through airport inspection, thereby allowing the camera bag to go through x-ray and limiting the hand-inspection to the film bag. For this purpose, it also makes a difference if one arrives early at airports and talks to supervisors if necessary. The only airport in the world where the author has failed to convince the officials of the importance of hand-inspection is Charles de Gaulle outside Paris, where the authorities worship the x-ray unit in much the way that the ancients believed in the spiritual powers possessed by the baobab tree. (Drawing on such a metaphor is probably being overly kind.)

Packing film in checked luggage is not safe, because virtually all luggage today is x-rayed. If one must pack film, the special lead pouches should be used, and their placement varied throughout the luggage.

Technique

This chapter is not intended to serve as a basic photography course, and the author is hesitant to speak of obvious matters to photographers. Nonetheless, I feel compelled, based on my own experience, to point out two common mistakes that must be avoided on safari. We all make these mistakes, which are annoying in the backyard but disastrous halfway around the world. And, all too often, the traveling photographer returns home to find that the exciting images that he recollects catching on film are simply not there.

The first mistake is easily avoidable, but shooting with the wrong ASA occurs frequently enough to be regarded as almost inevitable. Ordinarily, this error results from loading into the camera a roll of film that has a different speed from the previously used roll. Hastily and thinking of something else altogether, the photographer proceeds to close the camera and shoot without making the necessary adjustment. The solution is, *always* set the ASA *before* actually loading new film. Another time that this mistake comes about is when a mechanical ASA compensation is made while shooting and the photographer fails to return the dial or lever to normal after the special shot(s). A possible solution here is to lift the rewind knob or make another visible (but non-operative) adjustment at the same time as the ASA compensation is made that will serve to remind the photographer of the change. The newest cameras have their own indicators of adjustment.

If an ASA error is noticed while still shooting the roll in question, the photographer can correct the setting, continue, and have the roll split-processed by a professional

___

400, and the colors are virtually as good as those achieved with 400 film. I have found the same tendency to shift to blues in overcast situations characteristic of Ektachrome 400. I have not pushed the film to 3200, though professional labs can process this. The film has little to no exposure latitude, so accurate exposure is critical. One should bracket toward overexposure; on underexposure, the colors are dark and dull.

Plate 1. Twilight at Kariba.

lab. To refrain from ruining good pictures, however, the photographer ought to make two or three blank exposures where the film is to be split (always an approximation anyway). Or, should the difference between the two ASA figures not exceed one or two stops — the usual margin of error — the photographer may elect to continue and have the processing done on a "push" or "pull" basis. If the difference is but one stop in either direction — doubled or halved — a professional lab can do a clip-processing to see what would be the ideal exposure. As might be expected, the 'mistaken' exposure sometimes proves better! Clip-processing works best, however, when the entire roll was shot under similar conditions. Some photographers who shoot a great deal under tricky exposures or who are having equipment problems always use clip-processing (at an extra expense, of course) to ensure the best exposure possible under the circumstances. If one does follow this course, it helps to make a habit of reshooting the first two or three frames of every roll, as clip-processing inevitably involves cutting one frame and possibly over- or underexposing the first couple of frames.

The photographer should also develop the habit of checking the ASA 'again' when unloading the camera, so that any error observed then can immediately be noted on a small label pasted onto the film cartridge. Finally, clip-processing should always be attempted when the photographer, for one (embarrassing) reason or another, has lost complete track of the shooting ASA of a particular roll.

The second common mistake is actually best described as a compendium of errors that the photographer can make while loading, winding, and rewinding film. It is tempting on safari to rush film loading and just as easy for the film leader to slip off the take-up spool unknown to the photographer. Or, in another variation, the film may break for some reason during shooting. The photographer therefore should be checking periodically to see that the rewind knob is rotating. One trick in this regard is to leave the rewind lever up during shooting, thereby making the rotation of the knob easier to see. Again, the newest cameras have a variety of gimmicks that also keep efficient track of a roll's progress, unwinding or rewinding.

Despite the temptation to rush, good loading technique should always be followed. At a minimum, the photographer should never attempt to load a camera while the vehicle is moving, notwithstanding the frequent "need" to do so. Such a practice invites serious problems, not the least of which is dust accumulation inside the camera and on the film. The solution: begin loading when fully stopped (and the dust has settled) and finish the process before moving on.

Another poor, but common, misjudgment is to try to squeeze out one last frame at the end of a roll when resistance is felt on manual advancing. The culprit risks dislodging the entire roll, and trying to change such a roll outdoors, no matter what the manuals offer as possible

techniques, will inevitably fog the film. Furthermore, manual *re*winding should be slow and steady so as not to create a discharge of static electricity that results in lines appearing in the film image. The photographer should always stop rewinding immediately after the film leader disengages from the take-up mechanism. When the full width of the film is thus left showing, the light seal on the cartridge will work to maximum advantage. Because exposed rolls will then resemble new rolls, if this technique is followed, the author recommends never opening a new film package until actually loading the film. Alternatively, one could unfailingly and clearly mark exposed rolls. Finally, it is always a good practice to rewind a roll as soon as possible after exposing the last frame. No good, and possibly much harm (to the film), will come from carrying around cameras with exposed rolls of film inside that have not been rewound.

Beyond remarking on these common faults, the author would like to offer some pertinent advice in two broad categories: how to improve sharpness and what to do with exposure on safari.

Improving image definition, as suggested earlier, has to be a priority of any wildlife photographer. There are many relevant considerations in this regard while on safari. Camera shake is, of course, an important villain. Using a tripod or other support is the ideal solution but not always feasible. Ironically, the difficulty of hand-holding equipment has increased with the modern cameras and lenses. Both smaller and lighter, they have little inertia or resistance to movement. In fact, they need more careful handling and higher shutter speeds than their older, heavier counterparts. One answer is to add weight by using an attached but folded mini-tripod as a stabilizer. A camera bag or other object might also serve the same purpose. The author believes that the best advice for improving hand-holding steadiness is to press the camera into the face and squeeze the shutter release slowly with gentle, even pressure. For the really critical shot taken at marginal speed, the photographer is encouraged to take a deep breath, exhale, and shoot at the bottom of the exhalation, with elbows consciously held into the sides of the body. Whenever hand-holding, the photographer should concentrate on cradling, not grasping, the lens. Ultimately, hand-holding is, of course, a highly individual practice. Experts recommend choosing a speed of 1/125 or better, but the author and many other photographers frequently get by with 1/30.

One should always note how securely the lens is attaching to the camera. If the lens barrel moves once mounted, it should be remounted. Additionally, a photographer does not always notice an increase in wind, but any such change will require higher shutter speeds. Wind is definitely a potential photographic villain on safari. The breezes off the savannah will turn a long telephoto into a sail. At times, the tripod-cable-release combination is insufficient by itself; the photographer should then press down on the top of that part of the camera/lens located

PHOTOGRAPHY GUIDE

[The following information is a summary guide and, as such, is only an approximation. Wildlife acts predictably more often than not, but "not" is never predictable. Further details can be found in the chapters that follow.]

	Early Morning	Midday	Late Afternoon
	(Before sunrise, light has a cool, shadowless, pearly, and flat quality. After sunrise, the light is warm — with an orange to reddish cast. The soft light yields subtle effects and pastel colors and also increases the effect of a telephoto lens in compressing perspective. Shadows look blue. Directional lighting permits side, front, or back illumination.)	(Assuming a clear, cloudless day, the light is white and harsh. The greatest contrast exists between and among colors. Shadows are black. Haze subdues distant backgrounds. Reflected glare is common. Flat lighting permits widest use of color film's limited exposure latitude.)	(Much the same as early morning. Shadows lengthen. Surfaces are strongly textured. At twilight, light reflects the sunset colors from clouds. Shadows disappear, and the contrast between colors is reduced. At first, sky has a pink cast, then richer color. Skyline silhouettes are a strong feature.)
[in book order]			
Lion	Easy to find, by driving or scanning. Tends to be very active early; hunting and kill scenes (look for sequences). If not eating, the pride will be moving around. Do not crowd youngsters while adults are moving. When pride has stopped, photographer will be able to get extremely close and, though remaining alert, can take his time and choose his shots. Later in morning, slow film may be used. Mating. The safarist should resist the perfectly natural temptation to shoot every nuance of the first lions seen. He will see many others. Standard lens often quite satisfactory. Zoom helpful.	Occasional waterhole dramas. Pride generally seeks out shade and sleeps. Need depth of field to encompass large prides. Cubs will alternate sleep with play. Lions in trees. Mating. Lion prides in the popular parks are used to virtually any type of vehicular approach. Safarists must always exercise reasonable caution in the presence of lions up close. Leaving a vehicle or even hanging out a window is stupid. Experiment with polarizer.	More active as afternoon wears on. Often enjoying the breezes on knolls. Mating. Much preening. Cubs very active (motor drive helpful). Look for sequences. Medium-speed film is adequate until late afternoon. Alternate perspectives and formats.
Leopard	The only time to *look* for a leopard, as he moves to his daytime position, drinks etc. Scanning usually more effective than driving, but leopards require the photographer to react quickly once seen. Long lens and high-speed film needed. Shoot first to capture animal (the safarist may never see another) and bracket extensively; then attempt to improve position and shooting. Focus on whiskers, pupils, or the clear break-up of rosette spots.	Usually inactive; lying in trees or on rocks.	Virtually impossible to find, except in forests. Always start with fresh film and pre-set exposure.
Cheetah	Not always easy to find — must drive and scan at same time and cover great distances. Active but cautious *re* other predators. Preening. Photographer must be patient in approach and allow cat(s) to accept vehicle's presence. Standard lens possible. Try polarizer. Alternate perspectives and formats.	Frequent hunting. Use fast lens or high-speed film to capture action. Motor drive very useful, as is zoom. Proper positioning is critical. (Photographer must develop feeling for location of actual prey.) Whether eating or sleeping, cheetahs do not lose their wariness. They never fall into the stupor of lions. Try polarizer and think in terms of sequences.	Inactive until twilight, except that cubs will romp and play. High-speed film or fast lens required. Zoom helpful. At end of day, single cheetahs will hunt. Positioning is everything. Be alert for 'second round.'

	Early Morning	Midday	Late Afternoon
Serval	Hunting early in morning. Photographer cannot crowd; must shoot with long lens. As with all cats, patience is required.	Inactive. Difficult to see.	Hunting — occasionally.
Caracal	Hunting very early. Photographer must maintain distance to witness leaping (for which motor drive is critical).	Inactive. Difficult to see.	Hunting — occasionally.
Genet	Inactive. Will not see.	Inactive. Will not see.	Activity begins at twilight. Very fast film and fast lens needed. Focus on eyes.
Mongoose	Active foraging. Mongooses are out and about during much of the day and in and out of the many termite mounds scattered over their range. They move as a group but find food individually. Very jerky in movement, the animal requires high-speed film to capture. Best to try in the morning, when a certain amount of sunning and grooming takes place. Long lens required. Careless approach will send back to dens.	Active foraging. Try polarizer.	Moderately active, returning to dens by nightfall.
Hyena	Often active, returning to the den or scavenging at a lion kill (or harassing lions at a kill). Difficult to get close to, unless at carcass or immediately outside den. Whatever film the lighting will allow.	Generally inactive. Possible scavenging. Sunning outside lairs. Cubs moderately active near den entrance. Always act prudently in presence of hyenas.	Activity begins again at twilight.
Jackal	Actively following predators or hunting on his (or their) own. Long lens helpful; so is zoom at kills.	Active cleaning up at kills. Jackals are seen all day.	Reasonably active.
Bat-Eared Fox	Inactive and rarely seen.	Inactive. Rarely seen.	Basking outside den. Must approach carefully. Fox is moderately to very shy, requiring substantial patience by photographer.
Wild Dog	Active — hunting. Long lens and support usually imperative. Will cover enormous ground in a day.	Active — generally on the move, unless raising young pups.	Active — hunting. No way to anticipate direction. Must react quickly.
Vulture	Active all day: in the air, in trees, or at kills. Standard lens at last, long lens for other locations.	Active, but frequently cooling off.	Active until nightfall. Alternate perspectives.
Marabou Stork	Moderately active. Easy to photograph.	Moderately active, especially at water.	Moderately active.
Elephant	In early morning, moving towards water. Later, moving towards shade to avoid heat of midday. Casual, relaxed wandering and grazing. Slow film usually adequate; elephants act deliberately. The larger the group, the more difficult to approach. Patience required: follow and observe. Never crowd mother and calf. Long lens good with group to emphasize density. Focus on eyelashes or skin wrinkles.	Resting in shade, dusting, limited grazing. Mudbaths. Effective exposure not always easy in bright sun. Bracket.	Return to purposeful eating. Calves very active and photogenic. Alternate perspectives and formats.

	Early Morning	Midday	Late Afternoon
Hyrax	Moderately active. Tree hyraxes inactive during day but will see. Rock hyraxes not much of a photo study.	Basking on rock or in tree.	Sitting on rock or in tree.
Giraffe	Active; eating. Very photogenic. Use slow approach. Zoom lens useful to vary animal in picture.	Active; good time to see. Eating. At waterholes. Include landscapes.	Active; eating. Necking.
Hippopotamus	In the pool (or mudhole). Mild activity. The photographer must be patient — the gaping yawns will come.	Reasonably active. Babies shifting positions. Sunbathing on banks of the pool.	In the water. Increasingly active. Best time to photograph. Inevitable fighting. Much submerging and surfacing.
Rhinoceros	Best chance to see: feeds and walks about. Must be very slow and careful in approach. Keep respectful distance and use long lens. Once spotted, easy to find for days.	Heads for cover. Sleeps, often lying down in the shade at midday. Occasional mudbath.	Browsing. Mud-wallowing. Look for humorous tick-birds.
Buffalo	Moderately active. Grazing. Females essentially herd animals, reacting accordingly. Use caution *re* males, especially older bulls standing or grazing off from herd. Focus on texture of boss of horns.	Herd dozing. Often lying down.	Grazing. Mudbaths.
Antelopes	Antelope behavior varies widely. Careful, methodical approach always in order. Early morning good for all forest antelopes. Long lens and motor drive very useful; preparation (exposure and action considerations) essential. Constant decisions on whether to include environment or concentrate on animal by itself. Proper positioning is critical. Elands, bongos, bushbucks, oryx, reedbucks, klipspringers, and dik-diks are all very shy and likely to be stationary only briefly. Births may be witnessed — often seasonal. Early morning good for impala youngsters. Need current information to catch wildebeest migration. Fast film to capture action. Good time for statuesque portrait. Bracket. Focus on eyes. Must be patient for unusual picture or special portrait.	At waterholes; positioning key. Best chances to see most plains antelopes. Very difficult to see forest antelopes and dik-diks at midday. Waterbucks easy to photograph anytime — try polarizer. Oryx herds standing in sun — long telephoto needed. May see bushbuck but must be quick (and prepared). Gerenuks, impalas, and gazelles in sight all day long. Medium-speed film to capture action; most antelopes are "jerky," even when quietly grazing.	Best for forest antelopes (which are often nocturnal and really only begin activity late in day), especially bongos and Lesser kudus. The latter rarely leave their cover. Fast film necessary. Try different perspectives and formats. Look for sequences, especially among males (fighting/challenges).
Zebras	Active. Relatively easy to find and photograph. Use long lens to emphasize density or to pull out individual from herd. Normal TTL exposures (white and black even out). Look for sequences. Focus on "line" dividing black from white or the hair in ears.	At waterholes. Frequent dusting. Moderately active; zebra do not seek shade. Much contact between family members: grooming and resting together. Good time to isolate youngsters.	Look for stallions fighting. Alternate perspectives and formats.

	Early Morning	Midday	Late Afternoon
Warthog	Active. Will find them with antelopes. Long lens, fast film, and motor drive helpful: warthogs will not allow a photographer to approach too near. Focus on grains in tusks or on whiskers.	Seeks shade. Sometimes hunted by old lions.	Active. Same considerations apply as at early in day.
Giant Forest Hog	Difficult to find; see mostly by chance. Likely to catch up close, but not much time for photography (be prepared when in montane forests). Zoom is helpful.	Same.	Same. Best chance to see.
Bush Pig	Will not see.	Will not see.	May see at dusk.
Monkeys	Baboons are late risers. All monkeys are active in the morning. Zoom or telephoto helpful. Patience required, especially with Colobus.	Moderately active. Eating, drinking. Young are active, but difficult to approach.	Baboons retire early but active for most of the afternoon. Vervets and Sykes active.
Gorilla	Fast filter critical for low light prevalent in rain forests. Try unipods.	Gorillas often nap at midday.	Moderately active.
Chimpanzee	Active. Group dynamics. Look for sequences.	Active.	Active.
Prosimians	The diurnal varieties are active early. Basic forest photography. Bracket.	Moderately active.	Moderately active. Follow sequences.
Crocodile	Crocs come to land early in morning. By mid-morning, they have moved back into water or sought out shade. Try polarizer around water. Approach quietly. Focus on eyes.	Not active: in water or under shade.	Basking in sun.
Lizards	Active.	Active.	Active.
Snakes	Rarely seen.	Rarely seen.	Rarely seen.
Birds	Most active. Small, wary, and quick, birds are a challenge. Most bird shots on safari are spontaneous, not planned. Anticipation, fast shutter speeds, telephoto, constant refocusing, zoom, and motor drive all essential. Recording flight and movement requires *patience*. Pay attention to position of perch and direction in which bird is facing; do not try to encourage flight (bird will then usually fly directly away). Note that a bird in flight will fill more of frame than at rest — choose perspective/framing with margins. Colonies generally are easier to approach than single species. Keep distance at nests and at courtship displays. Raptors hunt now. Shoot a lot of film.	Less active. Many birds, like mammals, seek relief from the sun. Two basic problems *re* exposure: 1) skies will dominate readings (use manual or compensation controls; bracket) and 2) tree branches or forest will cast tricky shadows (think). Try polarizer when plumage stands out or for water shots. Most birds are frequently attracted to or need water, and waterhole is good bet at this time. Shoot for texture of feathers or bird's eyes in portraits.	Moderately active. Panning bird movement difficult (*e.g.,* wing movement in different direction than forwards) —better to observe patterns and anticipate. Difficulties *re* proper perspectives; frame carefully. Raptors tend to sit high in trees. Ground birds are small enough to cause "looking-down-upon" feeling in shots. Pay special attention to background and foreground elements for arboreal species. Ground birds head for nests in late day.

directly over the support or attach a second tripod to the camera (or lens, if the primary tripod is screwed into the camera). Pistol grips are also handy in this context. One time-tested trick for measuring the wind is to dangle a thread from the camera with a small feather attached to the other end.

To the extent that wildlife photography is action photography, the fastest shutter speeds that lighting and film will permit are used as a matter of course. Fast subject motion, if reasonably steady and predictable, can more-over be captured by panning the camera. Successful panning, however, definitely takes practice. The subject should constantly be kept in the same part of the viewfinder, the photographer must move his entire upper torso and not just the camera, and proper follow-through is critical. When panning, the photographer should also keep both eyes open to look out for any upcoming obstructions (like a tree) appearing just outside the viewfinder. And one has to bear in mind at all times that an animal could well be running for cover of some kind, thereby allowing only a limited opportunity to shoot. If the photographer has the time to plan the shot and the route of movement is predictable, he should pre-focus on a reference point, then pan to that point.

If subject movement is erratic, however, the only solution is to increase shutter speed. In any event, whatever adjustments are made for action, the photographer has to realize that some parts of the animal (normally, the legs) may be moving faster than the subject as a whole. More often than not — but not always — the photographer will wish to freeze all movement. In the same vein, it must further be emphasized that even panning often allows only marginally slower shutter speeds, if any, as an animal's legs will be moving in different directions. Panning for an impala is not the same as panning to follow a sportscar. Moreover, it helps to concentrate on the principle that the smaller the image in the frame (and on the film), the less shutter speed is needed to stop action; conversely, using high magnification and filling the frame only adds to the problem of movement. Finally, a slight change of angle toward a head-on shot will often prove considerably beneficial to freezing action in the photograph, though, if the shift of angle is too great, keeping the head-on animal in focus will quickly become a headache.

As a very general guide, a walking animal can probably be stopped at a speed of 1/125; a steady trot at no less than 1/250; and a full run or gallop in the 25-30-mph-range at 1/500. The swiftest antelopes, cheetahs, some birds — all these will take the photographer to the fastest end of the scale.

When using a long lens, the photographer often works at close to full aperture and at the slowest practical shutter speed. A slight change in lighting could cause an automatic camera to set a shutter speed too slow to stop movement, another example of the need to be constantly aware of the camera's settings and their practical results, despite automatic features. Of course, some modern cameras do everything but reach out and grab the photographer by the throat should the shutter speed drop to 1/30, but action may be lost far above that setting.

The soundest advice on focusing is to find the eyes or facial hair or whiskers. With a zoom, the photographer ought to focus at the closest setting,[15] then zoom to the focal length desired. Sometimes, it helps to change the focusing screen in those SLR cameras that feature interchangeable screens. The split-image microprisms arranged in a central "collar" that come with most cameras as standard issue — and which work well with standard and wide-angle lenses — do not always suit a photographer when he uses long focal lengths and can be especially distracting when trying to focus on moving animals. A plain or clear matte Fresnel screen often works better, allowing quick focusing with little distraction. The simple, unadorned Fresnel is, however, not ideal at dusk, looking into deep shadows, or during other low-light times.

The final word on "movement" concerns another factor altogether: one's fellow passengers. In a group safari, the photographers had better establish some reasonably clear ground rules, so to speak, so that the photography is not spoiled by thoughtless passenger-movement about the vehicle. An inopportune jostling, even less, can cause friction, shall we say, out-of-proportion to the contact (but not necessarily the result).

Depth of field or zone of *relative* (or acceptable) sharpness is a function of many factors. For a start, the film has to be lined up properly when loaded to ensure accurate calculations. Then, all photographers learn early that the smaller the aperture, the greater the depth of field. But stopping down the lens all the way for increased *sharpness* is fallacious. Most lenses, because of their diffraction, are not terribly sharp at the smallest apertures — most are, in fact, sharpest at two or three stops from the largest aperture.[16] Besides, a small aperture usually calls for a compensating slow shutter speed, which compensation is counter-productive for image definition if it emphasizes camera shake. On the other hand, the restriction of a really fast lens is that, when used at its widest apertures (the whole point to choosing a fast lens), depth of field is very shallow and focusing especially critical. In addition, when using a very long lens — for example, 600mm or beyond — depth of field is so shallow that stopping down the aperture (assuming the light permitted) is of relatively little help in increasing the zone of sharpness. The conclusion: aperture is often the wrong horse to ride for the purpose of manipulating depth of field.

---

15. As already noted and further discussed in the text below, the closest setting on a zoom also provides the most accurate metering.

16. The widest apertures, on the other hand, tend to show up the aberrations that exist in many lenses, aberrations that increase toward the edges.

The photographer also learns that the greater the focal length of the lens and the shorter the distance between the camera and subject, the smaller the depth of field. Or, as magnification increases, depth of field drops off dramatically. Thus, depth of field decreases when using a teleconverter, which adds, in effect, focal length and magnifies the image (even though it also "increases" the f-number and effectively makes the aperture smaller). In the field, these two factors—lens focal length and camera-subject distance—play the most significant part in determining, or changing, the relative zone of sharpness.

Unless the photographer is focusing on very close subjects, depth of field extends one-third before a focused subject and two-thirds behind. Thus, when focusing on infinity, two-thirds of the potential zone of sharpness is lost. Phrased another way, depth of field on the "far side" of infinity is wasted. If maximum depth of field is desired, the photographer should focus closer than infinity to include more of the foreground (while retaining the background). When photographing a distant scene, to place the farthest part of the picture at the far edge of the zone of sharpness, the best point on which to focus is not the most distant point, but at a point about one-third of the way between the nearest part of the scene that has to be sharp and the most distant part, as seen through the camera. Technically, this technique is known as focusing on what is called the "hyperfocal point" and will give more total depth of field than any other setting. Depth of field will, in fact, extend from a distance halfway between the hyperfocal point and the camera all the way to infinity. If such focusing proves difficult to do by eye, there is a more mechanical approach: simply line up the infinity mark found on the lens focusing ring with the depth-of-field color-coded line drawn on the lens barrel that corresponds to the color of, and represents the *far* limit (in a depth-of-field calculation) of, the aperture setting used. This will be the line on the left, looking out from the camera. The photographer should bear in mind that, at great distances, heat haze (including the mirage phenomenon), mist or rain, dust, and other atmospheric conditions encountered on safari all adversely affect sharpness and depth of field.

One of the most useful — and least used — tools on good cameras is the depth-of-field preview button or lever; this control closes the lens down to the actual shooting f-stop, so that the photographer can verify in the viewfinder what will come out sharp in the photograph. But depth of field is difficult to verify precisely when using a telephoto lens, because the focal distinctions from foreground to background are miniaturized.[17]

Handling the many exposure questions that arise on safari requires close attention to frequently complex lighting conditions. Indeed, achieving proper exposure is probably the biggest single headache for photographers. The safarist must learn to see, not with the naked eye, but as the camera sees. He must also not allow himself to become so caught up with auto-exposure that he neglects to think about the light and how the camera is adjusting to that light. The human eye selects, censors, and adjusts; it adapts quickly to changes in brightness to maintain what it regards as "normal" light — and hence is not always a reliable judge of the amount of light actually present. (The eye also adapts to color in the same way — it does not always register actual changes in "normal" color.) On the other hand, the camera and film are neutral and see everything indiscriminately. But they also "see," thanks to the camera's metering system and the restrictions of film emulsions, much less. Photographs reproduce a much smaller range of brightness or illumination than the eye records. The photographer must learn to pay attention to exactly what appears — and only what appears, figuratively speaking — in the viewfinder.

Many of the exposure aids normally available to a photographer are impractical to use on safari — for example, fill-flash and hand-held meters. Through-the-lens metering is the available exposure tool.[18] Camera meters are usually designed to give a reading that will cause the subject to appear average or middle-toned in the final picture, regardless of the brightness of the setting. "Middle-toned" is defined as a reading that reflects eighteen percent of the light striking it. Today, with cameras that have more sophisticated metering than ever before and increased automation as well, the amateur photographer is tempted to concentrate solely on composition. But the photographer yields his judgment to the meter at his own risk. Forgetting or ignoring the finer points of lighting and depending solely on the camera's readings will not produce elegant portraits nor avert the mistakes caused by an unusually bright sun or by substantial contrast in the scene (prevalent, for example, with backlit subjects).[19] Even the amateur photographer should know whether his camera's meter is "center-weighted" or "averaged" (or

17. If the photographer is following correct focusing techniques, if all vibrations are under control, and if the images are still turning out fuzzy, the cause might be traced to a dirty lens, front or back; film not properly seated in the back of the camera; a faulty prism or finder; or a lens that itself is faulty or not coupling securely to the camera mount.

18. On safari, with respect to metering, simplicity and speed are essential. But the author also feels like a faith healer on the subject of hand-held meters: "Throw down that crutch and. . ." Indeed, the sophistication of today's TTL metering, joined with a proper grounding in the fundamentals of outdoor exposure (including the technique of bracketing), makes — or should make — extra meter readings a total waste of time, even were the time available. On the question of fill-flash, I must be equally direct: it bothers many animals, the photographer rarely achieves that kind of intimacy with his subjects, and, in the absence of reflective surfaces, very little flash will ever strike the subject — the outdoors soaks up such artificial light like a sponge.

19. "Contrast" is an expression of the degree of separation surviving between the tones of an image. Contrast here refers to the difference existing between the darkest and lightest areas of a

whatever) and he should *understand* his own system. He must know where to aim his camera and he must understand what compensations have to be made in such very bright or contrasty situations as exist on safari. Large areas of sky appearing in the picture, to pick just one common example on the African plains, always calls for some allowances. Plains' lighting in East Africa generally is consistently bright, from roughly 10 a.m. to 3 p.m., because of the low horizon existing at or near the equator. (The day appears brighter at midday, but the effect is caused mostly by the heat.) But animals moving rapidly in front of changing backgrounds or between sunlit and shady areas definitely will challenge auto-exposure systems. The author knows of no camera meter that fails to overcompensate in the face of a very bright subject. Furthermore, correct exposure in shade is always troublesome, and side-lighting frequently needs thoughtful attention as well.[20]

At certain times, the photographer is forced to meter off something other than the shooting subject if he wants a reading that will produce "normal" results. Should time permit, he must follow a strict procedure for accuracy: first, he focuses on the shooting subject; then, *without* changing focus, he meters off a "middle tone"; and, finally, once the reading is taken and locked in, he returns to photograph the desired scene. Changing the focus will alter the length of the lens and thus alter the light reaching the meter (and, eventually, the reading), unless the lens is "internal focusing." The IF lens has already been described; if an IF lens is used, the first step — focusing on the subject — is unnecessary, making the entire process that much quicker. The photographer must, of course, ultimately focus on his subject, but no light is lost or gained as he does so. Exposures for sequences are a snap with IF lenses: the photographer is free to concentrate on the action (assuming that the lighting conditions remain the same). In any event, for the suggested procedure to work, the light on the metered middle tone must be the same as that falling on the shooting subject. Should it prove difficult to find a middle tone, the photographer can use the palm of his hand, which is usually one stop *brighter* than a true middle tone, and *open up* the lens one stop from the reading given.

Film type is an important exposure factor. Color films generally are balanced for average subjects in good light (say, between 10 a.m. and 3 p.m.). The author's experience is that higher-rated films should be set to their exact ASA rating but that the lower-speed films should be set one-half stop faster. Moreover, most new equipment seems consistently to overexpose color slide film, so that

slower color slide film could profitably be set even one full stop faster. "Pushing" film slightly as a matter of course should produce better color saturation as well. Pushing ASA does place a premium on correct exposures thereafter, or the shadows will be closed-up into total darkness. When using slide film, however, the photographer should expose for highlights — not the brightest parts of a picture, but the brightest parts of the subject whose texture is hoped to be recorded with color — and let the shadows fall where they may. Only when shooting outdoors under very dull, overcast conditions — not the typical safari postulate — should the photographer try overexposure, as many transparency films produce oversaturated results under these circumstances. Of course, with slide film, the final goal is a critical consideration: are the slides for projection or reproduction? Slides for reproduction can be dense and highly saturated — printers can "punch through" dark areas of underexposure to regain obscure details when preparing color separations.[21]

Generally, the photographer should err slightly toward overexposure with negative film, which is relatively easy to correct if need be in custom printing. Print film should, in fact, be exposed for shadow areas; the detail can be controlled in the final print by following a number of darkroom techniques. But, although color print film has a greater latitude than color transparency film — negatives have a range of about five stops; even the best transparency films have a comfortable latitude of only one f-stop in either direction — neither has the latitude of black-and-white film. On safari, as elsewhere, correct exposure has no completely satisfactory substitute.

In the final analysis, a photographer on safari ought to know enough about exposure so that i) he can compare what the camera's meter is telling him to what he believes to be correct; ii) he can operate his camera manually in the event of an emergency, such as a meter or battery failure, and still have a fair opportunity to succeed; and iii) he can pre-set both aperture and shutter speed in effectively anticipating shots. If one is looking for a shortcut in this regard, the old rule of "sunny f/16" is available: an aperture of f/16 combined with a speed of

$$\frac{1}{\text{shutter speed nearest to the ASA rating,}}$$

or any equivalent combination, equals the correct exposure on a bright, sunny day.[22] The rule is reliable for a frontlit subject (a subject in direct sunlight) of basic colors. From this starting point, one can determine virtually any daylight exposure as follows:

---

picture and not to colors that "contrast" with each other. Low-contrast film has a wider range between its bright and dark tones than medium-contrast film. High-contrast film has a narrow range or latitude.

20. Another fact to keep in mind while on safari: on a cloudy day, the sky relative to the land is even brighter than normal.

---

21. There is, however, no way to recover details in highlights that are completely washed out by overexposure. The film is just blank; a separator will not find any detail, because it does not exist.

22. Thus, an ASA of 400 becomes f/16 at 1/500; an ASA of 64 becomes f/16 at 1/60 or f/11 at 1/125; and so forth.

- when the subject is white or any other highly reflective color or surface or when a bright or hazy sun is shining on white sand, snow, or still water, change the rule to "sunny f/22" or use the next higher shutter speed;

- when the subject is backlit, open up one or two f-stops or use the next or two slower shutter speeds (two stops or speeds if the subject is a close-up);

- when the subject is sidelit or when shadows are soft, open up one f-stop or use the next slower shutter speed;

- when the lighting comes from a hazy sun producing no distinct shadows, open up one to two f-stops or use the next one to two slower shutter speeds;

- when the sky is heavily overcast, open up three f-stops or use a shutter speed three stops slower; and

- under dark clouds or when raining, open up four to five f-stops or use a shutter speed four to five stops slower.[23]

Whenever a serious question as to correct exposure exists, the photographer on safari should resort to bracketing. Bracketing is not, or does not have to be (as some have suggested), a sign of ignorance. One of the few ways to control the emotional impact of a color picture is to bracket — again, the technicians simply cannot do to color pictures in the lab what is possible with black-and-white film — and the mood of a color picture can change dramatically with a very slight shift in color hue and intensity. And bracketing is the only strategy to provide a degree of insurance under varying light conditions, in the event of inconsistent meter readings, or when faced with the inevitable variations in color-film emulsions. Bracketing is not an inexpensive technique, since considerable film may be used. But to try to save money here is, to repeat, false economy during a once-in-a-lifetime trip (or, even more likely and more to the point, when shooting a once-in-a-lifetime scene). After all, the errors will not become apparent until the safari is long behind. Film is inexpensive, compared with the cost of the trip, and infinitely cheap, when compared with lost opportunities halfway around the world.

Bracketing should not, however, be indiscriminate, and subject or photographic conditions do not always call for bracketing. That is, bracketing should not replace automation on the altar of laziness. Exposure increments on *both* sides of a metered norm are, normally, a waste of film and reflect poor technique. The exceptions would be a truly fast-changing situation (for example, at sunrise)

and a really important picture. The author uses the lens aperture ring to bracket, which technique permits easy half-stop bracketing. Use of the exposure override controls is often too slow and clumsy. The same can be said for ASA index-scale bracketing. When depth of field is a critical consideration and a particular aperture setting is all-important, a not-too-likely event in view of what has been previously said concerning depth of field, I switch to shutter speed. Some cameras have an "exposure compensation" button that the photographer simply presses as he takes a picture — a very nifty feature. If color saturation compensation has been made, as suggested earlier, by pushing the ASA setting, bracketing should probably be limited to half-stops favoring underexposure.

The photographer on a game drive may all too frequently find that he has the "wrong" film on hand for the existing lighting conditions. Lighting has diminished, subjects are more active or farther away, or any combination thereof — he needs faster film. The solution is to push the film by doubling or quadrupling (or perhaps more) its manufactured ASA rating. A custom developer will process the film accordingly. For decent results, only the higher speed films should be pushed more than once; slow or medium-speed film will not react as well.[24]

The *quality* of light is as important as the quantity. For example, color balance will change in shady areas on a clear day (producing a blue tinge on film), beneath the shade of a green, leafy tree (green hue), over long distances (blue), or on cloudy or rainy days (blue). High altitudes offer excessive ultraviolet radiation, producing casts of blue and purple on the film. Most important, color balance changes at different times of the day. Before 10 a.m. and after 3 p.m., the sun penetrates the atmosphere at a steeper angle and passes through a denser volume of atmospheric gases, eliminating some of the blue end of the spectrum by "scattering" and causing the light that emerges to appear with an orange or reddish tinge. The photographer may want to use color correction filters under these circumstances — but the use of a light blue filter (no. 82 series) or a darker blue series (no. 80) to reduce the reddish cast of dawn or dusk will ruin the natural effect of this time of day. The end result of using light-balancing or conversion filters is to adjust the daylight hues to the colors of the midday sun, a result not necessarily desirable.[25] "Normal" color to the human eye

---

23. Thus, for example, with an ASA of 64, shoot 1/30 at 2.8.

24. Ektachrome may, however, need a blue color correction filter if it is to be pushed by two stops or more. A yellow filter could be required if it is "pulled" by even one stop. On the other hand, these color correction filters can be used in the lab at the time of producing enlargements — this author's preference, at least. Kodak labs have the reputation of refusing to push or pull Kodachromes (25 or 64) — the process is difficult — but polite pressure and a degree of patience usually carry the day.

25. High-speed Ektachrome may, as suggested earlier, balance the extreme warmth of early morning or late day.

includes at least some of the color changes that occur in a day. In fact, the nature photographer has to exercise extreme caution in using color correction filters of any kind. The most serviceable are likely to be 81A and 81B (both amber-tinted), which are often employed to reduce the cool blueness of a picture taken under cloudy or overcast conditions or in open shade under a blue sky. Filters for large lenses are apt to be quite expensive — one suggestion is to make do with a (homemade) thin gelatin filter fitted over the smaller rear element.

An added complication for the safarist is that color and exposure considerations have to be weighed against various animal habits, which activities are themselves often tied to various times of the day. The chart accompanying this chapter attempts to pull all these factors together in an easily understandable manner. The chart is, of course, an approximation only. Animals, creatures of habit though they may be, expend a great deal of time doing the unexpected. A more thorough examination of what one should expect from a particular species is found in the chapters that follow.

The photographer should know that he has, at most, only approximately a half-hour after the sun goes down before he loses all detail for the day. Darkness comes quickly in the African bush, and it waits for no safarist.[26]

One final "trick of the trade" with regard to anticipating exposure is to keep aware of how many frames in a given roll of film have been shot. If the lighting has changed or is soon expected to change and the frame-counter shows only a few shots remaining on a roll, the photographer should sacrifice the unused film and reload with a more appropriate choice. As obvious as this advice may seem reading it here, photographers often neglect to follow it, even when anticipating important photographs ahead.

A safari is an exciting — and, for most, an unusual — time, and the author hopes to stimulate the photographer to focus on these considerations beforehand. They will never occur to him for the first time speeding across the savannah grasslands as dusk approaches and the Landrover heads toward a final rendezvous for the day.

Special Problems

1. Dust.

Of the four "special problems" that the photographer encounters on safari, perhaps the most annoying — certainly, the most pervasive — is the fine African dust. If dust penetrates the camera to any great degree, it might jam the film-advance mechanism, slow down the shutter,

---

26. The author has offered no advice on nighttime photography, because the distances to the animals are beyond normal portable flash or other light units. Night game drives are highly entertaining and should not be missed, but the cameras are best left behind.

or even coat the inner surfaces of the lens, thereby impairing light transmission. Moreover, dust that reaches film can cause speckled pictures. Dust is more of a problem with the older mechanical equipment, as opposed to the newer electronic gear; the same is true for the older helical-focusing lenses, as opposed to the newer internal-focusing systems. Simply stated, moving parts attract dust. In the final analysis, there is no way to keep the dust sneaking into practically everywhere; the object is to manage the problem as best as one can:

- Canned (compressed) air — larger cans for use back at the lodge or tent, pocket-sized for the field — is the primary instrument of salvation. One should exercise care, however, never to spray air directly onto the camera's shutter curtain.

- A very small vacuum, if one can be found, would also be useful.

- A rubber hand-squeeze bulb blower with a good camel hair brush is a handy supplement to canned air. (Lung power, incidentally, is not recommended because of the accompanying saliva!) A toothbrush or small typewriter cleaning brush for outside crevices and corners will also prove beneficial.

- All equipment should be cleaned (and checked) at the end of each game drive, this task accomplished without exception and meticulously (inside and out). Lens paper and cleaning fluid should be used as well. The proper cleaning sequence is very important. Never risk the chance of scratching surfaces with gritty particles: always blow and brush (in that order) before wiping.

- Several protective filters should be included in the photographer's kit; a filter can easily be damaged when subjected to the hurried dust cleaning frequently required in the field.

- Special attention should be given to cleaning regularly the film-loading chambers for dust and film fragments that will scratch film. In addition, the metal runners at the back of the camera should also be wiped clean regularly.

- Lens caps should be employed when the lenses are not actually being used, depending on how easily the caps go on and off (it helps to be quick: screw-ons can be a real hassle). Many lens hoods do not accommodate the caps, an annoying oversight by manufacturers. Photographers therefore may find it necessary to rig up homemade covers (*e.g.*, plastic wrap and a rubberband). Lens caps must be used on both sides of a lens, if the lens has been removed from the camera. Do not delay for any reason covering the rear lens

Plates 2-5. Photographer's Portfolio.

element once the lens has been removed from the mount — dust here has immediate access to inside the lens.

- Ziplock plastic bags to enclose equipment when not in use are most helpful. It is not always practicable to keep moving equipment in and out of a closed camera bag. Besides, the less that one has to revert to the basic bag (or kit), the less that dust will pervade the entire system.

- All equipment should be checked and cleaned professionally after a safari.

One would do well to note that dust is made far worse by vehicle movement, one's own or others'. A special effort should be made to protect the equipment at those times.

2. Heat.

Humidity is rarely a serious problem on safari — extreme, sustained humidity is found only in the dense rain forests on the coast. Heat is another matter altogether. And the problems are not just those of film. The African sun is hot, and the equipment itself can suffer. The camera lens is a particularly efficient conductor of heat; a few minutes of direct exposure pointed straight at the sun can damage a camera's shutter mechanism. The lens acts like a magnifying glass, and the image of the sun might even burn a hole right through the shutter. Lens cement can also soften in strong sun, and the lens elements separate. And lubricants in the camera itself will be adversely affected in intense heat.

The photographer knows that color film is sensitive to high temperatures. Consequently, he must look after both the film inside the camera and all the new and processed film kept in the film pouches. The basic rule for film carried under field conditions is to keep it as cool as possible at all times. A loaded camera should not be left in the direct sun; black camera bodies are especially good absorbers of heat (the temperature inside can rise rapidly to 120° F or more in the full sun). This precaution is easy to forget as the safarist rides around standing through the roof hatch with his camera hanging on a neck strap. The camera(s), when not in use, should be covered by clothing or, preferably, a white towel. Neither the camera nor any film bag should ever be left in a car trunk, glove compartment, inside any enclosed vehicle left in the sun, or on a car dash or back window ledge. Neither camera nor film should ever be placed directly onto the floor of a car. And, on a particularly long game drive, the film is best stored in the cold box.

Pictures developed from film that overheated will have a reddish cast. Heat-damaged slides also look pale and fogged, whereas negatives produce flat-looking pictures with little color saturation.

3. Brightness.

The severe brightness discovered throughout the middle of the day going about on game drives, including the reflected light off vehicles (especially off the white roofs) and off grass in the dry season or the bare ground when the sun is high, requires special attention. Most of the necessary or available precautions — or compensations — have already been mentioned:

- Slow film or neutral density filters are essential at midday to cope with the light.

- A lens hood is an absolute necessity at all times.

- One should always load film with one's back kept to the sun, while remaining in as much shade as possible. Moreover, a lens cap should always remain on when loading film.

- Err on the side of underexposure.

- Keep developed film out of direct sunlight (or any strong light).

- Use a rubber eyecup and keep the eye close to the finder. When the photographer works with a cable release or uses the time-release mechanism and, in either instance, takes his eye from the finder, the window should be blocked with the hand or black tape. (Some advanced cameras have a view-finder shutter that the photographer can close.)

The photographer may want to experiment with a neutral gray graduated filter, which will darken a bright sky to bring it closer to the brightness of the main subject — and avoid the burnt-out white sky that an averaging meter will often produce.

4. Vibration.

Next to dust, the *constant* vibration of the safari vehicle is the greatest enemy to photographic peace of mind. Equipment that is not being immediately used should remain in a well-padded camera bag or wrapped in specially designed protective material. One should do one's utmost to ensure that the equipment does not fall off the seat onto the vehicle floor. Equipment banging against other equipment is also a common concern. A lens hood and a protective filter will help protect at least the lens glass in the event of falls or equipment being jostled together. For a lens that has taken a severe jolt, one must check the glass surfaces and the diaphram connections. Internal unobservable damage may, of course, have occurred, and such an impaired lens may not produce excellent pictures thereafter. Aside from what has already been said, all that the photographer can do is to check the focusing (usually, at infinity) itself and, secondarily, the smooth operation of the barrel-focusing ring.

When cleaning inside a camera itself that has taken a beating, the photographer should always look for dents or holes in the shutter by holding the camera up to the light with the back open and firing a sequence of exposures. And the camera mirror should be checked for scratches. Moreover, the prism head on a camera often absorbs the impact of a fall. Thus, a second camera from which a similar prism could be cannibalized in the event of damage may be helpful. If the camera has sustained any injury to its back, the slightest dent may affect focus by misaligning the film pressure plate: once the relationship between the film plane and the lens has fallen out of sync, focus could easily fail. Finally, all components suspected of injury should be subjected to a 'sound' inspection as well: shake the part and listen for the rattle of loose bits inside.

Even well-protected equipment can be adversely affected; the steady vibration can loosen screws and damage precision mechanisms, and the photographer should periodically check every observable connection. Reasonable care and forethought, combined with rugged equipment, will lift all but the most unlucky photographers over the hurdle of equipment damage.[27]

Without question, the safari photographer wastes his time attempting to take photographs while the vehicle engine is running; vehicle vibration will ruin definition.[28] This fact causes a few problems for the photographer on safari. Drivers are inclined to be lazy in this regard, and too many vehicles are not in the proper condition for constant shutting off and restarting the engines. On his part, the photographer must remain (tactfully) persistent — first, by letting the driver know in advance of the game drive that he (the driver) will be expected to maneuver the vehicle into the best position, stop, and shut off the engine; and, second, by following up during the drive itself and continually reminding the driver to cut the motor. Occasionally, the driver will be understandably reluctant to switch off the means of escape. These are times when the animals threaten the vehicle. In reality, such moments are few, and some drivers (the tour operators hold the drivers responsible for any damage caused to the vehicles) tend to be excessively nervous in this regard. But moving very near an elephant matron with calf is genuinely dangerous. Solitary old buffalo bulls are maniacally unpredictable and should never be approached too close. A rhino rarely attacks a vehicle to the point of contact, though a fake charge or two may give everyone a thrill. Again, if the driver has taken proper care of his vehicle's electrical system — most important, he has periodically checked the electrical connections, which do have to withstand continual vibration and jostling on safari — there is usually enough time in a true predicament to start the vehicle and scamper away, if necessary.

The best strategy to keep from irritating the animals is to approach them slowly and to *remain quiet*. The author has sat for hours in the very middle of a huge elephant herd, with pachyderms young and old grazing right up to the Landrover. No one in our vehicle said a word, and, aside from a snort or two and the toss of a trunk, the elephants hardly appeared to notice. If the vehicle must be kept running or is actually moving, the photographer can chance a shot or two, but the better advice under those conditions is to forget the camera and simply enjoy the view.[29]

The author has mentioned the importance of cleaning the equipment at the end of every drive. That time should also be devoted to checking for any vibration or other damage. Indeed, at day's end, all the components should be gathered together back in the tent or lodge, inspected, and thoroughly cleaned. And everything for the next day should be prepared and laid out. The safarist will be rising early, and it is easy to forget a critical piece of equipment while staggering to the vehicle at 6:00 a.m.

Composition Notes

Up to now, this chapter has focused primarily on equipment, film, and technical skills. The basic goals have been to prepare the photographer for safari and to encourage him to handle and use the camera in an almost instinctive fashion — the photographic equivalent, so to speak, of quick reflexes. We now turn to the subjects themselves: finding, approaching, and observing the animals.

Conventional safari wisdom says that the early mornings, followed by the late afternoons, are the best times for photography, because the animals are most active then. A glance at the accompanying chart supports this testimony, to a point. Many animals, to be sure, avoid the heat of the day when they can and move around more when the air is cooler. Nonetheless, the observant and knowledgeable photographer will find much to watch and photograph in the middle of the day as well.

When photographing animals, it might be helpful to think in terms of two basic opportunities: one, to produce an elegant, full-color portrait; and, two, to capture the decisive moment of stopped action. The former presents a particular challenge vis-à-vis animals that have been photographed many times. The latter takes considerable

---

27. Without intending to be churlish, the author also should warn the traveling photographer against the polite and almost instinctual reach of all porters, drivers, and other native helpers on safari to carry the camera bag or equipment. The desire to be helpful should not be confused with the exercise of due care: the safarist is advised to carry his own gear and alertly (but kindly) to deflect attempts to relieve him of the burden.

28. Vibration caused by engines on a boat also plays havoc with definition, but stopping and restarting a boat on safari is often an impractical request.

29. An expensive option for the photographer who needs to get good results in a moving vehicle is a gyro-stabilizing system. The most reliable cost $2,000 or more.

skill. Of course, the new photographic technology that has solved most (but not all) problems of distance and subject motion has changed the emphasis of animal photography to predominantly action pictures. But, just as the best portraits show physical features that illuminate some important ingredient of the animal's character or life, the action depicted should show some similar insight as well. Taking the dichotomy further, the photographer may then want to regard the two ends of the day as opportunities for portrait sittings and midday as the time most favorable for capturing the action. The low, soft light of morning or late afternoon is as "flattering" to animals as it is to human beings, emphasizing as it does the animal's contours and textures. The warm color balance prevailing at these times also produces natural and healthy-looking portraits. Alternatively, the strong light of midday gives the edge to the photographer trying to stop a timid and fast animal. Unfortunately for such neat characterizations, the task is rarely quite that simple. Indeed, the photographer must be prepared at all times to capture action. This is, in fact, the great challenge of a photo-safari: the photographer must shoot under conditions dictated by the habits of the animals. He takes what comes along. Thus, the ideal dichotomy espoused above simply becomes one consideration among many.

One purpose of this book is to help the safarist gain some insight into the habits and characteristics of the most important or photogenic animals encountered (from the perspective of the "average safarist"). Careful planning, proper anticipation, and even quick reactions on the part of the wildlife photographer all presuppose a working knowledge of the animals and their environment. The first objectives are to locate the animals and then approach to bring them within optimum photographic range. The photographer as a consequence becomes a sportsman or hunter of sorts as he stalks his "prey." Indeed, the photographer shares much in common with the old safari trophy hunter, though it is undoubtedly far more difficult to secure a good picture than to kill the subject.

In the first instance, the visitor will frequently rely on the driver-guides, and the best of these are worth their weight in gold. Some parks have their own rangers, and one of them should probably be taken along as well — the local rangers "network" among themselves (some even use radio contact, when local vehicles are driven) and are excellent guides to recent animal movement. The local ranger will know, for example, that a certain pride of lions will likely be hunting early one morning, because he also knows that they did not feed the day before or the day before that. First-time visitors never cease to marvel at the "eyes" of the guides and rangers: how did he see that cheetah sitting under the tree before the rest of us even spotted the tree! Good eyes notwithstanding, the secret of the professional guide's success is more often the intelligence network and his familiarity with a particular reserve.

But the guides are also effective because they know many of the animals' habits. Neither guides nor rangers are infallible, of course, and, if the safarist himself has taken the trouble to learn something about the animals, he may recognize some pretty weird misinformation. At any rate, one should talk to the guides and gain their confidence — let them know of one's priorities and preferences, encourage them to "network," and show an interest in their country. Although he may retain the services of excellent guides, the photo-safarist himself should also understand the basic game-drive techniques. There is, in fact, much that the safarist can do to increase the success of locating interesting wildlife. The basic role is to set a full agenda.

The early morning drive should begin around 6 a.m.[30] — this is when many of the animals, including the big cats, are going to be the most active. The idea is to put in a good two or even three hours before breakfast. After returning to the camp or lodge for (a late) breakfast, the safarist then has a choice: he may wait until later in the day to go out again, a practice positively urged by most tour operators (and drivers); or he may venture forth with a boxed lunch to explore the far reaches of the park or to observe at greater length certain animal behavior. The author cannot understand why someone would travel all the way to Africa to pass each midday in a game park away from the animals. Occasionally, a nap or swim in a pool, will, to be sure, provide a much needed, refreshing break. Or someone might want to work with all the birdlife and small animals found in the proximity of the accommodations. But listening to the tour operators and more than a few lazy drivers, one could quickly come to believe that the entire animal kingdom itself naps through midday. This is wasteful information, indeed! Moreover, the drivers know that a visit to the hippo pool or local waterhole, to name but two of many choices, would prove rewarding. And, although they may well prefer to rest or visit with friends at midday, the drivers will also respect a safarist who knows enough about what he wants to see to insist upon going back into the bush at this time.[31]

In all these respects, whether the safarist is duly setting out at the crack of dawn or deciding what to do midday or scouring the bush for wildlife, the beginner should realize that a certain level of knowledge can be misleading. In particular, one needs to examine carefully "common lore." Knowing that lions, for example, lie under bushes or in the shade of trees when it's hot, or on a high open

---

30. All the camps or lodges will provide wake-up coffee or tea.

31. Drivers receive gratuities at the conclusion of safari. Those who work a long day deserve an extra tip, but this marginal expense will never be a burden to the safarist. The tour operators themselves, who have a professional interest in seeing that their drivers are well treated but not overtipped, are reliable guides to proper current gratuity payments.

spot when it's cool, appropriately concentrates one's attention at the right time of day. Nevertheless, an animal is not a robot, and the African bush is not some gigantic zoo, with corresponding feeding hours, visiting hours, and so forth. The safarist should not translate knowledge, much less anecdotes, into rules that can cause him to miss the "unexpected." Many a hungry lion has waited expectantly at the local waterhole at midday. Both the antelope *and* the safarist may be surprised to learn of his presence, but that is the whole point (at least, from the lion's perspective). Moreover, the range of one's knowledge must extend to many animals. Thus, the presence of one animal is frequently signaled by the presence or behavior of other animals. Perhaps, the best example of this "inductive reasoning" is the activity of a prey species in revealing the presence of the predators. The unmistakable profiles of several circling vultures is another classic signal, on one level, but lead to a possibly misleading inference, from the safarist's perspective, if seen during the huge migrations, when the ground is littered with rotting carcasses from many causes, diseases among others. The circling-vulture "signal" is also discussed in Chapter V.

The safarist makes a further contribution toward his own safari by setting the tone of the individual game drives. One may race through the bush like Lewis Carroll's White Rabbit or may adopt a more measured approach. Indeed, along with knowledge and good eyesight, as critical game-spotting elements, go patience and perseverance, two sides of the same coin. A second look, a third look from a different angle — these can make all the difference. The animals are out there, but luck is really the major player if they are revealed by a mere first glance. A more sure methodology requires work. In general, game-spotting from vehicles combines two search methods: looking on the move and scanning while stopped. The second, scanning (best accomplished with a good pair of binoculars), has the advantage of detecting shy animals at a great enough distance to prevent frightening them. The choice of a particular method has much to do with the terrain traveled by the vehicle and the vista afforded to the safarist at any given time, as well, of course, as what the safarist wants to see. And it should be obvious that the faster that one is traveling, the less that one is likely to see. Only the most obvious features of a reserve are visible at speed.

Earlier, the author suggested relying upon the guides or rangers who are familiar with a reserve to take the safarist to the choicest spots, as it were. Certainly, this is a reliable strategy on a short schedule. Like most people, the guides are, however, capable of varying levels of effort and attention. The easiest path is to slip into the "standard" approach: a great deal of random driving in certain areas, stops at the most reliable points, and tracking down other parked vehicles. But the safarist who takes the time to study a particular reserve and discuss a proposed game drive beforehand with the guide will benefit from a heightened enthusiasm and more focused procedure.

Parenthetically, the safarist ought to think about preserving his eyesight by avoiding excessive eye-strain. A break is recommended, now and then, to prevent loss of concentration and physical discomfort. Sunglasses worn throughout the middle of the day — to ward off the intense sun, heat waves from the ground, and dry, dusty winds — are also essential. And eye drops taken at the end of the day make sense as well. When planning a circuit in the late afternoon, the safarist, insofar as possible, should not travel in a westerly direction, when the sun is low. Both the eyes and the camera will appreciate a setting sun over the shoulder and behind the back.

The approach to animals, once they are spotted, is likewise a matter of applying proper technique. Hours of diligent searching are sometimes wasted by only a few minutes of approaching improperly shy animals. Again, the matter is essentially one of patience. The approach should normally be gradual, as the vehicle proceeds slowly and carefully. Abrupt action frightens most animals. Brief pauses are recommended to monitor the reaction of the game, but, if the vehicle is within the animal's hearing, the engine should never be switched off until the photographer is as close as and positioned where he wants to be. The sound of a car motor starting is far more likely to upset some animals than the sound of an engine gradually approaching. Finally, driving closer to the animal in a circling or oblique manner is preferable to driving straight at it.

As the author has already noted, the photo-safarist should always bear in mind that moving too near to many animals will cause them appreciably to modify their behavior. One often sees more interesting (and natural) behavior from a distance. Furthermore, a frequently encountered problem on game drives is that a stopped safari vehicle will eventually draw a "crowd." Where off-road driving is permitted, one many times sees animals completely encircled by cars: gleaming metal, excited human beings, many noisy cameras, and a blocked view of their environment — all guaranteed to make the animals exceedingly nervous, if not drive them away altogether. The author has just as often fooled the "pack" of other safarists by keeping a discreet distance from an animal and feigning ignorance when approached by another vehicle. Most other drivers will not bother to stop if they themselves do not see the animal. One can, in fact, think of many ploys to evade the other tourists, but, as previously indicated in Chapter I, the "crush" is never really oppressive over an entire vacation, despite an occasional disappointment caused by too many converging vehicles.[32]

---

32. Tour operators can make the problem truly oppressive by caravanning large groups in four or five (or more) minivans that follow each other like lemmings. The only benefit of dust on safari that the author can think of is that it encourages these minivans to stagger or alternate their routes. The problem is further explored in Chapter X.

The safarist has spotted the game and has carefully made his approach. The final compositional notes concern the practice of observation. (The reader will by now realize the broad context in which the author uses the term "composition.") The first principle is that the animals should never be purposely disturbed. Slamming the door of a vehicle to get "Leo to stand up" is simply boorish,[33] and photographically unhelpful behavior, besides. Even more seriously moronic are active attempts to influence nature. Trying to rile an old elephant by driving at him may be condemned by most people as revolting, or at least more resembling the comic insolence of a Peter Sellers movie, but the reader might be surprised at the number of times that well-intentioned tourists take it upon themselves to speed up nature's rhythms by attempting to drive game toward a carnivore in order to force a kill. Such tactics never work and many times succeed only in driving the actors off the stage altogether. On the positive side, keeping relatively silent is critical, especially when standing through a roof hatch or occupying an otherwise open vehicle. The sound most jarring, most threatening, to many wild animals is a human voice. It may help at these moments to think of Wodehouse's phrase: "Oysters garrulous and tombs chatty by comparison." On rare occasions, it is even advisable to wrap the camera in a dark cloth to muffle the sound of the shutter and to prevent reflections.

If the photographer is patient enough and the animals become accustomed to the presence of his vehicle, the good shots will come. For example, tourists must be willing to take sufficient time waiting for a carnivore to make a kill. And to allow enough space. If the animal is indeed hunting, the visitor who keeps a respectful distance may well be rewarded. Crowding the animal, however, will alert the prey and kill the hunter's opportunity.

Once the photographer is in place and looking for that "decisive moment" of action, he can begin to think about sequential shots. A picture can tell a story, but a photographic sequence invariably tells one better. And the faster the action, the more effective the sequence. In addition to a beginning, middle, and end, many sequences have a certain rhythm, and capturing that rhythm is usually desirable.

The importance of remaining alert during observation cannot be overemphasized. Anticipating possible changes in lighting and periodically checking the camera's settings have earlier been stressed. The animals themselves need the same attention. And, for essentially the same reason as keeping his eye on the camera's frame-counter when the lighting is changing, the photographer should anticipate a possibly important behavioral sequence coming up by changing a roll of film that may be near its end. The chapters that follow are full of tips relative to the behavior of many species, but one overriding observation may prove valuable at this point: the more frequently that any animal interrupts what it is doing to look at the safarist, the more likely that it will flee (or, at least, significantly alter its behavior).

The photographer should also concentrate when framing his composition. Special care is needed when filling a frame. Slide mounts, for example, will cut off about ten percent of the picture evenly all around (this missing photography does not cause any problem when the camera/lens shows through its viewfinder only ninety percent of the resulting picture, a feature of older equipment). Printing from slides can permanently lose that ten percent. This kind of loss should encourage the photographer to pay close attention to the location and position of the subject pictured in the viewfinder.

Previously, the author discussed the two basic vehicle perspectives: from the roof hatch and at window level. The photographer should try both angles and alternate between them frequently over the course of the entire safari. The lower angle of window level often provides more realistic or more dramatic photographs, because the photographer operates virtually on the same plane that the animals themselves are found. The animals tend to dominate the photographs. Of course, the most effective window shots must be taken from a position reasonably close to the animals. Generally, the photo-safarist will, however, prefer the undoubted convenience of the roof hatch and especially so when the grass or other vegetation obscures the animals or, even more important, when an animal is moving. Furthermore, whatever level or angle is used, the photographer should also alternate the horizontal and vertical formats. Surprisingly, perhaps, many photographers do not experiment enough with the vertical format. In fact, the author has looked at several safari collections that contained not one vertical shot! Nature has never been that orderly!

The photographer on safari deals with the question of creativity, of imaginative seeing, of escaping what has been called in the photographic context "the Tyranny of the Familiar" often belatedly. Most wildlife photographers attempt to shoot "authentic" pictures that are biologically truthful — accurate, clear, in a natural setting. Ideally, one should be able to identify unequivocally an animal from its photograph; to classify the animal, that is, show enough of its pertinent characteristics to enable a comparison with other fauna; and to help understand that animal's life from the clues pictured. On safari, the first instinct is simply to "get" the animal, with as much sharpness as possible. The confident photographer also looks for beauty; concentrates on effective framing of the subject; keeps space in front of moving objects;[34] avoids

---

33. This is the specialty of the one-week 'grand' safari, three or more parks in seven days (never more than two days in one place), with the driver playing the role of ringmaster in the circus. "Oh dear! Oh dear! I shall be too late!" complained the White Rabbit.

---

34. Animal movement can be "implied." Thus, an animal

distracting shadows; and searches for striking patterns, geometric designs, special color (in nature, nearly all colors "go together"), the blending of textures, and leading lines to guide the viewer or to emphasize distance. The notorious "rule of thirds" is never far from his mind. And one must, of course, always keep an eye open for manmade features that will jar human sensibilities in viewing portraits of nature — vehicles, roads, poles, signs, discarded bottles, and so forth.

Although the photographer may be concentrating on a single species, wildlife photography often turns into habitat photography — at least, the animal often benefits from a more varied or complete look at its surroundings. The immediate ecology may include a range of "photographic subjects" that could all stand on their own — flowers, insects, birds, and so forth. But, to understand an animal, one must know a great deal about its habitat — and photographers need to see and photograph the complete ecological unit in much the same fashion as they are inclined to do with respect to the animals standing by themselves. The relationship between land, weather, flora, and fauna can make for coherent — and brilliant — photographic images.

But the creative nature photographer may want further to act as an interpreter of nature's form, its beauty, integrity, mystery, power, and immensity. He will attempt primarily to convey esthetically exciting images that communicate his own, perhaps peculiar, appreciation for the natural world. This effort may lead to special perspectives, harsh contrasts, silhouettes, extreme graininess, the use of color correction filters, and severe under- or overexposure. Sharply lit horizons, the filtering effect of dust, the shadows provided by clouds and hills, bands of light and shade in the forests, and threatening storms — all can be used to advantage. And much, much more. But such creativity must always work within the impinging realities of safari: a limited to virtually non-existing capability of manipulating either the lighting or the subject at any one time.

The author usually draws the creative line at trying to convey a heightened sense of reality by frequently concentrating on the animal's environment, as well as the animal itself. The spontaneity, simplicity, and inherent harmony found on safari frankly appeal to the author. In my opinion, nature needs little artistic or inventive help. The zoom lens is my most creative tool. But the free use of imagination depends almost entirely upon the photographer's feeling for his subject. In the end, "creativity" is as uniquely personal as one's signature.

. . . .

The pictures in this book have been chosen in large measure for the information that they can give concerning the animals photographed: portraits that show a clear view of the entire animal or that emphasize key traits of that animal; group shots of prides, herds, flocks, or the like; the depiction of basic action or movement; animals gathering food or hunting, eating, drinking, or supplying meals to their young; courtship displays or rituals, as well as special mating coloration; mating itself; birth and the caring for the young; migration; den or nest building; greetings and other social activities; aggressive displays and actual attacks; predation, as well as repelling or fleeing from predators; and the animal living in its habitat or surroundings. The captions do not, however, give such photographic information as shutter speed, aperture, focal length, and ASA. The author has always found this latter practice slightly ridiculous. Are readers supposed to memorize such information? Does the successful photographer carry a hundred or more examples of film speed and camera and lens settings with him into the field? The practical value or such numbers is probably nil. The author has always suspected that many were made up after the fact, anyway; a photographer in the wild writing down all this information would miss fully three-quarters, possibly more, of the relevant shots.

The photographs contained in this volume, instructive though they may be relative to the animals themselves, are also meant to be enjoyed. At best, their ultimate message should be that pictures of this quality and interest — and better — are possible. Possible to photographers who will sharpen their skills, learn about the animals, and devote the time and patience necessary to do a proper safari. No doubt many of the most spectacular wildlife pictures — often seen in the popular magazines and later in book collections — are taken by professionals with sophisticated equipment that includes elaborate blinds, electronic flash, remote controls, and, most important, nearly unlimited time. But the amateur today has access to all the technology that one needs to shoot really fine pictures. Nor are the best pictures always made using complicated gear. The reader with sufficient interest to come this far, who appreciates the importance of a firm grounding in the basics just covered, will go on to learn about the animals. Armed with that knowledge, he will then be prepared to take advantage of all the opportunities that will arise on safari. He will expose many rolls of film. And the great shots will come.

which does not effectively fill a frame should ordinarily *look* into that frame. Several exceptions exist: for example, a herd animal looking outwards for danger, and all animals looking at the photographer. In general, wildlife needs room to "live in," and the photographer errs in framing his natural subject too tightly.

Plate 6. Cheetah Resting.

III. The Literary Setting

Nothing can really prepare you for Africa: it is too full of extremes and contrasts, too immense — a spectrum of creation so much wider and more vivid than anywhere else that it seems to require a new set of senses, or the rediscovery of lost ones. Also, if you live as close to the animals and nature as we did, the unconscious is stirred at levels deeper than anything "remembered": you are returned to times and experiences to which we have lost all other access.

Starting out, we felt like children again. The questions we asked! As the safari proceeded, they were to become less in number and more discriminating, but that first day they came as thick as the dust that boiled away behind us or encircled an oncoming car. What was the name of that tree? What did the secretary bird live on in such desert? Giraffes, here?

Evelyn Ames, *A Glimpse of Eden*[1]

Most of us, at one time or another, have read the fascinating tales of others' African safaris: the discoveries of the early explorers; the ofttimes miraculous treks of missionaries; the adventures of the white hunters; the trials and tribulations of the dilettante travelers; the reports of seemingly harassed administrators; and the observations of the dedicated, if occasionally somewhat amateurish, naturalists. What has not actually been witnessed first hand, the novelists have supplied. Africa has not lacked for the literary touch, however exaggerated or romanticized. Indeed, writers over the years have found it difficult, if not impossible, to be neutral about Africa. Until fairly recently, the vicarious pleasure of traveling through another's eyes was the closest that most of us could experience the continent. Today, when many people can, in fact, seize a part of the real thing for themselves, the choicest of anecdotes, though certainly rarely qualifying as scientific observation, can still set the scene or fire the imagination. Some of the author's favorites — sense and nonsense, perception and imagination — follow.

We thought we knew what to expect. Several friends had been there and told us about it; some, even, had made the same trip we were...going to make, but we discovered that nothing, really, prepares you for life on the East African Highlands. It is life (I want to say), making our usual existences seem oddly unreal

and other landscapes dead; that country in the sky is another world. . . .

It is a world, and a life, from which one comes back changed. Long afterwards, gazelles still galloped through my dreams or stood gazing at me out of their soft and watchful eyes, and as I returned each daybreak, unbelieving, to my familiar room, I realized increasingly that this world would never again be the same for having visited that one. Nor does it leave you when you go away. Knowing its landscapes and sounds (even more, its silence), how it feels and smells — just knowing it is there — sets it forever, in its own special light, somewhere in the mind's sky.

Ames, *A Glimpse of Eden*, pp. 1-2. Mrs. Ames, a poet and novelist, recorded the experiences of a month-long safari taken in East Africa in this book, which in many pages captures the magic of Africa.

ELEPHANTS HAVE RIGHT OF WAY

— frequent notice in game preserves

6.00pm   The sun is about to set when a large herd of elephants appears. The animals rush forward into the water, some just drinking, while others spray water over their backs with much excited trumpeting. But they don't stay long. We had not expected anything to happen, and had left the cameras in the van. By the time Günter returns, the elephants are already leaving the water-holes. Günter is just saying that he will never get such a chance again when a second herd appears. They behave much like the first group, rushing into the water and then drinking thirstily, and bathing with a lot of noise. This

1. Houghton Mifflin, 1967, p. 9.

Plate 1. Zebra and Gazelle Tableau.

time we capture the scene on film. . .

Günter Ziesler & Angelika Hofer, *Safari: The East African Diaries of a WildLife Photographer,* p. 61. This volume has been recommended in Chapter I for its magnificent pictures.

One's first encounter with a pride of lions in such a setting is an unforgettable experience. It is a late afternoon in the Mara Reserve. The weight of the equatorial sun has begun to lift. The air is clear and golden. The Land Rover bounces gently across the plain. Irregular clumps of wildebeest, zebra and gazelle extend to the horizon, their outlines brought to an unbelievable sharpness in the low level light. Suddenly someone says: "lions!"

It is as simple as that. There they are, 15 of them, a couple of fine males, half a dozen females and an assortment of cubs — all lying in a stupor, scattered over the ground like tawny bolsters, drunk with sleep, sun and food. They lie sprawled in every conceivable attitude, like dead soldiers on a battlefield, and they might as well be dead for all the attention they pay to

the approaching Land Rover. Long familiarity with those noisy, smelly machines in the game reserves has taught lions that they are neither edible nor dangerous, and their attitude toward them goes far beyond contempt — it approaches utter indifference.

The Land Rover stops 20 feet away. The man standing in the roof-hatch busies himself with his camera. One shaggy head may rise up. There will be a momentary glitter of a brilliant amber eye, a prodigious yawn that gives a glimpse of two fearsome canines and a foot or so of pink throat, and the head will fall again with an audible thump on the ground. The other members of the pride will not stir. And even the yawner will somehow have managed to get across the idea that the vehicle's approach had nothing to do with him. He was going to yawn anyway.

Thus, the lion, once again a king in his own country, relaxed to a degree of regal languor incomprehensible to humans — interested in other lions, in eating when he gets hungry, in nothing else.

The watchers settle down to wait. For a while nothing happens beyond a yawn or two. Then two small cubs wake up and begin to explore the nipples of a lioness who is stretched on her back, one paw stuck straight up in the air. Nothing doing there — the well is dry. But the female gives a grunt and rolls over on her side. Her tail twitches and instantly the cubs attack it. The next five minutes are given over to an enchanting display of baby-lion fun, ambushes and pounces, miniature growls, collapses on rubber legs.

Maitland Edey & John Dominis, *The Cats of Africa*, p. 33. This book was also recommended in Chapter I and is one of those rare 'picture books' with a superb text.

I used to watch all these animals come down to the Uaso Nyiro in the afternoon, and this perhaps is the best of Africa: to sit very quietly on the banks of a river through the last hot hours of the day and watch (as one might watch from a café chair in the Champs Elysées) the local life go by. For quite long periods nothing happens. The crocodile (very pale green ones up here) slithers off the sandbank and leaves the river a blank. You are being watched, you know, from all around, and from the branches up above, by many different eyes, and it's just a mat-ter of sitting still until the birds and animals are reassured that you are not dangerous. . .gradually you become an accepted part of the scene along the river; you breathe with it, you vibrate, as it were, at the right slow tempo. Then anything can happen.

Alan Moorehead, *No Room in the Ark* (Hamish Hamilton, 1959), pp. 103-4. A classic of its type. This book chronicles three journeys made in Africa in the 1950s. As expected today, many mistaken theories of animal behavior are propounded, but the basic perceptions and wisdom are nearly unrivaled. Moorehead also wrote *The Blue Nile* and *The White Nile*, brilliant and immensely entertaining studies of African exploration.

The views were immensely wide. Everything that you saw made for greatness and freedom, and unequalled nobility.

Isak Dinesen, *Out of Africa* (Random House, 1938; Vintage Books Edition, 1972), p. 4. "Isak Dinesen" was the pen-name of the Danish Baroness Karen Blixen. ("Dinesen" was her maiden name.) Born in Denmark in 1885, she and

Plate 2. Uaso Nyiro in the Afternoon.

her Swedish husband-to-be, attracted by the promise of the "riches" waiting there, went to live in British East Africa in January 1914. They established a coffee plantation outside Nairobi. Although she was divorced from her husband in 1921, she continued to manage the plantation for another ten years, until economic hardship forced her to sell the property and return to Denmark in 1931. *Out of Africa*, one of the great memoirs of the twentieth century, is Blixen's tribute to those seventeen years. A superb storyteller, Blixen's deep love for Africa shines through every moving, lyrical page. The book, first published in English in 1937, has become a classic. Blixen was nominated for the Nobel literature prize. Hemingway, who took the prize that year (1954), always maintained that she should have won. Rarely does a movie ever duplicate the poetry of literature, but the film "Out of Africa" is faithful to the beauty of the original.

During my ramble I noticed the remains of a lion, buffalo, and crocodile, lying together in a heap, and was told a curious story to account for this strange sight. It was said that when the

Plate 3. Savannah Vista. The grasslands of Africa — savannahs, veldt, plains — sometimes support sixty or seventy animal species in a particular locale. Nearly half of Africa's total land surface is grassland of one type or another; a virtually unbroken prairie stretches from the chilly steppes of South African Cape Province to the Sahara desert, feeding the greatest concentration of large mammals in the world. Indeed, the largest group of herbivores, the grazing antelopes, has colonized every diverse grassland habitat from the inundated swamps of the Nile to the heart of the barren Namib Desert and up to the exposed montane pastures found on Mt. Kilimanjaro. The dominant grass throughout the deciduous woodlands and open savannah of East Africa is usually red oat, resistant to drought, grazing, and fire — all which cause damage down to the ground surface and are indistinguishable to the grass. The grass makes quick use of rainfall and grows rapidly from ground level, at the base of its leaf.

buffalo came to drink a lion sprang upon him, and, both rolling into the water together, they were seized by a crocodile. He in his turn was dragged about twenty yards from the bank by the struggles of the two beasts, and there the trio perished in an inextricable entanglement.

Verney Lovett Cameron, *Across Africa*, 2 vols (Daldy, Isbister, 1877; Johnson Reprint Edition, 1971), Vol. I, p. 204. Cameron led an expedition sent out in search of Livingstone. Livingstone died with the relief expedition en route, but Cameron kept on to undertake exploration on his own. He was the first European to cross the African continent from east to west and was considered a hero in his time. *Across Africa* is a traveler's tale that truly is wilder than fiction, impossible to summarize adequately, and must be read in its entirety to be fully appreciated.

Terry is twenty-one and about to shoot his first elephant. He has paid dearly for the license, but if he is successful that $15 investment will launch him into his chosen career of professional hunter. For four days he and a friend have been scouring the Ukambani country in Southern Kenya. Today, at last, they spot four bull elephants, asleep on their feet, in the shade of a lone tree. The wind and the terrain are all perfect. Terry drops to a crouch and creeps forward, holding the .404 off the ground, his neck hurting, his nose sniffing for a change in the wind. At thirty yards, Terry raises his gun and sights in the earhole of the largest elephant. Terry has heard much about brain shots and he knows them to be the best recipe for assassination. Slowly, he squeezes the trigger.

Bedlam. As the elephant's forelegs collapse and it falls onto its stomach, Terry's companion adds two rounds of .577 lead to the elephant's brain.

While the three other elephants scatter, the two partners shake hands and offer congratulations, in the manner of hunters. As the men head for the carcass, however, the three departing bulls suddenly stop in mid-flight, look back and, slowly at first but with increasing speed, return to their fallen comrade. From a safe distance, the hunters watch in bafflement as the three elephants lift the carcass to its feet and march it off into the distance.

Terry fires off four more rounds into the wounded elephant's brain, but the shots only raise puffs of dust on his skin. By dusk, having followed the bizarre retinue for four hours, Terry sits on his haunches, soaked in doubt. He lights a cigarette and wonders what he did wrong.

At first light on the following morning, Terry rediscovers the elephants' spoor [a Dutch word for trail or foot print]. Between the surefooted tracks of the "stretcher-bearers" is a furrow, rimmed by blood, where the corpse was dragged. Here the two hunters come upon a place where the corpse fell; a pool of blood six feet wide is flecked with splinters of pumicelike bone. Here is where the others raised him up. Here he fell by an anthill. Surely, this parade will soon end. But the blood becomes a trickle and then vanishes altogether; the furrow dug by the trailing legs also disappears. From time to time, the hunters can see where the "dead" elephant lost his balance, where he stood with support of his comrades and finally where he proceeded without any help whatsoever. The spoor shows that the four elephants have now joined a larger herd of cow elephants and young. On the third day of tracking, Terry climbs a small hill and sees, far in the distance, a herd. He approaches and with his field glasses he examines each one individually. One of them must have a gaping head wound. Terry looks for congealed blood, for a telltale unsteadiness, for a sunken stomach. For two hours he scans the elephants and, in the end, he sees nothing.

The hunt is over, Terry. . .with a career now in doubt, in debt and no longer sure of his heavy rifle, or any rifle, returns home.

Today [thirty years later] Terry stands at the window, looking into a tree for a weaver nest he first discovered yesterday afternoon. "A wounded elephant, I was sure, would never be able to feed." He sips his first coffee of the morning. "That was, of course, my mistake. Today, I'm sure my wounded elephant was in that herd feeding, just like the others. Elephants feed when they're wounded. Age twenty-one and I was a horse's ass. What didn't make any sense to me then makes perfectly good sense to an elephant."

John Heminway, *No Man's Land: The Last of White Africa* (Harcourt Brace Jovanovich, 1983), pp. 58-60. Heminway, a conservation and natural history writer, film producer, and a frequent traveler to Africa, has written a romantic, evocative portrait of some of the better known (or more notorious, depending on one's view) whites who have chosen to remain in Black Africa after independence. Readers might also enjoy Heminway's evocative *The Imminent Rains: A Visit among the Last Pioneers of Africa* (Little, Brown, 1968; with superb illustrations by sister Hilary).

Now it was man who sat completely still. In the shade of the great fig, a soft hooting of a dove — coo, co-co, co-co. The dove, too, had been waiting for me to go, blinking its dark liquid eye and shifting its pretty feet on the cool bark. Now it had calmed, and gave its quiet call. Bushes at the kopje base began to twitch where mousebirds and bee-eaters stilled by the hush were going on about their bright-eyed business, and agama lizards, stone eyes glittering, materialized upon the rock. The males were a brilliant blue and orange, heads swollen to a turgid orange-pink (kopje agamas have been so long isolated on their rock islands that color variations have evolved; those at Lemuta Kopjes, in arid country, are mostly a pale apricot), and they were doing the quick press-ups of agitation that are thought to be territorial threat display. Perhaps man lay across the courtship routes, for they seemed thwarted and leapt straight up and down, whereas the females, stone-colored, skirted the big lump that did not concern them.

As if mistrustful of the silence, a kongoni climbed to the crest of a red termite mound to look about; I focused my binoculars to observe it only to learn that it was observing me. The long-faced antelope averted its gaze first. "The kongoni has a foolish face," an African child has said, "but he is very polite." Not far away, a Thomson's gazelle was walking slowly, cocking its head every little way as if to shake a burr out of its ear. It was marking out its territory by dipping its eye toward a stiff prominent blade of grass, the tip of which penetrates a gland that is visible under the eye as a black spot; the gland leaves a waxy black deposit on the grass tip, and the gazelle moves on a little way before making another sign. Once one knows it is done, the grass-dipping ceremony, performed also by the dik-dik, is readily observed, but one sees why it passed unnoticed until only a few years ago.

In the still heat that precedes rain, a skink, striped brown, raised its head out of the rock as if to sniff the flowers and putrefaction. A variable sunbird, iridescent, sipped from a fire-

colored leonotis, blurred wings a tiny shadow on the sky; it vanished, and the plain lay still.

Peter Matthiessen & Eliot Porter, *The Tree Where Man Was Born/The African Experience*, p. 109. This volume has been recommended in Chapter I. Porter took the pictures ("The African Experience"), and Matthiessen wrote the text ("The Tree Where Man Was Born"), which, though frequently a confusing mélange of anecdotes, history, analysis, and whatever, manages to weave its own inimical spell on the reader.

Once upon a time...there lived a Parsee from whose hat the rays of the sun were reflected in more-than-oriental splendour. And the Parsee lived by the Red Sea with nothing but his hat and his knife and a cooking-stove of the kind that you must particularly never touch. And one day he took flour and water and currants and plums and sugar and things, and made himself one cake which was two feet across and three feet thick. It was indeed a Superior Comestible. . .But just as he was going to eat it there came down to the beach from the Altogther Uninhabited Interior one Rhinoceros with a horn on his nose, two piggy eyes, and few manners. In those days the Rhinoceros's skin fitted him quite tight. There were no wrinkles in it anywhere. He looked exactly like a Noah's Ark Rhinoceros, but of course much bigger. All the same, he had no manners then, and he has no manners now, and he never will have any manners. He said, 'How!' and the Parsee left that cake and climbed to the top of a palm-tree with nothing on but his hat, from which the rays of the sun were always reflected in more-than-oriental splendour. And the Rhinoceros upset the oil-stove with his nose, and the cake rolled on the sand, and he spiked that cake on the horn of his nose, and he ate it, and he went away, waving his tail, to the desolate and Exclusively Uninhabited Interior. . .Then the Parsee came down from his palm-tree and put the stove on its legs and recited the following Sloka, which, as you have not heard, I will now proceed to relate:—

> Them that takes cakes
> Which the Parsee-man bakes
> Makes dreadful mistakes.

And there was a great deal more in that than you would think.
Because, five weeks later, there was a heat-wave in the Red Sea, and everybody took off all the clothes they had. The Parsee took off his hat; but the Rhinoceros took off his skin and carried it over his shoulder as he came down to the beach to bathe. In those days it buttoned underneath with three buttons and looked like a waterproof. He said nothing whatever about the Parsee's cake, because he had eaten it all; and he never had any manners, then, since, or henceforward. He waddled straight into the water and blew bubbles through his nose, leaving his skin on the beach.
Presently the Parsee came by and found the skin, and he smiled one smile that ran all round his face two times. Then he danced three times round the skin and rubbed his hands. Then he went to his camp and filled his hat with cake-crumbs, for the Parsee never ate anything but cake, and never swept out his camp. He took that skin, and he shook that skin, and he scrubbed that skin, and he rubbed that skin just as full of old, dry, stale, tickly cake-crumbs and some burned currants as ever it

could possibly hold. Then he climbed to the top of his palm-tree and waited for the Rhinoceros to come out of the water and put it on.
And the Rhinoceros did. He buttoned it up with the three buttons, and it tickled like cake-crumbs in bed. Then he wanted to scratch, but that made it worse; and then he lay down on the sand and rolled and rolled and rolled, and every time he rolled the cake-crumbs tickled him worse and worse and worse. Then he ran to the palm-tree and rubbed and rubbed and rubbed himself against it. He rubbed so much and so hard that he rubbed his skin into a great fold over his shoulders, and another fold underneath, where the buttons used to be (but he rubbed the buttons off), and he rubbed some more folds over his legs. And it spoiled his temper, but it didn't make the least difference to the cake-crumbs. They were inside his skin and they tickled. So he went home, very angry indeed and horribly scratchy; and from that day to this every rhinoceros has great folds in his skin and a very bad temper, all on account of the cake-crumbs inside.

Rudyard Kipling, "How The Rhinoceros Got His Skin," *Just So Stories* (Chatham River Press Edition, 1978). Kipling needs, of course, no introduction. *Just So Stories*, originally published in 1902, has been entertaining children — and adults — for generations.

When the Almighty issued the various species of animals with their uniforms or hides (so runs the Bantu fable) he also issued them with a needle apiece with which to sew them on. The rhino, always a bundle of nerves, carried the needle in his mouth while looking for a convenient place in which to sit down and sew on his skin. On the way he got a fright and accidentally swallowed the needle. This explains why he is so uncomfortable and bad-tempered and why there are creases and folds in his ill-fitting skin. It explains also why rhinos...will always paw and scatter their manure about, scrutinising it and studying it as they do so. They are said to be still looking for that needle. . .

Roy Campbell, *Light on a Dark Horse: An Autobiography (1901-1935)* (Henry Regnery Company, 1952), p. 42. *Dark Horse* is a charming reminiscence of a life spent partly in Africa and a youth filled with memories of animals and birds of all kinds.

I was, however, in no mood to admire the views as I uncoiled myself from the red-hot interior of the lorry and jumped to the ground. What I wanted most in the world at that moment was a drink, a bath and a meal, in that order. Almost as urgently I wanted a wooden box to house the first animal we had acquired. This was an extremely rare creature, a baby black-footed mongoose, which I had purchased from a native in a village twenty-five miles back when we had stopped there to buy some fruit. I had been delighted that we had started the collection with such a rarity, but after struggling with her for two hours in the front seat of the lorry, my enthusiasm had begun to wane. She had wanted to investigate every nook and cranny in the cab, and fearing that she might go and get tangled up in the gears and perhaps break a leg I had imprisoned her inside my shirt. For the first half-hour she had stalked round and round my body, sniffing loudly. For the next half-hour she had made several determined attempts to dig a hole in my stomach with her exceedingly sharp claws, and on being persuaded to desist from this occupation, she had seized a large portion of my abdomen in her mouth and sucked it vigorously and hopefully, while irrigating me with an apparently unending stream of warm and pungent urine. This in no way improved my already dusty and sweaty appearance, and as I marched up the steps of the U.A.C. manager's house, with a mongoose tail dangling out of my tightly buttoned, urine-stained shirt, I looked, to say the least, slightly eccentric. Taking a deep breath and trying to seem nonchalant, I walked into the brilliantly-lit living-room, and found three people seated round a card table. They looked at me with a faint air of inquiry. 'Good evening,' I said, feeling rather at a loss. 'My name's Durrell.'

It was not, I reflected, the most telling remark made in Africa since Stanley and Livingstone met. However, a small, dark man rose from the table and came towards me, smiling charmingly, his long black hair flopping down over his forehead. He held out his hand and clasped mine, and then, ignoring my sudden appearance and my unconventional condition, he peered earnestly into my face.

'Good evening,' he said. 'Do you by any chance play Canasta?'

> Gerald Durrell, *A Zoo in My Luggage* (Viking Press, 1960), pp. 20-1. Durrell, the brother of novelist Lawrence Durrell, is a dedicated conservationist and a gifted raconteur in his own right who lives on the Island of Jersey located in the English Channel, where he runs his own zoo. In his various connections with several zoos, Durrell has led a series of animal-collecting expeditions to Africa. His exploits fill many books.

Once I was charged when climbing through tall vegetation... Suddenly, like a pane of broken glass, the air around me was shattered by the screams of the five males of the group as they bulldozed their way down through the foliage toward me. It is very difficult to describe the charge of a gorilla group. As in the other charges I have experienced, the intensity of the gorillas' screams was so deafening, I could not locate the source of the noise. I only knew that the group was charging from above, when the tall vegetation gave way as though an out-of-control tractor were headed directly for me.

Upon recognizing me, the group's dominant silverback swiftly braked to a stop three feet away, causing the four males behind him, momentarily and ungracefully, to pile up on top of him. At this instant I slowly sank to the ground to assume as submissive a pose as possible. The hair on each male's headcrest stood erect...canines were fully exposed, the irises of ordinarily soft brown eyes glinted yellow — more like those of cats than of gorillas — and an overpowering fear odor permeated the air. For a good half-hour all five males screamed if I made even the slightest movement. After a thirty-minute period, the group allowed me to pretend to feed meekly on vegetation before they finally moved rigidly out of sight uphill.

> Dian Fossey, *Gorillas in the Mist* (Houghton Mifflin, 1983), p. 55. Fossey spent some fifteen years struggling through the Virunga Mountains studying the Mountain gorilla and warring against poaching. The poachers called her Nyiramachabelli, "the old lady who lives in the forest without a man." Such insults bothered her little, and her efforts were often successful, as she destroyed snares and traps, confiscated weapons, organized anti-poaching

patrols, and encouraged prosecution of the trophy hunters. Fossey first went to Africa on safari taken in 1963 and soon followed the footsteps of Carl Akeley and George Schaller. She carried a camera as well as a notebook, and the book contains many excellent photographs (the problems of photography under such circumstances are discussed in Chapter VIII). Fossey, a remarkable and dedicated zoologist, but disdainful of most human beings with whom she came into contact, made many enemies, not all of them poachers. She was brutally murdered the day after Christmas 1985 in her remote mountain cabin situated in the Rwandan Virungas. *Gorillas in the Mist* is a worthy tombstone.

[Photography] demands more patience and endurance of heat and other torments, more knowledge of the habits of animals — in a word, better sportsmanship than a mere tube of iron with a trigger; and when a successful picture of wild life is obtained it is a higher achievement, even in the realm of mere sport, than a trophy, however imposing. Thus, though I do not pretend to the rôle of a reformed game-slayer, I hope that my pictures will not be the less attractive that the birds and beasts here portrayed are, as far as I know, still living their life in the same surroundings.

> Edward North Buxton, *Two African Trips* (Edward Stanford, 1902), p. vii. Fine words, but most of Buxton's pictures were taken of animals shot by hunters (including Buxton). Buxton was the first notable camera-hunter in Africa. He was followed shortly thereafter by C.G. Schillings. Of Buxton's two holiday trips, the first was made to British East Africa, the second to the Sudan.

Soon,...it would be time for fire. Fierce fires fueled by the quantities of dried vegetation which the grazing animals and the termites and the ants and beetles and other grass-eating animals had been unable to consume would, in fact, become obligatory in many parts of the plains and woodlands, if only to ensure virile growth during the next wet season. In the wake of such superabundance, the fires might be awesome, traveling miles without halt and gripped by seasonal winds that could hurl them forward with devastating strength, or they could burn for twenty days in leisurely consumption of everything: the humus of the soil, the roots of still-living trees, the abodes of insect and reptile and warm-blood alike.

These fires might, in the end, catch the anthrax-ridden survivors of the elephant migration from the north. The elephants, reduced now to a group of only five animals, would be moving back toward the north in response to the call from familiar territories. But the fires would certainly spread, and burn particularly fiercely where elephants had traveled in the previous year, and in years before that, where they had destroyed groves of trees and left dead trunks supine in dead grass. In these places, the elephants might be tempted to linger, and there the flames would burn brighter and higher as they consumed both undergrowth and grass, both living shrub and dead tree. It was not uncommon for such fires to encircle animals, and elephants were not infallible. Perhaps fire was allied to the parasites of the elephants, the only force capable of reducing their great bulks and returning them to the soil. In the smoke and crackling stench of the long drought, the screams of distant elephants would be just another measure of long adjustment. . .

Fires would certainly drive lions into reluctant flight and fill the air with fleeing winged insects, falcons, flycatchers, and other birds darting through the smoke to catch them. Fires would sweep the woodlands and test the mettle of trees and grasses, of shrubs and herbs, all of which had to resist in manifold ways in order to survive. The bark of some trees was corky, receiving the heat, absorbing it and blackening, but not actually burning.

Some grass would burn to the ground, but the roots would live on. Others produced seeds that were fire-resistant enough to survive the scorching. The fires would suggest death and would ravage landscapes and fell trees, but the devastation would presage the distant season of green when trees would show new leaves before the rains began. The rains would come again and the woodlands would be dotted with orchids and the plains smothered with flowers.

> Franklin Russell, *Season on the Plain* (Penguin Books, 1975), pp. 309-10. This unusual book tries to recreate the dynamics of animal and plant life on the ecological islands known as kopjes — from the perspective of the animals themselves. Inevitably anthropomorphic, the effort nonetheless succeeds as a genuine "inside" look; Russell obviously has a wide familiarity with the subject and combines a poetic feeling for nature with a scientific understanding of its complex relationships. *Season* is in the same mold as the author's *Watchers at the Pond*, published in 1961, which book has become extremely popular.

We rode west all morning, and at noon we came to an open pan where fine, soft grass as fine as hair was blowing, and we saw a lion there, a big male with a black, tangled mane growing all the way down his neck and ending between his shoulders. He had the muscled neck and shoulders and the wide, swelling jaw of male creatures, and when he raised his head to look at us we saw that he was old. His face was wrinkled and massive, and he looked straight at us with a direct, indifferent look, the blind gaze of cats. His paws were enormous, his fur was the color of gold. He seemed so huge and bright in the sunlight, his eyes so cold and pale, that he fascinated us the way a cat fascinates birds. At that moment he could have walked up to us and carried one of us away.

Bushmen believe that certain famous sorcerers, once medicine men who chose to be poisoners and magicians instead of healers, have taken the form of certain lions, which can always be distinguished from ordinary lions by their great size and their ability to float in the air. Also, Bushmen say, the eclipses of the moon are caused by lions, as on very bright nights a lion may cover the moon's face with a great paw, given himself darkness for better hunting.

Usually, when a lion sees you, he skulks away or bounds off in great, ungainly leaps, in clumsy dodges, making a fool of himself because he is frightened; but when one raises his head and looks right at you, then turns as this one did, and walks off without even looking back, you understand at once why Bushmen believe the things they do.

> Elizabeth Marshall Thomas, *The Harmless People* (Random House, Vintage Books, 1958), pp. 34-5. The Marshall family began its study of a primitive people, some of the last hunter-gatherers left on earth, in 1950 in the Kalahari

Desert. Along the way, the many experiences with animals helped to punctuate this remarkable account. The reader might also enjoy *Warrior Herdsmen* (Alfred A. Knopf, 1965), concerning a tribe in Uganda.

The survival of Africa's wildlife is for all of us a matter of great significance. These wild creatures [and] the wilderness they inhabit are not only an important source of wonder and inspiration but are also an integral part of our natural resources, of our future livelihood, and of our well-being.

By holding our animal world in trust, we solemnly declare that we shall do everything within our power to ensure that our children and grandchildren, too, will be able to enjoy this rich and precious heritage.

The preservation of wild animals and their environment calls for specialized knowledge, skilled workers, and financial support, and we urge other nations to share with us in this important task, whose success or failure will affect not only the African continent, but the entire rest of the world.

> President Julius Nyerere of Tanzania, *Arusha Manifesto of 1961.* Tanzania has devoted a higher percentage of its land to national parks and conservation than any other nation on earth.

Baboons have their ways of asserting themselves against the human race...we were walking through a copse of acacias when we suddenly heard the shrill bark of a mature baboon overhead, and at the same moment a shower of faeces fell all about us, as thickly as cherry blossom in a springtime wind. We were not aware of sustaining any direct hit, or not at the time; but the smell of manure clung to us unpleasantly, and Robert found later that his bush-hat was liberally anointed. After that he made a great point of never forgetting to wear it when he went out in the bush at night. This was not the most gentlemanly way of repelling intruders, but it made great sense from the baboons' point of view, since it was likely to deter predators. In particular the elegant leopard — who is one of their chief enemies — would think twice before getting his velvety coat sullied in this way.

> Jeremy Mollinson, *Okavango Adventure* (W.W. Norton, 1973), p. 166. The author collected animals in Africa for various zoos located in the British Isles.

The silence of the glade was soon broken by the swish and thud of bush knives as the natives cleared a space for the tent and an area for a camp fire. The tent was pitched; a huge pile of faggots was stacked; a fire built between three stones for cooking; the hurricane lamp trimmed and my chair unpacked. As the sun dropped towards the horizon, silhouetting the five peaks of the Ngong Hills in a black-and-gold frieze, the boys returned to the mission, and left me there in solitude.

Solitude? How loosely we used words. I have been lonelier in the crowded streets of a city than in the great open spaces of Africa, with all wild things for companions.

> H.K. Binks, *African Rainbow* (Sidgwick and Jackson, 1959), p. 78. Lured from England by tales of gold, Herbert Binks, twenty years old at the time and trained as a chemist, arrived in Rhodesia in 1900. Making his way to

Kenya (then British East Africa), when Nairobi was little more than a few shacks, he took up farming but subsequently turned to hiring out as a photographer for big-game safaris. Later, he became an ivory hunter. He lived to age ninety-one and was buried in Kenya. *Rainbow* is a sensitive and frequently informative account of those years when British East Africa was the promised land to pioneers. Land itself was "dirt cheap," and adventure and a fresh start were assured. It was a time of great romance.

The lions that I was watching at the kopje rested most of the time, hour in, hour out. It can get pretty boring watching lions sleep and at times I would have liked to follow their example. Even if my conscience had let me, however, I wouldn't have been able to; there were too many flies which had the nasty habit of walking over my face. . .as I remained still. . .They bothered the lions, too, for I could see their skin twitch and they continually flicked their ears to chase away the flies behind them. In addition, the lions usually slept with one paw draped protectively over their sensitive noses. Then I discovered that the lions had directions, at first hesitantly. . .but finally jumping on the resting cats and catching the flies off them. The lions ignored them, even when the lizards caught flies from behind their ears.

I was to see this type of behaviour again but the outcome was somewhat different. I was watching a large pride resting in the shade of a tree. In seeking the maximum of shade one of the lionesses had pushed right up against the trunk. In spite of the many flies crawling on her back, she was fast asleep. After a while I noticed an Agama Lizard creeping down the tree trunk, its body almost the same colour as the bark of the tree.

Suddenly it noticed the flies on the lioness's back and rushed forward. On reaching the lioness it remained motionless but, when a fly came within reach, it snapped it up with its powerful jaws. However, in doing so, the lizard nipped the sleeping lioness, which jumped straight into the air with a roar. At this the other twenty resting lions jumped to their feet and there was considerable confusion. I couldn't help laughing at the puzzled expression on the lioness's face as she looked around, trying to determine who had pinched her bottom.

Hugo van Lawick, *Savage Paradise: The Predators of Serengeti* (Collins, 1977), pp. 19-20. This book is recommended in Chapter I. Van Lawick was a pioneering photographer of the Serengeti, arriving first in 1960 as an assistant to the Belgian animal photographers Armand and Michaela Denis. For many years, he served as the *National Geographic's* man in East Africa and he has produced a unique collection of photographs. In addition, he brought to this volume a sympathetic and inquiring mentality, postulating in the process many new, if not always precisely scientific, theories about his subjects. Van Lawick has produced several films for television and has been involved directly or indirectly in countless projects undertaken by naturalists in East Africa. His latest effort, just published, is *Among Predators and Prey* (Sierra Club Books, 1986).

One season there was an old jackal and vulture who decided to draw up a [p]act of friendship and dwell under it. As a measure of sureness they decided to dwell close to each other.

Thereby the jackal moved into the bottom of a tall tree on which his new friend placed [a] nest.

It was not long before each one had a family and were [sic] busy collecting food. One day when the jackal was out hunting, his friend flew down below and grabbed the jackal children, returning high up to his hungry family. When the jackal came home again, he entered his empty house and became sad with great sorrow. And then a rage burned red inside him and he cursed himself that he was a four-footed beast and could not follow a bird, and be revenged. And he waited at the bottom with a heavy feeling.

Not more that several meals later, the vulture flew to his lofty house with burning hot goat meat from a village fire. Flying air gave life to dark embers in the goat meat. When it was all in the nest with dry grasses and feathers, a wind that was blowing earnestly gave flames and fire. The high house and the children burned in the wind and it blew them cooked to the bottom. The old jackal who had eaten nothing since his loss was thin with hunger. High in a cloud he saw the vulture circling the tree, and within his sight he ate the cooked meal.

"To violate friendship safe from revenge is not to escape the punishment."

Peter Beard, *Longing for Darkness: Kamante's Tales from Out of Africa* (Harcourt Brace Jovanovich, 1975), "Kamante's Fables." Kamante was Isak Dinesen's cook and servant, a prominent character in *Out of Africa*. Beard transcribed from Kiswahili some of the fables that Kamante told Dinesen, who in turn had taught them in her Karen Coffee Farm School. *Longing for Darkness* is an unusual collection of recollections, stories, watercolors, and photographs.

After a day or two...one begins to realize that one must reassemble one's ideas about the wild animals in Africa. Somewhere in the tangled background of one's education something seems to have gone wrong; and now it is not the strangeness of the things that one is seeing that is so impressive — it is their false familiarity. . . .my wife and I had grown up with the legend of Africa, the danger-legend of the explorer and the white hunter, of Rider Haggard's tales and many a movie star on safari. The lion springs, the elephant charges with a terrifying bellow, and it is always some poor human devil who is going to get the worst of it unless he shoots quick.

Here in the Kruger Park, however, we were confronted with something quite different, the legend, as it were, within the legend: the animals reacting not to human beings but to themselves and to the surrounding forest. In other words, once you remove the human element — and in particular the emphasis on human danger — an entirely new world emerges. You see that an elaborate and subtle skein of influences is at work; that, for instance, there was a very good reason why these zebra and impala and other antelopes should have been grazing together; one species excells in hearing, another in smell, and another in sight, and together they establish a very effective warning system against their common enemies, the lions, the leopards and other carnivora.

These discoveries tend to create in one a simply unaffected pleasure. It is, of course, an obvious escape-entertainment, but there is nothing really synthetic about it because one quickly realizes, however calcified and disillusioned one may be, that this is a world that we knew very well when we were young; the dream world of the jungle stories to which we listened in a trance of sympathy and fear and quite definitely wanted to believe. And although this world has nothing to do with human beings it is often more moving, more entertaining and much more terrible than anything which has been dreamed of in the movies or the sportsmen's notebooks.

Moorehead, *No Room in the Ark*, pp. 15-6.

Never be a pioneer. It's the early Christian that gets the fattest lion.

"Saki" (H.H. Munro), *Reginald* (1904), Reginald's Chair Treat. Of course, as a naturalist will testify, better a fat lion than a hungry one.

But the numbers of grazers were not measurably influenced by the meat eaters. Instead, they were controlled by creatures who killed with invisible stealth.

. . .

Both young and old died in this time of change. The obvious deaths came in the struggle for power, territory, food. But by far the most common cause was the work of the creepers and the crawlers. These creatures — organisms — infested almost every part of every body. Livers, kidneys, lungs, nostrils, eyes, stomachs, intestines, bones were all vulnerable. An old animal, still relatively strong, still anxious to live, found his vital forces diminished enough to give that final parasite that final foothold which would kill him. Here was a stealthy world of silence. Instead of the noisy, yelping hyenas and the dramatic leaps of leopards, there was only the hidden sucking, biting, burrowing, poisoning, consuming work of the parasites. They had such power that entire nations of animals could be wiped out by them, thousands killed in quick successes of a single kind of parasite.

The wildebeests trudged along, maned heads stolidly down, lungworms working inside their bodies. Some resisted the worms' work, others sickened and stood helplessly while their fellows passed on. Ticks teemed everywhere, vectors of countless blood parasites which moved from animal to animal by unplotted roadways. Tapeworms worked through the livers of impalas and reduced their soaring leaps to feeble stumbles, bringing the graceful animals within reach of hyena and leopard. Giraffes hosted nematodes in their livers, parasites in their bloodstreams, and a swarming of skin parasites which sent clinging birds — the oxpeckers — exploring all over their bodies in search of ticks, eggs, larvae.

The island and the plains waited for the rains to begin and for the visitors to arrive. What stood between the antelope and horse and their journey to the land of promise? Gedulstia flies...

Nothing escaped the parasites. But the animals had lived so long in woodlands and plains that they had learned to function even with heavy infestations. Ticks smothered buffalo and eland, giraffe and antelope. Lice were everywhere. The moment an animal sickened slightly, their parasites flourished responsively so that they, rather than the original disease, might kill the animal. . . .

. . .

Wherever the host animals moved the parasites followed on wings, or traveled inside them, or fastened themselves to fur

and hide as the hosts passed through shrub and grass. Parasite competed with parasite for a share of the victim. . . .

. . .

The work of the parasites sent regular, rhythmic shock waves across the plains and woodlands. They were one of the oldest forms of life and skilled performers, functioning with subtlety and success. Their hidden power helped to maintain the impenetrable mystery of life here. Elephants bulking through the dry woodlands and smashing down a hundred trees a day in search of foliage might not fall to lions, but they could not repel the parasites. . . .The parasites respected nothing. Their ageless task was to monitor all life. Whenever their host animals became too numerous, were weakened by other diseases, or otherwise disobeyed the orders of a balanced life, they surged forward to restore equability. And so there were never too many lions, too many wildebeests, too few gazelles. The balance appeared precise.

Woodlands and plains thus contained a perfect deception where the eye saw nothing but lies. The leopard's bark sent terrified gazelles spinning away in the night, and that appeared to make the leopard important. The rumble of lions agitated the grazing animals, and the sound, being powerful, appeared to signify powerful animals. But such externals did not resemble the internal order, the invisible rules and unfathomable imperatives.

Russell, *Season on the Plain*, pp. 40-5.

The beauty of it all was breathtaking. The sunlight filtered through the foliage; there were moss-covered trees with masses of mistletoe and vines the thickness of man's arm draped from the overhead branches to the ground.

Squirrels darted for safety; birds of brilliant hue flew noisily from tree to tree. Butterflies, in a myriad of colour and form, rose in swarms from the mounds of elephant dung. Gauzy-winged dragonflies poised on trembling wings, darting, hovering. Here and there a crystal, icy torrent from the mountain's glaciers plunged through the green valleys and we caught an occasional glimpse through the foliage of the shining snow and ice of the peaks of Mount Kenya.

Binks, *African Rainbow*, pp. 136-7.

The best hunters in Kenya generally avoided the Hunters' Bar in the Hilton, and soon after its creation by the Professional Hunters' Association it became the lair of those out of work — the ones who like to boast about trophies and trysts. Liam Lynn, the Irish white hunter, will never have anything to do with the Hunters' Bar unless, of course, he is very thirsty.

Today he is just that. His thirst began the evening before, lasted through the night and allowed him to go without sleep and breakfast. Even after he has consumed two bottles of Martell brandy, Liam still retains the unique talent of being able to entertain listeners with the awful truth.

Today, at lunchtime, he is lurching as he pushes open the glass door. His clients, just arrived from Philadelphia, are waiting for him in one of Nairobi's hotels. His safari crew has already been posted to one of the hunting blocks to set up camp, and a chartered aircraft is standing by to fly Liam and his clients there in comfort, but poor old Liam looks as if he will

Plate 4. Elephants at Noon.

never make his way even to the bar stool. He spots someone else's clients sitting at the banquet table, and he weaves toward them. His eyes have fallen on the daughter of these nice eager people. She is a sixteen-year-old blonde with the hopeful looks of a recent convert to the sexual revolution. At first, the parents are not quite sure how to deal with Liam, but their hunter, John Painter, lets them know he is all right, one of Kenya's more lovable rogues, a great success as an elephant hunter but rather his own best enemy whenever he arrives in Nairobi. Liam considers this introduction a bit excessive. He leans onto the daughter and whispers, in a voice loud enough to be heard throughout the bar, that John Painter was well known to have wet dreams. "No," says the girl, quite horrified.

"And did you hear what came of his last wet dream?" Liam continues, his County Antrim brogue stronger than ever.

"No," says the girl once again, this time her face flushed with color.

"On his last wet dream he produced Uganda. The Republic of Uganda, that is. Quite a splash it was too."

John Painter is howling with laughter. The girl is still too nervous to laugh. But the parents are looking pained.

At the far end of the counter, one of the regulars of the Hunters' Bar yells: "Liam, tell us about your .458."

The Irishman affects a look of excruciating pain. "Awful thing," he grumbles. "Makes a terrible bang in me ear." Clearly Liam does not want to talk about guns or be egged on by any bullshit artist in the Hunters' Bar. He looks at the sixteen-year-old. His leer makes her smile. "How long have you been a virgin?" he asks at last.

John Painter, as tough as any hunter in the profession, blushes. "Tell us about elephants," he pleads, desperate to change the subject.

"Elephants," Liam says with a look of contrived puzzlement. "You mean those things with the big ears and long noses?" He has at last made the girl's parents smile. "So you call them elephants, do you?"

Suddenly, Liam no longer wants to keep up the patter of his one-liners. Even his interest in the girl has waned. He looks at his watch. "Time to leave. I've only a half-hour left on my twelve-hour deodorant."

Painter successfully changes the table talk to one of Kenya's more sober subjects — the calculation of death figures. "What does it look like?" he asks rhetorically. "Last year one client accidentally shot by his hunter, another killed by a rhino. The year before, one professional killed by an elephant, another taken from his tent by a lioness, and then what do you think, about half a dozen maulings and gorings? Quite a few record years..."

Liam has been listening with interest. "I'm always pleased," he says, "to hear about hunters being killed by elephants. It restores my faith in Africa."

Heminway, *No Man's Land: The Last of White Africa*, pp. 69-71. By ordinary standards, most 'white hunters' were certifiable lunatics, who drifted, grudgingly to be sure, in-to the popular safari game for lack of other jobs to do. One wag despairingly called them "white hunters in living color," as pictures of their safaris spread. They speak with authority and style (often taken for the same thing) on African wildlife and make the most ridiculous pro-nouncements (and, indeed, hold the most absurd opinions). Consequently, they are well represented here.

Or it may be said that hunting is ever a love-affair. The hunter is in love with the game, real hunters are true animal lovers. But during the hours of the hunt itself he is more than that, he is infatuated with the head of game which he follows and means to make his own; nothing much besides it exists to him in the world. Only, in general, the infatuation will be somewhat one-sided. The gazelles and antelopes and the zebra, which on safari you shoot to get meat for your porters, are timid and will make themselves scarce and in their own strange way disappear before your eyes; the hunter must take wind and terrain into account and sneak close to them slowly and silently without their realizing the danger. It is a fine and fascinating art, in the spirit of that masterpiece of my countryman Sören Kierkegaard, The Seducer's Diary, and it may, in the same way, provide the hunter with moments of great drama and with op-portunity for skill and cunning, and for self-gratulations. Yet to me this pursuit was never the real thing. And even the big game, in the hunting of which there is danger, the buffalo or the rhino, very rarely attack without being attacked, or believing that they are being attacked.

Isak Dinesen, *Shadows on the Grass* (Random House, Vintage Books Edition, 1974), pp. 53-4. *Shadows* was originally published in 1961, and Dinesen once again recreated the Africa that she had left behind thirty years earlier.

I suppose, if there were a part of the world in which mastodon still lived, somebody would design a new gun, and men, in their eternal impudence, would hunt mastodon as they now hunt elephant. Impudence seems to be the word. At least David and Goliath were of the same species, but, to an elephant, a man can only be a midge with a deathly sting.

It is absurd for a man to kill an elephant. It is not brutal, it is not heroic, and certainly it is not easy; it is just one of those preposterous things that men do...

Elephant, beyond the fact that their size and conformation are aesthetically more suited to the treading of this earth than our angular informity, have an average intelligence com-parable to our own. Of course they are less agile and physically less adaptable than ourselves — Nature having developed their bodies in one direction and their brains in another, while human beings, on the other hand, drew from Mr. Darwin's lot-tery of evolution both the winning ticket and the stub to match it. This, I suppose, is why we are so wonderful and can make

movies and electric razors and wireless sets — and guns with which to shoot the elephant, the hare, clay pigeons, and each other.

Beryl Markham, *West with the Night* (North Point Press, 1983), p. 205. Markham was born in England in 1902 and was taken by her father to East Africa in 1906. This autobiography was first published in 1942, a remarkable story of a life formed in the wilderness of an Africa that no longer exists. Markham learned to fly and carried mail, passengers, and supplies in her small plane to remote areas of East Africa. In September 1936, she became the first per-son to fly solo across the Atlantic from east to west (England to Nova Scotia). As a memoir of poetry, adven-ture, destiny, friendships, animals, and passion, *West with the Night* ranks on the same level with *Out of Africa*.

[An "*Elephant's Child*," full of " '*satiable curiosity*," — a trait that so far had earned him nothing but spankings from all and sundry — sets out for the banks of the "*great grey-green, greasy*" Limpopo River to find out what the crocodile has for dinner. At this time, the elephant had no trunk. Finally arriving at the river, the elephant child soon found himself in a tug-of-war for his life, as the crocodile dragged the elephant by the nose ("*no bigger than a boot*") and tried to pull the gullible child into the water, where the answer to the dinner query would have been all too clear. Aided by a sympathetic "*Bi-Coloured-Python-Rock-Snake*," the elephant, after a tremendous struggle, frees himself.]

Then the Elephant's Child sat down most hard and sudden; but first he was careful to say 'Thank you' to the Bi-Coloured-Python-Rock-Snake; and next he was kind to his poor pulled nose, and wrapped it all up in cool banana leaves, and hung it in the great grey-green, greasy Limpopo to cool.

'What are you doing that for?' said the Bi-Coloured-Python-Rock-Snake.

' 'Scuse me,' said the Elephant's Child, 'but my nose is badly out of shape, and I am waiting for it to shrink.'

'Then you will have to wait a long time,' said the Bi-Coloured-Python-Rock-Snake. 'Some people do not know what is good for them.'

The Elephant's Child sat there for three days waiting for his nose to shrink. But it never grew any shorter, and, besides, it made him squint. For, O Best Beloved, you will see and under-stand that the Crocodile had pulled it out into a really truly trunk same as all Elephants have to-day.

At the end of the third day a fly came and stung him on the shoulder, and before he knew what he was doing he lifted up his trunk and hit that fly dead with the end of it.

' 'Vantage number one!' said the Bi-Coloured-Python-Rock-Snake. 'You couldn't have done that with a mere-smear nose. Try and eat a little now.'

Before he thought what he was doing the Elephant's Child put out his trunk and plucked a large bundle of grass, dusted it clean against his fore-legs, and stuffed it into his own mouth.

' 'Vantage number two!' said the Bi-Coloured-Python-Rock-Snake. 'You couldn't have done that with a mere-smear nose. Don't you think the sun is very hot here?'

'It is,' said the Elephant's Child, and before he thought what he was doing he schlooped up a schloop of mud from the banks of the great grey-green, greasy Limpopo, and slapped it on his head, where it made a cool schloopy-sloshy mud-cap all trickly behind his ears.

' 'Vantage number three!' said the Bi-Coloured-Python-Rock-Snake. 'You couldn't have done that with a mere-smear nose. Now how do you feel about being spanked again?'

' 'Scuse me,' said the Elephant's Child, 'but I should not like it at all.'

'How would you like to spank somebody?' said the Bi-Coloured-Python-Rock-Snake.

'I should like it very much indeed,' said the Elephant's Child.

'Well,' said the Bi-Coloured-Python-Rock-Snake, 'you will find that new nose of yours very useful to spank people with.'

'Thank you,' said the Elephant's Child, 'I'll remember that; and now I think I'll go home to all my dear families and try.'

So the Elephant's Child went home across Africa frisking and whisking his trunk. When he wanted fruit to eat he pulled fruit down from a tree, instead of waiting for it to fall as he used to do. When he wanted grass he plucked grass up from the ground, instead of going on his knees as he used to do. When the flies bit him he broke off the branch of a tree and used it as a fly-whisk; and he made himself a new, cool, slushy-squshy mud-cap whenever the sun was hot. When he felt lonely walking through Africa he sang to himself down his trunk, and the noise was louder than several brass bands. He went especially out of his way to find a broad Hippopotamus (she was no relation of his), and he spanked her very hard, to make sure that the Bi-Coloured-Python-Rock-Snake had spoken the truth about his new trunk. . . .

One dark evening he came back to all his dear families, and he coiled up his trunk and said, 'How do you do?' They were very glad to see him, and immediately said, 'Come here and be spanked for your 'satiable curiosity.'

'Pooh,' said the Elephant's Child. 'I don't think you peoples know anything about spanking; but I do, and I'll show you.' Then he uncurled his trunk and knocked two of his dear brothers head over heels.

'O Bananas!' said they, 'where did you learn that trick, and what have you done to your nose?'

'I got a new one from the Crocodile on the banks of the great grey-green, greasy Limpopo River,' said the Elephant's Child. 'I asked him what he had for dinner, and he gave me this to keep.'

'It looks very ugly,' said his hairy uncle, the Baboon.

'It does,' said the Elephant's Child. 'But it's very useful,' and he picked up his hairy uncle, the Baboon, by one hairy leg, and hove him into a hornet's nest.

Then that bad Elephant's Child spanked all his dear families for a long time, till they were very warm and greatly astonished. He pulled out his tall Ostrich aunt's tail-feathers; and he caught his tall uncle, the Giraffe, by the hindleg, and dragged him through a thorn-bush; and he shouted at his broad aunt, the Hippopotamus, and blew bubbles into her ear when she was sleeping in the water after meals. . . .

At last things grew so exciting that his dear families went off one by one in a hurry to the banks of the great grey-green, greasy Limpopo River, all set about with fever-trees, to borrow new noses from the Crocodile. When they came back nobody spanked anybody any more; and ever since that day, O Best Beloved, all the Elephants you will ever see, besides all those that you won't, have trunks precisely like the trunk of the 'satiable Elephant's Child.

Rudyard Kipling, "The Elephant's Child," *Just So Stories*. Kipling had himself actually traveled to the banks of the Limpopo, also known at the time as "Crocodile River."

That evening, sitting in front of my campfire and smoking my pipe, I thought back over the many years I'd spent in Africa as a hunter. When I first came to Kenya, the game covered the plains as far as a man could see. I hunted lions where towns now stand, and shot elephants from the engine of the first railroad to cross the country. In the span of one man's lifetime, I have seen jungle turn into farmland and cannibal tribes become factory workers. I have had a little to do with this change myself, for the government employed me to clear dangerous beasts out of areas that were being opened to cultivation. I hold a world's record for rhino, possibly another record for lion (although we kept no exact record of the numbers shot in those early days) and I have shot more than fourteen hundred elephant. I certainly do not tell of these records with pride. The work had to be done and I happened to be the man who did it. But strange as it may seem to the armchair conservationist, I have a deep affection for the animals I had to kill. I spent long years studying their habits, not only in order to kill them, but because I was honestly interested in them.

Yet it is true I have always been a sportsman. Firearms have been my ruling passion in life and I would rather hear the crack of a rifle or the bang of a shotgun than listen to the finest orchestra. I cannot say that I did not enjoy hunting, but looking back I truly believe that in most cases the big game had as much chance to kill me as I had to kill them.

I am one of the last of the old-time hunters. The events I saw can never be relived. Both the game and the native tribes, as I knew them, are gone. No one will ever see again the great elephant herds led by old bulls carrying 150 pounds of ivory in each tusk. No one will ever again hear the yodeling war cries of the Masai as their spearmen swept the bush after cattle-killing lions. Few indeed will be able to say that they have broken into country never before seen by a white man. No, the old Africa has passed and I saw it go.

This, then, is a record of the last great days of big-game hunting. Nowhere in the world was there game to equal the African game. Nowhere were there animals so big, so powerful or so numerous. Now that is almost over, there may be some who wish to hear about the greatest hunting era in the world's history.

J.A. Hunter, *Hunter* (Harper & Brothers, 1952), pp. 11-2. Most publishers liked to trot forth their *soi-disant* authors as the 'most renowned white hunter' or the like, but Hunter's name indeed matched his reputation; few were his equal with a gun. Hunter's life was spent taking out sportsmen to shoot big game and killing "dangerous" (today, we would recognize them as more 'inconvenient' than 'dangerous') animals at the request of the local government.

The mornings greeted us with wispy clouds that drifted under a blue-black sky, looking as if it had been badly bruised by thunder. The Park was now thickly covered in rich, deep green that spread along the ground and up into the trees. Heavy rainstorms broke, usually in the afternoon, and lasted for an hour or more. The clouds swept past and the sun heated up the wet ground until it steamed and rich smells rose from the damp earth. On the crest of the hills along the ridges and tumbling down the sides of the gulleys, the yellow-leaved sterculia and commiphora trees shivered and sparkled. Even the acacia woodland with its thick covering of blossom had a lush look, and around the bushes and the wild flowers butterflies danced in circles.

A visitor would be unaware of any problems, but to a scientist there were problems and they were serious, for under the thick green cover, and behind the shelter of the green bush, the elephants were digging with their tusks into the indigo-coloured bark of the *Acacia tortilis*. They were ripping off thick slices, chewing and sucking out the juices, often leaving the trunk white and bare as if the tree's clothes had been torn to pieces. In

We stepped behind the bole of a tree and peered at the feeding gorillas about one hundred feet away. Without warning, a female with infant walked toward our tree, a large male behind her. I nudged Doc and quietly climbed up on a branch without being seen by the animals. The female stopped some thirty feet from us and sat quietly with her large infant beside her. Once the infant glanced up at me, then stared intently for fifteen seconds without giving the alarm. But when the female inadvertently looked in my direction, her relaxed gaze hardened as she saw me. She grabbed her young with one arm, pulling it

Plate 5. Elephant Work in the Yellow Fever Trees (Acacia Xanthophloea).

a month or less one tree after another would fade to a paler colour, its thin branches would become barren and finally die. Year after year Iain had seen these trees turn into skeletons. "Soon there will be none left," he said.

Iain & Oria Douglas-Hamilton, *Among the Elephants* (Viking Press, 1975), p. 175. A fascinating book, written by a couple studying elephants in East Africa (principally at Lake Manyara in Tanzania), *Among the Elephants* has become the leading 'biography' of Africa's most imposing animal. Most of the book's photographs were taken by Oria Douglas-Hamilton. This is one of those unique stories of scientific discovery, perseverance, and personal involvement that inspires generations of graduate students, as well as providing a firm basis for years of further work.

to her, and with the same motion rushed away, emitting a high-pitched scream. The male answered with a roar and looked around, and Doc, having failed to interpret the purpose of my nudge, was surprised to see me in the branches above him. The members of the group assembled around the male after a moment of tense alertness. The animals were still within about one hundred feet of us, and we wondered what would happen. To our relief, one face after another turned toward us in a quiet, quizzical stare as curiosity replaced alarm. They craned their necks, and two juveniles climbed into the surrounding trees to obtain a better view. One juvenile with a mischievous look on its face beat its chest, then quickly ducked into the vegetation, only to peer furtively through the screen of weeds as if to judge the effect of its commotion. Slowly the animals dispersed and went about their daily routine. I particularly remember one *female who left the deep shade and settled herself at the base of a tree in a shaft of sunlight. She stretched her short legs in front of her and dangled her arms loosely at her sides. Her face was old and kind and creased by many wrinkles. She seemed utterly at peace and relaxed as she basked in the morning sun.*

George B. Schaller, *The Year of the Gorilla* (University of Chicago, 1964), p. 38. The popular version of Schaller's monumental work on the Mountain gorilla, this volume is probably the best introduction to the Virunga Volcanoes and the shy giant who lives there. Schaller is a sensitive and articulate observer.

The highlight of the day was watching a pride of lion hunting, a scene I had always hoped to see. It was about 4.30 p.m. in thin bush, over which we were able to have a good view from a slight eminence. The whole procedure was most deliberate. When we first saw the pride they comprised 2 lion, 4 lionesses and 3 half-grown cubs, and they were all more or less in a bunch and looking in all directions. About 500 yards from them and upwind was a herd of 15 zebra. From the stealthy movement of all the lion it was clear that they were on the hunt and that they had spotted the zebra; the two lion with two lionesses and the three cubs then made a wide detour, using every possible fold in the ground and bushes to keep hidden from the zebra, with the clear intention of getting round them and stampeding them by giving them their wind. The two lionesses left behind separated and took up crouching positions some 100 yards apart, both intently watching the zebra. Meanwhile the main body of lion had reached a position where the zebra should have got their wind. Suddenly up went the zebras' heads in alarm and they stampeded downwind, while the lions with cubs lay flat with only their heads erect. The herd of zebra passed between the two crouching lionesses but only some 20 yards from one of them; she lay very flat in a ready-to-spring attitude; it was most exciting. As the herd of zebra got more or less level with the lionesses they suddenly stopped and looked back. At that moment the nearest lioness launched her attack at full gallop and sprang at her victim. It was all over in a moment. She leaped at the zebra, knocked it over, and quick as lightning got a hold on the throat; the zebra scarcely struggled. The herd, now thoroughly alarmed, dashed away in panic towards the second lioness, who launched her attack as they passed her at about 30 yards; she apparently had no difficulty in overtaking one, sprang on it and, like the first lioness, seemed to grip the throat all in one movement — spring and catch hold. The rest of the pride now came up at a trot, the two lion and one lioness joining one kill and the other lioness and the cubs joining the other kill.

The whole hunt was beautifully timed and executed.

Richard Meinertzhagen, *Kenya Diary (1902-1906)* (Hippocrene Books, 1983), pp.174-5. Originally published in 1957, some fifty years after its composition, *Diary* is mostly an honest but shocking record of killing — of animals for sport and humans for duty. All, apparently, with pleasure. Meinertzhagen was a young officer attached to the King's African Rifles, stationed in the East Africa Protectorate, as Kenya was then called. This particular passage is a brief respite in the astonishing tally of slaughtered animals. Later in life, in a familiar pattern followed by several hunters, Meinertzhagen was recogniz-

ed as an excellent naturalist and became a world-famous ornithologist.

During the night I managed to chase a hyena — not out of but into my tent. The only casualty was a canvas shoe. The animal bit off the toe-cap as cleanly as if it had been sliced off with a pair of shears. I don't know whether my foot would have been treated the same way had it been inside; I remember only my annoyance at being wakened up at midnight and the ridiculous scamper round the tent.

It had been erected in a gap between two large bushes. When the hyenas began to call with growing insistence I got up and saw two pairs of bright green eyes in the light of the torch. I threw a brick at them. When another animal started to yowl behind me I went round to the back of the tent to investigate. The hyena stood there — ashen grey in the bright light. It seemed so unabashed that I chased after it angrily. The animal swerved round the bush and disappeared. Walking round the bush to the front of the tent I saw it disappear through the back flap. It seems that I had chased it in. In the morning I found the chewed-up shoe and marvelled that it could have snatched at it so quickly.

John Hillaby, *Journey to the Jade Sea* (Grenada Publishing, 1973), p. 65. "One of the world's greatest walkers," Hillaby walked the length of Britain, through Europe from the North Sea to the Mediterranean, and across parts of Canada. *Journey to the Jade Sea* is an account of an 1100-mile walk through Kenya's Frontier District, from Wamba to Lake Rudolf (Turkana) and back, essentially "for the hell of it." If one stays in the African bush long enough, one will manage to share accommodations during at least a part of a night with a hyena, the latter in search of a shoe or boot or other choice leather morsel.

One of the most amusing incidents I witnessed with jackals concerned the eating of mushrooms. This took place in the Ngorongoro Crater when I was watching a family of two adults and four cubs. The whole family had been eating mushrooms of various types, but one day I saw one of the cubs eat a species I had not seen jackals eat before. Ten minutes later the cub seemed to go mad. He rushed around in circles and then, to my amazement, charged flat-out, first a Thomson Gazelle and then an adult wildebeest. Both animals stared at the tiny creature and hurried out of its way. Unfortunately I could not find another mushroom of that type for identification. I feel convinced the cub was suffering from hallucinations.

van Lawick, *Savage Paradise*, p. 37.

High above our camp, on the topmost crags, where the baboons barked all day long, the magnificent dark-chestnut fish-eagles with their snowy heads, necks, and shoulders, soared with their laughing cry, from their nests in the forks of the highest trees. Klipspringers perched against the sky on pinnacles and pin-headed footholds: or leaped from rock to rock with an amazing sense of balance. Baboons are the most mischievous and wantonly destructive animals on the bushveld. They will always insist on harming more of a maize or millet crop than they can ever eat, though they do a certain negative good by eating scorpions and insects which they find by over-turning the loose rocks and boulders with which that part of the bushveld is always covered. The bushveld is littered in many places with recently-upturned stones.

Campbell, *Dark Horse*, p. 71.

When a cow rhinoceros came out of a thicket with her calf she faced the ancient problem of many mothers on the plains: how to break the bond to her youngster so that she could resume her sexual life. Her calf had become relatively enormous, but he was still dependent on his mother and beginning to be jealous of her sexuality. The hot sun splashed her dusty hide as she follow-ed her predictable path toward her next grazing ground, her next lavatory. There, at the edge of the plains, she was accosted by two bulls. Immediately, both began demonstrating before her.

The cow was not yet fully in season and she looked at the demonstrations without responding, but the young rhino sensed the significance and he could not contain himself. Enraged, he charged the courting bulls despite the disparity in size. They stood fast and might have killed him if the mother had not charged the bulls only paces behind her youngster. The collision of the four animals was a bizarre accident; none real-ly wanted to fight the others, but all were forced into a comic melee. The young rhino ineffectually butted the bulls with his horn while they tried to parade before his mother, intending no harm either to cow or calf. The ground turned to dust under the pounding feet, and inexplicably, both bulls fled. The slower of them was severely gored in his hindquarters as the enraged female caught him on her horn.

Russell, *Season on the Plain*, pp. 265-6.

God made the hippopotamus and told it to cut the grass for the other animals. But when the hippopotamus came to Africa and felt how hot it was, he asked God for permission to stay in the water during the day and to cut the grass only at night. God hesitated to give this permission, for the hippopotamus was apt to eat fish rather than cut grass. But the hippopotamus promis-ed not to eat fish and was thus allowed to remain in the water. Now when the hippopotamus leaves a pile of dung, it scatters the pile with its tail, thereby showing God that there are no fish scales in it.

Schaller, *The Year of the Gorilla*, p. 64.

I took Abel Chapman out the whole day and found him charming, though I fear he was tired out at the end. We saw every variety of game between Nairobi and the Athi River south of Nairobi in an area of about 16 square miles. It amounted to:

3 rhinoceros	1267 wildebeeste
18 giraffe	1654 haartebeeste
42 ostrich	432 Grant's gazelle
31 warthog	234 Thomson's gazelle
42 eland	66 impala
568 zebra	11 wild hog
8 great bustard	1 cheetah
34 baboon	9 lion

We shot nothing.

Meinertzhagen, *Kenya Diary (1902-1906)*, p. 174.

I was much taken one day by a sick elephant. He was stand-ing there quite alone, ankle-deep in the muddy water in the mid-dle of the river, his trunk curling just an inch or two above the surface, and for a good fifteen minutes he never moved at all. He made no attempt to drink or wash himself. The river flowed down on him, hornbills and bright kingfishers swooped past, baboons in dozens ran past on either bank and tall palms and acacia trees rose overhead. But none of it was any good to this elephant. It may have been that he was suffering from toothache or some gargantuan stomach disorder, and quite clearly life for him was hell. He stood there ruminating, merely enduring ex-istence, until at last some dull hope made him think that he would feel better if he got back to the bank; and then he painful-ly pulled himself up through the reeds on to the high ground on the opposite side. He disappeared slowly through the bushes, and it was unnatural that he was not even bothering to feed.

Moorehead, *No Room in the Ark*, p. 104.

Then the sunset blossomed in full. The beauty of that evening still lives with us. Fourteen well-known predators galloped through the rising orange dust, backlit by the nearly horizontal rays of the setting sun. Apache, Comanche, and Sioux seemed to be stretched and elongated in their earnest race after the prey, and we still see their white-tipped tails glowing around the edges, like the silver lining on clouds. Plovers rose crying from the plain at their approach, and the rumbling of gnu hooves vibrated up through the tires of the car.

Fourteen wild dogs then stood eating, crowded shoulder to shoulder, shoving a little, but excusing themselves with in-gratiating nods and begging in soft twitters. The red sun went down through dust. We watched the feeding pack first through a golden haze and then, as the light failed, through a gray one, until the animals seemed to dissolve into the night itself. The sounds of eating went on.

George & Lory Frame, *Swift & Enduring: Cheetahs and Wild Dogs of the Serengeti* (E.P. Dutton, 1981), p. 225. The authors spent four years at the Serengeti Research Institute in Tanzania. *Swift & Enduring* is an intelligent research popularization.

...there in the grass beside the track lay a fine male lion. For a few seconds he looked directly at us, chin lifted, amber eyes half closed, then his attention abruptly shifted and focused on another big male walking toward him through the trees. When only ten feet or so of sparkling grass divided them, the nearer lion stood up, advanced and the two greeted one another — rubbed their huge shaggy heads affectionately against one another, over and over, uttering little moaning grunts of endearment like those we had heard between the mothers and cubs of our big pride. With a last placing together of their wide foreheads, they separated and looked about consideringly, then walked off, side by side, into the rising sun. The tenderness of their meeting and the radiance of the newly created day brought us into that blissful sense of harmony which more and more we were discovering was Africa's gift. The walls inside you, and those between you and the world, dissolved and disappeared; whatever it is that divides ceased to exist; it had never been real in the first place, you felt — it was some kind of conjuror's trick. One felt sustained by, and sustaining, a live, fluid matrix as pervading and boundless and unfamiliar as love.

Ames, *A Glimpse Of Eden*, p. 115.

It had started the night before when he had wakened and heard the lion roaring somewhere up along the river. It was a deep sound and at the end there were sort of coughing grunts that made him seem just outside the tent, and when Francis Macomber woke in the night to hear it he was afraid. . . .

"Sounds like an old-timer," Robert Wilson said, looking up from his kippers and coffee. "Listen to him cough."

"Is he very close?"

"A mile or so up the stream."

"Will we see him?"

"We'll have a look."

"Does his roaring carry that far? It sounds as though he were right in camp."

"Carries a hell of a long way," said Robert Wilson. "It's strange the way it carries. Hope he's a shootable cat. The boys said there was a very big one about here."

"If I get a shot, where should I hit him," Macomber asked, "to stop him?"

"In the shoulders," Wilson said. "In the neck if you can make it. Shoot for bone. Break him down."

"I hope I can place it properly," Macomber said.

"You shoot very well," Wilson told him. "Take your time. Make sure of him. The first one in is the one that counts."

"What range will it be?"

"Can't tell. Lion has something to say about that. Won't shoot unless it's close enough so you can make sure."

"At under a hundred yards?" Macomber asked.

Wilson looked at him quickly.

"Hundred's about right. Might have to take him a bit under. Shouldn't chance a shot at much over that. A hundred's a decent range. You can hit him wherever you want. . . .

. . .

Plate 6. Old Man in the Stream.

They climbed into the motor car and, in the gray first daylight, moved off up the river through the trees. Macomber opened the breech of his rifle and saw he had metal-cased bullets, shut the bolt and put the rifle on safety. He saw his hand was trembling. He felt in his pocket for more cartridges and moved his fingers over the cartridges in the loops of his tunic front. He turned back to where Wilson sat in the rear seat of the doorless, box-bodied motor car beside his wife, them both grinning with excitement, and Wilson leaned forward and whispered, "See the birds dropping. Means the old boy has left his kill."

. . .

They were driving slowly along the high bank of the stream which here cut deeply to its boulder-filled bed, and they wound in and out through big trees as they drove. Macomber was watching the opposite bank when he felt Wilson take hold of his arm. The car stopped.

"There he is," he heard the whisper. "Ahead and to the right. Get out and take him. He's a marvellous lion."

Macomber saw the lion now. He was standing almost broadside, his great head up and turned toward them. The early morning breeze that blew toward them was just stirring his dark mane, and the lion looked huge, silhouetted on the rise of bank in the gray morning light, his shoulders heavy, his barrel of a body bulking smoothly.

"How far is he?" asked Macomber, raising his rifle.

"About seventy-five. Get out and take him."

"Why not shoot from where I am?"

"You don't shoot them from cars," he heard Wilson saying in his ear. "Get out. He's not going to stay there all day."

Macomber stepped out of the curved opening at the side of the front seat, onto the step and down onto the ground. The lion still stood looking majestically and cooly toward this object that his eyes only showed in silhouette, bulking like some super-rhino. There was no man smell carried toward him and he watched the object, moving his great head a little from side to side. Then watching the object, not afraid, but hesitating before going down the bank to drink with such a thing opposite him, he saw a man figure detach itself from it and he turned his heavy head and swung away toward the cover of the trees as he heard a cracking crash and felt the slam of a .30-06 220-grain solid bullet that bit his flank and ripped in sudden hot scalding nausea through his stomach. He trotted, heavy, big-footed, swinging wounded full-bellied, through the trees toward the tall grass and cover, and the crash came again to go past him ripping the air apart. Then it crashed again and he felt the blow as it hit his lower ribs and ripped on through, blood sudden hot and frothy in his mouth, and he galloped toward the high grass where he could crouch and not be seen and make them bring the crashing thing close enough so he could make a rush and get the man that held it.

Macomber had not thought how the lion felt as he got out of the car. He only knew his hands were shaking and as he walked away from the car it was almost impossible for him to make his legs move. They were stiff in the thighs, but he could feel the muscles fluttering. He raised the rifle, sighted on the junction of the lion's head and shoulders and pulled the trigger. Nothing happened though he pulled until he thought his finger would break. Then he knew he had the safety on and as he lowered he rifle to move the safety over he moved another frozen pace forward, and the lion seeing his silhouette now clear of the silhouette of the car, turned and started off at a trot, and, as

Macomber fired, he heard a whunk that meant that the bullet was home; but the lion kept on going. Macomber shot again and everyone saw the bullet throw a spout of dirt beyond the trotting lion. He shot again, remembering to lower his aim, and they all heard the bullet hit, and the lion went into a gallop and was in the tall grass before he had the bolt pushed forward.

Macomber stood there feeling sick at his stomach, his hands that held the Springfield still cocked, shaking, and his wife and Robert Wilson were standing by him. Beside him too were the two gun-bearers chattering in Wakamba.

"I hit him," Macomber said. "I hit him twice."

"You gut-shot him and you hit him somewhere forward," Wilson said without enthusiasm. The gun-bearers looked very grave. They were silent now.

"You may have killed him." Wilson went on. "We'll have to wait a while before we go in to find out."

"What do you mean?"

"Let him get sick before we follow him up."

"Oh," said Macomber.

"He's a hell of a fine lion." Wilson said cheerfully. "He's gotten into a bad place though."

"Why is it bad?"

"Can't see him until you're on him."

"Oh," said Macomber.

. . .

"Can't we set the grass on fire?" Macomber asked.

"Too green."

"Can't we send beaters?"

Wilson looked at him appraisingly. "Of course we can," he said. "But it's just a touch murderous. You see we know the lion's wounded. You can drive an unwounded lion — he'll move on ahead of a noise — but a wounded lion's going to charge. You can't see him until you're right on him. He'll make himself perfectly flat in cover you wouldn't think would hide a hare. You can't very well send boys in there to that sort of a show. Somebody bound to get mauled."

"What about the gun-bearers?"

"Oh, they'll go with us. It's their shauri. You see, they signed on for it. They don't look too happy though, do they?"

"I don't want to go in there," said Macomber. It was out before he knew he'd said it.

"Neither do I," said Wilson very cheerily. "Really no choice though." Then, as an afterthought, he glanced at Macomber and saw suddenly how he was trembling and the pitiful look on his face.

"You don't have to go in, of course," he said. "That's what I'm hired for, you know. That's why I'm so expensive."

"You mean you'd go in by yourself? Why not leave him there?"

Robert Wilson, whose entire occupation had been with the lion and the problem he presented, and who had not been thinking about Macomber except to note that he was rather windy, suddenly felt as though he had opened the wrong door in a hotel and seen something shameful.

"What do you mean?"

"Why not just leave him?"

"You mean pretend to ourselves he hasn't been hit?"

"No. Just drop it."

"It isn't done."

"Why not?"

"For one thing, he's certain to be suffering. For another, some one else might run onto him."

Day's End

The Photograph in Lieu of Trophy

A Study in Eye Contact

Basking Hyraxes

Jumbos Emerging from the Shadows of Kilimanjaro

The Combined Extravagance of Sunset and Giraffes

A Good Climber for a Few More Months

The Languorous Exit from·the Waterhole

Lord and Mistress

One Predator's Day Ends (Another's Begins)

Jackal Portrait

For the Family Album

Sponge Bath

Watching the Progress of a Hunt: Is Dinner Ready?

The Arrival of "Tai"

A Falling Out Within the
Sanitation Department

Roof-Hatch View of Ngorongoro at Day's End
(Courtesy Ricardo Sanchez)

"I see."

"But you don't have to have anything to do with it."

. . .

"I'd like to," Macomber said. *"I'm just scared, you know."*

Thirty-five yards into the grass the big lion lay flattened out along the ground. His ears were back and his only movement was a slight twitching up and down of his long, black-tufted tail. He had turned at bay as soon as he had reached this cover and he was sick with the wound through his full belly, and weakening with the wound through his lungs that brought a thin foamy red to his mouth each time he breathed. His flanks were wet and hot and flies were on the little openings the solid bullets had made in his tawny hide, and his big yellow eyes, narrowed with hate, looked straight ahead, only blinking when the pain came as he breathed, and his claws dug in the soft baked earth. All of him, pain, sickness, hatred and all of his remaining strength, was tightening into an absolute concentration for a rush. He could hear the men talking and he waited, gathering all of himself into this preparation for a charge as soon as the men would come into the grass. As he heard their voices his tail stiffened to twitch up and down, and, as they came into the edge of the grass, he made a coughing grunt and charged. Kongoni, the old gun-bearer, in the lead watching the blood spoor, Wilson watching the grass for any movement, his big gun ready, the second gun-bearer looking ahead and listening, Macomber close to Wilson, his rifle cocked, they had just moved into the grass when Macomber heard the blood-choked coughing grunt, and saw the swishing rush in the grass. The next thing he knew he was running; running wildly, in panic in the open, running toward the stream.

He heard the ca-ra-wong! of Wilson's big rifle, and again in a second crashing carawong! and turning saw the lion, horrible-looking now, with half his head seeming to be gone, crawling toward Wilson in the edge of the tall grass while the red-faced man worked the bolt on the short ugly rifle and aimed carefully as another blasting carawong! came from the muzzle, and the crawling, heavy, yellow bulk of the lion stiffened and the huge mutilated head slid forward and Macomber, standing by himself in the clearing where he had run, holding a loaded rifle, while two black men and a white man looked back at him in contempt, knew the lion was dead.

Ernest Hemingway, "The Short Happy Life of Francis Macomber," *The Snows of Kilimanjaro and Other Stories* (Charles Scribner's Sons, 1927). On the next day's hunt, Macomber was shot and killed by his wife as a buffalo seemed about to gore him. Whether his wife was shooting at the buffalo or Macomber is one of those unanswerable Hemingway subtleties.

It is a curious fact that some people lose their heads when they go into the bush and forget ordinary conventions. . . . There is much of the savage in all of us, but a man will work out his primitive instincts by shooting while a certain type of woman often turns to sex. Usually the white hunter is the object of her devotion. In the bush a white hunter cuts a fine figure. He is efficient, brave, and picturesque. These ladies never stop to think how this dashing individual would appear on the dance floors of London or in a Continental drawing room. One of the greatest scandals of Kenya came about as the result of a lady's unwise attachment to a white hunter.

This tragedy occurred near the turn of the century. The white hunter involved was internationally known, having established a reputation by killing several man-eating lions. One of the parties he guided consisted of a wealthy man and his attractive young wife. When the safari returned to Nairobi, the husband was not with them. The hunter announced that his client had shot himself with a revolver while delirious. However, the hunter could not stop his native boys from talking and the story got around that the man had met with foul play. The government sent a police officer to investigate. The officer backtracked the safari and found where the client had been buried. He dug up the body and discovered that the man had been shot in the back of the head by a heavy-caliber rifle. Meanwhile, the hunter and the dead man's wife had left the country. As far as I know, they were never heard of again. I believe that the American writer Ernest Hemingway based his famous story "The Short and Happy Life of Francis Macomber" on this incident.

Hunter, *Hunter*, pp. 53-4.

The cheetah is a blur across the plain. Fifty, sixty, seventy miles per hour, the living missile streaks toward its target. At this moment, as it draws near the flashing rear quarters of its prey, the awesome beauty of their contest is inescapable. Each is a sculptor who, using eons of time as its maul and evolution as its chisel, has created, in the other, something of such form, such vitality, such truth that it can never be duplicated. This relationship is the best Nature has to offer; the ego of the natural world.

Mark & Delia Owens, *Cry of the Kalahari* (Houghton Mifflin Co., 1984), p. 6. A recent popular best-seller, *Cry* is the story of two young Americans who spent seven years in the little-explored Kalahari desert. In reading this remarkable saga, one is alternately caught up in the adventure or annoyed with the naïveté of the principals. Much solid research resulted, however, from their efforts.

Yet it is not on an enemy so recently acquired as man that the baboon lavishes panic. This he reserves for his more ancient enemy; the leopard, at nightfall.

. . .

. . . one night the leopard came early. It was still dusk. The troop had only just returned from the feeding grounds and had barely time to reach its scattered sleeping places in the high-piled rocks behind the fig tree. Now it shrilled its terror. . . .

[The leopard] appeared from the bush and took its insolent time. So vulnerable were the baboons that the leopard seemed to recognize no need for hurry. He crouched just below a little jutting cliff observing his prey and the problems of the terrain. And. . . two male baboons [were] edging along the cliff above him.

The two males moved cautiously. The leopard, if he saw them, ignored them. His attention was fixed on the swarming, screeching, defenceless horde scrambling among the rocks. Then the two males dropped. They dropped on him from a height of twelve feet. One bit at the leopard's spine. The other struck at his throat while clinging to his neck from below. In an instant the leopard disemboweled with his hind claws the baboon *hanging to his neck and caught in his jaws the baboon on his back. But it was too late. The dying, disemboweled baboon had hung on just long enough and had reached the leopard's jugular vein with his canines.*

...Night fell. Death, hidden from all but the impartial stars, enveloped prey and predator alike. And in the hollow places in the rocky, looming krans a society of animals settled down to sleep.

> Robert Ardrey, *African Genesis* (Dell Edition, 1967), pp. 81-3. First published in 1961, *Genesis* was later joined by the *Territorial Imperative* and *The Social Contract* as provocative and stimulating platforms for Ardrey's evolutionary theories. One of Ardrey's centerpieces was the apparent violent streak and brutality of modern man — the 'Mark of Cain,' over which philosophers have long agonized. Ardrey popularized a theory originally propounded by Raymond Dart, a professor of anatomy in South Africa, that man evolved from "killer apes," whose murderous instincts remained deeply embedded in us, whatever our veneer of civility. Ardrey's books were read or discussed by millions, but few scientists of note have accepted either the premises or the consequences of man's depravity, as proposed by Ardrey. Ardrey himself first visited Africa as a reporter during Kenya's Mau Mau uprising in the early 1950s, and that experience seems to have had an exaggerated effect on his writings (what might be labelled "The Robert Ruark Syndrome").

The silver sands of the rivers, powdered quartz, served us daily as news sheets where we could read whatever had happened in the dark and where we could actually reconstruct the story of what we had heard in the night. Sand is a wonderful news sheet. For instance, once near the Sabi river, I saw the spoor of three lions and a small hippo, with some blood. The hippo's spoor disappeared into the water and that of two lions emerged from the water a few yards further downstream, telling of an unsuccessful attempt on their part to get the hippo before it reached its native element. In our camp by the Sabi we had heard all the splashing, the grunts, and the general uproar, as two of the lions had ridden their intended victim into the crocodile-haunted water from which they were lucky to escape.

> Campbell, *Dark Horse*, p. 70.

Soft hills inset with outcrops of elephant-colored boulders rose beyond a bright stretch of blue river, and elephants climbed to a sunrise ridge from a world that was still in shadow. More than a hundred moved slowly toward the sun; the landscape stirred. . . .

. . .

To the south, on a rise that overlooks the Albert Nile where it bends away into Uganda, a herd of kob antelope stepped along the hill — some sixty female kobs and calves led by a single male with sweeping horns and fine black forelegs — and the delicate oribi, bright rufous with brief straight horns, scampered away in twos and threes, tails switching. A gray duiker, more like a fat hare than an antelope, gathered its legs beneath it in low flight, and a sow wart hog with five hoglets, new sun glinting on

the manes and the inelegant raised tails, rushed off in a single file at the scent of man. Here and there a stately waterbuck regarded us, alert.

Kob and waterbuck would be large animals elsewhere in the world, but here they seemed almost incidental, for to the east of them, the entire hillside surged with elephant, nearly two hundred now, including a few tuskers of enormous size. And to the north, on a small hillock, stood four rhinoceros, one of these a calf. The askaris approached the rhino gradually, hooping downwind — not always a simple matter, as the light wind was variable — and eventually brought us within stoning distance of the animals; they were astonished that we had no cameras, but simply wished to see. The rhinos were of the rare "white" (weit, or wide-mouthed) species, a grazing animal that lacks the long upper lip of the black rhino, which is a browser; mud-crusted, with their double horn, their ugliness was protean. The cow and calf having moved off, two males were left, and these, aware of an intrusion but unable to detect it, moved suspiciously toward each other, stopping short at the last second as if to contemplate the risks of battle, then retreating simultaneously. Having just come to Africa, I did not know that the white rhino is gentle and rarely makes a charge; buffalo in herds are also inoffensive. . .

Beyond the rhino, dry trees rose toward the dusty mountains, and beyond the hills hung the blue haze of Africa, and everywhere were birds — stonechats and silver birds, cordon bleus and flycatchers, shrikes, kingfishers, and sunbirds. Overhead sailed vultures and strange eagles and the brown kite of Africa and South Asia, which had followed me overland two thousand miles from Cairo, up the Nile.

> Matthiessen & Porter, *The Tree Where Man Was Born/The African Experience*, p. 29.

A foutra for the world and worldlings base!
I speak of Africa and golden joys.

> Shakespeare, *Henry IV, Part 2* (1600), Act V, Scene iii. The "swaggering Pistol."

"I speak of Africa and golden joys"; the joy of wandering through lonely lands; the joy of hunting the mighty and terrible lords of the wilderness, the cunning, the wary, and the grim.

In these greatest of the world's great hunting-grounds there are mountain peaks whose snows are dazzling under the equatorial sun; swamps where the slime oozes and bubbles and festers in the steaming heat; lakes like seas; skies that burn above deserts where the iron desolation is shrouded from view by the wavering mockery of the mirage; vast grassy plains where palms and thorn-trees fringe the dwindling streams; mighty rivers rushing out of the heart of the continent through the sadness of endless marshes; forests of gorgeous beauty, where death broods in the dark and silent depths. . .

. . .

The land teems with beasts of the chase, infinite in number and incredible in variety. It holds the fiercest beasts of ravin, and the fleetest and most timid of those beings that live in undying fear of talon and fang. It holds the largest and the smallest of hoofed animals. It holds the mightiest creatures that tread the earth or swim in its rivers; it also holds distant kinsfolk of these same creatures, no bigger than woodchucks, which dwell in crannies of the rocks, and in the tree tops. There are antelope smaller than hares, and antelope larger than oxen. There are creatures which are the embodiments of grace; and others whose huge ungainliness is like that of a shape in a nightmare. The plains are alive with droves of strange and beautiful animals whose like is not known elsewhere; and with others even stranger that show both in form and temper something of the fantastic and the grotesque. It is a never-ending pleasure to gaze at the great herds of buck as they move to and fro in their myriads; as they stand for their noontide rest in the quivering heat haze; as the long files come down to drink at the watering-places; as they feed and fight and rest and make love.

The hunter who wanders through these lands sees sights which ever afterward remain fixed in his mind. He sees the monstrous river-horse snorting and plunging beside the boat; the giraffe looking over the tree tops at the nearing horseman; the ostrich fleeing at a speed that none may rival; the snarling leopard and coiled python, with their lethal beauty; the zebras, barking in the moonlight, as the laden caravan passes on its night march through a thirsty land. In after years there shall come to him memories of the lion's charge; of the gray bulk of the elephant, close at hand in the sombre woodland; of the buffalo, his sullen eyes lowering from under his helmet of horn; of the rhinoceros, truculent and stupid, standing in the bright sunlight on the empty plain.

These things can be told. But there are no words that can tell the hidden spirit of the wilderness, that can reveal its mystery, its melancholy, and its charm. There is delight in the hardy life of the open, in long rides rifle in hand, in the thrill of the fight with dangerous game. Apart from this, yet mingled with it, is the strong attraction of the silent places, of the large tropic moons, and the splendor of the new stars; where the wanderer sees the awful glory of sunrise and sunset in the wide waste spaces of the earth, unworn of man, and changed only by the slow change of the ages through time everlasting.

KHARTOUM, *March 15, 1910*　　　　THEODORE ROOSEVELT

Theodore Roosevelt, *African Game Trails: An Account of the African Wanderings of an American Hunter-Naturalist* (Charles Scribner's Sons, 1910), Foreword. When Roosevelt left office in 1909, he was fifty-one years old and faced a difficult transition from President to private citizen for so active a personality. He immediately left for Africa on one of the most elaborate and publicized hunting safaris of all time. In fact, the itinerary was much discussed even before the election of 1908. One evening at a dinner held at the White House, Carl Akeley was amusing the guests with stories of Africa. One anecdote concerned sixteen lions. On hearing the tale, President Roosevelt turned to a member of the House of Representatives present: ''Congressman, I wish I had those sixteen lions to turn loose on the House.'' The Congressman, suitably horrified, protested: ''Might not the lions make some mistakes and eat the wrong members.'' T.R., in his best Churchillian manner, snapped back: ''They would not make any mistakes if they stayed long enough.'' In American politics, Presidents do not, however, always have the last word. The dinner conversation made the rounds, and, when the term of office was up and final preparations were made for the trip, certain Senators remarked to the press that

America expected every lion to do its duty. The cartoonists had a field day.

Our aim being to cure and send home specimens of all the common big game — in addition to as large a series as possible of the small mammals and birds — it was necessary to carry an elaborate apparatus of naturalists' supplies; we had brought with us, for instance, four tons of fine salt, as to cure the skins of the big beasts is a herculean labor under the best conditions; we had hundreds of traps for the small creatures; many boxes of shot-gun cartridges in addition to the ordinary rifle cartridges which alone would be necessary on a hunting trip; and, in short, all the many impedimenta needed if scientific work is to be properly done under modern conditions. Few laymen have any idea of the expense and pains which must be undergone in order to provide groups of mounted big animals from far-off lands, such as were seen in museums like the National Museum in Washington and the American Museum of Natural History in New York. . . .So our preparations were necessarily on a very large scale; and as we drew up at the station the array of porters and of tents looked as if some small military expedition was about to start. As a compliment, which I much appreciated, a large American flag was floating over my own tent; and in the front line, flanking this tent on either hand, were other big tents for the members of the party, with a dining tent and skinning tent; while behind were the tents of the two hundred porters, the gun-bearers, the tent boys, the askaris or native soldiers, and the horse boys or saises. In front of the tents stood the men in two lines; the first containing the fifteen askaris, the second the porters with their headmen. The askaris were uniformed, each in a red fez, a blue blouse, and white knickerbockers, and each carrying his rifle and belt. The porters were chosen from several different tribes or races to minimize the danger of combination in the event of mutiny.

Here and there in East Africa one can utilize ox wagons, or pack trains of donkeys; but for a considerable expedition it is still best to use a safari of native porters, of the type by which the commerce and exploration of the country have always been carried on. The backbone of such a safari is generally composed of Swahili, the coast men, negroes who have acquired the Moslem religion, together with a partially Arabicized tongue and a strain of Arab blood from the Arab warriors and traders who have been dominant in the coast towns for so many centuries. It was these Swahili trading caravans, under Arab leadership, which, in their quest for ivory and slaves, trod out the routes which the early white explorers followed. Without their work as a preliminary the work of the white explorers could not have been done; and it was the Swahili porters themselves who rendered this work itself possible. To this day every hunter, trader, missionary, or explorer must use either a Swahili safari or one modelled on the Swahili basis. The part played by the white-topped ox wagon in the history of South Africa, and by the camel caravan in North Africa, has been played in middle Africa by the files of strong, patient, childlike savages, who have borne the burdens of so many masters and employers hither and thither, through and across, the dark heart of the continent.

Roosevelt, *African Game Trails*, pp. 20-3. T.R. was a hunter, loved the outdoors, and was an incurable romantic to boot. The thrill of the hunt, the smell of camp, the activity and adventure of travel in an Africa that was still "wild" — all were utterly irresistible. African hunting by European royalty and wealthy businessmen had begun in the previous century, but the safari (and Africa) was still more or less unknown to Americans. Roosevelt was not wealthy and sought sponsorship of his trip by the Smithsonian Institution's National Museum and the American Museum of Natural History. When camped, the assorted assemblage stretched out over an entire football field of land! T.R. neglected, of course, to mention the cases of champagne. The trip itself lasted roughly a year. By T.R.'s own account, the safari exceeded all expectations. As extensive as Roosevelt's safari was, however, the personnel in terms of numbers were no match for some of the expeditions undertaken in the 1800s.

Perhaps I should explain at this point just what the normal personnel of a safari in British East Africa is. First, there is the headman, who is supposed to be in charge of the whole show, excepting the gun-bearers and tent boys, who are the personal servants and under the immediate direction of their masters. The askaris *are soldiers who are armed and whose duties consist of the guarding of the camp at night and looking after the porters on the march. There is one* askari *to from ten to twenty porters. The cook and his assistant or assistants, the number of whom is determined by the size of the party, are important members of the safari. Then there are tent boys, one to each member of the party, whose duty is to look after the tents and clothing, and to serve their masters or mistresses at table. The* syces *are pony boys, whose duties are to look after the horses and equipment. In addition to those already named come the rank and file of porters whose duties are manifold, carrying loads on the march, gathering wood under the direction of the* askaris *and the cook, bringing in game, beating for lions, setting up the tents under the direction of the tent boys, and so forth.*

Carl E. Akeley, *In Brightest Africa* (Garden City Publishers, 1923), pp. 136-7. Actually, the *askaris* were included primarily to keep porters from deserting. The whole affair was quite a spectacle, and the residents of the departure point always lined the route out of town to see off the safari. Before Akeley's time, each retinue also included a safari clown, a sort of court jester employed to joke, mimic, and revive spirits that flagged under the hardships of the journey.

Suddenly a commotion from the track above. Four gazelle raced along as if running in front of a bush fire. They were followed by two or three bushbuck and a small antelope, probably a duiker. All were apparently terrified. At points in their flight they dislodged little cascades of stones that tinkled down among us. With my mind on the possibility of lion I cocked the rifle. But the animals were not being chased by lion. The hunters were more fierce than any of the big cats. Through field-glasses I caught a glimpse of speckled shapes, fanning out to strike down a bushbuck some way behind the others. They were hunting dogs, the most formidable pursuers of game in the whole of Africa.

Like army ants, they have their home everywhere and nowhere, suddenly pouring into territory where they may not have been seen for years. We could only speculate on the outcome of the chase. The hunters and the hunted swept round a bluff and disappeared from sight. What seemed certain was that at least one bushbuck would be torn apart and devoured before dusk.

Hunting dogs never relent. In Ruanda on the borders of Tanzania some years earlier I had seen a pack chase an impala for about ten minutes. The antelope, utterly exhausted, had dogs on both flanks. From time to time one of the pack detached itself from the rest and sprang at the animal, tearing out a chunk of flesh from the quarters until the desperate antelope fell over and had its entrails ripped out. By the time we drove up to within fifty yards of the kill in a Land-Rover, the impala was not dead. One leg feebly rose and fell. But it had been eviscerated and as the dogs swung round at our approach they looked as if they had been bathed in blood.

The presence of hunting dogs can often be detected by an eerie, repetitive call which sounds like the last note in the call of the European cuckoo. It is usually heard about a dozen times and seems to be a rallying cry like the long-drawn ooo-ah-ooo of the hyena.

What impressed me most about the gruesome hunt I had seen in Ruanda was the discipline of the pack. When we first came across the dogs they were resting on the brow of a hill. They were in no sense put out by our presence but continued to gaze intently down on the plain below. After a time we saw a solitary dog racing up the hill towards them and the pack rose to greet it. There was a great deal of tail-wagging and excited chatter and then all the animals ran off in the direction from which the scout had come. We followed the animals in the Land-Rover and, as I remember the occasion, there were about a dozen vultures flying overhead. I felt as if we were taking part in a mediaeval hunt with hawks and hounds.

When the chase was over and the impala dead, the pack leader took possession of the carcass, accompanied by two bitches. The rest of the animals stood aside, expectantly. The leader ate his fill and retired to the shelter of some bushes with a bone. As soon as he had turned his back on the remains, the other animals slunk forward in twos and threes in accordance with some obscure hierarchy of place. They ate until there was nothing left of the antelope except the horns and a little patch of blood-stained grass.

John Hillaby, *Journey to the Jade Sea*, pp. 68-9.

There is a vast sweep of dry bush desert lying in South-West Africa and western Bechuanaland, bordered in the north by Lake Ngami and the Okovango River, in the south by the Orange River, and in the west by the Damera Hills. It is the Kalahari Desert, part of a great inland table of southern Africa that slopes west toward the sea, all low sand dunes and great plains, flat, dry, and rolling one upon the other for thousands of miles, a hostile country of thirst and heat and thorns where the grass is harsh and often barbed and the stones hide scorpions.

From March to December, in the long drought of the year, the sun bakes the desert to powdery dry leaves and dust. There are no surface waters at all, no clouds for coolness, no tall trees for shade, but only low bushes and grass tufts; and among the grass tufts grow brown thistles, briers, the dry stalks of spiny weeds, all tangled into knots during the rains, now dry, tumbled, and dead.

The Kalahari would be very barren, very devoid of landmarks, if it were not for the baobab trees, and even these grow far from each other, some areas having none. But where there is one it is the biggest thing in all the landscape, dominating all the veld, more impressive than any mountain. It can be as much as two hundred feet high and thirty feet in diameter. It has great, thick branches that sprout haphazardly from the sides of

the trunk and reach like stretching arms into the sky. The bark is thin and smooth and rather pink, and sags in folds toward the base of the tree like the skin on an elephant's leg, which is why a baobab is sometimes called an elephant tree. Its trunk is soft and pulpy, like a carrot instead of wooden, and if you lean against it you find that it is warm from the sun and you expect to hear a great heart beating inside. In the spring, encouraged by moisture, these giants put out huge white flowers resembling

Plates 7-9. Baobab Views. The baobab can be used by man in many ways: the leaves boiled and eaten as vegetables; the seeds ground and roasted to make a coffee-like beverage; the pollen to fashion a glue; tartaric acid from the fruit pod used for sherbets; and the soft wood made into paper and rope. On occasion, a baobab, which holds moisture like a large sponge, will absorb too much water and collapse in on itself from the weight and rot. Baobabs mostly endure: the explorer Livingstone carved his initials inside a large hollow baobab in 1858, which signature was discovered by a photographer in 1958. Subsequently, the government of Mozambique made that tree a national monument. Large baobabs may have a girth of fifty-five feet or more, but the soft wood does not permit an accurate count of its growth rings. We really do not know whether the tree is thousands of years old or "merely" hundreds.

gardenias, white as moons and fragrant, that face down toward the earth; during the summer they bear alum-like dry fruits, shaped like pears, which can be eaten. In the Kalahari there is no need of hills. The great baobabs standing in the plains, the wind, and the seasons are enough.

Thomas, *The Harmless People*, pp. 3-4.

Much of this chapter is about death, but a death so that others may live, death because of need, not pleasure. There is neither cruelty nor compassion in a lion's quest for food and this impersonal endeavor strikes a responsive cord in man the hunter. I enjoyed watching most hunts as struggles of life and death at their most elemental. It is a time when each animal uses to the utmost those attributes with which evolution has endowed it. It is also a moment when man, weak of body and slow of foot, can watch his limits transgressed, a moment which engenders not only humility for his own lack of prowess but also pride and exultation that he has managed to survive at all.

George B. Schaller, *Golden Shadows, Flying Hooves* (University of Chicago, 1983), p. 137. This study was first published in 1973. The golden shadows are the Serengeti lions, and the flying hooves are the wildebeests, zebras, and gazelles who are their prey. The beauty of the Serengeti, harsh in the dry season and lush during the rains, is the backdrop. *Golden Shadows* is one of the great animal behavior and ecology books and is further discussed in the Bibliography following Chapter X.

Our route lay across bare plains thickly covered with withered short grass. All around us as we marched were the game herds, zebras and hartebeests, gazelles of the two kinds, and now and then wildebeests. Hither and thither over the plain, crossing and recrossing, ran the dusty game trails, each with its myriad hoof-marks; the round hoof-prints of the zebra, the heart-shaped marks that showed where the hartebeest herd had trod, and the delicate etching that betrayed where the smaller antelope had passed. . . .Africa is a country of trails. Across the high veldt, in every direction, run the tangled trails of the multitudes of game that have lived thereon from time immemorial.

Roosevelt, *African Game Trails*, p.101.

Eleanor stands nearly ten feet tall and weighs just under four tons. When I stand beside her the top of my head just reaches the top of my foreleg. Her skin is like upholstered leather; a patchwork quilt that is prickly to feel because it is covered in short, stiff hairs. Mostly it is coarse and grainy to the touch, yet in some places it is pliable and spongy, especially where it hangs in loose, baggy 'pants' above her back legs; behind her ears it is soft and cool and as smooth as silk.

Her ears are one of Eleanor's most outstanding features. They are enormous. Round and wafery, they fan slowly ever backwards and forwards, stirring the hot still air of her arid homeland into a gently cooling breeze, and flapping softly as they slap against her flanks. Hers are probably the most sensitive ears in the entire animal kingdom; huge sounding boards that trap the faintest whisper borne in a breath of wilderness

wind, enabling her to unravel the symphony of different sounds that reach her and decipher their significance and meaning. For her world is different from ours, and one where every sound has a meaning.

Her legs are tall, straight columns, that easily support her massive bulk. Her feet, tipped with shiny round toenails, have cushioned soles that, despite her great size, enable her to move with uncanny silence through the bush covering the ground swiftly and easily in measured strides that appear deceptively deliberate and slow.

Two gleaming cream coloured tusks protrude from her head. Between them hangs her most unique feature — her long, rubbery trunk, its twin projections at the tip serving her very ably as a hand. Her trunk fulfils a multitude of functions besides that of breathing. It is flexible and strong, and like an arm, immensely powerful and supple. It is also extremely sensitive to scent, so can tell her more about her world than either her ears or her eyes. Raising it like a periscope, she can reach high in the air to test the wilderness wind. In this way she can determine by scent who moves beyond the field of her vision, and whether they be friend or foe. She is therefore usually forewarned of danger, and can easily trace a missing friend. Eleanor can determine where the rain has fallen in the hot thirstland that is her home; even if it be far away, she can tell where dry depressions in the landscape have been transformed overnight into life-giving drinking pools by rain, and where the bush will soon be tinged with green. She uses her trunk to fondle and feel, punish or help, rub an itch or remove a thorn, but mainly to select by smell what she should or should not eat, and convey both food and water to her mouth without having to lower her head, as do most other animals. With it she can pluck a tender shoot from the topmost branch of a tall tree, or delicately pick up a single fallen leaf without even having to look; and she can as easily break down a branch in order to peel off its bark as fell a tree if the mood so takes her. With her trunk she showers water over her body in a cooling spray during the heat of noon, or powders herself at bath time with puffs of blown dust. Her trunk also adds a very distinctive trumpet tone to her voice when she calls, making it quite different from any other voice in the wilderness.

Soft brown eyes fringed with lashes as long as a hand gaze downwards calmly and steadfastly with a deep intelligence mirrored in their tawny depths; haunting eyes of an animal which thinks and understands. As an elephant, Eleanor sees things that we never see, and hears sounds we never hear. She also knows of things that we will never know, and can predict events important to her with a mysterious certainty we would call 'eerie' long before they have even happened. For she has been endowed by nature with that mysterious sixth sense we know of only as instinct which gives her the perceptive ability denied us when we took a different turning in the road of life.

Daphne Sheldrick, *An Elephant Called Eleanor* (J.M. Dent and Sons, 1980), pp. 8-10. Daphne Sheldrick was born in East Africa. Husband David was the first warden of Tsavo National Park in Kenya. One of the most knowledgeable of the "amateur naturalists" who have spent their lives in East Africa and written about their many experiences there, she has published materials on several African animals. In common with many of those in similar positions, she would from time to time take a wild animal as a pet. A pet invariably shows the inherent potential for individuality that lies mostly dormant in a wild species. Eleanor was an orphan elephant raised by Sheldrick, ultimately to become famous in the wildlife film "Orphan Animals of Tsavo."

There is in African custom an essential harmony, an equilibrium with the land which seems to be lacking in our lives.

The people show this most clearly in the strength and propriety of their beliefs about, and their understanding of, the natural world. Many even identify themselves with a particular plant or animal, believing that there is a group spirit or soul, a collective identity that is equated in some way with this totem.

Each clan has its siboko, *around which it is united, and which distinguishes it from all other clans. The attributes of the totem become those of the clan and may be embodied in its ritual. "What do you dance?" the villagers asked when Boshier became a part of their lives. At first he did not understand, but later learned that this is always what people in Africa say when they want to know the origins of a stranger.*

The reply, "I dance the owl," for instance, means that the visitor comes from a community that recognizes the owl as its totem and is related not only to the bird, but historically to all other clans which know the same siboko.

Lyall Watson, *Lightning Bird: The Story of One Man's Journey into Africa's Past* (Simon & Schuster, Touchstone Edition, 1983), p. 38. This is one of those unusual books that deserves to be read by all readers having any interest in Africa, the story of man, or adventure generally. In 1955, a sixteen-year-old Englishman named Adrian Boshier ventured alone into the northern Transvaal bush — on foot, epileptic, and equipped only with a knife and a bag of salt — where he spent the next two decades. *Lightning Bird* is the "true story" of Boshier's struggle to stay alive and his many discoveries. The reader will hardly know what to believe as he progresses through this engrossing tale, so much of which is simply fantastic.

I had the most delightful experience today with a small bird known as the honey guide (Indicator). While working in the forest I became aware that a small bird was endeavouring to attract my attention by chattering at me from only a few feet away, evidently in a great state of excitement and often flying away into the forest but always in the same direction.

He was so persistent that I decided to follow him. His excitement then increased and he would keep some 20 yards ahead of me, usually fairly high up in a tree, but he never for a moment lost sight of me. After some 150 yards he was joined by two others, and their united chorus left me in no doubt as to the direction they wished me to take. The three birds finally came to rest in a smallish tree, and as they refused to leave it I was convinced that the honey they required was near at hand. A short inspection found the bees' nest under a strip of rotten bark, and my men soon laid it bare and spread the comb, rich with golden honey, on the ground.

As soon as it was clear to the birds that we had discovered the honey they sat fairly still in the tree within a few feet of us with very obvious feelings of satisfaction. Their little breasts were puffed out, and they would constantly throw their heads back and utter a low churning sound. But their greed was not untempered with jealousy, for with an angry call one would lift his head-feathers and make a dash at one of the others. Then would ensue a regular scurry through the surrounding trees, but the three birds would soon return to watch anxiously our operations. Having spread the comb out on a bare piece of ground we sat and watched from a distance of some 25 yards. The birds came down at once but did not feed on the ground. They each took a large bit of comb and flew off with it out of sight, and as soon as they had finished that bit they returned for more. I tried to follow one to see it feed, but could not locate it in the thick trees.

There is no doubt that these birds deliberately attracted my attention in order that I should follow their guidance to the bees which they had already located.

Meinertzhagen, *Kenya Diary (1902-1906)*, p. 268. We now know that the birds, the Black-throated African honey-guides (appropriately named *Indicator indicator*), seek the grubs and larvae in the hive and possibly the comb as well, which beeswax they can convert into nutrients by special enzymes found in their digestive tract.

We followed the honey-guide, which is one of those phenomena which you can never quite believe in until you see it with your own eyes. The bird makes a loud twittering over your head until you get up and follow it. From tree to tree it leads you on, twittering madly all the way, and the object of all this is some wild beehive which might be a few hundred yards or a mile or two away. The bird knows that human beings like honey and will open up the hive. Then it can feast on the young larvae of the bees (though some say it is really the wax that the bird is after). I followed a honey-guide for a quarter of a mile one day and then got bored and came back. At once the bird returned and started shrilling at me once more, shrilling so persistently that again I got up and followed. But it was too hot, and I wasn't as keen on honey as all that. I came back again. Saidi [the guide] did not approve of this at all. If one started a thing, he thought, one ought to go through with it. He added darkly that there was a legend that if you deceived the honey-guide too often it would grow mad and lead you on to a black mamba snake or some equally terrible reptile in the bush.

Moorehead, *No Room in the Ark*, pp. 97-8.

The chief feature of the landscape, and of your life in it, was the air. Looking back on a sojourn in the African highlands, you are struck by your feeling of having lived for a time up in the air. The sky was rarely more than pale blue or violet, with a profusion of mighty, weightless, ever-changing clouds towering up and sailing on it, but it has a blue vigour in it, and at a short distance it painted the ranges of hills and the woods a fresh deep blue. In the middle of the day the air was alive over the land, like a flame burning; it scintillated, waved and shone like running water, mirrored and doubled all objects, and created great Fata Morgana. Up in this high air you breathed easily, drawing in a vital assurance and lightness of heart. In the highlands you woke up in the morning and thought: Here I am, where I ought to be.

Dinesen, *Out of Africa*, p. 4.

The sun was high and hot, and flies were becoming bothersome. They concentrated on the old lion's left leg. Unless he kept his paw moving, they clustered there, sensing the corruption within and eager for a chance to deposit eggs. The lion watched the flies gather into a thick mass before jerking his paw away again and again. The flies were like the hyenas and the vultures of his old age: omnipresent and seemingly equipped with secret

Once vast herds of bison roamed North America's Great Plains. Some packs of wolves took their daytime ease on the grasslands like wild dogs do on the Serengeti. Perhaps groups of American lions followed the bison the way prides of African lions trek after migratory wildebeest and zebras. Golden pronghorn antelope dotted the plains in great numbers, looking very much like Grant's gazelles from a distance. Foxes and

Plate 10. Highland Vista.

information about him. They knew, somehow, when he felt sick or tired, or when minor injuries made him limp or lethargic. The previous night an old hyena, the moon glowing in the white disc of her one blind eye, had come boldly close to him and had stood there, sniffing, while the old lion had rumbled a warning to her. Now, he had forgotten his confrontation three days before with the young lioness over the carcass of the wildebeest. In the fight, she had hooked a claw into his left paw. The momentary pain had quickly gone but the lion was not to know that something more than a claw had entered his foot. He growled softly at the paw and licked it.

Russell, *Season on the Plain*, p. 67.

Hyenas are at home in the water. For some reason, wildebeest often try to escape hyenas by running into the lake or the Munge River. This manoeuvre merely seals their fate. Hyenas can even feed underwater. I once saw [hyenas] kill a wildebeest in the Munge River at a spot where the water was about six feet deep. Soon the carcass sank under-water. From then on the hyenas felt for the carcass with their feet, then dived underwater, emerging a moment later with a large chunk of meat in their mouths. With their coats all wet, smooth and dark, they looked remarkably like a colony of seals.

van Lawick, *Savage Paradise*, p. 36.

coyotes busily trotted through the grasslands, hunting and scavenging like jackals.

Today the picture is altered. A small population of bison survives on the National Bison Range — a grand name for a parcel of land barely thirty square miles in extent. Wolves and American lions have a chance for survival in some areas. But pronghorn antelope become trapped between the cattlemen's fences. Sheepmen bitterly resent the coyotes. Would you pay more for lamb so that the sheepman would stop demanding the "control" of the coyotes? Who are more important, people or animals? It is always the people who ask that question.

George & Lory Frame, *Swift & Enduring: Cheetahs and Wild Dogs of the Serengeti*, p. 226. The Frames now live in Utah.

...this first sight of wild animals in their natural surroundings really is something of a revelation, and although a thousand more lively scenes may overtake the traveller later on it is the first impression which will probably remain most clearly in his mind. The colours of the animals are brighter, their outlines clearer and their eyes more sprightly, than anything one could have previously imagined. There is a kind of tense vitality in their movements, an element of challenge in their glance, that immediately diminishes you, the observer, to a much smaller

stature than you thought you had before. That sense of privilege and superiority with which human beings approach another species suddenly forsakes you — you are simply another intruder in the bush on the same level as the animals themselves — and in a moment you comprehend how much human contact distorts wild creatures and destroys their proportions. While the zoo keeper forces on them an appearance that is much too soft and tame, the hunter (and incidentally the artist, the photographer and the taxidermist too) almost invariably makes them out to be too fierce and dramatic. Few animals in a natural state spend their lives in a state of panic or rage or in violent motion. They may be constantly on the alert, but for the most part you find them simply standing there under the trees, like this kudu, quietly munching leaves; and as a spectacle it is superb.

Moorehead, *No Room in the Ark*, p. 11-2.

As part of my duties I came to know many white hunters, the glamour boys of the wildlife world. Their hospitality was legendary and visiting their camps while on my rounds was invariably a pleasure. There was always a bed for a Game Ranger who became 'too tired' to get back to his own camp late at night. Many of these hunters became lifelong friends.

As a group they were somewhat misnamed, for few were actually good hunters. On their own most were incompetent trackers and couldn't find their way about the bush. Many found it difficult to approach animals easily and for actual bushmanship and hunting results they relied on their African staff of trackers and gunbearers. These were recruited from among the poachers, and many a safari depended upon their skills for its success. Of the few white men who were really competent bushmen and hunters, it was notable that almost all had grown up in rural Africa.

Above all else the white hunters were entertainers, accomplished actors and raconteurs. They were a select band, for their clients were the world's elite and very wealthy indeed. Through this clientele the hunters had the ears of prominent people in politics, business, films and theatre. Although the relationship between hunter and client was initially business, it gave rise almost routinely to firm friendships. Not since the days of the medieval court jesters has a guild of such modest pretensions had access to the pinnacles of power, with such licence to say what they would. In that sense the hunters were indeed latter-day court jesters.

As I went about my duties, ivory constantly impressed itself upon me. Listening to the hunters' tales I realised that great elephant tusks are keys to the romance of Africa. Ivory, big ivory, has a magical grip that can only be understood by those who had beheld and, above all, touched a great tusk.

The hope of sportsman and poacher was always to take a 'hundred-pounder': an elephant whose tusks weighed over 100 lbs each. The exceptional hunter, and the very lucky, occasionally obtained 'great ivory': tusks which weighed over 120 lbs apiece.

'Smith has got a hundred and thirty pounder.' That was enough to stop all conversation at any function in the Kenya of yore. Aficionados would wish to know where Smith had got his prize, to see the tusks, feel them, place their hands about them to judge the circumference, and stand and speculate. Never was there such rich material for speculation and fantasy. The

bearer of such grand tusks must have been, indeed could only have been, more than 100 years old — perhaps 200 and maybe even 300 and, having lived so long, must have covered great distances. Its travels might have encompassed hundreds, nay thousands of miles. Why shouldn't it have journeyed from the Knysna with the coming of the Boers, seen the rise and fall of the Zulus, skirted the Mountains of the Moon and dwelt beneath Kilimanjaro? And the hunters' yearnings became their fantasies, their own desires for longevity and their hope to go on and on wandering through all the hunting grounds from Agulhas to the Nile, from Cape Verde to Gardafui. Nothing stimulated their imaginations more than great ivory. Above all, it was felt, for an elephant to have lived for so long, it must have been wise — very wise. It was no coincidence that those who habitually took hundred-pounders and had more than one great elephant to their names were also held to be canny and sagacious and were much admired.

Ian Parker, *Ivory Crisis* (Chatto & Windus, 1983), pp. 17-8. One of the more controversial "expatriate" wildlife authorities in East Africa, Parker was a pilot, friend, and business associate of the Roots; a trader in animal hides, hair, and ivory; an associate of the British zoologist Richard M. Laws and proponent of animal cropping (for conservation and for food); and always a pragmatic businessman. *Ivory Crisis* is an opinionated, yet authoritative, study of hunting elephants for ivory.

In the forest of the table-land a mile back from the ocean old Kerchak the Ape was on a rampage of rage among his people.

The younger and lighter members of his tribe scampered to the higher branches of the great trees to escape his wrath; risking their lives upon branches that scarce supported their weight rather than face old Kerchak in one of his fits of uncontrolled anger.

The other males scattered in all directions, but not before the infuriated brute had felt the vertebra of one snap between his great, foaming jaws.

. . .

And then he spied Kala, who, returning from a search for food with her young babe, was ignorant of the state of the mighty male's temper until suddenly the shrill warning of her fellows caused her to scamper madly for safety.

But Kerchak was close upon her, so close that he had almost grasped her ankle had she not made a furious leap far into space from one tree to another — a perilous chance which apes seldom if ever take, unless so closely pursued by danger that there is no alternative.

She made the leap successfully, but as she grasped the limb of the further tree the sudden jar loosened the hold of the tiny babe where it clung frantically to her neck, and she saw the little thing hurled, turning and twisting, to the ground thirty feet below.

With a low cry of dismay Kala rushed headlong to its side, thoughtless now of the danger from Kerchak; but when she gathered the wee, mangled form to her bosom life had left it.

With low moans, she sat cuddling the body to her; nor did Kerchak attempt to molest her. With the death of the babe his fit of demoniacal rage passed as suddenly as it had seized him.

. . .

The young played and frolicked about among the trees and

bushes. Some of the adults lay prone upon the soft mat of dead and decaying vegetation which covered the ground, while others turned over pieces of fallen branches and clods of earth in search of the small bugs and reptiles which formed a part of their food.

Others, again, searched the surrounding trees for fruit, nuts, small birds, and eggs.

They had passed an hour or so thus when Kerchak called them together, and, with a word of command to them to follow him, set off toward the sea.

. . .

. . .And all the way Kala carried her little dead baby hugged closely to her breast.

It was shortly after noon when they reached a ridge overlooking the beach where below them lay the tiny cottage which was Kerchak's goal.

He had seen many of his kind go to their deaths before the loud noise made by the little black stick in the hands of the strange white ape who lived in that wonderful lair, and Kerchak had made up his brute mind to own that death-dealing contrivance, and to explore the interior of the mysterious den.

. . .

Today there was no sign of the man about, and from where they watched they could see that the cabin door was open. Slowly, cautiously, and noiselessly they crept through the jungle toward the little cabin.

There were no growls, no fierce screams of rage — the little black stick had taught them to come quietly lest they awaken it.

On, on they came until Kerchak himself slunk stealthily to the very door and peered within. Behind him were two males, and then Kala, closely straining the little dead form to her breast.

Inside the den they saw the strange white ape lying half across a table, his head buried in his arms; and on the bed lay a figure covered by sailcloth, while from a tiny rustic cradle came the plaintive wailing of a babe.

Noiselessly Kerchak entered, crouching for the charge; and then John Clayton rose with a sudden start and faced them.

The sight that met his eyes must have frozen him with horror, for there, within the door, stood three great bull apes, while behind them crowded many more; how many he never knew, for his revolvers were hanging on the far wall beside his rifle and Kerchak was charging.

When the king ape released the limp form which had been John Clayton, Lord Greystoke, he turned his attention toward the little cradle; but Kala was there before him, and when he would have grasped the child she snatched it herself, and before he could intercept her she had bolted through the door and taken refuge in a high tree.

As she took up the little live baby of Alice Clayton she dropped the dead body of her own into the empty cradle; for the wail of the living had answered the call of universal motherhood within her wild breast which the dead could not still.

High up among the branches of a mighty tree she hugged the shrieking infant to her bosom, and soon the instinct that was as dominant in this fierce female as it had been in the breast of his tender and beautiful mother — the instinct of mother love — reached out to the tiny man-child's half-formed understanding, and he became quiet.

Then hunger closed the gap between them, and the son of an English lord and an English lady nursed at the breast of Kala, the great ape.

. . .

Those of the apes who attempted to examine Kala's strange baby were repulsed with bared fangs and low menacing growls, accompanied by words of warning from Kala.

When they assured her that they meant the child no harm she permitted them to come close, but would not allow them to touch her charge.

It was as though she knew that her baby was frail and delicate and feared lest the rough hands of her fellows might injure the little thing.

Another thing she did, and which made traveling an onerous trial for her. Remembering the death of her own little one, she clung desperately to the new babe, with one hand, whenever they were upon the march.

The other young rode upon their mothers' backs; their little arms tightly clasping the hairy necks before them, while their legs were locked beneath their mothers' armpits.

Not so with Kala; she held the small form of the little Lord Greystoke tightly to her breast, where the dainty hands clutched the long black hair which covered that portion of her body. She had seen one child fall from her back to a terrible death, and she would take no further chances with this.

Edgar Rice Burroughs, *Tarzan of the Apes* (Grosset & Dunlap, 1927), pp. 16-22. (Originally published in 1914.)

Each day in Africa my heart had almost burst with Walt Whitman's outcry: "As to me, I know of nothing else but miracles."

Ames, *A Glimpse of Eden*, p. 204.

The evening was peaceful, the river-bed astir with life. Some ducks alighted, swam around and then took off again, leaving behind a gentle ripple. The harsh cackle of guinea-fowl came from the bush. Two giraffes with a half-grown child were browsing on thorn-tree tops. Suddenly came a sound of hooves thudding on dry, sandy soil overlying rocks: half a dozen male impalas, lyre-shaped horns laid back against their shoulders, leapt with effortless grace, like rufous waves surging over the bushes, as they chased each other in play. Unexpectedly, several elephants strolled down to the far end of the pool, sucked up water, sprayed themselves from their trunks and then retreated with their usual dignity into the bush. The ibises continued their fishing; a flock of sand-grouse alighted by the water's edge; a black-shouldered kite hovered overhead; doves ceaselessly cooed. Above the horizon, the sky reddened as the sun sank towards a steel-blue cloud stained with crimson.

The slanting light threw trees and bushes into dramatic relief, as though a spotlight had been switched on. Long, black shadows scarred the bush. Then the cloud swallowed up the sun, light faded quickly and a grey heron landing by the pool could scarcely be distinguished in the grey dusk. But the sky was still glowing when we jolted back to camp to see four giraffes move with their loping gait along the skyline, their heads and necks black against a smouldering sky. Their motion was like that of boats with masts awry sailing across a gently billowing ocean. They vanished down the slope below the camp and later, in the remnants of vanishing light, could be seen wading across the lake. Soon, frogs would strike up their nightly chorus.

Elspeth Huxley & Hugo van Lawick, *Last Days in Eden*, p. 11. This book is recommended in Chapter I.

She was really quite a girl, some while ago now, so we made a real effort and showed her around. She knew what she wanted. What she wanted was film, miles of film, of all the 'Big Five', not just pretty-pictures but real pictures of moving, killing, eating, fighting, mating, and not of animals like Gertie the Amboseli rhino that everyone had taken before.

That was a memorable safari, the girl dynamic and restless, always unexpected and never tired. We took her to...Marsabit for elephant film, and once were watching a cow herd and she said she'd like to film a calf being born so we said look, honey, that's something we've never even seen, so she said a naughty word and stepped aside — cow elephant and youngsters all round us — and gave a yell, then grabbed the camera and got a stampede scene. We had to act fast and when it was over she said she'd wanted to see what would happen, so we said if she did it again what'd happen would be with a slipper on a convex expanse, so she smiled and said that might be fun and we said don't bet on that.

Anthony Cullen & Sydney Downey, *Saving the Game* (Jarrolds, 1960), p. 124. Cullen, a former game warden in Samburu (Kenya), became a prolific writer who produced several books dealing with African wildlife. Downey was one of the most widely respected white hunters of his day.

Saving the Game was an early plea against the poaching and habitat encroachment threatening East Africa's animals, a statement made in the face of the bewilderment and waste caused by the changes sweeping Africa in the 1950s.

Women are astonishing creatures. American women, bless their hearts, especially so.

Downey was out once with an American client, a solid citizen who practically owned Illinois or wherever it was, enjoying his hunting vacation, roughing it out in the wilds. They went way down into the bottom of Tanganyika for a month or more, then turned back to the Kenya border, camping near a river like the one filmed in African Queen. *There was still some time to go, so Syd* [Downey] *sent off a lorry to Nairobi to fetch a load of petrol and supplies.*

Peace reigned. On the third day, in the mess-tent around noon, they heard a distant engine. Just the lorry, Downey thought. He got up idly — thinking of mail and wondering how the beer had travelled — to go and see. At the flap of the mess-tent he stopped abruptly, and an expletive born of simple astonishment fell from his lips. His client, whose thoughts had

Plate 11. Sand River.

not been on the Deity, tried to spring erect; in fact — from a position leaning back sipping a highball — he missed a hold of everything, poured all the ice down his shirt-front and collapsed in the ruins of a chair. It just wasn't going to be his day. . . .

Meanwhile, the engine noises subsided. It was the lorry right enough. But what had shaken Downey was the apparition that had been shepherded along by the lorry. It was a car, a particular sort of car. . . I'd better explain.

What happens in East Africa is that cars — maybe a Chev or a Ford or an Austin — get imported and sold. Whoever buys one — maybe a farmer or a magistrate or a hick journalist — runs it for about twenty years over the goat-tracks that we have learned to think of as 'roads.' Then it will be sent in for a spot of servicing — they might even change the oil — and a polish, and get [sic] put on a used-car stand where somebody else buys it because in the secondhand racket he can sometimes talk his own terms. About ten years later, it is again sold, perhaps to a farmer who wants somewhere for his wife's hens to get in out of the rain. Then farming hits bad times again, so the farmer digs out the derelict and tows it to a junk-yard in Nairobi, glad to exchange it for a dollar-and-a-half. The junk-yard proprietor tightens up a nut or two, breaks the last window for luck, tells junior to feel under the back-seat for puff-adders, then sends the vehicle out on hire at five dollars a mile. Thus a Nairobi taxi is born.

And it was a Nairobi taxi that Downey watched driving into camp, nearly two hundred miles from Nairobi, about a hundred from the nearest 'road,' way out in the African wilds!

The driver — a Kikuyu, his expression indicative of well-blended determination, unbelief, apathy and terror — took his hands off the wheel, and gazed at a tree. He had given his all. The back door of the vehicle opened, or at any rate sagged, and a vision emerged, immaculate, interested, chic. . . .

Downey had taken a pace forward, and was just about to offer a remark, when the client emerged. Perhaps emerged is an understatement. Holding the small of his back in evident anguish, he limped out, dabbing bitterly at an ice-crystal lodged in or around his navel, and expressing his thoughts in terms that would have made a Chicago meat-skinner blanch. Then he looked at the vision, and the flow stopped. His jaw fell. It fell so far that Downey thought he might have to use a jack to return it to his face.

'Why Elmer!' said the vision. 'Honey! Whatever is the matter?'

Elmer, his face contorted, managed a sort of stuttering yelp.

'Pearl!' he bleated. 'Thought you N'York,' he began. 'Left you N'York. How in the name of jumpin'. . . .'

'But, Elmer,' said Pearl. 'Honey! I was getting lonesome. So I just ran over to see how you were getting along. Now if Tarzan there' — an exquisite finger jabbed at Downey — 'will tell me where the powder-room's located, I'll wanna hear all about your wonderful vacation then we'll all have a wonderful time.'

Anthony Cullen, *Downey's Africa* (Cassell, 1959), p. 44-5. If hunting had a reasonably benign face, the expression was Downey's and Cullen's was its voice. Eventually, Downey joined with Donald Ker to form what became the premier hunting safari company in Africa.

There are so many vistas, so much unending sameness, so many sudden gems. But if Downey has a favourite bit of Africa it is the bed, the path of the Sand River, as it stretches its way

through uncanny, pristine wilderness to meet so unexpectedly, and even modestly, the swirling, muddy Mara. It is peculiarly Downey's own.

Sometimes it is dry. Sometimes down the middle, or flung from bank to bank, flow the remnants of a plaintive, fickle stream; pockets are trapped — by rocks or bunkers — and lay gasping, and when this happens the butterflies in hundreds cluster round these water-pools. Sometimes it is torrent, raging and irrepressible, beginning with a distant rumble that in seconds sweeps on by, tossing in its crisis a puny mass of boulders and stricken trees, and leaving the watcher humbled by the awful wildness of such water unconfined.

That is thrilling, tempering. But the Sand River is at its most rewarding season when it is practically dry.

Downey can lead one there through thickening bush towards the river's edge, dipping or swerving as the game-trail dictates, until the last corner is turned, then the last slither and a noiseless landing, eyes watchful and ears straining, and one is on the river floor.

It is cool and quiet. A God-made cathedral of the wilds, where humility knowing no human design can seek understanding of Him. There are trees on either bank, verdant, entwining, sometimes huge, dwarfing bush and creeper, sometimes meeting to form a vaulted canopy above, where movement merges into the silence of shade. Sometimes the river broadens and shafts of sunlight slant across cloistered scene, before evening foreshadows the softness and the fearsomeness of night and, distractingly, the fireflies play.

It is a place where every sound is sharp, staccato, clear. Each is a signature of Africa: forest hornbill, plantain-eater; monkey and baboon; a rustle in the forest screen — buffalo? waterbuck? leopard? an elephant's squeal. . . .

It is place of infinite variety, its simple wonderment cloaking the guises, the ardour of manifold life. Constantly parading, beckoning, offering — the flash of wings, strange shapes and gaudy colours, the gift of daintiness, the wine of sudden incident, the shock of eyes. There are birds and monkeys, bushbuck, a rhino, or a discernment of creatures unknown. Tracks and pittings that embalm their narrative, the message of the sand. There — the elephants so delicately digging tiny holes, scooping out the sand with trunks and funnelling into the cool, clean draught below. There — bushbuck moving gracefully down or over the river to feed; precise, engaging hoof-prints becoming — there! — galvanic, because — over here! — of a leopard's track beneath a looming tree. There — the scuffle of buffalo or rhino, slithering ungainly and uncaring, down the bank. There — pulse-quickening always, the imprint of a lion.

Widening and more querulous the Sand River moves to the Mara, and the calibre of incident will change. Baboon may bark more urgently, an iguana moves, strange ribbon-fish and catfish pulse out their unimpassioned lives, bereft in haphazard sanctity within clear, shallow pools. And at last the Mara, the swirl of crocodile affrighted, the astonished gaze of hippo; the muddy, passive, dangerous Mara, heart and climax of it all. . . .

Cullen, *Downey's Africa*, pp. 35-6.

As if through the eyes of a lion or leopard, an eloquent yet wordless film could be made of the changing scenes and seasons of the African plains. From a perch on one of the rocky outcrops which characterise these areas the moods of the surrounding countryside could be dramatically recorded by a movie camera, especially during April or October when the landscape is transformed by the onset of the short and long rains.

In the dryness and heat, with nothing but oceans of grass in every direction, the silence itself can be a unique experience. The human voice comes instinctively in a whisper. Mile upon mile of grey brownish grass which crackles ominously underfoot threatens to burst into flame. The sky is cloudless and seems endless. Directly overhead the sun pierces with its heat. Yet within hours, as if some mammoth colour-slide has been projected across the earth, the scene can change. Gigantic cloud formations appear, first white and golden, then turning grey-blue and black. Tension is broken by searing forks of lightning. An encircling thunder rumbles from afar and explodes overhead. The wind whips up the dust and dry grass in spiralling whirlwinds. The rains have come, suddenly, torrential and bitterly cold. Miraculously the sun continues shining through the clouds and etches golden islands of light which throw rainbow bridges linking land and sky.

Within two weeks these same grey-brown plains become bright green and yellow, blue and red flowers miraculously bloom out of the once parched and cracked earth. Swallows wheel and dive overhead, and below our rocky perch gazelles and wildebeest cavort and play with their young, their birth perfectly timed to enrich their young bodies on the milk which the females derive from the fresh shoots of grass and the leaves of shrubs. This awe-inspiring drama of rebirth has been re-enacted on these same plains every season since the pleistocene era...

Harshad C. Patel, *Vanishing Herds*, Chapter 4 (no page numbers). This volume is introduced in Chapter I.

Two miles from camp, one great mass of wildebeests unaccountably split into two columns. They began to trot, sidestep, and move ahead more briskly. Suddenly we saw the reason for their uneasy behavior. Two male lions, their manes gleaming orange in the first low rays of the sun, stood motionless studying their prey. It was a memorable tableau. Fortunately the pair did not run, but seemed only slightly annoyed when we approached near enough to photograph them at a favorable distance. For several moments, through a long telephoto lens, we could see every detail in the amber eyes of those splendid cats. Almost certainly those lions were siblings, bachelors with no other family ties and without membership in any pride. They are among the many lions that spend a lifetime following the ungulates, living off the fat of the land.

There is no way to estimate accurately the number of animals we saw on this day's crossing of the southern Serengeti. Once we stopped to photograph a pair of Thomson's gazelle bucks fighting, heads lowered almost to the ground. From east to west, an unbroken line of wildebeest trekked in slow motion, suspended in heat waves, and at the same time a squadron of vultures funneled down to a point out of our sight. Zeroing in on the large birds, we drove to where several spotted hyenas were tearing apart the remains of a wildebeest carcass. Two jackals tried to share the kill, but were driven away.

Erwin & Peggy Bauer, *Wildlife Adventures with a Camera* (Harry N. Abrams, 1984), p. 152. Erwin Bauer is one of the world's most enduring and widely published outdoor photographers. This extravagant volume is a compendium of the Bauers' anecdotes and superb photos from around the world.

...the small herd of a dozen tuskers arrived. In single file, they approached along an old path, which had become a trench from years of elephant passage. One of the arrivals was a cow followed by a half-grown calf. With the camera and telephoto lens resting on a foam pad and poked through the open cab window, I focused on the calf, which hurried ahead toward the water in high spirits. It was having a good time. . . .

Apparently the cow had no interest at all in us, and she barely glanced our way while drinking and giving herself a muddy shower bath. But she did keep shuffling ever so slightly to the right, feeling her way carefully along the muddy bottom of the waterhole, still not looking toward us. But suddenly, on solid ground again, she trumpeted once, flattened her ears, tucked her trunk under her body, and came lumbering in our direction. Mildly surprised, we backed away from the pond and lost a photo opportunity.

Erwin & Peggy Bauer, *Wildlife Adventures with a Camera*, p. 137.

One day when we were on a photo-safari in Southern Kenya there was great excitement when someone sighted a leopard that had been chased up a sausage tree by a lioness whose family of cubs was nearby. This was a rare opportunity to see the two biggest African cats together. When I got to the scene I found the leopard posing with dignity among the dangling "sausages" and the lioness sitting on the ground staring about her furiously, thrashing her tail and ready to take on all comers.

After showing a proper lack of concern, the leopard glided through the branches without effort or sound. He instantly blended with the convoluted limbs and mottled colouring of the bark. The coolness of his attitude in his green, airy world reminded me in a strange way of the atmosphere of a tropical café, exotic and relaxed. For some reason Casablanca, with Humphrey Bogart, came to mind. The surface atmosphere was cool and comfortable, but there was an undercurrent of menacing power.

Ramsay Derry, *The Art of Robert Bateman* (Allen Lane/Madison Press, 1981), p. 154. Robert Bateman, a Canadian, is a wildlife artist who has lived in Africa and produced paintings of African animals characterized by "superb naturalistic observations, by great technical skill, and by a powerful artistic imagination" (Roger Tory Peterson in the "Introduction," at p. 13). Bateman and Derry have collaborated on a new volume, *The World of Robert Bateman* (Random House/Madison Press, 1985), equally satisfying.

While even the sight of a resting lion contributes to the authenticity of an African scene, a hunting lion adds that edge of vital tension which changes a mere experience to a revelation.

Unfortunately the majority of tourists never see a hunt in the Serengeti because they do not have the patience, or the interest, or the knowledge to wait with some predator for a few hours. They rush, rush, rush along in convoys of cars, shrouded in dust, halting a minute by some resting lions and the cameras go click, click. Then the cars race on.

"How many lions did you see today?"

"Twenty-two."

"I saw twenty-nine!"

Many tourists cruise from park to park, spending half a day in each one, just as they would go from cathedral to museum to castle in Europe, quite bored with it all, concerned with the quantity rather than the quality of their experiences. Their recreation is mileage. The following incident reveals this attitude:

Tourist: "We saw an ostrich being attacked by a leopard."

Lodge Manager: "What happened?"

Tourist: "I don't know. It was lunch time and we had to leave."

Schaller, *Golden Shadows, Flying Hooves*, pp. 152-3.

Many visitors and scientists find elephants the most interesting animals to observe. There is the constant feeling that the elephants too know something, understand, make decisions, have feelings, contacts, friends. Stories of elephants are legion, many of them very well authenticated. Modern hunters say elephants know the boundaries of the National Parks and will smartly step inside when hunters are around. Would that the poachers knew the rules and stuck to them as carefully as their victims.

David Keith Jones, *Faces of Kenya* (Hamish Hamilton, 1977), p. 50. Jones is an English writer and photographer living in Kenya. *Faces* is a magnificent picture-book on Kenya, more focused on the land and people than the animals.

About a hundred years ago, a Danish traveller to Hamburg, Count Schimmelmann, happened to come upon a small itinerant Menagerie, and to take a fancy to it. While he was in Hamburg, he every day set his way round the place, although he would have found it difficult to explain what was to him the real attraction of the dirty and dilapidated caravans. The truth was that the Menagerie responded to something within his own mind. It was winter and bitterly cold outside. In the sheds the keeper had been heating the old stove until it was a clear pink in the brown darkness of the corridor, alongside the animals' cages, but still the draught and the raw air pierced people to the bone.

Count Schimmelmann was sunk in contemplation of the Hyena, when the proprietor of the Menagerie came and addressed him. The proprietor was a small pale man with a fallen-in nose, who had in his days been a student of theology, but who had had to leave the faculty after a scandal, and had since step by step come down in the world.

"Your Excellency does well to look at the Hyena," said he. "It is a great thing to have got a Hyena to Hamburg, where there has never been one till now. All Hyenas, you will know, are hermaphrodites, and in Africa, where they come from, on a full-moon night they will meet and join in a ring of copulation wherein each individual takes the double part of male and female. Did you know that?"

"No," said Count Schimmelmann with a slight movement of disgust.

"Do you consider now, Your Excellency," said the showman, "that it should be, on account of this fact, harder to a Hyena

than to other animals to be shut up by itself in a cage? Would he feel a double want, or is he, because he unites in himself the complementary qualities of creation, satisfied in himself, and in harmony? In other words, since we are all prisoners in life, are we happier, or more miserable, the more talents we possess?"

"It is curious thing," said Count Schimmelmann, who had been following his own thoughts and had not paid attention to the showman, "to realize that so many hundred, indeed thousands of Hyenas should have lived and died, in order that we should, in the end, get this one specimen here, so that people in Hamburg shall be able to know what a Hyena is like, and the naturalists to study from them."

They moved on to look at the Giraffes in the neighbouring cage.

"The wild animals," continued the Count, "which run in a wild landscape, do not really exist. This one, now, exists, we have got a name for it, we know what it is like. The others might as well not have been, still they are the large majority. Nature is extravagant."

The showman pushed back his worn fur-cap, underneath it he himself had not got a hair on his head. "They see one another," he said.

"Even that may be disputed," said Count Schimmelmann after a short pause. "These Giraffes, for instance, have got square markings on their skin. The Giraffes, looking at one another, will not know a square and will consequently not see a square. Can they be said to have seen one another at all?"

The showman looked at the Giraffe for some time and then said: "God sees them."

Count Schimmelmann smiled. "The Giraffes?" he asked.

"Oh yes, your Excellency," said the showman, "God sees the Giraffes. While they have been running about and have played in Africa, God has been watching them and has taken a pleasure in their demeanour. He has made them to please him. It is in the bible, your Excellency," said the showman. "God so loved the giraffe that He created them. God has Himself invented the square as well as the circle, surely your Excellency cannot deny that, He has seen the squares on their skin and everything else about them. The wild animals, your Excellency, are perhaps a proof of the existence of God. But when they go to Hamburg," he concluded, putting on his cap, "the argument becomes problematic."

Count Schimmelmann who had arranged his life according to the ideas of other people, walked on in silence to look at the snakes, close to the stove. The showman, to amuse him, opened the case in which he kept them and tried to make the snake within it wake up; in the end, the reptile slowly and sleepily wound itself round his arm. Count Schimmelmann looked at the group.

"Indeed, my good Kannegieter," he said with a little surly laugh, "if you were in my service, or if I were king and you my minister, you would now have your dismissal."

The showman looked up at him nervously. "Indeed, Sir, should I?" he said, and slipped down the snake into the case. "And why, Sir? If I may ask so," he added after a moment.

"Ah, Kannegieter, you are not so simple as you make out," said the Count. "Why? Because, my friend, the aversion to snakes is a sound human instinct, the people who have got it have kept alive. The snake is the deadliest of all the enemies of men, but what, except our own instinct of good and evil, is there to tell us so? The claws of the lions, the size, and the tusks, of the

Elephants, the horns of the Buffaloes, all jump to the eye. But the snakes are beautiful animals. The snakes are round and smooth, like the things we cherish in life, of exquisite soft colouring, gentle in all their movements. Only to the godly man this beauty and gracefulness are in themselves loathsome, they smell from perdition, and remind him of the fall of man. Something within him makes him run away from the snake as from the devil, and that is what is called the voice of conscience. The man who can caress a snake can do anything." Count Schimmelmann laughed a little at his own course of thoughts, buttoned his rich fur-coat, and turned to leave the shed.

The showman had stood for a little while in deep thoughts. "Your Excellency," he said at last, "you must needs [sic] love snakes. There is no way round it. Out of my own experience in life, I can tell you so, and indeed it is the best advice that I can give you: You should love the snakes. Keep in your mind, your Excellency, how often, — keep in mind, your Excellency, that nearly every time that we ask the Lord for a fish, he will give us a serpent."

Dinesen, *Out of Africa*, pp. 300-4.

Dr. Schofield had the best lion story, and told it far more delightfully [than] I can, but the gist of it was that his gun jammed and the lion charged him so he fell flat on his face and the lion jumped clean over him, so he quickly sprang up a tree and looked down and saw the lion jumping back and forth over the same spot so that he would not miss him next time!

Olivia Stokes Hatch, *Olivia's African Diary: Capetown to Cairo, 1932* (Washington, D.C., 1980), p. 126. This book recounts the reminiscences of a six-months' trip taken by the Stokes family from one end of Africa to the other — "over 14,000 miles: some 3041 by motor, 2058 by boat, 221 by air and some 9,000 by rail." A picture of a colonial Africa that no longer exists, the diary is a work of undeniable charm. Olivia's father was the Reverend Anson Phelps Stokes, Canon of Washington Cathedral and for many years President of the Phelps-Stokes Fund, an organization established for, among other things, the education of Blacks, both in Africa and the United States. Stokes was asked to go to Africa as Visiting Lecturer and eventually report his findings on the educational scene, as well as on "the rights and well-being of the Negroes."

Before the war, one notorious beast had lived on the escarpment of the Zambezi valley where both road and railway began the plunge down towards the Victoria Falls. It had piled up a score of eighteen lorries and buses, catching them on a steep section of road where they were reduced to a walking pace, and taking them head-on so that its horn crunched through the radiator in a burst of steam. Then, perfectly satisfied, it would trot back into the thick bush with squeals of triumph.

Puffed up with success, it finally over-reached itself when it took on the Victoria Falls express, lumbering down the tracks like a medieval knight in the jousting lists. The locomotive was doing twenty miles per hour and the rhinoceros weighed two tons and was making about the same speed in the opposite direction, so the meeting was monumental. The express came to a grinding halt with wheels spinning helplessly, but the rhinoceros had reached the end of his career as a wrecker of radiators.

The latest deposit of dung on the midden had been within the preceding twelve hours, Craig estimated with delight, and the spoor indicated a family group of bull and cow with calf at heel. Smiling, Craig recalled the old Matabele myth which accounted for the rhino's habit of scattering its dung, and for its fear of the porcupine — the only animal in all the bush from which it would fly in snorting panic.

The Matabele related that once upon a time the rhino had borrowed a quill from the porcupine to sew up a tear caused by a thorn in his thick hide. The rhino promised to return the quill at their next meeting. After repairing the rent with bark twine, the rhino placed the quill between his lips while he admired his handiwork, and inadvertently swallowed it. Now he is still searching for the quill, and assiduously avoiding the porcupine's recriminations.

Wilbur A. Smith, *The Leopard Hunts in Darkness* (Heinemann, 1984), p. 38. When *The African Safari* was being written, this instant novel was the latest work of Smith's prodigious output. Smith, a great storyteller, has infused most of his novels with the landscape and wildlife of Africa. One critic called this book "a thundering good read."

'When the world began,' Kibii said, 'each animal, even the Chameleon, had a task to do. I learned it from my father and my grandfather, and all our people know this fact.'

'The world began too long ago,' I said — 'longer than anybody could remember. Who could remember what the Chameleon did when the world began?'

'Our people remember,' said Kibii, 'because God told it to our first ol-oiboni, and this one told it to the next. Each ol-oiboni, before he died, repeated to the new ol-oiboni what God had said — and so we know these things. We know that the Chameleon is accursed above all other animals because, if it had not been for him, there would be no Death.'

'It was like this,' said Kibii:

'When the first man was made, he wandered alone in the great forest and on the plains, and he worried very much because he could not remember yesterday and so he could not imagine tomorrow. God saw this, so he sent the Chameleon to the first man...with a message, saying that there would never be such a thing as death and that tomorrow would be like today, and the days would never stop.

'Long after the Chameleon had started,' said Kibii, 'God sent an Egret with a different message, saying that there would be a thing called Death and that, sometime, tomorrow would not come. "Whichever message comes first to the ears of man," God warned, "will be the true one."

'Now the Chameleon is a lazy animal. He thinks of nothing but food, and he moves only his tongue to get that. He lagged so much along the way that he arrived at the feet of the first man only a moment before the Egret.

'The Chameleon began to talk, but he could not. In the excitement of trying to deliver his tidings of eternal life, before the Egret could speak, the Chameleon could only stutter and change, stupidly, from one colour to another. So the Egret, in a calm voice, gave the message of Death.

'Since then,' said Kibii, 'all men have died. Our people know this fact.'

Markham, *West with the Night*, pp. 106-7.

...it is something of a miracle how quickly everything here is transformed by the rain; the Ngong Hills...burned to the likeness of a doormat...now brilliant with the finest, most glorious green. . .If only it will go on. . . .It is so beautiful here, a paradise on earth, when there is enough rain. . . .I have a feeling that wherever I may be in the future, I will be wondering whether there is rain at Ngong.

Isak Dinesen, *Letters from Africa, 1914-1931* (The University of Chicago Press, 1981), p. 98. Letter to her mother of 26 February 1919. The Ngong Hills lie directly southwest and just outside Nairobi.

Ahead of us the brown waters were broken in many places by rocks. At any other time they would have looked exactly like rocks but now each one looked exactly like the head of a hippo, a cunning, maniacal hippo, lurking in the dark waters, awaiting our approach. Ben, presumably remembering his tale of daring with the bush-cow, attempted to whistle, but it was a feeble effort, and I noticed that he scanned the waters ahead anxiously. After all, a hippo that has developed the habit of attacking canoes gets a taste for it, like a man-eating tiger, and will go out of his way to be unpleasant, apparently regarding it as a sport. I was not feeling in the mood for gambolling in twenty feet of murky water with half a ton of sadistic hippo.

The old man, I noticed, was keeping our craft well into the bank, twisting and turning so that we were, as far as possible, always in shallow water. The cliff here was steep, but well supplied with footholds in case of emergency, for the rocks lay folded in great layers like untidy piles of fossilized magazines, overgrown with greenery. The trees that grew on top of the cliffs spread their branches well out over the water, so that we travelled in a series of fish-like jerks up a tunnel of shade, startling the occasional kingfisher that whizzed across our bow like a vivid blue shooting-star, or a black-and-white wattled plover that flapped away upstream, tittering imbecilically to itself, with its feet grazing the water, and long yellow wattles flapping absurdly on each side of its beak.

Gradually we rounded the bend of the river, and there, about three hundred yards ahead of us on the opposite shore, lay the white bulk of the sandbank, frilled with ripples. The old man gave a grunt of relief at the sight, and started to paddle more swiftly.

"Nearly there," I said gaily, "and not a hippo in sight."
The words were hardly out of my mouth when a rock we were passing some fifteen feet away suddenly rose out of the water and gazed at us with bulbous astonished eyes, snorting out two slender fountains of spray, like a miniature whale.

Fortunately, our gallant crew resisted the impluse to leap out of the canoe en masse and swim for the bank. The old man drew in his breath with a sharp hiss, and dug his paddle deep into the water, so that the canoe pulled up short in a swirl and clop of bubbles. Then we sat and stared at the hippo, and the hippo sat and stared at us. Of the two, the hippo seemed the more astonished. The chubby, pink-grey face floated on the surface of the water like a disembodied head at a seance. The great eyes stared at us with the innocent appraisal of a baby. The ears flicked back and forth, as if waving to us. The hippo sighed deeply and moved a few feet nearer, still looking at us with wide-eyed innocence. Then, suddenly, Agustine let out a shrill whoop that made us all jump and nearly upset the canoe. We shushed him furiously, while the hippo continued its scrutiny of us unabashed.

"No de fear," said Agustine in a loud voice, "na woman."
He seized the paddle from the old man's reluctant grasp, and proceeded to beat on the water with the blade, sending up a shower of spray. The hippo opened its mouth in a gigantic yawn to display a length of tooth that had to be seen to be believed. Then, suddenly, and with apparently no muscular effort, the great head sank beneath the surface. There was a moment's pause, during which we were all convinced that the beast was ploughing through the water somewhere directly beneath us, then the head rose to the surface again, this time, to our relief, about twenty yards up-river. It snorted out two more jets of spray, waggled its ears seductively and sank again, only to reappear in a moment or so still farther upstream. The old man grunted and retrieved his paddle from Agustine.

"Agustine, why you do dat foolish ting?" I asked in what I hoped was a steady and trenchant tone of voice.
"Sah, dat ipopo no be man...na woman dat," Agustine explained, hurt by my lack of faith in him.
"How you know?" I demanded.
"Masa, I savvay all dis ipopo for dis water," he explained, "dis one na woman. Ef no man ipopo 'e go chop us one time. But dis woman one no get strong head like 'e husband."

Durrell, *A Zoo in My Luggage*, pp. 28-30.

Can the Ethiopian change his skin, or the leopard his spots?

Bible, *Jeremiah 13:23*

In the days when everybody started fair, Best Beloved, the Leopard lived in a place called the High Veldt. . .the 'sclusively bare, hot, shiny High Veldt, where there was sand and sandy-coloured rock and 'sclusively tufts of sandy-yellowish grass. The Giraffe and the Zebra and the Eland and the Koodoo and the Hartebeest lived there; and they were 'sclusively sandy-yellow-brownish all over; but the Leopard, he was the 'sclusivest sandiest-yellowest-brownest of them all — a greyish-yellowish catty-shaped kind of beast, and he matched the 'sclusively yellowish-greyish-brownish colour of the High Veldt to one hair. This was very bad for the Giraffe and the Zebra and the rest of them; for he would lie down by a 'sclusively yellowish-greyish-brownish stone or clump of grass, and when the Giraffe or the Zebra or the Eland or the Koodoo or the Bush-Buck or the Bonte-Buck came by he would surprise them out of their jumpsome lives. He would indeed! And, also, there was an Ethiopian with bows and arrows (a 'sclusively greyish-brownish-yellowish man he was then), who lived on the High Veldt with the Leopard; and the two used to hunt together — the Ethiopian with his bows and arrows, and the Leopard 'sclusively with his teeth and claws — till the Giraffe and the Eland and the Koodoo and the Quagga and all the rest of them didn't know which way to jump, Best Beloved. They didn't indeed!

After a long time — things lived for ever so long in those days — they learned to avoid anything that looked like a Leopard or an Ethiopian; and bit by bit — the Giraffe began it, because his legs were the longest — they went away from the High Veldt. They scuttled for days and days and days till they came to a great forest, 'sclusively full of trees and bushes and, stripy, speckly, patchy-blatchy shadows, and there they hid: and after another long time, what with standing half in the shade and half out of it, and what with the slippery-slidy shadows of the trees falling on them, the Giraffe grew blotchy, and the Zebra grew stripy, and the Eland and the Koodoo grew darker, with little wavy grey lines on their backs like bark on a tree trunk; and so, though you could hear them and smell them, you could very seldom see them, and then only when you knew precisely where to look. They had a beautiful time in the 'sclusively speckly-spickly shadows of the forest, while the Leopard and the Ethiopian ran about over the 'sclusively greyish-yellowish-reddish High Veldt outside, wondering where all their breakfasts and their dinners and their teas had gone. At last they were so hungry that they ate rats and beetles and rock-rabbits, the Leopard and the Ethiopian, and then they had the Big Tummy-ache, both together; and then they met Baviaan — the dog-headed, barking Baboon, who is Quite the Wisest Animal in All South Africa.

Said Leopard to Baviaan (and it was a very hot day,) 'Where has all the game gone?'

And Baviaan winked. He knew.

Then said Baviaan, 'The game has gone into other spots; and my advice to you, Leopard, is to go into other spots as soon as you can.'

And the Ethiopian said, 'That is all very fine, but I wish to know whither the aboriginal Fauna has migrated.'

Then said Baviaan, 'The aboriginal Fauna has joined the aboriginal Flora because it was high time for a change; and my advice to you, Ethiopian, is to change as soon as you can.'

That puzzled the Leopard and the Ethiopian, but they set off to look for the aboriginal Flora, and presently, after ever so many days, they saw a great, high, tall forest full of tree trunks all 'sclusively speckled and sprottled and spottled, dotted and splashed and slashed and hatched and cross-hatched with shadows. (Say that quickly aloud, and you will see how very shadowy the forest must have been.)

'What is this,' said the Leopard, 'that is so 'sclusively dark, and yet so full of little pieces of light?'

'I don't know,' said the Ethiopian, 'but it ought to be the aboriginal Flora. I can smell Giraffe, and I can hear Giraffe, but I can't see Giraffe.'

'That's curious,' said the Leopard. 'I suppose it is because we have just come in out of the sunshine. I can smell Zebra, and I can hear Zebra, but I can't see Zebra.'

'Wait a bit,' said the Ethiopian. 'It's a long time since we've hunted 'em. Perhaps we've forgotten what they were like.'

'Fiddle!' said the Leopard. 'I remember them perfectly on the High Veldt, especially their marrow-bones. Giraffe is about seventeen feet high, of a 'sclusively fulvous golden-yellow from head to heel; and Zebra is about four and a half feet high, of a 'sclusively grey-fawn colour from head to heel.'

'Umm,' said the Ethiopian, looking into the speckly-spickly shadows of the aboriginal Flora-forest. 'Then they ought to show up in this dark place like ripe bananas in a smokehouse.'

But they didn't. The Leopard and the Ethiopian hunted all day; and though they could smell them and hear them, they never saw one of them.

'For goodness' sake,' said the Leopard at tea-time, 'let us wait till it gets dark. This daylight hunting is a perfect scandal.'

So they waited till dark, and then the Leopard heard something breathing sniffily in the starlight that fell all stripy through the branches, and he jumped at the noise, and it smelt

Plate 12. "Halftime."

like Zebra, and it felt like Zebra, and when he knocked it down it kicked like Zebra, but he couldn't see it. So he said, 'Be quiet, O you person without any form. I am going to sit on your head till morning, because there is something about you that I don't understand.'

Presently he heard a grunt and a crash and a scramble, and the Ethiopian called out, 'I've caught a thing that I can't see. It smells like Giraffe, and it kicks like Giraffe, but it hasn't any form.'

'Don't you trust it,' said the Leopard. 'Sit on its head till the morning — same as me. They haven't any form — any of 'em.'

So they sat down on them hard till bright morning-time, and then Leopard said, 'What have you at your end of the table, Brother?'

The Ethiopian scratched his head and said, 'It ought to be 'sclusively a rich fulvous orange-tawny from head to heel, and it ought to be Giraffe; but it is covered all over with chestnut blotches. What have you at your end of the table, Brother?'

And the Leopard scratched his head and said, 'It ought to be 'sclusively a delicate greyish-fawn, and it ought to be Zebra; but it is covered all over with black and purple stripes. What in the world have you been doing to yourself, Zebra? Don't you know that if you were on the High Veldt I could see you ten miles off? You haven't any form.'

'Yes,' said the Zebra, 'but this isn't the High Veldt. Can't you see?'

'I can now,' said the Leopard. 'But I couldn't all yesterday. How is it done?'

'Let us up,' said the Zebra, 'and we will show you.'

They let the Zebra and the Giraffe get up; and Zebra moved away to some little thorn bushes where the sunlight fell all stripy, and Giraffe moved off to some tallish trees where the shadows fell all blotchy.

'Now watch,' said the Zebra and the Giraffe. 'This is the way it's done. One — two — three! And where's your breakfast?'

Leopard stared, and Ethiopian stared, but all they could see were stripy shadows and blotched shadows in the forest, but never a sign of Zebra and Giraffe. They had just walked off and hidden themselves in the shadowy forest.

'Hi! Hi!' said the Ethiopian. 'That's a trick worth learning. Take a lesson by it, Leopard. You show up in this dark place like a bar of soap in a coal-scuttle.'

'Ho! Ho!' said the Leopard. 'Would it surprise you very much to know that you show up in this dark place like a mustard-plaster on a sack of coals?'

'Well, calling names won't catch dinner,' said the Ethiopian. 'The long and the little of it is that we don't match our backgrounds. I'm going to take Baviaan's advice. He told me I ought to change; and as I've nothing to change except my skin I'm going to change that.'

'What to?' said the Leopard, tremendously excited.

'To a nice working blackish-brownish colour, with a little purple in it, and touches of slaty-blue. It will be the very thing for hiding in hollows and behind trees.'

So he changed his skin then and there, and the Leopard was more excited than ever; he had never seen a man change his skin before.

'But what about me?' he said, when the Ethiopian had worked his last little finger into his fine new black skin.

'You take Baviaan's advice too. He told you to go into spots.'

. . .

'I'll take spots, then,' said the Leopard; 'but don't make 'em too vulgar-big. I wouldn't look like Giraffe — not for ever so.'

'I'll make 'em with the tips of my fingers,' said the Ethiopian. 'There's plenty of black left on my skin still. Stand over!'

Then the Ethiopian put his five fingers close together (there was still plenty of black left on his new skin still) and pressed them all over the Leopard, and wherever the five fingers touched they left five little black marks, all close together. You can see them on any Leopard's skin you like, Best Beloved. Sometimes the fingers slipped and the marks got a little blurred; but if you look closely at any Leopard now you will see that there are always five spots — off five fat black finger-tips.

'Now you are a beauty!' said the Ethiopian. 'You can lie out on the bare ground and look like a heap of pebbles. You can lie out on the naked rocks and look like a piece of pudding-stone. You can lie out on a leafy branch and look like sunshine sifting through the leaves; and you can lie right across the centre of a path and look like nothing in particular. Think of that and purr!'

. . .

So they went away and lived happily ever afterward, Best Beloved. That is all.

Oh, now and then you will hear grown-ups say, 'Can the Ethiopian change his skin or the Leopard his spots?' I don't think even grown-ups would keep on saying such a silly thing if the Leopard and the Ethiopian hadn't done it once — do you? But they will never do it again, Best Beloved. They are quite contented as they are.

Kipling, "How the Leopard Got His Spots," *Just So Stories.*

Terry is now by the window of his studio. "Everybody these days talks about principles. The so-called principles of hunting." Terry turns to me. "My ass. There never were any principles in hunting. I doubt whether there were even four or five hunters in the whole country who knew how to conduct a hunt without their Land Rover and their African tracker. And even the good ones, sooner or later, got lazy.

"We called it a sport too. Really. What kind of sport is it when a client pays a man to follow the spoor, to select the trophy, even to help him shoot it, to protect him from anything with teeth or a sting and in the evening to provide for his entertainment? It's like someone at a country club, hiring the tennis pro for a partner and then going on to win the club championships. Sport, you call it?" Terry rubs his eye under the patch. "And now my son wants to be a white hunter. Believes it to be a noble career."

Heminway, *No Man's Land: The Last of White Africa*, p. 69. In several moments of real candor, one professional hunter, Alexander Lake, entitled *his* book: *Killers in Africa — The Truth About Animals Lying in Wait and Hunters Lying in Print* (Doubleday, 1953).

Watching the game, one was struck by the intensity and the evanescence of their emotions. Civilized man now usually passes his life under conditions which eliminate the intensity of terror felt by his ancestors when death by violence was their normal end, and threatened them during every hour of the day and night. It is only in nightmares that the average dweller in civilized countries now undergoes the hideous horror which was the regular and frequent portion of his ages-vanished *forefathers, and which is still an every-day incident in the lives of most wild creatures. But the dread is short-lived, and its horror vanishes with instantaneous rapidity. In these wilds the game dreaded the lion and the other flesh-eating beasts rather than man. We saw innumerable kills of all the buck, and of zebra...it being evident that none of the lion's victims, not even the truculent wildebeest or huge eland, had been able to make any fight against him. The game is ever on the alert against this greatest of foes, and every herd, almost every individual, is in imminent and deadly peril every few days or nights, and of course suffers in addition from countless false alarms. But no sooner is the danger over than the animals resume their feeding, or love making, or their fighting among themselves. Two bucks will do battle the minute the herd has stopped running from the foe that has seized one of its number, and a buck will cover a doe in the brief interval between the first and the second alarm...*

   Roosevelt, *African Game Trails*, p. 239.

Now I had met baboons before and although I took a great interest in their behaviour and would have liked to have returned to camp with a fine specimen such as now sat complacently before me, I remembered that discretion was always the better part of valour when in their presence. I therefore stood up to go, trying to be as unhurried as I imagined I would be at a vicarage tea party, though I have never attended one. This simple movement, however, was heralded by unmistakable complaints from all sides in the form of the most unpleasant grunts. The old lady (or gentleman) before me also rose, but on all fours so that his or her posterior came into view. It happened to be bright pink at this time of the year, and I thought absurdly of the homeric description of the dawn as "rosy-fingered."

This display had remarkable effects. The bushes parted on all sides and a surprising array of subhumanity presented itself, ranging from one obvious male of quite alarming proportions, to the merest toddlers with pale, flat faces quite unlike their dog-nosed, black-visaged elders and betters. Their movements were leisurely, as if they were taking their places for a boxing match; they chattered and grunted exactly like any crowd of pleasure-seeking human beings preparing for an entertaining display.

While all this taking of seats was going on, I was retreating gingerly backwards up the path, while trying to learn the rules of monkey ethics in the raw. The outsize gentleman seemed to have been appointed as doorman. He trotted into the path behind me and stood squarely upon three boulders, one for each back foot and one for his gnarled hands. This was all very unpleasant and I found myself waiting with some trepidation to see what was the next item on the agenda. As they continued to sit and grunt to each other, it appeared to be up to me.

I don't expect you have ever been surrounded by a troop of expectant baboons, but if you have, you will probably agree that it becomes extremely difficult to think up any parlour tricks. My mind was a blank, especially as each part of the circle to which my back was turned in succession seemed to think its chance had come to grab a ringside seat, and since one can't face all ways at once, the ring began to diminish rapidly. I remember thinking stoically and hopefully that [baboons] are vegetable feeders and that I was not a vegetable although I doubtless looked like one. When the old gentleman yawned, and I had a glimpse of his three-inch fangs, I began to doubt the words of wisdom uttered by the worthy professor of my late

and, at that moment, greatly lamented university. I did remember that almost any animal, even a surprised tiger, will shy away if one stoops to pick up a stone and makes pretence of throwing it. This I instantly put to the test, but in my excitement I accidentally did pick up a stone and hurled it at the big yawning male with a force of which I did not believe myself capable. We were all greatly surprised when it found its mark in a glancing blow. This, combined with my sudden action, made the spectators jump backwards with some emphasis so that I was given quite a lot of room to move about in. My target seemed quite angry, as might be expected, and as I stooped to gather more missles, he waltzed about and returned the compliment with some vigour, scraping the ground with his hind feet, gathering up a small boulder in the process, and projecting it straight at me with considerable accuracy.

This heralded a great commotion. Apparently the show had begun. I hurled more stones in all directions, and although the admiring onlookers retreated each time, those on the opposite side advanced, the gentleman who had yawned so indulgently most of all. He was now very angry indeed, projecting stones and big blobs of spittle at me alternately as he waltzed about, presenting first his revolting, dog-like visage and then his still more revolting and quite uncanine other end.

These tactics, combined with more stones and the fast-descending dusk, made me not only definitely frightened, but inexplicably angry too. Once I nearly put a charge of lead into him, but luckily checked myself, realizing that this trump-card would be even more useful later on when the difference of opinion became general. Matters appeared to be rapidly drifting in that direction.

During one of the periodic lulls between these diplomatic interchanges, now carried on in a more or less tense silence, one of the smallest and most youthful of my audience uttered a peevish squeal and bowled a small lump of earth at me, just as an underhanded lob-bowler in a juvenile cricket match would do. The action was so ludicrous that in my decidedly agitated frame of mind I burst into roars of laughter. Why it seemd so screamingly funny I don't know; perhaps it wasn't really so at all. But my action proved a most fortunate one.

The brat's mother made a dive at her now cowering and shivering prodigy, gathered it to her bosom, and bolted, followed by several other mothers and their offspring. The remaining "stag party," numbering some dozen, began running to and fro looking surprised and angry. I continued laughing and shouting as if I were at a football match, and soon became quite incoherent from sheer nerves. I advanced on the old male, shouting: "They've made a goal; run, run, you old idiot; bonjour, mademoiselle cochon; nunca cafe con leche," at the same time executing a spine-rocking rumba combined with all the other outlandish dances in my repertoire. He stopped dead in his tracks. His eyes opened wide and his whole face took on a quite ludicrously human expression. He muttered to himself. "Standing aghast" is the only way to describe his poise, as if he was just as much shocked at my behaviour as he was bewildered and frightened at what he saw. A few seconds he stood his ground, amazement written all over his face; then his nerve gave way and he shied like a dog. His final rout was accompanied by a flood of the choicest swearing from my Cockney vocabulary. He fled.

   Ivan T. Sanderson, *Animal Treasure* (Viking Press, 1937), pp. 52-6.

In very old days the elephant, upon the roof of the earth, led an existence deeply satisfying to himself and fit to be set up as an example to the rest of creation: that of a being mighty and powerful beyond anyone's attack, attacking no one. The grandiose and idyllic modus vivendi lasted till an old Chinese painter had his eyes opened to the sublimity of ivory as a background to his paintings, or a young dancer of Zanzibar hers to the beauty of an ivory anklet. Then they began to appear to all sides of him, small alarming figures in the landscape drawing closer: the Wanderobo with his poisoned arrows, the Arab ivory-hunter with his long silver-mounted muzzle-loader, and the white professional elephant-killer with his heavy rifle. The manifestation of the glory of God was turned into an object of exploitation. Is it to be wondered at that he cannot forgive us?

Yet there is always something magnanimous about elephants.

Dinesen, *Shadows on the Grass*, pp. 55-6.

Plates 13-15. Giraffe Portraiture.

And recently I was driving through Kenya with a friend of mine. It was dusk, an explosion of red shot with gold, and the setting sun and the red air seemed to be pressing the acacias flat. Then we saw a giraffe! Then two, three, four — about ten of the lanky things standing still, the silhouettes of their knobby heads protruding into the red air.

I brought the car to a halt and my friend unsheathed his camera and cocked it. He snapped and snapped while I backed up. I was so busy looking at giraffes that I zig-zagged the car all over the road and finally into a shallow ditch.

The giraffes moved slowly among the trees like tired dancers. I wanted them to gallop. Once you've seen a giraffe galloping — they gallop as if they're about to come apart any second, yet somehow all their flapping limbs stay miraculously attached — you know that survival has something to do with speed, no matter how grotesque, double-bellied and gawky the beast may be.

My friend continued to fire his camera into the sunset, and pretty soon all the giraffes had either loped away or had camouflaged themselves in the trees. Both of us, rendered speechless by beauty, nodded and we continued along the road.

Paul Theroux, *Sunrise with Seamonsters* (Houghton Mifflin, 1985), p. 15. Theroux's name is synonymous with sophisticated travel literature. *Sunrise* is a collection of journalistic pieces written over twenty years. Many of the early years were spent in Africa.

I was having breakfast when Iain brought me a vulture to add to my collection. The bird was young and must have fallen out of his nest before he could manage to open his wings. When Iain picked him up he was walking on the road in a half-dazed state. We perched him on the windowsill, where he spent that day looking down into the valley.

We called him Auda Abu Taii, after the famous Arab chieftain who swooped out of the desert to pounce on the Turks during Lawrence of Arabia's campaign in the First World War. Somehow, after he had been given that name and despite his bald head and loose purple skin, he took on a certain air of magnificence and lost his repulsive appearance. His eyes were almond shaped and bright as rubies. People and animals alike respected and feared him. If we walked past his perch without shoes he would swoop down and thrust his head towards our toes, hopping after us, pushing himself along with his wings and pecking at our feet until we caught him and put him back on to his perch. I could never leave the genets alone when he was around. Widgey, who didn't approve of this intruder, would stand on her hind legs and growl as loud as a mongoose can, giving out her alarm signals to inform us that something big, bad and nasty was about. She would then dart under a table or a chair and wait for Auda to pass by, so as to get a good nip at him. As for the chickens and birds they listened attentively when they heard Widgey's alarm calls, and immediately went into hiding.

When it came to feeding time, and all the different saucers and meals were ready, Auda would make a flying leap and land with a heavy crash on the table and then totter towards the food. Ruffled out like a furry porcupine Widgey would fling herself at him with her high-pitched attack cry and bite him wherever she could.

In time Auda Abu Taii became a magnificent ornament to our camp, and we grew very attached to him. Then one day he suddenly took off from his perch, flew across the river to the opposite bank, sat on a tree for a while looking at us, and disappeared into the haze where the Lake meets the sky.

Iain & Oria Douglas-Hamilton, *Among the Elephants*, pp. 169-70.

Natures great master-peece, an Elephant,
The onely harmlesse great thing; the giant
Of beasts; who thought, no more had gone, to make one wise
But to be just, and thankfull, loth to offend,
(Yet Nature hath given him no knees to bend)
Himselfe he up-props, on himselfe relies,
And foe to none, suspects no enemies,
Still sleeping stood; vex't not his fantasie
Blacke dreames; like an unbent bow, carelessly
His sinewy Proboscis did remisly lie:

John Donne, *The Progresse of the Soule* (Stanza XXXIX). Written in 1601, the carefree "Progresse" showed a witty, if not entirely accurate, stab at natural history. In stanza XL, a mouse, the latest transformation of the "soule," walked into the elephant's trunk and surveying the "roomes of this vast house" made its way to the brain, where it killed the elephant by gnawing on "life cords there." But, when the "slaine beast tumbled downe," the mouse died as well: "And thus he made his foe, his prey, and tombe[.]" And the soule ("bent on gallant mischief")

went on to its next incarnation, a wolf, in this elaborate joke.

. . .I saw four majestic koodoo bulls on the edge of a wood of brilliant golden mimosa trees. Their beautiful shaggy silver beards, manes, and tails flushed electrically in the pure morning sunlight; and so did the dazzling white stripes that harnessed their red-golden bodies. They were pretending to fence and foil with their huge horns that rolled over their backs in magnificent spirals to a length of four or five feet. I have seldom seen an Arab or English horse, or a Spanish bull, that could equal them in their graceful and aristocratic carriage. They played and bounded in the sunlight as if they had just sprung forth from the hand of the Maker on the fifth day of Creation. When they caught sight of us, with their noble heads flung back, their horns undulating level with their backs, their great white bushy tails erected, their manes and beards streaming out, and their bodies bounding and scattering dew and pollen, they galloped off barking loudly into the labyrinths of flowers that closed behind them, firing off clouds of golden smoke in their wake.

Campbell, *Dark Horse*, p. 74.

The great story of Bowker and the lion comes from the Mara District. My father and Bowker were working through a bushy valley some three hundred yards apart, in search of the biggest of all lions. This lion was said by the trackers to be black-maned and so huge that he looked like a buffalo. His long hair covered his body like a colobus monkey, and he had killed a large number of people. A legend, no doubt, but obviously an objective for any hunter.

Suddenly Bowker saw the monster charging straight at him. He fired, but the lion came on like a dragon, roaring like thunder. He flattened Bowker to the ground, and set about chewing him into pieces. My father was barely within range, but had to face that terrible decision which is a crisis in many a hunter's life. Could he shoot accurately enough to kill the lion and not the man? There was no time to lose. The chance had to be taken. Bowker was probably already dead. At some two hundred yards he fired, and the great monster collapsed on top of Bowker. As my father hurried along, as best he could with his limitations, towards the tragic remains of his colleague he saw movement. The lion was getting up again. To his utter amazement, he saw the lion roll over, and Bowker sit up in an unrecognizable mass of blood and froth. As he approached, Bowker scooped the gore from his face and eyes, and, with some derision, merely said, "Wouldn't mind a bath."

The explanation of this amazing incident is that Bowker had smashed the lion's lower jaw with his one and only shot. The lion, enraged by the shock, but not fully aware of its disablement, tried in vain to bite Bowker into pulp. All that it achieved was to cover him in blood and inflict only a few ineffective bruises and cuts.

When Bowker had finally cleared enough gore and mess from his face both men sat down and laughed. For the huge monster, the largest of all lions, the killer of hundreds of people, the very embodiment of Satan himself, was nothng more than a normal black-maned lion, old and somewhat toothless, his appearance admittedly embellished by very long hair.

Mervyn Cowie, *I Walk with Lions* (MacMillan, 1963), pp.

9-10. This volume was originally published in London in 1961 as *Fly, Vulture*. Cowie was Kenya's first Director of the National Parks, and the reader can imagine the number of stories that he had to tell. He was especially fond of lions, as the American title demonstrates, and as shown by the following two entries.

...I was chugging along in the rain slowly and carefully, skidding on every muddy turn, when my interest was attracted by a family of seven lions, sitting on a bank some eighty yards above the road. So intrigued was I with this scene that I missed my pathway, and the motorbike slipped over onto its side. Worse still, my foot was caught underneath in such a way that I could not move it, nor could I get up to lift the heavy bike. After struggling for some time, I realized it was quite hopeless, and merely thanked my luck that my leg was not being scorched by the hot engine.

This was too much for the lions, and they became fascinated by a human being in a most undignified position, struggling on the road. I was not very impressed with their decision to come closer for a proper inspection. First one stalked forward a few yards and sat down, and then the rest followed to form a new front line.

Curiosity was their main motive, but I was not very sure this would be the rule in the hours of darkness. I tried to work out what to do. There was no siren on my motorbike, as I relied on the noisy exhaust to announce my presence. There was no way of sounding an alarm except by shouting. I thought it better to keep silent and still until the lions got really threatening, and then to give them a sudden fright. This I hoped would convince them that I was a proper human being worthy of some respect, even if my leg was entwined under my piki piki, *as the Africans called it. I began to realize that I was in a nasty predicament, as the lions grew more aggressive in the failing light. One lioness walked around below wind, and had a good sniff at the combined scent of sweat, gasoline and a joint of meat strapped in the saddle bag for the family dinner.*

At this stage I resorted to my prearranged plan of a sudden movement and a lot of shouting. To my dismay, it had little effect. Several of the lions drew back a few yards but gave no sign of a general retreat. Strangely enough, in these circumstances one never seems to accept the inevitable, and I couldn't believe that one of the lions would spring at me.

Suddenly all the lions jerked to the alert position, on their haunches, but instead of looking at me, they fixed their gaze on the road behind me. By craning my neck in the same direction, I could just make out the dark forms of six Africans walking toward me down the muddy road. I let out another shout, and this time the lions made off into the undergrowth. My saviors turned out to be some Maasai... They had heard my earlier shouts at the lions, and had abandoned a short cut in order to investigate the noise.

Cowie, *I Walk With Lions*, pp. 35-6.

...once coming back from Nairobi on my motorbike, [I] stopped at a place where the grass was long, and where I had often just missed running into some animal bounding across the road. I decided to burn the grass, so I put the bike on its stand and walked forward about ten yards. As I bent down to put a match to the road fringe, I heard an ominous growl. About five yards in front of me was a lioness, crouching, her tail lashing, and her teeth shining as she snarled. I never discovered which of us was more frightened, but I reached the absolute zenith of terror.

Instinctively, I knew it would be wrong to make any sudden movement and certainly to run away, for I was within springing distance. I could see the powerful muscles in her hindquarters rippling and tense, waiting only for her to set off the trigger. I was so overwhelmed by this sudden entry into trouble, I could not think reasonably.

The match went out. She blinked, and so did I. This gave me a thread of confidence. We both blinked again. She stopped lashing her tail. She also stopped baring her teeth and blowing through the back of her throat. This went on for a long time. I would have thought at least two hours, but I suppose it was only two minutes. Perceptively she calmed down and relaxed, and I wished I could do the same, but by now my muscles were trembling. Quite normally, she sat up on her haunches, and even glanced in another direction. Then, with an air of dignity, she strolled off without looking back — until she disappeared in some thick bush. I moved quickly off to my motorbike, and after an enthusiastic kick on the starter, the noise of the engine was one of the most welcome sounds I could have wished to hear.

Cowie, *I Walk with Lions*, pp. 43-4.

One hears men tell of staring a lion in the face — which of course, except in a zoo, is utter nonsense. To look or stare a lion in the eyes is a challenge a lion quickly responds to. . . .One may pass close to where a lion is lying up by, while watching the spot, avoiding its eyes. Once the eyes meet, a flag of recognition passes like an electric current — something happens, and quickly. I have at times had to work round to a position in order to get in a killing shot, conscious that the lion's eyes were on me all the time. I had to keep my eyes down on the ground and watch it, without meeting its eyes, till I got to the desired spot; when ready and in position to meet it, I raised my eyes and met the charge which more often than not followed, or shot it getting away. Once the eyes meet, there is no such thing as staring a wild lion out.

Marcus Daly, *Big Game Hunting and Adventure, 1897-1936* (MacMillan, 1937), p. 15. Daly was the son of pioneer settlers in Rhodesia. When his father and brother were killed during a native uprising at the turn of the century, Daly became a "professional hunter," as distinct from those "white safari hunters" who lived in Nairobi and who led a "life of comfort and luxury" guiding "these big rich American parties hunting along well-used tracks in civilized areas by motor car and lorry, with trap-guns, drags, spring-hooks and cameras" (p. 93). The following passages illustrate Daly's distinctions.

My tracker reported a large bull with very big ivory which he had seen not far over the French frontier. Though it was then afternoon, I called my boys and followed the tracker. The bull had moved well inland roaring, smashing and breaking bushes. It evidently had no fear of hunters, and had perhaps met them before. We followed on, into the long matteti reeds — a terror, as one can only move where an elephant has passed on account of the thick growth of the reeds, and then, even after an elephant has passed, many of the reeds shoot up again at all angles, and one is obliged to pass very carefully and noiselessly over and under these reeds, a difficult and trying task with a wakeful and dangerous bull near. Then, to increase the danger to the hunter and their own safety, they cut the figure eight many times, so that the bull or bulls that one may be following are perhaps just beside one, divided by only a yard or two of reeds, or just behind one. The game is full of unexpected dangers and sudden attacks from one or other of the hunters' numerous enemies; and hundreds and thousands of hunters of all colours, shades and nationalities have been killed...

We followed on and the big bull now roared on my left. All my boys fell back, and I was now, as so often before, quite alone, so moved quietly and quickly as possible forward, hoping to keep in line of the bull rather than have him on one side or the other. I thought of the possibilities of another bull; but it was too late now, and so on I went. A large, treble-decked blackthorn tree appeared in sight and I knew the bull would make for that if he didn't know of my presence, so followed on the winding and twisting trail. Hearing a slight crack behind me, I looked and saw my stout-hearted tracker just at the back of me, who, pointing to the tree, whispered, "Hurry, hurry before they get scent of us here." The great tree shook, indicating the bull against it. I slipped in and at the tree saw two large bulls, one facing me and the other standing at right angles, head to the tree, both brain-shots, and I quickly got into action with my .416 Magnum rifle; the first one had not hit the ground before the second one was on its way down — but then, unknown to me, I was standing right under the tusks of the big bull we had been following, which, with a roar, had me in the twinkling of an eye. As a last hope, as he lifted me in his trunk to pull me on to his tusks, I loosed off straight, as I judged, for his chest, and then away I went up clean through the tree-top, now, of course, quite unconscious.

The trackers seeing the two bulls come down and the third one throw me and also noticing that the third one had taken the shot, and me up in the tree slowly breaking my way through the heavy, thorn-covered, treble roof, paused to watch the finish, while my bull raced roaring round the two dead elephants and the tree. To finish with, this bull fell dead beside the others, while at the same moment I landed full force on to its stomach, and tumbled over unconscious to settle with my head resting against it, just behind the front legs. It was now late, my camp five miles away...My tracker, as related later, wanted to pull me away; he was alone, and the elephant kept moving its eyes, and, as he said, he dare not approach. By keeping away, he explained, the elephant would more likely die quietly, whereas to try and get me away might arouse him to a last effort, and if I were not already dead, it would surely kill me. So he watched on. The elephant made a few convulsive movements, the eyes still blinking. It was getting dark, lions were about; he could only return by the way he had come; he was unarmed and alone, and still the big crocodile-infested river to cross at the end. So he went, as he related, ran as hard as he could, and left me there for the night alone and unconscious against the elephant. Next morning early he returned with a party of my boys, and found me in exactly the same place and position, still unconscious, with both my eyes and side of my head plastered with congealed blood, while my mouth and chest were also blood-covered. The elephant had not moved, but lions, and plenty of them, had fed on all three carcasses of the elephant [sic] that night without in any way disturbing me. At sight of me

and the elephant my bush boys wanted to run away, but my stout-hearted tracker prevented them, and, using the tin of water he had brought with him, bathed my head. This revived me and, though still unable to move, I soon took in the whole position. In a faltering, weak whisper I asked him to make a stretcher of weeds and get me back to camp...After many stops and hours, for progress was necessarily slow, we reached the river and crossed and, a few hundred yards further in the bush, reached my camp.

Daly, *Big Game Hunting and Adventure*, pp. 139-42. The Real McCoy was not without a sense of humor: "A disappointed lady friend, reading an account of my escape from death in which it was said 'that only the angels of God saved me that night from the hungry lions' wrote me a letter after many years of silence saying that 'it was not the angels of God that saved me, only that the lions preferred clean meat'." (p. 143).

Watching [the elephant herd] *for some three minutes, I decided on a plan of action. They were both engaged in turn in reaching up with their trunks and pulling down chunks of dry wood and branches which they let fall on their backs. Seizing such a moment, I slipped through under the stomach of the big cow, got in a quick brain-shot on the bull, and passed on beyond him some twenty yards before he crashed to earth. The big cow rushed out the side I had entered and made off, after scattering my party in every direction.*

Passing under an elephant is an art I learnt in the Kalahari, and there are many factors to study before such an attempt can be made, such as ground surface under the elephant and beyond, the approach, the light inside and manoeuvring room, the occupation of the elephant at the moment of moving forward, and the relative position of other elephants about with the one required. Any carelessness in observing all and acting accordingly will mean the destruction of the hunter. Wind is no factor here, as in such jungles at certain times of the day the air is to all appearance still, and the fact of having got so close up unobserved rules it out.

A thin vine-string unobserved, the cracking of any twig in passing, will mean disaster.

I only mention this as an example of what can be done among elephants and what I have done in East Africa, the Kalahari and Equatorial African jungles many times.

Daly, *Big Game Hunting and Adventure*, p. 159.

...a well-known white hunter...followed his trackers along to an elephant standing three-parts in the bush with his back to them [and] *beckoned to the American millionaire, pointing out the brain-shot, covering the selected spot with his own heavy double to support the American shot. The American raised his rifle and tried by his best geometrical mental calculations to locate the brain centre. "No, no," said the gun-bearer in broken English, "dit no be de head, dit be the tail." American's rifle lowered. "Damn you," he roared in wrath to the confused white hunter as the great elephant shot away, "don't you know an elephant's tail from its head when it sticks it out through the bush looking at you?"*

The term "white hunter" is a purely Nairobi manufacture and was never heard of in Rhodesia where all the best hunters were found, or anywhere else in the big game countries, except

East Africa.

Daly, *Big Game Hunting and Adventure*, p. 160.

Five bands of vicious-looking creatures scuttled backwards and forwards like armoured columns, looking for a weak point to attack. The bands were about two yards in length with big-jawed soldiers on the outside and workers between them. The marauders were army ants or siafu, *probably the most formidable insects in Africa. They have been known to devour a large python which was so gorged after a meal that it could not escape. A warden had told me that if a horse is left tethered among these ants it will be eaten and left a skeleton where it stands. This may or may not be true. In the Congo some years ago I met a Wanande hunter who owed his life to the fact that if a soldier ant once closes its pincer-like jaws on a piece of skin it is very difficult to prise them apart.*

. . .At supper one night I noticed that his upper arm was furrowed by a scar which stretched from his shoulder to his elbow…[H]e had been walking through a forest track some miles from his village when a leopard sprang out and pinned his dog to the ground. The hunter lunged at the leopard with his spear and wounded it but before the animal made off it raked him with its claws. Blood poured from a large, loose flap of skin below his shoulder. Realizing he was in danger of bleeding to death, the hunter looked round until he found a trail of army ants. By holding the big-jawed specimens over the wound, one by one, he induced them to close their pincers on the flap of skin, in such a way that they clasped the edges of the wound together. Once the bodies has been nipped off, he was left with a row of 'stitches' composed of ant's jaws.

Hillaby, *Journey to the Jade Sea*, pp. 35-6. Also called driver or safari ants, the purely carnivorous *siafu* have been known to take lion cubs left down in a den and trapped leopards (though I am not suggesting that the reader should believe the surgery story).

…safari ants are so called by the natives because they go on foraging expeditions in immense numbers. The big-headed warriors are able to inflict a really painful bite. In open spaces, as where crossing a path, the column makes a little sunken way through which it streams uninterruptedly. Whenever we came to such a safari ant column, in its sunken way, crossing our path, the porter in question laid two twigs on the ground as a peace-offering to the ants. He said that they were on safari, just as we were, and that it was wise to propitiate them.

Roosevelt, *African Game Trails*, p. 325. Raiding swarms usually forage at night. Emigration, typically in a long column, goes on day and night until completed.

…Elsa was buried under the acacia tree where she had often rested (it stands on the river bank, close to the camp); at George's command the game scouts fired three volleys over the grave. The reports echoed back from Elsa's rock; perhaps somewhere in the sea of bush her mate may have heard them and paused.

It was 24th January, 1961.

Joy Adamson, *Forever Free: Elsa's Pride* (Collins & Harvill, 1962), p. 40. There are few people who do not know, at least vaguely, the unforgettable story of the lioness Elsa. Begun in *Born Free: A Lioness of Two Worlds* (Pantheon Books, 1960), continued in *Living Free: The Story of Elsa and Her Cubs* (Harcourt, Brace & World, 1961), and concluded in the volume whose quotation is given above, the trilogy of Elsa and her cubs, and the resulting movie, caught the imagination of animal lovers everywhere. Although she had (has) her numerous detractors and no doubt was a difficult person for many to appreciate, Joy Adamson was a truly extraordinary individual. She arrived in Kenya in 1938 from Austria. She married Peter Bally, an outstanding botanist, who introduced her to the flora of Kenya. Consequently, she produced some 700 magnificent illustrations of Kenya's indigenous wildflowers. These unsurpassed studies were subsequently used to illustrate many books on Kenya's flowers and today hang in Kenya's National Museum. For this work, she earned the coveted Grenfell Gold Medal of the British Royal Horticultural Society. In 1947, after a divorce from Bally, she married George Adamson, who was employed by the Kenya Game Department and stationed in the remote Northern Frontier District. Traveling through these outlying areas, she realized that she was observing the last use of tribal costumes and probably the end of an era and determined to provide a pictoral record of the tribes and their traditional dress. The result, spread out over some six-and-a-half years, were more than 400 fascinating paintings that today hang in Kenyan museums and government buildings. Some of the paintings were reproduced in her book, *Peoples of Kenya*, which provides an extensive tribal and cultural background of today's Kenya. But, when she and George found three orphaned lion cubs, the Elsa saga — the rearing of the cubs, their rehabilitation back into the wild, the subsequent breeding of Elsa to produce a wild litter, and the intimate relationship between Joy and Elsa — unfolded and dominated her life. Probably, no other single impetus has so benefitted the cause of wildlife conservation than the spread of this story. Later, concern for the plight of cheetahs led Adamson to consider rehabilitating into the wild captured or human-reared cheetahs. She focused on a captive cheetah named Pippa, which she tried to introduce into Meru National Park. This effort was chronicled in two books: *The Spotted Sphinx* (Harcourt Brace World, 1969), and *Pippa's Challenge* (Harcourt Brace Jovanovich, 1972). Finally, she turned to the remaining of the African big cats, in the form of a leopard named Penny, whose story was published as *Queen of Shaba: The Story of an African Leopard* (Harcourt Brace Jovanovich, 1980). On January 3, 1980, Joy Adamson was killed in the bush by a disaffected former worker. A legend in her lifetime, she lives on through the Elsa Wild Animal Appeal. Many are forever in her debt; President Moi of Kenya paid her this tribute: "Her death is a great loss, not only to her husband, but to Kenya as a whole." Not the slightest exaggeration. On the other hand, as suggested earlier, Joy did not always dance to the same tunes as the rest of us — she believed, for example, that animals communicated with her through mental telepathy. Ian Parker, long the iconoclast, has subjected both the Adamsons to a biting criticism contained in Chapter 6 of his book, *Oh Quagga!* (Ian Parker, 1983). While trenchant in part (as Parker is likely to be), much of the inconsistency noted and ultimately the criticism itself is irrelevant (as Parker is also wont to be) to the "Elsa message."

Every man in our party stopped dead as he arrived at the top and looked down on the vast crater, stretching away fifteen miles to the far edge of the encircling lip. All the tales I had heard of Ngorongoro were as nothing compared to the great herds spread out over those green fields as though shaken out of a giant pepper pot. The crater seethed with game. The grass was cropped as fine as a lawn by the thousands of beasts. In the distance the herds seemed to melt together into a trembling mass of white and fawn. There were zebra, eland, giraffe, topi, waterbuck, reedbuck, bushbuck, steinbok, Thomson gazelles, Grant gazelles, impala, wildebeest, duiker, oribi, and ostrich. This was how all the African veldt must have looked before the coming of the white man. Here in this isolated crater was the last great stronghold of game.

My two clients behaved like children suddenly turned loose in a candy store. They shot until their rifles were too hot to hold. The daylight hours were all too short to enable them to satisfy their passion for more hides and horn. "Trigger itch" had them in its grip. Later I was to discover that this is a common trait among Americans when first confronted by the abundance of African game after the shooting restrictions in their own country.

Hunter, *Hunter*, pp. 41-2.

. . .Ngorongoro Crater, an extinct volcano whose rim of near-perfect symmetry encloses, like the walls of an amphitheatre, a tiny peaceable kingdom two thousand feet below filled with one of the heaviest concentrations of large animals in Africa per square mile, all wandering about a lilliputian soda lake, acacia forest and grassland plain — a Fabergé version of the Serengeti outside...

Harold T.P. Hayes, *The Last Place on Earth* (Stein and Day, Scarborough Books Editions, 1983), p. 17. Originally published in 1976, this essay on one level is an account of a safari made by the author in the company of the great German zoologist Bernard Grzimek. On another level, the book is a revealing and important look at the politics of conservation. Highly recommended.

My hope was to get as close as possible to the zebras and wildebeest, the jackals and baboons which were all around the area between our camp and the deep forest of fever trees where, day and night, elephants could be heard at their noisy browsing. I also wanted to find again if I could, and see close to, a group of eland the Land Rover had frightened away — noble, archaic-looking creatures and one of the biggest of the antelopes. Up to a point I succeeded but with every encounter the same thing happened: as soon as I came within what seemed a certain magic distance of the creatures, no matter how quietly and gently I moved, they drifted away — politely, unhurried, and sometimes with a look over a shoulder that seemed to be saying "If you don't mind, I've got to be going along now," but always away. A baby zebra, still hazed over with a chestnut-brown fuzz, hung back longer than the rest of his herd, then

painted on his one-inch-thick hide, he was taken back to the plains and released.

Undoubtedly T.D. had shown that the first reaction, whether of man or beast, was to gain release. Retaliation was a secondary consideration. If T.D. and his boys had been on foot, the United States would have lost seven colourful citizens, because it was the quick turn of the horse which evaded the infuriated charge of the animal.

They captured every kind of game except wildebeeste (or gnu). That sloppy-looking wise-beard had them beat. He was the horses' equal at "turning on a dime", and could gallop all day after the horses were blown.

Binks, *African Rainbow*, pp. 103-6. For further rope tricks, the reader should consult Guy H. Scull, *Lassoing Wild Animals in Africa* (Frederick A. Stokes, 1911), the fairly wild tale of a safari taken by "Buffalo Jones, the Last of the Plainsmen, and his two cowboys, Loveless and Meany." Paul J. Rainey, to whom reference was made in the excerpt, had been recruited to hunt lions with dogs — in the U.S., he had used hounds to track cougars and bears. (Binks was taken on as Rainey's chief photographer.) The dogs so harassed the lions that the hunters had ridiculously easy shots at close range — indeed, this hunting method proved so successful (though a number of dogs were killed) that using dogs was later banned for safaris as unsportsmanlike.

Plates 17-19. Termite Mounds. The three examples shown are the author's basic "Moslem," "Cathedral," and "Las Vegas" versions. Surface termitaria — on the outside, apparently inanimate hills — are engineering masterpieces inside and house a highly sophisticated, complex form of life. An elaborate honeycomb structure — with its own ventilation system, fungus farms, and underground shafts that reach 150 feet (mostly horizontal) — the mounds are home to as many as three million termites. Termites ("mehwa" in Kiswahili) are winged insects (not closely related to ants but distantly related to cockroaches); some 400 species of termite are found in Africa, not all which, however, build these mounds. Simple anatomically, termites have survived basically unchanged for over 100 million years: thin-skinned, blind, slow, and weak. The hard-shelled fortresses serve essentially two functions: on the one hand, to protect the highly vulnerable insects from floods, drought, and predators, especially ants, their archenemies, and, on the other hand, to maintain the constant temperature (always between 84-86° F) and humidity required for the termites to live. Most of the inhabitants are sterile workers, who do all the construction and stand in constant attendance of the queen (feeding her, removing her excrement, and distributing her eggs). Aggressive soldiers exclusively defend the mound, and sexual males and females eventually leave the nest in a nuptial flight to start their own colonies. Last comes the large queen (the size of a human index finger), little more than an egg-laying machine, who resides at the center of the nest, three feet or more below ground, attended by her consort-king. A termitary operates on a strict caste basis, and the division of labor is so exact that some naturalists have called the entire colony a sort of "super-organism," in which the individual termites are analagous to cells. Termites communicate by saliva; pheromones, or scent messages, are passed from mouth to mouth.

The intelligence of lions is acknowledged and was demonstrated by a most extraordinary happening which took place when George was asked to kill two man-eaters. For the killing of man-eaters no methods are barred, so he put a small dose of strychnine into pieces of raw meat and placed these in the lions' latest pugmarks. They were soon taken. Observing this, George followed the lions' spoor which led him to a bush covered with small red berries: Cordia quarensis. *They are a violent emetic and Africans eat them when they wish to be sick. The lions had apparently laid up behind the bush, eaten the berries and vomited the whole content of their stomachs, including*

through the camp without even pulling out or tripping over a single tent-rope. The exception was a zebra that collided fully with a small tent, fortunately empty, and having rolled itself into a sort of animated sausage by the fury of its struggles, it lay like a mummy swathed in canvas with only its head protruding. When we plucked up courage to come out of our tents after the hurricane of snorts and hoofbeats had passed, we flashed our torches around and found the trussed-up zebra. By pulling at the tent ropes, we gradually unrolled the beast which got up and seemed to be either dazzled or stunned, for it remained standing and trembling in the camp all night until just before the

Plate 20. Kikuyu Cultivation.

the strychnine. Then they had walked off across rocks where it was impossible for George to track them. Though hardly credible, it appeared that when the lions felt ill they deliberately ate the berries, presumably knowing this would make them vomit.

Joy Adamson, *The Searching Spirit,* (Harcourt Brace Jovanovich, 1978), p. 26. Autobiography.

Both wildebeest and zebra love wheeling round in circus-like formations. A mixed herd of these was stampeded through our camp once, near the Athi river, by a pride of lions who had sent their killers round to the other side of the camp to intercept the fugitives. All except one of both species managed to thunder

dawn when it suddenly made off at a gallop.

Campbell, *Dark Horse,* pp. 77-8.

According to [a Turkana tribesman] the lion's roar translated into English goes: "WHO IS LORD OF THIS LAND?...Who is lord of this land?...I am!...I am!...I am!...I am!...

George Adamson, *Bwana Game: The Life Story of George Adamson* (Collins & Harvill, 1968), p. 309. Reading George Adamson's autobiography (published in the United States by Doubleday as *A Lifetime with Lions*), the reader realizes that the Elsa saga was really a shared experience, with George and Joy Adamson working closely together. When Joy's life turned to new directions, George remained preoccupied with the rehabilitation of lions. This book contains an excellent description of making the film "Born Free."

Masai Spearmen: The Bravest of the Brave

I saw my first spear hunt when I was staying in a small Masai community not far from Lake Magadi. The night before, a lion had jumped the twelve-foot boma that surrounded the village, seized a cow, and leaped back over the barrier with the cow in his mouth. I know this feat sounds incredible, as the lion weighed no more than four hundred pounds and the cow probably weighed nearly twice that. Yet a male lion can perform this exploit with no more trouble than a fox has in carrying off a chicken.

A lion shows a special knack in getting partly under the carcass and shifting the weight onto his back while still holding the cow's throat in his mouth. When jumping the barricade, the lion's tail becomes absolutely rigid and seems to act as a balance. The Masai have assured me that a lion without a tail could not possibly perform this feat.

I was prepared to start out on the lion's trail the next morning, but the moran in this community told me somewhat contemptuously that my help was not needed. They would handle the situation themselves. At that time, I found it hard to believe that a group of men could kill an adult lion with spears. I asked if I could go along...

We started off at daybreak. I followed the spearmen. There were ten of them. Magnificent-looking men, slender but finely muscled, not one under six feet. To give their limbs free play, each man removed his one garment, the long piece of cloth they wear draped over their shoulders, and wrapped it around his left arm. They carried their brightly-painted shields balanced on their shoulders. Their spears were in their right hands. The warriors wore their ostrich-plume headdresses as though going into battle and bracelets of fur around their ankles. Otherwise, they were completely naked.

We picked up the spoor of the lion and the moran began to track. The lion had gorged on the cow during the night and was lying up in some dense cover. They threw stones into the bushes at random until the savage growls of the lion showed he had been hit. When the moran had spotted the cat by his angry grunts and snarls, they began to throw stones in good earnest; then the bushes began to shake. Suddenly the lion burst out a hundred yards from us and went bounding away across the plains, his gorged belly swinging from side to side as he ran.

Instantly the Masai were after him, giving their wild cries as they sped through the tall, yellow grass. The lion, still heavy with his great meal, did not run far. He stopped and turned at bay. The spearmen spread out to encircle him. The lion stood in the middle of the ring, looking this way and that, snarling in a way to make one's blood run cold as the spearmen slowly closed in.

The lion allowed the men to come within forty yards. Then I could tell that he was preparing to charge. His head was held low, just above his out-stretched forepaws. His hindquarters were slightly arched so he could bring his rear legs well forward and get the maximum spring behind his rush. He began to dig his claws into the ground, much as a sprinter digs in with his

spiked shoes to make sure he does not slip when he makes his first jump.

I concentrated on the sinister inverted curve of the lion's tail. Just before he charges, a lion always twitches the tasseled tip of his tail three times in rapid succession. On the third twitch he comes for you at amazing speed, going so fast he seems only a small part of his real size.

The spearmen knew as well as I did that the lion was preparing to attack. By what seemed to be a single impulse, all their spear arms moved back together for the cast. The men were so tense with excitement that their taut shoulder muscles twitched slightly, making ripples of sunlight play along the spear blades. You could have driven a nail into any one of them without his feeling it.

Suddenly the tip of the lion's tail began to twitch. One! Two! Three! Then he charged for the ring of spearmen. At once half a dozen spears leaped through the air toward him. I saw one plunge into his shoulder and the next instant the spear head broke through the hide on his other side. The lion never paused in his stride. In his path stood one of the moran, a youngster on his first hunt. The boy never flinched. He braced himself to meet the charge, holding his shield in front of him and swaying back slightly so as to put the whole weight of his body into his spear thrust. The lion sprang for the boy. With one blow he knocked the young moran's shield out of his hand as though it were cardboard. Then he reared up, trying to sweep the boy toward him with his out-stretched paws.

The boy drove his spear a good two feet into the lion's chest. The mortally wounded beast sprang on him, fixing his hind claws in the boy's belly to insure his grip while at the same time he seized the boy's shoulder in his jaws.

The young warrior went down under the weight of the great cat. Instantly all the other moran were around the dying lion. It was too close quarters for spears. The men used their double-edged simis, heavy knives about two feet long. Shouldering each other out of the way, they hacked like madmen at the lion's head. In a matter of seconds, they had sliced the head to pieces. . .

Hunter, *Hunter*, pp. 101-3. Even the genuine article cannot resist the exaggeration and romantic nonsense endemic to his profession. No lion ever hoisted an 800-pound cow onto its back and leaped over a twelve-feet-high stockade, absurd fox-and-chicken comparisons notwithstanding. Actually, the account of lions jumping over barriers with cattle held in their mouths is an old canard, a *tour de force* "seen" by any number of early travelers. The problems with such reports are many, not the least of which is the physical impossibility of the feat itself, even given a much reduced size for East African cattle. Not only does a lion not possess this strength (a leopard perhaps is strong enough to manage a similar feat, in proportion to its own weight, but not a lion), it certainly does not possess the inclination to behave this way. Lions do not leap fences; they push through barriers. Occasionally, a lion might leap onto a barrier, then bound down to the other side. Moreover, a lion does not carry even a small animal but always drags it. Returning to Hunter's yarn, perhaps only slightly less remarkable are men throwing stones a hundred yards at a lion, even "in good earnest." And "three twitches of the tail," indeed! As for the "bravest of the brave" Maasai, the author recommends the following counterweight.

Plate 21. One Reason for Taking a Safari.

Not all encounters, of course, are between lion and other animals. Sometimes there is a two-legged foe. About five years ago, in Tanganyika, I was invited to witness at close quarters the spearing of a lion by Masai. What must be said of this feat will be entirely contrary to those eulogies written all too frequently by passing visitors or professional hacks, about the bravery of this 'noble savage.' In a letter written immediately on return from this safari, I said: 'My own personal feeling is that this is the most disgusting and brutal cruelty that I have ever seen. I would never have anything to do with this again. A good maned lion was singled out, then surrounded by about 25 Masai, apart from the vehicles in which we and the film-party were driven to the scene. The wretched animal was so terrified and bewildered by the numbers of its enemies that it seemed unable to attempt to save itself. It showed no fight whatever, and was simply hacked to death. . .People may think that the spearing of a lion is a brave act — but I only hope to be able to erase the whole thing from my mind.'

This is not a philosophical treatise, but surely true bravery must be conscious and deliberate. Surely, too, it must fly in the face of odds. In many instances, of course, individuals of the Masai or other pastoral peoples have most courageously defended their stock and property against carnivores. But nothing in the organization of a Masai lion-hunt conforms to any such standards. In unsavoury practice, first of all, these nonpareils go out and gather essential supplies of the bark of a certain tree, and this they boil until it resembles a kind of turgid soup. They drink this potion; I am not versed in the medical terms for its influence, but it fills them with false courage, hysterical zest, making them immune from sensitivity, from reason, from fear. Twenty, thirty, or forty of them then dash out to find their lion. This animal — bewildered, frightened, hemmed in — stands not a chance against the menace and assault of this ring of frightful spears. And after the exertion, the wild and drugged excitement, the Masai one by one become seized with some kind of fit. They foam at the mouth and fall in a heap, then arise in an eye-staring wildness, and have to be restrained.

Cullen, *Downey's Africa*, pp. 86-7. Indeed, this passage is offered as an antidote to all the hopeless accounts written about the Maasai young male achieving manhood status by killng a lion.

"What man dare, I dare:
Approach thou like the rugged Russian bear,
The arm'd rhinoceros, or the Hyrcan tiger..."

Shakespeare, *Macbeth* (1606), Act III, Scene iv. Macbeth is shouting his defiance at the ghost of the just murdered Banquo, which apparition has appeared at a banquet in the palace. The "arm'd rhinoceros" rated, then, as one of the terrors of the natural world.

I have no idea why these animals [rhinos] are so ill-natured although a client of mine once had an interesting theory. This man had an unfortunate brush with an infuriated cow rhino and, as the beast attacked him without any provocation, the man considered her conduct most unreasonable. Afterwards I noticed him carefully examining all the rhino droppings we passed. At last he said solemnly to me, "Hunter, do you know why these beasts are so irritable? It's because they are always constipated." I never forgot this remark and indeed there may be something to it as rhinos swallow their food partly chewed, leaving large quantities of undigested matter in their droppings.

Hunter, *Hunter*, p. 177. The old constipated-alligator theory!

The light of evening, Lissadel,
Great windows open to the south
Two girls in silk kimonos, both
Beautiful, one a gazelle.

W.B. Yeats, "In Memory of Eva Gore-Booth and Con Markiewicz"

So geographers, in Afric-maps,
With savage-pictures fill their gaps;
And o'er unhabitable downs
Place elephants for want of towns.

Jonathan Swift, *On Poetry* (1733), 1. 177. Even in the early part of the Eighteenth Century, critics commented (adversely) on the tendency of explorers and Africanists to exaggerate the savagery and danger of the "Dark Continent."

There is a strange thing about the elephants, said Jordan. In a storm I have seen them covering their tusks with their ears, bringing the great flaps forward like a cape. The lightning can strike their ivory. I believe this because once I saw a lone bull taking shelter in a storm, his ears forward over his face, yet this did not save him. When the storm had gone and the sun came out I went to where he had [b]een standing, and there I found a tusk newly broken off, and it weighed sixty-four pounds.
. . .
They are wonderful animals and I have a great love and admiration for them, which may seem odd to you, thinking that I shot them for their ivory. But you have to see them to understand what I mean, when a herd of them is bull down on a yellow ridge and then something sets them moving and the sun comes suddenly on their tusks, and a bull trumpets, and that is a sound like nothing else you have ever heard, for it is a sound you feel as much as hear. You feel it in your stomach, you feel it as it moves up and catches your throat. Once the world must have been full of more terrible sounds, when the elephant was outnumbered and outmastered by animals that are now only Latin names and plaster casts in a museum. But the elephant has survived them all and trumpets his pride.

The herd comes on slowly, gently, ears like great sails, like a great fleet of great frigates, coming down, swaying and swinging until they halt again, and now there is no sound but the wrench of grass as they tear it up, and, if you like impudent paradoxes, the rumble of their stomachs. All elephants have indigestion, and this is the most uncharitable practical joke in zoology.

John Alfred Jordan, *Elephants and Ivory* (Rhinehart,

1956), pp. 11-2. Jordan was a white hunter in Kenya during the early part of this century, when most of Kenya was still "frontier." All hunters — and fishermen — are congenital liars (or trained thespians, depending upon one's view); perjury comes with the territory and ammunition (or bait). In Africa, the canvas of life is a large one, and, as the reader by now has discovered for himself, the lying is proportionate.

I have never seen any of the carnivores except cheetahs go out of their way to teach their young to hunt. A mother cheetah will take a young gazelle alive to her cubs and let them play with it, quickly rushing to their aid if it should try to escape. She will also catch a wildebeest calf and hold it until her cubs join her, after which she may leave it to her cubs to finish off.

The most extraordinary lesson I ever saw of this kind involved a mother cheetah and her five half-grown cubs. With the mother in front and the cubs spread out behind her, they crept over the short grass plains towards a lone male Thomson Gazelle which was peacefully grazing about two hundred yards ahead. When the gazelle suddenly looked up, the mother cheetah immediately froze, but the cubs were a bit slow in following her example. I couldn't help laughing, for each froze in turn, one almost bumping into its sibling. They must have been very obvious, yet the gazelle continued grazing. Almost immediately, however, it looked up again and caught the cheetahs in mid-stride. Again the cubs froze in their haphazard way. The gazelle stared in their direction, then once more continued feeding. The cheetahs were too far away to be a threat and so the gazelle was not worried. In fact it seemed almost to make a game of catching the cheetahs out — sometimes even turning its back, only suddenly to look round. As the cheetahs advanced over the next hundred yards or so the scene was repeated time and time again, then the gazelle calmly walked away, its tail wagging jauntily.

van Lawick, *Savage Paradise*, p. 29.

I took the first film safari into Africa, said Jordan, the first real one, that is.

It was over forty years ago, and some moving pictures had been made there, and screened at the bioscopes, but they were tame, a few hundred feet shot by Norfolk-jacketed sportsmen. As I remember them they showed dogs chasing lions, or lions chasing dogs.

I was in New York arranging to trap some animals for the Ringling Brothers and for Barnum and Bailey, and I saw some films in the little Broadway theaters, and I thought that someone should put Africa on to that flickering screen, a film that showed Africa as it really was, and not as a coursing match between a lion and a dog.

I organized a party. It was not a large party. There was myself, a cameraman and his assistant. The cameraman was...called Pete....[W]e bought a camera and a tripod and several thousand feet of film, and we set out for Africa.

As soon as we started upcountry from Mombasa I saw that the one real worry of this safari was going to be Pete. He knew all about filming, or said he did, and nothing about Africa. I knew all about Africa, or he thought I did, and nothing about films. The safari could have done with more balanced knowledge.

To Pete, very French and very European, Africa was a nightmare, a very hot and sunlit nightmare with appalling things coming at him out of the grass. He was very unhappy and it was no comfort to him to be told that he was a pioneer in his profession. There are people who just do not want to be pioneers.

His camera weighed fifty pounds, and had to be set up on the heavy tripod. Where it stood it had to stay. Yet all Pete had to do was to supervise this simple action and wait for animals. My problem was to get such animals past the camera slow enough for Pete. . . .

. . .We decided to film elephants first; only they were large enough to satisfy our ambitions. And I thought we could do this with the least inconvenience either to the elephants or to Pete.

We went out at dawn with our porters and our spearmen, and we went through elephant grass higher than our heads. The ground was thick with vetch that snatched at our feet, and Pete looked up at the sky with the expression you might see on the face of a man who has suddenly fallen down a well. It was noon when we topped a hill and saw the herd below. They were going down to the swampland, a long, gray caravan, moving slowly, and there was fine ivory among them. I wanted to cheer. Pete looked at them. He got off his pony and lay down and put his hat over his face.

I said, "We'll go down to the swamp and find grass high enough to hide us, but low enough for the camera to clear." And this was a good idea, even Pete thought it was a good idea, particularly the part about the grass hiding us. So we went down, flanking the herd, and we set up the camera. The elephants came on and Pete looked at them through the camera and across the camera, and at last he began to crank the handle.

Perhaps I had overlooked many things, for this was the first safari of its kind, but this one thing I could not have overlooked for I knew nothing about it. As Pete cranked the handle there was a noise like a Gatling gun. It did not worry him for he was accustomed to it. The elephants, however, had never heard it before and a young bull shouldered his way to the edge of the herd, swung up his trunk and trumpeted. The other bulls took up the protest, and the cows added their treble notes, until the noise was like a gigantic but undisciplined brass band. The herd began to swing and sway irritably in the mud.

Pete stopped cranking, hand still on the handle, his face white.

Robby [the assistant] was just as frightened, but he decided that the thing to do in a case like this was shoot something. So he fired at a big bull, and a brave shot it was. It did not kill the bull, and the herd, which up to then had been looking for somewhere to escape this irritating clanking, went over to the offensive. They shuffled in an eddying circle, their trunks up, searching for us.

I shouted to the bearers, slapped Pete on the back to arouse him, and retreated up the rise. . . .

The herd charged aimlessly over the spot we had left, and then split into small parties, circling, searching the air with their trunks, trying to catch our scent. Two stayed close to the bull that Robby had wounded, and it was these three who were determined to find us. They went about it patiently, circling in slow, shuffling movements, narrowing the circle until something stopped them forty yards from us. I wetted the wind. It was blowing our scent toward them.

Then up stood the brave Robby and gave them another shot with the .500. He brought down the bull he had wounded and it went over and shook the earth. The other two screamed. I was using a light 9 mm. which could not have stopped an elephant charge, so I aimed at the trunk of a cow that was standing unhappily in the dust by the fallen bull. Before I could fire, her little eyes saw the glint of Pete's camera, and she charged.

Pete said something short and breathless in French, and fainted.

The cow came in and picked up the tripod with such ease and grace that she reminded me of a lancer tent-pegging. She stood there swinging the tripod around her head, and beyond her I saw Pete's rump crawling into the grass.

Robby and I fired together and she went down like a noble ship. On her haunches first, and then on her forelegs, and you could see the strength slipping out of her. She trilled sadly, but the camera she kept aloft, until her head touched the ground and her trunk at last brought the tripod down gently.

We ran around her and picked Pete up, and we had to hold him up for his legs could not. It was three days before we could get him from his tent, and then he came out dapper in his bush-jacket, his polished boots and slanting topi, and he said, "How about filming something?"

I decided to go down to the Loita plains, where there were many gazelle and antelope and zebra in the yellow scrub, and there would be no charging elephants to worry Pete. We found giraffe on the edge of the plain, but they cantered away from the shining camera, with Pete shouting, " 'Old zem.' " We followed them for two hours until, in disgust, I told Pete and his naked bearer to get into the bushes. Robby and I would go out on our ponies and drive the giraffe in. They would pass him, all he need do was crank.

He said, "Vraiment?" And I said, "Of course."

We circled the giraffe, coming in a wide sweep behind them and then driving hard, standing in our stirrups shouting. The giraffe went on smartly, with their stupid necks jugging. They not only stampeded past the brush where Pete was cranking, but through it, lurching away from him at the last second. We rode up through their dust and there was Bwana [Pete] with a wide grin. He said he had taken three hundred feet of film and had been too busy to be afraid. He explained that it was like that with a man. When he had something to do he had no time for fear. That was how it was, I agreed.

In that month the Loita plain was thick with game. You could stand on a rise and pick them out by the curl of horn or flash of rump fur. It was the scene that sportsmen dream about before they come to Africa and which, if they are very, very lucky, they do sometimes see. And I knew that all we need do was build a blind for the camera, in a thicket by a trail, and drive this game past Pete's camera.

I stayed with him and helped him set up the tripod. He fussed about it like a woman, crouching, bending, sighting. The beaters were out, and they scudded round several herds, bringing them gently together until the whole plain was moving toward us with the sun on flank and horn, and the air trembling. Even Pete was caught by the wonder of it. He stared at this river of animals and I knew that he had already filmed them, that he was now sitting in the theater with his legs crossed, and seeing this drive filmed at geat risk and great expense by Pierre Sirois [Pete]. There was a faint smile on his lips. He was being modest about the applause.

I had my glasses on the herd. There were two, maybe three thousand animals out there, coming fast under a red dust cloud. They were coming straight for the blind, and they were not yet frightened. Then something alarmed them and they stampeded. I saw the stampede as a sudden lurch forward, so violent that it was as if they had been stationary until that moment. Now they were a torrent of red and white and black and gray and sweeping horns. Some were racing low on the ground, some bounding, and the beat of the zebra's hoofs, as they ran in a striped cloud on the flank of the stampede, was a rapid, desperate drumming.

I wondered why I could not hear the Gatling crank of the camera handle.

I saw why. Pete was determined to sell his life dearly. He had picked up a rifle.

I shouted, "For God's sake take the picture!"

He looked at me. He said, "Comment?" as if we had never met.

I shouted, "Shoot!" And since there could be some ambiguity about this I said, "The camera!"

He started cranking. He was lucky. He must have filmed several feet of the last gazelle as the herd swerved past us.

For a month Pete behaved nobly and nonchalantly. He filmed several hundred feet of placid impala, of hyena and vulture, of the camp and our boys, and I decided that perhaps he was now ready for something more exciting. We went to the Amala River to film hippo, but there was only an old bull in the water and he wouldn't come out. However, he blew water through his nostrils and flicked his ears at the flies, and these things Pete faithfully filmed, and I suppose that for an audience who had never seen a hippo blowing water and flicking his ears this could be very interesting.

We looked for buffalo, and I thought that here we would either have very good pictures or a very dead cameraman. It was hard to find buffalo. The land was lonely, rolling parkland as green as England except that the earth in the dongas was red. But the trees were spaced like orchards and the hills were barred with thickets as straight as hedgerows. Pete rode by my stirrup with his...bearer trotting behind us, and Pete was very content. He talked of buffalo as if they were some sort of wild cow.

We rode thus until the bearer stopped and smiled. He had heard the honey bird, and he put down the tripod and went off into the thicket with his friend. They both came out quickly and behind, the thicket crackling, came twenty black buffalo.

Their horns were down and they were moody, but they were not going to charge.

Robby and the bearers went down in the grass. I got Pete off his pony and behind a tree. "Crank!" I said.

The buffalo were in a line along the grass, with an old black bull as their troop leader. The crank of the camera brought their heads up and they sniffed the air, they pawed the ground. The old bull saw Pete and began to kick the ground back. The noise of the camera puzzled him. I thought, if he charges the whole line will be up here like heavy cavalry.

So I fired, and the bullet struck back of the bull's shoulders and burned him along the spine. He snorted and led the herd at a gallop across our front. Pete filmed 250 feet of them before they had gone, and nothing had happened to convince him that the buffalo was not a cow, albeit très formidable.

. . .

Then my bearer called and pointed, and we saw a bull in the bushes. We rode at it, but he circled the bush, keeping his horns down toward us, and I saw the blood-line along his back. It was my wounded bull.

I told Pete to dismount and set up his camera, and then I rode at the bush and called my dogs up to drive the bull out. They went in yelping, but the bull came out before they reached the thicket, head down, bushed tail like a standard.

He went straight for Pete, and Pete's pony rose up, came down, turned and bolted. Pete decided to leave it, going round twice in the air before he touched the ground. The bull went at him, and I saw the turn of its head as it bowed for the toss. My bearer, who was carrying my .500, fired it into the bull's flank, and the buffalo turned and took the bearer on its horns. It threw him fifteen feet.

Pete screamed. On his hands and his knees he scra[m]bled toward a gully. The bull heard the scream, turned sweetly and came quickly at [Pete].

Now my dogs went for the bull! The Airedale snapped at the nose and the buffalo sabered it. The other three he played with, and they kept clear of him, snapping, and I knew another would be killed soon. But the buffalo saw my pony and put his head down again in a charge. I kicked the pony and led the bull away. I took it down the plain and across the stream into the forest, where I lost it.

I could not talk to Pete that night. My bearer had been a good man. Yet it was wrong to blame Pete.

Now Pete wanted lions.

I wanted lions too. What would a film of Africa be without lions? We heard them around us at night, but we never saw them. We met a Dutch hunter in the valley who said he had seen rhino in the bush, and he asked us what was in the shiny box. Pete explained the rudiments of cinematography, and the Dutchman smiled and said again that there were rhino in the bush. He said it with an air of I would like to see more of this.

We shot a big-horned rhino the next day before Pete had time to film anything, and we were following the blood-spoor when the Dutchman, who was up ahead with the tracker, shouted, and came back with the brim of his hat flapping. He said — and he breathed heavily saying it — that there was a troop of lions asleep on the other side of the grass.

But they were asleep no longer. The shout of the great Bwana Mkuba Dutchman had seen to that, and when we got through the grass they were standing up, swinging their tails and watching us without malice. Pete clattered with his camera and then pushed up his shoulders in disgust.

I said, "What's the matter?"

He said, "Too much shade."

I said, "Shall I ask the lions to move?"

He said, "Thank you, no. We are in too much shade."

We moved over to better light, but the lions grew tired of posing for their pictures and they yawned and went away into the brush. Since it was only a narrow patch I told the boys to beat it. I stationed six spearmen around Pete and we waited.

We heard the high shouts of the bearers, the clash of spear on shield. The noise came closer, and still with no sight of the lions, and I began to think that they had slipped away to the flanks. Then one of my spearmen raised his spear and beckoned to me. I went over. He did not move his head. He said softly, "Simba!"

Twenty-five feet away was a magnificent black-mane, half out of the brush, tail twitching. Nervous, but not too nervous, the muscles of his hind quarters were slack. I flipped my fingers at Pete, and he came up reluctantly. He pushed the toes of the tripod into the earth and sighted the camera on the lion.

The black-mane coughed, and behind him in the bush the others roared. It was a magnificent sound.

Pete cranked twice, and ran for a tree.

Black-mane saw the movement and turned. He was too big, too good to lose, and I stood up and dropped him pleasantly with a shot in the brain. The others roared back at the shot and then turned on the beaters. I saw the bushes swaying, and one by one the [bearers/beaters] leaping up into the trees to let the lions pass beneath them.

That was the end of the lion hunt. It was also the end of the big film safari. Pete had run out of film. I asked him where it had all gone and he explained. We had films of natives, of the camp, of a hippo in a pool, of giraffe, yes we had fine films of giraffe, and there was the stampede, of course. I said, of course. At that we had more film than had ever been taken in Africa. Pete was going to be a great man. Pete was going to be a very great man once he got his film to Europe. It occurred to me that I might well be famous myself.

We went to Nairobi and Pete found a dark room where he could process his films.

He was undoubtedly a good cameraman. I took his word for the fact that in a studio there was not his equal. But he had never filmed in the open before. He had taken thousands of feet of film with his camera set for indoor work under brilliant light.

Our elephant, buffalo, giraffe and gazelle were dim blotches on an almost opaque stretch of celluloid, four miles long.

Jordan, *Elephants and Ivory*, Chapter Eight (pp. 133-44).

It has been said that a white hunter must combine "the expert lore of an Indian scout, the cool nerve of a professional soldier, and the ability to mingle easily with the rich and aristocratic." One of the most successful white hunters...put the matter to me somewhat differently. "Hunter," he said, "You must always remember that only ten per cent of your work is hunting. Ninety per cent is keeping your clients amused."

Hunter, *Hunter*, p. 52.

Among my first aristocratic clients were a French count and his countess who wanted a few African trophies for their château in Normandy. It was fashionable for the European nobility to be able to say that they had been big-game hunting in Africa and we white hunters profited by the fad. . . .The couple had eight trained native boys as their personal servants and I took along enough supplies to stock a small hotel. Before we left, the count made it clear that the only commodity he was interested in was a plentiful supply of whiskey. I took along more whiskey bottles than I did cartridges and it was well I did so. We could have done without the cartridges, but without the whiskey I fear I'd have had a dead count on my hands and no mistake.

A few days out, I spotted a fine black-maned lion and took my clients over to him. When the countess saw the lion, she screamed and wanted to go back to Nairobi. The count lifted his gun with shaking hands and then asked anxiously, "Suppose I shoot and don't kill, what does he do, eh?"

"He may charge, but I'll stop him with my rifle," I told the gentleman.

The count shook his head. "I think I need a drink," he said and off we went back to camp. That was all the lion hunting the count did. But that evening the couple called me in to have drinks with them.

"I have thought of a clever idea," said the count. "You are a hunter, no? So you go and hunt. I will stay here and you get me nice trophies to show my friends."

I agreed that this was an excellent suggestion, saving us all time and worry. I got them several good trophies and the countess posed on each one for photographs wearing her shooting togs and holding her rifle. She always asked me anxiously, "Hunter, how do I look?" I knew little about such matters but I always told her she looked very well indeed and my answer seemed to please her. The countess wanted her husband to pose on a few of the trophies, but he was seldom in a condition to sit up long enough for the camera to click.

Hunter, *Hunter*, pp. 52-3.

The wicked flee when no man pursueth: but the righteous are bold as a lion.

Bible, *Proverbs 28:1*

The slothful man saith, There is a lion in the way: a lion is in the streets.

Bible, *Proverbs 13*

The wolf also shall dwell with the lamb, and the leopard shall lie down with the kid; and the calf and the young lion and the fatling together; and a little child shall lead them.

Bible, *Isaiah 6*

Be sober, be vigilant; because your adversary the devil, as a roaring lion, walketh about, seeking whom he may devour.

Bible, *1 Peter 5:8*

...I was resting on the rifle, contemplating the novel and striking scene — the Lake, with its broad blue waters — its finely-wooded shores — the varied and vast herds of animals — ...when I saw, a little ahead of me, two magnificent stag lechés [lechwes] approaching each other, evidently with no friendly intentions. I was right in my conjecture, for in a few seconds afterward they were engaged in combat. Taking advantage of this lucky incident, I approached, unperceived, within a dozen paces, when I quickly dropped on one knee and took a deliberate aim at the shoulder of the nearest; but, just as I pulled the trigger, he received a violent thrust from his antagonist, which made him swerve to one side, and the consequence was that the ball, instead of piercing his heart, merely smashed one of his hind legs. The animals, nevertheless, were so intently engaged, that, notwithstanding the report of the gun, and the wounded state of one of them (he probably attributed this to his adversary), they did not observe me. Throwing aside the rifle, I drew my hunting-knife, and thus armed, rushed upon the combatants. Just, however, as I was about to bury the fatal weapon in the flank of one of the animals, they both suddenly became aware of me, and fled precipitately. The wounded beast at once made for the river, which was hard by, and though it was running very swiftly at this point, perhaps not less than four or five miles an hour, he plunged into the water.

Not being then aware of the aquatic habits of this species of antelope, I was very much astonished, and for a while thought the beast would surely be carried away by the violence of the currrent and drowned. But I was soon undeceived; for he struck bravely out for the opposite shore, his course being marked with streaks of crimson. On gaining the bank, he gave one glance behind him, shook his bloody and drizzling coat, and made off. I was determined, however, not to be beaten; and, as I had nothing on but a pair of trousers and a flannel shirt, I threw myself, as I was, into the stream, and soon succeeded in reaching the opposite bank, when I at once started in pursuit.

In this way, swimming and wading alternately, several rivulets, swamps, and dikes were crossed and recrossed; but, for a long time, the result was doubtful. At last, however, the poor animal slackened his pace, staggered, and lay down, but again proceeded, though apparently with pain and difficulty. Seeing this, I redoubled my exertions, and having succeeded in turning him toward the Lake, I drove him right into the water, which was here shallow, and where he several times stuck fast in the mud. I now felt sure of my quarry; and, having approached sufficiently near, I seized him by the wounded leg, and severed the tendon at the knee-joint. The struggle between us now became severe. On trying to lay hold of his horns, which were most formidable weapons, with the intentions of cutting his throat, he struck out with so much violence as to upset me, and I was nearly smothered with mud and water. But the poor creature's course was run. His loss of blood and crippled state soon enabled me to put an end to his miseries. He was a noble old stag — the finest antelope of the species that I ever shot, and they were many; he well rewarded me for all my exertions.

Charles John Andersson, *Lake Ngami; Or, Explorations and Discoveries During Four Years' Wanderings in the Wilds of Southwestern Africa* (Harper & Brothers, 1856), pp. 458-60. Half-English, half-Swedish, Andersson led two expeditions to Africa. Typical of the kind of 'lunatic fringe' who found their way to the 'Dark Contintent' in those times, the intrepid Andersson had quite the time of it, shooting indiscriminately at anything that moved. Whether to believe half of what he wrote is another matter altogether. Even imagining visually the "exertions" described in the quoted passage is difficult. More lunacy in *The Okavango River* (Harper & Brothers, 1861).

Many wildebeest, streaming toward the highlands, cross the south end of Lake Lagarja, the headwaters of the Olduvai stream that cut the famous gorge; like almost all lakes of this volcanic region, it is a shallow magadi or soda lake of natron — native sodium carbonate in solution. In the low woods by the donga that drains the plateau to the west, a family of five cheetah lived that winter in the airy shadow of umbrella thorn, and greater and lesser flamingos, drawn to the soda lake's rich algal broth, rose in pink waves between the dark files of animals crossing the water. Since gnu are ever willing to stampede, the crossing is a hazard for the calves, and one morning of early winter more than six hundred drowned. Death passed among them like a windstorm, and its wake was awesome, yet the carcasses littered along the lake shore were but a third of one per cent of this antelope's annual regeneration in the Serengeti. Bloated calves had been dragged ashore by lions and hyenas, and others floated, snagged on mud reefs in the foamy shallows. In the thick heat of central Africa a stench so terrible clings to the throat; death had settled in the windless air like a foul mist. Among the carcasses, probing and sweeping, stepped elegant avocets and stilts, ignoring the taint in the stained water, and vulture and marabou in thousands had cleared the skies to accumulate at the feast. These legions of great greedy-beaked birds could soon drive off any intruder, but they are satisfied to squabble filthily among themselves; the vulture worms its long naked neck deep into the putrescence, and comes up, dripping, to drive off its kin with awful hisses.

Matthiessen & Porter, *The Tree Where Man Was Born/The African Experience*, p. 88.

Once upon a time a warthog took shelter in a cave. A lion suddenly entered the cave. The warthog immediately pretended to support the roof of the cave with its tusks and called plaintively: "Lion, lion, help me hold up the roof for it is falling and we shall both be killed." Thereupon the lion held up the roof with his paws. The warthog then said to him: "You are much stronger than I. Just hold up the roof while I fetch some logs to prop it up." The vain lion was flattered and agreed to stay. And the warthog escaped.

Schaller, *Golden Shadows, Flying Hooves*, p. 174.

The Serengeti Plains spread from Lake Nyaraza, in Tanganyika, northward beyond the lower boundaries of Kenya Colony. They are the great sanctuary of the Masai People and they harbour more wild game than any similar territory in all of East Africa. In the season of drought they are as dry and tawny as the coats of the lion that prowl them, and during the rains they provide the benison of soft grass to all the animals in a child's picture book.

They are endless and they are empty, but they are as warm with life as the waters of a tropic sea. They are webbed with the paths of eland and wildebeest and Thompson's [sic] gazelle and their hollows and valleys are trampled by thousands of zebra. I have seen a herd of buffalo invade the pastures under the occasional thorn tree groves and, now and then, the whimsically fashioned figure of a plodding rhino has moved along the horizon like a grey boulder come to life and adventure bound. There are no roads. There are no villages, no towns, no telegraph. There is nothing, as far as you can see, or walk, or ride, except grass and rocks and a few trees and the animals that live there.

Markham, *West with The Night*, p. 33.

As elephants go there was, I suppose, nothing very remarkable about this couple: they were medium-sized beasts with rather short tusks, and they were feeding on a clump of bushes with that quiet aldermanic dignity that one usually associates with the species. But this hardly describes the sensations that are almost bound to overtake anyone on first seeing elephants from close at hand in their natural surroundings. One has a moment of panic, of course, but it soon passes, and presently you find yourself absorbed in the simple act of watching. Elephants, when they are not hunted or disturbed, create a curious area of calm in the bush. A kind of a hush surrounds them, an air of quiet inevitability; and this in turn seems to have a reassuring effect not only on you yourself, the observer, but upon all the other animals — the water-buck, the

wildebeest and even the warthogs — that may happen to be grazing in the same valley. It is not the dull calm of the herds of munching buffaloes. There is here a certain fastidiousness, a sense of great power used very gently and deliberately. All this no doubt can be noticed in any circus or menagerie, but nothing can quite describe the delicacy with which the wild elephant selects and breaks off the exact bunch of leaves he wants, and then stows it neatly into his tricorne mouth with a rhythmical pendulum motion of his trunk. When he has had enough of one tree and moves on to the next his footfalls never make a sound.

…He stands there lording it out in the open plain for everyone to see, and his perambulation to the river for his midday bath is progress in the grand manner, not a stealthy nervous business as it is with the other animals.

…As you drive up to a herd every member of it will turn and face in your direction, and for a few moments, like a ballet in slow motion, there are a series of changes in the pattern of their position.

Moorehead, *No Room in the Ark*, pp. 46-7.

They [the jackals] had just entered the duneslope woodlands when Mate [the female jackal] began dancing around something on the ground ahead, her tail waving in the air. Captain [the male] rushed to her and found a nine-foot black mamba, one of Africa's most poisonous snakes, its body reared three feet off the ground and ready to strike. The mamba's tongue flicked in and out, its sinister coffin-shaped head drawn back like a crossbow ready to fire.

Captain feinted this way and that, trying to get past the snake's defenses. But the beady eyes tracked him like a missile. Wherever he moved, the mamba adjusted itself, waiting.

Mate moved around until she was opposite Captain, with the snake between them. She darted toward it, and for an instant it was distracted. With a motion too quick to follow, Captain lunged for the mamba, but it had recovered its attention and it struck. Several feet of its long ropy body sprang off the ground as Captain dodged away in a shower of sand, the lethal head barely missing his shoulder.

Instantly he was back on the attack, pouncing again and again, and each time the mamba struck, he jumped away. He would not let up; after each strike, the snake was taking a little longer to rear and prepare for another attack.

It was when the mamba was trying to recover after a miss that Captain managed to nip it hard on the back. Tired and injured, it tried to crawl away. But Mate blocked the retreat, and it raised itself and made another thrust, just missing Captain when he charged forward. Before it could escape, he bit it hard about three feet back from the head, and then again. It was writhing now. Finally, after several more bites, he held it for a split second and shook it violently, its coils squirming about his legs. Then he dropped it, and grabbing the dangerous head, crushed it in his jaws.

At that point the perilous hunt became a comedy. As soon as Captain seized the mamba's head, Mate grabbed its tail. In contrast to their supreme cooperation of just seconds before, they now began yanking at either end of the snake in a tug of war, each trying to run off with the prize. They glared, eyes blazing and ears laid back, along several feet of reptile. Their hackles bristled and their tails slashed as they seesawed back and forth, until finally the snake was yanked into two equal lengths of stringy white meat. Each began feeding feverishly; it took them nearly ten minutes to finish. Then they rolled in the grass, sniffed noses, rubbed faces, and trotted off together on a border patrol of their territory, their bellies round and bouncing.

Mark & Delia Owens, *Cry of the Kalahari*, pp. 62 3.

released my thoughts to roam the past, back to a time when this land still lay waiting for the first human voice. It is a Pleistocene vision, which imparts a primordial feeling of well-being as if one's existence still depended on these animals.

Schaller, *Golden Shadows, Flying Hooves*, p. 27.

Plate 22. Motherhood.

Within a day after a rain, shoots of grass emerge to impart a soft sheen of green to the somber terrain. These blades of grass, so fragile and modest, are the foundation of the Serengeti's character, for without them the vast aggregations of hoofed animals would not be able to exist. The Serengeti holds many pleasant memories: of silence on the plains at night, of the last streak of evening gold on a hill, but, most of all, memories of the immense herds. Standing on a rise and seeing the inexhaustible vigor of life — the wildebeest and zebra, the gazelle, wherever my eyes came to rest — made my heart leap with delight. In the words of Shakespeare: "O wonderful, wonderful, and most wonderful, wonderful! and yet again wonderful..." The sight

At the present time big game photography has largely superseded big game shooting.

In my youth, the only animals that were photographed were dead animals. This made the problem of animal photography very simple. After your client had shot his trophy, he posed on the dead beast while you clicked the camera. But today people are determined to secure pictures of living animals. The animals seldom care to cooperate. A white hunter guiding a photographer has a difficult task.

At first, photography was combined with shooting. This never gave good results. A man must use either a camera or a gun — not both. The requirements of the two sports are very different.

A sportsman wants his trophy. He cares nothing about weather conditions or the pose of the beast. A photographer must have the sun in a certain position and the animal out in the open so he can get a good, clear picture. . . .

. . .

Photographing game animals is frequently far more difficult than shooting them. Shooting an animal only takes an instant, but getting satisfactory pictures requires a long time.

Hunter, *Hunter*, pp. 232-3.

The visible time levels of Serengeti are unexpected. In one corner of the Ngorongoro Crater there are mysterious graves of a long-faced, long-headed people dating back three thousand years; to the northwest of the plain there is a Beau Geste-style fortress built by the Germans during their occupancy of Tanganyika at the turn of the century; at the center, near Seronera, pottery remnants from thirty thousand years ago have been traced to ancestors of the Wanderobo, a tribe still living in Serengeti; the giraffe, leopard, and hyena have lived there for two and a half million years without significant evolutionary change, the crocodile for a hundred and forty million years. Some of the rocks near Banagi are the oldest on earth — three thousand million years old. It is the sense of space, however, that is most immediately striking: sky traces the flat, green horizon for three hundred and sixty degrees, at once frightening and oddly liberating, as though one could wander for days in any direction without coming to the end of it.

Even the dirt underfoot is exotic; a kind of clay called black cotton soil, it is nonporous and does not immediately absorb the crashing rains that may fall with only a moment's notice. At the end of the dry season when the plain is grazed out or leveled by brushfires, rain summons the green shoots to reassemble; the red oat grasses grow an inch in the first two days of rainfall. Winds descending from the active Lengai volcano swirl loose lava sediments into huge black hills some twenty feet in height; the hills inch their way across the grass. Otherwise the plain is impeccable, policed by a chain of scavengers from lion through maggot flies, each taking its turn, so that a buffalo dying will be reduced in a matter of days to horn and skull glistening white against the dark-blue sky. One feels an instinctive sense of identification, of having felt the place even though never before having seen it. Once, when we wandered off the road and slowly over the plain, with hundreds of thousands of animals all about us parting leisurely to make an avenue for our vehicle to pass, the sky suddenly turned black and the rain pounded down in opaque flats turning the plain almost instantly into a shallow sea bottomed by the stubborn cotton soil. We made it back to the road but that, too, was quickly flooded out, and to go forward, one of us had to walk shin deep through the new sea to guide the road's edge. At such times is the wrenching strength of the place frighteningly visible; where the streams run, bridges are washed down, and water snaps white at elbows of the raging streams.

Another time, tenting out near Seronera west of the center of the plain, I was by myself fixing breakfast when I heard a low rumble, like thunder, off across the plain to the east. There were yellow-fever trees between me and the source of the noise, and as I squinted into the sun, I saw the first of an enormous herd of wildebeest emerging from behind the trees on a course directly across the right front of my camp site. On and on they came, thousands of them, and they were running at full stride, all out, shoulder to shoulder. When at last they had gone, the sense of

quiet and space returned, and Serengeti's sense of timelessness.

Serengeti's wildebeest are the last substantial gathering of the animal on earth, the last vast herd of any land mammal, and there are so many of them, they directly condition all forms of life on the plain. They are everywhere, feeding the lion at one end of the food chain, and at the other, tiny larvae inside the decaying wildebeest skull which, emerging as caterpillars, feed on the inner stuffs of the horns before they turn into moths and fly away. In the west, where the wildebeest churn the lakeshores to mud, fish come near the surface seeking clearer water; awaiting them are a variety of birds that have trailed the wildebeest in anticipation of the feast.

Hayes, *The Last Place on Earth*, pp. 57-8.

In one way, photographers are much like sportsmen. No matter how fine a trophy a sportsman secures, he always wants to get one a little bit better. So it is with a camera fiend. No matter what pictures he takes, he keeps trying for something more startling. The lengths to which these men will go is amazing. I took out one party that spent weeks photographing lions in every conceivable position. After they had pictured lions feeding at a kill, resting under thorn trees, and trotting after the lorry, they wanted the beasts to take still other poses. I tried every trick I knew. I hung an antelope carcass from a tree limb so the lions would jump for it. I had a carcass dragged past the lorry so the lions, following the scent, would walk parallel to the camera, thus affording a different type of shot. But all this had been done before by other photographic safaris and my party wanted to surpass their rivals. Finally one man had a brilliant idea.

"Why don't we get a picture of lions and humans at dinner together?" he suggested. "It'll be terrific! Never before photographed!"

No sooner said than done. We set up a table with a linen cloth and a vase of flowers. Places were laid and chairs put in place. Vegetable salad, fruit, and beer were the bill of fare. A zebra was shot and dragged alongside the table. I had it carefully staked down to make sure the lions did not pull it out of focus of the camera. The three cameramen took their positions in the truck while the rest of the party sat down at the table.

I fired my rifle a few times to attract the lions. Shortly, a pride came hurrying along toward us. In a few minutes they were hard at work on the zebra. Now the cinema cameras began to purr. Shaking natives in white robes served the meal, their courage having been much strengthened by a liberal distribution of baksheesh. The two meals progressed within a few yards of each other, the lions caring not a whit what we did as long as we left them alone to finish their meal.

Hunter, *Hunter*, pp. 237-8. Has anyone ever *seen* these photographs?

I have watched a herd of elephants a mile long in single file head to tail in the water crossing together a river in the Congo, appearing like a long line of porpoises. Sometimes the whole head of one would appear above the surface, but more often only the point of the trunk as they passed through deep water; then their heads and more and more of the body as the water got shallower, all keeping perfect line not in any way affected by the current, strong enough to take a good swimming horse a mile down-stream or more before effecting a crossing, and too strong to row against. At the landing side a big bull or two will be there to meet them, just to let them know that all is clear that side and welcome them.

Daly, *Big Game Hunting and Adventure*, p. 177.

But it was the flat-topped acacias over which we exclaimed aloud and which made us look up from the animals grazing underneath them to the branches above. Clean in outline as a wineglass, the ribs flare upward with such harmonious variations that approaching a tree, passing, looking back, is like circling a perfectly conceived sculpture — never quite the same from any two points yet always in balance. The flat top is no more than a single layer of lace against the sky from which hang — on one side of the tree only, and like decorations from a Christmas tree — the round golden balls of the weaverbirds'

longest. They met at an appointed spot and set to work; about noon, the elephant, whose hunger was satisfied, lay down to rest; he awoke after several hours' sleep, and with great surprise observed the cock still scratching and pecking amongst the grass. He then again began to eat in the pasture, but once more he was satisfied and retired, still leaving (with growing astonishment) the cock eating. The sun was near setting, when the cock jumped upon the elephant's back, who had been lying down for some time; soon after the elephant felt his skin pecked.

" 'What are you doing?' said he, half frightened.

" 'Nothing. I am only seeking the insects that are in your bristles.'

"The great pachyderm, terrifed at such persistent voracity, rose and fled as if he were mad; from that day the elephant flees whenever he hears the cock crow."

Belief in this story is so firmly rooted in the minds of the Dinka, that they provide themselves with a cock every time they

nests; they are the perfect finishing touch to the trees' straight-stemmed, clean-branched austerity. They must love the earth at Seronera, for they grow forty, fifty feet tall there and gather into the circumference of their shade large herds of gazelles...

Ames, *A Glimpse Of Eden*, p. 106.

"*Once upon a time, there was a challenge between an elephant and a cock as to which could continue eating the*

make a journey by night.

Gaetano Casati, *Ten Years in Equatoria*, 2 vols (Negro University Press Edition, 1969), Vol. II, p. 49. A nineteeth-century fable, in which the poor elephant is pressed into its usual role: straightman to all the other creatures of the forests or plains.

[Conscientious big-game hunters whenever possible tried to ensure that the animal that they had shot was really dead. This was a matter both of humaneness and of safety. Wounded lions or leopards especially often attacked or lived on to become man-eaters, because their wounds prevented them from catching wild game. But finishing off a wounded animal provided the principal danger in hunting; a wounded cat, for example, often concealed itself in a thicket, and the hunter had to go find it. If the quarry had been only slightly injured and was determined to kill the hunter, a deadly game ensued. This is what happened to Carl Akeley, the famous American naturalist and collector, in the semidesert country of Somalia. Dusk was descending, while Akeley was reconnoitering for a dead hyena.]

...a faint sound attracted my attention. Glancing quickly to one side, I got a glimpse of a shadowy form moving stealthily behind a bush. . . .Then I did a very foolish thing.Without a clear sight of what I was shooting at, I fired hastily into the bush. Immediately came an answer. The snarl and guttural profanity of a leopard told me, in no uncertain words, what kind of customer I was taking chances with.

Now a leopard is one of the most formidable of antagonists.

Plates 23 & 24. Flat-Topped Acacia. The most characteristic trees on the plains of East Africa, these acacias, once they are grown, confine by their very shape browsing by giraffes to their edges. The acacia's surface offers little resistance to (or attraction for) the drying wind. Its shade helps the soil below retain moisture and also attracts ungulates in the heat of midday, which animals deposit manure. Vegetation therefore thrives under these trees, plants in turn eventually harvested by these same ungulates (and others). Of the fifty or so acacia species found in Africa, the three best known are the yellow-barked fever trees, the whistling thorn, and the acacia tortilis (pictured).

He has every one of the nine lives attributed to the cat. To kill him you have got to kill him from the tip of his nose to the tip of his tail, and at that to 'kill him dead' as the old hunters say. Added to his 'nine lives,' a leopard, unlike a lion, is vindictive, and a leopard when wounded will fight to an absolute finish, ninety-nine times out of a hundred, no matter how many chances he has to make his escape. When once he is aroused, a leopard displays the most marked determination to fight. And fight he will if he ever takes hold. He claws and bites, without stopping, until his victim is torn to shreds.

Now, when I heard the leopard growl all these things flashed through my mind, and I began to look about for the best way out of it. I had no wish to force an issue with a possibly wounded leopard when it was so late I could not see my gun sights and when there was no second gun.

I now determined to leave the leopard until morning. If it had been wounded there might then be a chance of finding it. . . .

But what I had started, the leopard was now fully determined to finish. With my eyes straining at the base of that bush, I suddenly became aware...of a shadow moving slowly across the bed of the tug. It was the beast crossing the tug only twenty yards away from me. I began to shoot at once, though again I could not see to aim. It was so nearly dark that all I could see was where the bullets struck as the sand spurted up beside the leopard. My first bullet was beyond the target, the second was lower but still too high, but at the third shot, the leopard stopped. I had scored at last.

The leopard stopped in her tracks and I thought she was killed. My pony boy, of whose presence I had become totally unconscious, now broke into a wild song just behind me — the Somali song of triumph which they chant loudly whenever the master has killed a dangerous animal. But the native's song

quickly came to a sudden end. Another song burst forth on the evening stillness. It sealed the Somali's lips and it paralyzed me with terror. It was the voice of an enraged and vicious leopard, the snarling, cursing and guttural coughing, which it emits at the moment of its swift and fearful charge. In that moment when I still stood there benumbed with fear, I caught a glimpse of a lithe and yellow body springing up out of the gray sand. She was coming straight for me. For just a flash I was gripped with horror at the sight of the furious beast, then I was suddenly possessed with power for the quickest action. I worked the bolt of my gun. No answer! The magazine was empty. At the same instant, I realized that the solid point cartridge rested in the palm of my left hand, the one which as I had come up to the dead hyena, I had intended to replace with a soft nose. Now, if I could only escape the leopard until I could get that cartridge into the chamber! As the leopard scrambled up the left bank of the island, I dropped down the other side and ran toward the point from which she had charged — shoving the cartridge into my gun. Now all this took perhaps twenty seconds but in those few seconds I thought of many things — but not the misdeeds of my past life. There was no time for that. But I did think very clearly of what I was up against.

Around the camp fire we had discussed the possibilities of such an encounter and it had been agreed that if a man were attacked by a leopard the best thing was for him to fall on his face in order to avoid being disemboweled by the terrible action of the leopard's strong, knife-like hind claws. This would put it up to the gunbearer or companion to take care of the leopard. But I now realized that I must face the leopard the instant I could get that blessed cartridge in place because the [Somali] had no gun, and I also thought that the big cat might easily attack the [Somali] and that it would be my job to go to his assistance.

As the twentieth second ticked off and with my gun ready, I wheeled. Immediately I was face to face with the leopard in mid-air. My trusty rifle was knocked flying from my hands and in my arms was the leopard — eighty pounds of furious blood-thirsty cat. I knew she intended to sink her teeth into my throat and hold me tight in the grip of her jaws and forepaws while with her hind paws she dug out my stomach — for this practice is the pleasant way of leopards. But unexpectedly enough and most happily for me, she missed her aim. Instead of clutching my throat she struck me high in the chest and caught my upper right arm in her mouth. Thus not only was my throat saved but her hind legs were left hanging clear where they could not reach my stomach.

With my left arm I seized her throat and tried to wrench my right arm free, but this I could do only little by little. When I got grip enough on her throat to loosen her hold just a bit, she would seize and set her jaws again in my arm an inch or two further down. In this way, I drew the full length of my arm inch by inch through her slavering poisonous mouth. During all this time I was not conscious of any pain whatsoever but only of the sound of the crushing of tense muscles and the choking, snarling grunts of the infuriated beast. As I pushed her jaws farther and farther down my arm, I bent over and finally, when my arm was almost free, I fell to the ground — the leopard underneath me. My right hand was now in her mouth, my left hand clutched at her throat, my knees were on her chest, my elbows in her armpits which spread her front legs so far apart that her frantic clawing did nothing more than tear my shirt. Here we both struggled for life, man and beast. We were both determined to die hard. The leopard writhed and twisted her

body in an effort to get hold of the ground and turn herself over, but the loose shifting sand offered her no hold or purchase.

For a moment there was no change in our positions; and then after a little, I had a glimmer of hope. For the first time, I began to think I had a chance to win this strange and deadly flight. Up to that moment, I had been fighting a good fight in which I had expected to lose, but now I began to be aware that I had the advantage. Now if I could only keep my vantage ground, perhaps the pony boy would come to my assistance with his knife. I shouted and called to him but to no avail. The boy was out of earshot or else he was too frightened to answer.

Now during all this time, my original state of abject, helpless terror had changed utterly into one of complete physical anaesthesia and of the greatest mental activity. All dread of death had vanished and the only sense of physical hurt I had at all was toward the end, when with my hand shoved down her throat, my thumb was pinched by the animal's molars. And as the leopard was crunching my arm I recalled vividly a day at the World's Columbian Exposition in Chicago when I had stood with a medical friend before a bronze sculpture of a man in a death struggle with a bear. The bear was crushing the man's arms between his jaws. We had speculated on the probable sensations of a man under such conditions. Would he be sensitive to physical pain or not? And I now thought, "At last I have the answer to our question!" How I longed to tell my doctor friend. But there would never be a chance, for I should soon be killed, I thought as I fought on with a fierce joy — an exultation that can come only in a hand-to-hand battle for life where there is at least a fighting chance.

I still held on to the leopard. I contiued to shove my right hand down her throat so far and so hard that she could not close her jaws. With my other hand I gripped her throat in a strangle hold. Then I surged down hard upon her with my knees, putting all the power in them I could muster. To my surprise, I felt a rib break. I began to feel sure of myself. I did it again. Another rib cracked. Then I felt her relax, a sort of easing up and letting go, though she continued to struggle. Now, at the same time I felt myself weakening in like manner. I had done my utmost. Soon it would become a question as to which one would give up first. But I re-summoned my failing strength and held on to the big cat and thrust my knees down on her chest again. Little by little her struggling ceased. The fight was finished. My strength had outlasted hers.

. . .

As I later looked at the leopard, I concluded that what had saved me was the first shot I had fired at the beast when she went into the bush. That shot had hit and shattered her right hind foot. It sas this broken foot which threw out the aim of her first spring at me and made her seize my arm instead of my throat. It was also this wounded foot which made it difficult for her to use her legs effectively in an attempt to disembowel me.

Carl E. & Mary L. (Jobe) Akeley, *Lions, Gorillas and Their Neighbors* (Dodd, Mead, 1932), pp. 221-8. This famous passage, embellished from the first telling in Akeley's *In Brightest Africa* (pp. 96-101), has become one of the most repeated leopard stories. In addition to being a naturalist and conservationist, Akeley was a photographer, inventor, sculptor, and taxidermist. In these last two guises, Akeley was the man most responsible for mounting and displaying animals for the first time in natural poses, using plaster casts and real preserved skins. Faithful to the true skeletal and muscular underpinnings of his subjects, Akeley revolutionized taxidermy. He planned the African Hall in the American Museum of Natural History, which display was ultimately named after him. The leopard attack occurred during his first trip, in 1896, to Africa. On his second trip, ten years later, he was mauled by an enraged elephant, a description of which follows. On a subsequent collecting trip, he fell ill with fever and died. He was buried at Kabara on Mt. Mikeno in the Volcanoes in what was then the Belgian Congo.

While still warming my hands, inspecting the cartridges, and standing with the gun leaning against my stomach, I was suddenly conscious that an elephant was almost on top of me. I have no knowledge of how the warning came. I have no mental record of hearing him, seeing him, or of any warning from the gun boy who faced me and who must have seen the elephant as he came down on me from behind. There must have been some definite signal, but it was not recorded in my mind. I only know that as I picked up my gun and wheeled about I tried to shove the safety catch forward. It refused to budge, and I remember the thought that perhaps I had left the catch forward when I inspected the gun and that if not I must pull the triggers hard enough to fire the gun anyway. This is an impossibility, but I remember distinctly the determination to do it, for the all-powerful impulse in my mind was that I must shoot instantly. Then something happened that dazed me. I don't know whether I shot or not. My next mental record is of a tusk right at my chest. I grabbed it with my left hand, the other one with my right hand, and swinging in between them went to the ground on my back. This swinging in between the tusks was purely automatic. It was the result of many a time on the trails imagining myself caught by an elephant's rush and planning what I would do, and a very profitable planning, too; for I am convinced that if a man imagines such a crisis and plans what he would do, he will, when the occasion occurs, automatically do what he planned. Anyway, I firmly believe that my imaginings along the trail saved my life.

He drove his tusks into the ground on either side of me, his curled-up trunk against my chest. I had a realization that I was being crushed, and as I looked into one wicked little eye above me I knew I could expect no mercy from it. This thought was perfectly clear and definite in my mind. I heard a wheezy grunt as he plunged down and then — oblivion.

The thing that dazed me was a blow from the elephant's trunk as he swung it down to curl it back out of harm's way. It broke my nose and tore my cheek open to the teeth. Had it been an intentional blow it would have killed me instantly. The part of the trunk that scraped off most of my face was the heavy bristles on the knuckle-like corrugations of the skin of the under side.

When he surged down on me, his big tusks evidently struck something in the ground that stopped them. Of course my body offered practically no resistance to his weight, and I should have been crushed as thin as a wafer if his tusks hadn't met that resistance — stone, root, or something — underground. He seems to have thought me dead for he left me — by some good fortune not stepping on me — and charged off after the boys. I never got much information out of the boys as to what did happen, for they were not proud of their part in the adventure. However, there were plenty of signs that the elephant had run out into the open space again and charged all over it; so it is reasonable to assume that they had scattered through it like a covey of quail and that he had trampled it down trying to find the men whose tracks and wind filled the neighbourhood.

Usually, when an elephant kills a man, it will return to its victim and gore him again, or trample him, or pull his legs or arms off with its trunk. I knew of one case where a man's porters brought in his arm which the elephant that had killed him had pulled off his body and left lying on the ground. In my case, happily, the elephant for some reason did not come back. I lay unconscious for four or five hours. In the meanwhile, when they found the coast was clear, the porters and gun boys returned and made camp, intending, no doubt, to keep guard over my body until Mrs. Akeley, to whom they had sent word, could reach me. They did not, however touch me, for they believed that I was dead, and neither the Swahili Mohammedans nor the Kikuyus will touch a dead man. So they built a fire and huddled around it and I lay unconscious in the cold mountain rain at a little distance, with my body crushed and my face torn open. About five o'clock I came to in a dazed way and was vaguely conscious of seeing a fire. I shouted, and a little later I felt myself being carried by the shoulders and legs.

> Akeley, *In Brightest Africa*, pp. 47-50. This trip, whose primary purpose was to collect a family elephant group for the New York American Museum of Natural History, proved a nightmare for Akeley. He repeatedly fell ill — the succession of ailments included meningitis and blackwater fever, often fatal at that time — and was nursed throughout by his wife Delia. It is no exaggeration to say that Delia repeatedly saved Akeley's life, and, indeed, it was Delia who rescued him after the elephant mauling. The Akeleys were divorced in 1923. Carl remarried (to Mary Lee Jobe) in 1924 and died two years later. Delia's contributions thereafter tended to be belittled by commentators, including Akeley's second wife, who wrote prodigiously (and always omitted serious mention of Delia). The remarkable story of Delia Akeley is brilliantly sketched in a chapter of Elizabeth Fagg Olds, *Women of the Four Winds* (Houghton Mifflin, 1985).

Worn out from a rough morning hunt, we returned to camp on the Sand River in Masailand around noon. My two Mexican clients had just shot a rhino each, and everyone was ready for a nap. . . .

For many days we had been trying to attract a big leopard by hanging game carcasses in trees...That morning, I had promised my clients we would spend the late afternoon waiting near a bait that had been fed on, but at 5:00 P.M., when I woke up with a start, it was almost too late. But I decided to try anyway. In my rush to get moving, I didn't take my favorite rifle but, rather, a .475 double ejector that happened to be lying on the mess table. I hustled my clients into a safari car, and we all tore off to the leopard bait.

It was almost six o'clock [ed. — about forty-five minutes from complete darkness!] when the three of us crawled into our blind and settled in at the little "window." I was convinced we had missed our big chance when suddenly a blurry movement caught my eye. The leopard, a hulking, burly old tom, had just streaked up the trunk of the bait tree. Next moment he was perched on a heavy branch, staring crankily down at the game carcass dangling below.

Motionless and in plain view, the cat was a perfect broadside shot. He looked like the biggest, easiest target in a shooting gallery. Both clients had agreed to fire at the same time; surely one of them would hit him right.

Both clients fired. The leopard streaked down the tree, growling, raced across forty yards of open ground, and disappeared into thick bush...

I immediately sent a man up the tree to look for blood spots or bulletholes in the wood. One shot had splintered the branch on which the leopard was standing. Whichever of my clients fired that bullet had, at twenty yards, missed his mark by two feet. . . .

The other client had missed the tree, so at least there was a chance he had hit the leopard — somewhere. But not one speck of blood could we find.

. . .

While my clients waited in the blind, I sent [the skinner] to search for blood...He was just approaching the nearest thicket when suddenly I heard growling, followed by a shout, and saw the leopard streak. . .straight toward him. . . .

Unarmed and completely surprised, my poor skinner spun around and ran. He never knew what real running was until he heard that leopard growling right behind him. As they both rushed past me, I threw the .475 to my shoulder and let off both barrels in quick succession. The big cat buckled up and went down with a bullet in the belly, just as my panicky skinner tripped over his own feet into the knee-high grass. They both disappeared as though the ground had opened under their feet.

At first I thought the cat was dead. He had collapsed immediately on being hit; and the bullet I had slammed through him was made for killing elephant. I watched the grass where he had fallen and saw no movement, heard no growling.

Then, as I was about to reload, I saw his head appear above the grass. He was coming for me in a way that didn't leave any doubt about what he wanted.

I didn't even have time to eject the empty cases from my rifle, let alone push in two more shells. I grabbed the weapon and, using it like a cricket bat, clobbered the leopard just as he sprang at my chest and knocked me down. . . .

I landed face down with the cat on my back, but immediately rolled over and started to grapple with him. . . .we fought it out, thrashing about on the ground, yelling, growling, rolling back and forth. The leopard bit and clawed my arms, hands, and clothing to shreds. . . .

I finally managed to get on top of the leopard and tried to wring his neck. But with both my hands around his throat I couldn't control the rest of him, and his claws tore deep furrows in my arms. I tried to hold his front legs down with one hand while choking him with the other. But one hand wasn't enough to do either. I ended up getting badly bitten and scratched at the same time. . .

By now the two Mexicans had left the blind and joined [my skinner]. They all stood a short distance away, jabbering frantically in Spanish and Swahili. Suddenly the skinner yelled in Swahili, "You don't kill my bwana!" I shot a quick glance over my shoulder. One of the Mexicans was aiming in my direction, and the skinner was trying to wrestle the rifle away from him. This was the chap who had missed the leopard at twenty yards with a solid rest to shoot from. He now wanted to shoot the animal from standing position at twice that range — with me sitting on top of it! I was fighting a wounded cat with my bare hands, while expecting any second to get a super-high-velocity quick-expanding bullet up the arse.

My bout with the leopard lasted less than a minute. While I sat on him, still trying to wring his neck, he suddenly weakened. My .475 bullet was taking effect at last.

"My First Leopard Mauling," by Eric Rundgren, "professional hunter," as quoted in James Mellon et al., *African Hunter* (Safari Press, 1975), pp. 157-60.

Hunting, from the earliest antiquity, has formed no less the favourite pastime of the mightiest monarchs, than the chosen exercise of the most exalted heroes. Poets and minstrels have made the merrye greene-wode the theme and burthen of their wild song. Philosophers and sages have lauded the sylvan craft, as combining exercise to the body, with delight and entertainment to the mind; whilst painters and sculptors have made it the subject of the noblest creations of their skill and genius. The ancient schools instructed those who were destined for deeds of high emprize, to contest with the swiftest of the wild beasts in speed, with the boldest in strength, and with the most cunning in craft and subtilty...Victories gained over the savage tenants of the forest constantly formed the prelude to heroic exploits in war; — and the splendid monuments which transmitted to after ages the military achievements of the Emperors of Rome, not unfrequently blended with their most celebrated triumphs, the glories of the chase. The pages of history record the high estimation in which our own ancestors, from the rudest periods, have regarded this noble diversion. Princes and statesmen have alike been its protectors; and whilst men of the greatest genius in Europe have not disdained to share in the excitement it affords, oriental potentates have far eclipsed the more civilized nations of the glo[b]e, in the splendour and magnificence with which they have indulged in the engrossing fascinations of the field.

Of those who have taken up the unpretending Narrative of my recent adventures in the wilds of Southern Africa, to which the present volume may be considered to form an amplification, few will deny that to wander through a fairy-land of sport, among the independent denizens of the wide wilderness, — realizing, as it were, a new and fabled creation amid scenes never before paced by civilized foot, — is in itself so truly spirit-stirring and romantic, that in spite of the many hardships and privations which are inseparable from a campaign directed against the ferae naturae, the witchcraft of the desert must prove irresistible. Nor will any one who reflects that the regions I traversed were either totally depopulated, or very sparingly inhabited, complain, that my attention should have been so exclusively directed to the brute creation, which presented to the traveller the most prominent as well as the most engrossing objects of contemplation. In a region "where the grim lion prowls monarch of all he surveys," my interviews with the wild races of the human species were necessarily few and far between; and it seldom fell to my fortune to have opportunities of studying the natural history of those primitive children of the desert.

Africa, it is well known, is the great nursery of many of the most noble and interesting forms that exist in the animal kingdom. Her southern regions, which extend into the temperate zone, are surrounded on three sides by the ocean; and being divided from the milder climates of the northern hemisphere by the torrid belt that intervenes, are tenanted by a vast nation of indigenous quadrupeds. The grizzled Monarch of the forest — the stupendous Elephant — and the shapeless River Horse; — the mailed Rhinoceros — the gaily painted Zebra — and the richly arrayed Ostrich; — all claim alike some portion of her savage soil as the lot of their inheritance. An endless variety of grotesque and bulky ruminants also, offer to the keen disciple of "the mighty Hunter," quarrees *no less glorious than eccentric. The towering Giraffe, by whose lofty side man dwindles to the stature of a pigmy: — the malevolent and stately Buffalo,*

> *"With fiery eyes and angry roar*
> *And feet that stamp, and horns that gore." —*

the mild, though ponderous Eland, enveloped in a goodly garment of its own fat; — the fantastic Gnoo, with its scarcely less terrific-looking congener — the Unicorn-resembling Oryx, and the regal Koodoo; — the proud group of Aigoceri, and the graceful family of star-eyed Gazelles; — together with a whole host of subordinates, descending by fair gradations, link by link, to that tiniest of sylvan denizens, the Caerulean Antelope, and collectively filling the place which in other countries is occupied by the cervine race — all advance their hereditary title to a share in the trackless plateaux *of that mighty portion of the earth.*

. . .

..."To study animals with accuracy," *says the observant Buffon,* "we ought to view them in their savage state; — to accompany them into the retreats which they have chosen for themselves; — to follow them into the deep caverns, — and to attend them on the frightful precipices where they enjoy unbounded liberty." *Devoted to wood-craft from the craddle, my predilection for sylvan sports has afforded me all the opportunities, alluded to by the great Naturalist, of waxing intimate with the dappled denizens of the grove and waste to an extent, which abler artists and more finished Zoologists have necessarily been denied. I have beheld the venerable and half-reasoning Elephant browsing in native majesty among his own contemporary trees,* "in his huge strength impregnable;" *— have torn the much-prized ivory from his giant jaws, and plucked the horn from the saucy nose of the Rhinoceros. I have stripped the proud* spolia *from the shaggy shoulder of the* "king of beasts, who clears the desert with his rolling eye;" *— have humbled the haughty head of the forest bull; — and though* "she scorneth the horse and his rider," *have despoiled the fleet Ostrich of her costly plumes. More — I have dragged forth Behemoth,* "whose ribs are like bars of iron," *from his hiding place under the shady trees, in the covert of the reed and fens, — and have ridden familiarly by the side of the towering Zamor, the colossal glory of the wilderness, long classed with the wild chimeras of men's brain.*

W. Cornwallis Harris, *Portraits of the Game and Wild Animals of Southern Africa* (originally published in 1840; A.A. Balkema Edition, 1969), pp. 1-3. This was the first work entirely devoted to big-game hunting in Africa. An amazing, erudite, rambling dissertation, with notable artistry included, this volume more than any other in its time influenced many a man to go to Southern Africa to hunt.

My days [in the parks] *of East Africa gave me unforgettable glimpses of the world of nature as it was before the coming of modern man. To see African wild life in all its abundance and variety, living as it has always lived, was one of the most priceless experiences I have ever had. When I spotted a pride of lions resting lazily in the shade of a bush, when I watched warthogs trotting away, ugly yet curiously appealing with their self-*

important air, when I enjoyed the spectacle of hundreds of hissing vultures covering a cadaver and jackals and hyenas dashing into the seething mass to snap up some morsel, when I saw these and many other sights it was difficult to realize that most of the large game herds of Africa have been exterminated or drastically reduced and that very little wild life remains outside national parks and reserves.

Schaller, *The Year of the Gorilla*, p. 67.

...when a man approaches a herd looking for ivory, he is not likely to see much excepting tusks. It is natural, therefore, that from the ivory hunters we learn comparatively little of the more intimate things that we should like to know about the every-day life of the elephant. The world has no record of the knowledge of wild life that their experience should have given the ivory hunters.

It is for this reason that the camera hunters appeal to me as being so much more useful than the gun hunters. They have their pictures to show — still pictures and moving pictures — and when their game is over the animals are still alive to play another day. Moreover, according to any true conception of sport — the use of skill, daring, an endurance in overcoming difficulties — camera hunting takes twice the man that gun hunting takes. It is fortunate for the animals that camera hunting is becoming popular.

Akeley, *In Brightest Africa*, p. 155.

Yet I must admit that animals are sometimes remarkably tolerant of picture taking. I have watched in amazement while a group of photographers ducked in and out of brush within thirty yards or so of a herd of elephants, taking light readings, changing lenses, and assuming the most incredible poses to get unusual "angle shots." The elephants must have known that they were there and still the big brutes put up with their antics very patiently. After considering the matter carefully, I am convinced that the elephants thought that the photographers were a herd of baboons. Elephants are short-sighted, so this is a natural mistake for them to make under the circumstances.

Hunter, *Hunter*, p. 243.

He thought he saw an Elephant,
  That practised on a fife:
He looked again, and found it was
  A letter from his wife.
'At length I realize,' he said,
  'The bitterness of life!'

Lewis Carroll, *Sylvie and Bruno* (1889), Chapter 5. The introduction of the Mad Gardener.

Churchill in his journal tells us that if, while unarmed, you meet six or seven lions unexpectedly, all you need do is to speak to them sternly and that they will slink away, as you throw stones at them to hurry them up. "All the highest authorities recommend this," *he writes. But I doubt if he expects us to take him literally, and I for one would hesitate to put his theory to the test. I doubt also that my voice would carry the necessary authority. Something tells me that there would be a slight tremor.*

Roderick Cameron, *Equator Farm* (William Heinemann, 1955), p. 54.

The light fades in a display to surpass anything the immense sky has shown during the long African day with its many changes. The sun gets bigger as it falls faster. There is no slow decline to the day on the equator. A fireball stands on the horizon, dropping behind as you stand and stare. The last arc slips out of view and the sky is shot with the brief splendor of twilight. There is a flare and a glow, as is in the nature of this land of the brilliant and the transient.

Night falls. An hour ago there was full sunlight. Now there is darkness. The day ends suddenly with a glory that matches the sun's rising; how long ago the dawn seems now, much more than a day. Yet it is a day complete as a day ought to be, if one has not gotten too much out of touch with the rhythms of the natural world. Nothing essential has been left out. It takes time and a readiness to watch and see and listen, to learn what is new and not just what confirms "old-hand" beliefs. And then it

takes more time, and still more. Time passes; it is not chased. That is the attraction of Africa: it follows real time, not a clock-kept ticking.

Norman Myers, *The Long African Day*, p. 372. See Chapter I.

Breasting into the dawn, where the plains lay silent under the tears of dew, I wondered how I might find words to express that big, surrounding protection. It was as though everything had harmony of form and colour so that you were wrapped about with music, and a love so deep and vibrating that it flowed in upon one's consciousness continually, given by the trees, the sky, the very earth you walked upon. Uplifting was it to feel at last simplified, able to sail out of oneself on the wings of understanding; so that like a tree or a mountain you might look out untroubled above the world, no longer outside nature, but a part of it.

Vivienne de Watteville, *Out in the Blue* (Methuen, 1927), p. 219. Miss de Watteville began an East African safari with her father, not so much for sport as for collecting specimens for the Berne Museum in Switzerland. During

Plate 25. Fireball on the Horizon. Night falls quickly over most of Africa. Sunrise and sunset are two of nature's greatest spectacles.

the trip, the father was badly mauled by a lion and died shortly thereafter. The daughter managed to complete the safari, no small accomplishment in those times. The book is a testament to courage and determination but also a vivid description of the wild and beautiful character of the country traversed and its wildlife.

The elephant-hunters, or aggageers, exhibited their swords...[which] were bound with cord very closely from the guard for about nine inches along the blade, to enable them to be grasped by the right hand, while the hilt was held by the left; the weapon was thus converted into a two-handed sword. The scabbards were strengthened by an extra covering, formed of the skin of the elephant's ear.

In a long conversation with these men, I found a corroboration of all that I had previously heard of their exploits, and they described the various methods of killing the elephant with the sword. Those hunters who could not afford to purchase horses hunted on foot, in parties not exceeding two persons. Their method was to follow the tracks of an elephant, so as to arrive at their game between the hours of 10 A.M. and noon, at which time the animal is either asleep, or extremely listless, and easy to approach. Should they discover the animal asleep, one of the hunters would creep stealthily towards the head, and with one blow sever the trunk while stretched upon the ground; in which case the elephant would start upon his feet, while the hunters escaped in the confusion of the moment. The trunk severed would cause an haemorrhage sufficient to insure the death of the elephant within about an hour. On the other hand, should the animal be awake upon their arrival, it would be impossible to approach the trunk; in such a case, they would creep up from behind, and give a tremendous cut at the back sinew of the hind leg, about a foot above the heel. Such a blow would disable the elephant at once, and would render comparatively easy a second cut to the remaining leg; the arteries being divided, the animal would quickly bleed to death. These were the methods adopted by poor hunters, until, by the sale of ivory, they could purchase horses for the higher branch of the art. Provided with horses, the party of hunters should not exceed four. They start before daybreak, and ride slowly throughout the country in search of elephants, generally keeping along the course of a river until they come upon the tracks where a herd or a single elephant may have drunk during the night. When once upon the tracks, they follow fast towards the retreating game. The elephants may be twenty miles distant; but it matters little to the aggageers. At length they discover them, and the hunt begins. The first step is to single out the bull with the largest tusks; this is the commencement of the fight. After a short hunt, the elephant turns upon his pursuers, who scatter and fly from his headlong charge until he gives up the pursuit; he at length turns to bay when again pressed by the hunters. It is the duty of one man in particular to ride up close to the head of the elephant, and thus to absorb its attention upon himself. This insures a desperate charge. The greatest coolness and dexterity are then required by the hunter, who now, the hunted, *must so adapt the speed of his horse to the pace of the elephant, that the enraged beast gains in the race until it almost reaches the tail of the horse. In this manner the race continues. In the meantime, two hunters gallop up behind the elephant, unseen by the animal, whose attention is completely directed to the horse almost within his grasp. With extreme agility, when close to the heels of the elephant, one of the hunters, while at full speed, springs to*

the ground with his drawn sword, as his companion seizes the bridle, and with one dexterous two-handed blow he severs the back sinew. He immediately jumps out of the way and remounts his horse; but if the blow is successful, the elephant becomes disabled by the first pressure of its foot upon the ground; the enormous weight of the animal dislocates the joint, and it is rendered helpless. The hunter who has hitherto led the elephant immediately turns, and riding to within a few feet of the trunk, he induces the animal to attempt another charge. This, clumsily made, affords an easy opportunity for the aggageers behind to slash the sinew of the remaining leg, and the immense brute is reduced to a standstill; it dies of loss of blood in a short time, thus positively killed by one man with two strokes of the sword!

Samuel White Baker, *The Nile Tributaries of Abyssinia and The Sword Hunters of the Hamran Arabs,* (MacMillan, 1867), pp. 171-3. The enthusiastic and wealthy sportsman-adventurer Baker (with his ''wife,'' Florence, whom he had purchased at a Turkish slave auction held in the Balkan town of Widdin located on the Danube!) was one of the early explorers at the time of Speke, Burton, and Grant striving to find the source of the Nile. Avoiding the controversies and emotions that embroiled the others, the practical and 'conservative' Bakers nevertheless undertook very hazardous and daring journeys. Love of big-game shooting originally led Baker to Africa, but his explorations and subsequent books earned acclaim from the English public desperate for vicarious danger, suffering, and success. But Baker was also an accurate, comprehensive, and scientific observer. He (or, possibly, Florence) discovered Lake Albert, a lesser source of the Nile. He was awarded the gold medal of the Royal Geographical Society and was knighted — to one and all, ''Baker of the Nile.'' Many of the early explorers had a pronounced tendency to overstate the hazards of their journeys and exaggerate the savagery of wild animals to represent themselves as even greater heroes than they obviously were, but not the reliable Baker.

The reader will be rather tired of this endless killing...

W.D.M. Bell, *Karamojo Safari* (Harcourt, Brace 1949), p. 119. A rare moment of sanity in the endless annals of big-game hunting. Bell was another of those, dare one use the word, ''legendary'' African hunters. Known as ''Karamojo Bell'' from the wild and inaccessible region in Africa (at that time — but Karamojo is still the wildest, least developed district of Uganda) chronicled in this volume, Bell's name was synonymous with elephant hunting. (''There is nothing more satisfactory than the complete flop of a running elephant shot in the brain.'')

[The local country] *there goes in for grotesque and savage-looking rock formations, their summits generally occupied by swarms of gigantic baboons and jutting abruptly and nakedly from rugged vegetation as scarred and worn as the hills themselves. Even its denizens had something of the same character. The elephants were hoary and massive, the buffalo numerous and contemptuous of man, while down below the escarpment rhino were swarming and aggressive. Everywhere were great elephant roads worn deep into rock or clay. Great bathing pools showed where the massive beasts took their pleasure in the rainy season. Almost oppressive evidence of bush devastation met the eye on all sides. Scarcely one tree or bush could be found that did not bear upon it the sign of having been violated by the tree-browsing pachyderms. Only the euphorbias with their poisonous juice stood unharmed in the desolate landscape.*

Impressive as "Nabwa" was in the dry season, in the time of thunderstorms it transcended itself. Instead of bright sunlight there was a greenish purple gloom overhead. Sudden winds of hurricane force sprang up, dying away in torrential cloud-bursts. Lightning flashes supplied the chief illumination. Thunderclaps of the most appalling intensity shook an earth still quivering from the preceding discharge, while the miserable hunters, pale, cold, and depressed, cowered dithering under the shelter of an elephant ear cut from their latest victim. After a night of acute misery the sun would burst upon the soaked, torn, and horrible scene and transform it into one of surpassing beauty. Lilies that had pushed up through the moist earth in the night burst forth into glorious color, projecting into the now gentle atmosphere their heavy sweet perfume. Graceful tiny dik-dik played daintily about while that most beautiful of African antelope, the lesser kudu, lent contrast to the more massive forms of animal life as the hunters hurried away once more upon their blood trail. The effect on my boys of this peculiar country was to reduce them to silence; they spoke in whispers. Such was "Nabwa," the native name for this primordial wilderness.

Bell, *Karamojo Safari,* pp. 163-4.

For more than ten minutes David Graybeard and Goliath sat grooming each other, and then, just before the sun vanished over the horizon behind me, David got up and stood staring at me. And it so happened that my elongated evening shadow fell across him. The moment is etched deep into my memory: the excitement of the first close contact with a wild chimpanzee and the freakish chance that cast my shadow over David even as he seemed to gaze into my eyes. Later it acquired an almost allegorical significance, for of all living creatures today only man, with his superior brain, his superior intellect, overshadows the chimpanzee. Only man casts his shadow of doom over the freedom of the chimpanzee in the forests with his guns and his spreading settlements and cultivation.

Jane van Lawick-Goodall, *In the Shadow of Man* (Houghton Mifflin, 1971; Delta Edition, 1974, photographs by Hugo van Lawick), p. 3. Goodall began as a secretary in Nairobi, then worked for the famous anthropologist and paleontologist Louis S. B. Leakey at the local museum of natural history. Soon thereafter, however, she went to live and study the chimps at Gombe Stream on the shores of Lake Tanganyika located in Tanzania, where she remained off and on for ten years. This volume — the result of her careful, honest, and insightful field work — is a unique study in the history of research made on animal behavior. A classic of its kind, the book is further discussed in the Bibliography following Chapter X. Flo, the matriarch of Goodall's study group, was given an obituary in the London *Sunday Times.* The research effort is still going on, probably the longest continuous field work on any mammal extant today.

"Going up that river was like travelling back to the earliest beginnings of the world, when vegetation rioted on the earth and the big trees were kings. An empty stream, a great silence, an impenetrable forest. The air was warm, thick, heavy, sluggish. There was no joy in the brilliance of sunshine. The long stretches of the waterway ran on, deserted, into the gloom of overshadowed distances. On silvery sandbanks hippos and aligators sunned themselves side by side. The broadening waters flowed through a mob of wooded islands; you lost your way on that river as you would in a desert, and butted all day long against shoals, trying to find the channel, till you thought yourself bewitched and cut off [forever] from eveything you had known once — somewhere — far away — in another existence perhaps. There were moments when one's past came back to one, as it will sometimes when you have not a moment to spare to yourself; but it came in the shape of a unrestful and noisy dream, remembered with wonder amongst the overwhelming realities of this strange world of plants, and water, and silence. And this stillness of life did not in the least resemble a peace. It was the stillness of an implacable force brooding over an inscrutable intention. It looked at you with a vengeful aspect. . . .["]

["]...We penetrated deeper and deeper into the heart of darkness.["]

Joseph Conrad, *Heart of Darkness* (W.W. Norton, Norton Critical Edition, 1971), pp. 34-5. Based upon Conrad's own experiences in the Congo, *Heart* is the second of his "Marlow" tales. As the reader can discern from this passage, *Heart* is far from an ordinary light travelogue, but one of the great dark psychological meditations in literature. At the turn of the century, when *Heart* was published, Conrad's (the writer was by this time an established literary figure) exotic words defined Africa for generations: primitive, instinctual, black, savage, and incomprehensible.

Only when you reached the hotel did you begin to understand the charm of Kisumu. . . .its lounge was full of travellers from the ends of the earth. . .

In the small panelled bar airmen from Singapore swapped yarns with airmen from South Africa, Englishmen from Kenya talked to Belgians from the Congo, Germans from Tanganyika smoked cigars and swallowed lager. I found myself next to an elderly Frenchman with a beard who was gathering material for a book. "Inch by Inch through Darkest Kavirondo I shall call it," he shouted, and began a torrent of scientific explanation which left me breathless...

Eileen Bigland, *The Lake of the Royal Crocodiles* (Hodder and Stoughton, 1939), p. 47. Kisumu was a stop on the traditional air route into safari Africa. Bigland was the paradigm dilettante traveler.

When I first went to Africa I had the same experience as everyone else. Rhinos getting wind of me would charge me and to save myself I'd shoot. I suppose I had stood off twenty of these charges with my rifle before I discovered that if I did not shoot it would not necessarily be fatal. I discovered the fact, of course, quite by accident. I was going along the bank of the Tana River

Plates 26 & 27. River Vegetation.

one day with my camera. My gun boys were some distance behind so as not to disturb any animal that might afford a picture. Suddenly I was set all a-quiver by the threshings and snortings of a rhino coming through the bushes in my direction. I very hastily took stock of the situation. There was nothing to climb. Between me and the thicket from which the rhino was coming was about twenty-five feet of open space. Behind me was a 30-foot drop to the crocodile-infested waters of the Tana. The only hope I saw was a bush overhanging the brink which looked as if it might or might not hold me if I swung out on it. I decided to try the bush and let the rhino land in the river, trusting to luck that I wouldn't join him there. The bushes were thrust aside and he came full tilt into the opening where he could see me. Everything was set for the final act. He suddenly stopped with a snort. His head drooped. His eyes almost closed. He looked as if he were going to sleep. The terrible beast had become absolutely ludicrous. While this was going on I felt a poke in my back. I reached behind and took my rifle from the gun boy who had come up with equal celerity and bravery. I drew a bead on the old fellow but I could not shoot. A stupider or more ludicrous looking object I never saw. I began talking to him, but it did not rouse him from his lethargy. There he stood, half asleep and totally oblivious, while I, with the gun half aimed, talked to him about his ugly self. About this time my porters came into hearing on a path behind the rhino. He pricked up his ears and blundered off in that direction. I heard the loads dropping as the porters made for the trees. The rhino charged through the safari and off into the bush.

Akeley, *In Brightest Africa*, pp. 107-8.

The short twilight had passed and he was still riding towards camp when a lion sprang at his horse. Unseated, he was jerked almost into the jaws of another lion which ground its teeth into his right shoulder, dragged him a hundred yards, and then settled down to worry him. His mouth was smothered against its chest, his legs dragged below its belly and his spurs were torn off as he was dragged along.

A lesser man would have fainted. Wolhuter instead grew angry. "What an end for an old hunter!" he growled to himself.

With that he thought of the sheath knife on his belt. He groped for it with his left hand, hoping that it had not been flung out by his toss from the horse.

It was there. He sneaked it out. He slid his left arm under the lion's chest. He dare not alarm it.

For a moment the beast let go his shoulder. Wolhuter stabbed deeply with a backhand stroke, once, twice, and then a third time into his throat. The lion spurted blood.

Dripping, he leapt to his feet. He shouted and swore at the lion. Eye to eye it stared at him, then turned and padded into the shadow of the bush.

Wolhuter, weak as as a new-born impala, hoisted himself into a tree and tied himself to a branch. He shouted until his frightened boys came running to the tree and scared away the lion's mate, which was prowling around below. They lent him an arm for the eight miles' walk to his camp, and then helped him to dress his wounds with permanganate of potash. At dawn he mustered his boys for the two days' march to Komatipoort, where the nearest doctor was to be found.

How Wolhuter lived through that ordeal no doctor knows. His shoulder and arm were black and gangrenous — the foul teeth of a lion means certain blood-poisoning — but the thong-

taut fitness of the frontiersman carried him through. To-day Wolhuter still cannot raise his arm above his head. But as men in the game reserve say — men unborn when Wolhuter killed his lion with a pocket-knife — he can still reach the trigger when he raises his rifle.

Carel Birkby, *Limpopo Journey*, (Frederick Muller, 1939), pp. 237-8. Birkby is a journalist who wrote extensively about Africa. The Wolhuter story is a famous one, retold many times. Naturally enough, the retelling varies: compare the incident as related by J. Stevenson-Hamilton, *Animal Life in Africa* (E.P. Dutton, 1912), pp. 185-7, to that described by Wolfhunter himself in Alfred E. Pease, *The Book of the Lion* (St. Martin's Press Edition, 1987), pp. 185-9.

The water was rather shallow at this point, so the larger elephants merely walked across, wading up to their shoulders. The baby stayed on shore, eying the water dubiously; he was too small to wade and apparently too afraid to swim. His mother, the last adult to start across the river, gave me the very strong impression that she was steeling herself to ignore him. It was about time, she must have felt, that he attempted it on his own.

The baby elephant took a few steps, then hastily retreated to the shore and cried shrilly, swaying his trunk from side to side. His mother returned and watched for a couple of minutes — hoping perhaps that he might calm down and give it another try — but the baby kept wailing. When she couldn't stand it anymore, she waded back. I wondered what she would do, since he was much too big to carry in her trunk, but she soon showed me. Kneeling on her forelegs, she lowered her head and placed her tusks very carefully beneath the squalling baby's belly. He stopped crying immediately. Holding her head high to keep her tusks horizontal, she waded slowly into the water. Ecstatic, the baby smacked at the surface with his trunk, splashing like a human baby in his bath. She reached the shore and, very carefully, she put him down.

I had watched the whole scene, astonished, but what happened next was even more amazing.

Smacking his mother's leg with his trunk, the baby elephant started squalling again. She stared down at him with obvious disgust, then turned and moved away toward the herd. The baby screamed, flinging himself on the ground and rolling on his back, but scrambled to his feet, looking expectant, as soon as she returned. She nudged him with her trunk, pushing him a few steps away from the shore. He screamed and once again started rolling on his back. His mother made a deep throaty rumble — a sort of elephant sigh — and kneeled on her forelegs, lowering her great head. This time the baby didn't wait to be fork-lifted; he simply hopped aboard.

The patient cow waded back into the river and walked in a little circle while he splashed. Then, as she came back to the shore and lowered her head, he started a new bout of caterwauling. She raised her tusks and, for a moment, I thought she was going to dunk him in the river. Instead, she marched in the opposite direction toward the waiting herd, carrying him at least two hundred feet before she put him down, this time a little less gently. He started to cry but she paid no attention, moving away without turning her head. He kept crying, and then, apparently deciding he had pushed her to the limit, he followed quietly.

Jean-Pierre Hallet, *Animal Kitabu* (Random House, 1967), pp. 117-8. Despite its *many* hopeless absurdities, Hallet's book is recommended reading. Very critical of the vast amount of misinformation concerning safari Africa and its animals prevailing in the 1960s, *Kitabu* is also highly entertaining — at times, too much so. If the reader wants to read an almost nauseating account of a Maasai lion hunt (with Hallet cast in the role of a young *moran*!), this book should satisfy.

Then suddenly I heard the high-pitched stirring cry of the bee-eaters, and, looking up, I was more than delighted to find that there was a great swarm of two or three hundred carmine bee-eaters, like a shower of roses falling out of the heavens. They were about to do us the honour of visiting our grass fire, and of giving us the most wonderful display of aerial fireworks that I've seen since Peace Night in Hyde Park in 1919. We sat back against the baobab sipping our cool drinks and revelled for nearly an hour in their beauty, skill, and courage.

The roses that fell from the sky on the day of the canonisation of Saint Thérèse of Lisieux can scarcely have excelled these birds in colour, because, with the almost level rays striking them at a great altitude, they seemed to outshine the most wonderful flowers, as much as most flowers outshine their leaves. The flames were now crackling on the long grass and palmettos, and sending up an inverted cataract of sparks and black smoke, filled with scorched and stupefied insects. Then, from the height of about a hundred and fifty feet, the birds all simultaneously inclined their flight and swooped like dive-bombers, hurling their seraphic streaks of ruby and sapphire at the curtain of smoke and flame, striking through which, they seemed to ricochet at a steep angle to the same height on the other side, where they revolved, without pausing, in their own length, and repeated the process. They could have hawked an equal number of escaping insects outside the zone of fire: but they obviously took a real delight in the danger, and in matching their own solar flames against the plumes of the conflagration, which they outshone in brilliance as they outglanced it in nimble flight. They emerged from the smoke unsullied. . .

Campbell, *Dark Horse*, p. 123.

I was guiding a rajah who never moved without his personal secretary and doctor. The doctor carried a regular medical clinic around with him, most of the drugs being potent aphrodisiacs as the rajah was afraid of losing his manhood from the hardships of African life. In the bush, the doctor became a sort of general factotum, struggling along under a heavy cinema outfit to record the rajah's triumphs, while his pockets bulged with bottles of medicines, packets of herbs, and pills.

On one occasion, we were hunting buffalo. The rajah and I were in front while the doctor and the secretary lagged behind. We came on a herd with a fine bull and the rajah fired. At the sound of the shot, the herd panicked and dashed off through the thorny bush. The rajah was sure he had hit the bull and I was equally sure he had missed. . . .

Eager to prove their patron right, the doctor and the secretary set off to look for bloodstains on the ground. While they were wandering about, a bull rhino came trotting out of the bush toward the doctor. The animal had evidently been disturbed by the stampeding buffalo and was looking for a quieter spot. If the doctor had stood still, all would have been well, but instead he screamed and raced for the startled secretary, apparently

hoping the rhino would take off in pursuit of the other man. The secretary quickly realized what was happening and made for the nearest tree. He flattened himself against the stem like a poster and yelled "Go away! Go away!" to the frantic doctor.

The rhino had stopped for a moment when the doctor began to run. Then he started after him, making rooting motions in the air with his horn. The doctor put up a fine sprint, for his heart was in it, but the rhino easily overtook him. The doctor was in line with the rhino so I could not shoot but I soon saw that the beast was not making a serious charge. . . .The doctor ran through the thorn trees screaming "Help!" while the rhino galloped behind, encouraging his victim to fresh efforts by an occasionsal jab of his horn. As the doctor became so weak he could only stagger, the rhino slowed down to a trot, still keeping behind him. I became so interested in this performance that I forgot all about shooting the bull and watched with curiosity while the rhino chivvied the man through the scrub. At last, tiring of the sport, the rhino trotted off and the doctor returned to us, sweating and exhausted. His first earnest words were, "I have had much troubles."

Hunter, *Hunter*, pp. 60-1.

Back in the early days, they [Downey and a friend named Grafton] *were out together after buffalo — a third man, E. Robson, making up a week-end party. Most illegally, Downey had brought his dog on the expedition, fearing that it would not be properly fed and cared for at home; the animal was, of course, tied up at the camp.*

On the first morning they got to the entrance of Hell's Gate, in the Kedong Valley, when Grafton glanced back and saw a yellow object bounding through the bush. The dog! When it caught up with him, Syd felt it unthinkable that he should return to camp and miss the hunt. So did the other two, so they pressed on. The dog kept to heel some of the time, showing only a fatheaded tendency to chase dikdik; Downey remarked on this, whenever he could catch the animal's attention, in some thoughtfully chosen words.

It all happened so suddenly, as things in the bush often do. The smell of buffalo became quite overpowering — and the dog dashed ahead. A few seconds later, the three hunters found themselves at the edge of a clearing; there was the dog, regretting his impulse, streaking back with his tail tucked between his legs — and followed by practically every buffalo in East Africa in a solid, determined stampede. An insurance company would have developed an ulcer on the spot.

The courage and quick action of Grafton saved this day. As cooly as though the juggernauts coming at him were clay pigeons, he took aim and fired. The leading buffalo stumbled, then skidded on his nose and collapsed right in front of the trio, quite dead. Following buffalo tripped over or veered away from the carcase, and the whole herd thundered past the three hunters. 'What, literally at arm's-reach?' I asked Downey.

'Hell,' he answered, 'We wouldn't have had to reach.'

Cullen, *Downey's Africa*, pp. 8-9.

Next thing I knew, a large male chimpanzee had hoisted himself up out of the underbrush and was hanging out sideways from the tree trunk, which he was clutching with his left hand and left

foot.

Looking down my barrel at ten yards was man's closest relative, an ape, which, when mature, has the intelligence of a three-year-old child. Wouldn't I feel like a murderer if I shot him? I had some misgivings as my globular front sight rested on the ape's chest and my finger on the trigger.

But then, gradually, insidiously, my thinking took a different turn. I thought of the gorge-lifting sentimentality — most of it commercially inspired — that has come to surround chimpanzees. I thought of the long list of ridiculous anthropomorphic books about the "personalities" of these apes. I thought of that chimp who fingerpainted on TV and sold his "works" for so much money he wound up having to pay income tax. I thought of one ape who was recommended for a

knighthood, the ape who was left his master's yacht, the ape who was elected to parliament in some banana republic; and various other apes who were made astronauts and honorary colonels. Gathering like storm clouds in my mind, these thoughts roused me to such a pitch of indignation that there appeared to be only one honorable course of action. I blasted that ape with downright enthusiam and have felt clean inside ever since.

James Mellon, in James Mellon et al., African Hunter, pp. 320-1. What a piece of work! Hide the dog! The author and Mr. Mellon graduated within a year of one another at Yale. The "Mother of Men" could produce wildly different sons.

Lions take an occasional elephant calf which has strayed from the family circle, but there is always a danger that the mother elephant may retaliate when she realises what is happening. A lioness in Murchison Falls Park killed an elephant calf. Discovering this, the elephant followed the lioness into a patch of long grass where her own cub was hidden. Immediately she saw the cub the elephant killed it. She then picked it up, carried it back to where her own dead calf was lying and placed foliage on top of them until they were completely covered. Then she moved off after the lioness which had wisely withdrawn from the fray.

Rennie Bere, *The African Elephant* (Arthur Baker & Golden Press, 1966), p. 71.

Out on the plains, in the beginning of the rains, where the vast stretches of burnt grass begin to show fresh green sprouting, there are many hundred plovers. The plains always have a maritime air, the open horizon recalls the Sea and the long Sea-sands, the wandering wind is the same, the charred grass has a saline smell, and when the grass is long it runs in waves all over the land. When the white carnation flowers on the plains you remember the chopping white-specked waves all round you as you are tacking up the Sund. Out on the plains the plovers likewise take on the appearance of Sea-birds, and behave like Sea-birds on a beach, legging it, on the close grass, as fast as they can for a short time, and then rising before your horse with high shrill shrieks, so that the light sky is all alive with wings and birds' voices.

The Crested Cranes, which come on to the newly rolled and planted maize-land, to steal the maize out of the ground, make up for the robbery by being birds of good omen, announcing the rain; and also by dancing to us. When the tall birds are together in large numbers, it is a fine sight to see them spread their wings

Plates 28 & 29. The Calm of Twilight: On the Plains and over Water.

and dance. There is much style in the dance, and a little affectation, for why, when they can fly, do they jump up and down as if they were held on to the earth by magnetism? The whole ballet has a sacred look, like some ritual dance; perhaps the cranes are making an attempt to join Heaven and earth like the winged angels walking up and down Jacob's Ladder. With their delicate pale grey colouring, the little black velvet skull-cap and the fan shaped crown, the cranes have all the air of light, spirited frescoes. When, after the dance, they lift and go away, to keep up the sacred tone of the show they give out, by the wings or the voice, a clear ringing note, as if a group of church bells had taken to the wing and were sailing off. You can hear them a long way away, even after the birds themselves have become invisible in the sky: a chime from the clouds.

The Greater Hornbill was another visitor to the farm, and came there to eat the fruits of the Cape-Chestnut tree. They are very strange birds. It is an adventure or an experience to meet them, not altogether pleasant, for they look exceedingly knowing. One morning before sunrise I was woken up by a loud jabbering outside the house, and when I walked out on the terrace I saw forty-one Hornbills sitting in the trees on the lawn. There they looked less like birds than like some fantastic articles of finery set on the trees here and there by a child. Black they all were, with the sweet, noble black of Africa, deep darkness absorbed through an age, like old soot, that makes you feel that for elegance, vigour and vivacity, no colour rivals black. All the Hornbills were talking together in the merriest mood, but with choice deportment, like a party of inheritors after a funeral. The morning air was as clear as crystal, the sombre party was bathing in freshness and purity, and, behind the trees and the birds, the sun came up, a dull red ball. You wonder what sort of a day you are to get after such an early morning.

The Flamingoes are the most delicately coloured of all the African birds, pink and red like a flying twig of an Oleander bush. They have incredibly long legs and bizarre and recherche curves of their necks and bodies, as if from some exquisite traditional prudery they were making all attitudes and movements in life as difficult as possible.

Dinesen, *Out of Africa*, pp. 284-6.

'There was a full moon and I was sitting in my Land-Rover with a crash helmet on my head, my safety belt firmly fastened, and with a thick padding of foam-rubber stuffed all around me for extra protection. I was about to embark on one of my more dangerous but also most exciting jobs. Without using the car lights, I would try to keep up with a pack of wild dogs as they raced across the African landscape in pursuit of their prey. Only the moon would light my way and warn me of the dangers ahead — potholes, rocks, and even water-holes and precipices — for if I used the car headlights I would temporarily blind the hunters and their prey and I did not wish to influence the behaviour or affect the chances of either.

'Outside on the moonlit Serengeti plain, I could see the dim shapes of twelve African wild dogs. . .Suddenly, the dogs were off into the night and I raced after them. At first, it looked as if I might lose the pack, for they quickly left me behind, but as the car gained speed I caught up with the last two dogs and drove parallel with them. They were used to my following and so took no notice, concentrating instead on a Thomson's gazelle which fled in zig zags across the plain ahead of them.

'I glanced at my speedometer. We were going at 30 miles per hour, but the dogs were gaining on me and so I increased my speed. I know from experience that if I could not keep up, I would probably lose them in the dark and might not find them again for a month or more. This is because a pack normally covers ten to twenty miles in a night, going in any direction, and roams over an area of about 1500 square miles. Searching for African wild dogs is almost as bad as searching for a needle in a haystack, and so once I did find a pack, I tried hard to keep up with it. That night, as I raced across the moonlit plain, I kept a close eye on the two dogs running next to me. As a result I did not give enough attention to the ground ahead, and suddenly, without warning, the front of my car bucked violently sideways into the air and then crashed to the ground again. In spite of the foam-rubber, I banged my shoulder hard against the side of the car and at the same time the steering wheel spun out of my hands, twisting my thumb as it did so. Then one of the rear wheels hit the pothole and the car came to a shuddering halt. At some stage, I had jabbed my feet onto the clutch and the brake and so the engine was still running. I cursed, quickly put the car into four-wheel drive and first gear, and tried to climb out of the hole, but the back wheel spun and dug itself in deeper. I threw the gear lever into reverse, accelerated and let the clutch go. The car shot out backwards. As it did so, I quickly turned the steering wheel slightly so that both front wheels missed the hole. All this had only taken seconds and I could see the dogs vaguely but far away. I raced after them, and soon I was going at 40 miles per hour and catching up, but twice I was delayed as I had to swerve around two more potholes. Finally, I caught up, but almost immediately I came to a screeching halt amid a cloud of dust. The dogs had suddenly caught the gazelle and were tearing it apart, making strange bird-like twittering sounds as they did so.

'They had not been feeding for long when two larger shapes, attracted by the sounds, came racing across the plain — two spotted hyenas. Boldly, the hungry hyenas dashed in among the dogs and tried to steal some meat, but moments later they were giggling nervously as the dogs surrounded them, and then they growled and roared and screamed as the dogs bit at their bottoms. Moments later, the two hyenas retreated and the dogs continued to feed. Within the next five minutes, however, more and more spotted hyenas appeared, arriving in ones and twos from all directions, and finally the dogs were outnumbered and had to leave the last scraps of their kill to the hyenas, which started to approach with closed ranks, whooping and growling as they did so.'

Huxley & van Lawick, *Last Days In Eden*, pp. 46-7. This is vintage van Lawick and not, the would-be safarist should realize, standard *modus operandi* for normal visitors.

Buffalo and a solitary rhino took mute note of us; the world stood still. Flat wet dung raised its reassuring smell in halos of loud flies. We turned west across wild pasture — cropped turf, cabbage butterflies, and cloven prints filled with clear rain — that rings the sedge swamp in the pit of the caldera. A hawk rose on thermals from the crater floor, and white egrets crossed the dark walls; in the marsh, a golden sedge was seeding in the swelling light of afternoon. More buffalo lay along the wood edge at the western wall, and with them rhino and an elephant. The rhinos lay still, but the elephant, a mile away, blared in alarm, and others answered from the galleries of trees, the screams echoing around the crater; the elephant's ears flared wide and closed as it passed with saintly tread into the forest. Bushbuck and waterbuck lifted carved heads to watch man's coming; their tails switched and their hind legs stamped but they did not run. Perhaps the white-maned bush pig saw us, too, raising red eyes from the snuffled dirt and scratching its raspy hide with a sharp hoof. Another time I glimpsed it from the rim at twilight, a ring of white in the dim trees, and one night a year later, descending the mountain, my headlights penned a family band, striped piglets and all, between the high sides of the road, but today it remained hidden.

Matthiessen & Porter, *The Tree Where Man Was Born/The African Experience*, p. 173.

...a day in the bush is never dull...

Adamson, *The Searching Spirit*, p. 205.

Out of its farthest edge the forerunners of a huge herd of impala, wildebeest, and zebra plunged in flight before the shadow of my wings. I circled, throttled down and lost height until my propeller cut into the fringe of the dust, and particles of it burned in my nostrils.

As the herd moved it became a carpet of rust-brown and grey and dull red. It was not like a herd of cattle or of sheep, because it was wild, and it carried with it the stamp of wilderness and the freedom of a land still more a possession of Nature than of men. To see ten thousand animals untamed and not branded with the symbols of human commerce is like scaling an unconquered mountain for the first time, or like finding a forest without roads or footpaths, or the blemish of an axe. You know then what you had always been told — that the world once lived and grew without adding machines and newsprint and brick-walled streets and the tyranny of clocks.

Markham, *West with the Night*, p. 38.

That night we reached the home of the hyenas. . . .One of the animals began to call as we walked into the shadow of the rocks. It was the usual insistent ooo-ah-ooo, haunting and strangely beautiful. The hyena is a hideous-looking animal but it is also one of the most useful and its call is the keynote of night life in the bush. 'Fisi,' said Lelean. During his army days a fisi had carried off his highly polished belt. He was not well-disposed towards them. Another animal started to moan. It was echoed by two more. Before we halted for the night under the face of a cliff the canyon rang with a chorus of calls. 'Manyatta ya fisi,' said Karo.

Some districts are infested with hyenas. On my way down to Wamba I heard a strange story of a plague of the animals on the edge of the Turkana escarpment. It was told to me by the game warden at Moroto in Karamoja. He said that among the Karamajong there is a belief that at night the Imuron, the tribal witchdoctors, can either turn themselves into hyenas or travel from one place to another on the backs of the animals. Imuron are not among the most popular members of the tribe.

During the great drought in East Africa the cattle began to die in thousands and hyenas became a menace. With an abun-

dance of carrion they increased in numbers and, instead of scavenging in twos and threes, a pack of thirty or forty animals would gang up together and attack living animals. The warden killed them by pouring a tin of cattle dip into the stomach of a dead cow and leaving the poisoned carcass in the bush. In this way he sometimes collected twenty or thirty dead hyenas in one night.

After one successful onslaught his chief scout told him with evident satisfaction that he had killed an Imuron. Among the dead hyenas they found an animal decorated with the sacred ear-rings of the soothsayers. They could not have been put on after death. The bone rings were embedded in the pierced ears and the flesh had grown around them. The animal was also wearing a sacred necklace and its chest was painted with the characteristic stripes of the medicine men. The warden could offer no explanation for the decorated animal but the tribe considered he had done them a good turn.

Hillaby, *Journey to the Jade Sea*, pp. 157-8.

Once upon a time there was an elephant and a canary who lived in the same part of the forest. The elephant was very big and strong, and the canary, of course, small and cunning. They each in turn claimed to be king over the same part of the forest. They often submitted themselves to feats of skill to prove their own superiority. The elephant generally got the worst of it because the little canary was so ingenious.

One day, however, the elephant said to the other:

"Look here. I've thought of something that will decide once and for all which of us will be the boss. Will you promise to do whatever I say and abide for ever by the result of this test?"

The canary agreed and listened with excited interest.

"Now," said the elephant, very pleased with his idea, "this is the test. The one of us who can drink the most will be king."

The little canary thought for a moment and said:

"Good. We must find some water."

And he led the way. The elephant followed as he flitted on ahead or perched on a bough of a tree hard by and waited for him to catch up. As soon as the elephant caught up the canary again flitted on and once again rested till the other came up. On went the canary, and again and again, leading the elephant through great forests, over mountains far away from big rivers and lakes, until finally after many days' journey they arrived at the sea.

The tide was coming in and the cunning canary said to the elephant:

"Look, there is plenty of water here. You are the big boy, now you begin." And so, delighted, the elephant put his trunk into the water and drank and drank and drank.

"Go on," said the canary encouragingly. "I can do better than that. Drink some more."

So the elephant did his best and drank and drank yet again.

"But," said the other, "you are not drinking, you are making no impression, you are blowing into it. Look, the water is rising, it is getting higher."

Desperately the elephant drank, but the water still rose and drove him back, until he fell over from sheer exhaustion.

The canary waited to allow him to recover until the tide had turned. Then down he went to the brink of the lapping sea, dipped his beak into it, pretended to drink and waited a little while. Then he waded out after the receding water and again pretended to drink. Once more he waited a little while, and so on until the tide had gone right out. He then flew back to the astonished elephant and exclaimed:

"Do you see how much I have drunk?"

And the canary is still king of that forest.

Richard St. Barbe Baker, *Africa Drums* (George Ronald, Wheatley Revised Edition, 1951), pp. 82-3.

I was camping on the southern Masai plains of Kenya, a beautiful area of rolling country cut by numerous water courses and carrying at times vast herds of 'plain's game' such as zebra, wildebeest, and so on; it is also famous for its large number of lions, many of which carry big manes. It had been raining all afternoon but by the evening it cleared and the stars twinkled while the game warden and I enjoyed a welcome supper, superbly cooked on three stones by a wizard of an African cook. As we sat listening to the frogs and crickets, we also heard the unmistakable grunts of some lions. We at once set off to find them, the main object being to get a tape-recording of lions roaring. After bumping across the plains for a couple of miles, we saw several pairs of eyes reflecting the headlights of our Land-Rover. There seemed to be lions in every direction and we were so interested in watching them, turning the car this way and that to focus them in the lights, that we failed to avoid a bog — a shallow circle of swampy ground not much bigger than the Land-Rover, filled with water by the recent rain. The car plunged in — down to its axles in mud — with no hope of driving it backwards or forwards. This intrigued the lions and they crowded round the edge of the pool. Some ventured into the shallow water to examine our car more closely. The night was cool and calm and the lions were curious but silent. Still intent on getting a good recording I tried to provoke the lions to roar by imitating the noise made by a cub in distress. One lioness who went by the name of Sally responded and I recorded a few growls and grunts on the tape. Then, by playing this back, more lions took notice and one roared with some vigour. Again I played this back and it must have suggested to the lions that others were about to invade their territory, for there was then the most enormous noise. It developed into a full leonine choir at a range of only a few yards — the most thrilling of all wild sounds in Africa. After an hour or more of this exciting performance I ran out of tape and was feeling very satisfied with the evening's work; it then dawned on us that we were not in a very happy situation. Stuck in the mud in an open-sided Land-Rover with thirteen very rowdy lions all round us, there was little prospect of a good night's sleep. Each time a lion ventured too near we shouted and banged the side of the car with a tyre lever. My final weapon of defence was a can of fly-spray which I had to bring into action when a young lion came up to sniff my side of the car. The fly spray got him squarely in the face and he wrinkled his nose in disgust and retreated.

We began to feel some concern that the battery of the Land-Rover would not last much longer, as we had to use the lights frequently to see what the lions were doing. It was then about 2 a.m. and we did not cherish the prospect of spending the rest of the night in this predicament, but we had to accept that it would not be wise to walk back to camp without even a torch and with thirteen lions to challenge our progress. Our camp was too far to attract any attention by shouting or blowing the horn, and so we just waited. Our rangers back at camp grew anxious and manfully set out in a lorry to look for us. We saw their lights and flashed with ours so there was no difficulty in making contact. They brought the lorry up as far as the soft ground would allow, and, with hardly a thought for the lions, everyone got down to the task of pulling out the Land-Rover. A long tow-rope was produced and the lorry driver bent down to make it fast. A mischievous lion promptly caught hold of the other end of the rope and started to pull. Other lions joined in until there was a regular tug-of-war. The driver cursed his colleagues for pulling on the rope, not knowing that he had several lions on the other end. Everybody laughed, but I realised that there was a real danger of losing the rope. One of the rangers shared my thoughts and decided to take action. He walked towards the opposing team while the driver held the rope twisted round the axle of the lorry and shouted until the lions reluctantly dropped their new toy. After that we gained control of the tow-rope and fixed the chewed end to the Land-Rover. With engines whirring and more shouting, out came the Land-Rover, backwards, while the lions sat watching and obviously still sorely tempted to have another go at the rope.

...Although six people and thirteen lions were all muddled up, the task of salvaging our car from the bog became so important that nobody had time to feel afraid. Moreover we had been closely associated with these lions for the greater part of the night, and we had got to know each other fairly well.

I wonder what the explorers and pioneers of the last century would say if they could have a glimpse of this scene — this new order — this age when people no longer treat wild animals with contempt, or as potential enemies, and when, in consequence, wild animals have developed a new attitude towards man, that is man as a kindly member of the animal kingdom.

Mervyn Cowie, *The African Lion* (Arthur Baker, 1966), pp. 85-8. Vintage Cowie. Later in this volume — in Chapter Five, "Lion Men and Witchcraft" — Cowie turns to the story of young girls allegedly being raised as "lions" and used by witchdoctors to kill other people. This extraordinary tale, even beyond the pale of the outer reaches attracted by this compendium, has to be read in its entirety.

He pawed a twig, then chewed on it. When another cub passed by, he lunged and bit it in the lower back. The assaulted cub whirled around, slapped our hero in the face and walked off. He sat as if planning some new devilment. Suddenly he crouched and slowly, very slowly, stalked toward an unsuspecting cub. Finally he rushed. The two tumbled over and grappled before separating amicably, our cub now biting a tuft of grass instead. Tiring of this, he flopped first on his side, then rolled on his back and waved his paws in the air. Several cubs played near him and these he watched intently. When one cub ambled closer, our cub hugged the ground behind a tuft of grass and waited. Bounding out of hiding with exaggerated jumps, his mouth open and lips drawn back in a smile, he swatted at one cub and after that turned on another and nipped it in the flank, a form of greeting which led to his being clouted on the head. Two cubs wrestled gently nearby and he entered the fray enthusiastically, only to be slapped in the face, rebuffed again. A cub trotted by, intent on some errand. He lunged and tried to grab it with his forepaws, but missed. Both cubs then reared up on their hindlegs, and, leaning into each other, cuffed clumsily until the other one fell on his back, our cub on top trying to bite its throat with mock severity. Then they sat side by side, looking for new worlds to conquer, unaware that they were being stalked until our cub was hit on the head from behind. Failing to see the humor of the situation, he turned with a snarl and swiped the air in futile fury as the silent intruder vanished in the grass. He then reclined, his playful mood seemingly dampened, but suddenly he grasped a twig with both paws and bit it, shaking his head from side to side. The twig at least would not hit back.

The most common form of play among cubs consists of chasing wildly through the grass, of wrestling, pawing, and stalking. Small cubs, those less than six months old, are particularly fond of wrestling, but as cubs grow older they seem to prefer games with less body contact, such as stalking. Sometimes a cub picks up a branch and runs with it, and others then acquire an irresistible urge to posses it too, with the result that several may pursue, the chase ending with a tug-of-war during which each cub hangs on grimly as the branch is pulled this way and that. From a cub's point of view, males must be surly brutes, for most attempts to draw them into play are rebuffed with a slap or growl. Yet cubs are strangely drawn to these strong and withdrawn members of the pride. They like to sit by males and imitate them by, for example, yawning or sharpening claws when they do. The lionesses are more tolerant of playing cubs than are males, although their patience must be severely tested at times. A cub may leap onto a sleeping lioness with a thump that audibly knocks the air out of her, it may drape itself over her face, almost smothering her, it may pull her leg, bite her tail, and in general make a nuisance of itself without eliciting more than a mild reprimand. In fact, a lioness may reciprocate by slapping a cub hard but with restraint, first feinting with one paw and, when the cub's attention is diverted, clouting it with the other; she may cover it with her 250-pound body, lying as if dead, waiting for it to squirm free after much straining and wiggling; and she may pummel, maul, and chase it until it finally reclines on its back, exhausted, begging for peace. At night, when the moon stares in silence at the earth, a whole group of lions may gambol on the plains, sometimes dark shadows, sometimes shimmering silver spirits, the magic of such scenes never growing less with repetition.

Schaller, *Golden Shadows, Flying Hooves*, pp. 73-4.

At daybreak, through the tent fly, I could see giraffe heads swaying over the small rises around camp, like giant flowers shot up overnight; the bell note of a boubou shrike distills the windless morning. Giraffes gaze raptly, one ear flicking, before moving off in that elegant slow rhythm that is tuned to the old music of the elephants. Elephants, too, convene here in the night, and sometimes buffalo, chewing their cud as they contemplate man's habitations. Below the camp, the water trails of courting coot melt the surface of Momela, and beyond the lakes, in a realm of shadow, Kilimanjaro's base forms a pedestal for its high cumulus. Birds fly from this dark world into the sunlight of Momela — a quartet of crowned cranes, wild horn note calling from across the water, and ducks that hurry down the clouds — pintail, Cape widgeon, Hottentot teal. In rain, the lakes have the monotone alpine cast of mountain lakes across the high places of the world, but here the monotone is pierced by fierce rays of African color — a rainbow in a purple sky, an emilia blossom, tropic orange, or a carmine feather, drifted down from a diadem of birds crossing the heavens in the last shreds of sunset.

Matthiessen & Porter, *The Tree Where Man Was Born/The African Experience*, p. 169.

I do not regret my early contact with David Graybeard; David, with his gentle disposition, who permitted a strange white ape to touch him. To me it represented a triumph of the sort of relationship man can establish with a wild creature, a creature who has never known captivity. In those early days I spent many days alone with David. Hour after hour I followed him through the forests, sitting and watching him while he fed or rested, struggling to keep up when he moved through a tangle of vines. Sometimes, I am sure, he waited for me — just as he would wait for Goliath or William — for when I emerged, panting and torn from a mass of thorny undergrowth, I often found him sitting, looking back in my direction; when I had appeared, he got up and plodded on again.

One day, as I sat near him at the bank of a tiny trickle of crystal-clear water, I saw a ripe red palm nut lying on the ground. I picked it up and held it out to him on my open palm. He turned his head away. When I moved my hand closer he looked at it, and then at me, and then he took the fruit, and at the same time held my hand firmly and gently with his own. As I sat motionless he released my hand, looked down at the nut, and dropped it to the ground.

At that moment there was no need of any scientific knowledge to understand this communication of reassurance. The soft pressure of his fingers spoke to me not through my intellect but through a more primitive emotional channel: the barrier of untold centuries which has grown up during the separate evolution of man and chimpanzee was, for those few seconds, broken down.

It was a reward far beyond my greatest hopes.

van Lawick-Goodall, *In the Shadow of Man*, p. 268.

A buffalo when drinking at a waterhole was bitten on the tongue by a turtle. The buffalo left the water, and blood started to gush out of its mouth. Shortly afterwards it fell down and died. A later investigation of the carcass showed that the buffalo's tongue was indeed damaged. This waterhole — out in the bush in Toro district — is not used by the local people on account of the large number of turtles permanently in it.

Uganda Game Department Reports, 1947, as quoted in Anthony Cullen, *Window onto Wilderness* (East Africa Publishing, 1969), p. 181.

And the animals are everywhere. It is not like looking for sheep in Rocky Mountain National Park. All that afternoon I spent looking for lions, wherever the plain spread flat to the horizon there were beasts in view — a stem-legged ostrich at the least, or a splash of burning zebra stripes; or scores or hundreds of kongoni and wildebeest, the edges of the herds set with elegant gazelles, and with half a dozen other kinds of antelopes sprinkled about singly or in little bands. A bataleur eagle was there, up among the rolling clouds; and close over the plain the cry and swooping of hawks told of a different scale of life, *diverse as the antelopes themselves, down among the grass stems. Baboons trooped at the roadside; jackals, francolins, and plover ran ahead in the wheel tracks. In three separate acacia clumps, giraffes were browsing at the top shoots; their sides a pattern of fantastic chainwork among the feathery leaves. And always there was the fine, fair country to see, with the warm wind rippling the veld, smoothing the snowgrass on the hilltops, and stirring a thin song in the pipes of the whistling-thorn.*

Archie Carr, *Ulendo — Travels of a Naturalist in and out of Africa* (Alfred A. Knopf, 1964), p. 6. "Ulendo" is the equivalent of "safari" in Chinyanja, the language spoken in former Nyasaland, now Malawi. Carr's literary gifts were well matched by his acute observations.

One night in September, the Ranger shone his torch on the grass in front of his camp, and saw a female oribi lying down with what appeared to be two young ones. When he approached, the oribi stood up and started to move off, followed by the two young animals and three others which had not been noticed before. It was then clearly seen that all five young animals were jackal cubs. The six moved off together, and it was quite obvious that the cubs were definitely accompanying the female oribi, which appeared to encourage this strange relationship.

Uganda Game Department Reports, 1953, as quoted in Cullen, *Window onto Wilderness*, p. 182.

[We] were slightly taken aback when the D.C. [District Commissioner] told us that chitinde *meant manure in Chibemba.*
"But why call a village manure?"
"Because the chief had many cattle."
After that logical explanation I demanded to know the name of every village we passed.

Bigland, *The Lake of the Royal Crocodile*, p. 217.

One early morning I walked along the thicket of rapphia palms at the edge of the Kingupira forest, keeping an eye out for the lions that we heard each night, and listening to the sunrise plaint of the hadadas and fish eagles and trumpeter hornbills, the shrieking parrots, the squalling and explosive chack! *of four boubous chasing through a bush. High in a riverrain forest tree, four brown-chested barbets sat very still, gathering heat from the new sun in their crimson breasts, and not far away on a bare limb, a scarlet-chested sunbird preened itself with staccato energy, as if dealing with an attack of biting ants. Beside the track, a songbird came to perch just near the silhouette of what I had assumed was a Gabar goshawk, which will take such unwary birds wherever it finds them; looking more carefully, I saw that the hawk was a lizard buzzard. Interestingly, the lizard buzzard does not take birds, perhaps because it is too slow and lethargic, and more interestingly still, songbirds have learned to distinguish this raptor from the others, and will perch beside it without fear.*

Peter Matthiessen, *Sand Rivers* (photography by Hugo van Lawick; Viking Press, 1981), p. 61. In late 1979, Matthiessen and van Lawick joined a safari led by Brian Nicholson into the Selous Reserve in Tanzania. *Sand Rivers* is the account of this trip. Matthiessen, whose other book on Africa has been extensively quoted, is an award-winning and best-selling novelist and author of some of the best nonfiction work published dealing with naturalist subjects (e.g., *The Wind Birds* and *The Snow Leopard*).

The most remarkable task a client ever asked me to perform was to crawl down a hole after a wounded warthog. I was guiding the Earl of Carnarvon when he shot and wounded a big boar warthog. The animal took refuge in a hole. When a warthog enters a hole, he always turns and backs in so as to have his tusks pointed in the direction of a possible pursuer. The earl wanted the animal badly but I could think of no way to get at him. We had no digging tools and there was no way of smoking the pig out.

I asked my scouts if they would go down the hole after the boar. They explained that they were all of the Islam faith and were forbidden to touch a pig, otherwise they would have been delighted. There was nothing for it but do the task myself. I peeled off my coat and after telling the boys to drag me out by the legs when I began to kick, I started down the burrow.

The hole was a fairly tight fit for my waistline and the stinking breath of the pig nearly stifled me. With my body blocking the entrance the hole was pitch dark. I wriggled along, feeling ahead with my right hand, until I touched the boar's snout. Then I grabbed him by the tusk. The boar promptly tried to jab my hand against the top of the burrow but I hung on, kicking madly. I was close to fainting from the lack of air and the heavy odor of the pig. The boys pulled me out and I dragged the smelly beast with me.

When I stood up, wiping my face, the earl said, "Splendid, Hunter. I don't want the boar as a trophy. I just want his hide for saddle leather. Are you sure you didn't damage it getting him out of that hole?"

Hunter, *Hunter*, p. 70.

On one occasion, when we were in bad lion country and there was a risk of losing [a particularly valued] mule, I armed a sentry whose duty it was to keep watch all night and to shoot at anything approaching the camp without waking me up first. I told him that would be enough to drive the lions away if they ventured near. Next morning one boy was reported ill. On asking what was the matter with him I was tactfully informed that the top of his head was loose and a part of it had come off. Amazed at this statement, I went to where he was lying and found a dead man with the upper part of his skull shot away. It appeared that he was a practical joker, and, trusting to the notorious inability of Native marksmen to hit anything, he had crept into the bush near by and roared like a lion. By a miracle the sentry had this time hit the target in the dark, and the boy had paid for his amusement with his life.

John Boyes, *The Company of Adventurers* (East Africa Ltd., 1928), p. 100. Nineteenth-century England produced the most extraordinary individuals, even more odd than the usual quotient of perennial migratory Englishmen and women born with a romantic hunger to escape the constricting physical and cultural horizons (and wet climate) of the British Isles. Africa proved the perfect hideout for these immortal English eccentrics, and Boyes was one of the more eclectic of an already irreplaceably peculiar collection. Opinions in the white settler community concerning Boyes, known far and wide for his strong, uncouth (almost unbelievable, apparently) language, ranged from "that awful little man" to high praise as a "most remarkable early settler." Boyes began his odyssey by running away from school to sea. He sailed first to Brazil, eventually arriving in the East African port of Mombasa in 1898 carrying only the clothes on his back. At one point, Boyes wandered (the word is used advisedly) beyond the "usual" hunting and exploration routes into the most remote parts of British East Africa, where he was captured by Kikuyu warriors and nearly killed. But he survived and lived among the tribe, supplying meat to the Mombasa-Uganda railway teams. When he cured some wounded Kikuyu warriors by using a disinfectant (never seen before by the natives), he was given the honorary title "King of the Wakikuyu." (Actually, the Kikuyu had no kings — a particular village was ruled by a council of elders.) Boyes trained a small army of natives and armed them with guns. As his village gradually achieved ascendancy over its neighbors, Boyes became practically the supreme ruler of the Kikuyu tribe. This experience was described in Boyes' *King of the WaKikuyu* (Methuen, 1911), published in the U.S. as *A White King in East Africa* (McBride, Nast, 1912). One hesitates even to quote from that text; truly, it is one of those stories that must be read in its entirety to be believed (even in part). Boyes was subsequently arrested by the English Administrators for waging war, making treaties, impersonating government, leading punitive expeditions, and "dacoity" (stealing — in this instance, poaching ivory). The reader can imagine what the linguistically creative Boyes did with "dacoity" at his trial. Eventually, the charges were dismissed. Boyes was released, sailed for England, returned on a Nile expedition a few months later, and was soon back in Nairobi (1904). By the time of *The Company of Adventurers*, he had settled into the relatively prosaic life simply of shooting at anything that moved on four legs.

A favourite companion on my Congo trips was an Airedale dog. . .He was a good watch-dog, but I never took him out hunting, as he did not keep to heel well enough. One day, however, he broke loose and turned up at the critical moment; in fact, just as I had spotted a big bull elephant and was waiting for him to turn in order to get in the ear-shot. The dog rushed up and bit the elephant in the leg, or tried to. The elephant at once turned on him and in a moment the Airedale came sprinting towards where I was hiding. The elephant was on top of me before I could do anything and I was as near as possible killed, but just managed to dodge out of its way. I got that elephant later.

Boyes, *Company of Adventurers*, p. 101. Easier to shoot the dog.

At about noon the first heavy drops of rain began to fall. The chimpanzees climbed out of the tree and one after the other plodded up the steep grassy slope toward the open ridge at the top. There were seven adult males in the group, including Goliath and David Graybeard, several females, and a few

youngsters. As they reached the ridge the chimpanzees paused. At that moment the storm broke. The rain was torrential, and the sudden clap of thunder, right overhead, made me jump. As if this were a signal, one of the big males stood upright and as he swayed and swaggered rhythmically from foot to foot I could just hear the rising crescendo of his pant-hoots above the beating of the rain. Then he charged off, flat-out down the slope toward the trees he had just left. He ran some thirty yards, and then, swinging round the trunk of a small tree to break his headlong rush, leaped into the low branches and sat motionless.

Almost at once two other males charged after him. One broke off a low branch from a tree as he ran and brandished it in the air before hurling it ahead of him. The other, as he reached the end of his run, stood upright and rhythmically swayed the branches of a tree back and forth before seizing a huge branch and dragging it farther down the slope. A fourth male, as he too charged, leaped into a tree and, almost without breaking his speed, tore off a large branch, leaped with it to the ground, and continued down the slope. As the last two males called and charged down, so the one who had started the whole performance climbed from his tree and began plodding up the slope again. The others, who had also climbed into trees near the bottom of the slope, followed suit. When they reached the ridge, they started charging down all over again, one after the other, with equal vigor.

The females and youngsters had climbed into trees near the top of the rise as soon as the displays had begun, and there they remained watching throughout the whole performance. As the males charged down and plodded back up, so the rain fell harder, jagged forks or brilliant flares of lightning lit the leaden sky, and the crashing of the thunder seemed to shake the very mountains.

My enthusiasm was not merely scientific as I watched, enthralled, from my grandstand seat on the opposite side of the narrow ravine, sheltering under a plastic sheet. In fact it was raining and blowing far too hard for me to get at my notebook or use my binoculars. I could only watch, and marvel at the magnificence of those splendid creatures. With a display of strength and vigor such as this, primitive man himself might have challenged the elements.

van Lawick-Goodall, *In the Shadow of Man*, pp. 52-3.

During those last days, I began to understand the attraction of the Nile. . . .

It flowed by so placidly, neither hurrying nor tarrying, and the little Nile cabbages floated down, eddying in the current, and slipping by and out of sight. Thus might you muse upon it for a few brief hours, or for a thousand years; and it might stand almost for a symbol of time itself, running down through the ages; here still in its beginning, its banks wild and untrodden, its people primitive as the first man; anon flowing through the desert till it flows at last under bridges, and past great civilisations, old and new. About it, and about those natives who sat watching it, there was the same strong patience that would finally conquer all. It is this very patience that is at first so exasperating about Africa and Africans, a kind of apathy and indifference that is callous, and a fatalism that enrages one. Yet there, perhaps, lay the solution. Africa is too mighty for anything so brittle as impatience, and one's strength lies not in

pitting oneself against it, but in ranging oneself upon the same side.

de Watteville, *Out in the Blue*, p. 239.

Elephants were drifting into the forest from all directions. The sun was just coming up over the hills and was shining upon the forest, which sparkled in the sunlight — morning greetings to the forest people. The monkeys greeted one another with barks and coughs. Everything was waking up — it was a busy day. There was not a breath of air. I had gone back a million years; the birds were calling back and forth, the monkeys were calling to one another, a troop of chimpanzees in the open screamed, and their shouts were answered from another group inside the forest. All the forest life was awake and moving about as that huge herd of elephants, singly and in groups, flowed into the

hands, to the extremity of the bough that at a considerable height overhung the river; from this post they had a bird's-eye view, and reconnoitred before one of the numerous party descended to drink. The sharp eyes of the young one at once detected the crocodile, who matched in colour so well with the rocks, that most probably a man would not have noticed it until too late. At once the young one commenced shaking the bough and screaming with all his might to attract the attention of the crocodile, and to induce it to move. In this he was immediately joined by the whole party, who yelled in chorus, while the large old males bellowed defiance, and descended to the lowest branches within eight or ten feet of the crocodile. It was of no use — the pretender never stirred, and I watched it until dark; it remained still in the same place, waiting for some unfortunate baboon whose thirst might provoke his fate; but not one was

Plate 30. *Midday Drink.*

forest from the plain. There was one continuous roar of noise, all the wild life joining, but above it all were the crashing of trees and the squealing of the elephants as they moved into the forest on a front at least a mile wide. It was the biggest show I ever saw in Africa.

Akeley, *In Brightest Africa*, pp. 23-4.

The large tamarind trees on the opposite bank are generally full of the dog-faced baboons...in the evening, at their drinking-hour. I watched a large crocodile creep slyly out of the water, and lie in waiting among the rocks at the usual drinking-place before they arived, but the baboons were too wide awake to be taken in so easily. A young fellow was the first to discover the enemy; he had accompanied several wise and experienced old

sufficiently foolish, although the perpendicular banks prevented them from drinking except at that particular spot.

Baker, *The Nile Tributaries of Abyssinia, and The Sword Hunters of the Hamran Arabs,* pp. 177-8. Baker was a fluent writer, and the reader would also enjoy *The Albert N'yanza* (Macmillan, 1886) and *Wild Beasts and Their Ways* (Macmillan, 1890). Undoubtedly, a strong motivation behind all Sam's traveling was his nervousness about bringing the young and beautiful Florence back to face the scrutiny of Victorian England (indeed, the couple was snubbed by Queen Victoria, who somehow suspected Flo's origins). A confident and fearless explorer, Baker's volumes are well worth reading.

Giraffes too, I must say, are always surprising, with their beautiful markings reaching up and around their long necks and their funny flat heads that should really belong to a sea serpent. Their soft black muzzles are irresistible; so also are their great Landseer-like eyes, fringed with lashes as heavy as a crêpe curtain. . . .The strange thing about them is that they hate getting wet. They appear to be especially sensitive about their heads. When it rains, you will see them standing miserably, their heads stuck into a tree-top. If there are no trees they do the best they can to shelter under each other's necks. The lucky ones are presumably those who had the idea first.

Cameron, *Equator Farm*, p. 56.

to the conclusion that the timelessness of the continent — endless desert, endless bush, endless tortoise-like movement towards that which had been seized by puny man — was the root cause of it when we ran over a puff-adder and pulled up with a bang.

Bigland, *The Lake of the Royal Crocodile*, p. 160.

As a prince must be able to act just like a beast, he should learn from the fox and the lion; because the lion does not defend himself against traps, and the fox does not defend himself against wolves. So one has to be a fox in order to recognize traps, and a lion to frighten off wolves.

Niccolo Machiavelli, *The Prince (1532)*, XVIII.

Plate 31. Elephant Bull on the Shores of Lake Kariba.

We were later still, but it didn't do to say so. "Schedule" was the favourite word in all Africa. The English used it, and the Afrikanders, and the Boers, and the Belgians, the French, the Portuguese; even the Egyptians used it, heaven knew why, and the one thing in life which really mattered was to be not before or behind but on schedule. Nobody ever achieved this necessity, but the penalty for admitting they hadn't was complete and devastating ostracism from society. Indeed, when I told someone I was glad my publishers didn't live in Africa he studiously ignored me for the rest of my stay despite the fact that he was even later than myself for any appointment. So with the lorry-driver I held my peace, nodded when he reiterated "schedule", forebore to mention buffalo or lion, and cogitated the why and wherefore of this strange absorption with time. I had just come

*Olim quod vulpes aegroto cautal leoni
espondit referam: "quia me vestigia terrent,
omnia te adversum spectantia, nulla retrorsum."
(Let me remind you what the wary fox said once upon a time to the sick lion: "Because those footprints scare me, all directed your way, none coming back.")*

Horace, *Epistles*, I. i. 73.

One evening a group of us sat round old Brittlebank's camp fire on the banks of the Nile, fanning ourselves to keep away the mosquitoes. A full moon shone out of the beautiful African night, the attraction of which can be fully felt only by those who have experienced it. The only sounds which broke the stillness were those of the hippo disporting themselves and the occasional boom of the bull-frogs.

For a time we sat and smoked and swopped yarns about elephant hunting. Then, as none of us felt disposed to turn in, it was agreed that each in turn should tell a story of a strange or interesting happening within his experience. . . .

* * *

"Blowed if I know what to tell you blighters," began the unfortunate who had first suggested that each should spin a yarn in turn. "My experiences have been much more genteel than yours!"

When the jeers that greeted the remark had died down, "Tell us about jails," one man urged encouragingly. "You ought to know a lot about them."

"Jails! It's an idea, anyhow, for it reminds me of chain-gangs. For the sake of some of you newcomers (more chaffing), I'll recall that in the early days jails naturally did not exist in the up-country bomas, which had to be content with grass huts. Any Native prisoner who wished — but they [sic] were too well off to wish anything so silly — could easily have escaped on a dark night, even though an askari patrolled outside. To prevent escapes the system of chaining them together started. Then, as now, the chain-gang usually consisted of about ten prisoners, who did the usual jobs of bringing wood, water and grass to the boma, keeping it clean, attending to the garden, et cetera.

"One day, when I was at a boma, a chain-gang was sent out in charge of an askari to fetch firewood. The prisoners had not been gone long when out of the long grass charged an old rhino, who, scenting the shackled Natives, threw his tail up straight, stuck down his snout, and made straight for them. The askari stood his ground and fired his old Snider rifle, but that only wounded the beast and infuriated it more than ever. The prisoners, recognising their danger — and thinking no doubt of freedom, home, and more cattle-raiding — lit out quick and lively, with the rhino in full pursuit.

"But the race, though swift, did not last long. In a minute or two the rhino had got his horns entangled in the chain, and it is a solid fact that he disappeared into the bush dragging the whole chain-gang with him. When he arrived back at the boma minus the men, I heard the askari tell the D.C. the story, and I believed every word of it.

"When you beauties go to jail ..." The rest of the statement was lost in the uproar.

* * *

"Talking about chain-gangs," chipped in a usually taciturn fellow, who probably meant to pay his score in the fewest possible words, "I can tell you an equally true story of a whole chain-gang that disappeared in Lake Victoria. This also happened some years ago. A number of prisoners were sent down to the Lake to obtain water for the boma. The first man had no sooner stepped into the water...when an old croc. came along and swept him off his feet with one blow of his tail. Gripping him immediately he had lost his balance, and pulling him into deep water, the others had, of course, to follow. The askari went nearly frantic but was powerless to do anything as he saw his prisoners disappearing into the lake one by one — eaten up like a stick of celery.

"As the last prisoner was being dragged to a most unpleasant grave, the askari grabbed him, and a brief tug-of-war followed; but soon the Native had to let go, in order to save himself being pulled in. I too happened to be at the boma when the askari came

back, soaked to the skin, to tell the tale to the D.C. I'll leave you fellows to decide whether a rhino is a better kidnapper than a croc."

Boyes, *The Company of Adventurers*, pp. 109-11.

That later we, though parted then,
May still recall those evenings when
   Fear gave his watch no look;
The lion griefs loped from the shade
And on our knees their muzzles laid,
   And Death put down his book.

W.H. Auden, "A Summer Night."

Apeneck Sweeney spreads his knees
Letting his arms hang down to laugh,
The zebra stripes along his jaw
Swelling to maculate giraffe.

T.S. Eliot, "Sweeney Among the Nightingales."

. . .I once saw, at the Queen Elizabeth National Park in Uganda, a free-living, perfectly healthy, and even well-fed elephant without a trunk. I had been sitting behind the wheel of my pickup truck, watching a small herd of elephants move through heavy bush about a hundred yards away. There were seven of them, and they seemed like any other elephants until one of the bulls emerged from a thicket of false bamboo. . .

. . .His trunk ended in a huge scar just below tusk level: he had probably been tabbed through the trunk while fighting with a rival bull and, following severe infection, the lower part had sloughed away. The scar appreared to be several years old, but the elephant was still very much around.

There was only one logical explanation I could think of, but I had to trail the herd for nearly two hours before they finally confirmed it. As they settled down to browse in a thicket of mimosa, I watched the trunkless elephant stand idly while the herd tore at the trees, gathering twigs and leaves. None of them ate so much as a single leaf but moved instead toward their handicapped companion, bearing bundles of food, as they must have done for several years. He opened his mouth expectantly. Eager to feed him first, two of the elephants jostled each other. The rest waited their turns patiently. In all, they brought their trunkless welfare case so much food that he hardly had time to chew it; he gulped furiously for awhile, then closed his mouth tight and shook his head from side to side, rejecting any more leafy bundles. Only then did the other elephants move away and at last start to feed themselves.

Hallet, *Animal Kitabu*, pp. 110-1.

'This was certainly a hyena night. At 7.30 pm a herd of over forty buffalo started to leave the glade in a long line, when two hyena suddenly appeared and singled out a calf of about eleven months. They drove the calf into dense bush, and the mother turned to defend it. The rest of the herd carried on.

'For the next half hour a raging battle could be clearly heard: the calf's bellows of pain, the grunts of the mother, and crashings in the dense bush. During this time nine more hyena came loping across the glade and joined in.

'The fight then moved much closer to The Ark, its passage being marked by the continuous noise and the waving bush. A stand was made near the glassed-in viewing lounge. From time to time a hyena came out of the bush and howled. Eventually this was answered and a second pack of thirteen appeared at the end of the glade. Immediately half the first pack came out of the bushes and raced to greet them, stubby tails held high.

'Meanwhile a number of the old resident bulls came from the valley and joined in. Twice the milling animals came into view and we could see the calf clearly. Its tail was completely bitten off, a section of meat was missing from just below, and there were numerous wounds right down to the hocks. It followed close behind its mother.

'The fight settled down. Sometimes as many as six hyenas could be seen resting, with heads on paws. Twenty-five hyenas, nine buffalo bulls and the mother appeared to be involved. From time to time hyena would dance right up to the lowered head of one of the bulls but they were rarely tempted to move more than a few paces in retaliation. Nevertheless renewed bellowings always indicated that other hyenas were breaking through the cordon.

'About midnight, four and a half hours after the start of the fight, the bellowing ceased, and shortly after this the nine bulls came into the open and dispersed. Probably one was the herd bull but this could not be confirmed. The cow doubtless remained with her dead calf.

'The periodic howlings of the hyenas now changed to the cracklings, squeaks, and diabolic laughs associated with feeding.[']

R.J. Prickett, *The African Ark* (Drake, 1974), pp. 155-6.

Everywhere we looked, there was game. Wart-hogs ran off snorting, tails held high and dainty Thompson's [sic] gazelles, with the white flash on their flanks and long graceful horns, were quite near to us. A herd of very plump zebra looked at us inquiringly, their white stripes faintly pink from rolling in the wet mud. We saw two giraffes, and Loderic spotted four lions across a valley, lying up by some bushes. The grass was lush and covered with pretty white flowers which grew close to the ground. The short rains were just ending and the animals were in superb condition.

We drove to a pool on the Athi River where to our delight, the large dark bulk of a hippo slid into the water and swam slowly along to stop with just his eyes, ears and nostrils showing beneath the over-grown bank. A crocodile made an arrowlike wake as he crossed the pool and a tall giraffe looked down rather disdainfully as he nibbled the choice top leaves of a tree across the pool from us. On our side were lots of small grey vervet monkeys climbing the trees and swinging on the branches above our heads.

Madge Mayall, *Safari: Kenya-Uganda 1968* (1970). Mayall's account is a delightful, unassuming little story of what could be anyone's typical first-time safari.

The spreading of civilisation far into the interior of the once Dark Continent of Africa has progressed so much of late years that the ever-increasing occupation of large tracts of veld by enterprising settlers threatens to imperil the very existence of the larger mammals of East Equatorial Africa. It is likely that the elephant, the lordly master of the bush-covered tracts of Kenya Colony, will be one of the first of the African pachyderms to vanish from the world. I venture, therefore, to suggest that it now becomes to some extent advisable for the present day sportsman in search of adventure to preserve all possible records of the life of these beasts in their natural surroundings. What better instrument could be employed for compiling such a collection of records than the camera, equipped with a careful selection of the best modern lenses?

Marius ("Marcuswell") Maxwell, *Stalking Big Game with a Camera in Equatorial Africa* (Century, 1924), p. vxi. Maxwell, an Englishman who lived in the United States, brought back from the Serengeti Plains the first close-up photographs of live animals. (His few predecessors had closed the distance only by shooting the game.) In particular, a series of lion pictures showing prides at a kill or resting under acacia trees caused a sensation and were republished in many illustrated papers (especially *The London Times*) all over the world. Considering the bulkiness of Maxwell's camera and the fact that he was frequently on foot, the shots of bull elephants from ten or so yards away(!), the close-ups of buffalo, rhinos, and hippos, and the catching of giraffes at full gallop are all remarkable, indeed.

...directly [the wounded elephant] *emerged from the bush she saw me plainly in the open before her and came on two yards to my one, screaming shrilly all the time.*

I did not hesitate an instant what to do, but resolved to sacrifice the horse and try to get away myself in the grass. Catching him by the mane, when he instantly stopped dead, I jumped past him and ran forwards through the grass as hard as I could, which was not very hard, as I was now much exhausted. I had got some forty yards beyond him when the elephant suddenly stopped screaming and commenced making the rumbling noise I have spoken of...Turning my head I saw that she was standing...alongside of the horse, who remained perfectly motionless, but that she had not yet touched him. I instantly ducked down in the grass and watched her. I was very much afraid lest she should get my wind and come on after me, and at the same time feared to fire at her, as I felt so terribly shaky after my run that I knew I should only give her a bad shot and let her know where I was. I was very much surprised at her leaving the horse alone. Had she been unwounded,...I should have thought nothing of it, as there are many similar cases on record; but, irritated as the poor brute must have been from the wounds she had received, I made [sic] sure she would have killed him instantly. She would most certainly have killed me had she caught me, and I think she showed more magnanimity than sagacity in sparing my horse, for, although he had taken no part in injuring her, he had, at any rate, been instrumental in bringing me within shot of her. However that may be, the fact remains that this wounded and furious elephant ran screaming up to my horse, and, finding his rider gone, stood alongside of him without touching him. After a space of half a minute, perhaps, she turned and walked back into the bush, and I then went back to my horse, who had never moved his feet since I placed my hand on his mane and sprang from the saddle.

Frederick Courteney Selous, *Travel and Adventure in South-East Africa* (Hippocrene Books Edition, 1984; first published by Rowland Ward, 1893), p. 177. Selous was the most renowned big-game hunter of his day, a boyhood hero to most of the hunters who followed. A relentless killer when the animals seemed endlessly abundant, Selous was undoubtedly the model for Rider Haggard's Allan Quartermain character. Most of his hunting was done from horseback, the horse, as this passage suggests, perhaps not an altogether happy partner in the many escapades.

The Lion alone of all wild beasts is gentle to those who humble themselves unto him, and will not touch any such upon their submission, but spareth what creatures soever lieth prostrate before him. As fell and furious as hee is otherwhiles, yet hee dischargeth his rage upon man, before that hee setteth upon women, and never preyeth upon babes unless it be for extreme hunger.

Pliny, *Natural History* (trans. John Bostock & H.T. Riley, 1855, 6 vols). Pliny the Elder (Gaius Plinius Secundus, c. A.D. 23-79) was easily the most learned Roman of his day. His passion for collecting information resulted in the great compendium of ancient science, *Natural History* (*Historia Naturalis* appeared in A.D. 77), of which zoology forms only one — but surely the most entertaining — section. The preface states that the work contains 20,000 facts collected from 2,000 volumes and 473 authorities. *Natural History* is a digest whose value depends entirely on the reliability of its sources and the discrimination exhibited in quoting them. Though a careful and industrious writer, Pliny was hardly an original thinker and as a compiler suffered from credulity. One supposes that his reading was so extensive that he had little time for reflection or judgment. Certainly, his preoccupation with entertaining anecdotes led him to include all sorts of nonsense and to elevate the curious to the same level as the significant. He was, for example, convinced that lionesses occasionally mated with hyenas (afterward giving birth to horrible monsters). To keep the male lions from discovering this infidelity, the lionesses always followed the males at some distance behind and often washed their faces, both tactics to keep the smell of hyenas from the males. Pliny's various legends lasted for centuries. Pliny himself died while commanding a Roman fleet at Misenum (close to Naples), when scientific curiosity (and a desire to assist civilians in danger) led him to approach too near an erupting Mt. Vesuvius; he was suffocated by poisonous gases thrown off in the eruption.

...we had scarcely paddled three hundred yards, and had just rounded a small island, when we were stopped by yells and shouts behind us, and soon one of the paddlers belonging to my canoe came running along the bank, calling out, "The canoe is dead! the canoe is dead! a hippopotamus has killed the canoe!"

Selous, *Travel and Adventure in South-East Africa*, p. 259.

...I suppose it is no wonder the plight of the Pleistocene seems far away in Africa, where an unreal aura hangs anyway, part gin, part cordite smoke, part sex on a canvas cot. And anyway, *you can easily see from the movies that animals are all over the place out there — the ground is crawling with fauna. So with plenty to worry about at home, and with no real understanding of what is happening in Africa, the usual American says, oh, what the hell, the British will look after the animals.*

Carr, *Ulendo*, p. 236.

The chief aim of the camera hunter must, of course, be to obtain a result that will be of value alike to the naturalist, to the sculptor, and to the painter.

Maxwell, *Stalking Big Game with a Camera in Equatorial Africa*, p. xvii.

To all of these creatures I simply said something like "Boo!" in a very loud and peremptory manner and they shoved off at the double.

. . .

As a matter of fact, after nearly forty years of meandering about jungles under the most vulnerable conditions. . .I have yet to be actually jumped by anything larger than an ant.

Ivan Sanderson, *Ivan Sanderson's Book of Great Jungles* (Julian Messner/Pocket Books, 1965), p. 230. Most animals, even the most dangerous predators, avoid man, given an opportunity to do so. Notwithstanding all the Tarzan movies and the many reports of adventurers to the contrary, a man yelling "Boo" to a wild animal is strange enough not to be trifled with.

. . .[the owl] opened its wings and flew for two or three yards. As it did so I saw that there was something attached to one of its legs, and on catching it found that a large chameleon was fast secured to it, having its tail firmly twisted two or three times round one of the owl's legs. How they had got into this position I cannot say, but I fancy that the little owl must first have attacked the chameleon, though upon detaching it I could find no wounds or scratches of any kind upon it. Neither was there anything amiss with the owl, which, as soon as I had released it, flew away and perched in a neighbouring thorn-tree.

Selous, *Travel and Adventure in South-East Africa*, p. 249. Selous was a keen observer, and it is this sort of tidbit that makes him worth reading today. Recommended as well are *African Nature Notes and Reminisences* (MacMillan, 1908) and *A Hunter's Wanderings in Africa* (MacMillan, 1907).

The mornings were magical. Long before the sun appeared a green light slanted across the lake from the east, and through this the pelicans came flying. They flew in batches of anything from five to fifty birds, and either in a vee formation or in line, but always with one bird leading. They gave one the impression that they were ascending and descending a series of invisible hills in the sky. When they flapped their wings, a lazy casual motion, they rose together in a line; then together they went into a long glide which almost took them to the surface of the lake. Then again in unison they flapped and rose like galleons from the waves. Often one would see as many as a thousand birds flapping and gliding in this way, and their wings made a pleas-

ant sighing in the air. They landed a little awkwardly, like elderly gentlemen stepping off a moving bus.

Moorehead, *No Room in the Ark*, pp. 178-9.

A lot of humorous remarks are made at The Ark, either sub-consciously or because the person has no knowledge whatever of game. Consider these priceless comments, mostly heard in the darkness of the viewing lounge.

One night a lady was staring long and earnestly into an empty glade. Suddenly she looked up and said: 'Now I know the difference between a male and female bush...'

One man had been looking at two of the rarely seen, beautiful bongo, quite close to the building for a full twenty minutes. Suddenly he turned to me, saying: 'Say, when are the big cats coming in?'

One woman to another: 'You know there are two kinds of hippopotamuses, one that lives in water and one that lives on the land. The one that they have here is the one that lives on the land.'

A black rhino was walking into the glade one night and a lady guest said: 'There's a white rhino coming in.' 'That isn't a white rhino' came an answer out of the darkness. 'Well, if it isn't white it's beige.'

. . .

One very noisy lady had a lot to say, and the Hostess warned her a number of times. A big bull elephant came on to the salt in front of the glassed-in viewing lounge and the buzzer was sounded. The noisy lady came tripping along with her husband tagging behind. A moment later she saw the elephant and fell absolutely silent. As the long-suffering husband came past the Hostess he smiled and said: 'If it only takes an elephant to make her quiet then I'll buy a couple from you.'

A big herd of elephants once stood in front of The Ark with a huge bull in their midst. A dear old lady sitting with her back to the scene said to the Hostess: 'How do you tell which are boys and which are girls?' Before the Hostess could think of a suitable answer the bull decided to demonstrate to the whole world that he at least was not a girl. Blissfully unaware of this, the dear old lady repeated her question, to the uncontrollable merriment of all assembled. The Hostess fled. As the comment was voiced later, that big bull was well endowed.

One night a lady came into the darkened viewing lounge. There were six buffalo standing placidly at the waterside. From some angles they were reflected in the glass of the far side of the room. Not looking at the people sitting quietly there she spotted the reflection and screamed: 'The elephants are coming,' and, before she could be stopped, ran back and roused the whole building.

Some of the moths at The Ark are big. A gentleman had been watching the genet pounce on one in fairly long grass, and it took a little while to eat, the wings falling on each side of the genet's mouth. Later he was heard describing the event to a friend. But the story went something like this: 'I saw a mongoose catch a snake and eat it. There was such a big fight.'

Prickett, *The African Ark*, pp. 169-71.

Once, when a large herd stampeded toward me — probably panicked by a prowling lion — there was far more danger. Had I tried to run away across that stretch of open savannah near Rutshuru, south of the Albert National Park's Rwindi Plains, I certainly would have been overtaken, trampled, and crushed beneath four or five hundred thundering hoofs — buffaloes can travel at a speed of thirty-five miles per hour versus twenty for the fastest man alive (which I am not). So instead of taking suicidal flight, I waited quietly for the oncoming herd with arms outstretched, trying to look like a new species of baobab tree.

Fleeing as they were from some kind of danger, there was no good reason for the panic-stricken animals to waste their time investigating an immobile object that presented no real menace, even a bearded, very phony-looking tree. The buffalo stampede split into two, streaming by on either side of me. There was a great deal of noise and dust, plus a strong, sweet, bovine scent, far more powerful than that of native cattle — but that was all.

Hallet, *Animal Kitabu*, pp. 83-4. Vintage Hallet.

...the zebras were quite bright too. The Doctor discovered that these intelligent beasts had ways of marking and twisting the grasses to show where they had smelled lions about...

Hugh Lofting, *Doctor Dolittle's Post Office* (Lippincott, 1923), p. 97. This volume in the famous Dolittle series chronicles the Doctor's trip to the African kingdom of Fantippo and has always been the author's favorite.

And now it came, at last, to the pushmi-pullyu's turn for a story. He was very shy and modest and when the animals asked him the following night he said in his very well-bred manner:

"I'm terribly sorry to disappoint you, but I'm afraid I don't know any stories — at least none good enough to entertain you with."

"Oh, come on, Push," said Jip. "Don't be so bashful. We've all told one. You don't mean to say you've lived all your life in the African jungle without seeing any adventures? There must be lots of yarns you could tell us."

"But I've mostly led such a quiet life, you see," said the pushmi-pullyu. "Our people have always kept very much to themselves. We mind our own business and don't like getting mixed up in scandals and rows and adventures."

Lofting, *Doctor Dolittle's Post Office*, p. 229.

African Hall [of the American Museum of Natural History] is one of those projects which cannot be delayed. . . .twenty-five years ago, with innumerable specimens at hand, its development would have been an impossibility. Even if a man had had all the animals he wanted from Africa, he could not have made an exhibit of them that would have been either scientific, natural, artistic, or satisfying, for twenty-five years ago the art of taxidermy and of museum exposition of animal life hardly existed. Likewise, in those days much of the information that we had about animals through the tales of explorers, collectors, and other would-be heroes was ninety-five per cent. inaccurate.

Twenty-five years hence the development of such a hall will be equally impossible for the African animals are so rapidly becoming extinct that the proper specimens will not then be available. Even to-day the heads that are reaching London from

British East Africa are not up to the old standards. If an African Hall is to be done at all, it must be done now. And even if it is done now, we must have men to do it who have known Africa for at least a quarter of a century. Africa to-day is a modern Africa, the Africa of the Age of Man. Africa then was still the Africa of the Age of Mammals, a country sufficiently untouched by civilization to give a vivid impression of Africa a hundred years ago. By the time other groups are in place in African Hall, some of the species represented will have disappeared. Naturalists and scientists two hundred years from now will find there the only existent record of some of the animals which to-day we are able to photograph and to study in the forest environment. African Hall will tell the story of jungle peace, a story that is sincere and faithful to the African beasts as I have known them, and it will, I hope, tell that story so convincingly that the traditions of jungle horrors and impenetrable forests may be obliterated.

Akeley, *In Brightest Africa*, pp. 253-4. The exhibits have been mentioned in Chapter I. Fortunately, the full extent of Akeley's pessimism has not yet been realized.

In East Africa, hunters have ever been great liars, and except as fuel for nostalgia, their exploits make repetitious reading, clogged as they are with stupefying lists of the carcasses left behind and encounters with death so constant as to cancel one another out. Nevertheless, a great many of the adventurers were extraordinary men, and much of the seeming exaggeration in their accounts comes less from inflamed imaginations than from the compression of the inevitable adventures into a few pages, unleavened by all the quiet days in between.

. . .

Most professionals agree that a hunter who takes no risk is no hunter at all; since he lives by violence, he ought to be prepared to die that way. Yet they also agree that in the modern hunting safari there is virtually no risk to anyone but the professional, who may have less to fear from the wild animals than from his clients. A story is told of one of the Greek shipping magnates who took with him a bodyguard of three hunters, then damaged his expensive gun by dropping it when an elephant screamed; the gun's discharge sent it skidding across the rocks, and the bullet just missed one of his guards. Latin Americans, especially, think themselves unmanly if they do not pursue their own wounded animals into dangerous situations, and one hunter speaks of a Brazilian who...had wounded a lion [and] handed the hunter a movie camera, instructing him to film the inevitable charge and the destruction of the lion. "Don't shoot," he begged, "unless he has me down." The hunter refused, on the grounds that the loss of the client meant the probable loss of his own license. (In the good old days, when hunters were not penalized in this way, one of their number obeyed such rash instructions to the letter, and the filmed record of his client's demise, together with his personal effects, was duly sent home to his loved ones.)

Matthiessen & Porter, *The Tree Where Man Was Born/The African Experience*, p. 117.

The air in Africa is more significant in the landscape than in Europe, it is filled with loomings and mirages, and is in a way the real stage of activities. In the heat of the midday the air

oscillates and vibrates like the string of a violin, lifts up long layers of grass-land with thorn-trees and hills on it, and creates vast silvery expanses of water in the dry grass.

We were walking along in this burning live air, and...[a]ll at once the plain at the horizon began to move and gallop with more than the atmosphere, a big herd of game was bearing down upon us from the right, diagonally across the stage.

I said to Farah: "Look at all these Wildebeests." But a little after, I was not sure that they were Wildebeests; I took up my field-glasses and looked at them, but that too is difficult in the middle of the day. . . .

. . .

It is very difficult to judge distances on the plains. The quivering air and the monotony of the scenery make it so, also the character of the scattered thorn-trees, which have the exact shape of mighty old forest trees, but are in reality only twelve feet high, so that the Giraffes raise their heads and necks above them. You are continually deceived as to the size of the game that you see at a distance and may, in the middle of the day, mistake a jackal for an Eland, and an ostrich for a Buffalo. A minute later Farah said: "Memsahib, these are wild dogs."

The wild dogs are generally seen three or four at at time, but it happens that you meet a dozen of them together. The Natives are afraid of them, and will tell you that they are very murderous....The wild dogs are not as big as a Hyena. They are about the size of a big Alsatian dog. They are black, with a white tuft at the tip of the tail and of the pointed ears. The skin is no good, it has rough uneven hair and smells badly.

Here there must have been five hundred wild dogs. They came along in a slow canter, in the strangest way, looking neither right nor left, as if they had been frightened by something, or as if they were travelling fast with a fixed purpose on a track. They just swerved a bit as they came nearer to us; all the same they hardly seemed to see us, and went on at the same pace. When they were closest to us, they were fifty yards away. They were running in a long file, two or three or four side by side, it took time before the whole procession had passed us. In the middle of it, Farah said: "These dogs are very tired, they have run a long way."

. . .

I have told this tale to many people and not one of them has believed it. All the same, it is true, and my boys can bear me witness.

Dinesen, *Out of Africa*, pp. 312-5.

[Bicycling along the main approach road to the park,] *suddenly I found myself amidst a herd of elephants — there were elephants on my left, right, front and behind me; elephants were everywhere. I got off my bicycle and remained motionless; my presence did not appear to have caused alarm. After a short while the beasts began to move away and my fear was fading; then all of a sudden, a mother elephant charged from the side and another one attacked from the front. I threw down my bicycle and took to my heels at a speed such as I have never attained before in my life.*

The elephant did not want the bike, so I threw her my greatcoat. She did not seem to want that so I threw a shoe; but she did not want that either. I picked up a stick and the elephant got hold of the other end; so we were on the run. I thought I was flying but this proved to be untrue as I got tired very quickly. I was losing ground rapidly while the elephant was gaining at double speed. I felt that her trunk was almost touching me, and then I fell down between her front legs. She bent down her mighty head and her tusks got stuck into the ground. I was pinned between them.

In despair, somehow I took off my coat and pushed it right into the mouth of the determined beast which then kicked me and dashed off. I was left half unconscious on the ground but managed to crawl away for about 200 yards on my knees. When I had fully regained my wits I walked back to Wairingo ranger post, where I got someone to carry me on his bicycle to Masindi hospital...

Bere, *The African Elephant*, p. 94. This account was written by a Ugandan road supervisor who worked in a Ugandan national park.

The family life of the elephant intrigued me. The bull lumbered on by himself, scorning the cows and calves who travelled together, the babies playing and fighting among themselves while their mothers nuzzled and slapped them with their trunks, and encouraged them to imitate grown-up ways. Anyone who has hunted big game will tell you that one of the most enchanting occupations is to lie hidden on an ant-hill watching the calves solemnly copying their mama's habits. For myself, I found a strange resemblance in elephantine customs to those of the average English family out for a Sunday afternoon stroll when father, scorning to be seen with a perambulator, goes ahead and his slightly harassed wife bustles along some distance behind him restricting the antics of her young.

Bigland, *The Lake of the Royal Crocodiles*, p. 244.

I can watch elephants (and elephants alone) for hours at a time, for sooner or later the elephant will do something very strange such as mow grass with its toenails or draw the tusks from the rotted carcass of another elephant and carry them off into the bush. There is mystery behind that masked grey visage, an ancient life force, delicate and mighty, awesome and enchanted, commanding the silence ordinarily reserved for mountain peaks, great fires, and the sea. I remember a remark made by a girl about her father, a businessman of narrow sensibilities who, casting about for a means of self-gratification, traveled to Africa and slew an elephant. Standing there in his new hunting togs in a vast and hostile silence, staring at the huge dead bleeding thing that moments before had borne such life, he was struck for the first time in his headlong passage through his days by his own irrelevance. "Even he," his daughter said, "knew he'd done something stupid."

Matthiessen & Porter, *The Tree Where Man Was Born/The African Experience*, pp. 150-1.

A place the size of Nairobi is unique in having a national park adjoining the municipal boundary, and the park's proximity to a large centre of civilisation, although such a valuable asset to Kenya, brings many problems for those charged with the duties of its administration. The park is fenced on the two sides nearest to Nairobi with heavy chain-link wire-netting, but in spite of this lions occasionally get through a hole in the fence, made perhaps by a wart-hog or by a wash-away, and then

trouble starts.

...Two famous lionesses, 'Blondie' and 'Brunette'...and their families caused...trouble by moving out of the park one Saturday night, in pursuit of game seeking better grazing areas across the airport road. They made a kill and stayed with it until daylight. In the early hours of the morning travellers on their way to the airport were astonished to see some lions sitting by the roadside, quite unperturbed, still enjoying their meal. The airport road is a popular route for sight-seers and in no time large crowds gathered in their cars to watch the lions. By midday so many cars had assembled that it was impossible for any traffic to get through to the airport. The police and the park staff were summoned, and the airport authority, in a final note of despair, threatened to divert all international air traffic to Entebbe in Uganda.

The wardens, on arriving at the scene, were baffled by the sight of some two hundred cars clustered in a disorderly array, many of them blocking each other. The police tried to clear a way through but the people were so excited and keen to watch the lions that they paid no attention to traffic rules or to the police. The wardens then attempted to move the kill across the road towards the park, hoping that the lions would follow. This provoked great disfavour from 'Blondie,' normally a placid and tolerant lioness, who savaged the warden's Land-Rover and bit a hole through the metal wing. This pleased the excited crowd all the more, and made it almost impossible for the police or the wardens to do anything at all.

The police were compelled to stop all traffic from both approaches and take forceful action against any motorists who disobeyed orders. It was then possible, although difficult, for the wardens to coax the lions back to the park, and 'Blondie' and 'Brunette,' without any sign of repentance, condescended slowly to return home. One of the young cubs did not go back until the following day. Comments on this performance poured in from all parts of the world. Some people took great delight in telling their friends in London that they had been delayed by lions. Others protested about the monstrous way wild animals are allowed to impede the progress of modern communications. I have a feeling that 'Blondie' and 'Brunette' contributed more to the fame and eventual prosperity of Nairobi by their misdeeds than if the air-liners had sedately operated on schedule.

Cowie, *The African Lion*, pp. 89-92.

The traveler moving across the sundown savannah has witnessed a world going about its day's activities in accordance with its hourly needs, in accordance with the patterns of a thousand such mornings, a million such middays, a billion such evenings. They are all similar yet not the same. By infinitesimal shades of difference things are moving in fresh directions. The balance of evolutionary pressures has been shaping the animal life and its environment toward new forms of living. The visitor can hardly discern the slightest trend, but it is there and it is going on all the time: it is part of the experience of Africa, and you sense it is possible. One African day is the merest flicker in another long African day, and you are in both together.

The watcher puts away his binoculars and his camera and puts himself away for the night. Among the boundary trees there is a lion coughing. The sound sets off zebras a little way farther off. The safarist cannot see either; his watching is over for the day. But the day has not ended for most of the denizens of the area. For almost every creature but one the day merely enters another phase, for many the most active phase of all. As the tourist makes toward the light of the lodge he notices how the shadows streaming across the plain are matched by herds of antelope moving out into more open country. The aardvark emerges from its burrow to go on its evening exploration. The galano, better known as the bushbaby, swings around the branches of a tree looking for insects just as it has been doing for the last two hours of Africa's long day. The cheetah and wild dog are now at rest; they cannot exploit their skills at night unless there is a full moon. The hyenas and jackals are on the move, however, and on the move as they rarely are during daylight.

The dark uncovers another side to the creatures, and a fresh side to a fresh set of creatures. Across the wild areas of East Africa there are doings at night that you can only visualize, even if you can hear them well enough. The visitors around the campfire listen to the excited barkings of zebras, or pick up the distant trumpetings of elephants (and wonder how distant). They hear the snort of a wildebeest, and wonder what can be upsetting it. There is a grunt from a leopard, and everyone draws nearer the fire.

Myers, *The Long African Day*, p. 372.

When Chui had fled, she was not trying to divert the attention of the dogs or the Masai youth from her cubs. Chui had moved away as quickly and stealthily as she could in the hope of avoiding detection. To have stayed with the cubs in the lugga would have been a futile gesture, for the drought had robbed her of cover: there was nowhere there for her to hide, no caves large enough to protect her from dogs, or a man on foot. . . .

Chui's own safety was ultimately more important than that of her cubs, who were still far too young to fend for themselves in the event of her death. At five months, the cubs had nothing to contribute reproductively to the leopard population. Chui, however, would be able to produce another litter of cubs within a relatively short time if her young were killed or died. Avoiding injury is essential to any solitary predator. Chui knew her own limitations. When and if she were forced to defend herself she would prove to be a formidable adversary. Until that time, running away was the most obvious means for ensuring her own survival. There is no such word as cowardice in the animal world.

Jonathan Scott, *The Leopard's Tale* (Elm Tree Books, 1985), p. 131. The book is highly recommended in Chapter I.

At sunrise, a pair of big male hippos squared off in the river just in front of camp...One contestant was dark brown, the other flesh-colored. I favored Old Brown over Big Pink (who looked new and raw, and a bit vulgar) although I sensed that Brown was going to lose; as in mankind, it is ordinarily the weaker individual that makes most of the noise, in Brown's case a cacophony of fearful groans and blarts and roars and grumbling, interspersed with deep watery gurgles. On the far bank, a yellow crocodile lay nerveless as the dead, coldly oblivious of all this hippo nonsense, as a pair of small falcons — African hobbies — watched for big flying insects from their high perch in a dead tree, and a few impala, hind legs kicking

nervously, stepped discreetly to the water's edge, and wandered away again. The hippos hurled waves of water at each other, bluffed and skirmished, huge mouths wide, then sank from sight, perhaps to make the other nervous. But each time Old Brown went down, he surfaced again a little further off, or faced ever so slightly the wrong way, as if something upriver had captured his attention; he appeared to be giving signals that, for all of his continuing uproar, he had lost interest in leadership and might abdicate gracefully if young Pink, stout fellow, would not hold out for total victory, would not insist on driving his old boss out of the herd. Now both hippos sank again, the river flowed on; somewhere below, I thought, Old Brown was considering a surfacing maneuver that would bring his hind end into play, thus confronting his opponent with a delicate ethical decision as well as a big faceful of manure. The titanic argument went on for several days, until the night when something huge, presumably Old Brown, came running through the camp with thunderous blows of big round feet. The next day, when big Pink led the herd a short distance upriver, Old Brown was left alone, still and silent as a rock in the sinking river.

Matthiessen, *Sand Rivers*, pp. 89-90.

One evening we came on a magnificent lioness on a rock, gazing out across the plains. She was sculptured by the setting sun, as though she were part of the granite on which she lay. I wondered how many lions had lain on the self-same rock during countless centuries while the human race was still in its cradle. It was a thought which made me reflect that though civilised man has spent untold treasure on preserving ancient buildings and works of art fashioned by the hand of man, yet he destroys these creatures which typify the perfection of ageless beauty and grace. And he does so for no better reason than to boast of a prowess achieved by means of a weapon designed by man to destroy man, or to use its skin to grace some graceless abode.

Adamson, *Bwana Game*, p. 73.

...we couldn't do anything except think about getting back to Africa. We talked Africa, we dreamed Africa, we even held African parties.

Charlotte was every bit as eager to get back to the bush as I was, even keener maybe. She once said to me that she has tried to analyze what it is about Africa that holds such an appeal for her, but she just can't pin it down — and neither can I.

It's something in your blood. A combination of the climate, the landscape, the wildlife, the whole atmosphere. You somehow feel that you're missing everything when you're not there.

Chris McBride, *The White Lions of Timbavati* (Paddington Press, 1977), p. 71. The extraordinary white lions — not albinos, but normal, healthy lions — were discovered by McBride. McBride and his family spent several years studying the pride that produced them.

Why should there not be a remote wilderness where hunters pursue and are pursued? Where crocodiles eat people and people *eat crocodiles? Why not a flat earth to contain the wilderness, and a life of no spiritual importance? Why shouldn't warriors throw their spears into the unplummable depths of an inscrutable lake, rather than trawl for fish in its croc-free waters? Why should there not be famine and fighting and pestilence — and spiritual peace?*

It seems to be the destiny of all Walden Ponds, Lake Rudolf included, to be consumed by technological man. It is not for the Turkana to say yea or nay. He does not even have to submit or flee. He will not be butchered for his balkiness or haughtiness, as the Indian was. Instead he will be inundated with benevolence. Sociological religious, political, economic, scientific, medical and technological benevolence will flow over him like lava: a creeping, choking, inexorable mantle of civilization will bury him forever. The crocodile, because of its helpless hostility to man, will be traded with, made into a public spectacle, and finally exterminated without even the benefit of benevolence. The prophecy of Leonardo da Vinci will be fulfilled: "A countless multitude will sell publicly and without hindrance things of the very greatest value, without license from the Lord of these things, which were never theirs nor in their power; and human justice will take no account of this."

Alistair Graham & Peter Beard, *Eyelids of Morning: The Mingled Destinies of Crocodiles and Men* (New York Graphic Society, 1973), p. 224.

That airy platform of the East African Highland is our earth — the mothering abundance of Creation. But if, on coming away, I had lost it, I knew, now, that it is, there. I knew that high in the blazing bright, herds gallop and graze in the open plains; lions lie deep in the lion-colored grass, leopards rest in the sun-spotted shade. I knew that baboon families cluster like fruit in the fever trees along banks of streams, barking with alarm, screaming with dismay; that touraco open hibiscus wings to carry them to the next tree, and hippos send a wash of muddy ripples up the banks of rivers as they move under their own bow waves to fresh pastures. The whole concerto is still being played. It is only that I am no longer there to hear.

Ames, *A Glimpse of Eden*, p. 208.

The day may come when the camera will take the place of the gun in African hunting. In many ways, it will, no doubt, be a fine thing. Yet I am glad that I lived in a time when a man went out against the great animals with a rifle in his hands instead of a device to take pictures. Sometimes I think the animals themselves may have liked it better too.

Hunter, *Hunter*, p. 245. Not the slightest chance.

Considering the leopard's stealthy and largely nocturnal habits, deliberate or organized leopard hunts are just about impossible, either in Africa or India. But strictly to satisfy their clients' insatiable desire to get a leopard, professional hunters often stage a sorry little farce that has neither dignity nor danger. They take an antelope or zebra quarter, hang it in a tree for bait, and build a boma, *or hunting blind, at a safe distance. Sometimes, as a variant, they stake out a goat or dog on the ground. If the leopard rises to the bait toward sunset, as he often will, he can be picked off by the hunters' telescopic-sight rifles with no risk at all to their concealed persons. Somehow or other they manage to call it sport.*

Such a baited "leopard hunt" from a concealed blind was featured in January, 1967, on the documentary television series American Sportsman. *Movie actor John Saxon played the role of intrepid amateur hunter, crouching in the* boma *with his guide, squinting through his scope, and getting off a killing shot; but like most novices in Africa, he let the hunting talk convince him that the leopard hunt was for real.*

Hallet, *Animal Kitabu*, p. 29. This is what is maddeningly called the "thrill of the chase."

He could not blame these people for their fears: a man had to believe in nothing if he was not to be afraid of the big bush at night. There was little in the forest to appeal to the romantic. It was completely empty. It had never been humanized, like the woods of Europe, with witches and charcoal burners and cottages of marzipan; no one had ever walked under these trees lamenting lost love, nor had anyone listened to the silence and communed like a lake poet with his heart. For there was no silence; if a man here wished to be heard at night he had to raise his voice to counter the continuous chatter of the insects, as in some monstrous factory where thousands of sewing-machines were being driven against time by myriads of needy seamstresses. Only for an hour or so, in the midday heat, silence fell, the siesta of the insect.

Graham Greene, *A Burnt-Out Case* (Viking Press, 1961), p. 63. Greene's novels often take place in an African setting, Greene's voice always that of Western Civilization's.

Let me attempt to enumerate the more common of the sounds and noises which they make, and allot to each the probable meaning, or cause, as far as I could gather. On the approach of a solitary, contentedly feeding animal that feels completely safe and secure in the dense tropical vegetation, one may distinguish among the noises produced by the animal, apart from the snapping of twigs, swishing of leafy branches and other extraneous noises, the following: —

(1) The low intestinal rumblings at certain intervals, due to natural causes in the digestive organs.

(2) The intermittent voiding of wind and parting with dung; the latter occurs with fair regularity every forty minutes or so, and is at times quite a useful indication to the tracker.

(3) The occasional flap of the huge ears against the withers.

(4) The noisy chewing and munching of young twigs, leaves and bark.

(5) A low squeaking sound from the mouth, which is rarely heard when an animal is feeding in solitude, but may now and again be detected on the close approach of a cluster of feeding members among the herd. This particular noise indicates contentment or pleasure, and similar emotions are also expressed by a low purring rumble, apparently from the throat. A courting bull may at times utter the latter noise on approaching its mate.

The most common sounds from a mixed herd of cows, calves and herd bulls may briefly be enumerated as follows: —

(1) An occasional short and distinct roar from the lungs conveys an expression of resentment or fear. Anxious cow

elephants utter this occasionally to collect or reprimand their stray-ing calves when the herd is busily feeding in dense bush. An elephant struck by a bullet at close range and startled by the sudden shock may produce a deep, short roar.

(2) A continued rumbling noise often occurs when the members of a feeding herd are about to become alarmed. This noise undoubtedly signifies apprehension of some unknown danger and resembles at a distance the drone from muffled drums.

(3) A shrill trumpet at intervals, when uttered by the cows of a herd, may mean either resentment or anxiety. An elephant advancing towards an intruder sometimes uses the same sound for intimidating: with an alarmed herd, when the members are crowded together some distance from cover, the loud trumpetings convey their anxiety, or they may also be intended as a threaten-ing demonstration.

(4) Shrieks from the cows are generally uttered to warn off their unruly calves. A feint attack is invariably preceded by a shriek or a succession of short and shrill trumpet-like sounds. The same noises occasionally precede an assault in earnest.

(5) One of the most common noises in an alarmed herd is the loud, continued rumbling sound, presumably coming from the animals' throats, expressing apprehension of immediate danger. When a severely disturbed herd is scattered in the open, I have known the elderly cows to strut about making this continuous sound until the widely separated individuals are collected previous to a retreat into cover. A wounded animal, or one brooding in anger from some other cause, will at times express its agony or resentment by producing a similar sound, but in a somewhat deeper and lower tone.

(6) Short coughing sounds and other throaty noises are frequently heard from the calves, and apparently serve to convey their wants and feelings to their mother. Similar throaty noises uttered by sub-adult, or adult members, may be prompted by mild irritation against some brother individual. Baby elephants squeal at times when they are terrified, and creep instinctively for protection under the bellies of their parents, and that is the reason why they are seldom visible among a gathered herd.

Maxwell, *Stalking Big Game with a Camera in Equatorial Africa*, pp. 101-3. A taste of scientific observation in the 1930s.

As some of our best and most interesting work was done around the waterholes, it might be well for me to describe a day at one.

By June the heat is terrific and dries up all standing water except the larger oases. Our plan is usually to build a blind of thorn bushes. Thorn branches are also put in spots around the water where the camera cannot reach. This keeps the game before us. We go in early and wait for the animals to come. It is tedious work.

I am out at five, eat breakfast, and call the boys to get the cameras. Lunch has been put up by the assistant cook. Osa and I go afoot to the blind, which is some distance away, just as the sun is coming up. It is the most delightful part of the day. During our two or three mile walk we pass hordes of all kinds of game. Hyenas and jackals scurry out of our way. Zebras screech and cough. Lions often roar nearby; a lion seems to enjoy giving a few defiant roars at daybreak just before he goes to sleep for the day.

We reach the blind in about an hour. The boys have put it together the day before with thornbush, piling up the sides and top to cut out the light. For successful camera work an animal must not be able to detect any movement inside the blind. We go in the blind and set up the camera, arranging the different lenses so that I can get to any of them quickly. . . Having focussed my lenses on the waterhole I wait until something shows up.

. . .

From nine in the morning until eleven, and from two-thirty to four-thirty is the best time for photographic work, for the light is good. In dry weather the atmosphere seems to catch dust to such an extent that in the late afternoon the light becomes murky. A light rain settles the dust and washes the air. The trouble is that rains are few and far between in the waterhole season. In the rainy season there is so much water that the game does not need to gather at any particular oasis.

Impalla and Grant come and go all day. They walk right to the water without looking around very much. Zebra and oryx come slowly and stop every few feet to look around. Sometimes it takes them two hours to get to water from the time I first see them. This badly wears one's patience.

Giraffe are the most shy of all. They will hang around sometimes for hours without taking a drink. The slightest thing that frightens them sends them off never to return that day. Other game can get many frights but still keep coming back.

. . .

Little game comes along in the morning unless it is a very hot day. On a cloudy day few animals come at any time; but on hot days they come in groups separated by a hundred yards or so. As they amble along they stop now and then and stand dully with their heads down. Apparently the heat makes them sluggish.

Zebra and oryx are always fighting with other members of their own species. These idiots tear around after each other, kicking and snorting and fighting. Of course this stirs up the alkali dust in big clouds. As the fighting animals run through the herds they are snapped at by the others who are much irritated. But hardly has one pair finished their fracas when another pair starts off.

All during the day birds come down to drink. These are fine Kavarando crane, several varieties of storks, heron, hawks, and others. Big vultures come down and stand in the water. They are very picturesque with their fine six-foot spread of wings. For hours they hold their wings out, apparently to cool off their bodies.

When some animal decides to venture to water, all stir. Often I have counted many hundreds of head grouped about. Zebra, [sic] especially follow the lead of a courageous one like so many sheep. If he starts to drink then they all try to drink with him. But let one get the slightest start and away go the whole herd in a cloud of dust. Some days the game is so nervous that a fly or a bee will set them all moving. I have never been able to get a big bunch drinking at the same time.

Of course the reason for this nervousness lies in fear of carnivorous animals which are never far away. Lions, leopards and hyenas live on the plains. Their bread and butter consists of zebra and giraffe. None can tell which will be the next victim in the daily slaughter. As a result, when giraffes, zebra or oryx are drinking they prick up their ears at the slight first sound of the camera handle turning. I try to have my machines noiseless, for the slightest click or murmur of gears reaches the ears of these shy animals.

The minute I start turning the handle the animal looks around. But as the sound continues and nothing happens, he goes ahead drinking. When I stop, he gets another start and looks around again. Strange to say, the click of the still camera frightens him more than the whirr of the movie camera.

The larger the herd the less chance there is of getting a picture

*of common game. The opposite is true of elephants. A single
elephant is always on the alert. He knows that the slightest noise
may mean danger. But when a herd of elephants come together
they are unlikely to stampede. They seem to take it for granted
that any noise is made by one of the other elephants. Thus I can
always get closer with less danger to a herd of elephants than I
can to a single one.*

   . . .

*Now comes a long line of fifteen warthogs in single file. They
all trot along at about the same speed, their tails in the air; they
have a comical self-satisfied look about them. They stir up a lot
of dust with their little feet. I hope they will come close to me; but,
as luck has it, when they reach within ten feet of the water they
swerve off and trot away without changing speed or seeming to
be frightened. "Waterhole luck" Osa calls it.*

*I can always tell when ostriches are coming up even before I
see them. Our animals pay no attention to different species of other
four-legged game. They rub shoulders and all seem to be friends.
But the minute an ostrich comes along, the ranks part. I have never
seen an ostrich kick at another animal. Yet he seems to be feared.
Also he is fearless. When he starts for water and there is other game
in the path he never swerves or goes around it. He marches along
with a slow dignified gait and the game makes way for him.*

*One of my troubles is from animals coming up behind the blind.
They get my scent and frighten away the game in front. It wouldn't
be so bad if they went completely away. The trouble is they just
back off a hundred yards or so and keep the other game in a
nervous state for hours.*

At 1 P.M. I have lunch. . . .

*About 2:30 the animals start again for water. Around 4 o'clock
they drink more and frighten less than at any time of the day.
I suppose it is because many have put their thirst off all day and
have decided to take a chance even if there is danger. . . .*

I leave the blind about 6 P.M. and get back to camp near 7. . . .

   . . .

*I shall never forget the moonlit night we spent there . . . just
Osa and I, in our blind. About ten o'clock two full-grown rhinos
came down and drank for fifteen minutes without stopping. These
animals certainly have large tanks in their insides, for they drink
without once pausing and the noise they make during the operation is like that of a Chinaman eating soup. This pair got through
drinking, turned and went away as if they had important business
elsewhere.*

*Not ten minutes later a big rhino came down all alone for a
drink. He consumed gallons and gallons of water and then, like
the earlier ones, briskly departed. About midnight I was asleep,
when Osa gently awakened me. I heard a scraping of feet and
stones falling on the trail. A moment later buffalo came into view.
They poured down by the score, crowding about, sniffing the air
and advancing to the water so closely packed that they pushed
one another into it. Altogether there were over two hundred drinking there at one time and the noisy quenching of their thirst must
have been audible for a mile in the still night.*

*I went back to sleep again; but Osa can never sleep while in
a blind. She is always too excited and curious about what is going
to happen next. She wakened me again about 4 A.M. when a herd
of elephants came to water from behind us and caught our scent
before they had their drink. They snorted and trumpeted for half
an hour in expressing their annoyance. But in the end they went
away without touching the water.*

   Martin Johnson, *Safari: A Saga of the African Blue* (G.P.

Putnam's Sons, 1928), pp. 73-82. Despite Roosevelt's safari
and the intervening books of photographs by others, it was
the intrepid husband-and-wife team of Martin and Osa
Johnson in the 1920s and '30s that really introduced African
wildlife to the American public. In several full-length
documentaries and many shorter films — complemented by
a slew of adventure books (eighteen between them) — the
couple provided a basically ignorant public with sensational
nature and travel adventure. Their most productive work was
done from what amounted to a miniature village created on
Mount Marsabit in Kenya's remote Northern Frontier District.
Osa named the camp "Lake Paradise" (the area is now in
Marsabit National Park). Financially backed by The American
Museum of Natural History and George Eastman, of Kodak
fame, the Johnsons spent four years (off and on) at Lake
Paradise. The Johnson films, including the first talking film
made entirely in Africa (titled "Congorilla," in the spirit of
the times), were far superior in quality to the other expedition films of the day; Martin was a pioneer in the use of special
lenses, tripods, and remote-control photography. Slow
motion and other special effects gave the work a truly
innovative quality. As a daredevil, Martin was the Alan Root
of his day, often putting himself (and Osa) into serious danger
to secure the desired pictures. In the '30s, the couple spent
over a year flying two amphibious aircraft ("Osa's Ark" and
the "Spirit of Africa") over Africa and took the first aerial
photographs of Mt. Kenya and Mt. Kilimanjaro.

*Here gather men from all parts of East Africa, from Uganda, and
the jungles of the Upper Congo. At one time or another all the
famous hunters drop into its canvas chairs — Cuninghame, Allan
Black, Judd, Outram, Hoey and the others; white traders with the
natives of distant lands; owners of farms experimenting bravely
on a greater or lesser scale in a land whose difficulties are just
beginning to be understood; great naturalists and scientists from
the governments of the earth, eager to observe and collect this
interesting and teeming fauna; and sportsmen just out and full
of interest or just returned and modestly important. More
absorbing conversation can be listened to on this veranda than
in any other one place in the world. The gathering is cosmopolitan;
it is representative of the most active of every social, political, and
racial element; it has done things; it contemplates vital problems
from the vantage ground of experience. The talk veers from pole
to pole — and returns always to lions.*

   Stewart Edward White, *African Camp Fires* (Doubleday,
Page, 1913), pp. 121-2. White was writing of the redoubtable
Norfolk Hotel. All safaris in East Africa of the time began and
ended here, and visitors today to Kenya could scarcely
improve on this itinerary. Luxurious, in a colonial sort of way,
the Tudor façade, bougainvillaea-decorated verandah, and
bird-filled courtyard hide an exotic history (and guest list)
second to none.

*What it will cost, no words can express,
What is its object, no brain can suppose.
Where it will start from, no one can guess,
Where it is going to, nobody knows.*

What is the use of it, none can conjecture,
What it will carry, there's none can define.
And in spite of George Curzon's superior lectures,
It clearly is naught but a lunatic line.

Editorial poem that appeared in a London magazine (*Truth*) in 1896. The cynicism was a fair gauge of public opinion concerning the imperial scheme to build a railroad line from the port of Mombasa on the Indian Ocean to Uganda, a plan that eventually altered the natural balance that had been struck in East Africa over thousands of years. The original purpose of the Uganda Railway was predominantly military — to transfer troops to conquer Sudan (and secure the source of the Nile) from the south — and secondarily to enforce the suppression of the slave trade. When the nearly 600 miles of rail finally reached Kisumu on the shores of Lake Victoria, in 1901, the Sudan campaign was over, but the 'lunatic line' became, in effect, the backbone of European settlement in British East Africa and the foundation of the Asian community there as well. The five-year task of completing the railway across scorched deserts, over volcanic escarpments, and through the quagmire swamps of equatorial forests was an audacious and remarkable engineering feat. But the natural world objected over the entire route. Not the least of the many obstacles were the man-eating lions who occasionally fed on the hordes of imported Indian coolies and native Africans working on the line. One of the chief actors in the lion drama was Lieutenant Colonel J.H. Patterson, an English engineer and army officer brought over from India, where he was accustomed to hunting tigers. In his epic, best-selling account, *The Man-Eaters of Tsavo and Other East African Adventures* (originally published in 1907 by Macmillan; reprinted by St. Martin's Press, 1986), Patterson described in (excruciating) detail what has come to be regarded as the most extraordinary stalk in the history of big-game hunting. Certainly, the celebrated eight-months ordeal was one of the most protracted efforts on record. The notorious quarry were two marauding males who had slain twenty-eight Indians and probably 100 or more Africans before they were finished, eating most of them. Need one point out, morale among the workers during this time was not high. The melodrama of Patterson's account is more than a little thick — Victorian "scoundrels," "brutes," "demons," "foul play," "heartrending shrieks," "poor wretches," "treacherous-looking villains," "devils," and "dreadful monsters" populate the pages. And Patterson's own superiority begins to grate after only a few pages. Many regard this book as a must 'read' (the author prefers Patterson's *In the Grip of the Nyika: Further Adventures in British East Africa* (MacMillan, 1909)), but the entire tale — and a full account of the history of the railway — is beautifully captured in the fascinating, humorous, and eminently readable book by Charles Miller, *The Lunatic Express: An Entertainment in Imperialism* (Macmillan, 1971). The lions themselves received tributes in the House of Lords from none other than Lord Salisbury, then Prime Minister, and in newspapers across the world and today may be found (in rather ragged condition) in Chicago's Field Museum.

One day I asked my laboratory boy why he didn't take a bath, once, say, in six months. In the warmth of the little room in which we worked I found his body smell particularly offensive.
"God made water for hippo, not for black man," he explained smilingly.
"But you smell," I told him frankly.
He turned on me a serious liquid brown pair of eyes.
"Bwana," he said, quite without any intended rudeness, "to the black man you smell too and very bad. Even the elephant not like your smell as much as black man's."

Johnson, *Safari*, pp. 66-7.

He [Johnson's chief tracker] had a lot of queer maxims. If he failed for a considerable time to find elephants he would say one of three things was the cause:
"Shauri ako" . . . Business caused by you (the white man).
"Shauri Muunga" . . . Business caused by God.
"Shauri mvua." . . . Business caused by rain.

Johnson, *Safari*, p. 110.

A grey mist made a fitting background for the most monstrous and unearthly landscape that I have ever seen. Vague outlines of peaks and precipices towered around us. Here were plants which seemed more like ghosts of past ages than ordinary trees and herbs. They appeared as a weird and terrible dream to me, a botanist and hunter of strange plants. It all seemed unreal, like some imaginary reconstruction of life in a long past geological age, or even upon another planet. Our own familiar common herbs seemed to have gone mad. We saw groundsels, swollen and distorted with woody trunks twenty feet in height, lobelias like gigantic blue and green obelisks, heathers mighty as great trees. Most alpine plants are reduced to extreme dwarfness, but these have rushed to the opposite extreme and exhibit an exaggerated gigantism. On the ground grew a thick carpet of mosses. Some were brilliant yellow, others deep crimson in colour. Every shade of green was represented. The tree trunks were also clothed in thick moss, often tussocked into the semblance of faces, while from their branches dangled long streamers of a pale, sulphurous yellow lichen, the old man's beard.

Patrick M. Synge, *Mountains of the Moon* (Waterstone Edition, 1985), Introduction. *Mountains* is a personal account of a 1934 British Museum expedition to the mountain regions of equatorial East Africa. Synge was a botanist ("a hunter of strange plants") and an inspired observer. Classical writers told of a source of the Nile beginning on a silvery mountain range found in the heart of Africa. The legend grew in Herodotus, Aristotle, and others, especially Ptolemy, who labeled the source "the Mountains of the Moon,"and survived for many centuries, through the Middle Ages, on into the late nineteenth century, when Stanley named the great white peaks Ruwenzori ("rainy mountain"). At that time, the local Africans, who naturally enough knew nothing of snow, believed that the white substance was possibly salt. In Synge's hands, the mountain flora takes on as much life as the fauna.

There is something particularly fine about the oryx. Though not by any means the most graceful of the antelope, they make up for it by their vigorous build, their curious, soft, warm, dove-grey colour, with the relief of the strongly-defined, black markings on the face, side and legs, and by their remarkable, rapier-like horns, so long, straight and finely-pointed. As I watched the oryx playing

bring foorth yoong ones: neither are they great with yoong, but onely from seven yeeres to seven yeeres. This creature is saide to live 150 yeeres; hee is of a gentle disposition; and relying upon his great strength, he hurteth none but such as do him injurie; only he will in a sporting maner gently heave up with his snowte such persons as he meeteth. He loveth the water beyond measure, and will stande up to the mid-body therein, bathing the ridge of his backe, and other parts with his long promuscis or trunke.

Joannes Leo Africanus, *The History and Description of Africa and of the Notable Things Therein Contained* (Hakluyt Society, 1896; trans. John Pory, ed. Robert Brown, 3 vols),Vol. I, pp.73-5. A Moor from a wealthy Granada family that had settled in Northern Africa, Africanus ("Al-Hassan Ibn Mohammed Al-Wezaz Al-Fasi") was captured by Christian pirates in the Mediterranean and was sent as a slave to Pope

We agreed, and soon I found myself lulled to sleep by that interminable roar which has gone on for thousands of decades; the sound that Livingstone first heard seventy-nine years ago.

Early the next morning Renshaw and I went again to the garden, but in spite of sun and blue sky, a white mist hovered above the falls; the roar we had become accustomed to, like the traffic in some large city. After breakfast, dressed in open shirts and shorts, we started out down one of the numerous small paths that lead through the hotel grounds to the railway bridge.

From there we beheld the sight which people have travelled many miles to see; the full force of power and beauty, crashing, hurtling from its four hundred feet into a cauldron of swirling water with rocks below, unrestrained, untainted, untouched — as yet — by the hand of man. Crashing, thundering, all the words of Dante fail utterly to express the magnificence of that sight. On the bridge we stood — silent: three atoms of humanity facing a creation of nature too terrifying for words. In its grandeur one could only

Plate 34. Marabou Silhouettes on the Mara.

Leo X, who set him free and baptized him "Giovanni Leone." He was popularly known as "Leo Africanus." *History* was originally written in Arabic, published in Italian in 1550, (*Della descrittione dell'Africa*) and first translated into English in 1600. The wildlife described in this passage was found in the Congo. Africanus himself was widely regarded as an undisputed authority on Africa north of the equator for nearly three centuries.

think of the Judgment Day, when we shall be summoned from the grave by trumpets, and then, perhaps, those unrepentant sinners will be hurled into the abyss of that seething mass below!

In the afternoon we crossed the bridge and explored along the Northern Rhodesian side. We climbed down into the palm grove to the level of that restless cauldron we had seen from above; where the waters beat endlessly against the rocks. Then we walked very cautiously out on to an overhanging cliff, and watched the main

falls come thundering down. The spray soaked us, as if we were standing in a storm of rain. The falls danced with colour, the sun touching the water as it slid over the edge, to break at the bottom in a mass of white foam. As a background, dotted here and there along the lip, are the islands which, when the Zambezi is low, can be visited in canoes — vivid green with the constant sun and spray, looking as if at any moment they might slip over the edge. And then to see the falls from yet another angle we crept out on to Danger Point, where, on a rock jutting out into the gorge, we

Plates 35-37. Victoria Falls. Victoria Falls is the most impressive waterfall in the world — to the author, only the Iguaça Falls at the border of Brazil and Argentina have comparable grandeur. Zimbabwe and neighboring Zambia share the African natural wonder. Condensing such astonishing majesty with a 35mm camera is difficult, at best. Even the mind has trouble digesting what is so overwhelmingly beyond human scale. The visitor will want to devote several hours catching the many angles and views. He may never see the same view twice, as the light changes and the water pressure constantly ebbs and flows. Every day brings forth the most fantastic rainbows.

On November 16, 1855, Livingstone, the famous missionary-explorer, was taken by local residents to see the falls, which he promptly named after Queen Victoria. He is reputed to be the first white man to have seen the spectacle. The native (Tonsa) name for the falls is *Mosi-oa-Tunya,* popularly translated as the "smoke that thunders," but more literally "smoke does sound there," in any event an apt description of the white cloud of water particles that hangs over the thundering chasm. In fact, the force of the falling water can send a spray as high into the sky as 1600 feet or more during the rainy season. The rainy season is, however, not the best time to visit Victoria Falls, because the spray is so heavy that it drenches the tourist, who can barely see anything, anyway, or hear, for that matter, so loud is the roaring, tumbling water. The spray richly nourishes year-round the surrounding "rain forest."

Collectively twice as tall as Niagara Falls and half against as wide, Victoria Falls is actually five distinct waterfalls: the Devil's Cataract, the Main Falls, Horseshoe Falls, Rainbow Falls, and the Eastern Cataract. The flat, broad Zambezi River, which gives birth to the falls and has cut the zigzagging gorges over millions of years, approaches the lip in the most leisurely, smooth-flowing fashion, only to plunge unexpectedly into the vast abyss. The river is, of course, still at work as sculptor.

Livingstone was quite taken by the beauty of the falls; he wrote that the scenes there, "never . . . seen before by European eyes," were "so lovely [that they] must have been gazed upon by angels in their flight" (Livingstone, *Missionary Travels,* p. 558). Appropriately, the charter airplane trip over the falls offered to tourists is today called the "Flight of Angels."

A large bronze statue of Livingstone gazes east along the lines of the falls. His bible and field glasses are held in his left hand, his walking stick in his right, and his trousers are tied by string around his shins. At day's end, the receptive visitor can feel the lonely man's spirit — and perhaps sense his utter determination. Indeed, little seems to divide what stands before the visitor from what existed a century ago. But, just as Livingstone's guides could never have prepared him for the sight of Victoria Falls, so too the reader has to see this marvel for himself.

seemed cut off from all civilization — flicked by spray like the foam of an angry sea.

We drank our sundowners that evening on the front verandah of the hotel, surrounded still by Rhodesian veld, but the silence broken by the roar of water, and a distant haze of spray on which to feast our eyes.

Randon Hoare, *Rhodesian Mosaic* (John Murray, 1934), pp. 210-11.

All the mystery about elephants was a lot of bumf, Peter thought. An elephant cut his life into three parts just as a man divided his life. He had about twenty-one years to grow up in, and about thirty years to be a prime breeding male in, and another twenty to twenty-five years to grow old and grumpy and die in. He kept his own counsel and watched his elders for the first quarter century and minded his manners, and then if he were lucky he went out of the herd with the old, deposed bull as an askari, and, in return for running errands for a few years, he learned all the things there were to know from the old gentleman. When his knowledge was complete and he was about forty or fifty years old he went back and challenged the herd bull and they had a hell of a fight and the askari usually won. The newly deposed bull went off with two more neophytes and lived alone, as a bachelor, while the new chief mounted all the cows and left his issue behind him. Then there would come a day when another bull would challenge him and defeat him and drive him off from the herd, and he would then roam about with his own acolytes, growing older and sourer and fuller of malice toward everything. His feet would hurt and his teeth would ache from decay in the mammoth nerve, and ants would crawl up his trunk and drive him mad. He would run amok and trample native shambas and crush in the water holes, and finally somebody from the Game Department would come along and shoot him and take his tusks . . .

Ruark, *Something of Value*, p. 55.

Incredible numbers of crocodiles on the mudbanks. They lie flattened out close against the ground, mud- and bug-coloured, motionless, and looking as if they were the direct issue of the quagmire. A rifle-shot and they all disappear — swallowed up in the water of the stream, as if they had melted.

André Gide, *Travels in the Congo* (Alfred A. Knopf, 1929; Penguin Travel Library Edition, 1986), p. 159. First published in France as *Voyage au Congo and Le Retour du Tchad* in 1927, *Travels* was dedicated to Joseph Conrad and like *Heart of Darkness* was a strong indictment of the injustices and excesses of French colonialism.

It will be found with absolute certainty that one learns more about animals in a year's photography than in ten years shooting. When one gets within range of a shootable beast and a trophy is the object, the rifle is fired as soon as a steady shot at a vital point can be obtained. If the animal lifts its head to stare in the sportsman's direction, he will often assume that it is about to run away, so fires hurriedly. The camera does not frighten the subject away, and many a beast, photographed with lifted head, staring at the camera, later drops it to continue feeding.

C.H. Stockley, *African Camera Hunts* (Country Life, 1948), pp. 6-7.

I should like to know when it is that a hippopotamus can possibly sleep. It grazes all day. And in the night it lives in the water and is obliged to put its head up every five minutes to breathe.

Gide, *Travels in the Congo*, p. 202. I assume that Gide just inadvertently reversed the hippo's schedule. Individual species differ considerably in their sleeping postures. Each species has adopted a position or positions that is or are best suited to its anatomy, physiology, and environment. Several large animals sleep standing up, permitted by special skeletal adaptations. Water provides, of course, a measure of buoyancy to help relieve muscle tension.

A waterfall is, perhaps, the most dominating of all Nature's spectacles, the only one in the face of which it is absolutely impossible to say anything at all . . . . too dominating a spectacle to permit any consecutive thought. The noise, coupled with the sight, seems to shatter the brain into submission to its power.

Synge, *Mountains of the Moon*, pp. 84-5.

[During a hunt to dispatch a man-eating lion, Livingstone had wounded a lion.] *Starting, and looking half round, I saw the lion just in the act of springing upon me. I was upon a little height; he caught my shoulder as he sprang, and we both came to the ground below together. Growling horribly close to my ear, he shook me as a terrier dog does a rat. The shock produces a stupor similar to that which seems to be felt by a mouse after the first shake of the cat. It caused a sort of dreaminess, in which there was no sense of pain nor feeling of terror, though quite conscious of all that was happening. It was like what patients partially under the influence of chloroform describe, who see all the operation, but feel not the knife. This singular condition was not the result of any mental process. The shake annihilated fear, and allowed no sense of horror in looking round at the beast. This peculiar state is probably produced in all animals killed by the carnivora; and if so, is a merciful provision by our benevolent Creator for lessening the pain of death. Turning round to relieve myself of the weight, as he had one paw on the back of my head, I saw his eyes directed to Mebalwe, who was trying to shoot him at a distance of ten or fifteen yards. His gun, a flint one, missed fire in both barrels; the lion immediately left me, and, attacking Mebalwe, bit his thigh. Another man, whose life I had saved before, after he had been tossed by a buffalo, attempted to spear the lion while he was biting Mebalwe. He left Mebalwe and caught this man by the shoulder, but at that moment the bullets he had received took effect, and he fell down dead.*

David Livingstone, *Missionary Travels and Researches in South Africa* (Harper & Brothers, 1858), pp. 12-15. No European did more to open up Africa to the white man than Livingstone, a Scottish missionary who became one of the most famous explorers in history. For thirty-two years, between 1841 and 1873, he led expeditions throughout Southern and East Africa, primarily for the purpose of suppressing the slave trade (Christianity and 'civilized trade,' which included ivory, were thought to be antidotes to the Arab-controlled traffic in human beings), which had reached staggering yearly numbers in the early 1800s. Livingstone, a keen observer and eager to learn about the customs, character, and institutions of the peoples whom he encountered, always traveled slowly and frequently "disap-

peared" for years at a time. Indeed, he often traveled "in a circle," as it were, living and eating with the Africans as he went. Unlike many of his contemporaries, who organized complex and massive expeditions, Livingstone usually traveled with a small party — in fact, one cannot escape the impression that he would have preferred to wander completely alone, had that been possible. Stubborn — even pugnacious — and demanding, the Scot drove himself and his companions to the very limits of human endurance. The first European known to have walked across the African continent, he was always more an explorer by nature than a missionary (he despised the image of a "dumpy sort of man with a bible under his arm") and named many African lakes and rivers. It is fair to say that Africa came to possess Livingstone, and, in common with other explorers of his day, he developed an obsession with finding the true source of the Nile.

Despite Livingstone's many personal flaws (his vindictive grudges ruined more than one man who disappointed), he was regarded by Africans, Europeans, and Arab slavers alike as a hero, even a saint. He dominated his contemporaries, as his legacy came to dominate his successors. When he died, in the swamplands of Central Africa, his attendants cut out his heart and buried it there. What remained of his body was eventually shipped to England, where, nearly a year after his death, Livingstone was buried in Westminister Abbey. The funeral service rivaled that normally reserved for royalty.

During the course of his wanderings, Livingstone's close call with the lion was repeated with hippopotami, a buffalo, rhinoceros, and an elephant. The lion wounds bothered him for the remainder of his life: he could never again raise his left arm above horizontal.

At night the valley resounded with gruesome shrieks and screeches, which seemed to herald the approach of some dreadful monster or the conversation of a party of prehistoric ghouls. They seemed so uncanny that I, at least, felt momentarily cold and shivery, until I remembered what a fearsome noise even the domestic cat can make at night. We found that they were made by the rock hyrax . . .

Synge, *Mountains of the Moon*, p. 50.

. . . Selim [Stanley's interpreter] said to me, "I see the Doctor, sir. Oh, what an old man! He has got a white beard!" And I — what would I not have given for a bit of friendly wilderness, where, unseen, I might vent my joy in some mad freak, such as idiotically biting my hand, turning a somersault, or slashing at trees, in order to allay those exciting feelings that were well-nigh uncontrollable. My heart beats fast, but I must not let my face betray my emotions, lest it shall detract from the dignity of a white man appearing under such extraordinary circumstances.

So I did that which I thought was most dignified. I pushed back the crowds, and, passing from the rear, walked down a living avenue of people, until I came in front of the semicircle of Arabs, in the front of which stood the white man with the grey beard. As I advanced slowly towards him I noticed he was pale, looked wearied, had a grey beard, wore a bluish cap with a faded gold band round it, had on a red-sleeved waistcoat, and a pair of grey tweed trousers. I would have run to him, only I was a coward in the presence of such a mob — would have embraced him, only, he being an Englishman, I did not know how he would receive

me; so I did what cowardice and false pride suggested was the best thing — walked deliberately to him, took off my hat, and said:
"Dr. Livingstone, I presume?"
"YES," said he, with a kind smile, lifting his cap slightly.
I replace my hat on my head, and he puts on his cap, and we both grasp hands, and I then say aloud:
"I thank God, Doctor, I have been permitted to see you."
He answered, "I feel thankful that I am here to welcome you."

Henry Morton Stanley, *How I Found Livingstone* (Sampson Low, Marston, Low and Searle, 1872), pp. 411-2. Stanley's "rescue" of Livingstone was the greatest journalistic sensation of its time and possibly the single most celebrated event in all African exploration. The irony must have been obvious to insiders: Stanley, one of the greatest promoters of all time, finding Livingstone, who hated publicity. The *New York Herald* in 1869 had dispatched Stanley with a sort of adventurer's wish list (even by today's standards): attend the opening of the Suez Canal, travel up the Nile, visit Jerusalem, Constantinople, the Crimea and the Caspian Sea, travel through Persia to India, and then have a look around Africa for Livingstone, suspected dead as early as 1868. Within fourteen months or so, Stanley had accomplished all but the last task and had arrived in Africa to search for the missionary.

Stanley himself could only have been invented by Central Casting. Born in North Wales John Rowlands, the illegitimate son of Welsh parents, he escaped a terrible Dickensian workhouse straight from the pages of *Oliver Twist* to Liverpool, where he shipped out for New Orleans on a packet ship as a cabin boy. Once Stateside, a wealthy American merchant-benefactor adopted him as a son and gave him the name Henry Stanley. He later joined the Confederate Army in the American Civil War, was captured, enlisted on the Union side, and was later discharged for medical reasons. Rejected by his mother on a return made to England, he joined and then deserted the American navy. Thereupon, he accompanied expeditionary forces sent against American Indians in the West. By the ripe age of twenty-four (!), Stanley was working for the *New York Herald,* a roving reporter fresh from the British campaign against the Emperor of Abyssinia and various assignments in Europe, when he received the Livingstone quest.

At the end of a 236-day trek, Stanley found a sick and haggard Livingstone at the Arab trading post of Ujiji located near the shores of Lake Tanganyika. The two men remained together for four months at Ujiji — for Stanley, a father-son rapport developed; for Livingstone, the relationship was, no doubt, more that of teacher-disciple. When the missionary died soon thereafter, Stanley resolved to complete the former's work and returned to explore the watersheds of the Nile, Congo, and Zambezi rivers. All together, Stanley made four trips to Central and East Africa and died one of Africa's greatest explorers in his own right. (Mark Twain compared him to Columbus.) Stanley's huge expeditions (one included a portable boat hauled about in sections) inevitably produced maximum danger — drownings, dysentery, fevers, starvation, constant fighting with natives, and run-ins with the wild animals always insured heavy losses. But the forever unrepentant Stanley repeatedly managed to avoid total annihilation. The aggressive Welshman was a frequent favorite of a sometimes fickle American public but generally snubbed as a bit of a trespasser by Victorian England —

Queen Victoria referred to him as that "determined, ugly little man — with a strong American twang." He ended his explorations in the services of the Belgian king. In a world often dependent upon Africa for its adventure, Stanley inspired book after book.

The land appeared more romantic than anything we had seen. We had wound around wild amphitheatral basins, foliage rising in terraces one above another, painted in different shades of green, and variegated with masses of crimson flowers, and glistening russet, and the snowdrop flowerets of wild mangoes, or the creamy silk floss of the bombax, and as we looked under a layer of foliage that drooped heavily above us, we saw the sunken basin below, an impervious mass of leafage grouped crown to crown like heaped hills of soft satin cushions, promising luxurious rest. Now and then troops of monkeys bounded with prodigious leaps through the branches, others swinging by long tails a hundred feet above our heads, and with marvellous agility hurling their tiny bodies through the air across yawning chasms, and catching an opposite branch, resting for an instant to take a last survey of our line before burying themselves out of sight in the leafy depths. Ibises screamed to their mates to hurry up to view the column of strangers, and touracos argued with one another with all the guttural harshness of a group of Egyptian fellahs, plantain-eaters, sunbirds, grey parrots, green parroquets, and a few white-collared eagles either darted by or sailed across the leafy gulf, or sat drowsily perched in the haze upon aspiring branches. There was an odour of musk, a fragrance of flowers, perfume of lilies mixed with the acrid scent of tusky boars in the air; there were heaps of elephant refuse, the droppings of bush antelopes, the pungent dung of civets, and simians along the tracks, and we were never long away from the sound of rushing rivulets or falling cascades, sunlight streamed in slanting silver lines and shone over the undergrowth and the thick crops of phrynia, arum, and amoma, until their damp leaves glistened, and the dewdrops were brilliant with light.

Henry M. Stanley, *In Darkest Africa* (Charles Scribner's Sons, 2 vols , 1890), Vol. II, pp. 44-5. Goaded on by the newspapers to find someone else to rescue — preferably in Africa — Stanley hit upon the obscure Emin Pasha, the governor of Equatoria, the southernmost provinces of the Sudan, who had been effectively isolated by Egyptian revolutionaries in the north and a powerful Ugandan king in the south. Stanley's expedition, during which he himself was given up for lost, à la Livingstone, by the public, enlisted the help of the celebrated Arab-African trader (and slaver) Tippu Tib and is chronicled in *In Darkest Africa.*

Night was now fast setting in, so we descended, from the hills, and made for home. Cantering along, we observed what we took to be a herd of quaggas [pale red, zebra-like animals with stripes limited to the head and neck and extinct by the turn of the century] *and a bull wildebeest standing in front of us, upon which we jumped off our horses, and, bending our bodies, approached them to fire.*

It was now quite dark, and it was hard to tell what sort of game we were going to fire at; Strydom, however, whispered to me they were quaggas, and they certainly appeared to be such. His gun snapped three times at the wildebeest, upon which they all set off at a gallop. Strydom, who was riding my stallion, let go his bridle when he ran in to fire, taking advantage of which the horse set

off at a gallop after them. I then mounted 'The Cow,' and after riding hard for about a mile I came up to them. They were now standing still, and the stallion was in the middle of them. I could make him out by his saddle; so, jumping off my horse in a state of intense excitement, I ran forward and fired both barrels of my two-grooved rifle into the quaggas, and heard the bullets tell loudly. They then started off, but the stallion was soon once more fighting in the middle of them. I was astonished and delighted to remark how my horse was able to take up their attention, so that they appeared heedless of the reports of my rifle.

In haste I commenced loading, but to my dismay I found that I had left my loading-rod with Hendrick. Mounting 'The Cow,' I rode nearer to the quaggas, and was delighted to find that they allowed my horse to come within easy shot. It was now very dark, but I set off in the hope to fall in with Hendrick on the wide plain, and galloped along shouting with all my might, but in vain. I then rode across the plain for the hill, to try to find some bush large enough to make a ramrod. In this, by the greatest chance, I succeeded, and, being provided with a knife, I cut a good ramrod, loaded my rifle, and rode off to seek the quaggas once more. I soon fell in with them, and, coming within shot, fired at them right and left, and heard both bullets tell, upon which they galloped across the plain with the stallion still after them. One of them, however, was very hard hit, and soon dropped astern — the stallion remained to keep him company.

About this time the moon shone forth faintly. I galloped on after the troop, and, presently coming up with them, rode on one side, and dismounting, and dropping on my knee, I sent a bullet through the shoulder of the last quagga; he staggered forward, fell to the ground with a heavy crash, and expired. The rest of the troop charged wildly around him, snorting and prancing like the wild horses in Mazeppa, and then set off at full speed across the plain. I did not wait to bleed the quagga, but, mounting my horse, galloped on after the troop, but could not, however, overtake them. I now returned and endeavoured to find the quagga which I had last shot, but owing to the darkness, and to my having no mark to guide me on the plain, I failed to find him. I then set off to try for the quagga which had dropped astern with the stallion; having searched some time in vain, I dismounted, and laid my head on the ground, when I made out two dark objects which turned out to be what I sought. On my approaching, the quagga tried to make off, when I sent a ball through his shoulder, which laid him low. On going up to him in the full expectation of inspecting for the first time one of these animals, what was my disappointment and vexation to find a fine brown gelding, with two white stars on his forehead! The truth now flashed upon me; Strydom and I had both been mistaken; instead of quaggas, the waggon-team of a neighbouring Dutchman had afforded me my evening's shooting!

Roualeyn George Gordon-Cumming, *Five Years of a Hunter's Life in the Far Interior of South Africa* (John Murray, 2 vols, 1851), Vol. I, pp. 78-81. Were one to draw up a short list of lunatic hunters, Cumming would be at or near the top of anyone's effort, just before or immediately after our friend Charles John Andersson, quoted earlier. (Livingstone himself tagged Cumming as a "mad sort of Scotchman.") The incident described in the passage, in which Cumming nonchalantly wipes out a farmer's string of horses (and, incidentally, promptly decided not to inform the poor Boer, who Cumming was persuaded was very "avaricious" and who would seek "treble" the horses' value, and instead to blame the slaughter on lions or "wild Bushmen"!), occurred at the *beginning* of a series of trips through the South African veldt that began in 1844 and resembled, more or less, a war on all living things. A giant of a man physically (for that time), the ferocious Cumming usually ran around in the tartan kilt of his homeland shooting everything. At one point, fearful of losing a hippo that he had wounded, Cumming plunged into the river, cut 'hand-holds' in the animal's hide with his hunting knife, and steered the animal to shore. Illustrated in his book, this episode is entitled "waltz with a hippopotamus." Enthralled by the excitement of the chase, he spoke often of the "perfume" discharged by frightened animals. He returned to England in 1848 with thirty *tons* of souvenirs, in large part collections of skins and stuffed heads. The booty (and a live bushman) was put on display at the Great Exhibition of 1851 and, together with the racy and all but incredible accounts of Cumming's adventures, encouraged English gentry by the hundreds to try their luck. Regarded in his lifetime everywhere as an authority on Africa, and known by the sobriquet "the Lion Hunter," Cumming died of drink in 1866.

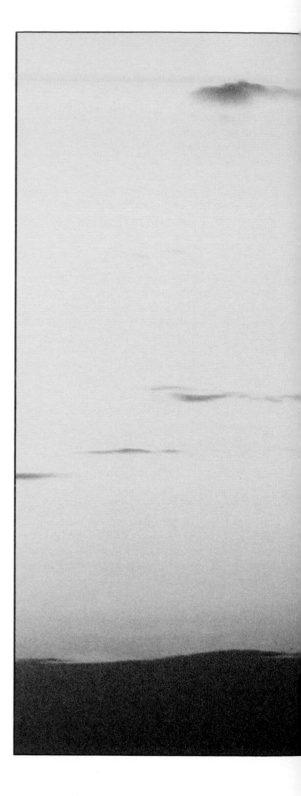

At last we were rewarded by the sight of a couple of buffaloes feeding some distance ahead. Gliding up warily till I got within fifty yards, I gave one of them a bullet close to the region of the heart. This was not sufficient to bring the animal down, and off it lumbered. Following it up, we were soon once more at close quarters, with the result that a bullet from my Express passed through its shoulder. With the obstinacy and tenacity of life characteristic of its kind, however, it did not quietly succumb. I next tried it with a fair header. This obviously took effect, for after it had struggled forward some distance it lay down, clearly, as I thought, to die. My belief was quite correct, only I should not have disturbed its last moments. Concluding, very foolishly, that the buffalo was completely hors de combat, *and that the game was mine, I, with the jaunty air of a conqueror, tucked my rifle under my arm, and proceeded to secure my prize. Brahim, with more sense, warned me that it was not finished yet; and indeed, if I had not been a fool — which the most sensible people will be sometimes — I might have concluded that with so much of the evil one in its nature the brute had still sufficient life to play me a mischief, for it still held its head erect and defiant, though we were unseen. Heedless of Brahim's admonition, I obstinately went forward, intending to give it its* quietus *at close quarters. I had got within six yards, and yet I remained unnoticed, the head of the buffalo being turned slightly from me, and I not making much noise. I was not destined to go much further. A step or two more and there was a rustling among some dead leaves. Simultaneously the buffalo's head turned in my direction. A ferocious, blood-curdling grunt instantly apprised me of the brute's resolution to be revenged. The next moment it was on its feet. Unprepared to fire, and completely taken by surprise, I had no time for thought. Instinctively I turned my back upon my infuriated enemy. As far as my recollections serve me, I had no feeling of fear while I was running away. I am almost confident that I was not putting my best foot foremost, and that I felt as if the whole affair was rather a well-played game. It was a game, however, that did not last long. I was aware of Brahim tearing away in front of me. There was a loud crashing behind me. Then something touched me on the thigh, and I was promptly propelled skyward.*

Plate 38. Kariba Sunset. Kariba is a man-made lake, but the special splendor at day's end belongs to nature.

My next recollection was finding myself lying dazed and bruised, with some hazy notion that I had better take care! With this indefinite sense of something unusual I slowly and painfully raised my head, and lo! there was the brutal avenger standing three yards off, watching his victim, but apparently disdaining to hoist an inert foe. I found I was lying with my head towards the buffalo. Strangely enough even then, though I was in what may be called the jaws of death, I had not the slightest sensation of dread; only the electric thought flashed through my brain, 'If he comes for me again I am a dead man.' It almost seemed to me as if my thought roused the buffalo to action. Seeing signs of life in my hitherto inanimate body, he blew a terrible blast through his nostrils, and prepared to finish me off. Stunned and bruised as I was, I could make no fight for life. I simply dropped my head down among the grass in the vague hope that it might escape being pounded into jelly. Just at that moment a rifle-shot rang through the forest, which caused me to raise my head once more. With glad surprise I found the buffalo's tail presented to my delighted contemplation. Instinctively seizing the unexpected moment of grace, I with a terrible effort pulled myself together and staggered away a few steps. As I did so, I happened to put my hand down to my thigh, and there I felt something warm and wet; exploring further, my fingers found their way into a big hole in my thigh. As I made this discovery there was quite a volley, and I saw my adversary drop dead.

Joseph Thomson, *Through Masai Land: A Journey of Exploration among the Snowclad Volcanic Mountains and Strange Tribes of Eastern Equatorial Africa* (Houghton Mifflin, 1885), pp. 517-19. While not deserving to be regarded as one of the giants of African exploration, Thomson was still an important figure. He opened up several trade routes, compiled detailed maps, and wrote two books on his travels — all before his twenty-seventh birthday. Much impressed by the exploits of Burton and Speke and equally by Stanley's quest for Livingstone, Thomson, a young Scottish geologist, accepted an offer by the Royal Geographic Society to accompany an East African expedition in 1878. The leader of the expedition died of fever soon after the group entered Africa, and Thomson, all of twenty-one years old, led the caravan to Lake Tanganyika. The young Scot developed a genuine liking for Africans and managed to avoid the violence that plagued other expeditions of his day. The trip was an enormous success, both to science and as an example of common-sense exploration. Not a single man was lost under Thomson, save one porter who died from disease; no shots were fired in anger. Moreover, the trip was concluded under budget, unheard of at that time. Thomson's account of this trip was entitled, *To The Central African Lakes and Back* (Houghton Mifflin, 1881). A few years later, Thomson was back, traveling through the heart of Maasai country (1883-84). On the last day of 1883, bent on shooting something for a New Year's feast, the by now part-time zoologist had his fateful confrontation with the buffalo. The goring left him semi-conscious for six weeks. Indeed, this incident was probably the closest anyone came to a violent end; again, the second trip was accomplished without the loss of a single man by violence or shooting a single native.

Thomson was to make three more trips into Africa and died at the age of thirty-seven following an expedition into Zambia undertaken for Cecil Rhodes. Over half of his relatively brief adult life was spent in Africa; before he was finished, he walked about 15,000 miles, climbed mountains, sailed lakes, and suffered from every imaginable African disease.

Thomson represented both a curiosity and a pattern that ran through much of Victorian exploration of Africa. The curiosity was that an inordinate number of early explorers were Scotsmen — Bruce, Clapperton, Park, Livingstone, Paterson, Grant, Cameron, Cumming, and Thomson, among others. The pattern was the irresistible pull that lured the men back to Africa. Thomson was, however, one of the few explorers who genuinely liked the Africans themselves (though he might appear a little racist to today's readers); many of the explorers professed great disgust at the "brutality" and "debauchery" of the natives, and all emphasized noble missions for returning again and again to the "Dark Continent." The truth was, however, that these men were, one and all, footloose wanderers, restless adventurers, for whom the romantic panorama and the matchless wildlife of Africa proved intoxicating and utterly irresistible. They were, in short, enchanted and obsessed with Africa. Alan Moorehead has likened them to the men who went to sea. Thomson, perhaps the most honest of the group, wrote just before he died: "I am doomed to be a wanderer. I am not an empire-builder, I am not a missionary. I am not truly a scientist. I merely want to return to Africa to continue my wanderings." (Quoted by Moorehead in his dedication to *No Room in the Ark*.)

There, towards the base of Kilimanjaro, are three great herds of buffalo slowly and leisurely moving up from the lower grazing-grounds to the shelter of the forest for their daily snooze and rumination in its gloomy depths. Farther out on the plains enormous numbers of the harmless but fierce-looking wildebeest continue their grazing, some erratic members of the herd gambolling and galloping about with waving tail and strange uncouth movements. Mixed with these are to be seen companies of that loveliest of all large game, the zebra, conspicuous in their beautiful striped skin, — here marching with stately step, with heads down bent, there enjoying themselves by kicking their heels in mid-air or running open-mouthed in mimic flight, anon standing as if transfixed, with heads erect and projecting ears, watching the caravan pass. But these are not all. Look! Down in that grassy bottom there are several specimens of the great, unwieldy rhinoceros, with horns stuck on their noses in a most offensive and pugnacious manner. Over that ridge a troop of ostriches are scudding away out of reach of danger, defying pursuit, and too wary for the stalker. See how numerous are the herds of hartebeest; and notice the graceful pallah [impala] springing into mid-air with great bounds, as if in pure enjoyment of existence. There also, among the tall reeds near the marsh, you perceive the dignified waterbuck, in twos and threes, leisurely cropping the dewy grass. The wart-hog, disturbed at his morning's feast, clears off in a bee-line with tail erect, and with a steady military trot truly comical. These do not exhaust the list, for there are many other species of game. Turn in whatever direction you please, they are to be seen in astonishing numbers, and so rarely hunted, that unconcernedly they stand and stare at us, within gunshot.

Thomson, *Through Masai Land*, pp. 91-2. For all his goodwill, Thomson (on foot, basically, with only a few donkeys) did not have an easy time of it. The Maasai constantly hassled him and his party and frequently stripped young Joseph for an inspection of one kind or another, including thorough examinations of his privates by Maasai women. He escaped one jam by pulling out his two false teeth and uttering a magical incantation (an idea that so impressed Rider Haggard that he used it in *King Solomon's Mines*). Another time, when confronted by a chief's demand that he immediately impregnate the chief's daughter, Thomson filled a mug with water and added some effervescent fruit salts that made the water fizzle. (Eno's salt crystals were a fizzy laxative made of baking soda and cream of tartar — invented for sailors in the 1850s by an English chemist named J.C. Eno.) Thomson then told the girl to drink the mixture, explaining that this was how white people conceived! Such a fine bit of imagination was not entirely unbelievable to Africans, who, when they first saw a white man, likened the latter to an unfinished fetus who had prematurely left the womb.

Thomson, profoundly disappointed by Haggard's inaccuracies in *She* and *King Solomon's Mines*, later sought to write (in collaboration with a Miss Harris-Smith) his own novel of Africa. Thus eventually appeared *Ulu: An African Romance*, with the dashing hunter Tom Gilmour, disappointed in love, sailing off to Africa, where he settled in with the Chagga tribe and . . . (the reader can take it from there).

There was no wind any more. There was no cloud or mist in the sky. I have never known such stillness. The only sound was the sound of one's blood murmuring like a far sea in one's ears: and that serene land and its beauty, and the level golden sunlight seemed to have established such a close, delicate, tender communion with us that the murmur in my ears seemed also like a sound from without; it was like a breathing of the grasses, a rustle of the last shower of daylight, or the swish of the silk of evening across the purple slopes.

Suddenly Karramba touched my arm. We could hardly believe our eyes. A very big male leopard, bronze, his back charged with sunset gold, was walking along the slope above the pool on the far side about fifty yards away. He was walking as if he did not have a fear or care in the world, like an old gentleman with his hands behind his back, taking the evening air in his own private garden. When he was about twelve yards from the pool, he started walking around in circles examining the ground with great attention. Then he settled slowly into the grass, like a destroyer sinking into the sea, bow first, and suddenly disappeared from our view. It was rather uncanny. One minute he was magnificently there on the bare slope and the next he was gone from our view. . . .

We waited attentively. About five minutes passed: not a sound anywhere, except this remote music of all our being. I was lying with my ear close to the ground when I heard a new sound that made my heart beat faster: it was the drumming of hooves far away. It was a lovely, urgent, wild, barbaric sound. It was getting louder and coming straight for us. I caught a glimpse of Michael's face, shining with excitement. The drumming of the hooves came towards us from somewhere behind the far slope, like a great Pacific comber, like a charge of Napoleon's cavalry at Waterloo, and then out of midst of this drumming, this surf of sound, there was thrown up like a call on a silver trumpet, or the voice of an emperor born to command, a loud, clear neigh. It was one of the most beautiful sounds I have ever heard, and it established itself in all my senses like the far silver fountain that I had once seen a great blue whale throw up on a South Atlantic horizon after a storm. Now, as the sun tinted the horizon, the wave of sound rose towering into the air and then crashed down on

to the summit of the slope opposite us. A troop of about forty zebra, running as if they had never known walking, the rhythm of their speed moving in waves across their shining flanks, charged over the crest and made for the pool where the leopard lay.

I wondered how it was going to end. I could not believe a leopard would attack such a lusty group of zebra, although I had never seen a leopard behave quite as this one did, so frankly, so openly. At that very moment, the leader of the troop with his mane streaming from him like the strands of the Mistral itself, stopped dead. At one minute he must have been going at thirty-five miles an hour, at the next he stopped without a slither in his tracks, two fountains of steam shooting out of dilated nostrils.

The rest of the group stopped with him. Had they seen the leopard or seen us? For about five minutes we saw a group of zebra, not fifty yards away, in earnest consultation. I saw Michael raise his gun and then put it down again. He had, I knew, to kill one zebra because it was his duty to examine them for parasites. I saw him take aim several times but always he put his gun down again.

Meanwhile the consultation went on, soundlessly and ceaselessly. Some invisible, some electric exchange of meaning was going on between those vivid creatures on the darkening slope. They looked so heraldic, like unicorns who had just had their horns pared. They had beautifully marked golden skins, with black blazonings. For five minutes they stood, their steaming heads close together, and then somewhere in the magnetic depths of themselves, their meaning fused and became one. They whirled swiftly round and charged back over the crest straight into the dying day and we did not see them again.

'I am sorry,' Michael said to me, breathing hard: 'I am sorry but I just could not shoot; they were beautiful.'

'I am glad you didn't,' I answered.

Laurens van der Post, *Venture to the Interior* (William Morrow, 1951), pp. 246-8. Van der Post is the author of many exceptional books on safari Africa, including *Flamingo Feather* (William Morrow, 1955), *The Heart of the Hunter* (Chatto & Windus, 1969), *A Story Like the Wind* (William Morrow, 1972) — this author's favorite — and *First Catch Your Eland* (William Morrow, 1978). Sir Laurens has achieved recent notoriety as a sort of guru to Prince Charles of Britain and recently accompanied the Prince of Wales into the Kalahari on safari.

At last the great moment came. Two large bulls walked to the edge of the pool, straddled their legs, put down their heads and drank, unconscious of the fact that I was turning the handle of the cinema camera and recording their every movement. Behind the two the others were standing about, looking or feeding and apparently posing for the film. Need I say that my excitement was so keen that my hand trembled violently and my knees shook so that I seemed to hear them. What I had longed for and worked for during the past years was at last realised, and more than realised, for in my wildest dreams I had never expected such a picture. Everything was in my favour, fine light, fairly good background, and all those wonderful, reticulated giraffe. Surely there is no animal more beautiful and certainly none that seems more in keeping with an African landscape. I was enjoying the most interesting experience in all my photographic hunting, and felt repaid a thousand-fold for all the hardships and disappointments of the past. How much better this was than shooting! No man with his rifle had ever had such perfect thrills of satisfaction and clean pleasure. Life was certainly worth living. Yard after yard of film was registering the scene, was being changed from mere celluloid, coated with chemical, to a moving picture of interest and beauty that required but the magic touch of the developer to bring it into being. But, was I giving the correct exposure? Was everything working properly? Was the focus right? These and a thousand other questions and doubts ran through my mind as I turned the handle at what I hoped was the proper speed. In my excitement and nervousness it was difficult not to turn too fast and to keep it going evenly during the various phases of the animals movements. When they moved fast I wanted to do likewise, and when they stopped still, almost unconsciously I did the same. The beautiful group moved about, some drinking, while others fed, not only on the thorny branches of the trees, but on the ground, which is rather unusual, but all of which the camera was faithfully recording.

As I watched the long-necked creatures making their meal of the fine leaves of the thorn bush I could not help wondering how they avoided lacerating their mouths and tongues with the sharp, claw-like thorns which grow both ways, so that they catch you coming and going.

One large bull, who seemed to be the leader, decided that the bush under which I was hidden, and which formed the support of my "blind," was capable of furnishing him with food. I had not counted on this, and felt sure that even if he did not see me he would be sure to get my scent. I had not yet made all the photographs I wanted, so the probability of the alarm being given made me most uneasy. On he came, until he stood against my bush, so close that I could have touched him, and then, without having seen or smelt me, he quietly fed directly over my head.

Dugmore, *The Wonderland of Big Game*, pp. 187-8.

Every baobab, every knobbly butte of clustered green with gold outcroppings of rock, every umbrella thorn, every mottled fig, every sweep of lovely curving hill, every harsh cruel drop of escarpment, every animal and every cloud of weaver birds, rolling and dipping and twisting like a tornado, every flock of guineas pacing, all the lions you didn't shoot, and all the herds you did not molest — all of this was so special that you gazed greedily, anxious to see all of it before anybody else saw it. There was no time for talk and no necessity for it. Talking was for when you got back to the fire . . . Then you talked. You babbled, with all the words you had saved up all day pouring out of you in a great welling rush.

Ruark, *Something of Value*, pp. 344-5.

"Any luck in the blind this evening?" I ventured to ask after a while.

"Wart-hogs!" Martin replied disgustedly.

I thought the pictures of the wart-hogs were extremely interesting. We were back at our home in Nairobi. Martin had developed and printed them and was projecting them along with some other odds and ends of things he'd photographed at the Athi River.

"Why, that's simply wonderful photography, Martin," I said. "Just look how the cross lighting hits the bumps on those hogs."

"Yes," Martin growled, "and just look at three months in Africa with nothing but wart-hogs to show for it — look how that hits

our pocket book!"

The little bit of film was ended — he snapped off the projection lights.

"Wart-hogs," he muttered to himself.

Osa Johnson, *I Married Adventure* (J.B. Lippincott, 1940), pp. 223-4. Osa was a full partner in the Johnson saga. Though far more conventional than Martin (easily done), she shared her husband's love of travel and adventure, operated the camera with gusto, and was an enthusiastic hunter and superb shot. (Indeed, Martin dedicated one book, *Lion: African Adventure with the King of Beasts* (G.P. Putnam's Sons, 1929), "To Osa, My Wife, Who Holds the Gun. . .") Though her books today have a fair bit of "gee-wiz" text, we can readily join the President of the American Museum of Natural History who wrote the Foreword to *I Married Adventure:*

Here, in a story about everywhere else in the world, is romantic Americana that will one day be history. These pages are themselves adventure. Here the watchmaker's boy from Independence out in Kansas meets the Santa Fe engineer's daughter from Chanute, plain people from the prairies. Against that homespun background is woven a life and career filled with exotic color.

Many a story is called a saga. This is one — in all the meaning of that word from the language of Martin Johnson's Scandinavian forebears. Martin was as born to adventure road as Lief-the-Lucky, and when Osa married Martin she married his destiny, too. It was to be always a-going, always a-seeing. Home was to be a schooner in the South Seas, a raft in Borneo, a tent on safari, a hunt in the black Congo, sometimes a dash of Paris, interludes of an apartment on Fifth Avenue — but always a place to be going from.

No matter where or how, through it all, the telling is no mere travelogue and picture album, but rather the intimate tale of their two lives — boy and girl from Kansas, pushing their horizons into far places. The bigger story is of their life, sometimes to be read between the lines, and not quite so much of the world they went to see as of the hearts they took with them.

The American Museum of Natural History with its great halls of exhibits and its laboratories has also a great invisible collection of careers in the lives of those who have associated with its projects, intangibles of tradition. To this Martin and Osa have contributed richly. And this is set down by one who has broken bread with them by the campfires of safari.

We followed Carl [Akeley] into a shallow depression between two hills. Here he stopped and motioned us to be silent, and a lion crossed our path not ten yards away. If it was aware of us, it didn't even bother to look around. And then, to our astonishment, eleven full grown lions emerged.

We hadn't the remotest idea what to expect. Eleven great lions not ten yards away. All I could do was hope they weren't hungry. Martin's eyes fairly popped, and Mr. Eastman went to work at once with his 16mm Cine. This reminded my husband that he also had a camera with him and as quietly and speedily as might be, he set it up. To our amazement the tawny beasts still paid little attention, though the click of the camera seemed to tickle their ears a little and they twitched them slightly. It was I, of course, who *bad to grow noisily excited. Up to now they had merely turned their heads toward us and blinked lazily; several had yawned, but at sound of my voice they faced us sharply, their muscles bulging under their shining coats. Several switched their tails and growled, and while I don't know about the others of our party, I do know that I was goose bumps from head to foot.*

The lions, however, after a moment or two of consideration seemed to conclude either that we were not good food or that we just didn't matter one way or another, so, rolling over, they stuck their feet in the air and went fast asleep.

We were all so happy we could scarcely contain ourselves, and exchanged congratulatory grins.

My husband ground hundreds of feet of film of the lovely big cats, Mr. Eastman's camera buzzed and finally we all decided to leave, when a twelfth lion, bigger than any of the rest, meandered into the scene, eyed his sleeping companions whimsically for a few moments, then apparently decided to tease them a little. He mauled and mouthed them, every last one, until he had them all awake. The donga resounded with their growls and snarls of irritation and then, as suddenly as he had started his little game, the big fellow thought he too would like a nap and presently twelve kingly beasts lay, feet in the air, snoring blissfully.

We tiptoed away and, selecting a shady spot under a mimosa, we ate our lunch and for two hours talked lion. I've since been so glad to have that memory of Carl; it was one of his happiest moments, I think, to be able to prove a tried and fond theory of his, that the lion will not molest man unless he is first attacked.

We were to have made another visit to the lion valley early the next day, but when we called for Carl we found him desperately ill.

He was smiling when we went into his tent, but his face looked very flushed against the white pillow, and Mr. Eastman's physician took charge immediately.

"Go ahead, Martin," Carl said to my husband. "Go ahead with your work. Get all the data and the pictures you can — through them better than any other way the world will come to know about animals — about lions. Sportsmen, so-called, too; I want them to know how unsportsmanlike it is to slaughter animals simply for the sake of slaughter."

He was quiet for a minute then smiled again. "An even dozen, like so many tabby cats, fast asleep on their backs and we only ten yards away."

> Osa Johnson, *I Married Adventure*, pp. 302-3. One particularly remarkable feature of the Johnsons' books is that husband and wife rarely seemed to agree on the details of a vivid remembrance. According to Martin, for example, Osa was not even present at the close sighting of the twelve lions described in the above passage — she was back in camp! One might infer that there was at least a moment or two of tension in Paradise . . .

Yes, Peter had learned a lot from his apprenticeship to old Dan. Over the two years . . . they had had a lot of peculiar clients. There was the queer Englishman who insisted on sleeping in trees, so they had to build him a platform in a tree in every camp and hoist a bedroll up into it. He swam naked in every stream they came to, against all warnings, and bought a thriving case of bilharzia as a result. But he was a jolly good chap and he didn't like to kill things. He puttered with cameras and seemed sincerely fond of lions. Oddly, or rather stupidly, he was completely fearless. He seemed to think that he was living in a large, controlled, airy zoo. . . .

They were a rare lot, all right. There was the old Duchess of Denton, who cursed like a man and smoked cigars and who had one aim on the safari, which was to eavesdrop lions and elephants and giraffes, especially giraffes, making love. . . . while they never caught any elephants copulating, they did manage to sneak up on some lions and giraffes. The giraffes were fantastic, all planes and right angles.

There was the pansy chap, a lawyer from Los Angeles, who tried to do all the black boys. Peter caught him with one of the porters, who seemed to think that there was nothing very unusual about it. Peter beat the porter with a kiboko [whip made from rhino hide] and sacked him, and Dan drove the pansy chap back to Nairobi and refused any payment for the safari.

Funny, the types who came to Africa to keep doing whatever it was they had always been doing in the States or in England or wherever. Peter first learned about lesbians on safari. One, the male part of the show, was a horsy-looking Englishwoman, very rich, who shaved her upper lip every day and who called herself Bill, though her name was Helen. She had a curious rubber contrivance with her. She kept it in a box and made great secret jokes about it with her girl friend. They called the contrivance Lord Derek, and they used to chuckle when they took it out of the box to "give Lord Derek a breath of fresh air." Bill, or Helen, was very jealous of her girl friend, a wispy little thing with enormous sad brown eyes and a weak, petulant mouth. The girl friend made a few tentative motions toward Peter and excited a great deal of jealousy in Bill. The jealousy got so bad that although, God knows, Peter felt nothing but loathing for the girl friend and tried to avoid her, the safari ended in utter disaster, with Dan and Peter eating apart from the women and speaking only in monosyllables when an order to the clients was necessary.

God, but some of them were funny. There was the Yankee book writer who came all the way out to Africa to hunt, and then refused to hunt. He stayed in camp all day long, drinking gin and talking seriously to the baboons who came curiously to visit him. There was the Cambodian prince, a decent little brown fellow, who had a big blond music-hall-type Englishwoman with him, who didn't want to hunt or take pictures or even look at game. What he liked to do was to stay in camp in his tent with the Englishwoman. They made some very peculiar sounds in the tent.

There was the rich spoiled son of a wood-pulp merchant who started the safari with one wife and finished it with another, puzzling the native boys no end. Then there was the cold murderer, who would ask each morning, "How many of what can I shoot today?" . . .

. . .

There was the rich Michigan manufacturer who ordered Dan to shoot it all and then blandly described how he had shot it all himself. Peter could understand how the man might fake it at home, but to sit on the veranda at the Norfolk, in Nairobi, with Peter and Dan present while he described his imaginary feats of bravery, was just a touch too thick. Especially the part in which the rich man told how he had plunged into the bush after the wounded buffalo —which, as he pointed out, Dan had wounded.

> Ruark, *Something of Value*, pp. 155-7. While Africa has always provided a spectacle to visitors, the visitors in turn often supply an equal dose of entertainment.

We next came upon a herd of eland. . . . On our approach they stampeded in a cloud of dust, the calves racing in front and the

*big cows vaulting five feet into the air like frisking calves and look-
ing for all the world like the picture in our nursery books of the
'cow that jumped over the moon.' These antics are one of the sights
of Africa, and one not to be expected from such [a] large antelope.*

Mary L. Jobe Akeley, *Carl Akeley's Africa* (Dodd, Mead,
1929), p. 139. Mary L. Jobe was Akeley's second wife and
accompanied him on his last (and fifth) expedition to Africa
(a honeymoon of sorts), where he died in the Belgian Congo.
She gamely carried on and led the expedition — principally
on behalf of the American Museum of National History and
its new "African Hall" — to a successful conclusion. Mary
Akeley was an explorer in her own right (principally in
Canada) before marrying Carl. She wrote several books concerning her brief time with Akeley and her own subsequent
adventures in Africa. Aside from those quoted here, the
author recommends *Rumble of a Distant Drum* (Dodd,
Mead, 1946), the story of a young native child who accompanied Mary on the expedition completed after Carl's death.

*Shortly after dawn we started . . . The indescribable blue of the
morning sky was streaked with rose; the whistling wind was crisp
and chill; and as we drove our little open camera car across the
level stretches of the veldt, we felt grateful for warm sweaters and
top coats for the sun had not yet touched the summit of the eastern
hills. Two secretary birds, rare and beautiful in form and color
and of amazing dignity of motion, were sitting by their nest on
the top of an acacia tree, feeding their young. Herds of wildebeest,
quietly grazing in long lines across the landscape, stampeded
noisily at our approach. Statuesque grown-up 'Tommies' looked
us steadily in the eye without giving an inch, the flick, flick of their
little tails being the only indication that they were living and not
sculptured animals. Their little ones, for all the world like the little
wooden animals in a toy Noah's ark, shy as young fawns, went
jumping across the landscape, stiff-legged, and on all fours.*

*Topi stood gazing quietly in groups of twos or threes, their
brown, satiny coats gleaming in the morning light. A cheetah
walked cautiously through the tall grass, herding her two little cubs
ahead of her toward the shelter of a low growing tree. Two fennec
foxes playing on a brick red ant hill, whisked their fawn-colored
bodies suddenly out of sight, only large ears and little beady eyes
showing that they watched us as we passed. Three or four miles
from camp, a large band of hyenas — we counted thirty-eight —
were fighting over the half-devoured carcass of a wildebeest,
apparently their recent kill.*

M.L.J. Akeley, *Carl Akeley's Africa*, pp. 134-5.

Why the Hippopotamus Left the Forest

*In the forest lands of Rhodesia, in the long years gone by, there
lived a large and hairy creature, Mvuu the hippopotamus.*

*In those days the hippopotamus lived as the other creatures liv-
ed, in the forest lands. Mvuu was the owner of a very fine coat
of nut-brown hair, of which he was extremely proud.*

*With bushy tail waving grandly, regularly at noontime Mvuu
would take his daily stroll to the river for his midday drink. He
nodded and chatted to all the creatures whom he met on the way.
And day after day he would ask them if they did not consider that
his was the most beautiful coat and tail in the forest.*

The monkeys in the treetops were foolish enough to agree with

*anything if they heard it often enough. They would answer the
hippo in chorus, "Well said, O noble friend. Great is your beauty.
Strong are your limbs, and beautiful is your silky brown hair.
Justified is your pride. O exquisite, beautiful one!"*

*The monkeys would throw garlands of vines from the treetops,
and these Mvuu would wear around his foolish neck, taking in
their flattery and praise.*

*Day by day his pride increased. Finally it became clear to the
forest dwellers that Mvuu would become completely insufferable
if he were not taken down a peg or two.*

*After a long and deep drink, Mvuu would sit at the side of his
favorite pool and gaze with joy at the reflection in the water of
his beautiful hairy coat.*

*Now, this was nobody's business but his own. But Mvuu brought
about his downfall by not keeping his very large mouth shut.*

*"Ha-ha-ha," he would laugh as he sat there. "The monkeys are
right. I certainly have decent-sized ears, a decent-sized tail, legs
of a decent length, and a beautiful figure. Not like that foolish
hare, Vundhla, who has a ridiculously small tail, foolishly long
ears, completely unbalanced legs, and what a starved little body!"*

*Unfortunately for the hippo, the hare's long ears often caught
the sound of Mvuu's hearty laughter and mocking remarks about
him. These remarks annoyed the hare more and more, until one
day he could stand it no longer. Vundhla decided to teach this
rude fellow a lesson.*

*With very great cunning, the hare started to make his plans.
First he laid in a store of tinder-dry grass. This he carried and
stacked in a big circle around the patch of forest in which the hippo
had made his sleeping quarters.*

*"What are you doing that for?" the hippo asked suspiciously
when he saw the hare putting a large armful of grass in place one
evening.*

*"Well, winter is nearly upon us," answered the hare, "and I
thought that a wall of this grass around your sleeping quarters
would keep the cold wind from ruffling your beautiful coat."*

*"Very thoughtful of you," agreed the hippo. "Of course a coat
and tail as beautiful as mine should, in the interests of everybody,
be protected against all bad weather. I am glad to know that you
realize your responsibilities. Good night." And the hippo settled
down with a yawn.*

*Now the hare went away still angry, but looking very smug and
determined. "Just you wait, my friend," he muttered to himself.*

*His first stop was at a small village in a little clearing up a hill
nearby. Here he hid himself among the brushwood that formed
part of the goat kraal. Soon he saw the people gather around the
evening pot of food, while the village dogs waited expectantly for
the porridge scrapings.*

*"This is my chance," said the hare. With a hop, skip and a jump,
he made for the doorway of the nearest hut. Yes, he was lucky.
Just what he wanted.*

*There was a smouldering fire in the middle of the hut. And, joy
of joys, a broken clay pot was lying nearby. He carefully selected
two bits of broken pot and clapped a glowing piece of wood
between them. With these tucked safely under his arm, he made
all speed for the forest.*

*With great care, so as not to put out the precious embers he was
carrying, he crept to the hippo's resting place. With equal care,
he set fire at many points to the circle of dry grass that he had
so carefully laid. There was a soft breeze blowing, and soon a
loud crackling began.*

*With a grunt and a roar the hippo woke up and dashed wildly
from side to side, only to be met at each turn by the tall, licking*

flames.

At last Mvuu was pressed to the very center of his resting place, and there the flames caught his beautiful nut-brown coat. Like a ball of flames, he rushed through the now-blazing forest. Into his favorite pool the hippo plunged, just in time to save his life.

With terror in his heart, Mvuu stayed under the water for as long as his breath lasted.

When his lungs were close to bursting for air, Mvuu rose to the surface, putting only his eyes and nose above the water. But he ducked down again in haste as the hot breath from the fire seared his burned nose and face.

In time, when the fire had died down,` and the hissing and crackling had ceased, Mvuu ventured to crawl out onto the bank.

He was very stiff and sore; but he was alive. He could almost afford to laugh at the hare for his clumsy trickery.

But could he? What was that?

Mvuu caught sight of himself in the mirror of the pool from which he had just risen. Could he believe his eyes? What were those silly little blobs where his silky ears had been? All the hair gone, and the edges frizzled away! No wonder they had been so painful.

He turned to look at his lovely tail. Not a hair left on it either, or on his bare gray body!

In shame, Mvuu quickly returned to the pool once more. As he sank out of sight, Mvuu breathed all the air out of his body so that he would sink more easily. The noise this made was as though he had said "Mvuu." And forever after, that has been the hippo's name.

And thus Mvuu has spent his days, leaving only his eyes and his nose above the water, lest the animals that had known him in his glory, should laugh at him in his shame.

From that day to this, Mvuu has been a creature of the rivers and lakes, coming out of the water only at nighttime to walk and to graze on the fringes of the forest.

Phyllis Savory, *Lion Outwitted by Hare and Other African Tales* (Albert Whitman, 1971), pp. 17-23. The author grew up on a farm in Rhodesia (now Zimbabwe). She collected folk stories from many sources, and this volume is a selection from four previous books. Not surprisingly, these tales resemble folklore from many lands — moralistic, clever, and humorous. Interestingly enough, several of the stories bear a strong resemblance to Uncle Remus stories. This particular story comes from the Matabele (or Ndebele) people.

Our ship was under way. We had cleared Mombasa harbor. That little spot of black I had watched so long — Bill in a red dhow, shoreward bound — Bill smiling and cheering and waving me farewell to the last, had finally mingled with the glowing sea. The one familiar fragment of the past had faded like a dream. It was indeed farewell. Soon twelve thousand miles of ocean would separate me from the land I had grown to cherish — from the land which for more than a year had borne witness to imperishable dreams and accomplishments and friendships and love — to the eternal motive that drives men on. Now, I was leaving Africa as we had entered, under the benediction of the sun.

Again the 'day star' slowly glided down the western sky, suffusing the great continent in the witchery that never fails to lure the wanderer to return. I stood by the rail watching it gild the broken, palm-fringed shore line, rising black and jagged from the reddening sea. I knew the great orb was rolling on, enveloping in magic the hinterland.

Suddenly, I seemed no longer on the ship. I was back again in the country I had unwillingly left behind. As if portrayed in a series of shifting canvases against a wall of gray, I saw again the high spots of our experiences in sharp contrast with the somber days of loneliness and toil. Again I saw the flower-filled meadows circling the rocky kopjes high above the Athi and the graceful leaping antelope that linger there; the northern desert, red with dawn, and herds of prehistoric, voiceless ungulates that crop the sweet and thorny herbage of the veldt; the golden, far-extending swales below Mt. Kenya's icy peak, where silvery herons show where wild and wary cattle hide; the rolling plains and shaded dongas, spreading eastward in unbroken vastness from Tanganyika's inland sea, where peaceful lions play and herds of gentle antelope travel ever onward seeking grass; the Great Rift, cleaving as a gigantic trench the central high plateau, in whose depths a turquoise, saline sea, decked with fluttering fowl like billows of pink foam, lies fervid in the sun.

And beyond it all in the very heart of Africa I saw a land in rare degree made fair by God — a land with gift of peace for shaggy man-like beasts that long have called that spot their home. I saw the ward for them throughout the ages yet to come — the sanctuary [Parc National Albert] a gentle, reasoning mind had planned; I glimpsed the lode of wealth for science, through the perpetual truce made certain by a gracious sovereign [King Albert of Belgium] who himself had borne the scar of dreadful war. I gazed again on that primordial land — its volcan mass, its widened vents, its billowing wald, its rain and sleet and sunset glow. I saw it all again, the 'fairest spot on earth' — a temple in the uttermost, on whose high altar a devoted sacrificial spirit had offered up the total of the man he was.

And as I gazed, the pall of darkness swiftly crossed the fading sky, wrenching my soul back to the enigma of the hour. A freshening, off-shore breeze brought perfumed presage of the waiting night. And with it came a message to my heart — I knew that Africa would never cease to call — I knew my work had only just begun — throughout the years, in every task my eager hands might grasp, I would keep faith with him who ever had such trusting faith in me and in all the steadfast family of mankind.

M.L.J. Akeley, *Carl Akeley's Africa*, pp. 296-7. Despite their disdain for one another, the truth is, Carl Akeley had two remarkable wives. Interspersed in the parade of African explorers were a number of women who traveled on their own, not accompanied by husbands, mentors, or the like. Without diminishing the contributions of the Florence Bakers and the Osa Johnsons, whose roles were frequently monumental, these women on their own — Alexine Tinne, May French Sheldon, Mary Kingsley, and the Akeley women, among the most famous — deserve a special place in the pageant.

[Speke is calling on the wife of the native king's brother] She was another of those wonders of obesity, unable to stand excepting on all fours. I was desirous to obtain a good view of her, and actually to measure her, and induced her to give me facilities for doing so, by offering in return to show her a bit of my naked legs and arms. The bait took as I wished it, and after getting her to sidle and wriggle into the middle of the hut, I did as I promised, and then took her dimensions, as noted below [Round arm, 1 ft. 11 in.; chest, 4 ft. 4 in.; thigh, 2 ft. 7 in.; calf, 1 ft. 8 in.; height, 5 ft. 8 in.] All of these are exact except the height, and I believe I

could have obtained this more accurately if I could have had her laid on the floor. Not knowing what difficulties I should have to contend with in such a piece of engineering, I tried to get her height by raising her up. This, after infinite exertions on the part of us both, was accomplished, when she sank down again, fainting, for her blood had rushed into her head. Meanwhile, the daughter, a lass of sixteen, sat stark-naked before us, sucking at a milk-pot, on which the father kept her at work by holding a rod in his hands, for as fattening is the first duty of fashionable female life, it must be duly enforced by the rod if necessary. I got up a bit of flirtation with missy, and induced her to rise and shake hands with me. Her features were lovely, but her body was as round as a ball.

> John Hanning Speke, *Journal of the Discovery of the Source of the Nile* (William Blackwood and Sons, 1863), p. 231. Speke and the notorious Richard F. Burton were co-venturers searching for the sources of the Nile who later fell out and enlivened the Victorian landscape in an acrimonious debate over the true source and each other's relative contributions. It was Speke who found and named Lake Victoria; Burton was given credit for Lake Tanganyika. Burton himself simply defies all ordinary definition. A man of enormous intellect, surpassing erudition, and remarkable linguistic talents (he was supposed to have eventually mastered over thirty languages, though we have to take his word on this feat, as no one was around to speak them all with him), Burton was a soldier, inventor, author, poet, noted Arabist, anthropologist, geographer, and botanist. Mostly, he was the most eccentric — the maverick *enfant terrible* — of the Victorian explorers. He prided himself on looking like Satan and took delight in frightening children. Whenever he traveled in Africa, he adopted native dress and participated with enthusiasm in local sexual life. He happily promoted rumors that he was a cannibal and worse. The personal argument with Speke ended tragically when Speke accidentally or suicidally killed himself while partridge shooting in England. Burton was a prolific writer, but his books are rough going — a single paragraph is likely to contain many words taken from several foreign languages, plus some inventions of his own. Perhaps, the most accessible volume is *The Lake Regions of Central Africa* (Harper & Brothers, 1860).

Tilly paused for so long before replying that I thought she had forgotten my question. But at last she said: 'The baby's all right. It is Kate who is lost. If you see Mr Crawfurd, you mustn't mention her. He is half off his head.'

I was muzzy with sleep, and could not understand how Kate had got lost. She had never walked far, or wandered off alone. Perhaps the Dorobo had led her in search of something in the forest, and then deserted her.

'She needed a doctor,' Tilly added, 'and if he had got there in time, she might have been saved. If only she had gone to Nairobi, as Humphrey wanted her to. . . .'

If I had been there, I would have saddled the pony and galloped so fast to Nakuru that he would have fallen dead at the doctor's feet, his nostrils flecked with bloody foam, like the horse that brought the good news from Ghent to Aix; the doctor would have galloped through the night and reached Kate Crawfurd in the nick of time.

'It wasn't the doctor's fault,' Tilly added. 'He came as soon as he got the message. But the boy they sent with it spent four hours up a tree to escape a wounded buffalo.'

The marks of its horns were on the tree-trunk, Tilly said, to confirm his story. And he had seen a half-healed wound on the buffalo's shoulder, suppurating and fly devoured. So no one could blame the messenger, or even the buffalo.

'It was that Dutchman — that young brute who stole their pony and was always blazing off with his gun. He wounded the beast and let it get away. And then it did for Kate. I'd like to do for him. . . .'

'It wasn't Dirk's fault,' I said. I remembered that wounded buffalo, and how Dirk had tracked it nearly all day, even with

Plate 39. "And another thing..."

his stiff leg. It was the Dorobo who had found the buffalo, and I who had found the Dorobo, and it struck me suddenly that I was to blame for this disaster, in a roundabout way. If I had never told Dirk about the Dorobo, he would never have wounded the buffalo; and if I had not stood that morning in the forest looking at the dikdik and the butterflies, and wanted to get tobacco for the Dorobo, none of this would have come about. This sudden glimpse of a pattern of events in which one had a part without knowing it, in which some force beyond all comprehension moved one about like a counter on a board, was very frightening, and I lay still without saying anything more, and thinking that the deepest magic of the Kikuyu would be needed to keep one out of reach of these malignant powers that controlled a sequence starting with butterflies in a forest glade and ending with the death of Kate Crawfurd.

Elspeth Huxley, *The Flame Trees of Thika* (William Morrow, 1959; Penguin Books Edition, 1962), pp. 276-7. Huxley has

Mottled Lizard. Many readers undoubtedly saw the wonderful PBS series, staring Hayley Mills. Even so, they should read the book or, rather, both books.

My attitude towards recreational hunting, or culling for that matter, may seem anomalous but it is not. In principle I am not against either, in fact, for strictly pragmatic reasons, I am all in favour. The arguments in their support are irrefutable. I don't hunt myself because of a suggestion put to me by my grandfather

perhaps written more books in English about Africa (many of them fiction) than any other writer. A good number positively brilliant. Indeed, an anthology of quotable Huxley would fill a sizeable volume all by itself. In a fit of discipline, I have limited her contribution here to this book, one of the author's favorites. A masterful storyteller, with an extraordinary gift for detail and humor, Huxley lived her childhood in Kenya, recounted in *Flame Trees* and its sequel, *The*

when I was still young.

My grandfather died years ago, but I remember him as a Disneyesque idealisation of the archetypal wise old man. He had a full and successful life. When I was a child he could thrill me with tales of hunting adventures during World War I while stalking von Lettow-Vorbeck's elusive army against the vast splendid backdrop of what was then German Tanganyika.

He smoked a pipe as he talked, staring all the while into the middle distance, as if dredging up those kind memories from the deepest recesses of his mind. He had a habit of punctuating his stories with thoughtful pauses, which lent an air of precision, of concern for accuracy to the telling and heightened the drama.

It was because of his hunting yarns that I felt confident of an ally in a quarrel I was having with my parents. They objected to my turning my pellet gun on the flocks of doves inhabiting the scrub behind our house. I felt sure of his approval for by restricting myself to doves, a quarry difficult to stalk in the first place, once the shooting was done the felled bird could be ceremoniously plucked, grilled over an open fire and eaten. For those reasons my hunting forays seemed to me to be not only justifiable but righteously commendable.

When I presented my case, my grandfather brought out his pipe, fired it up, then sat sucking contemplatively. Finally he said, 'Next time you go out shooting I want you to try something. Once you've got the dove lined up in your sights and you know that all you have to do is squeeze the trigger and it'll drop dead — don't fire. Lay your gun down and watch what it does now that you've given it a chance to go on living.'

He said no more and although I promised to do as he asked I was uneasy. I suspected what the outcome would be and foresaw an end to my hunting career almost before it had started.

And so it was. Having set my gun aside I watched as the dove ruffled its wings and began preening, the black ring of feathers circling its neck straining against a full crop. Then it called that harsh 'coo' so characteristic of the African bush. I understood the message for what it was — a celebration of life. To this day, whenever I hear that poignant pure song, there comes a deep wave of memory, almost an echo, of that moment of revelation. As I had anticipated I never hunted again and have never had cause to regret it.

Mitch & Margot Reardon, *Zululand: A Wildlife Heritage* (C. Struik, 1984), p. 9. An elegant photographic book, with a sensitive and informed text, *Zululand* should have been included in the recommended list of Chapter 1, but the volume, published in South Africa, is difficult to find here.

The other thing is [the rhino's] habit of sweeping [its] horns or a forefoot through [its] droppings to spread them about. This practice is not confined to fresh droppings only, for I have seen an old bull come mooning along through the bush until he got to a place where several sets of droppings lay in hollows scraped out with his predecessors' feet at the base of trees beside the game path. He stopped at each and swept them about with his 30-inch front horn.

There are two African stories about this habit. One is that the rhino and the elephant had a competition as to which could make the biggest pile. The rhino found that he was likely to lose, so spread his about to make them look larger; but was caught cheating by the elephant, since when [sic] there has always been bad blood between them.

The other, which was told me by a Rhodesian, is that when the Almighty issued hides to all animals for their suitings, he also gave them a large needle with which to sew them together. The rhino was pondering over cutting-out problems with his needle in his mouth, when the hyaena passed and made some ribald remark. In the ensuing explosion of violent temper the rhino swallowed the needle and has been looking for it ever since. This also explains why his hide fits so badly, for he had to carry on with an acacia thorn.

I do not like rhino. They have spoiled too many photographic opportunities, ruined too many nights' sleep by their habit of snorting offensively at one's tent, thus making it necessary to get out of bed to deal with a possible attack, while they have frightened me considerably at times, and kept me on the strain whenever hunting with the camera in their territory. The elephant is not so dangerous, though one has to be careful with him too, but he is a gentleman, whereas the rhino is a cad!

Stockley, *African Camera Hunts*, pp. 34-5. The reader may want to compare the rhino lore on page 52.

. . . I waited amongst the reeds at the water's edge for the vehicle to collect us. It was out of a reed, according to Zulu legend, that man and animals came. The Great Great-One made the reed to open and they stepped forth. It might well have happened here — the components were perfect to nurture new life.

As I sat there [the] sun fired the wings of a dragonfly probing the bank's shaded overhang. Adept as the dragonfly, a pied kingfisher, its wings a blur of motion, hovered above the swamp's refractive surface, then tipped over and dropped straight down, plunging into the water with a reverberating splash. A second later it re-emerged, without a catch, but, with an optimistic chirp climbed again to seek another target. At my foot, on a cushion of leaf mould, lay a set of butterfly wings, paired as neatly and carefully as if placed in a display cabinet — only the thorax was missing, surgically excised by a predatory bird.

The water lured all the birds in the district and the broken, overgrown nature of the place provided sanctuary and lent an air of confidence to their comings and goings. Flocks of starlings, red-billed helmet shrikes and an assortment of doves with individual nicators, square-tailed drongos and a single bearded robin arrived in a hurry, drank, and departed just as precipitously. The persistent rhythmic tapping of a superb golden-tailed woodpecker probing perished bark in search of insect larvae combined with winter warmth to induce a pleasant drowsiness that was hard to resist.

My feeling of wellbeing in these surroundings put me in mind of the secret places of my childhood, to which only my dog Kerry was invited. Then too there had been thick bush and water and the scurry of birds and small rodents. Kerry would stare up at me with quick pants of excitement, waiting my command to ferret them out. But I acted the spoilsport, taking a restraining grasp on his scruff until he subsided with small whines of frustration. He was a creature of the bush and that's how I remember him. Although he came with us when we moved to the city he couldn't adapt. He died on the street, under a car, confused and out of his environment, reacting to instincts that no longer held true. I wonder if my fate will be so very different — or yours — times are changing so fast.

Reardon, *Zululand*, p. 153.

I had seen the royal lion, before sunrise, below a waning moon, crossing the grey plain on his way home from the kill, drawing a dark wake in the silvery grass, his face still red up to the ears, or during the midday-siesta, when he reposed contentedly in the midst of his family on the short grass and in the delicate, spring-like shade of the broad Acacia trees of his park of Africa.

Dinesen, *Out of Africa*, p. 15.

The Kikuyu believed that when a man died, his spirit could enter an animal, and it seemed quite likely that the spirit of Ian, who was so much a part of the wild and silent places, would choose a forest creature like a bushbuck for a habitation. As for his body, I knew it would be eaten by maggots and hyenas; but if in time its remnants turned to dust, as the funeral service said, his dust, I thought, would not be quite the same as other people's, but would shine like those little specks of brightness that sometimes glitter in the sand.

Huxley, *Flame Trees*, p. 262.

Eventually the sun stayed too high too long, it seemed, without rain falling at all. The main channel of the river began to form into its smaller streams, creating again islands of sand exposed to the sky. The herds left and the prides spread out. There were fewer and fewer carcasses that could be of any use to a scavenging animal of Simba's size, even though that size had begun to shrink. He was down almost a full hundred pounds from his former weight when the hyenas decided to test him.

They followed him for almost twelve hours and then determined, however such signals are given, that come dark they would try. They did try and they were successful, and Simba, the cub born in the cut in the hills known as *E-Mururuai*, went back to where he had come from. All of the chemicals that had been in him at birth and all that he had borrowed from the system during his life and not already returned in the form of body wastes now were reclaimed. His breath was part of the clouds, his urine was part of the rain, his scats had been broken down by bacteria and lesser animals. His body bulk would be digested in hours and deposited by the hyenas.

He had created cubs, many of which were even then hunting across the savannah of which he was a part. The herds of hoofstock whose paths he had crossed for over fourteen years were stronger because he had so often chosen the weak among them and the surplus. All of the cycles imagined in the beliefs of people who have always lived close to the earth were realized.

It had all been true, none of it had been sad, and all of it was now over. The only thing that was left intact was the mightiest substance Simba had been born with, the ability to be a lion — that had gone forward. That would remain intact.

Roger Caras, *Mara Simba: The African Lion* (Holt, Rinehart, and Winston, 1985), pp. 207-8. A work of undeniable charm, the full life story of a single African lion, *Mara Simba* unfortunately (for 1985) repeats a long litany of popular misconceptions (leopards leaping from trees onto prey; lions hunting together with military-like precision; the Maasai on many matters; leopards hunting lion cubs in the presence of the lioness; and several more). The format — dramatic integration of an animal with its ecosystem — is a popular one (cf. Russell, *Season on the Plain* and Scott, *A Leopard's Tale*) and rarely totally successful. Caras does it better than most.

A troop of vervet monkeys played on the forest perimeter where it gave way to the grasscap we rested on. The vervets scampered and quarrelled, groomed and foraged, sometimes remembering to harangue us but without conviction. I watched them past the bulk of the old man who sat a little ahead of me. He too was looking towards the vervets but I wondered if he really saw them. He had lived all his life with such scenes and doubtless had domestic worries to occupy his mind. Anyway, I had been told on more than one occasion (by so-called 'experts') that Africans have no aesthetic appreciation of wildlife. Then he turned to me and on his face was a smile of pure delight. He was as charmed by the vervets as I.

Reardon, *Zululand*, p. 131. The Reardons also wrote (and photographed) the book *Etosha, Life and Death on an African Plain* (C. Struik, 1981), a worthy companion to *Zululand*.

But at home one is bound with petty regulations and irksome restraints. Instead of being a free wild man of the woods, one has become a herd animal. One's individualism is less apparent because there is less scope for it. People do not understand that a wanderer returned views things from a different standpoint, as his life has been spent away in the vast spaces where simplicity is the rule, and not complexity. He feels lost even in great crowds, for nothing and no one seem in sympathy. The people he knows may be good fellows, but they do not understand him, and he does not understand them. Environment (a favourite word with parsons) is at fault, because it has become foreign to him, and he longs to get back to the bush, the hills, and the plains, where he spent some of the happiest days of his life, for there he felt an exaltation that no civilized land can possibly supply.

Denis D. Lyell, *Memories of an African Hunter* (T. F. Unwin, 1923; St. Martin's Press Edition, 1987), pp. 238-9. In the early years of this century, the white hunter flourished in East, Central, and Southern Africa. In a world of adventure, gore, heat, dust, fever, comaraderie, and imagination, the list of the "greatest hunters" is a lengthy one — Selous, Neumann, Baden-Powell, Finch-Hatton, Sutherland, Norton, Pearson, Lyell, Stigand, Percival (Philip), Hunter, Millais, Smith, Chapman, Schindelar, Hoey, the Hill cousins, Cuninghame, Downey, von Blixen-Finecke, Newland and Tarlton, Bell, Pretorious, Salmon, Powell-Cotton, Ionides, the Greys, Pitman, Black, Cottar, Burger, Stevenson-Hamilton, Simpson, Alden, Oswell, Goss, Jackson, Bell, Rainsford, Pretorius, Layard, Finnaughty, and von Schellendorff, among others — but Denis David Lyell, part of the Scottish-African pipeline, stood near the top of the profession. No other hunter, save the legendary Selous, was so esteemed by his peers. It would, no doubt, be unfair to lump all these Nimrods together in a common mold. How and why they arrived in Africa varied considerably. But they all loved the aroma of canvas and the campfire, they loved shooting, and they loved killing animals. Most were 'gentlemen' of the times, even the most flamboyant were men of integrity, and several were keen amateur-naturalists as well. Earlier hunters had been mostly explorer-sportsmen, trigger-happy army officers, or settlers reacting to the endless difficulties (and boredom) of pioneer life. Encouraged by the blessings of missionaries, a few had eagerly sought profit (in ivory). The succeeding generation represented an institutionalization of sorts and was immortalized in fiction by such writers as Rider Haggard and (later) Ernest Hemingway and in too many films to mention. Many of the white hunters wrote their own tomes. Big-game sport hunting soon took on a repetitive and almost ritualistic quality: the same hair-raising stories, repeated over and over; constant reference to difficult "brain shots" and the velocities and thuds of bullets; and "large bags" of game. Above all, danger galore! Occasionally, someone *was* killed by a wild animal; as Voltaire once remarked, *'l'animal est très méchant; grand l'on attaque, il se défend.''* But exaggeration nearly always carried the day. Lyell was a prolific writer and wrote or co-authored eight books; *Memories* is reputed to be his "best."

As to the correct way to measure lion, tiger, and leopard, there is only one method which can be called really practicable, and that is to put a peg in at the nose and another at the end of the tail just after the animal is dead. All measurements taken from skins, which may have been soaked in water for some time, are fictitious and should never be accepted, as a lion skin (or any skin), when soaked for a night in a tub, can be pulled out quite a foot longer than the skin measured when stripped off the carcass. Curve measurements of animals are also unsatisfactory, as the tape cannot be kept tight, and some men keep it as slack as they can when they are looking for a record. For standing height a peg should be put in at the top of the shoulder, and another under the pad or hoof when the leg is held in a natural position.

Most people who know the proportions of the skin of any animal can soon see when a skin has been stretched, as naturally the more it is pulled out, the more is the width reduced. Only steel tapes should be used, as they do not stretch or shrink so much as cloth ones.

There is a story of an old Indian Colonel who was boasting in a smoking-room of shooting a 12-foot tiger. An angler sitting near immediately told a story of catching a skate a quarter of an acre in extent. The Colonel promptly challenged him to a duel, so the angler said, "If you'll take two feet off that tiger, I'll see what can be done with the skate."

Lyell, *Memories,* pp. 96-7. The safari clients arrived en masse, from damp and chilly Europe first, America later. A few were men of courage and real hunting ability. More were simply fools, an enormous number of jilted lovers and aristocratic black sheep — the English called them "bounders." Some were bloodthirsty; some simply wanted their trophies in the shortest possible time. The safari became a ritual of upper-class life and a logical extension of colonial empire. Africa's natural world a playground invented for sport. Soon, influential Americans would be entertained as well, as the English showed off empire. The motorcar ushered in the truly luxury safaris that reached their zenith in the 1920s. Money was no object, and, as J.A. Hunter later remarked, the safaris resembled "small circuses . . .[and] when two of these great safaris met, the chefs competed to see who could arrange the most elaborate meal, and some of these banquets I have eaten in the heart of the African bush were better than any I have ever had in London" (*Tales of the African Frontier* (with Daniel P. Mannix; Harper, 1954), p. 228). The Great Depression ended these affairs, though certain standards of luxury have survived to the present day, for a price.

One night my camp-bed, which was rather groggy in the legs, came down, and the mosquito-net got over my face and body. Being suddenly awakened, I thought a lion had broken in and was worrying me, and it took a few moments to discover the cause of the catastrophe, as my arms, legs, and head were all mixed up in the net.

Lyell, *Memories,* pp. 91-2.

I should have liked to have seen the cavalcade of nearly fifty wagons and teams setting off from Nakuru; but although I was born then, I was only about a year old, so would not have seen much. While most of the Boers had been training oxen, a few others had gone ahead on horseback to spy out the land. They had climbed three thousand feet, using elephant tracks through the forest, and had stood at last upon a rock (so Dirk's brother, who was one of them, had told him) silent with wonder, so noble did their promised land appear, teeming with animals who lacked the fear of man. Herds of kongoni, he said, browsed on the sweet green grasses, he saw wildebeeste and zebra by the thousand, and oribi wandering about wagging their tails, and the loping giraffe, like tiger-lilies bending with dignity before a gusty breeze, and the big biscuit-coloured eland with their drooping dewlaps and striped withers, and the red, nimble-footed impala walking in single file. And many birds: spurfowl, francolin, and guinea-fowl, as well as pigeons cooing in the trees; and smaller animals like reedbuck and duiker, all feeding together without enmity or fear. Even the lions excited no alarm unless actually hunting, and were ignored, and sunned themselves peaceably. A man had no need to stalk and crawl, he had only to stand still and shoot and something would fall.

Years later, I saw a picture of the Garden of Eden, with all the beasts consorting together in a park of great beauty, painted with meticulous richness and care. I thought at once of this vision of the Uasin Gishu plateau as the Dutch first saw it, and as no one was ever to see it again. The difference was that in the picture, Adam and Eve walked at peace with the animal creation; but that was only a vision. The artist should have painted Adam setting a trap, and Eve chewing a morsel of liver. The Dutch, of course, had rifles, and fingers that itched to press the triggers. This they did as soon as they had recovered from their astonishment. They shot a kongoni, and had a good meal.

Huxley, *Flame Trees,* pp. 238-9.

A few years ago I had pitched my temporary camp by Lakes Baringo and Hannigan in Kenya. I was assisting a moving-picture expedition which had made it its task to film the amazingly rich bird life which flourishes there among the hippopotami and crocodiles.

I had the opportunity of making many interesting observations; but I remember particularly one morning when I had gone out at dawn to conceal myself in the reeds opposite a sandbank and watch animal life at the moment when the crocodiles crawl up on the sand to rest in the morning sunshine after their night's fishing.

First they come floating like tree-trunks on the surface of the water; they lie still for some time till they have made sure that no danger is at hand. Then a big crocodile, a twelve-foot giant, crawls out. He walks slowly and stumblingly on his weak legs, lies on his stomach, and opens his jaws, which get fixed, so that they remain open even when he is asleep. The gray-speckled crocodile birds come hopping up; they flutter round, approach carefully, and, with a dentist's skill, pick out of the sleeping monster's jaws all the fragments of food which have become lodged during the night's meal.

Suddenly a hippopotamus poked his bright brown head up out of the water, winked once or twice with his little eyes, pushed his head farther out, looked hard at the crocodile on the sandbank, climbed up slowly, and quietly emerged on the sand. He stood looking about him in the warm sun and then slowly approached the crocodile, which closed his jaws suddenly, although the birds had not completed his morning tooth-brushing. The hippopotamus went right up to the crocodile and gave him one blow across the tail with his great head. The crocodile turned round and hissed at the insolent disturber of the peace; but the hippopotamus quietly took another step forward and, with a swiftness of which one would have not thought the clumsy beast capable, gave the giant crocodile a fresh blow with his head amidships, which flung the monster, certainly four hundred pounds in weight, out into the

Dinesen's) profligate husband and for the ignominy of having transmitted syphilis to her. Indeed, in terms of promiscuity, Bror was rivaled only by the notorious Fritz Schindelar (and *he* was eaten by a lion). It is said that Hemingway based his character Robert Wilson, the hunter in *The Short Happy Life of Francis Macomber,* on the congenial and durable Blixen. Between the wars, "Blix" (to his friends) squired many a notable of the day across the savannah. And not everyone joined the parade for shooting (or photography):

Plate 40. Classic Hippo Profile. Hippos thrive in water, and the benefit is reciprocated, especially in swamps and shallows. The large animals churn the bottom and the water encouraging circulation and oxygenation. Hippos help to keep flowing water from clogging up with vegetation. Where hippos have been driven off or shot out often quickly turns into marshland.

lake like a pebble.
I never saw anything like it before or since . . .

Baron Bror von Blixen-Finecke, *African Hunter* (Cassell, 1937; St. Martin's Press Edition, 1986), pp. 217-9. Since the film *Out of Africa,* Bror Blixen will probably suffer the obscurity of being remembered simply as Karen Blixen's (Isak

. . . not long ago I happened to hear a lady complaining bitterly about her white hunter. "I was three months alone in the bush with him," said the lady indignantly. "And all he did was show me animals. Did he think I came six thousand miles to look at a bunch of damn rhinos?" Hunter & Mannix, *Tales of the African Frontier,* p. 229.)

But not all animals that hide and want to be in contact with their surroundings in the most intimate way are tiny. At least one is a magnificently handsome giant of startling proportions. The Maasai have long known the glistening beauty of en-tara, which science has named Python sebae. It is the African rock python, a monster that can grow to thirty-two feet in length and be almost as big around as a grown man. The python is a sly hunter of immense power and unblinking eyes.

Nowhere in the world are giant snakes worshipped as they are in Africa. People not far from where the Maasai wander speak of the god Danhg-bi when they speak of this snake. It has been revered since times so ancient no one can reckon their place in the evolution of culture. Captive specimens are kept in temples of glass and wood and consulted, propitiated, and tenderly cared for as long as they live. Virgins serve them; priests and keepers with secret powers speak with them about matters of eternity.

The python of E-Mururuai was a wild, free hunter who depended on his glossy light-brown scales marked with blendings of darker brown and random speckling to hide him until he was close enough to strike his virtually irresistible blow. He could dart forward from his own giant coils at nearly six miles an hour. Although tales of his kind butting prey and knocking it down with the force of the strike are almost certainly nonsense, the python is equipped with immensely powerful jaws, and once it clamps down on prey with its inward-curving teeth, the victim seldom escapes. Prey is chosen with care, for like all snakes the python is fragile, subject to infections and parasites; to live it has to avoid wounds that could be invaded and become septic. A snake, too, even a giant snake, has muscles like steel bands, but they are supported by a relatively light skeleton. A python is a giant that can be torn as well as broken.

. . .

The largest of the four cubs, the one that weighed five pounds at birth, was the last still in its place of birth when the python slipped out of the deep grass twenty feet away. Instantly sensing movement ahead, the python increased his speed, tasting the air as he went until he was only a few feet away from the cub. At that point he lunged, for he had already identified his target. He dragged the cub toward him as he moved his own coils forward and lashed them around the barely struggling infant. In seconds his first coils closed over the cub and began drawing in like an enormous knot. No bones were broken; the cub was not crushed, for that is not the way the constricting snakes kill. As the little cat exhaled, the coils tightened, leaving less room inside for the lungs to expand. In less than two minutes the heart of the already unconscious cub stopped beating.

Before the python could position himself to swallow the cub headfirst, the lioness arrived to retrieve the last of her young. The cub was gone. It took her less than thirty seconds of casting around the area to locate the python. Her snarl came like an exploding boiler. Her lips were back and it was as if fire came from her yellow eyes. The python sensed his dangerous enemy as soon as she saw him and uncoiled, abandoning the cub he had just killed. Two killers were now stalking each other, one no less dangerous than the other. To be certain of victory each needed the advantage of surprise. A python, unseen, can drop on even an adult lion and perhaps kill it. A cat coming upon a python that has just fed and is semi-torpid might surprise it and win. But these two killers were alert, awake, facing each other. Although neither could feel hate as an emotion, they could manifest rage. They were dangerously aroused adversaries. The hormones that had seen the lioness through her pregnancy and birth turned her into a dragon at the

disturbance of her nest site, while the true dragon, the mighty python, had been disturbed at his meal.

The snake lashed out, his jaws gaping, but he was far slower than the enraged lioness. On his first thrust the python was met with the smashing impact of a great paw. Before the paw was withdrawn claws had curved out of their sheaths, making the first raking cuts that would spell death for the snake eventually, even

Plate 41. Zebra Combatants.

if the cat withdrew. But the cat moved forward and hammered the snake again and again with a rage born in the mists of ancient times. The snake writhed, tried to strike out at the cat, threw his coils into loops and piles. But his spine was broken not far down from his neck. His beautiful shiny scales were matted with his own fluids, were ripped and soiled with blood-soaked earth, and still the lioness hammered. Finally, as the snake's movements slowed the cat moved close enough to take the snake's head in her mouth. There was a crunching sound. The primitive nervous system would keep the snake writhing there, twitching and jerking, for hours.

Hyenas, jackals, and vultures would eat the snake and scatter his light, fragile bones. In less than twenty-four hours there would be nothing left but disturbed grass and some blood mixed with soil.

The lioness walked over to her largest cub, sniffed and prodded him, and then picked him up by the head as she had her other young. This cub did not draw up his hind legs but hung limp, his legs dragging as his mother moved out across the soggy marsh.

Halfway across she abandoned her dead infant and moved off without him, breaking into a trot to reach her remaining young sooner. She made a low, moaning sound as she moved. Later in the day a hyena would find the cub and carry it back to her underground den to feed her own cubs. The first cub had died without ever seeing light, but three more remained. Who can say what, if anything, the lioness felt? We have neither the insight nor the language. She would have killed the python if she had encountered it under any circumstances. If she did not have cubs waiting unattended, she might have eaten some of the snake,

although she would have left most of it for scavengers to use.

Caras, *Mara Simba*, pp. 23-8.

'It would be very bad to shoot the python. Then we should not get any rain.'

'What has the python to do with rain?'

'Have you not seen the big snake of many colours that lies across the sky when the rain falls? That is the snake who lives in the waterfall. If you look down into the waterfall you can see him there sometimes. His colours are many, like the flowers your mother grows.'

'But the python is black,' I objected.

'When he goes into the waterfall he puts on his bright clothes. They are so bright that they shine up into the sky. If you kill the snake there will be no colours and no rain.'

Robin, I recalled, had said that he would give the python's skin to Tilly, and she could have shoes and bags made from it. I was glad that I would be able to warn him, as we needed rain for the young coffee, and if Tilly wore shoes made from such a magical creature she might disappear.

Huxley, *Flame Trees*, p. 188.

Elephants are most interesting animals to watch in a wild state, and, having seen large numbers (at least two thousand), I have spent some enjoyable hours when near them. Elephants will help others off when wounded, as I have seen them do so on two occasions. On one of these instances I hit a bull in the head, and he fell dead as I thought, but was only dazed, and lay motionless with his tusks fixed deeply in the ground, as he fell directly downwards and not on his side. He lay quiet for about a minute, and two of the other elephants came and began prodding him and stroking him with their trunks. Then he awoke and tried to get up, but failed at the first attempt, and I could not get another shot in as the two others were in the line of fire. At last he got on his feet, but was dazed and silly, as he rocked about like a drunken man. I had become so interested that, instead of trying to fire, I stood watching them closely. As the elephant showed signs of collapsing again, the other two got one on each side, and every time he lurched over, the elephant he came against would give him a bump to steady him.

This all took place as they retreated at a slow walk, and I was so fascinated that, instead of running in and trying for another shot, I forgot all about killing him. Once the wounded beast stopped, still dizzy with the hard rap on his skull, and the two hustled him on until they were in the timber, gradually getting up a faster pace, though as long as they were in sight they never broke from a walk. As I was certain this elephant would recover, I did not go far after him, but I went far enough to know that the three of them had run at last.

Lyell, *Memories*, p. 140.

This wonderful feminine courage [of a lioness] recalls to my memory — I make no comparisons, of course — another episode which also happened some years ago. During the war I was acting as a scout on the Tanganyika front, and on one occasion it became necessary to move off in haste. It was impossible to take the whole camp with us at once; I hurried on ahead, while Tanne, my wife, took command of the transport wagon, drawn by sixteen oxen, which was to follow rather more slowly.

On the third evening, just as they were preparing to pitch camp, there was a fearful disturbance among the oxen, which had been left quite alone for a few moments. Tanne hurried up and saw two lions, each of which had jumped on an ox's back. It need not be said that the teamsters had disappeared like phantoms, and my wife faced the two lions alone and unarmed, for, through an oversight, the rifles had been carefully stowed away among the baggage. But she had the heavy stockwhip, and with it she literally whipped the lions away from the oxen.

My wife made light of the incident.

"What else could I do?" she asked. "If I'd had a gun I'd have used it, of course; but the stockwhip isn't to be despised, as you see."

One of the oxen had been so severely mauled by the lion in those few seconds that it died of its wounds, but my wife's care succeeded in saving the life of the other.

> von Blixen-Finecke, *African Hunter*, pp. 91-2. This famous incident in Isak Dinesen's life was brought to life as only film can do in the movie *Out of Africa*. I can assure the reader that tackling two full-grown lions in the middle of their hunt armed only with a bullwhip would be no small matter.

For until you actually saw it and travelled across it on foot or on horseback or in a wagon, you could not possibly grasp the enormous vastness of Africa. It seemed to go on for ever and ever; beyond each range of hills lay another far horizon; always it was the same, pale-brown grass and bush and thorn-trees, rocky mountains, dark valleys, sunlit plain; there was no break and no order, no road and no town, no places even: just marks on a map which, when you got there, turned out to be merely an expanse of bush or plain exactly like the rest of the landscape.

> Huxley, *Flame Trees*, p. 28.

Many people scoff at shooting now, so they take telephotos of game, sometimes pretending that a beast is charging when it is not, as an expert can see at once. They get up quite a reputation for courage amongst people who do not know the ropes, and who admire their fine pictures (some of them are certainly good). As a matter of fact, there is seldom much danger in approaching game with a camera, because the first instinct of any beast is to bolt.

On the other hand, it is much more dangerous to follow a wounded animal into thick cover with a rifle, for one is much more likely to be charged when doing so, than by taking a photograph of the same beast when unwounded.

In mentioning this, I have no wish to decry the pluck of the telephotographers, as they are brave men, but I do wish to dispel an erroneous idea which is prevalent amongst people who know nothing about hunting. Some of these "charging" photographs give themselves away at the first glance, as the beast is seen at an angle, whereas a real charge is straight on, if photographed from the front. Of course a charge at someone else could be taken from the side, but one does not often see that kind in books or magazines. Few animals charge unless wounded, except, possibly, a female with young. When game has been much molested, instead of wanting to charge at sight, they want to run away as quickly as possible.

> Lyell, *Memories*, pp. 157-8.

As we descended the last bit of hill above the Blue Posts, we saw the safari passing just below. The porters were marching smartly with their morning strength and chanting a vigorous song. Their loads were of all shapes and sizes: long tent-poles which, though jointed, poked out such a distance fore and aft that to manoeuvre them through bush must have presented appalling difficulty; a tin bath full of lanterns; folding-chairs and tables; rolls of bedding; chop-boxes of food; everything you could think of. It was a miniature army on the march, guarded by three or four askaris looking fierce and superior with nothing to carry but their rifles and water-bottles. The porters wore all sorts of nondescript clothing — tattered shorts, vests consisting mostly of holes, football stockings, discarded greatcoats, red blankets. This was a working safari, not one of the de luxe affairs equipped by the firm of Newland, Tarlton & Co., whose porters marched forth in long blue jerseys, like those worn by police askaris, with the letters 'N&T' stitched on in red. It was a rule or custom, I do not know which, among safari outfitters to present each porter with a pair of boots — much too good a pair to spoil by wearing, which in any case cramped and distorted the feet; so every man set forth with a pair of boots tied round his neck.

As the porters swung by with their bobbing loads, their song of challenge rose among the rocks, a dusty halo hung about the backs of the rear-guard askaris, two men left behind with slipping loads half-walked, half-ran after them, and the column wound out of sight along the wagon-road that dipped to cross the river by a log bridge. They were gone, marching to far romantic places beyond the last farm, the ultimate shamba, where the wild game of Africa had their wide plains and secret reeded water-holes all to themselves, and when you camped among the thorns beside a dry sand-river, and dug for moisture in the hot sand, it might be that you were treading where no man, white or black, had ever set his foot before. It was a moment to lift the heart, but also to fill the mind with anguish because the others were going, and I was left behind, and would never see these far imagination-torturing places, or taste the solitudes where nature keeps her pure and intricate balance free from the crass destructiveness of man.

'You shall come on a safari when you're older,' Tilly promised, noticing my state of mind.

'I shall never be older,' I said gloomily.

'You will be older tomorrow. You will even be a bit older when you get back to the farm.'

'How wonderfully lucky you are', Lettice added, 'to be glad of that, and not sorry!'

'Children are always being told they are lucky to have things they hate,' said Robin, 'like plenty of time ahead of them, and expensive educations, and healthy food, and considerate parents. It must be very annoying.'

'Perhaps it's as bad to feel one isn't getting old fast enough, as to know that one is getting old too fast,' Lettice agreed. 'We are always trying to make time go at a different pace, as if it were an obstinate pony. Perhaps we should do better to let it amble along as it wishes, without taking much notice of it.'

'That is what the natives do,' Tilly said.

> Huxley, *Flame Trees*, pp. 181-2.

We could not, unfortunately, relive *African Game Trails* entirely. We will have no memories of the laden caravan nor of the lion's charge; a Land-Rover is neither as romantic nor as companionable as a horse; and there is too little left, even in East Africa, that is "unworn of man." But there is still much to share . . . I tried to sum up something of the feeling in my diary: "The drive back to camp, in the brief equatorial twilight and early dark, is one of those entrancing moments one wishes to cling to and possess forever. You journey along over the open plains, down and up the steep donga banks, weaving between the thorn bushes or sometimes riding right over them, jolting over chunks of lava, and as the sun sinks behind the now black hills, the sky has a strong translucent quality, like fine mother-of-pearl. We don't have hundreds of porters singing the lion chant (which TR transliterated as "zou-zou boule ma ja guntai; zou-zou boule me ja guntai"); too much of the time it is our spines and rear-ends, not our feet, that feel the rough ground; but this is nonetheless a timeless experience that we can essentially share with TR and KR and hundreds of other hunters who have preceded us."

Kermit Roosevelt, *A Sentimental Safari* (Alfred A. Knopf, 1963), p. 286. The grandson of T.R. in 1960 returned to the highlands of Kenya to retrace the famous safari of his grandfather and father.

On the whole, elephants do not worry other species of animals around a waterhole, but we did watch one cantankerous old bull which really had a "chip on his shoulder". It was just after noon on an extremely hot day when the lone tusker arrived to drink. He had no sooner waded into the shallow water and begun to drink when he noticed a single warthog trotting down to the waterhole. Turning his attention on the little warthog, the elephant rushed towards it, his trunk swinging viciously from side to side and flaying the water. The warthog halted in amazement, then raced off to safety with its tail held stiffly erect like a flag. After the warthog had disappeared, the elephant waded into deeper water to cool off. Time after time he rolled completely over on his back, with much tossing of his head. Watching this unusual performance we noticed, through binoculars, that his left tusk had been broken off short, and realized that his grumpy behaviour must be due to agonizing toothache. By rolling over in the waterhole he packed the broken tusk with mud which may have relieved the pain, although it was impossible to know if this action was deliberate. While the elephant was still in the water, a beautiful bateleur eagle alighted at the edge of the hole to drink. Again the elephant splashed through the water and was almost on top of the bateleur before it realized the danger and flew off. His quarry having vanished, the elephant stood dejectedly on the bank, his trunk curled up over his head with the tip delicately caressing a ticklish spot behind one ear. Slowly, he began to plod round the edge of the waterhole when three warthogs approached the water. As they were about to pass twenty feet behind the elephant he suddenly wheeled about with an ear-splitting scream, ears spread wide, and swiped at the nearest with his massive trunk. Within seconds the warthogs had vanished and the elephant slowly moved off. A lonely figure without a friend in the world, he soon disappeared in the shimmering heat haze.

Jen & Des Bartlett, *Nature's Paradise* (Collins, 1967), p. 102. *Paradise* is another of those excellent picture books that should have been included in the brief list recommended in Chapter I. The Bartletts worked for many years with Armand and Michaela Denis. This volume has some excellent pictures of "Operation Noah," the rescue of trapped animals from the islands caused by the rise of man-made Lake Kariba, as well as interesting coverage of the Tree Hotel "Treetops."

All the afternoon it rained, but in the evening the sky cleared and we wandered out along the path, hoping to see the first giant groundsels (Senecio). The reality, however, surpassed our expectation. There he stood at a twist of the path, where it descended into a dip to cross a small stream by a rickety bridge; a veritable tree over twenty feet high, branched, gaunt, and with a certain pathetic, bizarre and indescribable look of unreality as of an old man, transported from another planet or age and set down to confront the present world. 'Senex', indeed, means an old man, and these trees are veritable 'Old men of the Mountains'.

The trunks are twisted and contorted often into all manner of weird shapes, so that some become almost more animal than vegetable; they are surmounted by mops of foliage, like great lax cabbages. The leaves are very large, sometimes three feet in length, and of a rather fierce shade of metallic green. The old leaves do not fall, but remain attached to the tree, dangling as a dead, slowly-decaying mass around the trunk below the rosette. Sometimes they are so numerous that the whole trunk becomes a pillar of dead leaves with a central core.

At Bulambuli there were none in flower, but higher up in the alpine moorland zone we found the giant groundsels flowering frantically. From the centre of the cabbage crown would emerge a vast spike, sometimes three or four feet high and branched repeatedly. The flowers of the higher species were very similar to those of the common English groundsel, except for size and number, but those of the lower species were always much more ornamental, having long ray florets (petals to the non-botanist) like the ragwort or yellow garden daisy. Some of these flowers would be an inch and a half in diameter, and one spike would bear a hundred or more, so that the effect was very striking.

At first the sight of the giant groundsels dominated us, and their bizarreness seemed an ever-exciting and thrilling wonder, but after a few days we began to accept them as part of the landscape, to expect their presence rather than their absence. Even so soon does habit dull over the sense of wonder.

Synge, *Mountains of the Moon*, pp. 68-9.

Millions feared Hitler and millions were enthralled by him. Millions laid down their lives for him and other millions died fighting against him. Today when German school children are asked questions about Hitler, most of them know very little about him and cannot even name his henchmen.

The same applies to Napoleon, to the Anabaptists, the Hussites and the protagonists of the first World War.

Men are easily inspired by human ideas, but they forget them again just as quickly. Only Nature is eternal, unless we senselessly destroy it. In fifty years' time nobody will be interested in the results of the conferences which fill today's headlines.

But when, fifty years from now, a lion walks into the red dawn and roars resoundingly, it will mean something to people and quicken their hearts whether they are bolshevists or democrats, or whether they speak English, German, Russian or Swahili. They will stand in quiet awe as, for the first time in their lives, they watch twenty thousand zebras wander across the endless plains.

Is it really so stupid to work for the zebras, lions and men who will walk the earth fifty years from now? And for those in a hundred or two hundred years' time . . .?

Bernhard & Michael Grzimek, *Serengeti Shall Not Die* (E.P. Dutton, 1961), p. 334. The world-famous zoologist Bernhard Grzimek actually wrote *Serengeti* after the tragic death of son Michael occurred in a plane accident (over the Serengeti; he was buried on the rim of Ngorongoro Crater). Father and son were working on a wildlife survey and a film to promote the Tanzania park and the cause of conservation. Audrey Moore's *Serengeti* (Charles Scribner's Sons, 1939) had earlier brought some attention to the area, but Professor Grzimek's book and film (and the martyrdom of Michael) and the resulting publicity proved a turning point in the popularity of the park, creating a surge of tourism. The technical information in the book itself has to be carefully sifted; for example, the migratory patterns described are incorrect.

Pioneer Mary pulled from the enormous pocket of her bushshirt an untidy parcel, saying that she would have bought me something fine and entertaining, a toy or a book, if she had known there was to be a child, but this was all she could find. It turned out to be a very small crocodile, about eight inches long, stuffed with grass and clumsily skinned, but engaging because it was a complete reptile in miniature, down to its tiny claws and little bumps along the backbone and prickly teeth jutting from ferocious jaws. It was extraordinary to learn that crocodiles were born like this, complete: little, snapping, predatory creatures from their moment of introduction on to this earth. I cherished my baby crocodile, and kept it for several years until it was eaten by a puppy.

Huxley, *Flame Trees*, p. 87.

The land immediately across the river was taken up by a Scot called Jock Nimmo who was always away shooting elephants. After a while he dumped a wife there to make a show of development. The regulations required every settler to spend a certain sum on his land within, I think, the first five years, and to do a certain amount in the way of clearing bush, fencing, cultivating, and putting up buildings. Anyone who failed to do this lost his land. As Mr. Nimmo was a hunter, not a farmer, he left all this to his wife. Tilly thought that was why he married her. Why had she married him? It can hardly have been for security or for companionship, and must have been a disappointment if it was for love. She was a nursing sister from Edinburgh who had come out to the Nairobi hospital, and that was where Jock Nimmo had met her. Soon after their marriage he had left her in the bush with a drunken headman, a few unreliable Kikuyu, and some implements and untrained oxen, and had gone off to poach ivory in the Belgian Congo, with a promise that he would take her to the races on his return.

Huxley, *Flame Trees*, p. 54. Just as the first decade of this century was drawing to a close, King Leopold of Belgium died, and a large piece of land spreading for thousands of square miles and consisting mostly of forest and swamp, known as the Lado Enclave, suddenly launched the African equivalent of a gold rush — for white gold. The Lado Enclave, located between the Belgian Congo and British Sudan, was one of those disputed pieces of the imperial pie that had temporarily fallen off the plate. Claimed by the British and leased to King Leopold (who treated the Enclave and, indeed, much of the Belgian Congo as his personal fiefdom), the Lado was due to revert to the British sometime after Leopold's death. When the King died, the Belgian officials there abandoned their posts for the more secure Congo proper. Actual British takeover was, however, approx-

imately a year in the future. Without immediate administration, the Enclave itself was reportedly the largest, if not last, stronghold of big-tusked elephants left in Africa. An ivory paradise for the taking! Every Nimrod who ever dreamt of profit from white gold, led by none other than the wild John Boyes himself and apparently including Huxley's Jock Nimmo, now stampeded to Lado. Thousands of elephants were killed — many renowned hunters taking a significant part of their lifetime total — in less than a year, and hundreds, if not thousands, of tons of ivory were removed from the Enclave. The large-scale poaching, less massive after British takeover but hardly eliminated, continued until the outbreak of the First World War.

A big male baboon was sitting in the open, busily starting to eat a baby Grant's gazelle it had just killed. Suddenly it was chased by an irate female Grant's gazelle, which pursued it across a stretch of open ground until the baboon found sanctuary in a large yellow thorn tree. Cautiously the baboon would descend the tree, only to be forced up again by the female gazelle. Time passed, and the mother Grant started to graze away from the tree. Not needing a second opportunity, the baboon was down the tree like a flash, looking back over his shoulder as he raced towards another tree. As he climbed to safety, the sharp horns of the charging female Grant's gazelle only missed him by inches. The conflict went on for three hours, with the baboon no sooner descending one tree than he had to race for the safety of yet another. This personal battle raged back and forth between three trees in the open and, in the meantime, the rest of the baboon troop moved out of sight. What would be the outcome of all this? The baboon was definitely frightened of the female Grant, and yet it was obvious that the gazelle did not want to risk a fight with the powerful male baboon. She worried and tormented him without actually drawing blood. The end came suddenly and unexpectedly! The battle brought the female Grant back to the place where her dead baby had been dropped in the grass by the baboon, and she looked at it without moving for perhaps half a minute. When the bereaved mother realized that the baby was dead, and therefore past her help, she walked off slowly towards the herd without a backward glance at the baboon, which was now racing off in the opposite direction. It had been a very touching and moving scene and it was hard to believe that a female antelope would remember and hold a grudge against another animal for so long . . .

Bartlett, *Nature's Paradise*, p. 139.

[This book] *is concerned with the "end of the game," the end of an era; the elephant reaching desperately for the last branch on a tree, rhinos rushing across a dusty horizon, stately giraffes plodding slowly out of the picture, their legs lost in mirage. The game is both the hunt and the hunted, the sport and the trophy. The game is killing the game. There was a time when the hunter killed only for his life and food, when wild animals were driven from one area into another instead of being shot or poisoned. Now there are few places left to drive the game. Fifty years ago men had to be protected from the beasts; today the beasts must somehow be protected from man.*

In Africa, life has been abundant, so death has abounded; but only in natural balance. The whole system has participated in an eternal rhythm, a timeless harmony. Nature devoted eons to perfecting her equilibrium, her infinitely complex "niche" structure. Time and again we see examples of evolution probing to the fullest every conceivable niche, fitting in the widest possible range of animals, allowing a vastly differentiated use of vegetation, resulting finally in balanced, mutual conservation of habitat. The elephant, with his great stride, broke paths for the other game; with his trunk uprooted trees, aiding fertilization and irrigation; and with his huge feet in swamps or his trunk in sand left holes providing water for the lesser fowl, small fish, and tadpoles.

It is nature's immutable law that individuals die but species and cycles live on . . . Death has always been the patiently awaited, unfeared fact of delicately poised African life; it is swift and silent. Its agents lurk everywhere, and its legacy is final; its beneficiaries circle gracefully overhead.

Then there is another death mirrored in these pages. This is the final dying, the end of all nature's processes, patterns, cycles, and balances. Equilibrium is dislocated, harmony destroyed; cement slowly suffocates the land. The great herds move into new and strange habitats. Unable to live off the land, they diminish, and, as they diminish, the land too begins to die. Imbalance is compounded. The land loses its game, and thus its life. This book chronicles that final dying, recording in words and pictures the gradual, remorseless removal of the central symbol of African life, the animal.

Peter H. Beard, *The End of the Game* (Viking Press, 1965), pp. 21-3. As the title suggests, Beard's well-known study is essentially pessimistic. A provocative text (among other ideas, Beard supported game-cropping and culling), striking photographs, and the interesting graphics that have become a Beard hallmark, all make this effort well worth reading in its entirety.

My earliest meeting with a lion was during my very first expedition in Africa, when I was out collecting workers for my coffee plantation. We had pitched camp near a water-hole — a quiet, peaceful place it seemed, but nevertheless the night was a trifle disturbed. The tropical night symphony was in too full blast. The crickets chirped more furiously than usual — it sounds like a thousand bows at work behind the bridge of a violin; the jackals howled far off, and at times the air resounded with the beating of heavy wings. Suddenly there was a moment's silence. The invisible conductor had silenced the music for a fraction of a second to make the famous solo singer's interjection the more effective. There came the long-drawn, melodious roar of a lion, ending in a staccato "huh-uh-uh."

I listened to the sound with every nerve drawn tight, as when I used to lie in bed at Näsbyholm and listen to the thunder; and I wondered, just as I had done then: would the sound come nearer? Another rumbling sound, duller, angrier than the first, but at the same distance from the tent. What was the royal route tonight? There — for a third time! Right by the tent, if you please! Were we to receive a nocturnal visitor?

I glanced towards the corner where Fara Aden, my Somali boy . . . had his sleeping-place. Fara was awake too; I could see in the faint starlight that he had raised himself on his elbow. I nodded, and with noiseless movements we made ready to go out. While I was making sure that my rifle was in order I heard the lion again; the roaring suggested that he had turned and gone off in another direction.

Outside, it had become silent all at once; the tropical night was holding its breath, waiting for the sun. The stars were paling, the

air had grown thinner. The black velvet curtain had been replaced by a dark, steel-gray silk veil which might be swept aside at any moment by the breaking of day.

Fara and I set off towards the line of rocks from which the last roar had come. But we had not gone many steps before the miracle happened. A red flame spurted up behind the rocks to eastward, and against the fiery background there stood out the silhouette of a splendid male lion, striding towards the rocks slowly, with head erect, to seek there a well-earned rest after the night's exertions. He did not honor us poor human reptiles with a look; he carried his admirably proportioned body with majestic strength and dignity — the King of Beasts.

"Piga, bwana, simba!" Fara whispered, and I knew very well that it meant: "Shoot, master, lion!" But I could not. The rifle remained under my arm.

One could not shoot a vision like that to pieces.

von Blixen-Finecke, *African Hunter*, pp. 85-7.

I forget which kind of trap was first constructed, but I do remember that instead of the leopard it caught a hyena, which none of the Kikuyu would drag away. Hyenas were unclean because they ate corpses, but more than that they were a favourite haunt of dead men's spirits; the creature whose baleful eyes you saw glinting in the darkness just beyond the halo of firelight might, for all you knew, be your grandfather or your uncle, come perhaps to embody retribution for some insult or injury inflicted on him while he was alive.

The fur of this dead hyena was a dingy sort of grey with dirty white spots. Its powerful shoulders tailed away towards long, sloping hind-quarters, a structure that gave it a curious loping motion. Njombo looked at the beast with distaste and said that all hyenas were lame. When I asked why, he pointed at some piebald crows hopping about at a safe distance beyond the vultures, and told me one of his children's tales. Long ago, it appeared, the father of all the piebald crows possessed a gourd with white stuff inside which the hyenas saw, and thought was fat.

'Where did you get that fat?' asked the hyenas. The crow answered: 'In the sky, beyond the moon.' 'Take us there,' said the hyenas, 'and we will get some of the fat.' 'Very well,' replied the crow. 'Catch hold of my feet, and my neck, and my wings.' The hyenas did so, and the crow took them up, up, up among the stars. 'Can you see anything below?' asked the crow. 'No, we can see nothing.' 'Very well.' The crow gave a big kick and flapped his wings and all the hyenas fell off, and dropped to the ground and were killed. All except one. This was a female, and her legs were broken. She gave birth, and the totos *[infants] were born with broken legs, and hyenas have limped ever since that day.*

Huxley, *Flame Trees*, pp. 166-7.

'We are coming now to the country of the cannibals,' [Juma, the cook] said facetiously, and quite untruthfully. 'These Kikuyu, they scavenge like hyenas, they will dig up corpses and eat them. Sometimes their women give birth to snakes and lizards. They have never heard of Allah. They eat the intestines of goats and circumcise their women. They—'

'Silence, Juma.' Tilly commanded. She was hot, tired, dusty, and in no mood for anatomical gossip, and her understanding of the Swahili tongue was still shaky. Although she had studied it with her usual energy and grasp on the voyage out, her phrase-book,

acquired from the Society for the Propagation of the Gospel, had not always suggested sentences most helpful to intending settlers. 'The idle slaves are scratching themselves'. . . 'Six drunken Europeans have killed the cook'. . . turning these over in her mind, on top of the ox-cart in the sun, she doubted if their recital, even in the best Swahili, would impress Juma favourably.

After his remarks I stared at the passing Kikuyu with a new interest. They looked harmless, but that was evidently a pose. We passed a woman carrying a baby in a sling on her back, as well as a load. I could see the infant's shiny head, like a polished skittle ball, bobbing about between the mother's bent shoulders, and looked hopefully for the glimpse of a snake or lizard. But no doubt the mothers would leave these at home.

Huxley, *Flame Trees*, p. 15

. . . Carr Hartley always keeps a few half-tame lions, leopards, hyenas, buffalo and giraffes on his farm however, so that American and German companies can film their adventure stories without too much effort or loss of time.

. . . One Sunday an American arrived and insisted on filming a fight between an African and a leopard. In reality this was only a tame, immature leopard playing with his keeper, a teenage boy, photographed in such a way as to look very dangerous. Carr Hartley does not work on Sundays, but the American kept offering so much money that Carr finally capitulated. Since the leopard boy was at church, a substitute had to be found. This boy did not really trust the leopard, got frightened during the play, and started to run away. The animal at once gripped his neck, started to bite in earnest and clawed the boy's chest. Gordon [Hartley's half-brother, a game ranger] *put his hands in the leopard's mouth, pressing the lips over the teeth. The farther the animal's mouth was forced open, the harder it lacerated the black skin with its claws. The film people did not dare to intervene. Finally Carr Hartley had to shoot the tame leopard and the black boy had to be stitched up in hospital.*

Grzimek, *Serengeti Shall Not Die*, p. 142.

There is a place on the Serengeti Plains, where the Seronera River is only a trickle of water connecting a series of secluded pools beneath stately yellow thorn trees, which is especially peaceful and beautiful — far removed from civilization. There are lovely places in other countries, but nowhere else can one find an idyllic setting where nature abounds in such profusion — where perfect peace changes to violence within seconds and returns just as quickly. Nothing could be more peaceful than a herd of delicate-looking Thomson's gazelles grazing in the open, with picturesque yellow thorn trees in the background. The newly born babies are so full of joy that they gambol amongst their elders with a stiff-legged action that is a joy to watch. Tired from the exercise, they pause near their mothers for a quick drink of milk, then lie down in a clump of grass, instinctively flattening their large ears so that they cannot be seen from even a few yards away. Equally peaceful is a nearby scene of two young hyena cubs playing together at the entrance to their underground home, their black baby coats glistening in the sunshine. Not far away their mother is quietly walking amongst the Tommies, large dark eyes ever alert, her shaggy coat constantly ruffled by a cool breeze. Everything is peaceful, and

the Tommies take little notice as she passes within yards of where they are quietly grazing. A baby Tommy, flattened and perfectly still, its fawn coat blending with the brownish grass, is passed unnoticed by the hyena. Twenty yards away its playmate of half an hour ago is also hiding, unseen by the hyena. But alas, the second baby loses its nerve and dashes off with the hyena in hot pursuit. The mother gazelle, until this moment apparently unconcerned and taking no notice of the passing hyena, now races ahead of her baby in a series of rapid zigzags, vainly trying to draw off the hyena. But the hyena cannot be sidetracked. In a flurry of dust the drama is over. There is no noise and the end is quick. The other Tommies, which have been watching the chase, resume their grazing. Two jackals appear from apparently nowhere to follow the hyena hopefully. There is peace on the plains once more . . .

Bartlett, *Nature's Paradise*, pp. 138-9.

What a good rain had done to the desert of the Northern Frontier was something impossible to believe. It was entirely unrecognizable. In areas that normally receive less than ten inches per year, over twenty had fallen in a matter of weeks. Rivers rushed through the barren sand; Lake Rudolf had risen thirteen and a half feet. From the driest, roughest rocks sprang bits of greenery and flowers. The tough, sun-baked acacia thorn twigs that had remained dead and gray for generations broke out in tender green leaves, and suddenly the whole desert was alive. After being dormant in hot sun and dry sands baking year after year, nature's rugged plant organisms sprouted with variety and profusion. The recovery startled everyone who saw it and served as a reminder that African life is first of all tenacious, never really dead. A road unused in southern Kenya is back to jungle in a few years. The seeds of life that have persisted in this toughest of lands throughout its millions of centuries of evolution remain underground or in secret places until a hut, a building, or a tarmac road changes just enough to let them take root and push upward into daylight. And in every bit of fresh green grass, on every branch of every tree, in every bush and around every flower, are the spikes and prickles and poisons and ticklers that protect this hard-earned, delicate greenery. It is a life that has learned in time the lesson of survival. The extremes of hot and cool, dry and wet, sharp and soft, balance each other with both delicacy and toughness. It is a complex structure designed for permanence that seems only lately to be threatened by the intrusion of missile projects, oil companies, and politicians.

Beard, *The End of the Game*, p. 202.

Crocodiles, crocodiles, crikey what a lot of crocodiles! In serried ranks they lie, rank upon rank, almost belly upon belly, covering the mud banks to the side of the river and gliding, loglike, through the water.

Synge, *Mountains of the Moon*, p. 132.

The lake was all hazy and very pale soft blue. Against it the pink flamingoes made a wonderful symphony of colour.

The birds rose in a glorious cloud when we got near. The sky became pink instead of blue. They seemed so numerous that it was impossible for them all to rise together. The air immediately above the lake was full, and some had to wait until the first birds had moved off a little way. They are so large that before rising each bird has to take a comical little run like an aeroplane taking off. In flight they look like gigantic pink crosses, tipped with black on the laterals. The head, legs, body, and upper surface of the wings are all pink, but the under part of the great wings, particularly near the tips, is dark. In flight they stretch both their legs and neck out straight.

The flamingo is an ungainly and rather grotesque bird. His legs are like two thin sticks about three feet long, while his neck is equally long and scraggy, twisting snakelike down to the water. He paddles perpetually in the shallow places with his long neck bent down and his fat beak resting on the mud. With this beak he sifts the water and mud, feeding, like the whale, on the small organisms so obtained. During feeding the beak is pointed backwards so that the bird looks through its own legs. There is hardly any sound, no raucous shrieks or hog-like grunts, but just a little murmuring noise made by the feeding flamingoes and the gentle lapping of the water. All is peaceful, until suddenly the birds rise. Then the sky is overfilled with a brief pandemonium.

Synge, *Mountains of the Moon*, p. 141.

To understand this last era in Africa we must first speak of the white man — his coming and his conquest. In the old days the white man was either an eccentric or an explorer. He hunted upon and opened up a new continent. He battled enormous odds, equipped with a child's dreams and a man's courage. This white hunter was the advance scout of the Western World, bringing the light of his background and curiosity to the darkness, the lush and the arid darkness where natives and animals lived in a brutal harmony of short life and sudden death. When J.A. Hunter, the famous game officer, worked on the Mombasa Railroad in 1908 the advance scouts were finishing up. They had made their romantic reports, and the vanguard moved in. Railroad tracks were laid, steel shafts through the shadows. The advance of civilization demanded the removal of dangerous game, and one page of Hunter's notebook records the shooting of 996 rhinos. No questions were asked; men acted out of necessity. In the African vastness, everything seemed inexhaustible.

What now of the white hunter? He is still with us, but the march has continued; the scouts are dead, the vanguard is on its way out, and the camp followers have come. The white hunter is now a licensed hired hand whose sole function is to conduct sportsmen through the bush, keep peace in camp, and make sure his clients get sizable heads, and elephant feet suitable for wastebaskets. He spends much of his time in Nairobi, bemoaning the politics that has frightened off the game. And so his game will come to an end.

Beard, *The End of the Game*, p. 23.

One morning I surprised two dikdik in the glade, standing among grass that countless quivering cobwebs had silvered all over, each one — and each strand of every cobweb — beaded with dew. It was amazing to think of all the untold millions of cobwebs in all the forest glades, and all across the bush and plains of Africa, and of the number of spiders, more numerous even than the stars, patiently weaving their tents of filament to satisfy their appetites, and of all the even greater millions of flies and bees and butterflies that must go to nourish them; and for what end, no one could say.

In the middle of this field of silver splendour stood the two dikdiks with their tiny heads lifted, their nostrils dilated and their unwinking eyes, as bright as blackberries, looking straight into mine. I never ceased to marvel at the delicacy and brittleness of

their legs, slender as reeds; it seemed impossible that the dikdiks should not break them as they bounded over tufts or hummocks, even with their leaf-light weight.

These dikdiks had the charm of the miniature. They were perfectly made, not a single hair or sinew less than immaculate; little engines of muscle and grace, more like spirits than creatures. One always saw them in pairs. So long as I stood still, so did the dikdiks; I wondered what would happen if I never moved at all. Would they stand and stare all day? Should we all be there at evening, still motionless? But it was hopeless to try to out-stare the dikdiks; after a while I took a step forward and, with a movement of superb ease and elegance, the little buck sprang away to melt into the trees.

Huxley, *Flame Trees*, p. 228.

Women, when quarrelling, often tell each other that their father or mother was a baboon, and the retort usually is that the other's parents were hyenas or warthogs. I never heard a native say a good word for a baboon or a hyena. They have a good reason with the latter beast, as many a native has been injured with his terrible jaws.

Lyell, *Memories*, p. 216.

One day, when Tilly was riding through an uncleared part of the shamba, a large red Masai in pigtails, who Tilly said was stark naked — in actual fact he probably wore the little short cloak of the warriors, which fell short of the waist — a red Masai stepped out of the bushes and raised his travelling spear. Her pony stopped dead and snorted, and she stared at him in surprise. This was some way from Masai country and she had never before seen a warrior so far from his native plains. He seemed to be alone, not with a party of cattle-raiders, and gave the normal greeting, 'Jambo!' in clear warrior tones.

She returned the greeting. 'This is my bwana's shamba. What do you want?'

'I want to be your cook,' the warrior replied.

Even Tilly was surprised at this. 'Do you know how to cook?' she inquired.

'For two years I have looked after seven hundred goats.'

At the time, she reported, this had struck her as an adequate reply.

Huxley, *Flame Trees*, p. 198.

There is a wonderful exhilaration about these happy first days and the glamour with which one starts out for a shoot, and the amount of energy one will expend in tramping miles to get some small animal which is new to one.

Lyell, *Memories*, p. 185.

In the last five or ten years rifle-shooting has given place more and more to camera-shooting, for which nothing but good can be said. For my own part, I must admit that I am one of those who decidedly prefer a good animal photograph of living game to the finest skin on the floor or horns on the wall. A successful photograph demands of the individual much finer sporting qualities than a gun-shot, better nerves, greater patience and endurance.

von Blixen-Finecke, *African Hunter*, p. 36.

Plate 42. "I'll take spots, then" . . . "and look like sunshine sifting through the leaves . . ."

Plate 43. "Think of that and purr!" (Kipling)

One of the most characteristic of all performances "under the big top" of Africa is the sight of the carrion-eaters around a kill. The noise, fighting, dust and confusion are appalling.

I remember coming one day upon the carcass of a zebra which had evidently been killed and half devoured the night before by a lion. Now it looked like the meeting place of all the devils in hell. Gaunt hyenas wedged bloody jaws far into the entrails. Dozens of vultures, with dripping hooked beaks and glistening, naked necks, skirmished about them and darted in now and then for a choice morsel. Solemn marabou storks, that looked like scholars and behaved like ghouls, pushed into the confusion whenever they saw an opening. Daring little kites, tempted beyond all fear, hopped and swooped in and out of the dusty battle. From the scene there rose grunts, scoldings, hissings and shrill cries that made one's blood run cold.

First the zebra was reduced to pitiable rags of flesh; and then, in the space of a few minutes, there was nothing left but bones. Whereupon the hyenas lost themselves in the grass; one or two little jackals trotted away with that full feeling; and the funereal vultures hopped heavily for a few steps, hardly able to rise after their feast. Several waddled around the bones with an air of sinister gravity before flapping slowly up into the blue.

Federick B. Patterson, *African Adventures* (G.P. Putnam's Sons, 1928), p. 40.

I had been pursuing three elephants for a long time in a dense forest without being able to catch sight of them for long enough to decide whether their tusks justified a shot. My only hope was that they would at last come out into more open country, and they did so late in the afternoon, after a nerve-racking chase. In the midst of a primeval forest they found a glade, perhaps a few acres in extent, pale-green in the evening sun and charming to the eye. The giants looked round, spread out their big sail-like ears, and trumpeted loudly several times. Then they began to move solemnly to and fro, with tails up and trunks in air. I thought they had got wind of me.

Then one of the beasts suddenly went up to one of the others, laid his trunk on his forehead, and set his tusks against the other's. Then began a wrestling match which made the earth shake. Both combatants faltered and took new grip. Ivories clinked, muscles quivered, the beasts' huge strength was strained to the uttermost. Then one of them fell at full length on his side, while the victor delivered a deafening fanfare.

Number three, who during the conflict had displayed his enthusiasm by waving his head, flinging huge sods of grass up in the air and rushing to and fro, now approached the conqueror. They met forehead to forehead; all their strength was exerted. Not a sound was heard, but their bodies quivered with the exertion; their feet slipped away when they took purchase; every nerve was at full strain. The whole surroundings seemed to be charged with a strong nervous tension while the two giants measured their colossal strength. I wonder if even the birds were not silent.

Then one of the champions fell on his haunches, and the fresh triumph was greeted with a fanfare. But at the same moment there came a gust of wind, this time from the wrong quarter, and when the elephants saw that a human being had been watching their play, they rushed panic-stricken into the jungle.

I stood there alone with a sight I shall never forget struck into my memory.

von Blixen-Finecke, *African Hunter,* pp. 71-3.

We pitched our tent just back from the lake shore in a clearing on the forest fringe. A lone hippo, submerged except for bristly ears, protuberant eyes and nostrils, mutely watched while we worked. At sunset, on short thick legs, the old bull ponderously hauled his huge bulk ashore to stand motionless on the beach, his whiskered chin resting on the ground, as if drained by the effort or lost in deep contemplation. His flanks were puckered by old scars and recent wounds gaping pink in raw relief against the old battleship grey hide. There would be no more wars in that old warrior's future — he had fought his last and lost. In defeat, he had come away from the herd to live out his days as a solitary outcast.

As last light faded into night, the fresh breeze coming off the lake seemed to revive him. Marshalling his reserves he plodded with solid assurance a familiar path to private pastures, passing from sight into the gathering dusk. Later that night I heard his turgid grunts, like the hollow laughter of a very old man nursing a bitter, personal joke. When his call went unanswered he did not repeat it. Perhaps unaccustomed to loneliness he had learned to accept it.

The next morning he was back in the water, silhouetted black and imperturbable in the fiery track that reflected the rising sun.

Reardon, *Zululand,* pp. 81-2.

I am often haunted by the beautiful forms that symbolised those free happy times camping in the veld. Whenever I doodle absent-mindedly, I find the koodoo, eland, sable, waterbuck, impala and bushbuck nostalgically bounding on to the paper from the old index-finger, whose trigger has now become a pen.

Campbell, *Dark Horse,* p. 75.

On our right the tawny plain stretched away, a bowl of sunlight, to the Tana river and beyond: you felt that you could walk straight on across it to the rim of the world.

Huxley, *Flame Trees,* p. 13.

At Amboseli it was . . . the mornings that I remember best. They were always cold and opaque when [a staff member] *brought in the coffee. A little voice would murmur "Jambo bwana" and in came the* cahowa. *It was a short and simple ritual. Then the sun from dawn until evening dictated our ways.*

Beard, *The End of the Game,* p. 77.

When we come across such esoteric gems as Warden Hale's assertion in an annual report that animals come out more when it rains because humans are likely to be indoors at such times, we are left in no doubt as to the Department's need of technical advice.

Alistair D. Graham, *The Gardeners of Eden* (George Allen & Unwin, 1973), p. 78. Few of the traditional tenents of conservation and animal preservation are spared in this acerbic, brilliant, and (highly) confused book. People as well are relentlessly attacked — Pitman, Uganda's first and most famous game warden, will, for example, probably never recover — often with strong justification (Pitman being an obvious example). Anyone who professes to have a strong interest in the subject should read both this volume and that of Graham's partner, Ian Parker, *Oh Quagga!* (noted in the commentary on the Adamson books) — and then think the matters through for himself. Gloomy. Pop psychology run amuck. But important insights.

On some recent film safaris that I conducted, doubles were used to replace the stars who were eventually filmed in Hollywood . . . .

On one of these safaris, the script called for a charging lion. Now naturally, if one abides by the game laws, as one must even for Hollywood, it is most difficult to get a lion to charge the cameras, and the film director was informed of the obstacles involved in staging such a performance. He eventually decided to fake the sequence, coming to the amazing conclusion that a long shot of a person springing out of a bush in a horizontal position into tall grass would resemble a charging lion. I was to star as the King of Beasts (the nearest I have ever come to playing the role of a royal imposter!) and dressed in a

Plate 44. Colobus Monkey in the Forest.

khaki jacket spread over my head with my arms stretched out through the sleeves, I was to leap out of the bushes in imitation of the animal springing. I was then to get shot stone dead by the hunter. The cameras were set up one hundred yards away. Three men were placed at intervals of about ten feet in the low bush, with instructions to shake each bush in turn violently, starting at the furthest. This was to make it appear that the lion was charging through the scrub.

And then the fun begins. As the last bush is shaken, I leap into the air with arms and legs stretched out and dive on to some cushions hidden in the grass. The two doubles wait for me to spring; the "white hunter" shoots; and the "client," who is supposed to be a coward according to the story, runs away down the rocky slope of the hill. But during several rehearsals and takes, my limbs become bruised, the "client" sprained an ankle in running over the rocks, and the many onlookers could no longer restrain their mirth at the ridiculously unrealistic scene. Eventually the director called "cut" and decided to figure out another way to get pictures of a charging lion.

Donald I. Ker, *African Adventure* (Stackpole, 1957), pp. 112–3. The other half of "Ker & Downey," Ker was a founding member of the Professional Hunters' Association (begun in 1934). He later turned exclusively to photographic safaris. His best stories deal with the various filming parties that descended upon Africa.

Later, on my cot in tent number 10, I listened for the last time to the sounds of the bush, the sounds of Africa . . . . Could they not be arranged into a sort of "symphony safari" for the blind? The sunset prelude, the increase in sound volume as the darkness comes on, the rising in a crescendo of hoots, moans, mutterings and howls, and then a final coda that might be the single death shriek, or cough, or groan of an animal brought to ground by the predator. As I lay there with eyes closed, "seeing" Africa through its sounds, I heard its leaping

Plate 45. Recognition Distance with a Primate.

life going on all around me out in the great darkness of Amboseli's deceptively lifeless bush.

A baboon screamed in a hair-raising voice of a man being murdered. The dreadful sound went on for several seconds, then stopped abruptly mid-scream. I guessed that a lion or leopard, the only carnivores strong enough to take a fierce-fighting baboon, had got him. This peculiar awareness of the events in an African night did not seem in the least strange to me. Anyone who had entered into the safari scene as I had, with love and total attention, would have developed it, like a sixth sense. I wondered only, like a possessive member of his family, what the devil my baboon brother was doing down on the ground, out of the safety of his sleeping tree at this time of night!

Kathryn Hulme, *Look a Lion in the Eye* (Little, Brown, 1974), pp. 222–3. The story of a one-month and twenty-five-hundred-mile ''bone-shaking'' safari through Kenya and northern Tanzania.

During the night, a few hours later, when the full moon was setting, its pale light would filter dimly through the leaves of stunted flat-topped thorn trees in front of the tent. The cold and watery light accentuated the chilly frostiness of the night wind, and even in the warm blankets it was often difficult to close all the numerous openings down which cool trickles of air seemed persistently to find their way. If one was disturbed by the cold, and awake, there would be nothing to do but listen to the sounds of night.

Down the valley the sharp whistle of a reedbuck could sometimes be heard, the sound ridiculously like the sharp squeak of a squeezed rubber doll. Eddies of air may have carried some scent of the camp to him, or possibly a rival male may have threatened invasion of his private domain. Up on a ridge, back of camp, a zebra might bark, making a shrill, querulous sound like the yelp of a sea lion, mellowed by distance to clear, musical tones lending enchantment to the African chorus.

Night was always a time of fascination, and sounds from the throngs of game came through the quiet air with greater clarity than during the day. Often the distant, melodious baying of a hyena roused us from sleep, and for several minutes the sounds would come regularly, growing fainter with the distance until the silence settled down again, heavy and mysterious. Although there was no actual danger, it was at such times that one most fully appreciated the basic survival value afforded by fire and felt glad that man had learned to make homes and keep fires burning through the night.

For one attuned to catch every sound, the night become full of mystery; vague rustlings heard here and there close to camp, or the sounds of a heavy body slowly and cautiously moving through the bush twenty yards away, and again faint snorts in the distance — or long, tense moments of absolute stillness.

> Raymond B. Cowles, *Zulu Journal: Field Notes of a Naturalist in South Africa* (University of California Press, 1959), p. 25. If the reader can suffer through such stupidities as the opinion that a black man's skin color is the evolutionary adaptation of concealing coloration (camouflage — remember Kipling's Ethiopian?), this is a good introduction to South African wildlife by an early authority. The volume is especially valuable for its discussions of the small game and bird life.

We turned in early, generally before 10 P.M. Then began the nightly adventure of listening to the thousands of wild animals surrounding us.

One never thinks of Africa after the first visit without remembering vividly the thousand and one sounds that float in from the wilderness at night. And many of them come from rare birds and animals that one never sees even if the visit be extended to years. Besides the pronounced noises of the larger game, there are innumerable little scurryings, rustlings, and squeaks all about that strain the imagination to a breaking point.

Out on the plains or in the bush, all is one great disjointed chorus of wilderness voices. A jackel barks at the evening star. A herd of zebras stampedes suddenly in terror of a stalking lion. There is the steady slow tramp of some wandering file of game going down to water. A hyena says something to himself in a deep bass, and then laughs at his own grisly joke with a weird treble screeching.

The song of insects is endless, and multiplies itself until it seems to fill the world. Cicadas chirp in the thickets. Mosquitos buzz in a steady volume of sound. On the edge of the marshes or streams, millions of fireflies light their tiny lamps against the sinister thickets.

Suddenly the night is shattered by the hoarse cry of a baboon or monkey that a leopard has chosen in the lottery of death. Zebras drift back again and bark nearby. Somewhere in the distance an ostrich lifts its voice in a hollow booming.

Even the birds seem eternally awake. From somewhere in a thorn tree is heard the melancholy note of a cuckoo; the busy nightjar buzzes and hums outside the tent repeating his monotonous drowsy song. Thousands of little birds uttering high, plaintive cries, stir restlessly in the trees near marsh or water. If the camp is in the vicinity of a swamp dusk brings long wavering lines of beautiful crested cranes flapping their wings against the smoky light with a noise like the creaking of rusty hinges.

Then comes the first roar of the lion. This is the climax of the African night. It begins with a low moan that gradually increases in volume till the real roar is heard. After several of these, the last one ends with a rasping sound that dies away in short but noisy coughs growing fainter and fainter. It is impossible to judge where the lion is. He is a ventriloquist and sounds as though he were always close at hand. His roar only indicates his direction. But he is conveying a message to other lions of his whereabouts: for lions usually hunt in co-operation when they can. Probably he is in the act of driving a herd of game towards his mate which crouches in the velvet distance. Sound of a new stampede comes faintly. Or perhaps one can hear the series of short, sharp grunts that mean the King of Beasts is actually stalking.

Dawn sounds also have a character all their own. The tropical day is at its best in the early morning. As one prepares for the day and drinks that welcome cup of tea or coffee, from the semi-darkness outside come the liquid notes of the bush-cuckoo. In the distance rises the last roar of a lion which is leaving his kill and seeking a lying-up place for the day. Doves fill the air with their clear soft calls: and francolins whistle to each other in the grass.

Suddenly the whole veldt becomes a silver expanse of dew in the early light. The breeze is cool and refreshing. Night creatures are going home; hyenas, jackals, and the smaller animal species. Herds of game out on the plains begin to scatter. It will not be until it gets really hot that they will form into real masses. Clouds of multicolored birds are rising in swift flight like confetti tossed up from the veldt and caught by the wind.

Another day on safari has begun!

> Patterson, *African Adventures*, pp. 23–5. Patterson's guide on his safari was Denys Finch Hatton, the mysterious love-interest woven through Karen Blixen's *Out of Africa*. Patterson took along two moving-picture cameras and over 100 porters. After five months, he apparently won Finch Hatton over to the desirability of photographing animals rather than bagging them as trophies. Patterson made a film of his safari, footage from which was pirated by a film company. Patterson later filed suit and won a plagiarism case.

Although the analogy is, I fear, hardly a complete one, yet there has always seemed to me a certain resemblance between the story of how the Sabi Game Reserve became the Kruger National Park, and the old fairy tale of Cinderella. At any rate I liked to play with the idea of the little handmaid, whom no one recognized for what she really was, sitting unregarded among the ashes, while her big half-sisters, the important government departments, received all the attention, and the money wherewith to buy themselves fine clothes.

> J. Stevenson-Hamilton, *South Africa Eden* (Cassell, 1952), Foreward (p. vii). *Eden* is a detailed history of the transformation of Sabi Game Reserve into Kruger National Park and the subsequent development of that world-famous reserve. Stevenson-Hamilton was uniquely qualified to tell the story: the first warden, he presided over the park for more than forty years, retiring shortly before his eightieth birthday. Stevenson-Hamilton's Bantu name was "Skukuza" — "the man who changed everything" — and this book is a reminder of the extraordinary dedication and human effort that underlay the establishment and survival, if not prosperity, of all the African parks.

However often you journey into the wild, each experience brings new impressions, new kinships and renewed astonishment at the marvellous beauty and intricate pattern of Nature's realm. As you listen to the night under a bushveld sky or lie hidden in the sun-scorched grass, the dynamic, vibrant world around you engulfs and enchants so that you long to return again and again, as I did, to search, to listen and to absorb.

Here, then, is a touch of the wilderness, the merest fragment of the diversity, the magnificence and the mystery that is yet to be discovered, surely an intricate part of our innermost soul.

> Sue Hart, *Back in the Wild* (Collins and Harvill, 1977), Introduction. Under the name Sue Hart or Susanne Harthoorn, the author has written several sensitive books reflecting on her experiences in Africa as a veterinarian and keen observer of the wildlife. *Back in the Wild*, as did its predecessor, *In The Wild* (Africana Book Society, 1974), contains the added benefit of Leigh-Voight's phenomenal illustrations. This volume is a collection of popular articles that appeared as weekly features in the *Rand Daily Mail* in the 1970s. The chapters treat 'every imaginable subject,' from insects to George Adamson, with a distinct penchant for the avian side. Reading Hart's autobiography (also recommended), *Too Short a Day: A Woman Vet in Africa* (Geoffrey Bles, 1966), I am reminded of James Herriot and am moved to reflect on the special understanding that some vets develop for animals, the power of life and death being what it is.

Other popular animal vocabulary concerns collective nouns. There is a "pride of lion," a "troop of baboon," a "pack of hyena or wild dog," a "colony of ants," a "herd of elephant" and a "herd of buffalo, zebra, antelope" and so on. (It is not a "herd" of birds, but a "flight of duck," a "gaggle of geese," a "flock of starlings.") If you are uncertain, remember you can always get out of it by saying, "Look at all those giraffe," or by employing the numerical exactitude dodge, "I saw eight hundred and thirty-seven wildebeeste."

> Betty & Jock Leslie-Melville, *Elephant Have Right of Way* (Doubleday, 1973), p. 154. Like the better known and later *Raising Daisy Rothschild*, this volume is a delightful, frivolous account, filled with humor (see, for example, Chapter XV, "Tenthold Hints or Minding Your Manners on Safari") and enough misinformation to fill several TV talk-shows (tellingly, the Introduction to *Elephant* is written by Jack Paar . . .). When the reader, in a book about safari Africa, reads on page 6, "I would rather go on safari in Bloomingdales than in East Africa, and I prefer the supermarket to any game park," he knows that he is in for a bit of a ride, shall we say.

One of the many times Jock and I were going to Treetops the hunter was explaining to his new group of tourists that each tree, on the short walk from the Land-Rover through the forest to the tree house, had a ladder, and that if he blew his whistle once, it meant there was a rhino about and everyone must climb ten feet up one of the ladders. (These have now been replaced by little stockades in which to hide.) If he blew it twice it meant an elephant, and everyone must climb to eighteen feet. One elderly lady said, "My dear sir, I couldn't possibly climb that ladder," and he answered, "Madam, you'll be surprised how fast you learn when you hear the whistle."

> Leslie-Melville, *Elephant Have Right of Way*, pp. 144–5.

Awaking before sunrise, Myles and I liked to drive out for an hour or two to see the early morning light on the plains. Herds of wildebeest stood in stark relief against an opalescent background, the sun streaming through their beards and turning them to silver. With the mists from the highlands lying in thin veils across the country, nothing seemed quite real, and the animals appeared to hover above the ground in a magical world of their own. There was an ethereal quality about the light, while all around us the pastel shades of distant hills faded to infinity and merged with a sky that held the last pale blush of dawn. As yet there was no heat in the sun and it shone in long shafts of gold through the dewy grass, occasionally touching a lion's mane or the burnished flank of a gazelle. The animals seemed to welcome each new day, tossing their heads and pursuing one another high-spiritedly. Sometimes they paused with startled expressions to watch us pass at such an early hour, and we would speak in whispers to try to lessen our intrusion upon them; in our noisy Land Rover we felt like interlopers into their primeval world.

Once we came on two lions in the morning twilight, stirringly noble as they stood side by side against a delicate sky. Their breath steamed in the cold air and one of them began to scuff the earth with his hind legs. Then they moved together towards a horizon that glowed with the first light of the rising sun.

As the heat intensified and the colours deepened, the magic of early morning faded, and it was time to return to our camp for breakfast.

> Kay Turner, *Serengeti Home* (George Allen & Unwin, 1978), pp. 183–4. Kay Turner's story of her life in the Serengeti (husband Myles was game warden there) is a personalized, hence passionate and anecdotal, account of her complete change of life and the development of the famous park. A simple, yet evocative story.

In the evening I discovered an enormous jigger in my small toe, and one of my Watonga boys skilfully removed it; the bag of eggs was the size of a marrowfat pea, and as there was only the bone and top part of my toe left, I was afraid that I should lose it; however, after giving me some trouble, it yielded to the persuasive influence of that panacea for all African ills, permanganate of potash, and healed.

> Ewart S. Grogan & Arthur H. Sharp, *From the Cape to Cairo: The First Traverse of Africa from South to North* (Hurst and Blackett, 1900), p. 106. While still an undergraduate at Cambridge University, Grogan and a small party *walked* (actually, the trip to Salisbury in Rhodesia was mostly by ox cart) from the Cape of Good Hope to Cairo. Ostensibly to map a possible route for a railway

running the length of the continent, the trip was essentially a vacation lark. This book is a wild tale of hardship and adventure; the travelers suffered every imaginable ailment while crossing every conceivable terrain but explored uncharted territory, named mountain peaks after loved ones, and dabbled in local native politics whenever the opportunity arose. Grogan mingled with the broad spectrum of local tribes, from Watusis to forest pygmies. He hunted animals like mad and barely survived himself one human ambush after another. Grogan subsequently moved to Kenya and was an early settler and later fixture in the annals of Nairobi's development. Known everywhere as "From Cape to Cairo" or more simply as "The Great Grogan," his disdainful view of native Africans eventually took a heavy toll. The author had the good fortune to talk to Grogan before he died only a short while ago in Nairobi: he was imperialist to the core and unrepentant to the end.

On this steep climb there was no possibility of asking the driver to stop that I might photograph the tree and try to discover what it was trying to say. As we ground our way upward, I could only stand on my seat and watch it from the hatch. The side away from the low sun was now drained of its rosy glow. The smooth, heavily folded bark was again gray and ghostlike, as if something in the baobab had died with our unresponsive passing. Now I realized why the baobab had been an object of worship and awe to the primitive African since the most ancient prehistoric times.

It is indeed a ghostly tree, especially when it bears neither leaves or blossoms, which are due to come forth in October. Seeing it bare-branched as we did, one could understand why David Livingstone had described it in his journal as seeming to have been "planted upside down," thus suggesting an outsized carrot with its roots in the air. As for me, seeing it in a Manyara sunset, the baobab would forever seem a gigantic creature of sorts, with a bombacaceous trunk twenty-five feet in diameter, multiple armlike branches of lesser girth and a final crest of terminal twigs resembling what used to be called "a windblown hair-bob." A tree trying to resemble man — a mutant between the vegetable and animal worlds!

Hulme, *Look a Lion in the Eye*, pp. 213–4.

The rain and the grass: these were the fundamental elements on which the plains depended. The rain fed the grass and determined its growth, which regulated the numbers of herbivores the land could support. They in turn, according to their abundance, dictated the number of predators. So it had been since the Pleistocene; a precarious paradise, beautiful to behold, both in its economy and complexity, stabilised by the extraordinary diversity of interacting life forms that maintained its continuity.

In the wake of the rains, when storm clouds trailed their dark veils beyond the Mau escarpment, the Mara was a glittering emerald shot through with the gleam of water that lay everywhere, in pool, marsh and lugga. Cycnium flowers sprang up as if from nowhere, stippling the plains with delicate white blossoms. The spicy scent of shrubs and marsh plants prickled in the nostrils, and over everything hung the rich meadow smells of warm grass and wet earth.

★ ★ ★

A similar fate had overtaken the giant acacia whose silver-grey carcass lay on the grassy shores of the Marsh not far from the spring. The tree had fallen many years ago. Too many elephants had pushed against its trunk, trying to shake down the succulent seed pods, until one day it had come loose from its roots and had crashed to the ground, smashing the eggs of a tawny eagle which had been nesting in the canopy. Now, stripped of its bark, weathered and polished by wind and sun, it lay at the water's edge like a discarded antler whose crooked tines offered a convenient perch for rollers, vultures, marabous and hammerkops.

★ ★ ★

On their second day in the valley, the cow and calf found themselves at the forefront of a group which had spent the day grazing far out on the open grasslands. Now they were coming in to drink, led by a bull who had completed the migration at least half a dozen times. Immediately behind him was a mother with a yearling female; then came the cow and calf. As always the bull was cautious; he had seen too many of his companions pulled down by cats or drowned by crocodiles. As he approached the river, the deceptive tranquillity of the fever glades filled him with a sense of unease that deepened when he saw a pair of giraffes staring fixedly into the trees. The bull stopped abruptly, recognizing their behaviour as a signal that predators might be lurking. For several seconds he froze, straining his eyes to see into the shadowy tangle of fallen branches and rank matted grasses. But his hoarse snort of alarm came too late to save the yearling. Even as he whirled, the grass exploded past him in a wicked yellow blur.

Brian Jackman & Jonathan Scott, *The Marsh Lions* (Elm Tree Books, 1982), pp. 54, 58–59, 70. A sampling from a superb book, a work that is all the more enjoyable when read on safari, where it will provoke tears of recognition, so strong and accurate is the poetry.

Below Olifants camp, visitors were fortunate enough to observe a large crocodile which had been basking in the sun on a sandbank next to the pool, suddenly being chased by an elephant. Apparently the elephant was seen moving in the direction of the crocodile but seemed completely unaware of its presence, when all of a sudden the elephant scented it and charged with a series of trumpeting sounds. According to our visitors the crocodile just made it to the water in time and even after it had disappeared beneath the surface the elephant continued to give chase until the water reached his belly. He still continued to sweep the water with his trunk and seemed absolutely determined to locate the crocodile. He was, however, unsuccessful, and after a while he decided simply to enjoy the water and once he had refreshed himself with a drink, he ambled off into the bush again. Not long afterwards the crocodile crawled out of the water onto the bank to continue its sunning routine, this time with no rude interruptions!

Gus Adendorff, *Wild Company* (Books of Africa, 1984), pp. 118-9. The job of ranger is an interesting and rewarding one

African Treasury
II

Afternoon Pachyderm Tussle

The Proper Distance from Man

Zebras in Water

Hillside Lighting

A Gallop on the Savannah

You're Too Close

Cat on a Stroll

"The Odor of Dust Filled the Nostrils"

Front Row Seat

Lake Manyara on a Busy Day

Where Are My Sentries When I Need Them?
(To Be Continued Later in the Text)

Long Odds to Adulthood

Rick's Big-Tusker at Forest Edge

Colors

The Jackals' Turn

New Arrivals: Wildebeest in Tall Grass

Expectant Safarist (Courtesy Ricardo Sanchez)

and witness to intriguing happenings 'behind the scenes.' Adendorff, a formidable amateur botanist, zoologist, and ornithologist, was a ranger in Kruger Park for twenty-seven years. *Wild Company* is a true inside-look at the life of a national park. The book contains some nifty art work *and* a short recording(!) of sounds of the African night.

. . . we disturbed thousands upon thousands of vultures and a sort of brown bush eagle, which had been flocking to the feast from miles and miles away. Often have I watched these great and repulsive birds, and marvelled at the extraordinary speed with which they arrive on a scene of slaughter. A buck falls to your rifle, and within a minute high in the blue ether appears a speck that gradually grows into a vulture, then another, and another. I have heard many theories advanced to account for the wonderful power of perception nature has given these birds. My own, founded on a good deal of observation, is that the vultures, gifted as they are with powers of sight greater than those given by the most powerful glass, quarter out the heavens among themselves, and hanging in mid-air at a vast height — probably from two to three miles above the earth — keep watch, each of them, over an enormous stretch of country. Presently one of them spies food, and instantly begins to sink towards it. Thereon his next neighbour in the airy heights sailing leisurely through the blue gulf, at a distance perhaps of some miles, follows his example, knowing that food has been sighted. Down he goes, and all the vultures within sight of him follow after, and so do all those in sight of them. In this way the vultures for twenty miles round can be summoned to the feast in a few minutes.

> H. Rider Haggard, *Allan Quartermain* (Longmans, Green, 1887), pp. 89-90. Haggard turned out tales of Africa that were 'made' for movies — non-stop dangers and adventure, great battles, exotic peoples, characters larger-than-life, beautiful women, and on and on — and so the movies followed: *She; King Solomon's Mines;* and *Allan Quartermain.*

Amusing incidents frequently happen when a hunting party is startled by the sudden crashing flight of a troop of monkeys. . . .

Sometimes the hunter will begin to stalk an imaginary herd of elephants and then, much to his chagrin, discovers that it is after all only a runaway troop of colobus. Once when we were hunting elephants in the bamboo forests on the Aberdare Range, we had for guide a fine old man of the Wakikuyu tribe. I nicknamed him "Joey" after a well-known British statesman whom he resembled in features as well as in his aristocratic manner. Joey was very sensitive and extremely proud of the fact that he knew every inch of the forests and the habits of the wild animals which inhabited them.

In the early evening when the icy wind swept across the mountain top and eerie sounds came up from the dark canyons, the bare-legged old man would come and squat beside our rousing camp fire to enjoy the warmth and smoke our tobacco, which he dearly loved. Usually after a few puffs he would throw his head back and stare for a few moments into the feathery bamboo leaves which were dancing over our heads in the heat of the fire. Then pulling the hyrax skin cape about his lean shoulders he would hitch himself a little closer to the flame and tell us fascinating stories of elephants and other wild animals.

With an enviable gift for mimicry and a native's love for storytelling he would describe the thrilling and narrow escapes he had while hunting them. He would argue with our gun bearers over the strange and various sounds that filled the night. And he insisted that he knew every sound made by bird or beast so well that he could not be deceived by any of them. When, in unison, the gun bearers ridiculed this statement he would glance at us to learn our attitude and then with a sly smile point with convincing pride to the gray hairs that sprinkled his kinky locks, and grandly toss his cape back from his shoulders to show us his unscarred body as evidence that his wisdom had saved him from injury.

But like many people who love to boast he finally met his Waterloo, in what to him was a most embarrassing way. One day we were following him silently through the forest, on a path that was made soft as a velvet carpet by gray-green moss and damp bamboo leaves, when suddenly just ahead of us there came the crashing of branches and the loud rattling report of hollow bamboo trees striking against one another.

Instantly our hearts flew to our throats and our hands to our rifles. Only Joey was calm. With all the assurance of one who is used to such breath-taking situations he whispered the one magic word tembo *(elephant) and raised his slender hand to enjoin silence. Then, as we followed close at his heels, he stalked carefully and cautiously forward. As we were entering a dense clump of trees, about thirty yards from where we started there was a sudden crashing of branches over our heads, and a shower of icy water and debris descended upon us as a troop of colobus monkeys went leaping in every direction. It was too humiliating for the old man, and when we laughed over his mistake he burst into tears. That evening when the gun bearers goodnaturedly burlesqued the little comedy and made Joey the butt of their jokes he began to cry again, and grasping a firebrand in one hand and his spear in the other he started for home. It required some tact to coax him back to the fire and then it was only by the most blatant flattery — by presenting him with tobacco and by mimicking our own terror when the monkeys frightened us — that we finally induced him to remain and continue the hunt.*

> Delia J. Akeley, *Jungle Portraits* (Macmillan, 1930), pp. 20-2. Delia returned to Africa on her own in 1924, sponsored by the Brooklyn Museum of Arts and Sciences. It is likely that she became the first (white) woman to traverse the African continent from the Indian Ocean to the Atlantic. (*Portraits* was published in the same year as Mary L. Jobe Akeley's *Carl Akeley's Africa.*) Delia was a forerunner to contemporary women primatologists Jane Goodall and Dian Fossey. Indeed, her obsessive absorption with a pet vervet monkey ("J.T."), captured while a baby during the second Akeley expedition and brought back with Delia to New York, undoubtedly helped lead to the breakup of her marriage with Carl. Of special interest in *Portraits* is Delia's own story, found in the last chapter (VIII), of the difficulties experienced in reaching Akeley the night of his fateful elephant encounter (quoted earlier here, on p. 109).

I woke up one night to a terrible, loud hissing sound and I could also hear my two dogs. I found that they had caught a honeybadger which had somehow got into the garden. Klaas, the kitchen help, slept on the premises a little way from the house and had also woken up with all the rumpus. He came to offer assistance and I told him the dogs had cornered an animal and that we should try to save its life. When he saw that it was a honeybadger, he immediately dropped his arms between his legs and warned me that we were looking for trouble because of that animal's habit of attacking the testicles.

Adendorff, *Wild Company*, p. 52.

My actors learned to climb trees and climb fast in Africa. These are real African elephants . . .

W.S. van Duke, *Horning into Africa* (van Duke, 1931), p. 61 (picture caption). The story of shooting the MGM motion picture *Trader Horn* on location. Hilarious stuff.

The following is copied directly from my diary:

. . .

But the worst was over. . . . when we pitched our tent once more at our starting point, Ibanda, the chief himself was there to greet us, dressed in a white cotton nightshirt and a tuxedo.

"Have you any message for the people of America and Britain?" I asked the Kimbugwe, as he is called, whereupon he posed before the movie camera and made the following speech:

"Tell the people of America and England that the elephants are eating up all our crops, and our people are starving. The safaris come here and ask me to feed them. How can I feed them when the elephants eat everything. Come and kill the elephants, or we shall starve."

Carveth Wells, *In Coldest Africa* (Doubleday, Doran, 1929), pp. 228-9. A member of the Cudahy-Massee-Milwaukee Museum African Expedition, Wells is the paradigm English dilettante traveler-explorer, poking fun at a century or more of African myths, Hollywood style, but in the process missing the mark (perhaps purposely) by an equally wide margin. An amusing book.

My favourite guest was one of those charming, resourceful, single American ladies whom one meets relentlessly ticking off a list of the more exotic places on earth as she visits them. This one was packed with personality to the frames of her narrow, upswept, brilliant-decorated glasses. Wilf [Lodge Manager at Murchison Falls National Park] had just gone into the lodge bar after lunch to check the takings before closing down, when this lady, whom he had never seen before and did not even know was arriving, tottered in, leaned breathless against the counter and gasped: 'Do you serve blood?'

Wilf, who was once on the boards as a Yorkshire comedian, sensed that here was a story worth bearing. 'Sit down, madam,' he said, 'and I'll send out for some.'

'Well,' the lady said, 'you won't get far, I guess. There's an elephant leaning against the door.' By and by, the American, soothed not by blood but by a large Scotch on the rocks, told her story.

Having nothing much to do, she said, she had taken the Dakota up from Entebbe, not really intending to stop off anywhere but simply to have a look at the country. Every seat in the aircraft was taken and since the atmosphere inside the Dakota was a little stuffy she had decided when the aircraft rolled to a stop on the park airstrip to get out and take a breather. This had been her mistake.

'I'd hardly set foot on good old Murchison,' she said, 'when this little fat guy with a red face comes up to me and says: "Welcome to the Uganda National Parks, madam."

'I looked at this little guy and said: "Well, that's fine, but I don't

Plate 46. *Yellow-billed Storks and an Egyptian Goose.*

Plate 47. *Lilac-breasted Roller.*

Plate 48. Somali Ostrich.

Plate 49. Crowned Cranes.

happen to be staying."

' *"You'll regret it all your life if you don't," he says. "The Nile at night, the grunts of the hippos, the roar of a lion. It's an experience you will want to tell your grandchildren about."*

'*Well, while I was figuring on telling this little guy that I didn't have any grandchildren, the pilot kinda buzzes his engines, the little fat guy touches his hat and nips up the gangway, and, before I can say a word, the door slams and* zoom, *there they are, off down the runway.*'

Wilf Wolfenden nodded gravely. He recognized the description of the little fat guy as being a reasonably accurate portrait of Bombo Trimmer, Director of the Uganda National Parks. He knew too that Bombo had been extremely anxious to get back to Kampala for a conference. Only that morning the Director had expressed the fear that, since he had not made a booking on the East African Airways DC3, there might not be a seat for him. Well, now he had one.

'*What happened after the plane took off?*' Wilf prompted gently. The airstrip is fourteen buffalo-dotted miles from the lodge and because he was expecting no one on that flight he hadn't sent a Land-Rover to meet the plane.

'*After the plane disappeared,*' said the lady, '*I kinda sat down and looked around. There isn't a lot to look at out there,*' she explained, '*But by and by I saw this house thing, only it couldn't have been a house because it moved and kind of gave a squeal and then, goddam it, I realized the sort of place I'd gotten myself into. And I thought to myself: that little old fat guy was right: this is something to remember the rest of your days — if you manage to live 'em. Well, this elephant moved away and then a great big black guy with a lot of white teeth came up and then a whole lot of other black guys came up, so we all sat around and* ugged *a little.*'

'*You what?*' said Wilf.

'*Ugged. You see they didn't have much Milwaukee and I didn't have any of what they talked. So we kinda ugged at each other.*'

'*I see,*' said Wilf. '*And how did you get here?*'

'*Well, this bronzed guy as handsome as hell came along in a Jeep thing and I'll tell you that I wouldn't have minded just then if he'd been as ugly as hell.*'

'*So Roger Wheater found you.*'

'*That's the guy and he brought me down here except that then there was this elephant. Say, do you have another half-pint of blood around?*'

It was only then that Wilf saw that the American lady really was shaking. She stayed four days and became a great success. Roger Wheater took her everywhere and she even got to like elephants.

Three American women whom I met at Paraa on my last trip there were of the right stuff, too. They had, it seemed, gotten this snake. The centre-piece of this trio was a remarkable, powerful and, I sensed, rich mother on tour with teen-age daughter and teen-age daughter's girlfriend. They were touring with an African chauffeur from one of the big hire agencies and an American automobile as long as a locomotive. They had been down in the south in the Q.E. and had driven up the three hundred odd miles to Murchison. There had been a violent tropical storm the night before they had left and this, they supposed, was when it had happened. It was only when they pulled in at Masindi a little after lunchtime on the following day that the petrol attendant went, if this is the word, white and pointed hysterically at the underneath of the car. The mother had gone into the nearby hotel to get some iced drinks, but both girls were cooling their feet by dangling them *out of the open car door exactly where the African attendant now pointed and gibbered. They quickly withdrew their feet and slammed the door without knowing why they should be required to do so. Why soon became clear. An eight-foot black-lipped cobra was travelling with them. In all likelihood it had climbed up to wind itself round the warm exhaust and to get out of the rain the night before at Q.E. Now it was inextricably coiled round the chassis members. Its head had been within six inches of the girls' bare feet.*

The mother came out of the hotel to find quite a crowd round the car and to hear a disgusted British voice saying (her version): 'Those terrible Americans have gotten themselves a snake.'

'As if,' she said to me with a certain amount of rancour, 'we went around scooping up black-lipped cobras just everywhere.'

Colin Willock, *The Enormous Zoo: A Profile of the Uganda National Parks* (Harcourt, Brace & World, 1965), pp. 152-4. An excellent account of the establishment of the main Ugandan parks (Queen Elizabeth and Murchison Falls) and their early years.

17-8-05, 1 hr. 45 mins.

Simba (1)
The Traffic Manager
Lion is on the platform. Please instruct guard and driver to proceed carefully and without signal in yard. Guard to advise passengers not to get out here and be careful when coming in office.

17-8-05, 7 hr. 45 mins.

Simba (2)
The Trafic Manager.
One African injured at 6 o'clock again by lion and hence sent to Makindu Hospital by trolley. Traffic manager please send cartridges by 4 down train certain.

17-8-05, 16 hrs.

Plate 50. *Red-and-Yellow Barbet.*

Plate 51. *Little Bee-Eater.*

Simba (3)
The Traffic Manager,
Pointsman is surrounded by two lions while returning from distant signal and hence pointsman went on top of telegraph post near water tanks. Train to stop there and take him on train and then proceed. Traffic manager to please arrange steps.

20-4-08, 23 hrs. 35 mins.

Tsavo (4)
The Traffic Manager,
2 down driver to enter my yard very cautiously points locked up. No one can go out. Myself Shedman Porters all in office. Lion sitting before office door.

W.S. Rainsford, *The Land of the Lion* (Doubleday, Page, 1909), p. 457. These are telegrams sent by Hindi railway station masters to their traffic manager on the "Lunatic Line." The stations, "Simba" (well-named!) and "Tsavo," were situated between what are now Tsavo and Amboseli parks. As the reader can see, August 17, 1905, was a harrowing day!

Another rhinoceros incident is just as fresh in my memory. Alfred Vanderbilt was the chief actor on that occasion, and heaven knows who would have become entitled to the Vanderbilt millions if a certain rhinoceros had been a bit quicker. We were at the time — it was early evening — out after nothing more dangerous than guinea-fowl. I had just shot a pair with my short-range practice rifle and sent two of our gun-bearers to pick up these valuable

additions to our rather monotonous bill of fare, when one of our black boys began to shout and yell:

"Look out, look out, sir!"

Then I saw. Two rhinoceroses were making straight for us at a jog-trot. My practice rifle was loaded, but that was of no use to me. I might as well have let off a pea-shooter at them. The gunbearer had taken my proper rifle when he went to pick up the guinea-fowl. I shouted and waved my hat to make the beasts alter course. No good. Stronger measures had to be applied; I rushed to the gun-bearer, snatched my rifle, and blazed away. The rhinoceroses altered course at once; but so had Vanderbilt, and I saw him disappear unarmed into the brushwood for which the rhinoceroses were now making in single file.

For all his millions Vanderbilt could not in that crucial moment purchase his life, which really hung upon the cheap bullet in my rifle. I fired, and one rhinoceros fell stone dead scarcely two yards from Vanderbilt's heels. The other, terrified by his companion's fate, turned about and vanished in a cloud of dust. The whole affair was a matter of thirty seconds, and when it was over we could not help laughing.

von Blixen-Finecke, *African Hunter*, pp. 112-3.

There is a vast difference between being an expert hunter and a capable observer, for a man may have shot a hundred or more elephants and know less about their habits than a man who has only shot a quarter of that number, because the former may be after the ivory for the cash he gets for it, and the other may be more interested in the natural-history side of the subject.

Lyell, *Memories*, p. 126.

Plate 52. *Secretary Bird.*

Plate 53. *Flamingoes on Magadi.*

'There was once a cock who loved the fairest of all the whydah-birds — the darkest, perhaps I should say, the darkest and the kindest; but another cock, a cock with blacker wings and longer tail-feathers, had made her his own. So she shared the nest of another, and sat by his side, and when her chosen mate danced before her, she nodded her head at him to say bravo, bravo. The first cock knew that she could not be his, because he came too late, and hadn't got such black wings, or such a long tail. So he flew far away into the mountains and looked for worms and beetles and things like that. Sometimes he found them, but they did not taste very good, and he knew that they never would, so long as he had to eat them all by himself, with his lady-love so far away.'

Ian Crawfurd paused, I thought to collect words for the ending; but that seemed to be all. I did not like inconclusive stories.

'What happened then?'

'Nothing happened — and that's the way to tell a true story from a made-up one. A made-up story always has a neat and tidy end. But true stories don't end, at least until their heroes and heroines die, and not then really, because the things they did, and didn't do, sometimes live on.'

'Does every story', I wondered, 'have to have a hero and a heroine?'

'Every story, since Adam and Eve.'

That story, I reflected, if you came to think of it, scarcely had an ending either; it started well, but tailed off into Cain and Abel, and I could not remember what had happened to Eve. Ian Crawfurd, I supposed, was right, but it was unsatisfactory, for everything ought to have a beginning, a middle, and an end.

Huxley, *Flame Trees*, p. 105.

A giraffe was encountered lying dead with a python under it, also dead. It could only be surmised that the python must have coiled itself around the giraffe's neck and strangled it, and that the great weight of the giraffe pinned the python to the ground.

Adamson, *Bwana Game,* p. 117.

Anyone who has watched a bull elephant breaking down a good-sized tree, or twisting off a branch the thickness of a man's leg, is bound to think a bit when he goes close up to a large tusker with the intention of waging a life-and-death struggle with a weapon shooting a bullet the diameter of a slate pencil. He begins to wonder if he should have made his will before starting out on the trip; though probably all he has to leave will be a rifle or two, perhaps a few cattle, some very ragged garments and boots, a copy of Rowland Ward's Records, *and a few notebooks of his wanderings, and game-bag.*

Lyell, *Memories,* p. 127.

I heard an amusing yarn about an old headman who came to a missionary and asked to become a member of his church. The evangelist asked him how many wives he had got, the first question a parson would naturally ask. The native, being a truthful man, said, "Three," and was told that his request was quite impossible as a Christain [sic] is only allowed one squaw. He was told that when he had only one wife there might be a chance for him, so he departed, musing deeply on the quaint ways of white men.

In three months he returned with a benign smile on his countenance, and again made his request, so the parson said, "And how many wives have you got now?" "One," said the beaming native. "And where are your other two wives?" said the missionary. "Oh, I've eaten them," said the headman as he gently patted his tummy.

Lyell, *Memories,* pp. 122-3.

Everyone (he went on to explain) had some affinity with a bird or beast or reptile — and not always the one that you would think. Doves, for instance, were unpleasant characters who squabbled, scolded, and were greedy and cross, whereas eagles were very shy, and cobras liked nothing better than to curl up in someone's bed and go peacefully to sleep in the warmth, and only spat when they were terrified.

I thought Mrs Nimmo might become an ostrich because she had a large behind which waggled when she hurried, and he assigned to Captain Palmer the giraffe because he was long and thin and had large feet and a thick hide. A bat-eared fox for Alec Wilson for his large ears and big brown eyes; for Victor Patterson a greater bustard with whom he shared a long stride, long neck, and toughness — 'and both need to be hung,' Ian Crawfurd said.

When I mentioned Lettice Palmer, he laughed and shook his head.

'We must leave her out of it,' he said.

'But why?'

He pointed with his whip at the sun, which was climbing quickly above the tawny ridge towards some fluffy clouds as light as meringues. 'Suppose the sun entered the sign of Virgo, the tide turned, and an eagle perched upon the Sphinx all at the same moment, it might really happen; and we should look fools if we

got back to breakfast and found our hostess had become a wallaby.'

I felt disappointed in Ian; like nearly all grown-ups, he had started something sensible and let it tail off into stupidity.

Huxley, *Flame Trees,* pp. 102-3.

There is a saying in Africa that somewhere there is a place where the grass meets the sky, and the name of that place is 'the end.'

Alan Root, *The Great Migration: Year of the Wildebeest* [film].

[A collection of this kind must necessarily omit many interesting and appropriate passages. Experts or lovers of Africana will, no doubt, wince to see *their* favorites absent, though the remaining chapters repair a few deficiencies. Further treatment must await another day. For secondary sources, readers could profitably begin with these volumes: Richard Hall, *Lovers on the Nile: The Incredible African Journeys of Sam and Florence Baker* (Random House, 1980); Sir Reginald Coupland, *The Exploration of East Africa 1856-1890* (Northwestern University Press, 1967); Robert I. Rotberg, *Joseph Thomson and the Exploration of Africa* (Oxford University Press, 1971); Heinrich Schiffers, *The Quest for Africa: Two Thousand Years of Exploration* (G.P. Putnam's Sons, 1957); Donald Simpson, *Dark Companions: The African Contribution to the European Exploration of East Africa* (Harper & Row, 1976); Valerie Pakenham, *Out in the Noonday Sun: Edwardians in the Tropics* (Random House, 1985); Errol Trzebinski, *Silence Will Speak* (University of Chicago Press, 1977); Timothy Severin, *The African Adventure: Four Hundred Years of Exploration in the 'Dangerous Continent'* (E.P. Dutton, 1973); Elspeth Huxley, *White Man's Country: Lord Delamere and the Making of Kenya* (Chatto and Windus, 1935); Alan Moorehead, *The White Nile* (Harper and Row, rev. ed. 1971); Alan Moorehead, *The Blue Nile* (Harper and Row, rev. ed., 1972); Peter Capstick, *Death in the Silent Places* (St. Martin's Press, 1981); Eric Axelson, *South African Explorers* (Oxford University Press, 1954); John Gallagher, *The Decline, Rise and Fall of the British Empire* (Cambridge University Press, 1982); Frederick Pedler, *The Lion and the Unicorn in Africa* (Heinemann, 1974); Christopher Hibbert, *Africa Explored: Europeans in the Dark Continent, 1769-1889* (W.W. Norton, 1983); and Errol Trzebinski, *The Kenya Pioneers* (W.W. Norton, 1986).]

IV. The Big Cats

I have...just emerged from the depths of the great wide open spaces, from the life of prehistoric times, today just as it was a thousand years ago, from meeting with the great beasts of prey, which enthrall one, which obsess one so that one feels that lions are all that one lives for...

. . .

...it was my first meeting with a lion and I shall never forget it. In their build, carriage and movements lions possess a greatness, a majesty, which positively instills terror...and makes one feel later that everything else is so trivial — thousands of generations of unrestricted supreme authority, and one is oneself set back 6,000 generations — suddenly comes to feel the mighty power of nature, when one looks it right in the eyes.

Isak Dinesen, *Letters from Africa 1914-1931*[1]

Lion

The lion ("simba" in Kiswahili) is neither a great hunter nor the most dangerous animal negotiating the African plains. Indeed, from a strictly scientific view, a naturalist might well question the appropriateness of Aesop's title "King of Beasts." But few animals have captured man's imagination and esteem as have all the big cats, and, among them, the lion reigns supreme. If for no other reason, the monarch's mantle is today deserved for the lion's stately bearing and his utter insouciance exhibited in the presence of man and the safari vehicle. Of course, lions have always been the animals most sought-after by visitors. Consequently, those lions living in areas frequented by tourists have become quite accustomed to the vehicles. On safari, the photographer can sometimes maneuver close enough to lions to touch them. Acclimated or not, however, no other African animal retains this confidence, this aloof *sang-froid*.[2] Indeed, the lion manages to be dramatic even while doing nothing *(1 & 2)*. The cliché "masterly inactive" comes to mind.

---

1. University of Chicago Press, 1981, pp. 18-21.

2. Some observers have asserted that the lions in national reserves do not associate the safari vehicles with human beings and do not actually see or recognize man. This nonsense has gained recognition by mindless repetition, as ignorance often does. In fact, lions, unlike many other animals, can distinguish all the passengers in a safari vehicle. They have simply come to trust the situation, repeated over and over since birth. Were a passenger to leave the vehicle, another story would develop dramatically.

The lion, with all his regal and imposing nonchalance, has long adorned Western war banners and decorated coats-of-arms, the most prominent figure in national heraldry. When Churchill rose to give a speech on his eightieth birthday (November 30, 1954), he recalled the ordeal of World War II in leonine imagery: "It was the nation and the race dwelling all round the globe that had the lion's heart. I had the luck to be called upon to give the roar." In Africa as well, the lion historically has served as a symbol of power and dignity. Many a strongly fortified city was called "Lion Town" and many strong kings "The Lion." The Emperor of Abyssinia (Ethiopia) was formally known as, among other appellations, "The Lion of Judah." The strongest charms and talismans were necessary to protect one against lions, and eating a lion's heart was generally thought to give the diner great courage.

Plates *1, 2,* and *3* show mature, black-maned males living in the Masai Mara. Some manes turn partially black in adult males and some do not. The black usually appears in the thick part of the mane, on the chest, and in tufts on the elbows. The mane itself sometimes extends in a fringe along the belly. Some naturalists believe that the male with the most impressive mane, because the excess hair serves to protect the vital throat areas against attack by rivals, is likely to be dominant. It is a fine theory, logical and no doubt supported by an anecdote or two, but how do we really know? More probably, a prominent mane helps a male to intimidate an opponent — by making its owner appear larger — and thereby to avoid fights.

These three magnificent adult males, each about six years old, are enjoying the prime of their physical powers. The adult male can grow to ten feet long, measured from

Plates 1 & 2. Monarchs. Throughout history, man has regarded the lion as a symbol of strength and majesty. Ultimately, this admiration may simply be one ranking predator's respect for another. Mutual homage at the top of the food chain. The lion is, however, the second largest feline predator, smaller on average than the tiger.

Plate 3. Dominant Male. The dominant male in the pride strikes an imposing figure. Pictured is a prime example of the mature black-maned lion found in Masai Mara. Its broad, heavy head and luxuriant mane set it apart from the females. Enormous muscles in the thighs, shoulders, and upper forelegs attest to immense power. This lion has the relatively straight back of youth and does not show the scars and wounds that all older lions carry. He is probably about five or six years old.

nose to tail tuft, and weigh in excess of 450 pounds. The average is closer to nine feet and 400 pounds. Males are considerably larger than females; the pronounced difference *(4)* is more than that found in most animal species. A midday yawn *(5 & 6)* reveals the tremendous canine teeth of lions and the primary characteristic of the species: lions are carnivores. These teeth are there for killing and tearing meat from bone. A large male may eat as much as fifty pounds or more in a single sitting (reports of one-hundred-pound meals are exaggerated), though lions normally eat only once every three or more days. Extremely large prides, with additional mouths to feed, are forced to hunt more often. Cats do not chew; they rip, tear, and swallow.

The long, sensitive whiskers supposedly help the animal to negotiate at night, when lions are active. One suspects that they need their whiskers very little, actually, finesse not being the lion's style, but all cats have them.

Plates 5 & 6. Midday Yawns. Constant or excessive yawning is a sign of restlessness — the animal is about to move. The large cats are the most strictly carnivorous among the animals called carnivores. Cats do not grind their food like dogs: feline jaws move only up and down. The female pictured has a broken canine, a common accident. The teeth of all carnivores are similar: three small incisors, one large canine, and various cheek-teeth on each side of the upper and lower jaws. One cheek-tooth on each side is enlarged and has a sharp cutting edge: the *carnassial* or flesh-tooth.

Plate 4. Simba Dume and Simba Jike. Simba dume (male lion in Kiswahili) is half again as big as *simba jike* (lioness). Among the cats, only in lions is the difference between male and female so extreme and instantly recognizable. The contrast is evolutionary and results from the fierce rivalries among male lions: in all nature, males that compete physically tend to grow significantly larger than females of the same species, particularly if the species is a highly social one.

The female is the more athletic of the species, sleek and sinuous, with a sense of controlled power that one can easily see and appreciate *(7 & 8).* The adult female can

Plates 7 & 8. Female Power. The mature lioness is a picture of grace, streamlining, and controlled power. She also is the workhorse of the pride.

attain a size of eight feet and 300 pounds and usually retains some of her youthful spotting on her belly and legs. From throat to abdomen, her underparts are virtually white. Like the turn-of-the-century woman featured in the Virginia Slims' advertisements, she also does most of the work required within the family. The prides are female-oriented: the ancestry of any pride is based on a matriarchal continuity. Its nucleus is a group of related females born and reared together. The mature males, always including a dominant male, found with a pride are often brothers themselves but are not related to the females and probably originated in another neighboring pride. The males that grow up in a pride are expelled at about two to three years of age — nature's protection against inbreeding — and form bachelor groups or live as nomads until old and strong enough to fight for a pride of their own (the normal tenure as master of a pride lasts only a few years, at most). Some males never join a pride and remain nomads until they die.

It is the female who does most of the hunting for the pride. (In bachelor prides, of course, the young males do the hunting; nomads also obviously have to look after themselves.) Naturally, many features make up a hunter. Sensitive noses and ears, for example. But, in lions, none is more important than the eyes *(9)*. Cats have eyes set wide apart, giving them a broad field of view. The pupils expand and contract rapidly in response to light and quickly adjust to seeing in the dark, when much of the hunting is done. All cats have reflectors in their eyes that help them to make the most use of whatever light is available. The eyes must be able precisely to judge the distances to moving prey and consequently face forward rather than sideways. The field of view of each eye overlaps, and the animal is able to focus upon an object with both eyes simultaneously, giving the cats "binocular vision" and extremely good depth perception.[3] Cats never look out of the corners of their eyes — as shown in plate *9,* they swivel their heads and stare directly at the object of their interest.

Contrary to popular estimation, most lions are, however, remarkably clumsy hunters. The athletes miss an embarrassingly high number of times: as many as an estimated four out of five attempts under cover of darkness, and an even higher percentage during daylight hours. The two most important causes of failure — apart from the skill of evasion possessed by the quarry — relate to a fault in stalking and to the characteristic lion charge. Lions can be remarkably clever stalkers, making do with available cover in a highly efficient manner. As low to the ground as possible, the lion crouches and sneaks forward, always approaching head on (to reduce its apparent body size), in virtual silence, and avoiding any sudden movement. So far, so good. But lions, for reasons not fully understood (as cats, their sense of smell is good), do not hunt by scent and consequently pay little attention to wind direction. Animals who hunt primarily by scent automatically approach from downwind, because they pick up the smell of their prey in the air and turn to face it. Lions, on the other hand, frequently approach from up-

---

3. The text is a convenient oversimplification. The degree of three-dimensional and depth-of-field perception exhibited by an animal relates to its stereoscopic vision (stereopsis), which often accompanies binocular seeing. Stereopsis results from the fact that spatially separated eyes each receive a slightly different view of a solid object. We know that certain animals have binocular vision, but their degree of stereoscopic vision is usually unclear and extremely tricky to determine by field studies. The big cats, for example, seem to need to see motion in their prey for accurate spatial judgments.

Plate 9. *Hunting Eyes.* The reflectors in cat eyes lying outside the retina cause them to receive at least a double dose of the light that enters, like a sophisticated camera lens. Cat eyes "glow" in the dark ("eyeshine"), because they reflect back the light shining at them. In daylight, lions see about as well as man, including color vision; in poor illumination, they see up to six times better than we do. The unwavering stare from this lion, with nothing more than a bland expression, should be taken as a mildly aggressive warning.

wind, thereby eventually alerting the prey and losing a dinner. Second, the lion's charge is more ballistic than either a leopard's or a cheetah's — that is, a lion launches itself directly at its quarry and rarely alters the path of attack. Success therefore depends on the initial aim and the choice of the path but most of all on the distance remaining to the prey: the longer that distance, the more likely that the intended victim will depart from the line of attack established by the lion. If a lion misses its target on the initial charge, it does not give pursuit — it quits and begins again.

The safarist's best opportunity for witnessing lions hunting is early in the morning, a prime reason for setting out on the game drive at the crack of dawn. Much imaginativeness has gone into the stories of a pride hunting together, each lion supposedly taking up a designated position, all working with military-like precision to produce a logical victim. Indeed, the literature is full of drawings and long-winded sagas of pincer-like movements, males roaring to drive prey into the ambush of waiting females, and any number of possible upwind-downwind combinations. Such descriptions, though perhaps not quite as absurd as the "Ceremony of Courage" in the

1953 *Mogambo* classic,[4] rank high on the scale of inventiveness. The safarist will never see anything like this (albeit that imagination goes a long way in the bush). In fact, the reality is often substantially different. Frequently, for example, a younger, more inexperienced lioness will jump the gun, raise up too early, or otherwise blow the stakeout, leaving the real pro in the group undoubtedly wishing that the others would just wait at the table. Some attempts truly have more in common with the futile charge that historians attribute to the Light Brigade. The author's observations in the field lead to the conclusion, and some qualified naturalists would dispute this,[5] that the group approach succeeds, on the average, about as frequently (or infrequently) as a single lioness. My belief is that lions hunt together, not because this pursuit is a superior method, but primarily because as communal animals they do nearly everything together. Hunger plays an obvious part. Moreover, the hungry females are naturally willing to hunt, because being in on the kill gives them an opportunity to eat something before the male or males arrive.

Successful or not, communal hunts are great fun to watch. During an early morning stalk, especially when several lions are taking part, a certain electricity fills the air. The other animals present — including the intended victim — know that the lions are about and hunting. Antelopes will snap to attention and stand straight-legged with necks stretched upward. Unless a lion is in sight, in which event all eyes will be riveted, the prey will be glancing about nervously. Other animals will react as well: non-prey "scolding," and all food candidates acting just as fearfully as the neighborhood antelopes. As is usual in nature, the predator is smarter than its habitual prey, and the lions have the initiative. The problem with early flight is that the prey does not know where all the lions are; indeed, how many they are; or how they will strike. The better plan accordingly seems to be to wait until the lions commit themselves. Acting prematurely, and in confusion, the prey will only "fall prey" to the waiting lions. Thus, like a football play, the offense begins the action. At times, the lions can be remarkably patient stalkers. The safarist must also exercise patience (and hope that his vehicle's presence does not attract another vehicle into the middle of the hunt); hunting cannot be artificially hurried.

The most common result of successful group hunting seems to be that larger prey is brought down. Two heads contain more teeth than one. And so on. Of course, there are also several lions to feed. Naturalists who support the view that the pride is a more effective hunting machine than the individual acting alone assert that the group frequently kills more than one animal at a time (not counting a mother taken in defense of her young). In all my years watching lions on the African plains, I have never seen more than one animal killed at a time. I have seen multiple carcasses being shared, but the additional animals had not died at the hands of the predators. Rather, disease or some accidental calamity had conspired to provide a large bounty. Nevertheless, some naturalists even insist on

---

4. To gain permission from the natives to proceed on safari, Clark Gable is forced to stand against a backdrop while the village warriors throw spears to see how close they can shave Gable without actually sticking him. An assortment of Ava Gardner, Grace Kelly, a priest, and the usual collection of chiefs anxiously look on, and, well, the reader can take it from there.

5. Even so eminent an authority as George Schaller has reported that lions hunting as a group were more successful in killing prey than those hunting alone. I have several problems with this conclusion and the implications often drawn from it. First, the environment studied — the open Serengeti grasslands — undoubtedly encourages large prides (or any collection of lions, for that matter) to hunt at the same time. More closed habitats would not. Second, hunting together does not necessarily entail cooperation. Close observation of lions hunting together leaves the distinct impression that each individual is really working on its own. Of course, a group of lions will necessarily spread out and stalk from different directions. And, in the course of stalking, several lions may indeed encircle a herd of ungulates. But the advantage offered by such positioning is rarely efficiently exploited. This is so, even though one lioness may well, for example, take advantage of her position to adopt an ambushing strategy. Certainly, a group of lions hunting in no way resembles the cooperation evidenced by hyenas, the virtual relay-running of wild dogs, or even the synchronization of a jackal pair separating a gazelle mother from her young fawn. Third, true group hunters maintain their community spirit right through the meal itself — a shared effort deserves shared rewards. But, as the text makes clear, lions do not (willingly) share at the table. Fourth, the question of extra efficiency that has been attributed (virtually automatically) to the group has to be approached with some care: to measure fairly the group result against single hunting, one should multiply every group effort by the number of active participants to get a true measurement of the net effort expended versus a single lion's attempt (though the multiple participants are, admittedly, not *equal* players). Finally, the overwhelming evidence throughout the natural world is that most hunters are solitary — of all predatory birds and land animals, the majority hunt alone. Not only does this method generally seem more efficient, evolution favors such a strategy in the following long-term sense: groups require by definition larger prey to satisfy the greater collective hunger (the alternative — more hunting — is probably far less efficient), and larger-prey requirements reduce the range of suitable species available,

---

thereby in the long run (unnecessarily) limiting the food supply.

This analysis is not to argue that group hunting does not confer certain advantages on some lions. Obviously, the poorer hunters make out better. Indeed, the author would agree that some lions join the hunt precisely to improve *their* particular chances. But, at the same time, their participation may — should — help negate to a degree the skill of the real pro(s) operating in the group. Some scientists have suggested that lion prides have actually evolved because of the need for — or, at least, efficiency of — group hunting. For the reasons already given, plus all the other non-predatory advantages accruing to lions living together, I regard this theory as erroneous.

reports that a single lioness has killed several tommies at one time. Should a safarist ever witness such an event, he is entitled to say that he has seen something special.

Another time for watching a kill, usually by a solitary lion, is midday — when tourists are often resting back at the lodge on the advice given them by tour operators. The author has personally witnessed several midday kills. The target is zebra or wildebeest or other antelopes who come to the local waterhole for a drink. *(10)* There, the prey is most defenseless: the head-down posture reduces vision, and attention switches to drinking. But, again, the prey is always, at least vaguely, conscious of the danger. In fact, most animals take an extraordinarily long time to have a midday drink, with numerous false starts and retreats; they never fully relax. The difference is very evident out on the plains, where herds of antelopes will graze, with no apparent nervousness and with what appears to be little concern, surprisingly near resting lions *(11)*. Those lions are, however, not hungry, not hunting, and the prey knows this. At the waterhole, however, the prey has good reason for concern: a lion has far more patience than desire to chase.

Lions are not particularly partial to what they consume. They will eat many animals, including warthogs (a favorite), baboons, snakes, crocodiles, and even an ostrich or two, but usually prefer those animals roughly their own size. Wildebeest and zebra, when readily available, are preferred kills — or so it seems to the author from surveys done at Nairobi National, the Serengeti, and other locations. I am aware that other preferences have been established in particular areas. We also have to remind ourselves that the larger kills are easier for us to detect and count. Lions will kill small animals when the opportunities present themselves, but it seems reasonably certain that only the old or infirm lions actually hunt such prey. In fact, feeding is never limited to a single prey species, even if that species is overwhelmingly abundant, and lions, in common with many other animals, select for palatability and nutritional requirements in the food that they eat.[6]

Killing is by far the most efficient detail of lion hunting, normally accomplished in one of three ways: a nape bite for small prey that severs the spinal cord, a throat bite for larger prey that kills by strangulation, and a muzzle bite that also suffocates the quarry. Over a short distance, a lioness can accelerate to 35 mph — the reader can imagine the stunning impact of *simba* colliding with its quarry, its massive forepaws and claws spread wide and digging into a rump or shoulder. Indeed, the lion simply bowls over anything but the largest prey. And many scien-

6. Lions, young and old, seem to have some fatal attraction for porcupines and are often found with quills stuck in their noses or paws. Although the quills themselves contain an antibiotic substance that prevents infection, the puncture wound is susceptible to infection from a variety of other sources and can be painful enough to hinder hunting and eating.

Plate 10. About To Strike. This waterhole drama is nearing a denouement. The lioness, who has been waiting patiently — so patiently that the omnipresent flies have settled on her nose — collects herself for the lunge.

Plate 11. Close Quarters. The plains animals graze quietly in the presence of lions when the latter are not hunting. The topis pictured here cannot, however, resist a wary peek or two at the young nomad. The reader should also look again at plate *12* in Chapter III.

Plates 14 & 15. *A Futile Game.* Despite the exhaustion caused by the exertions of her lone hunt and enormous meal (plate *13*), the lioness time and again interrupted her attempt to move the carcass to chase off the waiting scavengers. The vultures would come the closest but they could also escape the easiest. Lions do not expect to catch the vultures but seem nevertheless to be bothered by the presumption of the huge birds hovering too close to the food. The lioness here made no more than a perfunctory swat at the vultures — even when she knocked one down, which occasionally happens and happened here, she did not try to kill it. The hyenas, seen here in the background, are more wary, at least until their numbers significantly increase. Lions generally detest hyenas, and the lioness chased one here in deadly earnest for several hundred yards. If caught, the hyena probably would have been killed (but not eaten; lions only rarely eat hyena meat). The lioness ignored the little jackal pictured, who nonetheless kept his own respectful distance. After some two hours of this basically futile endeavor, the lioness finally abandoned the carcass.

a resting pride. The effort is slow and basically futile, and she is reduced to chasing off the scavengers, one by one. Well over two hours later, drowsy from the food and the effort, she is finally forced to admit defeat (encouraged by the arrival of several hyenas) and retreat, leaving the carcass to the next in line.

Aside from the lion's response to the waiting and anxious scavengers, the most interesting activity at a kill is the pecking order orchestrated among the lions themselves. Lions let it all hang out at a meal — the nose-to-nose, shoulder-to-shoulder competition in the group causes gorging and a not-inconsiderable amount of friction. The noise is fantastic: a real Tom Jones effort, with continual growling replacing the lechery. All are intent on seizing "the lion's share." And the reader should know that the "lion's share" was never meant to describe a little more than the next fellow's; indeed, strictly speaking, the "lion's share" is not even the greater part — it is all or nearly all. The mature males, if present, always eat first, while the females (including the provider herself) wait. Rarely, in fact, are the females tolerated in the initial feeding when the full pride is assembled. The dominant male sets the rules. The reader can guess whom he favors. After satisfying themselves, the older males retire a few yards off to rest, and the females come forward, with much bickering among themselves. Inevitably, a tug-of-war or some struggle ensues *(16)*. The dominant male nearly always eventually returns for a last bite or two, again chasing off the females *(17 & 18)*. In the sequence shown, the last bite is the *last* bite *(19)*.

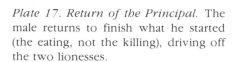

Plate 16. Tug-of-War. Females, who have been feeding for some time, fall out over the last bit of skin. The dominant male, having rested from *his* initial effort, stands and takes an interest. Additional members of the pride can be seen in the upper-left part of the picture.

Plate 17. Return of the Principal. The male returns to finish what he started (the eating, not the killing), driving off the two lionesses.

Plate 18. Phony Nonchalance. The male has no intention of sharing the final remains. Meantime, the still-hungry females engage in studied nonchalance of Oscar-winning proportions.

> *Always when the lion went out hunting he took Kanja, the jackal, with him, for Kanja was a much better hunter than he.*
>
> *But whenever the jackal had killed the game, he would say, "That is mine, Uncle Lion!" Then the lion would look at him with such an angry glare that Kanja would contradict himself at once, and say, "No, it is yours, of course!" Then Uncle Lion would eat it up, and Kanja would go hungry.*
>
> *"You see, I only take the lion's share," Uncle Lion would explain.*
>
> *"Yes, I have noticed it," replied the jackal.*
>
> *"What is your idea of the lion's share?" asked the lion, with one eye on Kanja.*
>
> *"Everything, Uncle Lion," answered poor Kanja.*
>
> *"Very well. You shall hunt with me again tomorrow," said the lion approvingly.* (Hartwell James (ed.), *The Man Elephant: A Book of African Fairy Tales* (Henry Altemus, 1906), pp. 91-2)

A brief homily on "the lion's share."

Plate 19. The Restaurant Is Closed. A sated male, whose distended belly hangs witness to a meal of fifty pounds or more, realizes that the plate is empty. A lion will take several days to digest this amount of food, which includes a fair part of the prey's skin as well. Consequently, this male will not be hungry nor attempt to eat again for at least three days.

In the meantime, the cubs are frequently left out altogether. A sad and all but inexplicable fact of lion life, given the generally social nature of the pride, is that the leading cause of cub death is starvation (the next two most important causes are predation by hyena and infanticide). If left to the females, including the very mothers themselves, the cubs would be forced to wait for scraps, if that. At a kill, the cubs are thus often compelled to amuse themselves in pursuits other than eating — like stalking the vultures and jackals that are also waiting for a turn (see plate 35 in Chapter V). Sympathetic observers are quick to point out that the adults cannot be expected to jeopardize the pride as a whole for the sake of the cubs: if the adults were to weaken from starvation and could not hunt, the entire pride would perish. Cubs in this view are readily expendable, in the interests of the pride, and later easily replaced. This thinking is academic and facile: the cubs

just do not require that much food to prosper, and too many other species place the highest priority on feeding their young, behavior fully "selfish" in a genetic or evolutionary sense.

Ironically, the males usually act as the cubs' saviors — the dominant male frequently allows the cubs to eat with him, even before the females. This tolerance may exist because the cubs do not eat enough to cause the male to worry much about his lion's share. The opportunity does not necessarily guarantee, however, a peaceful meal, as the dominant male will always find something calling for discipline (20-22). The ploys used by cubs and, indeed, all lions at the lower reaches of the pecking order to improve their mealtime opportunites are endless and amusing to watch. But the game ultimately has deadly serious overtones, starvation being as terminal as it is. At any rate, lions rarely eat in peace, whatever the flank-by-flank

Plate 20. The Head of the Table. The dominant male controls the eating order at a kill. This male's left paw is exerting more moral authority than actual physical leverage.

Plate 21. A Warning. A large pride *never* eats in peace. For some real or imagined infraction, the adult male here has a few words for the young female eating at the top of the picture. Her response is one of abbreviated submission: a twist of the neck, which is the prelude to rolling over, the display pictured in plate *22.*

combination. The males often fall out among themselves *(23),* and even the young cats bash away at each other *(24).* Most of the facial wounds and the injuries represented by the scars seen on lion heads (found for example, on the nose of the lioness pictured in plate *9)* are received at the table.

Plate *22* also illustrates another important feature of lion life. The uncertain temper and tremendous strength of the grown males makes an argument a risky business. The weaker members of the pride, especially the cubs, need an escape hatch. The solution is instinctual — and ingenious. The threatened member immediately adopts a fawning or cringing position and, by crouching or lying submissively on its back, deliberately exposes itself in such a fashion as to make killing as easy as possible for the superior lion. The aggressor, recognizing the appeasement gesture, does nothing. The moment passes.

Plate 22. Discipline. A young cub thinks it prudent to finish the entire submission gesture: rolling over on one's back. It should be noted that all submission behavior in lions is nevertheless accompanied by snarling or a forcefully extended paw of the errant party: it is important to lions to retain their dignity, to assert their "lion-ness." The male is not thereby threatened — the submission is clear — but instead realizes that this is another lion of which to be proud (and worth saving).

Plate 23. A More Serious Matter. A dispute between mature males can be a serious affair. The pride here senses the danger, and several members instinctively move toward the combatants in an attempt to diffuse the disagreement. Moments later, everyone was enthusiastically rubbing heads. Life in the pride is a mixture of relaxed social living and individual ferocity over food and sex.

By this time, the reader is forming some value judgments about the apparent monumental laziness of the pride's males, particularly the dominant male. Apologists are quick to point out that the males stay behind at the hunt to guard the cubs, a suspicious and in any event uninspiring excuse, and, more to the point, that the males are simply less efficient hunters — less agile, slower, and too conspicuous to camouflage easily. (25) Bolder chauvinists will explain that the males are conserving their strength — for copulating, organizing the meals, and fighting generally. A more pertinent remark perhaps is that the "life of Riley" lasts for a relatively short time. Soon enough, the once and future outcasts will be

Plate 25. A Difference in Conspicuousness. There can be little doubt as to who is best equipped to stalk like a lion. For a real lesson in camouflage, the reader is invited to find the *second* lioness in plate *4*.

Plate 24. Cub Bashing. Even cubs have a cross word or two for one another at mealtime. On the older lions, the safarist will notice that the left ears seem to be more beat up than the right. Lions, like people, tend to be right-handed. Thus, swatting at meals, where the bickering is fairly nondirectional or indiscriminate, is likely to be via a right hand — though in the picture, our combatant has thrown a left-hand punch. Of course, both ears over time show the wear-and-tear caused by the hourly contact with biting flies.

Plate 26. Lioness at the River. Lions ordinarily need a great deal of water and drink heavily after meals. Relatively inefficient drinkers, they take many minutes consuming a proper amount of water. It is said, however, that Kalahari lions go without drinking for long periods.

realization should come as no surprise, though many people are reluctant to recognize their psychological affinity with lower creatures. Describing an animal as "lazy" may thus be an excellent description of the animal's behavior, so long as we can accept that behavior on the animal's own terms and not also insist on adding the value judgments that pertain exclusively to man. This is not to say that value judgments cannot be made relative to the animals themselves — only that we must do so in the context of the animal's world. Infanticide, for example, may well be aberrant behavior, even on this level. Animals are, incidentally, guilty of the same "sentimentality" that causes people to misinterpret animal behavior: animals always attribute their own motivations to man's action. When a primate, for example, sees an advancing upright human being, it assumes that the posture is aggressive.

Lions have large, sharp-pointed papillae on their tongues — to cut through flesh and lift up water. The tongue of a lion is like coarse sandpaper and strong enough to scrape meat off a bone; a few swipes could, in fact, take the skin off the back of a human hand. Cat tongues to a degree make up for the lack of chewing molars and sideways jaw action. A lion must drink often and for a long time to take in sufficient water *(26)*. A drink follows most meals, and a thorough grooming session follows a drink. *(27)*

forced to hunt and make do on their own (again), without the catering service offered by the pride.

Actually, though the male lion easily assumes the role of a "gentleman" in cultivating his dignified appearance and the careful avoidance of work, the lioness, hunter though she may be, is also essentially "lazy." All mature lions in fact try to expend the least amount of effort absolutely necessary. Thus, the safarist will watch the comical performance of a lioness *dragging* a wildebeest calf or other small carcass in the same fashion as if she were lugging a full-grown zebra or buffalo body. Many other similar examples could be cited.

The use of the term "lazy," among others, requires a few words. Of course, a lion would not understand the term or the concept. All writers run the risk of anthropomorphism in describing animal behavior. The reader should appreciate, however, that a degree of anthropomorphism is not necessarily a bad thing — and probably inevitable. Indeed, criticism that a writer is ascribing human characteristics to animals can be unfair and miss the point entirely. Not only do we have to communicate in terms with which we are familiar, but man's own behavior is, after all, profoundly animal-like, which

Plate 27. Grooming. A lion's tongue is also useful in removing parasites during grooming and preening.

A mating pair is worth watching for awhile. During the period that the female is in heat, the pair is inseparable *(28-30)*. At this time, the lions mate frequently, as often as every twenty minutes or half hour for several days. The estrous cycle of a lioness lasts anywhere from three days to two weeks. The mating ritual itself is pretty standard. Between trysts, the male passes much of his time looking foolishly tender, smelling about for the female's scent and making the grimace known as "flehmen face" *(31 & 32)*,

Plates 28-30. Mating Pairs. A lion in love, so long as he is not harried by other males, assumes an almost pathetic protectiveness toward the female, a paradigm of the lovelorn male or of domestic bliss, depending on one's view.

Plates 31 & 32. Flehmen Face. Many male mammals make this characteristic grimace, named after a German scientist, when smelling the female's scent at the time of estrus. The male (lion, antelope, or other herbivore) raises his head, swills the female's urine in his mouth, and inhales deeply, drawing back his lips in a curl to expose his teeth and gums. Somewhat in the manner of a wine taster treating wine, this posture seemingly increases sensitivity and enables the male to assess the female's reproductive condition. Some scientists believe that the scent is passed through a structure in the nasal cavity known as Jacobson's Organ that can identify

hormones (the human male has a rudimentary Jacobson's Organ; the most developed form is found in reptiles, where it is, however, located in the roof of the mouth). The distinction between a sense of smell and a sense of taste cannot always be made with certainty in many animals. Both senses depend upon the ability to identify chemical substances, a sensitivity that is far greater in animals than in man. We can perceive more than 5,000 distinct odors (and our sense of smell is 10,000 *times* more sensitive than that of taste, though our tongue has 10,000 taste buds, each which in turn has ten to twenty recepter cells linked to the brain). Yet we can hardly comprehend how much greater is an animal's chemical sense. Flehmen itself remains something of a mystery. Females, as well as sexually immature subadults, have been reported making a flehmen-type gesture (common in giraffes, for example), which itself argues for regarding flehmen as related essentially to strong odors (not necessarily sexual in nature). The most reliable evidence indicates, however, that the behavior is primarily sexual. One possibility is that the males of those species who perform flehmen may not have as developed a sense of smell as the females and may therefore need this test as confirmation. One might seek support for this theory in the fact that females are the primary hunters among lions — until one recalls that lions do not hunt by smell. The males engage in flehmen only sporadically and not necessarily at the beginning of the courtship — sometimes only in the middle of mating, sometimes not at all — so that it is difficult to say that flehmen is strictly functional. The practice may simply give the male pleasure. Moreover, given the heightened chemical sensitivity of animals generally, and the always strong odors of estrus, so-called confirmation would seem unnecessary.

or asserting his authority against another male who has come too close to the pair. The female normally initiates the mating by approaching the male and nuzzling him (33). Should the male appear at all reluctant, she persists — to the point nearly of knocking him over, if need be. She will not be denied. The female then arches her back and assumes the submissive mating position on the ground, head stretched forward (34 & 35). Whereupon, the male mounts briefly, amid much growling and mild nape biting (36-39). The whole performance lasts no

more than a minute or two. Naturalists tell us that the lioness needs repeated intercourse to release fully the eggs from her ovaries. Even so, all that copulating does not always result in conception, and a lioness will come into heat every few weeks until she becomes pregnant. A lioness begins to reproduce by approximately four years of age and conceives a litter, on the average, every twenty to thirty months over a normal lifetime spent in the wild of some fifteen years.

Plate 33. The First Move. In all the matings witnessed by the author (a considerable number), the female played the provocative temptress and initiated actual intercourse, either by a clear signal (like rolling on her back) or, more often, by actually walking over and nudging her mate.

Plates 34-39. Mating Sequence. The mating pair takes a short walk until the female assumes the mating position. The male mounts. Copulation itself lasts from five to twenty seconds. The logical assumption underlying the fierce behavior shown is that nature is ensuring that only strong, aggressive males pass on their genes. The female herself plays nature's foil by snarling and requiring "submission." All cats behave this way, but, as they grow bigger (and stronger), the submission routine becomes more and more ceremonial. Otherwise, a male lion could seriously, if not fatally, injure his partner. Lions copulate many times in the course of courtship, and one may witness a relatively mild mating or two, but reports of an entirely peaceful romance may be doubted.

Like other animals, one lioness in season will bring other females into heat.[8] The results are that females find themselves in competition for the available males' attention *(40 & 41)* and several cubs are born at the same time within a given pride. Mating lions do not usually show any interest in hunting or eating, or much of anything else, for that matter. They do drink, out of necessity *(42)*. Other instincts can, however, produce the unexpected. A mating pair is not viewed as a threat by prey; experience has taught the potential victims that mating lions will not hunt. The author once watched a topi drift perilously close by a mating pair while advancing on his way to a nearby waterhole. The topi was obviously relying upon love to see it through. The surprised lioness hesitated

---

8. Some naturalists believe that lion-cub births are synchronized in a pride (a frequently observable fact) because of the threat that new dominant males may kill existing cubs (a practice discussed in the text below). Such sophistication is unnecessary as an explanation and unlikely: anyone with two female dogs in the house will recognize the force of imitation; when one comes in season, the other (often) quickly follows, no matter when the latter's last heat occurred. Pride living is at least as close as two or more pets occupying a home. The same naturalists will go on to insist that such imitation is functional; but such reasoning does not adequately deal with the "null hypothesis" (the simplest and least interesting explanation). In any event, the practice is not nearly as systematic and widespread in lions as in other species where functional considerations are clearly foremost.

Plate 40. No Privacy. Ordinarily, a mated pair will leave the immediate vicinity inhabited by the pride. Sometimes, however, the courtship will take place in the full company of the pride. Moreover, the whole business can become considerably more complicated when (as here) more than one lioness comes in heat at the same time, a frequent occurrence in large prides. Who mates with whom and in what sequence becomes a matter of constant negotiation and maneuvering.

Plate 41. The Other Side of the Coin. Another male is tolerated this close to the mating pair only when he is not actively seeking to mate with the female. The reader can appreciate here the studied non-interest exhibited by the second male. Some females manage, however, to cause all sorts of chaos by trying to mate with more than one male or to thwart generally the dominant male.

Plate 42. A Pause in the Schedule. Normally, the only respite from mating over the several days that the pair is together is the occasional drink of water.

only a second or two and rushed the topi in a flash. She ate, however, only a morsel (the male ate nothing at all). Her pride, on the other hand, a hundred yards off, enjoyed an unexpected but much welcomed meal that day.

The normal litter contains two to four cubs. Most cubs are born during seasonal dry periods, between June and October in East Africa. Gestation is a surprisingly short three months. The lioness usually leaves the pride to give birth to her cubs; she does so as a matter of safety to the cubs. Male lions will protect their own young cubs but will often kill others, particularly in a new (to the male) pride. A new dominant male, and a changeover in power can occur anytime, will likely slaughter any young nursing cubs sired by the deposed monarch. This causes the lactating female to come back in heat quicker and ultimately give the new male his own cubs. This infanticide is not true cannibalism, because the males rarely eat the young once killed. Moreover, it is important to emphasize that the practice in lions is not simply killing off the genetic stock of the previous pride leader and even further from simply disposing of potential competitors — if the cubs are already weaned, the incidence of killing is far less. The picture in plate *43* is unusual, because the father does not normally go off with the mother, as shown here.

Plate 43. A Full Family. This litter of two is only a few days old. It is most unusual for the father to be present at this time, as pictured here. The female ordinarily leaves the pride to bear the cubs alone. This family will rejoin the main group several weeks hence, after the cubs have become considerably more alert and mobile.

The mother rarely leaves her young cubs. *(44)* When she does, to hunt or drink, she risks losing them to other predators, like jackals or hyenas. The other big cats, cheetahs and leopards, will also kill lion cubs, if given a chance. Indeed, the hazards of infancy take their toll — perhaps, only fifty percent of lion cubs survive. Some would put the percentage even lower. Soon, the young cubs are having a look about for themselves *(45)* and trying to participate in mother's meal *(46)*. The young cats all have rosette-like spots, perhaps to increase their camouflage when they are most vulnerable. Before long, mother is devoting much time to retrieving the more adventurous youngsters *(47)*. A lioness carries a cub either by its neck or with its head gently but firmly held in her

Plate 44. A Mother and Nursing Cubs. A lioness has only four teats, and litters in excess of four encounter early survival problems. Under most circumstances, cub mortality is high. Cubs are born about a foot long and weigh less than a pound. More male cubs die than females — the males seem to be more active and more likely to turn up lost or in some (fatal) difficulty — which causes the male-female imbalance observed later in life. In many quarters, lionesses have earned a poor reputation as mothers, with several reports of cubs (especially one-cub litters) being just abandoned altogether. The author's own observations lead to the conclusion that lionesses as a rule make excellent, diligent mothers in an environment that is not always benign.

Plate 45. First Steps. This cub is less than two weeks old and is taking its first independent steps in the *lugga* (a Somali word for sand river or dried-up river bed) where it was born. Cubs sport very woolly coats and are born with their eyes open (and blue). The mottled spots found on young lions of both sexes and the legs and belly of older females are probably throwbacks to the day when lions were primarily forest animals.

Plate 46. First Taste of Blood. This lioness has captured a young gazelle and is eating the entire animal, bones (including the head) and all, presumably for the extra calcium. The author believes that such a diet is normal at this time, having witnessed a similar event on several occasions, but the scientific literature seems to be silent on this point. The lioness pictured here was exercising extra diligence and taking her meal in the presence of the cub (and not on the plains, where she had made the kill), because she had tragically lost her other cub (pictured in plate *44* opposite) to a jackal while she was hunting two days earlier. The surviving cub in turn got a purely inadvertent taste of blood long before he would normally know any sustenance other than milk.

mouth. After a month or so, the mother will take her cubs and rejoin the pride. They are affectionately received:

His introduction to a pride must be a momentous experience for a cub. Up to now he has known only one world, a tiny world of certain familiar tufts of grass, a few bushes and rocks populated only by his littermates and by the enormous and comforting body of his mother. Otherwise there is only the sun and the wind, crickets creaking at night, vultures and eagles soaring overhead by day. There will be little excursions, wobbly walks to new thickets and rocks. Then, one morning, there will be a longer walk than usual, and at the end of it a strong scent, familiar but strange, reassuring but a little frightening too — his mother's scent, but not his mother. Suddenly huge heads will rise up out of the grass. Big, shaggy faces will appear, some even bigger than his mother's, benign but with a hint of menace. Enormous bodies will look over him. He will be looked at, sniffed over, licked — all with great gentleness. Adult lions are fond of cubs, and the introduction of some new ones is an occasion for a good deal of solicitous examination. Thus reassured, the youngsters settle in very quickly, and in a few days they may not remember that there was ever a time when they were not surrounded by other lions of all ages and sizes.[9]

Plate 47. Retrieval. Once a cub is mobile, mother's problems mount exponentially. The only relief is to return to the pride.

9. Edey & Dominis, *The Cats of Africa*, p. 61.

Plate 48. The Wrestling Contest. Cubs engage in endless scuffling, much of it muscular in nature. Other play is more strategical and purposeful.

Plates 49-52. Cubs at Play. A cub seeking some diversion on its own, like a love affair with a tree, will invariably attract a sister or brother, and the game then changes to suit the newcomer(s).

Cubs in a pride are great fun to watch and photograph. Excruciatingly comical but always carrying that solemn expression fixed on their faces, they are quite irresistible. To an exuberant cub, its primary purpose in life is to gin up the pride. As a result, the pride — and all large prides have their share of cubs — is a gregarious mêlée of social interaction. Friendly lions greet one another by rubbing heads. The cubs want to rub heads with everybody, several times a day. The adults respond favorably. (The pride is truly a nuclear family: babysitting duties, even nursing in the case of strays or when mother is absent on a long hunt, are shared.) Cubs wrestle for hours and chase one another *(48-54)* well into young adulthood *(55-60)* and, somewhat more circumspectly, spar with mom *(61 & 62)*. Occasionally, courage will prevail, and a brave young soul will take on father's tail, with inevitably mixed results *(63)*. In nature's plan, all the playful tussling has a purpose: the young cats are, in part, exercising to develop their muscles and to sharpen their reflexes and, in part, working out the fighting techniques that they will need as adults to defend their territories and prides and food against rivals. In large prides, cubs will vary widely in age, ensuring that the youngest learn early the rules of rough-and-tumble. Watching cubs play, the safarist will also begin to notice the same techniques that adult lions employ in hunting: stalking, rushing, chasing (briefly), and pulling one another down from behind — all as will be used someday against prey. In fact, serious schooling begins early; cubs start to accompany mother on hunting expeditions when they are only about three to four

Plates 53 & 54. Rowdies in Search of Action. Leaving a scuffle is no guarantee of a rest: another combatant is as close as the nearby tree or clump of grass.

Plates 55-60. Play Continued. Older youngsters play roughly, and the competiton ranges over a considerable area. To a degree, a certain amount of play can be viewed as merely the release of surplus energy, but also serves as a safe method of establishing relative strength and dominance relationships that last into adulthood. Extensive play is regarded by naturalists as an indication of higher intelligence. The subject is further discussed in Chapter VIII.

Plates 61 & 62. Testing Mother. Mothers are remarkably patient in the face of persistent testing initiated by the youngsters. Rarely does a lioness lose her temper. Cub play with mother has a certain deliberate, almost slow-motion, quality about it. The youngsters seem to calculate every move, a mixture no doubt of training and judiciousness.

Plate 63. The Temptation of Father's Tail. The black-tasseled tail tufts are irresistible temptations to a cub: they twitch unexpectedly, just so, right down there on ground level, and turn out to be ideal for a pulling contest (with no chance of moving the 300 or more pounds attached to the other end). Father's patience is, however, not as reliable as mother's, and a warning curl of the lips is food for thought. Lion signals are many but clear (to lions) — subtlety is not the lion's style. The mature males must make a real effort to maintain their gruff dignity in the midst of tumbling cubs. The main rebuke turns out to be simply getting up and walking away. Lion males are, however, true individuals and never completely predictable.

months old. (The safarist cannot, unfortunately, expect to see this behavior; the initial forays nearly always take place at night.) Lions will not, however, kill their own prey until late in their second year.

Even at slower times, cubs, with or without mother, can be fascinatingly photogenic *(64-66),* and the observant safarist will have many opportunities to capture them practicing for their future Trafalgar role *(67),* studying intently a sportive possibility *(68),* snarling at the visitor who approaches too close *(69),* and smugly looking down from a hard-won perch in a nearby tree *(70).*

As lions are increasingly studied, we are learning that the pride is not quite as structured as once thought. Its size may be a neat family unit of three *(71)* or a jumbled convention of forty, twelve to fifteen members being a more characteristic figure. Rarely does a pride contain more than three adult males. As previously noted, the females are likely to be all mothers and daughters, sisters and cousins. Whereas a definite male hierarchy exists, flexible comings and goings create splinter groups (sub-prides, as it were), cast-offs rejoin, and the hierarchy itself readjusts at surprisingly short intervals. How many and who will hunt at any given time varies. Mating partners rarely repeat beyond the second year. On the other hand, some males and females do form lasting (for lions) relationships. Most females live their entire lives in the pride, but the males hardly ever do. Domination is non-existent among the females and transitory among the males. Nomadic challengers are always just around the corner *(72).* Interestingly, dominant males may have overlapping authority in more than one pride. The pride is, however, basically territorial, and members (including the females) will fight to the death, if need be, to preserve its bound-

aries against other feline intruders. The game-viewer should note a critical fact at this point: it is quite rare to see an entire pride of any real size together at one time. Thus, if the safarist finds the larger group, he should look for the others as well, and vice-versa. *(73 & 74)*

Lions have the reputation of being highly aggressive toward outsiders (*i.e.*, other lions). Non-pride lions represent competitors for food, a danger to the young cubs of the pride, and a threat to the integrity of the existing social structure. The dominant male and his cohorts cannot hope to keep all intruders from the pride's territory,[10] but, by driving out strangers when encountered, the pride can at least ensure that no other group manages to settle in permanently and offer serious competiton. The most efficient methods of defending one's territory — namely, without expending very much energy — are to ward off competitors by scent markings, vocalizations (*e.g.*, roaring), and displays of one kind or another. Lions frequently show notoriously little respect for ritual, however, and actual fighting is not uncommon. Moreover, we have seen that life inside the pride itself is not all curtsies and *politesse.* Aside from disputes erupting during eating and mating, a problem may also arise when the pride is disturbed from the outside — by another animal altogether.

---

10. In one day (in Masai Mara), I counted as many as ninety-five different lions! Others have seen even more in a day's ride. In this kind of density, pride territories — and possibly prides themselves — overlap, and interpride aggression is moderated. Such density is only likely to happen when prey is extraordinarily plentiful — and not merely sporadically available, as during a migration, for example.

Plates 64 & 65. At Rest. Life in the pride is, for the most part, a tactile experience. There is always a great deal of social grooming and long and intense rubbing of heads and bodies. Constant greetings and ingratiation are the orders of the day.

Plates 66 & 67. Posing. The youngster in plate *66* has a tick nestled in its eye, which passenger will soon drop off, thereby restoring unimpeded vision. Ticks and flies plague these animals all their lives — a source of constant irritability.

Plate 68. Thinking Up Mischief. Not until these cubs are fifteen to sixteen months old will they be ready to catch and kill their own (small) prey. Meantime, all the world's a stage for play and exploration. The curiosity of lion cubs is boundless. All three of these fellows eventually decided to investigate our vehicle, a process that ended with the trio asleep underneath the Landrover.

Plate 69. Annoyance. A cub can become annoyed, like older lions, when the photographer moves too close.

Plate 70. Proud Perch. Lion cubs love to climb trees. This youngster was as pleased with himself as it is possible for a lion to be, though cubs always seem to sport that solemn look of satisfaction.

Plate 71. A Family Portrait. A compact, immediate family unit, as pictured, is an unusual living arrangement among lions.

Plate 72. The Nomads. These young male nomads, probably brothers and only recently exiled, watch the game late in the day from a grassy knoll and wait for the time to challenge a dominant male for control of his pride. Unfortunately, nomads frequently wander from the reserves and are shot. The adult lion's mane begins to develop at about one year, but the real spurt begins around four years of age. Subadult males (brothers or cousins) leave their pride of birth in a group and are likely to remain together, whether they later take over a pride or continue as nomads.

Plate 73. *Their Majesties under the Shadow of Kilimanjaro.* The dominant male often seeks an alliance with another male. Such collaboration obviously further helps to control the pride and ward off would-be interlopers. These two males will often set up bachelor quarters away from the pride proper, joining the females only for meals and sex. The males will, however, actively patrol the pride's territory, mark the boundaries with their scent, and discourage marauding intruders.

Plate 74. *The Exile.* This old warrior has lost not only his pride but an eye as well. The older males are reduced to eating smaller mammals (even rats) and birds and digging warthogs from their burrows.

He had no destination and moved only because his victims were moving or because the territory was occupied by other lions who would not accept him. He saw the plains with new eyes, often resting on top of a ridge, with the moon high amid serried ranks of clouds, and with dust hanging in the air and obscuring the sharp outlines of the animals before him. He would sit motionless and watch packs of dogs standing with their big rounded ears protruding while the passive wildebeests trudged in the moonlight. He looked out into long gray ridges of land leading to yet another plain, yet another ridge, yet another day, and so on into an infinity of nights.

He wandered amid winds that were sometimes so strong they ripped up clouds of startlingly white soda dust from distant dried lakes, and by their force darkened the color of the sky. Then, the contrast between the white soda dust and the blackness of the sky gave the plains a starkness and a barrenness that matched his own aching feeling of loneliness.

He walked in dawn winds howling up out of the west and blowing into the eye of a cold white sun rising above the plains. He saw hunting dogs lying in long masses, one dog's body protecting the next from the force of the wind. He was humiliated when he sought to join other prides unobtrusively. He was thrashed when he tried to hunt with a young nomad.

He was repulsed by lionesses he found alone. He was chivvied by hunting dogs, pestered by hyenas, and dogged by jackals. He walked a long and lonely path after his fall from power. (Russell, *Season on the Plain*, p. 80.)

The aggression at this time takes the form of so-called "displacement activity."[11]

A recent example witnessed by the author will illustrate the point. A rhino charged a mating pair of lions that was lying on the outskirts of the local pride. Both lions scattered — there was little enough to be done with the nasty rhino — but the dominant male promptly jumped another nearby male lion and savaged him severely. Displacement activity can, of course, take many forms. Such dominance behavior is fairly common among lions.

Several years ago, when the author was a student, Robert Ardrey and Konrad Lorenz popularized the notion of man's innate bloodthirstiness. They made much of the idea that animals had developed rituals and signals that blunted their hostile energies, whereas man had not. One frequently heard (and still hears) the view that in all nature only man consciously murders another of his own species for reasons other than those of self-defense. In fact, we now realize that many animals are, by any standard, far more violent than man, and lions qualify as one species in which the tooth and claw is distinctly redder.

On the other hand, yet another myth needs to be laid to rest: Africans and non-Africans alike tend to view lions as man-eaters. But the real incidence of man-eating by lions is fortunately rare. Lions are opportunistic and lazy, and old age or some infirmity such as lameness could understandably drive them to capture and kill so easy a prey as man. Indeed, the first victim could even have been more or less accidental, but the relatively easy time of it could have encouraged the habit. The truth is, however, that the few authenticated accounts of lions who habitually attacked and ate human beings concerned strong, healthy, young male nomads. The most famous example concerned the notorious man-eaters of Tsavo, a story referred to in Chapter III. Such habitual behavior is, however, obviously pathological, far from the norm. Several African tribes, thinking it wrong to handle a corpse, did not bury their dead; they also believed that a person should not die in his own home and therefore carried sick, elderly, and mortally wounded relatives nearing death into the bush so that the wild predators could deal with the bodies. And, in fact, lions seem to have been the least interested of the possible scavengers, considerably behind the hyena, leopard, and even the jackal. All the best evidence shows that, though intense hunger and lack of other opportunities will occasionally cause a lion to attack and devour a man, lions do not acquire a "taste for human flesh."

Although lions tend to be most active early in the morning and late in the afternoon and the pride usually seeks out the shade at midday *(75)* for rest resembling a drunken stupor *(76-79)*, photographing these least private animals is actually a full day's affair. A large pride (twenty to thirty animals) can occupy the better part of a morning cleaning up a dawn kill. Mating and cub play can go on at all times. Lions are remarkable jumpers and do climb trees at midday (to avoid flies, for example, and to find the cool breezes at that time). Lions can infrequently be found in the trees at Lake Manyara and sometimes in Masai Mara and in Nairobi National Park. Writers have suggested that lions seek out the trees in Manyara as a precaution to keep out of the way of elephants (Manyara has a very high density of elephants). Nonsense: elephant herds would ordinarily avoid a pride of lions, unless unable to do so; the herds are not so large that the lions could not easily take evasive action of their own, if necessary; the lions do not rest in branches all that high off the ground; and rarely do the entire pride go up into the trees — many stay below on the ground. In all probability, if they were not so lazy, more lions would climb trees more often.

The author has experienced the surprise of a lioness leaping a considerable distance to the top of his vehicle — while he too was on the roof. I had maneuvered the Landrover to within twenty feet of a lioness who was in the process of enlarging a warthog burrow to accommodate her and her new cubs. I climbed to the roof and began to set up a full tripod for shooting down into the hole. The noise and movement upset the lioness; she wheeled and with no more than a half-step left to the roof in a single bound. I fell back through the hatch at the same

11. Displacement activity, common in conflict situations, is characterized by its irrelevance (to the human observer, at least) to the surrounding aggression (or motivating provocation) — the result of a tendency both to fight and to flee. A displacement activity itself may have the effect of resolving the conflict: one or both sides blowing off steam, so to speak. Displacement activities are not confined to instances of conflict and can occur whenever an animal is thwarted in some material way. Essentially, they are manifestations of frustration.

Plate 75. Heading for the Thicket at Midday. After feeding much of the morning, a well-nourished group heads out of the sun, trophy "in hand."

Plate 76. The Pride at Rest. The pride grouping in this picture, all adult females and cubs, numbers twenty. Lions devote an inordinate amount of time to sleeping, especially at midday on the plains once having found the shadow of an acacia tree. Every bit of shade is used. As social as they are, lions lie intertwined. When one shifts position, the chain-reaction affects half its bed partners. Twenty is only a fair-sized pride in some parks today. In the late 1950s, one authority reported that the largest pride that he had seen contained twenty-seven animals. Since the early 1970's, I have seen several prides of thirty-five or larger. (A large pride on the move is a dazzling display of feline grandeur.) As indicated earlier, the absence of adult males in the picture is normal. The cohesiveness and size of a pride depend to a large degree on its living accommodations. In open areas where there is much game (as here), the prides tend to be large and pretty much stick together.

prevented the loss of the headlights! Under so close an encounter, it is wise to stay off the roofs and keep the windows partly rolled up.

We have already spoken of the midday waterhole drama. In addition, lions love to menace warthogs and will even try to dig them from their burrows in the middle of the day. Even the sleeping pride occasionally stirs itself to some kind of dramatic action. The safarist is not likely, however, to see a lion roar — roaring is done mostly at night — an awesome, full-throated sound that surely has contributed substantially to his reputation as King of Beasts.[12] Few sounds in nature are more impressive. The lucky safarist who does hear the mighty roar out-of-doors will not forget the immediate impression: the roar invariably

Plates 77-79. Sweet Dreams. The adult lion fears no predator and thus can afford to sleep like this.

sounds very close, even though it may, in fact, originate up to four or five miles away. This characteristic might be more than mere romantic imagination; some writers maintain that a lion can deliberately "throw its voice" so that the sound seems to emanate from all directions at once.

time, but, had it not been for the tripod, which collapsed over the opening in the confusion, the lioness might well have joined me on the seat, with, no doubt, predictably unpleasant results. As it was, we were eyeball-to-eyeball, briefly, and she then jumped down to her hole and cubs.

Lions should, in fact, never be taken for granted. It is possible to maneuver oneself right into the middle of a pride, and young, curious lions will often stroll right up to the vehicle. I have also experienced — several times — lions actually slipping under my vehicle to avoid the hot sun and falling asleep. On one occasion, much to the distress of my driver, a young lion proceeded to strip the turn-signal lenses from the vehicle. The horn had no effect whatsoever on the marauder, and only driving away

---

12. When looking at pictures supposedly showing lions "roaring," the reader would do well to bear in mind that roaring is an effort — when the lion is standing, its head is lowered and back arched; the face is not relaxed but taut; the neck is stretched forward, and the muscles of the throat are evident; the eyes are (usually) open; the mouth is only partly ajar; and the nose only slightly wrinkled. When roaring while lying down, the lion raises its head up, like a barking dog or baying wolf. The lion is obviously pushing out the roar, which lasts a good thirty or forty seconds. One writer has reported seeing lions roaring in trees; this author does not believe that this happened. The truth is, most "roaring" on film started its natural life as a yawn, taking on a more ferocious mien in the processing room.

The exact function or functions of roaring are arguable, but a spacing or territorial call by a dominant male to warn away other adult males seems highly probable. If so, an omnidirectional sound would be especially effective. Of course, other lions are presumably more adept at deciphering the exact source of roaring than men or women sitting around a campfire. Roaring must serve other social purposes as well, as lionesses roar and several members of a pride also occasionally roar in concert. Unfortunately, it is impossible to monitor the visible reactions of other lions within hearing range.

The author would like to close the discussion on lions

the African bush. The lioness had recently eaten and was not particularly hungry. The fawn was hardly a meal, anyway, with the exception of those times when a lioness nursing cubs will specifically look for such prey to secure extra calcium for milk (and accordingly will eat everything, bones and all). Yet the little antelope was undeniably prey. On the other hand, the fawn, in a state of semi-shock, was making tentative steps toward what could be a new mother for all that it knew *(80)*. And the lioness, faced with this fragile package, indeed began to respond as a mother. The maternal instinct took hold. In plate *81,* the lioness is licking the youngster with the same

Plates 80-86. The Dilemma. This unusual sequence is discussed thoroughly in the text.

with a remarkable sequence of photographs shot one early afternoon. We saw in the distance what looked like a lioness playing with a cub. Being an inveterate cub-watcher, I instructed the driver to hurry over to have a look. When we drew closer, we saw that a very young antelope had somehow been separated from its mother (and herd) and had become entangled[13] with a lioness in one of those special mini-sagas that illuminate the unpredictable and photographically rewarding world of

tenderness and care that she would use with a cub. Over the next hour, as we watched, the lioness would exercise gentle restraint and no doubt thought about a meal from time to time *(82-84),* whereas the antelope never really tried to escape. At one point, the fawn did sprint off in one direction and was quickly retrieved by the lioness, who knocked the baby off its feet but gently cushioned its spill — much the same way that she might discipline an errant cub *(85).* At another point, the lioness warned off a second approaching lioness with a low-throated growl.

The scenario was broken by the arrival of a vehicle filled with tourists. Alarmed by the "plight" of the antelope (in their view, presumably, it appeared about to be eaten), the tourists prevailed upon their driver to honk

13. The infants of many species, when lost, show a tendency to move toward anything that moves, including their natural enemy.

the horn and drive directly for the lioness, in an attempt to free the baby. I feared that this action would surely cause the lioness to kill the young animal. But she responded by picking up the gazelle exactly as she would a cub and moving off some twenty yards or so *(86).* Unfortunately, the tourists and their driver persisted and eventually succeeded in driving the lioness away, placed the baby antelope in their van, and drove off to find a ranger. Such intrusions by man are most unwelcome in the reserves. But nothing could ruin the wonder of what we had seen that day.

Leopard

Seeing a leopard is a high point of any safari. Most visitors never do. The author knows many persons who live in East Africa and safari often and who have never seen the elusive animal. The leopard is truly Kipling's Cat that Walked by Himself — walked by his wild lone through the west wild woods. . .waving his wild tail: "all places are alike to me." No one really knows how many leopards exist in any given area; for awhile at least, some naturalists thought that the leopard was an endangered species. That view seems now to have been exaggerated, though the ban on real leopard coats indisputably has been beneficial to survival. The closest that even the most observant manage is often no more than to see the telltale kill in a tree *(87)*. It has always been so — thus, Carl Georg Schillings, the pioneer animal photographer who traveled East Africa at the turn of the century, wrote repeatedly that the leopard was far more common than the lion and would "long survive" the last King of Beasts, yet the former scarcely appeared in his photographs, leading him to despair, "the leopard is literally everywhere and nowhere."[14] On the other hand, blind luck sometimes rewards even the most casual tourist.

Solitary, shy, and nocturnal by nature, the leopard

Plate 87. The Evidence: A Leopard's Larder. Leopards seem to prefer to kill animals that will last for several days and more than one meal. On the other hand, unlike lions, who regularly kill prey larger than themselves, leopards as a rule will kill prey smaller than their own body size. The athletic cat deposits such prey (here, a warthog) in trees, where it can return unmolested again and again.

---

14. In his first book, *Flashlights in the Jungle* (Doubleday, Page, 1905), only one photograph caught the elusive cat, but that picture was much prized by Schillings. In his follow-up volume, *In Wildest Africa* (Harper & Brothers, 1907), Schillings hardly improved his bag: two pictures of dead leopards and one live animal caught in a steel trap!

("chui" in Kiswahili) is uniquely independent. Silent and smooth as running water, the leopard is much that the lion is not. It is, in fact, the leopard who is the hunter *non pareil*. He hunts by surprise and hunts anywhere. Both wasted effort and misses are surely rare, though the leopard, like the lion, suffers from ignoring wind direction. Leopards assume an *intimacy* with their victims. So incredibly stealthy is their stalk, they literally stumble across food en route — thus, leopards often find themselves eating wholly unintended meals. These cats are, in fact, the original opportunists. Watching a leopard *stalk* is to understand for the first time what the word was meant to convey *(88)*. Leopards are the most intelligent of the cats and the finest feline athletes by far. Their superbly proportioned bodies excel at running, jumping, tree-climbing, and swimming. Pound for pound, they are remarkably strong: a 120-pound leopard has been known to haul a large giraffe calf up a tree. I have seen a leopard leap at least nine feet vertically and a good twenty-five feet or more horizontally. It would be easy to take the view that

no other carnivore has reached such heights of evolutionary adaptation.

The safarist who is lucky enough to come face to face with this cat is not going to encounter the indifferent glance of the lion. The intense, cold, and unblinking stare of the leopard *(89 & 90)* will send a chill up anyone's spine. The eyes, like those of the other big cats, have round pupils that shrink to pinpoint size in bright light. But there is more, much more. A hint of savagery, malevolence, complete consciousness — all burn in this yellow glow. An experience like no other, the safarist will never forget the encounter.

Leopards pass much of their time in trees. Large prey is hauled into trees and wedged in crotches to keep it from lions and hyenas and very brave jackals. The tree larder is not easy to spot from the air, but vultures in any event will not touch a leopard kill in a tree. The more maneuverable bateleur eagle in a courageous moment might decide to tamper with a carcass, and baboons have been known, in the leopard's absence, to raid the pantry as

Plate 88. Assassin Stalking. The leopard moulds his body to the contours of the ground and the rocks. Its footsteps make no sound. African lore concerning *chui* — the Kiswahili itself conjures up a lithe, slinking body — is, not surprisingly, a mélange of anecdotes, rumors, glimpses, and fearful exaggerations.

Plates 89 & 90. The Look. The leopard's head is rounder than a lion's. Its magnificent whiskers are precise organs of touch that locate twigs, leaves, and other noisy impediments to its stealthy nighttime path. Whiskers also help avert the thorns in a tree. The small spots on the leopard's face gradually enlarge farther back on the neck and body and turn into the characteristic open rosettes.

well. Furthermore, the carcass must be placed high enough to protect it from an enterprising lion. Watching a leopard haul its kill into and about a tree *(91 & 92)* is to see logistical feats and astonishing agility almost without equal in the wild. And leaving a tree with a carcass is a head-first, straight-down affair that appears to defy the laws of gravity. Like lions, leopards enjoy putrid meat.

The preferred kill — impala, bushbuck, and reedbuck are favorites — is large enough to last for several days. Like their larger relatives, leopards also bury the stomach and intestines of their prey. Presumably, by burying those parts, some of the attraction for flies and other insects is removed. Or, perhaps, the intention is to fool interested scavengers.[15]

Plates 91 & 92. A Matter of Logistics. It is not just the weight but the dangling hooves and protruding horns that make maneuvering in the trees with such carcasses a remarkable feat. Leopards prey on a greater variety of animals than any of the other wild cats.

As indicated earlier, actually searching out a leopard during the day is almost an impossible proposition. Because leopards eat anything, their movements have meaning to most inhabitants of the forest or plains. Consequently, a leopard has no little difficulty moving undetected during the day. Even a trip to water for a drink, usually the sole daylight venture, sets off a raucous chain reaction. Therefore, the leopard simply stays put. The best advice for the safarist is to try to find the cat extremely early in the morning — at dawn — when he may be active, leaving his tree, for example, to take up a daytime position. Riverine acacia trees located in broken woodlands are a good start for an intelligent search, followed by areas that combine dense thickets and rocky crevices — wherever substantial cover exists. The more rugged the terrain, the better. The camouflage of a leopard is nearly perfect, as his spotted coat blends well

---

15. Leopards do not often cache their food in forests (at least, not above ground level), because the lions, hyenas, and jackals are mostly absent.

Plates 93 & 94. A Lesson in Camouflage.

with the patterns of light and shadow found in dense foliage *(93 & 94),* and, unless the animal is moving, the safarist will have to come extremely close to discover the

Plate 95. Discovery. Although trees and rocky ledges offer excellent vantage points to see prey, a leopard's choice of habitat is also meant as a refuge from lions (and man). Leopards have been known, however, to live concealed in areas densely populated by human beings. There is, for example, the notorious story of the leopard that escaped from a cage in Nairobi several years ago. When game wardens searched for him, they found tracks of *five other* leopards living in the parks and gardens of the city. Meanwhile, the escapee on its own returned unnoticed to its cage! The leopard occupies every habitat in Africa but the most arid deserts.

big cat. Contrary to the general guidance given earlier, no time should be wasted, when a leopard is spotted, in the approach. The odds are strong that the cat will move anyway when he knows that he has been discovered *(95 & 96)*, and the safarist must be prepared to give chase *(97 & 98)*. A good driver, a good vehicle, and proper anticipation ought to yield a shot or two, once the cat is flushed.

The author has spent considerable time on safari searching for the fanatically elusive feline. (It is unnatural to speak of leopards without using the word "elusive.") Look for the tail hanging from the tree limb, the old rangers will say. I have seen thousands of imaginary tails

Plate 96. Quick Exit. Spotting a leopard is a mixed blessing and in any event represents just the beginning of a hectic time, from the perspective of shooting some good photographs. The author many times has lost the animal, once it discovered that it had been seen. When the leopard begins to move, the photographer must close the distance between them as quickly as possible.

Plate 97 & 98. On the Run. Closing the distance with both vehicle and a change of lens.

hanging from tree limbs. To paraphrase (with apologies to the Bard) Theseus in "A Midsummer Night's Dream":[16]

> "In the bush, imagining some chance,
>   How easily is a tail made from a branch,"

or

> "In the trees, imagining some cat,
>   How easily is a branch supposed just that."

The ultimate indignity of this African version of a snipe hunt is the sure knowledge that the leopards *are* there, watching the safarist. A more sure sign of a leopard's home range are claw marks on tree trunks, where the cat has stretched its muscles and sharpened its claws. Such visual signals (and olfactory ones, as well) are, of course, clear to leopards. The safarist will, however, have a devil of a time figuring out which tree marks belong to leopards and which to lions, though the latter use trees in this manner far less frequently than the former.

Occasionally, fanaticism by the safarist produces a small victory for mankind. Once, the author discovered a leopard at daybreak but followed it for nearly one hour down a river bed without the cat showing itself long enough to allow squeezing off a decent shot. At one point, the leopard went into a clump of tall grass growing along the bank and disappeared. I was being careful to watch ahead and did not see him emerge up the bed. We drove right up to the tall grass and stopped, but the leopard was nowhere in sight. We waited; I was convinced that the cat was immediately below us. The wind blew the grass from side to side, and the silence was, as they say, deafening. No leopard. An hour passed. The clump of grass appeared to grow smaller and smaller. No leopard. The guide began making polite suggestions about moving on, to look for the cat farther up the stream, but I was betting that the leopard had not moved. But how could anything remain so still for so long? And in such minimal cover? Suddenly, with the low-throated, rasping grunt or cough that sounds a bit like sawing wood characteristic of leopards, he emerged from the grass *(99 & 100).* The victory was mine. In fact, he turned out to be a really large male and, thoroughly disgusted at our unnatural patience, made no further attempt to hide as he strolled off *(101),* a symphony of grace and strength. Karen Blixen again comes to mind:

> No domestic animal can be as still as a wild animal. The civilized people have lost the aptitude of stillness, and must take lessons in silence from the wild before they are accepted by it. The art of moving gently, without suddenness, is the first to be studied by the hunter, and more so by the hunter with the camera. Hunters cannot have their own way, they must fall in with the wind, and the colours and smells of the landscape, and they must make the tempo of the ensemble their own.[17]

---

16. The original, from Act V, is as follows:
    "In the night, imagining some fear,
      How easy is a bush supposed a bear."

---

17. Dinesen, *Out of Africa*, p. 16.

Plates 99 & 100. Leaving the Tall Grass. The cliché "disciplined inaction" comes to mind in describing how this feline athlete manages to keep so still for so long.

Plate 101. The Big Male Snarls. The underside of a leopard's tail, like the tip of a cheetah's, is white. This trait is supposed to be for the benefit of the young — a guide to cubs following in the tall grass. Male leopards have, however, nothing (good) to do with cubs.

There are other times, very different times, when luck takes a hand. Suddenly, one turns a corner, so to speak, and the cat is there, basking on a rock for all to see *(102)*:

> He [the leopard] lay sprawled. . .sunning himself — more impressive and regal and voluptuous than could be imagined of any animal. The pelt was so brilliant it seemed to shine from within, the spots night-black against the brushed gold, and there was so much of it — all those extra loose folds to take care of big kills. . .that it gave him a look of the most prodigal splendor. The tail, snowy underneath and dead black on top, waved continually at the tip like a weaving snake, as irresistibly in motion as consciousness itself, as if the leopard were thinking with it. One huge paw hung indolently over the edge. . . He turned his head our way, the long white whiskers spreading out from his face in two thick fans, gave us an uneasy look and poured slowly head first off [the resting place] and down into some bushes.

> In quite a different sense from what the lions had done, he left me feeling I had now seen one of the world's great — a feeling not unlike that which one has after an outstanding performance by a great actor or musician or dancer. It is as if you had come very close to the source of creative energy itself — had been brushed by its passing. The shock of excitement is partly surprise and partly recognition: so *that* is it! The earth is suddenly richer.

> What a contrast to a lion he was! Lions are animals of the sun, leopards seem to be of the moon. Though both hunt by night, the lion has always been associated with myths of the sun; he is shining and radiant; his mane frames him like the sun's rays. The leopard's coat is like the dapple of firelight and dark on the forest floor, his eyes are the pale gold of the hunter's moon. The natives say that his spots mimic the footprints of all the animals of Africa. More secretive, more sensual-looking than the lion, he belongs, you feel, to the Orient, in an exotic garden.[18]

As one can determine from the photographs, a leopard's body spots are actually rosettes or clusters of spots. No two richly studded skins are ever alike. The largest leopards can grow to eight feet long and 200 pounds in weight, but most are considerably smaller, averaging 80-120 pounds. A fully grown female can weigh as little as fifty pounds. All leopards are, whatever their weight, powerfully built. A leopard has a truly luxurious set of long whiskers, which appendages are far more utilitarian than the lion's. Sneaking about in the dark needs its tools. Leopards are the most adaptable of the large cats and are at home in the broadest range of environments — from the savannahs to dense rain forests. In the latter, their optimal habitat, they are the principal large predator and exist in relatively high density, perhaps as many as one per square kilometer. Leopards in the

18. Ames, *A Glimpse of Eden,* pp. 105-6.

Plate 102. Odalisque. Though the most widely distributed and abundant of all the big cats, the leopard is rarely encountered lounging in such splendor, gazing seductively into the distance like some detached ornamental concubine in a harem.

forest seem to have more heavily spotted coats. They are also smaller as a rule than their counterparts on the plains. In the rain forests at high altitude, melanism — producing the so-called "black panther," which is really a leopard — is also found. A small fortune undoubtedly awaits the photographer who succeeds in capturing the wild African melanistic leopards on film. (The famous black leopard used in filming the *Mogambo* epic came from Asia, via Milan, Italy!) Like the other big cats, a leopard's average longevity in the wild is about fifteen years.

Leopards in Africa have a legendary rivalry with baboons.[19] The two live in endless war. The day belongs to the troop of baboons. Several big baboon males, each of whom has canine teeth of his own that nearly equal a leopard's and each of whom is a pretty tough customer in his own right, are more than a match for a leopard (and sometimes kill one) during daylight. The night belongs to the leopard. The baboons congregate quietly in the tops of trees and huddle in utter terror. Lighter than a leopard, they sit as far out on the branches as feasible. Nevertheless, they wake frequently to find that one of their number was, in fact, snatched in the night by the big cat. But leopards also eat birds, snakes, hares, hyraxes, rodents, antelopes, warthogs — anything, in truth, that moves. To the cognoscenti, the unmistakable rasping grunt-cough of the leopard in the night instills more terror than the lion's roar. Most victims suffer the same surprise as the baboons. What they do not suffer is the surprise of finding a leopard on their backs, having dropped there from a tree. Although so immortalized in countless paintings and other artistic inventions, leopards ordinarily do not leap on prey from trees. There is apparently some evidence that an occasional leopard has indeed jumped from a tree onto a large antelope, but the same considerations that keep lions from attacking their prey from the top in this fashion apply as well to leopards. Reports to the contrary cannot be verified, and suffice it to say here that such behavior by the cat would be stupid, if not suicidal, and rarely successful. Strong swimmers, leopards often find food in or near water as well: fish, crabs, and several other water animals. Some leopards develop a taste for a particular animal and will ignore other opportunities to eat accordingly. Domestic dogs have always been so favored, and genuine man-eating leopards have been more common than their lion counterparts.

───────────

19. Based upon their own observations, some naturalists believe that the rivalry *is* legend. But, in places where leopards have been killed out, by poaching or poisoning by farmers, the baboon population has increased to levels disastrous for local agriculture. No observer will deny a baboon's hatred for a leopard; the reaction of the primate is unmistakable when a leopard is discovered. Nevertheless, given the efficient baboon social organization and the aggressive nature of the baboon male troop leaders, the best guess is that most leopards do not get fat on baboon meat.

If seeing a leopard is rare enough, seeing a mating pair is even rarer. As already indicated, leopards are strictly solitary and only come together to mate. The author does not know of anyone who has actually seen them mate in the wild, in contrast to the exhibitionist lions. The pair moves quickly and is highly evasive *(103 & 104)*. After mating, the female goes off to hide; the male would unfailingly cannibalize the cubs. Females may bear up to six young, three is probably average, but only one or two normally survive. Lions are the most frequent killers of leopard cubs. Those get that die in the first few days from natural causes are eaten by the mother to hide the telltale odors.

Plates 103 & 104. Mating Pair.

While mating leopards are so rarely encountered, seeing young cubs is purely "Shauri ya Mungu" — the business of God. I am told by those who have been blessed that the cubs play 'stalk-hunt-and-ambush' like all young cats. The reader is encouraged to look at Scott's *The Leopard's Tale*, to which reference was made in Chapter I.

One never sees a beat-up leopard, evidence that these cats, as befits solitary animals who know the necessity of staying healthy, are very cautious about fighting. All cats are territorial by nature, but the concept of "territoriality" is a bit deceptive. Strictly, two areas are associated with the idea: the entire area, or "home range," used by the animal to hunt, mate, sleep, and so forth; and the small portion of that former area habitually used, the "heartland." Only the heartland and its habitual pathways are deemed worth defending, sometimes to the death. A cat's "home range" usually overlaps with those belonging to others. Of course, both areas "float" over time — that is, they expand, contract, and shift as the animals respond to food availability and other lesser factors. Leopards apparently do not, however, actively defend even their "heartland" against other leopards; and they undoubtedly take care not to invade unnecessarily another's space. Extensive scent-marking is common.[20] As might be expected, a leopard's territory will "float" more than a lion's, but the evidence is also clear that leopards try diligently to avoid one another. Moreover, radio tracking has shown that leopards have utterly unpredictable movements.

The rocky outcrops (*kopjes*) or bushy gullies (*korongos*) of the Seronera region in the Serengeti are probably the best places in Africa for finding and photographing leopards. *(105)*

Cheetah

The Cheetah ("duma" in Kiswahili) is the least intelligent, most specialized, and least adaptable of the big cats — and the closest to extinction. Only a few thousand specimens remain in Africa and they have totally disappeared elsewhere where they once lived in abundance. Remarkable genetic uniformity greatly lessens the cheetah's chances of coping with the current threat to its survival — a shrinking environment.[21] Cheetahs are made

Plate 105. *Leopard under Tree.* The evidence seems to be growing that leopards are slowly becoming increasingly diurnal and tolerant of human presence in those national parks where poaching is under control and the cat can be assured of some security. Even Kipling's Cat that Walks Alone eventually made his accommodation with man, though few specimens are prepared to take up the habits of the leopard found in the Serengeti several years back and nicknamed "Good as Gold" in deference to its famous posing for tourists.

to run and they need space, lots of space.

Most of us have seen on television at one time or another film of a cheetah sprinting. On safari, seeing the same thing in person is akin to a religious experience. The animal is a speed machine, and, at least on land, nothing remotely compares. And little enough in the air; in fact, only the fastest birds are swifter. In repose, the cheetah sometimes appears gangling and awkward. But looking at one stretching *(106 & 107)*, we can see a good many parts of its functional "secret": small, rounded head; disproportionately long (for a cat), thin legs, in relation to its body; articulated vertebrae that allow the whole animal to flex like a bow; shoulder blades with remarkable rotation; and a deep chest for a sprinter's wind. So lithe is the entire body that one is tempted to believe it aerodynamically contoured — romantic but inaccurate imagery.

The cheetah releases energy (in proportion to weight) many times that of a racehorse. In two or three jumps, the cheetah approaches top speed. The fluid acceleration is something like 0-45 mph in two seconds; nothing on the

---

20. Mammals communicate in several silent ways. Cats mark territories by spraying urine on trees and rocks. The marked places are called scent posts. Such scents can, of course, also communicate sex, status, age, reproductive condition, and diet. Scent posts last for days at a time and they are efficient methods for reducing the chances of unexpected — and possibly damaging — meetings with another leopard, the last thing that most leopards want. (From time to time, naturalists report affectionate — but brief — reunions between mother and daughter leopards.) Claw marks also announce the leopard's presence to other leopards.

21. Genetic variation is the raw material for evolution; the cheetah's strikingly little genetic variety, rare in natural populations and unique in mammals, means that there are few individuals who can withstand ecological change or disease.

open road has ever accelerated like that. A horse reaches into a stride four times as long as its body (less the head and tail); a cheetah's stride turns out to be six times. The twenty-five-foot bounds are the same length as those of a horse, but a cheetah takes more than three strides per second! Think of a horse race on "fast-forward." At full speed, a racehorse is off the ground one-quarter of the time. A cheetah is nearly flying; for more than half the distance covered, no feet touch the ground. The puffs of dust rising up in its wake look like the result of machine-gun fire. Top speed: 70 mph — nearly twice as fast as a greyhound and half again as fleet as a thoroughbred. (A human sprinter runs 100 yards at roughly 23 mph.) At top speed, the moving body of a cheetah bends virtually into a circle, the hind feet striking the ground far in front of its head.[22] Watching this cat in action, the safarist expects to see the blurred, streaking poetry go on and on.

But the cheetah is a sprinter, not a runner. He goes no more than three to four hundred yards flat out (which is still farther than the leopard or lion can run at top speed), some fifteen to twenty seconds at most. The cheetah's

Plates 106 & 107. The Stretch. Simply standing there, the cheetah is beautiful, or not, depending on the eye of the beholder. To some, the head appears too small for its body, and the animal is all legs, sway-backed, and wasp-waisted. Others see a sleekness and a gentle, aristocratic bearing. When the cheetah runs, all opinions coalesce. It becomes one of the most dazzling, graceful creatures on earth. Or, as one writer has said, "one of nature's grandest exaggerations." "Cheetah" sounds as if it *ought* to mean a sudden explosion — chee-TAH — but the name comes from a Sanskrit word meaning "speckled body."

---

22. All cats normally gallop in a fashion known as the "half-bound," characterized by the hind legs thrusting in unison, while the forefeet in succession take the animal's weight. At lower speeds, the cheetah uses the half-bound motion, but, at full stride, cheetah movement is a bit more like that of a horse — a "lateral gallop," in which the trailing forefoot is followed by the hind foot on the same side, that is, the hind legs push sequentially.

"tommy" at slightly in excess of eight yards a second and given the length of its sprinting capacity, should start within 100 yards of the gazelle. It may well attempt to close the gap to 100 feet before launching its sprint. Actually, watching a cheetah begin a hunt, one soon realizes that the cat is also a careful and effective stalker. Unaccountably, unless they have not really witnessed the process itself, many writers play down the cheetah's stalking abilities. Although cheetahs do not make the same use of the available cover as a lion — an observation that perhaps has more to do with the lack of cover normally available to the cheetah than anything else — they can hardly be accused of adopting a casual approach. The cheetah ambles forward, sometimes crouching low, sometimes not, and freezes whenever the prey looks in its direction. As the prey resumes grazing, the cheetah patiently resumes stalking. *(108)* But the cheetah stalks only to get within a decent range, then it explodes. The reader should try to put all these figures and images into a practical context: you are a gazelle; one football-field length away, a killer starts after you; you quickly accelerate to just a little less than the maximum speed allowed on America's highways; and you will lose the *foot*-race in the next twelve to fifteen seconds! If all that were involved were this remarkable sprint, the gazelle would never escape; a cheetah can *always* stalk-lope to within 100 yards of its target. If a cheetah has, however, misjudged the distance and, having started too early, is not closing in on its prey fast enough, it will quit suddenly and begin again.

But the cheetah must also eat, and actually catching the prey is complicated by two factors. First, the gazelle knows that a straight line is suicide. The chase is instead a choreographed affair that zigs and zags at top speed. Using its tail for balance and as a sort of rudder and relying upon

favorite prey is the Thomson's gazelle, which is no slouch itself at a 50 mph peak speed.[23] The cheetah closes on a

---

23. The North American pronghorn deer is the cheetah's nearest competitor in the land speed derby. The pronghorn can run as fast as 55 mph and has been recorded maintaining 45 mph for four miles.

Plate 108. Cheetah Stalking. Not terribly different from other cats, the cheetah assumes a more or less traditional stalking posture. What might be interpreted as carelessness as the cheetah draws nearer to its prey is better viewed as confidence — confidence in its sprinting abilities.

its "dog-like" cleated feet[24] to provide the traction for quick turns, the cheetah still cannot swerve as well as the antelopes at top speed. Inevitably, the cat must slow down significantly to follow the quick turns. The antelope will often escape, if it times its fancy footwork just right. The cheetah wins only by anticipating a zig or zag. Indeed, the agile twisting of the prey can work to the cheetah's advantage if correctly anticipated: the cheetah 'cuts the corner.' (More on this contest in Chapter VII.) The second problem is bringing down the prey at top speed — the chase is not simply a foot-race nor even a game of tag. The prey must be caught and killed. The cheetah strikes larger prey above the legs with its forepaw, bowling over the animal. It then throws its weight on the forequarters of the downed animal and grasps the throat. Strangulation follows, unless the animal dies first from damage to its central nervous system. Smaller prey may be overcome from above and behind as the cheetah catches up. The cheetah has a dew claw on each front leg located just up from its claws, an appendage

that remains needle-sharp because it never touches the ground *(109),* and the cat uses the dew claw to hook into the galloping victim's side and help throw the animal off balance and to the ground. A cheetah has relatively small teeth and weak jaws (for a carnivore) and must aim accurately at the throat for the right killing bite. Of course, strangulation of the prey is made easier by the exertions of the chase: an antelope will build up a huge oxygen deficiency and also will struggle less after a full run. In addition, the theory that the animal goes into shock from the canine punctures has already been noted.

Plate 109. A Weapon of the Hunt.

24. Observers for years have supported an almost unanimous confusion about a cheetah's claws. The popular theory has been that the cubs, like other cats, were born with sharp, retractable claws but that adults developed like dogs, unable to retract their claws. Supporting the theory was the fact that the youngsters are good climbers, whereas the full-grown cheetahs are extremely clumsy climbers. It has now been shown that the claws in adults are also retractable. The difference between a cheetah and other cats is that the cheetah's claws are shorter and much straighter and no sheaths of skin cover the retracted claws (which therefore remain visible). The claws are blunted, because the cat chooses to use them as cleats during the chase, and thus serve as poor instruments for climbing.

The safarist should understand a few pointers, if he hopes to witness this blurring, spectacular performance. Cheetahs are not always easy to find: the base of trees that stand alone on the plains *(110)*, ant hills *(111)*, and fallen trees or stumps *(112)* are all fair bets. It helps to remember the cheetah's need for vigilance and a clear view of the horizon. Moreover, cheetahs must kill nearly every day, particularly if a female is feeding cubs or a pair (or threesome) is hunting. Thus, patience by the safarist will bring its own rewards. Proper positioning is everything. If one crowds a cheetah hunting, one definitely risks disrupting the hunt. Equally important, the safarist parked too close to the cheetah at the start will never see the ending, possibly three to four football-field lengths away. The best position is well off to the side and closer to the prey than the predator. The safarist must therefore try to pick

Plate 110. Sentinel of the Savannah. Safarists never fail to marvel at the ranger's eyesight when he picks out this cheetah from miles away. The rangers certainly know how to use their eyes, but it helps to know where to look and, furthermore, exactly what to look for — like this lone tree on the open plains with an unobstructed view extending to the horizon. The reader should note the cat's use of the available shade.

Plate 111. Standing on High Ground. For a long time, naturalists believed that a different species of cheetah, the King or Striped cheetah, existed in Rhodesia (now Zimbabwe). We now understand this animal to be a variant, the result of recessive genes, of the single cheetah species. King cheetahs can today be seen at De Wildt Cheetah Breeding Station in Transvaal, South Africa.

Plate 112. Cheetah Sitting. Because a cheetah's legs are so long, proportionately, the sitting position is more nearly vertical than that of other cats.

out a cheetah's intended target. In this regard, it helps to know that, despite some misguided reports, cheetahs do not rush a herd. They pick a target at the herd's edges or one off by itself, a straggler, and stick to it. Photographing the hunt poses one of the greatest challenges to the photo-safarist; most pictures of a cheetah at full stride are "stills" from a movie video.

Watching a cheetah chase a gazelle encourages some interesting speculation. The author has reserved a more detailed discussion of evolutionary theory for Chapter VII, but the reader might well ask at this point: are the cheetahs and gazelles engaged in some escalating evolutionary "arms race?" Are faster and faster cheetahs chasing faster and trickier gazelles? Should we not expect to see super-performers emerging? Not really. Too many variables, for a start. The environment throws up several pushes and pulls, in different directions and at different times. Moreover, we also know that an increase in speed or an improvement in some senses, already frequently so keen that we as human beings can barely comprehend them, is subject to physical and genetic constraints that act as roadblocks to simple, straight-line Darwinism. Moreover, predation by large cats is a doubtful choice as a major evolutionary influence. As a population check, predation is largely negligible. This has been shown again and again wherever prey populations expand dramatically because of significant improvements in the immediate en-

vironment (*e.g.,* the wildebeest and gazelles in the Serengeti). The predators thrive under such conditions but they cannot keep up. Given the normal targets of predation, the cats do serve as an excellent mechanism for selecting out old, crippled, or otherwise less than healthy animals. Such a result is beneficial to the breeding stock of a prey species. Whether the benefit ever rises to a level higher than "maintenance," relative to an entire local population, may, however, be doubted. And maintenance is not likely to serve as an engine of evolutionary change.

Cheetahs will normally hunt anytime in the morning, from early to midday. They need daylight to exploit their running power.[25] One would assume that a cheetah would prefer to hunt early in the morning or late in the afternoon and bypass the heat of the middle of the day. But other factors seem to be more decisive. In areas frequented by tourists, the cheetahs increasingly hunt at midday, when most tourists are off the plains.[26] Moreover, at midday, the lions and hyenas are sleeping — or should be — and the cheetah has less reason to fear their banditry. And the heat helps to dull the senses of the game.

The photographer is likely to find the cheetah sitting or lying with an authentic regal air and staring well into the distance *(113 & 114)*. The cat, assuming it allows the safarist to approach nearby, always seems to be looking past the visitor — indeed, only during a yawn or sleepy doze can the safarist be assured of any real, though still distinctly secondary, attention *(115-117)*. The cheetah has the best vision of all the cats but needs to find movement in the far distance to judge depth accurately. Thus, it must study the panorama stretching before it. Moreover, a cheetah's attitude is not all aristocratic bearing and

---

25. Some observers have reported cheetah hunting on moonlit nights. Others have seen cheetah hunting in the early evening, right after sunset. Although such things no doubt could happen, they hardly represent the norm. Naturalists have also recounted instances of cheetahs abandoning a particular hunt when the intended victims failed to run away, so used to the chase are the felines. The famous painting by George Stubbs that shows a cheetah belonging to King George III being "unhooded" in Richmond Park fails to record that the conveniently located stag pictured nearby failed to flee and the cheetah refused to hunt it. Some predators, especially those who do not scavenge, often need the stimulus of resistance to kill and eat prey animals. Thus, the possum escapes the wolf by playing dead. Risky business, however, for an antelope.

26. Contrary to many complaints, cheetahs can hunt effectively in the presence of tourist vehicles (excepting, of course, moving vehicles actually dogging a stalking cat), which are invariably in the wrong place for a hunt anyway, but the tourists sometimes crowd the cheetahs after their kills and scare the cats off before they are able to eat. Cheetahs are nervous eaters, and whether the human voice (and presence) is especially distracting or the vehicles regarded as just another "predator" arriving to deprive the cheetah of its kill is moot. Some cheetahs tend to be very shy toward safari vehicles and visitors, others very relaxed.

Plates 113 & 114. Cheetah Portrait: Imperial Feline Hauteur. The short muzzle and broad nostrils of cheetahs ensure quick delivery of oxygen to the lungs — of great help to a sprinter, whose peak oxygen demands are high. This cat's whiskers are of little help to an animal who hunts by sight and in daylight.

binocular eyes. In reality, the cheetah has much to think about; as it studies the plains, the cat is very much like a top billiard player who must plan well beyond the next shot and, indeed, worry about the game three or four shots away.

For the cheetah, the hunt and the kill are merely the opening shots. A cheetah will not — cannot — defend its kill against lions, hyenas, wild dogs, and leopards, any of whom may be drawn to the scene by the omnipresent vultures. The author has even seen a pair of jackals harass a feeding cheetah off its kill. Other observers report that aggressive vultures and baboons have had the same effect. Thus, for example, before launching its strike, the cheetah will itself be checking the sky for vultures signaling perhaps the presence of other predators close-by. Nor can the cheetah eat immediately after the kill is made *(118)*. Exhausted by the exertions of the chase, particularly if the day is hot, the hunter has to allow up to

Plates 115 & 116. Cheetahs Lying. A cheetah, despite his aristocratic mien, never projects total self-confidence. One cannot, of course, be positive, but one suspects that cheetahs think (not exactly comforting thoughts) about lions a good deal of the time.

Plate 117. Yawn. A cheetah has far shorter canines than the other big cats, and a yawn hardly disturbs its gentle expression.

half an hour recovery-time before eating.[27] Usually, immediately after the kill, the cheetah will move the carcass to what it considers a safer, more secluded place or to waiting cubs *(119)*. Once started, the meal is taken quickly

Plate 118. Cheetah with Prey. The hunter is cooling off after its sprint but also may still be in the process of strangling its prey. Sometimes, the cheetah's short teeth do not even pierce the antelope's skin.

Plate 119. Returning to the Cubs. A mother with weaned cubs must kill every day. The diurnal cheetah does not scavenge and must have fresh meat. It will not hide its food. Its hunting abilities normally confine it to prey no larger than its own body weight. Thus, the cheetah must hunt more frequently than other predators. Moreover, the hunting chase draws attention to the predator on the open plains, with the result that the cheetah is frequently deprived of its meal by the stronger carnivores. Indeed, with or without cubs, cheetahs often must hunt every day. They seem to do best in semi-arid conditions, where there is little other carnivore competition.

---

27. Strictly speaking, cheetahs do not "tire" — they overheat. Cheetahs cannot run farther than they do because sprinting generates so much heat in their muscles. Body temperature rises to a dangerous 105° F during a 400-yard chase; a higher temperature would cook their brains. The cheetah's respiratory rate more than doubles to supply the oxygen required; panting is not a sign of oxygen deficiency but a means of cooling off. On the other hand, the gazelle does not overheat — it has special cooling mechanisms that will be discussed in Chapter VII — but it does build up an oxygen debt. In many parks, Thomson's gazelles constitute ninety percent of the prey taken by cheetah.

and nervously. Cheetahs bolt their food. A mother eats only sporadically, as she maintains a lookout *(120-123)*. If more than one adult are feeding, one will always remain alert. Even cubs instinctively eat in spurts and stops. *(124-125)* Despite occasional minor disagreements, cheetahs eat in peace among themselves — indeed, compared to lions, they behave like saints. As fastidious as it is about what it eats, the cheetah is nonetheless a messy eater and rarely takes the time to clean a carcass in the way that lions do. Unlike lions or leopards, cheetahs eat only fresh meat. They will not even return at a later point to their own kill seeking a second meal. Whether this behavior is strictly a matter of taste or laced with a strong dose of caution is not exactly clear.

Mating is not usually witnessed; a cheetah mating pair copulate only once or twice a day and remain together but a day or two. The mating pair probably know each other from overlapping territories. Cubs are born year-round; cheetahs have no regular breeding season. Unlike the practice followed by other big cats, the male will sometimes assist in rearing the cubs. The cubs begin life, two to six in a litter, with a blue-gray mane that originates on the back of their heads and continues well down their backs (see the cubs eating in plates *124-128),* which

Plates 120-128. Mother and Cubs Eating. Two sequences of hurried meals. As the reader can determine, cheetah mothers are not at all selfish at the table — mother is as much a sentry as diner. Cheetah meals are never accompanied by the noisy quarreling that lions exhibit at the table.

Plate 129. Young Royalty. The "overcoat" of long, silver-blue hair on this cub has nearly disappeared. The exact purpose of this mantle is unkown. Some scientists have postulated that it gives the young, defenseless cubs crouched in the grass the appearance of a ratel, or honey badger. The latter is a particularly bellicose, fearless, sharp-toothed animal of the weasel family to which the other predators give a wide berth and who indeed has been known to route or re-route hyenas, wild dogs, and others. This mimicry theory is supported by the distribution of the ratel, which concentration is similar to the cheetah's. Others believe that the hair merely serves to provide extra warmth when mother is out hunting and the cubs are left alone and exposed to the cool winds that can quickly spring up on overcast days. Both theories raise as many questions as they purport to answer.

"body fur" gradually disappears with age. Plate *129* is a good portrait of a cub. All cats have a "tear stripe" that runs from the corner of each eye. This feature is most pronounced in cheetahs, as the stripe extends alongside the nose all the way to the mouth. Ultimately, the youngster may grow to seven feet and an average weight of 100 to 130 pounds as an adult. But cheetah-cub mortality is the highest among the big cats — half of all cubs born die before attaining three months of age, and seventy percent is the estimated mortality rate before adulthood. This statistic is a function of disease, malnutrition, and the female's inability to defend her young.[28] To offset this high loss, cheetahs have a much higher rate of reproduction than the other big cats and produce cubs far more frequently (approximately every eighteen months).[29] Mothers regularly move the young cubs about, like antelope mothers and their fawns, to keep the scent of the youngsters from building up and attracting predators. It has been suggested that the mother's high-pitched call, almost a bird-like chirp, to her cubs is also a mechanism for deceiving other predators.

Cubs tend to act like lions in their disregard for safari vehicles and, if the safarist is patient, the cubs will soon forget the vehicle and engage in their own versions of stalk *(130 & 131)*, roughhouse *(132-136)*, and king of the (termite) mound. The games are, however, considerably faster versions, requiring very high shutter speeds to capture — it is not just the adults that turn into blurs on the run. After eating, the cubs and mother engage in an elaborate and prolonged ritual of common preening and cleaning *(137)*. The safarist should notice that, although mother and cub do play together, they do not do so as vigorously as lions and for a much shorter period — life for cheetahs is just a more serious affair *(138)*. Among the carnivores, the cheetah works hardest to teach the juveniles to hunt. The mother will frequently bring a young gazelle or other small antelope that is still alive to her cubs and encourage them to play with it. The cubs frequently forget the object of the game, and mother has to intervene to direct the affair back to its logical conclusion. Eventually, the cubs learn (only too well, from the antelope's perspective) and are able to kill on their own by the end of their first year. The mother usually abandons them at fourteen to sixteen months.

Adult cheetahs are frequently solitary but they may also be found in groups of two, three, and sometimes four.

Plates 130 & 131. Stalking Practice.

28. The author has seen a cheetah mother attack and drive off a lone hyena who had wandered too close to the cat's cubs, but this success must be rare.

29. Some naturalists have extrapolated from the cheetah's exceptionally low breeding success in captivity to postulate a low rate of conception in the wild.

Plates 132-136. *Roughhouse.* Much of cheetah cub play is serious and related to hunting tactics. The cubs need extensive training from their mothers before they can hunt successfully. Cheetah cubs do not play with the reckless abandon of the katzenjammer young lions; as befits cheetah speed, however, the proceedings frequently turn into a blur for the photographer, as one can see in plates *134* and *135* found on the next page.

Plate 137. Preening after a Meal. Cheetahs do not engage in all the grooming that lions do, but, after eating or a rainstorm, a mother and her cubs, each in turn, will go through a thorough preening together, though the cleansing is usually confined to the face and neck. If the vehicle's engine is turned off, the safarist will hear the cheetahs purring at this time. Cheetahs seemingly do not drink as often as other cats and are said frequently to go without drinking for a week or so.

Plate 138. Mother and Cub "Playing." A mother and cub will play together but usually with rather constrained behavior — there is, for example, little of the constant, reckless rubbing of lions. Aristocrats might be expected to behave like this, call it 'affectionate distance,' but the cheetah has more serious concerns as well. In lion country, cheetahs simply cannot afford the insouciance of lions. Cheetahs also cannot afford the slightest injury that might interfere in any way with hunting.

These partnerships are either brothers or mother-and-daughter combinations that have not yet split up. *(139-144)* Questions of territoriality are made more complex with cheetahs because of the vast distances covered. Population density rarely exceeds one cheetah per sixty square kilometers — and is considerably less in marginal environments. "Home ranges" can significantly overlap — the author has, for example, witnessed three different groups operating in reasonable proximity in Ngorongoro Crater. Female cheetahs obviously try to avoid one another. Daughters are, however, permitted to occupy the same ranges as their mothers; young males leave their birth range and probably never return. Nevertheless, male cheetahs will defend their "heartlands" with deadly seriousness. Cheetahs sometimes hunt in pairs, with what appears to be impressive synchronization. One does not know, however, nor is it possible to determine, exactly what mistakes are covered up by sheer blinding speed. On the other hand, a "mistake" is a concept of man's and not much concern to a cheetah. Furthermore, the cats may be behaving more or less independently, quickly taking advantage of each other's efforts. In the Serengeti, cheetahs often migrate for a time with the herds. Cheetah groups are still somewhat shrouded in mystery and not nearly as well studied as lion prides.

The cheetah has none of the menacing mien of the leopard. Even if cornered, he will not attack man. Cheetahs are docile, easily tamed, and make excellent pets (except for the inordinate space and fussy food preferences ideally required). Only a few years ago, it was not uncommon to find them kept as household pets in Kenya among the white settlers. The Mongol leader Kublai Khan, according to Marco Polo, owned thousands. Ancient Assyrians and Egyptian pharaohs earlier and medieval French kings, Indian maharajahs, and Austrian emperors afterwards (all on a lesser scale) have done the same.

Amboseli in Kenya is widely known as cheetah country, and the permanence of Mt. Kilimanjaro in the background lends some credence to the hope that the cheetah lying in its shadow will somehow endure for our children and grandchildren to see *(145)*. But the dice are loaded — poaching, shrinking habitats, stronger and more numerous predators who steal their food and kill their young, hunting limited by darkness and bad weather (and the need to hunt often), the hazards of injury for a lone hunter who depends on speed, high cub mortality, and genetic uniformity that compounds all the other problems — against the cheetah.

Plates 139-144. Brothers. The cheetah stands somewhere between the lion, on the one hand, and the leopard, on the other, in terms of sociability. All females ultimately split off from any grouping and remain solitary. What look like "adult" groupings are either (i) young sisters, (ii) male brothers, or (iii) a mother and her older cub(s) before splitting up. A mother and daughter may remain together longer than normal or may briefly reunite under certain circumstances. Occasionally, male littermates will live together permanently. The pairs and the threesome pictured here are all brothers, a fact not discernible from the photographs but noted by the author at the time. The boys in plate *143* are annoyed with themselves: they have just lost a hare down a hole. The pair in plate *144* are attempting to hide from the photographer.

(the lost hare)

Plate 145. Cat of Kilimanjaro. One reason for the solitary nature of cheetahs is that the increased visibility associated with a group and group-living would definitely not serve the interests of the weaker cheetah vis-à-vis other predators. Cheetah density rarely rises above one to sixty square miles and is more like one to 150 square miles in marginal environments.

V. Other Noteworthy Hunters and Scavengers

The sight of the jackal had brought to mind the scarcely comforting speculation that in Africa there is never any waste. Death particularly is never wasted. What the lion leaves, the hyena feasts upon and what scraps remain are morsels for the jackal, the vulture, or even the consuming sun.

Beryl Markham, *West with the Night*[1]

Smaller Cats

Among the smaller cats found in Africa, the alert safarist is most likely to see a **serval**, a beautiful animal who looks like some domestic cats, though it is larger than the normal house cat and has a sharply pointed muzzle instead of the usual flat cat face. A pale yellow-buff or tawny color, its black spots run together into stripes on its back, shoulders, neck, and tail (*1 & 3*). Servals stand on long legs some twenty to twenty-two inches at the shoulder, grow to about three-and-a-half feet in length (with tail), and weigh some thirty-five pounds. In common with all small cats, its pupils are slit or elliptical in appearance when contracted and not rounded as are a large cat's. The most distinguishable characteristic is, however, a set of oval oversized ears. These ears, almost clown-like in size and appearance, are the key to understanding how the serval hunts and, as a predator, survives.

The visitor will undoubtedly see the serval — *if* he does find one; there are no guarantees, and a sighting is a rare treat — hunting in thick grass, where it is well concealed *(2)*. Indeed, all the small African cats spend much of their lives hunting, far more than their large relatives. A serval (called "mondo" in Kiswahili) is also an incredibly patient predator: the author has watched more than one serval stand "frozen" for up to thirty minutes or more in the tall grass, apparently just staring into the tangled depths ahead *(3)*. But the little cat, though he has the excellent eyesight common to all felines, is not looking so much as listening. As befits the relative size of his auditory equipment, he can hear virtually anything worth hearing — like the vibrations of a rodent's shudder, according to some

Plate 1. Serval Dozing. Servals are said to be mainly nocturnal but they can be found in some areas hunting during the early morning and late afternoon. Small nocturnal carnivores generally seem to have high metabolic rates and thus forage extensively.

1. At p. 23.

Plate 2. Superb Camouflage. Servals frequent well-watered habitats of grass savannahs, river beds and swamps, bush and open woodlands, and forest edges.

Plate 3. Listening. The smaller cats have a well-deserved reputation for viciousness and are almost impossible to tame. Their constant hunting obviously keeps them more wound up than their larger relatives. A serval feeds primarily on birds, rodents, and hares. The cat can climb well, and many servals hunt regularly in the trees, where they exhibit extraordinary balance. A serval kills by a deep neck bite.

experts.[2] If the safarist looks closely, he will notice that, although the serval at these times stands perfectly still, the ears will frequently rotate — they are, in fact, capable of turning nearly 360°.[3]

One sometimes sees a serval executing a series of very agile and seemingly choreographed leaps through tall grass. Some observers have stated that the serval leaps to improve his field of view — that is, to see over the tall grass. This conclusion is incorrect; what the serval is supposedly looking for he has already heard, *under* the grass, and the view is no better, and possibly worse, several feet in the air looking down rather than on the ground staring forward. Actually, the serval is flushing his game, forcing his intended meal to move. The process is both fascinating to watch — the leaps are organized in a tight little circle — and skillfully efficient.

The serval will also climb to search out nests and will augment his diet of small mammals with an occasional egg, fledgling, or full-grown bird. Sometimes, the young of the smallest antelopes provide a meal.

The other prevalent small cat, though less common than the serval, is the **caracal** or African or Desert lynx, a sleek, golden brown cat that sports even more spectacular looking ears than a serval, with long black hairs on their tips. The caracal (called "simba kali" or "simba mangu" in Kiswahili, which translates to fierce lion; "caracal" itself means "black-eared" in Turkish) is one of the few unpatterned cats. The author has seen a few caracals but has never photographed any. Caracals, who weigh up to thirty-five pounds or more, are also nimble jumpers and frequently hunt by jumping into the middle of a flock of birds and knocking them down as they fly up. Like some quick-shot artist of the Old West, a caracal can perform the remarkable feat, leaping as high as six feet straight up, of knocking several birds out of the air from the same flock by using its dexterous forepaws. Some reports have the agile cat killing as many as ten birds in a second or two. In addition to being very ferocious, a caracal is fast

2. Sounds are essentially vibrations in the air. Animals detect them through delicate membranes that respond to the moving air. The vibrating membranes in turn send signals to the brain. A cat's ears, like all mammalian ears, are very complex, but mammals that use their ears for hunting often have large "flaps," or outer ears (called pinnas), that act as a funnel guiding as much sound as possible down the ear canal to the ear drum itself (one of the membranes). The human ear is so sensitive that we can detect sound waves having an energy of only one ten-quadrillionth of a watt. A serval's hearing is so perceptive that it probably picks up the 'background' noise of molecules colliding in the air, though there is no way of knowing what (if anything) the cat's brain selects out to ignore.

3. Further confirmation of a leopard's incredible stealth, if such corroboration were needed, is provided by the fact that leopards will occasionally kill a serval (one may rest assured that no serval would loiter or vacillate long if he knew that a leopard were near).

enough easily to outrun a small gazelle.

Servals are found in the bushy cover of marsh areas or close to streams and lakes, caracals in dry desert country. Both are predominantly nocturnal but occasionally hunt in early morning or late afternoon. One of the more entertaining stories of African folklore, as related by Hallett,[4] concerns the origin of the small cats (and some other smaller carnivores). According to legend, Madame Leopard and her family once met a lady python in the forest. The leopardess was proud of her handsome cubs but complained bitterly that they were very difficult to manage. The python smugly replied that she simply laid her eggs and left the hatchlings to fend for themselves. The envious cat decided to try out the python's system; she went to her cave, deposited a clutch of eggs, and then departed. Returning some months later to check on the progress of her grand experiment, she was horrified to discover a caveful of starving, stunted cubs. For their part, the cubs were just as surprised at their first glimpse of the large cat and exploded from the cave in all directions to become servals, genets, civets, caracals, wildcats, African golden cats, and whatnots. Unaccountably (assuming that the tale makes sense to this point), the story progresses, leopards continue to lay eggs every other year, just to keep up the population of the lesser cats.

Civets and Mongooses

Civets are frequently referred to as cats and do exhibit many cat-like characteristics but, technically, they belong to another family (Viverrids). The most commonly encountered civet is the **genet** *(4)*,[5] a solitary woodland or forest animal[6] that safarists are likely to find around the mountain lodges or forest stations. The genet pictured, with nighttime eyes that look like soulless buttons, is the Large-spotted or Bush variety, which is both nocturnal and arboreal (descending to the ground only for breeding or to catch certain prey). Several species of genets (all called "kanu" or "fungo" in Kiswahili) live in Africa, all sleek and slender like the Large-spotted. Their diets run from insects, snakes, and lizards to rodents and birds. Although they are basically predatory, they also eat fruit. The author has watched a genet hunting roosting birds loose its grip and fall a considerable distance to the ground, landing with cat-like agility and without being injured (though no doubt thoroughly disgusted with itself) *(5)*. Very rarely, one sees an all-black genet, a melanistic mutation that also occurs in leopards and servals.

Plate 4. Large-spotted Genet. This genet was found outside The Ark, a mountain lodge for nocturnal viewing located in the Aberdares in Kenya. Genets can be found near most Tree Hotels; aside from the free scraps, they are quite fond of the moths that flutter around the lights and eventually fall exhausted to the ground.

---

4. *Animal Kitabu*, pp. 41-2.

5. Most writers treat the genet and civet as separate members of the same family. The author favors the minority classification of viewing a genet as another kind of civet.

6. The so-called Common genet is, however, found in open dry savannah.

Genets have incredibly supple bodies and can follow their heads through virtually any opening. The tourist should be careful when feeding the "pet" genets that sometimes come into the mountain lodges at night. Sharp teeth and powerful little jaws greet any culinary misunderstandings. Genets "spit" and growl like cats when angered.

Plate 5. The Question of Classification. The Large-spotted genet can be most easily distinguished from the Small-spotted, or Neumann's, variety by the dark tip on the former's tail. The rings in a Small-spotted genet's tail continue to the end. Telling a Large-spotted genet from a so-called Forest genet is another (virtually impossible) matter. Fortunately for the interested safarist, the latter lives primarily in West Africa. Classification of African mammals is often a complicated and debatable affair. The classification of many species is best regarded as tentative.

Plate 6. Banded Mongooses. Mongooses are famed for their snake-killing, but the belief that mongooses hunt mainly snakes is fallacious. In fact, snakes play a small part in a mongoose's life. Moreover, the hypothesis that mongooses are immune to snake venom is also apparently mistaken — the success of the mongoose, as Kipling himself noted, is due to lightning speed and accuracy (and thick fur) — though there is evidence that the suricate, or meerkat, a member of the mongoose family found in Southern Africa, has developed a degree of immunity to venom.

The **mongoose** is a member of the same family. Fabled in the Kipling story, ''Rikki-Tikki-Tavi,'' the brave little mongoose (''kicheche'' — plural: ''vicheche'' — or ''nyangau,'' or even ''nguchiro'' in Kiswahili) is found in many parts of the world. Worldwide, there are some forty different kinds. The six species most common to East Africa are the Banded, Dwarf, Slender or Black-tipped, White-tailed, and Marsh. The Banded mongoose, brownish-gray with conspicuous stripes across its back *(6),* and the smallest species, the Dwarf, sometimes called Pigmy, which is a dark reddish-brown and weighs but twelve ounces as an adult *(7),* live in large colonies or troops of thirty or more. The Dwarf troops do, however, tend to contain fewer members than the Banded mobs. The troops also seem to be organized along matriarchal lines. Both inhabit old abandoned termite mounds or ant-hills, rock crevices, and hollow trees. One troop may have a range as large as seventy-five acres, though the area will overlap with the ranges of neighboring troops. A

troop may use twenty or more termite mounds as den sites, bolt holes, and sentry posts. Diurnal, they are driven by insatiable appetites to forage during much of the day. By sunset, all have returned to their den where they pass the night. If two troops meet during the day, the safarist is likely to witness a pitched battle.

Mongooses are great fun to watch, as they pop out of their warrens, looking very much like the gaggle of clowns in the circus that magically climb from the little car, one by one, in apparently endless profusion. They scurry off, toe-to-tail in tight formation, resembling for all the world some huge snake, in search of food, whether that be the dung beetles and millipedes found in elephant and buffalo droppings, other insects, snakes, lizards, rodents, bird eggs, fledglings, or fruit. The mongoose is, in fact, virtually omnivorous and at heart an opportunist. Although they move as a group, generally led by a dominant breeding pair (usually, the oldest),[7] troop members normally find their food individually and do not really hunt cooperatively. Two individuals do, however, sometimes pair off and search the ground methodically together, turning over stones and logs looking for insects. The pair will share the results of their joint effort. Eggs of all kinds are favored by the little viverrid, but its diminutive jaws cannot always handle the larger sizes. The mongoose will then throw these eggs against a rock or another hard surface to crack their shell. If the eggs are too large or unwieldy to be picked up and thrown, the mongoose will toss stones directly at the shells. Such tool-usage is a sign of high intelligence in the animal kingdom. The Banded mongoose is particularly dependent upon the presence of large game, especially elephants, whose dung contains much semi-digested vegetation that in turn supports the big millipedes so desired. The foraging troop among itself is ordinarily amicable, but a good deal of brawling accompanies any meals taken together.[8]

When out and about, the mongooses are noisy — barking, whistling, growling, grunting, chattering in strident, high-pitched voices as they make their rounds. Whether eating or scurrying, the mongoose stops frequently to rise up on its hind legs to check the neighborhood for danger (see plate 7). Mongooses have sharp eyes and a well-developed system of sentries and alarm calls. One or more members of the troop at any given time — and the duty is usually shared among all subadult males — seek out an elevated position from which a sentry can scan the immediate environment while the remainder of the troop feeds. Variations in mongoose warning calls tell the troop whether a predator threatens from the air or from the ground. Danger often drops from the sky, as large raptorial birds frequently find the mongooses in greater profusion and hence easier pickings than other small mammals. Ironically, the sentry often turns out to be the most exposed mongoose and vulnerable to the raptors.

Beyond the early warning systems, mongooses will aid each other in defense against predators; the troop will, in fact, "mob" large predators when frightened and when no burrow or other hiding place is within easy striking distance. Bunching together like an old Macedonian phalanx, the mongooses face the aggressor as might a single, considerably larger animal. The combined biting power of twenty sharp-toothed mongooses acting in unison will cause a jackal or eagle (among others) to think twice about their intended prey.

Thus, the troop, which is flexible in number and always subject to much coming and going of both sexes, frequently displays an advanced social consciousness: efficient division of labor and individually altruistic behavior. Another interesting facet of Dwarf mongoose life that has only recently been reported is also pertinent in this regard. A safarist would never discover such a fact on his own but might recognize the behavior once he knew about it: mongooses often cooperate closely with hornbills in foraging and acting as guards against mutual predators (and even some predators who prey only on the viverrid). This relationship is discussed again in Chapter IX, but, basically, the mongooses flush food for the birds, in return for the hornbill's vigilance.

Both the Banded and Dwarf mongooses care for their young in totally communal fashion: while some adults hunt, others clean, feed, and protect the offspring. The roles change frequently, so that all can eat. The juveniles play rough; the safarist may see the equivalent of a Greco-

Plate 7. Dwarf Mongooses Foraging. It appears that nearly every young male mongoose in the troop takes a turn as lookout, normally lasting no longer than fifteen to thirty minutes, to insure that everyone eats. The safarist who pauses awhile will also see lots of reciprocal grooming and a novel method of drinking — mongooses dip their front paws into water and then lick the moisture off their paws. The mongoose pictured in the forefront here is sitting in a typical "tripod" posture, using its tail for balance. The "toe-to-tail formation" to which reference was made in the text is, functionally, *nose*-to-tail: the scent-gland secretions of one mongoose lead on the next in line, and so on.

---

7. Subordinate pairs mate but seldom produce viable offspring. The dominant pair can produce three litters a year.

---

8. Pliny somewhere picked up the afflatus that mongooses killed adult crocodiles by crawling down the reptile's throat while it was asleep and eating their way out through the stomach wall. One is entitled to wonder whether or not naturalists a thousand years hence will look upon the state of our knowledge with much the same humor that we read Pliny today. The prospect — or certainty — of more than a few guffaws is a sobering thought.

Roman wrestling match. The combatants leap-frog each other, somersault, and lock their mouths together in an attempt to throw the other party.[9] Mongooses habitually find themselves used as the favorite toys of young lions, in games too one-sided and deadly for the mongoose's taste, to be sure, but the courageous little fellow occasionally returns the torment with a very painful and vice-like bite to the nose. What works with a cobra, however, works only a brief time with a lion.

The Slender mongoose is generally solitary and can be recognized by the way that it carries its tail, which is also distinctively black at the tip, curved up like a Ground squirrel. The nocturnal White-tailed is the largest variety, weighing up to eleven pounds, and is often found in the mountain forests. Otherwise grey-brown, it has its own distinctive white shaggy tail. The Marsh variety (called Water mongoose in Southern Africa) has chocolate brown fur and a short tail. It swims well (all mongooses can swim) and feeds mainly on fish, other aquatic animals, and crocodile eggs. Additional varieties — principally, the Yellow or Bushy-tailed, Meller's, Cape Grey, Large Grey or Egyptian, and Selous' — are found in Southern Africa (the Egyptian is seen in East Africa as well). And Madagascar has several fascinating varieties all its own.

All mongooses, which have a lifespan of some eight years, have a musky, pungent odor that the safarist may well pick up at night in the tented camps. Well-developed anal scent glands located under the tail secrete a strong-smelling fluid. Mongooses are murderously difficult to photograph, with all their darting, jerky movements and scurrying about. Moreover, they are difficult to approach at close range. A mongoose's face is always "alert" *(8)*, and it is an excellent photograph that captures a decent portrait of that face.

Hyena

The first thing that should be said about the hyena ("fisi" in Kiswahili) is that the animal is, indeed, much misunderstood. One would be hard pressed to think of a more abused creature. The reader has already read in Chapter III a fair dose of typical vituperation. Thus, a pioneering conservationist of the sensitivity of Carl Akeley could still condemn the hyena as "a filthy villain." Teddy Roosevelt would characterize it as "foul and evil." For years, the commentary never improved: "stinking thief," "a living cemetery," and "a dirty joke on the en-

Plate 8. Mongoose Portrait.

tire animal kingdom." Not surprisingly, Hemingway well expressed the hunter's perspective:

> Highly humorous was the hyena obscenely loping, full belly dragging, at daylight on the plain, who, shot from the stern, skittered on into speed to tumble end over end. Mirth provoking was the hyena that stopped out of range by an alkali lake to look back and, hit in the chest, went over on his back, his four feet and his full belly in the air. Nothing could be more jolly than the hyena coming suddenly wedge-headed and stinking out of high grass by a *donga* [ravine or dry creek bed], hit at ten yards, who raced his tail in three narrowing, scampering circles until he died.[10]

The road back to sanity is a long one. To begin with, the hyena is as much an intelligent and fairly sophisticated hunter as a scavenger. The old image of "cowardly" scavenging from "noble" lions has recently been rehabilitated by fascinating nighttime research that teaches us much new information about a primarily nocturnal animal. Plains animals, hyenas live together in clans of commonly more than thirty and not infrequently as many as eighty or more. They hunt, mostly at night, in packs,

---

9. Such play helps to fine-tune later predatory behavior. A mongoose will lunge at a poisonous snake time and time again, eliciting retaliatory strikes that gradually exhaust the snake. The feints, surely honed in all the play of early life, are purely mock attacks, with no true biting intent. As the snake begins to tire, the mongoose dodges repeatedly to confuse the aim of the reptile and finally maneuvers into a position from which it can deliver a fatal bite to the lower back of the snake's head.

---

10. Ernest Hemingway, *Green Hills of Africa* (Charles Scribner's Sons, 1935), p. 37. Readers who find this paragraph a little extreme would not want to read the one immediately following. Hemingway's son, Patrick, atoned for Papa's itchy trigger-finger by serving as a game warden in Kenya.

though hyenas also can and do hunt alone, depending upon the size of the prey. Moreover, the size of the hunting pack depends very much on the character of the local environment. For example, when game is scarce, the large packs break into smaller groups. Hyenas regularly hunt and kill zebra, wildebeest, topi, and other large antelopes. But the hyena is one of nature's greatest opportunistic hunters — a sort of predatory goat — and, in the words of their closest observer (Kruuk), nothing between a termite and a buffalo is completely safe so long as hyenas, either alone or in groups, forage the plains.

At the same time, scientists believe that hyenas, at least occasionally, actually decide beforehand exactly what is to be the prey that night — one naturalist has described, for example, a recognizable 'zebra ritual' undertaken before the pack sets out — and stick to that decision regardless of the availability of other game. Concerning the zebra example at least, it seems more reasonable to the author that certain larger hyena clans have simply come to specialize in zebra hunting. Unlike other herds that tend to wind up strung out when fleeing hyenas, a zebra herd remains in a tight bunch for a considerable distance, with a dangerous stallion periodically attacking the pursuers. A mere half dozen hyenas may take out after a wildebeest herd, but a dozen or more are required to bring down a zebra. The so-called ritual could serve the same function as the wild dogs' pre-hunt ceremony: to excite the members present to reach a level of enthusiasm (and concentration) worthy of tackling large game.

In fact, the precision attributed to hunting lion prides is far more accurately employed in describing the work of hyenas, though there is still enough confusion and conflict to separate the hyena from the wild-dog packs (which last are truly organized group hunters).[11] Hyenas pick out a victim — usually, a single hyena or a pair will charge a herd once or even several times for the purposes of observation; something (which does *not* invariably appear to be sickness or another infirmity) about one member of the herd will attract attention and mark it as the target — and relentlessly run it down. Single-mindedly, the hyenas will stay with the original selection. They can run (at a fast lope, actually) for many miles at speeds approaching 40 mph, a pace that would leave a lion or leopard behind relatively early and even lose a cheetah after a mile or so. Some of the hyenas chase directly behind a herd; others 'cut the corner,' on both sides, in anticipation of the prey turning to the left or right. Few intended meals actually outrun hyenas — most animals that do escape (and the odds are not good) do so by crossing over into another clan's inviolate (usually) territory. This would be dicey strategy on the hunted's part, were it done purposely —

of course, it is done unknowingly — a bit like the bank robbers on the lam crossing the Rio Grande in a grade-B Western movie. Just as a relentless posse might keep right on going, one can also bet on hungry hyenas occasionally at least to break the rules. Then, it helps to recall the ending to Peckinpah's "The Wild Bunch."[12]

Hyenas attack from the rear, when they catch up with their prey, biting at the flanks and rump and quickly disabling and bringing the animal down. They kill simply by eating, that is, the hyenas begin to feed immediately once their prey is down. The victim eventually dies of bleeding and disembowelment, which gruesome procedure takes a certain amount of time, is frequently noisy, and always more than a little messy. Some naturalists have offered the opinion that the eaten are in a state of shock and do not feel all that much pain. The expression on their faces (at least, those that the author has seen), let alone some of the absolutely piteous noises that they make, would seem to indicate otherwise, but we simply do not know. I am not completely convinced that disemboweling produces the same result (shock) as the canine puncture, say, of the lion.[13] In any event, nervous tour operators welcome the fact that hyenas do most of their

---

11. The sheer numbers of and accompanying hunger within some hyena packs undoubtedly makes fancy coordination a little problematical.

12. The simile holds pretty well when the inevitable commotion of a kill rouses the resident hyenas — a frequent event. The appearance of the residents is often sufficient to send the invaders scurrying home, abandoning the uneaten or partly eaten carcass. Hunger can, however, lead to problems. As indicated in the text, crossing the border under normal circumstances is unusual; hyenas vent their aggression mostly by calling, displaying, and chasing one another around the borders without physical contact. If an invading group strays any serious distance into another clan's territory and hesitates to yield to the residents, a severe mauling or killing is sure to result.

13. The author is aware of research that would appear to prove that hyenas are, on average, more efficient killers — in terms of the time lapsed — than lions, leopards, or cheetahs, the so-called 'clean-killers.' Several writers have also remarked on the failure of the prey to struggle or attempt to escape, once hyena eating has begun. And the suggestion has followed that such acquiescence (attributed to shock) speeds up the killing process, in addition to being an evolutionary adaptation that, though sacrificing the individual, is good for the species. That is, if a prey animal managed to escape with these early wounds, it would only fall easy prey at a later time, in the interim consuming valuable food that could be used by unwounded, healthy individuals of the same species. Such convoluted logic apparently assumes that (temporarily) unsuccessful predators skip meals. In reality, the grass consumed would remain the same; if animal A were to escape, animal B would soon be eaten. In addition, given the maintenance function of predation on this level (already discussed in the last chapter), it would be more logical for evolution to encourage the selected prey — presumably chosen for some 'failure' in design or experience — to give up immediately once the chase has begun. But the author seriously doubts that evolutionary theory need be interposed this way into what seems obviously and simply an efficient way to kill.

hunting and killing under cover of darkness. The hyena has many traits that are more than suitable for tracking animals at night, including very sharp senses — keen hearing, eyesight, and sense of smell. Perhaps equally important, the hyena has an unusual determination, for which it is difficult to find even remote comparisons in nature.[14] The author has, for instance, seen a hyena race into the water and kill flamingoes before they could take off. I have also seen hyenas chase wildebeest into the water (the wildebeest no doubt thought that it was escaping) and begin feeding right there. On the other hand, there is also little question that a hyena functionally is built to be a scavenger. What has obviously happened over a great many years is that the unreliability of depending upon other carnivores (and natural causes), year in, year out, to leave enough behind has forced the hyena to hunt on its own. The proportion of time today actually devoted to hunting, as opposed to scavenging, varies according to local environmental factors.

As just stated, the average tourist will not see hyenas hunting. As also suggested, many tourists will probably not miss the gory drama. But the tourist has to learn to respect nature as he finds it; the predator-prey relationships of the African plains must be taken on their own terms and not overly weighed down by man's unrelated judgments and sensibilities. Unfortunately, popular attitudes toward a carnivore often turn on the method of killing its prey. Thus, the poor hyena stands to lose quickly its newly won respect as a hunter. But feeding is one of the basic features of all living things. A hyena disemboweling a zebra is engaged in the same function as a zebra cropping grass. And predation itself is not confined to large, 'fierce' animals. The song thrush hammers snails on a stone, the bee-eater uses a similar procedure on a bee, and robins pull worms from the ground. Ladybirds munch aphids. The basic process extends beyond the land, high into the air and deep into the oceans. Animals everywhere essentially use their natural tools to catch their normal food. Moreover, weeding out the weakest prey individuals and thus maintaining (or improving) the vigor of each new generation cannot be anything but beneficial in nature's scheme.

Accordingly, the author urges those who are able to do so to participate in nighttime game drives and also be prepared very early in the morning and late in the afternoon to follow the telltale hunting hyena — loping at speed, head held high, ears cocked forward, and tail up. At the very least, the safarist should imagine the hyena hunting as he watches a single hyena or small group travel during the day. And the safarist should be cognizant of the constant and subtle interplay that exists between hyenas and lions. He must recognize the fact that hyenas suffer far more from the banditry of lions than the reverse.

When the safarist comes upon lions finishing up at an early morning kill, with several hyenas warily circling the carcass, the odds are fair that the hyenas made the initial kill.

Only rarely, in fact, do hyenas actually reverse the process. Even in groups, hyenas will generally avoid directly challenging a single mature lion — almost never a large male and only slightly more frequently a single lioness. Hyenas are well aware that one swipe from those massive paws could easily snuff out a hyena life. And lions make no attempt to hide their sincere hatred for hyenas (when a lion occasionally happens to catch a hyena, the big cat is positively savage in its treatment, killing or mutilating the hyena without hesitation; and most lions will not eat a hyena that they have killed, a unique — for lions — policy). What usually happens is that hyenas will harass eating lions simply by their presence and, when the number of hyenas increases to the point when the harassment outweighs the remaining appetite, some lions simply pack it in, more out of disgust than fear. Obviously, the more hyenas present (and the total invariably increases as the minutes tick by — hyenas always call for help when confronting lions at a kill) relative to the aggregate of lions feeding at the carcass is an important psychological factor to both sides, the hyenas becoming more bold, the lions more inclined to yield. The truth is, the lions have the lion's share of respect in this on-going war of nerves. By comparison, a single hyena will ordinarily experience little problem in chasing off a leopard or a whole cheetah family. Nature does, however, reward the hyenas with the absolutely final word: old lions, especially those weakened by disease and starvation, are killed and eaten by hyenas.[15]

Objectively, hyenas also deserve respect for their scavenging function: they are, as asserted earlier, superbly fashioned for this task. In particular, the hyena's massive jaws and teeth are among the strongest in nature. Parenthetically, it is, in fact, an extremely unlucky tortoise who lies in the path of a hungry adult hyena. The latter will crack the tortoise shell the way that a macaw cracks a nut — pop! Hyenas can crack bones for the purpose of extracting the rich marrow lying within or crush them into digestible fragments. Moreover, the hyena's stomach and specialized digestive system can apparently digest virtually anything and extract whatever nutrients that might exist. Hyenas reject only horns, jaw bones, certain parts of a skull, and hooves. (9) Completely indigestible items are regurgitated as pellets. The hyena's droppings are little more than white powdery calcium. Because the animals of the same clan usually use a common spot for defecating over a long period of time, the watchful safarist will

---

14. Ancient Egyptians are reputed to have eaten the hyena's heart to gain courage.

---

15. The author several years ago saw what must be a very unusual sight: hyenas and a (young) lion actually, albeit uneasily, sharing a carcass. As inevitably happens when one spends a great deal of time on the plains, I had run out of film and could not record the event. I have never seen this again.

Plate 9. Hyena 'Trophy.' There is little left that the hyena can use. Hyenas, in the author's experience, except those found in Ngorongoro Crater, are normally elusive and wary of man. They are sometimes seen along roads, because they use the culverts that lie beneath the roads as dens. The hyena is more closely related to a cat than a dog but closer still to the viverrids. Interestingly enough (and logically, as well), hyenas seem to compete more vigorously among themselves at the scavenged meal than over carcasses provided by cooperative hunting. The point should not be exaggerated: scavenging, particularly if the meat has been looted from lions, often takes numbers and cooperation, and the large size of some hunting troops encourages more frenzy than respect.

discover telltale white patches on the ground.

Furthermore, hyenas waste little time feeding. A dozen hyenas will, if unimpeded, reduce a large antelope to a head and backbone within fifteen to twenty minutes! Another twenty minutes will permit the crushers to deal with the bones as well. Even the blood on the ground is cleaned up by hungry *fisi.* As it turns out, the voracious hyenas are the best housekeepers on the African plains, and most animals there at one time or another pass through their bowels. Not even the ubiquitous vultures are as thorough. Most safarists will still react adversely to the hyena; as we shall discuss, the animal naturally attracts little sympathy. But "hating" the hyena is about as pointless as hating the municipal garbage collectors; the game parks (and the city) would be unbearable without them.

Hyenas basically prefer to scavenge singly but will call for others if a carcass is found still populated by lions. The individual will also bury or cache excess food like a squirrel. Hyenas occasionally hide surplus meat underwater — hyenas enjoy wading in water — presumably to hide the scent of decaying carrion from other scavengers. It should also be noted that hyenas are one of the very few African animals liable to cause real danger to a man walking alone at night. They sometimes come into camp after dark, usually to raid the garbage, and will even attempt (though rarely) to go into a tent. A safarist staying in a tented camp should always therefore keep to the lit paths and retire with his tent well-zipped and fastened.

Having given the animal its due, I must admit that the common misunderstanding surrounding the hyena is quite understandable. The hyena, to man's eye, is a truly repulsive creature. And this reaction is not just typical anthropomorphism by tourists.[16] Africans themselves have long felt the same: local legend holds that the hyena acts as a carrier of witches on moonlit nights. To call someone "fisi" is a particularly strong African insult. Even in repose, the poor hyena looks like the devil's handiwork (*10*). In form, the animal is an ugly cross between a dog and a cat. Its sloping back, muscular shoulders, and massive head give it a misshapen symmetry (*11*). The hyena also has a generally scruffy look, which appearance its haphazard grooming (at best) and love for the mudhole (the most handy relief from the biting flies) hardly improve (*12 & 13*). Moreover, unless the female is nursing, it is virtually impossible superficially to distinguish males from females (even when they are cubs), as the females have mimic male genitalia — the basis for the African legend (itself echoed by ancient writers as old as Aristotle) that the hyena is a hermaphrodite who can change its sex at will. In fact, females tend to be somewhat larger than males (on the average, about ten percent larger).

In addition to its unattractive bodily appearance, the hyena sports a more or less cringing demeanor and

---

16. The hyena has never had an easy time of it. Pliny the Elder in his *Natural History* stated that hyenas were the only animals that dug up graves in search of corpses. Sir Walter Raleigh believed that God excluded hyenas from Noah's Ark, because they were hybrids, not purebred. After the flood (Raleigh still), hyenas again appeared, however, through the unnatural union of a dog and a cat.

Plate 10. Time Off. Even sleeping, the hyena looks as if it possesses some kinky secret. Adults weigh from eighty up to as much as 190 pounds.

Plates 12 & 13. Beauty Mask. Hyenas scarcely pass a day without wallowing in mud.

Plate 11. Beauty Contestant? The Spotted hyena is the species that most tourists will see. The hyena at its best looks like an unmade bed.

positively slinks about when it moves. This ungainly, slouching gait, coupled with furtive glances in every direction and what always looks like a salacious smile on eye contact, add up to the mannerisms of some gangster leaving the scene of a crime. The typical hyena raises the suspicion of what the criminal law calls "probable cause" just by putting in an appearance. Moreover, hyenas have a way of arriving from nowhere, suddenly issuing from the very heat and dust themselves, to converge from all sides on a carcass. The proverbial bad fairy (or, if one prefers, highway patrol) could not answer a summons any better.

If the hyena looks ugly and acts offensively, how does it sound? Worse. Scientists have catalogued at least eleven different noises, some would say seventeen, each more repulsive than the last. Aside from the familiar whooping cry that often fills the night on the plains and carries for several miles, the safarist will most likely hear the maniacal chatter at the kill, the high-pitched "laughing" cacophony that sounds more like a series of demented giggles. Another common noise heard at kills is what Lewis Carroll had in mind in the "Jabberwocky" when he invented the word "chortle," namely, a combination of chuckle and snort. In general, the deeper sounds are those of aggression; fear is expressed by sharp, distinct noises; and prolonged screams are usually a sign of recognition among members belonging to the same clan.

The average visitor will probably receive his best look at hyenas as they feed on a carcass, in ravenous competition with each other, the vultures, and the jackals (*14 & 15*). Most first-timers are quite unprepared for the incredible din and gruesome competition that ensues when the lions abandon a carcass to the waiting scavengers. Not to spoil its nasty image, the hyena, who may itself consume up to fifty pounds in the best carnivore tradition, has simply revolting eating habits, distributing blood and gore everywhere before it finally cleans up. Although hyenas do not squabble over a kill among themselves quite in the manner of lions, they do take advantage of every opportunity to better their consumption. One member is always wrenching off a leg or other chunk and trotting off to eat alone, followed by one or two companions who are determined to retrieve the prize. Such contests are,

Plates 14 & 15. Hyena and "Friends" at the Kill. Strangely enough, hyenas co-exist at the table rather peaceably with wild dogs, though predation of wild-dog cubs by hyenas is thought by some to be a major impediment to the dog population.

however, remarkably civil, and real fighting is extremely rare. Soon, the prey is literally torn to pieces, and the hyenas have scattered in all directions. Scavenger or hunter, hyenas definitely prefer to eat in semi-solitude and not side-by-side.

In mixed groups of scavengers, the contests between the jackals and hyenas present offer high comedy:

> After a time, most of the jackals moved off a few yards and lay down, except for Captain, who circled around and came slowly, almost nonchalantly in behind the feeding brown. The hyena freed a length of springbok leg, laid it at her feet, and continued to feed on the softer parts near the ribs. Lowering himself on wiry legs, Captain crept closer and closer to the unsuspecting brown hyena, until he was crouched with his nose to her rear. Still she continued to feed, unaware. Slowly he raised his muzzle to the base of the brown's flicking tail; he held it there for several seconds. Then, as the tail moved aside, he bit the hyena on the backside. She whirled to her left and Captain dashed to the right, seizing the springbok leg and a large swatch of dangling skin. It was almost more than he could carry, but by holding his nose high in the air he could run — and run he did.

> Hair streaming, her jaws open wide near the tip of Captain's tail, the hyena chased him in great circles across the riverbed. Whenever it seemed he was about to be swallowed up, Captain would make a turn too sudden for the lumbering hyena to follow. On he ran, his muzzle sagging lower and lower with his heavy loot, until finally he dropped it. Panting

heavily, he watched the hyena carry it back to the carcass. Once again the brown laid the leg at her feet and began to feed.

> Little more than two minutes later, Captain was back, sneaking up on the hyena again. It looked like an instant replay: Captain chomped the brown in the rear, stole the springbok leg and fled, his tail flying, with the hyena in hot pursuit. But this time he escaped into the bush at the edge of the riverbed.[17]

One especially grisly aspect of hyena life is a limited amount of cannibalism among adults. In the confusion of a crowded chase and also during a feeding mêlée, one hyena may be accidently bitten by an overzealous colleague. Or a hyena may be wounded by the prey itself. If the wound is serious enough, other hyenas may devour the injured animal. This practice is basically 'passive' cannibalism and seems to be more or less aberrant behavior brought on by stress. Again, such an event is not at all that common, though writers tend to exaggerate the incidence.[18]

---

17. Mark & Delia Owens, *Cry of the Kalahari*, p. 68. Equally amusing is the panic of the jackal who has succeeded in lifting a scrap from under a lion's nose only to find himself running like mad from a queuing hyena (and trying frantically at the same time to gulp down the morsel before he is forced to drop it).

18. A small group of 'experts' have written that seriously wounded hyenas are capable of drawing out and devouring their own protruding entrails, thereby killing themselves. This tale has more in common with the wisdom of Hemingway than science.

Plates 16 & 17. Hyena Cubs. Hyena cubs prove the point that *all* babies are irresistible.

Despite the alleged transgressions of the adult hyena, it is difficult *not* to be captivated by the young hyena cubs. (*16 & 17*) They are born furry and black and grow lighter coats and develop more prominent spots after ten weeks or so. For reasons not fully understood, hyenas have relatively poor reproductive success; they mate no more frequently than every couple of years — in a typically awkward, haphazard, and feisty fashion — and normally produce but two cubs. Rarely, a third or fourth cub is born, only to die quickly, as the females have only two teats for nursing. Again for reasons not totally understood, one of the cubs in a two-cub litter will also probably die. One possible explanation is that the intense competition of adults begins early and one cub usually develops at the expense of another. And, to make survival even more difficult, hyenas are also cannibalistic: every adult male in a clan poses an active threat to all the young cubs present. This behavior may be contrasted with the passive cannibalism previously noted.

About two weeks after birth, the mother will deposit the cubs in the communal den — usually a subterranean home of complicated burrows webbed by tunnels. Young hyenas develop slowly. Cubs nurse until they are eighteen months old and fully half as large as their mother. Unlike care within the lion pride, no communal nursing is practiced. Adults do not carry food back to the den, as some cats would do, nor regurgitate for the young, as some dogs would. Just when young hyenas actually join the hunt is a matter of controversy — some researchers say when the youngsters are several months old; others state one year. At any rate, the females, who control the kill, see that the cubs who are big enough to reach a kill site eat. Why then the cubs nurse for so long and whether milk or meat is their dietary mainstay after six months or so are not easy questions to answer. A logical theory argues that, were the young cubs fed entirely on meat, the stronger cubs would dominate their weaker siblings, taking the intra-litter competition to another level, with perhaps even higher mortality among the young resulting. According to this hypothesis, the extended dependence on mother's milk thus ensures a higher survival rate among juveniles.

If the safarist comes across the entrance to the den, he will often find the frisky, curious cubs having a look about. Or they may simply be sunning themselves (*18*). During playful moments, as they chase one another around, hyena cubs are as humorous and fun to watch as their feline counterparts.

Actually, three varieties of hyena are found in Africa.[19] The text has focused on the Spotted or "Laughing" hyena. The shaggy-haired Brown hyena, also called Beach or Strand wolf, who does not "laugh," is a rarer, very shy, and purely nocturnal variety found in Southern Africa,

19. The aardwolf (Dutch for "earth wolf") is a hyena-like animal (its Kiswahili name means "lesser hyena," but it is *not* a hyena nor particularly closely related — indeed, its nearest relative might well turn out to be the elephant or hyrax) that has changed its diet to insects, almost exclusively termites; its weak and widely spaced teeth and weak jaw are unsuitable for chewing meat. An animal unique to Africa, it is shy and never seen in daylight. Most Africans and all but a handful of tourists consequently have never seen one. The author has not found an aardwolf in the wild.

Plate 18. Sunbathing at Late Day.

particularly in the Kalahari in Botswana. The Striped hyena, also found in East Africa, is smaller and more of a loner than his more numerous spotted brother. Neither the Brown nor the Striped hyenas do any real hunting; both stick to carrion. One remarkable feature of the Spotted variety, not found in the other two, is the fact that the clan is strongly female-dominated, a real matriarchal society almost unique among mammals. Males do most of the killing — probably because they are the hungriest — but the females control the kill and divide the choicest morsels among themselves and their cubs. The males are positively subservient. Certain females are dominant, chosen we know not how (it does *not* seem to be by fighting or by pure size alone) but apparently passed on from mother to daughter. Moreover, the cubs of dominant females eat first (among cubs) and begin hunting at an earlier age than the others. The existing hierarchy is most obvious at carcasses where the meat and bone are not sufficient to feed all the clan at once. Nevertheless, the point should not be exaggerated: lower-ranking individuals not even in on the kill itself are always gate-crashing the meals.

Hyenas engage in elaborate greeting rituals — one sees a great deal of dog-like sniffing, licking, "grinning" and similar displays, and a number of submissive gestures like crawling and so forth. Not to mention the many different vocalizations. The life of the clan is, in fact, a somewhat complicated affair. A fair amount of ritualized (not deadly) fighting is included as well. As previously stated, more lethal activity takes place at the borders of adjoining clans; the females are fiercely territorial, and female hit-squads patrol and scent-mark a clan's borders. The rigidity of territories depends, however, upon the availability of game and how far the hyenas must travel to eat.

Females, of course, also guard the dens and the young (*19*), an equally serious matter; for extra safety, dens are usually located in the center of a particular clan's territory. Despite all this organization, a degree of shifting loyalties and coming and going exists between neighboring clans. Hyenas in this respect probably exhibit far more flexibility than lions. But, like lions, the males almost always wind up in clans different from those in which they were born.

Hyenas live approximately twenty-five years. The best

Plate 19. The Sentinel. The shrill shrieks, the yells, groans, gurgling, Wife-of-Bath chortles, and wild peals of maniacal laughter are all a memory — and all lie ahead. Only the young and the nursing mothers sleep in the communal dens.

Plate 20. Black backed Jackal. The jackal is a cunning and resourceful carnivore, closely resembling a dog or a lean wolf. The Black-backed variety is the most common East African jackal and is also widespread in Zimbabwe. The fruit-eating Side-striped cousin is more nocturnal, larger, and predominately coastal in orientation.

places to study the Spotted hyena are Ngorongoro Crater and the Serengeti in Tanzania. Behavior does vary significantly, however, depending upon which of these differing environments is chosen.

Jackals

Joining the hyenas at most kills are jackals, small coyote-like carnivores standing some eighteen inches at the shoulders, with long bushy tails, and weighing about twenty pounds. In the author's experience, the most commonly seen type is the Black- or Silver-backed, easily identified by the silver-streaked black saddle running from the neck to the tail (*20*). Relatively common as well is the Golden jackal (*21*), which is also found in Asia. A third type is the Side-striped, rarely seen by tourists. All three species overlap, to the best of the author's knowledge, only in Ngorongoro Crater. The jackal is a brave scavenger — not at all fitting the cowardly stereotype popularly ascribed to the word and much maligned in literature[20] — in the face of competition

20. The reader may recall that the whiny, despised jackal — "Tabaqui, the Dish-licker" — opens Kipling's *Jungle Book;* Tabaqui, who ran about "making mischief, and telling tales, and eating rags and pieces of leather from the village rubbish-heaps." Churchill, always handy with imagery at least theoretically lifted from the natural world, was fond of referring to Mussolini as a jackal: "This whipped jackal, who, to save his own skin, has made of Italy a vassal state of Hitler's Empire, is frisking up by the side of the German tiger with yelps not only of appetite — that could be understood — but even of triumph." (House of Commons Speech, April 1941).

Plate 21. Golden Jackal. Golden (also called Common) jackals seem to dominate the Black-backed variety when both are present at a carcass. The Golden prefers arid country and is rarely found below northern Tanzania. The bird in the background here is a Yellow-faced Egyptian vulture.

either overwhelmingly brawny or present in far greater numbers. The jackal makes do by patience and a series of lightning-quick mad-dashes for a scrap of meat or a bone. (22 & 23) Watching jackals work the edges of a kill is always a rewarding pursuit, definitely worth an hour of a safarist's time, as they test the patience and alertness of the larger carnivores. Competition with vultures (24 & 25)

Plate 22. Ambition. While his partner waits, no doubt a bit skeptical, a Golden jackal attempts to pull from the fray a large — rather too large for a jackal, who needs to preserve the utmost mobility — chunk of meat and hide.

Plates 24 & 25. The Competition Gathers. In these pictures, vultures (Egyptian, White-backed, and Rüppell's) and jackals, both a Golden and a Black-backed, have gathered at the edges of a kill to contest the outlying scraps. When scavenging, unlike hunting, jackals never cooperate; they squabble.

Plate 23. A More Realistic Prize. The jackal's playbook of stratagems would rival that of the most creative offensive coach in the National Football League.

Plate 26. Tug-of-War — Reprise. In nature, not always known for contests organized according to the Marquis of Queensbury Rules, a tug-of-war at the table is a recognition of equal bargaining power and little desire to strike a bargain. Occasionally, the spoils are physically difficult to divide satisfactorily among all parties.

leads to more direct challenges, oftentimes resulting in a fierce tug-of-war (26).

Jackals also hunt, though most safarists will not see this. In some environments, they may, in fact, hunt more than they scavenge. Indeed, in some locales, scavenging may account for only ten percent of a jackal's food. Thomson's gazelles, hares, dik-diks, rodents, and guinea fowl are the usual prey. Fruit is occasionally eaten, especially the fruit of the balanite tree, which food may serve as a natural "wormer." Highly prized as well by jackals are the afterbirths of wildebeest at calving time. Jackals will, in addition, kill cheetah, leopard, or lion cubs, if they find the cubs alone. Jackals have been observed regularly hunting in pairs, one distracting a mother gazelle, for example, the other going for the fawn,[21] but stories about jackals and cheetahs (or jackals and lions) cooperating in a hunt are products of an overheated imagination. Such tales usually take the form of suggesting that jackals will run into a herd of antelopes and begin barking to gain the attention of the herd, while

the large cat sneaks forward and makes its kill. In fact, cheetah will hunt and kill jackals, if given half an opportunity.

As a general rule, jackals carefully stalk their prey. Sometimes, they act more like hyenas or wild dogs and simply chase the quarry, hoping to wear it down. A Black-backed kills with a throat bite, the Golden by eviscerating its prey. Both species cache their surplus by burying it piece-by-piece over a large area. Presumably, this strategy is designed to foil the other participants in the scavenger sweepstakes.

Jackals ("bweha" or "mbweha" in Kiswahili) may be found almost anywhere — on the plains or in woodlands — on safari. Most active at night, with much howling or yelping at that time, they are often paired. Jackals act much like dogs, and strong bonds develop between males and females; a Black-backed pair frequently stay together for years and perhaps even for life. (27) Both mother and father help to bring up the pups. When the pups are first born, the mother remains with them in the den. The male feeds her by regurgitating partly digested food. Later, the cubs are also fed by regurgitation. Litters normally contain anywhere from one to eight pups — six is a common number. After a week or two in the den, females suckle their young outside standing up. The cubs are weaned at two to three months and at six months are hunting (or scavenging) on their own. Brothers and sisters from prior litters frequently help out in the raising of the young cubs

---

21. While the Black-backed jackal generally hunts in pairs throughout the year, the Golden jackal normally does so only during the whelping season (December through April in East Africa), when the parents are cooperating to feed their offspring. This time is also the rainy season (off and on), when the short-grass plains offer their greatest food abundance.

Plate 27. Jackal Pair at Their Den Entrance. Normally in the animal world, if the male is responsible for a large part in bringing up the young, the sizes of the male and female are nearly equal and the species favors monogamy.

— by standing guard at the den when the parents are absent, bringing back food to cubs and lactating mothers, and babysitting youngsters playing outside the den. Not surprisingly, naturalists call such jackals "helpers."[22] The young jackals are frequently moved to protect them from larger carnivores. A single jackal has been seen chasing away a hyena from a den full of pups by nipping the slower predator in the rear: too fast, too agile, and too motivated under the circumstances for a lone hyena, the jackal would nonetheless ordinarily prefer discretion. More dangerous in many respects are the rains, which flood the dens, drowning young pups or forcing them to the surface, where they may die of exposure on overcast and cold days. Incidentally, jackals have been seen burying their young who die.

Among themselves, jackals are strongly territorial. Not only will the male-in-residence drive off male outsiders, the female will chase away other females who stray onto the family plot. Jackals do not migrate at all. Consequently, a pair, once found, are easy to locate later, years later, if desired.

Colonial Englishmen,[23] the butt of not a few, however malicious, odd stories, imported fox hounds to Africa to introduce that favorite pastime, the fox hunt. (Continuity has to count for something!) The jackal was to be the orthodox quarry. Oscar Wilde, taking a hard look at the inbred, inimitable English country gentleman galloping after a fox, described the spectacle as "the unspeakable in full pursuit of the uneatable." One suspects that even Wilde would have been at a loss for words had he been confronted by the African version. One thinks vaguely of Noel Coward's song, "Mad Dogs and Englishmen." Pity the poor hounds, encountering such a huge variety of strange odors. Predictably, the hunt often ended with a cornered antelope, a warthog at bay, a treed cheetah, or any number of other possible, however unlikely, combinations. But, in the final analysis, the English eccentrics (and their eccentricities) are part of a universal currency, quite immune to ridicule. God-bless! (And Tally-ho!)

Jackals are quite sleek in appearance and certainly do not fit the mongrel-like mold popularly imagined. A "jackal" in a literary sense is a person who does someone else's dirty work. Nothing could be further from the real position assigned by nature to these tough and resourceful little fellows, honorable thieves looking out for themselves in the midst of some pretty tough customers. Jackals are the true "edge-players" — experienced dabblers in danger — of the African bush.

Bat-eared Fox

The Bat-eared, or Delalande's, fox is called "mbweha masikio" in Kiswahili, which means "eared jackal," but he is a true fox (and has, for example, the fox-like vertical eye pupils). Found only in Africa, this is the one fox — there are others in Africa[24] — that the safarist is likely to see. Classified as a carnivore, the alert Bat-eared fox does a little scavenging on the side but feeds mostly on insects, principally termites and dung beetles. Like the mongooses who also favor the insects that thrive in the herbivores' dung, the Bat-eared fox is often found near large herds of hoofed mammals and elephants. Mainly nocturnal, the fox appears in the late afternoon beside its burrow to catch the last rays of sun and enjoy the pleasant breezes that

---

22. Scientifically speaking, the "helpers" are not acting altruistically (engaging in behavior costly to themselves but helpful to others), for essentially two reasons. First, the period as "helper" can be viewed as simply a brief but hands-on apprenticeship before reproducing themselves. A helper is accumulating valuable experience in the difficult art of child-rearing. Second, in somewhat simplistic terms, such apparently individual altruism is really a manifestation of genetic 'selfishness.' Helpers in this respect resemble parents: the recipient, who shares a genepool with the samaritan, probably has the same gene for "helping." Thus, the helper is protecting that gene, which happens to be its own gene as well.

23. The same crowd who somehow managed to convince half the developing world of the virtues of hot tea drunk in hot climates; iced drinks, the indoctrination continued, provided only limited refreshment and were best enjoyed during the cool evenings, while seated around a fire.

24. Notably, the Cape or Silver fox, Pale fox, Rüppell's fox, Fennec fox, Sand fox, and Red fox.

blow across the savannah at that time (*28 & 29*). To see the fox reasonably close-up, the safarist must approach him very carefully: too fast or too close and he will pop back down into his subterranean lair. Should he so disappear during late afternoon, the safarist should simply park the vehicle at a respectful distance and wait quietly. He will soon come back out.

The Bat-eared fox's big ears not only help him hear his prey (insects) burrowing beneath the surface (experts believe that the fox can hear beetle larvae feeding underground!) but also operate as a cooling system, as he looses body heat through them. The little fox weighs only six to ten pounds. He is more sociable than other foxes and will mingle with others of his kind, though breeding pairs tend to be spaced widely apart. As previously indicated, the safarist is not likely to see the fox moving around much during the day, but the author has, from time to time, enjoyed watching the little hunter on a foraging expedition. He walks along, emphatically tipping his head from side to side — the reader may compare the tactics of the equally outsized-eared serval, who rotates its ears — as he picks up the subterranean activity below him. Suddenly, he will stop abruptly and without hesitation furiously begin digging.

Plates 28 & 29. Bat-eared Fox Outside His Lair. The lairs themselves are composed of networks of tunnels that remain cool even during the hottest days. The Bat-eared fox is the symbol of Botswana's Department of Wildlife, National Parks, and Tourism. One writer has termed the little fox the "ultimate adorable" animal, a Walt-Disney invention (were it not real). At any rate, *mbweha masikio* has up to fifty teeth, more than any other land mammal.

Wild (Cape Hunting) Dog

The author has not photographed wild dogs ("mbwa mwitu" in Kiswahili) and rarely sees them. Basically, pure luck is the predominant ingredient if the safarist encounters a pack[25] of these highly enigmatic vagabonds of the plains, animals who roam many miles every day over huge territories. Mangy and bad-smelling, with distinctive, large, rounded ears, the blackish or brindled-splotchy[26] wild dog — the wolf of Africa — is immensely clever. And the dogs, which are only slightly larger than jackals, can run at speeds of up to 35 mph. Hunting by these exclusively carnivorous animals is highly organized and always a genuine group effort. A sort of pre-hunt ceremony precedes the actual chase. The dogs gather amid much tail-wagging, nuzzling, and friendly licking of faces (derived, no doubt, from the habits of the young pups in begging for regurgitated meat). When the entire group is thus engaged and the moods of the individuals are suitably synchronized into coherent excitement, the pack sets off together. The prey herd is approached slowly, though no real stalking has been recorded,[27] while the dogs watch carefully to select appropriate targets. As soon as the herd starts to run — and the mere appearance of a pack of wild dogs is enough to send most herds into a panic — the pack gives chase. The dogs may initially single out a weak animal to pursue or the pack may run after several antelopes at once, attempting to scatter them from the security of the herd. In this latter sequence, the dogs will gauge each other's progress, and as soon as one dog is seen gaining on a quarry, the other pursuers will break off to concentrate on the one victim (to be). Ultimately, prey is relentlessly run down. No ambushing is ever involved. Tales of conscious relay-running are perhaps somewhat exaggerated; what happens is that a series of well-coordinated flanking movements, based on the antelope's tendency to run either in zig-zags or in a wide arc,[28] enable fresher dogs to come up from the rear (via 'short-cuts') to replace tired lead dogs. The entire hunt is conducted in silence.

The dogs regularly bring down large game. An adult wildebeest can, for example, be dispatched with remarkable ease, though a wildebeest calf seems to be the preferred meal. The dogs kill their harassed and exhausted victims like hyenas — by eating. Large prey is held by the nose and tail and disemboweled by formidable jaws and teeth while standing. The larger packs often hunt twice a day, early in the morning and again in the late afternoon. Occasionally, when there is a full moon and a clear night, they will also hunt after dark. The pack does not fail all that often — it is a genuine natural killing machine, as it were. One prominent observer (van Lawick) has set the success rate at only fifty percent, but most qualified naturalists would agree with a far higher figure. The hit-or-miss results of lion hunting are totally absent, and the dogs are even more successful than hyenas. Nor do the dogs readily give up a kill to larger predators. In fact, a little scavenging on their own is not unheard of: a large pack has been known to run hyenas from their kill (though the reverse is probably more often true) and even chase off a lion.

Despite the general excitement shown at kills, the successful hunters do not quarrel. There is no feeding frenzy. The younger dogs present seem to be given a priority, and those not eating more or less patiently wait their turn. Indeed, here is the essence of social hunting. The pack pools its talents to bring down game large enough to satisfy everyone, but if the available food is not sufficient to go around, the pack will hunt again that day. Each individual calmly waits its turn, knowing that it will be fed. No pride of lions ever behaves like this, and no clan of hyenas exhibits the same skill or confidence.

Only when members of a pack have young pups, which are raised in an underground den for about three months, are the Cape Hunting dogs temporarily stationary. And they frequently return to the same denning area every time that pups are expected (*i.e.*, yearly). Litters are large, ten is the average, and the practice of full communal rearing of the young is followed. The adult males do most of the work caring for the young after weaning, not the normal rule in nature. The author knows of no coherent explanation for this role-reversal.

In fact, wild dogs are extremely sociable creatures: there is little discernible friction ever within the pack. On the surface, no hierarchy prevails nor does there appear to be any truly dominant individuals. The most reliable evidence would seem to indicate, however, that the pack is strictly regimented when it comes to reproduction, particulary among the females. The dominant female may even kill another bitch's pups or so harass the other mother as to cause her to neglect her pups, thereby causing their death. The dominant pair will always attempt to monopolize reproduction. The hierarchy is not evident to the casual onlooker, because the lower echelons readily accept their reprimands from the dominant partners and the essentially cooperative nature of the pack keeps a tight

---

25. An average pack today contains seven to eight adults but can balloon to twenty or so. Formerly, the packs seem to have been considerably greater in number.

26. No two patterns are the same. The patches are, however, never evenly distributed or symmetrical in any way. Wild dogs have four toes, instead of the five found in true dogs — that is, evolution has selected out the dewclaw. For many years, the Cape Hunting dogs were thought to be a species of hyena.

27. The dogs do make use of whatever surprise is available. Even bunched together in a pack, they often move in ways that suggest, particularly at night, grazing animals. The effect is to enable them to move closer to their prey; whether such behavior is conscious strategy is another matter.

28. Zig-zagging or running in an arc makes sense as a strategy only when the predator is very close. Thus, some dogs constantly nip at the running prey's heels, encouraging the 'smart' antelope to take evasive action, its death warrant.

lid on aggression.[29] The dominant female can be recognized by "pee-marking" (common as well to aggressive bitches among domestic dogs): the bitch will half-squat and circle, dribbling urine the whole time. A male will then follow over the same area in similar fashion — he too is dominant and mated to the bitch. While the dominant female will usually remain on top for many years, the males rotate — frequently, a new male assumes the lead each successive breeding season. At any rate, not only the young but the old and lame as well receive regurgitated, semi-digested meat, and a wild dog pack is indisputably one of nature's most cohesive animal groups. The normal pack contains more males than females, often twice as many, quite unlike comparable lion or hyena congregations. Continuity seems to be maintained through the male line; all the males are normally related. Females periodically will go off (possibly, they are driven off) to establish new packs. Both sexes hunt.

It is somewhat of a mystery why such efficient and

_____

29. Once dominant relationships have been established, the overt submissions may be so subtle as to escape detection. Moreover, the subordinate animals may avoid any encounter that would require appeasement. And, in a secure social setting, no fear need be expressed. Thus, for many years, even the most reliable observers failed to discern any hierarchy within the wild dog pack. Indeed, typical dominant behavior appeared absent at the pre-hunt ceremony, during the hunt itself, or as the dogs fed. In many mammals, differences in body sizes and adornment (usually male) are reliable guides to dominance, but no such patterns exist with wild dogs. Adding to the difficulty of study was, of course, the transient nature of the pack, making extended concentration over any significant period virtually impossible. Finally, when one discovers a litter — and hence a stationary pack — everyone seems to be pitching in equally. Eventually, naturalists learned that females leave their natal packs in groups (*i.e.*, littermates leave together) and do compete for the right to breed in their newly established pack. How the dominant male partner emerges is not certain. Moreover, lesser pairs do occasionally breed successfully, and one has to know the pack well to follow exactly who is doing what to which pups.

Normally, in groups of relatively stable composition, dominance relationships tend to take the form of a durable linear hierarchy. In wild dog packs, there does not seem to be any hierarchy below the dominant mating pair — no ladies or gents in waiting, so to speak.

It should be noted that group cohesiveness is probably not the *cause* of such non-dominant behavior in wild dogs but could well be its *result*. It is not correct to assert, as some have, that constant and close social living removes the need to display dominance. Logically, and within the confines of our experience, the reverse could just as well be true. Rather, dominance here is not expressed — or, more likely, just not easily observable — because the animals find it advantageous to accept the position assigned (or assumed) and to cooperate as they do. To be sure, the success of such behavior may well encourage its continuation (or even an improved version). The reader is encouraged to reflect on these matters, because dominance relationships are some of the most basic social characteristics among species found in the African bush.

remarkably self-supporting communal animals are so rare. They have been seen in the sands of the Sahara and in the snows found on the summit of Kilimanjaro, neither environment associated with weaklings. Yet extinction seems inevitable. Disease, probably distemper, may be at least a partial answer. The selective breeding (and consequent limited genetic distribution) may also encourage disease to act as a limiting determinant. Failure to keep pace with hyena predation of pups must be a factor. Continual and determined persecution by man has also taken its toll over the years. Perhaps as few as ninety, certainly less than 200, wild dogs remain in all the Serengeti. The best place to see these animals, where they are called Cape Hunting dogs, is Kruger National Park in South Africa.

Vultures and Marabou Stork

Although an entire later chapter is devoted to birds, this pair of carrion eaters belong with the scavengers of this chapter.[30] **Vultures**, probably the most numerous and successful of all birds of prey, eventually seem to win the battle for the carcasses that lions abandon by sheer weight of numbers. The first-time safarist sees only a hopping, hissing, clawing *mob*, under which any prey soon disappears. (*30-32*) Actually, there are six main kinds of vultures in Africa, and each has a defined role at the carcass. Each goes for a different part: some tear, some peck, some rip, some clean. For convenience, the six species can be paired according to feeding behavior (and bill structure) as follows.

The first pair are the Lappet-faced (sometimes called Nubian), the largest and most aggressive vulture, and the White-headed, who is both the least numerous vulture and usually the first to show up at the kill. Lappet-faced vultures have fairly distinctive markings: a naked head and neck, both covered with fleshy pink caruncles (like the wattles of a turkey) that give them a slightly red look. (The large vulture standing off to the side in plates *15* and *32* is a Lappet-faced.) The bird also flushes bright red when angry or breeding. The White-headed vulture has a scarlet beak, a dark brown back (with considerable white on its wings), and an all-white face, crown, and neck.

Both species have deep, powerful beaks and broad skulls well adapted for twisting and tearing the tougher parts of a carcass, namely, the skin and tendons. If the dead animal died from sickness or other natural causes (and more than half do) and the vultures are the first scavengers to arrive, these two must do their work, tearing up the animal, before the others can participate.

_____

30. The choice of animals to be included in this chapter was considerably arbitrary. Many other animals included in this book — for example, the reptiles and several birds (other than vultures and Marabou storks) — hunt and scavenge. The divisions made primarily serve purposes of convenience and the author's notions of symmetry.

Plates 30-32. The Mob. The tourist first sees only a frenzied free-for-all. One wag compared the scene to a public meeting that has suffered a complete breakdown of law and order. A less casual observer begins to notice differences in feeding behavior and preferences for diverse parts of a carcass — thus, despite the boarding-house reaches, reducing the competition to a more orderly and all-round satisfying process.

Lappet-faced vultures often drive other vultures off until they have eaten their fill. Moreover, not as sociable among themselves as the others, only one, two, or three (rarely) Lappet-faced birds will join in at any given carcass. The White-headed will usually abandon the main carcass once a number of other vultures have collected and stand off at a distance, picking on an isolated bone or scrap. Both the Lappet-faced and the White-headed vultures occasionally kill their own prey, which include Bat-eared foxes, fledgling secretary birds, newborn antelopes, and even wild cats. Indeed, the basic reason

why the Lappet-faced and White-headed vultures frequently arrive first at a carcass is that they fly at relatively low altitudes, actively searching for prey, as well as carrion.

One should not expect too much of these two large vultures, however, when hunting on their own. Normally, only sick or infirm animals are seized: the vultures have a slow approach flight, and their weak feet are designed primarily for walking and running on the ground, not seizing and holding prey. Nor do these birds have the sharp eyesight of hawks or eagles. In fact, neither hawks nor eagles nor falcons nor other raptors — the list is long — have anything to worry about from their vulture competitors.

The second group is comprised of the White-backed vulture, the most common vulture in East Africa, and the larger Rüppell's Griffon. Both these birds have long, bare necks so that they can reach far inside the carcasses without collecting gore throughout their feathers (*33 & 34*). Blood congealed on the bare skin soon dries and quickly flakes off through exposure to the sun. The

potentially harmful coating of bacteria that climbs aboard has nowhere to breed and will be killed off by the sunlight. The same principle serves for the bare legs. All vultures, in fact, keep themselves scrupulously clean. It is not unusual to witness long preening sessions. White-backed and Rüppell's tear out large, soft pieces of muscle with sharp bills, and their tongues are specially adapted (lined with barbs) for ingesting slippery meat. Neither species hunts; both are exclusively scavengers. At a kill, many Rüppell's and a few White-backed are usually those vultures standing toe-to-toe, beak-to-beak, and causing the most commotion. Vulture arguments at the carcass resemble the Western barroom brawl in that one always has difficulty telling exactly who is "fighting" whom. A series of mock charges and hopping about, with wings widespread and necks extended, much of the action looks like Muhammed Ali's rope-a-dope. The cacophony is tremendous. The squawking of the Rüppell's manages to transcend the hissing and squeaking of the others.

The third and last pair are the modest-sized Hooded vulture, with a bald, reddish face and hooked beak (*35*),

Plates 33 & 34. Vultures Eating. These are the White-backed and Rüppell's Griffon vultures. The White-backed is best distinguished from the Rüppell's by the "collar" found at the base of the bare necks: the former has a brownish, long-feathered collar that does not extend all the way around the neck; the latter has a ruff of white down that encircles the neck. Rüppell's also have horn-colored beaks. In time, all life on the African plains ends up in their bellies, a sanitation department that, as another wag has remarked, never goes on strike. White-backed vultures live on the open grasslands and roost in trees along water courses. They are gregarious, roosting, feeding, and resting among their own. The Rüppell's are also gregarious and frequent both the plains and mountains. Rüppell's try to dominate the kills. In the Serengeti, the Rüppell's time their breeding season so that the young chicks are raised in February through May, the rainy season, when the main migratory herds of wildebeest are calving and grazing within easy reach of the nesting colonies located on the eastern escarpment of the Gol Mountains (see map on p. 428).

Plate 35. *Lion Cub Play-Stalking a Hooded Vulture*. The bare skin on the neck of a Hooded vulture turns a dark pink when the bird is excited (at a carcass, for example).

and the distinctive Yellow-faced Egyptian *(36)*. These are the smallest of the six species and they usually stay on the fringes of a kill, pecking at scraps — especially offal — and small bones with their thin, weak bills. They normally remain til last, and one or more can often be seen hanging around long after the other birds have gone. Both will also eat insects, termites, and lizards and will pick undigested or partly digested food from carnivore droppings. The Egypitan vulture, which is always seen singly, has the distinction of having been discovered on several occasions using rocks to break open tough ostrich eggs — an event often touted as one of the few genuine examples of tool utilization by birds, or any animal, for that matter. This is not the most successful example, however, as the vulture's aim leaves something to be desired: the bird usually misses the egg, and a direct hit seems more or less a matter of chance. (The author pursues the history of this discovery in the bibliography.)

The biggest vultures are really quite large birds. The Lappett-faced, a giant of a bird, has more than an eight-foot wingspan, but no vulture is small *(37)*. Despite their binocular vision, several times more powerful than man's, vultures cannot see at night and hence sleep. They return to the skies at early light, making use of rising currents of air heated at the earth's surface on a sunny day called thermals to attain their lofty stations. The heavier vultures often have to wait until the day has warmed up, giving the land-based carnivores a short-lived head start. The Rüppell's can, however, usually literally jump off to an

early start, because they nest in cliffs and can simply leap off the rock faces to catch the wind currents. As the day wears on, these silhouettes soaring in the sky can descend in a hurry, if need be *(38)*. During rainy seasons, vultures often lose the thermal updrafts — and can go for days without feeding.

Vultures find their food entirely by sight, but their much vaunted eyesight is not as good as several other birds and has frequently been exaggerated by writers. A large antelope or pride of lions or clan of hyenas or even jackals (it is said that vultures pay the most attention to the jackals; how a naturalist can know something like this is a

Plate 36. *Egyptian Vulture*. See also plates *21* and *25*. The Egyptian is distinctly smaller than the other vultures, save the Hooded. Most vultures move over the ground in gimpy skips and hops. The Egyptian does more of a *stroll*, as here.

mystery to the author) in daylight is not that difficult to see from a distance, even at the great soaring heights maintained by some of the birds. But most of the participants at the feast originally never saw the carcass. Vultures mostly watch each other. Thus, the "domino effect" will bring birds from great distances and ensures the large numbers actually seen at mealtimes. In this respect, the safarist should realize that a circling cloud of vultures is often more a sign of a strong thermal than a kill: the big birds do not eat in the air.

The formidable birds cool off in the heat of midday by spreading their wings *(39)*, or bathing in the nearest

Plate 37. Griffon Coming down in a Tree. Ugly, if not actually obscene, on the ground, the ''vile vulture'' is graceful aloft. Vultures take off with a pounding beat — an ancient sound of Africa. More than one writer has remarked that the birds are a powerful reminder of mortality.

Plate 38. Landing. A vulture lands with his long shanks pointed down at an angle, talons spread, looking for all the world like an aircraft's landing gear. Raptors generally have strong, curved, pointed claws that are used to capture, kill, and carry off their victims. The claws of a vulture are more blunt and not suitable for fully gripping objects but they nonetheless help in maneuvering on the carcass lying underneath the ''mob.''

Plate 39. Cooling Off.

stream and then sitting in a tree with their wings hung out to dry (40). Their feathers often become twisted out of shape, and sitting in the sun quickly straightens them out. After a big meal, some of the birds have a little difficulty in taking off and retire to the sidelines to wait for just that right gust of wind to put them airborne again.

One of the classic photographs of the African plains is that of the lone vulture perched high in a tree, a sentinel with hunched shoulders and sinister beak in profile, surveying the many miles of activity unfolding underneath (41 & 42). Along migration routes during the annual wildebeest trek, the vultures have almost more

Plate 40. Drying Out.

Plates 41 & 42. Classic Profiles. Vultures are called "tai" in Kiswahili, which is also the word for eagle. Indeed, many naturalists believe that vultures are descended from eagles. The "classic profile" here is not necessarily the most appropriate vulture posture: vultures earn their living in the air.

Plates 43 & 44. On the Migration Route. Before the day is over, this tree congregation will again become a squabbling mass on the ground.

carrion available to them than they can eat. Hence, the trees are full (*43 & 44*).

Without hooked beaks or talons, the **Marabou storks** ("korongo" in Kiswahili) cannot rip or tear. Whether they ever use their long bills to puncture carcasses may be doubted, but some writers have so reported. Like the Egyptian vultures, they usually hang around the outside of the main activity. They give the impression of sulking off to the side, waiting for permission from the vultures to come forward, but, in truth, they often steal from the vultures like jackals. And every now and then, one will see a Marabou actually insert itself right in the midst of the main mob. Nevertheless, the doleful-looking (or is it "solemn-looking"?) Marabou storks have small appetites, and therein lies the secret to their basic laid-back attitude. They simply have no need to eat every day and eat a smaller proportion of their body weight than nearly any other bird. In addition (or as a consequence?), they are generally lazy, easy-going, and non-aggressive.

Nice guys finish ugly in this instance, however, as Marabous look just grotesque and hideous standing there (*45*), all hunched down with their pink and raw, scabby heads, pallid legs (covered with excretal uric acid), and almost drunken, leering expressions. One writer has dubbed them "Boris Karloff" figures. Another has referred to their "Skid Row" eyes. Of course, such sentiments matter little or not at all to other animals, and a Marabou will always be appreciated by another Marabou. As

Plate 45. Marabou Close-Up.

Marabous become predators when nesting — they need to feed their young food containing bones to supply calcium for growth. Thus, they always nest near water, where they can pick off the small vertebrates such as fish, frogs, and baby crocodiles. Like all hunting storks, they spear frogs and fish. (*47*) Marabous have a murderous fondness for crocodile hatchlings, at all times, and the "duels" between the Marabou and a croc mother are notorious (see Chapter XIII). A few Marabous can, in the absence of the female crocodile, account for a whole brood of babies in short order, strolling along the river banks with that dignified, purposeful walk and picking up one life at a time.

Bigger than the largest vulture, the storks stand five feet tall and have a wingspan of ten to twelve feet. They require a sizeable running start, with strenuous flapping of wings, to become airborne (*48 & 49*). Once aloft, however, flight transforms these jumbo jets of the big flying birds into vessels of beauty (*50*), and, once captured by the thermal currents, their silhouettes above the tree tops speak eloquently (*51 & 52*).

Voltaire once observed, to a toad, beauty is pop-eyes, a yellow belly, and a spotted back. Marabou storks look as if they should be capable of a hearty, old-fashioned guffaw but disappointingly have no real voice, though they rattle their bills or upper throats and grunt in breeding colonies. Older adults have a distinctive, large air-filled sac hanging from their bill or upper throat (*46*).

Plate 47. Fishing. A Marabou is mainly a scavenger but will also feed on frogs, locusts, mice, and lizards. Marabous are often found at the edges of wild fires picking off the mice and lizards escaping the flames and heat. The storks also have become great camp-followers of tourists and can be found near most garbage dumps in an omnivorous frame of mind.

Plate 46. An Elder of the Tribe. The purpose of the large, air-filled (inflatable) pink pouch that hangs from the front of the neck apparently is to provide either a resting place for the heavy bill or a large surface area for dissipating heat. The pouch consists of a series of air sacs. When expanded, it turns magenta and may also serve as a sexual attraction. *De gustibus non est disputandum.*

Plates 48 & 49. Taking Off. Marabous take to the air with a rush and commotion of wings that remind one of a blowing, flapping shroud in the wind.

Plate 50. Gaining Altitude.

Plate 51 & 52. Graceful Silhouettes. Neck retracted and legs trailing, the Marabou sails into the distance, a true vessel of beauty.

All big birds in Africa have over-heating problems. Marabous stand in water to cool off (53). They also relax by resting on their lower legs and elbows (54). Marabous are sociable, roosting and breeding in large colonies.

Plate 53. Marabous in Water. "Marabou" is derived from an old French word meaning (as only French would) a priest, on the one hand, or an ugly misshapen individual, on the other.

Plate 54. Relaxation. The unhurried stork at rest.

VI. Land Giants (And a Tiny Relative)

Out on the Safaris, I had seen a herd of Buffalo, one hundred and twenty-nine of them, come out of the morning mist under a copper sky, one by one, as if the dark and massive, iron-like animals with the mighty horizontally swung horns were not approaching, but were being created before my eyes and sent out as they were finished. I had seen a herd of Elephant travelling through dense Native forest, where the sunlight is strewn down between the thick creepers in small spots and patches, pacing along as if they had an appointment at the end of the world. It was, in giant size, the border of a very old, infinitely precious Persian carpet, in the dyes of green, yellow and black-brown. I had time after time watched the progression across the plain of the Giraffe, in their queer, inimitable, vegetative gracefulness, as if it were not a herd of animals but a family of rare, long-stemmed, speckled gigantic flowers slowly advancing. I had followed two Rhinos on their morning promenade, when they were sniffing and snorting in the air of the dawn, — which is so cold that it hurts in the nose, — and looked like two very big angular stones rollicking in the long valley and enjoying life together.

Isak Dinesen, *Out of Africa*[1]

Elephant

The elephant furnishes as good a reason as any for taking an African safari; somehow, it is only fitting that people should travel thousands of miles to see one of the world's truly great travelers.[2] Over its lifetime, an elephant must, in fact, trek the equivalent of many transatlantic safaris. Man has directly benefited in this respect: any number of roads in Africa began as well-graded elephant migration routes, following the best alignment and most suitable gradient over difficult terrain. Of course, the original paths were very narrow; elephants travel virtually single-file in forests and on long journeys, huddling only in times of danger.

Indeed, the world's largest terrestrial animal will go where horses fear to tred; the more rugged the terrain and precipitous the incline, these engineers simply push on. Soon, the initial path becomes a regular trail, zigzagging around obstacles (some obstacles are, as might be expected, merely relocated) and up and down the most apparently inaccessible footing.[3] The secret to the elephant's remarkable locomotion is found in the structure of its foot, not outwardly visible, and the sponge-like, shock-absorbing pad found underneath, which cushion both absorbs the animal's great weight and adapts to the unevenness in the ground itself. These same characteristics permit some fairly delicate movement as well. Surely, one of the most unforgetable experiences of any safari is to wake in the middle of the night to find a herd of elephants grazing (or browsing) right outside one's tent — and throughout the campsite — carefully picking their way around the guy ropes and other impediments. By morning, all that will remain to remind the campers of their nocturnal visitors will be the enormous piles of dung. An only slightly less unnerving experience, but one that equally reminds the vulnerable visitor that he is not in a zoo, awaits the safarist in the bush, when he

---

1. At p. 15.

2. These behemoths do, however, present special photographic problems. On the surface, whatever they are doing, elephants lack expression. And their dull grey hides, with all that loose, wrinkled skin, soak up light in monotonous fashion. Extra patience and careful attention to lighting is often required to achieve an interesting photograph.

3. One of the more persistent fables in Africana is the "eyewitness" account of elephants purposely sliding down steep slopes on their haunches, legs extended into the air, much like kids on a park slide. At Samburu in northern Kenya, the rangers (with only the slightest trace of embarrassment) will even show the gullible tourists the "elephants' slide" on the local hill. Babar lives! Horses do have one advantage over elephants: the former can jump, the latter do not. Nevertheless, an elephant can probably outrun a horse over bad ground. In the typical elephant "amble," the hind feet are placed nearly exactly where the forefeet were, a considerable stride.

suddenly discovers that the huge animals are but a thicket away, so silently can they move, like rabbits in a forest. One wit has described the elephant as shuffling around like an embarrassed ballet dancer; minus the embarrassment, the simile is an apt one.

In any event, the elephant is a magnificent creature — great in stature, noble in bearing, loyal in behavior, and immensely intelligent. (*1 & 2*) Just as the lion stands at the head of African carnivores, the elephant represents the apex of all herbivores. In fact, it is the elephant who, over millennia and in many and complex ways, has altered the forest environment to support a huge variety of herbivores. From the destruction of the trees comes grasses and browse — food. And the migration trails of elephants provide the other herbivores freedom of movement.

Plates 1 & 2. The Noble Pachyderm. The African elephant is larger than its Asiatic cousin (one elephant shot in Angola weighed an estimated ten tons!) and has a flatter forehead (the African female has a flatter, more angular, forehead still than the male), a more concave back, and larger ears. The last are possibly the best means of differentiation at a glance: the Indian elephant's ears look like the African ears cut in half horizontally. In addition, the African elephant's trunk has two "fingers" on the end, the Asiatic's has only one. Asiatic elephants carry little ivory by comparison, and only the males have any tusks at all. Though the Carthaginian general Hannibal is supposed to have used them to cross the Alps and in the Pyrenees in the Punic Wars, the African elephants have not taken to domestication in the same way as the Asiatic elephants. Some authorities have suggested that the African elephant's reputation for being unmanageable is a product of circumstances and not nature. African elephants have been trained (in the former Belgian Congo, for example) successfully, but the Africans apparently have decided that the trouble outweighs the rewards. Whereas in Asia, the "partnership" has persisted for perhaps 5000 years. Evidence seems to point to the conclusion that forest elephants, like the Asiatic, are both smaller and more tractable than their wary, predominantly savannah brothers, and that the early Africans captured and used forest elephants then prevalent.

In any event, the Indian elephant is usually the variety found in circuses and in the zoos. Yet the most famous zoo elephant of all time was African. "Jumbo," as he was called and the origin of the popular nickname, was captured in Ethiopia or the Sudan and brought to the London Zoo in 1865. Riding on his back became a favorite treat of Victorian children; being photographed on his back became a much sought-after novelty for adults. Jumbo eventually turned a bit ill-tempered — perhaps suffering from all the junk, principally currant buns, fed to him by the crowds — and was sold in a highly controversial deal to P.T. Barnum, who established the animal in the United States in the 1880s. In Barnum's hands, Jumbo naturally became the "biggest" elephant in the world (Barnum both cooking the figures and resolutely refusing to allow a measurement to be made). Jumbo's stuffed body (mounted by Carl Akeley himself) was given to Tufts University in Boston; his skeleton is on exhibit at the American Museum of Natural History located in New York City.

Outside the forests, an elephant also provides water, directly by digging wells[4] or indirectly by creating reliable waterholes. This last is accomplished by repeated rolling in a shallow depression or pan, which practice eventually creates a sizeable pool, first, by carrying away each time no small amount of earth plastered on such a huge frame and, second, by sealing watertight a bed that will hold water even in times of drought. Furthermore, the concentrated weight of elephant feet sometimes brings up water just by the pachyderm traveling though a *lugga*, a Somali word for a sand river, most of which have water beneath the surface. (Indeed, in arid lands, the presence of elephants during dry season can determine whether or not many animals live or die.)

A baby elephant, after twenty-two months of gestation cradled in his mother's womb,[5] arrives in a world of giants. Normally, several elephants are present at birth to

---

4. An elephant can dig a hole three to four feet deep, using its feet as shovels, its toenails as spades, its trunk, and even its tusks. To dig with its tusks, the elephant must kneel down on its front knees. After watching elephants at length in the wild, I have to question the many accounts of elephants trampling their enemies and goring men knocked to the ground. An elephant is far more likely to try to crush something with its trunk or to *kneel* on an object of wrath — and it *must* kneel to reach someone on the ground with its tusks.

5. Elephant cows show little evidence of pregnancy — for example, no swelling is visible.

help, removing the fetal membrane or nudging the infant to its feet. Not one midwife, but many. Unfortunately, the safarist is not likely to witness the event; labor is short, and, although the mother does not go off to seek privacy,[6] the herd will shield her from any onlookers. The baby stands but two-and-a-half feet high and weighs a little more than 200 pounds. All around him are pillar-like legs that support, in gangs of four, up to seven tons and trunks that reach down from ten to eleven feet up (average adult shoulder height). Soon enough, the youngster realizes that these gentle giants mean him no harm: the many trunks will softly greet and caress him. From every direction, his blood relatives — grandmother, aunts, sisters, cousins, and adolescent brothers mostly — will gather to inspect him with great tenderness. But, as he totters to his feet and stumbles forward, it is the comforting shape of his mother that will dominate his early life. He will, in fact, pass most of his infancy, initially underneath and later glued to her side, as close as possible to mother (3) Every now and then, however, a more venturesome little

Plate 3. Matron and Calf. Calves are darker and hairier than older elephants, not particularly noticeable in this shot. A cow will produce an average of three to four calves in a full lifetime (biologically, she is capable of having up to ten). The calves remain close to their mothers for ten years or so, the longest period of child-parent attachment next to man. Normally, a mother will not abandon her calf under any circumstances. And there are several reliable accounts of mothers carrying around dead calves for days before finally giving them up. The alert safarist will hear soft, deep rumblings between a mother and calf. At one time, these noises were thought to emanate from the digestive tract, but elephants constantly 'grumble' (in the throat) to keep in touch and reassure one another as they browse, to express pleasure, and to greet one another. The sound, which might be compared to purring in cats, will cease immediately when the elephants are alarmed.

6. Occasionally, a female will leave a really large herd accompanied by her most immediate relatives. Only in the most unusual circumstances will a cow give birth alone.

individual jumps out front (*4 & 5*). As a general rule, if a baby elephant can still walk beneath his mother, he is but one year old or less (*6*).

Baby elephants and even adolescents sleep often, during the heat of midday and at night. They lie flat on their sides, with trunks coiled; at these times, the adults always crowd around in a circle of protection (*7*).

One of the youngster's most challenging tasks is to come to terms with his own trunk. What begins as a nuisance and an encumbrance — babies have been seen tripping over their own trunks — slowly becomes an indispensable appendage serving many needs. While perhaps not quite as versatile as a human hand, it certainly matches a human arm. Often used in combination with feet or tusks, an elephant's trunk actually is a combined upper lip and nose, possessing many thousands of muscles. Obviously, it takes a bit of getting used to. At the tip are tiny hairs useful for feeling the shape, temperature, and texture of things (or even locating the precise bearing of a scent in the wind) and two sensitive, finger-like protuberances. A baby elephant will suck the tip, much like a baby human being will suck his thumb. Eventually, the trunk will be used for drawing water and conveying it to his mouth for a drink (*8*) or blowing it out in a refreshing spray. The author has seen a young elephant employ its trunk as a snorkel to breathe while his head was virtually submerged. The trunk is also used for spraying dust (and even mud). It will pluck, scoop, or pick up leaves, shoots, branches, or whatever else that the elephant fancies. Even small trees can be uprooted. The elephant will apply it to shake fruit out of trees, as a sort of "radar" for rain, and in tugs-of-war started with rivals of the moment. Grass is harvested by the trunk holding the blades tautly in place and swinging the toes across as a scythe. In fact, the foot-trunk combination is capable of some serious "farming." As "hand-eye" coordination increases, the elephant will pick up a stick and use it to scratch himself, a rare but genuine utilization of "tools" in the animal kingdom. In short, the manipulation of the trunk is precise and delicate or forceful and efficient, as the need arises.[7] The author has even watched elephants place their trunks over their tusks, presumably for cleaning purposes.

The trunk is the main tactile tool and plays a large part in greeting ceremonies, when one elephant tenderly reaches into the other's mouth with its trunk, and many other forms of communication. Air can be expelled forcibly from the trunk to produce sounds of various pitches and intensities. Finally, its sensitivity is legendary. There is the apocryphal (but fun) story of the elephant in Egypt who was, they say, in love with a beautiful woman who sold flowers. One day in the market, he bought her some apples and put them in her bosom, leaving his trunk behind a long time to fondle her breasts. I suppose that, if one follows the tale as far as the elephant purchasing apples in the market, the rest follows naturally enough.[8]

The adult elephant does have one problem with its trunk that the youngster does not — what to do with it when sleeping. The main concern is to keep the tip off the ground and beyond the reach of ants. Thus, when the safarist comes across a napping elephant, he may well find its trunk draped across a tusk (*9*). On the other hand, the often-repeated wisdom that elephants suffer from a variety of creatures (including ants) constantly crawling up their trunks is nonsense. The reader has only to think of the powerful bellows that can propel dust, mud, and water with great force to realize that little of consequence not actually sucked up will attain the higher reaches of the proboscis.

The baby elephant will have to curl his trunk over his head to suckle (with his mouth) from his mother's teats, which, like woman's and unlike most other mammal's, number two and are located up-front between or just behind the forelegs. (Accordingly, some African tribes believe that elephants are really human beings who have been punished for one infraction or another by some vengeful deity.) Dependence upon milk is pretty much total in the first year. Thereafter, he continues to suckle intermittently until four to five years, when his own tusks become too painful for mother or when another calf is born.[9] Now begins the endless quest for vegetation; life turns into one long stand-up eating experience. (*10*)

As his confidence begins to grow, not to mention his size, the calf becomes more venturesome. Young elephants are among nature's most playful and mischievous juveniles. Calves certainly show a fondness for chasing birds. The herd itself gives them tremendous latitude for tomfoolery. Elders find their tails pulled in play and even suffer the "indignity" of having food snatched from their mouths. The teasing and roughhouse is especially apparent at waterholes and mudbaths, where play includes a lot of shrill trumpeting and rushing about with ears outspread in mock charges. This display often goes on for

7. Although the mother elephant frequently employs her trunk to control (or protect) her baby, the stories of cows carrying newborn babies in their proboscides [sic] may be doubted. Hauling around a dead body — referred to in the text — has, however, been authenticated.

8. In Pliny's (who else's?) version of the tale, the raconteur was at pains further to assure the reader that, so "nobody may think she was a vulgar choice [of the elephant!]," the girl was a "remarkable favorite of the very celebrated scholar Aristophanes."

9. Cows occasionally nurse two calves of disparate size, even simultaneously. And calves not born to the nursing cow are sometimes allowed to nurse as well. Some mothers also permit their young to suckle after reaching the age of six, seven, or even eight years. Weaning normally takes place, however, after birth of the next calf. Very rarely — there are only a few reported cases — a cow will have twins.

Plates 4 & 5. Little One out Front. Even if the calf were inclined to wander far, the elders would not permit it. Small calves could fall prey to lions and hyenas, but the older elephants have no natural enemies, unless, of course, one counts man. Indeed, the ivory trade — in "white gold," as it has always been called — is almost as old as man in Africa. Guns have, naturally enough, exacerbated the killing rates in this century. Africa's flagging economies help to accelerate poaching, which is further encouraged by corruption in high places. Over the years, millions of elephants have been killed for their ivory. Prized for its beauty, ivory has been used in many cultures as an artistic medium. Hard, durable, easy to carve, able to withstand severe changes in temperature, and polishable to a high gloss, ivory is unique as a medium for sculpture. But the greater emphasis has been on ivory as a precious material. Long a symbol of wealth, to Africans and foreigners alike, ivory is currently hoarded on a tremendous scale, presumably in anticipation (or fear) that the elephant is disappearing.

Plate 6. Field Test. A baby who can stand underneath its mother is less than one year old.

Plate 7. Midday Siesta. Adults themselves are infrequently seen sleeping on their sides. Most simply rest while standing. If an adult elephant does go down all the way, he will try to find a slight incline to aid him later in getting back up. Sometimes, this appears to take the form of seeking out a pillow — thus the reports of elephants napping like human beings. For years, elephant hunters swore that adult elephants did not lie down, because (so the majority thought) their ears would become "locked under the weight of the shoulder" and "hold their heads close to the ground." Such Archimedean logic was quite beyond our average *bon vivant* with a gun (though the author is not implying that all the field observations of the hunting fraternity were worthless, quite the contrary).

Plate 8. Youngster Drinking. A trunk has double hoses for suck-ing in and spraying out. Until they can master the coordination required, very young calves have to drink directly into their mouths. Elephants can exert great suction through their trunks because their lungs are bonded to their rib cages. But the trunk is, above all, a nose: the nostrils begin at the very tip and run the entire length. Elephants are born with so-called 'milk' tusks only a few centimeters long. These are replaced by the permanent tusks after a year or so, but the ivory does not begin to grow un-til well into the calf's second year and is noticeable only in the third year. Tusks are about six to ten inches long when the adolescent is five years old.

Plate 9. Proboscis at Rest. Arm, hand, pump, hose, mudsling, wind gauge, musical instrument, shovel, radar, lumber crane, and even weapon — the proboscis combines a fairly amazing brute strength with fingertip sensitivity. In addition to its ver-satility, the trunk saves a great deal of energy; the elephant's massive head does not have to be lifted each time that the animal gathers food. Of course, this observation begs the question, is not the head fashioned as it is to support the weight of the trunk (and tusks)?

Plate 10. Playmates. Sibling elephant calves are normally separated by at least four years, as females generally have no interest in sex during the first two to three years following birth, to which must be added the long gestation period (some twenty-two months). The two calves pictured are not separated by as much as four years and hence are playmates only, not siblings. Young elephants are difficult to sex — their genitals are well camouflaged in the cascades of slack and wrinkles.

hours. All elephants, young and old, find time to bathe at least once every day (*11 & 12*), roll in mud (if available), or make their own mud rolling in the dust. (*13*) Even the older elephants obviously relish the mud-wallowing and abandon themselves in delight. The entire herd joins the act; soon, the elephants are doing an excellent imitation of drunken sailors on leave (*14*).

More and more elephants kept arriving to coat themselves liberally with mud, as if to spruce up their gray old facades with fresh plaster. The wallow was soon overflowing with bodies — ears, trunks, legs, and tusks in wild profusion. A large bull came stalking up and elbowed in as if taking his right-of-way for granted, shoving the two adolescents aside and plopping down, the black slime oozing up around his groin. He, too, rolled over and plastered himself so thoroughly with mud that finally only the whites of his eyes were glinting through a mask of clay. After a while, he laboriously propped himself up like a dog

on his front legs, paused, drew his hind legs under him, and heaved himself into an upright position. At last he was standing safely on all fours, his legs looking like pillars of concrete arising from the bog.[10]

The reader might be surprised to learn just what constitutes a mudhole, given the dimensions of the more than Renoir-sized bathers. In fact, as plate *15* indicates, a two-square-feet hole will do — with great thoroughness, the elephant dips each part of his anatomy in turn. The trunk can distribute the rest.

Play-fighting among youngsters, which activity begins in earnest after a calf's first year, is also functional — it teaches an elephant his exact strength, relative to the

10. Reinhard Künkel, *Elephants,* p. 51.

Plate 11. Drinking in Lake Kariba. Reaching water seems to be the primary motivation for elephants traveling the way that they do. If the elephants actually go far into the water, the purpose is usually to bathe. Pliny suggested that the elephants' frequent trips to the river were rituals of purification and reverence for the moon and sun. Certainly, the sheer exuberance of an elephant bathing party impresses us today, as it must have the ancients as well. The animals jostle, splash, and squirt each other and trumpet with excitement. Calves save many of their most entertaining maneuvers for the water. The antics resemble those of children on crowded beaches during summer weekends. On a more mundane level, the trunks are particularly useful for drinking while standing in the water; the elephants can reach out and siphon in water not yet seriously muddied by their huge feet.

Plate 12. Crossing the Uaso Nyiro River. The meandering Uaso Nyiro ("Red River") is always shallow but also one of the most picturesque rivers in Africa. When fording rivers, the little elephants always go first, nudged along by mother or an elder relative. Pliny, with typical imaginativeness, declared that the herd put the youngsters in front so that the bottom of the river would "not be worn away by the tread of the larger ones, thus increasing the depths of the water." In fact, elephants are natural swimmers and frequently cross the Nile or Zambezi or other deep rivers at points where the water level is well over their heads. They have also been witnessed swimming in deep lakes.

Plate 13. The Mudbath. Daily hygiene always includes a dusting or, better, a mudbath (if available).

Plate 14. The African Hot Tub. If possible, elephants enjoy a wallow in muddy pools even more than a bathing expedition to a river or lake.

Plate 15. Determination. One way or another, this youngster is determined to gather his daily quota of mud from this little hole.

others, slowly developing over time a hierarchy in which everyone knows his place. Among adults, serious fighting is extremely rare. Mud and dust as well are important elements in the life of an elephant: by plastering the cool paste over his body, the elephant helps to keep his temperature under control and to protect his sensitive (or at least more sensitive than it looks) skin against biting flies. Once the dust or mud has been applied, the elephant thoroughly rubs himself against a termite hill or a tree, to pulverize or dislodge ticks and other skin parasites. The earthen coating acts a bit like sandpaper. (16) The author has enjoyed the experience of having a large elephant attempt to use his vehicle as a scratching post!

Elephant society itself is essentially matriarchal. The population is divided into small herds that are, in effect, family units (17). Herds frequently come together in larger related kinship or bond groups (18 & 19). When they do, the greetings are effusive and accompanied by great excitement: intertwining of trunks, ear flapping, and considerable trumpeting. These larger groups may number fifty or more. Family ties are thus lasting and widespread. Each herd is led by the dominant cow, the matriarch, and her sisters and daughters and their offspring comprise the unit.[11] The safarist should always try to pick out the matriarch — she is the unquestioned leader, and her herd follows her wherever she chooses to go. Each herd will, in fact, have a distinctive lifestlye, patterned after the matriarch. Such obedience is not so much a matter of size and strength, though size and strength abound; as befits cerebral creatures, this behavior reflects respect for experience and judgment — the matriarch will know where the water is, when to stand and when to flee, and where the best grasses and different food plants are. During a full lifetime, an elephant will wander over a range of many thousands of square miles, will experience several droughts, and will find itself challenged by poachers on more than one occasion. A young elephant could never hope to learn all the tricks of survival on its own — more efficient (and safer) to stay with its group and to learn from the experience of the old matriarch. Consequently, the group itself will move together, feed together, rest bunched together, rub up against one another several times a day, and answer one another's rumbling vocalizations.

Adult bulls are strictly transient and join the cow herds only on a temporary basis — for mating. The bulls typically show no lasting allegiance to any one cow or even to any particular group. The available evidence does indicate, however, that bulls do remember previous acquaintances and distinguish between strangers and one-time friends. The saying that an elephant never forgets is

grounded in fact, though one should make the distinction that Coleridge did: "Beasts and babies remember ... man alone recollects." The young bull severs his links with mother (and her herd) at the time of puberty (thirteen to fifteen years of age). Whether or not he leaves wholly of his own accord or is banished by the females is not entirely clear, although instances of young bulls trying to rejoin a family and being chased off by the older cows are common. The teenage males then seek the company of other bulls or wander alone (20 & 21).

The reasons for the matriarchal structure are not difficult to understand. Fundamentally, this society is nature's guarantee against inbreeding. Of course, that 'taboo' by itself is not entirely dispositive; once the newborns grow up and are assured of a decent opportunity at survival, the question becomes, who should leave home, brother or sister? The male is the logical choice. He is larger and better able to fend for himself alone. Moreover, the death of a bull is simply the loss of one elephant; the loss of a cow represents an opportunity cost of perhaps ten elephants. And the females should also remain behind to learn about child care, especially given the protracted childhood of elephants (as previously noted, the longest of any animal, except man). Besides, the males eventually would seek to mate with their mothers and other older relatives as well.[12]

Elephants by nature are even more social than lions. Babies are eagerly accepted not only by the members of their own groups but by all other elephants as well, including strange bulls — a phenomenon almost unique in animal behavior. There are many well-documented stories about unrelated bulls rescuing young calves in swamps, for example, and under all manner of other circumstances. Moreover, orphans are readily adopted by new families, even for nursing. Unrelated or only distantly related herds will intermingle and mix freely at waterholes, the adults greeting one another with quiet dignity and the youngsters frolicking together.

Plate 16. *Brick-Red Complexion*. One hears (or reads) a geat deal about "red" elephants. In reality, all elephants are grey. When covered with dust, however, they take on the coloration of the local soil.

---

11. Early in this century, reflecting the politics of the times, a particularly raunchy herd of elephants was referred to locally as a "suffragette herd," a commentary no doubt on the inevitable result following the absence of adult male company.

---

12. Leaving the herd at the time of puberty also directly benefits the young bull in the following manner. Although he may be sexually mature, he will not socially mature for another ten years, when size, strength, and experience will permit him for the first time to compete for cows in heat. Before then, instead of facing a barrage of rebuffs from older, larger courting bulls, the younger male will have an opportunity within bull groups to develop his position among his contemporaries.

Plate 17. Balloon View. At first, the family unit is merely curious at the strange shape looming overhead. As with all herd animals, however, it does not take much to throw the group into a panic. When the leader turns and runs, pandemonium breaks out. With elephants, the stampede always includes energetic ear flapping, indignant shaking of the heads, and shrill and angry trumpeting. Panic on a large scale is something to see. Really shrill trumpeting something to hear.

Plate 18. Samburu Kinship Group. Samburu in Kenya is an excellent reserve in which to study elephants. This large herd gathers under the trees along the river bank each midday to escape the heat and to rest. A kinship grouping is composed mostly of the nursery herds (adult females and their young; mature males only if a female is in heat) that usually number about fifteen, though they can vary from five to twenty members. Sometimes, bull herds — really best viewed as "clubs," with considerably looser, weaker social bonds and continually changing membership — join as well.

Some naturalists would carry the group classification further: several kinship groups that use the same dry-season range constitute a "clan." Really large populations remain together, however, only during wet months.

Plate 19. Kinship Group on the Move. Recent studies in Amboseli, another environment in which elephant families thrive, suggest that the behemoths may communicate with one another at sound frequencies too low to be detected by the unaided human ear. Such subliminal sounds may well carry several miles and account for how herds seem to be able to keep track of other herds' movements over vast distances and periodically come together in kinship groups.

At times, for reasons not always entirely obvious (stress is evidently one factor, another is the prospect of a distant rain interrupting a time of drought), many kinship groups will come together and form huge congregations. When such groupings move, a giant "train" is created, one of nature's greatest sights. Today, with the poaching and habitat constrictions prevalent, such sights are more properly regarded as miracles and are seldom seen. Indeed, few reserve habitats today could survive such biomass pressure for more than a short time. The train contributes greatly to the *mystery* that is the elephant. The author will never forget one late afternoon or early evening several years ago in Amboseli. My companions and I were sitting in a camp situated alongside a river bed. A little stream of water trickled by. Trees blocked our view more that forty or fifty yards in either direction, up or down the bed. Kilimanjaro loomed in the background, the cloud cover parting to make the summit dimly visible, a normal vista

for this time of day. Twilight enveloped us, and dusk was coming on. Up the stream, a commotion started, and elephants soon appeared, more or less in a single line. The leaders quickly reached and then passed us by and disappeared some distance down the bed, but the mass of grey shapes kept coming out of the tree line. No pausing or browsing, no significant deviations: an inexorable, steady march, the young ones trotting to keep up. Every now and then, their path led through some water, causing some splashing and the odd toss of the head or brief trumpet call. It was too dark for my available film and very dusty anyway, so we just watched. I recalled that as a youngster growing up in the Midwest I often found myself in an automobile sitting at a railroad crossing while a long freight train rumbled by. With great excitement and anticipation, we always counted the cars, hoping for a "record" of some kind or another. Trains of a hundred boxcars or more were then not uncommon. Now, after

Plate 20. The Trek in the Shadow of Kilimanjaro.
Perhaps the human mind cannot conceive of such
bulk simply wandering about, but elephants always
manage to convey the impression of *purposeful* trekking, of *going somewhere*. A healthy elephant can
cover thirty miles a day at a comfortable walk. The
nearly symmetrical cone-shaped Kilimanjaro, Africa's
"mountain of greatness," rises nearly four miles to a
perpetually snow- and glacier-capped summit, despite
its proximity to the equator. Kilimanjaro on a clear day
can be seen 100 miles away, rising in splendid isolation. The old volcano, one of the largest ever to explode through the earth's crust, is best seen in early
morning — at dawn, for about an hour, before the
cloud cover settles in. In common with all tall mountains, the heated air of day rises up the slopes where it
cools and condenses as a cloud. The mountain is,
however, more than just a dramatic background; the
snows are gradually melting, and Amboseli's underground springs begin on its slopes. Kilimanjaro was
once part of Kenya, but when the German Kaiser married, his British grandmother, Queen Victoria, made a
wedding gift of the entire mountain and transferred
Kilimanjaro to what is now Tanzania — at least so goes
a myth of long standing (but revealing nonetheless of
the often whimsical fashion in which the Europeans
carved up colonial Africa).

Plate 21. Alone But Not Aloof. Elephant bulls, despite their independence, are still sociable and are rarely found more than a mile or so from another bull or family unit. This is not evidence of permanent attachments, just a desire to be near other elephants. Adolescent bulls when they first separate from their natal herd are traumatized and reluctant to stray too far from their mother and the other older cows. But even adult bulls enjoy the proximity (and, one would suppose, comfort) of other elephants. Mature bulls do pass a lot of time alone, traveling among female family units, looking for receptive cows. Because of poaching, this bull has about as long a tusk as one is likely to see in East Africa. A full-grown mature bull, a really "big-tusker," has tusks that weigh in the 100-pound range (apiece) and are six feet or more long. Truly specimen examples have measured up to twelve to fifteen feet long and weighed over 200 pounds each. All big-tuskers are relentlessly hunted long before they reach full trophy proportions and are discouragingly difficult to find today. It should be emphasized, however, that no direct correlation exists between the length and weight of tusks, on the one hand, and the actual size of the mature elephant, on the other hand. Tusks are simply teeth (modified incisors). Elephants, like people, are left- or right-handed, in that they favor one tusk over the other — thus, one is usually shorter, more well-worn, than the other. Some experts say that elephants are predominantly left-handed; others categorically assert that most elephants are right-handed. (The Maasai apparently believe that all animals favor the left side in one sense or another.) The safarist will undoubtedly see both examples.

about five or ten minutes and with no end of this train of jumbos in sight, we realized that this was no ordinary collection of animals. We began counting. We eventually lost count, stopped, started again, stopped again, and finally gave up. At the half-hour point, we just sat transfixed.

Hundreds had gone by and still they came. The dust swirled around us. The great mountain seemed to grow larger, as the dim light slowly failed. We could not believe our eyes. I believe that we were all silently crying. The effect was overwhelming — as if Africa had reached back deep into its past and emptied before us all these magnificent beasts from the pages of history. None of our group will ever forget this indelibly carved experience.

Elephants are habitually peace-loving and tolerant of other animals and will as a rule go to great lengths to avoid trouble.[13] The severest tests of this goodwill are confron-

13. Stories of confrontations with hippos and crocodiles appear from time to time. But the paths of elephants and hippos rarely cross, and only a demented or astonished crocodile ever finds itself in a tussle with Jumbo, Kipling notwithstanding.

tations with cantankerous rhinos or buffalos at waterholes and with man on safari. The elephants ordinarily give way. About this and indeed all generalizations regarding elephants, however, one should add one broad caveat before also noting a specific and definite exception to each of the two "classic" confrontations and their results noted above. The caveat is that perhaps the single most distinguishing characteristic about elephants is their *individualism* (and hence relative unpredictability). The exception to the regular waterhole drama (see below, plates *100 & 101*) is caused by a very large elephant bull, who is accustomed to his own wide berth and who does not readily give way to anyone. And a particularly crusty buffalo bull, on the other hand, is just mean enough — and stupid enough — to play out the game to its mismatched conclusion.

The exception to the normal confrontation with man is provided by the matron with young calf standing at her side and limited (actual or perceived) freedom of movement *(22)*. The safarist who follows elephants will be treated to any number of threat displays — usually by adolescents *(23)*. Young bulls regularly let off steam by chasing monkeys, birds, jackals, and other small nuisances, and the safarist is but another petty obstacle to

Plate 22. Real Danger. With forest all around, the safarist blocks the logical exit at his own peril.

Plate 23. Cover Reprise: Threat Display. Pugnacious young elephants doing their thing. During intimidation displays, the ears are spread wide, the head is lowered and raised, and the animal shakes its trunk. A truly excellent work on elephants, centered on the inspired art of Paul Bosman, has recently been published in South Africa: Paul Bosman & Anthony Hall-Martin, *Elephants of Africa* (C. Struik, 1986).

bully during the passage to adulthood.[14] Occasionally, an older bull will make a more meaningful gesture: shaking his head violently from side to side, throwing the trunk up, flapping his ears, and trumpeting shrilly, he will charge the object of such opprobrium. (24) It takes a sturdy hand to record this latter event up close; the effect is a bit terrifying — lying in the path of an errant truck might be an equivalent. Invariably, the bull will pull up short or veer off at the last moment. Few fools will, however, be in a position to measure the exact remaining distance or the amount of the miss! And one never knows when the demonstration charge will be converted into the real thing, once the elephant realizes that the bluff is not having the desired effect! Moreover, a mother protecting her nursing calf is a different proposition altogether. The serious charge will come quietly, quickly, when the trunk is drawn in against the chest, the ears are folded back tight against the head, and the head itself is held high (with tusks parallel to the ground) and turned slightly sideways for a better view.[15] Advance warning is meager enough: a few lateral steps to improve an unobstructed path to the onlooker, a momentary rocking motion of the body, and a barely noticeable stiffening of the tail.

The villain of many popular adventure stories — the rogue elephant, vengeful and foul-tempered — is quite rare in the wild. Trouble with a decaying tooth, severe arthritis, or a poacher's wound may contribute to driving an elephant from the company of others to live a rogue's existence. Males, with looser social ties to the group structure, are far more likely to succumb to such a solitary life than females. An aggressive rogue does more than threaten, and to call him potentially dangerous is to understate the matter by at least half. But, again, very few individuals ever deserve such a label.

Among themselves, as previously noted, elephants rarely draw blood. Young bulls, again as noted, do their share of friendly sparring. Showing off and petty quarrels at waterholes are common enough, and adolescent exuberance sometimes ends in a lesson of one kind or another, but elephants ordinarily are, like the English, great respecters of the queue, and the sedate hierarchy (no doubt helped by a threatening gesture or two) holds together. At salt-licks, the equilibrium is invariably tested. The salt is much prized by all elephants — some seem positively to crave the sodium[16] — and, accordingly, an elephant tends to express any dissatisfaction about life in general at times of crowding at the lick. To a certain extent, the salt-lick experience becomes one of every elephant for itself. I once watched one elephant drive another away not just from the immediate area of the salt-lick but halfway around a large adjoining swamp and on into the nearby forest. The victim of this bullying reluctantly and slowly gave way but apparently not to the satisfaction of the aggressor (25 & 26). Having finally driven the *Loxodonta africana non grata* into the woods, the perpetrator returned to the salt. Whereupon, the victim furiously emerged from his forest exile and lumbered to the halfway point of the relinquished territory, trumpeting loudly, and shaking his head the entire way. He then reached down, hoisted a tree branch, flung it high over his head in a fit of utter rage, and loudly exited. For a good half-hour or so, we could hear him crashing about and bellowing in the deeper parts of the woods venting his wrath. The best moments of Italian light opera could not have been more comical.

The only really major — and sometimes fatal — conflict between elephants happens when two evenly matched (in body size and tusk length) bulls compete for a cow in estrus. Such battles are most unusual. A lesser conflict can also arise if a large bull comes into contact with a new (never before seen) group of bulls and feels compelled to establish his position.

Elephants seem to follow a practice of deliberate natural birth control. There is no specific breeding season, but heightened sexual activity ensues when the environment will support more elephants: plentiful food and water increases sexual relations. This fact alone causes, of course, no great surprise and certainly does not require any significant intelligence on the part of the elephant. If elephants have to wander less to eat and drink, they will, in common with other mammals, find more time for other matters. But, with elephants, there is more to the practice. Youngsters in herds that are forced into a predominantly nomadic way of life, roaming over huge areas of barely marginal existence and dependent upon the changing

---

14. An elephant herd that has been recently hassled by poachers will be especially touchy (and possibly dangerous) in the presence of man. Additionally, a particularly malcontent youngster might well have unwittingly let ants crawl up its trunk, a temporarily enraging experience. Pliny offered some typically remarkable insights concerning the interaction between elephants and man. For example, when an elephant accidentally met a human being who simply happened across its track, according to Pliny, the good-tempered leviathan actually showed the man the way. But should the elephant have noticed a human footprint before seeing the man himself, it began to suspect an ambush and worked itself into a belligerent mood. This last included digging up the footprint and passing it whole to other elephants, until a regular battle-line could be mustered. Furthermore, when surrounded by a party of hunters, elephants purportedly posted those with the smallest tusks in front, to fool the hunters into thinking that the herd had not sufficient ivory to warrant a fight. Failing all else, the exhausted elephants would break their own tusks against the trees and ransom the ivory for their freedom!

15. Elephants see better than rhinos, but their eyesight is not good. Their eyes are set too far to the sides of their heads for binocular vision. Like rhinos, they feel better if the "danger" is moving — preferably, away — and therefore more easily identifiable.

16. The salt may have purgative and anti-parasitic effects.

Plate 24. The Charge. Elephant feet have soft, spongy soles that absorb undue noise in the forest — a fact totally lost upon the object of a full charge. At 25 mph, elephants can easily outrun men but heat up quickly and, after a short burst of top speed, must slow down. They cannot run or gallop but move by a powerful trot, as shown here. Many of the pictures that one sees purporting to depict an angry, charging elephant merely show the animal having its dust bath or catch an animal (with trunk up and ears out) in an inquisitive posture. In the field, it is helpful to realize that most dummy charges by elephants remain just those — because the other animals (and people) *respond* to the threat by moving. Failure to take an elephant seriously may lead to the elephant upping the ante.

Plates 25 & 26. Salt-Lick Opera. Elephants will travel many miles for a lick of salt, a habit that contributes to the success of the "Tree Hotels," which are built overlooking salt-licks. Most proprietors then add their own salt to ensure the visitations. In any event, these places are an excellent choice to see the antics of all the pachyderms. Late afternoon is the best viewing time, but the fun goes on all night (the salt-licks are lit by floodlights after dark).

seasons for their very survival, actually seem to attain puberty later. And the intervals between estrus are longer for the females.[17]

Such nomadic existence is particularly difficult for elephants, whose vulnerability to suffering from poor habitat is magnified because of their size. The scarce vegetation, plus the low nutrition content of what vegetation there is, adds up to inadequate fuel, which does not easily support the trekking required to sustain the food search. The vicious circle produces starvation. To make matters worse, the elephant has a relatively inefficient digestive system; it digests less than half of what is eaten.[18] (In lush environments, the elephant thus becomes a sort of ambulatory fertilizer factory.) As the land dries up during a drought, elephants disperse in small units to spread their feeding load over the less rich pastures.

The effect that elephants have on an environment that is sustaining them is a subject of much (sometimes heated) dispute among scientific observers. An elephant maintaining good health will eat (if it can) 300 pounds of food each day or several thousand tons in a lifetime (while drinking water at the rate of thirty-plus gallons per day). On the average, Jumbo eats fourteen hours a day. The diet tends to be extremely varied: fruits, herbs, twigs, leaves, grasses (more than anything else), and bark, to name the most common foods. The reader can only imagine the perspective of a baobab tree as a "big-tusker" approaches — not exactly an exhilarating experience. Having undoubtedly survived all kinds of vicissitudes for several hundred years, the old tree might not survive the elephant (27). Simply stated, elephants love to destroy trees. What they cannot uproot or knock down, they hollow out with tusks. Just stripping the bark can be deadly, as bacteria and insects (especially the borer beetles) can then do their lethal work. Unfortunately, elephants do more damage than mere eating requires,[19] even allowing for larger elephants seeing to the needs of the youngsters with diminished trunk reach,[20] though 300 pounds per day per adult head is not to be minimized. Of course, a tree on its side provides convenient eating, and picking at the roots is perhaps the only way to satisfy a "sweet tooth," but, by any measure, the destruction is excessive and wasteful. In truth, elephants *enjoy* the harvesting, and an upright tree takes on a sort of challenge, becomes a matter of honor (28):

---

17. Many species, especially elephants, have developed behavioral and physiological mechanisms that detect resource deprivation and encourage individuals to respond early, before widespread famine sets in (a catastrophe likely to lead to more permanent damage to the environment and to the species). Whether the behavioral mechanisms, which themselves are fairly complex, are as important as the more simple physiological reactions (for example, endocrine stress) is a matter about which scientists disagree.

18. For most animals, vegetation is poor food compared to the flesh of other animals. Plants growing in the wild contain mostly cellulose, which animals can digest only with the help of bacteria and micro-organisms situated in their digestive tract. The process there of fermentation changes the cellulose to sugars, but that process is a difficult and time-consuming one, and the total energy released is low. (A plant's storage organs, in the form of tubers, bulbs, and rhizomes, and its seeds and fruits are, however, comparatively rich in starch or sugar.) Additionally, most plant tissues, other than seeds, are poor in protein and other vital chemicals. One result of the diminished food value of plants is that herbivores must eat a substantial amount of food relative to their body weight. Furthermore, an elephant is a "hindgut" fermenter, as opposed to a ruminant, that is, the site of fermentation is located in its large colon. The distinction is discussed in greater detail in the text below. The process of fermentation is identical to all herbivores, but hindgut fermentation is said to be less efficient because the food is retained for only half the length of time (roughly forty-eight hours) than that taken in by ruminants — this means that more food has to be consumed each day to accommodate the greater turnover rate. Typically, hindguters make use of only forty-five percent of the cellulose that they eat. Elephants probably digest even less. (Non-ruminants also need more water, to balance the urea in their urine; ruminants recycle urea.) Hindgut fermenters have an advantage where the food is high in fiber, thus necessitating a high intake to obtain sufficient energy and protein. And, as might be expected, coarse plants are more abundantly distributed (year-round and over the entire habitat) than more nutritious vegetation. Ruminants, on the other hand, thrive where the food quality is higher.

Thus, elephants require a huge intake of food (and water) each day. In fact, they eat for up to sixteen hours a day, seemingly nonstop to the casual onlooker, day and night. An elephant who lives for sixty-odd years will have devoted perhaps forty or so years of that time to feeding. Savannah elephants eat mainly grasses until the dry season, when they feed on the woody parts of trees and shrubs — twigs, branches, and bark. They will eat flowers and fruit when available (indeed, elephants have been said to become 'drunk' after consuming copious amounts of fruit, which then allegedly ferments into spirits) and frequently dig for roots, especially at the beginning of the rainy seasons.

Having said all this, it should be noted that an elephant actually eats *less* per body weight than other animals. Differences in metabolic rates enable a large animal to feed on less nutritious or a smaller amount of plant food proportionately than can a smaller animal. In other words, small animals require more food per pound of body weight than large animals. This phenomenon (the relationship of body mass to skin area — size — and the relative metabolic rates) is discussed in the text below.

19. It is thought that the bark and roots supply, in part, the great quantities of calcium required by the huge mass of bone and ivory. Possibly, other minerals and salts are included as well. In the absence of trees, elephants do not prosper. Nevertheless, elephants are remarkably adjustable and live in environments that range from rain forests to near deserts, where they wander aimlessly without actually seeming dilatory.

20. Ironically, the young elephants can be every bit as destructive as their elders, as they frequently imitate the adults by tearing off small branches and discarding them, content with the food-gathering experience without eating.

Plate 27. Jumbos and Baobab Tree: An African Drama. The elephant's path on its endless search for sustenance often resembles Sherman's march to the sea through Georgia: no quarter. In a few hours, the three elephants of varying sizes pictured here will do substantial damage to the baobab shown. The elephant, along with fire, is nature's most powerful tool for molding the environment: both bulldozer and gardener. They also work together — the damage that elephants do to trees makes the latter more susceptible to the ravages of fire. Baobabs — the famous ''upside-down trees'' (when leafless, they look as if their roots are pointing to the sky) — are thought to be 2500 years old or more, making them among the oldest living plants on earth. ''Mbuyu'' in Kiswahili, the trees are featured in the mythology of many African tribes — the bushmen, for example, say that, when the Creator made the world, He threw the baobab out of His garden and it landed with its head buried and ungainly roots pointing upward. The author believes that the most striking examples of the gargantuan tree, whose trunk can grow up to thirty feet in diameter, are found at Lake Manyara in Tanzania, but those located in the Kalahari look more dramatic in their isolation.

The elephants immediately threw themselves upon the fresh greens. In no time the torn branches were stripped nearly clean, and the lead bull reached for the treetop again. His first try fell short, and he lowered his trunk in preparation for a more strenuous tactic. Clutching the fork of a branch with the tip of his raised trunk, he took the tree trunk between his tusks and pressed his forehead against it with such force that the whole tree began to sway. The elephant pushed, stepped back, pushed again, three, four times. With each assault, the bull bent the tree a little farther before allowing it to swing back. After the fifth push, it swung back no more but arched in slow motion to the ground. The crash shattered the afternoon quiet for miles

around. Three more elephants left the tree on which they had been feeding a few hundred yards off to share in the new feast.

For the next hour the elephants were busy, tearing the treetop apart with their trunks, tusks, and forefeet, and chewing it up. Only rarely was there some minor trouble, when a low-ranking elephant plucked the choicest greens from under the nose of a higher-up, in which case the stronger animal simply shoved the weaker one aside, causing a chain reaction of rearrangements in the feeding order. But once or twice such an altercation led to serious confrontation, and then the higher-ranking elephant dealt his rival a blow with his heavy tusks that made their

Plate 28. Elephant Sport. There is no way that this elephant can readily knock down this tree by pushing in the opposite direction of its lean. Nevertheless, a push from this angle, a push from another angle — the elephant will eventually take its toll. So much for our initial reaction. But our sportsman deserves more credit: the elephant pushes against the lean to cause the tree to sway back and forth — by periodically releasing the forward pressure — thereby causing pods and fruit to drop to the ground. It is no wonder that baboons and impalas religiously follow elephants into the trees.

relative ranks and prerogatives unmistakably clear.[21]

Long ago, the damage to their environment caused by the elephants could be regarded as simple cyclical change — huge territories, continents even, could easily survive such long-term farming. The elephants do, after all, farm: by breaking up dense, unproductive woodlands, they create the right conditions for grasses; by felling trees, they also release nutrients and minerals locked in the wood, causing them to be recycled for the benefit of other plants and animals; and the break produced in the forest canopy allows the fallen trees' offspring (and immediate neighbors) to grow. Elephants additionally are great sowers of seeds; once the fruit is eaten, the seeds pass through the elephant unharmed and are scattered over a wide area in the droppings. With their outer shells softened by the passage, the seeds are thereby encouraged to germinate and further are packaged in a hefty application of fertilizer provided in the form of manure. Moreover, the seedlings that result would never have grown in the shade of the parents. Finally, research has shown that acacia trees, a favorite food, actually depend upon elephants (among others), whose digestive process kill parasitic beetle larva (found in the seed pods) that are specific and deadly to acacia. In other words, ''destruction'' eventually becomes enrichment. (*29*)

But a successful natural order requires a great deal of space and many lifetimes (in human terms) to work out on its own. Today, the damage in some reserves appears too severe where elephants have congregated in great numbers. Mortality within the parks is somewhat lowered because of favorable conditions, but the real villain is the constricting opportunities outside the reserves, forcing more and more elephants to limit their activities to the parks themselves. How then to deal with the problem is one of the thorniest questions for today's conservationists and game-keepers — leading to calls for (and opposition to) culling when the elephant density appears too high. The author returns to this question in Chapter X.

As suggested earlier and despite our research, much mystery surrounds elephants. In Africa, the elephant has, over time, achieved mystical status. To appreciate this wonder, the safarist must follow the herd for awhile. Patience will likely bring the same rewards achieved in watching the lion pride. The loyalty of elephants can, for example, be authenticated. They will assist — physically support, if necessary — old or wounded comrades. A herd will remain with a dying member to the end and even try to revive the animal once it has died. Elephants obviously grieve deeply over the loss of a fellow member. I have observed them standing for hours beside a dead body (the example of a mother carrying around a dead calf for several days has already been noted) and then burying it under earth and brush.[22] Elephants also will

21. Reinhard Künkel, *Elephants,* p. 19. In the forest or heavy thickets, the safarist is likely to hear the snap, crackle, and pop of elephants vandalizing the woodwork before actually seeing the giants. Dead branches breaking off in the still forest air often sound like pistol shots.

22. Elephants have also been known similarly to bury other animal carcasses that they find.

draw the tusks from skulls of dead elephants and bury the ivory elsewhere, along with other bones taken from the dead carcasses. This is one of the causes that may have given rise to the long-standing myth of the "elephant graveyard."[23] Another reason for finding many skeletons together in certain areas — and thus helping no doubt to feed the graveyard myth — is the proclivity of older elephants to collect in swamps, where many of them eventually die (see below). A third possible contributing factor was the old practice by some African tribes of hunting elephants by building a ring of fire around an entire group, thereby killing hundreds at one time.[24] Yet a fourth possibility was, of course, a natural catastrophe of some kind. Ironically, the stories of elephant graveyards may well, however, have received their greatest boost by the *lack* of bones lying around in those obvious places where elephants frequented. This deficiency must have puzzled the early travelers, looking at the giants while alive. We now understand that no bones, whatever their size, are indestructible on the African veldt; bones of all dimensions disappear quickly. What the hyenas and jackals leave, the beetles, termites, and ants take. What little these last leave is consumed by fire, rain, and rot.

Elephants are also great weathermen — they can

Plate 29. At Forest's Edge. Elephants prefer the tender new grasses at the forest's edge, an environment which they played a large part in creating.

23. The first European explorers who penetrated the interior of Africa returned with dramatic accounts of elephant graveyards, remote and secluded places chosen by aged tuskers for dying. Predictably, many adventurers, excited by the prospect of finding huge treasure hordes of ivory, set out to search for such burial grounds — in vain, as the ivory treasure became Africa's equivalent of the fabulous kingdom of El Dorado much sought after in South America.

24. Modern-day poachers find that they too often have to slaughter an entire herd or group in order to collect the ivory of just one or two elephants; any survivors would forbid the killers from approaching the dead.

"predict" rainfall in a region far away and will travel hundreds of miles to come together for just such an event taking place in times of drought. In spite of their interminable trekking, the evidence is strong that elephants return again and again to the same "home area," even zones of poor subsistence, and hence are in a certain sense "territorial," though they do not, as do the big cats, defend their territories.

In the meantime, our youngster, if he has reached ten years of age, is by now seven-and-a-half feet tall and approaching adolescence. He is pretty much able at this point to fend for himself. Males reach puberty at thirteen to fifteen years of age but, while physically capable of mating, are not yet "socially mature" and do not compete with the older males for estrous females until their early twenties. On the other hand, young females usually mate during their first estrous cycle — at approximately fourteen years. Females generally grow in size until they attain twenty years or so, but the males continue to grow for most of their lives and many grow to twice the magnitude of the females. Size is, therefore, a reliable guide to the relative ages of elephants in any given group. At thirty, the elephant is in the prime of life and can expect to live until sixty or so,[25] when its sixth and last set of teeth eventually wears down.[26] By then, it will be eating mainly the soft grasses found at the river's edge *(30)* or in swamps *(31)*. The elder jumbo will gradually starve (evidenced by extreme hollows seen in its skull), lose its strength, and eventually die of malnutrition or disease. Or it may die mired in the swamps themselves. Few diseases seriously affect elephants before the advent of starvation and malnutrition.

The best method for distinguishing between adult elephants is to study their tusks or large ears, no set of either of which are quite alike *(32 & 33)*. The large ears are the primary cooling mechanism of the elephant. Their surface area is roughly equivalent to one-third the rest of the animal! *Each* ear may have a surface of up to thirty square feet, and the total spread of both ears may well exceed the animal's height. The flap contains a great fan-like network of blood vessels located near the surface of the underside, where the blood is steadily cooled, a process encouraged by flapping the ears, by simply spreading them when there are breezes of any kind, or, less frequently, by spraying them with water. Thus cooled, the blood circulates to the brain and elsewhere. In the event of extreme heat, the elephant will burp up water from its stomach and use its trunk to hose the liquid over its ears and shoulders.

Heat is, of course, one of the primary characteristics of the African bush, and the safarist should understand some of the basic principles that govern how the animals cope with this aspect of their environment. A mammalian body dissipates heat primarily through its skin. A small mammal has a proportionately larger surface area to its volume, or mass, than a large mammal — simple math tells us that the surface area of a body increases by *squaring*, while volume increases by its *cube*. Thus, a bigger mammal has less skin area per unit of volume than a smaller animal and, all else being equal, loses heat more slowly. This is why small mammals have to eat incessantly — a mammal requires more energy the faster that it loses heat to the environment. Small animals need a higher metabolism (the reader may compare a furnace burning fuel) to maintain themselves. As implied in footnote 18, one large 7,000-pound elephant will actually eat far less vegetation than the equivalent biomass of hyraxes (for example). Relative size therefore obviously influences activity levels and the quality of food eaten, among many other characteristics. Smaller animals are pushed toward more nutritious diets; the bigger species can tolerate lower food value (but still need abundant amounts). And the bigger animals can clearly travel farther and faster to exploit widely separate resources. But, though large mammals have the advantage of conserving energy (and consequently do well in colder environments), they are at a considerable disadvantage when it comes to dissipating heat and staying cool under the African sun. Thus, even though the elephant's relatively sluggish metabolism means that it takes a long time to heat the great mass of the body to a critical level (helped further in the elephant's case by the insulation of one-inch thick skin), our elephant friend faces a potentially formidable problem at midday.

Aside from its ears, the elephant relies upon bathing, sweat glands liberally distributed over its body, and seeking shade during the hottest times of the day. At least one writer has suggested that all the wrinkles in an elephant's skin serve as cooling devices, each wrinkle creating a small shadow, its own 'shade,' so to speak, an assertion that seems more than a little fanciful. In truth, physiologically and behaviorally, the elephant is a thermally efficient animal — which helps to make him successful.

Elephant courtship has been typically romanticized in the literature beyond recognition in the wild. Writers have described a "very coy" and "playful" female, who "chooses" one mate; a "long courtship," during which the mating pair is "inseparable"; long, intimate, even

---

25. Some authorities believe that individual elephants have lived to 100 or more years, but the evidence for this proposition is scant.

26. Besides its tusks (enlarged incisors), an elephant has only four functional teeth at one time: two molars in the upper and two in the lower jaw. As the teeth wear down, they are gradually replaced by others, for a total of five replacements. The molars are huge — up to a foot long and eight pounds in weight! An elephant's skull is disproportionately large compared with the size of its brain — its size is required to support the mass of elephant dentition, including the tusks, and the trunk. On the other hand, the skull itself is relatively light (counting, however, the tusks and molars, its weight may reach twenty-five percent of body tonnage), thanks to an extensive network of sinuses and air cavities resembling a bony sponge (a picture of a skull is contained in Chapter IX).

Plate 30. *Along the River Bank.*

When people call this beast
  to mind,
They marvel more and more
At such a little tail behind,
So large a trunk before.
    Hilaire Belloc, *Bad Child's Book of Beasts*, "The Elephant."

Plate 31. In the Enkongo Narok Swamp (Amboseli). Young elephants, as well as their elders, enjoy the tender grasses of the swamps. Elephants are good swimmers, but the older bulls and cows eventually become stuck in the mud of swamps and die there.

Plate 32. A Big-Tusker. Tusks that grow so as to meet at the tips are of limited use; certainly, they no longer can be employed to strip bark and the like. The tusks of male elephants are far thicker than those of females; the male tusk is heavily tapered from the base, while female ivory is so slightly tapered as to look cylindrical. Differences in texture and shape also appear under varying environmental conditions — for example, tusks from Zaire and West African rain forests differ considerably from the softer, whiter ivory from East Africa. Ivory is essentially a mixture of dentine, cartilage, and calcium that covers a sensitive inner core comparable to a human tooth nerve. Only two-thirds of a living tusk is visible; one-third lies above the jaw level. Tusks are not a reliable criterion for judging age. Very rarely, one sees an elephant with more than two tusks, a condition that seems to result from damage to the tooth occurring in the second or third year.

Plate 33. Elephant Radiators. Every ear is different — each is full of holes and ragged from the business of living. The upper edge of an elephant's ear tends to flop over with increasing age. The ear flap of the African elephant is so much larger than that of the Asian because of its cooling function and the exposure to the sun experienced on the African savannah. (Accordingly, forest elephants in Africa have smaller ears.) Scientists also believe that the ears are an important tool for communication, and they certainly serve the additional varied purposes of increasing significantly an elephant's threat display and of chasing off flies.

"titillating" foreplay; and a quiet, gentle mating that takes place in the discreet privacy of the bush — all substantially misinformation. In reality, the bulls, either drawn to the nursery herd by scent or by circumstance, 'test' females' willingness to mate by touching the female genitals with their trunks. The females are reasonably cooperative and those in heat are quickly identified. Estrus lasts about four days, and the female is usually followed by several males and often mated by more than one. During part of that period, the female will, however, always be bred by the dominant male in attendance. That male in turn habitually establishes his primary right to mate. The mating itself lasts less than a minute. Although some mutual tender stroking by trunks and "kissing" accomplished by inserting their trunks into each other's mouth and then intertwining them above their heads happens, elephants do not devote much time to sexual activities. Quite unlike lions, for example, courtship does not interfere with the main business of every day: eating. (34) Far from being a private affair, all mating transpires in the open, among the herd members, and always causes great excitement in the group. During and immediately after each coupling, the herd excitedly mills around, bumping into one another and making as much noise as possible. Instead of a quiet, romantic interlude, the mating reality turns out to be a riotous pageant.

Furthermore, the sentimental honeymoon that supposedly follows the doting courtship is equally fictitious.[27] No permanent pair-bond is ever formed. While a bull may occasionally remain with a female's herd for as long as a month after copulation (he will certainly remain if other cows in the meantime come into estrus), this dalliance is inefficient and atypical behavior. Females remain in heat for only a few days, and bulls have to travel long distances each day to monitor the changing reproductive status of the cows in their home range.

The elephant ("tembo" or "ndovu" in Kiswahili) in many respects resembles man. At the very least, the jumbos are among the most intelligent animals, right up there with dolphins and whales and chimps.[28] The extended childhood, when compared to the human family, supports the theory that the longer the period of childhood, the greater the intellectual potential of the adult. That is, biologists believe that a close correlation exists between the length of youthful dependency and the level of intelligence of the species.[29] The elephants' fondness for their young and their family and social structures have much in common with ours. Elephants all their lives give the impression of decision-making,[30] deep feelings, and a capacity for goodness. They are certainly capable of quite varied and detailed personalities. The unswerving loyalty exhibited by elephants is quite rare among all animals. Even more rare — perhaps unique, with the exception of man — the elephant possesses some shadowy concept of death:

> For human beings and for elephants death remains significant in the behaviour of the survivors. In life individuals of both species are tied by strong family bonds and frantic attempts may be made to save a sick or dying relative.
>
> Many great zoologists including Charles Darwin have thought that animals possess strong emotions and I have little doubt that when one of their number dies and the bonds of a lifetime are severed, elephants have a similar feeling to the one we call grief. Unfortunately science as yet has no means of measuring or describing emotion even for human beings, let alone for animals.
>
> . . .
>
> Now I saw quite clearly a scene of great natural drama. The cow, an adult, was lying on her side down the slope;

to manipulate the trunk. As stated, elephant calves take some time, for example, to learn to drink with their trunks — for months, they kneel awkwardly to drink directly with their mouths. But conscious choice, initiative, and intelligent decision-making have to be evidenced by appropriate behavior. And, in many respects, elephant behavior indicates an intelligence that is surprisingly advanced. The safarist who watches closely how an elephant selects food, watches how an elephant overcomes a physical handicap, studies an elephant traversing difficult ground, and examines incidents of family and herd loyalty and devotion that he may be fortunate enough to witness (particularly the mutual aid or rescue of the type referred to in the text earlier), that visitor cannot fail to be fascinated by how an elephant *thinks*.

27. One "naturalist" has gone so far as to describe a long, tender honeymoon until the cow begins to feel her pregnancy in the ninth month, loses interest in the "romance," and grows cold to her "lover." The bull, according to this account, accepts the situation with gentlemanly calm and goes off to find another wife.

28. The subject of animals thinking is discussed at length in the next chapter. The elephant's reputation for intelligence is often based upon poor reasons: the size of its immense head, the dexterity of its trunk, and the fact that elephants have for centuries been successfully trained by man. In fact, an elephant's brain is but a small part of its skull and rather small for its body size as well. Nor do the muscular coordination of the trunk and all the training necessarily prove intelligence, though elephants undoubtedly have an extraordinary capacity for learning. And one should not automatically dismiss the *learning* process necessary

29. The reasoning is simple. If an animal is to rely on instinct — immutable behavior patterns programmed by heredity — there is little to learn after birth. But, if a species needs to react to a changing environment, for which a fixed number of behavior patterns would be inadequate to survive (or prosper), that species must have a more generalized intelligence, capable of learning. Nature's method of achieving this level of versatility is to expose the young to the world when their brains are immature and to allow them to develop in the 'real world,' as opposed to the security (and static environment) of the uterus.

30. Elephants even seem to know that they are "safe" within the national parks. There are many substantiated accounts of hunted tuskers making a beeline for the sanctuary of the reserves.

Plate 34. Elephant "Courtship." The safarist would have to follow this threesome awhile before learning that the big fellow is courting the female with calf. Male elephants that are breeding (*i.e.*, during periods of high testosterone hormone levels in the blood) often come into "musth," a condition difficult for safarists to recognize at a distance (the male secretes a sticky, oily fluid from the temporal glands, tiny slits located halfway between the eyes and ears that also become swollen and inflamed; up-close, the strong-smelling fluid can be seen slowly oozing down the side of the face, causing a dark, tarry stain). A male in *musth* can be aggressive toward other bulls, irritable (if not mean), unpredictable, and possibly dangerous. Some scientists have questioned the sexual linkage, asserting that *musth* occurs in females as well as in males and in males too young to breed, and also noting that sexual activity often takes place without any hint of *musth* whatsoever. Moreover, some animals in *musth* show no particular excitement or wildness. Indeed, for a long time, naturalists believed that the condition was peculiar to Asian elephants, in which, because of domesticity and close observation, *musth* was first noticed. These scientists (who support a non-sexual origin) believe that *musth* is more climatic in origin and usually suggest a connection with the start of the rainy season. They also believe that elephants in the wild are less liable to become deranged or disturbed, the natural environment encouraging the animal to stay on an even keel. Thus, because of *musth*, bull elephants are infrequently kept in zoos or circuses. In any event, *musth* can last as long as two to three months.

The ubiquitous egrets that accompany the herd in this picture are waiting for the insects stirred up when the elephants move. At the time of mating, the egrets are many — the "riotous pageant" described in the text produces a surfeit of food. Because of their sensitive skin, elephants will not tolerate tick-birds, unlike most other herbivores. Egrets are, however, permitted to ride like maharajahs and strut along the elephant's back with impunity. On the ground, they frequently appear about to be crushed by an ambling footstep, only to take appropriately evasive action at the last moment.

Plate 35. Leave-Taking. In truth, the study of elephants and their herds has only scratched the surface. The mystery is basically intact.

one of her hind feet was wedged between a boulder and a thick tree and she was hanging from it. Her head was bent backwards at an acute angle and she was stone dead. Next to her stood three calves of different sizes. The eldest was moaning quietly but every so often gave vent to a passionate bawl. The second just stood dumbly motionless, its head resting against its mother's body. The smallest calf, less than a year old, made forlorn attempts to suck from her breasts. Then the eldest knelt down and pushed its head and small tusks against the corpse, in a hopeless attempt to move it. I watched them for fifteen minutes repeating these patterns of behaviour until suddenly they caught my wind and wandered slowly away.

On closer inspection I found that the cow was still warm and that no flies had settled on her, so the accident must have happened only a short time earlier. Trees which had stood in the path of her fall were broken and boulders dislodged. I backtracked the path of her descent to a point about 400 feet up the slope where I found her last footprints. It appeared that she had stepped into a pig hole covered in vegetation, lost her balance and rolled out of control down the precipitous slopes. There were several cliffs and in places it looked as if she had bounced down them leaving the vegetation undamaged. The calves must have had some difficulty in finding her afterwards, for the nature of the terrain would have forced them to make a wide detour. It seemed that they were not aware that she was dead, although they must have known something was wrong. Perhaps they could not adjust immediately to the finality of her death.[31]

Some writers have simply but affectionately written off the elephant as "hopelessly bourgeois" and as nature's "solid citizen." Few animals are the subject of such unflagging interest around the campfires burning in safari Africa. A singular species, to be sure. Most safarists upon leaving the elephant would willingly join Elspeth Huxley in her prayer (35):

So goodbye, Manyara elephants. Another day is over, those big bellies filled with tasty fruit, with bark and branches, grass and seedpods, herbs and leaves, such a variety to chose from and to relish; mud-baths have been taken, children suckled, a drowsy siesta in the shade enjoyed, sunrise to sunset passed without alarums and excursions. May it so continue until the little calf we saw getting in the way of her elders, rolling under their bellies with her legs in the air, grows to be a matriarch with her grandchildren and great grand-children around her. May she live to lay her bones in peace when old age comes. May hunters with guns and poisoned arrows, may accident and mishap, may starvation as the woodlands shrink and wither, pass her by. May the hungry generations pressing in upon her sanctuary never tread her down.[32]

Hyrax

A very small mammal that nonetheless will be seen by most visitors on safari, the hyrax is perhaps best known as the closest living relative to the elephant, anatomically speaking. Even so, the relationship is a distant one in time: both may well have come from a common ancestor that lived many tens of millions of years ago. At one time, the hyrax was considerably larger and the elephant almost certainly equally smaller. The main similarities today

---

31. Douglas-Hamilton, *Among the Elephants,* pp. 44-7. Similar behavior has been reported by many other reliable sources. Few other animals react in any significantly observable fashion to the death suffered by a relative.

---

32. *Last Days in Eden,* p. 167.

(aside from some skeletal and cerebral parallelisms) are found in the toes and the flat, plate-like nails, on the one hand, and the tusk-like upper incisors of the hyrax that curve up from the skull, on the other hand.[33] (Both characteristics are sure to escape the observations of the average tourist.) Like tusks, these incisors are not used for eating *per se* but can be employed to perform several tasks, including fighting. Hyraxes look like large, furry guinea pigs but they are real ungulates, not rodents. The world's smallest hooved mammal, the hyrax preceded all hooved animals that we know today. The hyrax is indeed a living fossil.

Biblical scholars might also appreciate the fact that hyraxes, also known as dassies (especially in South Africa),[34] are the conies of the Old Testament, the only mammal included in the four "exceedingly wise" creatures (the other three were the ant, the locust, and the spider). Such excessive wisdom is, however, likely to be lost on the safarist.

There are three types of hyraxes in Africa: Rock, Bush, and Tree. All have short, thick fur, central dorsal hair patches,[35] and no visible tails. The Rock, or Johnston's, hyrax ("pimbi" in Kiswahili) is the largest species and is sometimes called a "rock rabbit," a good comparison for size at least (36). It has a mousy-brown color and feeds mostly on grasses. The Rock hyrax is a highly social animal (who engages in, for example, cooperative caring for the young) and lives in colonies of fifty or more but during the day spreads out through the immediate environment in groups of twos, threes, or fours to watch all parts of their rocky surroundings. Early in the morning, however, before the animals disperse, large groups huddle together for warmth. They also sleep in piles at night for the same reason. As a rule, a Rock hyrax feeds in the early morning and late afternoon. Midday, in common with all hyraxes, it basks in the sun. At this time, it appears to the safarist virtually frozen; a hyrax will hold the same position without moving for several hours. Rock hyraxes are easy to find on safari.

The Bush, or Bruce's Yellow-spotted, hyrax (also "pimbi" in Kiswahili) often lives side-by-side or in close proximity to the larger Rock variety and shares similar habits and features. More grey in color, it prefers abandoned termite mounds as homes and eats mostly fruits and leaves. The Bush hyrax, like all hyraxes, is a good climber. The soles of a hyrax's feet are well adapted to climbing: kept damp by glandular secretions, the elastic rubbery pads act

Plate 36. Rock Hyrax. All hyraxes look pretty much alike. The Rock hyrax varies from yellow-brown to grey-brown, always grizzled with black. Hyrax families have dominant males who fiercely defend their territories against intruding hyraxes. Families, however, live close to one another. The safarist will probably not notice, but males threaten one another by chattering their teeth. The safarist can easily tell where hyraxes like to sit in the rocks by the copious accumulations of droppings.

like suction cups. Thus, steep rock surfaces or vertical tree trunks are both easily traversed.[36] Thus, the little hyrax frequently manages to match the elephant's vertical reach.

The association between the Rock and Bush hyraxes is reputed to be the closest existing between any two mammalian species, except for certain primates. They do not compete directly for food, as the Bush browses primarily on leaves and the Rock eats mainly grass. They do not interbreed, because their mating behavior is significantly different and they also have distinct sex-organ anatomies.

The Tree hyrax (37) is shy, more nocturnal than other hyraxes, and, as the name indicates, arboreal. Basically grey, the Tree hyrax ("perere" in Kiswahili) is the smallest of the three types and also exclusively herbivorous, preferring seed from acacia trees. The little noisemaker (to put it mildly) comes into his own at night; his shrill, piercing scream carries for miles. If the safarist sleeps very near a tree inhabited by a hyrax, he is in for a surprise that could send him right through the sheets. The author recalls his first really close-up experience only a few years

---

33. A third member of what would probably be the most unlikely trio in the animal kingdom could be the aardvark, who also seems to be a distantly related "primitive ungulate," exhibiting similar flattened nails, elongated jaws, and specialized dentition.

34. Derived from *dasse* or "badger" in Dutch.

35. Hyraxes have a dorsal gland surrounded by a light-colored circle of hairs that stiffen when the animal is excited. The glandular spot is most prominent in Tree hyraxes.

---

36. Dassies defecate and urinate in specific spots, where the waste accumulates. Formerly, these droppings were collected and used as medicine for epilepsy and other diseases.

Plate 37. Tree Hyrax: Noisemaker.
Hyraxes are extremely adaptive: they are
found anywhere from sea level to high
up Africa's tallest mountains. Native
legend holds that hyraxes are the only
animals who are able to gaze directly at
the sun unharmed. Hyraxes do, in fact,
often scan the skies for predatory eagles
(especially Verreaux's eagle, who feeds
almost exclusively on hyraxes) and
hawks but apparently relax just long
enough for a number to be taken by
these birds of prey. If hyraxes become
visibly agitated and start to scurry about
in apparent panic, the safarist should
look to the sky. The other main enemies
are leopards and snakes. Tree hyraxes
are widespread, despite constant heavy
predation. Only deforestation has
significantly reduced their numbers.
Like elephants, hyraxes have long gestation periods. Also like elephants, males
carry their testes inside their bodies.

ago, as he settled down in a tented camp for the night.
The hyrax started in about 10:30 p.m. I had listened to
hyraxes in the night — far off — for years but was totally
unprepared for what followed. The disturbance at first
resembled the whirring, wind-up croak of a Halloween or
party noise maker or the harsh, magnified noise of the
typical Hollywood squeaky door. Then came the protracted and ascending scream. At close range, the effect
was blood-curdling. The repetition was then so exact that
it sounded almost mechanical. My initial reaction was to
blame the young tourists in an adjoining tent, and I sprang
to the path, flashlight in hand, to shut them up. And more
than a little curious as to how in the world they were making this awful noise. I was three steps from my tent and
directly under his tree when the hyrax let loose again.
Much chastened but also relieved that I had been spared
the embarrassment of mistaken accusations, I retreated to
my bed. The hyrax continued his relentless seesaw
serenade of rattling and high-pitched wailing, a sign that
he was moving around, descending and ascending the
tree, for several hours. He finally settled down and I finally went to sleep at about 2:30 a.m.

Rhinoceroses

This volume is not a book about wildlife conservation
and the rather desperate fight to save endangered African
species, though the author perhaps is justified in hoping
that the pictures and text will encourage a real appreciation for the animals and a corresponding sympathy for
their survival. But one cannot speak of the rhino without
addressing its problem: the most reliable recent estimates
indicate that only some 9,000 Black and 3,000 White
rhinos are left in all Africa, a staggeringly tiny number.[37]
Nor has some evolutionary failure doomed this sixty-
million-year-old survivor who walked the earth with the
dinosaur; instead, man's greed and a curious blend of
preoccupation with sex, Chinese folk medicine, and conspicuous consumption are responsible for consigning one
of evolution's greatest successes to such a precarious
status.

As indicated, there are two species of African
rhinoceros, the White and the Black, but they differ in
size, shape, and temperament, not in color. Both are, in

---

37. Plentiful at the turn of the century (the Black always greatly
outnumbering the White), the rhino was not doing so badly,
even into the mid-1900s. For example, the colonial government
of Kenya in the 1940s hired a hunter (J.A. Hunter) to shoot some
1,000 rhinos for the purpose of clearing just 50,000 acres for
agriculture. In 1968, reliable estimates put the total number in
Kenya at approximately 20,000, six to nine thousand in the
Tsavo ecosystem alone. Ten years later, only 1,800 Black rhinos
remained in all Kenya. Today (1987), that figure has dwindled to
600 or less; and only some 150 rhinos remain in Tsavo.
Elsewhere, the news is hardly more encouraging. The Luangwa
National Park in Zambia, long a rhino stronghold, now has 1,500
or less, down from 8,000 ten years ago. The largest Black herds
today are located in Zambia, Zimbabwe, and Tanzania. The
White rhino, found mostly in Southern Africa, was nearly extinct
in the early 1900s (probably no more than 100 were alive in the
1930s), but a concerted effort brought them back. Today, there
are some 3,000 in several parks established throughout South
Africa and in Zimbabwe and Botswana.

appropriate graphic terms, battleship-grey. The White rhino takes its name from its "wide" muzzle (*weit* in Africaans[38]). The upper and lower bony palates in the square mouth act like incisor teeth, which configuration makes it a short-grass grazer. It can also be distinguished by its large head and long face (usually held low to the ground) and a hump of muscle found at the base of the neck or top of the shoulder. The White rhino has an even, placid temperament and can safely be approached in

White is quite sociable and generally moves in small groups.

The Black rhino, on the other hand, is essentially a loner, quarrelsome, and unpredictably dangerous. It has a smaller head than the White, is more or less swaybacked in profile, and has no hump similar to the White's (*38*). Its snout is pointed, with an extended upper lip shaped like a parrot's or tortoise's beak and adapted for seizing and holding — "prehensile" — so it can browse on shrubs,

Plate 38. Antediluvian "Kifaru." The Kiswahili name for the prehistoric-looking rhino was used by East African troops in World War II to refer, naturally enough, to tanks. To distinguish the truculent Black from the peaceable White, more careful Kiswahili would be "kifaru kali" or "fierce rhino." Ugly but magnificent at the same time, the Black rhino (with head held high) is the insignia adopted by the national parks in Kenya. But, although the parks are doing reasonably well, the rhino is fast disappearing. If left alone by man, this rhino would live up to forty years old. The rhino in plate *38* is doing his best to be left alone on the open plains by seeking out rocky terrain, where the safari vehicles have trouble navigating. In Chapter I, the point was made that habitat reduction threatened most animals more than poaching. The rhino is, however, extremely adaptive and could easily live in much reduced quarters, if only we would stop shooting it.

those game parks that permit foot safaris. When compared with the Black, the White rhino is far larger, sometimes twice the size of the former. Weighing three-and-a-half tons or more and standing in excess of six feet measured at the shoulder, the White is the second largest land mammal in Africa, surpassing the hippo. The docile

---

38. Dutch settlers in South Africa named it "witrenoster," or broad-lipped rhino. English writers translated "wit" or "weit" to "white."

Plates 39 & 40. A Browser. The rhino is an odd-toed (three) ungulate, a category that it shares with the zebra. The white on this suspicious fellow's face is the chalk-like dust from the encrustation of salts where a lake has dried up. I have seen — many times — a rhino use its horn as a plough at salt licks.

leaves, and plants (39 & 40). The Black usually weighs about two tons or slightly less. Both sexes of Black rhino are roughly the same size, whereas the White bull is much larger than the female.

Both sexes of the two species carry the double horns[39] — which are not really horns at all but composed of closely compacted, hair-like keratinous fiber that does not fuse with the skull (41), as in other horned animals — that in India are so valued (in ointment and powdered form) as an aphrodisiac. More important, they are used throughout the Far East in a Chinese spurious pharmaceutical preparation primarily intended for treating fever but promoted for other maladies as well (from toothache to snake bite to insanity). Most recently, they have been carved in North Yemen (principally) into ornate ceremonial dagger handles, important symbols of wealth and manhood.[40]

---

39. Reports surface every now and then of animals that have three or four horns.

40. This last product has proved by far the deadliest (to the rhino) in recent years. In a real sense, the rhino may well be yet another victim of the rapid rise in the price paid for oil that began in the early 1970s. Rhino horn was worth about $35 a

pound in 1972. Today, one kilogram (2.2 lbs) brings more than $1000 (with the price going as high on occasion as $5,000) in Singapore or Hong Kong, traditional 'wholesale' hubs of the trade. When sold in final retail form to the public, that same kilo is worth $10,000 or more. (The average adult rhino has some six pounds of horn.) Yemen itself has no oil, but oil prices started neighboring Saudi Arabia on a massive development program, for which manual laborers in large numbers were needed. By 1978, nearly one million migrant Yemenis, one-third of North Yemen's adult population, were working in Saudi Arabia and sending home $1.5 billion a year. Soon enough, ninety percent of the male population in Yemen were wearing the (increasingly) expensive daggers (djambias). When a boy reaches the age of eleven or twelve years in Yemen, he becomes a "man" and must have his own djambia. Previously, the daggers, at least those beautifully carved in rhino horn, could be afforded only by the nation's aristocracy. Thus, they carry significant social status. They are also not strictly ornamental or ceremonial; in some areas of the country, they are both worn and used (to settle quarrels and the like)! Evidently, the Yemenis also believe in the sexual myths and other intrinsic qualities attributed to the horn itself. While substitute handles are available, none has the beauty, durability, or mythological status of the rhino's poor matted hair-like keratin. In 1982, a rhino-handled djambia cost at least $1000 in Yemen. By the end of 1982, Yemen under considerable international pressure formally banned the import of rhino horn. Whereupon, trade simply turned into smuggling, mostly from the Sudan. Earlier, in 1979-80, Hong Kong and Japan, the two largest consumers in Asia of rhino-horn products, stopped legal trade (in or out) of raw horn. Taipei then became a center of rhino-horn commerce, but Hong Kong eventually bounced back on a surreptitious basis. Trade in the horn is banned by CITES (the Convention on International Trade in Endangered Species of Wild Fauna and Flora), adhered to by as many as ninety countries. Presumably, today's oil glut and the current retrenchment in Saudi Arabia will help to preserve the few remaining rhinos left (but not, it is of course hoped, for future dagger handles). That still leaves the Chinese looking after their headaches, carbuncles, typhoid, hallucinations, devil-possession, and innumerable other real or imagined afflictions. Today, roughly half of all rhino horn sold is still used to prepare traditional Chinese "medicine." (Aphrodisiac sales are actually relatively small, though, to paraphrase J.A. Hunter, no doubt any man who has a harem of thirty or so beautiful women may feel the need for artifical stimulation from time to time.) Dried rhino hide also has considerable commerical value, but serious poaching could be organized around such a product only with considerable difficulty.

Rhino horn has, in fact, become the most costly animal product available — it might as well be gold, such is its value by weight. Ultimately, a single rhino, with two healthy but average horns, is worth more than $30,000 to the business chain. Of course, the poacher himself does not see nearly these sums, but the money paid for killing *one* rhino — say, $500 — is still many times more than the poacher would ever see in many months of alternative local employment, a powerful incentive for risk-takers. Moreover, the rangers assigned to guard the remaining rhinos are underpaid (and hence susceptible to their own economic pressures and temptations), armed with antiquated weapons, and short of vehicles and fuel. A handful of rangers patrol areas the size of states. They frequently face poachers who are more often than not well organized

Plate 41. The Unicorn's Stand-In in the Montane Forest of the Aberdares Salient. Rhinos once even roamed the forests of England! Today, they "hide" from Somali poachers in the depths of East African woodlands. The front horn can reach up to fifty-three inches long in the Black species, sixty or more in the White, worthy of anyone's unicorn. Although not that long, the horn pictured here is of impressive length. Females have longer and more slender horns than those sported by males. Amboseli was once famous for two cow rhinos — "Gertie" and "Gladys" (mother and daughter) — who both had perhaps the most beautiful (and most unusual) long flowing horns ever seen. Such pictorial notoriety was distinctly a mixed blessing. Today, a safarist would be lucky to see a rhino of any description in Amboseli.

into gangs and armed with modern automatic weapons.[41] This mismatch has brought the rhino to the very edge of extinction during the last twenty years, when better than 95% of the remaining African Black rhinos have been killed.

The rhino's "problem" is thought to have originated when men had difficulty locating the legendary unicorns, creatures credited with sexual powers and whose horns were believed to have a wide range of medicinal qualities, including the ability, when used as a cup, to discover poison in drink (the horn was supposed to shatter into pieces when brought into contact with poison of any kind). What potentate anxiously eyeing the future could do without such guidance? And man has probably dreamed of improving his sexual prowess since taking five steps or so out of the Garden of Eden. Apparently causing little or no gap in credibility, some industrious entrepreneurs substituted the rhino horn.[42]

Like the elephant, the adult rhino has no natural enemy. Nevertheless, as formidable as it is, the great armored mammal is almost ridiculously easy for man to kill — the easiest, in fact, of all big African game. In truth, the rhino is virtually blind (extremely near-sighted), and the presence of its horns only further obscures its vision. The rhino charge has to be reminiscent of Tennyson's *The Charge of the Light Brigade* — "Their's not to reason why" and so forth. An alert hunter can easily sidestep a charging rhino's tremendous surge — "alert," because the surge can attain speeds of 35 mph — even though the animal has the agility of a polo pony and can turn on a dime. Normally, it is no more than a blind juggernaut committed to a fixed direction. Despite the ubiquitous tick-birds found adorning most rhinos *(42)*, in theory providing an early warning system, Maasai warriors even have a game of each individual placing a pebble in turn on a sleeping rhino's back. One African tribe additionally uses a curse to the effect, "may you be killed by a rhino," the thrust (no pun intended) being that such a death would be a humiliation!

Compensating for its lack of sight, the rhino has keen hearing and one of nature's strongest senses of smell — much superior, in fact, to a bloodhound's. Human beings might have difficulty imagining the ability to detect scent more than several *miles* away (provided that the weather is good and winds favorable). A rhino's olfactory passages are larger than its brain! Mammals smell through their nasal cavities; scent molecules in the air come into contact with the sense organs and stimulate the many nerve endings there. Distinguishing between thousands of different smells is a process far from being completely understood. We know that the rhino has an extremely powerful sense of smell — and correspondingly far more nerve endings or receptors (perhaps, a hundred *times* more) than man — but we do not know that it is necessarily more discriminating than ours. That is, a rhino will easily detect much weaker smells than could man but whether or not it would recognize more distinct smells is open to question. The rhino also has a problem in this regard not ordinarily faced by man — the extreme dust. Dust particles are filtered out of the air that is headed for the receptors by a layer of mucus protecting the delicate olfactory sensory cells. The rhino must build up quite a collection of dust, and this accumulation is bound to affect adversely its sensory gift. A rhino probably chooses its food by smell and seemingly devotes a fair amount of time to scent-marking in the bush.

Much of this bush dreadnought's reputed irritability is, indeed, a response to its limited vision.[43] The frequent charging is the animal's way to force whatever is out there (discovered most likely by sound or scent) to move for better identification. A Black rhino will, in fact, charge anything remotely suspect without discrimination. Some report the pachyderm chasing butterflies! I have watched it take on a termite hill! Hallet described the rhino with characteristic insight and exaggeration:

> Insatiably curious, the black rhino is at the same time extremely timid and equipped with only limited mentality. His hearing and his sense of smell are superb, but his vision is abysmally defective. Each of his tiny eyes, set on opposite sides of his bulky, elongated head, gives him a different picture to look at; each picture is tantalizing in its wide-angle perspective but horribly frustrating in its perpetual fuzziness. An animal Mr. McGoo, nearsighted Kifaru cannot tell a man from a tree at distances of more than thirty feet, cannot see any object distinctly if it is more than twenty or even fifteen feet away, and has to cock his head sideways to see, with one eye at a time, around the bulk of his muzzle and his massive front horn. Moving forward with the horn lowered, he is running blind.
>
> By day as well as night, Kifaru hears and smells a whole world of fascinating objects which he cannot see. His curiosity drives him on to poke and probe among them ...

41. Nor does the legal process deal harshly with poachers arrested and tried in court: indifference and leniency characterize most convictions.

42. Marco Polo at least — on the island of Sumatra — found the substitution disappointing: " 'tis a passing ugly beast to look upon, and is not in the least like that which our stories tell of being caught in the lap of a virgin." This last reference is to the myth popularized by Leonardo da Vinci and others: only a young virgin could capture a unicorn and then only for a short time; she had to sit in a forest, quietly by herself, with one breast bared — the unicorn would then come and place its head in her lap long enough for her to pluck the horn from its forehead.

43. Orphaned Black rhinos have made great pets, and captured adults are apparently easy to tame. The hardened, chronic criminal turns into nothing more than, in one writer's phrase, a scatterbrained delinquent. Nevertheless, for something that has so little to *fear* (man aside), so few potential enemies, the untrained rhino, myopic confusion notwithstanding, is a bad actor, treating most every living thing as an intruder.

Plate 42. "Sentries." The Red- or Yellow-billed oxpeckers or "tick-birds," specialized starlings indigenous to Africa, accompany the rhinos everywhere. The oxpecker is known as "askari wa kifaru" in Kiswahili, or the rhino's policeman, or guard, and supposedly warns the rhino of possible danger. The author has always suspected that the oxpecker as a lookout (except perhaps on warthogs) was grossly overrated: the birds are gregarious and noisy at most times, and how does the rhino differentiate? Indeed, the oxpecker's reputation derives primarily from uncritical repetition passed from naturalist to naturalist over a hundred years or more. The birds patronize a wide range of ungulates, as we shall see, but the relationship with the rhino seems to be the most intimate. Nature cannot be said to have evolved a sentry system to protect merely against human poachers (for a start, there has not been enough time for evolution to work in this direction), and the birds do not seem to get very excited in the presence of natural predators, like lions or leopards. Moreover, the healthy adult fractious pachyderm really does not have a 'natural' enemy. Perhaps, the best commentary on the subject is a picture in the Patel volume, *Vanishing Herds* (recommended in Chapter I), of a tick-bird sleeping on the back of a sleeping rhino! In fact, the birds are undoubtedly tolerated primarily because they eat the parasites (especially ticks) from the rhino's skin, a true symbiotic relationship. The rhino helps by twisting its neck, for example, to expose new creases for picking and so forth. The tick birds do a fair amount of damage, however, as they also pick the flesh of the skin lesions that plague all adult rhinos (apparently initially caused by a bot fly and its hatching eggs). Although the birds probably keep the surface of the sores free of maggots and other parasites, the sores have little opportunity of healing under such attention. Indeed, the birds often enlarge a lesion. Moreover, the birds at times can be annoying pests, as they climb into ears and often try to drink the animal's saliva. The oxpeckers use the rhino as a perch, as a refuge, and as a platform for courtship displays and mating. They will hang on when the animal is galloping at full speed; as exciting as the ride must be, the destination must sometimes be a shocker. In fact, if a safarist witnesses two rhinos fighting, he will also probably see the highly amusing spectacle of ox-peckers hanging on both opponents for dear life. Having discounted the role as sentinel, one also has to question whether the birds can, in fact, significantly reduce the enormous amount of blood-gorged ticks present on any rhino. As we have already seen, elephants, uniquely among large ungulates, do not tolerate tick-birds — and have a trunk capable of enforcing their wishes. Less well endowed, rhinos, and others, may have come to accept the *inevitability* of tick-birds, whose needle-sharp, short curved claws (with stiff tailfeathers in a supporting role) enable the bird to cling tenaciously to the hide, even hanging acrobatically upside down (here, a sore has attracted some twigs and other matter). An anecdote from Kruger Park concerned a rhino who was found leaning its head against a tree trunk for long periods — to keep the oxpeckers from further opening a gaping hole in its head! (The rhino was eventually shot by a ranger to put the animal out of its misery.) Nature has other examples of possibly similar cross-species communication, for example, cleaner-fish and their hosts, but we know very little today about such things.

but his timid disposition makes him fear, and fear deeply, the very objects that he wants to examine. He hesitates, agonized, while the two conflicting instincts boil within him. Usually he runs away but sometimes rushes forward to investigate with the world's most farcical display of bluff, noise, wasted energy, and sheer ineptitude — the notorious rhino "charge."

Once ... I watched a typically addlepated rhino stage a typically silly charge. He was busy with a big mouthful of twigs when he heard a frog start to croak about a hundred feet away. He stopped chewing, cocked his head, and listened — with leaves fluttering out of his mouth — then trotted anxiously toward the sound. As he approached, the frog croaked loudly and hopped by chance in his direction. A ton and a half of spooked rhinoceros made an abrupt U-turn, retreating to "safety." He sulked for a few minutes before advancing again. This time the frog jumped in the opposite direction, making him feel more confident: he lowered his horn and charged, smashing the frog under his hoofs without even knowing it. He returned to the spot, sniffing until he found it, and pawed at the little blob of pulp with a puzzled expression.[44]

Unlike the vastly more intelligent elephant, a rhino is as likely to make contact on a charge as to pull up short — one never knows. Carl Akeley, the famous American naturalist, called the rhino the greatest bluffer in all Africa (the author would have chosen the elephant), but this is not sound practical guidance, whatever the probabilities. One helpful hint to ambitious safarists: jerky movements of head and tail and a powerful snort, like a steam engine, through dilating nostrils always precede the charge. It is wiser than not for the safarist to respect the rhinoceros; a safari vehicle is not as nimble as a hunter on foot, and the rhino weighs more than twice the Landrover. Insofar as possible, one should approach the rhino with the wind in one's face (rhinos are always likely to charge upwind, in the direction of an odor) and as quietly and gradually as practicable. Constant vigilance is also recommended. In the final analysis, there is no substitute for keeping a respectful distance and employing a medium telephoto lens. Forget the classic film duels of rhino and Range Rover; the author has been in a vehicle rammed by a rhino, and the experience is no fun.

As might be expected, Black rhino females are especially foul-tempered when accompanied by calves (43). On the other hand, a calf is equally protective of its mother

44. Hallet, *Animal Kitabu,* p. 86. High praise, considering Martin Johnson's views:

> The [Black] rhinoceros is a big, fat, stupid old idiot. He is always fighting, always in a bad humor, always grunting, always looking for trouble. I think he has the least desirable personality of any of the big beasts.
>
> I don't believe that the average rhino has a friend in the world, not even among his own kind. Rhinos don't go about in herds or mingle with other animals. When I meet them they seem to be always either fighting among themselves or making ready to fight us. On numerous occasions I have been treed by an angry rhino. (Safari, p. 96.)

and attacks anything that approaches the pair — including a courting (or, at least, curious) male. As the reader might imagine, these last confrontations can be the stuff of high comedy.

Rhinos are sedentary; they rarely wander far.[45] If a rhino is found on safari, it should be easy to find him again. Early mornings and late afternoons are the best

45. The Black rhino, for all its nastiness in the wild, is not territorially aggressive, while the peaceful White follows strict

Plate 43. Cow and Calf. For the safarist maintaining a respectful distance, a rhino usually presents a fairly non-demonstrative picture. Socially, Black rhinos avoid, when possible, potentially lethal intraspecific confrontations. And they have no need to herd. Consequently, they are often found alone. One's first encounter with a rhino always causes the pulse to quicken — the visitor knows that he is in the presence of something elemental, something not to be taken for granted. Soon enough, however, the safarist realizes that patience is required: hours can roll by with little happening — eating, repose, a sigh or two. A mother and calf are, on the other hand, a more lively discovery. During the cooler hours of the day, a calf will play with its mother. How do rhino calves play? Ah, yes, they butt.

territorial mandates (though subordinate males are allowed to remain within a given dominant's range). In large part, this behavior reflects food choice. The Black is a browser, and the density of accessible food is spread. The White grazes, and its food tends to be concentrated. Males and females of both species spray-urinate; probably, only the dominant White bulls elevate the practice to ritualized territorial demarcation. Rhinos frequently defecate on top of existing rhino dung, and large dung heaps — called ''middens'' — are a prominent feature of rhino landscape. Naturalists — and all serious naturalists are students of dung — are not absolutely sure why rhinos scatter their dung, as so many do, but dominant bulls using these middens as signposts may well be attempting to ensure that their smell covers any other's. I have never seen a rhino use its horn at this time, as reported by so many writers; it seems to prefer employing its hind legs, kicking backwards, in the same manner as a dog. The middens themselves are busy miniature ecosystems: mushrooms and plant life thrive; beetles and butterflies proliferate; termites harvest undigested matter; and insectivorous birds and assorted small carnivores congregate for lunch.

times for viewing. At midday, Kifaru often finds the shade to lie down. Basically, these animals lead a very routine life; they are real creatures of habit, with favorite walks, wallows, and feeding places, and they visit each haunt in the same order, day after day.

A regular trip to water is necessary — rhinos need to drink often but they can go four or five days without water, if necessary. (They also seem to prefer stagnant water.) Black rhinos, surprisingly enough to readers of the literature, do allow other rhinos into their territories, even right into their favorite mudholes. And a rhino loves his mudbath. The mud is a good cooling medium and is thus helpful for regulating body temperature. The daily mud-bath is also important for keeping the skin in decent con-dition. Of course, "decent" for a rhino is not what the reader would choose for his own body. And, despite what some writers believe, mud is only a limited prophylactic against ticks — the tick-birds know what they are doing. The mud coating does, for a time, offer limited protection against the ravages of biting flies. Watching a rhino bathe in something approaching a mere puddle is quite a sight, as he immerses first one part, then another, and so on — the whole, hilarious process can take an hour or more. The wallowing usually takes place in late afternoon, rid-ding the body of the heat accumulated during the day. Older rhinos sometimes become stuck during their mud-baths — and starve or fall to predators — a high price to pay for such contentment.

Rhinos rarely fight one another, but watching bulls play out a drama of mock charges and confrontation — serious only in the presence of a female in heat[46] — is a treat, sometimes a long treat. The modalities can last an hour or more. Dominance is usually established without blood-shed, though occasionally a horn is ripped off (it gradually grows back). Males approach females only for mating pur-poses. Both sexes begin mating when about six years old. The union is always tempestuous, Black or White, with much protest and simulated fighting. The female is par-ticularly aggressive and at the outset will often attack the male. Thus, the initial approach by the male under-standably is made with special caution — and seemingly endless circling and feigning — but the actual coupling lasts thirty minutes or more, even up to one hour, far longer than with most other animals. Worth the wait, so to speak. Such 'endurance' probably contributes to the unfortunate aphrodisiac myth.

Gestation normally takes fifteen to sixteen months. The calf, looking very much like an adult in miniature (44 & 45), nurses for about two years (46), by the end of which time, because of its size, it has to lie down to suckle.

46. Females in heat make whistling noises to attract bulls. If the safarist sees two Black bulls squaring off, he should look for a female standing nearby. White bulls may simply be engaging in a territorial encounter, normally non-violent (though noisy) and brief.

Plate 44. Young Calf. The tick-birds latch on at an early age. Ex-cept for ear fringes (in older animals), eye-lashes, and tufts on the end of the tail, a rhino, large or small, is hairless.

Plate 45. A Bouncing Trot. For an animal that weighs so much, its trot is remarkably buoyant. Of course, one's perspective is in-fluenced by extraneous factors: an early English writer com-pared the action to the "mincing gait of a French dancing master;" and the author, who has passed many an hour standing in the Non-Sporting Group ring at purebred dog shows, is always reminded of a bulldog rolling up and down going away. Calves usually keep in front of mother when moving ("calf at heel" is, in the author's experience, a misnomer). Calves appear to be more alert than adults and also seem to have marginally better eyesight. And, given the parent's poor eyesight, it would seem more logical for the cow to keep her youngster in front (at least until danger is confirmed). When a rhino runs off in fright, it car-ries its tail curled up over its back. The tail is dropped during an angry charge.

Plate 46. Mealtime.

Plates 47 & 48. Troika. From a distance, a rhino family such as that pictured in plate 47 looks like an outcropping of three rocks on the plains. During her most productive years, the female rhino is rarely solitary. In plate 48 (overleaf), one of the animals is an "orphan." In any group of rhinos, someone is always staring off furiously (we imagine) in the wrong direction.

(Mother herself will sometimes lie down to allow a calf to nurse.) Rhinos have a slow reproductive cycle, and, on average, the females produce a calf every four years or so. It is frequently said that a calf will leave its mother when its younger sibling is born, that the cow will then no longer tolerate the older offspring. This may be doubted as a strict rule. The author has frequently seen Black rhino groups of three, all absolutely inseparable (for more than several days, at least), which often seem to be the adult female and two immature rhinos of differing ages (47). It

is, of course, possible that the older of the two youngsters is another cow's calf, accepted by the natural pair. This must happen, as the author has also seen two juveniles of roughly the same age together with a cow (*48*), but is unlikely in every instance of a threesome exhibiting varying ages among themselves. In any event, if another calf does not come along, the original youngster apparently stays with its mother until nearly fully grown.

Giraffe

In the quotation heading this chapter, Isak Dinesen (as others had before her) wrote that giraffes looked like gigantic, long-stemmed flowers. Indeed, no more decorative animal inhabits the African bush (*49*). One African legend holds that God used leftovers from the antelope, camel, and the leopard to make the giraffe. The older writers frequently called the animal a "camelopard." Unlike some other creatures who suffer in man's eyes from a similar spare-parts reputation, like the wildebeest, the giraffe ("twiga" in Kiswahili) is a picture of incredible stately grace. And peace. Even head down,

during an awkward (for a giraffe) drink, the animal remains in beautiful and quiet harmony with the immediate environment (*50*). Its name is, in fact, derived from an Arabic word that means "one who is graceful."

The tallest animal in the world (*51*), reaching heights of eighteen to twenty feet (the legs are six feet tall, the neck even longer), the giraffe is one of those distinctive animals that have fascinated man for centuries. The unmistakable profile inevitably is enthusiastically received on safari by most visitors. And the appreciation is spontaneous, almost awestruck. One of the author's most fond safari experiences has been horseback riding among giraffes (at Lewa Downs in Kenya, a camp run by the ever-gracious Craigs). On the whole, giraffes tend to be very shy and ordinarily do not allow safari vehicles to approach too close, but a man on horseback stands a good chance of riding right in among a group and even immediately next to some juveniles. Nearer to the giraffe's natural plane on horseback, I felt a special affinity for these fascinating giants. Anyway, one always manages to feel more caught up in the rhythms of the plains once having left the confines of the vehicle, a rare enough possibility.

Plate 49. African "Flowers."

There are several types — some would go so far as to call them subspecies — of giraffe, just how many depends upon whom one relies for classifications.[47] Most of these giraffes successfully interbreed, making the distinctions even more difficult, if they are needed, or more tenuous, if one is skeptical, and the differences in any event are primarily ones of color and pattern. The average tourist will see Maasai giraffe, the largest variety, throughout East Africa; Baringo, or Rothschild's (also called "Ugandan"),

in western Kenya and Uganda; the Reticulated giraffe in northern Kenya; the Thornicroft's in Zambia; and Cape giraffes in South Africa. The most pronounced divergence occurs between the Maasai (also called Kenyan or Southern), which has dark- or light-caramel irregular blotches (with jagged margins, much like maple-leafs), each containing very dark-brown or black spider-like inner lines or "stars," set on a white or buff-colored background (52), and the Reticulated, which has large, regular, geometric patches, liver-red or deep chestnut in color, well-delineated by narrow white lines (53). The spotting on both varieties always extends down to the hooves. The markings of a Rothschild's appear to be a cross between the former two, with darker Maasai-like stars in dark, smooth-edged patches characteristic of a Reticulated pattern, little or no spotting below the knees, and broader buff delineating lines (54). Both the Cape and Thornicroft's are "similar." In any case, a giraffe's pattern is like a set of distinguishing fingerprints: no two markings are the same. (55-57) And, despite their bulk — adult giraffes weigh some one-and-a-half tons — the patchwork hides so nearly match the sun-dappled acacia trees of the

---

47. Not included in this volume is the okapi, an antelope-like animal belonging to the giraffe family but still a zoological mystery. The elusive okapi, hunted for millennia by Mbuni pygmies, was not known to scientists before the early part of this century. Nocturnal and solitary, it lives in the dense rain forests (mostly in the Ituri forest of eastern Zaire). Very little is known about its behavior in the wild. It has a glossy coat, with a dark liver-brown, almost chestnut coloring typical of forest animals, and zebra-striped black and white buttocks, each individual having its own distinct pattern. The okapi also has a short neck that more resembles an antelope than a giraffe.

Plate 50. A Drink in the Uaso Nyiro. When a giraffe was brought to Paris in the early 1800s, near riots broke out, as people rushed to see the unusual animal. It was Julius Caesar, having transported several giraffes to Rome after his African campaigns, who apparently first adopted the name "camelopard" (suggesting the cross between a camel and a leopard). Later, the scientists fell in line: the scientific name for the giraffe is *giraffa camelopardalis*.

Plate 51. World's Tallest. The Maasai giraffe, pictured here, is the tallest animal in the world. In parts of Kenya, the telephone lines had to be raised to allow the big boys to pass underneath. But the giraffe is no string bean. And images of delicateness can be misleading. The stilt-like legs have to support a great deal of weight — the giraffe with its thick chest, thick hide, and heavy elongated neck weighs more than a ton. Indeed, giraffes have to be cautious about where they step: great weight combined with small hooves is a recipe for sinking in marshland. The individual shown here has developed an infection in a front joint above the hoof, no small matter for an animal who stands practically its entire life on its feet.

Plate 52. National Emblem of Tanzania. Recognition of individuals is best accomplished by neck patterns. All giraffes have long tufted tails, very effective whisks against the tsetse fly.

Plate 53. Common Reticulated. Oxpeckers (the little jockey pictured on the shoulder here) work the giraffes as well. The notion that tick-birds could ever be ''sentries'' for giraffes provides the ultimate commentary on the sentinel theory: absurd. Two slightly different tick-birds thrive on the African ungulates. The yellow-billed oxpecker (bright yellow bill with a red tip) are said to prefer buffalos, rhinos, zebras, and hippos. The red-billed (all red bill with bare yellow skin around the eye) are supposed to frequent giraffes and the various antelopes.

Plate 54. Rothschild's, or Baringo. The Rothschild's is a more thickset animal than other giraffes. The Baringo males also have three to five "horns." One of these proturberances is a knob that is present to some degree on all giraffes, from a slight bump on the forehead to what appears to be another full-fledged "horn." These extra horns, some experts believe, are caused by the trauma of head banging during necking (discussed in the text). Giraffes can remain out in the open, strolling the savannah, all day long. Seemingly oblivious to the sun, they do not seek out shade, do not wallow in mud, and do not dust themselves.

Plate 55. A Dark Specimen. Some Maasai giraffes are so darkly marked as to appear almost melanistic. Bulls generally darken with age, though the pattern remains the same. Albino giraffes are also occasionally seen. The skin of most giraffes is smooth, bright, and glossy.

Plate 56. A Poser. Without knowing where this picture was taken, one would be hardpressed to classify this giraffe. It is also virtually impossible to identify Rothschild's giraffes without knowing their geographical location. In fact, each giraffe has its own unique pattern, and classifying giraffes by pictures alone is ultimately fruitless. Many have nondescript spots that could belong to any one of several "subspecies." The reasons for a giraffe's skin patterns have not been established — they may be the result of blood vessels lying near the surface of the skin.

Plate 57. Rich Chocolate. The pattern and rich chocolate color of this individual are unusual. It looks as if it belongs in an Easter basket.

Plate 58. Moving Trees. As the ethereal giraffes glide silently through the wooded areas, their markings provide a sort of camouflage — but not purposely. Giraffes do not try to conceal themselves even when standing behind a large bush; twiga can usually be seen hanging out over the top, looking at an intruder (the reader may recall plate *13* on page 84). Nevertheless, the visitor on safari will often not notice a giraffe standing amid vegetation until nearly right on top of the animal. Then, what at first appears to be but one giraffe frequently turns out to be a group.

African savannah that one sometimes fails to notice the animal until it moves *(58)*.

Like elephants, giraffes mostly just eat — sixteen to twenty hours a day are devoted to feeding. Because giraffes do not compete for food with grazers and barely overlap with other browsers at the heights at which they usually feed (only elephants can reach as high), they share their habitat with a wide range of other herbivores.[48] The giraffe's tongue, which looks blue, is extendable another eighteen inches, giving it just that much more reach. In-

deed, the tongue appears to take on a life of its own; like an elephant's trunk, it seems to choose or reject food with unerring dexterity and accuracy. A giraffe's prehensile upper lip is made for gathering in leaves; an average giraffe eats hundreds of pounds of leaves each week (the safarist might profitably reflect on what he thinks a handful of leaves weighs). And, in areas frequented by giraffe herds,

---

48. Naturalists are fond of referring to "niches" and the principal that species who live together (in the same immediate environment) tend not to compete with one another for food — different herbivore species each use particular parts of the same habitat for food. Each species develops, in other words, its own niche. And, in fact, most herbivores found together do have *preferences* for different foods. Specialization in eating is, of course, one way to conserve energy: the animal first looks where that food is normally found (plant food does not, after all, run away). Thus, a species chooses efficiency. Ultimately, the result

of such specialization is to increase the diversity of the animal community. But, insofar as the niche theory is meant completely to remove competition for food, it often simply overstates the fact. In particular, changing environmental conditions will cause animals to deviate from "normal" patterns. Drought will, for example, bring most browsers into direct competition with each other and also encourage browsers to encroach slightly on available grazing (and, to a lesser degree, vice-versa). Moreover, habitats are always in the process of change — not necessarily with the same degree of alteration as that caused by a drought, but important change nonetheless. The author returns to the subject in the next chapter, where grazing sequences and the like are introduced.

the trees frequently look like manicured hedges.[49] Unlike elephants, giraffes are "neat" eaters. Only now, however, are naturalists realizing that giraffes may be more harmful to a stand of trees than elephants: studies have shown that acacias will grow six times as fast if not browsed by giraffes, while elephants only pose the bigger threat to mature trees.

The favorite meal of these peripatetic Eiffel Towers is the tender leaf of the thorn acacia, but the giraffe eats some thorns as well (59 & 60), though the spikes are designed to discourage heavy browsing. Munching on this latter "delicacy" is helped considerably by the giraffe's thick, rubber-like saliva that protects the lining of the inside of the mouth and also by a horny skin covering the palate. The acacia trees, in turn, resort to another (more creative) defense to protect themselves against overbrowsing — by harboring throughout their upper branches colonies of ants that have painful bites! The

Plates 59 & 60. Favorite Meal. Most African acacias have evolved thorns or spikes to protect against browsing animals, particularly giraffes. (In dense forests, where giraffes rarely venture, the acacias generally do not have thorns.) Young growth has soft thorns that can easily be eaten. The older plants have formidable two-inch, needle-like spikes. The giraffe occasionally eats these, as well. So, the whistling-thorn, or black-galled or ant-gall, acacia has raised the stakes by developing bulbous galls the size of golf balls located at the base of each pair of thorns scattered throughout the tree. These hollow galls, which seem to result initially from attacks by insects, are usually inhabited by colonies of small but pugnacious ants. When the giraffe shakes these little 'forts,' armies of aggressive soldiers swarm out and attack the diner. A true form of symbiosis. (Other acacias have nectaries that contain a sugary solution attractive to ants and thus have their own special protection — the nectaries (and ants) are concentrated in the growing tips much favored by browsers.) The eerie, flute-like "whistling" that the safarist may hear in the presence of these acacias is caused by the wind blowing across the ants' entrance holes cut into the galls and by the wind likewise vibrating the long thorns.

---

49. The simile is even more than visual: like trimmed hedges, the trees respond with extra growth at the edges, which surface then provides greater leaf area for the giraffe to feed. It should be noted that the loss of trees themselves occurring on the outer edges of a forest — destruction caused by both giraffes and elephants — creates fire breaks that limit the entry of fires into the forest itself.

giraffe inevitably disturbs the ants and, when enough of the little warriors are scurrying about, eventually moves on.

The safarist is able to use the browsing style of a particular giraffe reliably to indicate its sex: the female usually bends over to take her vegetation, the male feeds at full stretch.

Like a cow, the giraffe is a ruminant. It first swallows its food and later regurgitates the vegetation in the form of a "cud" — a small wad of partly digested food — which is then chewed thoroughly and swallowed again. The problem of dealing with cellulose has been previously discussed. The ruminant's solution is to aid fermentation in its multi-chambered stomach by retaining the food for nearly four days. Maximum use of the available cellulose is thereby achieved (with about sixty percent utilization). The author and others have also seen giraffes chewing on bones and even the horns of antelopes, perhaps for minerals, but my own observations usually concerned youngsters seemingly playing rather than eating. (*61 & 62*)

Plates 61 & 62. A Giraffe and His Bone.

Here on these dry plains, and only here, the reticulated giraffe appears. Its skin is not a series of surrealist blotches but a very definitely marked network of lines with patches of dark chocolate colour in between: an effect such as you get with a crazy pavement. Giraffes are gentle creatures, and there is something virginal and modest about them all; but this particular breed in the north is so slim and pretty that it is the very essence of the jeune fille. They look at you timidly over the tops of the bushes, keeping just their heads in sight, like schoolgirls peeping out of a dormitory window. (Moorehead, *No Room in the Ark,* p. 103.)

Its neck is, of course, the giraffe's glory. Actually, like man and all mammals, the giraffe has but seven vertebrae, though these are elongated and attached to each other by ball-and-socket joints that permit both great flexibility and strength. A giraffe's long neck is usually regarded as a good example of natural selection influencing form: the taller animals could eat beyond the reach of shorter giraffes and thus enjoyed a larger food supply; the ability to feed more easily and exploit a basically untouched food source led to improved chances of survival during lean seasons; the taller individuals over time thus bred more successfully; and those genes that caused the giraffes to grow tall concentrated in the gene pool.[50] The advantages of such a stretched-out approach to life are not limited to eating. Matched with sharp eyesight, the neck offers the giraffe an early-warning system for predators. Consequently, a giraffe is frequently accompanied by all manner of antelopes at a waterhole. (63) An alert giraffe provides a measure of security for all wherever he goes and hence often finds himself saddled with many fellow-travelers. (If the safarist sees a group of giraffes all staring into the distance, he should expect a predator, most likely a lion.)

The neck also, naturally enough, provides the leverage to enable a giraffe to stand back up from lying down. (64) With impressive synchronization of neck, legs, and body, the animal throws its neck back sharply, producing the impetus to throw its forelegs out from underneath its body and get to its knees, then it swings the neck forward to allow its hind legs to straighten up, and finally back again as the animal rocks to its feet. All this takes about four seconds.

Plate 63. Early Warning System. Antelopes are noticeably more relaxed at waterholes when these "mobile watchtowers" are present. And, to elaborate, giraffes are rarely unescorted at waterholes.

50. Such neck length also necessarily requires a unique plumbing system. A large, powerful heart must pump blood a considerable (for a heart) distance uphill to the brain. Ten feet or more, in fact. The giraffe consequently has an aortic blood pressure several times that of man. The work that is done by the human heart each minute is the equivalent of lifting seventy

If the safarist is patient and donates some time to giraffes, he will see the interesting phenomenon known as "necking." (65) This activity always takes place between males, normally subadult males, leading some observers to comment on the giraffe's supposed homosexual behavior (whatever that means exactly, in giraffes). In reality, necking is the male giraffe's version of the ritualized mild sparring — to establish dominance or simply to release aggressive energy — in which the males of many species (and most mammals) engage. Certainly, a form of aggressive affection or camaraderie is also involved. The best analogy in human terms that the author can think of is arm-wrestling. Standing side-by-side and facing in either the same or opposite directions, the giraffes rub their necks and wrap and unwrap them around each other. Frequently, the participants will pause, gaze into the

distance, ruminate for a spell, then begin again. The contest often ends with one male attempting to mount the other, the final assertion of dominance.

Plate 65. Necking. Even a shoving contest is a graceful, almost caressing, affair with giraffes. At such times, the neck can be screwed around as if it were on a swivel.

pounds one foot off the ground; the giraffe by comparison is a gym housing an Olympic heavyweight competition. To prevent an unwanted rush of blood, however, the huge carotid artery in a giraffe that carries oxygenated blood from the heart divides into a great spongy network of smaller blood vessels before the blood actually reaches the brain. On the way, it is also cooled by blood draining from nasal sinuses. But more is needed, to prevent the giraffe from collapsing from a massive return rush of blood to the brain each time that the animal lowers its head (to drink, for example). Thus, the jugular vein, which sends blood back to the heart from the brain, has a series of one-way valves to prevent the blood flowing backwards. In nature's circular fashion, maintaining the elasticity of a giraffe's valves and blood vessel walls requires a diet taken from the higher branches of acacias, unreachable without the long neck.

Plate 66. Escalation. Serious dueling is still carried on in a leisurely fashion. A long pause punctuates each swing of the neck, and neither participant makes any attempt to avert the blow of his rival or to sneak in an extra lick. The atmosphere is one of calm, the combat more resembling the grace and poise of ballet. The contest over, the bulls will resume feeding peacefully.

Occasionally, the friendly jousting escalates into more serious fighting *(66)*. Vigorous buffeting ensues, and the neck and head are wielded with all the force of gigantic sledgehammers. The noise of impact can be heard for some distance across the plains. Still, the show is more sound than fury, and lethal or to all appearances even minor harm is rarely inflicted. An onlooker can usually recognize a really serious contest: the giraffes will face the same direction, spread their legs for better support, and attempt repeatedly to use their heads and horns, potentially formidable weapons. Some blows will also be aimed at the legs. Kicking or biting is never seen — these are reserved for predators. Fighting between mature adults is extremely rare.

At the top of the neck sits what could be viewed as an absurdly small head, but the irresistible long black eyelashes, dreamy eyes, and somehow appealing face only complete the portrait of elegance. As tall as the animal might be, the giraffe ascends to the very limits of style, never to topple over into distortion. The horn-like protuberances are actually layers of skin that harden. In females, these "horns" come to a point; in males, they are larger and do not taper. Female adults may and subadults of both sexes always have tufts of hair on top of the structures. One can look, but it is fruitless to challenge a giraffe to a staring contest. The giraffe's interminable stare is actually common to most ruminants (who may take hours just to chew their cud and thus always have something to do at these times), but he has also mastered the aloof superiority of a slightly affronted socialite.[51] With just the slightest hint of a mild reproach, he makes it clear that *he* belongs and that the only relevant question is, "why are *you* here?" Just waiting for a giraffe to blink during these moments could wear out the safarist, as the only movement, minute by minute, is the monotonous sideways rhythm of the jaw, working its cud.

Giraffes do lose a bit of their grace and *comme il faut* hauteur when they drink.[52] With uncharacteristically clumsy coordination, the forelegs are splayed wide apart to allow the head to reach the water. The giraffe accomplishes this task virtually inch by inch, edging the front legs apart wider and wider, until he can finally swing the long neck down to drink. In this way, the adult giraffe is exposed to his one serious predator — the lion. As a result, the "camelopard" takes its time drinking a full round — it drinks briefly, snaps back to attention, looks nervously around, and only when it is assured of safety

----

51. Other writers have interpreted the look as "wistful," the guise of "thoughtful genius," or, most often, just plain curiosity.

52. Drinking patterns are unpredictable. Because their food often contains natural water (in the acacia thorns, for example) and because vegetation usually collects dew, giraffes frequently appear not to need to drink for substantial periods. If the water is available, however, the giraffe normally drinks daily.

Plates 67 & 68. Drinking Scenario. Swallowing water is an engineering marvel; the water has to flow uphill for some ten feet. A very muscular esophagus does the trick. Armchair biologists for many years theorized that the giraffe raised its head slowly from a drinking position, so that the blood would not rush down to the heart. In reality, a giraffe lifts its head with a snap, several times during a drink. The network of blood vessels near the brain and a complex system of valves hold sufficient blood when the head is raised; the same system also reduces the rush upwards in an animal that has a blood pressure many times that of man. Giraffes apparently can manage with little to drink, if necessary, as their food contains much water. The real problem with drinking is, of course, not loss of face (awkwardness) but loss of life (lions), though the two are not unrelated. The author believes that the vulnerability of a giraffe drinking has been exaggerated in the literature; the animal can very quickly resume its standing posture. Moreover, only a very hungry lion or group of lions will go after an adult giraffe, a lot of throat for a throat killer. Unfortunately for the giraffe, very hungry lions are, however, not that rare. Old and weak giraffes are frequently taken by predators, hyenas as well as lions. But, aside from a waterhole mishap, the alert, healthy adult giraffe has little to fear from lions: it is too fast. Giraffes do have to exercise special caution at a lake's edge: they are one of the comparatively few animals who cannot swim naturally.

cautiously resumes. *(67 & 68)* The entire process can consume many minutes. Some scientists have voiced the opinion that all this jerking to attention is more than simply checking for possible danger — the movement may facilitate swallowing. Despite the obvious effort in bending down and struggling erect, the process recurs throughout the drinking session.

The giraffe's large size works to its advantage as an effective heat-dispersal body, unlike those of other large mammals. The long legs and neck create a larger surface area, proportionately, than have the other large animals. Thus, giraffes do not loll in deep water like the hippo, nor wallow in the mud like the rhino, buffalo, and elephant. The giraffe will, to the contrary, frequently stand out in the hottest sun even when shade is readily available.

One of the most memorable safari experiences is to witness a giraffe moving along at full gallop. Obviously, one never sees this poetry in a zoo, and it is, in fact,

Plate 69. *Fast Walk.* At a walk, the long-legged animal has a curious lopsided stride. Because both legs on one side are off the ground at the same time, the giraffe's weight is thrown onto the legs on the other side. The head and neck are, however, swung over in the opposite direction to compensate. Thus, the animal dips forward and rocks backwards and all at the same time sways from side to side. Huge, checkered pendulums in a strong cross-wind! The swaying action can also be seen at a canter, though in a more modified form. Giraffes "rack" instead of trotting, quite like five-gaited saddle horses (who must be trained; the "rack" is regarded as a man-made gait in horses). Perhaps, the best way to describe a four-legged animal racking is to visualize *two* men running *in step*. Actually, saddle horses differ in this respect: they rack in a 'single-footed' manner, each foot strikes the ground separately, whereas both giraffe feet on one side leave and return to the ground together. Giraffes do switch to single-footing when they gallop.

unimaginable until actually observed. Worth, one might say, the price of admission. At a fast walk, the giraffe paces or racks, that is, both legs on the same side move together in the same direction *(69)*. Given the length of its stilt-like legs and proportionately short back, the giraffe cannot walk or trot like a horse; it would trip itself. Stepping up the motion into a full run resembles turning a video-tape

on slow-motion, except that long, fifteen-foot strides are covering immense distances and in a hurry. Indeed, the animal can gallop as fast as a horse (*70*), or roughly 35 mph, but the dream-like, rocking-horse gait with neck and head swinging freely back and forth in a kind of delayed rhythm, gives the impression of effortless, undulating gliding. Technically, a galloping giraffe moves both forelegs and hindlegs together (not diagonally, like a horse) and makes contact with the ground with each foot placed in turn. The hindlimbs are splayed widely apart so

that the hindfeet can overreach the forelimbs by swinging outside them. The neck pulls the center of gravity forward when it is thrown in front just as the legs themselves move forward. The neck rocks back to prevent toppling over. Visually, the animal barely seems to touch the ground the whole time. The sight is breathtaking.

Giraffes are, the evidence confirms, gregarious animals, and one giraffe nearly always seems to be in the company of others. But they do not appear physically to interact very often, and the "herds" are haphazardly constituted, at best. (71) Individual bonds inter se are strictly temporary. (Females in particular show hardly any physical interaction.) Quite often, the loose, open giraffe grouping is interspersed with other herbivores — being able to see over a crowd tends to allow that — and who is doing what to whom becomes a little complicated. (72) For the most part, giraffe groups tend to be small, though it is difficult to tell exactly where one group ends and another begins. A giraffe's field of vision extends so far that giraffes a mile apart could well be part of the same constellation. On at least a random basis, the author has counted as many as sixty giraffes within sight of one another. Thirty-five is a large herd. Studies[53] have shown that there is no special sex or age consistency in giraffe groups — there are bull herds, mixed herds, so-called "nursery herds," and so forth — and that home ranges tend to be very large. Moreover, herd composition apparently changes daily. Naturally, given the lack of (obvious) coordination, the safarist will be hard pressed to pick out in a given grouping a real leader, though he may well see dominant males bully other males (principally by running them out of trees). Nor do we know for sure that a real group leader

Plate 70. Gallop in the Bush. Tail carried high (to prevent interference), the giraffe can run as fast as 40 mph. The young are said to run faster than adults (less inertia and wind resistance), but a bull can really move along. As it runs, the giraffe pumps with its neck, both gaining momentum and maintaining balance.

Plate 71. Beginning or End? One hardly ever knows whether or not a group like this is the beginning or the end (or all!) of a herd. The large bulls stroll their ranges looking for females in heat; no territoriality is evident, but a strict dominance hierarchy prevails.

53. The giraffe is probably one of the most understudied of the large African mammals. Much remains to be done before commenting conclusively on twiga's behavior.

Plate 72. Faces in (over) the Crowd.

exists. A strict hierarchy is, however, maintained at breeding time but without any territorial overtones.

Mating is rarely seen in the wild but reportedly is a brief and sedate affair.[54] Birth is also infrequently witnessed. The mother remains standing during delivery, and the foal consequently drops some five feet to the ground. "Drops" and "five feet" are both probably exaggerations, because the young calf, normally born singly (twins have rarely been reported), is virtually six-feet tall at birth. The practical effect of gravity may therefore be operative only during the last foot or so.

Giraffe females have a bad reputation as mothers, which infamy is somewhat undeserved. Nevertheless, a degree of carelessness, if not weak maternal instinct, cannot really be disputed. Although mother and calf for a short period after birth are almost inseparable, with much affectionate licking, nosing, and rubbing going on between the two, soon enough (often within a few weeks), the mother begins to browse farther and farther away (but see plate *73*). Indeed, there are reliable reports of "nursery herds," composed entirely of youngsters who have been left alone during the day while their mothers have gone off to feed elsewhere. These groups correspond to what ethologists call the "crèche" system, a form of day-care. On the other hand, the youngsters usually are at least kept in sight; a young giraffe in any event can frequently outrun his parent and hence a possible predator; and, during the middle of the day, when the nursery herd seems to be the most unattended, the lion is usually sleeping. Nevertheless, calves have a high mortality rate, thanks primarily to lion predation, and a mother racing back to defend a calf is not nearly as effective as on-the-spot deterrence. Overconfidence, "benign neglect," or even indifference, the result is the same. An adult giraffe has a deadly front and back kick, and no single lion and only the most dedicated (hungry) pride would risk initiating such a confrontation in the open. Employing its full leverage and muscular frame, a giraffe has been known to kick a full-grown eland bull off its feet, and many a lion has fallen to the same weapon (supplemented by trampling). Once lions have, however, committed themselves — "tasted blood," so to speak — the contest is on. The well-publicized recent reports of tourists seeing giraffe mothers attempting to defend their young against lions have all happened when the youngsters were first attacked alone and mother thereupon hastened back to the defense. Invariably, a classic case of too little, too late.

Young giraffes suckle for nine months at most (some can count on only one to two months). In the first few

---

54. Because of the comparatively high quality of their browse, giraffes breed all year-round. Moreover, they seem to return to traditional calving grounds.

days of life, the young giraffes grow at the remarkable rate of one-half inch per day! Even after this spurt, they grow with astonishing speed. Nursery herds or not, one youngster always seems to be in the company of at least one other. (74 & 76) Young giraffes are extremely curious, much less shy than their parents, and very photogenic. (75) Contrary to popular belief, the giraffe is not mute. If the safarist pays attention, he will hear youngsters moan, snort, and bleat (or at least something resembling a bleat).

Plate 73. Exception? It would seem that this mother, standing by her older calf in the absence of danger, is an exception to the rule. Young giraffes carry their necks in a more erect manner than do adults, as can be seen here: the neck tendons stretch with age.

Plate 74. Maasai Youngsters. The young have little tassels of hair growing from the tip of their short horns. In addition, their manes are longer and look softer than the stiff, brush-like manes of adults. Giraffes attain maturity at about four years, but the male does not reach its full height until seven years old.

Plate 75. Young Pacer. Normally, one can maneuver much closer to a calf than to an adult giraffe. The safarist should, however, always approach a giraffe slowly and be satisfied with a reasonable distance. With luck, a giraffe will live for twenty-odd years in the wild. Giraffes are increasing significantly in the Serengeti and in Masai Mara and perhaps elsewhere as well.

Plate 76. Reticulated Pair. As stated in the text, a giraffe's growth rate is phenomenal. Calves grow four feet in their first year and have been recorded as growing as much as nine inches in a single week.

Hippopotamus

It must be admitted at the outset that the hippo, the second or third largest land animal, depending on which rhino one is considering, and by far the largest river dweller, is a dull study (by human standards) for the average safarist. Hippopotamus is Greek for "river horse" (called "kiboko" in Kiswahili), but, from the time that it's born to the time that it dies, the hippo more closely resembles a huge pig *(77 & 78)*. In a more literary sense, all hippos are shaped like Nell, the kitchenmaid in "The Comedy of Errors": "spherical, like a globe." Undoubtedly, the Behemoth in the Book of Job is this same hippo, but the first white settlers in southern Africa described the animal as a nine-eyed monster, given the various features just barely visible above the surface of the hippo pool. True to the Greek, however, the hippos arrive at the water pool (or mudhole in drier times) before sunrise —

long before the safarist — and leave after dark. In between, they are mostly a collection of backs, eyes, ears, and nostrils — glistening backs, bulbous eyes, pig-like ears always wriggling free of water, and snorting nostrils *(79)*. The tourist sits, takes a stab at a count, waits briefly for the famous gaping yawn, listens to the "hoosh-ba-haw-haw-haw-haw" of the surfacing titan and the staccato chorus of answering grunts, and soon drives on.

Certainly, a more unusual way to meet the hippo is during a night safari, when the huge beasts have left their pool and followed well-worn pathways to pasture areas. Sometimes, the grasslands are near the pool, sometimes several miles away. Infrequently (a hippo should be so lucky), more than one pool is handy, which layout increases the available grazing radius and means that the W.C. Fields animal may not return to the main pool for several days. Hippo paths are unmistakable: deeply rutted and marked with copious amounts of dung. In the grass,

Plates 77 & 78. The River Horse. Our large friends here, with their balloon-like girth, are nearly as big around as they are long. A mature bull is about thirteen feet long, nose to tail, and measures five feet high at the shoulder. The pigmy hippopotamus is a different species entirely, rare, lives in West Africa, and is not discussed in this volume.

Plate 79. Lolling in the Pool. Africans have always hunted the hippo, both for food and for its superior ivory — softer than an elephant's and close-grained, the tusks are more easily carved. Most ivory tourist souvenirs are made from hippo ivory. But, in spite of the poaching and the inevitable and continuous habitat encroachment, hippos are not endangered. This situation is particularly ironic, because the early use of the rivers for transportation during colonial times led to the rapid decimation of the hippos for food and sport. Today, in some parks, they are even cropped by authorities to control the populations. Hippos practice natural birth control, like elephants, when they jump out of balance with their environment, but the natural way "takes too long" for man and his reserves. Culling is always controversial, but hippo 'management' seems to have worked well in Uganda for a short period.

the hippos spread out and graze alone, except for a female and her calf, who stay close together, most of the night. An adult hippo eats a prodigious amount of grass, more than 150 pounds a night (sometimes *far* more).[55] Lush habitats of many square kilometers are frequently grazed down to a short lawn. As Lewis Carroll's Mad Gardener observed in *Sylvie and Bruno*:

> He thought he saw a Banker's Clerk
>   Descending from the bus:
> He looked again, and found it was
>   A Hippopotamus:
> 'If this should stay to dine,' he said,
>   'There won't be much for us.'

The grazers tear up grass not with their teeth but with their lips. Coming upon a herd grazing at nighttime is an unforgettable acoustical experience — the cacaphony of all the tearing and chewing, the heavy breathing, and the periodic snorting is unbelievable, reminiscent perhaps of a *very* bad orchestra interminably tuning up for an evening's performance.

But it is at the river, lake, or stream that one must come to terms with the hippo. Here, the herd gathers in a group where, appropriate to its aquatic surroundings, it becomes a "school." Schools can easily comprise twenty or more (*80*), and the configuration or crowding depends significantly on the available space or depth of the water, as the hippo needs to submerge itself up to its ears, protruding eyes, and nostrils (all conveniently placed on top of its head, like a crocodile or a frog) without exposing much else to the hot African sun. Indeed, the hippo's iceberg imitation is its only lasting method of dispersing excess heat and keeping cool during a bright day and

maintaining a stable moisture balance throughout its virtually hairless skin. Hippos have a thin epidermis, and the rate of water loss through the skin in dry air is several times greater than in other mammals. Hence, the river horse must stay in the water or in a very humid habitat to prevent dehydration. In addition, the animal has no true temperature-regulating sweat glands. If the hippos are few or the available pool large, older adults, especially the bulls, will spread out and stake out aquatic territories off from the main group (*81*), but any sizeable school will have a core of females and youngsters who will congregate in a gregariously tight formation. The 'little' youngsters occupy most of their time in the water standing on the back of the adults (normally, their mothers). Otherwise, the effort to keep afloat would wear them out. All this is revealed in a few minutes from the vehicle window or roof hatch — the hippo that most people take home.

Actually, there is more, much more. The school is a rugby scrum ready to explode and never as benignly inactive as it frequently appears at first glance. Ideally, one should make a picnic out of hippo-watching — take a box lunch and, where permitted, leave the vehicle to sit on the banks (always at a safe distance) and follow the scrum in action. To begin to understand the hippo (and we all suffer from the relative lack of scientific data available), the safarist must realize that the animal is really semi-aquatic and truly amphibious. The water then is far from simply a convenient escape from the sun; to a large degree, it is home. Indeed, the hippo's day does not vary significantly when the weather is overcast or rainy (*82*). There is no way, for example, that a hippo's stubby little legs could support all that bulk, day in, day out, over an average lifetime of forty years or so, without the buoyancy of water to relieve the burden. Moreover, calves are often born *underwater* (and must swim to the surface for their first breath of air) and nurse mostly underwater.[56] In fact, hippos frequently even mate in the water, with the female wholly or partially submerged. The learning is that hippos can stay totally submerged for up to six minutes and, having a high specific gravity, they can easily walk or run along the bottom during a dive. The author has timed hippos apparently completely submerged for periods ranging up to twenty minutes. I cannot account for the discrepancy. When submerged, they close the valves of their nostrils and press their ears flat against the sides of their heads. The heart rate of a hippo also slows down, giving it more time underwater. When a hippo surfaces, it is usually with a loud hiss, a snort, or distinctive grunt that

55. Wherever hippos congregate, vast numbers of fish and birds follow. The hippos crop closely the grass at the water's edge, making it ideal for ground-nesting waterbirds, such as spoonbills, and White pelicans. Such close-cropping has other benefits as well — for example, by keeping the grass short, the hippo limits the spread of fires close to the rivers, thereby encouraging thickets of woody plants to expand along the water. As might be expected, some animals suffer; waterbuck and (to a lesser degree) bushbuck calves are quite vulnerable in the absence of long grass. They cannot hide from predators. A hippo will travel great distances, up to six miles (more typical is one to two miles) to establish his natural grazing area, but, if the grasses there do not grow during an especially harsh dry season, the hippo does not emulate other grazers and travel many additional miles searching for food. Above all, he will not emigrate. Basically, more like the rhino, who also will not leave his home range, he slows his eating and waits for the rains to return and the grass to grow again. (In part, he cannot, of course, move beyond the reach of water.) And despite what appears to be a massive appetite, a hippo eats, in relation to its body weight, only half as much as many other herbivores. The reader should recall the basic mathematics lesson regarding the elephant and body size. Moreover, the hippo expends far less energy during the day in the water than he would if he lived on land.

56. Of course, sliding underneath a hippo on land (a hippo cow must nurse standing up) can be a logistics nightmare; her belly nearly scrapes the ground. When a calf does nurse on land, and this location is preferred at the beginning, he acts as he would underwater: he automatically closes his nostrils and folds his ears to the sides of his head. Consequently, he must sporadically stop suckling to breathe.

Plate 80. A Large School. The author once counted sixty-two hippos in a school. (Counting a large school is difficult, because several animals at any given point are submerged and moving around.) Hippos have a low mortality rate, one key to their numbers today. In addition, both males and females reproduce into old age. The females usually have their first calf at about ten years of age and continue calving roughly every three years thereafter. Longevity is forty years or so.

Plate 81. Nature's Snorkler. Submerged, with most of its girth left to the imagination, the hippo looks like some gigantic frog. He will soon disappear altogether in a circle of shimmering ripples. At Mzima Springs in Tsavo, Kenya, visitors can watch hippos effortlessly tip-toeing across the bottom from the windows located in an underwater observatory. (In recent years, however, the hippos have tended to congregate in a different area of the pool.) A hippo is a good swimmer but it prefers to run on the bottom.

Plate 82. Hippo Tasting Rain. It takes real patience to watch the hippos in the rain(!), but they seem to enjoy this time. When the gaping jaw is open, the hippo's mouth looks like a huge cavern edged with ivory stalagmites and stalactites. Indeed, a full-grown man could sit down in a hippo's mouth. A hippo at this point is usually making a statement, something like, 'This part of the pool belongs to me' or 'Take a good look at this weaponry.'

sounds like a quick blast from a tuba. Watching a large school, one never knows where the next hippo will emerge, as they go up and down like errant corks.

In sum, much of the hippo's life is connected to the water; and far more is involved than simply escaping the heat. In fact, around midday and even in the hottest sun, the school usually adjourns to the shore, apparently for a sunbath. (83-87) Rangers have told the author of seeing hippos lying on their backs with feet held straight up in the air, but I have never witnessed anything like this. Eventually, after approximately an hour, the behemoths return to the water. (88-90)

If the mornings in the pool are relatively tranquil — eating the amount of food that it does the night before, the hippo deserves a little quiet digestion — the afternoon is another story altogether. Hippos might look docile, the little pig-like ears twirling in every direction. In fact, they are anything but. From the perspective of natives killed, hippos are probably the most dangerous African animals, well ahead of the crocodile and anything else. Hippos are not only aggressive and easily enraged, they are very unpredictable (and so, the mornings are not necessarily invariably peaceful). On land, this is a one- to three-ton animal capable of moving like a locomotive — a hippo can, over the short haul, easily outrun a man and stay with a rhino — who carries under a full head of steam whatever authority is needed to clear its way. And the sheer bulk — despite appearances, mostly muscle — turns out to be very agile as well. One writer has referred amusingly to hippos as walking with the ponderous grace of Sydney Greenstreet ("fetching his decanter of scotch"), and so they sometimes do. But woe to the person in the night who accidently blocks our sharp-tempered friend's access to the water. (A spooked hippo always heads straight for

the protection of his waterhole.) And, in the water, hippos frequently attack small boats, canoes, and the like, in addition to people bathing or swimming. Anything worth biting is bitten (off or in half). One assumes that many of the boating incidents involve mothers protecting calves. Canoes in particular must look threatening — perhaps even like crocodiles — to a hippo. And one cannot discount accidents in which hippos unwittingly surface under a small craft. Moreover, a submerged hippo can be remarkably inconspicuous in the water and undoubtedly does not appreciate being rammed by a boat of any size. Having noted all these factors — excuses — the safarist should still realize that the hippo is not the cherubic old wardboss, long affectionately regarded by all, but the mafioso don who is capable of serious mayhem.

But let us return to life in the scrum. As it turns out, the adult hippo's only real enemy (other than man) is his poolmate.[57] As indicated, the afternoon is the time to settle old scores and begin new feuds. After his sunbath, the hippo falls back into the pool with all the subtlety of a morning talk-show host and all the goodwill of Pete Rose arriving at home plate just ahead of the throw. The baby hippos, always looking to improve their position or footing on top of mother, often start the fireworks. Backs tend to look remarkably alike, and, whoops, suddenly baby is riding a 'stranger.' The new platforms are not necessarily pleased to support the additional weight and react accordingly. Whereupon, the mothers aggressively rise to the defense. But the real brawls break out between the males, and a patient safarist can always count on an incident or two — indeed, a hippo bull begins the day with a nasty disposition and passes the morning in the pool developing and then nursing an attitude. Much of the famous yawning that one sees in the pool is, in fact, one hippo (males *and* females) mildly threatening another (or others) or generally stating its negative intentions by displaying its tusks. As the yawning increases, the fighting is near. The afternoon can be filled with dozens of disputes. The bulls naturally fight over females in breeding season but quarrel over

Plate 83. Significant Biomass. To a degree, a hippo herd collapsed on a sandbar resembles a resting lion pride: the stupor is real, a body-on-body mass is the order of the day, and shifting or jockeying for a "better" position inevitably produces a domino reaction.

57. Lions, leopards, hyenas, or wild dogs will occasionally take a baby. Only man hunts the adult.

Plates 84-87. The Expandable Nap Midday at the River Bank on the Mara River. Eventually, one by one or in twos and threes, nearly everybody leaves the water. If hippos remain in the hot sun too long, they begin to ooze a pink or reddish oily (and highly alkaline) liquid through their pores. This is not "blood," as once promoted by P.T. Barnum, but a cooling agent that also protects against sunburn (and perhaps infections as well). Hippos do not possess sweat glands.

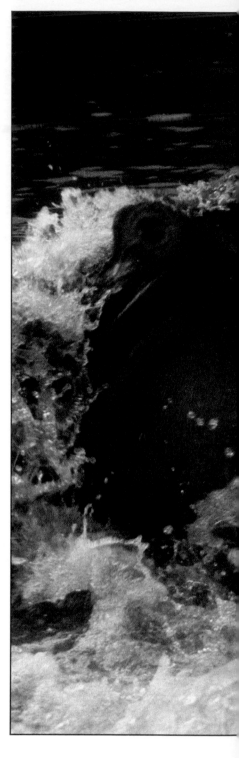

Plates 88-90. A Charles Laughton Version of a Cannonball Dive. A hippo is not designed for finesse. The belly flop into the water is far easier than the haul out of the water and *up* the banks.

Plate 91. War. A hippo fight is an impressive display of pink gaping mouths and gnashing tusks.

water space at all times, especially in dry season. Bulls are extremely territorial, and, though it is difficult for the safarist to see the distinctions, each bull has staked out his own particular spot in the pool. In large schools, the evidence indicates that a master bull of sorts emerges to run the show and set the boundaries. He then fights with everybody.[58]

---

58. An alternative theory, supported by a few naturalists, is that a hippo herd very much resembles an elephant herd —

Hippo fighting is not the ritualized choreographed affair engaged in by the males of many other species. Rather, this is an old-fashioned barroom brawl, a vigorous, incredibly noisy, no-holds-barred struggle nearly unrivalled among mammals in ferocity. (91) What makes one curmudgeon really dangerous to another is, of course, the set of massive, razor-sharp tusks found in the corners of each jaw and hidden away inside the folds of its fatty lips. The two tusks of the lower jaw can grow up to a foot or more.[59] Sharp incisors also line both jaws. Nevertheless,

organized along matriarchal lines, with a dominant female arranging the pool. The male, in this view, is a rugged individualist, without much authority within the herd. In any event, hippo schools are not as stable as elephant herds.

59. Really large lower tusks (canines) are visible and grow in a curved fashion, up toward the nostrils.

although the struggle is fierce and the weapons at hand often inflict significant wounds, the war is rarely carried to lethal completion. When it is (and at times when it is not), the pool turns blood-red. But the more normal result is yet another scarred hide. Thus, a good look at a hippo male usually reveals huge punctures in his skin that look as if they were made by mortar shells. This hide is tough and thick[60] and alone can weigh half a ton, so the reader can imagine that creating such holes takes more than a little nibbling. Actually, though the scars remain, the huge, lethal-looking wounds heal quickly; hippo skin seems to have strong healing properties. And why not? — they are obviously needed.

The epic nature of a struggle between two hippos is well described in this passage from Durrell:

When I was collecting animals in West Africa we once camped on the banks of a river in which lived a hippo herd of moderate size. They seemed a placid and happy group, and every time we went up or down the stream by canoe they would follow us a short distance, swimming nearer and nearer, wiggling their ears and occasionally snorting up clouds of spray, as they watched us with interest. As far as I could make out, the herd consisted of four females, a large elderly male and a young male. One of the females had a medium-sized baby with her which, though already large and fat, was still occasionally carried on her back. They seemed, as I say, a very happy family group. But one night, just as it was growing dark, they launched into a series of roars and brays which sounded like a choir of demented donkeys. These were interspersed with moments of silence broken only by a snort or a splash, but as it drew darker the noise became worse, until, eventually realizing I would be unlikely to get any sleep, I decided to go down and see what was happening. Taking a canoe, I paddled down to the curve of the river a couple of hundred yards away, where the brown water had carved a deep pool out of the bank and thrown up a great half-moon of glittering white sand. I knew the hippos liked to spend the day here, and it was from this direction that all the noise was coming. I knew something was wrong, for usually by this time each evening they had hauled their fat bodies out of the water and trekked along the bank to raid some unfortunate native's plantation, but here they were in the pool, long past the beginning of their feeding-time. I landed on the sandbank and walked along to a spot which gave me a good view. There was no reason for me to worry about noise: the terrible roars and bellows and splashes coming from the pool were quite sufficient to cover the scrunch of my footsteps.

At first I could see nothing but an occasional flash of white where the hippos' bodies thrashed in the water and churned it into foam, but presently the moon rose, and in its brilliant light I could see the females and the baby gathered at one end of the pool in a tight bunch, their heads gleaming above the surface of the water, their ears flicking to and fro. Now and again they would open their mouths and bray, rather in the manner of a Greek chorus. They were watching with interest both the old male and the young who were in the shallows at the centre of the pool. The water reached up only to their tummies, and their great barrel-shaped bodies and the rolls of fat under their chins gleamed as though they had been oiled. They were facing each other with lowered heads, snorting like a couple of steam-engines. Suddenly the young male lifted his great head, opened his mouth so that his teeth flashed in the moonlight, gave a prolonged and blood-curdling bray, and, just as he was finishing, the old male rushed at him with open mouth and incredible speed for such a bulky animal. The young male, equally quick, twisted to one side. The old male splashed in a welter of foam like some misshapen battleship, and was now going so fast that he could not stop. As he passed, the young male, with a terrible sideways chop of his huge jaws, bit him in the shoulder. The old male swerved round and charged again, and just as he reached his opponent the moon went behind a cloud. When it came out again, they were standing as I had first seen them, facing each other with lowered heads, snorting.

I sat on that sandbank for two hours, watching these great roly-poly creatures churning up the water and sand as they duelled in the shallows. As far as I could see, the old male was getting the worst of it, and I felt sorry for him. Like some once-great pugilist who had now grown flabby and stiff, he seemed to be fighting a battle which he knew was already lost. The young male, lighter and more agile, seemed to dodge him every time, and his teeth always managed to find their mark in the shoulder or neck of the old male. In the background the females watched with semaphoring ears, occasionally breaking into a loud lugubrious chorus which may have been sorrow for the plight of the old male, or delight at the success of the young one, but was probably merely the excitement of watching the fight. Eventually, since the fight did not seem as if it would end for several more hours, I paddled home to the village and went to bed.

I awoke just as the horizon was paling into dawn, and the hippos were quiet. Apparently the fight was over. I hoped that the old male had won, but I very much doubted it. The answer was given to me later that morning by one of my hunters; the corpse of the old male, he said, was about two miles downstream, lying where the current of the river had carried it into the curving arms of a sandbank. I went down to examine it and was horrified at the havoc the young male's teeth had wrought on the massive body. The shoulders, the neck, the great dewlaps that hung under the chin, the flanks and the belly; all were ripped and tattered, and the shallows around the carcase were still tinged with blood. The entire village had accompanied me, for such an enormous windfall of meat was a red-letter day for them. They stood silent and interested while I examined the old male's carcase, and when I had finished and walked away they poured over it like ants,

---

60. Immortalized by Belloc in these words:

> *I shoot the Hippopotamus*
> *With bullets made of platinum*
> *Because if I use leaden ones*
> *His hide is sure to flatten 'em.*
> *(Bad Child's Book of Beasts,*
> *"The Hippopotamus")*

screaming and pushing with excitement, vigorously wielding their knives and machetes. It seemed to me, watching the huge hippo's carcase disintegrate under the pile of hungry humans, that it was a heavy price to pay for love.[61]

In fact, love or not, I find hippo aggression somewhat of a mystery, given the current state of our knowledge. Surely, at least some of nature's "rules" appear to be ignored by the violence. Animals designed to pass on their genetic traits to their offspring — as all animals are, through natural selection — have to give the highest priority to survival. This quest means that the animal must ensure sufficient food, sufficient "housing," and sufficient mating opportunities. All these needs are therefore worth defending, fighting for, or possibly fighting to improve. A degree of competition in a finite world becomes inevitable. But the most efficient form of competition is to use threats, displays, vocalizations, scent-marking, and what-not to intimidate one's competition without having to expend great energy oneself by fighting. Thus, the hippo yawns, for example, many times a day. Males threaten males; females with calves threaten everybody.

So far, so good. The next step — escalation — is ritualized fighting, in which both competitors test each other without resort to the risk (and obvious costs) of real fighting. Most herbivores, who do not kill for a living, are quite content to let matters rest at this stage. Normally, a system of dominance, based on relative strength, is established; inferiors accept subordination, at least until their opportunity for challenging "up the ladder" comes up, and consequently have no desire to fight all the time. The hippo seems, however, to ignore this intermediate step altogether. Not only is it often unclear just *why* hippos fight in the first instance — what exactly is the provocation — it is even more of a mystery why they feel compelled to fight so *seriously*.

The mystery deepens. Normally, even in earnest fighting, the weaker of the two combatants finds a way to retreat, sometimes with honor, sometimes by the skin of its teeth. Hippos fight on, in titanic struggles. Why? Apparently, what specialists call "motivational cornering" is at work — that is, a situation is created in which the rival is trapped, not by physical barriers but by psychological concerns of one kind or another. We can only speculate now what are influencing the hippos at these times. Finally, animals generally use their most deadly weapons only against their enemies, not in intraspecific arguments. Thus, as we have just seen, giraffes do not kick other giraffes. They do kick — and kill — lions. Hippos bite, maim, and kill each other. Not invariably, but enough to wonder. In truth, the hippo possesses an innate aggression which is stronger than that found in most other species, and this aggression seems to be triggered even in

the absence of the normal stimuli and without recourse to the normal safeguards.

There are two, dare one say, "companions" that the hippos tolerate in their pool, aside, of course, from the fish, who were there first anyway.[62] First are all manner of birds, encouraged by the fish and insect 'by-products' of a hippo pool. Waterfowl use hippos as fishing platforms. *(92)* I have seen hammerkops, egrets, and storks fish off the backs of the river horses. And this tactic goes beyond the convenience of employing a handy diving platform: a hippo's strong smell and excretions attract fish (and fish will feed off the plants adhering to hippos), and the

Plate 92. More Than a Free Ride. Birds stroll around on hippos as though they were walking on rocks, without fear or hesitation. Gulls, terns, egrets, herons, plovers, stilts, jacanas, sandpipers, cormorants, geese, ibis, darters, and hammerkops fish from, rest on, dry outstretched wings on, and stalk insects along these huge platforms. More: the ill-tempered giant has also been known to tolerate turtles, monitor lizards, and other freeloaders.

61. Gerald Durrell, *Encounters with Animals* (Rupert Hart-Davis, 1958), pp. 55-8.

62. Although not necessarily in that quantity. When hippos defecate into the water, they also scatter their dung by rapidly whirring their tails. Naturalists believe that the dominant males purposely aim for their inferiors (not so subtle *noblesse oblige,* in our terms). The copious quantity of manure and organic matter and the blender action together combine to release into the water rich nutrients that dissolve and fertilize prolific algae and plant growth, which in turn feeds many aquatic animals. Thus, a large hippo pool always supports a large fish population. And insects. Undigested or partly digested plant matter in the dung also collects (by wave action) at the shorelines. Aquatic insects breed in this decay and insectivorous birds do very well, indeed.

Plate 93. A Little Scavenging on the Side. With remarkable equanimity, the hippos tolerate it all. Meanwhile, the fish below are "cleaning" the submerged surfaces.

Plate 94. African Tableau-I. Crocs, hippos, heron — and much that the eye cannot see. The reader should be able to find at least three crocs in this tableau.

churning caused by the hippo's feet below stirs up frogs and other tasty morsels. The inevitable oxpeckers and related birds hop around looking for food in the wounds or scars found on every hippo's hide. (92) They stalk and eat the insects and larvae in the skin and wounds and are, no doubt, helpful to a degree. But they also pick the flesh as well and invariably make the wounds worse. One supposes that the hide is so thick and tough that the hippo hardly notices. (93)

Second, surprisingly enough, are crocodiles. Although a croc will occasionally kill a hippo calf, the two species frequently live in close and peaceful proximity. (94) A croc that is seen feeding on an adult hippo carcass is simply taking good advantage of an already dead hippo. The living hippos might well appreciate the housekeeping. It has even been said that young crocs bask on the backs of hippos! I have never seen such behavior, nor have I ever been able to confirm such reports. The idea is, however, not so farfetched, given all the other jockeys in the sweepstakes.

As one might imagine, studying hippos is a real chore. Few of the standard techniques can be applied, and we know even less about the hippopotamus than we do about the giraffe. It will be many years before our knowledge of the river horse equals that of its more terrestrial neighbors.

Cape (African) Buffalo

The adult male buffalo[63] is regarded by many — the author included — as the most dangerous animal in Africa.[64] More vicious, more vindictive, and less predictable than anything else, the buffalo bull has proved itself a cunning and more than formidable adversary to hunters over the years. Buffalos have also proved to be dangerous animals when encountered on foot safaris. Virtually all the tourists killed by animals — and in all this time, including the many (recent) years of sport hunting, there have been only a handful — have involved miscalculations or surprises concerning buffalos. Throughout most of the nineteenth century, the buffalo was abundant in East and Southern Africa. At the end of the century, the virus rinderpest, probably first introduced into Somalia from Arabia or India, swept Africa and caused a catastrophic decline. The epidemic was a major natural disaster of recorded history, and its effects lasted well into our time. The buffalo slowly recovered, but rinderpest was not eradicated until the 1960s (by innoculation campaigns).

Ordinarily, one can readily tell the difference between a male and female buffalo (buffalo is "mbogo," or "nyati," in Kiswahili). Both are heavily built, but the cows have lighter horns that do not dip down in such heavy sweeps. And the cow does not have as heavy a boss (the center, raised part of the horn that on its underside lies flat on top of the head). In addition, the females (like calves) have more of a brownish or even reddish tinge to their coats (95). The bulls are dressed in basic black. (96)

It has been said that the cows are more alert than the bulls, but this opinion probably reflects a lack of understanding concerning the basic nature of the buffalo herd and the different functions assumed by the males from those carried out by the females. The females are usually bunched together, at the heart of the herd, and the slightest response by one member of the herd will throw the others into similar activity, or even an exaggerated version. Buffalo herds show a strong sense of cohesion and coordination. But, if one rarely sees a cow off by herself, the bulls frequently drift to the outer edges of the herd and beyond. The males in the herd show machismo — their function is to stand and test the "danger," however briefly. (97) When the herd bolts, the bulls are not supposed to head the charge, but to follow and protect the rear. In any herd, several bulls, as a rule easily distinguishable by an onlooker, will dominate and they will take an active role in protecting the herd against predators. It is not uncommon to see one of these bulls advance menacingly toward a lion, for example, and other males from the herd will join the leader(s) if actually under attack. But the herd, on the whole and like all herds everywhere, is easily spooked and basically timid. The group in a national park daily reinacts the saga of Chicken Little. The wary buffalos will not remain long lying down in the presence of a safari vehicle, and no herd will allow a vehicle to approach very close without exploding and thundering off. The animals never flee very far, however, and quickly stop and wheel about after fifty or sixty yards to look back.

To understand the buffalo, one must therefore know something about its herding behavior. Whether buffalos remain in closely compact groups principally to avoid predation or primarily to learn the essential features of their environment, most notably the food supply, is a question that naturalists will argue for many years. The author, for one, does not give much credit to the predation influence. Predation — almost entirely by lions, though a hyena pack can be a factor — compares well to a murder in our society: front-page stuff because it is so noticeable, but of little consequence in determining population. And the question that I always put to the over-enthusiastic Darwinists is, how can species behavior evolve when so little of the total population is affected? It is true that all the evidence clearly shows that lions overwhelmingly select buffalos that have wandered from the herd. The older males are, as a category, the most preyed-upon buffalos; the younger age groups are protected by remaining in the herd, and females, who remain in the herd all their lives, do not suffer significant predation at all. But these are relative statistics.[65] As a whole, buffalos are simply not efficient targets for lions. I realize that

---

63. Technically, no buffalo ever "roamed" — or did anything else, for that matter — in the United States. The American version of this animal is the "bison," a distinct species of its own.

64. Several writers have attempted to 'rise to the defense,' one supposes, of the buffalo by challenging this "quite unjustified reputation." The usual complaint is that these well-known characterizations of buffalo behavior are the result of hunters' tales and that the bovid, if left alone, is benign enough. But hunters exaggerated *everything* and probably on a more or less equal footing. Thus, as a comparative matter, we may give some credence to their admiration for the cunning and dangerous buffalo. And, second, the reputation obviously is stated relative to the presence of man. Man is, and has been for some time, very much a part of the buffalo's natural world. The herd itself will not charge human beings, unless its exit is blocked (as recently happened in Kenya, when a small herd under purely accidental conditions scattered a foot safari like duckpins), but the so-called rogue seems to recur with biological frequency.

65. The argument has been made by those favoring predation-oriented evolution that the old males are no longer subject to the "pressure" to stay with the herd, because, as sexually inactive members, they are no longer contributing to the survival of offspring (protection? numbers?) and thus are "free" to leave the herd. This line has even been carried to the extreme of suggesting that by remaining with a herd, the individuals could even decrease the survival possibilities of their progeny — *i.e.,* by removing easier prey (themselves) remaining outside the herd. The author will have something to say about such convoluted evolutionism in the next chapter, though rarely does the imagination rise to such levels of intricacy (and irrelevance).

Plate 95. Females and Egret. Needless to say, the "cattle" egrets are constant companions. The birds, small Buff-backed (so-called because of the darkening of the upper parts during breeding season) herons, are sometimes confused by novices with the tick-birds. But these herons do not groom (examinations of their stomach contents have never revealed more than the odd, isolated tick or two); they devour the insects stirred up by the bovids' movement. Too much movement, however, like a stampede, will send the egrets into the air like a snowstorm. Although naturalists have tried to renew the symbiotic argument familiar to oxpecker devotees, that the egret furnishes a warning system for its grazing partners, complete with gleaming white plummage to signal the alarm as it leaps into flight, the bird's behavior more likely is an instance of commensalism, in which the host remains unaffected. After a day of feeding, the egrets congregate and fly in flocks to roosting sites — forming temporarily (at lower levels) a beautiful white cloud against the dusky sky. Somehow, the bird crossed the Atlantic, colonizing the West Indies and South America in the 1930s. First seen in the United States (in Florida) in the early 1940s, it is now well-established throughout ranching country in the United States, where it travels about with the cattle (and, naturally enough, farm machines!). The expansion of its range (the bird has continued on to Australia, as well) is an astounding success story. Bird specialists estimate the world population of cattle egrets at nearly one billion.

some environments encourage bovid predation; lions at Lake Manyara live almost exclusively on buffalo. But killing even a lone buffalo can be a monumental task. I have personally seen a single bull ward off three apparently very hungry lionesses and have also witnessed a male who was obviously ill successfully defend himself against an entire pack of hyenas (perhaps as many as twelve to fourteen), once he had maneuvered his back to a tree. As one might expect, given the determination of hyenas, this

of vengeance. In sum, no predator tackles a buffalo, unless the odds heavily favor success — and nature does not provide such odds as a matter of course.

On the other hand, the business of earning a living makes herding attractive. Experience is required to learn how to find the best food at a given time in a certain habitat. Available food — especially if a variety is involved — will change with the season. Young, inexperienced animals will benefit by associating with experienced

Plate 96. Bull Head. These massive horns, which remind one of some magnificent Viking's helmet, are among the most formidable weapons in the natural world. Tip to tip, they can spread more than five feet in length. As trophies, they have drawn hunters from all over the world. When bulls fight, the greater part of the force of the blows received is absorbed by the broad bosses of the horns. The noise is striking, but little damage is done.

last was a Homeric struggle that lasted well over two hours. Moreover, females as well as males will defend calves against predation, and there are several reports of cows taking the intiative to chase off lions. Finally, scientists have recounted numerous incidents, in which herd animals have attacked lions *after* a member of the herd had been killed. Only elephants join buffalos in this sort

adults. And not only adults, but the same group of adults. Thus, we would expect to find that buffalo herds are relatively stable — and they are. We would expect adult males to begin to drift from herd life (the females, the reader should recall the elephant example, have motherly reasons for remaining) — and they do. The suggestion has been made that young males remain in the herd because they can thereby achieve an occasional mating — subordinate bulls generally do not mate — but this factor must be distinctly secondary, and probably a bit too sophisticated a strategy, as well, for buffalos. Having come this far, however, the argument should also recognize that herding behavior imposes limitations on the types of food that can be eaten. The closer that animals herd and the more members constituting the group — both factors limit the variety of fuel taken. A

both).

Herd life is both routine and highly coordinated. A herd, which occupies a basic home range, may well number in the thousands; herds of several hundred are common. Obviously, habitat characteristics influence herd size. Normally, forest herds are considerably smaller than those found on the open savannah. The size of home ranges is also directly related to habitat characteristics: small ranges are found in forested, high-rainfall regions,

Plate 97. Akagera Bull in Prime. Buffalos often stand motionless like this, as if carved from stone. In Akagera, in Rwanda, the male buffalos are among the largest in Africa, rivaling those found on the western side of Mount Kenya. These monsters are hardly ever challenged by predators and can live to twenty-five years or so. They are, however, ill-tempered and often charge safari vehicles. The African buffalo is very susceptible to rinderpest, which, though believed to be under control at this time, has periodically destroyed herds.

large, closely knit herd would lose more energy than it gained by walking any significant distance to obtain a scattered variety of plants; the food must be abundant, when found. And, when the abundance declines, as during a long dry season, for example, the herd must split up into smaller units or spread out among themselves (or

and larger ranges in open, drier savannahs. And the obvious fact that animal density will rise where the amount of food is plentiful is offset by the total size-limitation. Nevertheless, early one morning at Treetops, a Tree Hotel located in the Aberdares forest range in Kenya, the author counted a herd of nearly two thousand coming to drink and take the salt at the waterhole. The heavy early mist obscured the forest, except for the tree edge at the clearing that led to the water. Phalanxes of buffalos would suddenly step through the vapor like ghosts. The experience might have been more eerie were it not for the heavy bovine smell, reminding all onlookers that the obscure forms were real enough. The picture found in the front plates of this book was taken at that time. As the mist slowly evaporated, the tableau revealed more buffalos than trees, perhaps more than surface ground itself.

It is important to think of these large herds as entities and not as temporary aggregations — their members can identify one another as being of the same herd (probably by smell), and harmonization of activity is always evident. Although individual herds have their own home ranges, or preferred areas, these geographical expanses overlap. Little or no aggression has ever been noticed between herds. A kind of "passive" territoriality is observed, however, in that animals from one herd that wander into the range of another herd are not accepted by the residents (and thus lose the protection that herds afford). In fact, very little interchange between herds exists. Large herds do, of course, tend to form subgroups, and, as a herd grows larger, groups will drift apart, ultimately to form new herds. This is a normal method of extending the distribution of a species.

As noted earlier, the adult males often leave the herds during the dry seasons, usually in groups. They return at the beginning of the rainy season. This behavior usually begins at about four years of age. A hierarchy develops within the adult-male segment of a herd, but a true linear hierarchy is improbable within any significant-sized herd, which may have as many as 100 adult males. Females show little, if any, dominance; a herd has no lead cow, and mothers and daughters do not remain together once grown, making female relationships purely *ad hoc* affairs. Herd life represents, in fact, a military operation without anyone acting above the rank of sergeant, save for a few Pattons at the top. But the precision is there, and the herd moves around during the day with little fighting, pushing, or unruly behavior.

An observant safarist will see, however, particularly during the breeding season, threat behavior between two mature bulls. The typical aggressive posture consists of arching the neck (head held high, nose pointing to the ground), tossing the head up and down and making hooking motions in the air with their horns, standing sideways to emphasize size ("lateral display"), circling each other, and digging up (with the horns) and tossing clods of earth. Although one might expect a bovid to paw the ground, African buffalos generally do not. On occasion, two bulls will line up like champion medieval knights tilting in a joust: the impact — on the boss of the horns — of the resulting charge ends the "fight"! The loser turns and flees. Young males frequently spar by putting their heads together and twisting the horns from side to side, but the exercise is clearly benign. Subadult males will also fre-

quently mount each other during play fighting in an attempt to assert dominance. The submission by a young male to a dominant adult is equally obvious. The former will adopt a suckling posture, with head held low and extended, and may touch the belly of a dominant with his muzzle, completing the nursing gesture. The youngster may also adopt a more sophisticated appeasement display: "testing the wind," in which he sticks his nose in the air, giving the impression of trying to scent danger. In this way, he is sending the dominant male a message that he will flee if attacked.

The older males progress from sporadically leaving the herd for limited periods during the dry season to more or less permanent bachelor status. Some writers have assumed that the old malefactors simply turn so truculent that even their own herd ostracizes them. But the reality is that an old bull loses interest in the herd as his ability to breed declines. He then lives alone or in a small group, call it a gentleman's club, outside the herd mainstream.[66] (98) This is the buffalo of which the safarist has to be especially suspicious. Like any incorrigible recidivist, he must be approached only with the greatest caution. This fellow *always* feels like the late-afternoon hippo. And once he has made up his mind to charge, he cannot be distracted. The author remembers one day in a tented camp in Kenya, when I had remained behind for the morning. Returning a little too early for lunch, one of the camp's Landrovers looked as if it had taken one of those spectacular dives off a cliff that is seen in the movies. Three windows were broken, and one side and at least part of the front were completely collapsed. The passengers themselves were unhurt but looked a little white around the gills, so to speak. Their story tumbled out about as quickly as they alighted from the vehicle. Some two hours earlier, they had come upon two old bulls grazing together several miles from the camp. The driver had carelessly parked too close to the pair but, more to the point, had not remained alert. Shortly, two massive horns, propelled by nearly a ton of fury, were implanted in the side of the vehicle. According to the passengers (the driver by then was smiling solicitously...), the entire vehicle was moved first sideways and then up on two wheels before it fell back. The bull kept at it for a

---

66. The oldest bachelors collect in groups of two, three, or four animals and show their own hierarchy and have their own home ranges. In the author's experience, they remain in the general vicinity of the original herd, at least on the savannah. Not surprisingly, however, the herd animals cover far more territory than the bachelors, who are showing by this time increased difficulty in movement. Some bachelor bulls, despite increased predation, live to an old age. They eat the same food as before, but the far smaller groups can make use of considerably more limited patches of habitat than the herd. And the lack of harassment from dominant or would-be dominant bulls must relieve a great deal of stress, perhaps offsetting any stress added by neighboring hungry lions.

good fifteen minutes or so, while the driver frantically (no smile at that point, I can assure the reader) tried to restart his vehicle. One can picture the machine being rocked and thrown about by this beast; one can only imagine the story that will be told to grandchildren. At any rate, retreat was finally effectuated when the bull hesitated and pulled off for a few yards (undoubtedly to develop a better fix on the next point of impact). The vehicle took more than an hour to limp home.

The author, with more than a tad or so too much machismo himself, decided to set off with a driver to find

countless such Cold War diplomatic confrontations, and the number of times that the buffalo has given way can be ticked off on one hand. Most elephants come to accept such brinkmanship with the placid tolerance that is their wont; some protest and race around in an only half-serious fury; a few proud (and large) bulls will actually attack the buffalo. And there are reliable reports — the author has never witnessed this — of an elephant bull killing an especially truculant buffalo. Mostly, a *modus vivendi* is reached: live and let drink. *(101)*

In the long run, of course, even the fiercest old buffalo

Plate 98. Gentlemen's Lawn Party. Seconds after the picture was made, the warthogs were strutting off, and these bulls positioned just off from the main herd were standing. In a real panic, herd members can run at 30 mph. Once the herd pirouettes in unison and gallops away, the stampede is a solid, thundering mass of thudding hooves.

this rogue bull. The result is pictured in plate *99*, a medium-telephoto effort that tries to capture the mood of floating malice hanging in the air. Unfortunately, no good action shots resulted. As we got closer, my driver, in a fit of common sense, refused to kill the engine, and we thus played not matador but rodeo clown for the next hour or so, as the old codger chased us unmercifully whenever we got within thirty or forty yards. We finally retired to a late lunch, leaving the field of battle to the victor.

From a safer perspective, one can easily witness the same uncompromising behavior at one of the Tree Hotels overlooking a salt-lick. There, the old bulls yield to no one, not even an elephant *(100)*. The author has watched

is finally killed by predators or eaten by the scavengers of the plains. Ten years is the normal lifespan; a few individuals may see twenty years. But the law of the African bush — eat and be eaten — applies to all alike *(102)*.

Like ruminants everywhere, the buffalo needs to eat only a fraction of his body weight in food. It is said that buffalos are entirely grazers, and, though this must be nearly true, the author has seen examples of browsing in the forests. Buffalos prefer the longer grasses that grow near water, but this source is not abundant in the dry season, and the large animals may turn in part to the leaves of herbs and bushes. The buffalo can live in a wide variety of environments, from the dense forest to the open plains,

Plates 100 & 101. Typical Sequence: Stand-off at the Salt-Lick. Challenging an elephant is an act of stubborn foolishness, a specialty of buffalos. Among themselves, buffalos assume a threatening posture by holding their heads high and arching their necks (arching a bull neck is not all that noticeable to us). They will also stand so as to give a lateral view — to dramatize their size. A submission gesture is characterized by holding the head low and stretched out, in imitation of suckling. The reader should not be fooled, however, by plate *100*: confronting an elephant head-on (in this instance, the buffalo also stood between the elephant and the water) is never a sign of peace and goodwill. This buffalo did, eventually, have the presence of mind (and sense of well-being) to reach an accommodation.

Plate 99. Old Bull. Shot in the bright heat of midday, this particular kamikaze had already repeatedly attacked two safari vehicles that morning, sacking one. Spittles of fury dangling from his mouth and patent-leather nose, normally gleaming with moisture but today covered with a layer of dust, snorting short Hemingway sentences resonant with ill will, this old boy was in no mood for tourists. Bulls always charge with their heads up, keeping the enemy in clear sight, and lower the horns only at the last moment before impact. Old bulls come and go at will in their former herds, but they are unpopular, and a diminished sex drive ensures that any mixing is brief. On the other hand, they do remain in the general vicinity of their former comrades.

Plate 102. The End of All Buffalo Journeys. The buffalo's predators — lions, leopards, hyenas, and crocodiles at river crossings — are usually careful to pick out sick or wounded, old, or very young animals.

though it seems to prefer at least some bush, where, presumably, it can escape the heat of midday. In fact, buffalos midday tend to refrain from much of any activity, causing them to feed more at night. They are, moreover, never found in really dry areas — they must drink often and hence are always located within striking distance of a lake or river or permanent waterhole. (*103*)

The buffalo loves his mudbath. He has no sweat glands to speak of in his skin and thus cannot cool off by sweating. And mud is a good antidote for pesky insects. But, for the males, the mudhole has more than temperature-regulation and grooming purposes. The dominant males especially choose wallows that are fouled with their own dung and urine (such wallows are never used by females). Encrusted with such a mixture, the dominant bull seems thereby to have enhanced his status and further seems to have improved his disposition as well, however temporarily, as one will often see a buffalo sharing a mudhole with hippos and elephants alike. A buffalo bull who has just emerged from his daily bath is likely to be as sanguine as he ever manages. (*104*)

With regard to mating activity, the safarist should look for two especially notable traits. First, the male smells and licks the female's urine and frequently displays the *flehmen* grimace. Without reviewing the entire question here regarding the exact purpose of flehmen that was raised in the discussion on lions,[67] the act of flehmen in buffalos appears to close the nostrils, allowing the scent taken into the mouth and nose to pass into the Jacobsen's

organ. The second activity is called "tending." When a bull detects a female already in heat or approaching estrus, he remains close to her, virtually a second shadow. Such tending acts as a signal to other males, and a more dominant male will come over and displace the subordinate. The dominant males in a herd become quite proficient at observing the other males, displacing them, and securing the females in heat. The subordinates do not go off and attempt to establish their own herds; they simply bide their time.

Females give birth in the herd while the herd is at rest (morning or midday). A calf is weak at birth and cannot immediately follow its mother. Thus, the pair is temporarily left behind when the herd moves off to graze. At some point later in the day, the female will slowly lead her calf back to the herd — a deliberate, vulnerable process. Cows are most aggressive at this time — and will chase a vehicle that comes too close. The newborn buffalo calf is fairly underdeveloped compared to the calves of other grazing herbivores. But calves are appealing little creatures. (*105 & 106*) They are born throughout the year, but calving peaks in the wet season, when the improved level of nutrition on the land benefits females in late pregnancy and nursing mothers. The seasonal pattern is also ensured by the fact that the females must achieve (or, following a birth, recover) a certain threshold in body condition before they can conceive (again).

The buffalo juvenile is still very slow and clumsy well into its second month and can run only in a cumbersome fashion. This can be a frantic time for mothers, who are trying to keep up with the herd yet take care of their calves. They wind up shuttling back and forth. The bleating from a calf that cannot keep up or finds itself in distress brings the entire herd, as well as mother, to the

---

67. See page 201. Female giraffes have been seen exhibiting an entire flehmen sequence, but the practice with buffalos seems to be limited strictly to sexual courtship.

Plate 103. Slaking Thirst at River's Edge. Even a Cape buffalo is cautious at drinking time. Herds tend to drink at certain 'safe' places and at certain 'safe' times. Buffalos do not play in water as do elephants. Some observers have credited the buffalo with excellent sight and hearing; others take the exactly opposite view! The author's experience squarely supports the former. The animal also has a keen sense of smell and can run faster than a rhino.

Plate 104. The Pleasures of Mud. Buffalos are strong-smelling and attract an almost unimaginable number of flies. The males' habit of rolling in their own dung and urine contributes to both the smell and the flies but, for the buffalo, contributes to success (dominance).

rescue. Calves later are normally kept in the middle of a herd and closely protected.[68] A buffalo calf hangs pretty close to its mother for about two years. He will, of course, romp with other calves, tease his mother, and chase his own tail.

The Cape buffalo has several relatives elsewhere in the world — the American bison, the European wisent, and the Asian Water buffalo (also found in Latin America), for example — but, despite some regional variations (differences in color, body size, and in the shape of the horns, all relatively minor, but to be expected from changes in habitat), there is only one large buffalo in all Africa.[69] When the old white hunter sitting at the campfire at night, having perhaps taken that one-too-many sundowner, begins to expound on which is the more vicious, the Cape Water buffalo or the African Savannah buffalo (it happens!), it is time to doze off.

Plates 105 & 106. Buffalo Calves. Gestation in buffalos takes nearly an entire year. From the picture, studying the horn size and shape, this calf is no more than three to five months old. His reddish brown coat will grow darker and coarser with age. His little horns, along with the rest of him, will grow to full size in about five years. Interestingly, calves suckle from between their mother's hind legs rather than from the side. If the female is lying down when the calf decides to nurse, he will nudge her to her feet. Nursing continues until the next calf is born, fifteen to twenty-four months after the prior birth — that is, suckling continues; apparently, milk ceases to flow several months before nursing is no longer permitted.

---

68. This is the author's observation. At least some evidence exists that might point to the conclusion that calves and their mothers graze dispersed throughout the herd.

69. Indeed, horns, color, and size vary widely within a given herd. Another kind of African buffalo, the dwarf forest buffalo, is considerably smaller: standing three to four feet at the shoulder and weighing no more than 500 pounds in adults. It has a thick, reddish brown coat and short horns that lack frontal bosses, lay straight back, and end in sharp points. Said to exist in the forests at the equator, predominantly in West Africa, the author has never seen one in the wild and believes that they are fairly rare.

VII. The Remaining Ungulates

We climbed a low rise late in the afternoon of the fourth day, and I was walking ahead. Suddenly I stopped. "My God! Look at that!" The sounds and smells of animals, tens of thousands of animals, carried to us on the light wind. For as far as we could see, the plains beyond were covered with zebra and wildebeest, grazing placidly near a large water hole. Fighting zebra stallions bit and kicked each other, puffs of dust rising from their hooves. Wildebeest tossed their heads and pranced and blew their alarm sounds. The great herds stirred, and my skin tingled at the spectacular display of life. . . .this one glimpse of what much of Africa must once have been like.

Mark & Delia Owens, *Cry of the Kalahari*[1]

All the Land Giants, save the elephant, are hooved mammals, or "ungulates." The many antelopes, three zebras, and a trio of pigs (warthog, bush pig, and giant forest hog) constitute the remaining African ungulates and the subjects of this chapter. Africa has, in fact, nine-tenths of the hooved animals of the world; from an evolutionary perspective, most of these actually emerged in Africa and did not wander in from the outside.

Hooves are horny sheaths, strong but supple, that extend over and protect the toes, reducing to a minimum the area of contact existing between the foot and the ground. Hard-edged and basically keratinous, they provide the proper footing for hard terrain, rock or soil, and help cushion the legs over the many years and many more miles of trekking. And running — they also promote speed and rapid movement (at the expense, for example, of climbing and digging) away from the reach of predators. The acquisition of hooves also signals a commitment to a herbivorous diet.

Lumping all ungulates together this way is helpful as a logical popularization but somewhat unscientific. Even-toed ungulates and odd-toed ungulates (ungulates that have more than one toe have split or cloven hooves) actually fall into two distinct orders, *not* closely related to each other. In this chapter, only zebra represent the odd-toed order (technically designated the "Perissodactyla"). In Chapter VI, rhinos were also odd-toed. Today, the even-toed ungulates ("Artiodactyla") far outnumber the former, both in the variety of species and in total population; flourish much wider geographically and therefore inhabit ecological niches of great diversity; and, finally, exhibit the larger divergencies of form. This order includes the hippo, the giraffe, all the antelopes, and the pigs. Indeed, even-toed ungulates are among the most successful of all mammals, a success in large measure derived from the ruminant digestive system. All even-toed ungulates are ruminants, and the ruminant system generally is more efficient than the hindgut fermentation of odd-toed ungulates. Consequently, ruminants can choose relatively selective food sources, and a greater variety of animals can divide the available plant species found in a given habitat.

Antelopes[2]

"Every morning in Africa, a gazelle wakes up. It knows it must run faster than the fastest lion or it will be killed. Every morning a lion wakes up. It knows it must outrun the slowest gazelle or it will starve to death. It doesn't matter whether you are a lion or a gazelle: when the sun

---

1. At p. 13.

2. Antelopes have deerlike characteristics but are not strictly deer. Antelopes have hollow horns that, however shaped and in whatever length (the variety is amazing), are never branched and do not fall off periodically, as do a deer's solid antlers. The buffalo is also a hollow-horned ruminant and belongs to the same family (Bovidae) as antelopes. All male (and a few female) antelopes have horns, which are not critical for survival but rather play important social roles. Through ritualized "fighting," the males test their relative strengths and determine their hierarchical positions. Normally, the horns are used for self-defense only as a last resort. The females of those species that are basically gregarious and consort in large herds — these females are most

comes up, you'd better be running." The audience laughed appreciatively at the speaker's hyperbole.[3] Obviously, the participants were not naturalists — lions do not "wake up" in the morning nor do they favor gazelles as prey, and gazelles rely on more than pure speed to keep off the lion's breakfast table. As specialists in financial technology, the audience may be forgiven. Nevertheless, as we shall see, the popular mind is not the only intellectual plane on which the life-or-death struggle of the African plains is allowed (or encouraged) to cast the antelopes as prey and very little else. A French philosopher once said that life could be summed up in the conjugation of the verb "manger"; insofar as antelopes are concerned, many naturalists have simply added the passive voice.

Here at home (and, the author suspects, elsewhere), young children remark excitedly at the sight of a common squirrel — to a child, a squirrel is a marvelous work of nature, a small miracle. Adults hardly notice. The average tourist on safari reacts like the child; most animals that he sees are new and fascinating. But the safarist soon, very probably by the end of his second or third game drive, has seen thousands of antelopes, a veritable plethora of antelopes — nature's fungibles, as far as the eye can see in every direction, all apparently living the mundane lives of some other animal's meal. Indeed, a few days into his safari, the natural tendency of the visitor is more or less to take the antelopes for granted. And, to the extent that the safarist does look closer, the temptation is to break the "monotony" by imagining the lurking predator. The same thought has, of course, occurred to the antelope, and a full array of physical characteristics and behavioral patterns have evolved to help the antelope avoid predators. Thus, all antelopes, whatever the species, share the long, rotating ears, large nostrils, and protruding eyes that, together with fast reflexes, fleetness of foot, and endurance, militate against ending up as venison. Antelopes can hear a predator's cough or misstep at a great distance. And the ears can be rotated to help locate precisely the direction from which a suspicious sound comes. An even stronger sense of smell detects the big cats a hundred or

_____

likely to come into conflict with one another — also are equipped with horns. The great medley of horns in antelopes (long, short, straight, spiraled, u-shaped, v-shaped, forward- or backward-curved, or whatever) tells us much about evolution — and *not* that each different type supports some involved history of particular use. Rather, that natural selection is very tolerant of random mutation that "works." The spiral corkscrew of elands, the rapier of the oryx, and the lyre of impala males have all survived because they have not *failed* their owners. The import of this generalization (and distinction) is discussed in the text that follows. Some antelopes are found in Asia, but the antelope essentially is an African animal, found in virtually all habitats but especially in forests or on grasslands.

3. At a recent London conference, as quoted in *The Economist,* July 6, 1985, at p. 37.

more yards away, unless the wind is wrong. The bulging, oversize eyes (the word "antelope" means "bright-eyed"), set to the sides of the head, provide full wide-angle vision. Herbivores do not need the binocular vision of cats (or man) — their food is standing still. They do need, however, to look out for predators coming from every possible direction. We cannot really imagine what exactly antelopes see, but they can see forwards, upwards, backwards (though not, of course, directly behind), and sideways, in each of these directions with each eye without turning the head.[4] Finally, most antelopes are built for speed, dexterity, and fair endurance: long, muscular legs, strong hindquarters, and

_____

4. This different eyesight has led several naturalists (some, one presumes, by "blind" repetition) to the fairly bizarre speculation that the zigzag running by certain antelopes (the gazelles being the most obvious practitioners) is not "deliberately" evasive. Rather, the zigging and zagging is supposedly caused by the way that the antelope sees from its eyes set back on the sides of the head. The animal theoretically finds it easier to turn its whole body to secure a proper look at the ground in front, thereby causing it constantly to run at an angle to the line of escape. As proof, these naturalists point to the fact that *herds* flee flat-out in straight lines. But more than one misconception clouds this judgment. We do not, as the text indicates, know how clearly the antelopes see straight ahead. But, when an antelope *looks* in the direction of danger (a predator, for example), he turns his head and stares directly with both eyes; he does not cock his head to look with one eye. Cocking a head on the run to secure a better view of what is *following*, while maintaining a clear picture of the path ahead, makes far more sense. Moreover, there is little reason to believe that an antelope cannot run ahead in a straight line should he so want. Indeed, he often does. The herd behavior (especially of those individuals running on the edges of the herd who are not hemmed in), if such action proves anything in particular, would seem convincing testimony that the straight line is certainly an option. Additionally, the antelope cannot outrun a cheetah who has slipped within the former's "flight distance" — plan number two then is what? The comparison between an individual and the herd also simply ignores the realities of the hunt. Most predators do not chase herds. The herds flee out of instinct; the safety of being in the herd lies statistically in the sheer numbers and functionally in the confusion that a fleeing herd represents — multiple targets are confusing, distracting, and even dangerous (so many hooves) targets — not in any inordinately impressive speed derby. Certainly, no one has stepped forward to suggest that the herd runs faster than the individual. (On the other hand, a sort of "competition" between immediate neighbors may well act to ensure that a minimum pace is kept or to prolong a particular flight.) Predators work the edges of herds: they pick out stragglers or seek out "logical" individuals (the cheetah, for example, is looking for pregnant females, among others). The real drama of the chase on the plains is the single antelope zigging and zagging, doing all that he can to escape with his very life. Indeed, if the choreography were not necessary — it *is* frequently successful — evolution might ultimately make it so. If one drives into a herd of gazelles, some will resist being herded and instead of running away from the vehicle will run alongside exactly

angled hooves that help in leaping all come as standard equipment.

In the forests, safety ordinarily depends strictly on an individual effort. Indeed, the senses of forest antelopes, especially those senses that do the most good in heavy vegetation (like hearing), are even sharper than those of their counterparts on the plains. An alert safarist will note the difference. But, on the grasslands, where little cover exists, the grazers seek the additional protection of living and feeding in herds. Thus, a multitude of alert eyes, noses, and ears — and complex warning systems — spread out over the plains. Alarm signals (some noisy, some not) bring the herd to the point of acting. Not a few commentators have remarked on the so-called "altruistic" or "suicidal" behavior exhibited by individual antelopes in alerting the predator to their position. Other writers have responded that saving one's own immediate gene pool at the expense of oneself is not really, in nature's scheme, altruistic, even if technically suicidal. Both schools suffer from the ignorance of high places. Down on the savannah, the predator knows where the prey is long before the prey becomes aware of the carnivore's presence or intentions. Predators all know by heart Admiral Nelson's great recipe for victory: being there a quarter of an hour before the other fellow. For its part, the prey, once having discovered or suspected the presence of its enemy, must first alert the herd to benefit from whatever advantage that the herd eventually offers.[5] And the safety of the herd works. So much so, in fact, that the 'arms race' between most antelopes and predators is at a standstill, as we shall discuss. The predator does not bother with herds (nor with the alarm-giver or receiver) *per se* but takes the lame, aging, newly born, and unwary who have strayed too far from the edges.[6]

The safarist will also notice that the herd travels single file, thereby lessening the chances of stumbling upon a hidden predator. Moreover, most large antelopes use regular trails to move from one part of their range to another, and these trails avoid obvious danger spots or hazards. Furthermore, the safarist should realize that the quality of being a ruminant — and, again, all antelopes are — while not directly a reaction to predation,[7] at least serves the prey well. The ruminant system (a four-chambered stomach) is, as previously stated, highly efficient in breaking down plants for digestive purposes but it also allows a large amount of food to be eaten quickly, often simply swallowed whole. The antelope can then chew its cud,[8] head up and alert. Antelopes that herd, especially grazers, already benefit from the extra vigilance of numbers: individuals can devote more time to head-down feeding, if others are maintaining an effective lookout. The ruminant system simply increases the efficiency of the lookout system.

Birth and childhood also appear to be defined, at least to some significant degree, by the realities of predation. Usually, calving takes place in the morning, giving the antelope newborn (and its mother) a full measure of daylight to get organized, as it were, before nightfall and, under the cover of darkness, prime-time predation. Invariably, no calving occurs in the afternoon or later. Moreover, synchronized breeding in herds produces, at one time, large numbers of calves that even the most active predators in a given habitat could not totally devour. As we shall see, this last "strategy" is a primary characteristic of wildebeest organization, but most other antelope herds also show at least some synchronization.[9] Such unison would work to thwart predation only if the period of childhood (and special vulnerability) were short. It is. Indeed, antelope kids have relatively little to learn as children: neither flight nor eating at this stage is all that complicated. Soon after birth (within hours, not days), the fawn can run after its mother. Within weeks,

---

parallel, for some distance. Then, when the gazelle realizes that he is not outrunning the "pursuer," he will summon an extra burst of speed and take evasive action by suddenly bolting across the front of the vehicle. This strategy is obviously not the product of queer eyesight.

5. A warning call also acts as an invitation to the predator (or *suspected* predator — the predator himself cannot be sure whether he has actually been discovered or merely imagined) to give up the hunt, now that the hunter has been exposed.

6. The anti-predation value of the herd is confirmed indirectly by another fact: the males of most prey species that herd bear a disproportionate share of lion predation. One could postulate that all the fighting, ritualistic or not, in which males engage makes them more vulnerable than females to killing: the combatants are conspicuous, occupied, and, eventually, often exhausted. And this theory — especially with respect to certain species — must be correct, to a point. On the other hand, female pregnancy and the birthing of calves should be equally inviting to predators. As we have already seen, cheetahs clearly prefer to chase mothers-to-be, who carry the extra weight of the fetus. Lions, though they hunt differently from cheetah, could also benefit from the burden of prey-pregnancy, especially if that

---

condition slows the reflexes or hampers the quick dexterity needed to avert the ballistic charge of the lion. (Whether or not a predator will find it easier to recognize an affected male than a pregnant female is an interesting question. Certainly, the latter constitutes by far the more numerous category.) Thus, the more relevant explanation seems to be that the females remain well within the herd and take full advantage of herding, while the males tend to scatter and often prefer to remain slightly apart from the main body. Indeed, when animals, male and female alike, stay in cohesive groups, as zebras do, little or no predatory sexual differential exists.

7. Not all ruminants are threatened by predators in the way that antelopes are.

8. The cud is called a "bolus" and consists of partly fermented fodder. The bolus is rechewed into a pulp.

9. The costs of pregnancy and lactation are high. In seasonal environments, animals might be expected to time births to periods when food is most abundant. Moreover, as noted in the discussion on lions, female estrous periods are strongly influenced by the force of imitation.

the newcomer can look after itself, though it may nurse longer. On the other hand, some antelope young are "hiders," not "followers." These last take six months or more to achieve independence.

The safarist can turn anti-predation behavior to good advantage in staking out those waterholes likely to attract antelopes. Most ungulates exhibit a regular daily drinking pattern and prefer a few select watering sites devoid of surrounding vegetation or dense undergrowth (the larger, less vulnerable herbivores — like the elephant, buffalo, and rhino — are less selective). Park rangers, who not only know the usual sites but also know the seasonal changes that take place (as the feeding grounds shift), can guide the safarist. Rangers will, no doubt, be pleasantly surprised to learn of this interest; most safarists express a preference only for the showy big cats and the increasingly rare rhinos. Alternatively, the visitor may read the manual published on a particular park; the better ones will indicate watering holes. Close inspection on game trails and at waterhole localities — to find those that have recently been heavily trampled — should also enable the safarist to anticipate where large groups of animals will water each day.

Some naturalists would go so far as to define an antelope's whole being, in a real sense, in terms of its prey status: an antelope, according to this view, lives constantly on the verge of flight. Life may be a long period of "inactivity" followed by short bursts of very rapid movement, but the inactivity is filled with tension. Thus, the vitality of the prey species results from frequent predator pressure (made *constant* by uncertainty). And it becomes entirely logical, in this view, to regard predator and prey as dance partners in some evolutionary fandango that never ends. Thus, we come back, as promised, to the London speaker.

In reality, antelopes are, of course, more than mere prey. And the truth is, they may be prey only secondarily. Safarists who would like to achieve some deeper understanding of the animals must first come to grips with the behavioral and anatomical adaptations derived from a specific animal's environment. One logical *starting* point would be the animal's diet. Of course, an obstacle to a quick study is the amazing variety of antelopes. Rarely when he sees the teeming herds stretched out before him does the safarist see only one kind. Indeed, when the safarist takes in what George Schaller, an authority on many species of African wildlife, has called the "Pleistocene vision,"[10] he sees purposeful diversity. Although writers are apt to exaggerate the neatness of the 'herbivore system,' grazers for the most part graze selectively, each species taking grasses at different heights or different grasses altogether. Some, like the eland, eat the

taller, tougher (more fibrous) growth; some, like the wildebeest, eat shorter cover; still others, like the gazelles, prefer the new shoots. Kongonis eat the dry stalks rejected by the majority. The grazers do not, under ideal conditions, compete directly. Put another way, the animals *select* different types and growth stages of grass to reduce competition. Moreover, the extraordinary mass and variety of grazing animals *reinforce* one another — the heavy grazers (like the buffalo, hippo, and elephant) eat and trample large, coarse vegetation, thereby actually preparing the savannah for lighter grazers (zebra, topi, and wildebeest, for example), who in turn leave behind a more palatable menu for the lightest herbivores (for example, gazelles and warthogs).[11] Nor is the "system" limited to grazers. Browsers will browse at different levels and they also reinforce one another — they sow as well as reap, and large shrubs are reduced over time to levels that small browsers can reach. Yet a further complexity rounds out the picture: in studying the carrying capacity of a particular habitat, ecologists must pay attention to the feeding "calendar," as well as grazing successions and browsing levels. Different vegetation is taken at different times of the year, as climatic variations and extremes dictate.

This "ecological niche" theory — that each species has a unique combination of diet and thus habitat — serves well as a guide to an ecological description of a particular species: how, for example, one kind of animal affects others and what determines their distribution and abundance. But some ecologists — perhaps most ecologists in the last several decades — have assumed that competiton between species is the leading factor determining how many such species can coexist and what population levels will survive. Almost by definition, according to this view, each niche contains only one species, which species is (and has been) prevented from spreading into another niche by the competitive superiority of the animal already there. An obvious problem with this thinking is that many observable phenomena (we have already suggested climate and predation) prevent a given species population from reaching levels at which it would be tempted to compete with another. Another problem is the fact that both grazers and browsers do indeed overlap in their eating habits to a surprising degree.[12] More damaging still to a strict competitive theory is the facilitation that one

---

10. The quotation is given on page 104 in Chapter III. Teddy Roosevelt made a similar notation in his diary ("a Pleistocene day") many years before when on safari.

11. Wild ungulates cause comparatively little damage to the underlying pasture from trampling when they move through a habitat, when contrasted with domestic stock. Even antelopes participating in large-scale migrations travel in herds that move well spread out in single file formations. Maasai cattle, on the other hand, move as a mob and can quickly turn the grasslands into a dust bowl.

12. In part, some naturalists have confused 'preferences' with 'requirements,' imparting a rigidity to a system that is already arguably slightly artificial. Most species will, in fact, switch foods as circumstances dictate. If conditions permit, however,

potential competitor may offer to another. Thus, buffalo, eating identical food as waterbuck, will make it easier for waterbuck to graze in areas of heavy abundance. The point is, few populations reach the size at which competition would begin to sort them out.

Virtually since scientists have begun to reflect seriously on these issues, the most popular hypothesis has been that the more species that an environment supports (see, for example, plate *71* of the last chapter, where zebra, giraffe, topi, and wildebeest are all pictured, with several additional species grazing or browsing just outside the angle of view), the more stable the ecosystem. Indeed, this conclusion logically follows the niche thinking. Certainly, as a factual matter, the richer the natural pasture, in terms of its wealth of grasses, herbs, shrubs, and trees, the greater the diversity of animals found there. The Pleistocene vision — African wildlife at its wildest and most abundant levels — is thus a vision of interspecies harmony. Actually, antelopes roamed Africa in huge numbers even before the cataclysms of the Pleistocene, and, in that sense, the enormous herds found today in the parks gathered in all their numbers and diversity represent ghosts trekking through many, many millenia of undulating grasslands. Nevertheless, such visions of "harmony" and competitive equilibrium should not be allowed to obscure the enormous *complexity* of such ecosystems. And the more that one studies the ecology of nearly any area, the more one understands that very habitat's inherent complexity. The view that such intricacy is more stable than a simpler system is basically intuitive. It has not been proved. At the very least, the correctness of such an hypothesis in the field depends upon what exactly (in terms of generality or scope) one inspects at any given point and for how long. The contrary argument — that the more complex and intimately

interconnected the ecosystem, the *less* stable that it is — is attractive to an increasing number of specialists today.

But the basic point here, a fact to which we return again and again when discussing individual species, is that intricate and intimate relationships link food usage and social behavior. Antelopes are as much shaped by what they eat as by the fact that they are eaten.[13]

Of obvious importance for defining antelopes is the availability of water and the ambient temperature of the environment. Antelopes have developed special cooling systems to cope with the heat,[14] especially in the absence of drinking water. For example, the antelopes who struggle with prevailing arid conditions and continued temperatures rising well over 100° F have a nasal cooling system that can lower the temperature of the blood reaching the brain by 5° F or more, while body temperature remains at the higher mark. Simplified somewhat, the blood destined for the brain via the carotid artery first travels to the nose; as the animal breathes, the evaporation in the nasal cavity cools the blood. This evaporation is far more specific and hence directly useful than general perspiration. Thus, the large noses that smell predators at a distance, a periodic concern, also cool the body, a more continuous concern (during the day).

Coat color — a more visible characteristic than even the horns, when one considers that most females are hornless — inevitably has evolved, at least in part, as a reaction to

---

preferences will enable a significant variety to live together. The question of whether or not food competition can be considered a vital evolutionary force should be considered in the context of the discussion that follows in the text. Darwinists of the old school begin with one species and (eventually) a crowded niche. Divergence in the use of resources then increases the chances for survival. Ultimately (over eons), new species result and slip over into other niches. Evolutionists of the new school shrug off such intellectual constructions; the diversity, in their view, evolved by chance and was sustained by the ability of the ecosystem to accommodate the diversity.

When considering the validity and implications of niche theory — reduced competition between species, widest possible diversity of the animal community, and the harmonious conservation of a given habitat — the reader must realize that herbivores generally are no longer free to migrate as circumstances dictate and that available pastures today must support increased density pressures. The reduction of the horizon by man is probably more fundamental than any of the natural disturbances of the past.

What is certainly true today is that nearly every blade or leaf of vegetation is eaten by something.

13. The author would be remiss if he did not point out that the predation-oriented school looks at the grazing sequence in a slightly modified way. Putting aside matters of strict engineering or efficiency (for example, tall grass is physically unavailable to dwarf antelopes), the more important question of palatability or choice is determined by the danger quotient: zebra and wildebeest do not eat the tall strands of grass for fear that such food could conceal predators; leave the lurking lions to the elephants. And so on down the size ladder.

14. The heat load of an animal is determined in four ways: (i) radiation from direct sunlight; (ii) conduction from touching the ground, rocks, and the like; (iii) convection from wind carrying heat; and (iv) metabolic heat production, caused for the most part by fermentation (digestion) taking place in the stomach or by exercise (the expenditure of energy) within muscles. Mammals normally must maintain an even body temperature, regardless of the temperature around them. Their brain will function within only a few degrees either side of 100° F. Normal, or simplified, cooling mechanisms (physiological and behavioral) are somewhat the reverse of the determinants listed above: a) conduction within the body (spreading and dissipating heat) and between the body and an external surface; b) convection from cooling winds, by which it is to the animal's advantage to face *with* the wind so that the air blows against the angle of hair growth and more air strikes the body surface; c) the color and texture of the animals coat (discussed in the text); d) seeking shade, if available, but at least assuming a posture that minimizes the body area exposed to radiation; e) evaporation (sweating, breathing, and panting); and f) reduction in daytime activities (with, in most instances, a corresponding increase in nighttime activity) that expend energy.

the animal's needs in regulating body temperature. Antelopes who live in forests (bongo and kudu, for example) are dark in color, with stripes or spots. The sun and radiation are basically irrelevant. Those species that live in more open but well-watered terrain also tend to sport dark coats, but without numerous stripes or spots (like the waterbuck). Again, heat for these animals is something to manage by ducking under cover; failing that, they simply take another drink. Most of the antelopes that inhabit the open grasslands have, however, lightly colored coats that

times confers near invisibility.[15] We shall return to the persistent Mr. Thayer when the subject of zebras is discussed and later when dealing with flamingoes (in Chapter IX), where his theories, valuable though they may be (but hardly of overwhelming importance, as we shall see), were relentlessly and erroneously carried (by him) to one *reductio ad absurdam* after another. Thayer's theme was the concealment value of adaptive colors and patterns. As a committed Darwinian, he believed that color and patterns must serve some important, immediate

Plate 1. Wary Prey. All ruminants look up repeatedly when feeding. Recent research has shown that such interruptions increase once a predator has been spotted in the vicinity. This is not programmable behavior; this is an example of animals thinking.

reflect the heat. Moreover, they have white underparts that cast back the heat coming up from the ground. Finally, relatively dense coats help reduce heat absorption through the skin. The radiant *heat* is thus trapped on the surface, from which, incidentally, a part is radiated back into the air. In other words, some of the heat gained will always be dissipated as radiant heat loss!

The purpose of coat color is a subject that has always caused controversy among scientists. Re-enter predation. At the turn of the century, an artist-naturalist named Abbott H. Thayer elucidated the interesting principle of ''countershading'' — an adaptation of prey that some-

purpose in the unending struggle for existence. As a painter, he identified the primary method of concealment as countershading, a phenomenon that makes animals look flat. Naturalists before Thayer knew, of course, that many animals blended into their habitats but were unaware — in Thayer's view — of the sophistication entailed. While animals certainly needed the right color and pattern to blend in with their background, counter-

---

15. The author is indebted to an entertaining column on Thayer written by Stephen Jay Gould in *Natural History,* May 1985, at p. 12.

shading also provided a loss of dimensionality in a three-dimensional world. In countershading, an animal's colors are graded to counteract the effects of sunlight and shadows.[16] The animal is darkest on top, where sunlight falls, and lightest on the belly. The reversal between intensity of color and intensity of light cancels out shadows and produces a uniform color from top to bottom — the optical illusion causes the animal to appear flat or two-dimensional to the predator, thus guaranteeing the blending process.

When Thayer sought to apply countershading theory to all prey animals everywhere, naturalists went for his throat, which turned out to be all too three-dimensional.

would have responded in the affirmative. And, looked at in this way, the application of the theory to antelopes is only marginally less cockeyed than when applied to peacocks.

To begin with, it should be obvious that countershading depends to a significant degree upon the distance between the viewer and the object viewed. No amount of light and shadow legerdemain (on the open plains) is going to affect dimensionality twenty yards away. The longer the distance between predator and prey, the more the theory has at least a fighting chance (aided, the author hastens to add, by shimmering heat waves and other long-distance mirage effects). Thus, the cheetah must look for

Plate 2. Taking an Interest in the Proceedings. Lions do their thinking up front, as they choose their intended victims. Once the ballistic charge is launched, everything depends on the initial aim.

But many admired nevertheless the mental gymnastics and were (and are) at least willing to concede the field to the gazelles and other plains antelopes (among others), precisely, or perhaps ironically, the group in which heat seems to be at least a determining factor. Indeed, the coloration cooperated, and countershading as a phenomenon undoubtedly works. But the real question is this: is countershading of such importance to antelopes that it determines coat color? Did color really *evolve* as a result of the (relative) success of countershading? Thayer

movement in the distance to add dimensionality. But the interesting fact is that the prey invariably obliges, whether by the incessant tail-wagging of the Thomson's gazelles, the up-and-down neck action of alert grazing, or simply moving forward to take the next bite (or the bite after). Most predators are patient enough simply to wait out the effects of countershading; countershading with movement is self-defeating. Indeed, motion of any kind is the antithesis of all cryptic camouflage. In this sense, herding itself and countershading are mutually exclusive; in a herd, someone will be moving, and, when a predator finds one individual, he may quickly locate the others. Indeed, most truly camouflaged animals live singly and scattered.

Actually, in the presence of prey, the predator does not lack for opportunity, and the plains antelopes rely instead

---

16. An object of uniform color, even if placed before a background of similar color (and texture) will, because of the effect of unequal illumination falling upon its different surfaces, give an appearance of "relief," that is, will show the effect of light and shade.

upon anticipation, speed, and fancy footwork to escape. Moreover, one has to question why a real herd animal would *need* to be concealed, colorwise, though one could postulate that anything that brought the individual visually within the incoherent mass of the herd would be helpful.[17] Some antelopes, notably the small fawns of certain species and reedbucks of all ages, try to escape their enemies by dropping down into the bush or grass and hiding. Predators have been known to miss them even while walking only a few feet away. Surely, countershading at this distance is irrelevant[18] — old-fashioned blending and amazing stillness are the working principles here. In any event, seeking to escape notice by crouching flat clearly eliminates the subtlety of countershading.

And what of the night? The lion, the leopard, and hyena — the major predators of antelopes (in terms of number taken) — hunt mostly at night. Countershading under the moon? The answer is obvious. The waterhole drama — not a rare event by any means, hence the prey's nervousness when it drinks — is only slightly less inappropriate for countershading mechanics than nighttime. What of the smallest antelopes, whose predators frequently drop from the sky? The conclusion is inescapable. Had Thayer spent more time in a safari vehicle (or, in fairness, on a horse) and less time crawling on his belly in the mud playing alligator and looking at flamingoes (see below), he might have had a more productive intellectual life.

In fact, much of the coloration that exists in nature, among prey and predator alike, serves to *increase* visibility: adaptive colors and patterns may serve as a warning to frighten off potential predators, as a status symbol to maintain territory or social position, as a mating signal, and as disguise. This last may be to imitate unpalatable or dangerous creatures (the reader may recall the young cheetah's grey mantle and the ratel theory — Batesian mimicry) or to resemble an inanimate (and thus — for a carnivore — inedible) object. Although concealment certainly has a place in determining color, whatever the position that biologists ultimately assign countershading theory, but visibility may well prove to be at least as important.

Whether predation or temperature or, in fact, neither is the primary determinant of coloration in antelopes is, therefore, difficult to say. Apparently, no single motivation can explain all the variations in coat color and only with difficulty the basic coloration of a single species. The author's ultimate purpose here is to indicate the diversity of factors at work — and many factors beyond predation — in species commonly regarded as prey animals.

Indeed, one would also do well not to exaggerate the "constant fear" supposedly motivating all prey. Whereas antelopes live an undoubtedly wary existence, they also seem to know when a predator is not actually hunting. At such times, antelopes show remarkably little nervousness and even allow the carnivores to remain within the limit of the antelopes' "flight distance" (the distance at which a particular predator can normally close successfully on a particular prey when hunting). Sometimes, when the carnivore is discovered, the prey will actually move closer for a better look or "feel" for the situation. Members of a herd will often *approach* successful hunters who have just taken a fellow member of the herd.[19] The survivors actually watch for a time the resulting feast, then calmly resume their routine, secure in the knowledge that hunting is a function of hunger. Antelopes flee only as far as they have to in escaping a particular hunt; they never flee an environment, even one full of predators. And a well-fed predator makes a better neighbor than the unknown. No careful observer could doubt that, in the absence of predation, the herbivores would almost certainly lose some of their vitality — they would die anyway, of course, but the diseased, lame, malformed, and the like would survive longer and continue to contribute to the gene pool — but one should not exaggerate the point[20] or believe that nature's "arms race" will eventually produce supersonic (let alone "invisible") antelopes and super-powerful predators. Or everybody growing bigger and bigger, as well. Predation serves as one check to overpopulation, restricts to a degree the spread of disease, and reduces the birth of abnormal individuals; whether it is ever the primary engine of evolutionary change is another matter altogether. Predators and prey are essentially "evenly matched," and predators normally refrain from tackling the average members of the herd.

Ungulates form the staple diet of the carnivores because the hooved animals are the most abundant large mammals in those habitats shared with the predators. And that very abundance seemingly makes starvation a far more critical mortality factor than predation. A drop in the yearly car-

---

17. In addition, it seems reasonable to suppose that countershading works best on smaller antelopes as well. In any event, the larger herd antelopes, such as the wildebeest, kongoni, topi, and others, have dark, relatively uniformly colored coats and no white underparts.

18. Moreover, walking (that is, slow movement) nearly all the way around something — at least along one whole side and past one end, if not both ends (by glancing around) — seems an easy way to eliminate an object's apparent flatness.

19. Approaching a predator in this fashion has been compared to the mobbing behavior of birds, but the former's purpose is not to drive off or disturb the predator in any way. Nor can this behavior strictly be considered curiosity, which is a purely voluntary (and, directly, non-functional) reaction to novel situations or occurrences. And the practice is not free of risk; cheetahs have been known, for example, to make a sudden dash and catch gazelles who ventured too close.

20. Antelopes do not live long lives; ten-years-old is an old antelope. Antelopes who are not in the best of condition will find difficulties in securing a mate, anyway. Those very few non-prime individuals who survive a drought or two *and* succeed in covering females are going to have little enough impact on the gene pool.

rying capacity of the local plant community; the stress of lactation or contesting a position in the dominance hierarchy; finally wearing down one's teeth — does anyone doubt that these dénouements will bring the curtain down many times more often than the efforts of all the predators combined? And what of disease and parasitism? Yet, at the same time, predation can hardly be divorced from the mortality equation. Indeed, drawing the proper correlations among the ecology, the animal's behavior, and its physical make-up is immensely difficult and perhaps all too often quite impossible, given our current knowledge. The variables are, or could easily be, interrelated, and most arguments quickly turn circular. Or at least reinforcing. Clearly, all the defenses against predation, primary (built-in) or secondary (behavioral — after the predator has been discovered), are compromises with earning a living (finding and eating food) and reproduction (sexual performance). As we have discussed, herding has its drawbacks, but many benefits. In any event, as effective as the strategy may be, fully half the species population (the males) uses it only sporadically. Does food — that is, the nature of the diet consumed and the methods by which it is obtained — determine body size, which in turn produces social groupings from which a specified antipredatory behavior emerges? Or does predation force some species into certain behavior patterns? And certain body sizes? Does social organization itself — principally revolving around the imperatives of sexual reproduction — dictate body size, food choice, foraging, and predation avoidance? At this point, to deny the importance of any of these selection pressures in the abstract would be quite risky. And, in any event, detailed examination can proceed only on a species-by-species basis.

Accordingly, the safarist should take the time to look at antelopes as individuals, or at the very least as members of individual species — and enjoy the diverse shapes, sizes, colors, and behavior of the variety strung out before him. Idiosyncrasies abound. Africa has ninety ungulates, by conservative count (more liberal classification computes close to 100 antelopes alone), of which approximately seventy are antelopes. By comparison, North America has eleven species of ungulates, Europe has thirteen, Central and South America sixteen, and all Asia (including Japan, Indonesia, and the Philippines) can deliver but seventy. The unique variety of antelopes in Africa evolved only partly because of the size of the continent. Tropical lands achieved biotic maturity early and produced many species that originated in remote areas, primitive animals that became highly specialized. With no need to adapt to a whole range of environmental pressures caused by the season-to-season fluctuations that characterize temperate lands, the animals could manage in smaller niches. In Africa, the range of vegetation, a long history of semi-seclusion, and environmental stability all contributed to immense diversity.[21]

Obviously, an entire book could profitably be devoted to such an overwhelming assortment of animals. Surprisingly few have been.[22] The author has limited the antelope section of this chapter to sixteen different antelopes representing six broad groups, defined in terms of what they eat (browsers to grazers), their differences in size (here, from dik-dik to eland), habitats (rain forest to desert), antipredator behavior (hiders to runners), and social systems (single animals living alone in small, fixed areas to huge aggregations roaming over hundreds of square miles), as well as anatomical similarities.

But, before introducing the individual antelopes, two further complications to the discussion should be raised at this time. (Having lured the reader on board with the flash of big cats, curiosity toward the scavengers, and the magnificence of the land giants, the author now throws in a little homework.) We have raised questions of classifications, of the correctness of characterizing antelopes as essentially prey animals, and, indeed, all manner of issues concerning the adaptive function of form and behavior. Actually, there lurk two more fundamental matters. Evolutionary adaptation itself, as generally understood for a great many years, is now under attack within the scientific community. The curious safarist today finds himself thrown into the midst of issues that are stirring widespread debate. The reader might not be interested in all the details of the controversy concerning genotypic adaptation — how species originate and change — on the one hand, and animal intelligence, on the other, but an abbreviated (and necessarily simplified) version of the issues will help put into a more meaningful and useful perspective what he reads or hears about the animals.

The unrelenting intellectual curiosity of man has long encouraged an attempt to order and categorize the natural world around him. When the poet John Donne wrote the eternal truth that 'no man is an Island,' the lesson went beyond *homo sapiens*. Over many years, the evidence accumulated indicating linkages, ancestry, and causation among the animals on earth. In the late 1700s, French biologist Jean Baptiste Lamarck looked at this evidence and postulated that animals who responded creatively to their environment acquired small changes in form (and behavior) that were then immediately passed on to their descendants. Everything in fact acquired by an individual animal during its lifetime was transmitted to its progeny: "inheritance of acquired characteristics" is the biologist's jargon. Thus, the giraffe's neck grew longer and longer

---

21. By contrast, temperate lands contain species more recently

evolved and fewer of them — but the animals are more adaptable and within a species more numerous. Thus, North America has far fewer species of deer than Africa has antelopes but probably *many* more deer, in total numbers, than all the antelopes.

22. A book has recently (too late to be included in the recommended list of Chapter I) appeared — Gerald Cubitt, *Portraits of the African Wild* (Chartwell Books, 1986) — that has sixty photo-pages devoted to antelopes. Concentrating on Southern African species, the pictures are excellent.

simply by one generation after another stretching up, higher and higher, to reach for food, the food underneath having been eaten up, and passing on to the next generation the (increasingly) stretched-out version. Thus, the neck, tongue, and legs stretched over several generations to the higher realms of the trees (or at least to where food was again plentiful). Lamarckism was, however, generally discredited by the discovery of genes and the laws of heredity

Charles Darwin, influenced by Malthus, Lyell, and a host of others, filled the breech and put the giraffe's neck into a more lasting framework. Darwin argued that environments do not impose adaptive pressures directly. Instead, the process was more passive: animals whose makeup were better suited (quite fortuitously, initially) to the rigors of their local environment would live longer and produce and leave more surviving offspring. Eventually, the gene pool for that animal would come to have more and more of these "favorable" traits. Even more gradually, an accumulation of these characteristics might prevent interbreeding with the "original" types — thus producing a new species.[23] The whole process was called "natural selection" (it was, however, the converted-Darwinian Herbert Spencer who popularized the phrase "survival of the fittest" and the word "evolution"). The theory seemed so satisfyingly complete and so obvious that the scientific world quickly took to it. Later supported by Mendelian genetics, natural selection (or, rather, a synthesis of Darwinism and Mendelian inheritance known today as "neo-Darwinism") permeated the whole of biology, came to be regarded as the outstanding scientific achievement of the nineteenth century, and until recently remained the ruling dogma. Indeed, biologists proved beyond a reasonable doubt that small-scale evolution is the result of natural selection among members of a species and that life has evolved — diverse organisms have descended from common ancestors — over a very long period of time.

Darwinism over the years developed along some predictable lines but also took directions that might have surprised Darwin. The most obvious emphasis was on gradualism: big changes were made slowly but steadily, accumulations of many tiny changes over eons. Thus, continuous minute alterations gradually produced the diversity that we see today. A more questionable conclusion (more Lamarckian — Lamarck believed in constant improvement, even in the perfecting power inherent in nature — but also encouraged by Darwin) was the idea of perfection: the evolutionary chain, both within a species and along the chain as a whole, became synonymous with progress. Thus sprang the concept of nature's "master plan" — and natural selection as fine-tuning, fitting an animal perfectly to its environment. At the same time, Spencer's survival of the fittest took on a certain air of ruthlessness — Tennyson's "Nature, red in tooth and claw."[24]

A third distinct byproduct, perhaps the most questionable (but, for a long time, equally unquestioned) of all, was the belief that every part of an animal was explainable in terms of its evolutionary usefulness. In other words, all physical features fitted behavior that in turn reflected the environment. Every part of every creature was fashioned for some immediate use by evolution. This reasoning was, of course, encouraged by the human desire to find meaning in all things and, perhaps, by religious ideals as well. In the end, everything must fit, must have a purpose, must be for the best.

But questions about large-scale evolution — especially the formation of new species — continued to surface. No one, after all, had ever witnessed the emergence of a new species. Moreover, fossils proved as notoriously uncooperative as cooperative. Today, without going into detail, the complacency of the neo-Darwinian evolutionists has indeed been rocked by genetic evidence that the so-called "DNA codebook" (the instructions within a gene for making proteins, the building blocks of life) is too complex to support simplistic Darwinian evolution. Work on the internal cell development now convincingly points to both accidental instructions (evolution) and built-in constraints or limitations imposed by the genes themselves, by the necessities of genetic architecture, so to speak. At the same time, more rational observations in the wild — that is, observations derived from a more open, questioning perspective that does not *ipso facto* confine everything within the traditional Darwinian

23. Scientists define a "species," in a strict sense, as an animal distinct enough from any other so that, under natural conditions at least, it *cannot* breed successfully (to produce fertile offspring) with any different animal — it is "reproductively isolated," a byproduct of adaptive evolution through natural selection. In fact, many naturalists categorize animals according to significant deviations that still permit interbreeding. Lions and tigers will interbreed, for example. And "hybrids" of all kinds abound in nature. As already suggested, the entire business of classification is subject to as much strong, specific disagreement as mild, broad agreement.

24. Darwin's fitness, it should be emphasized, was measured strictly in terms of procreative proficiency — the contribution of a given individual's genes made to the gene pool of the next and following generations. Oversimplified somewhat, the "fittest" individuals were the parents of the largest number of children who survived to their own reproductive years. Fitness was, however, determined by the environment, and conventional Darwinism had no trouble explaining altruistic — even suicidal (for example, a mother defending to the death her offspring) — behavior *within* a species and especially within a common gene pool like a family unit. In the author's view, the most cogent and powerful analysis (particularly if one likes metaphor) and defense of current neo-Darwinism is Richard Dawkins's *The Blind Watchmaker* (W.W. Norton, 1986). The reader should be warned that evolutionary theory today, especially in its mathematical models, matches the complexity of life itself.

straight-jacket — have also pointed to conclusions that the vagaries of chance must play a role, that a species can be "overspecialized" to the point of contributing to its own extinction, and that the purpose for which a given characteristic was developed through evolution does not necessarily specify fully the capacity of that characteristic or associated development.[25]

The debate intensifies day-by-day, and little hope exists for agreement or consensus in the near future. The author offers the following as a fair synthesis to aid the interested safarist:

(1) The heart of Darwin's message remains intact: individuals within a species vary; those best fitted to their environment survive to pass their favorable (to the environment) traits on to their descendants; and, over generations, the selection of the "fittest" is a primary engine of change.

(2) Nevertheless, every trait, every characteristic, every form of behavior does *not* necessarily help an animal to survive or reproduce. An animal as a whole may seem well adapted to a habitat but it may also have traits that are more or less "accidental," possibly "unfavorable," or, more likely, neutral or irrelevant. Nature contains a lot of Rube Goldberg "solutions." Because the growth of different parts of an animal are obviously linked to one another, some of what we see is surely "accidental" (from the Darwinian perspective), a piggyback rider or offshoot, so to speak, of something else more important (and more adaptive). Indeed, even a current vitally useful feature may be little more than an evolutionary side-effect. Until recently, scientists could not grasp this simple point. African naturalists, as well as their brethren elsewhere, were plagued by what Stephen Jay Gould has usefully tagged "vulgar Darwinism." They resembled eager graduate English literature students reading sophisticated meaning into every line of Shakespeare.[26] The drive to atomize organisms into separate traits, independent and optimal parts, each with its own history and justification, becomes a caricature of Darwinian thought. Today, we should realize that fitting all physical features to environmentally influenced behavior via an endless array of subtleties is useless. Evolutionists are always asking the "why?" of things; the question is not always relevant. Ardent adaptationists insist on searching for the reproductive value of every evolved characteristic, an incorrect equation of utility (today or earlier) with history.

(3) In a similar vein, animals develop in many ways, in response to many pressures and, equally, parameters. Rather than perfection, the multiplicity of selective pressures may well result in a particular "stand-off"; evolution often yields "workable compromises" — for all practical purposes, "final forms" of evolution. (Mammals have, for example, four limbs, not because four is ideal but because they evolved from four-finned fishes and the number was difficult to change. Thus, neither prey nor predator run any faster because nutrition and structural engineering have established certain limits, notwithstanding the obvious benefit to either side of running faster.) Animals moreover do develop exaggerated characteristics that limit the flexibility of a species for future evolutionary change. And adaptations to particular ways of living rarely add up to "perfection." Indeed, an animal does not always have a beneficial effect on its own immediate environment. After all, animals may be more or less well-adapted; they are, in fact, at some intermediate stage of evolution, because all the living components of an environment — food, disease, parasites, predators, competitors, and so forth — are themselves undergoing change, adaptive change. The sheer number of variables also practically insures that the adaptions are doubtfully proportionate all the way around. The world has never been in "sync." To view nature as some giant version of symbiosis is to deny both complexity and reality. Some organisms are bound to achieve a 'technological breakthrough,' as it were; others will fall behind. If there is a "master plan" — and the evidence now is rather overwhelmingly against its existence — we are still so near the beginning that we have no idea what it may be.

(4) Again, in a related argument, evolution is a patchwork of both function and structure. The dichotomy dividing biologists — is function the mechanical result of form, or form the manifestation of function? what is the essence of life, organization or activity? which came first? — is an old one. The author could scarcely improve on the question as phrased by Stephen Jay Gould:

> Giraffes feed on leaves at the tops of acacia trees. But did their necks elongate in response to a need for such feeding (the functional view) or did giraffes grow long necks for reasons unrelated to utility and then discover that they could reach the succulent leaves at the tops of trees (the structural alternative)?[27]

25. Intelligent speculation long ago should well have pointed the way to the new genetic conclusions, if not their actual complexities. Genetic architecture of *some* kind obviously kept certain animals, for example, from developing "wheels" in place of legs.

26. This criticism is further elaborated in the preface to the bibliography supplied at the end of this book.

27. Taken from the column, "Archetype and Adaptation," *Natural History* (October 1986), at p. 16. Interestingly enough, though Lamarck is not always given the credit, the premise that animals first adopt a different mode of behavior to trigger an

It would seem irrefutable today that our adaptationist biases have prevented a proper appreciation for the structuralist insights. Thus, adaptation is not always the cause of good design; adaptation may also be, from time to time, the *consequence* of structural constraints. Both the starting point and the "rules" of transformation provided by the *nature* of organic life (the laws of form, as it were) specify permissible pathways. Nor would Darwin himself disagree.

(5) The new theories that seek to uncouple evolution and advantage altogether are surely on the wrong track, especially considering the *difficulty* of institutionalizing change, any significant change. The new evidence that argues for the complexity of genetic evolution also argues for the unlikelihood that *harmful* changes would survive the tests of natural selection over any meaningful period. Nevertheless, natural selection is no longer entirely a matter of "survival of the fittest"; now the process is as well (or, at least partly) one of "differential reproduction," that is, different (without more) combinations of genes produce different reproductive success.

(6) The recently propounded theory of "punctuated equilibria" — that evolution *between species* does not follow the Darwinian model of gradual change but rather comes in a process of fits and starts, of evolutionary "jumps," so to speak, true transitional stages that are relatively brief and followed by long periods of stability — is still hypothetical.[28] Indeed, many of the same problems of proof that hound inter-species Darwinism operate here as well. The most likely answer to the question of which model will prevail is that both processes take place.

In the author's view, the definite loosening-up of the Darwinian model has also reopened the door to our second complication: to refocus the question of "cultural evolution" in animals. If some traits do not lead directly to important (from the perspective of survival) behavior, might not some behavior be the result of more than animals simply playing genetic roles, more than strictly behavioral conditioning? In other words, can animals think? reason? remember? Sensitive people who have lived with or studied animals for long periods have never doubted the affirmative answers. In human beings, cultural evolution, unlike biological evolution, is truly Lamarckian: powerful and fast. What is acquired in one generation can be — and usually is — passed on to the next. The engine of change is learning, the "genetic" code is language. Can animals learn? Can they communicate with one another? The best evidence today — and the author returns to the issue when discussing primates in Chapter VIII and birds in Chapter IX — is that the human mind and capabilities are not unique in these respects.[29] Coleridge, quoted earlier in the discussion on elephants, was correct in that the basis for higher (man's) mental skills is memory, both the storage of information *and* the encoding of that information for accessible recall (Coleridge, of course, expressed it more poetically). But the dividing line between man and the rest of the natural world, be it a chasm or a creek, is not a straight line.[30]

Vulgar Darwinism encourages the belief that animals behave only in "successful" ways, make only "evolutionary choices." Many behavioral scientists therefore conclude that animal activity should be described only in terms of stimuli, responses, and adaptive advantages. In this view, animals cope with challenges — new situations — by following behavioral strategies obtained from their genetic instructions and individual experience. But, to those familiar with the seemingly endless challenges of the natural world and the significant varieties of animal behavior witnessed, the specific instructions needed under the Darwinian model to provide for all contingencies would reach a staggering number — and would surpass the capacity of the most sophisticated computer. Indeed, it is far more likely — particularly given the example of the highest animal, man — that more general instructions suffice. Certainly, the *efficiency* of conscious thinking is a compelling argument for its deployment.

People must, it is true, exercise care not to read too much in the behavior of their pets or any domesticated animals. Heavily influenced by their masters — by conscious training, by conditioning, and by genetic selection — domestic animals often appear inordinately "clever." On the other hand, many of the circumstances under which thinking would likely emerge in the wild — obtaining food or water and avoiding predators, for example, have been eliminated. Consequently, domesticated animals do not always give the impression of any self-

---

alteration in form — that is, a change in behavior must precede an alteration in form, and not vice-versa — is distinctly Lamarckian.

28. Such "catastrophism" implies that the natural selection of individuals is relatively unimportant; what matters is the selection of species. Perhaps ironically, the importance of such essentially random evolution would seem to rehabilitate (superficially, at least) Lamarck. It should be noted that neo-Darwinians such as Dawkins (see footnote 24 above) view punctuated equilibrium as a "minor wrinkle" and essentially as gradualist as the neo-Darwinian synthesis. And, indeed, it must be admitted that true Darwinian gradualism should not be confused with a *constant* rate of evolution.

29. On the other hand, sociobiology in recent years has sought to explain human behavior increasingly in genetic terms, though its champions have not gone so far as to raise the long-discredited banner of social Darwinism (in *its* day, sufficiently nebulous to be used by such unlikely bedfellows as the American "robber barons" and Karl Marx).

30. For a provocative essay concerning the conscious mental capabilities of animals, the reader should see Donald R. Griffin, *Animal Thinking* (Harvard University, 1984).

sufficiency. From either angle, wild animals under natural conditions are the best subjects for our inquiry.[31]

But the evidentiary problem with the wild is twofold. First, the evidence produced by amateurs (including the author) rarely leaves the anecdotal level and can easily (though not necessarily fairly) be dismissed by the scientists as "accidental" or simply the product of faulty observation. Given the devotion and diligence required by field zoologists to overcome the often immense practical difficulties in gathering detailed and objective evidence, as well as the endurance needed to survive the discomfort and inevitable frustrations present, one can sympathize with the scepticism, if not the outright rejection, shown by the professionals to the data offered by the amateur. Second, and the author knows this from many discussions with field naturalists, a great deal of evidence, particularly of a preliminary nature, that suggests conscious awareness of wild animals is actually suppressed by these field ecologists for fear of the presumed negative reaction that would be shown by the scientific community![32] Such inhibitions are only slowly dissolving.

The whole point to raising these issues here is to encourage the safarist, or even a reader from an armchair perspective, to look for what seem to be enterprising solutions to possibly new problems. For the alert safarist, the most obvious "problems" will arise in food gathering, predation, and the construction and use of tools. Other fertile behavioral patterns — communication, courtship and mating, the rearing of young, territorial defense, dominance and aggression, and habitat selection (particularly in the context of migration) — may well prove less revealing for the average safarist with limited time available. Ironically, considering that much of this introductory discussion has been triggered by the popular misconception that antelopes are essentially "prey" animals, the interaction between predator and prey offers one of the best opportunities on safari to gauge conscious thinking. We have already alluded to the subtleties of escape. Those who believe that only the simplest tactics — hiding, crouching motionless, fleeing — are employed to evade capture are not paying attention.[33] Nor should the reader forget that an individual antelope does not play this potentially deadly game every day. That is *not* the same

wildebeest that the lions keep missing! Playing the role of prey for keeps is very much a novel experience for most antelopes. And the successful player has made an intelligent series of decisions. Some of the latest evidence collected by naturalists in this regard concern the "flight distances" that antelopes set for different predators. Efficiency is a powerful motivation in nature, and it is hardly surprising that prey do not seek to escape the presence of predators who remain outside their range of effectiveness. Nor would it fall beyond programming capabilities to set a different flight distance for each of the major predators. What naturalists now realize, however, is that gazelles, for example, are periodically fine-tuning the flight distances to take into consideration their own age, sex, and condition. In other words, they are establishing (or speculating on) the proper correlation between the hunter's abilities and their own range of response. It may be seriously doubted that genetic programming could specify such complexity.

On the other end of the footrace (or ambush), though the predator obviously does participate in the business of earning a living frequently, if not daily, capturing such agile and elusive prey (or determining which prey is impaired) calls for flexible, intelligent choice in the face of changing and, more than likely, at least occasionally novel circumstances. From Chapter IV, the reader perhaps gained the impression that the cheetah simply wins the sprint — or not. That some gazelles zig (or zag) and escape. Not that simple![34] The cheetah knows only too well that the gazelle can and will take evasive action. Thus, a cheetah will sprint to come within a certain striking distance, then slow down to follow the quick changes in direction. At some point, when the prey is running directly away, the cat will accelerate into its final sprint. All this happens quickly. In other words, people who write about cheetahs as if they were missiles set on irrevocable paths of destruction, without a sophisticated pilot at the controls, are engaged in mythologizing. (The image of cheetahs sliding out of control past a turning antelope is a cartoon of reality — when cheetahs miss, they *barely* miss.)

The safarist should not, however, expect too much. One deals here with subtleties, not earthshaking observations. The dividing line between instinctive behavior and conscious thought on a case-by-case basis may not be all that great; both modes must frequently be mixed to some degree, anyway; and even the most "intelligent" versatility will always be limited by evolutionary adaptations.

Two final introductory notes concern photography. First, it is often useful to take careful notes as one photographs antelopes; the safarist may well have difficulty later in identifying the animal simply from the picture.

---

31. Laboratory animals have also been selected and conditioned in ways that encourage them to display far less social behavior than their wild counterparts — they normally behave in highly artificial ways and are emasculated to the point of uselessness when one is looking for reliable evidence of "thinking."

32. The most obvious examples almost always concern the differences between groups of the same species living in separate environments. Objectively, these differences can only be called "cultural" contrasts.

33. Earlier, the point was made that young antelopes grow up quickly, because they do not have that much to *learn*. There is no contradiction: no practical amount of additional time will teach an animal to *think*.

---

34. The reader should recognize that the dodging itself involves critical decisions: zigzags as a good strategy work only if the predator is *very* near — otherwise, such behavior simply offers the predator an opportunity to draw closer.

A strict view might question the value of a photograph in which the exact species or subspecies of antelope was not clearly evident, but this judgment would be a harsh one for first-timers. The beginning safarist may find it desirable to note down color and patterns (especially on the extremities), size, shape, movement, sound, and habitat of any antelope not obviously recognizable.

Second, proper positioning by the photographer, always important in the wild, is especially critical when shooting antelopes. If the photographer tries to maneuver too close to his subject, in particular to single individuals, the animal(s) will quickly disappear. On the other hand, the safarist must move reasonably close to the herd to extract the play, courtship, various social hierarchies, and tussling between males. Proper approach techniques were discussed in Chapter II; suffice it to say here that antelopes should be treated as the most wary of subjects.

1. *Patterson's Eland.*[35]

The ox-like eland (also known as the Cape or Livingstone's eland) is the largest antelope. Watching the eland move away at speed *(3)* — the usual experience with an eland — reminds the author of the five-gaited American saddlebred show horse trotting around the show ring. Head set for balance; stylish, unwavering leg-action for maximum animation; white pin stripes against a polished background — all combine to produce a portrait of collected authority, elegance, and graceful effort. The adult male elands also make a persistent click in the forelegs as they move that sounds like the noise made by the quarterboots which all gaited horses wear as protective devices (against overreaching with the hind foot). This popping or clicking, which is specific to males and probably originates in the tendons of the front legs, seems to get louder as the male gets older and can be heard up to a mile away in still conditions. Presumably, the clicking serves to let other males (and, possibly, females) know of the presence of a mature bull.

The eland, which once was called the "impoofu" and used to be regularly seen in large herds of several hundred, in many respects is an enigma today. Essentially a plains animal, it is not nearly as common as other large plains antelopes (the wildebeest, kongoni, or topi, for example).[36] Moreover, several individuals will appear in one area, then disappear altogether. In fact, elands roam over considerable distances, though the adult males are less nomadic than the females and the young, and the safarist can never be sure that he will sight the same eland twice. Samburu in Kenya is a good place to see eland; Nairobi National Park is even better. Although the eland moves around like a grazer and does eat some grass, it prefers leaves, berries, bushes, and available plains herbs (in the form of "wild flowers") and is therefore considered basically a browser. Such foods are nutritious, enabling the eland to bulk up; these high-quality plants are also relatively scarce, helping to hold down eland density and ensuring scattered distribution. Eland herds are only temporary in composition, changing daily. *(4)* There is little evidence of bonding between adults. Large groups that are occasionally found usually revolve around juveniles, suggesting a protective function. Small cow groups have been known to aggregate into herds of several hundred, accompanied by males, during peak breeding seasons. When juveniles join a herd after their early concealment (called "lying out" or "going to ground"), they frequently come together in nursery groups by themselves, again, one presumes, for protection. And, when calves are weaned at three months, they do continue to exhibit close bonding among themselves. Smaller, all-male groups of three or so are common among young adults.

The adult eland is a formidable animal and not greatly concerned about predators. Large plains antelopes, who are too big to hide or depend upon concealment, usually form herds for protection. But a bull eland can fend quite nicely for himself. In fact, eland bulls react like buffalo bulls in the presence of lions and will frequently challenge or threaten the predator if given an opportunity. Eland cows have even been known (in a group) to challenge a lion — a rare act among all prey species. Both sexes have sizeable horns that look as if they were made to be used.

---

35. As a matter of categorization, the eland may be lumped with other spiral-horned antelopes: kudus (Greater and Lesser), bongo, nyala, sitatunga, and bushbuck. Some reputable field guides distinguish between the Patterson's eland and a "Giant" or "Lord Derby's" eland. The Giant eland has broader and rounder ears, a dewlap that begins nearly at the chin (with the same tuft of black hair), more white stripes on its body, and longer, narrower, and more diverging horns. Despite the difference in size, the author doubts that two separate species exist and believes that the Giant eland is but a variant of the Patterson's. The best place (and one of the only reliable places) to see the Giant eland is the Lichtenburg Nature Reserve in South Africa. Small populations exist in the wild in West Africa and in the Sudan. Older texts attempted to establish the eland variants as follows: the Cape eland in the south, Livingstone's eland in Central Africa, and Patterson's (of *Man-Eaters of Tsavo* fame) eland in the east and north.

36. Two primary factors account for the relative scarcity today. First, of all the antelopes, and though resistant to tsetse fly, the eland is the most susceptible to rinderpest, which accordingly devastated the species from time to time in this century, until the disease was controlled in the 1960s. Second, the eland has traditionally been hunted for food (even the Maasai, who in principle do not hunt wild animals for food, hunt and eat eland in times of hardship and have been known to adopt orphaned eland calves into their herds), and this fact alone has virtually eliminated the animal from Southern Africa, with the exception of the Kalahari. No other animal, save the giraffe, appears so frequently in the ancient rock paintings of the Bushmen — in both hunting and apparently domestic scenes — and the quality of eland meat, which has a veal-like consistency and flavor, has today confined the antelope to the national parks.

Plate 3. Mature Bull. The male is humped and dewlapped like an ox and much heavier and bigger all over than the female (though the female also has a heavy bovine profile). The dewlap is not very obvious in this picture, because it is swinging from side to side as the animal trots. The eland is taller than a buffalo but on the average weighs less. Coat color varies from a rich chestnut to the pale fawn pictured here. Males darken with age, frequently becoming nearly black or blue grey. Both sexes have spiral horns, which are often longer in the female (and sometimes more than two feet in length). The long, thin tail ends in a brush of black hair. The tuft of coarse black hair found at the apex of the dewlap disappears with age, as the dewlap itself hangs lower and lower. Males sport another "brush" or curly mat of hair between their eyes that grows from the forehead down to the nose and becomes increasingly prominent with age. All elands have black bands across the back sides of the forelegs above the knees. Another black stripe along the back merges into a short mane. Their horse-like ears are smaller proportionately than those of other antelopes. The author has witnessed the agile elands leap a surprisingly long distance (probably as much as eight feet) for so heavy an antelope. I have even seen one large bull leap over another bull, a remarkable feat, when one considers that a bull stands six feet at the shoulder and weighs up to 2000 pounds.

Elands, often held in religious-like awe, have inspired many poetic descriptions. A small, three-part sampling:

The giant elands. . .have a majesty in common with Michelangelo's Day. . .In their best condition they are almost orange-coloured, with brilliant white stripes. A fine eland bull grazing peacefully among the flowers is the finest expression of tranquil majesty and harmless strength that it is possible to find in Nature. It recalls Jupiter, when he carried off Europa, as the daffodil-coloured bull, in Moschus. . .(Campbell, *Dark Horse,* p. 74);

Obesity forming one of the exclusive prerogatives of African royalty, it is not surprising that the Eland — more lusty, fat, and well looking, than any other wild quadruped — should assume unto himself an air of princely consequence. "Lord of an hundred does," amongst which he moves with all the pomp and self-importance of a nabob in his harem, the stately bull is at once the most corpulent, one of the most ponderous, and certainly the most magnificent, of all the ruminants. (Harris, *Portraits of the Game and Wild Animals of Southern Africa,* p. 34); and

. . .The mighty peaceful beasts. . .seem to have come out of an old Egyptian epitaph. . .(Dinesen, *Out of Africa,* p. 99).

Elands are totally non-territorial, in common with most spiral-horned antelopes, and real fights between eland bulls are almost never seen. A rare sparring episode over a female is really the only exception to the general lack of overt aggression exhibited among the adult males. Younger males in all-male groups will engage in ritual "tussling" — gently and carefully entangling their horns and then pushing and shoving each other, as they test their strength. Sometimes, they coat their horns with mud and sap from certain shrubs before engaging.

For some reason, the nomadic eland ("pofu" or "mbunju" in Kiswahili), unlike most other park animals, has not acclimated itself to the frequent vehicles. Possessed of exceptionally keen senses (sight, hearing, *and* smell) and very difficult to approach, the eland has assigned the safarist and his vehicle a "flight distance" of some 400 yards! The use of a telephoto is therefore essential to capture the animal on film.

Elands have remarkable systems for protecting themselves against heat when necessary under drought or arid conditions. In fact, the large antelopes can easily survive a ten-degree rise in *body* temperature during the day: they

Plate 4. Family Unit. Calves depend on mother for only a short period; they are fully weaned at three months. For the first month or so, however, they are vulnerable to large predators and so remain concealed in dense bush or tall grass. The mothers visit several times a day to nurse. Elands have perhaps the sharpest senses of the antelope family and are extremely shy. Many years ago, eland were seen high up on Kilimanjaro!

stop sweating, a relatively inefficient cooling mechanism, and, in common with many antelopes found in drier regions, they employ the same arrangement discussed earlier by which blood destined for the brain is routed first to the nose. But the eland also increases his breathing rate, by as much as seven times. As the air is then inhaled into the lungs faster and faster, evaporation (and cooling) increases. Moreover, the exhaled air contains moisture that also further cools the nasal cavity. Thus, rapid breathing through the nose (not panting) is a form of highly efficient sweating. Evaporative cooling is, however, still a relatively "expensive" method of conserving water, and the eland's needs of up to six gallons per day under normal conditions accordingly increase in hotter areas. He can stop drinking only if he can cover enough territory to substitute all the acacia leaves (more than half moisture in composition) required. An eland will also move into the shade at midday, if shade is available (particularly bearing in mind the animal's size), but this strategy helps only a little when the residual radiation characteristic of desert-like conditions is strong. During really hot days, the eland slows appreciably his eating and makes up the deficiencies at night.

The eland is often mentioned as Africa's answer to the protein shortage. Some believe that its food potential is even greater than American beef cattle because it does not need vast acres of grass to sustain its growth and existence. Apparently gentle and easily domesticated — a seeming contradiction to the extreme shyness shown in the wild — the eland yields meat that is highly palatable (and which contains large amounts of body fat compared with other antelopes). Its milk is also good. But the "impoofu's" natural way of life — nomadic, a selective feeder, and maintaining a low density — however docile the big antelope appears to be in captivity, clashes sharply with normal ranching procedures and resources. The many experiments, in Africa and elsewhere (especially in the Soviet Union), in domesticating and ranching the eland for milk and meat have produced mixed results.

2. *Lesser Kudu.*[37]

The Lesser kudu ("tandala ndogo" in Kiswahili) is a forest antelope, living in the *nyika*, the dry scrub or thornbush country of Eastern and Southern Africa. Forest antelopes do not congregate in significant herds, in part because the habitat does not permit group cohesion — visibility is poor, communication is muffled by the vegetation, and there is often not enough room — and in part

because large groups would give predators much easier opportunities. Consequently, kudus are seen singly *(5)*, most often in pairs *(6)*, and in small bands that include juveniles. The safarist has to remain alert to see the kudus; they remain in dense cover during the day, and the biggest herd is likely to be six or so animals (unless mating season "swells" the ranks by another four or five individuals). The evidence seems to indicate that kudus also have a larger home range than do most forest antelopes.

Forest antelopes are essentially browsers, but the Lesser kudu will occasionally eat some grass. Extensively hunted for its horns (the Greater kudu has always been the most sought-after trophy of all the antelopes), the regal-looking kudu profile serves as an emblem favored by many sporting bodies. In real life, the magnificent horns also mostly serve in an ornamental capacity: as an added embellishment used in lateral displays to guard territorial or breeding rights. Male hierarchy is based on age, and horn wrestling, despite the kudu's reputation for pugnacity,[38] is infrequent.

3. *Bongo.*

"Bongo, Bongo!" the attendants announce in hushed but earnest tones, as they move quickly through the corridors of Kenya's Ark or Treetops or Mountain Lodge late at night. Seeing the elusive, nocturnal bongo is a possibility that the resorts promote, but the occasions when the antelope actually appears in the spotlights trained on the salt-licks are rare.[39] Perhaps, a more sure approach to finding a deep-forest animal that almost never leaves its isolated mountain environment is to pass a few days deep in the bamboo forests of the Aberdares Salient or on the slopes of Mt. Kenya or in the Mau Forest in Kenya. The most likely times for a sighting are early morning or dusk, when the "ghosts" of the forest, as they are often called, actively browse.[40]

37. The Greater kudu, mostly a larger version of the Lesser, is more nocturnal and has grand, divergent horns, measuring along the curve four feet or more. It also has a prominent fringe of hair along the underside of its neck. The Greater is the largest antelope after the eland. Nevertheless, it is shyer than the Lesser kudu and, though it lives in larger groups and moves around less, is infrequently seen by safarists.

38. Hunters have always found killing fierce animals less offensive than killing milder-acting creatures. There do appear to be one or two reliable reports of kudus whose elaborate horns were so intertwined that the combatants could not pull free and consequently died from subsequent predation or starvation. Most such accounts are, the author believes, extrapolations from experiences with other species having less magnificent horns.

39. At one of the Tree Hotels, a lengthy fight between two bongo bulls that left one dead has entered the permanent mythology of the area. Forest antelopes do crave minerals (especially salts), which can be difficult to find in humid forests. Thus the relative success of the Tree Hotels in drawing out these elusive creatures.

40. Forests vary considerably, depending upon altitude and rainfall. The major forests in Africa tend to be geographically isolated and thus have their own distinctive fauna. Experts divide forests into two broad categories: upland or mountain (above 5400 feet) and lowland. Within these two main divisions, the species of trees, saplings, shrubs, herbs, and grasses determine several different zones. In the upland forest, the middle

Plate 5. Female Lesser Kudu. The female has no horns (the male's horns can reach three feet in length) but is a beautiful, elegant creature decorated in white: thin vertical body stripes, a chevron between the eyes, cheek spots, and patches on the neck. Indeed, the Lesser kudu is sometimes referred to as the Apollo of antelopes. The vertical white stripes simulate streaky sunlight in thick cover.

Plate 6. Young Male and Female. These may well be young Greater kudu, distinguishable from their Lesser cousins having the same age by fewer vertical stripes, the absence of two white throat patches, a fringe of throat hairs running from the chin to the bottom of the neck, and frequently (but not always) redder coats. Lesser kudus are more common in East Africa, Greater in Central and Southern Africa (and often in rocky or mountain terrain). Lesser kudu can live in very dry country, Greater need more water. These youngsters are browsing on the shores of Lake Kariba in Zimbabwe. All kudus are good leapers, though thick bush requires other skills. A Lesser kudu calf hides for a month or so after birth, then joins its mother on browsing excursions and links up with one or two other cows with calves. Kudus share many habitats with bushbucks.

Like all true forest antelopes, bongos are built higher in the haunch than at the withers, a configuration that allows the animal to run at speed in a sort of crouching position, navigating undergrowth and beneath low-lying obstructions, head up and horns laid back along the neck. Bongos, as the reader can see *(7-9)*, are also brightly colored, with large white body stripes set against a bright coat that ranges from chestnut-red to mahogany and white markings on the face, neck, and legs (along with contrasting black markings). Bongo coloration is, in fact, a good example of the principle that underlies the theory of military camouflage, of what is called "disruptive coloring." Simply stated, the colorful bars, stripes, or splotches break up an animal's coherent outline and make it appear in the forest as a collection of curious and unrelated patches. This results in true concealment, the opposite of mimicry, in the haphazard lighting that filters through the forest.

4. *Bushbuck.*

The bushbuck is found in most of sub-Saharan Africa where dense cover exists. It is the most widely distributed of the spiral-horned antelopes, and as many as forty different variations, distinguished mainly by striping and coloration, have been recorded. Although it is small, shy, frequently nocturnal, and elusive at all times, the bushbuck is so common that the safarist will undoubtedly see the adult version of this antelope if he spends any significant time in the bush. *(10)* Bushbucks are territorial and remain in one spot for years, the only spiral-horned antelope so to behave. The most common places to look for them are at the edges of clearings *(11)* or at a waterhole or stream *(12)*. In fact, if one stakes out a waterhole in the forest, sooner or later, a bushbuck shows up, step by dainty, nervous step. The bushbuck is solitary — the safarist usually sees the species singly, sometimes in breeding pairs, and rarely in threesomes.

Plate 7. Bongo Male. Bongos inhabit dense rain forests but occasionally will briefly come into a clearing. At the salt-licks, they are best seen at dawn. For a reason not yet known, they show a definite predilection for bamboo groves but eat little bamboo. Bulls can weigh up to 900 pounds, which size makes them the heaviest forest antelope after the Greater kudu. The bulls live alone, except when breeding. They have dark coats and a dark muzzle; some older bulls are nearly black. Adults sometimes have bare patches on their backs where the tips of their horns, laid back during running through the forest, have rubbed away the hair.

zone (often called "montane") is frequently dominated by bamboo thickets, where most bongos are found. An important feature of montane bamboo forests are large patches or breaks in the canopy (the more or less continuous leafy layer formed by the crowns of the trees intermingling). It is on the edges of these glades where one is likely to spot the bongo.

In the Mau Forest in Kenya, an interesting discovery has been reported: the bongo population is controlled naturally by a forest vine known as setyot. The vine is a favorite food of the bongo, but two-year old vines are toxic and periodically kill significant numbers of bongos (and giant forest hogs).

The females do not have the stripes and markings of the males — they retain the spots of youth *(13)* — which suggests that coloration has sexual, as well as disruptive, implications. The male has a reputation for pugnacious behavior and for turning on a pursuer.[41] One of the most reliable pursuers is, however, the leopard; but it does not detract from the courage of the valiant bushbuck to note

41. Some hunters have reported a bushbuck hiding until they were nearly on top of it, then being attacked!

Plate 8. Bongo Ewe. The female has horns, shorter than the male's and closer to parallel. Bongos, occasionally called "forest elands," are entirely browsers and make very little noise in the forest. A measure of just how little the bongo has been observed in the wild is the native legend that the bongo's dislike for mud and dirt is so strong that the antelope at night hangs itself in a tree by its horns to sleep to avoid lying down. Most such legends at least are based on observable phenomena; it is the motivations that are a bit fanciful. This particular fable goes awry at the start: bongos are, in fact, nocturnal creatures, who are also fond of wallowing in the mud!

Plate 9. Calf. Once considered a great hunting trophy when grown, this little youngster will pose a similar challenge to photographers.

The author and others have noticed that bushbucks are often found in the company of baboons, and both animals appear to have established some kind of a working relationship, though baboons will sometimes kill and eat young bushbuck. No one seems to have any plausible theories about this observation.

The bushbuck is made like the bongo and other forest antelopes, that is, slightly higher at the rump than shoulder, and also sports typical "forest" ears — large and broad. In the forest, hearing is more important than eyesight; sounds communicate more than images. If the bushbuck does not hear the leopard (or smell him), he will be eaten. Naturalists tell us that, indeed, the young bushbuck (who also has pythons about which to worry) grows its big ears first, then the remainder of its body catches up.

5. *Beisa Oryx.* [42]

The oryx belongs to a group of antelopes that are found in open country and light woodland and in the desert. *(14 & 15)* Some texts have distinguished the Beisa oryx from the so-called "Fringe-eared" oryx, [43] but the author has seen the two side-by-side in the same herd and believes that they are essentially variations of the same species. The Beisa variety is the more common of the two and is

that turning on a leopard is a losing proposition. The underside of a bushbuck's tail is white, and the antelope will flash the conspicuous white tail at a pursuer. This so-called "flash coloring" is meant to disorient the hunter: the predator momentarily has a clear signal on which to fix, then the bushbuck immediately covers it up and vanishes.

42. Grouped with the oryx are gemsbok (found on South Africa's coat of arms), Roan antelope, Sable antelope, and addax. Some naturalists believe that all varieties of oryx are conspecific (belonging to the same species), but the Scimitar-horned (or White) oryx found in the southern Sahara seems sufficiently different to warrant treatment as a separate species.

43. The Beisa oryx is the greyer of the two; the Fringe-eared has a tassel of black hairs on the ears.

Plate 10. Bushbuck. Only the males have horns, which are short with a single spiral when mature. The Kiswahili name for the bushbuck is "mbawala" or "pongo." Swahili legend (with a leavening of the Old Testament thrown in) tells us that the bare "necklace" at the base of the neck was caused by the collar with which Noah was forced to tether the recalcitrant animal on the Ark. Some of the male bushbucks living in forest areas that also produce melanistic leopards, servals, and genets are nearly black.

Plate 11. At Clearing Edge. Like the bongo, the bushbuck is found in dense forests but it also emerges frequently into clearings or at forest edge and will eat young grass. The bushbuck is sometimes referred to as the "prince of the forest."

Plate 12. Resting at the Stream. The bushbuck's chief enemy is the leopard. Lying in the open during the day is not as dangerous as it might appear, though a youngster may be taken by a python.

Plate 13. Bushbuck Ewe. Obtaining a decent photograph of a bushbuck ewe is a real challenge.

found predominantly north of the Tana River in Kenya, the Fringe-eared to the south. Large antelopes, with well-developed distinctive stiletto horns in both sexes, the oryx ("choroa" in Kiswahili) lives in herds of up to fifty or sixty animals *(16).* Given the open, low-resource character and vast size of the oryx's habitat, single herds containing all ages and both sexes are significant energy-savers. An oryx herd is a highly ordered and structured society — both bulls and cows show a fairly strict linear hierarchy — that remains constant over long periods of time (some males emigrate elsewhere). Within the herd, both males *and* females spar a great deal among their own sex, although tolerance is widespread and the animals tend to remain reasonably close physically to one another. Newcomers are allowed to integrate, but slowly, and remain on the periphery of the social system, as "satellites" for several weeks. Stud males also do something that territorial males of some other antelopes do — they place a front leg between the female's hind legs and touch the knee to her belly. Called "laufschlag," this gesture is part of the mating ritual, a test of sorts of female receptivity.

An oryx herd, particularly one whose ranks have been swelled by a local rainstorm, is worth watching for awhile. Very little serious fighting is ever observed, but the younger members always seem to be engaged in some on-going tournament. Several young males will run around the rest of the herd in wide circles, frequently slowing to an exaggerated, high-stepping trot with head carried high and tipped slightly back (the facial stripes and horns in a horizontal line). Other males then emerge from the herd to accept these challenges, leading to a brief, inconsequential horn clash, then disengagement.

Oryx graze on coarse grasses but will browse when no grass is available. Naturalists have established that oryx

Plates 14 & 15. Oryx. The oryx is a distinctive antelope, horse-like in outline, with a variety of black stripes. Facial patterns are each unique; the fancy head-markings, to the extent that they are functional, probably emphasize head gestures. Coat color varies from grey to brown, as shown here.

Plate 16. Oryx Herd. During the heat of midday, an eland will often seek out the shade. The oryx does not bother; it stands in the sun all day long, no problem! In extremely hot and arid country, an oryx might take advantage of any available shade and at the same time excavate a slight depression in the sand with its hooves to reduce radiant heat and lie down. (Lying down also reduces the surface area exposed to drying winds.) But the most significant cooling or heat-avoidance systems are built-in. Individually, the oryx is a highly decorative animal, and a herd is a magnificent sight. Unusual among antelopes, the oryx herd normally contains males, as well as females, of all sizes.

can go without drinking for extremely long periods, obtaining their water needs from vegetation and dew found on the grass at dawn. Even when there is no dew, technically speaking, the nighttime drop in temperature common under desert conditions causes a rise in humidity and dew-like water to condense on plants — which suits the oryx well, because it prefers to eat mostly at night. Writers often make the statement that an oryx can go a lifetime without drinking water. Logic may support the thesis, but the experience may be doubted; no one has spent a lifetime with an oryx, and such learning is basically speculation. The related assertion sometimes made that an oryx just does not drink at all is demonstrably false — in the author's experience, oryx will drink often enough (sometimes, once a day), if water is available *(17)*. It is, however, certainly true that the oryx is well adapted to desert conditions. Oryx have, for example, the same special cooling systems as the eland, only even more

developed, and additionally can actually reduce their basic metabolism at midday. Indeed, the oryx is said to be better adapted to withstand heat than a camel. Its light coat reflects heat, and the farther that one travels into the desert, the lighter the coats become.

An oryx's hooves are large and somewhat splayed, an adaptation for sure-footedness on sandy surfaces. As a consequence, the oryx cannot run quite as well as some other antelopes but it will trek non-stop with long strides for huge distances, usually at night. (One of the benefits of the ruminant system is the ability to walk and ruminate at the same time.)

Fairly typical of naturalists who hew to the strict Darwinian line and sometimes leave the track of common sense is the suggestion that the impressive horns of an oryx might be an adaptation to conserve water. The theory is, an oryx does not have to flee from a predator (and generate heat from such exertion) and can simply

Plate 17. The Antelope "Who Never Drinks" Drinking. Animals arrive at the Uaso Nyiro River in Samburu to drink like desert travelers at an oasis — indeed, one of Africa's most scenic rivers is the only water for many miles. The oryx is an extremely wary animal, very wild, and a drink is a big production. Contrary to popular opinion, desert antelopes do not "store" extra water (nor, incidentally, do camels).

410   African Safari

stand to defend itself. Even the reader who is a novice in such matters could guess otherwise. One can imagine the energy that a joust with a lion would entail. Actually, an oryx's environment contains few predators; that environment itself serves to limit oryx population without significant help from predation. Moreover, the most cursory look at oryx behavior would reveal that oryx are extremely skittish in the presence of predators and are quick to gallop away at the first sign of danger.

Oryx can be, however, quite pugnacious when cornered and have been known to impale an enemy — including lions — by lowering their heads between their

6. Waterbuck. [45]

Everyone leaves Africa having selected a favorite antelope, and the waterbuck ("kuru" in Kiswahili) has always been the author's. The lordly males absolutely define the term statuesque: proud, erect carriage culminating in handsome pitchfork horns *(19 & 20)*. The female simply has to be one of the most exquisite creatures on earth *(21 & 22)*. Two variations exist: the Common waterbuck, which has a dark brown coat and a white ring on its rump *(23)*, and the Defassa waterbuck, whose coat is more grey and shows a broad white patch on the hindquarters (see plate *22*). The Defassa is the

Plate 18. Oryx Standing Against the Sky. Oryx horns vary significantly in shape and length but all appear to be too long and set at the wrong angle for practical use. When the forehead is, however, lowered parallel to the ground, between the forelegs, one can see what formidable weapons that these stiletto spikes become. In strict profile, the straight and virtually parallel horns appear as one; the oryx was thus frequently used as the model for unicorns in sculptured bas-reliefs, carvings, and insignia.

forelegs. Somewhat more suspect are stories of oryx (or gemsbok) spearing a predator who has leaped on their backs by throwing their heads up.[44] They have keen sight and are extremely shy toward safarists. Consequently, one normally must use a telephoto to capture a decent photograph. *(18)*

more numerous. The two subspecies interbreed where their ranges overlap; the offspring show a great variety of intermediate rump color patterns.

As their name suggests, waterbucks are never found far from water. At times of danger, the waterbuck will take refuge in a stream or lake and will run to the deepest parts

---

44. The author has made the point earlier that predators virtually never leap onto an antelope's back.

45. Allied with the waterbuck are the kob, lechwe, reedbuck, rhebok, and puku. Waterbucks closely resemble the European red deer.

Plates 19 & 20. Male Waterbuck. Whether a waterbuck is sighted in lush or arid country, a river, stream, or lake is nearby. Waterbucks, which have always brought to the author's mind the image of Santa Claus' reindeer, are entirely grazers.

Plates 21 & 22. Female Waterbuck. The female has no horns. Both sexes have coarse, shaggy coats that help to keep the skin dry after a swim.

Plate 23. Common Ring. At least one wag has remarked that the Common variety looks as if it had sat down on a freshly painted toilet seat.

or all the way up to its head. Not surprisingly, waterbucks are powerful swimmers. The thick, shaggy coat is an unexpected feature for an equatorial mammal but it helps to keep the skin dry (and warm) for an animal who passes so much time in the water. Such a covering is also difficult for a crocodile, who may well be sharing that same water, to penetrate.

Waterbucks are not nomadic; living near water usually ensures a plentiful supply of rich grass growing at all times of the year. Only mildly gregarious, waterbucks live in herds of five to roughly twenty-five. *(24)* A typical herd comprises a master bull, assorted females, young, and a sub-adult or two. Young bucks also congregate in bachelor herds. Master bulls are strongly territorial. The

Plate 24. Normal Waterbuck Herd. The females are dispersed throughout a male's territory. Consequently, the male will rarely collect more than five or six females together at any one time.

Plate 25. Mother and Baby. Waterbucks lead fairly casual lives and are not difficult (relative to most other antelopes) to approach. A ewe with young is, however, typically nervous. Waterbuck breed year-round; calves are hidden in tall grass.

females wander into a given territory and graze at random; they do not move about as a close-knit group. The stronger males take the best and largest grazing lands and over time attract more females. Fighting between bulls tends to be less ritualistic than with most other antelopes, and serious encounters are common, though the combatants generally stop short of causing death to one side. At Lake Nakuru in Kenya, the density of waterbucks is so high that social behavior common elsewhere has been modified. Territories are relatively small, territorial ownership tends to be short, and the dominant bulls accept one or more satellite males within their territories. Indeed, these subordinate males often themselves protect the territory and act as surrogates of the dominant bull against outsiders. Occasionally, a satellite male will cover a female in heat, and, as might be expected, it is common for satellite males to succeed dominant bulls.

To all appearances, waterbucks give the impression of leading relaxed lives. *(25 & 26)* In most environments, they are not favored as prey by the carnivores. In fact,

Plate 26. Never Far from Water. Water is also the waterbuck's source of protection. Most antelopes head for the open spaces at night. Waterbucks make for the thickets along a water source.

little of their behavior seems predator-oriented. For example, individuals frequent the same spots all the time and they drink with little of the tension or obvious nervousness common to other antelopes. The author has frequently come upon a buck dozing on its feet in areas not exactly secure from stalking predators. Why waterbucks

enjoy this relative security is speculative. Their skin glands give off an oily secretion that imparts a strong musky odor which is at least mildly repulsive.[46] The coarse, shaggy coat is undoubtedly at least a minor impediment to throat killers. Perhaps more significant, the waterbuck's horns are set at a very practical angle and make formidable weapons, capable of inflicting serious damage. On the other hand, in Kruger Park, lions favor waterbucks among all prey. (27)

7. Bohor Reedbuck.

"Tohe" in Kiswahili, reedbucks are more nocturnal than diurnal. Like waterbucks, they are usually found near water; on the other hand, they are not nearly as common as waterbuck. Normally, there are no reedbuck herds as such (28); pairs (29) or small family groups are sometimes seen. In those rare instances where high local densities occur — for example, at Akagera in Rwanda — a loose herd of up to fifty or more is occasionally found, behavior so uncharacteristic that no one has offered a cogent explanation to account for it. Many variations of reedbuck can be described; the light and graceful Bohor is the most prevalent in East Africa.

Reedbucks are hiders — they will crouch in the grass when predators approach, lying quite flat and still, muzzle stretched between forelegs, ears laid back, and bolting only when almost stepped upon. They run with a distinctive rocking-horse motion. Even when it knows (or suspects) that it has been spotted, the feeding reedbuck resorts to strategy: it pretends to graze unconcerned, in the hope of encouraging the nearby predator to relax in over-confidence — then, suddenly, it bounds away. Risky business, in the author's view, but who is to say that zigging and zagging at top speed is any more effective? Plenty of reedbuck survive.

8. Topi.[47]

The classic image of a topi on safari is that pictured in plate 30, the Solitary Sentry standing on an ant or termite hill. Whether looking out for predators or simply surveying his territory and warning off other male topis, the topi buck will stand motionless for hours. Or, if the safarist drives slowly past, the animal will sometimes pivot deliberately on its forelegs to keep the vehicle in sight.

In an antelope group noted for its bizarre features, the topi ("nyamera" in Kiswahili) is probably the most "normal," or least exaggerated, of the lot. (31) Topis have

Plate 27. African Tableau in the Mist of Early Morning. Waterbucks are only mildly gregarious among themselves but always seem to be in the company of numerous other species. Living near water undoubtedly accounts for the "popularity."

46. The suggestion sometimes heard that the odor repels crocodiles is a myth. The safarist in light winds will get close enough to waterbuck to smell the distinctive scent.

47. The topi's allies are the various hartebeests, wildebeest, sassaby (tsessebe), blesbok (bontebok), and Hunter's antelope. Of all the large plains antelopes generally living in large herds, this group in anthropomorphic terms is distinguished by nature's most "stupid" expressions.

Plate 28. Male Bohor Reedbuck. The Bohor reedbuck has a reddish fawn, even yellowish coat, a short bushy tail with a "white flag" underneath, a white belly, white eye rings, and forward-hooked horns (males only) and is principally a grazer on floodplains and inundated grasslands. Reedbuck are most active at night and are the favorite prey of leopards: a match-up of stealth versus stillness, a test of immense patience.

Plate 30. Solitary Sentry on Ant Hill. Half of Dr. Dolittle's Pushmi-Pullyu. Some naturalists have suggested that topis stand on the mounds to enjoy cooling breezes and to allow the savannah drafts to blow off annoying flies, distinctly secondary (but possible) motivations. An ant hill, which occurs in all types of habitats, is worth contemplating. Antelopes may use them as observation points and for scent-marking (to indicate territorial boundaries, dominance, and sexual attraction). But their importance to animal life is far more extensive. Pangolins and aardvarks eat the ants and dig out holes that are later occupied by warthogs, mongooses, and others. Primates sit on them. Elephants, rhinos, and buffalos use them as rubbing posts. Finally, dense clumps of thicket frequently originate as isolated ant mounds. An active ant colony stores dead vegetation in the underground chambers directly beneath and radiating from the hill. A rich soil results, followed eventually by shrubby germination. Because of ant activity and the trampling caused by the various visitors, the ground surrounding the mound becomes bare and acts as a firebreak. Thus, the bushes survive and grow into thickets. The dense clumps in turn sometimes provide protection for young trees.

Plate 29. Females. The female is hornless. All reedbucks have a prominent round bare glandular patch below each ear, clearly visible in the photograph.

beautiful, glossy chestnut-red coats, with boldly contrasting blue patches on the face, shoulders, and hindquarters. Topi herds can be huge — at one time, the topi was probably one of Africa's most numerous antelopes and is still widely distributed across the continent's grasslands — and the topi is frequently the most conspicuous herbivore in an area. During times of migration, when the topi joins the wildebeest, zebra, and kongoni, many thousands are in evidence *(32)*. Topis follow the typical social pattern for large herd antelopes. The males stake out domains, females freely wander in and out of particular territories, and mating takes place within the boundaries when the females are in estrus. During rutting, the males engage in the usual scent-marking, visual displays, and ritualistic fighting *(33)*.

Topis eat both the green leaf and the dried-up stalk of grasses. This latter diet prevents the build-up of dead vegetation, of immense importance in controlling fires. Without the topis or other antelopes that eat the roughage, fires feeding on an accumulated blanket of such combustible matter would blaze like furnaces and incinerate the fallen seeds and root systems lying just below the surface. After the topis *et al.* have done their work, the fires merely sweep quickly and lightly over the surface, cleaning the ground, rather than baking it.

Topis (and their immediate relatives, the tsessebes) are probably the fastest of all antelopes, with great endurance as well. All that awkward-looking form manages to produce a powerful running machine that will outrun and outdistance even the little speed demon, the gazelle. At full gallop, the topi will keep its head well forward and hence is able to change direction without losing much

Plate 31. Pregnant Female. With its long head and ungainly sloping back, the topi is only slightly less exaggerated than the hartebeest or kongoni, for which it is often mistaken (naturalists frequently referred to the topi as the "bastard hartebeest"). Topis have a "stop" in their muzzle line between the eyes. Kongonis have Roman noses; the muzzle line is straight from the base of the horns to the nose. A topi's horns curve gently backwards. Kongoni horns have a hitch somewhere (usually bending forwards before twisting backwards). The high angle of the head and relatively high, lateral position of the eyes provide topis with a greater field of vision than that of wildebeests, which are roughly the same size. Female topis have shorter horns and are lighter in color than the males but still retain the rich bay hue with blue black markings on the hips, thighs, and upper forelegs.

speed. Like all the large plains antelopes of its group, with the exception perhaps of the kongoni, the topi will drink (at least once) each day, if water is available. *(34)*

9. Hartebeest.

The hartebeest (a Boer word for "tough ox") is known in East Africa by its Kiswahili name, "kongoni." *(35)* Not as numerous as topis, kongoni herds can still run into the hundreds. Nonetheless, kongonis manage to give the impression of being loners at heart, and herds are loose associations that maintain a semblance of communal organization but which do not seem to count for much, except at migration times. Old bulls are particularly solitary. Younger males form detached bachelor herds. Kongonis are mostly sedentary and occupy relatively small home ranges but will join migrations in the dry season. At all times, the safarist will frequently see them in the company of zebra and wildebeest. Like topis, kongoni "scouts" will take up prominent positions on termite mounds. Kongonis prefer the coarse grasses and thus must eat a great deal, often for ten hours or more, to take in sufficient nutrients. They are exclusively grazers.

Plate 32. Migration Mixture. Topis thrive on dry grasses not eaten by other antelopes. Such a preference leads to seasonal use of habitats and at least a semi-nomadic life cycle; in large ecosystems like the Serengeti, the topi will thus join the seasonal migration.

Plate 33. Ritualistic Fighting at Rutting. When one sees antelopes squaring off on their knees, the safarist knows that he is witnessing some harmless post-Camelot (actually, pre-Camelot) ritual.

Plate 34. Topis at Water.

Kongonis have a low juvenile mortality rate, perhaps the lowest among antelopes. Calves appear throughout the year, though seasonal peaks are encouraged by the needs of mother and calf for fresh green grass.[48] The calves are hiders, not followers. Indeed, kongonis seem to have written the textbook on "lying out." One key element of the strategy: mothers scrupulously eat the young calf's urine and feces to remove any smell that might give the hiding spot away to predators. Mothers will also use "pronking," a bouncy, stiff-legged gait discussed thoroughly in the text below (under "gazelle") to distract passing predators.

The alert safarist, if he takes sufficient time on the savannahs, will notice that kongonis play the part of professional mourners. Not only will they stand for hours over a dead or dying kongoni, they will likewise hover over other dead antelopes and mammals generally. Every now and then, one may find a kongoni side-by-side with an elephant mourning a dead elephant. One is obviously tempted to make a comparison to elephants, but kongonis do not have the jumbo's mental equipment, and the apparent concern may be nothing more than a mixture of Kipling's 'satiable curiosity and a general inability to put the pieces together.

Indeed, the odd fopdoodle, fairly or unfairly, reminds the author of those strange people in my youth who hung around station houses or newspaper offices complaining that communists were poisoning the drinking water with fluoride. Even a penguin seems to have more purpose and a better grasp of what's going on than a kongoni.

48. Antelope breeding cycles generally follow predictable patterns. The larger species tend to calve at the beginning of the normal rainy period, when the ground is green with the tender shoots of new grass. Feeding conditions are then optimal. On the equator, where there are two wet seasons, some species (but not, of course, individuals) will calve at least twice a year. Forest antelopes and the smaller antelopes, who both live in areas where feeding conditions vary little, drop calves year-round. The ages at which breeding starts and the lengths of gestation periods themselves vary widely, generally dependent upon body size: large antelopes tend to breed later and have longer gestations than small antelopes.

Plate 35. The True Gomer Pile of Nature. A more literate reference in a non-TV age would be to the elongated and exaggerated forms of El Greco. With its long, drawn-out locust face and doleful expression, its extreme sloping shoulders, matchstick legs, and exaggerated rocking-horse gait, the kongoni is surely one of nature's most preposterous creatures. Even the bracketed horns, apparently poised to fight each other, seem to make little sense. The horns rise from a bony, skin-covered basal support or pedicel attached to the skull. The variation shown here is Coke's (pronounced ''cook's'') hartebeest, found predominantly in Kenya and Tanzania. The Coke's is essentially fawn-colored, but, on each hindquarter, a line appears that extends across the lower body and front legs below which the coat assumes a whiter shade.

Plate 36. Mother with Young. Kongonis have extremely pliable necks and can look back directly over their shoulders. The female has more slender horns than the male. Mothers hide their calves when the latter are very young and graze well away from them to detract attention.

Plate 37. Billiard Table. After the rains, when the grass is green, kongonis in a group look like improbable toy animals standing upon a billiard table. These are Jackson's hartebeests, which are taller than Coke's, redder in coat color, and which have v-shaped horns. From a distance, kongoni ears, set on the same angle as the horns, look like the third and fourth horn.

10. *Wildebeest*.[49]

Everyone makes fun of the prehistoric-looking, absurdly proportioned animal known as the Blue (or White-bearded) wildebeest or Brindled gnu ("nyumbu ya montu" in Kiswahili; "gnu" is derived from the Hottentot expression describing the typical loud bellowing of the animal) pictured in plate *38*. A popular adjective applied is "grotesque." One writer described the animal as the four Marx Brothers stuffed into the same costume. Another compares it to a gypsy. The Zulus believed that the wildebeest was the progeny of a cross between a buffalo and a zebra. Local Swahili legend relates that after God made all the animals on earth, He paused to contemplate the result. Once He realized that He had some leftovers (and being adverse to waste), He gathered all the bits and pieces and hurriedly threw them together in haphazard fashion, thereby creating the wildebeest. In his superb film, *The Great Migration: Year of the Wildebeest*, Alan Root, in a more secular mood, introduces the wildebeest as "an animal apparently designed by a committee and assembled from spare parts."

The author's favorite description is George Schaller's:

> The wildebeest is a strangely fashioned antelope, looking as if assembled from the leavings in some evolutionary factory. Its head is heavy and blunt, and it has a shaggy white beard and knobby, curving horns that give it a petulant mien. Its stringy black mane is so sparse that it seems to compensate for this thinness by having several vertical black slashes on its neck, an arrangement comparable to someone simulating a toupee by drawing black lines on his pate. The bulky shoulders give way to spindly hindquarters and a plumed tail that flails about as with

Plate 38. Wildebeest Portrait. The fairly unbelievable-looking males are distinguished from the equally incredible females by their more massive size, heavier horns, and conspicuous genitalia. Wildebeest have changed very little over the past million years — they are true living fossils.

---

49. "Wildebeest" is Afrikaans for "wild cattle." A White-tailed gnu, or Black wildebeest, once one of the most numerous antelopes in South Africa but hunted to the very brink of extinction and now very rare, can be found in small herds in South Africa (mostly on private ranches and in a few small reserves). The largest herd apparently is that of the Willem Pretorius Game Reserve, located in the Free State of South Africa.

a will of its own. Wildebeest alone seem rather woeful, but *en masse* they convey a strange beauty and power. Occasionally I walked among them. Retreating a few hundred feet to let me pass, the animals near me stood silently, their horns shining in the sun. Those farther back continued their incessant grunting, sounding like a chorus of monstrous frogs. Now and then several animals dashed off in apparent panic only to halt and stare back at me. The air was heavy with odor — earth and manure and the scent of trampled grass.[50]

Of course, it is the wildebeest who is primarily responsible for the most "Pleistocene vision" in Africa, the greatest assemblage of grazing animals left on earth (39). The huge annual migration in the Serengeti ecosystem, the heart of Africa's grasslands, the only phenomenon of its kind anywhere,[51] is essentially a wildebeest affair, though smaller armies of zebras, gazelles, topis, and (locally) kongoni participate as well. Little that the reader will read or hear can prepare him for the sheer grandeur of the migration spectacle. In fact, the experience — in the sights, the sounds, and the smells — is difficult to imagine beforehand, so grand is the scale and so different from anything remotely familiar is the spectacle. The Alan Root film is, as previously indicated, worth seeing as often as one has the chance, but no film can truly capture the personal first-hand experience. And even those who have seen the migration many times, like the author, never fail to be thrilled by the latest run-through.

The migration is better viewed not as a self-contained event but as a continual year-round cycle of movement, and, indeed, the evidence strongly suggests that the wildebeest have been covering roughly the same cycle within the ecosystem[52] for at least a million years, looking for water and fresh green grass. Today, with the control of the rinderpest virus[53] by introducing successful cattle immunization programs in the early 1960s, the number of wildebeests in the Serengeti system have swelled from 260,000 in 1961 to the almost unimaginable number of at least two million today, increasing during this time at an annual rate of roughly ten percent, probably more than what existed when European settlers first began to colonize Africa. In total numbers for ungulates, the wildebeest now is second only to the White-tailed deer of North America. The increase in animals has been encouraged and supported by a sizeable extension of the grasslands (at the expense of woodlands) and thus the carrying capacity of the ecosystem. In addition, the wildebeests today use more of the ecosystem than when their numbers were considerably fewer, traveling to the farthest reaches of the grasslands.

These statistics (and the increase) are even more remarkable when one realizes that catastrophic droughts, which occur with some regularity in East Africa, will upset the calving rhythm and set a herd back for several years. Thus, the increase was not spread out evenly over the intervening years; during certain periods, the multiplication must have been absolutely spectacular. Although climate and rainfall were the primary favorable factors, the decline of the ungulates during the rinderpest pandemic ironically paved the way for the later explosions: as the grass grew higher, the fires[54] burned with a vengeance,

---

50. *Golden Shadows, Flying Hooves,* pp. 30-1.

51. In the nineteenth century, the Serengeti migrations were rivaled by the great springbok migrations in South Africa. The *trekbokke,* during which literally millions of antelopes were on the move — packed so densely that everything in the path was either swept along or trampled — was periodic, not seasonal. It was unpredictable then, and, today, we still do not know the reasons for this particular migration; the mystery endures to the present time.

52. In the natural world, every plant and animal is part of a constantly changing but interdependent community called an ecosystem. Within the ecosystem, the basic materials of life keep circulating. The most fundamental ecology of the Serengeti is the ungulate-grazing-grassland-fire-climate-forest cycle. Natural boundaries, like large bodies of water, mountains, or other dramatic environmental phenomena, impose limits that help define the outer boundaries of an ecosystem. The Serengeti ecosystem (see map) comprises the Serengeti and surrounding areas in Tanzania and Masai Mara in Kenya. Fittingly, "Serengeti" (deriving from the Maasai language) means "an extended place." The Serengeti Park is nearly the size of Connecticut; the ecosystem is about twice the size of the park. Highlands and escarpments bound the ecosystem on all sides. At least twenty species of large herbivores (some count as many as twenty-eight species of antelopes alone) work the Serengeti system, eleven are grazers, five are browsers, and four eat both grass and shrubs. No part of the vegetation is ignored.

53. Rinderpest, introduced in the 1880s with cattle imported by Europeans, is a virulent disease that kills virtually all the calves and yearlings in a herd. Until 1960, periodic epidemics kept the wildebeest population down to around 250,000 animals. In addition to the successful immunization program referred to in the text, the wildebeests themselves had begun to develop natural immunities and tolerances by the early 1960s.

54. Fire is a major modifying ecological factor in grassland areas. On one level, fire is an integral part of the "normal" Serengeti cycle; up to three-quarters of the park burns each year. After a burn, the grass plants put out new shoots, depending on the reserves of moisture and nutrients stored in their roots. The fires remove the straw or dry stems and leaves that have accumulated during the dry season, which dead matter would inhibit photosynthesis and hence growth. Continued growth depends, however, on the rains: if the annual rains do come, vigorous regeneration of the grasslands follows; should the rains fail, the vegetation will suffer accordingly. In the Serengeti, the climate favors grasses because there are two wet seasons, two annual chances for regeneration. Grasses, unlike many other plants, can survive the roller-coaster climate, as their fibrous root system penetrates deep into the ground and they grow from their base, not at their tips. Or they hold over in seeds. The usual short grass fires have the same effect as grazing or trampling (both which help to insure that the withered grass — the fuel — is short and that the fires are of limited intensity and duration): the grass roots survive, as do the seeds, and new growth comes quickly with the rains. This new growth is high in quality or crude protein content. Normally, the trees in a forest can tolerate the effects of short-grass fires — indeed, the forest acts as a firebreak (certain tree species have even developed fire-resistant bark and especially thick root stocks). The fires will, however, prevent the growth and encroachment of thicket and woodland

Plate 39. *"A Pleistocene Day."* On days like this, the safarist can reach out and touch the distant past. Many antelopes, the wildebeest included, can take advantage of periods of high nutrition to store fat. Wildebeest mow their way across grasslands like lawnmowers. Nevertheless, the gnus (in common with other antelopes) never overgraze an area as domesticated cattle might. The latter will simply destroy a grassland, if not driven on; the former instinctively stop short of causing such destruction and move on voluntarily. Indeed, antelopes graze to the point of *stimulating* grass production (like lawnmowers).

invaded the forests, and killed the trees. Thus, the grasslands spread as the woodlands diminished.

The migration story begins — as all true cycles do — when and where one wants to begin, but the preponderant part of the calving takes place in the southeastern treeless, short-grass plains (see map) within a three-week period falling in January-February. The earth here is enriched with calcium and phosphorus, minerals essential for healthy bone growth. The fresh new grass — this

period is the rainy season — in these ancestral calving grounds supplies these minerals needed by the young calves. Moreover, the flat vistas enable the herds — especially the slower pregnant females and, soon thereafter, the calves themselves — to see the predators coming from a long distance. But the main anti-predator device is simply the overwhelming number of calves delivered in such a short space of time.[55] Considerably

___

into the great expanses of grasslands (grasslands that are maintained by regular fires and grazing are called "derived"). The complexity of the cyle is enormous — obviously, the short-term benefit (to the resident herbivores) of the fires depends on the timing of the following rains and a host of subsidiary factors. The natural cycles are, of course, centuries long.

55. Fully eighty percent of the calves arrive within a three-week period; the female wildebeests are able to synchronize delivery, as if the herd itself had a collective communal womb. It should be understood that the glut of births is not likely *caused* by predation pressures. The basic point of seasonal breeding is usually to deliver calves into a world containing an adequate food suppy. The cycle does *serve* the wildebeest well in its "relationships" with its predators, and antipredator strategy probably

more than one-half million calves are born! Eventually, only one calf in five or six survives the first year, but that percentage suffices. Even working overtime, the lions, hyenas (especially the hyenas), wild dogs, and other predators can kill only a meager percentage of the initially helpless newcomers.[56] The glut of calves simply swamps the predators.

And the precocious calves develop quickly: a youngster can walk within minutes of birth, is nursing within ten minutes, can run within half an hour, and, within a day or two, can keep up with the herd. In a remarkable two to three days, the baby can run nearly as fast as an adult! Moreover, the juvenile is grazing some ten days later. The reader can only imagine what an incredibly noisy, confused time calving represents — a deafening cacophony of honking, bleating animals. The air is full of the joy of new life and the ululation of distress. The pregnant mothers do not seek seclusion like most other antelopes and simply lie down, dozens at a time in closely packed maternity herds, and give birth right in the middle of the herd. Suddenly, the plains are dotted with tottering light brown calves. A few predators dart in and out of the herds, dramatically increasing the bedlam. A newborn calf has to "imprint" on its mother by suckling. Mothers come to recognize their calves by smell. The calves recognize their mothers by sound. Considering the vast numbers involved, both systems, when they work, are nothing short of miraculous. In the great confusion of calving, newborns often separate from their mothers and wind up totally lost, especially if separation comes before imprinting. To make matters worse, a nursing mother will not accept an orphan calf. Lost calves are a pitiful sight and will follow or trot toward anything that moves — including safari vehicles *and* predators.

_____

is responsible for squeezing the actual calving into such a short period of time. The same considerations may well apply to the *statistical* result that herding reduces the odds of ending up on a carnivore's plate; certainly, herding has significant motivations other than anti-predatory concerns, as noted earlier.

56. The placentas or afterbirths are devoured by vultures, eagles, and jackals. The jackals are, in fact, tolerated within a few yards of calving mothers, because they do not threaten the calves themselves. The months of January and February in the southeastern Serengeti are as close to heaven as the predator population ever experiences in Africa. The predators do not, however, dramatically increase their numbers, because they are essentially non-migratory and must also sustain themselves in the absence of the vast herds. It should also be emphasized that the largest part of calf mortality is due to the rigors of the trek and not predation. When considering the migration experience, one needs to modify slightly the assertion made in Chapter IV that the predators kill only when hungry and consequently eat (when they can) what they kill. Lions in particular, when confronted by the surfeit of prey, seem to kill more often, eat less of a given carcass, and leave more to the scavengers. The author has not seen a satisfactory study that deals with the interrelationship here between opportunity or temptation and instinct.

Only mothers — and they only occasionally — come to help a wildebeest calf caught or threatened by predators at this time. A sense of destiny settles over the calving grounds, but mother and newborn calf normally can count on the remainder of the day to organize themselves. As indicated earlier, births take place primarily in the morning; every moment counts on the savannah. The most popular calving time coincides with the end of an early morning grazing sequence. Predator pressure each day wanes by mid-morning; the safarist will see the predators basking in the early morning sun, their distended bellies testimony to the previous night's hunting.

By the end of May,[57] most of the vegetation in the short-grass plains has dried up — the grass withers quickly at the onset of the dry season — and, just as important for the wildebeest, drinking water is rapidly disappearing. There is no permanent water in the short-grass plains, only surface water lying in hollows and natural depressions. If not replenished by rainfall, the hot sun and millions of drinking antelopes (and zebras) make quick work of what drinking water is left. Calves are suckling, and mothers in particular need substantial amounts of water. Thus, huge herds begin to mass in preparation for the trek to the wetter west and north. This is the time of the greatest concentration and an absolute wonder to see. And hear. Wildebeest are never silent; even when grazing, the constant mumbling and grunting, as well as the very noise of harvesting and chewing grass, causes the large herds to sound from a distance like the drone of active beehives.

The wildebeest have just spent several months of grazing up to eighteen hours a day, storing up food and energy. The bounty of the short-grass plains has brought them into peak condition for their long journey. The Burchell's zebras leave first, perhaps as many as a quarter million strong, followed by well over a million wildebeest, and, finally, some 500,000 gazelles (mostly

_____

57. It should be emphasized to those planning to take in some part of the migration that the actual times of various movements change from year to year. After all, natural phenomena such as rainfall trigger the activity and these are never precise. Some naturalists speak mysteriously about factors (presumably genetic) other than grass or rainfall that drive the wildebeest. That may be, but the natural factors set the genes in motion. No two migrations are exactly alike, and only the general drift is predictable. Sometimes, the wildebeest even doubleback when a freak rainstorm occurs behind them, and, as discussed later in the text, some wildebeest herds are practically sedentary where food and water are available all year. The approximate dates given in the text represent historical averages, so to speak. Furthermore, the migration in some years will be more pronounced than in others — again, the severity of the natural conditions causes modifications. The safarist on a one-time shot must secure expert advice to ensure the best opportunity of pinpointing (within the usual *week* allotted) what he wants to see.

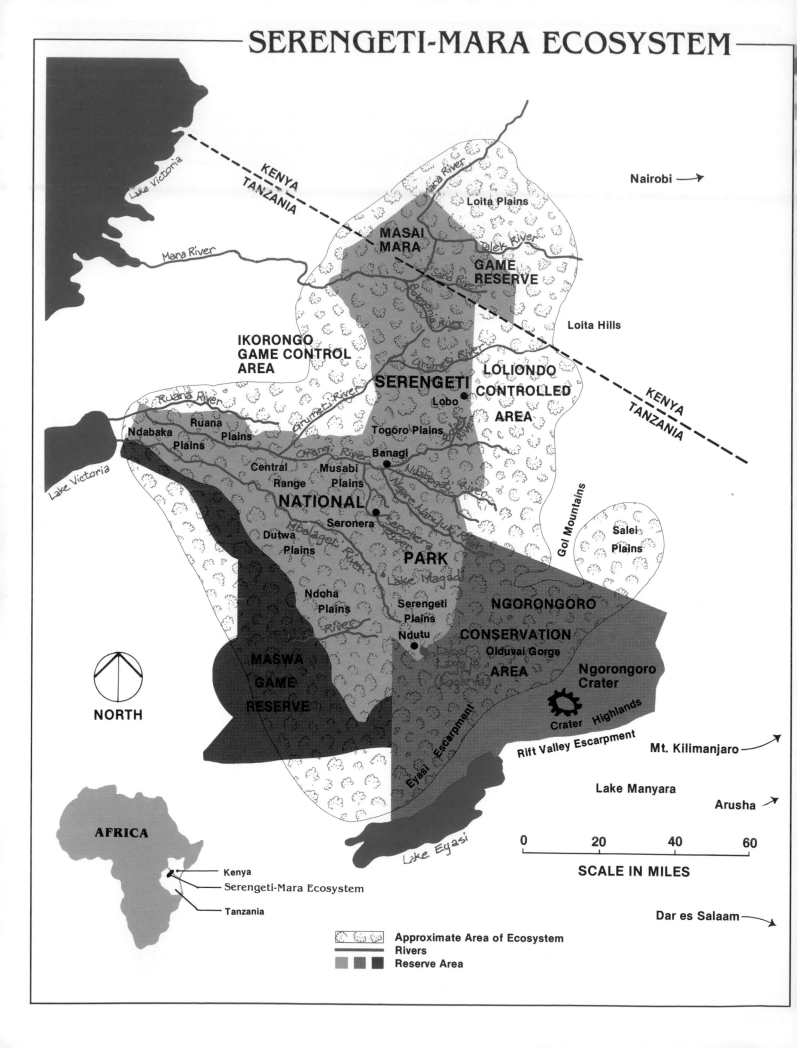

SERENGETI-MARA ECOSYSTEM

Lake Victoria

Mara River

KENYA
TANZANIA

Nairobi →

Loita Plains

MASAI
MARA

Mara River

Talek River

GAME
RESERVE

Loita Hills

IKORONGO
GAME CONTROL
AREA

Sand River

Bologonja River

SERENGETI

Grumeti River

LOLIONDO
CONTROLLED

KENYA
TANZANIA

Ruana River

Lobo

AREA

Ndabaka

Ruana
Plains

Ruana
Plains

Togoro Plains

Grumeti River

Lake Victoria

Central
Range

Orangi River

Musabi
Plains

Banagi

Ndabegati River

Gol Mountains

Salei
Plains

NATIONAL

Seronera

Seronera River

Mbalaget River

Dutwa
Plains

Ndoha
Plains

River

Lake Magadi

PARK

Serengeti
Plains

Ndutu

NGORONGORO

CONSERVATION

Olduvai Gorge

AREA

Ngorongoro
Crater

MASWA

GAME

Lake Ndutu
(Lagaja)

Crater Highlands

RESERVE

Eyasi Escarpment

Rift Valley Escarpment

Mt. Kilimanjaro →

NORTH

Lake Manyara

Arusha →

AFRICA

Lake Eyasi

Kenya
Serengeti-Mara Ecosystem

Tanzania

Dar es Salaam →

0   20   40   60

SCALE IN MILES

Approximate Area of Ecosystem
Rivers
Reserve Area

"Tommies") trail behind. The order of movement is influenced by the grazing cycle: the zebras eat the grass tops and the taller, coarser grasses, low in protein and high in fiber; the wildebeest eat the lower, more nutritious parts of the grasses; and the gazelles prefer the fresh shoots of new, replacement grass. The initial movement heads into the long-grass plains and woodlands to the west and north, reaching well into the so-called "Corridor," where permanently flowing rivers that eventually empty into Lake Victoria have their headwaters (see map). By July, a large contingent of zebras (again, first) and wildebeest — the gazelles for the most part remain in the central woodlands and western Serengeti — head north and northeast all the way to Masai Mara, which has the highest rainfall in the system, permanent water in the Mara River and its tributaries, and frequent out-of-season rainstorms. (The rainfall gradient for the entire ecosystem runs from the drier southeast to the northwest.) The animals on the trek usually follow clearly defined routes, where millions of trampling hooves over the years have cut deep grooves in the ground (shifting rainfall patterns may cause the trek route to vary in a given year).

Coinciding with the start of the physical migration that begins in late May is the beginning of the mating or rutting season. Wildebeest seem to prefer utter chaos, and the breeding season is no exception. Rutting begins as the wildebeest are milling about, preparing to move off the short-grass plains. The transformation of a gregarious, placid male, who ordinarily has no stomach for fighting anyone (and who, for example, will not even spar with his male companions, as do other antelopes), into an aggressive and arrogant territorial male at rutting time is a metamorphosis worthy of cocoon-butterfly comparisons. Apparently, it is primarily the acquisition of property that stimulates to the fullest the aggressive and sexual hormones, though challengers begin, of course, with only high hopes. Once a bull has been expelled from his particular territory, for instance, he loses his aggressive behavior and sexual attitude. Making a "comeback" is, incidentally, pretty much unknown among wildebeest. Once deposed, retirement is the norm. Only the most vigorous and tenacious bulls succeed in winning prime space. Those who do become determined warriors, intent on maintaining their hard-won superiority. The territorial bull will now stand erect, his head held high to advertise his status — a posture known to naturalists as "static-optic marking." John Wayne aficionados know it as "standing tall." He will also cavort with abandon — racing around in circles, kicking up his heels, bucking, and spinning — an important ritual announcing his status and warning would-be intruders.

Some observers have focused on the relationship between status and territory to conclude that the notion of males fighting during rut for the favor of females is an anthropomorphic fallacy. But the conclusion that the competition for status and territory takes place irrespective of sexual dynamics is more than a little confused. The same

stimuli (whatever they are, exactly[58]) that send the males into the property market send the females into heat. Males confirm by scent what their activated hormones have already told them. The females convey identical messages through *their* behavior. Moreover, the fighting at rut — in the first instance to win and defend a piece of territory — is ultimately nature's selection of the strongest, quickest, most tenacious, most cunning fathers. Nor do wildebeest males acquire territory for food (they actually eat little during rut).

The females wander at random into the piece of territory that the male wildebeest has staked out as his own, and the bull tries to round them up and encourage them to congregate for servicing. The safarist can always recognize herding — the males will be cantering purposely about with their heads erect and with tails stiff, and some females will usually be attempting to escape. The aggressiveness of the territorial males extends even to regulating the number of females allowed into their territories; the males will often chase out female newcomers when some limit has been reached. Strong bulls with a desirable patch of land will nevertheless collect over 100 females at a time. This territorial system ensures that only the strongest males breed with the females. In theory, such a system should also impart a degree of order and discipline, limiting sexual competition in lieu of a grand free-for-all. But, naturally enough, the territorial bulls are continually challenged by roaming bachelors and neighboring bulls. Roaming bachelors are summarily dealt with; most exit without a great fuss, though they do make the initial challenge. Occasionally, a territorial bull will permit one or two additional male 'partners' to help service his herd.

Thus, the herding, challenging, and breeding bring life to a mad pitch. Rutting continues into the actual trek itself, so that the bulls are forced regularly to establish new temporary territories wherever the aggregations come to rest (and remain for about a day). Bulls during this time become so worked-up and excited that many foam at the mouth. Nomad bachelors are so overcome with frustration that they wind up ejaculating in the midst of wild, involuntary pelvic thrusts. Imagine a savannah full of Elvis impersonators.

The patch of territory held by a bull is usually no more than a football field in size. The actual boundaries, surely well-known to the male inhabitant and his closest neighbors and marked with waste and glandular secretions, are impossible for the safarist to determine, but the visitor can easily pick out the so-called "stamping ground," a relatively small bare patch of ground located in the center

---

58. We simply do not know exactly what *triggers* the production of sex hormones in the males. Environmental factors, such as length of daylight, temperature, or food availability, may be critical. Or the female coming into heat may do the trick all by herself — through communication not yet known to us.

WILDEBEEST MIGRATION

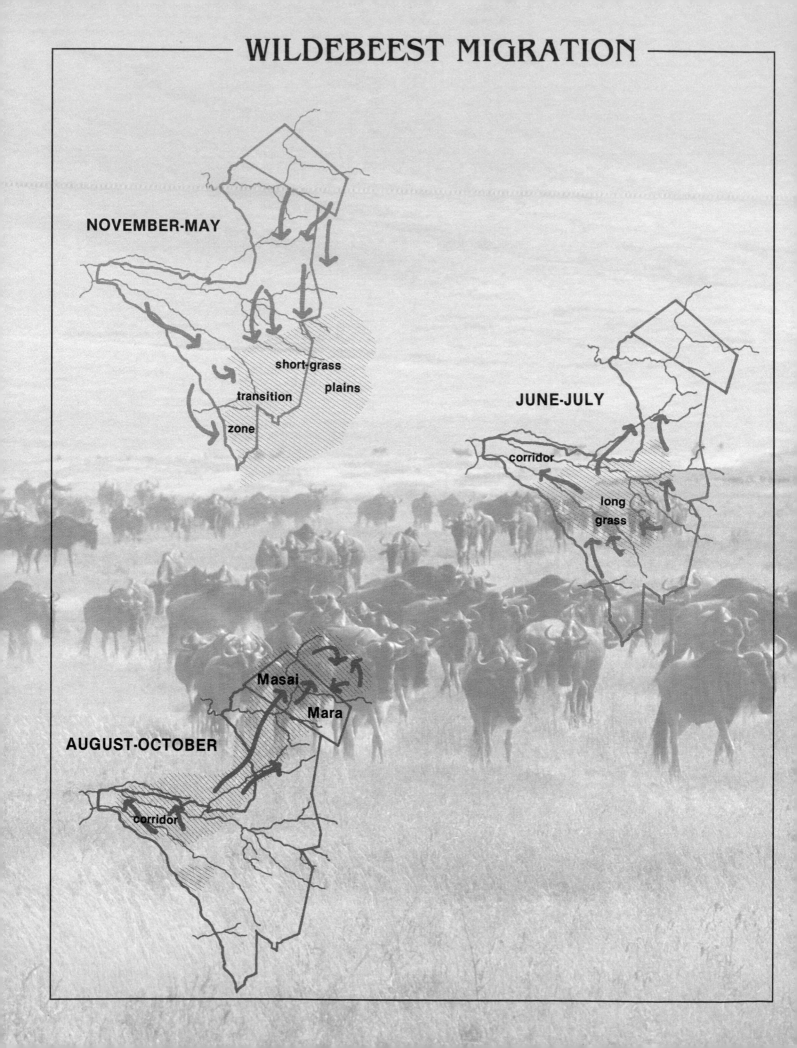

NOVEMBER-MAY

short-grass

plains

transition

zone

JUNE-JULY

corridor

long
grass

Masai

Mara

AUGUST-OCTOBER

corridor

of the bull's territory, where the male passes most of his time. The grass is quickly worn away by constant pawing, kneeling, and horning of the ground — all part of the territorial-courtship ritual. Further purely territorial behavior includes rubbing their faces on the ground (thereby leaving a scent from the secretions released by their preorbital glands; there are also scent glands between their toes) and actually rolling in their own excrement to saturate themselves, each with his own distinctive scent.[59] At other times, the males are content to advertise their presence simply by standing for long periods with head held high, staring into the distance (static-optic marking).

To the onlooker, the most interesting behavior is likely to be the challenge ritual engaged in between neighboring territorial bulls. These fairly complex rituals appear to be simply benign ways of checking on each other, without

bull will move into a position standing sideways in front of the invader in what is called a "lateral presentation" to emphasize the former's size. The two then change into a reverse parallel position and rub their heads on each other's rumps, a sort of aggressive grooming. Both urinate and one or both will test the urine of the other (each is thereby testing the other's hormone levels and thus territorial status) and exhibit the flehmen face or expression. After a round of slow circling, both drop to their knees in the classic rutting combat position *(40)*. They may or may not actually touch heads. If the heads are butted together, the noise from the clashing horns can carry a great distance. Alternatively, they may not touch at all but instead horn the ground, tearing up bits of turf in what appears to be redirected aggression.[60] The challenge is often ended by both jumping up and staring into the distance at some imaginary threat, snorting in mock alarm. This

Plate 40. The Challenge Ritual. Endless variations and all bluff.

having to resort to real combat, and maintaining the dominance status quo. Each day, each immediate neighbor enters the territory of another bull. Were the intruder simply a nomad bachelor, he would be ejected without ceremony. A neighbor of equal rank and status requires more tact. The ritual lasts anywhere from a minute to a half-hour and always varies. There is no set pattern or series of postures — the variations are many, their order is variable, and any sequence can be repeated (or not) — but the following is a representative progression. The invader approaches the stamping ground slowly, grazing nonchalantly the whole time. The challenge is not, however, performed on the actual stamping ground itself. The resident

disengagement reduces tension and allows a mutual release without surrender or loss of face. One or both may then go into a typical wildebeest cavort, bucking, kicking, spinning, and leaping about. One or both may even react by suddenly and completely relaxing, perhaps going so far as to lie down, and chewing its or their cud. Soon, the

59. Most antelopes do not roll in the mud and dust like other ungulates.

60. All antelopes in fact engage in what naturalists call "displacement activity" — concentration on some commonplace activity that results when (here) there is a conflict between the natural tendency either to fight or to retreat. Such behavior is most likely to happen at points of equilibrium. Although common in conflict situations (and, indeed, it often becomes a part of the ritual), displacement activity is not confined thereto — it may arise whenever an animal is thwarted in some meaningful way.

invader retreats as he entered: grazing peacefully as he goes.[61]

The dominant male wildebeest at the height of rut has more than just a busy day: he may be trekking, he may be establishing his newest territory, he may be actively marking his stamping ground, he may be herding 'his' females together, he may be covering as many females as possible, he may be chasing out a bevy of nomad bachelors, he may be involved in up to six challenge skirmishes with neighboring bulls. In addition, he has to eat and drink and he has to contend with predation (during rut, the wound-up males are quite aggressive toward possible predators).

Wildebeest rutting actually represents a special opportunity for the casual (but alert) safarist to witness first-hand the establishment of dominance relationships, no matter how short-lived. In regard to many species, the safarist so often faces a *fait accompli:* a dominant relationship has already been created, from which point further fighting (certainly on a regular basis) and possibly even overt aggressive displays decline dramatically. Subordinates generally give dominants a wide berth; status frequently confers the advantage of *un*challenged access to food, water, females, and so forth.[62] In any event, the subtleties often escape the safarist's notice (and field ethologists, I hasten to assure the reader).

Breeding transpires over a short period — thus permitting calving at roughly the same time every year. Gestation takes eight to nine months. Under favorable conditions, more than ninety percent of the cows actually covered conceive (health permitting, a female will give birth each year for the rest of her life); many are bred by several males over a week, the females showing little, if any, preference for any particular male.

Rutting is over by late June, and the breeding groups are

absorbed into highly amorphous larger herds that show little social structure while on the move. In fact, the same individuals rarely share one another's company for more than a couple of days; there are no well-defined subgroupings. The males return to their normal, docile state. The emphasis now is on movement; at this time, the migration can cover thirty miles a day. In July-August, the main migration splits into two groups: one stays in the Corridor region, drifting more and more toward Lake Victoria; the second, broken down into many smaller groups, turns northeast in innumerable, closely packed chorus lines and crosses into Masai Mara (see map).

By August-September, the Mara is normally jammed with the pewter-colored, white-bearded wildebeest (with a significant increase in the zebra and topi populations, as well). The wildebeest graze in scattered formation (41), some cross and recross the Mara River daily, and most engage in mini-migrations of one kind or another seeking more secure areas for nighttime or simply looking for local rainfall. The main social organizations at this time are nursery herds of related females with their young and bachelor herds of bulls.

One remarkable feature of the migration that a safarist may witness at the right time, having obtained the help of a knowledgeable ranger who can guide the visitor to the right spots, is the crossing of water. (42 & 43) No writer whom I have ever read nor any naturalist with whom I have spoken has ever favorably remarked on a wildebeest's intelligence. Indeed, there are times when wildebeests give every indication of occupying the lowest rungs of the I.Q. ladder. One suspects that the animal lingered too long in Darwin's waiting room. Surely, one or two A.C. wires are attached to D.C. terminals. If crossing water were an exam, all wildebeest (who survived) everywhere would be held back, as they say, year after year.[63] For a great many, it would be the final exam.

Wildebeest refuse to go around lakes and refuse to search for intelligent ways to cross streams. Blind and immutable instinct simply drives them to press forward, to swim for it. Wildebeest arrive at the water's edge, like poor souls desperately late for a blind date with chaos, lemmings on their mindless journey prepared similarly to hurl themselves into some Gadarene plunge. Sometimes, it is simply a matter of too many animals trying to cross at one time, resulting in a back-up of bodies attempting desperately to scramble out of the water, thrashing about wildly, rearing up, and climbing over each other and up the bank lying on the opposite side. Many animals simply drown, or are trampled to death, or suffocate, or die

61. As repeatedly emphasized, fighting among all antelopes is rarely fatal — murder on any significant scale would be self-destructive, not adaptive. Intraspecies aggression is instinctive and usually healthy in nature (not only does the competition ensure the breeding of "qualified" males, it helps space individuals beneficially over an available habitat, as well as guarantee the survival of juveniles, and the resulting hierarchy additionally provides leadership and discipline). Nature also ritualizes (and inhibits) actual fighting. Thus, the individual animal benefits from aggressive values, while the species is preserved from aggression's possible toll.

62. Logically, dominance does not need to be demonstrated regularly (of course, in several species, certain physical characteristics signal dominance) for animals that live together. Most animal societies enjoy stability and presuppose the tendency of most members to subordinate themselves. But acceptance of a dominance relationship does not mean that a subordinate will never fight again. A young animal usually fails to oust a mature, experienced rival, but the tendency to fight is innate and the initial failure will not prevent the young adult from trying again against a different, and perhaps weaker and less experienced, opponent (and, ultimately, against a dominant who has aged or otherwise weakened).

63. In fairness, the submersion of the individual into the collective will of the migration "herd" may well remove whatever sense the wildebeest may be predisposed to exhibit in less crowded conditions. The old springbok migrations also contained their share of repeated examples of crowd imbecility. Indeed, thousands similarly were always killed at waterways like the Orange River.

Plate 41. Board of Directors Meeting. Midday during non-rutting times, and with the latest leg of the trek behind, is devoted to lying down and ruminating. The grazers follow fairly routine days. Wildebeest are more social than almost all other antelopes. They frequently rub against one another and lie with rumps and backs touching. This contact is worth a moment's reflection, as much of an antelope's life is devoted to separating itself from rivals and predators. Indeed, the wildebeest's "non-antelope" behavior here may help account for the amazing sexual success of the migratory wildebeest population— that is, the huge increase where the carrying capacity of the grasslands has permitted. Courtship normally is devoted, at least in large part, to reassuring females, who ordinarily share the male antelope's aversion to closeness, as to the good intentions of the suitor. The typical appeasement process may prove more successful with these wildebeests, who obviously have their strong streak of sociability.

shortly thereafter hampered by a broken leg. Equally without reason, wildebeest will try to negotiate a raging, swollen river. They plunge in, disregarding all dangers. Massive drownings inevitably result. For weeks, the waters are darkened by bloated corpses. Often, wildebeest will arrive at the edge of a steep embankment, too steep to negotiate intelligently. But pressure from behind keeps building up, and, eventually, some bellwether — not necessarily a leader; it may even be a sub-adult — jumps and, within seconds, wildebeest are literally flying off the top of the embankment, looking for all the world like pre-Wright Brothers would-be aviators jumping off

their barns. *(44)* An incredible mêlée results — again, dead and dying wildebeest collect in large numbers, bewildering chaos rules in the choking dust — all this *before* the water is reached. Exhausted, the survivors (still a horde) hit the water, many only to drown in the slightest current. Crocodiles wait below the surface to take their victims but, in the final analysis, hardly need to bother. The corpses will collect without any outside help. And the mass confusion continues on the other side, as wearied wildebeest drag themselves from the water only to confront the steep, slippery slopes of the opposite banks. *(45)* After a crossing, one always sees mothers frantically searching for lost calves and lost calves pathetically running from cow to cow (as explained earlier, no cow will accept a calf not her own). The searches go on for days, but failures far outnumber reunions.

Plate 42. *Crossing Water.* Pictured is the most orderly crossing of water by wildebeest that one is ever likely to see. Nevertheless, despite the shallow water, the animals in the single-file column are still trying to climb over one another in their haste and confusion.

Plate 43. *Date with Chaos.* Wildebeest are far from remarkable swimmers. They simply attack water and attempt to thrash their way through. As if frightened by the water, the wild-eyed animals appear to be trying to run on the surface!

Plate 44. *Gadarene Plunge.* In the instance pictured here and typically, a perfectly safe crossing lay only twenty yards away. In the dust, the reader should be able to make out wildebeest tumbling over the edge. Wildebeest have a definite knack for "choosing" the most unlikely crossing spots. This particular group of animals included some topis. In time, they too plunged over the edge. Early witnesses thought that wildebeest panic on river banks was the result of lions engaging in military-like maneuvers, driving the antelopes over the edges. The author can assure the reader that this theory gives too much credit to both predator and prey.

Plate 45. *The "Rewards" of the Other Side: More Dust, Steep Banks, and Sacrifice.*

The author has seen the same group of wildebeest cross and re-cross the Mara twice in the same day. A ritual of calves looking for mothers, mothers looking for calves, and fellow travellers just participating aimlessly. In either direction, the same idiotic route was chosen, only reversed; each day, many died, and many orphans bleated hopelessly into the night.

In September-October, thunderclouds slowly begin to build up over the plains leading southward, thunder can eventually be heard in the distance, and lightning appears on the horizon. Even the smell of rain drifts northward. By November-December, the "short rains" have started, and the movement south (and east from the Corridor) back to the short-grass plains has begun. Long columns of tightly grouped wildebeest can be seen for miles, females heavy with calf, all trudging along in single file or several abreast. (46) Despite the fandangle of the occasional frisky male, the pace is steady: they walk or suddenly all begin to canter, which sometimes turns into a run. (47) The onlooker will not see any reason for running; the wildebeest are not being chased but are quintessential herd animals, so the relentless urge to keep up, to stay with the others, makes the leader the pacesetter or a pacesetter the leader, as the case may be. All the while, as Schaller noted, the deep frog-like grunting continues.

By year-end, the travelers are back in the short-grass plains, where the mothers receive the fresh grass essential to add weight onto the fetuses growing in the last months of pregnancy and the males begin to build themselves up for the rut and all the activity of the coming year. The dramatic rebirth of the short-grass savannahs is one of nature's most impressive miracles. The first tropical rainstorms after a long dry season bring much more dramatic changes than the first day of spring weather in temperate zones. A mere shower of rain in Africa can transform a burnt plain into an emerald-green carpet nearly overnight. Lest the reader take this for exaggeration, the grass shoots can actually grow an inch or more in only twenty-four hours.

The cycle, as we have described the pageant here, closes just before calving. The tapestry of sun — at its brightest when the rains pause — of the bright green grass of the plains, of a powder-blue sky dotted with immaculate white thunderclouds, and of water lying on the top of the land everywhere is the most impressive that nature has to offer.

The entire trek — an eerie combination of age-old biological programming and practical response to hardship conditions — can cover more than 1000 erratic miles, though 400-500 is probably more the average. Despite the huge size of the animal biomass, the great migration imparts a stability to the entire ecosystem: the migrants survive to find new food and water, abandoned areas have time to regenerate, and the predator population along the route is, periodically at least, well fed. To give the migration its proper due, the reader should think of the saga as a fantastic Cecil B. DeMille epic: award each of the in-dividual animals a name and a character and think of the enormity of the sacrifice — to the trail, to the rivers, to the predators — so that millions may live. *Every year.*[64]

Some areas have permanent, essentially non-migratory groups of wildebeest, for example, Ngorongoro Crater,[65] where social behavior follows predictable wildebeest patterns but varies accordingly. The dominant mature males are even more territorial and generally so all year-round. The herds comprise either females and their young, or bachelor (non-territorial) males. The latter are often confined to the poorer parts of the habitat. The female herd is normally accompanied by a single adult male in whose territory the herd happens to be at the time. A young male is ejected from the female herd at sixteen to eighteen months of age and joins a bachelor herd of males-in-waiting or -in-retirement. At four to six years, in its sexual prime, the wildebeest male will attempt to acquire a territory of its own by defeating a dominant male (a defeated male returns to a bachelor herd and "retires") or by squeezing out a territory of its own between existing bulls. The first try is rarely successful, but the young bull perseveres. His chances for piecing together a territory of his own by seizing parts belonging to others improves markedly during the chaos of rut. The network of territories extends over most of a given wildebeest range, more dense in the best grazing areas, less dense in woodlands and other less favored areas. The most desirable territories, in terms of the rut or in terms of grazing (usually coincidental), are held year-round for many years; the dominant males do not choose to risk losing their hard-won positions. That is, the land is far easier to hold than to regain each year during rut. Thus, though the migratory wildebeest's territorial aggressiveness is centered on breeding, the sedentary counterpart exhibits territorial instincts all year. The safarist can, in fact, determine the quality of the habitat at any time by noting the spacing of the territorial males. When a territorial male moves from his own territory to water, he must normally cross other territories. To avoid troublesome encounters, he shows submission by holding his head low and uses well-worn trails. During rut (and sometimes outside rut), challenge rituals develop much the same as described earlier for the migratory animals. A territorial bull must always be up to dealing with his immediate neighbors, who seek constant verification of his adequacy and confirmation that he is their equal.

Even with relatively stationary wildebeest, calving is limited to a few weeks each year between January and April. The calves are born brown and gradually over a few

---

64. All parks have seasonal migrations of some kind (migration being defined as group movement that follows fairly regular environmental patterns): zebras, wildebeests, kongonis, gazelles topis, elephants, oryx, elands, ostriches, and giraffes are all animals that migrate when conditions so dictate.

65. Small, sedentary populations also exist within the Serengeti ecosystem.

Plate 46. Northward. With the Gol Kopjes and the peaceful munching in the Serengeti's verdant short-grass plains long behind and the excitement of rut but a dim memory, after months of dodging ravenous predators from raptors gliding silently through the air to crocs gliding silently beneath the water's surface, and having lived through several frantic massed river crossings, the survivors head into Masai Mara. Different soils, different grasses, *more water* lure them on. The comforting feeling of numbers holds them together.

Plate 47. Southward. On the run, migratory wildebeest stir up dust that rises like clouds from the trails. Most of the running takes place on the return legs of the trip — why, exactly, no one knows. Wildebeest scatter in disorderly groups when alarmed but run single file during migration. Meanwhile, the monitoring vultures sit in the trees — and wait patiently.

months turn grey. Like the zebra foal, a young wildebeest's neck is short relative to his legs, and, to graze the short grass, he must either splay his legs or kneel. (Even adult wildebeest sometimes kneel when they graze.)

For years, casual safarists have been watching the wildebeest earn its nickname "clown of the plains" by going through its bizarre, animated gyrations — flinging itself on the ground, dashing about, leaping, bucking, and spinning with all the abandon of a mad dervish. To the uninitiated, the rodeo routine comes without warning. Then, suddenly, the wildebeest will stop and look back, as if to say, "How am I doing?" The other wildebeests do not, however, seem to pay any heed. Some observers have jokingly (I hope) seen in this "frivolous" activity a faulty sense of balance. Others have written about a "shameless recourse to the melodramatic." The comparison has also been made to circus clowns trying frantically to escape the trained spotted dog around and around the sawdust arena. Many serious naturalists insist that the mad gyrations are instinctive practicing for the next assault by a cat. There may well be some truth in this last explanation — from time to time, at least. Certainly, when a wildebeest runs from danger, it invariably pauses to buck, twist, and lash out with its rear hooves in the manner of a horse. Females do not, however, seem to cavort nearly as frequently or with the same animation as males, and they too would need to brush up on their escape tactics (though the reader may recall the peculiar predation burden borne by the males). In fact, a particularly nasty bite from a tsetse fly or a driver ant (up the nostril) might well explain the same number of sudden cavorts.[66] As we have seen, during the rut for migratory wildebeest and at all times for sedentary wildebeest, territorial bulls cavort to threaten potential competitors, to advertise their claim to a particular patch of ground, and probably also to attract females. A certain amount of activity may even be just a way of letting off steam. Indeed, when a rainstorm begins, wildebeest do a sort of ecstatic rain dance. Whenever the author goes up in a balloon, I look forward to an opportunity to descend on a herd of wildebeest (48). The effect is very much like watching the Yale Marching Band take the field at halftime. Of course, the peculiar form of the basic action, giving the impression of moving in two directions at once, as the animal ducks to the right, say, and then gallops off to the left, is open to interpretation. One interesting hypothesis is that the wildebeest wants to see what is going on behind it without stopping to turn its head; wildebeest do not have the broad angle of vision that most other antelopes have.

In spite of the huge multitudes stretched before him, the safarist should take a moment or two to study the closest individual animals — he may see the scars of an unsuccessful lion attack, or some oddity that makes an already preposterous animal seem even more silly. (49)

Moreover, before leaving the wildebeest, the visitor should realize that the Serengeti, in common with all ecosystems, will change in the future, perhaps dramatically. Today, the area is probably at or near the maximum carrying capacity for wildebeest. But the woodlands may well eventually regain their previous position, replacing large areas of grasslands. An adjustment in climate, agriculture on the park's boundaries, the incidence of fires, the elephant population, and so on — any or all could promote such a result. Nor can one count out the bovine virus rinderpest, which once decimated nearly ninety percent of all wildebeest in East Africa. Today, few (if any) individual wildebeest have been naturally immunized against rinderpest — the last animal to have survived "yearling disease" is gone. In 1982, as Tanzania's economic difficulties curtailed the country's veterinary services, there was yet another outbreak of the deadly virus, though it was confined to cattle and buffalo. And, who knows, if not rinderpest, perhaps something else.

From a tourist perspective, the main "beneficiary" of the increased migration has been Masai Mara in Kenya. Slowly, as the trek has reached farther and farther north and has also increased so in size, more and more wildebeest and zebra inevitably have appeared year-round in Masai Mara. The truth is, not all the migrants return from whence they came. The local carnivore population, mostly lion prides, has correspondingly increased. Earlier, I emphasized that a larger migration per se would not lead to a proportionate rise of predators, principally because the hunters do not migrate and have to make do twelve months a year. Moreover, the territorial systems[67] of the big cats and hyenas (and most other predators, as well) even prevent large numbers of predators temporarily gathering to take advantage of any short-term glut in the market. Nevertheless, the Mara has the ability to sustain a larger permanent herbivore population that heretofore (in our lifetime), and the lion prides have grown in response. Finally, it is not difficult to draw a fairly direct correlation between lions and tourists.

11. Gerenuk.[68]

Gerenuks, sometimes called "Waller's gazelles," usually surprise the first-time safarist: more often than not, the visitor finds these antelopes nimbly upright on their hind legs feeding (50). In fact, gerenuks are perfectly comfortable in this stance, their normal dining posture. They frequently remain upright for hours. The front legs are used for balance or to reach up and pull branches within reach.

---

66. A more deadly explanation might be a botfly or another parasite eating into the brain.

67. Of course, the territorial behavior is, in large part, a *consequence* of the need to ensure the residents that their homes can sustain them through lean as well as fat times.

68. Allied to the gerenuk are the many different gazelles, springbok, impala, and dibatag.

Plate 48. Under a Balloon. The gyrations are guaranteed to be spectacular. Wildebeest stamp, prance, gyrate, snort, and buck at the slightest provocation. The vigorous activity is so frenetic, complex, and unorthodox that it defies categorization. The legs are kicked out at angles that belie anatomical study. Suddenly, one or more will stop dead and stare at the safarist, legs quivering, as if to ask: "How am I doing?" Posturing? Nerves? Practice? To be continued.

Plate 49. Upside-Down Horn.

Gerenuks very seldom graze but rather browse on prickly bushes and thorn trees, eating the tender leaves and green shoots. Reaching up to seven or eight feet, they feed below the giraffe and above most other browsers. Gerenuks live mostly in open, dry country that contains little grass but a fair amount of scrub. They have adapted so well to a desert-like environment that they absorb all their moisture requirements from browsing. To the author's knowledge, no one has ever seen a gerenuk in the wild take a drink. The gerenuk moves around a great deal as he eats — indeed, he is a very selective feeder. The author has never seen, in person or in pictures, a gerenuk that was anything but sleek and fat, even in extremely arid conditions, a testimony to the high quality of a gerenuk's varied diet.

Gerenuks live singly or in small groups of up to seven

Plate 50. Giraffe Gazelle. The gerenuk is known as "swala twiga" in Kiswahili, or "giraffe gazelle." "Gerenuk" itself is a Somali word for "giraffe-necked." The point is, of course, the animal's exceptionally long neck and elongated limbs. Gerenuks also have a long tongue, delicately pointed muzzle, and mobile lips, in the same manner as giraffes. And, like giraffes, they occupy a distinctive eating niche. Samburu in Kenya is the ideal place to locate these antelopes; they are easy to see there but notoriously difficult to find elsewhere. Triangular front hooves can help brace the gerenuk during its acrobatic search for food, but, as the reader can see here, the animal can balance itself quite nicely, without propping itself against anything substantial.

head. The males are strongly territorial and individually hold territories a few square miles in size. A group of females (up to six) and young habitually live and feed within a given area; additional females may wander in from time to time. The territorial male is usually found feeding with one or two resident females *(51)*. Gerenuks can mate at any time of the year when the females come into heat; no particular breeding season has been noted. Gestation lasts about seven months. Adult females frequently conceive soon after giving birth, so that many females remain in virtually continuous pregnancy — further testimony, incidentally, to the variety and quality of the gerenuk's diet. *(52)* Newborns are hidden from predators; the mothers feed during the day well away from the fawns and return to nurse only in the evenings.

We do not know whether the borders of territorial males are static or whether they overlap. Territories may not even be contingent — the gerenuk males seem well spread out and apparently fight each other very little, if at all. They do, however, take extensive time to scent-mark their territories (boundaries?) with secretions from anteorbital glands situated at the outer corner of each eye. Chemical substances secreted for signaling purposes are called pheromones.[69] Such communication can be far more effective than sound, especially as the pheromones can be expected to last for awhile. Obviously limited by the prevailing winds, such scent-marking can nevertheless be used to demarcate extensive territories without the necessity of expending frequently huge amounts of energy.

Plate 51. Male with Friends. The female gerenuks have no horns. Gerenuks have a white ring around their eyes, extending as a streak toward the muzzle. Of all the antelopes, gerenuks are probably the closest to exclusive browsers. The does seem to lead in selecting new browse; the male follows. All ungulates can rear up on their hind legs (especially to mate), but the gerenuk is unique in assuming a nearly straight vertical stance at full stretch. Moreover, this is true bipedal maneuverability, as the antelope steps sideways around a bush, all the while continuing to feed.

Plate 52. Picky Eaters. The long neck is most noticeable when the antelope has descended from its bipedal stance and is strolling off to find its next meal. Gerenuks will eat nearly 100 different plant species, changing with the seasons. The safarist will see them carefully investigate a shrub before eating; often these picky eaters will wander considerable distances to find what they want. The short tail of the gerenuk is invariably tucked between its legs.

---

69. Feces and urine can also be used for scent-marking but are not considered pheromones. In addition, the latter normally are much stronger smelling, and their scent endures longer. One should not, however, draw the conclusion that animals using pheromones are more seriously territorial than those who rely upon waste material. These last may simply have different strategies for imposing their claims. Nevertheless, the extensive use of pheromones probably signals less reliance upon physical aggression.

A medium-sized antelope, the impala is also an extremely versatile, and hence successful, animal that can thrive in several different environments. (So successful that in some areas it is unflatteringly referred to as the "bush cockroach.") It can be found in large numbers from South Africa to Kenya. Impalas prefer to live in "transition zones," areas that represent a transition from one kind of habitat to another but that always have some cover. Thus, they generally do not live on the open plains or in dense forests but do, for example, inhabit thick woodland savannah.[70] Of all the ungulates, with the possible exception of the bushbuck, impalas ("swala pala" in Kiswahili) are the most specific to a particular habitat and show no seasonal movements. *(56)*

Social organization is intricate but highly flexible at the same time. The impala's range — whose total size is determined by the availability of water or food — is divided up into a series of plots each occupied by its aggressive male defender. For many years, observers reported males leading permanent (large or small) "harems" of ewes (or does) without regard to particular territorial considerations. We now know that capturing a patch of ground comes first and that the females themselves are far from passive. Only by obtaining a territory does the male gain

Plate 53. Tsavo Vista. The gerenuk's first reaction to danger (or possible danger) is to freeze. If the safarist is close enough when the gerenuk is discovered, he will capture a good photograph. This photograph was taken in Tsavo East, along the Voi River. Rising some 3,500 feet in the background are the Chyulu Hills, a volcanic chain forty miles long and one of Africa's newest mountain ranges (many of the cones are so young that they remain virtually free of vegetation). Water flows underground from the Chyulus to Tsavo's several springs, including the well-known Mzima, which alone produces some fifty million gallons daily.

12. *Impala*.

To most people, the impala probably represents the quintessential *antelope*, what they think of when the word is mentioned. The impala moves on its own stage with all the incredible grace and clarity of a typical Balanchine dancer. And looks like the animal world's equivalent — lithe, leggy, and fair-haired. (Does one call an impala a ballerina or a ballerina an impala?) With its smooth, glossy red orange coat (punctuated with white underparts, buttocks, chin, and upper throat), velvet black eyes, and fantastic s-shaped, or lyrate, horns *(54 & 55)*, the impala is surely one of the most visually satisfying animals in nature. And the astounding energy, zest, and athleticism of these delicate porcelain figurines never fails to engage the safarist.

---

70. Wooded savannah, so characteristic of Kenya, Tanzania, and Central Africa, is known as "Miombo." This habitat is also favored by elephants and buffalo and supports a great weight of animal life, or biomass, perhaps more than any other environment. Impala also prefer the edges of "gallery forests" found along major rivers.

Plates 54 & 55. Lyrate Impala Horns. Every pair of heavily ring-ed horns is different. The longest horns are two to three feet in length. Only the males carry horns, which break easily and are too angled and long for really effective fighting. Indeed, large horns do not correlate directly with hierarchical position. The thickness of a male's neck and the general condition of the animal count for more than the size of its horns. Horn growth, incidentally, is not, after youth, a reliable guide to age. One theory for the spirals and ridges of horns is that they are "safety devices" which keep the horns from slipping during ritual head-wrestling and causing injury. Such a function would emphasize the social significance of horns, as opposed to effective weaponry. Impalas may, however, not be the best examples to use here; males *do* try to stick one another.

looking around for lions! At the peak of a rut, an impala ram may roar nearly 200 times in an hour!

The territorial male vigorously defends his territory against other males. He distributes his unique smell over the ground by frequent defecation and urination and by rubbing an oily secretion produced by skin glands found on his forehead directly onto the area's vegetation. (Impalas also have scent glands located just above the heels of the hind legs concealed in tufts of black hair.) Territorial males — because fighting tends to be a serious affair with impalas and because it is important to preserve energy — will, however, allow bachelors to pass through or even feed in their territories, so long as the visitors ignore the females and exhibit the proper deference to the land-holders. In other words, challengers are readily joined, tourists receive a free pass. Young males — distinguished by their small horns — frequently joust (mild butting and horn "rotation") among themselves. By one year of age, they have normally been ejected from their herd of birth by the territorial male. They wander alone for a period,[71] then join a bachelor herd. Thereafter, through a sort of continuous elimination tournament within the bachelor herd, winners about three years old emerge to challenge the territorial males (58 & 59).

Contrary to some reports, estrus in females is not strict-ly limited to certain seasons,[72] and a large herd will keep a male in rut pretty much the entire time that he retains his territory. As previously indicated, fighting between males in rut nearly always involves physical contact, unlike, for example, wildebeest contests. The usual sequence is for the two combatants to stand head to head, lock horns, and push and twist trying to throw the other off balance. This challenge sounds benign enough; indeed, males seldom seriously injure one another. But not for lack of trying. Underneath the apparent ritual, the struggle is

access to females for mating — in fact, females in estrus will assiduously avoid non-territorial males. The females, usually in herds *(57)*, enter a particular male's territory, and the game is on: the resident male actively tries to herd the females to retain them within his territory, but the females sooner or later intend to leave. Female impalas normally traverse the entire impala home range in search of food and water. An individual male's territory does not hold enough food for a sizeable female herd. But even a small group will not remain to the point of exhausting a given plot. Consequently, the males have to forgo the proud posturing and work hard to hold the fleet-footed does for any serious length of time. The strategies are many, including professing alarm at some non-existent predator supposedly lurking just outside the boundaries (the safarist will see the male suddenly stop and look off). The active chasing becomes a bit frantic as the females near the boundaries. The safarist often hears at this time a deep "roaring" or honking call from the male — the visitor is hereby forewarned not to embarrass himself by

71. At this time, the male impala is most subject to predation. The heavy toll taken may well account for the far greater number of adult females than males. Males are sexually mature at twenty months.

72. The reproductive cycle of all herbivores is, to some degree, linked to the annual pattern of rainfall. The reader by now is well aware of the dynamics involved: a female must build up her fat reserves to cope with the stress of lactation — thus, a substantial delay necessarily intervenes between births, a delay that in turn places a premium on calving at a time when food will be plentiful and the calf has the best chance of surviving. Even in species (like impalas) where estrus individually occurs in all months, births tend to be at least concentrated around the rainy seasons. In equatorial East and Central Africa, peak calving periods are associated with the two wet seasons. In Southern Africa, which has a single rainy season, an obvious peak lasts for approximately one month. Synchronized calving necessarily presupposes syn-chronized breeding. As might be expected, an intense period of rut among impalas leads to a concentrated display of chasing, roaring, and fighting. But, as explained in the text below, where rutting is truly concentrated by climatic extremes, the "impala" social system breaks down.

Plate 56. Ewes on Forest Edge. The reader sees six impala, but this particular patch of riverine forest contained sixty-six of the animals, too dispersed for the camera to record. Golden tan herds this large moving through the thicket are an unforgetable sight. The antelopes here look especially alert, but a member lying down is a giveaway to a relaxed posture. Impala prefer trees for cover but like grasses as food (with supplemental browsing).

Plate 57. Female Herd. Female or breeding herds can, in fact, number in the hundreds. There is a great deal of social activity within a herd: individuals will lick one another on the head, throat, and chest, and their activities are closely coordinated. Nevertheless, the females do not exhibit permanent bonds, and a herd is best viewed as a gregarious but loose association. This small group also contains a young male. He appears to be more than a year old, making his presence unusual and surely temporary. Impalas are mixed and somewhat opportunistic feeders: they eat the short grass and browse on flowers, fruits, seeds, and the leaves of trees. Especially preferred are acacia; like elephants, impalas eat the seed pods of *Acacia tortilis,* and the seeds pass through the animal's system, where gastric juices soften the outer covering of the seed, allowing it to germinate later. Impala feeding patterns are important clues as to why the does appear so restless, why they refuse to remain for

long within a given male's territory. Moreover, the physical condition and number of impala present is always a fair indication of the general health of the prevailing habitat.

Plate 58. Mercutio and Tybalt. Like Shakespeare's proud young aristocrats, impala males fight frequently and for more than sport. (The female Grant's gazelle pictured is an innocent bystander and not the object of this conflict.) But even the territorial males are not uniformly aggressive. Indeed, impalas are complex and flexible animals. The male impala lives a life webbed with both submissive and aggressive relationships. A subordinate male traversing a piece of territory and not there for a challenge approaches the dominant member with his neck stretched forward in a vulnerable gesture, sniffs the latter's forehead, and is permitted to bound off on his way. As might be expected, the territorial males are most aggressive during rut.

Plate 59. Typical Displacement Activity. A part of all antelope ritual, even between the more serious fighters.

serious and fierce. Each animal is not simply attempting to "throw" its rival in some antelope version of a sumo-wrestling match. Rather, any advantage gained in balance is followed immediately by an attempt to impale the loser. The surprising paucity of deaths (and, even more remarkable, serious injury) results from the protection afforded by the especially thick layer of skin that covers a male's head and neck. Thus, the most successful males are usually not those with the most impressive horns, but those with the thickest necks and toughest hides.

The life of the territorial male is not easy. The queue of bachelors, battle-wise from intra-herd skirmishes, is long. For their part, the females seem to appreciate little the effort that goes into winning a territory: while they will not mate with any other than a territorial male, they drive him to exhaustion much of the time by trying to escape. The males quickly lose condition as the energy spent on fighting, evicting bachelors, herding, courting, and mating make holding a territory a costly proposition. Consequently, the males do not maintain their territories longer than three to four months. Even shorter in peak rutting periods. Unlike wildebeest males, however, many defeated impalas rest up and later stage a comeback (after working their way up the bachelor-herd hierarchy again), often to regain their precise former territory.

The availability and dispersion of food and water affect not only the size of the impala home range and individual territories. Rainfall has profound effects on the basic social system as well. In areas where predictable and prolonged dry seasons exist, the females come into heat on a more seasonal basis. Thus, rutting tends to be concentrated, and a system of full territoriality, which works best under good environmental conditions, is not maintained throughout the year. As the dry season lengthens, and food and water become scarcer, females have to pick up the pace of their wandering and cover more ground daily. Normally highly gregarious in herds that often swell to 100 or more, the females now divide into many smaller groups. Obtaining water especially becomes a problem. During the dry season, an impala must find water to drink nearly every day. Thus, more and more groups of females move rapidly through the males' territories. Males who attempt to maintain a strong posture under these circumstances become strung-out in a hurry. Most do not try, and strict order breaks down. During really dry seasons, the bachelor herds will mix with the female herds, and boundary disputes are rare.[73] The territorial males take the opportunity to mobilize their fat reserves for the future rutting frenzy.

The safarist (and reader) should always realize that the broad social patterns described in the discussions on a certain species may give way to what seem like peculiar anomalies from time to time in the wild. We have just seen that normal impala social organization breaks down, logically enough, during a prolonged dry season. Ironically, a habitat of superabundance may have a similar effect. In Akagera Park in Rwanda, for example, impala density reaches as high as 1000 animals per square mile along the lakes. It should be clear that the level of 'normal' aggression that would be required to sort this lot out would be such as to inhibit any breeding whatsoever. Elsewhere in this book, the tendency of other animals to moderate their aggression and adjust their social patterns during periods and in environments of high local density is noted. Impalas also adjust and, under the circumstances just described, live in large mixed herds of many adult males, females, and young. Again, territoriality gives way to more communal living.

Impalas differ in some respects from other antelopes when it comes to anti-predator behavior. They herd and therefore rely upon the common principle of more eyes, ears, and noses for detecting danger. Only the most alert safarist will detect the more subtle forms of herd communication: sounds so soft that they are barely audible to the human ear;[74] scents from the glands on the face and feet; visual expression; and pantomime, where the orientation of the body has significant meaning — all these signals can ripple easily through a herd. And herding, as previously explained, causes difficulties for a predator trying to pick out an individual to attack. But impalas put a special gloss on this strategy. If a predator attacks, impalas do not scatter as a unified herd, rather, they explode into leaps in all directions simultaneously, like a violent billiard break. The intention is to confuse the predator and break its concentration. And the leaping ability of impalas is astounding: they can easily clear ten feet in height and thirty feet in length in a single running jump (60) and seventy or eighty feet in three consecutive strides. From a complete standstill, the distance is only slightly shorter and perhaps even more impressive.

Actually, impalas prefer environments where (it so happens that) the cover provides ample opportunities for predators. Thus, impalas necessarily lead very careful lives. They drink mostly at midday. They give birth mostly at midday (calving has not been observed in the wild).

---

73. One could remark that territories accordingly change ownership less frequently — but, at this point, the system of territoriality has taken on an altered meaning, and the comparison has little validity. Prolonged drought also enlarges the home range considerably (though impala are not migratory), and the (by that time somewhat nominal) territorial units increase as

---

well. One could postulate a different result — that the individual territories, limited in some measure by a male's ability to defend only a given amount of land (an obvious fact), would remain roughly the same and that more bachelors would emerge to assume the status of territorial males. This second possibility ignores, however, the sexual motivation underlying the territorial system. During a drought, the emphasis switches to survival.

74. Some of the sounds made are nasal as well as vocal; the front nasal cartilages have evolved into resonance chambers.

Plate 60. Prodigious Leaper. These athletic jumps, apparently made with no effort whatsoever, are equalled in nature perhaps only by porpoises. Many naturalists believe that the impala's distinctive rump markings — diagonal black stripes on white patches — act as a signal for keeping the herd together in times of flight. That is, the impalas behind or off to the side of the leader(s) can follow the direction of escape after the initial confusion. I find this explanation a bit thin. More likely, in my estimation, the markings make for excellent "flash coloration," as the tail, which is white on the underside and operates as a third stripe when lowered, is alternately raised (see plates *61-63*) or held down (as shown here). Indeed, the impala's entire defense mechanism at this time is "disruptive."

Females remain with their newborn hidden in thick bush for several days following birth — they do not leave the young "lying out," as do many other antelopes. The young fawns are subsequently weaned at six months and lose little time in forming nursery herds within the female herds. Despite these precautions, fully half of the newborn impalas are taken by predators during the first several months of life. To help insure survival, the female impalas take a page from the wildebeest book and periodically flood the market.

The safarist should make an effort to see impalas early in the morning, as the sun begins to warm the land. The herd will leave the thicket and come out into the open at this time. One of nature's most enjoyable displays of irrepressible energy and *joie de vivre* soon begins. The visitor must keep a respectful distance and watch the ballet from the back rows, as it were. The youngsters will execute their routines and gambol about with stiffened limbs, at times appearing suspended in the air, at times gliding over fifteen to twenty feet of ground without perceptible exertion. Indeed, one is always surprised when they come down, even if only nimbly to spurn the earth underneath again, so complete is the illusion of flight *(61-63).*

Plate 61. Morning Constitutional. Early morning is frequently a time for play and showing off — both which, for an impala youngster, mean jumping in gravity-defying arcs. In a relaxed gambol, a young impala will leap anything — another impala, ravines, a fallen tree, whatever lies in the path. One rarely sees an antelope of any kind break a leg — a testimony both to remarkable ability and internal engineering (laminated bones and the like).

Plates 62 & 63. Sheer Exuberance. Play behavior is important to all species; in antelopes, the opportunities for play and exploratory behavior are critical for the development of normal fear and avoidance responses.

One of the loveliest sights imaginable is the reddish-golden arc formed by the bodies of a herd of impala as they leap clean over a stream or (so as not to leave any tell-tale spoor) over a wide waggon road. They seem not so much to leap as to fly: and their aerial acrobatics compare with those of other smaller antelopes as the flight of swallows, swifts, or bee-eaters compare with the flight of other birds. (Campbell, *Dark Horse*, p. 75.)

13. *Thomson's Gazelle.*[75]

Joseph Thomson was a young Scottish naturalist (of sorts) freshly graduated from Edinburgh University when he first set foot in East Africa in 1878. "Set foot" is not a figure of speech: he walked across much of Kenya in 1879 and the early 1880s. Thomson was, in fact, the first white explorer to enter "Maasailand." In 1884, he shot an antelope near Lake Baringo that proved to be a new species, later given the name *Gazella thomsoni*. Known to all who live in or leave East Africa as "tommies" (even "swala tomi" in Kiswahili), these graceful little creatures sometimes dot the plains from horizon to horizon:

> Eye, gazelle, delicate wanderer,
> Drinker of horizon's fluid line.[76]

Far and away the most prolific gazelle, the tommy weighs at most sixty pounds. Its pattern is distinctive *(64)*: both sexes show a lateral jet-black band, in direct contrast with white underparts; and the white hindquarters are bordered by a narrow black stripe.[77] The side stripe possibly serves at least three distinct functions. It breaks up the outline of the animal when viewed at a distance, a camouflage of the same type as the forest bongo's. Second, it operates as an alarm signal when the animal uses special lateral muscles to vibrate its sides upon sensing danger. The stripe then looks like a flickering electric sign of some kind. Third, the marking acts as a visual signal to help keep the herds together.

Aside from their incessant tailwagging, tommies are famous for a characteristic gait called "stotting" or "pronking."[78] When alarmed, the antelope will frequently execute a succession of high, virtually vertical leaps, with all four legs held stiffly and the four hooves relatively close together (striking the ground at once), back curved, and the head held down. This wooden, trampoline or pogo-stick motion sometimes goes on for several minutes. (Some writers report seeing stotting for over an hour!)

---

75. There are several gazelles, but the Thomson's and Grant's are the most numerous. Tommies also show significant intraspecific variation. "Gazelle" is an Arabic derivation, originally meaning (like "antelope" itself, which is of Greek derivation) bright-eyed.

76. Stephen Spender, *Collected Poems* (1955), Preludes, 35.

77. A female Thomson's is sometimes confused with a young impala (indeed, the two are often found together). The vertical black rump stripe on an impala intersects the white hindquarter patch; on the gazelle, the same stripe borders the white. The distinction is not always easy to follow in the field.

78. The Southern African champion was the springbok. The early settlers called the antelope a "trekbok" because of the vast migrations witnessed. When agriculture and hunting ended the migrations (by the turn of the century), the "trekbok" became the "springbok," in deference to its pronking. Today, the springbok is South Africa's national animal. Impala and even kongoni pronk occasionally. And who knows what the gnu is trying to do!

Some have put the startling leaps at as high as fifteen feet. The author has never seen more than half that figure. Nevertheless, the auditions for "A Chorus Line" could not have been more impressive. At its high point, the animal seems to hover there, like a bird. The perpendicular rebounding — in William Cornwallis Harris' phrase, "with the elasticity of corks thrown against a hard floor" — betrays not the slightest perceptible exertion.

Naturally, the professional observers have developed many theories for this behavior, not all which (I fear) will survive a clear thought (or two). One school has main-

for ostentatious displays. Second, no evidence exists whatsoever that predators respond and go after a stotting individual, as opposed to some original target. Third, as discussed at the very beginning of this chapter, an active predator has seen and taken an interest in the gazelles long before the gazelles or a gazelle have noticed the carnivore. The most effective defense that a gazelle has is to join a fleeing herd and strictly observe its flight distances. The odds on individual bravado of any kind compare negatively with concerted herd behavior and flight. Gazelles must 'know' this.

Plate 64. Thomson's Foursome. A group of "hyper" tommies, though well spread out, is always a beehive of activity: someone is bound to be urinating, biting violently at flies, or jerking a head up to check the neighborhood (all pictured here). All tommies constantly wag their tails — not so much from side to side, but round and round. Even when the rapt attentiveness of early day gives way to noonday reveries under the hot sun, the tail is moving. One wag has drawn the analogy to windshield wipers out of control. Naturalists, characteristically in a more serious mood, have suggested that this behavior is a recognition signal, like the tail fluttering of certain birds, and possibly an alarm signal when halted. A simple (and thus more probable) explanation is that the tommy is doing what it can to prevent flies from taking their toll.

tained that by stotting an individual altruistically draws attention to itself, while warning the other members of a herd. At least three major errors haunt this analysis. First, gazelles, in common with all herd antelopes, have a great variety of subtle and sufficient communication signals. Tommies can and do, for example, effectively signal alarm simply by ceasing to wag their tails. If more were needed, a simple short snort, a foreleg stamp, and erect neck posture would do — again, I return to the analogy of comparing the herd to a school of fish; the effect of any signal would be nearly instantaneous. It takes so little to bring a herd of gazelles to full attention; there simply is no need

Another common explanation for stotting is that it is a mechanism for conserving energy, when compared to running at full tilt, until a final sprint carries the day. This theory is impossible to accept in its totality. Whether stotting does, in fact, conserve energy relative to running is unknown. Horses and other animals would frequently rather run than trot, the latter gait seemingly causing more wear and tear. Although stotting looks both athletic and effortless, the latter is surely an illusion. Moreover, the author has never seen stotting when the chase was really on and suspects those accounts that purport to have so witnessed. Stotting is basically an up-and-down activity, covers far more vertical distance than horizontal, and is certainly self-defeating if the goal is to move as far as possible, as fast as possible, from an attacking predator. Despite the romantic descriptions, stotting as a means of escape would quickly become a recipe for dinner. Only Jerry Lewis would seek to escape a villain on a pogo-stick. No gazelle would ever pronk in the presence of a closing cheetah, and, at the other end of the spectrum, only when a pack of wild dogs or hyenas is a long way off would the little antelopes still have sufficient doubts as to its intentions. And why take the chance with a slower or less determined lion? The antelope knows its flight distance. If a predator has slipped inside, conserving energy is the least of the target's concerns. With the predator still outside, no energy is strictly necessary, but a cautious individual if so inclined could increase the distance more easily (and effectively) by moving at any speed horizontally and closer to the ground. As we have previously noted, so long as the relevant flight distance is observed, an efficient way to learn a predator's intentions is to move *closer*. Thus, the territorial males often follow the progress of predators who move through their territories.[79]

No, the most logical explanation for stotting is this: the effort is a direct and entirely selfish *challenge* to a predator. Gazelles stot when their intensely acute senses tell them that a predator is near but they are unaware of just exactly where (or who) the carnivore is or (worse) where its partners are. Sprinting away under these circumstances could easily prove terminal. So, the gazelle turns to its springs of tension to announce to any waiting predator that (a) the killer has been discovered and (b) the gazelle is *very* healthy, strong, and fleet. Quite far from altruism, stotting is an intimidating invitation to choose another victim.[80] At least, the predator may hesitate, its concentration broken. The author has no idea of how effective stotting is — whether, in fact, predators are discouraged or do choose another target. In my experience, when predators have rushed toward a herd, it appeared at the time that non-stotting individuals were singled out. But this suggestion is not proffered as scientific observation and may be no better than the 'all-Indians-walk-single-file-at-least-the-five-that-I-saw-did' variety, itself only slightly more reliable than the Just-So-Stories. At least ten different meat-eaters (including birds and pythons) go after gazelles on a regular basis. Not all provoke stotting, of course, but a patient safarist will see the behavior.

Social organization resembles that of impalas: territorial males (the territories are small), bachelor herds, and female herds interact in similar fashion. Females hide their newborn after giving birth in secluded spots away from the herd and purposely graze off at a distance. The young lie hidden for several weeks, and the females return only to nurse and eliminate all waste (and its scent). In the face of danger, the female gazelle will do her best to draw attention to herself and away from the direction of her fawn. Thus, the safarist will sometimes see a gazelle excitedly jump, caper, and "approach" a vehicle. Or, it may pretend to be lame, unable to run away. These are all examples of a female whose fawn is concealed nearby. Meanwhile, the fawn will lie absolutely still — one could touch it, and it would not move. But, in spite of these tactics and precautions, the young are often taken by jackals, eagles, and vultures. Female tommies have been observed actually banding together to attack and drive off small predators, like jackals. By the time that the fawns join the herd, they can run like the wind.

These gazelles are almost entirely grazers (most other gazelles are essentially browsers). The safarist should note the difference, say, from wildebeest feeding. Wildebeest will use their broad muzzles to graze slowly and steadily forward. Tommies with their pointed muzzles will stop to graze in small patches at a time before moving on to another patch some distance away. In fact, the gazelles cover substantial amounts of ground during grazing. Thus, to take a good picture of a tommy, the photographer should get well ahead of the grazing pattern, then wait for the advance. Only a minimum degree of patience is required (65). Tommies will also drink daily, unless they can find sufficient moisture from grazing.

Like the males of most antelope species, the male tommy is worth watching. Males mark their territories either through exaggerated urination and defecation or by marking from the scent glands near their eyes. To the casual observer, this last maneuver looks as if the antelope is

---

79. Other theories of stotting — such as giving the antelope a better view of a predator (or the predator's allies) — do not deserve extensive treatment.

80. Within a large group of gazelles, several will stot at once in the perceived presence of predators. In a vague sense, the message then comes from the herd itself. Of course, several stotting antelopes may confuse a predator and almost certainly break the latter's concentration on any one prey, *provided* that the original target is one of the stotters. The text does not mean to

suggest that a gazelle does not become confused in the excitement of the moment and stot when it should be fleeing. Moreover, mild forms of stotting can frequently be seen in juvenile play. Juveniles probably also stot to improve their mothers' ability to keep tabs on their whereabouts (a lost juvenile will stot repeatedly). And mothers will frequently stot to *distract* (which is not necessarily the same as to *lure*) predators — or a safarist — away from a youngster lying out in nearby grass. The explanation of stotting offered here does raise the interesting question that often arises with regard to cross-species communication. The central dogma of modern ethology is that behavior, like any other aspect of animal nature, has evolved because it benefits the genes of the behaving animal. Stotting obviously benefits the gazelle. How does the behavior of understanding such intimidation benefit the receiver of the communication? The correct answer to this question — and some following speculations — might rewrite a few chapters of ethology.

sticking a blade of grass or twig directly into its eye. A black, sticky tar-like secretion is deposited. When the territories are closely spaced, males fight frequently. The fighting is more physical than ritual, though the close set of the horns help to avert severe skull wounds. Males approach one another in a stiff-necked posture, with horns vertical. When they spring straight forward, the horns clash. They retreat, then butt again. The thrusts and parries are lightning-quick, the horns are rarely engaged, and the result is much harmless banging together. The fighting is typically interrupted to relieve tension: either or both combatants will tear up tufts of grass, attack a nearby bush, defecate or urinate, stand in mock alarm, graze, scratch, or engage in one of several other diversionary tactics.

Plate 65. *Young Tommy.* A tommy always looks at the world (and visitors) with keen, interested eyes:

> *I never nursed a dear Gazelle, to glad me with its soft black eye, but when it came to know me well, and love me, it was sure to marry a market-gardener.* (Charles Dickens, *The Old Curiosity Shop* (1840), Chapter 56: thus spoke Dick Swiveller, Dickens' paradigm profligate young man.)

The male Thomson's horns grow short and straight and at first glance appear capable of inflicting definite harm (at least to another gazelle). The female has small horns; many females seem to have degenerate or misshapen horns, perhaps indicating a gradual evolutionary loss.

14. *Grant's Gazelle.*

Grant's gazelles ("swala granti" in Kiswahili) are often found mixed with Thomson's gazelles, and the safarist may initially confuse the two. Reasonably close observation will, however, readily show the many differences. Male Grant's are consistently larger, as much as three to four times heavier than Thomson's. Thomson's of both sexes are reddish, Grant's are pale fawn. Grant's have longer legs and necks, and the horns of the male Grant's are longer, heavier, and more curved (66). The female Grant's horns are also more developed than those of her tommy counterpart. Probably, the most common distinction made is that the Grant's do not have the black side stripe of the tommy, but this test often fails in the field: some female Grant's do have what appears to be a dark stripe. In fact, the Grant's "stripe," when present, is less conspicuous than a tommy's and also exhibits shading or a shadow band just below the primary band. A Thomson's stripe is, on the contrary, clearly bordered. Nevertheless, in the confusion of a herd, the stripes of both species can look alike. Actually, the most reliable guide[81] is to look at the white rump patch. On a tommy, the patch always ends exactly at the base of the tail (the tail of the tommy is entirely black). On a Grant's, it extends a few inches above the base of the tail (the tail itself is predominantly white). *(67)*

The Grant's gazelle lives on open plains that contain a certain amount of bush and also, less frequently, in thick bush, but never in long grass. The Grant's lives in a broader range of habitats than a tommy but is a far less numerous species. In northern Kenya, it lives in barren, semi-desert conditions and can go without water for several months (perhaps longer). Its nasal cooling system has already been described. Like an oryx, the Grant's frequently seems to ignore the shade and remains out in the sun. A Thomson's will wander great distances while feeding; the Grant's, by preference a browser, will generally stay in one place for quite some time.

The herds of Grant's rarely exceed thirty. The males also are territorial and organize their lives much like tommies, but the patches of territorial domain are much larger — up to a mile in diameter — and the female herds are thus more constant. Territorial encounters between males also are less frequent. Some naturalists believe that Grant's engage in more intimidation, mostly by dignified neck displays *(68)*, and less actual fighting than tommies, but the author has witnessed some serious scrapes, every bit as tough as those between impalas or between tommies, including one fight to the death.

---

81. The Grant's also has a blackish, tent-shaped patch or upside-down chevron on its nose; the tommy has none (or it is inconspicuous). But this last distinction is difficult to use as a field test. Grant's moreover do not wag their tails like tommies. Finally, a tommy has a distinctive jerky walking style, whereas a Grant's moves in a smoother, more upright fashion.

Plate 66. Standing Proud. A full-grown Grant's is an impressive antelope. The ram boasts the biggest horns in proportion to the body belonging to any animal in Africa. Its horns are, however, too grand to do the damage that its Thomson's counterparts can do. The Grant's gazelle is named after James Augustus Grant, another Scotsman, who spent considerable time in Africa (with Speke) searching for the source of the Nile. Primarily a botanist, he discovered the new species in what is now Tanzania. The torn ear pictured here may well be evidence of a previous territorial encounter.

Plate 67. Field Test. Distinguishing a female Grant's gazelle from a male tommy at a glance is not easy. The two gazelles often intermingle.

The redoubtable Samuel Baker has left us with this special description of what was probably a Grant's:

A buck gazelle weighs from sixty to seventy pounds, and is the perfection of muscular development. No person who has seen the gazelles in confinement in a temperate climate can form an idea of the beauty of the animal in its native desert. Born in the scorching sun, nursed on the burning sand of the treeless and shadowless wilderness, the gazelle is among the antelope tribe as the Arab horse is among its brethren, the high-bred and superlative beauty of the race. The skin is as sleek as satin, of a colour difficult to describe, as it varies between the lightest mauve and yellowish brown; the belly is snow-white; the legs, from the knee downwards, are also white, and are as fine as though carved from ivory; the hoof is beautifully shaped and tapers to a sharp point; the head of the buck is ornamented by gracefully-curved annulated horns, perfectly black, and generally from nine to twelve inches long in the bend; the eye is the well-known perfection — the full, large, soft, and jet-black eye of the gazelle. Although the desert appears incapable of supporting animal life, there are in the undulating surface numerous shallow sandy ravines, in which are tufts of a herbage so coarse that, as a source of nourishment, it would be valueless to a domestic animal: nevertheless, upon this dry and wiry substance the delicate gazelles subsist; and, although they never fatten, they are exceedingly fleshy and in excellent condition. Entirely free from fat, and nevertheless a mass of muscle and sinew, the gazelle is the fastest of the antelope tribe. Proud of its strength, and confident in its agility, it will generally bound perpendicularly four or five feet from the ground several times before it starts at full speed, as though to test the quality of its sinews before the race. The Arabs course them with greyhounds, and sometimes they are caught by running several dogs at the same time; but this result is from the folly of the gazelle, who at first distances his pursuers like the wind; but, secure in its speed, it halts and faces the dogs, exhausting itself by bounding exultingly in the air: in the meantime the greyhounds are closing up, and diminishing the chance of escape. As a rule, notwithstanding this absurdity of the gazelle, it has the best of the race, and the greyhounds return crestfallen and beaten. Altogether it is the most beautiful specimen of game that exists, far too lovely and harmless to be hunted and killed for the mere love of sport. But when dinner depends upon the rifle, beauty is no protection; accordingly, throughout our desert march we lived upon gazelles, and I am sorry to confess that I became very expert at stalking these wary little animals.[82]

15. *Klipspringer*.[83]

The klipspringer is rarely seen and then only in rocks. Stocky and powerful, yet extremely agile, this shy and nervous antelope is unique. Its feet are specially adapted to cope with its rocky habitat. The little antelope walks on the blunt tips of its conical-shaped hooves, in a kind of mincing gait, the animal world's equivalent of high-heels. It moves delicately but rapidly by leaping easily from rock to rock on its rubberlike hooves ("klipspringer" is Afrikaans for "cliff springer"). The hooves each have an elastic center and a hard outer ring. A famous jumper, it can land on ledges no bigger than a saucer, and one sees klipspringers scrambling around the most precarious footholds. The hoof tips, though blunt, are also quite narrow and hard-edged and thus dig into loose surfaces. A klipspringer's gait is also said to increase friction with the rocky surfaces, thereby providing better footing up or down vertical cliffs. In any event, the acrobatic klipspringer is a nimble, strong climber.

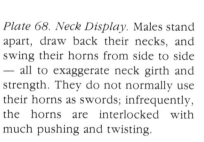

Plate 68. Neck Display. Males stand apart, draw back their necks, and swing their horns from side to side — all to exaggerate neck girth and strength. They do not normally use their horns as swords; infrequently, the horns are interlocked with much pushing and twisting.

---

82. *The Nile Tributaries of Abyssinia and the Sword Hunters of the Hamran Arabs*, pp. 47-9.

83. Klipspringers weigh no more than thirty to forty pounds and stand barely two feet at the shoulder. Other pygmy or dwarf antelopes are the many duikers (forest and bush), suni, dik-diks, oribi, Bate's Pygmy antelope, Royal antelope, steenbok, grysboks (Sharpe's and Cape), and beira. Some scientists would include the chevrotain ("mouse deer"), some would not.

Indeed, the "rock goat" negotiates the rocks about as well as its most common neighbors, the many lizards. All the precision-leaping has led to the speculation that a klipspringer, unlike other antelopes, has at least a form of binocular vision that would permit the precise perception of distance. And the facial configuration supports this conjecture: its eyes are large and widely spaced, and its nose is short and wedge-shaped — thus, the same object (say, the landing strip) can easily be viewed simultaneously by both eyes.

Klipspringers are not very gregarious and are found only in pairs or small family units. *(69 & 70)* The male may be distinguished from the female by its short, separated horns (although the females of one variety have small horns). The best places to look for klipspringers are the kopjes[84] of the savannahs, rocky prominences that jut up

Plates 69 & 70. Sure-Footed "Rock Goats." "Rock goat" is the translation of the klipspringer's Kiswahili name, "mbuzi mawe." Klipspringers can climb almost sheer cliffs. No taller than fourteen inches, they stand usually on a tip of rocks like statues, with all four feet placed close together like goats. Klipspringers have thick coats of fairly long, stiff hairs (the texture is quite brittle) unique to African antelopes. Their grey green color, mixed with reddish yellow, blends perfectly with the granite rock of their habitat. Its facial markings also help to make the Klipspringer inconspicuous in its natural surroundings.

84. Pronounced "cop-ee," and sometimes spelled "koppie," an Afrikaans-Dutch word for "small head," the kopje is also technically known as an inselberg. A kopje, which on occasion looks more like a man-made tower — even a castle — than nature's handiwork, can reach 100 feet above the ground.

from the plains, islands of stone anchored in seas of grass. These are among the oldest rocks on earth, formed millions of years before life began. Kopjes can be viewed as practically separate ecosystems, specialized environments whose inhabitants have made special adaptations. Some of those inhabitants, like hyraxes, agama lizards, baboons, snakes, and klipspringers, spend their entire lives within the kopjes. Others, who basically live elsewhere, find the rocks a convenient source of shade and food, a sometime sanctuary from predators and the ravages of fire and floods alike, and a natural place to nurse their young in seclusion. Many of the food-seekers are looking specifically for klipspringers. Fortunately for the little antelope, its thick, bristly hair comes away in tufts when one persistent visitor — the eagle — drops in for a surprise call and the talons take hold.[85]

The author has watched a leopard in effect pluck a klipspringer: the cat took one leg of the antelope between its teeth and shook the corpse violently through a thorny thicket. Soon, handfuls of the sharp, brittle coat hairs were flying everywhere and covered the undergrowth. The assasin changed its grip to another leg and repeated the procedure. The antelope was virtually bald when the leopard settled down to feed.[86]

Klipspringers are strictly monogamous. When the safarist sees one, its mate is usually only a few yards away. At least one writer has recently come to the conclusion that the animal's monogamy, like the tear-away fur of its coat, is solely a device to thwart predation. Superficially, such an assumption has much to recommend it. So small an antelope is inevitably susceptible to many predators, and the klipspringer must adopt a way of life that serves to increase its chances of survival. The basic observable pair behavior relative to predators is that, while one klipspringer eats, the other acts as a lookout. Of course, there are several other compelling reasons why an animal might follow a monogamous pattern. Monogamy is, for example, often associated with special male care for the young. But the male klipspringer neither carries around its young nor carries food back to the fawn (which is a "hider") or to a pregnant or nursing female. On the other hand, having a reliable sentry clearly enables the female to nurse more freely and eat more when pregnant. Furthermore, males are strongly territorial, and a male's territorial dominance extends over five to ten acres, surely enough room to support more than one female. And females come into estrus only once each year. These last facts would, in the absence of some other strong motivation, argue for polygamy; monogamy would be a highly

unusual strategy — requiring much effort and investment — to insure such brief mating.

The author has, however, cautioned earlier in the chapter against the predation-bias that some single-minded Darwinians have adopted when antelopes are discussed. Monogamy no doubt offers the same temptations vis-à-vis klipspringers that coat color offers in gazelles. But other animals that have at least similar profiles are monogamous (including the dik-dik, discussed below), and predation seems an unlikely motivation for all such instances — at least, unlikely as the sole or predominant motivation (dik-diks, for example, suffer high predation rates). In fact, as suggested here, the agile, fairly well-camouflaged klipspringer with its sheddable coat cannot be an easy target within its rocky habitat even without a nearby sentry. But the main problem with the predator-oriented approach in this species is the apparent assumption that three or four (or more) klipspringers would be less efficient lookouts than two. The klipspringer's immediate neighbor, the hyrax, who also relies on the sentry strategy, believes strongly in numerical strength. The klipspringer's normal environment, among other factors, would prevent significant herding, to be sure, but something approaching a gerenuk's social organization would be entirely feasible. In truth, monogamy is probably not the most efficient protection from predation and results from several converging determinants.

16. Kirk's Dik-Dik.[87]

We began the antelope section with the largest antelope and we end with one of the smallest species, named after its shrill, bird-like whistle, "dik-dik-dik." Of the six variations or species of dik-diks that exist today in Africa, the diminutive Kirk's is probably the one that the average safarist will see (71). All dik-diks are, however, shy and elusive and, though numerous, normally yield no more than a fleeting look.

Dik-diks live in dry and arid bush country, where trees are scattered but where enough thick undergrowth is available for shelter, yet their social system more resembles that of a forest-dwelling antelope. They mate for life and live in pairs; they inhabit a fixed territory (five or six acres normally, but this may vary considerably); they move around pretty much by definite paths; and they are mostly nocturnal. Dik-diks are essentially browsers, with eclectic tastes that cause them to eat throughout their entire range.[88] Dik-diks clearly manage a

---

85. The thick coat also acts as a natural cushion against the inevitable collisions with rocks and thorny bushes. Each follicle is hollow-shaped, with an air-filled core that also provides excellent insulation against the cold winds that can sweep the rocks at night and during certain seasons.

86. A similar event (with a novel twist) is described in Watson, *Lightning Bird*, pp. 29-30.

---

87. Other dik-diks include the Phillips's, Swayne's, Salt's, Darmara, and Guenther's (Long Snouted). The last is very similar to Kirk's but has no white ring around the eyes and a larger nose. The Darmara or Darmaraland dik-dik is the only species occurring in Southern Africa.

88. One occasionally sees dik-diks standing on their hind legs *à la* gerenuks to reach leaves at the top of a shrub. Dik-diks have low water requirements, acquiring what moisture is needed from their diet, and do not drink for indefinite periods.

very nutritious feeding; like the gerenuk, the females are virtually constantly pregnant and thus are lactating while pregnant. They produce two fawns each year and conceive within ten days of birth! The safarist will not witness a birth. The newborns barely weigh two pounds. They pass a period "lying out" in clumps of vegetation, while the mothers move around their ranges. The mother returns to the fawn some four times a day and nurses it for only two minutes or so. A fawn and a mother are actually together for less than one hour every twenty-four. Every few days, a new hiding place is chosen, to keep the smell of the fawn from accumulating in one location. The young are weaned at six to eight weeks. At one year, a dik-dik is fully grown.

Both sons *and* daughters are eventually chased out of the territory (often, the daughter goes before the son!). In common with many animals (including, perhaps, man), the smaller the antelopes, the more ferocious it seems to be. The male dik-dik is a tiny but high-strung terror. (One artist has labeled dik-diks "tremendously condensed,

Plate 71. Kirk's Dik-Dik: Mated Pair. The dik-dik is so small — weighing less than ten pounds and standing a foot to sixteen inches at the shoulder — that it is easy to miss. The second smallest antelope (the suni is smaller) does not herd and is seen singly or in pairs and only for seconds before disappearing. The photographer should not hesitate to take whatever shot is available. The dik-dik supports itself on tiny, pencil-thin legs. The conspicuous and large, dark, but luminous, eyes of the Kirk's are accentuated by a white ring. A large black spot that represents a preorbital gland is found below the inside corner of each eye. These and other glands — like the wildebeest, the dik-dik also has interdigital glands between its cloven hooves — produce a sticky substance used by the antelope to mark its territory. The elongated nose provides the animal with a particularly keen sense of smell. (The proboscis — most pronounced in the Guenther's variety — also aids cooling. Venous blood is cooled under normal breathing as moisture evaporates in the mucous membranes found in the nasal cavity; under great heat stress, the animal "pants" through its nose.) The prehensile upper lip aids browsing.

The female is slightly larger than the male. Only the latter has horns, but, when excited or alarmed, a crest of hairs on its forehead is erected and conceals the tiny horns. Adapted to areas least suitable for human habitation, dik-diks are likely to survive a long time. On the other hand, the dik-dik has a lot of predators about which to worry: eagles, other raptors, mongooses, pythons, small and large cats, hyenas, jackals, and wild dogs, among the most obvious. But dik-diks are great hiders, using to full advantage their size and coloration, and make a point of knowing intimately their ranges.

high-strung racehorses.'') He marks and patrols his territory (two to twelve acres) and aggressively repels intrusions by both male *and* female dik-diks. On the other hand, the rushing sequences between bucks that the safarist *may* see — the author has seen only two — do not usually result in real contact or actual use of the tiny, spear-like horns.

Dik-diks have the habit of defecating in one place, several times a day, always with great ceremony and near their territorial borders. Scientists explain that this practice is territorial demarcation. Bush lore offers another elucidation. Years ago, the king of the dik-diks found himself mired in some elephant droppings. Vowing revenge, as kings invariably do, the monarch issued an edict to all his subjects everywhere to teach the elephant a lesson: pile droppings together in the hope that an elephant will also stick fast. And, because no elephant ever has, the dik-diks keep trying.[89]

Zebras

Looking at the zebra (''punda milia'' in Kiswahili), the first question that comes to everyone's mind is, why stripes? *(72)* On one level, the question — and the ensuing speculation — results from a perfectly natural curiosity toward a unique animal. On another level, the question — and the different answers most often given — reveals much what is wrong with how naturalists for years have looked at animals.

The first reason sometimes heard — ''first'' not in terms of chronology or of widespread agreement but in terms of inventiveness — was that offered by our old friend Thayer. The reader will recall Thayer's mission: to prove that all animals preyed upon evolved ''disruptive coloration'' that permitted them virtually to disappear before their predators, by vanishing into their own backgrounds. Thus, a zebra's stripes were said to break up the animal's coherent outline, especially as it moved.[90] Thayer and subsequent apologists made much ado about stooping down to the lion's plane, where the vertical white stripes

Plate 72. *Oxpecker and Stripes.* Whether the zebra — once called a horse tiger — has black or white stripes and why are questions that do not concern the oxpecker, who is satisfied with a tick or two (or twenty). As zebras are infested with grass ticks, the oxpeckers are frequent and happy guests — and welcome, from the zebra's perspective. The tick-birds also remove fur (from antelopes as well) for use in their nests.

---

89. In yet another version, the dik-dik monarch tripped over rhino droppings as he was looking over his shoulder at a pursuing lion. Tripping up the rhino then became the goal.

90. The concealment aficionados generally had begun by suggesting that a zebra's stripes mimicked the reeds or tall grass of its habitat. (Kipling, as the reader will recall, had the zebra disappearing in the forest.) Thayer initially criticized the mimicry theory. He admitted that, when zebras went down to the riverbed to drink, their pattern indeed sometimes blended with the reeds and tall grass. But, as he pointed out, zebras usually sought out drinking places with as little cover (and lions) as possible. In fact, Thayer at first acknowledged that the striped horse depended upon its vigilance and fleetness of foot to escape its foes. The seductive power of disruptive coloration proved, however, too strong in the end.

supposedly ''vanish'' into the sky, blurring the line of the animal's back and leaving it without a distinct shape. Later observers have added the thoughts (one hesitates to call them ''observations'') that disruptive coloration is most effective in a heat haze at 300-400 yards or on moonlit nights. One may wonder just *what* were these people looking at, out there on the African plains. Quite aside from the (perhaps) minor point that even the largest tourist in a red shirt (and his vehicle!) begins to fade in a heat haze at that distance and that in any event lions do not begin the chase at 300-400 yards, the truth is, in *any* setting or light and against *any* background and from *any* angle or level, a zebra is impossible to miss. *(73)* This is unquestionably one of nature's most distinctive animals

one zebra end and another begin? In a sense, zebras in a herd create their own background, against which the individual loses its discrete form. The moment or two of confusion may cause the lion to hesitate and throw it off balance. That brief pause may be sufficient to give the zebras enough time to achieve speed and escape.[92] Nevertheless, the undeniable confusion is not primarily caused by stripes, and the fact that stripes play what is a distinctly minor part here cannot amount to evolutionary justification. Impalas employ the same strategy without the stripes — darting bodies by themselves create enough confusion. Indeed, stripes clearly seem too elaborate a solution to a problem shared by many ungulates. And the zebras have the added weapon common to all horses: hard hooves connected to a powerful kick. The predator knows that a well-directed hoof will put it out of business — perhaps, permanently. Thus, a predator cannot simply throw itself into a herd of zebras. Predators choose prey at least partly isolated from the mingling mass.

Although predation may have played no part in creating zebra stripes and Kipling notwithstanding, predators may well have helped to keep the zebra striped. In all probability, any zebra born significantly different, in a color sense, would more likely be chosen and picked off by a lion. Predators seem to equate a conspicuous animal among its peers with a defect, always a killing offense, and, besides, the predators would have been able more easily to recognize their target in any subsequent confusion.

Fundamentally, stripes cannot be camouflage because zebra behavior would cancel out any such advantage. Zebras are noisy, active, and alert. They never attempt to conceal themselves; they never "freeze" in response to predators. Even optical illusions work best in relative silence. The zebra prefers to rest, grouped, in exposed places where it has the advantage of a good view — even at the cost of conspicuousness.

Why stripes? Next in the queue is the "venetian blind" theory. Some naturalists have, mindful of a zebra's environment, suggested that stripes help the zebra withstand radiant heat from the sun. Indeed, zebras stand in the hottest sun all day long. But, though the white could be expected to reflect heat, the black would surely absorb an equivalent share. In fact, what keeps a zebra from overheating is its coat's thickness. The hide turns out to be a

— concealment theories, all of them, are simply ludicrous. If the needle in the haystack looked like a zebra, there would be no adage.[91]

A more subtle predation-oriented answer is that stripes are a form of "cryptic coloration," not like regular camouflage in which the animal is rendered inconspicuous but more like an optical illusion that confuses a predator's judgment as to the exact shape, distance, and speed of a fleeing animal. There is probably some truth to this theory, especially at dawn (the time of many hunts). When a herd is startled, the zebras will dart around in confusion, such mingling resulting in a mass of stripes and making it difficult to isolate a single animal — where does

---

91. Some concealment fanatics finesse the issue altogether by explaining that the zebra is often dusty and thus looks grey from a distance! And the historians among the converted note that Africa was once primarily covered by forests and, well, reread Kipling.

---

92. As a thinking reader may, however, realize, there is another side to a bunch of zebras tightly packed together acting in confusion — the ideal situation for "cryptic coloration." It is just as likely that such zebras stall in one another's way during the panic of an attack, giving a lion an extra second's or two's advantage! Some zealots in the optical illusion (or signal) school have hypothesized that stripes may be a deterrence to harmful flies. Aside from some evidence that flies are influenced by optical signals, I cannot find *any* evidence that flies are of significant concern to zebras.

real insulative barrier that allows little radiation to penetrate.[93]

Yet another answer proffered by some naturalists is that stripes serve to identify individuals. Superficially, this view is intellectually attractive. Selection pressures that "must" maintain stripes are far more liable to result from the behavior of those animals who *see* the stripes most often — zebras themselves, not passing predators. Thus, zebras recognize one another by differentiating stripes. But, though it is true that no zebra has exactly the same pattern as any other zebra — and that one side of a particular zebra moreover does not even mirror or match precisely the other side — the author is unaware of any evidence that zebras cannot behave like a great many animals whose social organization depends on personal

bonds and who do not have markings so spectacular as stripes. Black or white stripes are, in fact, not that unusual among African animals; as we have seen, ungulates of many descriptions have stripes somewhere. But nature has chosen to stripe completely only the zebra. On the contrary, the evidence is compelling that zebras use smell and sound, as well as sight, in recognition and greeting. Again, though stripes may possibly help zebras distinguish other zebras, this function can hardly rise to the level of evolutionary purpose. And Grevy's zebras, with narrow and numerous stripes, are more difficult for the safarist to distinguish and may be more difficult for zebras to do so as well (by sight).

Another, more subtle, variation of the communication adherents recognizes the weakness inherent in a dis-

Plate 73. Zebras "Disappearing" Against the Sky. Stripes are a zebra's "fingerprints" — no two zebras have the same pattern. With a little practice, the safarist can easily tell individuals apart.

93. Grevy's zebras have more white than other zebras (a Grevy's belly is always white) and live in a much hotter atmosphere — a fact that supports, again, a minor cooling role for (white) stripes. A zebra's coat is also quite shiny, which characteristic aids its reflective ability. Another variation to temperature-regulation emphasis is that striping is somehow (as yet unexplained) a chemical device that adjusts the body's temperature. This hypothesis is difficult to accept, simply because the striped patterns show no variations that can be attributed to climatic changes.

crimination function and states instead that stripes simply offer visual stimulation and attract one zebra to another. That is, stripes — with their tonal contrasts, edges,[94] and spatial frequencies automatically provoke attention from other zebras and cause the equids to approach one another, quite indiscriminately. Furthermore, the patterns may even be, in a sense, restful to zebras. But such an intellectual construction depends upon herding zebras behaving in unique ways — unique relative to other wild horses and other ungulates — that further can be linked to striping. The evidence is simply not there.

In some respects, we can be more sympathetic with Thayer than later naturalists when we realize that zebras — and other strikingly marked animals — represented the biggest challenge to his theories and had to be addressed directly (and creatively). The average Darwinian naturalist has an even larger ax to grind but should know better. When one talks to naturalists in the field — as the author has for years — few (if any) will admit to the "vulgar Darwinian" approach, namely, that natural selection is so powerful and hence pervasive that animals become, in effect, collections of perfect parts. Yet the fairly Byzantine methodology of searching for meaning by analyzing every part of an animal is grounded precisely on such a premise. Thus, a giraffe's neck, a lion's mane, and a zebra's stripes all must have an optimum function, having evolved through natural selection. Thus, "only very strong selective pressure could maintain such crisp, evenly spaced black and white stripes."

The stripes have, however, proved to be a formidable stumbling block; indeed, no theory adequately dispenses with the feeling of most safarists that stripes are so *unnatural*. One is always, well, *startled* to see these "highly varnished" black-and-white animals, who look as if they were made to adorn a carnival merry-go-round, trotting around instead on the plains. And zebras are always at or near the top of the menu chosen by lions. For example, lions eat more zebra in the Serengeti than any other prey. One has the distinct impression that predators would not do any *better* with 'regular' horses (or ponies). And "visual grooming" theories — stripes as conspicuous socializing mechanisms — are interesting but die on the altar of the null hypothesis ("keep it simple").

Let us begin again. Unencumbered. Why stripes? The best answer is probably this: *purely by accident*. The argument begins by turning the question to a slightly dif-

ferent direction: *what* are stripes? Most of us regard the zebra as a white animal with black stripes. It will, no doubt, surprise many readers to learn that Africans believe the animal to be basically black with white stripes. The author used to think that the white underbelly was determinative (in favor of a white background), but logic really does not support this thesis.[95] If the striping results from an inhibition of melanin — that is, the striping mechanism inhibits natural pigment formation — the zebra is a black animal with white stripes. If striping results from a deposit of melanin — the striping mechanism stimulates natural pigmentation — the zebra is a white animal with black stripes. We also now know that broad stripes indicate rather different embryonic development from that provided by the narrow stripes. The same is true for the varying interspecies patterns. All these considerations seem to take us further and further from functional possibilities.

The mechanics of striping do not, of course, altogether eliminate functional or evolutionary motivation. But there is not just one zebra. There are three: the Burchell's or Common zebra, the Grevy's, and the Mountain or Hartmann's zebra. All differ notably in the number of stripes, the basic patterns, and the configuration of the stripe itself. Subspecies merely increase the differences. Functional justifications offered for this diversity quickly strain the imagination. All zebras belong to the family *Equidae* and the genus *Equus,* together with horses, asses, and donkeys. Indeed, the different zebras appear to be more related to horses generally than to one another. "Zebras" then may simply be horses with black-and-white stripes,[96] and all horses may have the capacity for stripes. Three types of horses — "zebras" — thus either availed themselves of the genetic opportunity, quite accidentally, or the common ancestor had stripes and most horses lost them, probably accidentally, only the zebras retaining the original characteristic.[97]

---

94. Most true body stripes in animals — the reader should recall the Thomson's gazelle — have a "flicker" effect (moving edges) that reinforces *any* signal theory. Of course, a zebra's markings extend all the way to its muzzle. Indeed, some writers have suggested that the stripes on the face may be useful as a threat display, drawing attention to powerful teeth in a black muzzle. I suppose that the next step in this absurd process is to observe that the declining circles (and optical spiral) on the legs serve to emphasize powerful hooves. . .

95. And I have seen some zebras that were essentially black, with only a few white stripes.

96. Zebra foals have been born to quarter horses by means of embryo-transfer. And zebras have been successfully bred with some horses and ponies.

97. The distinction between these last two broad alternatives is rather technical but significant. The interested reader is advised to begin with Stephen Jay Gould's, *Hen's Teeth and Horse's Toes* (W.W. Norton, 1984), Chapter 7. The strict Darwinists do not give up here: they assert that stripes can be maintained only in tropical areas, because the annual moulting in colder climates would eliminate the advantages of distinct striping, and that desert-dwelling asses lost their stripes, because low herd densities made striping irrelevant (assuming that conspicuous socializing lay behind the patterns). On the other hand, the process of rationalization can keep going to posit why in cold climates year-round socializing is not critical or, if necessary, is encouraged by certain cold-season factors and so forth. And the Grevy's species is not one of high density.

1. Burchell's Zebra.[98]

The Burchell's or Common or Plains zebra (74) is the most widely distributed of the three species; its range overlaps that of both Grevy's and the Mountain zebra, from the southeastern Sudan to the Cape Province of South Africa. Generally, the Common zebra is an inhabitant of grasslands, the open savannah, the more lush the better. Zebras are thus essentially grazing animals and the only non-ruminant ungulate found in large numbers on the plains. When pasture is scarce, the zebra will, however, browse and, although the Burchell's usually remains in one general area most of the year, it will also migrate when there are seasonal shortages of vegetation on which to graze. The same wanderlust arises when there is a shortage of water, as zebras must drink every day and are seldom found far from water. (75) The most spectacular migration — within the Serengeti ecosystem — has already been discussed earlier in this chapter.

One outstanding feature of zebras is that, whatever the environment and even under extremely poor conditions, they all look sleek, fat, and contented. Their well-developed barrel-shaped bellies and full hindquarters give the impression of a life of prosperity.[99] Why this plump, sassy appearance prevails is not exactly clear, and, indeed, logic would seem to dictate otherwise. The zebra shares its food resources with ruminants. But the nutritive value of fibrous vegetation is never high, and the extraction of sufficient nutrients is no simple matter. All herbivores depend upon symbiosis: micro-organisms (bacteria and protozoa) in the digestive tract convert the plant's cellulose content. Even the mightiest elephant depends upon its tiny partners for sustenance. Many scientists are emphatic that, among the herbivores, ruminants have a superior digestive process. Certainly, ruminants are more efficient. By comparison, a zebra's digestion appears somewhat ar-

chaic. All odd-toed ungulates, of whom the zebra is one, are hindgut fermenters. The comparison to ruminants or foregut fermenters was made in the discussion on elephants and need not be repeated here. In summary, hindgut processing is rapid but incomplete, compared to rumination. The zebra has to eat far more — probably twice as much — than comparably sized ruminants. A mature zebra will eat up to thirty pounds of grass a day, twice that consumed by a wildebeest. Zebras also make other "adjustments" to reduce the physical costs of harvesting. In any event, the only explanation for a zebra's inevitably prime condition is that it somehow absorbs more protein into the body than do (most) ruminants.

Additionally, zebras play an important part in the total herbivorous system by grazing down the taller (and older), more fibrous parts of the grass — the wildebeest and other antelopes follow to graze at the shortened grass that has been encouraged to regenerate in fresh, protein-filled sheaths and leaves. As Norman Myers has stated so

---

98. William John Burchell, an Englishman, became the most renowned of Southern Africa's explorers and pioneer naturalists in the early 1800s. A remarkable man, Burchell traveled modestly with Africans and was responsible for numerous animal and plant discoveries. Although certainly best known in his day as a botanist, the meticulous Burchell also "discovered" the White rhino, Blue wildebeest, sassaby, and a large number of birds. (Burchell was also the first man to import live hyena to England.) His book, *Travels in the Interior of Southern Africa*, published in two volumes in 1822 and 1824, became a classic of English travel literature. Burchell literally lived for his work; at the age of 82, when he had completed classifying and cataloguing all his specimens, he committed suicide, because, as he said then, he was too old to begin a new project.

A number of subspecies for the Plains zebra have been identified: Boehm's, Selous', Chapman's, Grant's, and Damara. Some scientists have also classified the Burchell's as a subspecies (now more or less extinct), not the terminology favored here. All the distinctions are pretty technical.

99. The tapered striping pattern also contributes an illusion of roundness and sleekness.

Plate 74. Plains Zebra. Zebras are never far from water. Although the Common zebra favors the open savannah, it can also be found on swamp edges, in woodlands, and in bushed grasslands. Serious attempts have been made from time to time to domesticate zebras. Early settlers in Africa hoped to take advantage of the zebra's natural immunities to horse-related diseases and, of course, its abundance. Tried as well were crosses between a zebra and a mule or donkey. Most of the experiments failed. Domestication proved difficult, and successfully broken zebra could not stand up to sustained transport work. Moreover, in captivity, high infestations of intestinal worms became a serious concern. The crosses were sterile.

well, "There is more to a zebra than just a zebra."[100] But this high cellulose diet of the zebra,[101] compared with the more protein-filled and soluble carbohydrate selections of the wildebeest and gazelles, only adds to the mystery of why the zebras seem to do so well.

Plains zebras are normally seen in large aggregations that can contain from several dozen to several hundred to several thousand in some areas. But all these large groups are made up of small, highly stable and cohesive units — either a family *(76)* or a bachelor group *(77)*. A family consists of one dominant stallion and two to six mares and their foals, all linked by strong personal bonds among

themselves. Over time, only the young born into the group eventually disperse. The mares establish a strict hierarchy, most evident when the group moves. The dominant mare (usually the eldest) always leads, and the others follow in a single file, according to their rank. Sometimes, a threatening gesture or two is needed to maintain the order, but the queue is invariably respected. The foals follow their mothers, that is, the lower-ranking mares honor the position of the foal of a higher-ranking mare. The male, on the other hand, will stay to the rear or off to the side, occasionally coming alongside the lead mare only to change her direction. The stallion will actually challenge any pursuing or threatening predators and is successful, more often than not, in warding them off. Adult females remain in the family throughout their lives; if the stallion dies or leaves the group for some reason (usually, severe illness or old age), the group will then be taken over whole by another stallion.

When female foals are about thirteen to fifteen months old, they come into estrus for the first time and are abducted by young stallions starting families of their own or simply augmenting their existing harems. The male foals also leave the family between the ages of one to four years; they do not appear to be forced out but leave voluntarily because of the proximity — and temptation — of a bachelor group containing playmates and because of the greatly diminished attention received from their mothers who eventually turn to newborns to look after.

The male foal joins a bachelor group, which contains anywhere from two to ten stallions — three to four being the average. The stallions are usually friendly and maintain strong interpersonal bonds (at least some of which endure after members leave to establish their families). These bachelor herds are fairly stable over long periods because of the low turnover of males possessing harems and the slow birth rates among zebras generally. The bachelors do not seem to be stictly ranked, but an adult

---

100. *The Long African Day,* p. 270. Astoundingly enough, the safarist may read (elsewhere) that zebras are often the first animals to graze young grass shoots and hence lead migrations. A fairly complete misinterpretation.

101. As a general rule, crude protein is inversely related to the amount of lignified fiber found in grass.

Plate 75. Zebras at the Stream. The safarist will most likely never see a skinny zebra. And a zebra, the size of a wild pony, is never so impressive as when encountered in its natural habitat. Males are recognizable by genitals (not always easy to see) and thicker necks, heavier hocks, often a shorter mane, and more distinctive black and white markings than females. All zebras like company and are rarely found alone. Adults often remain in their group for a lifetime.

always leads the group. The younger animals of the club are very high-spirited and playful. Their day inevitably includes mock fights, races, and anything else that horses can dream up. This is the best (most active) zebra group for a safarist to watch. The visitor can always distinguish play from real fighting by the fact that the mock combatants take turns chasing each other.

The close fondness among zebras in all groups is illustrated by the extensive body contact when resting, most notably when two zebras place their heads on the backs of each other,[102] and the very evident and elaborate grooming, in which two animals stand facing shoulder to shoulder and with their teeth systematically work each other over simultaneously. Obviously, grooming has a utilitarian side — the close attention rids the coat of external parasites and extracts loose hair, helping the skin and hair maintain a healthy appearance — but a strong element of socializing is present as well. The most frequent grooming partners are mares and their foals, stallions and their younger mares, and young bachelors among themselves fairly indiscriminately.

Zebra mares are slow breeders. Gestation can last as long as a year and will take at least eleven months. Birth usually takes place between October and March in East Africa, that is, just before or during the rainy season, when both the quality and quantity of forage are nearly optimal. The process of giving birth lasts no more than seven or eight minutes. A foal is remarkably developed (precocial) at birth, and the newborn will, after some initial falls and clumsiness, move with the herd within an hour, at most. Morning is the preferred time of birth — the foal has some eight hours of light to organize its locomotion and stay alive. Pictures of the process are included in Chapter X. During delivery, mother and foal are completely vulnerable to predation but are frequently closely guarded by the stallion. As noted many times in this volume, most predators are active at night, and the stallion has a far better chance of protecting his charges during the daylight, when he can see clearly. For a good two days following birth, mothers try to keep other zebras away from their foals to insure proper imprinting. Thereafter, mothers and their youngsters remain inseparable during the first seven months of nursing *(77 & 78)*. The young zebra looks just like a picture lifted right out of a children's book, the kind with raised fuzz that is meant to be stroked, or, in Alan Moorehead's phrase, like a rocking horse (with stripes) taken off the shelves of a toy shop. *(79)* Newborn animals are short in the neck, long in the legs, and have long, furry hair. Their coloration is basically brown and white, the brown gradually changing to black when they are weaned (no connection exists, however, between the change of diet and the change in color). Some females retain patches of brown as adults.

---

102. A posture that also gives a 360° view of a predator-occupied savannah.

Plate 76. Family on the Run. Like most horses, zebras love to run. A young zebra will not allow an antelope to run past without offering a challenge dash of its own. Zebras, in common with other equids, "run" in ascending fashion as follows: a "canter" or slow gallop is a three-beat gait with "leads," and a full gallop more resembles a bound from the pair of hind legs to the pair of forelegs. In a canter — the word is unique to English and probably derived from the deliberate, smooth pace adopted by medieval pilgrims traveling to Canterbury Cathedral — either the left foreleg or the right foreleg "leads" or appears to reach forward to initiate the stride (the appearance is slightly deceptive; the impetus really comes from the rear legs pushing off, and the "leading" front leg is actually the last leg to touch down in the sequence). The inside foreleg leads on turns, which causes the body weight to remain in balance. When it changes direction, a zebra will naturally change leads. In a straight line, just as people are naturally right- or left-handed, zebras generally prefer one lead to the other. When a zebra canters, it starts the movement with one hind foot pushing off (beat one), then the other hind leg and the diagonal front leg touching down (beat two), followed by the opposite front foot (beat three). After a slight hesitation, the sequence starts over. The full gallop maintains a "transverse" cadence, but the hind and forelegs in turn touch ground almost simultaneously, giving the impression that the zebra is bounding from the hind legs to the forelegs. (Antelopes gallop in a rotatory fashion: the feet hit down in counterclockwise sequence.) The speed of a full run can exceed 35 mph. There is a brief period during every full stride when all four legs are completely suspended in the air. The reader is also invited to review footnote 22 on p. 242 and the accompanying text.

Zebra families resemble elephant families in their sociability and cohesiveness. Strict cohesion is, however, always dependent upon food and water availability.

The stallions fight frequently.[103] *(80-82)* Much of the effort is harmless sparring, however painful and vigorous it always appears to onlookers. In truth, the teeth doing all the loud chomping are blunt, and the skin receiving all the rough attention is extremely tough. When one party in at

---

103. Some writers have asserted that zebra stallions fight less than almost all other male mammals. Whenever the author has stopped to watch any sizeable group of zebras, he has, however, witnessed at least one scuffle. Slight hostility between mares also flares up on occasion: dominant mares will displace subordinates from a particular feeding area. Normally, a threatening gesture — head held low and ears laid back (like horses) — will suffice.

Plate 77. Mother and Foal. The safarist may see the birth of a foal (particularly in January or February) in a large herd. The safarist should look for a zebra showing signs of discomfort: walking only a few steps at a time and not eating. The early morning is the likely time, and the pregnant mare simply lies down. If disturbed for any reason, a female can, however, delay a birth once started for several hours. The stallion often stands guard over the mare during birth. Zebra foals are not taken by predators in the way that wildebeest young are, even though abundant at roughly the same time and of comparable mobility. The zebra family unit keeps reasonably tightly bunched when fleeing, never outrunning the slowest member, and the stallions actively fight off predators.

Plate 78. Nursing. For several days immediately after birth, a mother will keep other zebras away from the foal to insure imprinting.

least a semi-serious quarrel has had enough, he has only to quit and break away; the victor almost never chases. Chasing is mostly play between young males. (Indeed, the most dangerous time of a confrontation would be the risk of catching a flaying hind hoof thrown by the retreating loser.) There is no territoriality among the males, and mature herd stallions generally behave amicably toward one another. Each family has a home range, which varies in size and location according to rainfall and which overlaps with the areas favored by other stallions and their harems. In fact, in a typical day, a family stallion might meet and greet in a friendly way some thirty other stallions in the vicinity. Nevertheless, some serious fighting does occur during the abduction of young female foals. The family stallion always tries to prevent the abduction and always (eventually) loses, primarily because the challenge is invariably mounted by more than one young would-be abductor.[104]

Unlike ruminants, young zebras will lie flat on their sides when sleeping. Nor do ruminating ungulates roll on their backs — which action would apparently disrupt their system of filtering and fermenting food — but zebras make rolling in a common dust patch a standard part of most days, undoubtedly a means of ridding themselves of parasites. *(83)*

There are further interesting comparisons between zebras and the other ungulates that share their plains habitat. All plains animals exercise caution when taking a

Plate 79. Storybook Animal. If it survives the first week of life, the chances for a zebra foal are good. Young zebras play a great deal, especially as they begin to venture from mother's side, with much nipping, nuzzling, and running games. They will also chase gazelles, birds, and other innocents.

---

104. We now know that many young female foals are abducted not just once but several times before they "settle in." The foals advertise their availability by adopting a provocative stance — legs apart, tail lifted — that all the males recognize. As long as a foal does this, she will be an object of attempted kidnapping. As she grows older and approaches the age when she can conceive for the first time (at approximately three years, despite the much earlier estrus), she gradually lessens the provocation and eventually limits the display for the benefit of her dominant stallion immediately before breeding. Incidentally, the introduction of a young mare into an existing harem is not without excitement; the other females make life difficult for a time. And courtship itself includes much chasing about and nipping.

drink, but zebras, who drink often, take the greatest care when approaching water. *(84)* The approach is literally inch-by-inch, and even an excited bird has been known to startle zebras into a panic retreat (what startled the bird?), the latter only to begin again, slowly, ears twitching, nostrils flaring, and with multiple glances in every direction. The patient safarist soon feels like Jackie Gleason in the classic "Honeymooners" sequence in which Art Carney sits down to write a letter and proceeds to go through a dozen or so introductory maneuvers that quickly drive Ralph Kramden to the breaking point.

On migratory routes, zebras exhibit none of the energetic mindlessness of wildebeest. For example, the

Plates 80-82. Stallions Fighting. Those readers familiar with horses will recognize the biting of the legs and neck, the half rearing, and all the rest, characterizing not exactly ritualistic posturing but something less than serious antagonism. Zebras (and horses) always go down on their knees (what is usually called the "knee" in a horse is really the equivalent of our wrist; the hock corresponds to our ankle) or haunches to protect the vulnerable and all-important lower legs. Zebras also engage in 'neck wrestling,' one zebra putting the full weight of its own neck onto the top of the other's neck, attempting to force the opponent downward. All combat, which can last for *hours,* is accompanied by a great deal of squealing and barking.

Plate 83. Dusting. Zebras queue up to roll in a communal dust patch.

Plate 84. Zebras Down for a Drink. A vanguard slowly approaches the water. Individuals stop nearly every step, look around, test the wind, and allow their brains to process their senses. Then, another step. Eventually, the entire herd will follow, and soon, other herbivores as well, trusting the good judgment of the striped donkey. The waterhole is a good place to see family groups separate slightly from the larger herd. The zebra who normally leads the family to and from the water is the dominant mare.

zebra always chooses the best times and most functional crossings over water. *(85 & 86)* Some naturalists have suggested that one reason why zebras pass so much time in the company of wildebeest is that lions seem to find the gnus easier prey. Others give the wildebeest more credit — the gnus may have sharper senses (at least, sense of smell) than the zebras.[105] Surely, zebras associate with giraffes and ostriches to take advantage of the others' superior eyesight. In fact, zebras seem to strike a pretty

---

105. The simplest explanation is that the two species eat the same kind of vegetation, though zebras prefer the coarser parts.

Plates 85 & 86. A Course in River Crossing. Zebras pick the best available crossings. They check the footing carefully. They usually cross at the narrowest points. They swim relatively spread out and avoid the panic at the far banks that greets all wildebeest crossings. Foals cross with their mothers. (Note the resting crocodile in plate *86.*)

Plate 87. Temporary Casualty. A safe passage is not guaranteed. This foal collapsed on the other side from exhaustion and perhaps a hurt tendon. Its mother returned several times to lend encouragement. After an hour or so, the youngster slowly got to its feet and cantered off. Youngsters do occasionally get separated from their mothers in mass crossings (or migrations). The call sounds made by mothers searching for their foals resemble the high-pitched bark of a dog. If a safarist will listen closely, he can distinguish between the barks of different animals. In a real panic, the bark becomes more like a shrill yelp. At night, zebras are restless and noisy; a nearby safarist will hear much exciting braying and the characteristic querulous barking whinny. "Qua-ha, qua-ha, qua-ha-ha-ha" — day or night, the contact call is one of the common sounds of the African plains.

fair balance where predation is involved. *(87)* They are, as indicated earlier, popular prey for both lions and hyenas. On the other hand, as a statistical matter, a single zebra probably runs about as much a risk of being eaten by a lion as the reader does of being killed by a car. Those Burchell's zebras that do not fall victim to predators usually live for at least twelve years and have been known to reach thirty.

Plate 88. More than Idle Curiosity. These zebras are viewing a pride of lions (not pictured) with the same intensity as the jackals. The lions are eating another zebra. The jackals are waiting for a chance to snatch some scraps. On their part, the zebras are not behaving ghoulishly; before they resume their grazing, they want to make sure that the lions are satisfied with their meal. Soon enough, a zebra being devoured by lions takes on the aura of a traffic accident — the traffic (zebras, among others) just flows around the obstruction; everyone does some rubbernecking, but life goes on.

2. Grevy's Zebra.[106]

The Grevy's is the largest (tallest and heaviest) of the three species and probably the largest wild equid: it stands four-and-a-half to five feet tall at the shoulder and weighs nearly 1000 pounds. *(89 & 90)* The Grevy's is confined to northern Kenya and adjacent parts of Ethiopia and Somalia. Grevy's zebras do not congregate in large herds like the Common zebra *(90)*, though several hundred may be seen at waterholes during the dry season. In fact, Grevy's zebras seem to have a social organization markedly different from that of all other zebras. In particular, no permanent bond exists between any two adult individuals. Groups are purely informal affairs without leaders or dominant males or females. No stable hierarchy of any kind is apparent; indeed, a group, such as it is, rarely stays together longer than a few months. Mutual grooming is rare. Grevy's stallions tend to be territorial, and the largest among them occupy and defend individual territories. But a given territory may be as large as four square miles (identified by dung piles and the stallion's presence),[107] and other subordinate stallions are permitted to remain within the borders. The mares enter and leave territories at random, and the stallions try to hold them whether or not they are in estrus. A stallion apparently will not defend his territory unless a mare is present.

Grevy's zebras prefer the semi-desert, arid scrub country in Kenya (nicknamed "orchard savannah," after an unkempt orchard), and their highly flexible social organization reflects the availability of grazing in this environment. That is, the zebra must move over a large area to gain sufficient nutrition. Moreover, a Grevy's can go without drinking water for several weeks.

The Grevy's in most respects looks more like a horse (to the author, at least) than does the Common zebra. Its head resembles that of an Arabian. Its ears are larger proportionately and rounded; the stripes are narrower and set close together, running vertically down the flanks (the

Plate 89. Grevy's Zebras. Even the Grevy's zebra, known to be considerably less social than its cousins, likes the company of other zebras. Grevy's are sometimes found mixed with Common zebras, though no interbreeding takes place in the wild, and stallions of one type do not fight with stallions of the other nor show interest in the estrous mares of the other species. In captivity, the two species have been bred, but the offspring is sterile.

---

106. The species was first described from Abyssinia, now Ethiopia. The Emperor Menelik II (before he was emperor) sent a living specimen to Paris in 1882. The President of France at that time was François Paul Jules Grévy. The animal died a short time later and was stuffed for display in the local museum of natural history. A noted French zoologist, perhaps forgetting who was ultimately responsible for the gift, named the animal in honor of his president.

107. These are the largest male territories recorded among herbivores. A stallion will maintain the same territory over several years. The territorial stallions leave their domains only to drink, though a critical drought will cause them to migrate. They will not, however, establish new territories during migration and will not mate with mares. Because mating takes place only back in the established territories and because rains are unpredictably sporadic where the Grevy's lives, the species' reproductive rate is low.

Plate 90. Grevy's Foal. A Grevy's foal is as magical as a Burchell's foal. The stripes on the upper hind legs of the Grevy's form a trigon or triangle. On both the Plains and Mountain species, the stripes curve gradually from vertical (on the belly) to horizontal. All zebras have a trigon on the forequarters.

belly is unstriped); and the mane is taller (sometimes, it stands up even higher than pricked ears).

Recognition of individual Grevy's zebras is difficult, because their stripes are so numerous, narrow, and drawn close together. A Grevy's sometimes appears almost grey from a distance, but this zebra is still a distinctive animal.

3. Mountain Zebra.

Mountain (either Cape or Hartmann's) zebras are restricted to dry regions of Namibia (especially Etosha) and Cape Province of South Africa. They are the smallest zebras, with a little dewlap under the throat and long, narrow ears. Their stripes are broader than those of other zebras. Mountain zebras are not the usual tourist fare. Hartmann's zebras are very wild, nervous animals and notoriously difficult to photograph. Indeed, the author has neither seen nor photographed one in the wild. The Cape Mountain zebras are almost extinct. Both types seem to resemble Plains zebras in social organization.

Plate 91. Storm over Samburu. Pictured is an average Grevy's group in size. Grevy's zebras were extensively poached — many leather goods were made from their hides. Naturalists for awhile thought that the species was, in fact, endangered. Subsequently, an error was discovered in the statistics: a zero had been lost, and the population was increased from 1,500 to 15,000. Any visitor to Samburu in Kenya should have suspected the error, given the profusion of Grevy's zebras seen there, the heart of the species' last real stronghold.

Wild Pigs

The African wild pigs are the warthog (''ngiri'' in Kiswahili), the Giant Forest Hog (''numera''), and the bush pig (''nguruwe''). In form, all may be as old as forty-five million years. Each species occupies essentially different habitats, though they frequently overlap, and does not compete in any way with another. All are omnivores and will eat virtually anything that their snouts can reach.

1. Warthog.

Alan Moorehead, in his wonderful classic, plaintively asked, ''Who, for example, ever writes about the warthog?''[108] Indeed, the warthog is everywhere and has — in Moorehead's words — a ''small trotting-on part in every other scene.'' Nearly all safarists come away with a new friend in the little Lewis Carroll character:

> The warthog is the clown of the jungle, and he has a certain awful charm. He is an extremely bothered animal about the size of a small pig, and he is furnished with two enormous tusks, a lion's mane and a tail and hindquarters which are quite uncompromisingly bare. He roots about the ground in family groups, and if surprised he stands and stares for a moment with deep concern written all over his appalling face. Then with a flick of his head, his tail rising like a railway signal bolt upright behind him, the father of the group is off into the scrub. The rest of the family follow in line, the biggest first and the smallest drawing up frantically in the rear. The warthog is not really ugly — it is the sort of countenance that is covered roughly by the French phrase *'une jolie laide'*...[109]

Another writer has commented favorably on the warthog's bravery:

> I know animals more gallant than the African warthog, but none more courageous. He is the peasant of the plains — the drab and dowdy digger in the earth. He is the uncomely but intrepid defender of family, home, and bourgeois convention, and he will fight anything of any size that intrudes upon his smug existence. Even his weapons are plebeian — curved tusks, sharp, deadly, but not beautiful, used inelegantly for rooting as well as for fighting.
>
> He stands higher than a domestic pig when he is full grown, and his hide is dust-coloured and tough and clothed in bristles. His eyes are small and lightless and capable of but one expression — suspicion. What he does not understand, he suspects, and what he suspects, he fights. He can leap into the air and gut a horse while its rider still ponders a strategy of attack, and his speed in

emerging from his hole to demonstrate the advantage of surprise is almost phenomenal.

> He is not lacking in guile. He enters his snug little den (which is borrowed, not to say commandeered, from its builder, the ant-bear [aardvark]) tail foremost so that he is never caught off guard. While he lies thus in wait for the curiosity or indiscretion of his enemy to bring him within range, he uses his snout to pile a heap of fine dust inside the hole. The dust serves as a smoke screen, bursting into a great, enshrouding billow the moment the warthog emerges to battle. He understands the tactical retreat, but is incapable of surrender, and if a dog is less than a veteran, or a man no more than an intrepid novice, not the only blood spilled will be the warthog's.[110]

Thus, if the quality of expression makes up for the lack of attention, the warthog has received its due in the literature. (The pig would have been content with simply a literary misrepresentation or two; out on the plains, he was known to a class of arrogant hunters as the ''poor man's rhinoceros,'' not exactly a healthy appellation.) Nearly all visitors today arrive in safari Africa with a kind of animal-shopping list, as it were, in mind: the best known creatures are sorted by preference. One wants to see a lion first, for example, then an elephant, a rhino, and so on. Not everyone has the same list, of course, and few could explain their preferences in any detail. Konrad Lorenz, the famous ethologist, years ago argued that human beings respond favorably to animals whose faces resemble human countenances or features in some significant way. Perhaps that is why the warthog initially appears on so few lists. But, when safarists leave Africa, the warthog has a prominent spot in everyone's inventory.[111] Especially women — and I do not want to be misunderstood on this, as I do not pretend to know why — who fall madly in love with the little fellow. Harry Truman once stated that ''no man should be allowed to be President who does not understand hogs.'' Aside, of course, from deftly whittling down the electorate's choice, Truman's *bon mot* may have hidden insight for the visitor to Africa's savannahs.

Only the male has noticeable warts, a pair of large ''handle bars'' protruding just behind and under the eyes and a smaller but still prominent set positioned down the snout. (The female has a small and barely obvious pair located

---

108. *No Room in the Ark,* p. 17.

109. *Id.* Moorehead goes on to describe some local examples who had developed a passion for a kind of green apple growing wild that fell to the ground in summer: ''In this African heat the fruit ferments quickly and the warthogs sometimes become quite drunk. Instead of bolting in the usual way they stand and

---

gaze at the intruder with a bemused and careless eye. Then the instinct for self-preservation dimly asserts itself, and they turn and make a befuddled rush for a few yards, stop, change direction and then plunge off again. Finally they subside to sleep on the ground to awake to heaven knows what sort of primeval hangover in the morning.''

110. Markham, *West with the Night,* pp. 90-1.

111. Well, nearly everyone. Martin Johnson was unimpressed: ''The African warthog is just plain pig; he looks like a pig, tastes like a pig and usually acts the way I think a pig would . . . '' (*Safari,* p. 93). As the text elaborates, Osa had quite a different view.

below the eyes.) The purpose of the warts is apparently to serve as a mask of sorts for protecting the face, especially the eyes, when fighting or rooting. (Fighting involves head-to-head pushing, while attempting to strike the opponent's head with the flat upper surface of the snout or with the long and twisted blunt canines. The facial warts cushion the blows.) Some naturalists believe that the warts also prevent fluctuations in body temperature, but the author has never understood how this is so or why, then, the female should be left lacking. The elongated snout serves as a shovel, useful for clearing a burrow or looking for roots and tubers, as all pigs do. The snout has

twenty-four inches, but the average length is closer to twelve inches. Warthogs seldom use their tusks for digging. The lower pair, normally about six inches long, are the practical and effective fighting tools — they become quite sharp through constant honing against the upper tusks. Tusks are present in both sexes, but the boars carry heavier ones than the sows.

The safarist can never win the approval of a warthog. The reaction is always the same: the animal stares at the visitor for a suspicious second, grunts in alarm, wheels in a huff, and, showing his backside, assuming an air of supreme self-importance, and pointing his tail stiffly at the

Plate 92. Warthog. Africa produces elegance *and* the compact warthog, the ultimate one-liner. By the end of safari, the entertaining pig will have endeared itself to all but the hardest of hearts. (Albeit the harbored affection is often kept secret.) A warthog's legs are surprisingly slim for such a portly animal (weighing up to 200 pounds), which feature promotes a minimal area of contact with the ground and hence rapid movement. In other words, a warthog can really scoot along. Each foot has four toes: two touch the ground, and the other two are used only in soft terrain.

special bones that help make it exceptionally tough and resilient for such a task. The tail goes up like a car radio antenna when the warthog senses danger. (92)

Two pairs of powerful canine tusks protrude from the mouth, similar to those of a hippopotamus. The upper pair, shaped like scimitars, have been recorded as long as

sky, trots briskly away in jaunty strides. Fresh meaning to the phrases, "turn tail" and "hightailing it." An entire family, strung out single file in the same manner, is a preposterous ensemble, making its way across the savannah like some miniature train (93). And the faster the hog runs, the stiffer the erect and tufted tail, which serves, at least in a popular view, as a beacon for those family members following. The raised pennants may well serve that purpose, though the family stays close enough to follow an entire backside, but the warthog probably holds his tail up primarily to prevent it from being uncomfortably struck by his running back legs.

The warthog trots, however, with purpose and not for fun. Despite its well-deserved reputation for fierceness — few animals of comparable size can fight so effectively — the warthog is considered a culinary treat by lions, leopards, and wild dogs, a trio of predators not easily intimidated and rarely defeated. Scurrying off obviously makes more sense. And, even with its eyes placed high on its head and the broad vistas afforded by the open plains, the warthog has a dangerously low view. The pig compensates by maintaining strict alertness, by paying close attention to antelopes *(94)*, baboons, oxpeckers,[112] and other birds, and by seizing a quick start, without paying too much concern to exactly what it is that causes suspicion. A warthog has noteworthy stamina and, provided that it manages a good jump on its tormentors, can outlast most of them at thirty miles per hour.

Plate 93. Toy Train on Track. Safarists go crazy trying to secure pictures that capture both the fact and the spirit of the warthog group on the run. Like most visitors, I have been only mildly successful.

The warthog rarely ventures more than a few hundred yards from its burrow, usually a modified aardvark hole, where it settles in for the night, during the hottest parts of the day, and at times of danger. Burrows are, however, not necessarily a safe haven; indeed, the big cats can dig

the pigs out, and dangerous (to warthogs) would-be roommates not infrequently try to use the same dens.[113] Thus, the ever-ready adult warthog backs down into the hole and covers itself with dust; as such, the burrow represents a kind of loaded cannon.

Plate 94. Relying on Gazelles. Gazelles (and others) help the warthog monitor his environment.

The author has had firsthand experience with this phenomenon. Early one morning, I was watching a leopard from my Landrover. We had discovered the leopard in a tree finishing off an old antelope carcass. The cat then decided that a nearby clump of bushes afforded more privacy, descended from his airy platform, and proceeded to take his meal on the ground. In time, our vehicle attracted two other early rising groups in their vehicles. We were all, including the driver-guides, pretty excited: one hardly ever sees a leopard like this, and we were positioned only twenty yards away. On its part, the leopard was making quite a commotion — leopards can be rough eaters and really shake and rip up a carcass. After about one hour of what seemed like the noisiest ceremony in memory, the big cat finished its meal and settled down to

---

112. The author has seen warthogs nearly covered with tickbirds!

---

113. The aardvark's hole has been called Africa's motel: warthogs, snakes, mongooses, lizards, hyenas, and many other animals all check in (and out) on occasion. If a warthog goes to ground, the safarist should pause a few minutes. 'Warters' frequently reemerge within a short time, almost as if they do not trust the hole of choice. Indeed, some predators successfully just wait them out.

cleaning itself on the spot. Suddenly, without the slightest warning, the very ground underneath the leopard exploded. Something resembling a squealing cannonball emerged from a cloud of dust and shot off between two of the vehicles. The leopard was thrown straight up, recovered in mid-air, and itself streaked back to and up its tree. The human beings in attendance all uttered a collective surprised cry of alarm and jumped in our seats. The effect was reminiscent of seeing the shark for the first time in the film *Jaws*. But without any warning music! Only after a few seconds and seeing the famous rear-end with upright tail moving well off in the distance did we realize what had happened. The leopard had taken its meal lying *on top of* an occupied warthog burrow, unknowingly of course. Apparently, the warthog feared discovery when the eating stopped and the grooming began. The reader can imagine how *still* the warthog must have been, for over an hour, yet how wound like a spring to effect such an escape! And Mr. Stealth himself embarrassed! We looked up into the tree: our leopard had collected his composure and had resumed grooming but not without a nervous glance or two outward and an annoyed twitch of the tail — he may never have realized exactly what happened. The pig had disappeared into the horizon, no doubt looking for another burrow. The *petite histoire* ended quickly, but lives were enriched for the experience.

In Chapter II, I stressed the importance of staying alert for pictures of the unexpected. But, to secure a shot of our cannonball-warthog, I would have had to have been playing the fool and shooting the ground with motor drive on 'burst' — before the action started! Even the best photographers soon realize on safari that they are going to capture only a part of the experience on film. A safarist will never succeed in converting the African bush into a studio. Every now and then, a photographer will see, in a magazine somewhere, 'tips on safari' or something to this effect. A few are insightful; a few are beyond the pale. One of my 'favorites' included an explanation for using fill-flash to "manipulate" the image of a leopard who had gone down into a "dark hollow"! At such times, I am reminded of the White Hunter Jordan and his French photographer "Pete." Now, I also recall the cannonball. And suppress a guffaw.

Baby warthogs, piglets, come two to six in a litter. They are ridiculously tiny as infants and very appealing. *(95)* Characteristically curious, they venture from their dens early in life, whirling around their mother with abandon. Half are eaten by predators in the first six months. Females share in raising one another's youngsters and will nurse piglets other than their own (physically, a sow can suckle up to eight).

A warthog group of any size is called a "sounder." Though never very large, a sounder may include a couple of families, or some other social combination. Father and mother warthog are devoted parents, but the reported monogamy of pigs has been exaggerated. Males seem to fight over territory and females during mating season.

Plate 95. *Piglet: A Little Carbon Copy.* Baby warthogs are appealing little creatures and dash around, making little excited grunts as they go. Nairobi National Park is the best place in Africa to come reasonably close to a sounder with youngsters. Sows are very prolific and repeatedly produce large litters.

Warthogs are frequently seen grazing on their knees,[114] even shuffling along without bothering to stand *(96 & 97)*. Assuming or remaining in this posture is not a matter of reach but of voracious appetites: the prayer position compensates for a short neck and allows them to eat more, quicker. The pig has few sweat glands in its skin, so it cannot cool off by sweating. Consequently, it seeks the shade at midday *(98)* and is a frequenter of the mudbath. The old boars live alone and eventually forgo the deep dens for shallower depressions, where they are particularly vulnerable to predators with a taste for pork *(99)*. *(100)*

No animal in Africa escapes its share of anecdotal "science," and the warthog is certainly no exception. Occasionally, the learning is further embellished by a local legend, squaring the circle, so to speak. Thus, the warthog is supposed to approach waterholes hindfirst, kicking at the edges with its back feet before turning to drink. The backward approach is supposed to be a carry-over from going to ground. The kicking is for the purpose (we are told) of knocking some salt into the drinking water. In an unusual twist, the native legend makes more sense: the first warthog saw this hideous-looking beast lurking in the still water; thereafter, the timid animal always stirs his drinking water before facing it (so that he does not have to

---

114. Again, this is more accurately the carpal, or wrist, joint.

look at his own reflection). I have seen many warthogs take a drink and, quite unlike many other ungulates, they usually stride jauntily right to the water's edge, with little or no hesitation. None has ever backed in or kicked anything. Perhaps, the reader will have better luck.

Plates 96 & 97. The 'Prayer Position.' All warthogs have hardened pads or callosities on their forelegs for kneeling — even newborn piglets have them. Some naturalists have suggested that warthogs assume this position principally to root or drink. In the author's experience, the purpose is primarily to graze — voraciously, with a minimum of wasted effort. Warthogs are virtually omnivorous. In a world of finite resources, would not every animal want to be an omnivore? Not necessarily. Certain environments encourage specialists, and specialists (with appropriate adaptations) may have a competitive advantage in a given area. Often specialists lead safer lives, avoiding poisonous food and the like. In fact, being an omnivore requires high intelligence: there are too many possible foods, on the one hand, *and* dangerous substances, on the other hand, for strict hereditary programming. Thus, as we might expect, the pig is considered one of nature's most intelligent animals, inferior only to primates and dolphins. Some mutual grooming usually goes on within a family, but the basic order of the day for any sounder is the industrious and methodical exploration — called rooting — of the land ahead and determined eating.

Plate 98. Sounder at Midday. Most sounders are either bachelor groups or matriarchal family groups. Among warthogs, the mother-daughter bonds are especially strong. Until they grow old, warthogs are basically gregarious. Although ''sweat like a pig'' is embedded in our language (indeed, the pig generally does not fare too well in English expressions, from ''piggish'' to ''pigheaded'' to ''pig-in-a-poke'' and more), pigs have only a few sweat glands and sweat very little. In order to cool off, the warthogs must seek relief in the shade, a pool of water, or a mudhole.

Plate 99. Old Boar. Warthogs lead lives filled with peril. Aside from predation, rinderpest and the tsetse fly have been deadly. Surprisingly, at least to this author (who in his right mind would want to shoot a warthog?), sport as well has taken its toll. Warthogs consistently have been among the five mammal species most frequently imported into the United States as hunting trophies. The old boar shown here is a genuine survivor but is destined for some predator's table.

Plate 100. The Problem of a Low Profile: A Midday's Drama. There are two warthogs, one standing and one lying, and a lioness in this picture. With the patience of Job, the lioness has, in virtually no cover and by moving glacially no more than an inch or so off the ground, placed herself just to the right of the warthogs' bolthole. Another couple of feet and she will have sealed off their escape. The reader can now appreciate the danger of having a limited field of vision on the savannah. The hogs seem vaguely aware that something is amiss, but the midday heat has dulled their senses; a sort of alert stupor prevails (note the limp tail on the standing hog). Had the lioness charged, she would undoubtedly have enjoyed a pork dinner. But the tableau remained unchanged for another thirty minutes; perhaps, she wanted that last two feet of surprise. She had taken almost two hours by now (we had watched the entire, laborious process from a distance), when a breeze suddenly swept the tops of the grass with her scent. In a blink, the warters were off and running. The element of surprise fell to the prey, and they escaped. The lioness, caught flat-footed, could only watch them go.

2. Giant Forest Hog.

The Giant Forest hog was the last mammal discovered by the scientific world.[115] Its biology is still basically unknown. A forest animal, the heavily built hog is relatively abundant in Virunga National Park and the Aberdares but rarely seen. Mostly nocturnal, it normally emerges at dusk; perhaps, the best time to see the animal — certainly, the only likely time to see a family — is under the lights at one of the Tree Hotels in Kenya. Nevertheless, the hog is capable of appearing suddenly in the middle of the day — the photographer must remain alert in the forest. The males are distinguished by large, swollen crescent-shaped growths located below their eyes. *(101)*

I have seen a sounder of Giant Forest hogs at the Ark numbering nineteen: the scene honestly resembling some imaginative horror movie! *(102)* Again at the Ark, on a different night, I witnessed a fight between two huge boars. They charged at each other from a distance of eight to ten feet, and the resulting thunderclap of skulls could be heard, I imagine, throughout the nearby forest. After five

---

115. Richard Meinertzhagen, introduced in Chapter III, confirmed its existence in 1904.

Plate 101. *Giant Forest Hog.* On average, the hog weighs about 300 lbs. Some reports assert that weights reach 600 lbs. This seems a high number, until one realizes that farmers in the United States routinely fatten some breeding hogs to 800 lbs. or more (a select few in excess of 1000 lbs.).

Plate 102. *Down to the Salt-Lick.* In recent years, huge sounders of Giant Forest hogs have been turning up regularly at the Ark in Kenya.

Plate 103. A Romp with No Clear Winner.

jousts, the parties retired to their respective haunches, exhausted but apparently unscathed. The ranger assured me that these mock "brawls" (he said) were not serious: if either boar had meant business, he would have used his tusks in a sideways swipe. *(103)*

As befits a forest animal, the hog is built higher in the rump than in the shoulder, its eyes are small, and its ears are large and flexible (for a pig). As expected, its senses of smell and hearing are keen. The tail, long and tufted, is never carried upright like the warthog's. The author is content to give Isak Dinesen the last word:

> In the Ngong Forest I have also seen, on a narrow path through thick growth, in the middle of a very hot day, the Giant Forest Hog, a rare person to meet. He came suddenly past me, with his wife and three young pigs, at a great speed, the whole family looking like uniform, bigger and smaller figures cut out in dark paper, against the sunlit green behind them. It was a glorious sight, like a reflection in a forest pool, like a thing that had happened a thousand years ago.[116]

3. Bush Pig.

Though common and frequently found in large sounders, most visitors will not see a bush pig. The author does not have a clear photograph of one; the animal is strictly nocturnal. Easily distinguished from the warthog, the bush pig has much smaller (but sharper) tusks, a more elongated muzzle and a Roman nose (little or no 'stop'), protuberances below the eyes (but not nearly as large as a warthog's), and tassels of long hairs on the ears. The bush pig's long, thin tail hangs down when the animal runs. Several subspecies exist; the most common is the Red River hog, which has a bright, rust-colored coat and a long white dorsal crest of hair and white markings on its head and ears. It is a handsome pig.

Even more widely distributed than the warthog, the bush pig inhabits nearly any forest, woodland, or extended patch of bush. It is a serious nighttime pest to farmers (the extensive crop damage caused by the bush pig is often unfairly blamed on the warthog). In large sounders, a "master boar" usually emerges to lead the group.

A Gallery of Ungulates
(Plates 104-130)

---

116. Dinesen, *Out of Africa,* pp. 65-6.

Plate 104. Bongo Head Study. Bongos are the most secretive of all antelopes, congregating in small parties only when lying up during the day.

Plate 105. Leaping Blur. When an impala takes the time to gather itself and then leap, the result resembles an archery shot.

Plate 106. Eland Bulls. Appearances can be deceptive: the animal on the right has two horns, but the second is bent down along the neck.

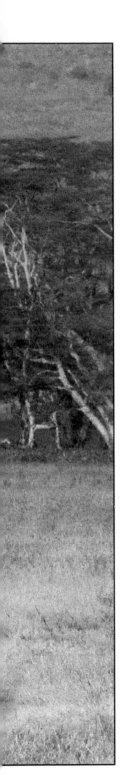

Plate 107. Waterbuck Young. Some safarists fill their carousel trays with lions and elephants. The author has four trays of waterbucks.

Plate 108. The Author and Bushbuck Doe at Mt. Kenya Safari Club. The animal orphanage here is a special place, not-to-be-missed by visitors stopping over.

Plate 109. Young Jumper. Adult zebra have few occasions to jump. Youngsters look for any little excuse to take off. Jumping a stream that one could easily walk across or go around is pure play: "wasteful" action in the face of the familiar.

Plate 110. Dik-Dik Pair. Slow down, look closely: the little dik-diks are everywhere. The safarist has, however, the same problem as the predators. Indeed, the dwarf antelopes themselves rely upon scent, rather than visual displays and encounters, to demarcate and maintain their exclusive territories.

Plate 112. Wildebeest on the Run. At migration times, the columns moving northward can reach fifteen miles long.

Plate 113. The Chase Phase. This particular tournament joust lasted an entire morning.

Plate 111. Oryx Jousting. Medieval heraldry in a Camelot display.

Plate 115. Wildebeest and Zebra at Water. Why is the wildebeest the dominant herbivore in the Serengeti? Why, indeed, does the wildebeest outnumber its buddy, the zebra? Some naturalists have pointed to the gnu's wide row of incisor teeth, tools that can harvest more grass per mouthful than any other grazer.

Plate 114. Tommy Leaping. Running, zigzagging, stotting, or leaping, the tommy is an impressive little athlete, the Olga Korbut of the animal world.

Plate 116. Flehmen.

Plate 118. More Exercise than a Quarrel. Unless present at the Serengeti-Mara migration, the safarist will see more of the irrepressible tommies than any other ungulate.

Plate 119. Impala Doe with Newborn.

Plate 117. Non-Migrant at Home. Amboseli wildebeest are essentially non-migratory. Interestingly enough, non-migratory herds lose more of their population annually to predation than migrants, over twice as many victims.

Plate 120. A Grevy's Tapestry of Hindquarters.

Plate 121. Unicorn. A one-horned impala ram makes as good a unicorn as any.

Plate 124. Herding. Males will run their (temporary) females in herding exercises to keep them within the designated territories.

Plate 122. The Mad Scramble. A herd of impala fleeing danger, real or imaginary, reminds the author of the at-home Fourth of July celebration when younger brother managed to set off the entire *box* of fireworks.

Plate 123. A Suspicious Brood. Most ungulate females bear one large, well-developed juvenile at a time. Pigs are an exception and produce several piglets to a litter.

Plate 125. Fear. This youngster has just realized that a leopard is advancing not ten yards away, a realization that might well bring the reader's hair to stand on end under similar conditions.

Plate 127. Bachelors on a Spree.

Plate 128. Grevy's Mating. With the distinct disapproval of the little fellow (though he will enjoy the playmate soon enough!).

Plate 126. Wildebeest and Dust. The safarist, who for a brief time fights the problem, will sympathize with the improbable gnu, who lives with the pervasive dust all its life.

Plate 129. The Colors of Africa. And perhaps the best reminder that asking the ''why?'' of things is a reliably important question only if one is prepared to accept an occasional answer, ''no special reason.''

Plate 130. A Run Through the Tall Grass. Ungulates are never so spectacular as when they run.

VIII. Primates and Reptiles

Each time I entered the Ground Water Forest in Manyara it always made me feel as if I were living in a fairy tale. It was magical with its tall, naked, grey-limbed trees standing next to yellow-barked fig trees, racing each other up to the sun, covered in an iridescent canopy. Baboons and monkeys jumped through the branches, swishing the leaves like rustling taffeta, and called to each other with chuckles and barks. Crystal clear springs emerged from below the cliffs and flowed in little streams under a shiny, emerald carpet of plants, which looked like tiny palm trees. When one walked through the forest, the sun streamed down like long spider-spun threads. It was cool and translucent, with the same damp smell as an old cathedral. Sweet flowers and the strong scent of elephants mingled and blew in the wind. Anyone who walks through the Ground Water Forest must stop and look and feel the wonder of it, for it is unique. It is alive.

Douglas-Hamilton, *Among the Elephants*[1]

Primates

The primates of Africa, man excluded, divide into three groups: Old World monkeys, apes, and prosimians. These primates share obvious characteristics. Most are mainly vegetarian, though some eat insects, few eat meat, and fewer still eat considerable quantities of meat. Primates usually produce only one young at a time and virtually never more than two. All have well-developed brains (though there are many levels of 'higher' intelligence within the primate order). The arrangement of their teeth is generally similar to that of man — a continuous row of incisors, canines, and cheek-teeth (molars and pre-molars). Their hands and feet usually contain five digits, including an opposable thumb, and are capable of grasping. Consequently, most primates have adapted to an arboreal existence. And they tend to adopt an upright posture, at least when sitting. Apes and monkeys are active by day; by contrast, the prosimians are generally nocturnal. Sight and hearing, rather than smell, are a primate's most important senses. And binocular vision enables it to judge distances.

In keeping with the theme of this study, only those animals that are most likely to be seen by the average tourist are emphasized here. Gorillas and chimpanzees are briefly discussed, because they are frequently the objects of special-destination safaris. The lemurs of Madagascar are also noted.

Watching primates in the wild can be a special treat for many of us: here, before the safarist, are — so the many scientists testify — man's closest relatives. But, in the most profound sense, the African primates are simply a gloss on the entire safari experience. On safari, the visitor confronts *life* in many more of its manifestations than one sees at home — whether home is the concrete jungle that we have created or something closer to Our Town. And the primates, man included, represent, in any view of evolution, only a fraction of the many participants in life. Many of the African animals can be seen in zoos. Why therefore spend several thousand dollars and take the time to travel halfway around the world? In Chapter X, we will look at the question of just how "wild" are the inhabitants of game reserves — a question that may well have particular relevance to those primates who have been studied seemingly to the point of domestication — but the distinction between one's local zoo and the African bush should be clear enough by now to admit that the former is no direct substitute for the latter. Zoos, whatever their justifications (and there are, in the author's view, several), are not "home" to the inhabitants. The observant and sensitive safarist is going to see special, dare one say "miraculous," things on safari. And the magic of confronting life, other life, at *home* is worth whatever it costs and however long it takes.

1. *Monkeys: Baboons.*

Baboons undoubtedly are the most studied creatures in Africa (though chimps run a close second). For years, scientists have eavesdropped on and spied upon the intimate details of baboon life. But, as might be anticipated, the usual controversies of classification and behavior are stronger than ever! Indeed, why should naturalists argue any less than, say, economists? Certainly, the complexities of baboon life rival obscure economic formulae, graphs, and equations. If they were capable of expressing an opinion, the baboons themselves would probably welcome both the attention and the blessings of such controversy. For years, the Africans and the white settlers

---

1. At p. 170.

alike treated baboons as "vermin." Such infamy resulted from the monkey's periodic onslaughts against man's agriculture. The "thief of Africa" was a "born bully, a born criminal, a born candidate for the hangman's noose."[2] Only slowly (and successfully only recently) did baboons achieve the status of "wildlife." In truth, before going to Africa, the author found monkeys in zoos mildly to overwhelmingly repulsive — and boring, to boot. But monkeys where they belong are another matter altogether — fascinating, charming, intelligent, challenging, and worthy of many hours of the safarist's time. Without necessarily experiencing the excitement level of Ivan Sanderson,[3] no one easily forgets a lengthy encounter with a large troop of baboons.

For convenience's sake (that is, without attempting to settle scientific controversies), one can point to eight "species" of African baboon, the largest of the so-called Old World monkeys,[4] but only three need concern us here[5]: the Anubis or highland Olive baboon of nothern Tanzania, western and central Kenya, Uganda, Sudan, and Ethiopia; the lowland Yellow baboon of Mozambique, Malawi, Zambia (north of the Kafue River), Tanzania, and eastern Kenya; and the Chacma baboon of Southern Africa, principally found in South Africa, Zimbabwe, and southern Zambia. Many taxonomists and scientists believe that these three baboons are actually races of one species, the Anubis baboon ("nyani" in Kiswahili), ranging therefore from the tip of South Africa all the way to the uppermost parts of Ethiopia and the Sudan and extending as well into Central Africa and even farther west. Indeed, the social organization and behavior of all three are quite similar, and, in zones where the different baboons overlap, they interbreed, producing a wide range of gradations. Physically, there are superficial divergencies. The Olive baboon is the largest and most stocky. The males have a thick mantle or mane of hair extending over their head, upper back, and shoulders very much in the manner of lions. Coat color is olive-green and grey. *(1)* The Yellow baboon has a generally rangy and leggy appearance and a more dog-like head. The males have a less prominent mane. Yellow and brown, the Yellow baboon also has predominantly white underparts. Chacma baboons are nearly as large as their Olive counterparts but also are slim like their Yellow cousins, have the small mantles of the latter, and are colored dark olive-grey, with black heads, hands, and feet. But, as indicated earlier, beneath these assorted distinctions, the anatomies of all three types show great similarities.

The baboon is as widespread as it is because of its extreme adaptability. Among primates, only man inhabits more ecological zones or separate environments. Until fairly recently, in fact, baboons outnumbered human beings in Africa. And, although slaughtered for years as a pest, the baboon still survives in significant numbers. Along with the vervet (discussed below), the baboon thus may be considered the most "successful" of the world's monkeys. In South Africa, the Hottentots maintain that the baboons can speak but refrain so as not to encourage man's proclivity to put them (the Chacmas) to work. Indeed, the baboon has been trained to perform a variety of menial tasks — the most famous example was "Jack the Signalman," who actually learned to pull the levers that operated the rail switches in response to a designated number of toots. He performed flawlessly, without supervision, for years.

Baboons[6] live in troops ranging from ten to 200

<hr />

2. Robert Ardrey, *The Territorial Imperative* (Dell Edition, 1966), p. 246. Ardrey continues: "He has the yellow-to-amber eyes that one associates with a riverboat gambler. . .he enjoys nothing better than killing and *devouring* the newborn fawns of the *delicate* gazelle. And he will steal anything." (Emphasis added — the reader can just feel the venom dripping from such a description.) Ardrey also credits the monkey, as befits one's casual conception of the riverboat gambler, with immense cleverness. In his earlier study, *African Genesis,* he wrote:

> If while he [the "bandit of Africa"] is plundering a man comes out of a farm-house, he will flee. If a woman comes out, he will ignore her. But if a determined male human enemy dresses in woman's clothes, the baboon will instantly take to the woods. And South African farmers are convinced that the baboon can count to three. When a troop of chacma baboons raids an orchard and the enraged farmer appears, the troop will withdraw to return of course the instant he leaves. If three farmers enter the orchard, and two withdraw, the baboons are not to be deceived; they will keep their distance. Only if four farmers enter the orchard, and three withdraw, will the baboon's mathematics fail him. He will return to the orchard and fall into an ambush. (*African Genesis* [Dell Edition, 1967], pp. 78-9.)

The reader can only imagine the prodigious research that backs up this piece of wisdom.

3. See Chapter III, p. 83.

4. New World monkeys have a prehensile tail that can be used for gripping. New World monkeys also have nostrils that are wide-open, set far apart, and face outwards; the Old World species have nostrils that are narrow by comparison, close together (the septum between them is very thin), and point downwards. Old World monkeys have ischial callosities — bare, leathery buttock or sitting patches — whereas, their New World counterparts have none.

5. The other five are the terrestrial drill and the strikingly colored mandrill (the largest living monkey) of West and Central Africa; the red-faced and heavy-maned Hamadryas baboon (the sacred baboon of Ancient Egypt) found in Ethiopia, Sudan, and Somalia; the mountain Gelada baboon of Ethiopia; and the reddish Guinea or Western baboon of West Africa. (The Guinea baboon may well be a western race of the Hamadryas species.) Closely related to the baboon are mangabeys, large, diurnal forest monkeys found in many parts of Africa.

6. The text from this point refers to the Anubis baboon, broadly defined. Two picture books that have recently appeared contain particularly outstanding photographs of baboons: Gerald

Plate 1. Olive Baboon. According to one writer, the baboon has a rather Lincolnesque face; indeed, Abe Lincoln's enemies reviled him with the epithet "baboon." Naturalists are quick to note that baboons provide an instructive example of how social behavior relates to environment. A long time ago, baboons probably lived primarily in forests and in trees (as most primates do today). As these forests declined, the baboons chose to live on the resulting savannahs, a decision encouraged by food availability and living space. The savannah — an essentially open environment — presented, however, a far less safe habitat; the number and size of the potential predators increased dramatically, as raptors and snakes gave way to lions, leopards, cheetahs, hyenas, and wild dogs. The baboons responded by organizing themselves in troops that grew to larger and larger units, the individual members totally coordinated their lives, and a common front by the strongest males was adopted as a defense against most danger. A better early-warning system and statistical probabilities did the rest. But, after Chapter VII, the reader should be leery of such predation-oriented emphasis. Monkeys, unlike most other forest dwellers, have always congregated in groups: the ability to go *up*, as well as *out*, makes a big difference. Herding then becomes a viable strategy for avoiding predation, and food supplies, sparsely distributed for most forest species, increase dramatically. In fact, the author has never seen convincing evidence that baboon troops were particularly smaller at some previous time.

individuals.[7] The maximum number sometimes grows even higher, though the largest groups become too cumbersome and strain available food resources — the primary determinant of troop size — and eventually split into two smaller troops. Roughly fifty is probably a typical unit, which would then ordinarily break down pretty much as follows: eight adult males, sixteen adult females, and twenty-six subordinates, juveniles, and babies. For many years, scientists believed that the troop was organized as a strict hierarchy, ruled under a regime of stern discipline maintained by a senate or junta composed of powerful, dominant males. No single male ever stood alone at the top of any sizeable group. The oligarchy, once established, was thought to remain stable for long periods, with little fighting within the clique itself. All troop life was organized by these elite males. The movement of the troop, protection from predators, discipline, and mating, for example — these were thought to be controlled by the aristocratic patriarchs at the center. For their part, the females were believed to have a fairly unstable hierarchy among themselves and to quarrel frequently. A female's status within the troop depended, in this view, entirely on her current relationships with the dominant males, and, as might be expected, the overlords always elevated the importance of females in estrus and females with newborns.

The latest studies show (at times) a far more subtle and even (at other times) a widely variant picture of group dynamics. The stable core, the real anchor, of the troop now appears — not unlike that of a lion pride or an elephant herd, for example — to be female, that is, focused on mothers and their descendants and collateral offspring. The troop is still viewed as a coordinated and predominantly exclusive group, in which everyone is actively assigned a place and a rank. The members — one hesitates to use the word "individuals" — travel, feed, and sleep together. No matter how large the troop, every baboon seems to know every other baboon; all interact frequently. In a typical troop, adult females outnumber adult males two or three to one; it is the female who remains with the troop into which she was born for her entire life. And female relationships now appear to be remarkably stable. On the other hand, males voluntarily move out of their natal troop as they mature, between the ages of two and three years. Some form new groups, most

join existing troops. In fact, the adult males tend to shift around, switching troops from time to time, though they are always more than simply fringe members of a particular troop. The frequency of such maneuvering apparently depends significantly on the local environment and varies considerably from one area to another. Moreover, the dominance relationships among the males frequently change. The so-called "senate" periodically readjusts its own hierarchy and rules of procedure, causing a certain measure of instability among the mature males.

Nevertheless, the new learning is mostly a change of emphasis, not a wholesale invalidation of earlier studies. One can still pick out a "senate" of sorts, and the adult males indeed receive their due by the remainder of the troop. A mature male will, for example, displace a female or an immature male at a resting place or water source. Rank is always reflected in priority access to food. Without doubt, the adult male is a powerful animal by any reckoning, about twice the size of the female. His mantle of hair, which can be bristled when excited, makes him look even larger and more impressive. *(2)* The notable three-inch dagger-like canines have been remarked upon earlier. Of the entire troop, these adult males, as they stroll among all and sundry, are the most likely to attract the attention of the fast-moving safarist.[8]

What is now clear is that, despite the presence of several of these formidable males living in the average troop, the old emphasis of social cohesion promulgated by fear and sexual attraction has been seriously challenged by the available evidence. Not only does the

---

Cubitt, *Portraits of the African Wild* (Chartwell Books, 1986), pp. 69-79 (Chacma baboons); and Hugo van Lawick, *Among Predators and Prey* (Sierra Club Books, 1986), scattered throughout, but where the monkey finally makes the "big time" — a (spectacular) cover!

7. Instances of finding solitary baboons (invariably, males) have infrequently been reported, but such occurrences might be nothing more than transitional, brief interludes between troop lives. A baboon is simply not an individual in an ordinary sense; a single baboon is the ultimate "organization man" and has little identity apart from its place in the troop.

8. Throughout nature, significant size differential between males and females of the same species usually signals intense sexual competition: the largest males can normally defeat more rivals and sire more offspring; and the females in turn prefer the bigger mates, whose sons will accordingly prosper because of *their* increased size. In baboon society, relative size is, however, only one factor among many in determining status and may not even achieve importance in some troops. (Throughout all nature, males are generally smaller than females, a pragmatic result of the relative roles of the sperm and the egg: the sperm is essentially a "messenger boy" delivering DNA, while the egg carries all that is required for embryonic or larval growth, including early food. Moreover, females usually provide the primary care of the egg and young. In mammals, males often become larger because they compete as *individuals* for access to females — a strong argument for Darwinian evolution, evolution for individual advantage alone.) Moreover, it is generally believed that male "weaponry," such as canines and manes, are very pronounced in competitive polygamous species. Again, the male baboon has both impressive canines and a distinctive ruff, but the corresponding intense sexual competition is lacking. This is not to say that adult male baboons do not physically compete for mating rights — they do and, in some troops, quite often, especially for priority in the queue. The females are not, however, the passive objects of male competition; in large measure, the females establish both the permissible competitors and the boundaries of the competition.

Plate 2. Adult Male. The safarist can easily distinguish the adult male from the female: the male is roughly twice as large, has a thick mantle of hair around the shoulders and face, and has large canine teeth and an elongated muzzle to house them. Adult males stand nearly three-and-one-half feet tall on all fours. Baboons walk by putting their "hands" flat on the ground, not supporting themselves on the knuckles like apes. The most specialized ground-walkers of all the monkeys, baboons stand higher in the shoulder than hips when moving forwards. The impressive mantle grows in at about eight years.

female-female matrix, known as a "matriline,"[9] seem more likely to define the social life of the troop, but males in reality do not act as aggressive despots. Perhaps, the best proof of a fundamentally matrilineal outlook within the troop is mating behavior. During estrus, pair formation is both temporary and, most strikingly, not directly related to any male hierarchy prevailing at the moment. The estrous female will invariably mate with at least two, and frequently more, males; paternity of newborns is, in fact, impossible to determine. Moreover, the females obviously make their own choices of partners. Finally, the females often appear (to human eyes, at least) fairly unpredictable as to which males they will choose.[10] In this

and preference groupings define the on-going social life of the troop. The male immigrant thus has to penetrate a fairly dense network of relatives and friends. This he does, as discussed in the text, by catching the eye, so to speak, of a particular female or females. The process of establishing a relationship takes months but eventually serves to incorporate the male into the troop. What is important to note here, is that both sides to a relationship have made a significant *investment* of time, energy, and available social flexibility. Females pass much of their adult lives either pregnant or nursing (lactating) and accordingly are not sexually receptive over ninety percent of the time. With so limited a love life, the female naturally turns to the limited number of males, usually two to four, with whom she has (jointly) invested the time and energy in establishing a prior social bond (and, who knows, the female may well have chosen her social bonds with 'sexual' characteristics in mind). Thus the observation of naturalists who report that mating preferences extend to grooming, feeding, traveling, and other social activities. While this behavior falls far short of monogamy, it is a social strategy that generally promotes efficiency and 'equitable' troop cohesion. (Male friends in turn offer the female and her kin additional protection, against predators and other troop members.) It also ensures that mating partnerships are well spread throughout the troop: different females will obviously choose different males. And males that have, as most do, more than one mating bond will generally mate within the same matriline or preference group. Thus, from all the potential disorder and conflict emerges a working society based upon "families," or at least the derivative concept of "familiarity." Courtship itself is not elaborate, as the mates know each other too well to make a big fuss. Copulation is brief, and the mating pair can count on frequent interruptions by juveniles.

9. Matrilineal cohesion among baboons has some additional "rules": the rank of different members of the same matriline follows birth order, that is, daughters rank immediately below their mothers but *above* older sisters. Furthermore, matrilines themselves are ranked inter se: all members of high-ranking matrilines outrank all members of low-ranking ones, irrespective of individual ages. In other words, new matrilines follow the mother and share her status in the troop.

10. What exactly is the basis for female choice is a complicated question and beyond the observations of a casual safarist. The answer, in simplified form, seems to be as follows. The maternal kin network, or matriline, noted in the text extends down through several generations and out to include at least first cousins. In addition, females will form other "preference" relationships (and groups), especially between or among females that have (or have had) infants of similar ages. These matrilines

respect, among others, "dominance" is too strong a term and implies too simplistic an advancement by males to the front of the mating queue. Something akin to "friendships," the establishment of preference relationships, is more accurate. Kinship is, as suggested, crucial, and troop identity derives in large measure from the matrix of family relationships that exists, but, among the separate families and between males and females, the cultivation of preference relationships will determine much in the way of social life. While size and strength have a bearing, a male's broad social strategies seem more important in achieving status — a classic example of 'brains (or personality) over brawn.' Nor are the lines of preference or authority or leadership strictly linear. The entire troop is better viewed as a union of interlinked circles, some larger and intersecting more circles than others. Indeed, the richness and complexity of baboon life — and the intricate relationships that result — resemble man's societies. *(3)*

If a safarist were to take sufficient time to follow a troop, he would witness several disputes, during which various baboons would obviously take sides. Indeed, the outcome of a given argument normally depends on which party is the most "influential" and who can garner the most support. Kin groups naturally tend to support their own members, but non-kin reciprocity is often determinative. Females (and, by extension, their families) achieve definite spheres of influence within the troop. And, although the intervention of adult males often settles severe controversies, the early belief that a female's status was elevated (by the dominant males) when she was in estrus now appears unfounded. Each time that a new male enters a troop, he does not fight his way into the senate but begins a process of maneuvering and cultivating social relationships with important or influential females (after a brief period sitting on the sidelines, presumably to locate target females). At this point in our education, one has to wonder whether the adult males ever form strong relationships among themselves. The senate seems neither to meet nor to vote! The connection among these mature males is dynamic, and "dominance," such as it is, shifts continually. Certainly, in dispute settlement, the males choose sides (not respective merits) along with everyone else. The most successful males become social fathers to a female's family.[11] Some males fail and rather quickly move on to another troop.

For the safarist, an obvious indication of a preference relationship takes place during grooming — who grooms whom. Grooming is conspicuous and, apart from ridding the animals of parasites, plays an important part in social bonding. Constant grooming is prevalent among most primates: a practical, hygienic measure and an important social ritual. Grooming is also used as a weaning tool — that is, during the weaning, grooming of the youngster is significantly increased. During a grooming session, relatives will typically gather round the oldest female of the matriline.

Throughout the day, the troop can deal effectively with most would-be predators. Little escapes a baboon's vision, probably the best of any terrestrial creature anywhere (with the possible exception of the ostrich): stereoscopic (like man's), far-ranging (said by some to equal eight-powered binoculars), and capable of judging distances and focusing on motionless objects far away with great accuracy. A baboon also has color vision, rare among all animals. In addition, baboons have a good sense of hearing.[12] Baboon troops frequently employ scouts or sentries, sending monkeys to nearby trees or the tops of ant hills to reconnoiter and maintain a lookout. When the alarm is raised, the big males often come forward to investigate. In the presence of predators — hyenas, jackals, cheetahs, or leopards — the males may advance in a threatening manner, flashing their long canines, grunting, and screeching. The literature sometimes records some surprising encounters:

> Down in the south-west [of Africa] where the leopards are smaller and the baboons are very big, a troup of baboons will hunt down a leopard and kill it by tearing it to pieces, at every possible opportunity. From an elevated position up on top of a mountain range in Gordonia, South-West Africa, I watched a troop of great baboons drive a leopard down off the mountain to the sand flats below, and down an ant-bear hole. As soon as the leopard disappeared down

---

11. Interestingly enough, young baboons seek out their mother's male friends (and, perhaps, their fathers) from an early age. The relationship resembles one of hero-worship: the safarist may see a little baboon sitting for quite awhile and staring adoringly (so it seems) at an adult male. To a large degree, the males reciprocate, and a bond is formed. As with all baboons, however, friendships mean different things to individual baboons, so clear patterns are difficult to describe.

---

12. The normal rule in nature is that the lessening of one sense is usually associated with intensification of another or others. All the higher primates — essentially non-predatory, active primarily in the daylight, and originally forest-dwelling — developed acute sight (and, to a lesser extent, hearing). Many observers think that antelopes seek out the company of baboons; the combination of baboon sight and hearing with the antelope's strong sense of smell is, indeed, a formidable early-warning system. As noted earlier, in Chapter VII, baboons are often found in the company of impalas, gazelles, waterbuck, and even bushbuck. Especially at waterholes. Some authors have suggested that the antelopes additionally are taking advantage of the baboon's fighting abilities. It may be doubted, however, whether the antelopes would, in fact, wait around for a contest! Moreover, it would seem a moot point whether the antelopes choose the baboons' company or vice-versa. In any event, the association commonly is one of good will; the author has, for example, observed several instances of what appeared to be baboons and antelopes playing together. Baboons also turn up frequently with zebra herds, but no one has suggested a basis for a formal relationship. Warthogs for some reason (possibly fearing predation of their young) seem to chase baboons, given half a chance.

Plate 3. The Troop. To the casual safarist, troop life is chaotic. Squabbles abound. Different baboons appear to be eating different foods. Indeed, the baboons are, in a sense, always looking out for Number One. For example, if a baboon discovers just enough fruit for one, he will quickly eat it — he will signal for his friends only if there is enough food for many. Confronted by such scenes, commentators have been moved to stress baboon individuality and to contrast a troop with an antelope herd. To the extent that such theorizing de-emphasizes the collective nature of baboon life, it is misdirected. The relationships among troop members are, however, undoubtedly more intricate than those prevailing throughout an ungulate herd. Grooming is the most obvious and time-consuming form of primate social behavior. Obviously, grooming keeps the animals clean — baboons are virtually free of ticks and other parasitic insects. Dead skin and dirt are also removed. But, equally important, grooming helps to develop and reinforce bonding among individuals. Both teeth and hands are used, with great delicacy and dexterity (like birds preening), to rake the hair. The expressions found on the faces of the recipients of this attention are relaxed and blissful, almost comical really, and the whole process can take an hour or more. Socializing is, of course, greatly influenced by the environment and the size of the troop. For example, where food is plentiful and appetites satisfied relatively quickly, baboons have more time for grooming.

the hole, the biggest baboon took up a position just behind the hole; while on each side of it and a little back two big baboons posted themselves . . . on each side: further back the rest of the troop waited. Not a move was discernible from any of the baboons and perfect silence reigned for quite half an hour, when the leopard, thinking all was clear, came slowly out. As soon as its head protruded out of the hole and below the central baboon, the baboon grabbed it by both ears, pulling its head back against the roof while the others rushed in, and dragging it out to the surface, tore it to pieces.[13]

Perhaps slightly more reliable, yet still remarkable, are the observations of Jonathan Scott recorded in his *Leopard's Tale* (a book highly recommended in Chapter I), including witnessing the scavenging by baboons of a

---

13. Marcus Daly, *Big Game Hunting and Adventure: 1897-1936* (MacMillan, 1937), p. 228.

leopard's kill lodged in a tree. Under most circumstances, 'mobbing' a predator is a sufficient deterrent. Mobbing commonly consists of a sequence of mock attacks, alternating charging and retreating, with loud vocalizing (screaming) all the way (some monkeys will even throw branches at a predator). The monkeys, torn between aggression and fear, frequently stop and engage in reassuring behavior among themselves, then resume. The predator, robbed of all surprise, hunts elsewhere.

Naturalists once thought that the troop traveled in an anti-predation formation organized with military precision: lower-ranking adult and subadult males marched at the front and rear of the troop, acting as scouts; mothers with infants and younger juveniles moved in the center of the troop guarded by the big males; and the remainder of the troop scattered to buffer the center. We now know that such precision is mostly imagination. Baboon movement depends on whether a troop is feeding along the way, when no discernible formation normally is evident, or moving primarily to cover ground, when some organization is obvious, though the alignment varies without assuming a definable pattern. Sometimes, the troop moves as a tight unit in columns of several abreast, each animal positioned only a few feet from the next. At other times, the monkeys are spread out virtually single-file over several miles! The males are, however, always obviously handy for perceived trouble. The troop can travel as far as twelve miles a day foraging for food, but one to two miles is more like an average day's journey. A large troop, forty members or more, will occupy up to fifteen square miles of home range.

The one predator that baboons never advance to challenge is the lion, alone or in the company of other lions. Baboons flee lions in a great raucous mêlée, every baboon for itself, like duckpins hit by a bowling ball. Occasionally, baboons react in the same way to the approach of man. But, even in times of flight, as soon as safety is reached, the troop comes to resemble a political meeting at Hyde Park Corner — hissing and screaming with frenzy, the monkeys alternate between threats and mockery from the safety offered by their perches.

The author is not suggesting that baboons unnecessarily challenge their many predators. In fact, mobbing is an effective deterrent. And, all in all, baboons lead reasonably cautious lives. Aware of the various hazards found in their home ranges, they avoid potentially dangerous areas. Nor do they fall victim to the "Andrea Doria syndrome" so common to lower animals: once in familiar territory, baboons do not drop their guard.[14] Baboons tend to congregate where they can take immediate refuge, if need be, in the event that a predator strikes. They show extreme caution when approaching a permanent waterhole or river, both which are usually surrounded by vegetation tall or thick enough to hide a predator. (4) In the presence of zebras or antelopes, a real Alphonse-Gaston routine develops: the baboons keeping a close watch on the activities of the ungulates, the ungulates waiting for the baboons. A warning bark from a baboon or a quick snort from an antelope will freeze everyone into a full ten minutes of suspicion. Only the presence of a giraffe can accelerate the proceedings. When baboons do drink, they drink hurriedly, to reduce their exposure.

At night, the monkeys sleep in tall trees or on the sides of steep cliff faces or at the tops of the large kopjes. Baboons are conscientious about retiring before twilight (the East African plains are dark by 6:30 p.m.) and on cloudy days will always settle down by 5:00 p.m. The most inaccessible roosts are chosen, limited only by the weight that the perch will support. The adult males thus usually find themselves, intentionally or not, positioned

between the troop and possible danger on the ground. In any event, the members of the troop also sleep as close as possible to one another. Baboons sleep sitting up (apes and New World monkeys do not have ischial callosities and sleep horizontally). And it is thought that they sleep fitfully, waking frequently to listen for leopards (neither the trees nor rocky cliffs are completely safe from leopards or snakes) and to keep from losing their balance and falling. Finally, the troop does not rise early, thereby giving the early hunting or late-retiring predators a wide berth. Indeed, by 9:00 a.m., the baboons may still be in the trees, looking to the earlier-rising safarist like Dinesen's "overripe fruits ready to drop."

The adult males save their most virulent aggressiveness for the predators; the senate has few real quarrels itself. Adult males do, however, fight occasionally but they rarely go to lethal lengths. In fact, a dispute is mostly noise and threat rituals. A real fight is an eye-opener: the safarist sees what looks very much like a wild dance, complete with hair-raising screams. Actual contact is sporadic. And the losing side has many ploys to inhibit the belligerency of the other combatant and gracefully[15] end the conflict. One of the more common appears a bit bizarre at first glance: the losing side will snatch up a young infant and hold the baby to its stomach (as a mother would do) or even thrust the captive before the opponent of the moment. An aggressor must then choose between incurring the wrath of the baby's mother (and the entire matriline, bolstered by its male friends) or halting. This use of "buffers" occasionally extends to seizing small females as well and normally stops the fight at once. The fun begins when an uncooperative buffer is chosen; panic-stricken and complaining vociferously, the buffer attracts its family and friends in defense, and chaos results.[16] This chain reaction emphasizes an important lesson concerning baboons: relations are rarely one-to-one affairs, social life involves networks of families and friends, and reciprocal balancing is the norm. Troop life becomes far more complicated than that of a lion pride or even an elephant herd.[17]

Baby baboons are born after a gestation of some six months. Only a few trained researchers who have devoted years to baboon study have witnessed a birth in

---

14. The Andrea Doria sank in regularly traveled shipping lanes in 1956.

15. Some retreats are not so "graceful." A submitting male may assume the posture of a sexually receptive female. The dominant male will then simulate the act of copulation (called "socio-sexual mounting," a term the reader may someday want to drop in casual conversation) before allowing the other baboon to rejoin the troop. The intimidation ritual may be repeated at short intervals for some time, until honor (or whatever) is fully satisfied.

16. At other times, when a dispute arises between females or between juveniles, an adult male may sometimes step forward to calm the difficulty.

17. The most complex primate troop structures are those of the male-dominated Hamadryas baboons found in Ethiopia.

the wild. Most births take place at night, which fact might be expected, given the mobile life of baboons during the day. Few young animals face life as helpless as does the baboon newborn. It has a black coat and pink face and ears. These conspicuous babies are irresistible to the other females of the troop; all "friends" of the mother take a great interest either in touching the infant (sometimes resulting in unfortunate tugs of war, when a mother resists, or outright kidnappings at other times) or grooming the new mother to achieve a position nearer to the infant. The baby at first clings to the hair of its mother's chest when moving about during the first month. It is not unusual at this time to see mothers walking three-legged, holding with one hand the young baboon that is clinging underneath. To the safarist, this sight indicates that the young baboon in question has only recently been born. After the first month, the youngster rides jockey-style on top of mother's lower back, hanging on with all fours *(5 & 6)*. Gradually, the young monkey ventures a few steps away from its mother to eat a little solid food and to begin to play with older kin. At four to six months, the black

coat turns a light brown, and the pink face and ears grow darker. More and more time is spent with its peers and exploring its immediate world. Like lion cubs, young baboons are great mischief-makers and soon assume a high-octane life. Naturalists regard such playfulness as a strong indication of animal intelligence. And all the running, chasing, and wrestling helps in the development of muscles and reflexes and provides a rehearsal for adult situations. More like human babies than other mammals, the young baboons are capable of great temper tantrums. A visitor cannot watch a large troop for long without experiencing a shattering round of clamor. And the screeching accompanying punishment is something else. All in all, the youngsters are responsible for much of the noise and commotion of the troop.[18]

---

18. Young baboons are incorrigible pranksters, on the one hand, and serious students, on the other hand. Watching them, the safarist might want to distinguish between exploration and play — both dominate the youngster's life — and to reflect on the nature of genuine curiosity. Both exploration and play

Plate 4. Male Drinking. Baboons prefer to drink daily, unless sufficient moisture is available from dew or succulent vegetation.

Plate 5. Jockey. A normal female passes half her adult life with a dependent infant and one-third of that life pregnant. Females reach social and sexual maturity earlier than do males. In their third or fourth year, young females come into estrus for the first time. Estrus is highly conspicuous, distinguished by pronounced swelling of and bright pink coloring in the "sexual skin" around the tail and the hard callous pads (technically called ischial callosities). The skin also stays pink during pregnancy and turns bright red shortly before birth. The females are not monogamous and mate with several males. Copulation is a quick affair — ten seconds is normal. A female usually has her first baby at about four-and-a-half years old. A female's breeding life is roughly ten to twelve years, during which time she will produce on average seven infants.

demand physical exertion that ultimately promotes healthy physiological development. Exploration is purposeful — goal-oriented or at least consciously exploratory — and thrusts the juvenile into its environment to learn information and skills necessary to survive and soon enough, as an adult, to perpetuate its species. All species "explore"; the function or trait is exaggerated in primates. (Or it may be that the activity is simply more recognizable to us when performed by primates.) Watching baboons "explore," one is hard-pressed to avoid the conclusion that something very much like human curiosity is at work. And exploration is closely associated with learning.

Play is more or less spontaneous (no enemy to flee, obstacle to overcome, or object to attain) and normally involves a higher level of exertion than does exploration. Thus, critical physical skills like running and jumping are developed. Social play also promotes bonding with peers and, to a lesser extent, integration with adults. Play helps the juvenile eventually to separate from its mother, complete the weaning process, and achieve a measure of independence. Play is also perhaps the quickest way to initiate young baboons into the rules of the troop (establishing dominance, controlling aggression, developing cohesion, etc.). Play, more frequent and more varied in primates than in 'lower' species, declines significantly in adults. The dangers and costs of such energy expenditure (outwardly "wasteful" or superfluous or paradoxical) generally outweigh the additional benefits of continued play. To the casual observer, play is often difficult to distinguish from exploration. One hint: play often involves manipulating familiar, exploration novel, objects. Recognition of and distinguishing between the two presupposes a fair degree of knowledge about the species. The casual safarist has another problem: he may be seeing incomplete or out-of-sequence behavior. Displacement activity and rituals, discussed earlier in several chapters, are easily mistaken for play. Exaggerated forms of normal movements are also difficult to classify.

Plate 6. Fancy Riding. The infants at first will attempt to pick food from the "saddle." When disturbed, they will also revert to the lower side, where they lived for the first month following birth. During the first year of life, infant mortality is high, at least fifty percent. Mothers vary in the amount of wandering allowed their youngsters. Consequently, young baboons achieve independence and develop at different rates, much like human children. Young baboons have irresistible expressions — highlighted by an old man's eyes and such serious, worried wrinkled brows.

The older juveniles and subadults seem to take a degree of perverse pleasure in tormenting the youngsters. A favorite tactic is to force the younger animals to the farthest flimsy tips of a branch, where they hang helplessly, screaming bloody murder all the while, or simply fall — this last eventuality the result of the branch breaking or the youngster actually being shook loose by his tormentor(s). The pitiful howling will often bring mother and friends to the rescue to control a game about to get out of hand. Or one of the dominant males who fancies himself a disciplinarian will perhaps intervene. Actually, most of these marquises of mayhem know just how far they can go before provoking severe discipline from some quarter and exercise restraint at that point. These constant minor altercations are great fun to watch, but the safarist has to linger to see (and hear) the whole *petite histoire* played out. The younger baboons also take malicious delight in chasing smaller creatures other than fellow monkeys, like hyraxes.

Apparently, infanticide is a feature of baboon life, as it is with lions and some other animals. This characteristic has only recently been observed,[19] and scientists are divided

as to whether this behavior is "normal" or a pathological aberration. With lions, the behavior appears to be a reproductive strategy (with other animals, it may also be a form of population control or the result of food competition). Some naturalists have been tempted to attribute the same motivation to baboons. Indeed, the only young that have been killed (or seen killed) by the adult males were still suckling and not even close to weaning. Thus, the mother was not on the verge of another heat, which event would presumably have made a killing unnecessary. But a closer look at baboon dynamics casts considerable doubt on the analogy. Baboon mating is indiscriminate, and dominance alone does not determine pairing. Bringing a particular female into heat for only the *chance* of mating and an even more remote gamble of fathering young seems a low-probability strategy. And, if baboon males practiced this strategy to any serious extent (like lions), infanticide would be widespread, given the flexibility of mating, which demonstrably it is not. Nor does baboon infanticide include "takeovers" or instances of chasing off adult males.

The author's suggestion for explaining infanticide here is that the males occasionally simply lose control when disciplining an infant or its mother. The forms of stress that could lead to such loss of control are many. Indeed, males are also sometimes seen violently attacking, apparently without immediate provocation, females, presumably a form of punishment for some prior infraction. The females are bitten, shaken violently, and occasionally thrown bodily several yards. Youngsters would not fare well under such rough handling. And do not.

The young are weaned at roughly the end of their first year. The business of feeding themselves then begins in earnest. On the one hand, baboons are picky, selective eaters. On the other hand, they are truly opportunistic omnivores. The list of foods *not* eaten by baboons would be shorter than the list of foods regularly consumed. Most nutritious items at hand are taken. The usual fare: roots, bulbs, eggs (bird or croc), small reptiles, scorpions (after removing the sting) and other insects (such as ants, termites, and grasshoppers), large quantities of grass (at different stages, in various seasons), acacia blossoms and pods, vines, leaves, and tree sap. Baboons are obviously

19. There is always the basic problem of relying upon faulty observation, even (apparently) photographs. *Time* magazine in the issue of September 6, 1982, ran two pictures purporting to show a male baboon killing a small infant. The photography appears to support the text. But the same pictures were used in a four-part sequence in the *Time-Life* book of the "Wild, Wild World of Animals" series titled *Monkeys and Apes* (1976) that illustrated an "obstreperous youngster" receiving a "painful but non-wounding bite on the neck" from a "dominant male disciplinarian." The editors cannot have it both ways.

fond of fruits, especially figs. The author has frequently seen them also pluck and eat the ant galls from whistling-thorn acacias. Very strong hands adept at digging up rhizomes and bulbs help them live through severe droughts. Most of the feeding is done while patrolling on the ground. Although the basic diet is overwhelmingly herbivorous, baboons will kill small prey and eat meat. Accounts of bloodthirsty baboons in the literature are, however, wildly exaggerated; there is little evidence that baboons ordinarily search for or systematically stalk prey. A baboon, usually a male, while foraging may fortuitously[20] come across a young dik-dik, gazelle fawn 'hiding out,' a hare, or a fledgling and catch it before it has an opportunity to escape. From time to time, baboons will also eat vervet monkeys[21] and have been known to fish, eating small fish and crabs caught in shallow water. The practice of meat-eating varies from place to place, and the baboons in some locations seemingly have recently acquired a more pronounced taste for meat, which trait undoubtedly presages real hunting. Deliberate stalking under these circumstances by baboons is liable to be an intelligent and well-coordinated effort, against which the prey is not apt to be really prepared.

The alert safarist should be cognizant of a baboon's body language and vocalizations — all subtle and not-so-subtle forms of communication. Scientists have identified more than thirty meaningful postures and some fifteen sounds. Many in each category are self-explanatory. Grinning, holding the body prone to the ground, facing away, glancing sideways, scratching, or shoulder shrugging are all signs of fear and submission. Presenting one's rear end can be a sign of submission or of amicability. Presenting a foot-palm, front or back, exhibiting a "fear-grin," and raising one's tail to a vertical position are all submissive greetings. Lip-smacking and grooming are, without question, indicators of satisfaction and amicability. Yawns with teeth exposed (7), head-bobbing with ears flattened and eyebrows raised, steady staring, or slapping the ground are all signs of aggression or threats. Charging and biting need no explanation. Yawning in which the teeth are covered by the gums is considered a play threat. When the troop is spread out, vocal communication is constant, but baboons are noisy at most times during the day.

Each troop occupies a definite and limited home range that may overlap those of adjacent troops. At times, when troops meet, considerable aggression may result, but home ranges are not defended in the way that ungulates or other territorial animals behave. When possible, troops apparently try to avoid one another, and the usual reaction upon meeting is for each baboon to ignore its counterpart. Several troops often share the same drinking place, with little intermingling, except that youngsters from different troops might briefly play together. Travel is normally a function of obtaining food and water, though baboons have also been known to change their usual haunts in response to a heavy predation onslaught, and hence varies considerably. Baboons are restricted by how far they can go and still return to the fixed, safe community sleeping sites before nightfall. A normal day's trek is one or two miles. Movement during the day tends to be predictable and conservative: the troop concentrates its activities in certain "core areas" that have water, food, and safe places to sleep. Zoologists have, in fact, encountered considerable difficulty in attempting to lure baboons away from their natural domains. (The Maasai have an old saying: "Baboons will not leave their own ground.") And the progress of a straggler is always noisily remarked upon by the rest of the troop (disapprovingly, one assumes).

Visitors should be especially wary of baboons and not underestimate their cunning, strength, or ferocity. One is always tempted in the presence of a troop to try to feed them from the vehicle or while visiting one of the Tree Hotels, where they may become a real nuisance. Some animals have come to expect tidbits from tourists and will clamber expectantly onto the vehicles or porches of the lodges. Many a careless driver has had the unpleasant experience of attempting to eject from his automobile a baboon that has jumped in through an open window. Many an amusing session on the balcony of a Tree Hotel has quickly turned sour, even ugly, as a baboon steals a pocketbook or other personal belonging and perhaps attacks the pursuer. Photographers should be especially careful about their equipment. Baboons are notorious collectors of fine photographic gear. Early in my safari career, I had a running confrontation with a large male at Treetops. The malingerer with a classic feint had managed to snatch a camera body and promptly began to parade his prize on the roof, with me in close pursuit. Breaking the rules, I followed my antagonist to the ground, where he simply resorted to a deft forward pass to an ally and so on into the thicket. I lost the camera.

2. *Monkeys: Vervet.*

"Tumbili" in Kiswahili seems a good name for the agile, tumbling vervets, probably the most abundant monkey in Africa and hence the world.[22] (8) Indeed, wherever there are substantial collections of trees in East and Southern

---

20. At least, the baboons appear to be acting inadvertently; moving across the plains eating grass and looking for insects and the eggs of ground-nesting birds does not ensure that the primates are not at the same time ever on the lookout for baby gazelles hiding in the grass.

21. Interestingly enough, the vervets show little fear of baboons and sometimes even mingle. Similarly, champanzees occasionally kill and eat young baboons in certain areas, but the monkeys do not seem to shun contact with the apes and frequently live in proximity to the larger primates.

22. Vervets are also called grivets, or Green, Grey, and (inexplicably) Grass monkeys. Technically, they are one of the Guenon family of monkeys.

Plate 7. Weaponry Display. When a baboon yawns like this, accompanied by mantle hairs bristling and the white-eyelid display, he is threatening someone — another baboon, a possible predator, or a human being who has come too close. This formidable Treetops male eventually stole a camera from the author.[23]

Africa, there are likely to be vervets:

Here, high above the ground, lived a garrulous restless nation, the little grey monkeys. Where a pack of monkeys had travelled over the road, the smell of them lingered for a long time in the air, a dry and stale, mousy smell. As you rode on you would suddenly hear the rush and whizz over your head, as the colony passed along on its own ways. If you kept still in the same place for some time you might catch sight of one of the monkeys sitting immovable in a tree, and, a little after, discover that the whole forest round you was alive with his family, placed like fruits on the branches, grey or dark figures according to how the sunlight fell on them, all with their long tails hanging down behind them. They gave out a peculiar sound, like a smacking kiss with a little cough to follow it; if from the ground you imitated it, you saw the monkeys turn their heads from one side to the other in an affected manner, but if you made a sudden movement they were all off in a second, and you could follow the decreasing swash as they clove the treetops, and disappeared in the wood like a shoal of fishes in the waves.[23]

Vervets are fantastic climbers and can move many times

---

23. Dinesen, *Out of Africa.* p. 65.

faster through the trees than can a man on the ground.

In general, vervet groups resemble baboon troops in composition and behavior. The little monkeys live and travel in relatively stable and closed communities, numbering as a rule from six to twenty-five, though groupings as large as 100 can be found in localities of high food availability. During the day, vervets forage widely within a home range but return each dusk to a particular sleeping grove of trees. Actually, vervets are not true forest monkeys in that they prefer the edges of a forest,

tion, the author has never seen vervets far from water.

The vervet group is extremely sociable and organized into echelons. A small troop often has a single dominant adult male, but, as with baboons, a new male's success in a larger troop depends on his "charm," as much as (if not more than) his fighting ability. Male status turns in large measure on female support. Also like baboons, male vervets switch troops at adolescence, whereas females remain in their troop of birth. Female status is, in fact, basically inherited. One is born into a family niche. Of

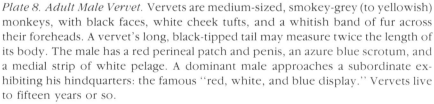

Plate 8. Adult Male Vervet. Vervets are medium-sized, smokey-grey (to yellowish) monkeys, with black faces, white cheek tufts, and a whitish band of fur across their foreheads. A vervet's long, black-tipped tail may measure twice the length of its body. The male has a red perineal patch and penis, an azure blue scrotum, and a medial strip of white pelage. A dominant male approaches a subordinate exhibiting his hindquarters: the famous "red, white, and blue display." Vervets live to fifteen years or so.

trees standing alone along streams or rivers, and wooded grasslands. A foraging expedition will venture several hundred yards into the savannah, so long as it can retreat to trees in the event that sudden danger threatens. In addi-

course, some flexibility is always introduced by the contingencies of predation or disease, but the average female is essentially locked into the status of her kin group. What then is the practical effect of being, for example, low-born? A female may be pushed off food, denied access to tempting infants, drafted into the tougher grooming tasks and denied the more desirable grooming positions, and hard pressed to find a grooming partner for herself. Even more problematical will be obtaining widespread support in a dispute.

Unlike baboons, vervet groups are territorial and will defend their ranges against neighboring troops. Defense may mean hurling branches at intruders; it may also take the form of defecation and urination (with appallingly accurate results). However intense the threat gestures and vocalizations, physical contact between troops is rare.

young receive a large measure of attention from the troop and are handled by a wide range of females and subadults. *(10)* When the older monkeys pause in their fawning, to eat for example, the younger set keeps the attention going by snatching food from the elders. And any overzealous discipline will quickly bring down the collective defense of mother and her matriarchy.

Resembling their baboon neighbors, vervets are opportunistic omnivores with seemingly insatiable appetites. They eat a wide variety of plant food *(11)*, fruits, insects, and occasionally eggs and chicks of small birds. They are, in addition, most fond of the gum or glue-like resinous sap

Plate 9. "Leapfrog." Many of the vaudevillian maneuvers have a serious side: practice in motor skills and coordination and teaching social strategies in a relaxed and friendly context. But, as the safarist watches that day's version of 'King of the Mound,' he cannot help but conclude that the monkeys are simply having fun. When food becomes scarce (for example, during a long dry season), play declines considerably — to preserve energy and as more time is devoted to the business of earning a living.

As the Dinesen passage suggests, safarists may hear the vervets above or around them before actually seeing the monkeys. The cacophony can be likened to coming into a bingo hall between games: not a raucous roar exactly, but a series of bird-like twitters, hisses, clicks, and only an occasional sharp bark, all that one would expect from such a gallery of eccentrics whispering their forest gossip. The gallery also offers the visitor a great variety of visual mimicry and gestures.

Much of the commotion is, as the reader might guess, caused by the juveniles in their endless play. *(9)* The

that exudes from the bark of acacia trees. In common with many monkeys, vervets have expandable cheek pouches. This anatomy is slightly reminiscent of the ruminant system — a protective adaptation for ground-collecting monkeys that enables the storage of food during foraging for leisurely chewing (and, as a Madison Avenue ad exec might add, "double the pleasure") later in the trees.[24] Vervets can be serious pests to crops and

---

24. The author is not suggesting that cheek pouches are simply — or even primarily — devices to prevent predation. The

Plate 10. Mother and Infant. The infant has a light face that turns dark with age. Early on, an infant is carried by its mother pressed to her chest. Rarely do the youngsters ride on the backs like baboons. After the first week or so of life, the young are also carried around by related subadults and juveniles, in addition to mother. The vervet's insatiable appetite begins early in life. The female has two teats that sit close together, and the infant will suck from both at the same time! Occasionally, a mother will have twins, both whom grow up presumably somewhat frustrated. An infant will nurse until the next offspring arrives, a year or so after its own birth.

equally accomplished when stealing from unwary tourists. In the author's experience, vervets show even

pouches may be an adaption for foraging in the face of competition (for a limited food source). It also appears likely that the saliva of monkeys plays an important part in digestion (as in man); vervets, even when hungry, do not seem to swallow their food immediately, preferring instead to fill the cheek pouches with chewed food before swallowing. Another theory is worth noting, one that originated vis-à-vis rumination but not discussed previously in this volume. Some scientists believe that rumination developed not as a "more efficient" system but to help herbivores protect themselves against poisons which plants use to thwart their own destruction. In this view, rumination is a detoxification step before full digestion. So, too, by analogy, cheek pouches — particularly apropos, one might add, for omnivorous and voracious eaters.

more 'cheek' than baboons and are amazingly quick.[25] Picnicking near vervets, in or out of one's vehicle, is the same as inviting the block at home to dinner: good luck!

The major enemies of vervets are leopards, the smaller cats, pythons, and large birds of prey, such as the Martial eagle or Verreaux's Eagle owl. As the reader can readily realize, the predators must exhibit exceptionally deceptive features (in the form of stillness and cryptic coloration) or possess great speed and maneuverability in the trees (or both) to capture these alert and agile monkeys. Vervets have only slightly less acute vision than baboons and probably better hearing. Little escapes their attention.

25. The visitor should also exercise some care in the presence of 'pet' vervets, common throughout safari Africa. Like pet macaws, a pet vervet specializes in biting the unsuspecting.

Plate 11. Picking Flowers.

Plate 12. Instructions for a Topi: Sentry Stationed on Termite Mound. A dominant male often acts as lookout.

One of the most reliable clues to a leopard's daylight whereabouts is an excited troop of vervets. The monkeys will "mob" a leopard during the day, that is, they will follow a leopard on the prowl, chattering and scolding raucously from the safety of the treetops. It is this kind of attention that keeps the leopard 'at home' when the sun comes up. *(12)*

Vervets have different alarm calls for leopards, for snakes, and for eagles — a vervet needs to know which way to run, especially up or down. An air-raid is one thing, a leopard on the prowl is quite another.[26] These various signals are clearly learned. Babies screech indiscriminately. Juveniles begin to make critical distinctions. Adults have the system down pat. This is but one example of behavior that has convinced cognitive ethologists that primates can *think* in surprisingly sophisticated ways. And communicate more than crude messages. One also is led to speculate that primates can

hardly be unique, though primate behavior is perhaps easiest for us to recognize, because we are primates as well. The evidence is overwhelming that animals are not simply stimulus-response machines in which behavior is strictly a matter of direct, pre-programmed responses to environmental stimuli or clues. Observed in their natural setting, animals — primates surely, others at least partly — *routinely* face choices too complex for rote responses. Instead, these animals are consciously engaged in mental activity that leads to decisions between alternatives and among goals. The truth is, few environments are so "simple" that animals may forgo decision-making. To survive and obviously to prosper, the inhabitants must daily

---

26. That the calls actually describe the predator has been established by careful observation and experimentation under natural conditions. Many ethologists once argued that the separate alarm calls conveyed only degrees of fear and that the

listeners quickly determined the identity of the predator for themselves simply by looking at the caller and then in the direction in which the caller was looking. The evidence today is reasonably clear: in response to a leopard alarm, the vervets climb high in the nearest trees; the eagle alarm causes them to head for ground and thick vegetation; and the snake alarm makes all present stand on their hind legs to determine the exact location of the python. Several other similar subtleties of social communication have been discovered.

Plate 13. "Kima." The Kiswahili term applied to a Sykes' monkey is also used casually for all monkeys. The ordinary safarist is not likely to see many Sykes' monkeys, and the species is probably more numerous than appearances would indicate. Heavier than vervets, the Sykes' looks black from a distance but is really dark bluish grey with several white markings. Coloration does, however, vary widely among individuals.

balance costs and benefits. Such evaluation is a form of thinking: I do not believe that the decision strategy for a complex and changeable environment could ever be "programmed." Consequently, human consciousness may well be unique only in degree.[27]

3. *Monkeys: Sykes'.*

The Sykes' monkey is the East African version of the Blue monkey.[28] Bigger than a vervet but not nearly so common, the Sykes' is shy and remains mostly in the true forest. *(13)* A Sykes' normally lives in a small group organized around the harem principle — a core of related females with their young and one resident (temporarily) adult male. Groups of all males are also seen.

The Sykes' monkeys are most active just after sunrise, late in the morning, and again in the late afternoon. They are not particularly noisy, but an alert safarist in the forest will hear an abrupt, single cough — "jack!" — or a "nyah-nyah-nyah" cry. A Sykes' is quite amusing to watch, even for a short time, if the visitor can maneuver close enough to see the great variety of facial gestures produced during just a few minutes — the constant lowering and raising of

---

27. The learning process is not all one-way. Primates themselves show a sophisticated understanding of human behavior when they are thrown into lasting contact: crop-raiders descend when people are predictably absent (for example, in heavy rainstorms or during the hottest times of the day) and will assiduously avoid men, who experience has shown are likely to be armed, while sometimes challenging women, who are not.

28. Several authors divide the Sykes' and Blue monkeys in a different way, identifying geographic (limited to East Africa) variants (Blue, Silver, Golden, Sykes', and Samango). However the classification is made, the Sykes' or Blue monkey is another guenon. Still other guenons, all long-tailed and forest-living, are the Allen's (Swamp) monkey, Talapoin (some believe this to be a separate group), Moustached monkey, Red-eared Nose-spotted monkey, Black-cheeked White-nosed monkey, Golden monkey, Mona monkey, Diana (Roloway) monkey, De Brazza's monkey, L'Hoest's monkey, the Owl-faced (Hamlyn's) monkey, Lesser White-nosed (or Lesser Spot-nosed) monkey, the Crowned guenon, Red-tailed monkey (Coppertail or Schmidt's), Dent's guenon, Campbell's (Lowe's) monkey, Dryas monkey, and the Red-bellied monkey. Some are genuinely rare, others just infrequently seen. Africa has, in fact, hundreds of different kinds of

Plate 14. The Quizzical Sykes'. A Sykes' always, at least if allowed a few seconds, looks as if he has a ponderous question for the intruder. His *long* tail is used mainly for balance.

eyebrows, perhaps the most active in nature; the furtive glances, followed by a wide-eyed look, alternating between guile and innocence; the puffing of the shopping-bag cheek pouches; and all the rest. *(14)*

4. Monkeys: Colobus.

Africa has several species of Colobus monkeys, but none more striking than the Abyssinian Colobus found in Kenya, Ethiopia, and Tanzania.[29] *(15 & 16)* "Kolobus" is Greek for mutilated or stunted, and this monkey has the unusual (for an advanced primate) anatomical feature of

lacking a thumb.[30] Its Kiswahili name is "mbega." Almost entirely arboreal, the Colobus is not always easy to spot, and the safarist must look carefully in the heavy mountain forests, in woodlands along rivers, and in tropical rain forests to find the first specimen. *(17 & 18)* In spite of its striking coloration, a Colobus "disappears" in the trees: the animal in the presence of outsiders can remain quite still for long periods, its black body initially merges in the

___

monkeys. The Patas monkeys, though not strictly guenons, are closely related. Shy and elusive, the long-legged, dog-like Patas (sometimes called "red hussars") live primarily on the ground (but sleep in trees) — they are the fastest monkey on the ground and run like cheetahs — and range from the savannahs to far into the Sahara. Co-territoriality between guenon species is common. They will defend boundaries together, act in concert against predators, and collectively harvest food. Occasionally, hybridization will occur, despite the color patterns presumably designed to help keep variants apart.

29. The spectacular black-and-white Abyssinian Colobus, also known as the Guereza, is one of many kinds of Colobus. Others

include the (Satanic) Black Colobus, Angolan Black-and-White Colobus, Red Colobus, Western Red Colobus, Western Black-and-White Colobus, and Olive Colobus. A rare, small population of entirely white Colobus monkeys has also been found near Mt. Kenya. The existence of common or very similar forest monkeys in widely separated areas is compelling evidence for the view that forests at one time were connected over vast expanses, probably covering most of the African continent.

30. Arm-swinging in trees is called "brachiation." Frequently, one reads that the loss of the thumb is a modification that helps brachiating monkeys to prevent snagging in branches and impeding movement. On the other hand, the champion in any brachiation competition would be the orangutan, who like all apes has a well-developed thumb.

dark leafy background characterizing the topmost parts of the forest canopy, and the long, ornamental white tail can easily be mistaken for a hanging vine. But, after the first monkey is found, the safarist has only patiently to look for the many others that are undoubtedly nearby. The author has counted as many as fifty Colobus monkeys "together," though, like giraffes, it is not always easy to know when one group ends and another begins. (Apparently, social organization is limited.) Once the safarist becomes accustomed to picking them out, the monkeys are fascinating to watch in their element, the most acrobatic and agile of all forest animals. These daring, ef-

fortless aerialists can even change direction in mid-air, putting to shame the most dramatic NBA superstar, and, leaping spectacularly from branch to branch, they look as if they were flying *(19)*. A Colobus is able smoothly to clear thirty feet more or less horizontally and will drop vertically forty-five to fifty feet without concern. The long silky hair and tail are said to act like a parachute.

The rapacious grasp of man in the face of such extreme natural beauty has, unfortunately, not bypassed the unmistakable Colobus. Some East African tribes historically have used the Colobus fur as part of their headdress or cape regalia. The silky pelts have also been prized by

Plates 15 & 16. The Wise Man of the Forest. The Colobus monkey is at the same time among the most striking animals in Africa and one of those creatures whose grave and serious demeanor radiates a sense of wisdom. One is tempted to sit down with this monkey and unburden one's concerns. Colobus congregations remain in specific areas; once located, they are easy to find again. A Colobus will sneeze when alarmed and shake branches at enemies. Colobus species do not have cheek pouches but have a compartmentalized stomach, where fermentation produces much methane and carbon dioxide. The resulting belching, for which all Colobus are well-known, does little, however, for the wise-man image.

poachers — at the turn of this century, as many as 150,000 skins a year may have been taken for export.[31] Such relentless hunting has caused the Colobus to be extremely shy, and many will flee the slightest human intrusion.

The very young are entirely white, with slightly wooly fur, and closely protected by mother *(20)*. Adult coat and coloration are acquired in about four to six months. Not much is known about Colobus social behavior; limited observation has been combined with what we know about "normal" primate activity to speculate on troop life.[32] Troop cohesion and interaction is slight: cohesion is not required to evade predators, and the requirement to eat for long periods to make up for the low nutritional content of their diet necessarily reduces socializing. Mating seems basically a random affair, casting doubt on one-male harem-group theories. Colobus monkeys appear territorially inclined, with defined routes during the day, but non-aggressive and not terribly status-conscious. Of course, arboreal creatures define territories in an extra-dimensional fashion: up (and down), as well as outwards. Volume — and the heights of trees — becomes the yardstick, a difficult measurement for naturalists to undertake.

---

31. Severe poaching is often accompanied by enduring myths of relatively benign capture — apparently (in the absence, of course, of a ferocious nature), it helps not to hear about slaughter when donning a garment made from some wild animal. Thus, the story gained recognition — and was uncritically accepted by some writers who ought to have known better — that, in their high altitudes, where the temperature drops significantly at night, the Colobus monkeys become so cold that poachers in the early morning simply shake the trees and capture the monkeys as they fall down. It is difficult to believe that intelligent people write these things. The reader is invited to look at the pictures and imagine how many Paul Bunyan-types would be needed to shake appreciably the tall trees and just how cold the temperature would have to be before such a long-haired, agile creature could be frozen into submission.

---

32. In a sense, several other monkeys are "catching up" with the Colobus. We thought that we could pinpoint typical troop sizes, home ranges, and social organizations of these species, but recent research has cast considerable doubt on any rigid notions and has revealed significant variation within most species and even within a given troop from time to time.

A little way into the forest we met a troop of colobus monkeys, the shyest and most acrobatic of the tree people. Moving with great rapidity and skill they travel through the forest, going out to the very ends of branches and hurling themselves into the air, to land with a great curtsying and swishing of boughs on a tree twenty or thirty feet away. All their lives they seldom go near the ground. They are stunning to look at: black with a white fringe draped low across the back, like an academic hood, tails a long bush of pure white, thicker than a fox's brush, and black faces severely framed in white, as though they wore the closest-fitting of nun's coifs. . . .

The family we found looked like so many fruit on the huge tree from which, one after another, they launched themselves to a smaller, lower tree and then on into the forest . . . Mythlike creatures they seemed; exotic as birds of paradise and a little catlike; at the furthest remove from apes and baboons, living like that in the air and the beautiful high trees. When their last rustling had died away, the forest was very silent, very full of their absence. (Evelyn Ames, *A Glimpse Of Eden,* pp. 146-7.)

A Colobus will tolerate other types of monkeys close nearby: safarists may find them in the same trees with baboons or vervets or Sykes' monkeys. Indeed, monkeys in trees mirror antelopes and the latters' grazing niches. Feeding takes place at different levels, different stages of growth are eaten, and so forth. Direct interspecies competition is rare. Much of a Colobus' food (nearly all mature leaves) is not very nutritious, and the monkey must eat a large quantity to prosper. Like antelopes, monkeys never completely deplete their food sources, branches are never stripped, and the feeders move around sufficiently to leave a healthy tree behind. In the absence of a thumb, the leaves are plucked with the lips.

Although a troop of Colobus monkeys can remain quiet for hours, once the safarist's presence is even partially accepted by a troop, he will hear the usual chatter perpetrated by forest monkeys reverberating through the treetops. One striking part of this chorus is a sort of fierce, gutteral roaring by certain adult males, one of the most distinctive sounds of the African forest. In sequences of five to fifteen seconds, this impressive display can last up to twenty minutes and be heard a good mile away. The roaring, which in any event is only intermittent, probably

identifies the species, the troop, and the individual and serves to encourage the congregation of a scattered group, to warn off non-troop Colobus (not from a given area per se but for the time that it is occupied), and to monitor the number and status of sexually active males. The loudest calls sound at dawn. The vocalization is often accompanied by dramatic leaping back and forth over a defined area. All the swaying and cracking of branches makes for quite a display (the reader should recall the comparison to elephants charging through the forest quoted in Chapter III) — and lends support to confrontational interpretations for the calling.

Despite reports that the Colobus monkeys never come to the ground, the author has frequently seen them forag-

Plate 19. Airborne. Its long, white hair spread out like a cape (or parachute), the Guereza executes really breathtaking leaps. The hair and bushy tail may actually have the aerodynamic effect of an air-brake, slowing downward speed. And landing is but a continuation of the excitement, as the branches bend perilously under their (considerable) weight.

Plate 20. Mother and Young. The Colobus mother is not likely to allow an unimpeded view of her baby; she carries her newborn so close to her chest that an onlooker can hardly distinguish it from her own body. Another long, white tail is usually the clearest evidence that a youngster is present. Colobus mothers lavish much care and affection on their babies. Constant grooming and minute inspection of all food taken are *de rigueur*. The mother also allows other adult females to handle the infant.

ing in mad dashes across forest clearings. Indeed, these are usually the only times to see a youngster clearly, as he scampers to keep up with his mother *(21)*.

5. *Apes: Gorilla.*

A gorilla safari is a specialized affair, a difficult trip to arrange and one that should be undertaken only with an experienced and established operator. The bamboo rain forests of the Virunga Volcanoes[33] do not offer a Sunday stroll: the visitor will frequently find himself on all fours, arduously crawling through the wet, dense forest habitat.

33. The Virunga chain of eight extinct (for the most part) volcanoes, extending twenty-five miles in length and in width varying from six to twelve miles at the extremes, forms the boundaries between Rwanda, Zaire, and Uganda. The game reserves are known as the Parc National des Volcans in Rwanda, Parc National des Virungas in Zaire, and the Kigezi Gorilla Sanctuary in Uganda. (A smaller gorilla population lives about fifteen miles north in the Bwindi (''Impenetrable'') Forest in Uganda. Once a continuous habitat, the Virungas are now

Plate 21. Mad Dash. The visitor assumes that some real delicacy must be the object of this safari by a primarily tree-dwelling animal. The Colobus hops and runs across open ground in what amounts to a graceful gliding motion, white coat and tail floating behind.

separated from Bwindi by cultivated land that the gorillas will not cross.) For tourists properly organized, authorized, and guided, a gorilla sighting is virtually guaranteed in Rwanda or Zaire. Rwanda today is probably the better choice. Once the gorillas are sighted, the duration of a visit in Rwanda is pretty strictly limited to one hour. The trips in Zaire are improving all the time, and the visitor generally can remain with a group for longer than one hour.

Indeed, a draining, uphill, two-hour-plus hike at elevations of 8,000 feet precedes most sightings. By comparison, even the roughest ride across the savannah in a Landrover seems comfortable. But tracking the great apes ("ngagi" in Kiswahili) through the misty forests of the Virungas is truly a unique wildlife experience. The Virungas today can handle only twenty or so tourists a day, and most groups are held to about six people. Furthermore, only one group of tourists is allowed close to a particular gorilla family each day — at this time, only five gorilla parties have been acclimated to tourists — and reservations must be made with the proper authorities. Anyone contemplating such a trip should read Dian Fossey's magisterial study, *Gorillas in the Mist*.[34] The death of Digit, Fossey's famous silverback (a mature male gorilla with a saddle of striking grey lower-back hair), killed by poachers for his head and hands,[35] was announced by Walter Cronkite on the "CBS Evening News."

The gorilla's manlike appearance, his tremendous strength, and reputed savagery have fired man's imagination for a century or more. The French-American explorer and big-game hunter Paul du Chaillu set the tone in the mid-1800s for the King Kong fantasy as he described a "half man, half beast" and "hellish dream creature" screaming in a "hideous roar."[36] (Reportedly, du Chaillu's publisher returned the first *and* second draft as "not lively" enough.) The naturalist Carl Akeley, who was in large measure responsible for the creation of Albert National Park incorporating the Virungas, began the process of setting the matter right. (Akeley often signed off as "The Old Gorilla.") Then came the fine study by George Schaller (quoted in Chapter III), who confirmed that the essentially vegetarian gorilla is a shy and reclusive animal, unless harassed. The reader has been treated to a taste of the literature in Chapter III, but the author's favorite passage concerning the initial sighting of a gorilla by a visitor is Alan Moorehead's:

He was a huge shining male, half crouching, half standing, his mighty arms akimbo. I had not been prepared for the blackness of him; he was a great craggy pillar of gleaming blackness, black crew-cut hair on his head, black deep-sunken eyes glaring towards us, huge rubbery black nostrils and a black beard. He shifted his posture a little, still glaring fixedly upon us, and he had the dignity and majesty of prophets. He was the most distinguished and splendid animal I ever saw and I had only one desire at that moment: to go forward towards him, to meet him and to know him: to communicate. This experience (and I am by no means the only one to feel it in the presence of a gorilla) is utterly at variance with one's reactions to all other large wild animals in Africa. If the lion roars, if you get too close to an elephant and he fans out his ears, if the rhinoceros lowers his head and turns in your direction, you have, if you are unarmed and even sometimes if you are, just one impulse and that is to run away. The beast you feel is savage, intrinsically hostile, basically a murderer. But with the gorilla there is an instant sense of recognition. You might be badly frightened, but in the end you feel you will be able to make some gesture, utter some sound, that the animal will recognize and understand. At all events you do not have the same instinct to turn and bolt.

. . .

And now abruptly he rose to his full height. Had I really been about to give expression to my sub-conscious desire to move towards him I expect that, at this moment, I would have paused, for he was tremendous in his great height and strength. It was a question now as to whether or not he would beat on his chest and charge, so as to give his family (unseen by us but certainly lurking somewhere there in the bush) further time to get away, but, in fact, he did neither of these things. He lifted his head and gave vent to another of those outlandish and terrifying barking-screams. Once again it seemed to bring every living thing in the bush, including one's own heart, to a full stop. Then he dropped on to his hands and melted away. There was, of course, no chance of following him; despite his size he could travel many times faster than we could."[37]

The Mountain gorilla[38] has, in fact, been poached to the brink of extinction; perhaps, less than 400 remain in all Africa, only 250 or so in the Virungas. Like virtually all primates, the Mountain gorillas are social animals that live in extended, fairly stable family groups dominated by a polygamous patriarch or silverback. Kinship bonds are strong. These family parties wander in reasonably well-defined territories, and five such groups in the Virungas are now accustomed to the presence of people, some having seen tourists almost daily since 1978, when public visits were initially organized. Careful tourists are

---

34. Although George Schaller effectively exploded most of the popular myths about gorillas, Fossey actually established communication with the apes. She went far beyond observation and by imitating ape behavior tried to become accepted as a member of gorilla groups, succeeding quite beyond the expectations of most zoologists.

35. The head to be mounted as a trophy, the hands used as "ornamental" ashtrays.

36. Du Chaillu was most probably born in Paris but became an American citizen in 1855. His first book, *Explorations and Adventures in Equatorial Africa*, described, to the astonishment of everybody, the new ape. Several books about Africa followed — the writings seem naive, boastful, and obviously exaggerated today but were enormously popular in their day. Traveling widely and lecturing and writing prolifically, du Chaillu led a romantic and extraordinary life, dying in Russia in 1903.

37. *No Room in the Ark,* pp. 133-5. Visitors are likely to hear the gorillas before seeing them, as they are relatively noisy.

38. The more familiar Lowland gorillas (the subspecies usually found in zoos), both western and eastern races, are smaller than the Mountain or Eastern gorilla and do not have the same long thick hair that protects the latter from the cool mountain temperatures. Gorilla safaris exclusively target the Mountain gorilla. There is no true Kiswahili name for gorilla, "sokwe mtu," "ngogi," or "ngagi" (used in the text) all being employed.

sometimes lucky enough actually to sit among the apes for an hour or so.

An adult male can stand more than six feet tall (the apes can walk upright for short distances), has an arm span of roughly eight feet, and weighs up to 500 pounds — an awesome physical specimen. Unfortunately, the author has never photographed gorillas in the wild, but most readers will have seen a picture or two of the real thing. Yet, despite their size and the reputation for treacherous belligerence, no gorilla has ever been reliably proved to have killed a man, and it may be doubted whether an unprovoked gorilla would even slightly harm a human being. Of course, "provocation" in the wild is not always intentional (or foreseeable); a recent poaching incident or the presence of a newborn, both unknown to a visitor, may set off some excitement. The dominant silverback will protect his troop in the face of a real or perceived threat by initiating a bluff attack that may include the famous fearsome chest-beating and hoot-screaming. The intimidating display is a mixture of intentional bluffing and of displacement activity (the gorilla is torn between fleeing and defending its family). Although the ape is probably as frightened as the visitors at such times, the display is absolutely terrifying. The guides will inform the tourist of the proper etiquette to avoid unintentionally provocative behavior: speak only in low whispers; avoid direct eye-to-eye staring, showing one's teeth, and any sudden moves — all considered by gorillas as threats; and know the important submissive gestures (like crouching down and pretending to eat leaves — never run from an angry gorilla — and clearing one's throat to simulate submissive grunting).

The great apes live in well-defined social groups, organized on the harem principle. Groups average about twelve members: a single, mature silverback male, a small number of younger adult males ("blackbacks"), several adult females, and juveniles. Silverback males also live alone. The silverback, who is at least twelve years old, is twice as large as the adult female, typical (if a bit extreme) sexual dimorphism (difference in body form between the sexes) exhibited by most polygamous mammal species. Once a male has established a successful harem, he remains ensconced relatively permanently. Competition between silverbacks for females can be severe: thus the large size and the fearsome-display capability. Female gorillas, unlike the females of most other social mammals, leave their natal groups. Therefore, the adult females in a silverback's harem are likely to be unrelated. And, in direct contrast with other primates, the social bonds between each female and the silverback, rather than ties among females, hold a group together. Indeed, social grooming among adult females is rare; mothers groom their children, and everyone (infrequently) grooms the silverback. During all rest periods, the safarist will see an entire group gather round the dominant male in affectionate socializing. A gorilla unit naps like a lion pride: all intertwined.

Gorillas eat a varied herbivorous diet. Their strong jaws can handle any vegetation desired, and the apes generally have no great difficulty in finding food,[39] though the relatively low nutrient content of their diet combined with their bulk ensures that a great deal of food (as well as time in eating) must be consumed. At night, the gorillas sleep in nests of grass, branches, and leaves built on the ground. A fresh nest is made every night, as gorillas soil their sleeping quarters.[40] The great weight of the males keeps them out of trees, but females and juveniles sometimes go aloft and swing on limbs.

Visitors will, interestingly enough, find that the gorillas are themselves highly curious and as interested in the intruders as vice-versa. Not infrequently, both sides wind up studying each other. Most of the body language of a gorilla resembles that of man, rather than monkeys. The more that one watches gorillas, the more human they seem. For example, gorillas stretch their arms and yawn in the morning when they wake up. They sit on logs or branches with their legs dangling down and frequently rest on their backs with their arms placed under their heads. They frown when annoyed and bite their lips when uncertain. Youngsters, who pass a long period dependent upon their mothers (three years or more), throw temper tantrums when thwarted but exhibit little of the bickering and screeching that characterizes baboons. Gorillas have also shown a large vocabulary of regularly emitted sounds, from soft, purring rumblings

---

39. Rain forests are among nature's most complex and intricate ecosystems. The climate there is generally stable; the absence of serious droughts or cold periods ensures that food is normally available year-round. Moreover, most African forests contain hundreds of species of trees and other vegetation, all supporting a varied animal population. By comparison, forests in the Northern hemisphere tend to be dominated by one or a few species of tree. African forests have been spared the periodic geological destruction of Northern forests and many are millions of years old! The competition for space, light, and water is intense, and the forests are a tangled riot of trees, bushes, shrubs, vines, and grasses fiercely asserting themselves in distinct layers. The bamboo, celery stalks, nettle and thistle, and vines that make up the gorilla's diet grow best in secondary and montane forests with open canopies that permit light to reach the forest floor. Gorillas feed extensively on leaf material and do not have to travel far to find suitable food. This abundance, the time needed for foraging and digestion, and a very conservative (contented) nature have helped keep the ape from expanding its range.

40. The "nests" keep the animals off the cold ground and prevent them from sliding down a hill or otherwise provide support. The lack of fruit in the gorilla's diet means that the dung is dry, and several naturalists have asserted that it will not foul a gorilla's coat. (They also point to the fact that in West Africa, where the diet includes fruit, gorillas rarely deposit their feces in the nests.) Nevertheless, the fact is, gorillas do not reuse the sleeping platforms.

(so-called "belch vocalizations") to staccato pig-grunts to loud hooting.

A gorilla safari calls for some special apparel: waterproof hiking boots (the guides travel barefoot!), tough trousers, and gloves. Insect repellent (lotion or spray) should be applied liberally, and *all* bites, cuts, and scratches promptly treated with an anti-bacterial ointment. Fast film is a must for photographers because of the low and sporadic available light prevalent in the forest, even at midday. ASA 64 film will generally be useless without a tripod, itself often too cumbersome (and sometimes unacceptable to the animals). Fortunately, the gorillas forage in areas where the break in the forest canopy allows some light to filter down to picture-taking level. Nevertheless, even with fast film, the shutter speed is likely to be marginal: an ASA 400 film with a 400mm lens shot as slow as 1/60 will still need an f-stop of 5.6 or wider. Lens speed thus becomes a critical factor, but lens size cannot be allowed to compromise mobility. A cumbersome lens obviously will not work on such a safari. A 300mm f/2.8 might only just be manageable; a 200mm would probably suffice, considering how close one may come to the gorillas. The animal's dark fur (and no reflectivity) and black face must be lit to capture texture, facial features, and wrinkles. The photographer must always bear in mind that his eyes will see what the film cannot. Flash is out of the question — realistically, photography is feasible only with habituated gorillas, and even they must not be unintentionally threatened. A unipod, not terribly difficult to lug along and, if carefully deployed, not likely to threaten unduly the apes, might prove well worth the trouble. Given the quality of the lighting, a warming filter would be recommended, but, again, a further reduction in the quantity of light is usually not permissible.

A head sweatband helps to keep perspiration off the camera body. A casual photographer will not be in the rain forest long enough to worry about excessive humidity, but typical conditions can be severe on equipment during a period stretching as long as a week or more. Humidity will cause film to deteriorate and can adversely affect the electrical circuitry of today's sophisticated cameras, as well as corrode metal parts. Over a slightly longer period, fungus may even attack lens surfaces. Insulated storage for equipment and film is recommended, and a dessicant, such as silica gel crystals, should be included in all storage, particularly if humid air is sealed into the containers. Blue paper indicators that turn pink when saturated can also profitably be stored with equipment or film to warn the photographer. The reader is further referred to Chapter II and the special precautions for heat mentioned there.

6. *Apes: Chimpanzee.*

The only logical place to look for chimpanzees is at Gombe (Stream) National Park, a reserve specifically established to protect them and located near Kigoma on the shores of Lake Tanganyika in Tanzania. Other possible destinations exist — the chimp has survived in small forest and woodland pockets throughout Africa — but most such sites cannot at this time be recommended for tourists (for a start, non-acclimated chimps are very shy and practically impossible to approach). In addition, before visiting the relatively new sanctuary at Gombe, one should definitely read Jane Goodall's *In the Shadow of Man* (quoted in Chapter III) and her remarkable new book, *The Chimpanzees of Gombe — Patterns of Behavior* (Belknap Press, 1986). Hugo van Lawick's film, *People of the Forest*, is also a masterpiece worth seeing. And, as with the gorillas in the Virungas, visits to Gombe are strictly regulated; reliable, advance arrangements are necessary.

The chimp — star attraction of zoos, circuses, and late-night television — is the most intelligent of the great apes and man's closest relative. Like gorillas, chimps generally use all four limbs in locomotion, treading on the knuckles of their "hands" and the soles of their "feet." But they can also travel just as fast on their hind feet, supported by one hand, and can run short distances (much more slowly) on their feet alone, if they are obliged, for example, to use both hands to carry fruit or some other object. It should help the safarist — particularly one on foot — to understand that the upright posture among most apes, if not clearly utilitarian at the time, is one of aggression. Unlike the considerably heavier gorillas, chimps pass a great deal of their time in trees, where they can move around quite rapidly.[41] The usual method of propulsion in the trees is swinging by their arms from branch to branch, one hand at a time, though a chimp is not nearly as handy with this technique as an orangutan or gibbon. Indeed, even when trees stand close together, chimps will frequently slide down one trunk to the ground and shimmy up its neighbor, instead of moving laterally through the branches. Chimps usually nest high up in the trees and, cleaner than gorillas, may use the same nest or one another's nest for several consecutive nights, if the sleeping sites are located close to a rich crop of food.

Physically, apes are mainly distinguished from monkeys by the absence of a tail and by having arms that are longer than their legs. From a behavioral perspective, chimps show many similarities to the other primates already discussed. They live in groups, perhaps as large as fifty animals at a time, which congregations are, however, not as structured or stable (varying in size and formation from day to day) as baboon troops; they are quite sociable; and they frequently act in relatively unselfish ways. Grooming is important, as might well be expected, but chimp life also includes a rich repertoire of physical touching in addi-

---

41. Chimps found in Tanzania seem gradually to be leaving the trees and evolving more and more to a life on the savannah (like baboons). Actually, chimp preference for either the branches or the ground varies significantly among different troops and sites. The availability of food and the status of predators in large measure determines the choice.

tion to grooming, such as clasping or holding hands, embracing, kissing, patting, and one chimp resting an arm on another chimp. Tickling is very popular, and the safarist is bound to be a bit taken aback by the laughter and such 'human' behavior. Social status is established by intelligence, as well as by displays of aggression. Various hierarchies exist, but alliances are more dispositive. Moreover, chimp life has a distinctly unpredictable character, as chimps are notoriously fickle.[42]

Mating is actively polygamous, though females mate only when in heat and are promiscuous only during the first week or so of estrus. In the last week, when ovulation happens, high-ranking males compete for mating rights, and an actual courtship leads to a more monogamous, consort union (for a brief period). The newborns are weak and helpless and receive special attention from the entire troop. Later, the antics of the juveniles are widely tolerated by the elders. Mother begins by clasping her baby to her belly, but the youngster soon moves to a jockey position on her back (though he will return underneath at the first sign of trouble). The young may be suckled for as long as four years and will stay with their mother until well into adolescence (age seven to ten).[43]

Typical of all higher primates, a mother will come to the defense of her child long after the latter has grown up. On the other hand, males seem to play no part in bringing up the young, though a youngster may be the object of discipline like any other member of the troop. Indeed, there is little physical discipline of the young chimps — a mother's main strategy is to distract the miscreant from its chosen course. Strong family attachments endure for a lifetime. Youngsters play with each other and alone in activities that are clearly less utilitarian than "play" of most mammals. Summersaulting is an obvious example, and especially observant witnesses have identified several recurring games, such as elders dragging youngsters on the latters' backs. Some of the play turns very rough — bouncing someone on his head is, for example, not uncommon! Growing up chimp is a complex business. Youngsters "ape" their elders and always tease the older

chimps to see how far they can go. A frequent target of such teasing are mothers carrying very young who presumably have difficulty in chasing the malefactors.

Chimps apparently are more territorial than other primates and will guard some territorial prerogatives jealously — although flexible chimpanzee social organization places an extra burden on observers who try to sort out such claims. Fighting sometimes leads to real biting and brutal physical contact, for that matter. Indeed, recent evidence has laid to rest the myth (promulgated in part by authorities such as the "early" Goodall) of the gentle, peace-loving ape. Chimps can be as violent as lions in defense of territory, with considerably more sophistication, and scientists now speak of precursors of human warfare. Mostly, a confrontation results in a "war dance" of sorts — threats and simulated battle — that lasts anytime up to an hour.[44] Separation and eventual reconciliation inevitably follow. Under some conditions, chimps will also cannibalize their own kind, though this behavior is rare.

Like many forest animals (and not just primates), chimps can be extremely noisy creatures, especially when food is discovered and eaten, when another troop is encountered, or simply at the beginning and end of every day (sunrise and sunset). At such times, the milling congregation sounds like a football crowd reacting to a big play. Many observers have referred to chimp "carnivals," periods when the apes set up a deafening hooting and barking and drum their hands against tree trunks in tom-tom style. Such carnivals probably represent periods of anxiety. A chimp's expressive face can also render a full range of common human emotion: fright, excitement, sadness, anguish, satisfaction, thoughtfulness, anger, peevishness, and much more. Chimpanzees also greet one another in much the same way that human beings do — in combinations of submissive and reassuring gestures.

The chimpanzee's favorite food is fruit, but the primate lives on (and craves) a varied diet, basically vegetarian supplemented by insects. Small groups (usually families) typically travel widely in search of food each day. Chimps (especially females) will insert a long stick or stem of grass into an active termite mound or ant hill, draw it out when it is covered with termites or ants, and lick off the insects. This behavior is not, however, merely another example of the use of tools discovered in the animal kingdom; the chimp will alter the shape of a branch or stem with its hands or teeth to conform to its purpose and thus is

---

42. The complexity of chimp society is particularly evident in the relationships between and among males. Males will gang together to attack other chimps. These same males can, however, quickly realign to fight one another. Adult males appear more "sociable" generally than the females, who remain, on the other hand, very family oriented. Nevertheless, one of the most distinguishing features of chimpanzee society is the individualism of each chimp and, concurrently, the relative autonomy of all mature individuals compared to other nonhuman primate societies. As might be expected, each chimp society is both unique and quite unstable over time.

43. Experiments in captivity, confirmed by field study, have shown that a baby chimp separated too early from its mother may well grow up excessively shy or aggressive and may not display normal sexual development. Physical development could also be markedly retarded.

---

44. Threats include charging with hair erect or dragging a branch, shaking trees, rolling on the ground, stamping, and screaming. Bluff attacks include throwing stones or other missiles and leapfrogging an antagonist! Amazingly enough (and a mystery for those who want to know why), threat displays can be triggered by heavy rain or strong winds or coming upon rushing water (a stream or waterfall) — interruptions, one might say, of the normal environment. The point is, chimps are quite capable of sudden violence.

engaged in primitive *tool-making*.[45]

Under some circumstances, chimps will kill monkeys smaller than themselves and other animals, like antelope fawns or baby pigs. Moreover, this behavior is not 'accidental,' as with baboons, but represents purposeful, thoughtful hunting. The killing itself often lacks, shall we say, a certain artistry: a chimp will, for example, catch a small monkey by one leg and beat the animal to death against the ground. Or, like hyenas, the killing is in the eating! The chimps that are most disposed to hunt are those living on the fringes of forests. If a visitor is lucky enough to witness several chimps hunting, he will recognize that the effort is truly cooperative. Afterwards, the meat is usually shared, though most naturalists believe that the sharing is grudging (the recipient has to "ask") and done purely to buy peace at the table. With a rare possible exception or two, chimps are not known to scavenge.

The author has not spent much time observing chimpanzees ("soko mtu" or "sokomutu" in Kiswahili, literally, "man of the market place," perhaps recalling the "carnival") in the wild and refers the interested reader to the bibliography, and especially the thorough Goodall books, for more details. A vast amount of information about man's nearest phylogenetic relative is available. Male chimps seldom leave the community into which they are born; females search out new troops. Mature chimp males weigh from 125 to 150 pounds and are said to be three to four times as strong as an adult man. Unlike gorillas, there is little size difference between males and females. The adult male chimp rises up and bristles his hair when sensing danger — and puts in a generally formidable appearance. Chimps will defend a troop in communal fashion and will also throw sticks and stones at predators. And some observers have even witnessed chimps advancing upon danger stick-in-hand!

Reference has already been made to evidence that primates depend not only on instinct but also on learning and communal experience passed down from generation to generation. "Cultural evolution" is clearly alive and well: the performance of a gifted individual can spread throughout his particular group and rapidly become part of its tradition, extending to the immediately following generations. Thus, for example, significant variances in behavior characterize the same species living in different areas. Chimps obviously weigh possibilities, assess choices, and make decisions. They plan for the future and draw upon sophisticated memories. They are adept at social manipulation and show a surprising (perhaps) understanding of others' behavior.

The even more fascinating question is whether apes can be taught to "talk." Non-verbal communication is required, because their vocal apparatus cannot produce the wide range of sounds that characterizes a spoken language. But researchers have asserted establishing dialogues through sign language used by the deaf (Ameslan or ASL) with chimps and, to a lesser extent, with gorillas (indeed, the gorilla "Koko" is perhaps the most famous of all these communicators). What appear to be rigorous scientific tests also seem to establish beyond doubt that these apes exhibit an extensive comprehension of spoken English words and have learned to use symbols somewhat like words. The issue now is whether apes can really master human language — word combinations, rhymes, metaphors, and complete (however simple) sentences and complex instructions. Skeptics, including some respected biologists, say that the animals do not show true spontaneity and are merely mimicking their teachers without having any real comprehension of syntax. A safari holds no answers to these questions but may stimulate a visitor to follow the controversy with more interest.[46]

7. Prosimians.

The African prosimians (literally, 'pre-monkeys') are the pottos, the galagos or bush-babies, and the lemurs of Madagascar. The **pottos** are thickset, teddy bear-like, round-headed animals, with wooly fur, exceptionally large protruding eyes, small round ears, and short bushy tails. They move very slowly and deliberately, hand over hand, like slow-motion rope climbers. They are also nocturnal and rarely seen by a safarist. The author personally knows of no casual tourist who has even seen one in the wild. The little **galagos** or **bush-babies** are similar-looking animals, though they have bigger ears and longer tails, and unique to Africa. *(22)* (The author suspects that bush-babies were the models for the friendly little gremlins of filmaker Steven Spielberg — before they "turned.") They too are nocturnal and arboreal, infrequently coming down to the ground. Bush-babies are,

---

45. This use of probes has been thoroughly studied and analyzed. The tool is chosen with considerable foresight and is frequently altered during its use. The whole process is never stereotyped. In fact, scientists who have tried invariably fail to gather as many termites or ants, both which bite on or attack the twig or grass in defense of their nest, as the chimps. Moreover, youngsters learn the art by watching their elders. Nor is this the only example of tool-making and use by chimps. "Cups" are often made of various materials for drinking water. Sticks are used and improved for enlarging holes and reaching objects. Fruits with shells are smashed against "platform" stones that have been altered to improve their use. Fly-whisks and contrived sponges have also been identified. Branches, frequently altered in one way or another, are used as weapons — to threaten, whip, flail, or club. More examples are sure to be discovered in the future.

---

46. The work with "talking" apes is, among other motivations, expected to help scientists understand how children learn to talk, as well as how human language originally developed. Apes do not appear to use these complex linguistic abilities in the wild, though the range of sounds, postures, and facial expressions equals a broad exchange of information.

Plate 22. A Pair of Lesser Bush-Babies. The most widely distributed bush-baby, the Lesser is also called the Senegal bush-baby. Its bat-like, membraneous ears help track the movements of insects (prey) in the dark. A strong sense of smell, aided by excellent night and binocular vision, also guide the agile leapers. In fact, prey can be seized as it flies past — to take one example, bush-babies can catch gnats on the wing. At night! Long hind legs and bushy tails that are used for balance complete the arsenal.

however, not uncommon — and very adaptable — pets *(23)*, so a safarist may well see one or two while in Africa. Many a staff pocket at a Tree Hotel contains a tiny bush-baby, who will occasionally emerge to lick its owner's face. Even more likely, the safarist will *hear* the bush-baby on its nocturnal rambles through the forest, as it utters an amazing variety of harsh, shrill wails and dramatic screams. Sounding uncannily like the wailing of a newborn child, the nickname "bush-baby" stuck a long time ago. The animal has changed little in twenty-five million years and passes its days hidden in the hollows of trees, nests abandoned by birds, or on branches well concealed by foliage. Several bush-babies often sleep clustered together (and are easier to find that way by flashlight on night safari). In contrast to the slow potto, most bush-babies are extremely agile, and some are capable of prodigious leaps of fifteen feet or more, when moving from tree to tree, much in the same manner as a kangaroo jumps. The largest bush-baby is no bigger than a small rabbit. All have enormous eyes for seeing in the dark and pads on the tips of their fingers and toes to help them cling to branches. No sound of any consequence in the forest escapes an alert bush-baby's sensitive hearing. But, when sleeping, the animal folds up its ears like fans and sleeps with them shut.

To see a **lemur,** the safarist must travel to Madagascar (or a few nearby islands), a romantic, magical island paradise lying about 250 miles off the southeastern coast of Africa, where lemurs live throughout the rain forests of the east coast and in the dry forests located on the western and southern sides. Madagascar is the world's fourth largest island,[47] more than a thousand miles long and covering more than a quarter of a million square miles. Not exactly on the beaten tourist track, Madagascar

Plate 23. Tortoise Ride. Bush-babies, in common with most other prosimians, have a retina with a reflective layer behind called a *tapetum,* a specialization for night vision. The *tapetum* is a flat stratum of crystals that shifts the wave length of available light to the sensitive, yellow range for the light receptors and reflects the light back through the retina. In the beam of a flashlight at night, the *tapetum* produces "eyeshine." The safarist is advised not to attempt to pet any of the prosimians within reach, despite their cute demeanors, except for the tame bush-babies. Sharp canines may make the would-be communication an unpleasant experience.

---

47. Only Greenland, New Guinea, and Borneo are larger. Australia is considered a continent.

— often called "L'Ile Rouge," from the color of its soil — is frequently referred to as the "naturalist's promised land." Indeed, it is a veritable mysterious Noah's Ark, bypassed by time. The most cogent geological theory is that Madagascar was once part of the African continent but broke away many millions of years ago. The encircling deep sea trench created an island fortress, biologically speaking. Isolated and protected in effect from the evolution taking place on the mainland — including, for example, the late evolution of large carnivores, antelopes, and monkeys — the island developed a unique and startling (today) assortment of flora and fauna. More than half of the 230-plus species of birds found on Madagascar exist nowhere else in the world.[48] Nearly ninety percent of the plant species of Madagascar are endemic.

Madagascar is, in effect, a continent in miniature and has a diverse topography consisting of three main geographic divisions or ecosystems: a narrow chain of mountains running along the entire eastern coast, pierced everywhere by dramatic, cascading waterfalls and trapping the warm, wet trade winds to create a closed-canopy tropical rain forest; a central highlands some 3,000 to 5,000 feet above sea level (with scattered peaks rising more than 9,000 feet), once completely forested but now denuded by slash-and-burn agriculture (called "tavy" locally) and overgrazing; and a wide western coastal plain, which is much drier than the east and which contains woodlands that range from deciduous forest in the northwest to hot dune desert and semi-arid thorn scrub in the south and southwest. Each ecosystem supports a distinct wildlife community.

The absence of predator pressure and of competition from more highly developed primates has enabled the

primitive lemurs to flourish on Madagascar.[49] And they evolved into a rich variety; no other family of mammals is so diverse. Some twenty different species and thirty subspecies range in size from that of a diminutive mouse to that of a large dog. Some superficially resemble monkeys, and one, the Indri, is tailless like an ape. Many are brightly colored, some as ornamental as fancy birds; most have long, wooly fur; and the majority are vegetarians or insectivorous, arboreal, and nocturnal. They are noisy and make distinctive cries. (The name "lemur" is supposed to have been coined by early European explorers from the Roman *lemures,* which term meant wailing ghosts.) Many also carry active scent glands for communication, and "stink fights" are common.

Mouse lemurs, some no longer than five inches and the smallest Madagascar primates, resemble bush-babies but cannot leap as far as the latter. They run about in the trees at night, whistling in shrill voices and fighting a great deal. Some Mouse lemurs become torpid in the dry season when food becomes scarce. They roll into a ball in a leaf nest or in a hollow tree trunk and remain inactive in a sort of suspended animation comparable with the hibernation of animals living in cold climates.[50] Except for the Ring-Tailed lemur, which habitually prefers bare, rocky terrain, lemurs are all active arboreal animals. So-called Gentle lemurs live in bamboo thickets and reedbeds. The True lemurs are larger specimens, about the size of a house cat, and usually strikingly colored, They have fox-like heads and fine, soft fur and carry long tails in an S-shaped curve. They act much like monkeys and engage in extensive grooming. Sifakas,[51] one of the Indri group, have achieved a special status with the local human population: they are regarded as the least ambitious progeny of man's direct ancestors, and to kill one would be considered the same as killing a "brother" or at least a "cousin." Moreover, Sifakas go to the tops of trees to sun themselves in the early morning with arms outstretched to catch the full warmth of the rays, a habit that has endeared them as more or less sacred "sun-worshippers." Finally, these same lemurs are said to bestow favors to supplicants, a practice (or myth, depending on one's perspective) bound to curry local favor.[52] The Indris as a

---

48. As a matter of zoogeography, there are two kinds of islands: continental and oceanic. A continental island is one that lies near a large adjacent "mainland," from which it received its fauna. Thus, the animals of the island resemble in significant ways those of the neighboring land. Oceanic islands get their animals by accidental distribution. Arising from the sea bottom, these islands have no historical connection with the old fauna of the continents. Animals arrive on the wind or by the currents or evolve from marine forms that invaded the land edge. As might be expected, freshwater fishes and amphibians are poorly represented, but birds and insects are likely to be unique. Madagascar confounds the specialists with animals that suggest *both* land connections (to Africa, to India, and, more surprisingly, to South America) and long isolation; it has, in other words, characteristics of both a continental and an oceanic island. In addition to lemurs, Madagascar is known for its tenrecs, chameleons, birds, giant fruit bats ("flying foxes"), boas, butterflies, spiders, palms, and orchids. Unfortunately, Madagascar is comparatively unknown as a tourist destination. The surge of interest in African wildlife that has drawn millions of visitors to other African countries has bypassed Madagascar. And, even on a scientific level, the study of lemurs is in its infancy.

---

49. Ancient forms of life usually suffer in the presence of man, and several large species of lemurs, probably weighing more than 200 pounds and one perhaps even as large as a gorilla, were wiped out by early human settlers. Massive environmental damage and habitat destruction — nine-tenths of the indigenous forests that once carpeted Madagascar have been destroyed by man — today threatens nearly all the existing species.

50. This seasonally lowered metabolism is preceded by intense feeding, during which large amounts of fat are stored, especially in the tail. One kind of lemur is, in fact, called the Fat-Tailed lemur, who remains dormant fully half the year.

51. Named after their distinctive cry: SEE-fakh! SEE-fakh!

52. Unfortunately, the taboos that have protected Indris are weakening. For example, Christian churches, in an attempt to

group are the largest of all lemurs, are diurnal, and some can leap fantastic distances of thirty feet or so while moving from tree to tree. They do come to the ground occasionally, where they leap from an upright posture (and look somewhat like a small person). Some Indris are partly carnivorous. Early in the morning and at night, the safarist may hear their extraordinarily loud wailing — a choir of high, almost human voices. Indris are confined to the rain forests of the east coast escarpment.

Perhaps, the most remarkable of all lemurs is the small, peculiar aye-aye, now nearly extinct. This highly specialized, squirrel-like animal survives in some forests and bamboo thickets located on the eastern border of the central plateau. Nocturnal and arboreal, the aye-aye feeds on insects, birds' eggs, and vegetation. It has chisel-like teeth completely unlike those of all other primates, more resembling a rodent's dentition. But its most remarkable anatomical feature is a freakish, elongated, slender middle-finger that looks like a spindly, dead twig and is used to locate (as a hammer) and extract (as a probe) the larvae of wood-boring beetles from logs;[53] as a meticulous self-grooming tool; and in drinking by literally flipping liquids into the mouth. The aye-aye is perhaps the most intelligent lemur. Nevertheless, the Malagasy people believe that the aye-aye is a harbinger of death. Consequently, it is both scrupulously avoided but also killed whenever it is found.

Lemurs exhibit many patterns of social life — troop activity, care for the young, and other behavior all differ enormously among the species and in fascinating ways. Scientists have made only a beginning in seeking to understand these facets of lemur existence; the possibilities of study are virtually endless.

The spectacular lemurs are one of the earth's great zoological treasures. And the thrill of seeing them is not limited to scientists: the author did not have his camera equipment along on his only trip to Madagascar, but that piece of foolishness (a long story) did not diminish the excitement of recognition across a gap amounting to millions of years, and who knows what evolutionary twists and turns, when I looked close-up at a lemur's hand. But all lemurs today are desperately vulnerable and defenseless against the ever-present, relentless human pressures. Their hold in the biotic miracle of L'Ile Rouge is tenuous.

Reptiles

When the subject of African wildlife is mentioned, the images that usually come to mind are the spectacular mammals. But a trip to Africa also represents an oppor-

tunity to view some of the world's most fascinating reptiles.

1. *Crocodile.*

If possible, the crocodile over many years has received even more bad press than the hyena. The accounts of Herodotus and Pliny, the references in the Bible (where the Leviathan of the Book of Job is almost certainly a crocodile), the descriptions brought back by the early explorers — all were filled with that special awe-inspiring dread reserved for these monsters of the cold, indifferent eyes. Alternating between pure fantasy and gross exaggeration, the seemingly endless stream of invective has clouded most people's judgment concerning these reptiles. The majority of the old game wardens, for example, carried on personal vendettas against crocodiles, poisoning, shooting, or trapping them and offering bounties for their eggs. Today's safarist will no doubt see a crocodile, and probably more than one, and should take some time to learn about them. As the reader might suspect, the reality is less threatening — and more interesting — than the myth.[54]

Crocodiles and their close relatives, alligators, caimans, and gharials, are the sole survivors of a great group of reptiles that included the dinosaurs. Essentially, the basic differences between alligators and crocodiles are the teeth and the shape of the snout. In a crocodile, the conical teeth in the upper and lower jaws fall in line. In the alligator, when its mouth is shut, the upper teeth lie outside the lower — that is, it has an overshot bite. A crocodile's fourth lower tooth (larger than the rest) is visible when the mouth is closed; an alligator shows no teeth when its jaws are shut. In addition, the alligator's head is broader and shorter, and its snout is correspondingly blunter. Otherwise, alligators and crocodiles are extremely alike and live similar aquatic lives.[55]

The main crocodile of Africa and the best-known species, the Nile crocodile ("mamba" in Kiswahili), has a long *and* broad snout *(24)*. Crocodiles, unlike alligators, are often found in brackish water, estuaries, and even swimming far out at sea. The saltwater or estuarine

---

eliminate such superstitions, have worked to convince congregations that the primates are merely beasts — even to the point, it is said, of priests killing Indris and roasting them for food!

53. Madagascar has no woodpeckers, and some naturalists believe that the aye-aye may have evolved to fill the predatory

---

role played elsewhere by these birds. The solitary aye-aye's large ears also help to detect the larvae hidden under the bark.

54. For a full review of the lurid prose, the author wholeheartedly recommends the Graham and Beard volume, *Eyelids of Morning: The Mingled Destinies of Crocodiles and Men*, noted in Chapter III. Most African adventurers found it obligatory to have witnessed at least one fatal "loathsome" croc attack when writing their diaries.

55. That two such alike reptiles should have been given different common names is purely accidental. The Spanish sailors who first saw the large animals in the rivers of Central America (and who presumably knew nothing of crocodiles) called them lizards — *"el lagarto"* in Spanish. English seamen who later followed adopted the Spanish name but ran the two words together to make "allagarter," which was subsequently further corrupted by American Colonials to "alligator."

version can reach truly impressive lengths of twenty-five to thirty feet and is considered the most dangerous crocodile. Despite fearsome exaggerations, the Nile crocodile can reach twenty feet in length but doubtfully more. Now, twenty feet of crocodile, which can weigh about a ton, especially when it draws up alongside a safarist in a boat, is sufficiently noteworthy, to be sure. But huge crocs, like big-tusker elephants, have been hunted pretty much to extinction. On the other hand, despite all the uncontrolled shooting and trapping of the past, the Nile crocodile as a species is widely distributed in rivers, lakes, and swamps throughout East and Southern Africa. The Nile itself no longer teems with them, but other parts of Africa seem to be holding their own populations. Recently, crocodiles appear to be making a comeback, in fact, on the Uaso Nyiro, Galana, Mara, and Tana Rivers in Kenya, along many stretches of the Zambezi River, in the Serengeti Corridor, and in parts of South Africa. But only on Lake Turkana, where the alkaline water reputedly has caused the skin to lose much of its commercial value, and possibly in Murchison Falls National Park in Uganda, which reserve used to be a well-regulated sanctuary but which has suffered extensive poaching in recent years, can one still see the large assemblages of the past. Wherever they live, crocs prefer sheltered areas.

Reptiles are "cold blooded" — that is, they cannot internally maintain their body temperatures within fine limits, as can mammals and birds.[56] A reptile's body temperature depends (within a few degrees) on that of its

immediate surroundings. The animal cannot shiver to keep warm nor sweat to cool off. Thus, reptiles such as crocodiles keep their body temperatures from varying too much by following a daily routine that avoids temperature extremes. In Africa, that strategy requires careful attention. Crocodiles come out of the water at sunrise to lie on the land and bask in the sun. (25) When their bodies have warmed up, they either move into the shade or drop back into the water to escape the full strength of the midday sun. They can usually be found basking again in the late afternoon, returning to the water by nightfall. By staying underwater at night, they conserve heat, because water is a better insulator than air. Crocodiles are, in fact, the most successful reptile in maintaining efficiently body temperature around a 'normal' range.

When crocodiles leave the water, they generally stay nearby. Some will, however, wander a fair distance from the water's edge, and a safarist may see any one or more of three distinct gaits. Given their bulky bodies and short (but strong) legs, crocs are generally sluggish but they are also capable of surprising bursts of speed. The normal "high walk" consists of moving with the legs directly under the body, which itself is lifted well off the ground. When dashing into the water, a croc may also use the familiar 'tobogganing' or "belly-run" motion — the animal slides on its belly, moving its legs as oars or paddles that are occasionally reinforced by lateral swishes of the tail. The third method is employed by young crocodiles, who will sometimes gallop along with the front and back legs working together, like the bounding run of a squirrel. To my mind, crocodile movement always has something 'voluptuous' about it.

Crocodiles float low in the water, usually showing little more than eyes, ears, and nostrils. They carry several pounds (sometimes as much as thirty pounds) of stones, gravel, or other hard objects in their stomachs, which "gastroliths," as they are called, apparently help to stabilize their bodies. The stones lie in the stomach, against the ventral body-wall and below the center of gravity, and work to counterbalance the buoyant lungs.

56. It might be helpful to define in more detail what "cold-blooded" and "warm-blooded" mean. Taken literally, the words are misleading. The body temperature of warm-blooded or "endothermic" animals (birds and mammals) is maintained internally by the oxidation of food (that is, the burning of fuel, or metabolism) or by increasing muscular activity (like shivering), independent of the outside environment. In other words, a warm-blooded animal's high metabolic rate provides it with an internal source of heat. Some warm-blooded creatures maintain a nearly constant internal temperature; others vary slightly. High metabolism and effective insulation of one kind or another enable birds and mammals to maintain a body temperature generally higher than that of the environment. Thus "warm-blooded." Their temperature is regulated by a "thermostat" in the brain. Cold-blooded or "ectothermic" animals cannot regulate their temperatures by internal means. Temperature rises or falls depending on the outside environment. Consequently, even more than a mammal, a reptile must adapt a lifestyle to offset extreme environmental temperatures. Even though a reptile can withstand wider swings in body temperature than a warm-blooded animal, too great a variance will kill it just as surely as its warm-blooded counterpart. Basking in the sun raises blood temperature and conserves energy (the consumption of energy causes blood temperature to fall). Crocs pass the night in water because water is a better insulator of heat than air, but, by morning, the croc has so cooled that it must warm up (to hunt, for example). Thus, the weather plays as much a role in defining a

croc's hunting ability as the availability of prey. (A crocodile simply does not hunt in cold weather.) Being cold-blooded does have its advantages; most notably, reptiles can survive in the absence of prey — at least for a time. The abundance of prey often varies with seasonal changes or the availability of water. Warm-blooded animals must eat all the time to sustain their high metabolism, and, when water becomes scarce and prey unavailable, a mammal must migrate or starve. A cold-blooded animal simply slows down, finally becoming virtually immobile. When prey returns, the cold-blooded animal slowly replenishes its energy reserves, returning to "normal" activity. (The matter is not always so simple: many small mammals and birds are able to economize on energy expenditure by periodically falling into a torpor.) Reptiles do not "play" very much — their metabolic rates are just too low for sustained activity and fast recovery from exercise (repaying oxygen debt).

Plate 24. Leftover Dinosaur. Nile crocodiles are little changed from their ancient ancestors who lurked in the waters of tropical lakes and rivers 140 million years ago, except that some of the extinct crocs were considerably larger. Fossils show skulls measuring six feet long and a total body length reaching fifty feet! When looking at a picture of a crocodile, the reader can often tell a wild specimen from one held in captivity: the latter will exhibit a broader head and splayed teeth (even more than normal), both resulting from a greatly increased time living out of the water. In addition, the scales on a captive animal are often worn down on the back from all the "buffing" that occurs when crocodiles frequently climb over each other in crowded conditions.

The principle is the same as ballast kept in a ship's hold, though some have questioned the sufficiency of the stones' weight for such a purpose. Nevertheless, the need for some such device is seemingly indicated by the top-heavy instability shown by the stoneless young crocodiles in deep water, as compared with the ease exhibited by their stone-bearing elders. In fact, the discovery of these stones has from the beginning caused controversy among scientists. Some have gone so far as to insist that the gastroliths serve digestive purposes — like the mechanical digestion accomplished by gizzard stones in birds — but crocs have nothing resembling a gizzard. Others suggest that the objects are simply incidental debris reflecting a croc's habitat and culinary habits. That is, crocs simply gobble up the rocks inadvertently. This explanation has the merit of avoiding possibly the "vulgar Darwinism" criticized in the last chapter. But the hydrostatic school seems, to this author at least, to be on the right track. Balance is also important to a crocodile who is struggling to hold a large prey underwater until the latter is drowned and additionally to help a crocodile prevent being tumbled in a strong current (while lying submerged, for example, on a river bottom). Again, this would not be a matter of extra weight — the crocodile needs little of that, and gastroliths never amount to a proportionately significant total, when compared with body weight — but where the dense, dead weight is placed.

Basically, crocodiles follow a leisurely path in life. Consequently, and contrary to popular opinion, a crocodile survives on surprisingly little food, relative to its size. Gastronomically, it is an opportunist (a polite way of saying that it eats virtually anything within reach and "small" enough to kill), and its diet changes with age. Very young crocodiles, who pass much of their time on land, feed primarily on insects, like dragonflies, mosquitoes, ants, and spiders. Young crocs have been seen collecting mosquito larvae in the water by curving their bodies and tails around such prey. As the croc grows older, the amount of insects in its diet declines, and it turns to eating crabs, snails, frogs, snakes, turtles, small birds, and rodents. The juvenile will stalk its prey, swimming stealthily forward and pouncing with a sideways snap of the jaws — sideways, because the croc's eyes are located to the side of its head and because it is far easier to move a snout sideways in the water than up and down.[57] Adults supplement a predominantly fish diet by trapping mammals that come down to the water's edge to drink. They also take a certain amount of waterfowl. The larger crocs will pull into the water some big animals, as large as a full-grown buffalo. (Indeed, a single croc can kill a buffalo far more efficiently than can a lion.) A more normal quarry would be an antelope who has dropped its guard or bogged down in mud. Like a lion, a croc that devours a sizeable prey will

then go for several days (at least) without eating anything more. As suggested earlier, croc hunting is more than power and speed. Cunning is very much a factor, and crocodiles sometimes cooperate in the hunt. Old crocs especially depend upon ambush.

Common sense and superficial observation would seem to argue that crocs hunt by sight and, up close, by taste, but several authorities have suggested that the reptiles find their prey by smell. This theory seems improbable, for at least three reasons. First, a crocodile closes its nostrils when submerged, so smell is hardly active a good part of this time. Second, the eyes are adapted to night vision — they show a slit pupil by day and a wide-open rounded pupil at night[58] — a tip-off to serious nighttime hunting. Third, experiments with dried blood put into tanks with crocodiles have produced no reaction.[59]

When a victim is seized in its vice-like jaws, the crocodile pulls the body underwater to drown. Crocodiles normally do not eat on land — they need the water to raise their heads for the swallowing angle, so to speak. But a croc also cannot swallow underwater[60] and must surface to raise its head out of the water to gulp down its meal. Nor do crocs chew. (Reptile jaw structure and musculature generally allow snapping and gripping but no grinding.) They must tear off pieces small enough to swallow whole. Thus, the safarist may see a crocodile roll over and over in the water in a violent thrashing motion to help dismember its victim. A croc may also tear a carcass held in its mouth with its feet. Finally, after drowning their prey, crocs sometimes wait for the corpse to bloat and 'ripen,' depositing the carcass in a convenient larder underwater. Presumably, a putrefied body is easier to tear into bite-sized chunks for bolting.

To a degree, crocodiles are "water vultures," and do in and for the water what hyenas, vultures and other scavengers do on and for the land. They clean up carrion. A croc's jaws are immensely strong — but in one direction only, upwards (only the *lower* jaw actually moves independently), to close. The "closing power" of the jaws has been measured at up to 1,200 lbs. per square inch! A man can, on the other hand, hold the jaws shut, preventing a croc from opening its mouth. (Forgetting for the

---

57. Some writers assert that a crocodile cannot turn its head sideways and must turn its entire body. Not true.

---

58. During a night safari, the safarist will see the telltale reflections of the croc's eyes, gleaming like bright coals, lying out on the water's surface. The experience is an eerie one and guaranteed to keep the safarist on land (though serious crocodile hunting, especially when live capture is the goal, is often accomplished at night). A crocodile can apparently recognize colors and can detect sharp movement made 100 feet or more away.

59. Hearing is probably a croc's most developed sense, but the animals do have a keen sense of smell.

60. A "valve" closes automatically in a croc's throat when underwater, allowing the reptile to capture things in its mouth (without taking in large amounts of water) but not to swallow them.

Plate 25. Jaws Agape. Tourists view this aquatic relic of the Age of Reptiles with a mixture of loathing and fascination, as it rests with its mouth open on a sandy river shore or small island, seemingly oblivious to all around it. The jaws at this time display an impressive array of sixty-odd sharply pointed, murderous teeth. Naturalists do not know for certain just why the croc holds its jaws open this way. The most popular explanation, in the alternative, is to cool themselves: either by allowing cool breezes to flow over the soft skin inside the mouth or by encouraging evaporation from mucous parts of the mouth. Proponents of the first alternative originally suggested that crocs also faced breezes at this time, which gloss proved demonstrably incorrect. Indeed, the hot air frequently coming off the bright sand and the utter lack of any breezes on occasion puts this theory in question. The second suggestion proposes a kind of substitute for panting. One apparently contrary observation: a croc generally has a very dry mouth. But the basic problem with the theory — either alternative — is that why would a crocodile leave the water to warm up and immediately open its jaws to cool off. Particularly when, to cool off, the croc has only to slither a few feet back into the water. (On the other hand, passing the day, falling into and hauling itself out of the water may qualify as inefficient energy use.) As a factual matter, crocs do not necessarily wait until they have been in the sun for a time before they begin the yawning routine. The purpose of basking is to maintain a higher temperature; a crocodile simply goes into the water or seeks out shade to cool off. Yawning in the shade (never seen by the author), especially if done exclusively in the shade, would be another matter. On the other hand, a croc frequently leaves its tail in the water, dissipating heat, as in this picture, and perhaps the yawn is indeed part of a complex temperature-balancing act. Some basking snakes and lizards also gape. Another possibility is that the croc may be taking a page from the hippo's book (or is it vice-versa?) and issuing a general warning gesture to interested passersby. Yet another theory is offered, one that also accounts for the whiteness and cleanliness of the teeth themselves: the croc basks with its mouth open to prevent algae deposits from forming. At all times in the water, the mouth and teeth are wet, conditions that would, so the argument runs, cause a quick coating of algae deposits. But, in the final analysis, the gaping jaws may simply be a relaxing posture associated with lying out of the water. Crocs look torpid in this state, but the slightest disturbance brings them back to life. Excessive noise by a safarist will send them back into the water.

moment the problem of getting to and from the croc. . .) The tales of crocs seizing all sorts of animals are legion. An absolutely extraordinary series of photographs appeared recently in *Animal Kingdom*[61] depicting a crocodile seizing a giraffe's muzzle when the watchtower bent down to drink. As the surprised giraffe jerked its strong neck back, the ambitious (and stubborn) croc was hoisted right out of the water and let go only from a height of several feet to fall back into the river. No less remarkable was an earlier sequence run in *National Geographic*[62] showing a baby hippopotamus snatched off the river bank.

As a man-eater in the water, the "sinister" crocodile's reputation rivals that of the shark. The truth of this infamy varies in different habitats, but crocodiles have definitely posed a threat to man in many parts of Africa. Undoubtedly, crocs have, for example, killed far more Africans than lions. Some writers have asserted that crocs have accounted for more human deaths than all the other African man-killers taken together! One crocodile alone in Central Africa was recorded as having killed 400 people over a period of several years. No infamous man-eating cat ever approached that figure. Of course, a hungry croc is not necessarily going to distinguish man from any other prey at the water's edge; certainly, a person's size is about right for a larger croc. In areas where streams and pools dry up or where fish are otherwise limited, a croc may welcome the opportunity to improve the immediate food supply. Little evidence exists, however, for believing that crocs kill anything other than other crocs for anything but food. A croc may be testy when guarding its young or its territory but is not likely to find lethal steps necessary. Reports of crocs attacking boats should be skeptically received — crocs are more apt to be timid in the presence of boats. The truth is far more likely to revolve around tourists menacing crocs while looking for a "little action." As incredulous as this last may seem, *homo touristicus* is capable of unbelievably stupid transgressions. Simple ignorance, perhaps less culpable, can also lead the unwary to a tragic rendezvous with a croc.[63]

Nile crocodiles begin breeding from approximately five years onwards and continue virtually until they die. Full-grown males stake out territories and share them with juvenile males and with females. Males will defend their territories, mainly in breeding seasons, first by aggressive displays such as head-slapping, then by fighting, if necessary. And one contestant will sometimes kill another. But fighting is not common and in any event is more ritualistic than physically harmful. Crocs are fairly docile — and live crowded together — even during mating seasons. And territorialism is always moderated within the large populations. Courtship itself, which a non-intrusive safarist may be lucky enough to see, though moderately tender, becomes something of a contest of strength. The affair is always an entirely aquatic one. The male approaches a female and displays to her by thrashing the water with his snout and tail. Additionally, he may offer something called the "bubble display" — in which a kind of tremor vibrated off the crocodile's back causes bubbles and spray to dance on the water's surface — or the "fountain display" — where air is ejected from the nostrils, causing a vertical jet spout of water. The pair swim in concentric circles with the male moving on the outside, but the male frequently turns, bumps the female, and slithers over her, trying to press her down in the water. She resists. Natural buoyancy and the business of copulating eventually win out. Isn't nature grand?

The female will lay a clutch of up to ninety or so eggs — fifty is a normal figure — during the dry season. Crocodiles have communal, ancestral laying grounds, usually in the sand or soil along the river banks or lake shores, and normally return to the same spot year after year to lay. The eggs, each which is an oblong, leathery white sphere roughly the size of a goose egg, will hatch three to four months later, during the rainy season when there are plenty of insects for the babies to eat. Eggs are also laid in the dry season (during receding waters) to keep the nests from flooding and then hatched at the time of rising waters to guarantee safer dispersal of the newborns into the water. The eggs are deposited in pits, dug one to two feet deep and invariably placed near water and shade, so the female can guard her brood and still remain cool, and covered by the sand or soil present. During the incubation period, the female stays by the nest, defending it day and night against all enemies, including cannibalistic neighbors, though in some colonies crocs nest but a few yards apart. Many nesting females will not even leave the eggs to feed and assume a sort of comatose vigil.[64] Indeed, she must try to remain as alert as possible, no easy task for naturally lethargic crocs. Monitor lizards, as discussed below, are the main enemy and are both bold and sneaky enough to dig right underneath the croc, as she naps over her nest. One monitor has, moreover,

---

61. December 1984/January 1985, at p. 19.

62. February 1972, at pp. 182–3. C.S. Stokes in his book *Sanctuary* tells the remarkable story of a very large (and over-reaching) croc who seized a large bull elephant by a hind leg as the latter was bathing. The result: one dead croc wedged into a tree crotch along the shore. A warning for the future? — one is tempted to compare the hanging of criminals in public places!

63. Not to make light of a potentially tragic occurrence, but the author is reminded of one of his favorite Larson "Far Side" greeting cards: two fat crocs are reclining on the shore talking; a battered canoe, paddle, shirt, hat, and pair of eyeglasses are scattered about; and one croc with an air of great contentment remarks: "That was incredible. No fur, claws, horns, antlers, or nothin'. . . Just soft and pink."

---

64. This fasting lethargy is duplicated by crocs who find themselves trapped on the bed of a lake or river during an unexpected dry period and who are content to lie in the mud until conditions improve months later. Indeed, scientists believe that a crocodile can go a year without food, if forced to do so.

been witnessed decoying a crocodile a little way from her nest, while another co-conspirator stole the eggs. Baboons and hyenas are also notorious diggers of croc nests — but strictly in the temporary absence of mother. Predation and flooding ensure that no more than half the eggs will survive.

While still in the egg, the baby crocodiles croak and grunt just before hatching — a signal for the mother to uncover the nest. The muffled noise is audible from some distance away. The eggs are hard-shelled, and the babies must break their shells with a special "egg-tooth" that is grown during incubation and quickly shed afterwards. But the youngsters will likely suffocate if mother fails to uncover the nest, particularly if the soil cover has hardened under the sun. A mother may aid overdue eggs by breaking some shells herself. Moreover, if an entire nest is overdue, a croc mother will sometimes open it up and take the unhatched eggs to the water's edge, where she gently cracks them open. In any event, the babies climb from their shells and stay as near as possible to mother, yapping if they get lost. The first excursion is normally to the water, and foraging for insects begins in earnest. The young all look and act exactly like miniature dragons, with golden eyes, gleaming olive and black skins, and hissing, grunting, and snapping at one another, as they run about or ride on mother's back. A female can also use her massive jaws like forceps and ever so delicately pick up the newborns and either carry them in her mouth or deposit them in a pouch that bulges prominently beneath her jaws. The youngsters disperse after a few weeks, but, at the beginning, both mother and the hatchlings have much about which to worry: the predators are numerous; other crocodiles,[65] herons, Marabou storks, mongooses, turtles, eagles, and predatory fish all eat baby crocs with relish. The safarist might be fortunate to see the drama played out by Marabous and crocs throughout the African waterways:

> . . . the marabou stork with his hard hangman's eye . . . stands in the shallows, and with the speed of swordplay flicks [the hatchlings] into his long bill; and if you care to watch you can descry the wriggling passage of the young crocodile down the bird's scraggy throat.
>
> Sometimes the mother crocodile will try to defend her young at this perilous moment. . . . The marabou, with elaborate unconcern, stands in about six inches of water waiting for the next tid-bit to come swimming by, and from about twenty yards away the mother crocodile watches: just two murderous eyes above the surface of the stream. Then silently she submerges and comes up again

about ten yards from the marabou. The bird takes no notice. And now, having carefully calculated her distance, the mother again goes down. This time she is coming in for the kill. It is a matter of about two seconds before the strike, but in those two seconds the marabou abstractedly and casually takes a backward step. At the same instant the tremendous jaws of the crocodile come rearing out of the river and snap together in the empty air at the precise spot where he was standing. Green water streaming off her back, the crocodile subsides into the river again; and the bird, with the same disingenuous air, never taking its eyes off the water at its feet, steps back to resume its meal.[66]

Parental care is brief, intense, and only moderately successful. Perhaps, one baby crocodile per brood will live to maturity.

Adult crocodiles also have a few enemies: lions, elephants, leopards, and hippopotamuses have all had well-publicized run-ins with crocs.[67] Friction arises over carcasses, over space, and as a matter of real or perceived self-defense. Hippos, who often share their immediate environment with crocs are particularly worrisome neighbors. Hippos have been seen strolling among basking crocs and knocking recalcitrant reptiles who failed to move quickly enough into the water. Hippos also can take a dim view of crocs during calving time. There are reliable records of large crocs found bitten completely in two by hippos. Of course, man has been the primary predator for at least a century. The crocodile and its relatives have been killed in large numbers for the skin (belly and sides) that is tanned and used in shoes, handbags, and other pricey ornamental goods. Crocs have also been regularly killed as dangerous animals, but most "defensive" killing is done by misguided fishermen, who hold the reptile accountable for depletion of fishing stocks. Actually, the crocodile normally serves a valuable purpose in controlling certain carnivorous fish populations. In the lakes and rivers, large fish (like catfish) eat most everything else and breed prolifically. Once the crocodile, who is the only serious predator of these large fish, has been eliminated or seriously reduced in number, the large fish take over, virtually exterminating all the edible fish species. And the crab population, itself deadly to fish eggs and fry, also

---

66. Moorehead, *No Room in the Ark*, p. 55. Baby crocodiles are about one foot long when hatched and grow at the rate of about ten inches a year for their first seven years. Thereafter, they normally add yearly about an inch to their length.

67. All too frequently, the reader of wildlife literature will come across an eyewitness account that stretches credibility to the breaking point. For example, Joy Adamson reported a croc "sharing" a carcass with some lions. From everything that we know about crocs (forgetting, for the moment, the lions), including the fact that they just do not eat on land, this story seems impossible to believe. That is not to say that a croc is above showing some interest in possible free meat and approaching such a carcass. But a commensal relationship is out of the question.

---

65. Crocs are notorious cannibals. The safarist will not likely witness this depravation but will notice that basking groups tend to be sorted into parties of nearly equal size. Small crocs — especially males — always keep their distance from bigger brethren. Older crocs tend to feed increasingly upon fellow crocs.

increases to dangerous levels. Finally, baby crocodiles are prevented from doing their share, eating predatory insect larvae. Thus, the whole ecosystem is disrupted. In fact, fishing problems are inevitably aggravated by killing crocs.

A crocodile's tail is primarily a swimming tool (and rarely used to knock down prey, notwithstanding the frequent exaggeration to the contrary), the sole propulsion organ, in fact, as the legs and webbed toes are held close to the flanks of the body when swimming. The reptile is a strong swimmer:

> The speed with which a crocodile can travel is amazing. My men once drew my attention to one that was passing underwater in the middle of the Abbai and against the stream, and had they not suggested what was causing the slight ripple on the surface that was travelling at such a pace it would not have occurred to me that any living thing could move so fast in the water, and I should have put it down to a peculiar form of wind eddy. We all stood fascinated and watched it till it was out of sight.[68]

But it is a still more remarkable diver. It can submerge for several hours, many times longer than a hippo. Mention has been made of the efficiency of having its sensory faculties arranged so as to lie almost totally submerged in the water, yet fully capable of seeing, hearing, smelling, and breathing. On diving, special valves close the nostrils, special transparent membranes ("nictitating membrane") lubricate and protect the eyes, a thick operculum seals the ear openings, and another muscular flap forms an hermetic barrier at the rear of the mouth cavity. In addition, the croc's spongy lungs are highly economical in their use of oxygen. But most spectacularly, a croc can lower its heart rate to one beat per minute. All in all, nature has developed a most extraordinary diving machine.

Crocs live a long time in the wild — perhaps as long as sixty or seventy years. They run through forty-five sets of teeth, then starve to death. They die in the water. Of course, all crocs, young or old, look old! A crocodile, like an alligator, is able to "roar" for several seconds — a growing, vibrant rumble, deep in pitch, that seems to tumble out of the stomach and empty through what appears to be a prodigious yawn. Naturalists have compared the bellowing sound to thunder or the roll of a big drum; its function is not totally understood, though it appears to be the exclusive province of males during mating season. Actually, little is known about crocodile social life, such as it is. We really do not even know that crocs recognize one another individually.

Although crocodiles are known to eat birds — feathers of herons, ducks, and other birds are frequently found in their stomachs — many winged species flock around crocs basking in the sun. The presence of these steady companions is often likened to the symbiotic association that oxpeckers share with rhinos and other ungulates. Early writers suggested that the crocodile lay with its mouth open to permit the "crocodile birds" (presumably, the Egyptian plover) to hop in and pick the leeches and other debris from its gums, teeth, and tongue. But crocs also continued to "yawn" indefinitely in the absence of the birds, and the cause-and-effect explanation for the behavior had to be revised. In truth, several kinds of birds — especially plovers and sandpipers — walk on, flit over, and pick from the sprawled crocodile bodies. And birds are often seen rummaging in and picking food from a croc's mouth or pulling out a leech. In addition to the sanitary function (from the croc's perspective), the birds may well also play the role of sentinel and warn the reptiles of danger. The author has earlier suggested that oxpeckers generally make poor sentries, but the plovers *et al.* may serve the lethargic crocodile better.

And what of a crocodile's tears — noted prominently in Chapter III? The idea that crocs shed hypocritical tears is an ancient one. As Francis Bacon proposed in his *Essays,* "It is the wisdom of the crocodiles, that shed tears when they would devour." The comparison to women also has a long lineage and was probably inevitable; Othello was not the first to complain of the supposed deception (by Desdemona).[69] One would suppose, as Bacon suggested and Spencer asserted, that the "cruell, craftie" crocodile's purpose is to lure the unwary traveler closer to learn the reason for such grief. Like many legends, the story of a croc's tears may have a basis in fact. Crocodiles do have tear glands to keep their eyes moist,[70] and tears or water trapped in their lids may occasionally run from the corners of their eyes. Together with the permanent — Lewis Carroll called it "cheerful" — grin of their jaws, these would have encouraged the myth.

2. *Lizards.*

Lizards as a group are the most diverse and adaptable of all the reptiles. Africa has several noteworthy lizards. Little **geckos** everywhere run up and down walls and even walk upside-down on ceilings, thanks to adhesive or suction pads on their toes. The safarist will share a lodge room or two with these ubiquitous insect harvestors,

---

68. R. E. Cheesman, *Lake Tana & The Blue Nile: An Abyssinian Quest* (Macmillan, 1936), p. 285. Major Cheesman was the British consul in north-west Ethiopia for a decade in the early quarter of this century and the first true geographer of the Blue Nile.

69. O devil, devil!
If that the earth could teem with woman's tears,
Each drop she falls would prove a crocodile.
(Shakespeare, *Othello, The Moore of Venice,* Act IV, Scene I.)

70. Marine crocodiles have large glands in their head whose function may be the same as the salt-gland found in certain sea birds — to enable the animals to eliminate salt (by "weeping") and live without fresh water.

which are most active at nighttime. The beautiful foot-long **Rock agama** (also called Rainbow lizard) also puts in frequent appearances at the lodges and camps and can always be found patrolling kopjes. *(26)* The dominant territorial males in breeding season are metallic blue green, with terra cotta to red heads and rainbow-colored banded tails — the colors grow intense or fade, according to the lizard's excitement level. The mature male with its red face and ferocious mien has been compared to the English traditional "peppery colonel" about to explode in some apoplectic rage. Indeed, quarreling among the colorful agama males is commonplace. Broken, shortened tails are familiar testimony to pugilistic encounters. The safarist will see as well the constant, rhythmic, and comical head-bobbing of these males, which exercise looks very much like push-ups. The safarist should look closer: if the triangular flap or dewlap under the lizard's chin is smooth, making his neck look slender, the effort is for the

horns and all which are perfectly camouflaged.[72] With its prehensile (gripping) tail and monkey-like opposable fingers or toes, which are, however, partially webbed or fused, the chameleon makes its slow, stealthy way along the branches, rolling first one large turret eye, then the other. This last, optical feature is unique in the animal kingdom. Although the geckos and agamas depend upon lightning-fast dashes and jaws, the chameleon rapidly flicks its long, muscular, sticky tongue to procure its insectivorous meal. Watching chameleons gobble down insects is worth a few moments. Once a chameleon has spotted a target, the eyes cease to swivel around independently and point forwards together: perfect aim requires binocular vision. The lizard may also rock its head gently from side to side, improving its stereoscopic range-finding capacity by looking at the prey from slightly different angles. The movement mimics a leaf swaying in a breeze. Zap! The target, almost always stationary, is

Plate 26. "Rainbow" Lizard. I have seen — but, unfortunately, not photographed — a Rock agama lying sprawled across two hyraxes basking in the sun! The reader may recall from Chapter III stories of agamas catching flies off lions. Fast and agile, these lizards can negotiate any rock face and make spectacular leaps from one rock to another.

benefit of the ladies; if the loose skin is let down, the agama is warning off would-be male competitors who have been bold enough to cross his own boundaries. A certain amount of head-bobbing is also evident whenever the lizard is excited or nervous.

Tree-living **chameleons** are represented by many species,[71] some of which come armed with helmets and

African Continent, south of the Sahara. (One species can be found in Southern Europe, the Middle East, and North Africa, and one in India and Sri Lanka.) The safarist has only to look carefully in the bush; he will see the lizards.

72. The highly successful cryptic camouflage of these ultimate mimics serves two purposes. First, the reptile can move closer to its insect meals. Second, a passive defense is established against the many snakes, birds, and mammals that are predators. Everybody knows that a chameleon is a quick-change artist, but chameleons do *not* dramatically change their color to match their background. Instead, they live in environments that suit their basic coloration (a green chameleon spends its time on

71. Some eighty species of true chameleons ("kinyonga" in Kiswahili) are known, more than half of which are found in Madagascar and all but two of the remainder located on the

Plates 27 & 28. Nile Monitor. The large Monitors ("kenge" in Kiswahili), which can reach six feet in length, are formidable lizards. At bay, they inflate their bodies and hiss and lash out with their powerful tails, like whips. They may also bite and claw. In a more cautious mood, whenever circumstances permit, the Monitor can outpace most anything in thick cover. Moreover, it is an expert tree climber. A Monitor's color ranges from brown to olive-green, with yellow and black spots of varying sizes and shapes. The spots disappear with age. The lizard swims powerfully and dives to catch fish, frogs, and mollusks. It will also jump into the water to escape predators. Most lizards, the Monitor included, are tricky to photograph: at rest, they are dull and motionless, but they tend to move in sudden jerky spurts. In the early morning, Monitors behave like most reptiles trying to shake off the cold-induced sluggishness of the previous night: they bask in the sun. Monitors are common all along the rivers of tropical Africa.

trapped on the sticky end. Chameleons can extend their elastic tongues (by a kind of catapult mechanism) nearly twice the equivalent length of their bodies. Only very high-speed photography can catch the entire sequence.

The largest of the African lizards is the **Monitor,** the African brother to the Komodo dragon of Australia, the

green leafy branches, and so on). Chameleons do, however, completely change color in response to temperature and certain other stimuli and to express emotion — such as warning or challenging an intruding chameleon. Thus, the strongly territorial males will rise to a challenge by changing color, puffing their bodies up, inflating their throat pouches, opening their mouths, and otherwise bluffing a credible imitation of a miniature dragon. Interestingly enough, chameleons tend to turn a pale color, almost white, at night, making them easy to capture with a flashlight.

largest lizard now in existence. The Monitor most often seen by safarists is the Nile Monitor (27 & 28), which prefers to live near water and especially near crocodile nesting grounds. A variant, called a Bush or Savannah Monitor, lives on the open plains. The safarist might see one crossing the road or standing alongside a vehicular track (the only places where the author has managed to spot one). A Desert Monitor also lives in the desert regions of Africa. The Nile Monitor has a blunt head, a forked tongue (more typical of a snake than a lizard), and a laterally flattened, crested tail that aides in swimming.[73] It is carnivorous and preys on turtles, insects, snails, frogs, crabs, fish, and even birds. But the Monitor lives to raid croc nests and the eggs of ground-nesting birds along riverbanks. It has been said that happiness to a dog is what lies just behind a door; to a Monitor, what lies buried in the sand is the equivalent. The long, forked tongue that the safarist will see darting in and out is actually sniffing out such nests. The tongue picks up scent-particles in the air or on surfaces and passes them to the Jacobson's organ located in the roof of the mouth, where they are smelled or "tasted." As well-hidden as the eggs might be from most would-be predators, they will not escape the sensitive sense of smell of Monitors. As do crocs or snakes,

Monitors swallow sizeable prey whole.

Monitors resort to an ingeniously secure plan of egg-laying and incubation. In the rainy season, the Monitor digs into the center of a termite mound softened by the downpours and lays its eggs inside. These mounds are made of hard, clay-like soil baked by the sun. When dry, they are impervious to most damage, give or take an excavation or two by an aardwolf or aardvark (ant-bear) or the indignity of an elephant's baggy trousers. And, because the mounds are roughly two-feet thick, ants and other potential egg eaters are also deterred. The termites themselves quickly block up the openings made by the female Monitor and simply go about their business, negotiating around the eggs! The eggs are, in fact, actually incorporated into the termite nest. The constant warm, moist conditions inside the nest are ideal for the developing lizard embryos. The young hatch after an incubation period of some nine months. Their first food consists, naturally enough, of freely available termites.[74] As the eggs hatch, excess liquid from within flows into the clay that surrounds the eggs and hatchlings. The softening effect of this liquid ensures the escape of the young — neither Monitor parent returns to the nest nor shows any interest in its progeny. Indeed, what could it do? As the clay inside the termite nest softens, the young Monitors, from six to forty or so, break down the surrounding walls and dig out a central chamber. From there, the young engineers gradually dig a narrow vertical passage through which they eventually escape, one at a time, into the nearby undergrowth.[75]

3. Snakes.

Many visitors expect to see snakes everywhere on safari — and are usually surprised at their apparent scarcity. In fact, most

---

73. Most lizards have tails that break easily (the tails have special 'zones' of weakness) to thwart predators. When the body scurries away, the attacker is left with the tail. In some lizards, the adaptation has been so honed that the tail can be detached at will when the reptile is simply touched or even merely menaced by a predator. A monitor's tail is more like that of a snake's: it stays on unless bitten off.

74. Not all interested naturalists agree that the Monitor hatchlings eat the termites, which are available by the thousands, either in live form or drowned by the mud caused by the hatching process. Logic would, however, seem to support those scientists who believe that the termites are eaten.

75. The nesting phenomenon just described is predominantly, though not exclusively, a Southern African practice. Many

safarists never see even one.[76] The few who do normally witness, from the safety of their vehicle, a specimen slithering across a road. Snakes are shy and sensitive, and many species are primarily nocturnal. They are difficult to find even when one is looking for them and tend to move quickly away when approached. The majority of the venomous snakes are ground dwellers and "hear" with a bony rod in their jaws that picks up vibrations of an approaching vehicle or person on foot. The author has been told by an expert that a cobra can detect a barefooted person walking 150 feet away!

The most dangerous snake in Africa is a toss-up between the **Black mamba** and the **puff adder.** Mambas are a form of cobra (or vice-versa), and the Black mamba is not really black — its color ranges from an olive-green to a sort of silvery khaki with a conspicuous pale belly. Color darkens with age. The Black mamba is the largest mamba; the usual length is eight to nine feet, but it may reach fourteen feet. Feared throughout Africa for its deadly venom, extraordinary agility, and reputed belligerency, the Black mamba is not, in fact, at all aggressive and will always attempt to escape from a human being. On the other hand, if cornered or provoked, this snake will attack in self-defence, and its neurotoxic venom may cause unconsciousness and death in a few minutes. As readers of this volume might guess by now, the reputation of the Black mamba is really the victim of imaginative narrators who could not accept the thought that *their* encounters did not live up to the best of the *previous* tales, which older stories themselves were intended to fill any possible gaps in the African odysseys of returning heroes, ordinary

---

Monitors in East Africa use sand pits similar to crocodile nests or hollow trees.

76. Nevertheless, snakes are present. The author offers the following practical advice:

(1) On foot safaris, one should wear (comfortable) boots, the higher the better.
(2) Always look where one is walking in the bush.
(3) Treat all snakes as venomous.
(4) Treat all snakes as alive, even if they look dead. Many snakes, especially cobras, feign death when disturbed and go limp. Moreover, even a dead snake can bite for up to six hours after death!
(5) If it is necessary to handle a snake, one should hold it by the head *and* the tail.
(6) Most bites occur at dusk or at night.
(7) Most large-headed, short, thick-bodied snakes are venomous.
(8) Green snakes three feet long or longer are likely to be mambas.
(9) A smooth black snake more than six feet long is probably a cobra.

Africa has fewer poisonous species than Asia or the Americas, and, in actuality, one has a greater chance in Africa of being killed by lightning or by an allergic reaction to a bee sting than dying from a snake bite.

hardship and adventure being what it was. Lions and other African animals have, of course, all suffered a similar fate; the truth inevitably seems just a tad too tame. Unlike lions, however, snakes are relatively fragile and easily killed and hence gain nothing by wanton aggressiveness that would only endanger them. In reality, extreme timidity is the rule. Even a Black mamba that has been forced to fight will remain alert to escape possibilities and will not continue the defensive aggression if an opportunity to flee occurs.[77] Nevertheless, the hair-raising stories about mambas will not die. Statements too silly for attribution — "Nature's diabolic genius has attained its pitch of perfection" — to stories of lunges that take men off their horses fill volumes. And, of course, nine of every ten large snakes seen in Africa are said to be mambas.[78] By far the most entertaining stories are those told by "Adrian Boshier," introduced to the reader in Chapter III. Of these, the author's favorite is the following:

> . . . the news that reached Boshier told of a large black mamba trapped in a termite mound. . . . So Boshier went to investigate.
>
> The termite mound was riddled with holes, all of them blocked with stones. There was no doubt that any large snake that happened to be inside the old fortress was well and truly trapped. Standing beside the mound was a man who had done the trapping, a weather-beaten black veteran who described the snake and said that he knew this particular animal well. It was definitely a mamba, one with an evil reputation in the area, known to be unusually aggressive, even for its kind.
>
> While they talked, other people began to arrive. A hundred or more black laborers came up from the tobacco lands nearby and, before long, trucks and cars filled with local white farmers and ranchers, most of them sitting securely behind rolled-up windows, formed up in a semicircle around the mound. The farmer who owned the land had called up all his neighbors and invited them over to watch the Englishman try to catch a mamba.
>
> "I was surrounded by the largest audience anyone ever had while catching a lethal snake," Boshier later reported.
>
> One of the vehicles parked closest to the scene bristled with armor, including a double-barreled shotgun pointed ominously in his direction. The occupants promised that, if the snake should bite, they would shoot both him and the mamba — the catcher in order to prevent any unnecessary suffering and the snake out of revenge.
>
> Boshier was able, only with difficulty, to persuade them to put their arms away.

---

77. In fairness to some storytellers, an attempt by a snake to escape into a hole located near the human intruder may easily be misinterpreted as deliberate aggression.

78. The Green mamba is smaller (six feet or so), extremely shy and elusive, its venom only half as poisonous as that of its 'black' relative, and basically arboreal (as are most forest-dwelling snakes). Nevertheless, it too has suffered from stories of aggression — usually lying in ambush on branches overhanging paths in the forest.

He then turned to the people gathered at a cautious distance and said he needed one man to stand beside him with a stick, while he used a pickax to demolish the mound. At first no one moved, then the same old man who had trapped the snake stepped forward. He promised to hold his ground and not run away, so the digging began. Boshier had just demolished the tough outer shell of the mound when the pick sank deeply into otherwise solid clay. Pulling hard on the handle, he displaced a large panel of earth, which dropped out leaving a window into an internal cavity. As the dust settled, he could see the heaped-up coils of a long snake and on top, an unmistakable narrow, steep-sided head with a hard dark eye, the pupil edged with silver.

"It was a mamba alright, a black one and as big as any I had ever seen."

He coaxed the farmer from the safety of a truck to see this snake in its refuge. It lay there with its long forked tongue flickering, sensing every vibration, fixing them with its glittering eye.

"It was extraordinarily evil. I don't normally feel that way about snakes, but this one was something different."

The farmer felt it too, for after staring at it in fascination for a while, he whispered, "Man, nobody can catch that snake. It can't be caught. Let me shoot it."

Although he tended to agree, Adrian Boshier hustled the man back to his truck and returned to the mound. The mamba followed his movements with a cold and deadly stare and he began to feel uncomfortable. An enormous force emanated from that snake. It was like no other he had ever experienced.

Eventually he summoned up all his nerve and slowly extended his stick toward it. The snake doubled back its neck, opened its jaws wide to show the dark bluish lining of the mouth, and produced a deep, eerie hiss that filled the cavity in the mound.

"I glanced at the old man who, with great courage, still stood beside me. He too was transfixed by this snake, by the power and the sense of pure evil which it generated."

He tried to pin the head down with his stick, but after a few tussles, the mamba slid down a hole that led to a deeper chamber. When several feet of snake had disappeared, Boshier stuck his hand into the hollow and grabbed its tail. All he got for this piece of daring was a handful of dead skin that the snake was in the process of shedding. Handing the stick back to the old man, he took up the pickax and once more attacked the mound. At length, the opening of a second cavity appeared and simultaneously the furious head and neck of the mamba reared up through the dust and rubble and began striking wildly.

"I grabbed the stick from my companion and entered into the fiercest battle with a snake that I have ever experienced. Rearing up to my own height, the mamba attacked with absolute fury, jaws agape and fangs cleaving the air as I leaped from side to side. I was completely oblivious of the audience. All my world at that moment was filled with a long black body, hissing and lashing at me."

When the snake hesitated after one forceful lunge, Boshier knew that his chance had come. He rushed at it, hooked it just under the raised neck, and carrying the charge through, forced it back and down until he had it pinned to the ground. Then, without giving it a chance to recover, he grasped it behind the head.

The snake erupted in rage. Flinging out its coils, it fought and strained and several times he was afraid that it would wrench its head from his grasp, even though he was holding it with both hands and exerting all his strength. He was acutely aware that if it did break free, there was no one who could save him.

"Just at the point where I became convinced that the snake was going to outlast me, it weakened and the battle was won. I hustled it into my waiting sack."

One by one the farmers climbed out of their vehicles and the postgame discussion began. An old black man came up to him and said with conviction that this was no ordinary snake, but one with a great and terrible spirit. And while everyone was milling about comparing notes, a lone figure appeared from the bush to ask what all the fuss was about.

Everyone turned to the old man who, with no further encouragement, launched into a wonderfully vivid account of the whole affair. He began by telling simply how he had passed the spot that morning just as the mamba was returning to its lair and how he had trapped it there. But, as the story progressed and a circle formed around him, the old man began to reenact the scenes with great skill and drama. Not only did he assume both human roles, but he also took the part of the snake, rearing up out of the mound and striking. Each time he lunged forward with his mouth open, the members of the crowd fell back and raised their arms and roared.

When the snake made its final attack, the catcher, in a nice bit of artistic license, nonchalantly took hold of its neck barehanded in midstrike. A great triumphant shout filled the air. As the old man stood there, proudly holding up the imaginary mamba, the crowed [sic] began a rhythmic chant in which Boshier, for the first time, heard the name Rradinoga — father of snakes.

From that day on Rradinoga was his name. It was a name whose fame preceded him across the land, a name that acknowledged Boshier's special powers and a growing belief that he and the snakes and the spirits of the snakes were all one.

The Africans still talk about the way in which he and snakes so often arrived at a village together; it was considered strange and unusual for one to be seen without the other.

But the reputation that grew up around Boshier also produced a great deal of ambivalence. He was made welcome as a man with *moya*, with spirit; but he was held in superstitious awe. . . .On one occasion, the rumor that he was coming and that he was angry was enough to shut down a whole street full of shops for the day. For better or for worse, the name was his and only his.[79]

---

79. Lyall Watson, *Lightning Bird*, pp. 48-52. The reader can just *imagine* what the "evil" mamba was thinking about during all this time. What might be called the "banderillero principle" applies generally in nature: persecution provokes aggression. Or, as Voltaire in his famous line declared (in translation): "This animal is very vicious — when you attack him, he defends."

This is truly a story difficult to beat!

The puff adder, which belongs to the viper family,[80] is almost as notorious and certainly just as deadly as a Black mamba, though the poison takes longer to act and therefore may be easier to counteract. But the adder is more widespread and more numerous than the mamba, and, because it prefers to hide and rely on its near-invisibility against its surroundings, a person may accidentally step too near. The puff adder actually is no more aggressive than a Black mamba, but provocation, the Adrian Boshiers of the world aside, is easier to supply. Most snake deaths are from puff adder bites. Fortunately, the snake usually gives a loud hissing warning before striking, or the toll would be much higher.

Both Black mambas and puff adders are swift moving, but not nearly so fast as the early exaggerated estimates of thirty or twenty miles per hour. Quite simply, the effortless-looking (and impressive) gliding motion can be quite deceptive. Having relatively inefficient circulation, neither snake, even if thoroughly warm, would really be capable of the effort needed to reach and sustain such speeds. Instead, the Black mamba, which is supposed to be the fastest snake alive, has actually been clocked at seven miles per hour. It is possible that ten to fifteen miles per hour could be achieved in a short burst.[81] Nevertheless, mambas are at a disadvantage on any relatively smooth surface and often are run over by a vehicle when attempting to cross a road, especially if the road surface is paved.

Striking is, however, far quicker. In the middle of its strike, a puff adder's head moves at a rate of about twenty-five feet a second — too fast for man (or most animals) to avoid by mere reaction. Striking distance varies between one-third to three-quarters of body length; the largest snakes can manage only the former. More is fantasy; accounts of fantastic leaps are all nonsense. On the other hand, a ten-foot snake lunging five feet in a split-second should need little embellishment.[82]

––––––––––––

80. There are at least eight species of puff adder in Africa, all stout-bodied snakes with short tails and broad heads. The text basically refers to the common puff adder, which is yellow to brown, with darker bars or chevrons on its back. To some degree, adders are ecological counterparts to the rattlesnakes.

81. Green mambas can negotiate the trees in a hurry and seem almost to "fly" through the branches.

82. At this point, the reader may want to revive his respect for the little mongoose. Though the mongoose's thick skin and dense hair absorb a good deal of poison before it can enter the blood stream and though the mongoose is possibly (this has not been proved) naturally resistant to venom, the contest is settled on the basis of strategy and quickness. The mongoose wears down his enemy with rapid feints and fast-circling movements. In may respects, the cobra is an ideal opponent because of its method of raising its body off the ground before it strikes. Mambas remain on the ground until lunging and are quicker — and mongoose rarely, if ever, challenge this snake.

Herpetologists are agreed that the Black mamba's venom is too strong and equally that the puff adder injects too great a quantity of venom merely for the purpose of killing. Both venoms also begin the process of breaking down blood and tissue for actual digestion. Large prey is often struck with the fangs and then allowed to run away, the snake later following to eat it at leisure. Obviously, a mamba's victim does not travel very far. As evidence of this digestive function, the body of an uneaten victim will change color quickly and putrefy far earlier than a normal carcass. Mamba venom acts differently on the body from that of a puff adder's: the principal ingredients of the former are neurotoxins that affect the nervous system and cause paralysis and the collapse of the lungs and heart, whereas vipers act principally on the blood system, destroying tissues.

Another snake that receives considerable notoriety is the celebrated **Spitting cobra** (also called the Black-necked cobra). All cobras are well known for their distinctive "hood," which serves to intimidate an adversary and to protect their own necks from a bite (by, for example, a mongoose), but this particular cobra is capable of propelling a jet of poison through its hypodermic-needle fangs. The process is not exactly "spitting," which implies lip participation, but a method of squirting or exhaling two streams of a finely vaporized moisture of saliva and venom.[83] The spitting range varies from six to ten feet, which is farther than the comparable striking distance. The Spitting cobra will normally "spit" only when cornered and will usually aim for the face of its presumed enemy. The theory explaining this choice is that the snake is aiming at the movement and reflection of the eyeball. The venomous mixture is a very strong irritant, causing intense pain and perhaps even temporary blindness, but rarely leaves any lasting injury.

The final contender for a significant place in the African pantheon of dangerous poisonous land snakes is the **Green Tree snake** or **boomslang**. A boomslang's venom, by weight, is supposed to be even more toxic than that of a mamba or viper. Moreover, the poison acts equally on both the nervous system *and* the blood system. But each boomslang secretes only a very small amount of venom and carries its poison fangs so far back in its jaws — the snake is called "back-fanged" — that a person would have to stick his finger into its mouth to receive any venom. And, like our other deadly friends, boomslangs are exceedingly shy and try to avoid people at all costs. Birds and tree-climbing lizards are, however, not so fortunate: the boomslang, whose average length is four feet, is very agile among the tree branches and can glide gracefully to their very tips, aided by its prehensile tail. Because of the location of its fangs, a boomslang must hold prey for many minutes, having to "chew" at the

––––––––––––

83. An extraordinary photograph of a Mozambique Spitting cobra in the act was published in *Natural History,* August 1985, at pp. 78-9.

wound to allow the venom to penetrate.

Without minimizing the terrible consequences of a lethal snake bite to man, this very rare loss of human life is more than compensated for by the immense amount of food saved by the snakes' control of the rodent population. Changing perspectives, a snake's two major enemies are man (directly and through habitat destruction) and fire. Also deadly are other snakes (snakes are voracious cannibals), large birds of prey (including the secretary bird), cats, mongooses, and monitor lizards.

The one non-venomous snake with which most safarists are at least vaguely familiar is the **Common** or **African Rock Python,** a magnificent reptile that grows to thirty feet long or more.[84] Pythons are the Old World equivalent of the New World boas. The Rock pythons are widely distributed in the forest, bush, and savannah. They prefer open woodlands (particularly near water), but the safarist has to be especially observant to find them at all. Ordinarily, the most likely place to spot a python is in a tree ((29), but pythons normally descend to the ground to find food.

Prey is ambushed: the python lies in wait along a well-trod game trail, then springs forwards. A blow from its muscular head lands with sledgehammer force, knocking over the victim, which is then seized with the snake's jaws[85] until the serpent can wrap its tightening coils around the victim's body. The prey is killed by constriction and strangulation. The coils then loosen somewhat but still hold the dead body steady while the python works the victim, apparently always head-first, into its mouth. All snakes have remarkable swallowing abilities, but pythons take first prize in that activity. Contrary to general belief, constriction does not smash the bones of large prey but is used simply to strangle and hold the target. Although constriction may, in fact, stretch a victim slightly or break off long horns, thereby making an animal easier to swallow, a python ingests antelopes and sundry completely whole and basically intact. Its jaws are loosely connected — not hinged, but joined by elastic ligaments — and can move independently, outwards as well as downwards and upwards, thus allowing a gape much wider than the snake's head. Indeed, a python can open its mouth proportionately more than four times as wide as can the reader. While swallowing very large prey, which activity may take quite some time, the 'breathing

tube' or glottis is deflected out of the way and extended like a snorkel, allowing the snake to continue breathing.

Obviously, the python must maintain this extreme flexibility right down the body. Snakes have no breastbones, so nothing initially prevents the ribs from spreading outwards. The skin's scales are not detachable like fish-scales but are formed by unfolding of the skin, resulting in great elasticity. The meal is gradually "walked down," as each row of teeth alternately grips and pulls. Much saliva is manufactured and used for lubrication. Significant digestion comes later; for awhile at least, the full outline of the prey's body can still be seen in the python's digestive tract.

Safarists who are lucky enough personally to witness the fantastic feeding sequence, pictured in the Zeisler & Hoffer book, *Safari*,[86] referred to in Chapter I, are always amazed to see the size prey that a python will tackle. In all nature, solitary hunters seldom kill prey bigger than themselves, but much of a python's diet is larger — often, far larger — in circumference than its own body. Of course, an adult python is no small animal — extending more than twenty feet long, weighing perhaps a hundred pounds, and having a girth as great as a man's waist. But prey regularly consumed — pythons are, as all snakes, strictly carnivorous — includes adult gazelles, other small antelopes weighing up to 100 pounds, large monkeys, and warthogs. A particularly ambitious (so one assumes, needless to say) python is reported to have caught and eaten a leopard. In other words, what Norman Myers has called this "consummate consumer" can double its size with a single mouthful! Mammals and birds are preferred — pythons have heat detectors near their lips, which organs are so sensitive that minute temperature differences can be noted, enabling the snakes to find warm-blooded prey and strike accurately. A large appetite does not, of course, insure good sense; occasionally, a python is found with porcupine quills or antelope horns that have pierced its stomach wall. But a python's voracious eating habits are sporadic, at best. After a particularly large meal, a python will not eat again for some time; waits between meals of months are not uncommon. Some snakes have been known to delay a year or more before eating again.

A safarist who spots a python on open ground will see one of four methods by which snakes move: large-bodied snakes "creep" in caterpillar fashion. In a slow, rhythmic procession, the muscles contract along the belly, with the large belly scales alternately sliding forward over the

---

84. The increase in the body length of snakes is not achieved by elongation of the vertebrae, as in a giraffe, but by adding vertebrae: several hundred in a python. Snakes grow quickly as youngsters and never stop growing, though the rate of growth slows appreciably in old animals.

85. A python has a formidable array of long, recurved teeth: six rows worth (100 total). Typically, the teeth of a non-poisonous snake all point backwards, ensuring a firm grip on prey. Such teeth are useless for cutting or chewing, and the snake has no choice but to swallow prey whole.

86. At p. 36. Some visitors (and Africans) have been foolish enough to tease a python apparently immobilized by a gargantuan meal, as shown here. Their reward has, often enough, been a dangerous bite. The snake can disgorge a carcass far more quickly than swallowing the same. Moreover, a python that is well along in digestion can still move its head rapidly.

Plate 29. Python. Snakes have evolved exploiting life underground and in thick cover, which early habits account for their shape and protective eye-scale (the eye is protected by a layer of transparent skin). This latter obviates the need for eyelids and gives snakes their cold, unblinking, hypnotic stare. A python's skin, like any other snake's, is dry and smooth, not slimy. "It's scales a sheen of spotted gold," wrote Virgil of the python. The forked tongue is flicked out to catch the scent molecules in the air and returns to touch the small organ (Jacobson's Organ) in the roof of the mouth. This gives the snake its sense of smell; snakes have no sense of taste, as such. Pythons are easier to find than most snakes because of their size and because they do not flee at the mere approach of man — vibrations do not travel well up tree trunks. But their camouflage makes them easy to miss. Early mornings or late afternoons are the best times to look for them, but speeding through a safari will not do.

the rear part again), or engage in side-winding, a modified looping gait characteristic of desert dwellers (in loose soil or sand).

Another characteristic feature of pythons is the mother's close care of her young. Among snakes, only pythons "incubate" their eggs in a manner resembling birds. A female will gather her clutch of eggs — up to 100 in number — into a pile and will then coil protectively around them until they hatch. Scientists are not agreed on whether the female is actually incubating the eggs — some studies have indeed shown a dramatic rise in the temperature of the female's coils, especially the inner-most coils, compared with the outside temperature — or merely guarding them. During all the time before the eggs are hatched, from two to three months, the female moves only infrequently to drink or eat.

Predictably, the best python story is Boshier's:

The first time Boshier saw a python, it was so big that he almost failed to recognize it. Then he noticed that the tree trunk in his path was moving. He stood entranced as yard after yard flowed by. It was unbelievable; somewhere was a head and, at some stage still to come, a tail. And in between, more snake than he would have thought possible.

When he plunged into the undergrowth in search of its head, the python began to coil its body. This seemed an undesirable situation, so he put his stick across its back and made a grab for its head. It was then that Boshier learned the difference between the strength of a snake that relies on poison, and one that depends on its muscle for a living. He was jerked right off his feet and forced to cling to its neck with both hands, whereupon it promptly behaved like a python and began to engulf him in its coils.

Boshier released one hand and tried to pull free, but could not even get a grip on the broad body. Then he tried unwinding the snake and found to his relief that this worked. Pythons seem to be unable to resist a strong centripetal force. As fast as it threw its coils around him, he unwound them. And there they remained in an animated embrace.

"We became acquainted," he said later. "We really did!"

After an hour of action, the python began to relax and Boshier released the pressure on its neck. He watched carefully for any sly maneuvers, but the snake lay without resistance. Boshier felt so certain of this change in attitude that he even stroked it. And it seemed to settle itself more comfortably, half of its enormous length cradled in his arms.

He wondered what to do next. The bags he had with him were far too small. He decided that he needed help, but the nearest village was more than a mile away. Stroking it for reassurance (his own as much as the snake's), he began to gather up its coils, draping the python's body about his own — doing deliberately that which he had so recently fought to prevent.

The python seemed to like it! They set off together, in this odd embrace, and Boshier soon discovered that the snake was extremely heavy. By the time they reached the village, he was exhausted. But help was a little hard to find. A fourteen-foot python is very thick and when draped around a skinny human, not much of the latter is visible. The sight was more than even the strongest hearts in the village could stand. Evacuation was virtually instantaneous.

ground, then anchoring and pulling the body forward in a ratchet-like action. Smaller snakes slither, the ordinary wriggling familiar to most everyone,[87] or move in the "concertina" method (drawing the body into tight, horizontal folds, pushing the head forward, and drawing up

---

87. Such looping, slithering locomotion depends upon friction, which accounts for a snake's difficulties on a smooth surface.

Standing there in the empty village, Boshier realized the futility of trying to hold on to his prize. So he staggered off into the bush again and, at a safe distance from the settlement, unwrapped this acquiescent burden. It slipped quietly away, but a legend had been born.

Boshier later heard several wildly different accounts of how he had "attacked" the village with the Great Serpent itself riding on his back. And with each telling, the size of the snake and its ferocity grew. In the minds of the people, he was beginning to be associated with the reptiles and given some of their attributes. He was being identified with his totem as a Snake Man. And Adrian Boshier was never loath to capitalize on his reputation.

As he traveled about, catching snakes for sale, he was always ready to stop in a village and hold an impromptu

Plate 30. Bicolored Python Rocksnake Fresh from Whipping the Elephant's Child. The rectilinear motion used by pythons enables them to glide smoothly forward in a straight line. On flat surfaces, the weight of the snake's body is sufficient ("gripping" by friction alone), but, on sloping ground, the scales can dig into irregularities to obtain greater purchase and move faster. This locomotion is silent, and pythons approach their prey unheard. The rectilinear method is also the least conspicuous movement to the eye.

show. He would haul out his captives one by one and drape them all over his body, allowing them to slither in and out of his pockets and shirt-sleeves. At first the audience held back in fear. But eventually fascination would get the better of even the most timid and each performance would end with everyone prancing about and shouting in excitement. Afterward, when the snakes had been returned to their bags, there was always food and drink and hospitality.[88]

The snake, cursed in Genesis for tempting Eve, has been given a unique mythology by Western man. A living, mobile phallic symbol, the reptile has often been portrayed as a seducer of women. Indeed, the sexual connotation may well have contributed to its unsavory reputation. But it is hardly difficult to predict what the human imagination would do with a creature without legs, that moves on its belly, can kill with one bite or swallows entire bodies, looks coldly at the world through a permanent window, smells with its tongue and hears with its jaws, *and* has been pronounced evil by the Bible.[89] For the snake, slander has long been a fact of life. Yet, in Africa, despite what may well be man's innate fear, snakes in general have been accorded a more positive, even sacred, role in mythology. A divine python, the Great Serpent, is said by some to be the first being and to have set the universe in motion. The Great Serpent then gouged out channels for rivers and can still be seen moving in the currents. Or arching in the form of a rainbow and flashing in the sky as lightning. The ability of snakes to shed their skin at regular intervals has led to the widespread belief in their immortality: the symbol of eternity in African lore is a coiled snake with its own tail in its mouth. Thus also, snakes are regarded as reincarnations of the spirits of ancestors, as representing forces of life and regeneration, of fertility and good fortune, and as having supernatural powers of wisdom (including the secret of eternal youth).

In truth, snakes are easily fascinating creatures — worthy of a lucky safarist's cautious interest.

88. Watson, *Lightning Bird,* pp. 45-6.

89. On the other hand, the snake has had a long connection in Western thought with medicine and has become a powerful figure of healing. Today, the symbol of the medical profession is still the snake, based on the serpents belonging to the Roman god of medicine, Aesculapius (or the corresponding Greek god, Asclepius, son of Apollo).

IX. The Birds

We came to the sandy mouth of a stream where a great concourse of pelicans and cormorants was gathered. The pelicans had spread out in the shallow water of the lake in tens of thousands. They surged into the air in great sweeping clouds tinged with pink, making as they took off a sound like booted armies treading the ground, against a background of dark blue storm-clouds and distant misty blue hills. These huge birds look clumsy and rather ugly on the ground, but fly most gracefully.

Cormorants in thousands lined the muddy river bank as if waiting for a supper-bell to summon them. Their eyes were green. Their white throats pulsated like bellows, in and out — a cooling mechanism? Marabou storks, who stand five feet tall, stalked to and fro amongst them, and amongst white and black wood ibises, white-all-over spoonbills gobbling with their spatulate bills, groups of gulls, and flocks of both spur-winged and Egyptian geese. The air was noisy with their mingled sounds — chatterings, wing-beats, landings and takings-off, air-beatings, honkings, splashings. Such a profusion of bird-life is overwhelming. I thought sadly of the English bird-table and its three or four pairs of tits, several sparrows, a few greenfinches, a chaffinch, a single robin. The appearance last winter of a solitary greater spotted woodpecker was an event, and the subject of telephone conversations with a neighbour whose bird-table competed with mine for his favours. How many birds were feeding on or near this lake-shore and in the lake? Half a million?

Huxley & van Lawick, *Last Days in Eden*[1]

The shores of its lake are rich in silence, lonely with it, but the monotonous flats of sand and mud that circle the shallow water are relieved of dullness, not by only an occasional bird or a flock of birds or by a hundred birds; as long as the day lasts Nakuru is no lake at all, but a crucible of pink and crimson fire — each of its flames, its million flames, struck from the wings of a flamingo. Ten thousand birds of such exorbitant hue, caught in the scope of an eye, is a sight that loses credence in one's own mind years afterward. But ten thousand flamingos on Lake Nakuru would be a number startling in its insignificance, and a hundred thousand would barely begin the count.

Beryl Markham, *West With The Night*[2]

Plate 1. Saddle-Bill Stork Landing in Tree.

If it needs to be said, Africa is a birder's paradise; birds are one of the glories of African wildlife. Most people visiting the game parks for the first time come to see the big game animals. Within a very short time, they realize that African birdlife is spectacular by any standard: beauty, abundance, diversity, the size of some birds, and exclusivity. Active bird watchers can see — easily —more than 100 species in a day on safari. And another 100 the following day. More, in fact, than one could find in an entire year in the Eastern United States or in the United Kingdom. Even the most casual, though observant, safarist should surpass what birders call a "big day" in North America. In a month's safari in East Africa, particularly at the peak of the spring migration (mid-March to mid-April), a diligent visitor could well compile a list of 700–800 species, more than a lifetime's results at home. Some 8,700 distinct kinds of living birds that ordinarily do not interbreed in the wild are known. Kenya alone has

1. At pp. 163–6.
2. pp. 160–61.

considerably over 1000 species.[3] So, too, Uganda. The Serengeti Park alone contains nearly 500 species. South Africa nearly equals Kenya. Moreover, Africa has many "pockets" of bird life, distinct areas not far apart geographically but differing greatly in the kinds of birds present. Thus, in one of the more extreme examples, Ngorongoro Crater has over 900 different birds, 100 which differ from the species encumbent at Lake Manyara only thirty miles away. Lake Manyara, in turn, has another 100 species not found in the Crater! One can only surmise that the Great Birder himself looked forward to a stint as a tour operator.

According to the National Audubon Society, some thirty million Americans watch birds, and the number increases significantly every year. Only gardening surpasses birding as the most popular American passive pastime. Of course, really "passive" birders — those who do not climb mountains, hike through forests, or splash through swamps — do not see much at all. But, once the trouble of organizing a safari has been taken, the ease of birdwatching in Africa is unsurpassed — and slightly overwhelming. Indeed, real birders, an obsessive lot by nature, leave safari Africa with a sense of accomplishment that other visitors find slightly condescending. The basic requirements are good binoculars and silence. Moreover, while the seasoned ornithologist will find a challenging diversity,[4] even the amateur without field guide will still see many conspicuous and interesting birds that are quickly identifiable: the ostrich, Crowned crane, Yellow-billed stork, Ground hornbill, vultures (and their cohorts, the Marabous), oxpeckers, Cattle egrets, Kori bustards, the secretary-bird, hamerkop, touracos, and mousebirds, among several others. Most of these birds are restricted to Africa. Finally, Africa offers to the lucky safarist — the timing is a matter of chance to visitors locked into a tight schedule — some bird spectacles unrivalled elsewhere.

The subject of African birds is, of course, worthy of an entire book, and, indeed, many a book has been written (some of the best are listed in the Bibliography). Limitations of space prevent the author, a bird enthusiast, from being overly ambitious, and this chapter serves only to introduce *some* of the more common distinctive, popular, colorful, and unusual various birds to the reader. Faced with the veritable riot of colors and profusion of types in the following pages, the reader may doubt the assertion that the chapter represents only the tip of a very large iceberg, but that is the simple truth of the matter. The author has left to the fieldguides the fine points of distinguishing birds of the same variety. Personally, I cannot imagine a happy safari without carrying along a reliable field guide to the birds. Moreover, the Kiswahili names are, in a departure from the previous chapters, not given in the text — most are not common and the safarist will have little use for them. Nevertheless, the names of the most well-known, provided a consensus exists, are listed in the Kiswahili guide at the back of the book.

---

3. A few countries — for example, Colombia and Equator in South America — may have more species than Kenya, but no country combines numbers with access to bird habitats the way that Kenya does. Kenya, because of its position astride the Equator and basically halfway between northern and southern Africa and also because of its amazing geographical diversity — tropical coast to glaciers, freshwater and saline lakes, semi-desert to closed-canopy forest, mangrove swamps and alpine zones — supports most of the more or less 1,500 species listed for the eastern half of tropical Africa (Mozambique to Sudan). On the other hand, South Africa also has most of the more distinctive birds found in Kenya.

4. The more serious bird watchers can find excellent orinthological collections (and libraries) at the National Museum in Nairobi and the Transvaal Museum in Pretoria. The Austin Roberts Bird Hall in the latter is truly unique in the world for displaying a country's avifauna — over 820 species (including variations in plumage) are represented, each species accompanied by a distribution map, an egg, and, where possible, a nest!

After lunch they took us down a farm track to Lake Nakuru . . . . We drove right down through the bush to the lake and it was an unforgettable sight. There is a wide grassy plain and a sandy beach. There were many gazelles and zebra all about us and a few perfectly beautiful golden-crested crane, which are royal game and the crest of Uganda. But most marvellous of all were the thousands and thousands of flamingoes walking in ranks along the shallow edges of the lake. They were a mass of pink until they rose in flight, when the black under their wings showed. There were also a few sacred white ibis among them. The flamingoes have graceful red legs and they make the most extraordinary sound with their beaks. They walk along in ranks all facing one way and then turn together as though by magic signal. A school of hippos was sporting out just beyond them. There was the most glorious light effect with both dark clouds and sunshine so that tearing up and down the beach right beside the birds, with others wheeling over head for a three-mile stretch, was indescribably beautiful and really thrilling. We picked up many feathers varying in shades from white and pale pink to deep rose. We then struck through the bush in the cars chasing warthogs, zebras and herds of impala. Father was nearly beside himself with enthusiasm, and it really was an unforgettable afternoon. (Olivia Stokes Hatch, *Olivia's African Diary,* pp. 111–2)

Plate 2. Flamingoes. Some bird naturalists believe that all the Lesser flamingoes in East and Southern Africa are really *one* highly mobile population.

considerably larger (taller by more than a foot) bird. Nevertheless, the ratio of Greater to Lesser is 1:100, and the safarist may have difficulty relying upon such characteristics to segregate a flock. More reliable and distinctive than plumage is the color of the bill: a Lesser has a bright red bill, the Greater a pale pink bill with a black tip (in the distance, the latter's bill looks solid black). Moreover, it helps to know that Lesser often swim away from the shoreline, as they can "graze" while swimming, while the Greater is more likely to be standing closer to shore when feeding.

The story of the flamingoes, including the 1962 near-disaster in Tanzania, is a fascinating one, and this brief introduction barely scratches the surface — readers are urged to pursue the matter elsewhere. It should help the safarist to know that the quick-exit migrations take place at night (sometimes 400 miles worth!) and that a huge flock reported at dawn will still be there by late day. But, before leaving flamingoes, re-enter, stage door left, Mr. Abbott H. Thayer, for the last time, still attempting to prove magic with colors.

Indeed, the straw that broke Thayer's back was his argument that natural selection made flamingoes red to mimic the sunset and conceal the bird from predators: "vanish" against the "rich-colored skies" of early morning and evening. Crawling on his belly in West Indian mud, Thayer wanted a 'birds's eye view,' so to speak, or at least a crocodile's or python's view. He saw, or thought that he saw, the entire flock assume the shape and color of a pink cloud. But Thayer had everything wrong — flamingo behavior, predator behavior, even color behavior (any object of *any* color viewed against

Plate 4. Taking Off. When taking off, flamingoes use their web feet to. "run" along the surface to gain speed. Flamingoes are both excellent swimmers and fliers. It is sometimes said that the Lesser flamingo cannot live on freshwater lakes. The truth is, flamingoes have to drink freshwater to survive and would welcome the change in environment, except that only *spirulina* can support the density of large flocks. Thus, birds that move off to freshwater eventually disperse.

Plates 5 & 6. Nakuru Late Afternoon. Esthetically, everyone talks of the breathtaking sight when a flock rises off the water. To this photographer, the muted tones of late day set a mood that is equally magical.

fading lighting *always* appears dark). Ah, nature likes nothing so much as taking a scientist-naturalist by the lapels and giving him a rough shake and the following command: start over!

Ibis. The *Sacred ibis* in the land of the Pharaohs was supposed to be a reincarnation of the scribe of the gods and itself a deity. No longer found in Egypt, the bird today is found throughout safari Africa in lakes, rivers, and swamp land areas. The bird is most attractive in flight. At nightfall, ibises adjourn to a tree, sharing it with herons and Marabous (and an occasional vulture!), thus forming large, mixed colonies. This association with other species lasts throughout the year, including breeding season and during nesting. The most distinctive feature of the ibis is probably the long, thin, down-curved bill used for probing in mud to capture prey.

Herons and Egrets. We have already met the Cattle egret (also known as the Buff-backed heron), the one notable exception to a group of large, wading birds that feed on fish and a variety of aquatic animals found in or around shallow water. The heron is a resourceful fisherman — it prefers to stand motionless, "knee-deep" in water, waiting for prey to come within striking distance (a special vertebrae structure permits it to thrust its head forward rapidly) to grasp (*not* spear), but it will also take matters in hand and walk very slowly through the water, looking for its meal. The bird is almost comical as it picks up its feet and puts them down again ever so carefully. Four long, spreading toes give it the balance needed for

Plate 7. Ibis Coming to Earth. *During breeding season, the naked skin under the wing, turns bright red.*

the muddy, slippery lake bottom. The most distinctive technique is, however, holding its wings outspread, thus forming an umbrella. The fish are attracted by shade and move in underneath. The technique probably also enables the bird to see better through the water, as bright surface reflections are eliminated. Herons have been known to hunt cooperatively on the shore itself (the birds do, however, like to dip any prey caught on land in the

Plate 8. Sacred Ibis Tree Colony. A loud, croaking congregation.

water before swallowing it). Herons and egrets are gregarious in the breeding season and nest in colonies. Pictured here are a variety of the most common and distinctive species.

Plate 9. Black-Headed Heron on Land. In the author's opinion, this bird is the most beautiful of the heron family. Whether fishing in water or looking on land, the herons exhibit unbelievable patience and will stand like stones, motionless for an hour or longer, looking . . . looking. Walking (or wading) as well is carried out with excruciating deliberation. Next to the Cattle egret, the Black-headed heron is the most terrestrial of the heron group, much less dependent upon water for its food than the others.

Plate 10. Heron with Frog. After catching this frog, the Grey heron methodically dipped the prey, wiggling to no avail, several times into the water to clean off the mud and sediment, then swallowed it whole (still wiggling).

Plate 11. Grey Heron on Shore. We do not know whether the heron waits so patiently for a fish or a fish large enough to be worthwhile.

Plate 12. Nest of Black-Headed Heron. The elders feed their offspring by regurgitation. The fledglings can fly about six weeks from birth but keep returning to the nest for food for another two weeks or so. The hunting and feeding of chicks is shared by both parents.

Plate 13. Goliath Heron with Fish. The largest of all herons, at roughly five feet tall, the Goliath heron can wade deeper into the water and catch bigger fish than its brethren. This fish was, however, caught in shallow water.

Plate 14. Grey Heron in Tree. A Grey heron is easily distinguishable by its black eye-stripe.

Plate 15. Great White Egret. The largest African egret feeds on crustaceans, fishes, frogs, snakes, and an occasional small mammal. Safarists usually think of lions as serious predators, but the big cats take a back seat to the opportunistic and voracious Great white egrets. If fish are plentiful, the egret will catch a new victim every two minutes or so. In my experience, this egret is not as patient as other herons and will move on within ten minutes, should the fishing prove poor. The bird is, of course, just as careful when walking not to disturb potential prey and not to stir up the bottom sediment, clouding the water. As the reader can see from the insert plate, the Great White flies with its neck tucked in and legs outstretched. One can easily distinguish herons and egrets in flight from storks: the latter fly with their necks stretched out, the former in the characteristic "S" shape.

Crowned Crane. The magnificent Crowned crane has been adopted as the official emblem of Uganda, and a more decorative large African bird there is not. It could be considered a terrestrial bird and is often found in open grasslands stamping for its supper like a secretary bird. The author has, however, never seen the bird very far from water of some kind. An ancient and noble family,

Plates 16–18. Crowned Crane in Various Moods. The tall, slate-grey bird, with its striking straw-colored fan of bristle-like feathers, black velvety crown, red wattles, and white cheeks, is right up there with the most decorative of African birds.

cranes are long-lived birds that remain paired for life and return to the same nesting site for years. Toward the end of the breeding season, they congregate in large mixed flocks, where youngsters form pairs and adults replace lost mates. Cranes are high-altitude fliers (sometimes out of sight from the ground), but the Crowned crane is best known for its elaborate nuptial dance displays. Both cock and hen take part — the larger of the two is the male — and each opens its wings wide, stiffly bows to the other, jumps two to three feet in the air, lands and runs around its partner, then begins again. Naturalists now believe that the graceful ballet may not be strictly courtship; it appears to be performed year-round and occasionally by juveniles. A pair of Crowned cranes usually appear to be synchronizing their movements anyway. The stately, long-necked and long-legged bird, also called a "Crested crane," superficially resembles a stork but is in no way related.

Ducks and Geese. Africa has its share of ducks and geese. One of the noisiest and certainly the most colorful (the male) is the *Egyptian goose.* From Egypt all the way south to the Cape, this goose (it looks more like a duck) is a common resident, found almost everywhere fresh water exists. The birds are seen in pairs (they pair for life), in small parties, and in large flocks. Mated pairs constantly honk at neighboring pairs and flocks of unmated

Plate 20. Fairy Tern. The Fairy tern here represents the family of **gulls** and **terns,** small water birds that frequent inland and coastal regions. Terns have forked tails, are generally gregarious, and eat fish and insects. The Fairy tern is also our representative of the amazing and beautiful birdlife of the Seychelles.

Plate 19. Male Egyptian Goose. The female, who incubates, is considerably less conspicuous all year round. Thus, she blends in with the environment and, when sitting, is almost invisible.

Plates 21 & 22. Grey-Headed Kingfisher. Kingfishers are readily identifiable with their large heads and short necks set on compact, powerful bodies. Beaks are proportionately large. Most kingfishers are brilliantly colored, including the legs. A Grey-headed looking for a meal sits on its perch with its head slightly cocked to one side, scanning the water with one eye. Perches are chosen with care: a thick, rigid platform is desirable. After an interval, the bird will cock its head the other way and use the opposite eye. The patient bird overcomes glare from the water's surface by having an efficient filter of sorts in its retina that counteracts glare.

Plates 23 & 24. Pied Pair Fishing. By kingfisher standards, *Pieds* are large birds. Kingfishers prefer shallow streams and pools. They will fish in deeper waters but do not dive deeply, always waiting for the fish to come to the surface. The bird will fish in muddy waters as well, but the fish must break the surface before they are seen. When Pied kingfishers hover over the water surface, they constantly utter their 'hysterical' tweeting cry. The safarist wishing to see a successful dive must be patient. Most of the dives are not completed: the birds change their minds and pull out. These feint attacks must be unavoidable — they are extremely costly in energy expended — and the shadow of the bird may alert the fish. The African sun is basically overhead most of the day. In any event, the simplest natural phenomena —rain, a breeze, and so forth —will complicate the life of the diver. The Pied kingfisher will also fish over the sea.

birds, and frequent bickering, including biting, wing-beating, and even dunking, all accompanied by much hissing, is the rule when pairs meet. Broods are large and evident throughout the year. The geese, even a hen with her brood, normally show little fear of man — perhaps because their unpalatability has kept them off the table. They often roost at night in trees. Although good swimmers and divers, this species is frequently encountered well away from water grazing on open plains, especially after the rains. The Egyptians regarded these birds as sacred and kept them in captivity.

Kingfishers. Although the great majority of kingfishers live far from water and eat mainly insects(!), the most famous of the freshwater diving birds are undoubtedly the kingfishers. The two representatives here signify two different strategies: diving from a perch and diving following hovering. The *Grey-headed kingfisher,* like so many kingfishers, a gorgeous and brilliantly colored bird, spies its prey from its perch, dives into the water with its eyes closed, and comes up immediately with or without its prey. Misses outnumber catches by a wide margin (perhaps as high as ten to one, but more often three to one). Small fish are swallowed in flight; large (relative to a kingfisher) fish are carried to the perch, where they are beaten

to death and swallowed head first. The prey is not torn up before swallowing. The Grey-headed will also take water insects and crustacea.

The *Pied kingfisher* uses the air as its platform: it hovers — head motionless and eyes trained on the water below, wings working furiously to hold its position — until a fish is spotted near the surface. The Pied drops like a dart, wings folded for added speed, to pluck its victim from the water. The details of the dive can only be appreciated in slow-motion film.

When it spots a fish, the kingfisher tenses itself and pulls in its feathers for streamlining purposes (and to

to break the dive. The bird actually swims (or is it "flies"?) underwater by flapping its wings and powers itself to the surface with sufficient speed to break through and rise into the air. The fish-catching ability of the kingfisher suggests that the bird can see underwater, but the exact mechanism for this feature is uncertain. Perhaps, the kingfisher has an eye similar to ducks and cormorants, an eye which has a lense that can be so distorted by surrounding muscles that its focusing power is increased dramatically when in the water. A Grey-headed kingfisher can go as deep as three feet into the water. A Pied kingfisher will dive from six to 100 feet above the water. The

Plate 25. Late Afternoon Stroll.

increase water repelling). In a flash, the metallic-colored missile is plunging head-first toward the water below. In the split-second prior to impact, the bird, stretched out to its full length, manages to compensate for the refraction of light in the water as it zeroes in on the fish. The wings close for the moment of impact but open again (with the beak) under water. The force of impact carries the bird to the fish. The prey is caught in the beak, *not* speared. With prey in beak, the kingfisher now spreads its wings wider

whole process lasts only a second and only one-third of the time is passed actually underwater (the reader might try blinking that fast!).

Pieds are often seen in small flocks. Grey-headed are, on the other hand, mainly solitary (in pairs). Kingfishers nest in holes along river banks, in termite nests, or in tree cavities.

Storks. The safarist cannot fail to see the ubiquitous *Yellow-bill* (or *Yellow-billed*) *stork* throughout safari

Africa. (This stork is also popularly known as a "Wood ibis," a misleading name, because it is decidedly not an ibis.) As the reader by now no doubt is aware, the African lakes and rivers are havens for birds. Most have resident populations of ibis, pelicans, kingfishers, Marabous, ducks and geese, herons and egrets, cormorants and darters, and fish eagles, among scores of other species. The rich variety must be seen to be believed. The Yellow-bill can normally be expected to round out any such tableau, except during June, July, and early August, when most

> *The Rift Valley, the outstanding geological feature of its kind on earth, is a huge trough slicing through Africa from Ethiopia to Mozambique, from the Red Sea to the Zambezi River. Half the length of Africa. It is known for its volcanos, lakes, and birdlife. Formed millions of years ago by a great fault in the earth's crust, the Rift Valley has created lakes of great variety ranging from shallow, highly alkaline lakes to deep, clear, freshwater lakes. The ecological relationship between the birds and the various lakes is fascinating and complex. Some species use different lakes for different purposes and migrate between them for feeding and breeding. For example, the flamingoes feeding in such huge numbers at Lake Nakuru in Kenya all breed on the barren, salt flats of Lake Natron in Tanzania, where there is little to no food but protection from predators.*

every (so it seems) Yellow-bill in East Africa has gone to nest at Lake Manyara. The Yellow-bill will go onto the grasslands for grasshoppers and locusts, considered a delicacy, but the bird is basically a fisherman. Storks are, with

Plate 26. Earning a Living Stork-Style. When feeding, the Yellow-bill walks in shallow water, probing the bottom with its bill held slightly open. Like some herons, it will extend one or both wings horizontally to shade the reflections of sunlight as it peers through the surface.

Plate 27. Collection. This stork is collecting sticks for its nest some ten trees away. The wings are spread for balance, as the nest-builder must break off the existing branches.

their long and broad wings, also efficient and strong fliers. They fly with head extended and are capable of fantastic glides and soaring.

Plate 28. Landing. Storks (and herons) have large alula feathers (the so-called ''bastard wing'') that sit immediately in front of the wing primaries to give maximum lift on landing, when they almost hover and gently touch down on their long legs. As it lands, a stork sways its wings forward to secure maximum lift with slow speed.

Plate 29. Colonial Nesting. Yellow-bill storks nest colonially high up in trees. They are frequently joined in the same tree by herons (pictured here is a Grey heron) and all manner of other water birds. These inland colonies of mixed fish-eating birds, which congregations spread throughout whole blocks of trees, are just as impressive as bird colonies on the coast or on islands. The same feelings of abundance and vigor prevail. In fact, the rates of breeding success, even at such designated nesting sites. are not all that high. Nevertheless, the numbers of these birds all along the waterways of the region show that enough herons, storks, and other birds are surviving to ensure the prosperity of future generations (man permitting).

Cormorants and Darters. The *African Darter* has an extraordinarily long egret-like neck that, even when fully extended is "S" shaped. Its head is so narrow that the pointed bill appears to be a natural extension of the serpentine neck, hence its early nickname, the "snake-bird." The name "darter" is a reference to its habit of thrusting out its neck in rapier fashion to spear its prey. The bird inhabits fresh and brackish waters throughout safari Africa. It feeds almost exclusively on fish, and its 'harpoon' is deadly. Large fish are carried back to the fishing platform and, in a neat juggler's trick, tossed into the air, caught head first, and swallowed whole. (Kingfishers do the same with especially large prey.) The quick flash of the head does not, however, always loosen the fish; the author has seen the bird hit the fish against a branch to jar it loose.

The water is the darter's element, and it swims partially submerged, only the narrow head and long neck showing. References to a miniature Loch Ness sea serpent are inevitable. It swims by the combined movements of the wings and webbed feet. In the air, the bird is an excellent flier, similar to the pelican, to whom it is distantly related, gliding on thermals with considerable grace in broad spirals. The long neck and stiffly held tail form the shape of a cross with the outspread wings. The silhouette is unique.

Plate 30. Snake-Bird Dressed in Basic Black and Browns.

Plate 31. Cormorant. A cormorant needs only a little time to secure its daily requirement of two pounds of fish. Thus, it can (and does) spend much of its day preening and displaying.

Birds   567

The *White-necked cormorant,* larger of the two African cormorants, is often confused with the African darter, who also has a conspicuous white neck stripe, but the cormorant can easily be distinguished by its shorter neck, stockier profile, and *hooked* bill. The last in particular is a quick field test. The cormorant dives from the surface for fish and amphibians: the White-necked variety actually leaps clear of the water before plunging headfirst. As might be expected from the bill configuration, a cormo-

rant does not spear its catch, but it is a master deep-water angler. Safarists turn up regularly at submarine observation tanks, such as the one at Mzima Springs in Tsavo (Kenya), to see hippos and, with the greatest of luck, a crocodile, but they should also look for the skillful cormorant diving for prey. A transparent nictitating membrane covers the eye during diving, enabling the bird to see underwater. The bird pictured in Plate *31* is not necessarily drying off, as one might surmise. Cormorants have more traditional waterproofing than darters and simply shake off most water drops from their plumage. The posture is more one of digestion, which is speeded up to reduce body weight and promote quick take-offs and easy, efficient flight. The bird is known as a powerful flier. If disturbed during digestion, the cormorant regurgitates undigested food. Thus, there are always a fair amount of dead, undigested fish lying around a cormorant's resting spot.

Plate 32. Darter Drying Out. Darters are often seen drying off their plumage in the sun, wings and tails spread wide. Their feathers are slightly porous — the oily protective covering that all water birds have serves a different purpose here: it reduces friction to aid swimming, which is virtually underwater, and helps prevent disturbance of the water (and prey). No bird glides through water quite like a darter. Thus, before the darter can fly, it must dry off, the sun slowly evaporating the water that weighs the bird down. In the sun, the feathers on the back

shine with metallic, iridescent gleams. Some authorities maintain that darters actually spend little time in the water, unless actually fishing or escaping territorial enemies. The author can hardly claim to have made a thorough study of such an assess-

ment but has seen darters in the water far more often than out (such evidence is not as anecdotal as it may sound, when one considers how easily the resting darter with wings spread is to see, as compared with the submerged "snake-bird").

Pelican. Every reader will recognize the pelican, a bird that, despite its rather ridiculous appearance and wobbly gait on land, is an expert in the water — as swimmer, diver, or fisherman. Its most characteristic feature is, of course, the enormous beak and the huge gular pouch hanging underneath. And whatever comic clumsiness holds this big bird back on land, the extraordinary grace and agility exhibited in the air make the pelican a supreme flier. Two out of three on nature's scorecard is more than respectable; the pelican by any measure is an extraordinary animal.

Two species frequent safari Africa: the *White pelican* and the *Pink-backed pelican.* Both are residents, but the population of White pelicans is considerably augmented in the 'winter' months by migrating birds from Asia and Europe. The White is the larger of the two. The adult is white with black flight feathers, a yellow beak, and slightly pink feet. Only during breeding season will the casual safarist be able to sex the birds: the male's plumage, which ordinarily has a slightly pinkish tinge, becomes a deep salmon-pink, and the bare skin on his face turns pinkish yellow; the female remains basically white, with a bright orange face. (No elaborate courtship display takes place: a shame, given the obvious humor that the awkward bird would have provided!) The birds nest in large colonies, whose inaccessibility to human beings, while a minus for the safarist, has been the most significant factor in the success of the species in Africa. The White is also one of the largest flying birds, weighing up to thirty pounds.

Plate 33. Pelican in Tree. With all its pompous dignity, the pelican needs to be reminded from time to time of the famous verse:

A wonderful bird is the Pelican.
His bill will hold more than his belly can.
He can take in his beak
Food enough for a week.
But I'm damned if I see how the hell he can.

Plate 34. A Pink-Backed on a Glide. A pelican does not favor rough water — a mirror-smooth inland lake is its ideal haunt.

Plate 35. Low Flying Through the Marshes. One would think that pelicans would have a time of it lifting themselves airborne. Actually, one or two flaps of the wing will do, and, for short distances at least, the pelican can maneuver quite nicely at water level.

The Pink-backed pelican is considerably smaller, and its basic plumage is more gray. The pink back is clearly visible when the wings are spread out. A Pink-backed also sports a pronounced crest on the back of its head. In many respects, its behavior patterns are quite similar to the White's, and White and Pink-backed will flock together. Indeed, most collections of pelicans seen on freshwater lakes are a mixture of the two species. On alkaline waters, the Pink-backed will be by itself. Small flotillas of pelicans mix freely with flamingo masses and most other water birds. Other swimming fish-eating birds, like the White-necked cormorant, will tag along on pelican fishing parties, and herons, storks, spoonbills, and others will turn up on wading expeditions. (Pelicans themselves have been known to steal a fish or two from other birds.) On their own, the pelican colonies in Africa may contain many thousands of birds; in fact, a colony sometimes is as large and dense as that of flamingoes.

Both species catch fish individually by diving, but the Whites more frequently will work as a group to fish. Ordinarily, a line of about a dozen to fifteen birds is formed, and fish are driven, with short, 'beak' dives and vigorous wing-flapping, into shallow water, where they are easily scooped up and swallowed, using the large pouches as fishing nets. Alternatively, the fish may be herded into the center of a u-shaped formation, the birds periodically — by a signal or formula unknown to us — dipping in unison to capture the prey. The procedure looks like synchronized water ballet. The popular belief is that pelicans use their pouches to store food. But the bird whose beak can hold more than his belly can does not, in fact, use his beak for storage. Even when carrying food

Plate 36. The Nighttime Roost. The Pink-backed almost always roosts in the branches of trees, in a small group such as pictured here; the White prefers the ground, in huge numbers at breeding time.

Plate 37. Mixed Signals. Pelicans are nearly mute, through adults will grunt on occasion. Body language can be equally effective communication. The White pelican on the right is expressing a combination of annoyance and appeasement to its more boisterous neighbor.

Plate 38. Leisure Time. Pelicans always look delightful among the shoreline vegetation. The huge beaks and saucy little round eyes lend a certain comical charm to any African waterside.

back to the chicks, the pelican will swallow the food in the usual way and regurgitate into the pouch at the nest. The pouch really is best viewed as a giant fishing net. Only when building nests do pelicans use the pouch for transporting (in this instance, sticks, grass, and other building materials). Such flotilla fishing does not depend upon the birds being able to see the prey. Many naturalists believe that the dipping is basically trial and error, with the probabilities on the pelican's side. Other believe that the pelicans somehow 'know' when the fish are present (by feel?). A lone bird fishing will likely do so in the morning, when the waters of the lake are clear and the glare from the sun does not severely hamper eyesight. Flotillas are likely to sail on fishing sorties later in the day; glare, algae buildup, winds, and so forth do not unduly hamper the fleet.

A pelican's daily ration of fish can reach four pounds. One interesting point is that the individual Pink-backed bird does about as well fishing alone as the White bird does in its armada. Single birds using sight catch more fish. Communal fishing brings in bigger fish, both because the diving activities of the birds seem to improve the chances of catching bigger fish and because the large fish come to the surface (where the pelicans can reach them) during the times of communal hunting. In other words, the White pelican either purposely hunts at times when bigger fish are about or the same conditions that cause the Whites to hunt coincidentally bring the big fish to the surface (turbidity of the water, climatic conditions, time of day, and so forth).

The safarist who pauses to study the pelicans — in water or in the air — will see remarkably synchronized

Plate 39. Flight. Pelicans in formation are as precise as schools of fish. Indeed, nature is replete with examples of what is, at bottom, a level of communication quite beyond human capabilities. With its extraordinary wingspan, the hollow, lightweight bones, and the many subcutaneous air sacs that serve to lighten the weight of the bird (and, incidentally, prevent deep diving in water), the pelican has it made in the air. Synchronization is, however, a more striking phenomenon. However many pelicans are up, they are stretched out in evenly spaced, straight or diagonal lines. All move their wings in perfect unison, and changes by the leader(s) cause not a ripple in the rhythm of the flight.

. . . the vulture awoke. No movement betrayed his awakening, only the reptilian glitter of a watchful eye. For some time the bird remained motionless, as if carved from the same volcanic rock that littered the surrounding slopes, while the sky grew brighter in the east and a tide of birdsong arose from the river.

Somewhere nearby a morning warbler began to sing. Dusky bulbuls chattered to each other, flaunting sulphur-yellow vents as they flitted among the rocks. Skulking unseen in the depths of a thorn thicket, a boubou shrike and its mate belled to each other in such perfect unison that call and response sounded like one bird.

Other voices joined in; the melodious fluting of black-headed forest orioles, the squeal of brown parrots flying over the treetops, the grating cries of guinea-fowl and francolin. And from all sides, over and over again above the mounting crescendo of chats and mousebirds, barbets, weavers, starlings and wood hoopoes, the joyful purring of ring-necked doves throbbed from every acacia top to greet the awakening African day. (Jackman & Scott, *Marsh Lions*, p. 13)

At all times of the year the Marsh was alive with the sounds and movements of birds, for whom the muddy waters provided a never-ending feast of snails, fish, frogs, dragonflies and other insects. Squacco herons skulked in the reeds. Sandpipers bobbed at the water's edge, where painted snipe probed for worms in the soft mud. Malachite kingfishers swung on the papyrus stems, blue and glittering like electric sparks, and armies of solemn storks - yellow-bills, saddle-bills, woolly-necks - slow-marched through the pools stabbing at catfish and tiny jewelled reed-frogs.

. . .

From dawn to dusk the great fen echoed to the incessant clangour of wild voices; the urgent chuntering of Egyptian geese, the mournful bugling of hadada ibis who cried their own name - ha-da-da *-as they circled overhead with down-curved beaks outstretched. Sometimes the dark shape of a harrier of fish eagle would drift across the Marsh, or a marsh mongoose would come stealing through the sedgy tussocks. Then the reed-beds would erupt with sky-rocketing wildfowl and the air would fill with a cloud of wings, only to subside moments later, falling like a soft blanket across another part of the swamp.* (Jackman & Scott, *Marsh Lions*, p. 58)

behavior. Not a few writers have compared the flotillas on the water to images of "old-fashioned frigates in full sail" and the like. Individually, perhaps, but, collectively, the precision belongs not to ponderous examples but to the performance of a corps de ballet. In the air, the birds glide and soar with such ease as to defy imagination. I once counted *one* flap of the wings per quarter hour over an hour and a half period! Moreover, it is difficult to believe that the aerial acrobatics in the thermal currents have any purpose other than pleasure.

Hamerkop. The Hamerkop (sometimes spelled hammerkop) is also known as the Hammer-headed stork, a name that reflects an earlier confusion: the bird belongs to its own family and only superficially resembles a stork. In either version, the name obviously is derived from the profile of the thick crest that points backwards together with the long bill (the two appear "in balance," with the neck as the handle). Endemic to Africa, the bird hunts mainly invertebrate food along the banks of slow rivers and streams throughout Africa. They are also found near springs in dry country. Frogs always constitute the favorite diet.

The bird is seen singly or in pairs and an occasional threesome. Semi-nocturnal, it is most active at twilight. A pair is supposed to remain mated for life. No other bird has inspired both the same dread and reverence in the African native. To disturb it, even to point at it, is said to court disaster. Known as the rainmaker, the hamerkop can command rain and fill rivers with fish. The magical qualities go on and on and serve the tranquil bird well — it is comparatively free of human persecution.

Plate 40. Hamerkop. In a family of its own, 'midway' between storks and herons (that is, the bird has a little of each in its own anatomy), the hamerkop is often encountered standing in or alongside water staring intently straight ahead and down, as if in deep thought or studying its own reflection. Looks are deceiving, as the bird is highly vigilant.

All photographers bring back from safari a list of disappointments (a mental list for all but the most compulsive) — of the lost shots, the equivalent to the fisherman's "one that got away." When one has taken as many trips as the author, the list unfortunately just grows to absurd lengths. Somewhere near the top is, however, a picture of one hamerkop standing (with legs outstretched, not squatting) on another, with the one underneath standing on a hippo, who was, at the time, out of the water! The impossible trio looked like a circus act.

Plate 41. Hamerkop Nest. A hamerkop pair build one of the most remarkable nests in nature. An inner core structure, the size of a football, consists of three chambers. This in turn is enclosed in a superstructure large enough to fill the fork of a tree. Countless twigs are woven with grass and mud to produce a nest several feet high and wide. An energetic pair might take at least four months to build such an edifice. The whole structure is five to six times the size of a larger stork's nest, with a diame-

ter exceeding six feet. An entrance hole is always placed in the most inaccessible lower side, impregnable to snakes and small mammalian predators. The structure is simply too large to be a practical solution to anything and represents a thumb in the eye of enthusiastic Darwinists and the petty restrictions of natural selection! The nest is often later appropriated by birds of prey or bees.

Ground Birds

This category comprises birds of the savannah — birds that spend a preponderant part of each day right down on the ground with the mammals. For the most part, these avion participants in the terrestrial pageantry are large, active, and an obvious addition to everyone's safari.

Ostrich. Fittingly enough, we begin the section with the curious, flightless bird that is such a familiar sight in many of Africa's national parks. The ostrich is peculiar to Africa, and no bird is better adapted to a life on the open savannahs, sharing the same pastures as zebras, wildebeest, and the other plains antelopes. (Some naturalists talk a lot about ostriches and antelopes combining in a sort of common early warning system against predators. Ostriches need little help in this department, and, as we shall see, their predation is almost unavoidable. Of course, an alert herbivore can monitor any other animal without resorting to a formal 'cooperative' strategy.) Although ostriches are omnivorous — and include insects, reptiles, and rodents in their diet — they prefer vegetable food, particularly tough plants that they tear up and swallow, roots and all. A specialized digestive system allows them to make the best use of such herbaceous material. It is widely believed that ostriches sometimes swallow stones and pebbles as an aid to digestion; it is true that ostriches swallow all sorts of odd things, including anything that glitters — whether this is helpful activity and exactly why are unclear.

The eight-foot tall birds are the sentinels of the open plains, their large dark eyes protected from the dust by thick eyelashes, scanning the far horizon for danger. Aside from keen eyesight, among the sharpest in the animal kingdom, remarkable speed and stamina help protect the birds in an environment known for its number and variety of predators. Each of the powerful legs has only two toes and only the inner toe, protected by a flat nail, is used when running. The reader will recall from the discussion on hooves that the least amount of contact between the foot and the ground translates into speed. An ostrich can run, in bursts, 40 mph and can maintain 30 mph for long distances (a half hour or more!) in huge strides, head high and wings slightly outstretched. A frightened ostrich has been seen overtaking a kongoni at full gallop. Indeed, an ostrich is the fastest animal on two legs.

Although the ostrich's wings are useless for flying, they do serve a purpose in permitting rapid swerves and sudden braking. They are also used to swish flies and to provide much-needed shade for young chicks. The ostrich lacks the distinctive keel-shaped breastbone of all flying birds.

Man has always exploited the ostrich for one thing or another. The vogue for its plumes led to widespread massacre and threatened the bird with extinction in the late nineteenth century. Fortunately, people learned to breed them in captivity, and ostrich farms sprang up in Africa (mostly in Algeria and South Africa), the United States, and Europe. The craze has now subsided, but active farms still exist in South Africa. Much of our knowledge of the breeding habits of ostriches comes from these farms (just saving the bird from extinction is, of course, its own, sufficient reward).

The call of the ostrich sounds like "mbuni" — hence the Kiswahili word for ostrich — and is said to resemble the throaty roar of the lion. Actually, the 'roars' that I have heard were far less powerful — and were in fact far more "visual" than vocal. It is the male who makes the noise, and his neck expands about two to three times its normal size (presumably acting as a resonance chamber). If a safarist approaches too near, the cock bird will cease the calling, so I always maintained my distance at fifty yards or more — and the wind managed to blow away much of the sound. In fact, the noise that I have heard most often resembled the hiss of a gander. Heard predominantly at sunrise and sunset, the purpose of the display seems clearly sexual (to attract females) and to warn off other males. Ostriches are extremely territorially aggressive in mating season — without a plot of his own land (usually, five to seven square miles in extent), the cock is out of luck — and cocks will fight among themselves.

The males also engage in extraordinary courtship rituals to attract the available females who wander through the competitive territories. The cock draws himself up to his full height and puffs out his feathers as he approaches a female. He then drops on folded legs before his intended and extends his wings, flapping them backwards and forwards, with tail lowered. Putting his head back and rubbing the nape of his neck against his back, he also proceeds to rock from side to side, rapidly fluttering the tail up and down at the same time. The red neck is also writhing from side to side. Additionally, the cock periodically stamps the ground with his feet. The wing and tail fluttering and all the rocking can last for ten minutes or so. To our eyes, the female appears totally bored with the entire operation. And, in fact, the ritual often has to be repeated. Eventually, the hen squats at the approach of the male and a brief mating takes place (accompanied by moderate wing waving as in the earlier display).

When the cock has selected a suitable site for laying the eggs, he clears and scrapes out a shallow depression in the earth or sand to make a nest some three feet in diameter. Each breeding cock partners several hens — he will mate with any hens that pass through his territory, often as many as five or six, but three is a more likely number. Each of these hens lays six to eight eggs, which are deposited in the communal nest at regular intervals every other day (a hen lays one egg every two days). The cock forms, however, a close liaison with only one hen, and this "major hen" together with the male will later be respon-

Plate 42. Maasai Ostrich. The Maasai race of ostrich has pink thighs and a pink neck, both which turn bright red during mating season (August to December). The legs themselves are long, unfeathered, and powerfully muscular. In a picture, the legs just look like oversized bird legs. In person, they look like small, knarled trees — the observer has a feeling of real sinewy strength. The feet also are formidable. The two toes are padded, the inner one with a strong, flat nail. The whole ensemble makes for a very effective weapon, whatever its individual purposes are. A large cock ostrich can stand up to nine feet tall and weigh more than 300 lbs., formidable prey by any predator's standard.

The ostrich is indigenous to Africa and similar to the emu in Australia and rhea in South America but not closely related to either (all three are in the same general order). Bushmen believe that the ostrich first brought fire to the world but jealously kept the secret tucked away under its wing to prevent anyone from stealing it. By a trick, man obtained the secret, but, to this day, the ostrich refuses to use its wings to fly for fear of losing fire to other creatures as well. The Greeks and Romans believed that the ostrich was a cross between a camel and a bird!

Ostrich breeding is tied to the arrival of annual rains, so that the growing chicks can make use of the rapid flush of new plant growth that follows the rains. But water can be hazardous to the youngsters: the filaments of their feathers do not cling together as do those of flying birds and, rather than repelling water, soak it up. Ostriches also lack oil glands that provide waterproofing in other birds. Consequently, chicks are susceptible to fatal chilling. At the first sign of rain, the parent or guardian bird squats down to cover the chicks present.

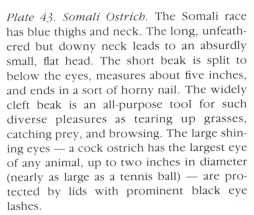

Plate 43. Somali Ostrich. The Somali race has blue thighs and neck. The long, unfeathered but downy neck leads to an absurdly small, flat head. The short beak is split to below the eyes, measures about five inches, and ends in a sort of horny nail. The widely cleft beak is an all-purpose tool for such diverse pleasures as tearing up grasses, catching prey, and browsing. The large shining eyes — a cock ostrich has the largest eye of any animal, up to two inches in diameter (nearly as large as a tennis ball) — are protected by lids with prominent black eye lashes.

sible for incubating the eggs and the rearing of the chicks. During this laying time, no ostrich stays near the nest sites to reduce the chance of detection by predators.

At the end of the laying period, the nests may contain a total of fifteen to thirty or so eggs. The major hen and male then share the incubating duties, the hen sitting on the nest during most of the day, the cock during the longer night period and part of the day. In fact, incubation is predominately the responsibility of the cock. Eager Darwinists jump forward to explain that the dowdy brown coloration of the female and the black (and white plumage, though the white is evident only when the male stands) of the male explain this division of labor (black goes well with nighttime and all that). The truth is probably only partially a matter of coloration; a black or brown rock, which is what the nesting ostrich looks like from a reasonable distance (provided that it keeps its head down) is equally convincing, but the black cock would undoubtedly soak up more solar heat during the daytime, perhaps a dangerous amount for the eggs. At any rate, the best method for an interested safarist to find a nest would be to follow an adult male (in nesting season) at dusk.

The incubation period lasts six weeks. Predation — on the nest, taking both adults and eggs — is common at this time and unavoidable. Jackals are the most significant egg eaters, even outdoing the hyenas, and Egyptian vultures also take a significant toll. Predators are remarkably resourceful, given the fortress that an egg represents. The creamy white oval eggs are, as might be expected, the largest of any bird (and the biggest single cell there is) — roughly six inches long, five inches wide, and as thick as china (an egg will support the weight of a man without breaking). They are also the smallest, relative to the bird's size and weight. Called a "clutch," the nest of eggs is composed of a middle of some twenty eggs and an outer, somewhat scattered circle of remaining eggs that sit more or less discarded, do not hatch, and eventually rot. Presumably, the outer eggs go some way towards satisfying the queue of predators. The pair can cover only about twenty eggs. Furthermore, the different laying females can apparently recognize their own eggs, and the major hen frequently yields to the temptation to roll her own eggs to the middle and displace others. There is evidence that the embryos in contiguous eggs can somehow communicate with one another and synchronize hatching, even though the eggs were all laid at different times. The unborn chicks alert their parents/nursemaids with chirps from within the eggs but they are on their own. Unaided, they peck their way through the shells, a process that can take days (for some unaccountable reason, ostrich hatchlings have no sharp egg tooth, as one would expect). They emerge exhausted, already a foot tall, and precocial to the point of being able to run once they catch their wind from all the pecking and digging. (They can run 30 mph in a matter of weeks.) The hatchlings grow at a rate of a foot a month and are guarded by concerned, alert adults, who moreover are vigilant, fast, and armed with

devastatingly powerful kicks (an ostrich can kill a lion, though the betting line is on the lion), but predation is high. Predators, from eagles to lions, regard the young birds with great favor, and the small size of the chicks makes them fair game. The reader can also imagine the difficulty of keeping twenty-odd chicks together when under attack from a determined (and hungry) carnivore. Perhaps, as much as eighty to ninety percent of the chicks are killed.

The strategy that saves the last ten to fifteen percent is called "crèching." The young of different parents or

Plate 44. Ostrich Breeding Pair. A clear lesson in the difference in male-female coloration. The ostrich courtship display is spectacular and perhaps a bit more individualistic than other comparable rituals (like that of the crowned crane, for example): flapping of wings, high-stepping, running, and pirouetting are simply the artistic touches. Authorities are divided about female behavior in the wild, despite years of observation in captivity. Some maintain that all the females mating with a cock ostrich lay their eggs in one nest. Others contradict this description and say that the females who are not major hens lay in more than one nest. A hen in one season can lay as many as thirty eggs.

The little pan near Gam was full of blue water, and was surrounded by yellow-leafed trees. We found two ostriches beside it. The ostriches stared mutely at us first, very wide between the eyes and square at the jaw, until it came to them that we were not ostriches; and with that they rushed headlong away, flapping their ostrich-feathered wings, working their naked thighs and knees like pistons, wildly out of control. They had an air of old people with tough, gray, varicose-veined legs, wearing nothing to hide their nakedness but little feather boas around their waists, which were the wings. (Thomas, *The Harmless People*, pp. 164–6)

An ostrich seen close-to in the bush looks like nothing so much as a preposterously enlarged chicken . . . and there is something a little indecent about its huge bare legs. (Moorehead, *No Room in the Arc*, p. 27)

And what of the ostrich? After growing accustomed to cautious safarists, he will probably accept the human visitors as harmless but grotesque passers-by!

Plate 45. "Mbuni" Troop (of Females) on the Move. This ancient and adaptable species can outrun giraffe. A racing ostrich in the United States was once timed over a half-mile course running at an *average* speed of 29 mph —with a jockey on its back. One myth that should be put to rest: ostriches do not bury their heads in the sand (for any reason), a fable that may have originated when early explorers witnessed, from a distance, the bird feeding, head-down, or trying to hide while roosting on the nest. In both postures, the head is frequently stretched out along the ground.

guardians tend to merge together into bands or crèches, to be cared for by one set of parents. A large crèche may contain as many as one hundred chicks. Though more conspicuous than a smaller group, the larger crèche has statistical realities on its side: the old advantage, raised again and again in this volume, of herding.

At nine months, the chicks are virtually fully grown, though they take about four years to mature fully.

The ancient Egyptians viewed the ostrich as a symbol of justice — something to do with the fact that ostrich feathers have the unique property of vanes of equal width. All other birds have feathers with a wide and a narrow vane — an "unjust" division. Ostrich eggs on their part were regarded as the emblems of watchfulness (why, exactly, is not clear). The fortunes of the ostrich, just or not, took a tailspin in the nineteenth century, when ladies decided that ostrich plumes were fashionable.

Plovers. Plovers are small- to medium-sized birds found throughout the tropics. They are strong fliers and very swift runners. On the ground, despite strong color patterns, they can be very difficult to see. Plovers simply deposit their eggs in the slightest indentation in the bare ground and rely upon camouflage or the ability to startle the large mammals and cause the latter to swerve from stepping onto the "nest." Sometimes, the eggs are deposited in the dried droppings of elephants or buffalos. In addition, plovers are masters of the distraction display, in which they divert the attention of an intruder by feigning

Plate 47. Plovers and Jackal. The plovers are not pleased with the presence of the jackal, who on his way to taking a drink has accidentally come within four feet of the nest. The birds will try distraction, if necessary, but will not hesitate to attack the jackal to frighten it away. The odds (if the jackal suspects a nestfull of eggs and is hungry): fifty-fifty.

Plate 46. Blacksmith Plover. Plovers are often surprisingly difficult to see until one is right on top of them. And, they frequently nest within a foot or two of the track or road in the parks. The bird takes its name from its loud, metallic cry, resembling a hammer hitting an anvil, when disturbed.

injury (spreading one wing as if it were broken, or hopping lamely and pretending inability to fly) to themselves. If necessary, plovers can also execute wicked dive-bombing attacks.

The ubiquitous *Blacksmith plover,* always trim and immaculate looking, ranges from Kenya to South Africa and perhaps is the best known of all plovers in Africa. Noisy and aggressive, it is most commonly found near fresh or brakish water — lakes, rivers, streams, mudflats, and swamps — where it finds its main diet of insects, worms, and crustacea.

Saddle-Bill Stork. One of the tallest storks, the Saddle-bill stork is included here because it habitually is encountered away from water in the open grass foraging and is rarely (in the author's experience) seen in the water itself, unlike all other storks. Like most large avian terrestrial feeders, Saddle-bill storks are drawn to the scene of bush fires to profit from the havoc of the flames. Little is known about the habits of this fancy bird. We do know that it is solitary and not gregarious, unlike virtually all other storks. Although its distribution is scattered throughout Africa, it is never numerous. Frogs and grass-hoppers are staple foods, but the bird is practically omnivorous.

Ground Hornbill. In open grassland, the safarist is liable to come across a group of large, black turkey-like birds, a family party of Ground hornbills. The largest of the African hornbills, the Ground hornbills are generally found in parties of two to eight, but a lone individual is sometimes seen. Nests are located in hollow trees or stumps or in small caves on rock cliffs and are used year after year. Unlike all other hornbills (see below), the female is not walled-in during incubation, does not molt, and is therefore still able to fly. She will leave the nest to search for food (she is also fed at the nest by the male), so a safarist may see a female on the savannah, as well as a male (most adult hornbills that the safarist sees, for reasons made clear below, will be males). Indeed, fairly recent studies undertaken in Kruger National Park indicate that the foraging groups are normally dominated by

Plate 49. Male Ground Hornbill. Throat and face skin are bare and bright red; in the female, the throat skin can be slightly red but more often is blue. The large bill is black in both sexes, and white primary feathers are conspicuous only in flight.

Plate 48. Saddle-Bill Stork. A purely African species, this bird stands some four to five feet tall and is distinguished by its white body, dark wings, jet-black neck, and heavy, black-banded red bill, onto which is grafted a yellow shield or "saddle." The solitary stork is normally shy, but this specimen allowed our Landrover to approach within fifteen yards.

an adult female. The feeding expeditions are searching for fruit, insects, small mammals, young birds, frogs (a favorite), and reptiles. Tortoises apparently are considered a delicacy and are picked clean with the same efficiency (and relish!) that we tackle lobsters.

The call of the Ground hornbill is a deep, rumbling series of lion-like gruntings. At a distance, a family sounds much like a group in human conversation. A Maasai folk tale reports the sound as a man speaking to a woman, "I want more cows," to which she returns "You'll die before you get them." The Maasai also believe that Ground hornbills should never be killed (bad luck) and that, if one lands on the roof of a house, the occupants must move at once or death will ensue. Many tribes in Africa believe the bird to be a rain prophet. The Kaffirs of South Africa took this last theory one step further: in times of drought, the "medicine man" would order the bird killed; Ground hornbills have a strongly offensive smell and throwing the corpse into the river was supposed to make the river sick, causing heavy rains to wash the stench away.

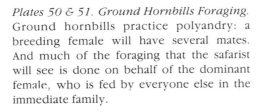

Plates 50 & 51. Ground Hornbills Foraging. Ground hornbills practice polyandry: a breeding female will have several mates. And much of the foraging that the safarist will see is done on behalf of the dominant female, who is fed by everyone else in the immediate family.

In Chapter VI, we noted how Cattle egrets used certain herbivorous mammals as "beaters," riding on the backs of buffalos, for example, to take the insects stirred up by their larger hosts. Interestingly enough, little bee-eaters (specifically, the Carmine bee-eaters) patronize bustards (and ostriches and Kori bustards, for that matter) in the same way.

Secretary Bird. The secretary bird could easily be classified as a bird of prey — indeed, these raptors who stalk on the ground have been called "terrestrial eagles." At the outset, it is desirable to correct an almost unanimous mistake made by writers and commentators on things African. The secretary bird is said to have received its name because of its crest feathers, which when erect supposedly resemble the quill pens that were stuck behind the ears, or in the wigs, of the office male secretaries and clerks of earlier days (before typewriters). Moreover, the bird's "primness" in dress and demeanor is said to resemble the old-fashioned frock-coat and black silk knee-breeches of that clerk-type. Actually, such imagination aside, the name is derived from the Arabic, "sagret-tair," which means "the hunter bird." In any event, to me, the bird looks far more like an Aztec warrior.

The secretary bird can grow to striking proportions: more than three feet tall, with a wingspan of up to seven feet. I have seen specimens in the Serengeti that were as large as bustards. These huges boys offered quite a formidable appearance stalking about with their deliberate, dig-

Plate 52. Hunter on the Plains. The secretary bird eats, in order of importance, insects, small mammals, and snakes. Equipped with long legs and short toes, the bird kills its prey by stamping. Thereafter, prey is handled exclusively with the beak; the bird's feet are not adapted for seizing or carrying. The secretary bird is another member of the congregation that shows up at the raging grass fires to feed on the escaping victims.

Plate 53. Early Morning in the Tree Tops. Distant relatives of hawks and falcons, secretary birds fly in long, undulating soaring patterns.

Plate 54. Nesting Pair. One pair of secretary birds requires as much as 10,000 acres of short grassland to support themselves. A pair will be aggressively territorial and will chase intruding pairs from their home range. A pair will use several nests at one time, the massive constructions frequently mistaken for vulture nests. Any one nest is likely to be used for several years and more than likely is placed in a flat-topped acacia. Adults of both sexes, as the reader can see, look identical.

Game Birds. The term "game birds" is today used loosely to refer to birds that are caught or shot for eating. Ornithologically, the term describes an order of birds that include quails, francolins, spurfowl, guinea fowl, and their allies. Their main food consists of seeds, insects, roots, and bulbs rooted out by scratching with their feet. When startled or threatened, most game birds prefer to escape on foot and will take to the air only if feeling desperate. One way or another, however, spurfowl form an important part of the diet of several small predators.

The *Yellow-necked spurfowl* is the most common spurfowl in East Africa, where it frequents the edges of forests and woodlands, on the one hand, and open bush country, on the other. The spurfowl is one of the first birds to greet the dawn — with a raucous call — and one of the last heralding the day's end. The most beautiful — at least the most striking — member of the family is the *Vulturine guinea fowl.* The cobalt-blue coloration, set off in black and white, is a severe contrast with the bird's usual environment.

The plump *Helmeted guinea fowl* figures significantly in the serval's, leopard's, and baboon's diet. The safarist may see a mixed flock of Helmeted and Vulturine guinea fowl, a not uncommon occurrence. Watching a flock, the visitor will see the purposeful, foraging stroll frequently interrupted by one bird dashing at another member of the assorted group and an ensuing brief chase in small circles. But there is no (easy) way of knowing whether this is a jealous male protecting his favorite hen, a courting manoeuvre, or simply greed at the table.

nified kind of stride for miles upon miles. A pair will divide their domain with great care and strutting at a steady pace will scrutinize the ground ahead every inch of the way. Hunting is signalled by a vigorous stamping, often with wings outspread for balance (and, possibly, as a distraction as well). The bird is an efficient snake killer and will tackle snakes up to six feet long. Specialized pads on the underside of the feet help the powerful pounding. In addition, the bird frequently takes a page from the serval's playbook and stamps the ground to frighten mice into moving and thus exposing themselves.

As we have seen, birds are not adverse to involving other animals in their food quests. A feeding association that is harmless to both parties is known as "commensalism" or "eating at the same table." Another mutualistic relationship only recently discovered (and which may need more study to verify) is an association between some hornbills and dwarf mongooses. The hornbills follow the mongooses and seize small animals (locusts, mice, etc.) that escape the latter. In return, the hornbills relieve the mongooses of some sentinel duties. The mongooses post fewer guards and forage more extensively. (See O. Anne Rasa, "A Taru Life Story," *Natural History,* September, 1985.)

Plate 56. Vulturine Guinea Fowl. Guinea fowl are native to Africa. The bare skin of its head and neck and the small (in relation to the remainder of its body) head have given it the name "vulturine." Look for these birds in abundant quantity at Samburu (Kenya).

Plates 57 & 58. Helmeted Guinea Fowl. These distinctively spotted birds gather in pairs or large and noisy flocks. The large flocks today are seen only in effectively protected game reserves. The stiffly erect carriage, precise if not mincing little steps, and dark plumage with white dots suggest a respectable elderly spinster out for a walk. Guinea fowl are very shy and will not allow the safarist to come very close.

Plate 55. Yellow-Necked Spurfowl. Both male and female look alike, except that the male has spurs on its legs, identifiable in this picture. At dusk, the throat looks like an artificial candle flame. Here, darkness is on the way.

Bustards. Bustards are essentially ground birds and walk with a hesitant but heavy gait, quite unlike the steady march, for example, of the secretary bird. The bustard never appears in a hurry, yet closing the distance between a bustard and the safarist is a matter entirely at the bustard's discretion. Most birds naturally prefer a "respectful" distance. Some individuals are quite shy and run or crouch at the first sign of danger, including man. Others exhibit almost total indifference to human visitors.

The *Kori bustard* is the largest African bustard and is famous for its bizarre courtship display. The elaborate ritual begins with the bird inflating its neck like a balloon. The "gular pouch," the extensible, air-filled sacs located at the front of the neck, may even touch the ground. Then, with the nuchal crest and extensive lax feathers of the neck ruffled out and the wings drooped, the male slowly lifts his tail, first to a vertical position, where it appears in profile as yet another head and neck, and soon forward, until the tail actually lays along the back and the tip touches the bird's (real) nape. The bird seems virtually to turn himself inside out — the white, outspread undercoverts are thereby fully exposed — and the effect on someone arriving at this point in the display is to appear like a white ball. One has to look carefully to distinguish a bird! The contortionist then begins to rock back and forth and strut about in tight circles. The whole odd, magnificent affair presumably impresses the female bustard — little bustards do eventually appear — but hardly more than the amazed safarist.

During a particular mating season, the males of many bird species engage in elaborate ritualized courtship displays. Of course, the details vary. The purposes are the same as for the equivalent behavior in antelopes and other animals, namely, to overcome the natural reluctance of the female to permit another individual such close access (a sexual matter) and to signal the male's (or perhaps both male's and female's) species identification for the purpose of efficiency.

Although bustards usually collect together in flocks, the Kori bustard is more solitary. Males can be quite territorially aggressive, and the bird is also known for a fearless attitude in the field toward dangerous animals:

> One day I was following a [hyena] when a shape crept through the high grass towards it. It was a Kori Bustard, a large bird but hardly a match for a hyena. However, much to my surprise, the bird suddenly fluffed out its feathers and approached in a threatening attitude. The hyena stopped and stared but slowly retreated when the bird got close. For a brief moment it turned and looked as if it was about to go for the bird but the Kori Bustard seemed fearless and the hyena hesitated, then fled.
>
> The courage and intelligence of these birds is indeed remarkable. Some years ago I saw a pack of wild dogs come across a wounded Kori Bustard. The bird staggered away from them, one wing limp. The dogs immediately

Plate 59. White-Bellied Bustard. Bustards are also found in southern Europe, throughout Asia, and in Australia. There are some sixteen species in Africa; East Africa is well represented with about a dozen. The white-bellied is one of the smaller types. The camouflage of this bustard well serves its shy instinct for concealment when first disturbed, but, like most of its relatives, the white-bellied will resume its dignified posture (and stately walk) when its confidence has been restored. A relaxed bustard is ever on the move, energetically pursuing the business of earning a living. As much of the activity takes place in tall grasses, photography is not always easy, and identifications from photographs not always sure.

Birds of several species meet danger from a predator or intruder who ventures near their nest by feigning injury: the distraction display. The parent draws attention to itself, and away from its young (or eggs), by fluttering on the ground, lying on its side, trailing a wing, or limping as if a leg were damaged. Always keeping just out of reach, the bird lures the enemy away from the nest. The only comparable behavior in mammals is the stotting of gazelles (discussed in Chapter VII).

---

chased it and, with an obvious effort, the bird managed to fly a short distance, collapsing on the ground forty yards further on. As the dogs raced to the spot, the bustard again tried to run, staggering from side to side. Yet, when the dogs were almost upon it, the bird effortlessly took to the air. It had successfully led the dogs away from its nest and had completely fooled me too. (Hugo van Lawick, *Savage Paradise*, p. 35.)

Plates 60 & 61. Kori Bustard Pairs. The reader can see from these two pictures the effect that different lighting (at different times of the day) has on the colors of nature. The top picture was taken at midday; the bottom shot was an early morning effort. The Kori bustard male can weigh nearly fifty pounds and stand some four feet high, making this one of the largest flying birds in the world, certainly the largest in Africa. The toe structure of birds varies according to their movement (and environment). Perching birds normally have four toes: three face forward and one backward. Bustards have dispensed with the rear toe, an adaptation for walking purposes. The bustard's diet includes grains, insects (especially locusts, which food makes the bustard a great favorite of farmers), and small mammals. In other words, the birds are essentially omnivorous. As such, food requirements can be varied according to seasonal cycles and the available natural resources.

Arboreal

This is perhaps the loosest classification of all. Akin to the non-sporting group in dogs, the arboreal birds simply cannot appropriately be placed in another category — and they all live, for the most part, in trees.

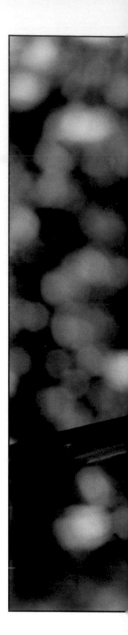

Plate 62. Hornbills. A hornbill's social life is characterized by elaborate cooperative behavior.

Hornbills. We have already introduced the Ground hornbills. The *Red-billed hornbill, Yellow-billed hornbill,* and *von der Decken's Hornbill* (among others) are smaller hornbills, mostly white and black, with a red, yellow, or partially red bill. These birds are conspicuous in dry, semi-desert districts, like Samburu in Kenya, but may be found anywhere in acacia woodlands. Their monotonous call or whistle resembles "tok-tok-tok-tok" (and so on), which sound is, I believe, the basis for their scientific name, *Tockus.*

The hornbill is justly famous for its nesting habits, which were beautifully depicted in the Alan Root film, *Secrets of the African Baobab.* Normally, hornbills are seen in pairs, but, during the breeding season, only males are evident. The females use their large bills to seal themselves in a natural hole in a tree by plastering up the entrance with a dung, mud, and saliva mixture. The male often supplies the raw materials, regurgitated in pellets to the female, who works from inside the hole. Soon, she can no longer leave at the end of a day's work. A narrow, vertical slit is left open, through which the male feeds her while she lays and then sits on her eggs. Three to six eggs are laid. The slit is large enough to permit the female to receive food and to defecate (to keep the nest clean), but too small for snakes and other predators to enter. While thus confined, the hen molts all her feathers during incubation. The molt is quick. When the young are only half-grown, the female breaks out of the hole (often with the male's aid) and helps her mate to feed the family left behind. Both parents are, in fact, needed to find the necessary insects to satisfy the hungry brood. Furthermore, the nest by now has become more than a little crowded.

Plates 63 & 64. Males on Feeding Expeditions. The nesting behavior detailed in the text may take place as often as twice a year. The male supplies geckos, berries, damsel flies, frogs, grasshoppers, caterpillars, beetles, and much more. A hornbill's enormous bill gives it a top-heavy appearance, especially when flying. When taking off, the hornbill flaps its wings strongly to keep from nose-diving.

An alert safarist can learn much from a bird's feet. The ostrich's two toes permit great speed on the ground. The heron's long toes distribute its weight to prevent sinking in the mud. Raptors grasp prey with sharp talons. Woodpeckers climb with two toes in front and two toes facing behind. Perching birds have feet adapted to grasping branches. Ducks swim with webbed feet. Game birds' toes are designed for scratching. And so on.

Meanwhile, the young chicks, remarkably enough, repair the damaged exit, replastering the hole with dung and saliva, until, again, only a feeding slit remains. The young, when they are ready to fly, tear down the entrance wall again and finally leave the nest. Normally, it is the elder of the chicks who initially rebuilds the wall. And the chicks usually leave singly: as each juvenile matures, it breaks out; with each breakout, the wall is rebuilt by the next in line; and so on, until the last young hornbill has left the nest. Each fledgling leaves exactly according to the order and interval of hatching. (In larger, forest species, predominantly fruit-eating, as opposed to their insectivorous cousins, the female molts slowly and will wait until the young —numbering only one or two —are grown and ready to fly together before actually leaving the nest. The male thus continues to supply food to the family for some three and one-half months by himself. He will carry tens of thousands of fruits in one nesting season!)

(plates 65 & 66 omitted)

Plate 67. Holub's Golden Weaver at the Breakfast Table.

Bird watching on safari differs from what birders might call a "big day" with Roger Tory Peterson in eastern Massachusetts. Many of the birds will be totally unfamiliar. Most of the time, the safarist will be limited to his vehicle. Birding per se will be rare; the normal *modus operandi* (birders favor Latin) will be to sandwich in birds between, say, a lion pride and a hippo pool. Of course, the birds are an integrated part of virtually all African tableaus — after all, the lions may be dining on an ostrich, and all manner of avian passengers may be found riding the river horse. Obviously, the bird enthusiast will benefit from learning about the physical make-up and behavior of the most prevalent species. Of primary initial significance is to learn to recognize shapes and silhouettes. While color is important, it may also be misleading (especially given lighting variables) or, at best, a blind alley. The visitor should also note the size, shape, and color of the bill, the size and color of the eye, specific characteristics such as crests or types of tail feathers, the color of the legs and feet, and any repetitious behavior. A *good* pair of binoculars (at least 8 x 30 magnification, with coated lenses) is essential, and this equipment ought to be treated as one would camera equipment.

Weavers. Weavers are small birds of the finch family (or closely related to finches, depending upon whom one relies). The most common birds in Africa, taken as a group, weavers are nearly exclusive to Africa (a few representatives live in Asia). Many varieties are separated by only the slightest difference in usually very bright colors. The safarist will have the devil of a time keeping the species straight in the field — and only marginally less difficulty in doing the same from photographs. I have included a little field exam below — out of necessity, I admit. Weavers occupy virtually every habitat, from forests to deserts. Forest dwellers usually live alone, but those that inhabit open savannahs often form huge colonies, many, many thousands of birds nesting in a single tree.

Their name derives from the way in which their intricate nests are woven. The central precept of nest construction is to locate the nests out of reach of predators.

Some species build their nests in thorn trees, where the spines discourage climbing predators; others hang their nests tied securely to the end of a fine branch using a single, long, slender support, frequently over water. The nests are further constructed with entrance holes on the sides or bottoms that are difficult for any predator who advances that far to enter. Access tunnels tend to be long and elaborate. In most instances, the males weave the nests from grass, and a few nests are unbelievably elaborate. All weaver-nest builders can tie a knot, holding one end of a long piece of grass with a foot and fastening the other end with their beaks, and the enclosed nest is always woven. Should a safarist have the opportunity to see the process, the work is well worth watching. The bird normally weaves the basket nest while standing in the middle of the ring; the progress is energetic but meticulous. The exact architecture varies from species to species, but the shape is typically globular (domed) or oval. Most weavers are polygamous, and the males build nests in the hope of attracting females. Should a male fail to entice a partner, he will destroy the nest and start over. There must be a lesson somewhere here for us bachelors. On the other hand, some species — notably, the *Holub's Golden weaver* and *Reichenow's weaver* — builds several nests, up to six, concurrently, but occupies only one. That lesson is obvious.

Plate 68. Golden-Backed Weaver at the Same Plate.

A bird called the *Social weaver* builds a vast edifice — the work often spans generations of weavers, as the colony grows — that serves as a communal, "apartment-house" home. Non-breeding birds share a chamber, but each mating pair has its own nesting chamber. Each room has its own entrance on the underside of the massive domicile. (These birds also forage and feed together.) The "world's biggest nest" exhibited in a museum is said to be a Social weaver's nest placed on display in The Museum of Natural History in New York City (in the Sanford Hall of Biology of Birds): some 400 cubic feet worth! Indeed, the largest nests in the wild are estimated to reach 2,000 cubic feet, and these nests occasionally grow so heavy (particularly in the rains) that they collapse, taking a part of the tree with them. The Social weavers formerly in residence simply begin anew.

Plate 69. Golden Palm Weaver.

Plate 70. Acacia with Weaver Nests. An acacia tree festooned with weaver nests, often placed but a foot apart, is a frequent sight in the bush. The nests here are those of the Black-headed weaver. During breeding season, the tree obviously becomes a center of tumultuous activity, as the males build and display for the females. In addition to the anti-predation safeguards noted in the text, weavers also purposely locate their nests close to stinging insects, large birds, and human beings.

Plates 71 & 72. Upside Down Builder. When he is finished, the male will hang upside down at the entrance and flutter his wings to attract a female. Assuming all goes well and the female likes what she sees, the woven basket will become a home. Newly born chicks are especially vulnerable neophytes in the animal kingdom — surviving the first several days of life unable to fly and not equipped with defenses makes this period the most critical time of a bird's life cycle. Would-be predators are many, and building a nest in a tree, even high in a tree, eliminates only a few of the voracious diners. The weaver bird's solution to the predation problem is obviously successful, given the numbers and distribution of the family. Nests also offer shelter from rain and sweltering sun.

Plates 73–75. Reader's Field Test. The reader is invited to consult a guide and make his own choices: Holub's Golden, Golden, Orange, Taveta Golden, or Golden Palm.

Turacos. Related to hornbills, turacos, also known as louries or plantain-eaters, are endemic to Africa. The *White-bellied Go-Away bird* is a conspicuous member of the family. Common throughout Kenya and Tanzania (its counterpart in Southern Africa is the Common Go-Away bird or Grey lourie), the Go-Away bird has been called a "congenital alarmist." Its sheep-like bleating call — "kay waay" — is said to resemble "go awayaaa," hence the name. Try as I might, I cannot "hear" this interpretation: the cry more resembles, to the author at least — a high-pitched laugh. Most members of the family have loud, harsh calls, many sounding, in fact, a bit like crows.

Hartlaub's turaco is the most prevalent forest turaco in the Kenyan highlands. All the forest species are remarkable for their brightly colored plumage and long tails. Indeed, the turaco is easily one of the most beautiful birds in the forest — and murderously difficult to photograph. The safarist will see a sudden flash of bright red as the bird lands or takes off. In the trees, the bird acts more like a squirrel than an avian member and is known for its running and hopping along the limbs. Rarely stationary, it certainly does not wait for a fumbling photographer struggling with forest lighting. Hartlaub's has a raucous, croaking call that is often confused with that of a Colobus monkey. All turacos are very noisy most of the time.

Plates 76 & 77. White-Bellied Go-Away Bird.

Plate 78. Hartlaub's Turaco. Forest turacos sport fantastic mixtures of blue, green, violet, and red colors. Hartlaub's, among others, is distinguished by its rich crimson flight feathers.

Hoopoes. The *African Hoopoe* is found throughout East and Central Africa. It feeds mainly on the ground, and a safarist cannot fail to recognize its unmistakeable profile and coloration. Nevertheless, the hoopoe is a shy bird, and a decent photograph is a rare treat. Its name is derived from its dove-like "hoop-hoop" sound at mating season.

Plate 79. African Hoopoe.

As the reader may recall from the discussion on vultures found in Chapter V, a bird watcher can tell a great deal about a bird's diet simply by looking at its beak. The hooked bill of a White-backed vulture is, for example, obviously designed for a different task than the long, straight bills of marabou storks, whatever the proximity of the two bird species at a carcass. Straight-beak hunters look for victims that can be captured easily by simple, downward jabs. Birds that eat hard seed or nuts have short, powerful bills suitable for cracking. Insect-eating birds collect their food in many different ways, all which are reflected in the shapes of their bills. Slender bills are used like tweezers to pick up small insects; stouter bills, hooked at the tip, substitute larger insects. Short bills with a wide base can be opened wide to collect flying insects (catching night-flying insects argues for an even wider gape). And so forth. Nevertheless, the safarist should not be misled into drawing correlations that are too restricting.

The ability to fly and visit so many places encourages a bird continually to assess possible food sources. Eating successfully is important: a bird's high metabolism requires more food proportionately than mammals and far more than reptiles — a croc for example may take from four to five months to eat its own body weight, but a bird may do so in a day or two. But eating is not simply a matter of quantity. A bird must *remain* light (to fly) and thus must choose food rich in caloric energy. The food must be burned quickly and efficiently (digestion usually lasts no longer than an hour, and birds use a far greater portion of ingested food than do mammals). Thus, even if known for filling a particular "niche," in a biologist's parlance, most birds tend to be opportunists of one sort or another.

Pigeons and Doves. Most safarists are familiar with the family of pigeons (normally used to refer to the larger species) and doves (the smaller members of the family); several hundred species populate the world. Africa has its share of this successful bird. The distinctive *Speckled (Rock) pigeon,* a large bird as pigeons go, is a strong flier and is often seen in large flocks. Its diet is vegetarian: seeds, berries, nuts, and grains. Unusual in birds, the Rock pigeon drinks by sucking up water, instead of putting its head up to swallow. The incessant, deep "coocoo-kukuroo" call of the pigeon is heard throughout the long African day; no bird cry of the African bush is more distinctive, save that of the fish-eagle.

The *Ring-necked dove,* also pictured here, is a common bird, the size of a domestic pigeon. The safarist will often see the plump forager on the ground searching for seeds or berries.

Plate 80. *Speckled (Rock) Pigeon.*

Throughout the Mara the rains unleashed a frenzy of activity among the birds. Red-necked with lust, hot-blooded ostrich cocks pursued their hens in absurd high-stepping dances. Kori bustards preened and strutted before their mates with swollen throats and uplifted tails. Buttercup clouds of weaver birds chattered and built their dangling raffia nests in riverside acacias. Larks and yellow-throated longclaws nested in the drier tussocks of the high plains, filling the air with plaintive cries. Crowned plovers laid freckled eggs in shallow scrapes on the bare earth and rose screaming around the heads of trespassing topi. My love, forget-me-not, crooned the red-eyed doves in the strangler figs, and fish eagles yelped as they sailed over the drowning Marsh. (Jackman & Scott, *The Marsh Lions,* p. 55.)

Plate 81. *Ring-Necked Dove with Berry.* The white belly of this bird distinguishes it from the similar Red-eyed dove.

Shrikes. The *Long-tailed Fiscal shrike* is a common bird found throughout Africa. Essentially carnivorous, the shrike will eat insects, the eggs and chicks of other birds, and small mammals. Known as the "butcher" bird or "hangman," a shrike will impale prey on thorns or twigs (or wedge the dead bodies in the forks of branches) until such time as the bird is ready to dine. Fiscal shrikes are bold, aggressive, and extremely territorial birds. They show little fear in taking on larger birds, and I have seen vicious and prolonged attacks against kites and even small eagles.

The Cattle egret, which bird was treated in Chapters VI and VII, has evolved feeding methods so successful that the bird has recently increased its range throughout South America, the American west as far as Canada, and is spreading through Asia and Australia! All that it needs, apparently, are ungulates, especially in the form of cattle ranching (and accompanying deforestation and swamp draining). On their own steam, the birds use a leapfrogging technique: individuals at the rear of a flock leapfrog to the front, and so on — all stirring up the grassland's insects.

Plate 82. Magpie Shrike. The Magpie shrike is fairly common in Central Africa and in the black-cotton/whistling-thorn parts of the Serengeti. This photograph was taken in Zambia.

Plate 83. Long-Tailed Fiscal Shrike. The shrike looks a bit like a miniature falcon, with its sharp, hooked bill.

Barbets. Related to woodpeckers, barbets constitute a striking-looking group of birds. The first two examples pictured, the *Red-and-Yellow barbet* and *D'Arnaud's barbet* are roughly robin-sized, with the former measuring slightly longer. Though it is primarily arboreal, the Red and-Yellow barbet is often referred to as a ''ground barbet,'' because the bird regularly locates its nests in tunnels hollowed out of termite mounds. Consequently, the safarist will frequently see the bird perched on termite hills.

D'Arnaud's is more exclusively arboreal, and the males of this species are aggressively territorial. Both species repeat over and over a strident, mechanical-sounding call — though each call is different. In fact, the repetitive cries are a duet between a mating male and female (called ''antiphonal'' singing) and are invariably accompanied by the pair displaying to each other. The pair singing in duet are usually so well coordinated that the listener hears only one bird singing. On occasion, several pairs will join in a chorus, all performing their curious, excited antics at the same time.

The third barbet pictured is the *Double-toothed barbet,* one of the largest species.

Plate 85. Red-and-Yellow Barbet. When not perched on a termite hill or some thornbush, the barbet will fly in an undulating fashion characteristic of woodpeckers.

Plate 84. D'Arnaud's Barbet. The name ''barbet'' comes from the tufts of bristles found at the base of the bird's beak, tufts faintly resembling a beard.

Plate 86. Double-Toothed Barbet. Most barbets are fruit-eaters.

Bee-Eaters. The colorful bee-eaters perch near the ground and dart forward to capture passing insects, with, as their name suggests, a penchant for bees. The insects are caught on the wing, in mid-air, and killed by returning to the perch and beating them to death on branches. Apparently, the bee-eater can distinguish between stinging insects and non-venomous types. The former are, in addition to the pounding, rubbed repeatedly against a hard surface to dispose of a stinger or to squeeze venom from the prey's abdomen. The latter are, however, often simply swallowed in flight. On the other hand, bee-eaters do carry natural resistances to most insect venoms that would poison other birds and do swallow, without apparent adverse effect, entire bees. Perhaps, the matter is one of degree, and the birds may also simply be trimming some insects down to swallowing size.

Only swifts and swallows, among small birds, can fly as well as bee-eaters. The aerial choreography is quite fantastic: the little masters can dart and soar at will, fly backwards, and rise and fall like a helicopter. After all, insects themselves have mastered flight and are not easy to trap in the air; an almost mathematical sense of movement is required.

Although honey bees are preferred, all actively flying insects — including wasps, dragonflies, butterflies, and locusts — are taken as prey. Birds that depend upon flying insects for food cannot survive cold weather. Consequently, those bee-eaters that originate and breed in Europe migrate to Africa at the end of the summer.

Plate 87. A Pair of Little Bee-Eaters. The widely distributed Little bee-eater is one of the smallest bee-eaters, probably the smallest living in Africa, and undoubtedly the most common African variety. The birds never remain still for long and, despite their abundance, are difficult to photograph well. Normally, only one species of bee-eater is found in a given (limited) habitat, and, when the safarist sees one, others soon appear. This is the way it is generally with birds on safari: the visitor goes for a long time without seeing this or that species, then suddenly sees several examples in a short period. The Little bee-eater seldom ventures far from its perch and its high success rate ensures that the bird can usually be found day after day hunting in the same general area. For photography purposes, it helps to know that the same perch is repeatedly used before the little bird shifts to another branch (itself not too far away).

Sunbirds. The safarist will see the small sunbirds erratically darting everywhere in flowering trees and shrubs. The brilliant, metallic plumage of the male sunbirds — the females are mostly drab and are extremely difficult to identify in the field, unless they accompany males — complement the shifting background. Sunbirds are found throughout the tropical world, but the largest collection lives in Africa, where some eighty species inhabit east, central, and southern environments. Moreover, the birds occupy all types of country, from forest to savannah, and most altitudes.

One is tempted to compare sunbirds to hummingbirds of the New World. Indeed, superficial similarities immediately suggest themselves: brilliant plumage, feeding on nectar from flowers, and long, down-curved bills and extendable tongues that can be thrust deep into flowers. Nevertheless, the two families are not closely related. And further study yields significant divergencies. Sunbirds do not hover while feeding (they can, however, hover), nor do they play as extensive a part in pollination as do hummingbirds. Indeed, sunbirds probably visit flowers as much for insects living in the corollas as for nectar. Moreover, the bird has learned to "cheat" the flower by poking holes in the base of the flower and drinking the nectar there without picking up pollen. And this last practice may do considerable damage and outweigh the benefits derived from the mere chances of pollination.

The reader should understand that plants have encouraged the nectar-drinking habits of birds by providing large amounts of nectar — enough for birds to live on exclusively, should they so choose. Flowers are, of course, colored to attract birds, and liberal and well-positioned perches are usually provided as well. The birds are supposed to repay the favor by carrying pollen from one flower to another. Moreover, pollination (and reproduction) requires that pollen must be transferred from stamens to stigmas of the *same* plant species. Thus, the plant must also try to prevent haphazard foraging by the birds — by, for example, restricting choice. Thus, only certain flowers grow in one place, and different plants flower at different times. Some African plants are more or less dependent upon sunbirds for pollination.

Plate 88. Eastern Double-Collared Sunbird. The exquisite beauty of these glittering gems is reflected in their species names: Superb, Splendid, Shining, Regal, Beautiful, Bronzy, Amethyst, and so forth. None is more striking than our friend pictured here; naturalists just ran short of 'wow' adjectives.

Plate 89. *Nubian Woodpecker*. The closest Southern African counterpart is the Bennett's woodpecker. Woodpeckers are known for eating insects, but many, including the Nubian, supplement their diet with vegetation.

Woodpeckers. The *Nubian woodpecker* is one of the most common and widespread of all woodpeckers. Dead and dying trees attract their share of insects, which in turn are hunted by the carnivorous birds who drill holes in the wood with their heavy, chisel-like bills to extract their meals. A woodpecker is a living hammer, superbly fashioned for such drilling. The heavy head is specially constructed: the skull is strengthened, and the brain cushioned to withstand all the shocks; a long tongue is attached to a retractable bone that will extend the bird's reach deep into the wood; and the tip of the tongue itself is covered with both a sticky mucous and fleshy 'barbs' for seizing insects (or at least moving the prey within range of the bill). Very short tails are used as braces when climbing vertically. The feet are, as expected, powerful aids, as well.

The safarist may be surprised to learn that the drumming heard is not necessarily feeding — woodpeckers also communicate in this way. Most woodpecker foraging takes place on the west side of a tree trunk, where the sun hits and keeps moist the resins derived from the tree holes.

Plate 90. *A Revenge of Sorts*. The extrovert of the bird world takes its "revenge" on an elephant skull: oxpeckers, thoroughly introduced earlier in the text, are, in fact, starlings, and the elephant is the only animal who routinely denies the tick-birds a ride.

Starlings. The safarist who is used to the drab starlings found elsewhere in the world will especially enjoy the glossy plumage and iridescent colors of the African varieties. More than forty species of these noisy, gregarious birds are represented in safari Africa. None is more handsome than the *Superb starling*. To say that the *Superb* is not shy is to understate the matter by half. Found in large numbers around most lodges (and throughout thornbush savannah), the bold and mischievous bird is not above jumping into the safarist's breakfast plate. The lodge managements always make a point of asking clients not to encourage the starling's "bad manners" by throwing it scraps of food. Unfortunately, the message does not necessarily filter down to the voracious and practically omnivorous bird.

The *Superb* has a spectacular courtship display but is busy at most times, always chattering, whistling, and running about — a casual safarist may have difficulty determining when ordinary daily life ends and love begins. A final note of interest: most starlings have well developed powers of mimicking other bird calls.

Plate 91. Impertinent Superb Starling. Both male and female look like this. The ubiquitous starling began in Europe and western Asia but today has multiplied all over the world. Such colonizing success indicates adaptability and opportunism, particularly in diet. Basically insectivorous, starlings will also eat small animals. Their bill and its muscles are adapted for what is called "open-bill probing": the bill is pushed into the soil, then forced open to create a hole, into which the starling peers for worms, grubs, or caterpillars. Such foraging is not easy work and requires intelligence to limit duplication and wasted effort. At other times, starlings also turn to vegetable food.

Rollers. Every picture book on African animals contains a *Lilac-breasted roller,* the most beautiful of all the rollers. Although the bird is fairly easy to photograph perched on a branch, the incredibly blue — an intense ultramarine blue — hue really strikes the visitor in flight. The bird takes its name from the spectacular rolling, twisting, acrobatic flight of courtship displays and, to a lesser extent, of chasing off competitive birds. At these times, the flash of color is blinding.

Rollers are noisy and call in raucous squawks that seem quite out of place in the presence of all this beauty. The Lilac-breasted roller (often called a "blue jay" in South Africa) is a hearty eater and in an hour will venture up and down from its perch many times to take large insects in the grass. The roller is but one of an enthusiastic pack (yes, hyenas do come to mind) of different birds that congregate at fires to enjoy the 'barbeque' of escaping and scorched insects. On the African plains, one animal's dilemma is, invariably, another animal's bonus.

Plate 92. Lilac-Breasted Roller. A photographer's delight. Both sexes share the fluorescent coloration.

Plate 93. Flight Display.

Plate 94. Speckled Mouse-bird. Long stiff tail feathers, small handsome crests, broad finch-like beaks, and a mammalian look distinguish these acrobatic feeders, usually found in all sorts of hanging positions. The safarist will often see hundreds of these birds feeding or roosting together in a small clump of thick shrub.

Speckled Mousebird. The mousebird is peculiar to Africa and receives its name from its mouse-like movements through trees and bushes foraging for berries and fruit (its loose and hair-like feathers undoubtedly helped supply the proper appellation). With its heavy, hooked claws, the brownish bird would rather climb and scurry than hop as it makes its way. Highly gregarious and widespread along forest edges and in bushy savannahs, the mousebird is usually found in follow-the-leader formations and activity. Suspected of chick and egg thievery, the benign-looking (to us) mousebird is not always tolerated by other birds and is frequently the target of a mobbing attack.

Lovebirds. The parrot family is not strongly represented in safari Africa. In certain areas, the safarist will, however, see lovebirds. **Fischer's lovebird** is confined to northern Tanzania; the author has never seen them outside the Serengeti. If one is making one's way from Seronera to Lobo Lodges via the main track, there is a long stretch where the birds are plentiful, picking on the road or flying from bush to bush in rapid, short bursts.

Plate 95. Fischer's Lovebird. This vividly colored bird is always part of a larger flock. A bushfull is, indeed, a colorful sight. Among the most sociable of birds — hence the name — lovebirds frequently huddle together, shoulder to shoulder. Mutual preening is common.

Birds of Prey.

Africa has some eighty species of diurnal raptors (literally, a "raptor" is one who "seizes") and a good representation of nocturnal raptors, namely, owls. Birds of prey as a category here is used to refer to birds that actually search from the air or at least use flight to capture their prey. Thus, for example, the secretary bird in this scheme has been placed with the "ground birds," though it certainly is, in a real sense, a bird of prey. Our birds of prey swoop down to take their victims from the ground or from the water, and, consequently, insectivorous birds are not included as well. Sight is obviously the most important sense of these hunters, but, like most predators who depend upon sight, they respond primarily to movement. Thus, prey "freeze" when they see a raptor dropping in for a meal. Moreover, the sight of some eagles is at least eight to ten times as strong as man's. Most birds of prey have the visual acuity to pinpoint the *movement* of a mouse at 100 yards.

Birds of prey rarely use their beaks to kill anything — their talons, very sharp and very strong, are the primary weapon for attacking prey. The stabbing action of the claws and the crushing grip of the toes normally kill quickly and efficiently. Pressure from an eagle's grip will, for example, crush a monkey's head. On the other hand, the beaks, sharp in their own right and strongly hooked in most species, are used for tearing prey after it has been caught. Some birds of prey eat entirely invertebrate food and many regularly feed on insects, but the majority concentrate on small mammals, birds, and fish. Most, if not all, raptors will scavenge — eat carrion — if the opportunity arises and if they are hungry enough.

Birds are specialists; the main specialty for all but a few is flight. The ability to fly is the single most important reason why birds are, numerically at least, the most successful animals. All that flying has resulted in very few and very desolate places in the world where one cannot find a bird. Virtually all bird biology relates in one way or another to an aerial existence, and most facets of bird behavior cannot be understood without reference to the benefits and costs of flight.

Although mammals vary widely, all birds designed to fly must have similar structures. A bird is actually a living airplane — or, put more chronologically, an airplane is an inanimate replica of a bird — and flies by the same principles. Sound aerodynamic design and engineering requires a biology that provides lift, forward progress or thrust, and control. Thus, birds have feathers, wings, a streamlined shape, thin hollow bones fused together, remarkable respiration, a large strong heart, internal air sacs, powerful pectoral muscles, and are warm-blooded. All non-flight organs are reduced to a minimum (for example, the female has only one ovary). In fact, the airplane analogy takes us only so far; fixed wings are easier to understand, and the mechanics of bird flight are not completely worked out! Both wings are shaped to generate lift when the bird or plane is moving forward through the air. But bird wings — by flapping — also act as propellers. The forward thrust comes from the flight feather's ability to change shape and position through the wind beat cycle. The cycle consists of an *upstroke* (whose stages vary with the type bird), which twists the feathers and starts the thrust and also separates the primary feathers (the large feathers in a wing) — the spaces between the feathers are called "slots" — to allow the air through and decrease resistance, and the *downstroke,* which acts primarily like an oar in water to give the bird an extra push forward. In addition, when taking off, hovering, or landing, a bird obviously loses its lift created by forward movement. The extra lift needed at these times is supplied by sweeping, exaggerated movements of the wings.

(continued on page 612)

Plate 96. Vulture Reprise: Lappet-Faced, Rüppell's, and White-Backed Species. Different shifts at the carcass (see Chapter V).

Plates 97 & 98. Vulture Reprise: Hooded Vulture. The hooded vulture is a picker of bones. The bare skin on its neck becomes a dark pink (the blood vessels dilate) when the birds are aggressive or excited.

Plate 99. Reprise Continued: A Pair of Egyptian Vultures. Much is made of the Egyptian vulture's use of stones ('tools') to break open ostrich eggs. It has been suggested that such behavior first arose accidentally (as "redirected behavior" — "kicking the cat," so to speak) and subsequently 'taught' other birds. But the practice is probably too widespread for such an explanation.

Plate 100. Marabou Double Take. I need not repeat here all the slanderous comments about the Marabous' looks. Perhaps it was this particular specimen's immediate environment, but this Marabou was strikingly sleek and well-appointed (even if I cannot bring myself to say "beautiful").

Plate 101. African Marsh Owl. Most owls hunt by night, and the Marsh owl is one of the few liable to be seen by safarists during the day in open country. Neither as common nor as varied as daytime raptors, owls hunt both by sight and by ear. They do not eat carrion: carrion is static, and owls, like all birds, have a negligible sense of smell. Noiseless flight completes this raptor's arsenal. It is not true, as sometimes heard, that owls have trouble seeing in daylight.

(continued from page 609)

The safarist can tell much about a bird simply by looking at its wing design. (Wings may be used for other purposes — in courtship displays or as sunshades while fishing, for example — but flying needs are paramount.) Birds that live in the forest and on the ground have short, wide wings with several variable slots between the primary feathers when the wing is extended, a configuration that equals high maneuverability in close quarters and rapid takeoffs. Birds that feed in the air or make long migrations have slim wings with minimum slotting for fast, level flight. Soaring seabirds have long, thin wings designed for high-speed gliding in strong, steady winds. On the other hand, soaring landbirds have long, wide slotted wings with the primaries spread (like fingers) — to increase lift at low speed, maneuverability, and efficient gliding.

Taking off is a strenuous, energy-consuming maneuver, and the bird has to generate enough power to get airborne without the aid of airflow over the wings to give it lift. Many birds jump straight up to give the wings room to beat (the tail is also used to increase the lifting effect). The loud ''claps'' made by some birds taking off this way are caused by deep wing beats and outstretched wings hitting each other above the body. Some birds cannot jump satisfactorily for these purposes — their legs are too short or set too far back — and prefer to drop from a perch of some kind, spread their wings and allow gravity to provide momentum. Still other birds, who cannot leap or drop, have to run along the ground (or water or snow or any other surface), wings beating rapidly but shallowly like an airplane gaining acceleration down a runway. If wind is available, these birds will take off into the wind (which generates extra lift). The safarist will witness the bird equivalent of a jumbo jet when after a full meal of carrion, the huge Rüppell's griffon labors to get airborne.

Plate 102. Pale Chanting Goshawk. This goshawk, whose name is derived from its melodious, piping chant repeated for hours during breeding seasons, is peculiar to Africa. A resident of dry bush, semi-desert and acacia country, the bird has a restricted home range and, once seen, can usually be found again relatively nearby. Favorite diet: lizards.

Plate 103. Black-Shouldered Kite. A thickset, medium-sized hawk often seen hunting at dawn or dusk. This meal is an early breakfast.

Birds do everything so miraculously that one should not be surprised that they are colored in the way that they are. Nevertheless, as I watch the feathered parade on safari, I am always reminded of a little girl and her mother standing by the cages located in the bird house of the St. Louis Zoo: "Oh, Mommy! Are they *real?*" Indeed, coloration in birds serves real functions, both to hide (cryptic camouflage) and to reveal (sexual attraction, age differences, inter-species differences, and so on). But the functional explanations often wear a little thin. In fact, there is no inherent reason why coloration should *not* run into the extravagant. Given the possibilities of evolution, it would have been extraordinary if such extravagance had not yet been realized. The bright colors and geometric patterns of the enduring harlequin in his multicolored costume became the theater's symbol of concern for character and setting. On the stage, this clown was always the great improvisor serving as a reminder that the stage was but a mirror reflecting the external world back to the theater audience. The bird is indeed a mirror of nature's extravagance (and, perhaps, comedy as well).

Plate 104. Black Kite. The omnivorous Black kite, which is, on close inspection, actually brown, is one of the most common birds of prey and is frequently found scavenging around towns and villages, as well as throughout the national parks. A deeply forked tail is a distinguishing feature.

Plate 105. An African Goshawk's Forest Meal.

Plate 106. Bateleur Eagle.

Eagles. The average safarist will see several noteworthy eagles. The *Bateleur eagle* is easily identified. In flight, both the white underparts of its wings and the short tail are distinctive (together). At rest, the brilliant scarlet beak, legs, and eyes contrast sharply with glittery, coal-black plumage. Such a short tail makes for high speed but reduces maneuverability. Thus, as it zooms along, the Bateleur displays a teetering, rocking motion in flight, sometimes mistaken for nuances of wind. Probably the most aerial of all eagles — that is, it passes most of the day on the wing, sometimes logging as much as 300 miles in a day back and forth over its territory — the bird will do somersaults like tumbler pigeons. It was these sensational aerial acrobatics that led the Frenchman LeVaillant to name them "bateleurs" ("tumbler" in French). (Alternatively, the French word was slang for tightrope walkers, and the reference could have been to the incessant gliding back and forth and constant balancing on the thermals.) The Bateleur is also a known pirate, who will bully and rob Ground hornbills and secretary birds, among others. He will also scavenge.

The *Martial eagle* is the most powerful predatory bird on the open savannah, specialized in killing game birds and small antelopes. Second in size only to Crowned eagles, the Martial casts a foreboding shadow across the veldt. The author has seen, several times, a Martial challenge a jackal for the latter's meal. On at least one occasion, the big eagle was the winner.

The *Long-crested eagle* is well known in East Africa but infrequent in Central and Southern Africa. It eats mostly rodents.

The *African Fish eagle,* Africa's equivalent of the American Bald eagle, is one of the most studied of big birds. This eagle is found near all large inland bodies of water — lakes, rivers, and mangrove swamps — and along the sea coast. Its piercing, high-pitched gull-like call, reminiscent of shrill laughter, is, like the whoop of the spotted hyena, the trumpet of the elephant, the roar of the lion, or the haw-haw-haw of the hippo, a distinctive and unmistakable voice of Africa and carries great distances over water. When calling, the head is thrown back like a dog baying at the moon. During flight, the call visibly contorts the eagle's whole body.

As suggested by its name, this eagle feeds mainly on fish, but not exclusively (as some writers have suggested). It will also prey on the young of many water birds and is especially fond of flamingo chicks. Fish eagles will scavenge (carrion, as well as dead fish) and will also steal from other birds. This latter piracy is often at the expense of pelicans and large herons, but fellow Fish eagles are not immune. As to its fishing, while impressive pictures (usually taken in baited situations) testify to the capture of large fish, some weighing three to four pounds, snatched from the surface of the water using only one foot, the bird misses fully eight out of ten times. The favorite fishing targets are catfish and lung fish, both which regularly come to the surface to breathe. The Fish eagle's feet have special spikes or hooks on the underside of its toes for grasping such slippery prey, so fishing is obviously of critical importance. Most fishing is done by making short sorties from a vantage point on a tree near the water. Only rarely does the bird search while soaring. Although the bird's success rate is disappointing (particularly if a camera is involved!), the author does not wish to minimize the skill and especially the strength necessary to hone in on prey, snag the fish at full stall with talons just

Plates 108 & 109. Martial Eagle.

Plate 107. Long-Crested Eagle.

on or below the water, and take off again with the extra weight of the bagged fish. All this, usually a ten-second drill, requires incredible timing and great strength.

Nevertheless, the Fish eagle spends little enough time fishing (late morning is the preferred time) and a good part of the day simply sitting on a perch. Indeed, the gorging on large fish, the piracy, the scavenging, and the long indolent periods suggest much of the lion. The king of the river and king of the savannah. Pairs show strong attachment extending beyond the breeding season. Where the fishing is good, the eagles have rather small ranges and pairs will nest close to other pairs. Where fishing is limited (for example, in fast-moving rivers) the bird is highly territorial. Indeed, a Fish eagle will resolutely chase all raptors from its own air space. In general, eagles are widely spaced, forced to divide the ground below into large territories to support a pair and its offspring. Fish eagles tolerate high densities near water because of the abundance of fish (as compared with the more inaccessible land-living food).

Plate 110. The Six-Foot Wingspan of a Fish Eagle Flying.

Plate 111. Normalcy: Paired and Perched.

Plate 112. A Lesson in Graphic Design.

Plate 113. Fish Eagle Portrait.

X. Concluding Thoughts

'Don't ask so many questions,' Tilly said. 'It is bad manners.'
'But if I don't ask questions, how shall I find out things?'
'You are not supposed to be a private detective.'
'All the same, that is quite an interesting point,' Lettice remarked. 'The best way to find out things, if you come to think of it, is not to ask questions at all. If you fire off a question, it is like firing off a gun; bang it goes, and everything takes flight and runs for shelter. But if you sit quite still and pretend not to be looking, all the little facts will come and peck round your feet, situations will venture forth from thickets and intentions will creep out and sun themselves on a stone; and if you are very patient, you will see and understand a great deal more than a man with a gun.'

Huxley, *Flame Trees of Thika*[1]

Now, looking back on my life in Africa, I feel that it might altogether be described as the existence of a person who had come from a rushed and noisy world, into a still country.

Dinesen, *Out of Africa*[2]

Still, now that my life is over, I am glad to have lived, glad to have known the dear breath of woman's love, and that true friendship which can even surpass the love of woman, glad to have heard the laughter of little children, to have seen the sun and the moon and the stars, to have felt the kiss of the salt sea on my face, and watched the wild game trek down to the water in the moonlight.

Haggard, *Allan Quatermain*[3]

We carry within us the wonders we seek without us: There is all Africa and her prodigies in us.

Sir Thomas Browne, *Religio Medici*[4]

Diary Notes

(In June 1987, the author and a fellow photographer traveled to Kenya and Tanzania on a one-month safari. What follows are some excerpts taken from a diary kept at the time. Editing has purposely been held to a minimum. Sympathetic readers — are there any other kind? — will forgive the grammatical infelicities for the extemporaneous flavor . . .)

It was pitch-black when we finally returned to the gate. Our late returns at the end of each day have become a topic of derision among the watchguards. We are known in some dialect or another as "those who come late." A quick shower and change of clothes. Twelve hours of dust shed miraculously. Dinners in the camp are fabulous.

The quality of the fare is exceeded only by our appetites — indeed, we would eat and relish food far inferior. The real fun of dinner is the conversation, the first real chance to test the triumphs of the day. I say 'test,' because no one ever sees exactly the same thing. We argue. We laugh. Mostly, we marvel at the day's events. In the Landrover, we talk little. The medium of observation is silence. Nor is it easy to talk during miracles, one right after another. There is time, on occasion, to curse violently at the camera equipment, but that is another story. At dinner, the day tumbles forth, and prayers, spoken and silent, are said for the photographs. Agony for the missed shots. Joy and thanks just to have seen. After dinner, the crackling, popping campfire. A broader group of conversationalists. An idiot or two. I feel like distributing bibliographies. But the sense of wonder is shared all-round. Drowsiness takes hold. Words start to rise with the smoke into the clear African night. And so to bed . . . I am following the path back to my tent. Rather, I am following the Maasai who is accompanying me, spear in hand, along the path. I have the flashlight and keep trying

---

1. At p. 264.
2. At p. 98.
3. At p. 270.
4 (1643), pt. i, 15.

Plate 1. The First Leopard. The first leopard that one meets in this way — close-up, eye-to-eye — is an experience that transcends all others on safari. I shared this moment (and many others) with an African guide, whose love for and appreciation of the animals was at least as great as mine. Thank you, Francis.

to shine it around him onto the path in front for his benefit. Realizing that he hardly needs it, I save my own feet. Suddenly, there is a rush across the path. Not two feet in front of us, a huge hippo (is there such a thing as a 'small' hippo?) has broken across the path headed back into the woods. Apparently, he found the closely cropped grass of camp a delicacy. I was overjoyed: a "close-call" with a hippo on the way to one's tent is enormously good for the soul. "Kiboko!" I exclaimed aloud. "Kiboko," the Maasai laughed appreciatively . . . Sunrises are awesome. No amount of early-morning blues could make me miss one. This morning is what I call a 'working sunrise.' We are determined to catch an elephant (or two) in the golden sphere as it breaks the horizon. Thus, we are driving like mad to find the elephant(s). For the last three days, the valley below us has been filled with elephants most of the time. This morning we are treated to a lesson on the trekking abilities of *Loxodonta africana.* Not a pachyderm in sight. A run four miles in both directions produces nothing. The sun is on the way. A tree is standing, as do many such trees on the savannah, absolutely alone. A testament to unbelievable fortitude, to survival at its most elemental levels. Fires, droughts, *elephants,* all manner of enemies. Yet, here it is. What draws our attention now is a magnificent secretary bird in the top of the tree, organizing itself for a day on the ground. The sun is ascending, and the bird is lit in colors unattainable on the ground. Our sunrise picture! And another prayer . . . The gazelles know nothing about the tranquility of early morning. Perhaps to make it through the predator-filled night is a cause for celebration. Perhaps the warmth of the early morning sun is provocation enough. We are, at any rate, parked in the vehicle watching the chorus line perform. One by one, the tommies leap a ditch. So far, so good: to get to the other side. Then the group turns and repeats the performance going the other way. And the occasion of our finally moving forward in the vehicle is seized for bedlam — or at least a cartoon of bedlam, which is what four or five gazelles stotting all at once look like . . . This is serious . . . most neck-wrestling in giraffes is a slow-motion version of a made-in-Hollywood brawl. But here there is some serious banging going on. The blows are solid, and the thuds have the ring of authenticity. Periodically, they stop and look at us, but we have the feeling that this is not so much a giraffe's curiosity as displacement activity or, understandably, an opportunity to clear one's head . . . Across the deep ravine are three lions. But not *just* lions. These are three of the finest black-maned lions that I have ever seen. Three males in the very prime of life, alone, and beyond close observation. We explored every inch of the *donga* for miles in both directions, but no crossing. We were in a part of the immense park (Serengeti) rarely visited by tourists, well off any beaten trail. And we were beaten, or so we felt. The lions were obviously shy. Our arrival — and we were no closer than five hundred yards — had brought them to attention, and an exit was imminent when we returned a second time. We speculated that they were brothers who were living as nomads without a pride and who had grown up in this area of the park with little human contact. I cannot recall seeing three males of this size and magnificence together before. The ranger is equally impressed. Suddenly, a fourth head! A foursome. Scarcely believable. Then they are gone. Here, I thought, were some males who would hunt (quite successfully) in the absence of the females. Four totally self-sufficient big boys. . . .

. . . Rick is determined to secure a close-up shot of the famous hippo yawn. Up to now, the effort has had a considerable touch of Charley Chaplin about it — the hippos yawn like crazy until Rick sets up, then quit for the duration. We have located an enormous pool of the river horses, some thirty to forty strong. Creeping to the edge of the river, big-game-hunter-style, we are spotted immediately by several members, and the hippos both back off twenty to thirty yards and begin long dives to the bottom. We wait patiently, and the hippos slowly accept our presence. Finally, three hours after the idea was initiated, a big yawn. I look over at Rick, who has turned ninety degrees to photograph a Yellow-bill stork fishing . . . The rhino and calf, were sound asleep when we pulled up to within twenty yards of their rock-like forms. We were trying to exercise the greatest care not to disturb the pair. The sound of the cameras wake, however, the mother, who jumps to her feet in an amazingly quick time for such a heavy animal. We expect her to test the wind. What she decides, without so much as a second's hesitation, is to test our fortitude: on a dead run, she is headed for the vehicle! Total panic in the Landrover. This is going to be one helluva collision! But

mother stops on a dime one inch from the side of the vehicle, nose to the metal. One snort, then a second. She turns and slowly makes her way back to the youngster. Within another twenty minutes, both rhinos had resumed sleep . . . We have been slowly making our way along one side of the Gol kopjes. Following a Lilac-breasted roller into the rocks, I notice . . . lion cubs. Suddenly, the rocks explode with cubs. After considerable difficulty, we make out a total of twelve, with two mothers accounted for. The cubs, we now realize, are everywhere, at levels up and down the hillside. There appears to be a massive game of 'capture the flag' about. The mothers are stoic, but the cubs seek periodic nourishment. The mothers seem to have cut a workable deal: drink your milk but leave us out of the game. Little brown bodies of fun are rolling down the hillside, the stuff of high comedy . . . I have with me the first half of *The African Safari,* which pages have been printed, and Rick is looking them over with a critical eye. Normally not a churlish fellow by any means, he marches

right up to the line with the suggestion that I somehow 'edit out' the shots taken of the mating pair of leopards found on p. 240. Whereupon, I launch into a lecture on the difficulty of getting *any* shots of a mating pair, etc., etc. (The shots are *not* very good, but I, for one, have never seen photographs of a mating pair.) . . . Every sound is a signature in the bush . . . This hamerkop business is getting out of hand. I want to secure a close-up of the bird for the book, not being satisfied with my existing efforts. But every time I whip out a camera, the bird flies off. The frustration level is mounting rapidly. Messing with a hamerkop is bad luck, anyway, and the driver is not exactly pleased with the campaign thus far. Finally, crossing a bridge, I notice a hamerkop directly below me. Without further ado, I take the picture . . . A group of several elephants is making a fairly fast safari across the savannah. It looks to be all business except that the last participant is a young bull who is not satisfied either with the formation, the pace, or the object of the march. He is venting his frustration by running up to the next in line, a decidedly bigger bull, and goosing him with a tusk. In my book, this is more than a gesture, but the large bull does not want to lose his place in line and is

Plates 2 & 3. Passengers on Safari.

trying his level best to ignore the provocateur. The later is, of course, not to be mollified by any such condescension. Somehow, honor has tangled up in what must have started as a game. Another goose. And the last straw. The older elephant turned, and for half an hour, the two elephants intertwined and released each other's trunks. Memories of the goosing notwithstanding, it looks like a love-in to me . . . The oryx tournament is in full swing. One male with exceedingly long horns is chasing a smaller version around. We don't know, of course, what the smaller has said (or done) to the larger, but it is quite clear that long horns is not going to let it pass. He is demanding satisfaction, and the small one can run but he can't hide, as they say. He is in for a long day, and the Samburu sun is at full strength. . . .

A grand night in the bunker! I am enscounced underneath the Ark in a concrete enclosure that allows me unimpeded viewing — at ground level. A male bushbuck has already made the tortuous (for a bushbuck) trip to the salt. A female steps forward to try. Extremely wary, soft nose testing, round eyes searching — the most appealing picture of cowardice that ever existed. A buffalo stomps to the water's edge, oblivious to left or right. Two elephants wander by, waving their trunks and enjoying a personal joke between them, unaccountably passing up the salt and water altogether. Tonight belongs, however, to the Giant Forest hog. A visitor might have taken the salt-lick for a movie lot, where casting for some horror picture was in progress. One huge, grotesque form after another, I had never seen so many, not together, not even altogether. At twenty-three, I stopped counting. Surely, even more walked shrouded in darkness beyond my view. At one point, I was only four or five feet from a boar, head to head. He must have sensed my presence; nothing lay between us . . . A certain affinity exists between the old-timers and the first-timers. If one has studied the animals as I have, one can anticipate action — to the point of enjoying the animal just standing there. I can look at a wildebeest and fill in all the blanks, as it were. The first-timer frequently has time and capacity for little else. Everything is new and time is needed to assemble definitions and boundaries. The net result is the same, pure enjoyment at the most simple sights and sounds . . . Amboseli is, as usual, a dust bowl. Wherever one went, the odor of dust filled the nostrils. Tourism is destroying this park but not in the way that is commonly written about. The tourists — and principally off-track driving — is blamed for the dust. This is fallacious. Amboseli has always been a dust bowl. Joseph Thompson, the first white man through these parts, complained of all the dust in 1883. What Amboseli could do without today are the huge day *coaches* from Mombasa who ferry up excursions from the beaches for a quick look at the animals. No park should be subjected to this kind of casual, hell-bent-for-leather "interest" nor, surely, these gigantic rolling leviathans! It's just ten a.m. and already I've been in two altercations with coach drivers. No park

in Africa will long survive a cadre of drivers, guides, and rangers who do not care passionately about *their* parks (*their* heritage). Steps have to be taken to ensure that those who are responsible for bringing people into the parks have the high ethical outlook that is required — and are prepared to do what is right, whatever the pressures raised by the tourists themselves . . . On the way to dinner, I pass a group of rock hyraxes who have come together in sleeping formation for the night. There are some sixteen bodies, all organized in a kind of cheerleading formation: the biggest on the bottom, the next size on top in another row, juveniles forming yet another layer, *followed* by the very young . . . I love the exhileration of speeding across the savannah at dusk, trying to make camp by dark . . . The views from the balloon, never predictable, today are mostly of birds — vultures, Marabous, herons, and storks along the Mara. High in a balloon is a good time to consider a feather, one of the many triumphs that go toward making up a bird. A partially hollow shaft forms the center. Radiating from the shaft are the barbs. Barbs are feathers in miniature, each bearing its own projections called barbules. There must be hundreds of thousands of barbules per feather, all overlapping in a web. On both the flight feathers and the body feathers, the barbules have tiny hooks that attach onto adjacent barbules, giving the feather a smooth, tight, windproof, and waterproof surface. (A bird effectively "zips" up its feathers when it runs them through its beak.) All feathers are made of kerotin — the same substance that makes up our own nails and hair and the scales of reptiles . . . Most animals are like complex detective stories; the "police" (the naturalists/scientists) have been examining the evidence bit by bit, but there is considerable digestion and synthesis ahead, and, though we may not know the conclusions, we know enough to want to continue to the outcome . . . The cheetahs were having trouble hunting, the primary impediment being the unusually tall grass. The mother led the way to the tree overlooking the Savannah, but the cubs were the first to bound up, one at a time, to survey the plains. Eventually, mother followed, but no sooner had she managed the trick than her primary concern switched from search for possible game to keeping from falling. She was obviously uncomfortable and came down quickly . . . In breeding season, a pair of goshawks are flying in slow circles over their territory, displaying and calling while on the wing . . . Whenever I pause and reflect on the time that I have spent on safari, I understand the poignancy of Haggard's Quatermain comment at the end of his life: to have lived . . . to have watched the wild game trek down to the water . . . It's been said that all sounds in nature are beautiful once you understand how to listen. "Natural" sounds have a special sort of reality. Africa assaults (in a pleasant, challenging way) all the senses, but most safarists are surprised by the renewed sense of hearing . . . The late afternoon sunlight catches the pelicans flying against approaching storm clouds . . .

5:30 a.m. The tent is alive with activity. In spite of the ungodly hour, we are late. Too exhausted the night before to clean the camera equipment, we agreed to get up "slightly" early this morning. A rigorous round of cleaning and organizing, prior to the day's game drives, goes a long way towards ensuring that missed photo opportunities will not result from equipment problems. A bitter lesson in the learning, too! It is black outside; the milky grey that precedes dawn is still several minutes away. One tea, one hot-chocolate (mine) arrive and galvanize our efforts. We cut a few corners. The imperative to be underway by 6:30 is cast in bronze . . . We discover the leopard as we round the turn. She is lying on a fallen tree trunk. As we draw near, hardly believing our good fortune, she looks quickly in our direction and flicks her tail. But she does not move, and the excitement level in the Landrover jumps fivefold. That's the way it is with leopards: they choose the meeting. She is gorgeous. The early morning light that is filtering through the canopy is playing hide-and-seek with the rosettes. We have been watching her for only ten minutes, when suddenly she pulls back and slides to the ground. She is tense, incredibly alert. And headed straight for the vehicle. "Oh, Jesus!" Rick says. The driver is muttering something under his breath. I put my hand on his shoulder to calm him; out of the corner of my eye, I saw movement in the bush ahead. The leopard is stalking, not us, but a dik-dik pair just twenty feet the other side of the vehicle. Incredibly (for a leopard), she is using the vehicle as a hide and pauses at our right rear tire. At this point, we are all — human beings and leopard — breathing the same air we are so close. The excitement is palpable. My heart — I cannot speak for the others — is racing. I am also worrying about lens length, available light, and the leopard is moving again. Progress from now on is in a flat-down, belly-to-the-grass posture. The dik-diks, who have temporarily moved into the open, appear only normally cautions. A hornbill utters a raucous cry. The tableau freezes. The dik-diks seem to drift in and out of focus like shadows. The leopardess continues forward. Progress is excruciatingly slow. The tiny antelopes continue to drift, step by dainty step, always away. Finally, she stops, sits up. The stalk is over . . . the serval is obviously hunting and pays little attention to the arrival of our vehicle. (Always in the past, I had to remain far off to the side; today, I am afforded a ring side seat.) There follows a series of well-planned leaps designed to stir up prey. The tall grass is full of rodents, and success is high. We are surprisingly close; to an outsider, it would appear that the small cat was giving us a demonstration. I begin to think just how spectacular these shots are going to be . . . The train of jumbos was stretched across the savannah like a fresco painting; little one, big one, little one, big one, little one, and on and on. The majesty of elephants is unbelievable. They dominate the landscapes in which they participate. They dominate photographs. Can anyone imagine a world without elephants? . . . I tell the driver to slow down. There is something obviously wrong with a zebra mare, obviously pregnant. She has dropped back a bit from her herd, is grazing only intermittently, and is raising and lowering her tail. Suddenly, I realize what's afoot — the mare is going to foal! A rare event at midday! Zebras, like many antelopes, can delay labor if disturbed, so we hang back a respectful distance. She sits, then stands, then sits again and rolls on her side. The contractions are swift (it seems), and the foal appears. Cautiously, we move slightly forward to take better pictures. The mare shows no concern at our presence and licks and nibbles at the remains of the fetal sac. Whatever exhaustion she feels, mother stands and moves to the baby. She licks it and nudges it encouragingly. The foal attempts to stand. He tries rising with the hind legs first, then collapses. Now the front legs first. Collapse. Finally, twitching and trembling all over with effort, the foal stays on his feet. The mother instantly moves away to encourage the baby to take a few following steps. She returns to his side and walks in another direction, keeping just ahead of the staggering shape off her flank, desperately trying to nurse. The mare is also trying to distance herself and the foal from the afterbirth, before it attracts predators. Progress from this point is swift. Within thirty minutes of birth, the foal is trotting alongside the mare! All signs of unsteadiness are gone! Other zebras are now approaching; but the mare places herself between the herd members and the baby — the foal must first be allowed to "imprint" on his mother to form a tight bond that will keep them together later in the mingling herd. We sit down in the Landrover, exhausted. Emotionally drained, our day is made, and it's just noon . . . We arrive at the hippo pool and unpack lunch. The snorting and wheezing and haw-haw-haw punctuate the stagnant midday air. The pool looks inviting. Then I see four legs sticking straight up from the water. What is going on? Again. A huge male, off from the crowd, is actually rolling over in the shallow water. Back and forth! I have never seen anything like this before. The entertainment continued through lunch. Only with difficulty was I pried away. Hippos are fascinating and I have always been a hippo follower . . . Coming to the edge of the lake, we are treated to a scene, a carousal, of almost unbelievable lewdness. There is no other word for it, anthropomorphism be damned. Four or five male hyenas are mating with a female in the water. Whoop, whoop, whoooop. The sound is so ribald as to defy retelling (in print). We are all laughing so hard that tears are streaming down our faces. Whoop, whoooo, whoop. The males are also fighting among themselves for position in the queue, and one male at least has sustained a nasty gash on his mouth. The female is obviously calling the tune. Whoop, whoop. Shallow water, deep water. Whoop, whoop. We stay there hours (with an occasional glance at the flamingoes) . . . The sun is hot when we find the mating pair of lions. The male partner is a worthy full-maned adult. Off to one side is a male almost identical to the consort.

Plates 4–9. *Birth of a Zebra.* Is the birth of a zebra foal any less of a miracle than the birth of a human baby? Is a mother's agony and joy not shared on some fundamental level? Is not the interest that the herd shows in the newcomer an equivalent of human parents' pride? And do not the dynamics, imperatives, and possibilities of *life* continue on parallel planes?

The sun was making ready to set behind the escarpment when we started to drive back to the hotel. There can be no more wonders, I told myself, I've had them all. An old baobab tree growing out from the Rift wall was a familiar sight by now, a halfway marker between the park and our hotel. It could have nothing new or startling to reveal, for we had passed it often going or coming, although never at this late hour. Casually I looked at it as we passed and now saw it as if for the first time.

The setting sun had called forth the pinkish tones of the baobab's gray bark and was causing it to glow as if from an inner flame. I seemed now to be looking no longer at a rooted member of the floral world but at some animal of flesh with its multiple arms outflung and its whole body twisted in a grotesque contortion, as if trying to communicate its state to anybody who passed by, to anyone who had eyes to see . . . (Hulme, *Look a Lion in the Eye,* p. 212–3)

I really thought those famous tree-climbing lions were overpublicized if *they existed at all. For who ever heard of a four-hundred-pound lion lying on its backside like a kitten in the treetops? Or, more improbably, slung over tree branches like a sack with head, legs and tail drooping inertly in air?*

So when we did at last see a lion sprawled sleeping in a tree, I still could not believe him real. He was contrary to all experience. He was at variance with the laws of nature. He was implausible, unimaginable, unreasonable. Also, he was the most touching sight I had seen in Africa because of his trust in man, for he allowed us to approach from underneath his great stuffed belly only thirty feet above our open hatch and photograph him at will. Indeed, he did not open an eye.

This was our first tree lion and we found him in a magical corner of Lake Manyara National Park, in woodlands of enormous old acacias, their gnarled branches overhead holding thorny canopies — the Acacia tortilis, *the preferred tree for the lions' siestas aloft.* (Hulme, *Look a Lion in the Eye,* p. 207)

Plates 10–14. The Hunting Serval. The serval has a distinctive hunting style. The safarist who takes the time to learn something about a serval will be enriched for the *understanding* of what he then sees — the nuances, intricacies, efficiencies (and, yes, *in*efficiencies) all begin to reveal themselves. A day in the life of a serval is like any day in the history of the world — far more than one would imagine from reading the headlines.

Plates 15–17. Arboreal Existence. It is not only a bird that lives in a tree.

Plate 18. Hippo on a Roll.

Plate 19. Dominant Female.

Plate 20. Dominant Male.

Plate 21. The Pack Sets Off To Hunt.

Plates 22–25. Balloon Vistas. I have been up in the Masai Mara balloons many times. Whenever, in fact, the opportunity arises. Repetitious? No, I always arrive in an expectant mood:

> *Africa, of course, never repeats itself. I should have learned that in the very beginning when I saw my second lion, my second savanna, my second sunset. No two of anything in Africa are alike and this lack of repetition is what makes the magic of the African chiaroscuro. (Hulme, Look a Lion in the Eye, p. 205)*

Plates 26–29. Hyenas Mating in Water. I can still hear the ''whoop, whooo, whoop.''

Obviously, these two beautiful specimens grew up together and share mastery over the pride. Even mating tends to slacken in the heat, and the female is sound asleep on her side. She wakes and shifts positions, slightly closer, it appears, to the other male. He in turn stands and looks around and takes no more than a half step in the pair's direction. Instantly, the mating male is on his brother. The suddenness of the attack is staggering. The two lions are on hind legs now, raking the other with massive claws. Lion violence can be frightening in its ferocity. In seconds, a lifetime of growth, hunting, rolling in the sun is being torn to shreds. The second male was as startled as we were and fortunately fell back quickly under the onslaught. His brother let him go. There is no telling whether the damage to the loser's face and body will allow him to participate again fully in the pride. It all happened so quickly that we were able to photograph only the departure from the field of battle. An air of sadness hangs over the scene . . . The hyena cubs appeared extraordinarily calm, as if they have been recently chastized and instructed to sit in a corner. Although at that age (different ages, to be sure) when they like to play, these two lay at the den entrance without more, just waiting. As we drove off, we discovered why. The body of a third cub, bloated by death and the heat, lay just twenty-five yards away. It looked to be the work of lions. Only a hyena corpse would rot for any length of time as this one had, untouched . . . We return to the fallen tree of our leopard. Amazingly enough, she has returned. We fancy a sign of recognition. She relaxes, head off to one side, looking below down into the grass. Is that a sound? Suddenly, fifteen years in the bush come together (Rick is, however, fifteen minutes into his second game drive . . .): leopard cubs are bounding up the log to join their mother! What a secret! Rangers had been reporting seeing this leopard for over a week, but no mention of cubs. My heart is in my mouth; I can barely work the camera. The leopard is telling me to take my time. She keeps them out for an hour or more. Not a roll of film remains in the Landrover . . . The dogs are stirring; our patience is about to be rewarded. We have stayed with the pack since discovering their presence at midday. Two or three of the animals are running around in great excitement, grinning feverishly and licking one another's muzzle. Within minutes, all seventeen dogs are excitedly milling about. Quite a remarkable change. Suddenly, they are off — lining up single-file with two leaders well in front. The horizon also comes alive. Way in the distance, some gazelles are stotting, other antelopes break into a dead run. We are amazed — these seem like impossibly long flight distances, and the dogs have not even committed themselves. At the same time, we are having trouble keeping up; the dogs are in high gear. They have, however, allowed themselves to become too spread out, making concerted action more difficult. Indeed, the rear dogs are no longer exactly sure where the leaders are; the leaders themselves have torn off in dead sprints. Their speed is amazing. There is no relay running here. Chaos prevails: the pack has split into three, perhaps four, subgroups, all chasing different animals. Two groups are chasing gazelles. One group of three has come to a halt under a giraffe: all parties seem unclear exactly how to proceed — the giraffe is staring down in disbelief; the dogs are having second thoughts. The fourth group of dogs has disappeared over the horizon, following, we believe, impala. The excitement is tremendous; we have been jostling across the savannah at breakneck speeds, this way and that. Then occurred one of those events that sets wild dogs apart as communal animals. The leaders have returned and they have blood on their muzzles; they have, in fact, killed something. Rather than devour the prey, however, they have returned to fetch their comrades. All the more remarkable, when we all arrived at the prey, is that the carcass is only a tommy, little more than a meal for two dogs, let alone seventeen. Needless to say, *every* scrap of that gazelle was gone within three minutes . . . The dogs are still hungry and are milling about, but it is too dark for further hunting. Night descends with great rapidity here. A sense of frustration — the realization of a hungry night — prevails. Suddenly, two dogs break off — a hyena, shuffling upon the scene in true Quasimodo fashion, has come too close. Thereupon ensued one of the most remarkable sequences that I have ever witnessed in the bush (all the while cursing the darkness and holding the camera helplessly). The hyena turned to run, not seriously, just enough to show respect. The dogs were not buying respect and bore down. The hyena, now in full panic and squealing with surprise, ran into a cluster of shrubs to wait out his tormentors. The entire dog pack then aggressively gathered round. From the hyena's perspective, the situation must have appeared grim. It was hardly credible that the dogs would try to kill him; if forced to fight, his superior strength was sure to kill or injure two or more dogs. Yet, here he was . . . The hyena made his break, and two dogs tore after him (no way of telling if these were the original two), nipping furiously at fisi's heels. The hyena was no match for their speed and was reduced to running in tight circles, half sitting, scooting, trying to keep the dogs from crippling him. The hyena was also going through his entire repertoire of hideous sounds. The dogs were chewing all over his backside, fur was flying from the rump and hocks — this was one misfortunate hyena! They were not, however, trying to kill the hyena, but had apparently decided on a lesson not to be forgotten. The remaining members of the pack were purely spectators at the disciplinary session. The dogs chased the hyena for ten minutes or more, in constant bedlam. The hyena would periodically turn on his pursuers, but they were too swift and always maneuvered to his rear. Finally, they fell back, and the hyena was allowed to limp off — his rear end looked as if it had been plucked. The disciplinarians rejoined the pack. We were three landrovers full, and most of those assembled gave the dogs a rousing hand.

Plate 30. Secretary Bird Game-Stalking Cheetah. At this point, the cheetah was guarding its secret well. What the bird was doing is anyone's guess.

Frankly, I felt sorry for the lone body dragging off into what was going to be a very uncomfortable night . . . The game was a complicated one, and we seemed to be the object of the fun. We were following a leopardess and her son, when they decided to split into two different trees. Neither was enamored with our attention, and when we went to one, the other tried to sneak off to another tree unnoticed. We had been through three sets of trees each and had managed to keep up. The mother finally broke the deadlock and disappeared up a ravine for good. When we returned to the tree where we had left the male, he, too, had given us the slip. Score: leopards 2, visitors 0 . . . The cheetah stretched and sat still. It was time. The air had cooled in the last hour, and this was his hunting time. He sat on a mound in the midst of a sea of gazelles. Flickering tails, flickering side-stripes, tommies in every direction. Gazelles who furthermore knew that the cheetah would be hunting now, as he had done every day for the past three months. Sentries stood on the edges of individual herds. These sentries maintained a short flight distance from the cheetah and moved with him — approached, as he moved away; retreated, if he came forward. The entire herd shifted with the sentry. But the cheetah possessed a secret. In time, he was loping toward one herd. We had tried to pick the most likely target group and, predictably, had guessed wrong. As we now tried to make up the distance, the cheetah broke into a sprint. Too soon, we all said, way too soon. There was no element of surprise, and the gazelles seemed in no danger. We did not know the cheetah's secret. We arrived at the place where the gazelles had formerly been only seconds after the cheetah itself. Exhausted, the cat was sitting, panting mightily. Disappointed that we had chosen such inexperience to observe, we watched, however, with fascination a secretary bird approach the resting cheetah. Unbelievably, the bird was 'game-diving' the cheetah, approaching the big cat in zig-zag fashion. What was the bird doing? He was coming to within yards of the fastest animal on earth. Possibly, the cheetah wondered as well as he followed the progress of the bird. Suddenly, the cheetah was moving again. The bird? No, it was now that the cat revealed his secret. The earlier rush had chased away the gazelles — all but one, that is. As he undoubtedly had for many afternoons, the cheetah had chosen a herd with young fawns. A little fawn had reacted to the charge by flattening out, motionless in the grass. Indeed, he could not be seen. The cheetah was banking on inexperience to cause such a young antelope

to rise up too early or otherwise give itself away. And so it happened. The cat nearly ran over the bird to get to the fawn. One had the feeling that this cat would live a full life . . . We sat in the Landrover waiting for the last sunset. No one spoke. It would be some time well into the future before most of us could return. One month on safari! We were awash with the colors of Africa, the golden colors of late day. The lion, long the symbol of African wildlife, resting on the nearby kopje calmly surveyed his domain. Breezes danced along the tops of the savannah stretching every direction as far as the eye could see. The author was reminded of a book in his youth — Rölvaag's *Giants in the Earth* — that had moved him from the opening pages: 'tish-ah,' said the grass. A gust ruffled the full black mane. Where were the poets? It is inconceivable that man could allow all this to disappear. The sun was dropping behind the escarpment. The last sunset was upon us. We drove slowly back to the lodge.

(End of diary excerpts)

Plate 31. A Train of Jumbos.

Plate 32. A Prodigious Yawn. And, given the number of poolmates, a bit of bravado, as threats go.

Plate 33. Reflections. Obviously a contest to see who can cast the largest shadow.

Plate 34. The Last Sunset.

Plate 35. Lioness Tensed to Spring.

Plate 36. The Loser. Only a few seconds are needed to turn upside down a life of majesty.

I am not sure that the reader wants to hear all that I have to say about the "significance" of the safari experience. In the final analysis, the experience is an intensely personal one. I purposely included in Chapter III a fair sampling of the personal views written by others far more eloquent than I. On my part, I could only reemphasize the importance of coming face to face with things irreplaceably precious. Natural beauty on this scale forces a

Plates 37 & 38. Visual Trickery. Despite the realism of photography, the reader is frequently left to rely on the honesty of the writer. Unfortunately, photographer-writers frequently feel compelled to follow in the footsteps of the early travelers and exaggerate the specifics of a given situation. The animals inevitability become more fearsome and dangerous. There is, of course, the problem of honest misinterpretation, but one would count on both hands the number of picture books released in the last ten years that deal with African game without exaggeration. These two plates (and the following plates) are instructive. For plate *37,* the author could write about a snarling lioness — threatening the photographer, about to strike, and so on. In plate *38,* the lioness appears to be growling at a cub or perhaps even attacking the youngster (though the juvenile does not appear particularly concerned). The truth is, in both instances, far different. (Turn the page.)

Plates 39 & 40. The Truth: Cubs Have Sharp Teeth. A mother's lot may be to suffer, but there is no requirement to do so in silence. When lion cubs begin to teethe, nursing will be painful. The lioness in plate *37* is simply expressing, to no one in particular, displeasure at the rigors of a cub taking a meal. The cub in plate *38* has a confederate pulling on a teat. The confederate, in plate *39,* in turn expresses his displeasure at being cut off (the result of too much pain to mom).

sensitive person to reflect on his own significance — *not* insignificance or triviality, but on a context of meaning. A sharing of life. A realization that our concerns are mirrored up and down (or *out*) the animal chain. A reminder of the persistence and adaptability and vigor of all life. There is more here than the freedom and relaxation that looking for game provides, though one should not underestimate the value of the change in perspective from the daily newspaper, the Dow Jones average, or the new stereo system to the question of whether one is going to

Plate 41. Elephants in Forest Tableau. Elephants are able to travel considerable distances in the course of a day. This family, whose red color establishes such a vivid contrast with the lush green of the forest, passed the early day miles and miles away rolling in the red mud of the "red river" (Uaso Nyiro). The coating dried, the elephants went on their way, and the safarist was later to marvel at the terra cotta pachyderms.

find a leopard that day. And Dinesen's "stillness." How conducive — and necessary — to Browne's inner voyage.

After a few days in the wild, the safarist will be using senses long underemployed. The smell of grass, burned or trampled, of fresh dung, and so forth will teach much. The ear will strain to hear the stories being told all around. And the eyes learn both to reach into the distance and to probe the midday shadows up-close.

And, of course, the animals themselves. Most people have a deep-seated sympathy for animals. We love our pets, and our perception of kinship is strong. Moreover, we try to understand them, with the inevitable result that immense intelligence or a particularly strong personality is credited to *our* dog, cat, horse, bird, fish, or what not. Most people come by their curiosity in this respect, and their empathy, naturally. And the interest extends outward to zoos, TV programs about wild animals, and picture books. A safari is, then, but an extension of such behavior.

Earlier, I spoke of the desirability of seeing animals in their natural habitats. Objectively, a zoo simply cannot provide the real thing. The visual differences are obvious, but the "feel" — the totality of senses — is what is

Plate 42. Can Anyone Imagine a World Without Elephants?

Plates 43–45. The Gol Kopjes Exploded with Cubs.

Plate 46. A Complicated Game — The Main Player.

Plate 47. The Mythology of Elephants. These remarkable animals will never cease to fire man's imagination, so extraordinarily beyond human scale are they. It has always been so.

The theme of a continual struggle between elephant and python was a popular one in Roman times lasting well into the Middle Ages. As might be expected, Pliny offered the most fantastic versions:

. . . the serpents also being of so large a size that they easily encircle the elephants in their coils, and fetter them with a twisted knot. In this duel both combatants die together, and the vanquished elephant in falling crushes with its weight the snake coiled around it . . . one difficulty that the serpent has is in climbing to such a height; consequently it keeps watch on the track worn by the elephant going to pasture and drops on him from a lofty tree. The elephant knows that he is badly handicapped in fighting against the snake's coils, and therefore seeks to rub it against trees or rocks. The snakes are on their guard against this, and consequently begin by shackling the elephants' steps with their tail. The elephants untie the knots with their trunk. But the snakes poke their heads right into the elephants' nostrils, hindering their breathing, and at the same time lacerating their tenderest parts; also when caught in the path of the elephants they rear up against them, going specially for their eyes: this is how it comes about that elephants are frequently found blind and exhausted with hunger and wasting misery . . . there is another account of this contest: that elephants are very cold-blooded, and consequently in very hot weather are specially sought after by snakes; and for that reason they submerge themselves in rivers and lie in wait for the elephants when drinking, and rising up coil round the trunk and imprint a bite inside the ear, because that place only cannot be protected by the trunk; and that the snakes are so large that they can hold the whole of an elephant's blood, and so they drink the elephants dry, and these when drained collapse in a heap and the serpents being intoxicated are crushed by them and die with them.

Plate 48. The Black-Maned Brothers. Beyond the grasp of man.

entirely different. A lion that roars in the zoo sounds little more than indigestion. In the wild, the roar will cause one's hair to stand on end. A zoo will, of course, be a less expensive option and clearly one more accessible to most people, but the African safari is, increasingly, a trip that more and more Americans, Europeans, and Japanese, among others, are contemplating. The cynical argument is sometimes heard that the natural parks are nothing but glorified zoos — giant zoos, to be sure, — and that the animals have somehow ceased to be "wild." Aside from the purist's natural hyperbole (good or bad) at finding forms of organization and facilities in the wilderness such as roads and Tree Hotels, the cynicism is one of the two principal legacies of the the big game hunter. (The second is, of course, all the stuffed heads, rows upon rows, adorning walls and mantles all over the world.) The hunter's stock-in-trade is the illusion that the wilderness is a dangerous place requiring a gun and a large quotient of bravery. Basically, hunting is finished in safari Africa, but this fallacious legacy lingers. That animals become

Plate 50. Zebra and Dust Storm: An African Tableau.

Plate 49. Hyena Cubs Chastised. More inclined today to wait patiently for the return of the elders .

acclimated to the presence of man and consequently permit a certain level of access does not make them any less wild. The thrill of the hunt — man ginning up the wildlife community — is hardly a matter of natural law, however "primeval" the experience. There is nothing unnatural about man appearing in nature's tableau, provided that he too gives way to the elephant's "right of way."

Conclusion   651

Plate 51. The Crater, Inside Looking Out. The magic of Ngorongoro, so overwhelming on the descent, remains with the visitor throughout the day. There is hardly any view that is less than breathtaking. And the animals thrive in such a place. By "thrive" is meant, for the most part, permission to develop their full potential in a wild, natural state. Such permission is granted (or withheld) today by man. This magnificent big-tusker is a rare sight in safari Africa and survives only in strongly protected areas.

Whither safari? Will the parks survive? The animals? The *experience?* The truth is, on the surface at least, the reserves are alive and well. I say this fully aware of the existing threat to several animals. The Black rhino today, for example, walks a tightrope between survival and extinction. And the circumstances that have compelled such an outstanding paradigm of life's endurance to march this line are positively obscene. Nevertheless, a fair analysis of the animal populations existing in the reserves and an objective view of the ecosystems concerned show, on balance, natural environments holding their own. And I speak as one absolutely steeped in the literature of problems, conflicts, and false starts but also from a perspective of fourteen years spent on the ground. Indeed, in some respects, the protected areas have never been healthier. The Serengeti, and its extension, Masai Mara, for example, teems with wildlife as never before. Optimism in the middle of rubble is little more than that —hope. Optimism in the midst of plenty, of at least relative success, is, on the other hand, the basis for a program, for next steps, and a future pleasing to contemplate.

But not a guarantee. The seeds of pessimism were sown long ago. Mankind, taken as a whole, does *not* have an enviable record of protecting existing life on earth. Indeed, man has progressed — and only the intellectually myopic would deny the comprehensive *progress,* as that term is properly used — at the expense of most other creatures here. One has to love mankind beyond reason (and, perhaps, love it to death) to be sanguine about this result. There are notable examples of a contrary outcome — the African national parks today are one — and, unless one carries neo-Darwinism to ridiculous extremes, the immediate future holds little that is inevitable. We will receive what we will to receive. As one writer has recently said so well: man will either become the brain guiding the earth to welcome destinies or the cancer that will destroy the organism altogether. African game will exist in our futures if the collective will to ensure such a result is strong enough.

To emphasize the precarious health of the African parks, one has only to reflect on one of the reasons why they contain so many animals today. In most instances, the animals have nowhere else to go. The parks represent, in fact, the *last* home for many species. As habitats beyond the reserves shrink, the animals are forced to regroup and remain within narrower confines. Most can manage (some cannot) — so long as the existing boundaries are not butchered.

Racists, big-game hunters, professional doomsayers, and other equally attractive elements predicted the collapse of the national parks when the Africans achieved independence in the 1960s. To the contrary, the parks are, generally speaking, better organized today than under colonial administrations. There are three reasons for *this* progress. First, the African governments have been able to secure the cooperation of their peoples in ways that the colonial governments could never have. In fact, a careful reading of the last twenty years reveals a series of amazingly 'tough' decisions in favor of the parks (obviously, the record is far from flawless). Second, the level of research directed toward better park management has improved dramatically. Retired British military officers with little more than a hunter's myth-dominated view of animal ecology have been replaced by professionals (African, for the most part) well-grounded in the intricacies of their task. Expertise without judgment is, of course, little better than useless. But judgment without expertise would have been positively dangerous.

Third, and perhaps most important, the national parks represent an economic resource — in particular, a source of valuable foreign exchange — that an African government ignores only at *peril* to its own existence. There is not space here for an economic lesson sufficient to explain the overwhelming importance of foreign exchange — *hard* currency — to today's young African countries. Suffice it to say that tourism-generated revenues have and will continue to have an importance to African economies that (will) rival if not surpass the earnings derived from their primary products (mineral or agricultural). There are, of course, other motivations for visiting Africa than seeing the animals. But the uniqueness of the animals resource can hardly be questioned. In purely developmental terms, the most productive use of an acre in the Masai Mara is to raise lions. The other options are not even close. In purely developmental terms, a pride of lions is worth many times an equivalent home range devoted to agriculture, even the most productive agriculture.

African governments know these things. Or, at least, the full import of this economic resource is fast sinking in. Moveover, the old learning that the Africans themselves were indifferent to their wildlife was never more than a misunderstanding (on a "less than" basis, such sentiments were basically racist rubbish). African folklore, *dominated* by the animals, speaks volumes. Ignorance is, on the other hand, hardly surprising. Ask an American child a question or two about grizzly bears. And, exploitation is hardly beyond human experience. Try the American bison. While it is true that there are pressures within African societies, as in our own, to develop in ways that are inimical to the health of the national parks, the governments and, ultimately, the peoples of Africa have it in their immediate and long-term self-interest to preserve and protect this unique heritage. The betting odds on whether that result will, in fact, occur are certainly no worse than elsewhere in the world and perhaps better — and, perhaps, with outside support, far better.

This last is an important point. A popular notion today is that Africa is a trustee of this wildlife heritage, that the animals belong to all the peoples of the earth, to the earth itself. Whatever philosophical truths can leap the hurdles of national self-interest, Africa deserves the support of the world community in exercising its guardianship.

Plate 52. The Reach of Man. Man has, it seems, the ability to reach into the sky and cast down even such a high-flier as the pelican. Captured for resale by poachers, this bird managed to escape, but the cord attached to its leg eventually caught in the treetops, hanging (upside down, but hanging nonetheless) the escapee. The subject of poaching is a controversial one in Africa. The discussion reminds the author of all the rhetoric surrounding crime in a disadvantaged neighborhood. Yes, there are compelling motivations for the behavior. The disease has causes as well as symptoms. But, whatever the long-term solution may be, if indeed any "solution" is likely, only rigorous measures will protect life today. The most severe symptom, extinction, is final.

The threat to the parks is, in fact, likely to come from within. That is, popularity breeds problems (popularity *breeds*, period). Tourism is not, unfortunately, a perfect mechanism. There is a great deal written about managing the parks — about, for example, the difficult questions of culling and other resource-management measures — and the thrust is always a balancing between laissez-faire and steps necessary to enable the environments to prosper in the short to medium-term. In the long term, as Keynes once wryly remarked, we are all dead. A sentiment of immediate importance to park administrations with a tourist facility to run — a perspective more naturalists directions . . . . in creative use of the resources, and the expansion of opportunities, not narrow restrictions. And, above all, in increased numbers of visitors. It is a truism that the parks must pay for themselves to survive. This itself will require a healthy flow of tourists. But the truth is rarely static: to survive, the parks will probably have to pay for *more* than themselves. And this will be the challenge for the future — which begins, incidentally, when you close this volume.

Plate 53. Finis.

should appreciate. More attention now needs to be paid to managing tourism. And, on this subject, the author has read very little of real value.

To the extent that professional ethologists or their allies have been drafted (or volunteered) into the task of rationalizing human intrusion, the results have been predictable: *limit* the intrusion. Forbid off-track driving, limit viewing in certain areas, and so forth. The elitist among us, and who if given half an opportunity would not take this high road, shudder at the thought of more vehicles, more dust, more *people*. The Africa experience easily becomes a secret to be shared with only a few. Thus, the circle is squared with the cynical crowd who castigate the "giant zoos." But survival, and prosperity, lie in other

Leopards at Ease

The Security of

Grooming

a Hilltop Vista

Royal Portrait

Cubs in the Rocks

Escape from the Tortured Air

A Mother with More
Than a Handful

Leopard up a Tree

Cheetah up a Tree (While Still Young)

Lions in Trees

Late Afternoon Trek to the Killing Grounds

Phillip's Cubs

On the Path to Pride Mastery

A Mother's Love

Immanuel's Good Sense

Flight Distance (the Gazelle's Perspective)
and the Beginning of Paul's Hunt

Inveterate Cat Watcher

BIBLIOGRAPHY

Bibliographical Note

What follows is a fairly comprehensive listing of popular sources for information relating to the animals included in this book. The list does not purport to be exhaustive. In the first place, the author has culled certain books that have no redeeming value whatsoever. Second, only books that are readily available, in libraries or elsewhere, are included. By "popular" is not meant a book designed solely for the mass market; many of the listed titles are sophisticated works, though the unreadable scientific treatises have been omitted. If the title does not clearly indicate the specific subject matter, the animal is included in parenthesis. If the title is not specific and there is no such parenthetical designation, the entry applies to the chapter under which it is listed as a whole.

Given the length of the listings, one could conclude that the animals benefited from exhaustive secondary materials. To the contrary, the literature, taken as a whole, is repetitive and not overwhelmingly intelligent. At least three problems are worth noting here (in a bibliographical note). First, many volumes suffer from the repetition of non-facts. Such repetition, usually quite innocent, is more dangerous than simply making things up *de novo,* because frequent repetition soon develops its own credibility. Thus, oxpeckers act as sentinels — a "fact" repeated by nearly every writer on African animals. To the extent that all noisy birds act, to a degree, as "sentinels" (providing strident warnings at times of general danger), such a statement would not be remarkable. But the "fact" is offered as the oxpeckers' contribution to a symbiotic relationship. That is, its significance is elevated to a defining facet of oxpecker behavior. Treated this way, and there is no need to repeat the book's text on this point, the assertion can survive only by blind repetition, not honest observation.

Another example of false repetition is the statement, first offered by van Lawick in the 1960s and repeated by any number of writers (some, first-rate) since, that he (van Lawick) discovered or first reported the use of stones by Egyptian vultures to break ostrich eggs. This surprising ignorance of the historical record should never have received the credence that it has: "Seemingly trustworthy settlers have assured us that vultures break the tough shells with stones." (T.R. Roosevelt in *African Game Trails,* p. 354, some fifty years earlier on what was then common knowledge among the white settlers).

Uncritical repetition also frequently loses sight of the original context. Thus, African folklore, hunter anecdote, or traveler fantasy become, in time, reportable fact.

The second problem is neo-Darwinism run wild. Considerable space was devoted to this subject in Chapter VII. This failure turns some books of potentially immense value into near caricatures. Thus John Reader and Harvey Croze, *Pyramids of Life: An Investigation of Nature's Fearful Symmetry* (Collins, 1977), where extremely lucid details of natural cycles are elevated to philosophical dogma. Another good example of the problem is Brian Bertram's *A Pride of Lions,* which book has some excellent research followed by logical speculation and conclusions. But *Pride* is capable of significant confusion as well, mostly traceable to "vulgar Darwinism." (See, for example, the discussion of predation on page 219.) And the author happens to believe that the success of someone like Jane Goodall is due in large measure to a mind uncluttered by theory and a willingness to look at data in an unbiased fashion. On the other hand, vulgar Darwinism, especially when the speculation outraces observable facts, often reaches flights of fancy equivalent to the Just-So stories. The problem is compounded by single-species researchers or writers not sufficiently grounded in animal behavior across a wide spectrum. And by the failure to test or verify conclusions in the field. In fact, most trained zoologists could do with *considerably* more field work.

The third problem is the *thinness* of the material. Despite the apparent length of the bibliography, most of the learning about African animals is supported by research that in many other fields would be regarded as terribly thin. That is, few researchers exist. The author certainly does not mean to question the bona fides of many of the researchers who operate today in Africa or who have worked there in the recent past. The dedication, in the face of innumerable difficulties and hardship, of this fraternity as a whole is legendary. Nevertheless, with the exception of certain species (mostly primate), the data on any given species is being collected by only a few people. Such a state of affairs leads to little cross-fertilization, so to speak, and exaggerates the flaws in individual methodologies. As with most subjects, the truth concerning the animals is more likely to emerge in the context of healthy specific debates. This is not an argument for quantity over quality — rather, a plea for *more quality.* Moreover, the dearth of research puts a significant burden on truth-telling. Fraud is typically considered a rare ingredient in scientific research. The author happens to believe that fudging of one kind or another is more prevalent than admitted. The argument here is that a certain background level of fraud should be expected in science as much as in any other profession, and only an active marketplace of ideas will ensure the sifting process necessary to remove the erroneous and misleading. Jane Goodall recently admitted some mistakes in her early work — and the interpretation of chimps as predominantly peace-loving has undergone significant modification as a result. At this time, we are quite dependent upon this kind of intellectual honesty. The reliance is not always necessarily well-founded or repaid in spirit.

Finally, a *broader* treatment of an animal species is particularly desirable because of the variations that exist from individual population to population — a fact often conveniently overlooked by the young biologist making definitive pronouncements based on his intensive (though geographically limited) research. Differences in behavior that may subsequently be found in another location are nearly always as important as the original research.

On a more positive note, I would like to make a number of specific recommendations. In Chapter I, several outstanding photo books were singled out and recommended. That list was supplemented by a few titles subsequently mentioned in the text. In particular, the names of Jen and Des Bartlett, Gerald Cubitt, and Mitch and Margot Reardon should come to mind for their excellent photographic work dealing with African wildlife. All are compiling some envious credits, combined, in several instances, with equally well-done texts.

A book has just appeared in English (it was previously published in Japan) by the Japanese photographer Mitsuaki Iwago, who presented a photographic portfolio in the May 1986 issue of *National Geographic*. Titled *Serengeti: Natural Order on the African Plain* (Chronicle Books), the volume simply consists of one stunning photograph after another. The text, unfortunately (but typically), is useless, but one hardly cares (it is mercifully short), so outstanding is the visual effort. As interpretive photography, Iwago's volume is likely to have set a standard for years to come.

For substantive reading, I would like to recommend again in the strongest possible terms the Myers book, *The Long African Day,* and Jonathan Scott's work, both *The Marsh Lions* (with Brian Jackman) and *The Leopard's Tale.* Surveying the list below, a few titles of monumental excellence stand out. George Schaller's *Golden Shadows* is all that a book on African wildlife could possibly be and represents the finest combination of scholarship and popular writing imaginable. It is, indeed, a pity that we could not give Schaller four hundred years and have him "do" each animal in turn. To continue to praise the Goodall books would be repetitive. I have also singled out other books in Chapter III. Cynthia Moss is justly well known for her work, *Portraits in the Wild,* a pioneering popularization. One hesitates to use the word "pioneering," I suppose, because there is very little original thought in *Portraits* (as Moss would probably be the first to admit), but pulling together the existing scientific literature and making it available to the general reading public is no small task and, to my knowledge, had not previously been attempted on this scale.

On a more general, reference-book level, I should like to credit David Macdonald (ed.), *The Encyclopedia of Mammals* (Facts on File, 1985), a superb book and surely the best of its kind (probably ever). Jonathan Kingdon's three-volume *East African Mammals,* (Academic Press, 1971–82) is frequently cited as a standard for African wildlife, but, while it should no doubt be consulted, I do not find it to be of the same caliber as the Macdonald

effort. Furthermore, no serious student of animal behavior can do without *The Oxford Companion to Animal Behavior* (edited by David McFarland, Oxford University Press, 1981), and I am greatly indebted to its clarity and exposition.

The subject of birds is of particular interest to the author, and, aside from (of course) the Karmali and Brown books, I cannot recommend too highly the book, Robert Burton, *Bird Behavior* (Alfred A. Knopf, 1985). Combining scholarship and photographs with this success is what the author is trying to do in the present volume. And to the handy, little field-guide-type volumes on birds mentioned earlier in the text, I should add John Karmali's *Beautiful Birds of Kenya* (Camerapix, 1985).

From a visual perspective, I should also like to single out the work of the artist Ugo Mochi, who is referenced a number of times below. Readers familiar with Mochi's work will perhaps recognize my zebra "logo" as being of the Mochi school. The recent book with Dorcas MacClintock, *African Images* (Charles Scribner's Sons, 1984), published just after Mochi's death, is probably the best single introduction to this master (the text by MacClintock is excellent).

To those with a more historical interest, there are two old works on the African game that even today I find instructive. One is T.R. Roosevelt and Edmund Heller, *Life-Histories of African Game-Animals,* 2 Vols. (Scribner's, 1914); the other is C.H. Stigard, *The Game of British East Africa* (Horace Cox, 1909). Stigard had any number of fantastic personal escapes and maulings from animals and was one of the colorful characters regrettably—and only reluctantly—omitted from Chapter III. Until nearly the present day, these works were more or less authoritative and were plagiarized on a regular basis by many naturalist writers.

Concerning the magazine listings, I have, of course, omitted the immense volume of scientific articles. The *African Journal of Ecology* (formerly, the *East African Wildlife Journal*) is a particularly fertile source for a serious student of African wildlife. Although a few notable exceptions were thought important enough to include (for example, the articles in *Scientific American* on birds), the references below are generally limited to *Natural History, National Geographic, Smithsonian,* and *Animal Kingdom,* the four most widely available popular magazines dealing with our subjects, and date from 1970.

As a final note, I should correct the book with respect to particular park guides. The African Wildlife Foundation has produced new versions of the old official guides to the Tanzanian parks. The author has now seen the volumes, edited by Deborah Snelson and illustrated by David Bygott and Jonathan Scott (a special bonus!), for Serengeti, Lake Manyara and Tarangire. More are planned. In the tradition of the older guides, these new books are truly superb. Finally, I neglected to mention two excellent books made available by the Zambia National Tourist Board: John Clarke, *A Guide to the National Parks* and John Hanks, *Mammals of Zambia.*

IV. The Big Cats

Adamson, George, *Bwana Game — The Life Story of George Adamson* (Collins & Harvill, 1968; published in the U.S. by Doubleday as *A Lifetime with Lions*)

Adamson, Joy, *Born Free: A Lioness of Two Worlds* (Pantheon Books, 1960)

———, *Living Free: The Story of Elsa and Her Cubs* (Harcourt, Brace & World, 1961)

———, *Forever Free: Elsa's Pride* (Collins & Harvill, 1962)

———, *The Spotted Sphinx* (Harcourt, Brace & World, 1969) (Cheetah)

———, *The Searching Spirit: Joy Adamson's Autobiography* (Harcourt Brace, 1979)

———, *Queen of Shaba: The Story of an African Leopard* (Harcourt Brace Jovanovich, 1980)

Akeley, Carl E. & Mary L. Jobe Akeley, *Lions, Gorillas and Their Neighbors* (Dodd, Mead, 1932)

Ammann, Kathrine & Karl Ammann, *Cheetah* (Avco Publishing, 1985)

Beadle, Muriel, *The Cat: History, Biology and Behavior* (Simon and Schuster, 1977)

Beebe, B.F., *African Lions and Cats* (MacKay, 1969)

Bertram, Brian, *Pride of Lions* (Charles Scribner's Sons, 1978) (also contains chapters on the leopard and cheetah)

Caras, Roger, *Mara Simba, The African Lion* (Holt, Rinehart and Winston, 1985)

Cowie, Mervyn, *I Walk With Lions* (Macmillan, 1961)

———, *The African Lion* (Golden, 1966)

Curio, Eberhard, *The Ethology of Predation* (Springer-Verlag, 1976)

Denis, Armand, *Cats of the World* (Houghton Mifflin, 1964)

Eaton, Randall L., *The Cheetah: The Biology, Ecology and Behavior of an Endangered Species* (Van Nostrand Reinhold, 1974)

———, *The Cheetah: Nature's Fastest Racer* (Dodd, Mead, 1981)

Edey, Maitland A. (text) & John Dominis (photographs), *The Cats of Africa* (Time-Life, 1968)

Ewer, R.F., *The Carnivores* (Cornell University Press, 1973)

Frame, George W. & Lory Herbison Frame, *Swift and Enduring: Cheetahs and Wild Dogs of the Serengeti* (E.P. Dutton, 1981)

Grindlay, Irene, *Velvet Paws: The Story of Mara, The Young Lioness* (Robert Hale, 1966)

Grobler, Hans, Anthony Hall-Martin, & Clive Walker, *Predators of Southern Africa* (Macmillan, 1984)

Guggisberg, C.A.W., *Simba: The Life of the Lion* (Howard Timmins, 1961)

———, *Wild Cats of the World* (Taplinger, 1975)

Haas, Emily, *Pride's Progress: The Story of a Family of Lions* (Harper & Row, 1967)

Hanby, Jeanette & David Bygott, *Lions Share: The Story of a Serengeti Pride* (Houghton Mifflin, 1982)

Jackman, Brian (text) & Jonathan Scott (photographs and drawings), *The Marsh Lions: The Story of an African Pride* (Elm Tree Books, 1982)

Jeaney, Bertram F., *Pride of Lions* (Longmans, Green, 1936)

Johnson, Martin, *Lion* (G.P. Putnam's Sons, 1929)

Kruuk, Hans, *The Spotted Hyena, A Study of Predation and Social Behavior* (University of Chicago, 1972)

McBride, Chris, *Operation White Lion* (St. Martin's Press, 1981)

———, *The White Lions of Timbavati* (Paddington, 1977)

Nett, Nancy, *The Big Cats, The Paintings of Guy Coheleach* (Harry N. Abrams, 1982)

Owens, Mark and Delia Owens, *Cry of the Kalahari* (Houghton Mufflin, 1984) (lion)

Patterson, J.H., *The Man-Eaters of Tsavo and Other East African Adventures* (Macmillan, 1907)

Pearson, John, *Hunters of the Plains* (W.H. Allen, 1979)

Pease, Alfred E., *The Book of The Lion* (John Murray, 1913)

Ricciuti, Edward R., *The Wild Cats* (Ridge Press Book, Newsweek Books, 1979)

Roosevelt, Theodore, & Edmund Heller, *Life-Histories of African Game-Animals,* Volume 1 (Scribner's, 1914)

Rudnai, Judith A., *The Social Life of The Lion* (Washington Square East, 1973)

Schaller, George B., *Serengeti: A Kingdom of Predators* (Alfred A. Knopf, 1972)

———, *The Serengeti Lion: A Study in Predator-Prey Relations* (University of Chicago, 1972)

———, *Golden Shadows, Flying Hooves* (Alfred A. Knopf, 1973)

Schick, Alice, *Serengeti Cats* (Lippincott, 1977)

Scott, Jonathan, *The Leopard's Tale* (Elm Tree Books, 1985)

Sinclair, A.R.E. & M. Norton-Griffiths (eds.), *Serengeti: Dynamics of an Ecosystem* (University of Chicago, 1979)

Singh, A., *Prince of Cats* (Jonathan Cape, 1982) (leopard)

Smuts, G.L., *Lions* (Macmillan, 1982)

Turnbull-Kemp, Peter, *The Leopard* (Howard Timmons, 1967)

Varaday, Desmond, *Gara Yaka, The Story of a Cheetah* (Ballantine, 1974)

Wells, Eric F. Vesey, *Lions Wild and Friendly* (Viking, 1934)

Wilson, Vivian, *Lions, Leopards, & Lynxes, Twenty Years with Wild Cats* (Books of Zimbabwe, 1981)

Wrogemann, Nan, *Cheetah Under the Sun* (McGraw Hill, 1975)

Articles

Abbott, Shep & Tex Fuller, "A Fresh Look at the Cheetah's Private Life," *Smithsonian* (June 1971)

Bartlett, Des & Jen Bartlett, "Family Life of Lions," *National Geographic* (December 1982)

Chadwick, Douglas H., Des Bartlett & Jen Bartlett, "Etosha: Namibia's Kingdom of Animals," *National Geographic* (March 1983)

Eisenberg, John F., "A Splendid Predator Does Its Own Thing Untroubled by Man," *Smithsonian* (September 1970) (leopard)

Estes, R.D., "Predators and Scavengers," *Natural History* (February 1967)

Frame, George W. & Lory Herbison Frame, "Cheetahs: In a Race for Survival," *National Geographic* (May 1980)

Hanby, Jeanette & David Bygott, "The Queen of Beasts," *Animal Kingdom* (June/July 1980)

Houston, Dick, "An Old African Hand Fights To Keep His Lions Wild & Free," *Smithsonian,* (July 1983)

Künkel, Reinhard, "Cheetahs — Swift Cats of the Serengeti," *GEO* (Premier Issue, Undated)

Myers, Norman, "A Leopard's Ways Prove Adaptable to Modern Haunts," *Smithsonian* (May 1982)

Pusey, Anne & Craig Packer, "Once and Future Kings," *Natural History* (August 1983)

Schaller, George B., "Life With the King of Beasts," *National Geographic* (April 1969)

———, "The Social Carnivore" (Part I), *Natural History* (February 1972)

———, "Predators of the Serengeti" (Part 2), *Natural History* (March 1972)

———, "The Gentle and Elegant Cat," *Natural History* (June/July 1970)

V. Other Noteworthy Hunters and Scavengers

Dinneen, Betty, *The Family Howl* (Macmillan, 1981) (Silver-backed jackal)

Edey, Maitland A. (text) & John Dominis (photographs), *The Cats of Africa* (Time-Life, 1968) (serval, caracal)

Fox, Michael W. (ed.), *The Wild Canids: Their Systematics, Behavioral Ecology, Evolution* (Van Nostrand Reinhold, 1975)

Guggisberg, C.A.W., *Wild Cats of the World* (Taplinger, 1975) (serval, caracal)

Hinton, Howard E. & A.M.S. Dunn, *Mongooses: Their Natural History and Behavior* (Oliver & Boyd, 1967)

Kruuk, Hans, *The Spotted Hyena: A Study of Predation and Social Behavior* (University of Chicago Press, 1972)

———, *Hyena* (Oxford University Press, 1975)

Moss, Cynthia, *Portraits in the Wild: Behavior Studies of East*

African Mammals (University of Chicago Press, 2nd ed., 1982) (Chapter VIII -Spotted hyena)

Neal, Ernest, *Uganda Quest: African Wildlife After Dark* (Taplinger, 1971) (genets, Banded mongoose)

Owens, Mark & Delia Owens, *Cry of the Kalahari* (Houghton Mifflin, 1984) (Brown hyena)

Pearson, John, *Hunters of the Plains* (W.H. Allen, 1979)

Rasa, O. Anne, *Mongoose Watch: A Family Observed* (Doubleday, 1986)

Schaller, George B., *Golden Shadows, Flying Hooves* (Alfred A. Knopf, 1973)

van Lawick, Hugo, *Solo: The Story of an African Wild Dog* (Houghton Mifflin, 1974)

   & Jane van Lawick-Goodall, *The Innocent Killers* (Houghton Mifflin, 1971) (hyenas)

Articles

Estes, Richard, "The Flamingo Eaters of Ngorongoro," *National Geographic* (October 1973)

Gould, S.J., "Hyena Myths and Realities," *Natural History* (February 1981)

Kruuk, Hans, "Hyenas, The Hunter Nobody Knows," *National Geographic* (July 1968)

Malcolm, James, "African Wild Dogs Play Every Game by Their Own Rules," *Smithsonian* (November 1980)

Moehlman, Patricia D., "Jackals of the Serengeti," *National Geographic* (December 1980)

Moss, Cynthia, "That Ugly Hyena Turns Out To Be a Superb Predator," *Smithsonian* (June 1975)

Myers, Norman, "Hunt of the Wild Dogs," *Animal Kingdom* (October 1971)

Owens, Delia & Mark Owens, "Hyenas of the Kalahari," *Natural History* (February 1980)

Pennycuick, C.J., "The Soaring Flight of Vultures," *Scientific American* (December 1973)

Rasa, O. Anne, "A Taru Life Story," *Natural History* (September 1985) (mongoose)

Rood, Jon P., "High Society," *Animal Kingdom* (April/May 1984) (mongoose)

Titson, Ronald L., "Carcass Protocol," *Natural History* (March 1983)

VI. Land Giants (And a Tiny Relative)

Beard, Peter, *The End of the Game - The Last Word from Paradise* (Doubleday, 1977) (elephant)

Bere, Rennie M., *The African Elephant* (Golden Press, 1966)

Blond, Georges, *The Elephants* (Macmillan, 1961)

Bosman, Paul (paintings and drawings) & Anthony Hall-Martin (text), *Elephants of Africa* (C. Struik, 1986)

Carrington, Richard, *Elephants: A Short Account of Their Natural History, Evolution and Influence on Mankind* (Chatto & Windus, 1958)

Carter, Nick (Bryan), *The Arm'd Rhinoceros* (Andre Deutsch, 1965)

Dagg, Anne Innis & J. Bristol Foster, *The Giraffe: Its Biology, Behavior & Ecology* (Van Nostrand Reinhold, 1976)

Davis, John Gordon, *Operation Rhino* (Joesph, 1972)

Douglas-Hamilton, Iain & Oria Douglas-Hamilton, *Among the Elephants* (Viking Press, 1975)

Eltringham, S.K., *Elephants* (Blandford Press, 1982)

Fernström, Gunnar, *Tembo* (Halls, 1966)

Freeman, Dan, *Elephants: The Vanishing Giants* (Gallery Books, 1980)

Garcia, Sanchez J.L., *Hippopotamus* (H.P. Books, 1983)

Grzimek, Bernard, *Serengeti Shall Not Die* (Hamish Hamilton, 1960)

   , *Rhinos Belong to Everybody* (Collins, 1964)

Gucwa, David & James Ehmann, *To Whom It May Concern; An Investigation of the Art of Elephants* (Norton, 1985)

Guggisberg, C.A.W., *S.O.S. Rhinos* (Andre Deutsch, 1966)

   , *Giraffes* (Golden Press, 1969)

Hanks, John, *A Struggle for Survival: The Elephant Problem* (C. Struik, 1979)

Holman, Dennis, *The Elephant People* (Murray, 1967; published in U.S. as *Massacre of the Elephants,* Holt, Rinehart & Winston, 1967)

   , *Elephants at Sundown: The Story of Bill Woodley* (W.H. Allen, 1978)

Jolly, W.P., *Jumbo* (Constable, 1976)

Künkel, Reinhard, *Elephants* (Harry N. Abrams, 1982)

Laws, Richard M., *Elephants and Men in East Africa* (University of Saskatchewan, 1970)

   , I.S.C. Parker & R.C.B. Johnstone, *Elephants and Their Habitats* (Clarendon Press, 1975)

Leslie-Melville, Jock & Betty Leslie-Melville, *Raising Daisy Rothschild* (Simon & Schuster, 1977) (giraffe)

MacClintock, Dorcas (text) & Ugo Mochi (illustrations), *A Natural History of Giraffes* (Charles Scribner's Sons, 1973)

Martin, Esmond Bradley & Chrysse Bradley Martin, *Run Rhino Run* (Chatto & Windus, 1982)

Mloszewski, Mark J., *The Behavior and Ecology of the African Buffalo* (Cambridge University Press, 1983)

Moss, Cynthia, *Portraits in the Wild: Behavior Studies of East African Mammals* (University of Chicago Press, 2nd ed., 1982) (Chapter I - elephant, Chapter II -giraffe, Chapter III - Black rhinoceros)

Muldoon, Guy, *The Trumpeting Herd* (Rupert Hart-Davis, 1957; with drawings by Ralph Thompson) (elephants)

Murray, Neil, *The Love of Elephants* (Octopus Books, 1976)

Parker, Ian & Mohamed Amin, *Ivory Crisis* (Chatto & Windus, 1983)

Player, Ian, *The White Rhino Saga* (Stein and Day, 1973)

Schenkel, R., *Ecology and Behavior of the Black Rhinoceros* (Paul Parey, 1969)

Scullard, H.H., *The Elephant in the Greek and Roman World* (Cornell University, 1974)

Sheldrick, Daphne, *The Tsavo Story* (Harville Press, 1973) (elephant)

   , *An Elephant Called Eleanor* (Dent, 1980)

Sikes, Sylvia K., *The Natural History of the African Elephant* (Weidenfeld & Nicolson, 1971)

Sinclair, Anthony R.E., *The African Buffalo: A Study of Resource Limitation of Populations* (University of Chicago, 1977)

Spinage, C.A., *The Book of the Giraffe* (Collins, 1968)

Sutherland, James, *The Adventures of an Elephant Hunter* (Macmillan, 1912)

Torgersen, Don Arthur, *Giraffe Hooves and Antelope Horns* (Children's Press, 1982)

Wilson, Derek & Peter Ayerst, *White Gold: The Story of African Ivory* (Taplinger, 1976)

Articles

Allaway, James, "The African Elephant's Drinking Problem," *Natural History* (April 1981)

Animal Kingdom (February/March 1980) (entire issue devoted to elephants)

Carr, III, Archie, "The Elephant and the I-Beam," *Animal Kingdom* (August/September 1982)

Douglas-Hamilton, Iain & Oria Douglas-Hamilton, "Africa's Elephants - Can They Survive?" *National Geographic* (November 1980)

Douglas-Hamilton, Oria & Iain, "Africa's Elephants, Can They Survive," *National Geographic* (November 1980)

Dozier, Thomas, "Our Elephant, How It Came Here," *Smithsonian* (March 1975)

Fisher, Allan C., Jr. (text) & Thomas Nebbia (photos), "African Wildlife: Man's Threatened Legacy," *National Geographic* (February 1972)

Foster, Bristol, Bob Campbell, & Thomas Nebbia (photos), "Africa's Gentle Giants," *National Geographic* (September 1977)

Goddard, John, "The Black Rhinoceros," *Natural History* (April 1973)

Hartmann, Frants, "Elephant Walk," *Animal Kingdom* (December 1973)

, "Saving the African Rhino," *Animal Kingdom* (February 1973)

Haynes, Gary, "Where Elephants Die," *Natural History* (June 1987)

Hiley, Peter, "How the Elephant Keeps Its Cool," *Natural History* (December 1975)

Isaac, Hussein Adan, "An African Ethic of Conservation," *Natural History* (November 1976)

Kaplan, Marion, "In East Africa, Poaching Worsens," *Smithsonian* (September 1974)

Langman, Vaughn, "A Poignant Sequel about Giraffes," *Smithsonian* (April 1982)

Lewis, Dale M., "A Problem of Mammoth Proportions," *Animal Kingdom* (March/April 1986)

Martin, Esmond Bradley, "The Conspicuous Consumption of Rhinos" (I), *Animal Kingdom* (February/March 1981)

Martin, Esmond Bradley, "The Conspicuous Consumption of Rhinos" (II), *Animal Kingdom* (April/May 1981)

Martin, Esmond Bradley (text) & Jim Brandenburg (photos), "They're Killing Off the Rhino," *National Geographic* (March 1984)

Moss, Cynthia J., "The Two and Only," *Animal Kingdom* (December 1980/January 1981)

Myers, Norman, "A Naturalist at Large: The People Crunch Comes to East Africa," *Natural History* (January 1973)

Patterson, Carolyn Bennett, "Rescuing The Rothschild," *National Geographic* (September 1977)

Pratt, David M. & Virginia A. Pratt, "Big Baby," *Animal Kingdom* (June/July 1980) (giraffe)

Reader, John, "Too Many Elephants: They Can Be Shot or Allowed To Starve," *Smithsonian* (July 1972)

Redmond, Ian, "Underground Elephants," *Animal Kingdom* (December 1984/January 1985)

Ricciuti, Edward R., "The Ivory Wars," *Animal Kingdom* (February/March 1980)

Root, Joan & Alan Root, "Mzima, Kenya's Spring of Life," *National Geographic* (September 1971)

Schaaf, Dietrich, "Elephants, Fire and the Environment," *Animal Kingdom* (April 1972)

Sikes, Sylvia, "Baby Elephants Cavort in Africa's Surviving Herds," *Smithsonian* (December 1970)

Weaver, Henry, "Animals and Man in East Africa, *Smithsonian* (August 1970)

Western, David, "Monitoring Africa's Megafauna," *Animal Kingdom* (May/June 1985)

VII. The Remaining Ungulates

Bateman, Graham (ed.), *All the World's Animals: Hoofed Mammals* (Torstar Books, 1984)

Bere, Rennie M., *Antelopes* (Arco Publishing, 1970)

Bronson, Wilfrid S., *Horns and Antlers* (Harcourt, Brace, 1942)

Cloudsley-Thompson, J., *Animal Migration* (Putnam, 1978)

Cronwright-Schreiner, S.C., *The Migratory Springbucks of South Africa* (T. Fisher Unwin, 1925)

Cumming, D.H.M., *A Field Study of the Ecology & Behaviour of Warthog* (Salisbury, 1975)

Dawkins, Richard, *The Selfish Gene* (Oxford University, 1976)

Fraser, A.F., *Reproductive Behavior in Ungulates* (Academic Press, 1968)

Groves, Colin P., *Horses, Asses and Zebras in the Wild* (David & Charles, Newton Abbot, 1974)

Jarman, Martha, V., *Impala Social Behavior* (Parey, 1979)

Jungius, Hartmut, *The Biology of the Reedbuck* (Paul Parey, 1971)

Leuthold, Walter, *African Ungulates — A Comparative Review of Their Ethology and Behavioral Ecology* (Springer-Vertag, 1977)

Lind, Edna M. & M.E.S. Morrison, *East African Vegetation* (Longmans, 1974)

McCarthy, M.L., *The Life of Animals with Hooves* (Silver Burdett, 1979)

MacClintock, Dorcas (text) & Ugo Mochi (drawings), *A Natural History of Zebras* (Charles Scribner's Sons, 1976)

, *Hoofed Mammals of the World* (Charles Scribner's Sons, 1953)

, *African Images* (Charles Scribner's Sons, 1984)

Mochi, Ugo, & T. Donald Carter (text), *Hoofed Mammals of the World* (Charles Scribner's Sons, 1971)

Moss, Cynthia, *Portraits in the Wild: Behavior Studies of East African Mammals* (University of Chicago Press, 2nd ed., 1982) (Chapter IV — zebras; Chapter V — antelopes)

Neary, John, *Wild Herds* (Time-Life Films, 1977)

Pratt, D.J. & M.D. Gwynne (eds.), *Rangeland Management and Ecology in East Africa* (Hodder & Stroughton, 1977)

Reader, J. & H. Groze, *Pyramids of Life* (Collins, 1977)

Scuro, Vincent, *Wonders of Zebras* (Dodd, Mead, 1983)

Shirka, Peter & Wendell Swank, *African Antelope* (Winchester Press, 1971)

Sinclair, A.R.E. & M. Norton-Griffiths (eds.), *Serengeti: Dynamics of an Ecosystem* (University of Chicago Press, 1979)

Spinage, Clive A., *A Territorial Antelope — The Uganda Waterbuck* (Academic Press, 1982)

Torgersen, Don Arthur, *Giraffe Hooves and Antelope Horns* (Children's Press, 1982)

Walther, Fritz R., Elizabeth C. Mungall & Gerald H. Grau, *Gazelles and Their Relatives - A Study in Territorial Behavior* (Noyes Publications, 1983)

Zaloumis, E.A. & Robert Cross, *A Field Guide to the Antelope of Southern Africa* (Wildlife Society of South Africa, 1974)

Articles

Bandler, Michael J., "I Call Myself an Evolutionist," *Smithsonian* (December 1970)

Bell, Richard & Jeremy Grimsdell, "The Black Lechwe Is an Antelope To Be Preserved," *Smithsonian* (March 1973)

Bell, Richard H.V., "A Grazing Ecosystem in the Serengeti," *Scientific American* (July 1971)

Bryceson, Derek N., "Visions of Paradise," *Animal Kingdom* (June/July 1980)

Campbell, Sheldon, "Noah's Ark in Tomorrow's Zoo; Animals Are A-Comin', Two by Two," *Smithsonian* (March 1978)

Dunbar, Robin, "Monogany on the Rocks," *Natural History* (November 1985)

Estes, Richard D., "Showdown in Ngorongoro Crater," *Natural History* (October 1973)

, "The Most Splendid Antelope Is Also One of the Least Safe," *Smithsonian* (January 1972)

, "Zebras Offer Clues to the Way Wild Horses Once Lived," *Smithsonian* (November 1974)

Heminway, John, "Despite Long Odds, Mighty Herds Still Plunge Across the Serengeti," *Smithsonian* (February 1987)

Hillman, Jesse Christopher, "The Bongos of Banganai," *Animal Kingdom* (March/April 1986)

Jarman, Mattie, "The Impala Imperative," *Animal Kingdom* (April/May 1976)

Kesse, Dmitri, "The River Across the Serengeti — A Yearly Floodtide of Wildebeest," *Smithsonian* (August 1971)

Myers, Norman, "Zaire: Nation with A Wild Future," *Animal Kingdom* (April/May 1976)

Pitman, Charles Robert Senhouse, *Common Antelopes* (Longman's, Green, 1956)

Pitman, Dick, "The Best-Kept Secret of Africa," *Animal Kingdom* (April/May 1983)

Reader, John, "A Cattle Trek, across the Wild Wide Kalahari," *Smithsonian* (April 1976)

Reader, John, "The Violent Rescue of Grevy's Zebras — a Controversial Operation," *Smithsonian* (January 1979)

Ricciuti, Edward R., "Paradise Lost," *Animal Kingdom* (June/July 1984)

Schaller, George B., "Predators of the Serengeti: Conclusion, The Endless Race of Life," *Natural History* (April 1972)

Sidney, Jasmine, *The Past and Present Distribution of Some African Ungulates* (Zoological Society of London, 1965)

Sinclair, A.R.E., "The Wildebeest Triangle," *Animal Kingdom*

(June/July 1984)

Talbot, Lee M., "Wildlife Quotas Sometimes Ignored the Real World," *Smithsonian* (May 1977)

Weaver, Henry, "Animals and Man in East Africa, *Smithsonian* (August 1970), pp. 32

Whittow, G. Causey, "Short Ungulates," *Natural History* (May 1978)

VIII. Primates and Reptiles

Abegglen, Jean-Jacques, *On Socialization in Hamadryas Baboons* (Bucknell University Press, 1984)

Adamson, Joy, *Friends from the Forest* (Harcourt Brace Jovanovich, 1981) (colobus monkey)

Akeley, Carl E., *In Brightest Africa* (Doubleday, Page, 1923) (Chapters XI–XIV)

    & Mary L. Jobe Akeley, *Lions, Gorillas and Their Neighbors* (Dodd, Mead, 1932)

Akeley, Delia J., *"J.T., Jr.," The Biography of an African Monkey* (Macmillan, 1932).

    , *Jungle Portraits* (Macmillan, 1930) (Chapter II: Gorillas and Monkeys)

Altmann, Jeanne, *Baboon Mothers and Infants* (Harvard University Press, 1980)

Altmann, Stuart A. (ed.), *Social Communication Among Primates* (University of Chicago Press, 1967)

    & Jeanne Altmann, *Baboon Ecology: African Field Research* (University of Chicago Press, 1970)

Annixter, Jane & Paul Annixter, *Monkeys and Apes* (F. Watts, 1976)

Ardrey, Robert, *The Territorial Imperative* (Atheneum, 1966) (primates)

Attenborough, David, *Zoo Quest to Madagascar* (Lutterworth Press, 1961)

Bannister, Tony & Franklin Russell, *Wild Creatures: A Pageant of the Untamed* (Simon and Schuster, 1975)

Baumgärtel, Walter, *Up Among the Mountain Gorillas* (Hawthorn Books, 1976)

Beebe, Burdetta Faye, *African Apes* (McKay, 1969)

Benchley, Belle J., *My Friends the Apes* (Little, Brown and Company, 1942)

Bourne, Geoffrey Howard (ed.), *Progress in Ape Research* (Academic Press, 1977)

    & Maury Cotten, *The Gentle Giants: The Gorilla Story* (Putnam, 1975)

Bradley, Mary Hastings, *On the Gorilla Trail* (D. Appleton, 1922)

Bramblett, C.A., *Patterns of Primate Behavior* (Mayfield Publishing, 1976)

Brewer, Stella, *The Forest Dwellers* (Collins, 1978)

Carr, Archie, *The Reptiles* (Time-Life Books, Inc., 1980)

Chalmers, Neil, *Social Behavior in Primates* (University Park Press, 1979)

Cloudsley-Thompson, J.L., *Crocodiles and Alligators* (Raintree Childrens Books, 1980)

Clutton-Brock, T.H. (ed.), *Primate Ecology: Studies of Feeding and Ranging Behavior in Lemurs and Apes* (Academic Press, 1977)

Desmond, Andrian J., *The Ape's Reflexion* (Dial Press, 1979)

DeVore, Iren (ed.), *Primate Behavior: Field Studies of Monkeys and Apes* (Holt, Rinehart & Winston, 1965)

Dixson, A.F., *The Natural History of the Gorilla* (Columbia University Press, 1981)

Doyle, G.A. & R.D. Martin (eds.), *The Study of Prosimian Behavior* (Academic Press, 1979)

DuChaillu, Paul Belloni, *Exploration and Adventures in Equatorial Africa* Harper, 1861)

    , *Stories of the Gorilla Country* (Harper, 1867)

Easterbrook, Mark S., *A Book of East Africa Snakes* (Coast Publicity, 1972)

Eimerl, S. & I. DeVore, *The Primates* (Time-Life, 1965)

Eri, Vincent, *The Crocodile* (Jacaronda Press, 1972)

Fitzsimons, V.F.M., *A Field Guild to the Snakes of Southern Africa* (Collins, 1970)

    , *Pythons and Their Ways* (George Harrap, 1930)

    , *Snakes of Southern Africa* (MacDonald, 1962)

Fobes, L. & James E. King (eds.), *Primate Behavior* (Academic Press, 1982)

Fossey, Dian, *Gorillas in the Mist* (Houghton Mifflin, 1983)

Freeman, Dan, *The Great Apes* (Putman's, 1979)

Garner, R.L. *Gorillas & Chimpanzees* (Osgood, McIlvaine, 1986)

Geddes, Henry, *Gorilla* (Andrew-Melrose, 1955)

Ghiglieri, Michael Patrick, *The Chimpanzee of Kibale Forest* (Columbia University Press, 1984)

Goodall, J. van Lawick & Hugo van Lawick, *Innocent Killers* (Houghton Mifflin, 1970)

Goodall, Jane, *The Chimpanzees of Gombe, Patterns of Behavior* (Belknap Press of Harvard University Press, 1986)

    , *In the Shadow of Man* (Collins, 1971)

Graham, Alistair & Peter Beard, *Eyelids of Morning: The Mingled Destinies of Crocodiles and Man* (New York Graphic Society, 1973)

Graham, C.E., (ed.), *Reproductive Biology of Great Apes* (New York: Academic Press, 1981)

Guggisberg, C.A.W., *Crocodiles: Their Natural History, Folklore and Conservation* (Stackpole Books, 1972)

Hamburg, David A. & Elizabeth R. McCown (eds.), *The Great Apes* (Cummings, 1979)

Healey, Tim, *The Life of Monkeys and Apes* (Silver Burdette, 1979)

Heatwole, H., *Reptile Ecology* (University of Queensland, 1976)

Ionides, C.J.P., *Mambas and Man-Eaters* (Holt, Rinehart, & Winston, 1966)

Isemonger, Richard M., *Snakes of Africa* (Books of Africa, 1968)

Itani, J., *Chasing Wild Chimpanzees* (Chikuma-Shobo, 1970)

Jay, Phyllis C., *Primates: Studies in Adaptation and Variability* (Holt, Rinehart & Winston, 1968)

Jolly, Alison, *Lemur Behavior: A Malagasy Field Study* (University of Chicago Press, 1966)

    , *The Evolution of Primate Behavior,* 2nd ed., (Macmillan, 1985)

    , *A World Like Our Own: Man and Nature in Madagascar* (Yale University Press, 1980; photographs by Russ Kinne)

Kavangh, M., *A Complete Guide to Monkeys, Apes and other Primates* (Jonathan Cape, 1983)

Kevles, Bettyann, *Thinking Gorillas, Testing and Teaching the Greatest Apes* (Dutton, 1980)

    , *Watching the Wild Apes* (Dutton, 1976)

Köhler, Wolfgang, *The Mentality of Apes* (Routledge and Kegan Paul, 1925; reprinted, Liveright, 1976)

Kummer, Hans, *Primate Societies: Group Techniques of Ecological Adaption* (Aldine Atherton, 1971)

Lane, Margaret, *Life With Ionides* (Viking Press, 1963)

Lorenz, Konrad, *On Aggression,* (trans. M.K. Wilson; Harcourt, Brace and World, 1963)

Maple, Terry L. & Michael P. Hott, *Gorilla Behavior* (Van Nostrand Reinhold, 1982)

Marais, Eugene N., *My Friends the Baboons* (Methuen, 1939)

    , *The Soul of the Ape* (Atheneum, 1969)

Martin, R.D., G.A. Doyle & A.C. Walker (eds.), *Prosimian Biology* (Duckworth, 1974)

Mattison, Christopher, *Snakes of the World* (Facts on File, 1986)

Merfield, F.G., & H. Miller, *Gorillas Were My Neighbours* (Longmans, 1956)

Midgley, M., *Beast and Man: The Roots of Human Nature* (Cornell University Press, 1978)

Minton, S.A. & M.R. Minton, *Venomous Reptiles* (George Allen and Unwin, 1971)

Morris, Ramona & Desmond Morris, *Men and Apes* (Hutchinson, 1966)

Moss, Cynthia, *Portraits in the Wild: Behavior Studies of East

African Mammals (University of Chicago Press, 2nd ed., 1982) (Chapter VI — baboons)

Napier, J.R. & P.H. Napier (eds.), *Handbook of Living Primates* (Academic Press, 1967)

, *Old World Monkeys, Evolution, Systematics, and Behavior* (Academic Press, 1970)

, *The Natural History of the Primates* (M.I.T. Press, 1985)

, *Monkeys Without Tails* (Taplinger, 1976)

Neill, Wilfred T., *The Last of the Ruling Reptiles* (Columbia University Press, 1971) (crocodiles)

Nicki, Peter, *The Crocodile* (Jonathan Cape, 1976)

Osman Hill, W.C., *Evolutionary Biology of the Primates* (Academic Press, 1972)

Parker, H.W. & A.G.C. Grandison, *Snakes — A Natural History* (Cornell University, 2nd ed., 1977)

Patterson, Francine & Eugene Linden, *The Education of Koko* (Holt, Rinehart, and Winston, 1981)

Poirier, F.E. (ed.), *Primate Socialization* (Random House, 1972)

Pooley, Tony, *Discoveries of a Crocodile Man* (Collins, 1982)

Porter, Kenneth E., *Herpetology* (Saunders, 1972)

Potous, Paul L., *My Enemy, the Crocodile* (Wilfred Funk, 1957)

, *No Tears for the Crocodile* (Hutchinson, 1956)

Premack, D. & A.J. Premack, *The Mind of an Ape* (Norton, 1983)

Reynolds, P.C., *On the Evolution of Human Behavior* (University of California Press, 1981)

Reynolds, Vernon, *The Apes, the Gorilla, Chimpanzee, Orangutan, and Gibbon* (Dutton, 1967)

, *The Apes* (Cassell, 1968)

, *Budongo: An Africa Forest and its Chimpanzees* (Natural History Press, 1965)

Rose, Walter, *The Reptiles and Amphibians of South Africa* (Maskaw Miller, 1962)

Rumbaugh, Duane M., *Language Learning by a Chimpanzee: The Lana Project* (Academic Press, 1977)

Sanderson, Ivan T., *The Monkey Kingdom* (Hanover Press, 1957)

Schaller, George B., *The Mountain Gorilla: Ecology and Behavior* (University of Chicago Press, 1963)

, *The Year of the Gorilla* (University of Chicago Press, 1964)

Schultz, A., *The Life of Primates* (Weidenfield & Nicolson, 1969)

Sebeok, Thomas A. & Jean Umiker-Sebeok (eds.), *Speaking of Apes, A Critical Anthology of Two-Way Communication with Man* (Plenum Press, 1980).

Sebeok, T., (ed.), *How Animals Communicate* (Indiana University Press, 1976)

Shuttlesworth, Dorothy Edwards, *The Story of Monkeys, Great Apes, and Small Apes* (Doubleday, 1972)

Simons, E.L., *Primate Evaluation* (Macmillan, 1972)

Smith, Euclid O. (ed.), *Social Play in Primates* (Academic Press, 1978)

Smuts, Barbara B. et al, (ed.) *Primate Societies* (University of Chicago Press, 1986)

, *Sex and Friendship in Baboons* (Aldune Publishing, 1985)

Struhsaker, Thomas T., *The Red Colobus Monkey* (University of Chicago Press, 1975)

Sussman, R.W. (ed.), *Primate Ecology: Problem-Oriented Field Studies* (John Wiley, 1979)

Tattersall, Ian, *Lemur Biology* (Plenum Press, 1979)

, *Man's Ancestors* (Murray, 1970)

, *The Primates of Madagascar* (Columbia University Press, 1982)

Taub, David M. (ed.), *Primate Paternalism* (Van Nostrand Reinhold, 1984)

Temerlin, M.K., *Lucy: Growing Up Human* (Science and Behavior Books, 1975)

Terrace, Herbert S., *Nim* (Knopf, 1979)

Tylinek, Erich & Gotthart Berger, *Monkeys and Apes* (Arco Publishing, 1985)

Visser, John, *Common Snakes of South Africa* (Purnell 1979)

De Waal, Frans, *Chimpanzee Politics: Power and Sex among Apes* (Harper & Row, 1982)

Watson, Lyall, *Lightning Bird: The Story of One Man's Journey into Africa's Past* (Simon & Schuster, 1983) (snakes)

Willoughby, D.P., *All About Gorillas* (Barnes, 1979)

Wykes, Alan, *Snake Man* (H. Hamilton, 1980)

Yerkes, Robert M., *Almost Human* (Century, 1925)

, *Chimpanzees: A Laboratory Colony* (Yale University Press, 1943)

Yerkes, Robert M. & Ada W. Yerkes, *The Great Apes, A Study of Anthropoid Life* (Yale University Press, 1929)

Zim, Herbert Spencer, *Monkeys* (Morrow 1955)

& James Gordon Irving (illustrator), *Alligators and Crocodiles* (Morrow, 1952)

Zuckerman, Solly Z.B., *The Social Life of Monkeys and Apes* (Harcourt, Brace, 1981)

Articles

Bandler, Michael J. & Robert Archy, ''I Call Myself an Evolutionist'' *Smithsonian* (December 1970)

Fletemeyer, John, ''A World of Their Own,'' *Animal Kingdom* (February/March 1978)

Fossey, Dian, ''Making Friends With Mountain Gorillas,'' *National Geographic* (January 1970)

, ''More Years With Mountain Gorillas,'' *National Geographic* (October 1971)

, ''The Imperiled Mountain Gorilla,'' *National Geographic* (April 1981)

Goodall, Jane, ''Life and Death at Gombe,'' *National Geographic* (May 1979)

, ''My Life Among Wild Chimpanzees,'' *National Geographic* (August 1963)

, ''New Discoveries Among Wild Chimpanzees,'' *National Geographic* (December 1965)

Gore, Rick (text) & Jonathon Blair (photos), ''A Bad Time to be a Crocodile,'' *National Geographic* (January 1978)

Harding, R.S.O. & Shirley C. Strum, ''The Predatory Baboons of Kekopey,'' *Natural History* (March 1976)

Hausfater, Glenn & Reed Sutherland, ''Little Things that Tick off Baboons,'' *Natural History* (February 1984)

Homewood, Katherine, ''A Well-Adjusted Monkey'' *Animal Kingdom* (December 1977, January 1978)

& Alan Rodgers, ''Treasures of Tanzanian Forest,'' *Animal Kingdom* (September/October 1985)

Jolly, Allison, ''Some Tall Tails: Remarkable Lemurs of Madagascar,'' *Smithsonian* (November 1978)

Kordlandt, A., ''Chimpanzees in the Wild,'' *Scientific American* (May 1962)

Luft, John & Jeanne Altmann, ''Mother Baboon,'' *Natural History* (September 1982)

Marsh, Clive, ''Patch of River, Ray of Hope,'' *Animal Kingdom* (December 1977, January 1978)

Martin, Robert D. & Simon K. Bearder, ''Radio Bush Baby,'' *Natural History* October 1979)

Milton, Oliver M.B., ''The Last Stronghold of the Mountain Gorilla in East Africa,'' *Animal Kingdom* (March/April 1957)

Patterson, Francine & Ronald H. Cohn, Ph.D., ''Conversations with a Gorilla,'' *National Geographic* (October 1978)

Rock, Maxine A., ''Gorilla Mothers Need some Help from their Friends,'' *Smithsonian* (July 1978)

, ''It's not easy to become a good Gorilla Mother,'' *Smithsonian* (September 1973)

Smuts, Barbara, ''What Are Friends For,'' *Natural History* (February 1987)

Starin, E.D., ''Monkey Moves,'' *Natural History* (September 1981)

Strum, Shirley C., ''Life With the Pumphouse Gang,'' *National Geographic* (May 1975)

, ''Baboons May be Smarter Than People,'' *Animal Kingdom* (April 1985)

, ''The Pumphouse Gang and the Great Crop Raids,'' *Animal Kingdom* (October/November 1984)

Stuart, Michael D., ''Island of the Lemur,'' *Animal Kingdom*

(February/March 1985)

Susman, Randall, "Acrobatic Pygmy Chimpanzees," *Natural History* (September 1980)

Tattersall, Ian, "Of Lemurs and Men," *Natural History* (March 1972)

Teleki, Geza & Lori Baldwin, "Breeding Programs Aim to Keep this Planet of the Apes," *Smithsonian* (January 1975)

Veit, Peter G., "Gorilla Society" *Natural History* (March 1982)

Vessels, Jane (text) & Ronald H. Cohn (photos), "Koko's Kitten," *National Geographic* (January 1985)

Washburn, Sherwood L. & Irwin DeVore, "The Social Life of Baboons," *Scientific American* (June 1961)

IX. The Birds

Adamson, Joy, *Friends From the Forest* (Harcourt Brace Jovanovich, 1981) (Verreaux's eagle owls)

Alston, Madeleine, *Wanderings of a Bird-Lover in Africa* (H.I.G. Witherby, 1937)

Benson, Constantine W., R.K. Brooke & Michael P. Stuart Irwin, *The Birds of Zambia* (Collins, 1971)

Boag, David, *The Kingfisher* (Blandford Press, 1982)

Britton, P.L. (ed.), *Birds of East Africa* (East Africa Natural History Society, 1980)

Brown, Leslie, *African Birds of Prey* (Houghton Mifflin, 1971)
, *The Mystery of the Flamingos* (East African Publishing House, 1973)
, *The African Fish Eagle* (Purnell, 1980)

Brown, Leslie & Dean Amadon, *Eagles, Hawks and Falcons of the World* (McGraw-Hill, 1968)

Brown, Leslie & Rena Fennessey, *Birds of the African Bush* (Collins, 1975)
, *Birds of the African Waterside* (Collins, 1979)

Brown, L., E. Urban & K. Newman, *The Birds of Africa* (Academic, 1982)

Burton, John A. & Philip Burton, et al. (eds.), *Owls of the World* (Dutton, 1973)

Clancey, P.A., *The Birds of Natal and Zululand* (Oliver & Boyd, 1964)

Cowles, Raymond B., *Zulu Journal: Field Notes of a Naturalist in South Africa* (University of California Press, 1959)

Curry-Lindahl, Kai, *Bird Migration in Africa* (Academic Press, 1981)

Dorst, J., *The Migration of Birds* (Houghton Mifflin, 1962)

Eastman, R., *The Kingfisher* (Collins, 1969)

Friedman, H., *The Honey-Guides* (Los Angeles County Museum, 1963)

Greenwalt, Crawford H., *Bird Song: Acoustics and Physiology* (Smithsonian Institution Press, 1968)

Griffin, Donald R., *Bird Migration* (Dover Publications, 1974)

Grossman, M.L. & J. Hamlet, *Birds of Prey of the World* (Cassell, 1965)

Hancock, J. & H. Elliott, *The Herons of the World* (London Editions, 1973)

Hinde, R.A., *Bird Vocalizations* (Cambridge University Press, 1969)

Hortshorne, C., *Born to Sing* (Indiana University Press, 1973)

Jackson, Frederick J., *Game Birds of Kenya & Uganda* (Williams & Norgate, 1926)

Karmali, John, *Birds of Africa* (Viking Press, 1980)

Moreau, R.E., *The Bird Faunas of Africa and Its Islands* (Academic Press, 1966)

MacDonald, Malcom, *Treasure of Kenya* (G.P. Putnam's Sons, 1966; photography by Christina Loke)

Newman, Kenneth B., *Birds of Southern Africa: Kruger National Park* (Macmillan, 1983)

Pasquier, R.F., *An Introduction to Ornithology* (Houghton Mifflin, 1977)

Penny, Malcolm, *The Birds of Seychelles and the Outlying Islands* (Collins, 1974)

Robert, Austin, *Robert's Birds of Southern Africa* (McLachlan, G.R. and R. Liversidge rev. ed., J. Voelcker Bird Book Fund, 1985)

Rowan, M.K., *The Doves, Parrots, Louries, and Cuckoos of Southern Africa* (Croom Helm Ltd., 1983)

Scott, Peter, *The World Atlas of Birds* (Random House, 1974)

Steyn, Peter, *Eagle Days* (Sable Publishers Limited, 1974)

Thorpe, W.H., *Bird Song* (University Press, 1961)

Tuck, G.S. & Hermann Heinzel, *A Field Guide to the Seabirds of South Africa* (Collins, 1980)

Turner, Ann Warren, *Vultures* (David McKay Company, 1973)

Van Someren, Vernon D., *A Bird Watcher in Kenya* (Oliver & Boyd, 1958)

van Tyne, Josselyn & Andrew J. Berger, *Fundamentals of Ornithology* (Wiley, 2nd ed., 1976)

Welty, J.C., *The Life of Birds* (Saunders, 2nd ed., 1975)

Zim, Herbert S., *Ostriches* (William Morrow, 1958)

Articles

Emlen, Stephen T., "The Stellar-Orientation System of a Migratory Bird," *Scientific American* (August 1975)

Emlen, Stephen T. & Natalie J. Demong, "Bee-eaters of Baharini," *Natural History* (October 1984)

Frame, George W., "Topknots and Tails," *Animal Kingdom* (April 1985) (Crowned crane)

Greenwalt, Crawford H., "How Birds Sing," *Scientific American* (November 1969)

Hailman, Jack P., "How an Instinct is Learned," *Scientific American* (December 1969)

Heminway, John, "An African Bird Makes Its Move Around the World," *Smithsonian* (May 1987) (Cattle egret)

Hess, Eckhard H., "'Imprinting' in a Natural Laboratory," *Scientific American* (August 1972)

Hurxthal, Lewis M., "Our Gang, Ostrich Style," *Natural History* (December 1986)

Kahl, M. Philip, "East Africa's Majestic Flamingoes," *National Geographic* (February 1970)

Kahl, M. Philip, "The Pink Tide," *Natural History* (May 1972)

Keeton, William T., "The Mystery of Pigeon Homing," *Scientific American* (December 1974)

Nicolai, Jürgen, "Mimicry in Parasitic Birds," *Scientific American* (October 1974)

Pasquier, Roger and Carl Jones, "The Lost and Lonely Birds of Mauritius," *Natural History* (March 1982)

Pennycuick, C.J., "The Soaring Flight of Vultures," *Scientific American* (December 1973)

Rahn, Hermann, Amos Ar & Charles V. Paganelli, "How Bird Eggs Breathe," *Scientific American* (February 1979)

Root, Joan & Alan Root, "Inside a Hornbill's Walled-Up Nest," *National Geographic* (1969)

Sauer, E.G.F., "Celestial Navigation by Birds," *Scientific American* (August 1958)

Schmidt-Nielson, Knut, "Salt Glands," *Scientific American* (January 1959)

Scholz, Christopher H., "Rifting in the Okauango Delta," *Natural History* (February 1976)

Stettner, Laurence Jay & Kenneth A. Matyniak, "The Brain of Birds," *Scientific American* (June 1968)

Storer, John H., "Bird Aerodynamics, *Scientific American* (April 1952)

Taylor, T.G., "How an Eggshell is Made," *Scientific American* (March 1970)

Temple, Stanley A., "The Seychelles Try Harder," *Animal Kingdom* (February/March 1986)

Thorpe, W.H., "The Language of Birds," *Scientific American* (October 1956)
, "Duet-Singing Birds," *Scientific American* (August 1973)

Tucker, Vance A., "The Energetics of Bird Flight," *Scientific American* (May 1969)

Welty, Carl, "Birds as Flying Machines," *Scientific American* (March 1955)
, "The Geography of Birds," *Scientific American* (July 1957)

ENCYCLOGPIDA BUSINESS WEEK

SAFARIST'S GUIDE TO KISWAHILI

[Note: Pronounce exactly as written, voice every syllable — vowels are syllabic; consonants are sometimes combined in unusual-looking ways and pronounced as one syllable — and *slightly* stress the penultimate syllable. One can manage well by stressing all syllables equally, without emphasis. Africans will appreciate the effort. The letter '*m*' is a frequent prefix letter and is pronounced as one syllable with the letter or letters immediately following — say "m" quickly, not "um" (thus, *mzee* sounds like "*mzay-ay*"). Kiswahili has many local variations, but what is given below is widely accepted.]

Mammals

Aardvark: *korongo* (see also "stork")
Antelope: *pofu* or *kulungu*
  small antelope: *paa*
Ape: *nyani*
Baboon: *nyani*
Bat: *popo*
Bat-eared fox: *mbweha masikio*
Blue monkey: *kima*
Bongo: *bongo* or *dongoro*
Buffalo: *mbogo* or *nyati*
Bush-baby: *komba* or *komba kubwa*
Bushpig: *nguruwe* or *nguruwe mwitu*
Camel: *ngamia*
Cape Hunting dog (see "Wild dog")
Caracal: *simba mangu*
Cat: *paka*
Cattle: *ng'ombe*
Cheetah: *duma*
Chimpanzee: *sokomutu* or *soko mtu*
Civet: *fungo* or *ngawa*
Colobus monkey: *mbega* or *mweupe*
Dik-Dik: *digidigi, dikidiki, saruya,* or *paa*
Dog: *mbwa*
Donkey: *punda*
Duiker: *nsya, fumo, mindi*
Eland: *pofu* or *mbunju*
Elephant: *tembo* or *ndovu*
Fox: *mbweha*
Gazelle: *swala* or *paa*
  Thomson's: *swala tomi*
  Grant's: *swala granti*
Genet: *kanu*
Gerenuk: *swala twiga* or *mdogo gerenuku*
Giraffe: *twiga*
Gnu (see Wildebeest)
Goat: *mbuzi*
Hartebeest: *kongoni* or *nyamera*
Hippopotamus: *kiboko* (also means "whip" made from dried hippo skin)
Horse: *farasi*
Hyena: *fisi*
Hyrax
  Bush or Rock: *pimbi*
  Tree: *perere*
Impala: *swala pala* or *mpala*
Jackal: *(m)bweha*
  Black-backed: *bweha shaba* or *mweusi*
  Golden: *bweha dhahabu*
  Side-striped: *bweha miraba*

Klipspringer: *mbuzi mawe*
Kongoni: *kongoni*
Kudu
  Lesser: *tandala ndogo*
  Greater: *tandala*
Leopard: *chui*
Lion: *simba*
  male: *simba dume*
  female: *simba jike*
  "lion's share": *fungu kubwa*
Mongoose: *nguchiro* or *kicheche*
Monkey: *kima, mkima,* or *tumbili*
  Sykes': kima
  Vervet: tumbili
  Colobus (see "Colobus monkey")
  large monkey: *nyani*
Oribi: *taya*
Oryx: *choroa*
Pig: *nguruwe*
Porcupine: *nungu*
Rabbit: *sungura*
Ratel: *nyegere*
Reedbuck: *tohe*
Rhinoceros: *ki faru* or *faru*
Serval: *mondo* or *ngawa*
Sykes' monkey: *kima*
Topi: *nyamera*
Waterbuck
  Common: *ndogaru*
  Defassa: *kuro*
Warthog: *ngiri*
Wild (Cape Hunting) Dog: *mbwa (wa) mwitu*
Wildebeest: *nyumbu (ya montu)*
Vervet Monkey: *tumbili*
Zebra (Common or Grevy's): *punda milia*

Birds

Barbet: *duduvule*
Bird: *ndege* (also means "plane")
Bustard: *tandawala*
Cormorant: *mnandi*
Crane: *korongo*
  Crowned: *kung'wani*
Crow: *kunguru*
Dove: *(see "Pigeon")*
Duck: *bata*
Eagle: *tai* or *koho*
  Bateleur: *mwewe*
  Martial: *mwewe*
  Fish: *mwewe samaki*
Egret: *yangeyange*
Flamingo:
  Greater: *heroe mkubwa*
  Lesser: *heroe ndogo*
Goose: *bata bukini*
Guineafowl: *kanga*
Hamerkop: *fundichuma*

Hawk: *mwewe*
Heron: *korongo*
Hornbill:
  Ground: *mumbi* or *hondo mtembezi*
  von der Decken's: *hondo hondo*
  Silver-cheeked: *hondo hondo kijivu*
Ibis: *kwarara*
Kingfisher: *mdiria*
  Pied: *deterpwani* or *kisharifu*
Marabon stork: *korongo*
Nightjar: *mpasuasanda*
Ostrich: *mbuni*
Owl: *bundi*
Parrot: *kasuku*
Pelican: *mwari*
  Pink-backed: *jahari* or *mwari pink*
  White: *jahari* or *mwari mweupe*
Pigeon: *njiwa*
Roller (Lilac-breasted): *kweru*
Saddle-billed stork: *korongo*
Sandgrouse (Yellow-Throated): *gargara mchanga*
Secretary Bird: *ndege karani*
Spurfowl: *kwale*
Starling (Superb): *kwenzi*
Stork: *korongo*
Sunbird: *chozi*
Vulture (all): *tai*
Weaver: *mzingi*
  Golden weaver: *mnama*
Woodpecker: *gogota*

Reptiles:

Agama Rock Lizard: *mjuzi kafiri*
Chameleon: *kinyonga* or *kigengeu*
Cobra (Spitting): *fira swilia*
Crocodile: *mamba*
Lizard: *mjuzi*
  Monitor: *kenge*
Python: *chatu*
Snake: *nyoka* or *omsoto*
  big snake: *joka*